Collins
FRENCH
DICTIONARY
ESSENTIAL EDITION

...ollins
...print of HarperCollins Publishers
Westerhill Road
Bishopbriggs
Glasgow G64 2QT

Second Edition 2018

10 9 8 7 6 5 4 3 2 1

© HarperCollins Publishers 2014, 2018

ISBN 978-0-00-827072-8

Collins® is a registered trademark of
HarperCollins Publishers Limited

www.collinsdictionary.com

Typeset by
Davidson Publishing Solutions, Glasgow

Printed and bound by
CPI Group (UK) Ltd, Croydon, CR0 4YY

Entered words that we have reason
to believe constitute trademarks
have been designated as such.
However, neither the presence nor
absence of such designation should
be regarded as affecting the legal
status of any trademark.

The contents of this publication are
believed correct at the time of
printing. Nevertheless the Publisher
can accept no responsibility for errors
or omissions, changes in the detail
given or for any expense or loss
thereby caused.

HarperCollins does not warrant that
any website mentioned in this title will
be provided uninterrupted, that any
website will be error free, that defects
will be corrected, or that the website
or the server that makes it available
are free of viruses or bugs. For full
terms and conditions please refer to
the site terms provided on the
website.

A catalogue record for this book is
available from the British Library.

If you would like to comment on any
aspect of this book, please contact us
at the given address or online.
E-mail: dictionaries@harpercollins.co.uk
 facebook.com/collinsdictionary
 @collinsdict

Acknowledgements

We would like to thank those authors
and publishers who kindly gave
permission for copyright material to be
used in the Collins Corpus. We would
also like to thank Times Newspapers
Ltd for providing valuable data.

TABLE DES MATIÈRES

CONTENTS

INTRODUCTION

Nous sommes très heureux que vous ayez choisi ce dictionnaire et espérons que vous aimerez l'utiliser et que vous en tirerez profit au lycée, à la maison, en vacances ou au travail.

Cette introduction a pour but de vous donner quelques conseils sur la façon d'utiliser au mieux votre dictionnaire, en vous référant non seulement à son importante nomenclature mais aussi aux informations contenues dans chaque entrée. Ceci vous aidera à lire et à comprendre, mais aussi à communiquer et à vous exprimer en anglais contemporain.

Au début du dictionnaire, vous trouverez la liste des abréviations utilisées dans le texte et celle de la transcription des sons par des symboles phonétiques. Vous y trouverez également la liste des verbes irréguliers en anglais, suivis d'une section finale sur les nombres et sur les expressions de temps.

COMMENT UTILISER VOTRE DICTIONNAIRE

Ce dictionnaire offre une richesse d'informations et utilise diverses formes et tailles de caractères, symboles, abréviations, parenthèses et crochets. Les conventions et symboles utilisés sont expliqués dans les sections qui suivent.

ENTRÉES

Les mots que vous cherchez dans le dictionnaire – les entrées – sont classés par ordre alphabétique. Ils sont imprimés en **gras** pour pouvoir être repérés rapidement. Les entrées figurant en haut de page indiquent le premier (sur la page de gauche) et le dernier mot (sur la page de droite) des deux pages en question.

Des informations sur l'usage ou sur la forme de certaines entrées sont données entre parenthèses, après la transcription phonétique. Ces indications apparaissent sous forme abrégée et en italiques (par ex. *(fam)*, *(Comm)*).

Pour plus de facilité, les mots de la même famille sont regroupés sous la même entrée (**ronger, rongeur** ; **accept, acceptance**) et apparaissent également en **gras**.

Les expressions courantes dans lesquelles apparaît l'entrée sont indiquées par des caractères romains gras différents (par exemple **retard** [...] **avoir du ~**).

TRANSCRIPTION PHONÉTIQUE

La transcription phonétique de chaque entrée (indiquant sa prononciation) est présentée entre crochets immédiatement après l'entrée (par ex. **fumer** [fymc] ; **knee** [ni:]). La liste des symboles phonétiques figure aux pages xi et xii.

Les traductions des entrées apparaissent en caractères ordinaires ; lorsque plusieurs sens ou usages coexistent, ces traductions sont séparées par un point-virgule. Vous trouverez des synonymes de l'entrée en italique entre parenthèses avant les traductions (par ex. **poser** (*installer: moquette, carrelage*)) ou des mots qui fournissent le contexte dans lequel l'entrée est susceptible d'être utilisée (par ex. **poser** (*question*)).

MOTS-CLÉS
Une importance particulière est accordée à certains mots français et anglais qui sont considérés comme des « mots-clés » dans chacune des langues. Cela peut être dû à leur utilisation très fréquente ou au fait qu'ils ont divers types d'usage (par ex. **vouloir**, **plus** ; **get**, **that**). L'utilisation de triangles et de chiffres aide à distinguer différentes catégories grammaticales et différents sens. D'autres renseignements utiles apparaissent en italique et entre parenthèses dans la langue de l'utilisateur.

DONNÉES GRAMMATICALES
Les catégories grammaticales sont données sous forme abrégée et en italique après la transcription phonétique (par ex. *vt*, *adv*, *conj*). Les genres des noms français sont indiqués de la manière suivante : *nm* pour un nom masculin et *nf* pour un nom féminin. Le féminin et le pluriel irréguliers de certains noms sont également indiqués (par ex. **directeur, -trice** ; **cheval, -aux**).

Le masculin et le féminin des adjectifs sont indiqués lorsque ces deux formes sont différentes (par ex. **noir, e**). Lorsque l'adjectif a un féminin ou un pluriel irrégulier, ces formes sont clairement indiquées (par ex. **net, nette**). Les pluriels irréguliers des noms et les formes irrégulières des verbes anglais sont indiqués entre parenthèses, avant la catégorie grammaticale (par ex. **man** (*pl* **men**) *n* ; **give** (*pt* **gave**; *pp* **given**) *vt*).

INTRODUCTION

We are delighted that you have chosen this dictionary and hope you will enjoy and benefit from using it at school, at home, on holiday or at work.

This introduction gives you a few tips on how to get the most out of your dictionary – not simply from its comprehensive wordlist but also from the information provided in each entry. This will help you to read and understand modern French, as well as communicate and express yourself in the language.

This dictionary begins by listing the abbreviations used in the text and illustrating the sounds shown by the phonetic symbols. You will also find French verb tables, followed by a final section on numbers and time expressions.

USING YOUR DICTIONARY

A wealth of information is presented in the dictionary, using various typefaces, sizes of type, symbols, abbreviations and brackets. The various conventions and symbols used are explained in the following sections.

HEADWORDS

The words you look up in a dictionary – 'headwords' – are listed alphabetically. They are printed in **bold** for rapid identification. The headwords appearing at the top of each page indicate the first (if it appears on a left-hand page) and last word (if it appears on a right-hand page) dealt with on the page in question.

Information about the usage or form of certain headwords is given in brackets after the phonetic spelling. This usually appears in abbreviated form and in italics (e.g. (*inf*), (*Comm*)).

Where appropriate, words related to headwords are grouped in the same entry (**ronger**, **rongeur**; **accept**, **acceptance**) and are also in **bold**.

Common expressions in which the headword appears are shown in a bold roman type (e.g. **inquire** [...] **to ~ about**).

PHONETIC SPELLINGS

The phonetic spelling of each headword (indicating its pronunciation) is given in square brackets immediately after the headword (e.g. **fumer** [fyme]; **knee** [niː]). A list of these symbols is given on pages xi and xii.

TRANSLATIONS

Headword translations are given in ordinary type and, where more than one meaning or usage exists, these are separated by a semi-colon. You will often find other words in italics in brackets before the translations. These offer suggested contexts in which the headword might appear (e.g. **rough** (*voice*) [...] (*plan*)) or provide synonyms (e.g. **rough** (*manner: coarse*)). The gender of the translation also appears in italics immediately following the key element of the translation.

KEYWORDS

Special status is given to certain French and English words which are considered as 'keywords' in each language. They may, for example, occur very frequently or have several types of usage (e.g. **vouloir**, **plus**; **get**, **that**). A combination of triangles and numbers helps you to distinguish different parts of speech and different meanings. Further helpful information is provided in brackets and italics.

GRAMMATICAL INFORMATION

Parts of speech are given in abbreviated form in italics after the phonetic spellings of headwords (e.q. *vt*, *adv*, *conj*). Genders of French nouns are indicated as follows: *nm* for a masculine noun and *nf* for a feminine noun. Feminine and irregular plural forms of nouns are also shown (**directeur, -trice**; **cheval, -aux**).

Adjectives are given in both masculine and feminine forms where these forms are different (e.g. **noir, e**). Clear information is provided where adjectives have an irregular feminine or plural form (e.g. **net, nette**).

abréviation	*ab(b)r*	abbreviation
adjectif, locution adjectivale	*adj*	adjective, adjectival phrase
administration	*Admin*	administration
adverbe, locution adverbiale	*adv*	adverb, adverbial phrase
agriculture	*Agr*	agriculture
anatomie	*Anat*	anatomy
architecture	*Archit*	architecture
article défini	*art déf*	definite article
article indéfini	*art indéf*	indefinite article
automobile	*Aut(o)*	automobiles
aviation, voyages aériens	*Aviat*	flying, air travel
biologie	*Bio(l)*	biology
botanique	*Bot*	botany
anglais britannique	*BRIT*	British English
chimie	*Chem*	chemistry
commerce, finance, banque	*Comm*	commerce, finance, banking
informatique	*Comput*	computing
conjonction	*conj*	conjunction
construction	*Constr*	building
nom utilisé comme adjectif	*cpd*	compound element
cuisine	*Culin*	cookery
article défini	*def art*	definite article
économie	*Écon, Econ*	economics
électricité, électronique	*Élec, Elec*	electricity, electronics
en particulier	*esp*	especially
exclamation, interjection	*excl*	exclamation, interjection
féminin	*f*	feminine
langue familière	*fam(!)*	colloquial usage
(! emploi vulgaire)		(! particularly offensive)
emploi figuré	*fig*	figurative use
(verbe anglais) dont la	*fus*	(phrasal verb) where the
particule est inséparable		particle is inseparable
généralement	*gén, gen*	generally
géographie, géologie	*Géo, Geo*	geography, geology
géométrie	*Géom, Geom*	geometry
article indéfini	*indef art*	indefinite article
langue familière	*inf(!)*	colloquial usage
(! emploi vulgaire)		(! particularly offensive)
infinitif	*infin*	infinitive
informatique	*Inform*	computing
invariable	*inv*	invariable
irrégulier	*irreg*	irregular
domaine juridique	*Jur*	law
grammaire, linguistique	*Ling*	grammar, linguistics

ABRÉVIATIONS

ABBREVIATIONS

masculin	*m*	masculine
mathématiques, algèbre	*Math*	mathematics, calculus
médecine	*Méd, Med*	medical term, medicine
masculin ou féminin	*m/f*	masculine or feminine
domaine militaire, armée	*Mil*	military matters
musique	*Mus*	music
nom	*n*	noun
navigation, nautisme	*Navig, Naut*	sailing, navigation
nom ou adjectif numéral	*num*	numeral noun or adjective
	o.s.	oneself
péjoratif	*péj, pej*	derogatory, pejorative
photographie	*Phot(o)*	photography
physiologie	*Physiol*	physiology
pluriel	*pl*	plural
politique	*Pol*	politics
participe passé	*pp*	past participle
préposition	*prép, prep*	preposition
pronom	*pron*	pronoun
psychologie, psychiatrie	*Psych*	psychology, psychiatry
temps du passé	*pt*	past tense
quelque chose	*qch*	
quelqu'un	*qn*	
religion, domaine ecclésiastique	*Rel*	religion
	sb	somebody
enseignement, système scolaire et universitaire	*Scol*	schooling, schools and universities
singulier	*sg*	singular
	sth	something
subjonctif	*sub*	subjunctive
sujet (grammatical)	*subj*	(grammatical) subject
techniques, technologie	*Tech*	technical term, technology
télécommunications	*Tél, Tel*	telecommunications
télévision	*TV*	television
typographie	*Typ(o)*	typography, printing
anglais des États-Unis	*US*	American English
verbe (auxiliaire)	*vb (aux)*	(auxiliary) verb
verbe intransitif	*vi*	intransitive verb
verbe transitif	*vt*	transitive verb
zoologie	*Zool*	zoology
marque déposée	®	registered trademark
indique une équivalence culturelle	≈	indicates a cultural equivalent

TRANSCRIPTION PHONÉTIQUE

CONSONNES		**CONSONANTS**
NB. **p, b, t, d, k, g** sont suivis d'une aspiration en anglais.		NB. **p, b, t, d, k, g** are not aspirated in French.
pou**p**ée	p	**p**u**pp**y
bom**b**e	b	**b**a**b**y
ten**t**e **th**ermal	t	**t**en**t**
din**d**e	d	**d**a**dd**y
co**q** **qu**i **k**épi	k	**c**ork **k**iss **ch**ord
ga**g**e ba**gu**e	g	**g**a**g** **gu**ess
sale **c**e na**t**ion	s	**s**o ri**c**e ki**ss**
zéro ro**s**e	z	cou**s**in bu**zz**
ta**ch**e **ch**at	ʃ	**sh**eep **s**ugar
gilet **j**uge	ʒ	plea**s**ure bei**ge**
	tʃ	**ch**urch
	dʒ	**j**udge **g**eneral
fer **ph**are	f	**f**arm ra**ff**le
ver**v**eine	v	**v**ery re**v**el
	θ	**th**in ma**th**s
	ð	**th**at o**th**er
lent sa**ll**e	l	**l**itt**l**e ha**ll**
ra**r**e **r**ent**r**er	ʀ	
	r	**r**at ra**r**e
ma**m**an fe**mm**e	m	**m**u**mm**y co**mb**
non bo**nn**e	n	**n**o ra**n**
a**gn**eau vi**gn**e	ɲ	**ch**urch
	ŋ	si**ng**ing ba**n**k
	h	**h**at re**h**earse
yeux pa**ill**e p**i**ed	j	**y**et
n**ou**er **ou**i	w	**w**all **w**ail
h**ui**le l**ui**	ɥ	
	x	lo**ch**
DIVERS		**MISCELLANEOUS**
pour l'anglais : le **r** final se prononce en liaison devant une voyelle	ʳ	in English transcription: final **r** can be pronounced before a vowel
pour l'anglais : précède la syllabe accentuée	'	in French wordlist: no liaison before aspirate **h** and **y**

En règle générale, la prononciation est donnée entre crochets après chaque entrée. Toutefois, du côté anglais-français et dans le cas des expressions composées de deux ou plusieurs mots non réunis par un trait d'union et faisant l'objet d'une entrée séparée, la prononciation doit être cherchée sous chacun des mots constitutifs de l'expression en question.

PHONETIC TRANSCRIPTION

In general, we give the pronunciation of each entry in square brackets after the word in question. However, on the English-French side, where the entry is composed of two or more unhyphenated words, each of which is given elsewhere in this dictionary, you will find the pronunciation of each word in its alphabetical position.

FRENCH VERB FORMS

a Present participle b Past participle c Present d Imperfect e Future
f Conditional g Present subjunctive

1 **ARRIVER a** arrivant **b** arrivé
c arrive, arrives, arrive, arrivons,
arrivez, arrivent **d** arrivais
e arriverai **f** arriverais **g** arrive

2 **FINIR a** finissant **b** fini **c** finis, finis,
finit, finissons, finissez, finissent
d finissais **e** finirai **f** finirais **g** finisse

3 **PLACER a** plaçant **b** placé **c** place,
places, place, plaçons, placez,
placent **d** plaçais, plaçais, plaçait,
placions, placiez, plaçaient
e placerai, placeras, placera,
placerons, placerez, placeront
f placerais, placerais, placerait,
placerions, placeriez, placeraient
g place

3 **BOUGER a** bougeant **b** bougé
c bouge, bougeons **d** bougeais,
bougions **e** bougerai **f** bougerais
g bouge

4 **appeler a** appelant **b** appelé
c appelle, appelons **d** appelais
e appellerai **f** appellerais **g** appelle

4 **jeter a** jetant **b** jeté **c** jette, jetons
d jetais **e** jetterai **f** jetterais **g** jette

5 **geler a** gelant **b** gelé **c** gèle, gelons
d gelais **e** gèlerai **f** gèlerais **g** gèle

6 **CÉDER a** cédant **b** cédé **c** cède,
cèdes, cède, cédons, cédez, cèdent
d cédais, cédais, cédait, cédions,
cédiez, cédaient **e** céderai, céderas,
cédera, céderons, céderez,
céderont **f** céderais, céderais,
céderait, céderions, céderiez,
céderaient **g** cède

7 **épier a** épiant **b** épié **c** épie, épions
d épiais **e** épierai **f** épierais **g** épie

8 **noyer a** noyant **b** noyé **c** noie,
noyons **d** noyais **e** noierai **f** noierais
g noie

9 **ALLER a** allant **b** allé **c** vais, vas,
va, allons, allez, vont **d** allais **e** irai
f irais **g** aille

10 **HAÏR a** haïssant **b** haï **c** hais, hais,
hait, haïssons, haïssez, haïssent
d haïssais, haïssais, haïssait,
haïssions, haïssiez, haïssaient
e haïrai, haïras, haïra, haïrons,
haïrez, haïront **f** haïrais, haïrais,
haïrait, haïrions, haïriez, haïraient
g haïsse

11 **courir a** courant **b** couru **c** cours,
courons **d** courais **e** courrai **g** coure

12 **cueillir a** cueillant **b** cueilli **c** cueille,
cueillons **d** cueillais **e** cueillerai
g cueille

13 **assaillir – a** assaillant **b** assailli
c assaille, assaillons **d** assaillais
e assaillirai **g** assaille

14 **servir a** servant **b** servi **c** sers,
servons **d** servais **g** serve

15 **bouillir a** bouillant **b** bouilli **c** bous,
bouillons **d** bouillais **g** bouille

16 **partir a** partant **b** parti **c** pars,
partons **d** partais **g** parte

17 **fuir a** fuyant **b** fui **c** fuis, fuyons,
fuient **d** fuyais **g** fuie

18 couvrir a couvrant **b** couvert **c** couvre, couvrons **d** couvrais **g** couvre

19 mourir a mourant **b** mort **c** meurs, mourons, meurent **d** mourais **e** mourrai **g** meure

20 vêtir a vêtant **b** vêtu **c** vêts, vêtons **d** vêtais **e** vêtirai **g** vête

21 acquérir a acquérant **b** acquis **c** acquiers, acquérons, acquièrent **d** acquérais **e** acquerrai **g** acquière

22 venir a venant **b** venu **c** viens, venons, viennent **d** venais **e** viendrai **g** vienne

23 pleuvoir a pleuvant **b** plu **c** pleut, pleuvent **d** pleuvait **e** pleuvra **g** pleuve

24 prévoir *like* voir **e** prévoirai

25 pourvoir a pourvoyant **b** pourvu **c** pourvois, pourvoyons, pourvoient **d** pourvoyais **g** pourvoie

26 asseoir a asseyant **b** assis **c** assieds, asseyons, asseyez, asseyent **d** asseyais **e** assiérai **g** asseye

27 MOUVOIR a mouvant **b** mû **c** meus, meus, meut, mouvons, mouvez, meuvent **d** mouvais **e** mouvrai **f** mouvrais **g** meuve, meuves, meuve, mouvions, mouviez, meuvent

28 RECEVOIR a recevant **b** reçu **c** reçois, reçois, reçoit, recevons, recevez, reçoivent **d** recevais **e** recevrai **f** recevrais **g** reçoive

29 valoir a valant **b** valu **c** vaux, vaut, valons **d** valais **e** vaudrai **g** vaille

30 voir a voyant **b** vu **c** vois, voyons, voient **d** voyais **e** verrai **g** voie

31 vouloir a voulant **b** voulu **c** veux, veut, voulons, veulent **d** voulais **e** voudrai **g** veuille ; *impératif* veuillez !

32 savoir a sachant **b** su **c** sais, savons, savent **d** savais **e** saurai **g** sache *impératif* sache ! sachons ! sachez !

33 pouvoir a pouvant **b** pu **c** peux, peut, pouvons, peuvent **d** pouvais **e** pourrai **g** puisse

34 AVOIR a ayant **b** eu **c** ai, as, a, avons, avez, ont **d** avais **e** aurai **f** aurais **g** aie, aies, ait, ayons, ayez, aient

35 conclure a concluant **b** conclu **c** conclus, concluons **d** concluais **g** conclue

36 rire a riant **b** ri **c** ris, rions **d** riais **g** rie

37 dire a disant **b** dit **c** dis, disons, dites, disent **d** disais **g** dise

38 nuire a nuisant **b** nui **c** nuis, nuisons **d** nuisais **e** nuirai **f** nuirais **g** nuise

39 écrire a écrivant **b** écrit **c** écris, écrivons **d** écrivais **g** écrive

40 suivre a suivant **b** suivi **c** suis, suivons **d** suivais **g** suive

41 RENDRE a rendant **b** rendu **c** rends, rends, rend, rendons, rendez, rendent **d** rendais **e** rendrai **f** rendrais **g** rende

42 vaincre a vainquant **b** vaincu **c** vaincs, vainc, vainquons **d** vainquais **g** vainque

43 lire a lisant **b** lu **c** lis, lisons **d** lisais **g** lise

44 croire a croyant **b** cru **c** crois, croyons, croient **d** croyais **g** croie

45 CLORE a closant **b** clos **c** clos, clos, clôt, closent **e** clorai, cloras, clora, clorons, clorez, cloront **f** clorais, clorais, clorait, clorions, cloriez, cloraient

46 vivre a vivant **b** vécu **c** vis, vivons **d** vivais **g** vive

47 MOUDRE a moulant **b** moulu **c** mouds, mouds, moud, moulons, moulez, moulent **d** moulais, moulais, moulait, moulions, mouliez, moulaient **e** moudrai, moudras, moudra, moudrons, moudrez, moudront **f** moudrais, moudrais, moudrait, moudrions, moudriez, moudraient **g** moule

48 coudre a cousant **b** cousu **c** couds, cousons, cousez, cousent **d** cousais **g** couse

49 joindre a joignant **b** joint **c** joins, joignons **d** joignais **g** joigne

50 TRAIRE a trayant **b** trait **c** trais, trais, trait, trayons, trayez, traient **d** trayais, trayais, trayait, trayions, trayiez, trayaient **e** trairai, trairas, traira, trairons, trairez, trairont **f** trairais, trairais, trairait, trairions, trairiez, trairaient **g** traie

51 ABSOUDRE a absolvant **b** absous **c** absous, absous, absout, absolvons, absolvez, absolvent **d** absolvais, absolvais, absolvait, absolvions, absolviez, absolvaient **e** absoudrai, absoudras, absoudra, absoudrons, absoudrez, absoudront **f** absoudrais, absoudrais, absoudrait, absoudrions, absoudriez, absoudraient **g** absolve

52 craindre a craignant **b** craint **c** crains, craignons **d** craignais **g** craigne

53 boire a buvant **b** bu **c** bois, buvons, boivent **d** buvais **g** boive

54 plaire a plaisant **b** plu **c** plais, plaît, plaisons **d** plaisais **g** plaise

55 croître a croissant **b** crû **c** croîs, croissons **d** croissais **g** croisse

56 mettre a mettant **b** mis **c** mets, mettons **d** mettais **g** mette

57 connaître a connaissant **b** connu **c** connais, connaît, connaissons **d** connaissais **g** connaisse

58 prendre a prenant **b** pris **c** prends, prenons, prennent **d** prenais **g** prenne

59 naître a naissant **b** né **c** nais, naît, naissons **d** naissais **g** naisse

60 FAIRE a faisant **b** fait **c** fais, fais, fait, faisons, faites, font **d** faisais **e** ferai **f** ferais **g** fasse

61 ÊTRE a étant **b** été **c** suis, es, est, sommes, êtes, sont **d** étais **e** serai **f** serais **g** sois, sois, soit, soyons, soyez, soient

VERBES IRRÉGULIERS ANGLAIS

PRÉSENT	PASSÉ	PARTICIPE	PRÉSENT	PASSÉ	PARTICIPE
arise	arose	arisen	cost (*work out price of*)	costed	costed
awake	awoke	awoken	creep	crept	crept
be (am, is, are; being)	was, were	been	cut	cut	cut
			deal	dealt	dealt
bear	bore	born(e)	dig	dug	dug
beat	beat	beaten	do (does)	did	done
become	became	become	draw	drew	drawn
begin	began	begun	dream	dreamed, dreamt	dreamed, dreamt
bend	bent	bent			
bet	bet, betted	bet, betted	drink	drank	drunk
			drive	drove	driven
bid (*at auction, cards*)	bid	bid	dwell	dwelt	dwelt
			eat	ate	eaten
bid (*say*)	bade	bidden	fall	fell	fallen
bind	bound	bound	feed	fed	fed
bite	bit	bitten	feel	felt	felt
bleed	bled	bled	fight	fought	fought
blow	blew	blown	find	found	found
break	broke	broken	flee	fled	fled
breed	bred	bred	fling	flung	flung
bring	brought	brought	fly	flew	flown
build	built	built	forbid	forbad(e)	forbidden
burn	burnt, burned	burnt, burned	forecast	forecast	forecast
			forget	forgot	forgotten
burst	burst	burst	forgive	forgave	forgiven
buy	bought	bought	forsake	forsook	forsaken
can	could	(*been able*)	freeze	froze	frozen
cast	cast	cast	get	got	got, (*us*) gotten
catch	caught	caught			
choose	chose	chosen	give	gave	given
cling	clung	clung	go (goes)	went	gone
come	came	come	grind	ground	ground
cost	cost	cost			

PRÉSENT	PASSÉ	PARTICIPE	PRÉSENT	PASSÉ	PARTICIPE
grow	grew	grown	mow	mowed	mown, mowed
hang	hung	hung			
hang (execute)	hanged	hanged	must	(had to)	(had to)
have	had	had	pay	paid	paid
hear	heard	heard	put	put	put
hide	hid	hidden	quit	quit, quitted	quit, quitted
hit	hit	hit			
hold	held	held	read	read	read
hurt	hurt	hurt	rid	rid	rid
keep	kept	kept	ride	rode	ridden
kneel	knelt, kneeled	knelt, kneeled	ring	rang	rung
			rise	rose	risen
know	knew	known	run	ran	run
lay	laid	laid	saw	sawed	sawed, sawn
lead	led	led			
lean	leant, leaned	leant, leaned	say	said	said
			see	saw	seen
leap	leapt, leaped	leapt, leaped	seek	sought	sought
			sell	sold	sold
learn	learnt, learned	learnt, learned	send	sent	sent
			set	set	set
leave	left	left	sew	sewed	sewn
lend	lent	lent	shake	shook	shaken
let	let	let	shear	sheared	shorn, sheared
lie (lying)	lay	lain			
light	lit, lighted	lit, lighted	shed	shed	shed
			shine	shone	shone
lose	lost	lost	shoot	shot	shot
make	made	made	show	showed	shown
may	might	–	shrink	shrank	shrunk
mean	meant	meant	shut	shut	shut
meet	met	met	sing	sang	sung
mistake	mistook	mistaken	sink	sank	sunk

PRÉSENT	PASSÉ	PARTICIPE	PRÉSENT	PASSÉ	PARTICIPE
sit	sat	sat	stride	strode	stridden
slay	slew	slain	strike	struck	struck
sleep	slept	slept	strive	strove	striven
slide	slid	slid	swear	swore	sworn
sling	slung	slung	sweep	swept	swept
slit	slit	slit	swell	swelled	swollen, swelled
smell	smelt, smelled	smelt, smelled	swim	swam	swum
sow	sowed	sown, sowed	swing	swung	swung
			take	took	taken
speak	spoke	spoken	teach	taught	taught
speed	sped, speeded	sped, speeded	tear	tore	torn
			tell	told	told
spell	spelt, spelled	spelt, spelled	think	thought	thought
			throw	threw	thrown
spend	spent	spent	thrust	thrust	thrust
spill	spilt, spilled	spilt, spilled	tread	trod	trodden
			wake	woke, waked	woken, waked
spin	spun	spun			
spit	spat	spat	wear	wore	worn
spoil	spoiled, spoilt	spoiled, spoilt	weave	wove	woven
spread	spread	spread	weave (wind)	weaved	weaved
spring	sprang	sprung	wed	wedded, wed	wedded, wed
stand	stood	stood			
steal	stole	stolen	weep	wept	wept
stick	stuck	stuck	win	won	won
sting	stung	stung	wind	wound	wound
stink	stank	stunk	wring	wrung	wrung
			write	wrote	written

LES NOMBRES

NUMBERS

un (une)	1	one
deux	2	two
trois	3	three
quatre	4	four
cinq	5	five
six	6	six
sept	7	seven
huit	8	eight
neuf	9	nine
dix	10	ten
onze	11	eleven
douze	12	twelve
treize	13	thirteen
quatorze	14	fourteen
quinze	15	fifteen
seize	16	sixteen
dix-sept	17	seventeen
dix-huit	18	eighteen
dix-neuf	19	nineteen
vingt	20	twenty
vingt et un (une)	21	twenty-one
vingt-deux	22	twenty-two
trente	30	thirty
quarante	40	forty
cinquante	50	fifty
soixante	60	sixty
soixante-dix	70	seventy
soixante-et-onze	71	seventy-one
soixante-douze	72	seventy-two
quatre-vingts	80	eighty
quatre-vingt-un (-une)	81	eighty-one
quatre-vingt-dix	90	ninety
cent	100	a hundred, one hundred
cent un (une)	101	a hundred and one
deux cents	200	two hundred
deux cent un (une)	201	two hundred and one
quatre cents	400	four hundred
mille	1000	a thousand
cinq mille	5000	five thousand
un million	1000000	a million

LES NOMBRES	NUMBERS

premier (première), 1er (1ère)	first, 1st
deuxième, 2e *or* 2ème	second, 2nd
troisième, 3e *or* 3ème	third, 3rd
quatrième, 4e *or* 4ème	fourth, 4th
cinquième, 5e *or* 5ème	fifth, 5th
sixième, 6e *or* 6ème	sixth, 6th
septième	seventh
huitième	eighth
neuvième	ninth
dixième	tenth
onzième	eleventh
douzième	twelfth
treizième	thirteenth
quartorzième	fourteenth
quinzième	fifteenth
seizième	sixteenth
dix-septième	seventeenth
dix-huitième	eighteenth
dix-neuvième	nineteenth
vingtième	twentieth
vingt-et-unième	twenty-first
vingt-deuxième	twenty-second
trentième	thirtieth
centième	hundredth
cent-unième	hundred-and-first
millième	thousandth

LES FRACTIONS ETC.	FRACTIONS ETC.
un demi	a half
un tiers	a third
un quart	a quarter
un cinquième	a fifth
zéro virgule cinq, 0,5	(nought) point five, 0.5
trois virgule quatre, 3,4	three point four, 3.4
dix pour cent	ten per cent
cent pour cent	a hundred per cent

EXEMPLES	EXAMPLES
elle habite au septième (étage)	she lives on the 7th floor
il habite au sept	he lives at number 7
au chapitre/à la page sept	chapter/page 7
il est arrivé (le) septième	he came in 7th

L'HEURE	THE TIME
quelle heure est-il ?	*what time is it?*
il est ...	*it's ou it is ...*
minuit	midnight, twelve p.m.
une heure (du matin)	one o'clock (in the morning), one (a.m.)
une heure cinq	five past one
une heure dix	ten past one
une heure et quart	a quarter past one, one fifteen
une heure vingt-cinq	twenty-five past one, one twenty-five
une heure et demie, une heure trente	half-past one, one thirty
deux heures moins vingt-cinq, une heure trente-cinq	twenty-five to two, one thirty-five
deux heures moins vingt, une heure quarante	twenty to two, one forty
deux heures moins le quart, une heure quarante-cinq	a quarter to two, one forty-five
deux heures moins dix, une heure cinquante	ten to two, one fifty
midi	twelve o'clock, midday, noon
deux heures (de l'après-midi), quatorze heures	two o'clock (in the afternoon), two (p.m.)
sept heures (du soir), dix-neuf heures	seven o'clock (in the evening), seven (p.m.)
à quelle heure ?	*(at) what time?*
à minuit	at midnight
à sept heures	at seven o'clock
dans vingt minutes	in twenty minutes
il y a un quart d'heure	fifteen minutes ago

Français – Anglais

French – English

a

a [a] *vb voir* **avoir**

⭕ **MOT-CLÉ**

à [a] (*à* + *le* = **au**, *à* + *les* = **aux**) *prép*
1 (*endroit, situation*) at, in; **être à Paris/au Portugal** to be in Paris/Portugal; **être à la maison/à l'école** to be at home/at school; **à la campagne** in the country; **c'est à 10 m/km/à 20 minutes (d'ici)** it's 10 m/km/20 minutes away
2 (*direction*) to; **aller à Paris/au Portugal** to go to Paris/Portugal; **aller à la maison/à l'école** to go home/to school; **à la campagne** to the country
3 (*temps*): **à 3 heures/minuit** at 3 o'clock/midnight; **au printemps** in the spring; **au mois de juin** in June; **à Noël/Pâques** at Christmas/Easter; **à demain/la semaine prochaine** see you tomorrow/next week!
4 (*attribution, appartenance*) to; **le livre est à Paul/à lui/à nous** this book is Paul's/his/ours; **donner qch à qn** to give sth to sb; **un ami à moi** a friend of mine
5 (*moyen*) with; **se chauffer au gaz** to have gas heating; **à bicyclette** on a *ou* by bicycle; **à pied** on foot; **à la main/machine** by hand/machine
6 (*provenance*) from; **boire à la bouteille** to drink from the bottle
7 (*caractérisation, manière*): **l'homme aux yeux bleus** the man with the blue eyes; **à la russe** the Russian way
8 (*but, destination*): **tasse à café** coffee cup; **maison à vendre** house for sale; **je n'ai rien à lire** I don't have anything to read; **à bien réfléchir ...** thinking about it ..., on reflection ...
9 (*rapport, évaluation, distribution*): **100 km/unités à l'heure** 100 km/units per *ou* an hour; **payé à l'heure** paid by the

hour; **cinq à six** five to six
10 (*conséquence, résultat*): **à ce qu'il prétend** according to him; **à leur grande surprise** much to their surprise; **à nous trois nous n'avons pas su le faire** we couldn't do it even between the three of us; **ils sont arrivés à quatre** four of them arrived (together)

abaisser [abese] /1/ *vt* to lower, bring down; (*manette*) to pull down; **s'abaisser** *vi* to go down; (*fig*) to demean o.s.
abandon [abādɔ̃] *nm* abandoning; giving up; withdrawal; **être à l'~** to be in a state of neglect; **laisser à l'~** to abandon
abandonner [abādɔne] /1/ *vt* (*personne*) to leave, abandon, desert; (*projet, activité*) to abandon, give up; (*Sport*) to retire *ou* withdraw from; (*céder*) to surrender; **s'~ à** (*paresse, plaisirs*) to give o.s. up to
abat-jour [abaʒuʀ] *nm inv* lampshade
abats [aba] *nmpl* (*de bœuf, porc*) offal *sg*; (*de volaille*) giblets
abattement [abatmā] *nm*: **~ fiscal** ≈ tax allowance
abattoir [abatwaʀ] *nm* slaughterhouse
abattre [abatʀ] /41/ *vt* (*arbre*) to cut down, fell; (*mur, maison*) to pull down; (*avion, personne*) to shoot down; (*animal*) to shoot, kill; (*fig*) to wear out, tire out; to demoralize; **s'abattre** *vi* to crash down; **ne pas se laisser ~** to keep one's spirits up, not to let things get one down; **s'~ sur** to beat down on; (*coups, injures*) to rain down on; **~ du travail** *ou* **de la besogne** to get through a lot of work
abbaye [abei] *nf* abbey
abbé [abe] *nm* priest; (*d'abbaye*) abbot
abcès [apsɛ] *nm* abscess
abdiquer [abdike] /1/ *vi* to abdicate
abdominal, e, -aux [abdɔminal, -o] *adj* abdominal; **abdominaux** *nmpl*: **faire des abdominaux** to do sit-ups
abeille [abɛj] *nf* bee
aberrant, e [abeʀā, -āt] *adj* absurd
aberration [abeʀasjɔ̃] *nf* aberration
abîme [abim] *nm* abyss, gulf
abîmer [abime] /1/ *vt* to spoil, damage; **s'abîmer** *vi* to get spoilt *ou* damaged
aboiement [abwamā] *nm* bark, barking *no pl*
abolir [abɔliʀ] /2/ *vt* to abolish
abominable [abɔminabl] *adj* abominable
abondance [abɔ̃dās] *nf* abundance
abondant, e [abɔ̃dā, -āt] *adj* plentiful, abundant, copious; **abonder** /1/ *vi* to abound, be plentiful; **abonder dans le sens de qn** to concur with sb
abonné, e [abɔne] *nm/f* subscriber; season ticket holder

abonnement [abɔnmɑ̃] *nm* subscription; (*pour transports en commun, concerts*) season ticket

abonner [abɔne] /1/ *vt*: **s'abonner à** to subscribe to, take out a subscription to; **s'~ aux tweets de qn sur Twitter** to follow sb on Twitter

abord [abɔʀ] *nm*: **abords** *nmpl* (*environs*) surroundings; **d'~** first; **au premier ~** at first sight, initially

abordable [abɔʀdabl] *adj* (*personne*) approachable; (*prix*) reasonable

aborder [abɔʀde] /1/ *vi* to land ▷ *vt* (*sujet, difficulté*) to tackle; (*personne*) to approach; (*rivage etc*) to reach

aboutir [abutiʀ] /2/ *vi* (*négociations etc*) to succeed; **~ à/dans/sur** to end up at/in/on; **n'~ à rien** to come to nothing

aboyer [abwaje] /8/ *vi* to bark

abréger [abʀeʒe] /3, 6/ *vt* to shorten

abreuver [abʀœve] /1/: **s'abreuver** *vi* to drink; **abreuvoir** *nm* watering place

abréviation [abʀevjasjɔ̃] *nf* abbreviation

abri [abʀi] *nm* shelter; **être à l'~** to be under cover; **se mettre à l'~** to shelter; **à l'~ de** sheltered from; (*danger*) safe from

abricot [abʀiko] *nm* apricot

abriter [abʀite] /1/ *vt* to shelter; **s'abriter** *vi* to shelter, take cover

abrupt, e [abʀypt] *adj* sheer, steep; (*ton*) abrupt

abruti, e [abʀyti] *adj* stunned, dazed ▷ *nm/f* (*fam*) idiot; **~ de travail** overworked

absence [apsɑ̃s] *nf* absence; (*Méd*) blackout; **en l'~ de** in the absence of; **avoir des ~s** to have memory blanks

absent, e [apsɑ̃, -ɑ̃t] *adj* absent ▷ *nm/f* absentee; **absenter** /1/: **s'absenter** *vi* to take time off work; (*sortir*) to leave, go out

absolu, e [apsɔly] *adj* absolute; **absolument** *adv* absolutely

absorbant, e [apsɔʀbɑ̃, -ɑ̃t] *adj* absorbent

absorber [apsɔʀbe] /1/ *vt* to absorb; (*gén, Méd: manger, boire*) to take

abstenir [apstəniʀ] /22/: **s'abstenir** *vi*: **s'~ de qch/de faire** to refrain from sth/ from doing

abstrait, e [apstʀɛ, -ɛt] *adj* abstract

absurde [apsyʀd] *adj* absurd

abus [aby] *nm* abuse; **~ de confiance** breach of trust; **il y a de l'~!** (*fam*) that's a bit much!; **abuser** /1/ *vi* to go too far, overstep the mark; **s'abuser** *vi* (*se méprendre*) to be mistaken; **abuser de** (*violer, duper*) to take advantage of; **abusif, -ive** *adj* exorbitant; (*punition*) excessive

académie [akademi] *nf* academy; (*Scol: circonscription*) ≈ regional education authority; *see note* **"Académie française"**

• **ACADÉMIE FRANÇAISE**
•
• The *Académie française* was founded by
• Cardinal Richelieu in 1635, during the reign
• of Louis XIII. It is made up of forty elected
• scholars and writers who are known as
• 'les Quarante' or 'les Immortels'. One of
• the *Académie's* functions is to keep an
• eye on the development of the French
• language, and its recommendations are
• frequently the subject of lively public
• debate. It has produced several editions
• of its famous dictionary and also awards
• various literary prizes.

acajou [akaʒu] *nm* mahogany

acariâtre [akaʀjɑtʀ] *adj* cantankerous

accablant, e [akablɑ̃, -ɑ̃t] *adj* (*chaleur*) oppressive; (*témoignage, preuve*) overwhelming

accabler [akable] /1/ *vt* to overwhelm, overcome; **~ qn d'injures** to heap *ou* shower abuse on sb; **~ qn de travail** to overwork sb

accalmie [akalmi] *nf* lull

accaparer [akapaʀe] /1/ *vt* to monopolize; (*travail etc*) to take up (all) the time *ou* attention of

accéder [aksede] /6/: **~ à** *vt* (*lieu*) to reach; (*accorder: requête*) to grant, accede to

accélérateur [akseleʀatœʀ] *nm* accelerator

accélérer [akseleʀe] /6/ *vt* to speed up ▷ *vi* to accelerate

accent [aksɑ̃] *nm* accent; (*Phonétique, fig*) stress; **mettre l'~ sur** (*fig*) to stress; **~ aigu/grave/circonflexe** acute/grave/ circumflex accent; **accentuer** /1/ *vt* (*Ling*) to accent; (*fig*) to accentuate, emphasize; **s'accentuer** *vi* to become more marked *ou* pronounced

acceptation [aksɛptasjɔ̃] *nf* acceptance

accepter [aksɛpte] /1/ *vt* to accept; **~ de faire** to agree to do

accès [aksɛ] *nm* (*à un lieu*) access; (*Méd: de toux*) fit; (: *de fièvre*) bout; **d'~ facile/ malaisé** easily/not easily accessible; **facile d'~** easy to get to; **~ de colère** fit of anger; **accessible** *adj* accessible; (*livre, sujet*): **accessible à qn** within the reach of sb

accessoire [akseswaʀ] *adj* secondary; (*frais*) incidental ▷ *nm* accessory; (*Théât*) prop

accident [aksidɑ̃] *nm* accident; **par ~** by chance; **~ de la route** road accident; **accidenté, e** *adj* damaged *ou* injured (in an accident); (*relief, terrain*) uneven; hilly; **accidentel, le** *adj* accidental

acclamer [aklame] /1/ *vt* to cheer, acclaim

acclimater [aklimate] /1/: **s'acclimater** *vi* to become acclimatized

accolade [akɔlad] nf (amicale) embrace; (signe) brace

accommoder [akɔmɔde] /1/ vt (Culin) to prepare; **s'accommoder de** to put up with; (se contenter de) to make do with

accompagnateur, -trice [akɔpaɲatœr, -tris] nm/f (Mus) accompanist; (de voyage) guide; (de voyage organisé) courier

accompagner [akɔpaɲe] /1/ vt to accompany, be ou go ou come with; (Mus) to accompany

accompli, e [akɔpli] adj accomplished

accomplir [akɔplir] /2/ vt (tâche, projet) to carry out; (souhait) to fulfil; **s'accomplir** vi to be fulfilled

accord [akɔr] nm agreement; (entre des styles, tons etc) harmony; (Mus) chord; **se mettre d'~** to come to an agreement (with each other); **être d'~** to agree; **d'~!** OK!

accordéon [akɔrdeɔ̃] nm (Mus) accordion

accorder [akɔrde] /1/ vt (faveur, délai) to grant; **~ de l'importance/de la valeur à qch** to attach importance/value to sth; (harmoniser) to match; (Mus) to tune

accoster [akɔste] /1/ vt (Navig) to draw alongside ▷ vi to berth

accouchement [akuʃmɑ̃] nm delivery, (child)birth; labour

accoucher [akuʃe] /1/ vi to give birth, have a baby; **~ d'un garçon** to give birth to a boy

accouder [akude] /1/: **s'accouder** vi: **s'~ à/contre/sur** to rest one's elbows on/ against/on; **accoudoir** nm armrest

accoupler [akuple] /1/ vt to couple; (pour la reproduction) to mate; **s'accoupler** vi to mate

accourir [akurir] /11/ vi to rush ou run up

accoutumance [akutymɑ̃s] nf (gén) adaptation; (Méd) addiction

accoutumé, e [akutyme] adj (habituel) customary, usual

accoutumer [akutyme] /1/ vt: **s'accoutumer à** to get accustomed ou used to

accroc [akro] nm (déchirure) tear; (fig) hitch, snag

accrochage [akrɔʃaʒ] nm (Auto) (minor) collision; (dispute) clash, brush

accrocher [akrɔʃe] /1/ vt (suspendre) to hang; (fig) to catch, attract; **s'accrocher** (se disputer) to have a clash ou brush; **~ qch à** (suspendre) to hang sth (up) on; (attacher: remorque) to hitch sth (up) to; (déchirer) to catch sth (on); **il a accroché ma voiture** he bumped into my car; **s'~ à** (rester pris à) to catch on; (agripper, fig) to hang on ou cling to

accroissement [akrwasmɑ̃] nm increase

accroître [akrwatr] /55/ vt: **s'accroître** vi to increase

accroupir [akrupir] /2/: **s'accroupir** vi to squat, crouch (down)

accru, e [akry] pp de **accroître**

accueil [akœj] nm welcome; **comité/ centre d'~** reception committee/centre; **accueillir** /12/ vt to welcome; (aller chercher) to meet, collect

accumuler [akymyle] /1/ vt to accumulate, amass; **s'accumuler** vi to accumulate; to pile up

accusation [akyzasjɔ̃] nf (gén) accusation; (Jur) charge; (partie): **l'~** the prosecution

accusé, e [akyze] nm/f accused; (prévenu(e)) defendant ▷ nm: **~ de réception** acknowledgement of receipt

accuser [akyze] /1/ vt to accuse; (fig) to emphasize, bring out; (: montrer) to show; **~ qn de** to accuse sb of; (Jur) to charge sb with; **~ réception de** to acknowledge receipt of

acéré, e [asere] adj sharp

acharné, e [aʃarne] adj (lutte, adversaire) fierce, bitter; (travail) relentless

acharner [aʃarne] /1/: **s'acharner** vi: **s'~ sur** to go at fiercely; **s'~ contre** to set o.s. against; (malchance) to hound; **s'~ à faire** to try doggedly to do; to persist in doing

achat [aʃa] nm purchase; **faire l'~ de** to buy; **faire des ~s** to do some shopping

acheter [aʃte] /5/ vt to buy, purchase; (soudoyer) to buy; **~ qch à** (marchand) to buy ou purchase sth from; (ami etc: offrir) to buy sth for; **acheteur, -euse** nm/f buyer; shopper; (Comm) buyer

achever [aʃ(ə)ve] /5/ vt to complete, finish; (blessé) to finish off; **s'achever** vi to end

acide [asid] adj sour, sharp; (Chimie) acid(ic) ▷ nm acid; **acidulé, e** adj slightly acid; **bonbons acidulés** acid drops

acier [asje] nm steel; **aciérie** nf steelworks sg

acné [akne] nf acne

acompte [akɔ̃t] nm deposit

à-côté [akote] nm side-issue; (argent) extra

à-coup [aku] nm: **par ~s** by fits and starts

acoustique [akustik] nf (d'une salle) acoustics pl

acquéreur [akerœr] nm buyer, purchaser

acquérir [akerir] /21/ vt to acquire

acquis, e [aki, -iz] pp de **acquérir** ▷ nm (accumulated) experience; **son aide nous est ~e** we can count on ou be sure of his help

acquitter [akite] /1/ vt (Jur) to acquit; (facture) to pay, settle; **s'~ de** to discharge; (promesse, tâche) to fulfil

âcre [ɑkr] adj acrid, pungent

acrobate [akrɔbat] nm/f acrobat; **acrobatie** nf acrobatics sg

acte [akt] nm act, action; (Théât) act; **prendre ~ de** to note, take note of; **faire ~ de présence** to put in an appearance; **faire ~ de candidature** to submit an application; **~ de mariage/naissance** marriage/birth certificate

acteur [aktœʀ] nm actor

actif, -ive [aktif, -iv] adj active ▷ nm (Comm) assets pl; (fig): **avoir à son ~** to have to one's credit; **population active** working population

action [aksjɔ̃] nf (gén) action; (Comm) share; **une bonne/mauvaise ~** a good/an unkind deed; **actionnaire** nm/f shareholder; **actionner** /1/ vt (mécanisme) to activate; (machine) to operate

activer [aktive] /1/ vt to speed up; **s'activer** vi to bustle about; (se hâter) to hurry up

activité [aktivite] nf activity; **en ~** (volcan) active; (fonctionnaire) in active life

actrice [aktʀis] nf actress

actualité [aktɥalite] nf (d'un problème) topicality; (événements): **l'~** current events; **les ~s** (Ciné, TV) the news; **d'~** topical

actuel, le [aktɥɛl] adj (présent) present; (d'actualité) topical; **à l'heure ~le** at this moment in time; **actuellement** [aktɥɛlmɑ̃] adv at present, at the present time

▌ Attention à ne pas traduire actuellement par actually.

acupuncture [akypɔ̃ktyʀ] nf acupuncture

adaptateur, -trice [adaptatœʀ, -tʀis] nm/f adapter

adapter [adapte] /1/ vt to adapt; **s'~ (à)** (personne) to adapt (to); **~ qch à** (approprier) to adapt sth to (fit); **~ qch sur/dans/à** (fixer) to fit sth on/into/to

addition [adisjɔ̃] nf addition; (au café) bill; **additionner** /1/ vt to add (up)

adepte [adɛpt] nm/f follower

adéquat, e [adekwa(t), -at] adj appropriate, suitable

adhérent, e [adeʀɑ̃, -ɑ̃t] nm/f member

adhérer [adeʀe] /6/: **~ à** (coller) to adhere ou stick to; (se rallier à: parti, club) to join; **adhésif, -ive** adj adhesive, sticky; **ruban adhésif** ou **adhesive tape**

adieu, x [adjø] excl goodbye ▷ nm farewell

adjectif [adʒɛktif] nm adjective

adjoint, e [adʒwɛ̃, -wɛ̃t] nm/f assistant; **~ au maire** deputy mayor; **directeur ~** assistant manager

admettre [admɛtʀ] /56/ vt (visiteur) to admit; (candidat: Scol) to pass; (tolérer) to allow, accept; (reconnaître) to admit, acknowledge

administrateur, -trice [administʀatœʀ, -tʀis] nm/f (Comm) director; (Admin) administrator

administration [administʀasjɔ̃] nf administration; **l'A~** ≈ the Civil Service

administrer [administʀe] /1/ vt (firme) to manage, run; (biens, remède, sacrement etc) to administer

admirable [admiʀabl] adj admirable, wonderful

admirateur, -trice [admiʀatœʀ, -tʀis] nm/f admirer

admiration [admiʀasjɔ̃] nf admiration

admirer [admiʀe] /1/ vt to admire

admis, e [admi, -iz] pp de **admettre**

admissible [admisibl] adj (candidat) eligible; (comportement) admissible, acceptable

ADN sigle m (= acide désoxyribonucléique) DNA

ado [ado] (fam) nm/f teen

adolescence [adolesɑ̃s] nf adolescence

adolescent, e [adolesɑ̃, -ɑ̃t] nm/f adolescent, teenager

adopter [adopte] /1/ vt to adopt; **adoptif, -ive** adj (parents) adoptive; (fils, patrie) adopted

adorable [adoʀabl] adj adorable

adorer [adoʀe] /1/ vt to adore; (Rel) to worship

adosser [adose] /1/ vt: **~ qch à** ou **contre** to stand sth against; **s'~ à** ou **contre** to lean with one's back against

adoucir [adusiʀ] /2/ vt (goût, température) to make milder; (avec du sucre) to sweeten; (peau, voix, eau) to soften; **s'adoucir** vi (caractère) to mellow

adresse [adʀɛs] nf skill, dexterity; (domicile) address; **~ électronique** email address

adresser [adʀese] /1/ vt (lettre: expédier) to send; (: écrire l'adresse sur) to address; (injure, compliments) to address; **s'adresser à** (parler à) to speak to, address; (s'informer auprès de) to go and see (: bureau) to enquire at; (livre, conseil) to be aimed at; **~ la parole à qn** to speak to ou address sb

adroit, e [adʀwa, -wat] adj skilled

ADSL sigle m (= asymmetrical digital subscriber line) ADSL, broadband

adulte [adylt] nm/f adult, grown-up ▷ adj (personne, attitude) adult, grown-up; (chien, arbre) fully-grown, mature

adverbe [advɛʀb] nm adverb

adversaire [advɛʀsɛʀ] nm/f (Sport, gén) opponent, adversary

aération [aeʀasjɔ̃] nf airing; (circulation de l'air) ventilation

aérer [aeʀe] /6/ vt to air; (fig) to lighten

aérien, ne [aeʀjɛ̃, -ɛn] adj (Aviat) air cpd, aerial; (câble, métro) overhead; (fig) light; **compagnie ~ne** airline (company)

aéro: aérobic nf aerobics sg; **aérogare** nf airport (buildings); (en ville) air terminal; **aéroglisseur** nm hovercraft; **aérophagie** nf (Méd) wind, aerophagia (Méd); **aéroport** nm airport; **aérosol** nm aerosol

affaiblir [afebliʀ] /2/: **s'affaiblir** vi to weaken

affaire [afɛʀ] nf (problème, question) matter; (criminelle, judiciaire) case; (scandaleuse etc) affair; (entreprise) business; (marché, transaction) (business) deal, (piece of) business no pl; (occasion intéressante) good deal; **affaires** nfpl affairs; (activité commerciale) business sg; (effets personnels) things, belongings; **~s de sport** sports gear; **tirer qn/se tirer d'~** to get sb/o.s. out of trouble; **ceci fera l'~** this will do (nicely); **avoir ~ à** (en contact) to be dealing with; **ce sont mes ~s** (cela me concerne) that's my business; **occupe-toi de tes ~s!** mind your own business!; **les ~s étrangères** (Pol) foreign affairs; **affairer** /1/: **s'affairer** vi to busy o.s., bustle about

affamé, e [afame] adj starving

affecter [afɛkte] /1/ vt to affect; **~ qch à** to allocate ou allot sth to; **~ qn à** to appoint sb to; (diplomate) to post sb to

affectif, -ive [afɛktif, -iv] adj emotional

affection [afɛksjɔ̃] nf affection; (mal) ailment; **affectionner** /1/ vt to be fond of; **affectueux, -euse** adj affectionate

affichage [afiʃaʒ] nm billposting; (électronique) display; **"~ interdit"** "stick no bills"; **~ à cristaux liquides** liquid crystal display, LCD

affiche [afiʃ] nf poster; (officielle) (public) notice; (Théât) bill; **être à l'~** to be on

afficher [afiʃe] /1/ vt (affiche) to put up; (réunion) to put up a notice about; (électroniquement) to display; (fig) to exhibit, display; **s'afficher** vi (péj) to flaunt o.s.; (électroniquement) to be displayed; **"défense d'~"** "no bill posters"

affilée [afile]: **d'~** adv at a stretch

affirmatif, -ive [afiʀmatif, -iv] adj affirmative

affirmer [afiʀme] /1/ vt to assert

affligé, e [afliʒe] adj distressed, grieved; **~ de** (maladie, tare) afflicted with

affliger [afliʒe] /3/ vt (peiner) to distress, grieve

affluence [aflyɑ̃s] nf crowds pl; **heures d'~** rush hour sg; **jours d'~** busiest days

affluent [aflyɑ̃] nm tributary

affolement [afɔlmɑ̃] nm panic

affoler [afɔle] /1/ vt to throw into a panic; **s'affoler** vi to panic

affranchir [afʀɑ̃ʃiʀ] /2/ vt to put a stamp ou stamps on; (à la machine) to frank (BRIT), meter (US); (fig) to free, liberate; **affranchissement** nm postage

affreux, -euse [afʀø, -øz] adj dreadful, awful

affront [afʀɔ̃] nm affront; **affrontement** nm clash, confrontation

affronter [afʀɔ̃te] /1/ vt to confront, face

affût [afy] nm: **à l'~ (de)** (gibier) lying in wait (for); (fig) on the look-out (for)

Afghanistan [afganistɑ̃] nm: **l'~** Afghanistan

afin [afɛ̃]: **~ que** conj so that, in order that; **~ de faire** in order to do, so as to do

africain, e [afʀikɛ̃, -ɛn] adj African ▷ nm/f: **A~, e** African

Afrique [afʀik] nf: **l'~** Africa; **l'~ australe/du Nord/du Sud** southern/North/South Africa

agacer [agase] /3/ vt to irritate

âge [aʒ] nm age; **quel ~ as-tu?** how old are you?; **prendre de l'~** to be getting on (in years); **le troisième ~** (personnes âgées) senior citizens; (période) retirement; **âgé, e** adj old, elderly; **âgé de 10 ans** 10 years old

agence [aʒɑ̃s] nf agency, office; (succursale) branch; **~ immobilière** estate agent's (office) (BRIT), real estate office (US); **~ de voyages** travel agency

agenda [aʒɛ̃da] nm diary; **~ électronique** PDA

┃ Attention à ne pas traduire agenda par le mot anglais agenda.

agenouiller [aʒ(ə)nuje] /1/: **s'agenouiller** vi to kneel (down)

agent, e [aʒɑ̃, -ɑ̃t] nm/f (aussi: **~(e) de police**) police officer; (Admin) official, officer; **~ immobilier** estate agent (BRIT), realtor (US)

agglomération [aglɔmeʀasjɔ̃] nf town; (Auto) built-up area; **l'~ parisienne** the urban area of Paris

aggraver [agʀave] /1/: **s'aggraver** vi to worsen

agile [aʒil] adj agile, nimble

agir [aʒiʀ] /2/ vi to act; **il s'agit de** it's a matter ou question of; (ça traite de) it is about; **il s'agit de faire** we (ou you etc) must do; **de quoi s'agit-il?** what is it about?

agitation [aʒitasjɔ̃] nf (hustle and) bustle; (trouble) agitation, excitement; (politique) unrest, agitation

agité, e [aʒite] adj fidgety, restless; (troublé) agitated, perturbed; (mer) rough

agiter [aʒite] /1/ vt (bouteille, chiffon) to shake; (bras, mains) to wave; (préoccuper, exciter) to trouble

agneau, x [aɲo] nm lamb

agonie [agɔni] nf mortal agony, death pangs pl; (fig) death throes pl

agrafe [agʀaf] nf (de vêtement) hook, fastener; (de bureau) staple; **agrafer** /1/ vt to fasten; to staple; **agrafeuse** [agʀaføz] nf stapler

agrandir [agʀɑ̃diʀ] /2/ vt to extend; **s'agrandir** vi (ville, famille) to grow, expand; (trou, écart) to get bigger; **agrandissement** nm (photographie) enlargement

agréable [agʀeabl] adj pleasant, nice

agréé, e [agʀee] adj: **concessionnaire ~** registered dealer

agréer [agʀee] /1/ vt (requête) to accept; **~ à** to please, suit; **veuillez ~, Monsieur/Madame, mes salutations distinguées**

(*personne nommée*) yours sincerely; (*personne non nommée*) yours faithfully

agrégation [agʀegasjɔ̃] *nf* highest teaching diploma in France; **agrégé, e** *nm/f* holder of the *agrégation*

agrément [agʀemɑ̃] *nm* (*accord*) consent, approval; (*attraits*) charm, attractiveness; (*plaisir*) pleasure

agresser [agʀese] /1/ *vt* to attack; **agresseur** *nm* aggressor, attacker; (*Pol, Mil*) aggressor; **agressif, -ive** *adj* aggressive

agricole [agʀikɔl] *adj* agricultural; **agriculteur, -trice** *nm/f* farmer; **agriculture** *nf* agriculture; farming

agripper [agʀipe] /1/ *vt* to grab, clutch; **s'~ à** to cling (on) to, clutch, grip

agroalimentaire [agʀɔalimɑ̃tɛʀ] *nm* farm-produce industry

agrumes [agʀym] *nmpl* citrus fruit(s)

aguets [agɛ] *aux* **~** *adv*; **être aux ~** to be on the look-out

ai [ɛ] *vb voir* **avoir**

aide [ɛd] *nm/f* assistant ▷ *nf* assistance, help; (*secours financier*) aid; **à l'~ de** with the help *ou* aid of; **appeler (qn) à l'~** to call for help (from sb); **à l'~!** help!; **~ judiciaire** legal aid; **~ ménagère** *nf* ≈ home help (BRIT) *ou* helper (US); **aide-mémoire** *nm inv* memoranda pages *pl*; (*key facts*) handbook

aider [ede] /1/ *vt* to help; **~ à qch** to help (towards) sth; **~ qn à faire qch** to help sb to do sth; **s'~ de** (*se servir de*) to use, make use of

aide-soignant, e [ɛdswanjɑ̃, -ɑ̃t] *nm/f* auxiliary nurse

aie *etc* [ɛ] *vb voir* **avoir**

aïe [aj] *excl* ouch!

aigle [ɛgl] *nm* eagle

aigre [ɛgʀ] *adj* sour, sharp; (*fig*) sharp, cutting; **aigre-doux, -douce** *adj* (*sauce*) sweet and sour; **aigreur** *nf* sourness; sharpness

aigu, ë [egy] *adj* (*objet, arête*) sharp; (*son, voix*) high-pitched, shrill; (*note*) high(-pitched)

aiguille [eguij] *nf* needle; (*de montre*) hand; **~ à tricoter** knitting needle

aiguiser [egize] /1/ *vt* to sharpen; (*fig*) to stimulate (: *sens*) to excite

ail [aj] *nm* garlic

aile [ɛl] *nf* wing; **aileron** *nm* (*de requin*) fin; **ailier** *nm* winger

aille *etc* [aj] *vb voir* **aller**

ailleurs [ajœʀ] *adv* elsewhere, somewhere else; **partout/nulle part ~** everywhere/nowhere else; **d'~** (*du reste*) moreover, besides; **par ~** (*d'autre part*) moreover, furthermore

aimable [ɛmabl] *adj* kind, nice

aimant [ɛmɑ̃] *nm* magnet

aimer [eme] /1/ *vt* to love; (*d'amitié, affection, par goût*) to like; **j'aimerais ...** (*souhait*) I would like ...; **j'aime faire du ski** I like skiing; **je t'aime** I love you; **bien ~ qn/qch** to like sb/sth; **j'aime mieux Paul (que Pierre)** I prefer Paul (to Pierre); **j'aimerais autant** *ou* **mieux y aller maintenant** I'd sooner *ou* rather go now

aine [ɛn] *nf* groin

aîné, e [ene] *adj* elder, older; (*le plus âgé*) eldest, oldest ▷ *nm/f* oldest child *ou* one, oldest boy *ou* son/girl *ou* daughter

ainsi [ɛ̃si] *adv* (*de cette façon*) like this, in this way, thus; (*ce faisant*) thus ▷ *conj* thus, so; **~ que** (*comme*) (just) as; (*et aussi*) as well as; **pour ~ dire** so to speak; **et ~ de suite** and so on (and so forth)

air [ɛʀ] *nm* air; (*mélodie*) tune; (*expression*) look, air; **paroles/menaces en l'~** empty words/threats; **prendre l'~** to get some (fresh) air; **avoir l'~** (*sembler*) to look, appear; **avoir l'~ triste** to look *ou* seem sad; **avoir l'~ de qch** to look like sth; **avoir l'~ de faire** to look as though one is doing

airbag [ɛʀbag] *nm* airbag

aisance [ɛzɑ̃s] *nf* ease; (*richesse*) affluence

aise [ɛz] *nf* comfort; **être à l'~** *ou* **à son ~** to be comfortable; (*pas embarrassé*) to be at ease; (*financièrement*) to be comfortably off; **se mettre à l'~** to make o.s. comfortable; **être mal à l'~** *ou* **à son ~** to be uncomfortable; (*gêné*) to be ill at ease; **en faire à son ~** to do as one likes; **aisé, e** *adj* easy; (*assez riche*) well-to-do, well-off

aisselle [ɛsɛl] *nf* armpit

ait [ɛ] *vb voir* **avoir**

ajonc [aʒɔ̃] *nm* gorse *no pl*

ajourner [aʒuʀne] /1/ *vt* (*réunion*) to adjourn; (*décision*) to defer, postpone

ajouter [aʒute] /1/ *vt* to add

alarme [alaʀm] *nf* alarm; **donner l'~** to give *ou* raise the alarm; **alarmer** /1/ *vt* to alarm; **s'alarmer** *vi* to become alarmed

Albanie [albani] *nf*: **l'~** Albania

album [albɔm] *nm* album

alcool [alkɔl] *nm*: **l'~** alcohol; **un ~** a spirit, a brandy; **bière sans ~** non-alcoholic *ou* alcohol-free beer; **~ à brûler** methylated spirits (BRIT), wood alcohol (US); **~ à 90°** surgical spirit; **alcoolique** *adj, nm/f* alcoholic; **alcoolisé, e** *adj* alcoholic; **une boisson non alcoolisée** a soft drink; **alcoolisme** *nm* alcoholism; **alco(o)test®** *nm* Breathalyser®; (*test*) breath-test

aléatoire [aleatwaʀ] *adj* uncertain; (*Inform, Statistique*) random

alentour [alɑ̃tuʀ] *adv* around (about); **alentours** *nmpl* surroundings; **aux ~s de** in the vicinity *ou* neighbourhood of, around about; (*temps*) around about

alerte [alɛʀt] *adj* agile, nimble; (*style*) brisk, lively ▷ *nf* alert; warning; **~ à la bombe** bomb scare; **alerter** /1/ *vt* to alert

algèbre [alʒɛbʀ] *nf* algebra

Alger [alʒe] *n* Algiers

Algérie [alʒeʀi] *nf*: **l'~** Algeria; **algérien, ne** *adj* Algerian ▷ *nm/f*: **Algérien, ne** Algerian

algue [alg] *nf* seaweed *no pl*; (*Bot*) alga

alibi [alibi] *nm* alibi

aligner [aliɲe] /1/ *vt* to align, line up; (*idées, chiffres*) to string together; (*adapter*): **~ qch sur** to bring sth into alignment with; **s'aligner** (*soldats etc*) to line up; **s'~ sur** (*Pol*) to align o.s. with

aliment [alimã] *nm* food; **alimentation** *nf* (*en eau etc, de moteur*) supplying; (*commerce*) food trade; (*régime*) diet; (*Inform*) feed; **alimentation (générale)** (general) grocer's; **alimenter** /1/ *vt* to feed; (*Tech*): **alimenter (en)** to supply (with), feed (with); (*fig*) to sustain, keep going

allaiter [alete] /1/ *vt* to (breast-)feed, nurse; (*animal*) to suckle

allécher [aleʃe] /6/ *vt*: **~ qn** to make sb's mouth water; to tempt sb, entice sb

allée [ale] *nf* (*de jardin*) path; (*en ville*) avenue, drive; **~s et venues** comings and goings

allégé, e [aleʒe] *adj* (*yaourt etc*) low-fat

alléger [aleʒe] /6, 3/ *vt* (*voiture*) to make lighter; (*chargement*) to lighten; (*souffrance*) to alleviate, soothe

Allemagne [almaɲ] *nf*: **l'~** Germany; **allemand, e** *adj* German ▷ *nm* (*Ling*) German ▷ *nm/f*: **Allemand, e** German

aller [ale] /9/ *nm* (*trajet*) outward journey; (*billet*) single (*BRIT*) *ou* one-way ticket (*US*) ▷ *vi* (*gén*) to go; **~ simple** (*billet*) single (*BRIT*) *ou* one-way ticket; **~ (et) retour (AR)** return trip *ou* journey (*BRIT*), round trip (*US*); (*billet*) return (*BRIT*) *ou* round-trip (*US*) ticket; **~ à** (*convenir*) to suit; (*forme, pointure etc*) to fit; **~ avec** (*couleurs, style etc*) to go (well) with; **je vais le faire/me fâcher** I'm going to do it/to get angry; **~ voir/chercher qn** to go and see/look for sb; **comment allez-vous?** how are you?; **comment ça va?** how are you?; (*affaires etc*) how are things?; **il va bien/mal** he's well/not well, he's fine/ill; **ça va bien/mal** (*affaires etc*) it's going well/not going well; **~ mieux** to be better; **allez!** come on!; **allons!** come now!

allergie [alɛʀʒi] *nf* allergy

allergique [alɛʀʒik] *adj*: **~ à** allergic to

alliance [aljɑ̃s] *nf* (*Mil, Pol*) alliance; (*bague*) wedding ring

allier [alje] /7/ *vt* (*Pol, gén*) to ally; (*fig*) to combine; **s'allier** to become allies; (*éléments, caractéristiques*) to combine

allô [alo] *excl* hullo, hallo

allocation [alɔkasjɔ̃] *nf* allowance; **~ (de) chômage** unemployment benefit; **~s familiales** ≈ child benefit

allonger [alɔ̃ʒe] /3/ *vt* to lengthen, make longer; (*étendre: bras, jambe*) to stretch (out); **s'allonger** *vi* to get longer; (*se coucher*) to lie down, stretch out; **~ le pas** to hasten one's step(s)

allumage [alymaʒ] *nm* (*Auto*) ignition

allume-cigare [alymsigaʀ] *nm inv* cigar lighter

allumer [alyme] /1/ *vt* (*lampe, phare, radio*) to put *ou* switch on; (*pièce*) to put *ou* switch the light(s) on in; (*feu, bougie, cigare, pipe, gaz*) to light; **s'allumer** *vi* (*lumière, lampe*) to come *ou* go on

allumette [alymɛt] *nf* match

allure [alyʀ] *nf* (*vitesse*) speed; (: *à pied*) pace; (*démarche*) walk; (*aspect, air*) look; **avoir de l'~** to have style; **à toute ~** at full speed

allusion [a(l)lyzjɔ̃] *nf* allusion; (*sous-entendu*) hint; **faire ~ à** to allude *ou* refer to; to hint at

🔵 **MOT-CLÉ**

alors [alɔʀ] *adv* **1** (*à ce moment-là*) then, at that time; **il habitait alors à Paris** he lived in Paris at that time

2 (*par conséquent*) then; **tu as fini? alors je m'en vais** have you finished? I'm going then

3: **et alors?** so (what)?

▶ *conj*: **alors que** (*au moment où*) when, as; **il est arrivé alors que je partais** he arrived as I was leaving; (*tandis que*) whereas, while; **alors que son frère travaillait dur, lui se reposait** while his brother was working hard, HE would rest; (*bien que*) even though; **il a été puni alors qu'il n'a rien fait** he was punished, even though he had done nothing

alourdir [aluʀdiʀ] /2/ *vt* to weigh down, make heavy

Alpes [alp] *nfpl*: **les ~** the Alps

alphabet [alfabɛ] *nm* alphabet; (*livre*) ABC (book)

alpinisme [alpinism] *nm* mountaineering, climbing

Alsace [alzas] *nf* Alsace; **alsacien, ne** *adj* Alsatian ▷ *nm/f*: **Alsacien, ne** Alsatian

altermondialisme [altɛʀmɔ̃djalism] *nm* anti-globalism; **altermondialiste** *adj*, *nm/f* anti-globalist

alternatif, -ive [altɛʀnatif, -iv] *adj* alternating ▷ *nf* alternative; **alternative** *nf* (*choix*) alternative; **alterner** /1/ *vt* to alternate

altitude [altityd] *nf* altitude, height

alto [alto] *nm* (*instrument*) viola

aluminium [alyminjɔm] *nm* aluminium
(*BRIT*), aluminum (*US*)
amabilité [amabilite] *nf* kindness
amaigrissant, e [amegrisã, -ãt] *adj*:
régime ~ slimming (*BRIT*) *ou* weight-
reduction (*US*) diet
amande [amãd] *nf* (*de l'amandier*) almond;
amandier *nm* almond (tree)
amant [amã] *nm* lover
amas [amɑ] *nm* heap, pile; **amasser** /1/ *vt*
to amass
amateur [amatœʀ] *nm* amateur; **en ~** (*péj*)
amateurishly; **~ de musique/sport** *etc*
music/sport *etc* lover
ambassade [ãbasad] *nf* embassy;
l'~ de France the French Embassy;
ambassadeur, -drice *nm/f* ambassador/
ambassadress
ambiance [ãbjãs] *nf* atmosphere; **il y a de
l'~** everyone's having a good time
ambigu, ë [ãbigy] *adj* ambiguous
ambitieux, -euse [ãbisjø, -jøz] *adj*
ambitious
ambition [ãbisjɔ̃] *nf* ambition
ambulance [ãbylãs] *nf* ambulance;
ambulancier, -ière *nm/f* ambulanceman/
woman (*BRIT*), paramedic (*US*)
âme [ɑm] *nf* soul; **~ sœur** kindred spirit
amélioration [ameljɔʀasjɔ̃] *nf*
improvement
améliorer [ameljɔʀe] /1/ *vt* to improve;
s'améliorer *vi* to improve, get better
aménager [amenaʒe] /3/ *vt* (*agencer*) to fit
out; (: *terrain*) to lay out; (: *quartier, territoire*)
to develop; (*installer*) to fix up, put in; **ferme
aménagée** converted farmhouse
amende [amãd] *nf* fine; **faire ~ honorable**
to make amends
amener [am(ə)ne] /5/ *vt* to bring; (*causer*)
to bring about; **s'amener** *vi* (*fam*) to show
up, turn up; **~ qn à qch/à faire** to lead sb
to sth/to do
amer, amère [amɛʀ] *adj* bitter
américain, e [ameʀikɛ̃, -ɛn] *adj* American
▷ *nm/f*: **A~, e** American
Amérique [ameʀik] *nf* America; **l'~
centrale** Central America; **l'~ latine** Latin
America; **l'~ du Nord** North America; **l'~ du
Sud** South America
amertume [amɛʀtym] *nf* bitterness
ameublement [amœbləmã] *nm*
furnishing; (*meubles*) furniture
ami, e [ami] *nm/f* friend; (*amant/maîtresse*)
boyfriend/girlfriend ▷ *adj*: **pays/groupe ~**
friendly country/group; **petit ~/petite ~e**
boyfriend/girlfriend
amiable [amjabl]: **à l'~** *adv* (*Jur*) out of
court; (*gén*) amicably
amiante [amjãt] *nm* asbestos
amical, e, -aux [amikal, -o] *adj* friendly;
amicalement *adv* in a friendly way;
(*formule épistolaire*) regards

amincir [amɛ̃siʀ] /2/ *vt*: **~ qn** to make sb
thinner *ou* slimmer; (*vêtement*) to make sb
look slimmer
amincissant, e [amɛ̃sisã, -ãt] *adj*
slimming; **régime ~** diet; **crème ~e**
slimming cream
amiral, -aux [amiʀal, -o] *nm* admiral
amitié [amitje] *nf* friendship; **prendre en
~** to take a liking to; **faire** *ou* **présenter ses
~s à qn** to send sb one's best wishes; **~s**
(*formule épistolaire*) (with) best wishes
amonceler [amɔ̃s(ə)le] /4/ *vt* to pile *ou*
heap up; **s'amonceler** to pile *ou* heap up;
(*fig*) to accumulate
amont [amɔ̃]: **en ~** *adv* upstream
amorce [amɔʀs] *nf* (*sur un hameçon*) bait;
(*explosif*) cap; (*tube*) primer; (: *contenu*)
priming; (*fig*: *début*) beginning(s), start
amortir [amɔʀtiʀ] /2/ *vt* (*atténuer*: *choc*) to
absorb, cushion; (: *bruit, douleur*) to deaden;
(*Comm*: *dette*) to pay off; **~ un abonnement**
to make a season ticket pay (for itself);
amortisseur *nm* shock absorber
amour [amuʀ] *nm* love; **faire l'~** to
make love; **amoureux, -euse** *adj* (*regard,
tempérament*) amorous; (*vie, problèmes*)
love *cpd*; (*personne*) in love; **être amoureux (de
qn)** to be in love (with sb) ▷ *nmpl* courting
couple(s); **amour-propre** *nm* self-esteem,
pride
ampère [ãpɛʀ] *nm* amp(ere)
amphithéâtre [ãfiteɑtʀ] *nm*
amphitheatre; (*d'université*) lecture hall *ou*
theatre
ample [ãpl] *adj* (*vêtement*) roomy, ample;
(*gestes, mouvement*) broad; (*ressources*)
ample; **amplement** *adv*: **amplement
suffisant** more than enough; **ampleur** *nf*
(*de dégâts, problème*) extent
amplificateur [ãplifikatœʀ] *nm*
amplifier
amplifier [ãplifje] /7/ *vt* (*fig*) to expand,
increase
ampoule [ãpul] *nf* (*électrique*) bulb; (*de
médicament*) phial; (*aux mains, pieds*) blister
amusant, e [amyzã, -ãt] *adj* (*divertissant,
spirituel*) entertaining, amusing; (*comique*)
funny, amusing
amuse-gueule [amyzgœl] *nm inv*
appetizer, snack
amusement [amyzmã] *nm* (*voir amusé*)
amusement; (*jeu etc*) pastime, diversion
amuser [amyze] /1/ *vt* (*divertir*) to
entertain, amuse; (*égayer, faire rire*) to
amuse; **s'amuser** *vi* (*jouer*) to amuse o.s.;
(*se divertir*) to enjoy o.s., have fun; (*fig*) to
mess around
amygdale [amidal] *nf* tonsil
an [ã] *nm* year; **être âgé de** *ou* **avoir 3 ans** to
be 3 (years old); **le jour de l'an, le premier
de l'an, le nouvel an** New Year's Day
analphabète [analfabɛt] *nm/f* illiterate

analyse [analiz] *nf* analysis; (*Méd*) test;
  analyser /1/ *vt* to analyse; (*Méd*) to test
ananas [anana(s)] *nm* pineapple
anatomie [anatɔmi] *nf* anatomy
ancêtre [ɑ̃sɛtʀ] *nm/f* ancestor
anchois [ɑ̃ʃwa] *nm* anchovy
ancien, ne [ɑ̃sjɛ̃, -jɛn] *adj* old; (*de jadis, de
  l'antiquité*) ancient; (*précédent, ex-*) former,
  old; (*par l'expérience*) senior ▷ *nm/f* (*dans
  une tribu etc*) elder; **ancienneté** *nf* (*Admin*)
  (length of) service; (*privilèges obtenus*)
  seniority
ancre [ɑ̃kʀ] *nf* anchor; **jeter/lever l'~** to
  cast/weigh anchor; **ancrer** /1/ *vt* (*Constr*:
  câble etc) to anchor; (*fig*) to fix firmly
Andorre [ɑ̃dɔʀ] *nf* Andorra
andouille [ɑ̃duj] *nf* (*Culin*) *sausage made of
  chitterlings*; (*fam*) clot, nit
âne [ɑn] *nm* donkey, ass; (*péj*) dunce
anéantir [aneɑ̃tiʀ] /2/ *vt* to annihilate,
  wipe out; (*fig*) to obliterate, destroy
anémie [anemi] *nf* anaemia; **anémique**
  adj anaemic
anesthésie [anɛstezi] *nf* anaesthesia;
  ~ générale/locale general/local
  anaesthetic; **faire une ~ locale à qn** to give
  sb a local anaesthetic
ange [ɑ̃ʒ] *nm* angel; **être aux ~s** to be over
  the moon
angine [ɑ̃ʒin] *nf* throat infection; **~ de
  poitrine** angina (pectoris)
anglais, e [ɑ̃glɛ, -ɛz] *adj* English ▷ *nm* (*Ling*)
  English ▷ *nm/f*: **A~, e** Englishman/woman;
  les A~ the English; **filer à l'~e** to take French
  leave
angle [ɑ̃gl] *nm* angle; (*coin*) corner
Angleterre [ɑ̃glətɛʀ] *nf*: **l'~** England
anglo... [ɑ̃glo] *préfixe* Anglo-, anglo( );
  anglophone *adj* English-speaking
angoisse [ɑ̃gwas] *nf*: **l'~** anguish *no pl*;
  angoissé, e *adj* (*personne*) distressed
anguille [ɑ̃gij] *nf* eel
animal, e, -aux [animal, -o] *adj, nm*
  animal
animateur, -trice [animatœʀ, tʀis]
  nm/f (*de télévision*) host; (*de groupe*) leader,
  organizer
animation [animasjɔ̃] *nf* (*voir animé*)
  busyness; liveliness; (*Ciné: technique*)
  animation
animé, e [anime] *adj* (*rue, lieu*) busy, lively;
  (*conversation, réunion*) lively, animated
animer [anime] /1/ *vt* (*ville, soirée*) to liven
  up; (*mettre en mouvement*) to drive
anis [ani(s)] *nm* (*Culin*) aniseed; (*Bot*) anise
ankyloser [ɑ̃kiloze] /1/: **s'ankyloser** *vi* to
  get stiff
anneau, x [ano] *nm* (*de rideau, bague*) ring;
  (*de chaîne*) link
année [ane] *nf* year
annexe [anɛks] *adj* (*problème*) related;
  (*document*) appended; (*salle*) adjoining ▷ *nf*

(*bâtiment*) annex(e); (*jointe à une lettre, un
  dossier*) enclosure
anniversaire [anivɛʀsɛʀ] *nm* birthday;
  (*d'un événement, bâtiment*) anniversary
annonce [anɔ̃s] *nf* announcement;
  (*signe, indice*) sign; (*aussi*: **~ publicitaire**)
  advertisement; **les petites ~s** the small *ou*
  classified ads
annoncer [anɔ̃se] /3/ *vt* to announce;
  (*être le signe de*) to herald; **s'annoncer
  bien/difficile** to look promising/
  difficult
annuaire [anɥɛʀ] *nm* yearbook, annual;
  ~ téléphonique (telephone) directory,
  phone book
annuel, le [anɥɛl] *adj* annual, yearly
annulation [anylasjɔ̃] *nf* cancellation
annuler [anyle] /1/ *vt* (*rendez vous, voyage*)
  to cancel, call off; (*jugement*) to quash
  (*BRIT*), repeal (*US*); (*Math, Physique*) to
  cancel out
anonymat [anɔnima] *nm* anonymity;
  garder l'~ to remain anonymous
anonyme [anɔnim] *adj* anonymous; (*fig*)
  impersonal
anorak [anɔʀak] *nm* anorak
anorexie [anɔʀɛksi] *nf* anorexia
anormal, e, -aux [anɔʀmal, -o] *adj*
  abnormal
ANPE *sigle f* (= *Agence nationale pour l'emploi*)
  national employment agency (*functions include
  job creation*)
antarctique [ɑ̃taʀktik] *adj* Antarctic ▷ *nm*:
  l'A~ the Antarctic
antenne [ɑ̃tɛn] *nf* (*de radio, télévision*) aerial;
  (*d'insecte*) antenna, feeler; (*poste avancé*)
  outpost; (*petite succursale*) sub-branch;
  passer à/avoir l'~ to go/be on the air;
  ~ parabolique satellite dish
antérieur, e [ɑ̃teʀjœʀ] *adj* (*d'avant*)
  previous, earlier; (*de devant*) front
anti... [ɑ̃ti] *préfixe* anti...; **antialcoolique**
  adj anti-alcohol; **antibiotique** *nm*
  antibiotic; **antibrouillard** *adj*: **phare
  antibrouillard** fog lamp
anticipation [ɑ̃tisipasjɔ̃] *nf*: **livre/film d'~**
  science fiction book/film
anticipé, e [ɑ̃tisipe] *adj*: **avec mes
  remerciements ~s** thanking you in advance
  ou anticipation
anticiper [ɑ̃tisipe] /1/ *vt* (*événement, coup*)
  to anticipate, foresee
anti: anticorps *nm* antibody; **antidote**
  nm antidote; **antigel** *nm* antifreeze;
  antihistaminique *nm* antihistamine
antillais, e [ɑ̃tijɛ, -ɛz] *adj* West Indian,
  Caribbean ▷ *nm/f*: **A~, e** West Indian,
  Caribbean
Antilles [ɑ̃tij] *nfpl*: **les ~** the West Indies;
  les Grandes/Petites ~ the Greater/Lesser
  Antilles
antilope [ɑ̃tilɔp] *nf* antelope

anti: antimite(s) *adj, nm*: **(produit) antimite(s)** mothproofer, moth repellent; **antimondialisation** *nf* anti-globalization; **antipathique** *adj* unpleasant, disagreeable; **antipelliculaire** *adj* anti-dandruff

antiquaire [ɑ̃tikɛʀ] *nm/f* antique dealer

antique [ɑ̃tik] *adj* antique; *(très vieux)* ancient, antiquated; **antiquité** *nf (objet)* antique; **l'Antiquité** Antiquity; **magasin/ marchand d'antiquités** antique shop/ dealer

anti: antirabique *adj* rabies *cpd*; **antirouille** *adj inv* anti-rust *cpd*; **antisémite** *adj* anti-Semitic; **antiseptique** *adj, nm* antiseptic; **antivirus** *nm (Inform)* antivirus (program); **antivol** *adj, nm*: **(dispositif) antivol** antitheft device

anxieux, -euse [ɑ̃ksjø, -jøz] *adj* anxious, worried

AOC *sigle f (= Appellation d'origine contrôlée)* guarantee of quality of wine

août [u(t)] *nm* August

apaiser [apeze] /1/ *vt (colère)* to calm, *(douleur)* to soothe; *(personne)* to calm (down), pacify; **s'apaiser** *vi (tempête, bruit)* to die down, subside; *(personne)* to calm down

apercevoir [apɛʀsəvwaʀ] /28/ *vt* to see; **s'apercevoir de** *vt* to notice; **s'~ que** to notice that

aperçu [apɛʀsy] *nm (vue d'ensemble)* general survey

apéritif, -ive [apeʀitif, -iv] *adj* which stimulates the appetite ▷ *nm (boisson)* aperitif; *(réunion)* (pre-lunch *ou* -dinner) drinks *pl*

à-peu-près [apøpʀɛ] *nm inv (péj)* vague approximation

apeuré, e [apœʀe] *adj* frightened, scared

aphte [aft] *nm* mouth ulcer

apitoyer [apitwaje] /8/ *vt* to move to pity; **s'~ (sur qn/qch)** to feel pity *ou* compassion (for sb/over sth)

aplatir [aplatiʀ] /2/ *vt* to flatten; **s'aplatir** *vi* to become flatter; *(écrasé)* to be flattened

aplomb [aplɔ̃] *nm (équilibre)* balance, equilibrium; *(fig)* self-assurance nerve; **d'~** steady

apostrophe [apɔstʀɔf] *nf (signe)* apostrophe

apparaître [apaʀɛtʀ] /57/ *vi* to appear

appareil [apaʀɛj] *nm (outil, machine)* piece of apparatus, device; *(électrique etc)* appliance; *(avion)* (aero)plane , aircraft *inv*; *(téléphonique)* telephone; *(dentier)* brace *(BRIT)*, braces *(US)*; **qui est à l'~?** who's speaking?; **dans le plus simple ~** in one's birthday suit; **~ (photo)** camera; **~ numérique** digital camera; **appareiller** /1/ *vi (Navig)* to cast off, get under way ▷ *vt (assortir)* to match up

apparemment [apaʀamɑ̃] *adv* apparently

apparence [apaʀɑ̃s] *nf* appearance; **en ~** apparently

apparent, e [apaʀɑ̃, -ɑ̃t] *adj* visible; *(évident)* obvious; *(superficiel)* apparent

apparenté, e [apaʀɑ̃te] *adj*: **~ à** related to; *(fig)* similar to

apparition [apaʀisjɔ̃] *nf* appearance; *(surnaturelle)* apparition

appartement [apaʀtəmɑ̃] *nm* flat *(BRIT)*, apartment *(US)*

appartenir [apaʀtəniʀ] /22/: **~ à** *vt* to belong to; **il lui appartient de** it is up to him to

apparu, e [apaʀy] *pp de* **apparaître**

appât [apɑ] *nm (Pêche)* bait; *(fig)* lure, bait

appel [apɛl] *nm* call; *(nominal)* roll call (: *Scol*) register; *(Mil: recrutement)* call-up; **faire ~ à** *(invoquer)* to appeal to; *(avoir recours à)* to call on; *(nécessiter)* to call for, require; **faire *ou* interjeter ~** *(Jur)* to appeal; **faire l'~** to call the roll; *(Scol)* to call the register; **sans ~** *(fig)* final, irrevocable; **~ d'offres** *(Comm)* invitation to tender; **faire un ~ de phares** to flash one's headlights; **~ (téléphonique)** (tele)phone call

appelé [ap(ə)le] *nm (Mil)* conscript

appeler [ap(ə)le] /4/ *vt* to call; *(faire venir: médecin etc)* to call, send for; **s'appeler** *vi*: **elle s'appelle Gabrielle** her name is Gabrielle, she's called Gabrielle; **comment vous appelez-vous?** what's your name?; **comment ça s'appelle?** what is it *ou* that called?

appendicite [apɑ̃disit] *nf* appendicitis

appesantir [apəzɑ̃tiʀ] /2/: **s'appesantir** *vi* to grow heavier; **s'~ sur** *(fig)* to dwell at length on

appétissant, e [apetisɑ̃, -ɑ̃t] *adj* appetizing, mouth-watering

appétit [apeti] *nm* appetite; **bon ~!** enjoy your meal!

applaudir [aplodiʀ] /2/ *vt* to applaud ▷ *vi* to applaud, clap; **applaudissements** *nmpl* applause *sg*, clapping *sg*

appli [apli] *nf* app

application [aplikasjɔ̃] *nf* application

appliquer [aplike] /1/ *vt* to apply; *(loi)* to enforce; **s'appliquer** *vi (élève etc)* to apply o.s.; **s'~ à** to apply to

appoint [apwɛ̃] *nm* (extra) contribution *ou* help; **avoir/faire l'~** to have/give the right change *ou* money; **chauffage d'~** extra heating

apporter [apɔʀte] /1/ *vt* to bring

appréciable [apʀesjabl] *adj* appreciable

apprécier [apʀesje] /7/ *vt* to appreciate; *(évaluer)* to estimate, assess

appréhender [apʀeɑ̃de] /1/ *vt (craindre)* to dread; *(arrêter)* to apprehend

apprendre [aprɑ̃dr] /58/ vt to learn; (événement, résultats) to learn of, hear of; **~ qch à qn** (informer) to tell sb (of) sth; (enseigner) to teach sb sth; **~ à faire qch** to learn to do sth; **~ à qn à faire qch** to teach sb to do sth; **apprenti, e** nm/f apprentice; **apprentissage** nm learning; (Comm, Scol: période) apprenticeship

apprêter [aprete] /1/: **s'apprêter** vi: **s'~ à qch/à faire qch** to prepare for sth/for doing sth

appris, e [apri, -iz] pp de **apprendre**

apprivoiser [aprivwaze] /1/ vt to tame

approbation [aprɔbasjɔ̃] nf approval

approcher [aprɔʃe] /1/ vi to approach, come near ▷ vt to approach; (rapprocher): **~ qch (de qch)** to bring ou put ou move sth near (to sth); **s'approcher de** to approach, go ou come ou move near to; **~ de** (lieu, but) to draw near to; (quantité, moment) to approach

approfondir [aprɔfɔ̃dir] /2/ vt to deepen; (question) to go further into

approprié, e [aprɔprije] adj: **~ (à)** appropriate (to), suited (to)

approprier [aprɔprije] /7/: **s'approprier** vt to appropriate, take over; **s'~ en** to stock up with

approuver [apruve] /1/ vt to agree with; (trouver louable) to approve of

approvisionner [aprɔvizjɔne] /1/ vt to supply; (compte bancaire) to pay funds into; **s'~ en** to stock up with

approximatif, -ive [aprɔksimatif, -iv] adj approximate, rough; (imprécis) vague

appt abr = **appartement**

appui [apɥi] nm support; **prendre ~ sur** to lean on; (objet) to rest on; **l'~ de la fenêtre** the windowsill, the window ledge

appuyer [apɥije] /8/ vt (poser, soutenir: personne, demande) to support, back (up) ▷ vi: **~ sur** (bouton) to press, push; (mot, détail) to stress, emphasize; **s'appuyer sur** vt to lean on; (compter sur) to rely on; **~ qch sur/contre/à** to lean ou rest sth on/against/on; **~ sur le frein** to brake, to apply the brakes

après [aprɛ] prép after ▷ adv afterwards; **deux heures ~** two hours later; **~ qu'il est parti/avoir fait** after he left/having done; **courir ~ qn** to run after sb; **crier ~ qn** to shout at sb; **être toujours ~ qn** (critiquer etc) to be always on at sb; **~ quoi** after which; **d'~** (selon) according to; **~ coup** after the event, afterwards; **~ tout** (au fond) after all; **et (puis) ~?** so what?; **après-demain** adv the day after tomorrow; **après-midi** nm ou f inv afternoon; **après-rasage** nm inv after-shave; **après-shampo(o)ing** nm inv conditioner; **après-ski** nm inv snow boot

après-soleil [aprɛsɔlɛj] adj inv after-sun cpd ▷ nm after-sun cream ou lotion

apte [apt] adj: **~ à qch/faire qch** capable of sth/doing sth; **~ (au service)** (Mil) fit (for service)

aquarelle [akwarɛl] nf watercolour

aquarium [akwarjɔm] nm aquarium

arabe [arab] adj Arabic; (désert, cheval) Arabian; (nation, peuple) Arab ▷ nm (Ling) Arabic ▷ nm/f: **A~** Arab

Arabie [arabi] nf: **l'~ Saoudite** ou **Séoudite** Saudi Arabia

arachide [araʃid] nf groundnut (plant); (graine) peanut, groundnut

araignée [areɲe] nf spider

arbitraire [arbitrɛr] adj arbitrary

arbitre [arbitr] nm (Sport) referee (: Tennis, Cricket) umpire; (fig) arbiter, judge; (Jur) arbitrator; **arbitrer** /1/ vt to referee, to umpire; to arbitrate

arbre [arbr] nm tree; (Tech) shaft

arbuste [arbyst] nm small shrub

arc [ark] nm (arme) bow; (Géom) arc; (Archit) arch; **en ~ de cercle** semi-circular

arcade [arkad] nf arch(way); **~s** arcade sg, arches

arc-en-ciel [arkɑ̃sjɛl] nm rainbow

arche [arʃ] nf arch; **~ de Noé** Noah's Ark

archéologie [arkeɔlɔʒi] nf arch(a)eology; **archéologue** nm/f arch(a)eologist

archet [arʃɛ] nm bow

archipel [arʃipɛl] nm archipelago

architecte [arʃitɛkt] nm architect

architecture [arʃitɛktyr] nf architecture

archives [arʃiv] nfpl (collection) archives

arctique [arktik] adj Arctic ▷ nm: **l'A~** the Arctic

ardent, e [ardɑ̃, -ɑ̃t] adj (soleil) blazing; (amour) ardent, passionate; (prière) fervent

ardoise [ardwaz] nf slate

ardu, e [ardy] adj (travail) arduous; (problème) difficult

arène [arɛn] nf arena; **arènes** nfpl bull-ring sg

arête [arɛt] nf (de poisson) bone; (d'une montagne) ridge

argent [arʒɑ̃] nm (métal) silver; (monnaie) money; **~ de poche** pocket money; **~ liquide** ready money, (ready) cash; **argenterie** nf silverware

argentin, e [arʒɑ̃tɛ̃, -in] adj Argentinian ▷ nm/f: **A~, e** Argentinian

Argentine [arʒɑ̃tin] nf: **l'~** Argentina

argentique [arʒɑ̃tik] adj (appareil photo) film cpd

argile [arʒil] nf clay

argot [argo] nm slang; **argotique** adj slang cpd; (très familier) slangy

argument [argymɑ̃] nm argument

argumenter [argymɑ̃te] /1/ vi to argue

aride [arid] adj arid

aristocratie [aristɔkrasi] nf aristocracy; **aristocratique** adj aristocratic

arithmétique [aritmetik] adj arithmetic(al) ▷ nf arithmetic

arme [aʀm] nf weapon; **armes** nfpl weapons, arms; (blason) (coat of) arms; **~ à feu** firearm; **~s de destruction massive** weapons of mass destruction

armée [aʀme] nf army; **~ de l'air** Air Force; **~ de terre** Army

armer [aʀme] /1/ vt to arm; (arme à feu) to cock; (appareil photo) to wind on; **s'armer** vi: **s'~ de** to arm o.s. with; **~ qch de** to reinforce sth with

armistice [aʀmistis] nm armistice; **l'A~** ≈ Remembrance (BRIT) ou Veterans (US) Day

armoire [aʀmwaʀ] nf (tall) cupboard; (penderie) wardrobe (BRIT), closet (US)

armure [aʀmyʀ] nf armour no pl, suit of armour; **armurier** nm gunsmith

arnaque [aʀnak] (fam) nf swindling; **c'est de l'~** it's daylight robbery; **arnaquer** /1/ (fam) vt to do (fam)

arobase [aʀɔbaz] nf (Inform) 'at' symbol; **"paul ~ société point fr"** "paul at société dot fr"

aromates [aʀɔmat] nmpl seasoning sg, herbs (and spices)

aromathérapie [aʀɔmateʀapi] nf aromatherapy

aromatisé, e [aʀɔmatize] adj flavoured

arôme [aʀom] nm aroma

arracher [aʀaʃe] /1/ vt to pull out; (page etc) to tear off, tear out; (légume, herbe, souche) to pull up; (bras etc) to tear off; **s'arracher** vt (article très recherché) to fight over; **~ qch à qn** to snatch sth from sb; (fig) to wring sth out of sb

arrangement [aʀɑ̃ʒmɑ̃] nm arrangement

arranger [aʀɑ̃ʒe] /3/ vt to arrange; (réparer) to fix, put right; (régler) to settle, sort out; (convenir à) to suit, be convenient for; **cela m'arrange** that suits me (fine); **s'arranger** vi (se mettre d'accord) to come to an agreement ou arrangement; **je vais m'~** I'll manage; **ça va s'~** it'll sort itself out

arrestation [aʀɛstasjɔ̃] nf arrest

arrêt [aʀɛ] nm stopping; (de bus etc) stop; (Jur) judgment, decision; **être à l'~** to be stopped; **rester** ou **tomber en ~ devant** to stop short in front of; **sans ~** non-stop; (fréquemment) continually; **~ de travail** stoppage (of work)

arrêter [aʀete] /1/ vt to stop; (chauffage etc) to turn off, switch off; (fixer: date etc) to appoint, decide on; (criminel, suspect) to arrest; **s'arrêter** vi to stop; **~ de faire** to stop doing

arrhes [aʀ] nfpl deposit sg

arrière [aʀjɛʀ] nm back; (Sport) fullback ▷ adj inv: **siège/roue ~** back ou rear seat/wheel; **à l'~** behind, at the back; **en ~** behind; (regarder) back, behind; (tomber, aller) backwards; **arrière-goût** nm aftertaste; **arrière-grand-mère** nf great-grandmother; **arrière-grand-père** nm

great-grandfather; **arrière-pays** nm inv hinterland; **arrière-pensée** nf ulterior motive; (doute) mental reservation; **arrière-plan** nm background; **à l'arrière-plan** in the background; **arrière-saison** nf late autumn

arrimer [aʀime] /1/ vt (cargaison) to stow; (fixer) to secure

arrivage [aʀivaʒ] nm consignment

arrivée [aʀive] nf arrival; (ligne d'arrivée) finish

arriver [aʀive] /1/ vi to arrive; (survenir) to happen, occur; **il arrive à Paris à 8 h** he gets to ou arrives in Paris at 8; **~ à** (atteindre) to reach; **~ à (faire) qch** to manage (to do) sth; **en ~ à faire ...** to end up doing ...; **il arrive que ...** it happens that ...; **il lui arrive de faire ...** he sometimes does ...

arrobase [aʀɔbaz] nf (Inform) 'at' symbol

arrogance [aʀɔgɑ̃s] nf arrogance

arrogant, e [aʀɔgɑ̃, -ɑ̃t] adj arrogant

arrondissement [aʀɔ̃dismɑ̃] nm (Admin) ≈ district

arroser [aʀoze] /1/ vt to water; (victoire etc) to celebrate (over a drink); (Culin) to baste; **arrosoir** nm watering can

arsenal, -aux [aʀsənal, -o] nm (Navig) naval dockyard; (Mil) arsenal; (fig) gear, paraphernalia

art [aʀ] nm art

artère [aʀtɛʀ] nf (Anat) artery; (rue) main road

arthrite [aʀtʀit] nf arthritis

artichaut [aʀtiʃo] nm artichoke

article [aʀtikl] nm article; (Comm) item, article; **à l'~ de la mort** at the point of death

articulation [aʀtikylasjɔ̃] nf articulation; (Anat) joint

articuler [aʀtikyle] /1/ vt to articulate

artificiel, le [aʀtifisjɛl] adj artificial

artisan [aʀtizɑ̃] nm artisan, (self-employed) craftsman; **artisanal, e, -aux** [aʀtizanal, -o] adj of ou made by craftsmen; (péj) cottage industry cpd; **de fabrication artisanale** home-made; **artisanat** [aʀtizana] nm arts and crafts pl

artiste [aʀtist] nm/f artist; (Théât, Mus) performer; (de variétés) entertainer; **artistique** adj artistic

as vb [a] voir **avoir** ▷ nm [ɑs] ace

ascenseur [asɑ̃sœʀ] nm lift (BRIT), elevator (US)

ascension [asɑ̃sjɔ̃] nf ascent; (de montagne) climb; **l'A~** (Rel) the Ascension

● **L'ASCENSION**

● The fête de l'Ascension is a public holiday
● in France. It always falls on a Thursday,
● usually in May. Many French people take
● the following Friday off work too and
● enjoy a long weekend.

asiatique [azjatik] *adj* Asian, Asiatic
▷ *nm/f*: **A~** Asian
Asie [azi] *nf*: **l'~** Asia
asile [azil] *nm* (*refuge*) refuge, sanctuary;
droit d'~ (*Pol*) (political) asylum
aspect [aspɛ] *nm* appearance, look; (*fig*)
aspect, side; **à l'~ de** at the sight of
asperge [aspɛʀʒ] *nf* asparagus *no pl*
asperger [aspɛʀʒe] /3/ *vt* to spray,
sprinkle
asphalte [asfalt] *nm* asphalt
asphyxier [asfiksje] /7/ *vt* to suffocate,
asphyxiate; (*fig*) to stifle
aspirateur [aspiʀatœʀ] *nm* vacuum
cleaner; **passer l'~** to vacuum
aspirer [aspiʀe] /1/ *vt* (*air*) to inhale;
(*liquide*) to suck (up); (*appareil*) to suck *ou*
draw up; **~ à** to aspire to
aspirine [aspiʀin] *nf* aspirin
assagir [asaʒiʀ] /2/ *vt*, **s'assagir** *vi* to
quieten down, settle down
assaillir [asajiʀ] /13/ *vt* to assail, attack
assaisonnement [asɛzɔnmɑ̃] *nm*
seasoning
assaisonner [asɛzɔne] /1/ *vt* to season
assassin [asasɛ̃] *nm* murderer; assassin;
assassiner /1/ *vt* to murder; (*Pol*) to
assassinate
assaut [aso] *nm* assault, attack; **prendre
d'~** to (take by) storm, assault; **donner l'~
(à)** to attack
assécher [aseʃe] /6/ *vt* to drain
assemblage [asɑ̃blaʒ] *nm* (*action*)
assembling; **un ~ de** (*fig*) a collection of
assemblée [asɑ̃ble] *nf* (*réunion*) meeting;
(*public, assistance*) gathering; (*Pol*)
assembly; **l'A~ nationale (AN)** the (French)
National Assembly
assembler [asɑ̃ble] /1/ *vt* (*joindre, monter*)
to assemble, put together; (*amasser*) to
gather (together), collect (together);
s'assembler *vi* to gather
asseoir [aswaʀ] /26/ *vt* (*malade, bébé*) to sit
up; (*personne debout*) to sit down; (*autorité,
réputation*) to establish; **s'asseoir** *vi* to sit
(o.s.) down
assez [ase] *adv* (*suffisamment*) enough,
sufficiently; (*passablement*) rather, quite,
fairly; **~ de pain/livres** enough *ou*
sufficient bread/books; **vous en avez ~?**
have you got enough?; **j'en ai ~!** I've had
enough!
assidu, e [asidy] *adj* assiduous,
painstaking; (*régulier*) regular
assied *etc* [asje] *vb voir* **asseoir**
assiérai *etc* [asjeʀe] *vb voir* **asseoir**
assiette [asjɛt] *nf* plate; (*contenu*)
plate(ful); **il n'est pas dans son ~** he's not
feeling quite himself; **~ à dessert** dessert *ou*
side plate; **~ anglaise** assorted cold meats;
~ creuse (soup) dish, soup plate; **~ plate**
(dinner) plate

assimiler [asimile] /1/ *vt* to assimilate,
absorb; (*comparer*): **~ qch/qn à** to liken *ou*
compare sth/sb to; **s'assimiler** *vi* (*s'intégrer*)
to be assimilated *ou* absorbed
assis, e [asi, -iz] *pp de* **asseoir** ▷ *adj* sitting
(down), seated
assistance [asistɑ̃s] *nf* (*public*) audience;
(*aide*) assistance; **enfant de l'A~ (publique)**
child in care
assistant, e [asistɑ̃, -ɑ̃t] *nm/f* assistant;
(*d'université*) probationary lecturer; **~e
sociale** social worker
assisté, e [asiste] *adj* (*Auto*) power-
assisted; **~ par ordinateur** computer-
assisted; **direction ~e** power steering
assister [asiste] /1/ *vt* to assist; **~ à** (*scène,
événement*) to witness; (*conférence*) to
attend, be (present) at; (*spectacle, match*)
to be at, see
association [asɔsjasjɔ̃] *nf* association
associé, e [asɔsje] *nm/f* associate; (*Comm*)
partner
associer [asɔsje] /7/ *vt* to associate;
~ qn à (*profits*) to give sb a share of; (*affaire*)
to make sb a partner in; (*joie, triomphe*)
to include sb in; **~ qch à** (*joindre, allier*) to
combine sth with; **s'associer** *vi* to join
together; **s'~ à** (*couleurs, qualités*) to be
combined with; (*opinions, joie de qn*) to
share in; **s'~ à** *ou* **avec qn pour faire** to join
(forces) *ou* join together with sb to do
assoiffé, e [aswafe] *adj* thirsty
assommer [asɔme] /1/ *vt* (*étourdir, abrutir*)
to knock out, stun
Assomption [asɔ̃psjɔ̃] *nf*: **l'~** the
Assumption

* **L'ASSOMPTION**

* The *fête de l'Assomption*, more commonly
* known as "le 15 août" is a national holiday
* in France. Traditionally, large numbers of
* holidaymakers leave home on 15 August,
* frequently causing chaos on the roads.

assorti, e [asɔʀti] *adj* matched, matching;
fromages/légumes ~s assorted cheeses/
vegetables; **~ à** matching; **assortiment**
nm assortment, selection
assortir [asɔʀtiʀ] /2/ *vt* to match; **~ qch à**
to match sth with; **~ qch de** to accompany
sth with
assouplir [asupliʀ] /2/ *vt* to make supple;
(*fig*) to relax; **assouplissant** *nm* (*fabric*)
softener
assumer [asyme] /1/ *vt* (*fonction, emploi*) to
assume, take on
assurance [asyʀɑ̃s] *nf* (*certitude*)
assurance; (*confiance en soi*) (self-)
confidence; (*contrat*) insurance (policy);
(*secteur commercial*) insurance; **~ au tiers**
third party insurance; **~ maladie (AM)**

health insurance; **~ tous risques** (Auto) comprehensive insurance; **~s sociales (AS)** ≈ National Insurance (BRIT), ≈ Social Security (US); **assurance-vie** nf life assurance ou insurance

assuré, e [asyʀe] adj (réussite, échec, victoire etc) certain, sure; (démarche, voix) assured; (pas) steady ▷ nm/f insured (person); **assurément** adv assuredly, most certainly

assurer [asyʀe] /1/ vt (Comm) to insure; (victoire etc) to ensure; (frontières, pouvoir) to make secure; (service, garde) to provide, operate; **s'assurer (contre)** (Comm) to insure o.s. (against); **~ à qn que** to assure sb that; **~ qn de** to assure sb of; **s'~ de/que** (vérifier) to make sure of/that; **s'~ (de)** (aide de qn) to secure

asthmatique [asmatik] adj, nm/f asthmatic

asthme [asm] nm asthma

asticot [astiko] nm maggot

astre [astʀ] nm star

astrologie [astʀɔlɔʒi] nf astrology

astronaute [astʀonot] nm/f astronaut

astronomie [astʀɔnɔmi] nf astronomy

astuce [astys] nf shrewdness, astuteness; (truc) trick, clever way; **astucieux, -euse** adj clever

atelier [atəlje] nm workshop; (de peintre) studio

athée [ate] adj atheistic ▷ nm/f atheist

Athènes [atɛn] n Athens

athlète [atlɛt] nm/f (Sport) athlete; **athlétisme** nm athletics sg

atlantique [atlɑ̃tik] adj Atlantic ▷ nm: **l'(océan) A~** the Atlantic (Ocean)

atlas [atlɑs] nm atlas

atmosphère [atmɔsfɛʀ] nf atmosphere

atome [atom] nm atom; **atomique** adj atomic; nuclear

atomiseur [atɔmizœʀ] nm atomizer

atout [atu] nm trump; (fig) asset

atroce [atʀɔs] adj atrocious

attachant, e [ataʃɑ̃, -ɑ̃t] adj engaging, likeable

attache [ataʃ] nf clip, fastener; (fig) tie

attacher [ataʃe] /1/ vt to tie up; (étiquette) to attach, tie on; (ceinture) to fasten; (souliers) to do up ▷ vi (poêle, riz) to stick; **s'~ à** (par affection) to become attached to; **~ qch à** to tie ou fasten ou attach sth to

attaque [atak] nf attack; (cérébrale) stroke; (d'épilepsie) fit

attaquer [atake] /1/ vt to attack; (en justice) to sue ▷ vi to attack; **s'attaquer à** vt (personne) to attack; (épidémie, misère) to tackle

attarder [ataʀde] /1/: **s'attarder** vi to linger

atteindre [atɛ̃dʀ] /49/ vt to reach; (blesser) to hit; (émouvoir) to affect; **atteint, e** adj (Méd): **être atteint de** to be suffering from

▷ nf attack; **hors d'atteinte** out of reach; **porter atteinte à** to strike a blow at

attendant [atɑ̃dɑ̃]: **en ~** adv meanwhile, in the meantime

attendre [atɑ̃dʀ] /41/ vt to wait for; (être destiné ou réservé à) to await, be in store for ▷ vi to wait; **s'~ à (ce que)** to expect (that); **attendez-moi, s'il vous plaît** wait for me, please; **~ un enfant** to be expecting a baby; **~ de faire/d'être** to wait until one does/is; **attendez qu'il vienne** wait until he comes; **~ qch de** to expect sth of;

▌ Attention à ne pas traduire attendre par to attend.

attendrir [atɑ̃dʀiʀ] /2/ vt to move (to pity); (viande) to tenderize

attendu, e [atɑ̃dy] adj (événement) long-awaited; (prévu) expected; **~ que** considering that, since

attentat [atɑ̃ta] nm assassination attempt; **~ à la pudeur** indecent assault no pl; **~ suicide** suicide bombing

attente [atɑ̃t] nf wait; (espérance) expectation

attenter [atɑ̃te] /1/: **~ à** vt (liberté) to violate; **~ à la vie de qn** to make an attempt on sb's life

attentif, -ive [atɑ̃tif, -iv] adj (auditeur) attentive; (travail) careful; **~ à** paying attention to

attention [atɑ̃sjɔ̃] nf attention; (prévenance) attention, thoughtfulness no pl; **à l'~ de** for the attention of; **faire ~ (à)** to be careful (of); **faire ~ (à ce) que** to be ou make sure that; **~!** careful!, watch out!; **~ à la voiture!** watch out for that car!; **attentionné, e** [atɑ̃sjone] adj thoughtful, considerate

atténuer [atenɥe] /1/ vt (douleur) to alleviate, ease; (couleurs) to soften; **s'atténuer** vi to ease; (violence etc) to abate

atterrir [ateʀiʀ] /2/ vi to land; **atterrissage** nm landing

attestation nf certificate

attirant, e [atiʀɑ̃, -ɑ̃t] adj attractive, appealing

attirer [atiʀe] /1/ vt to attract; (appâter) to lure, entice; **~ qn dans un coin/vers soi** to draw sb into a corner/towards one; **~ l'attention de qn** to attract sb's attention; **~ l'attention de qn sur qch** to draw sb's attention to sth; **s'~ des ennuis** to bring trouble upon o.s., get into trouble

attitude [atityd] nf attitude; (position du corps) bearing

attraction [atʀaksjɔ̃] nf attraction; (de cabaret, cirque) number

attrait [atʀɛ] nm appeal, attraction

attraper [atʀape] /1/ vt to catch; (habitude, amende) to get, pick up; (fam: duper) to con; **se faire ~** (fam) to be told off

attrayant, e [atʀɛjɑ̃, -ɑ̃t] adj attractive

attribuer [atribɥe] /1/ vt (prix) to award; (rôle, tâche) to allocate, assign; (imputer): ~ **qch à** to attribute sth to; **s'attribuer** vt (s'approprier) to claim for o.s.

attrister [atriste] /1/ vt to sadden

attroupement [atrupmɑ̃] nm crowd

attrouper [atrupe] /1/: **s'attrouper** vi to gather

au [o] prép voir **à**

aubaine [oben] nf godsend

aube [ob] nf dawn, daybreak; **à l'~** at dawn ou daybreak

aubépine [obepin] nf hawthorn

auberge [ober3] nf inn; ~ **de jeunesse** youth hostel

aubergine [ober3in] nf aubergine

aucun, e [okœ̃, -yn] adj, pron no; (positif) any ▷ pron none; (positif) any(one); **sans ~ doute** without any doubt; **plus qu'~ autre** more than any other; **il le fera mieux qu'~ de nous** he'll do it better than any of us; ~ **des deux** neither of the two; ~ **d'entre eux** none of them

audace [odas] nf daring, boldness; (péj) audacity; **audacieux, -euse** adj daring, bold

au-delà [od(ə)la] adv beyond ▷ nm: **l'~** the hereafter; ~ **de** beyond

au-dessous [odsu] adv underneath; below; ~ **de** under(neath), below; (limite, somme etc) below, under; (dignité, condition) below

au-dessus [odsy] adv above; ~ **de** above

au-devant [od(ə)vɑ̃]: ~ **de** prép: **aller ~ de** (personne, danger) to go (out) and meet; (souhaits de qn) to anticipate

audience [odjɑ̃s] nf audience; (Jur: séance) hearing

audio-visuel, le [odjɔvizɥɛl] adj audio-visual

audition [odisjɔ̃] nf (ouïe, écoute) hearing; (Jur: de témoins) examination; (Mus, Théât: épreuve) audition

auditoire [oditwar] nm audience

augmentation [ɔgmɑ̃tasjɔ̃] nf increase; ~ **(de salaire)** rise (in salary) (BRIT), (pay) raise (US)

augmenter [ɔgmɑ̃te] /1/ vt to increase; (salaire, prix) to increase, raise, put up; (employé) to increase the salary of ▷ vi to increase

augure [ogyr] nm: **de bon/mauvais ~** of good/ill omen

aujourd'hui [oʒurdɥi] adv today

aumône [omon] nf alms sg (pl inv); **aumônier** nm chaplain

auparavant [oparavɑ̃] adv before(hand)

auprès [opre]: ~ **de** prép next to, close to; (recourir, s'adresser) to; (en comparaison de) compared with

auquel [okɛl] pron voir **lequel**

aurai etc [ɔre] vb voir **avoir**

aurons etc [orɔ̃] vb voir **avoir**

aurore [ɔrɔr] nf dawn, daybreak

ausculter [ɔskylte] /1/ vt to sound

aussi [osi] adv (également) also, too; (de comparaison) as ▷ conj therefore, consequently; ~ **fort que** as strong as; **moi ~** me too

aussitôt [osito] adv straight away, immediately; ~ **que** as soon as

austère [ɔster] adj austere

austral, e [ɔstral] adj southern

Australie [ɔstrali] nf: **l'~** Australia; **australien, ne** adj Australian ▷ nm/f: **Australien, ne** Australian

autant [otɑ̃] adv so much; **je ne savais pas que tu la détestais ~** I didn't know you hated her so much; (comparatif): ~ **(que)** as much (as); (nombre) as many (as); ~ **(de)** so much (ou many); as much (ou many); ~ **partir** we (ou you etc) may as well leave; ~ **dire que ...** one might as well say that ...; **pour ~** for all that; **d'~ plus/mieux (que)** all the more/the better (since)

autel [otɛl] nm altar

auteur [otœr] nm author

authentique [otɑ̃tik] adj authentic, genuine

auto [oto] nf car; **autobiographie** nf autobiography; **autobronzant** nm self-tanning cream (or lotion etc); **autobus** nm bus; **autocar** nm coach

autochtone [otɔktɔn] nm/f native

auto: autocollant, e adj self-adhesive; (enveloppe) self-seal ▷ nm sticker; **autocuiseur** nm pressure cooker; **autodéfense** nf self defence, **autodidacte** nm/f self-taught person; **auto-école** nf driving school; **autographe** nm autograph

automate [otɔmat] nm (machine) (automatic) machine

automatique [otɔmatik] adj automatic ▷ nm: **l'~** ≈ direct dialling

automne [otɔn] nm autumn (BRIT), fall (US)

automobile [otɔmɔbil] adj motor cpd ▷ nf (motor) car; **automobiliste** nm/f motorist

automutiler [otomytile] /1/: **s'automutiler** vr to self-harm

autonome [otɔnɔm] adj autonomous; **autonomie** nf autonomy; (Pol) self-government

autopsie [otɔpsi] nf post-mortem (examination), autopsy

autoradio [otoradjo] nf car radio

autorisation [otɔrizasjɔ̃] nf authorization; (papiers) permit

autorisé, e [otɔrize] adj (opinion, sources) authoritative

autoriser [otɔrize] /1/ vt to give permission for, authorize; (fig) to allow (of)

autoritaire [otɔriter] adj authoritarian

autorité [otɔrite] nf authority; **faire ~** to be authoritative

autoroute [otoʀut] nf motorway (BRIT), expressway (US); **~ de l'information** (Inform) information superhighway

auto-stop [otostɔp] nm: **faire de l'~** to hitch-hike; **prendre qn en ~** to give sb a lift; **auto-stoppeur, -euse** nm/f hitch-hiker

autour [otuʀ] adv around; **~ de** around; **tout ~** all around

◯ MOT-CLÉ

autre [otʀ] adj **1** (différent) other, different; **je préférerais un autre verre** I'd prefer another ou a different glass **2** (supplémentaire) other; **je voudrais un autre verre d'eau** I'd like another glass of water **3**: **autre chose** something else; **autre part** somewhere else; **d'autre part** on the other hand
▶ pron: **un autre** another (one); **nous/vous autres** us/you; **d'autres** others; **l'autre** the other (one); **les autres** the others; (autrui) others; **l'un et l'autre** both of them; **se détester l'un l'autre/les uns les autres** to hate each other ou one another; **d'une semaine/minute à l'autre** from one week/minute ou moment to the next; (incessamment) any week/minute ou moment now; **entre autres** (personnes) among others; (choses) among other things

autrefois [otʀəfwa] adv in the past

autrement [otʀəmã] adv differently; (d'une manière différente) in another way; (sinon) otherwise; **~ dit** in other words

Autriche [otʀiʃ] nf: **l'~** Austria; **autrichien, ne** adj Austrian ▷ nm/f: **Autrichien, ne** Austrian

autruche [otʀyʃ] nf ostrich

aux [o] prép voir **à**

auxiliaire [ɔksiljɛʀ] adj, nm/f auxiliary

auxquels, auxquelles [okɛl] pron voir **lequel**

avalanche [avalãʃ] nf avalanche

avaler [avale] /1/ vt to swallow

avance [avãs] nf (de troupes etc) advance; (progrès) progress; (d'argent) advance; (opposé à retard) lead; **avances** nfpl

(amoureuses) advances; **(être) en ~** (to be) early; (sur un programme) (to be) ahead of schedule; **d'~, à l'~** in advance

avancé, e [avãse] adj advanced; (travail etc) well on, well under way

avancement [avãsmã] nm (professionnel) promotion

avancer [avãse] /3/ vi to move forward, advance; (projet, travail) to make progress; (montre, réveil) to be fast to gain ▷ vt to move forward, advance; (argent) to advance; (montre, pendule) to put forward; **s'avancer** vi to move forward, advance; (fig) to commit o.s.

avant [avã] prép before ▷ adj inv: **siège/roue ~** front seat/wheel ▷ nm (d'un véhicule, bâtiment) front; (Sport: joueur) forward; **~ qu'il parte/de partir** before he leaves/leaving; **~ tout** (surtout) above all; **à l'~** (dans un véhicule) in (the) front; **en ~** (se pencher, tomber) forward(s); **partir en ~** to go on ahead; **en ~ de** in front of

avantage [avãtaʒ] nm advantage; **~s sociaux** fringe benefits; **avantager** /3/ vt (favoriser) to favour; (embellir) to flatter; **avantageux, -euse** adj (prix) attractive

avant: avant-bras nm inv forearm; **avant-coureur** adj inv: **signe avant-coureur** advance indication ou sign; **avant-dernier, -ière** adj, nm/f next to last, last but one; **avant-goût** nm foretaste; **avant-hier** adv the day before yesterday; **avant-première** nf (de film) preview; **avant-veille** nf: **l'avant-veille** two days before

avare [avaʀ] adj miserly, avaricious ▷ nm/f miser; **~ de compliments** stingy ou sparing with one's compliments

avec [avɛk] prép with; (à l'égard de) to(wards), with; **et ~ ça?** (dans un magasin) anything ou something else?

avenir [avniʀ] nm: **l'~** the future; **à l'~** in future; **carrière/politicien d'~** career/politician with prospects ou a future

aventure [avãtyʀ] nf: **l'~** adventure; **une ~** (amoureuse) an affair; **aventureux, -euse** adj adventurous, venturesome; (projet) risky, chancy

avenue [avny] nf avenue

avérer [aveʀe] /6/: **s'avérer** vr: **s'~ faux/coûteux** to prove (to be) wrong/expensive

averse [avɛʀs] nf shower

averti, e [avɛʀti] adj (well-)informed

avertir [avɛʀtiʀ] /2/ vt: **~ qn (de qch/que)** to warn sb (of sth/that); (renseigner) to inform sb (of sth/that); **avertissement** nm warning; **avertisseur** nm horn, siren

aveu, x [avø] nm confession

aveugle [avœgl] adj blind ▷ nm/f blind person

aviation [avjasjõ] nf aviation; (sport, métier de pilote) flying; (Mil) air force

avide [avid] adj eager; (péj) greedy, grasping

avion [avjɔ̃] nm (aero)plane (BRIT),
(air)plane (US); **aller (quelque part) en ~** to
go (somewhere) by plane, fly (somewhere);
par ~ by airmail; **~ à réaction** jet (plane)

aviron [aviʀɔ̃] nm oar; (sport): **l'~** rowing

avis [avi] nm opinion; (notification) notice;
à mon ~ in my opinion; **changer d'~** to
change one's mind; **jusqu'à nouvel ~** until
further notice

aviser [avize] /1/ vt (informer): **~ qn de/
que** to advise ou inform ou notify sb of/
that ▷ vi to think about things, assess the
situation; **nous aviserons sur place** we'll
work something out once we're there; **s'~
de qch/que** to become suddenly aware of
sth/that; **s'~ de faire** to take it into one's
head to do

avocat, e [avɔka, -at] nm/f (Jur) ≈ barrister
(BRIT), lawyer ▷ nm (Culin) avocado (pear);
l'~ de la défense/partie civile the counsel
for the defence/plaintiff; **~ général**
assistant public prosecutor

avoine [avwan] nf oats pl

○ MOT-CLÉ

avoir [avwaR] /34/ vt 1 (posséder) to have;
elle a deux enfants/une belle maison she
has (got) two children/a lovely house; **il a
les yeux bleus** he has (got) blue eyes; **vous
avez du sel?** do you have any salt?; **avoir
du courage/de la patience** to be brave/
patient

2 (éprouver): **avoir de la peine** to be ou feel
sad; voir aussi **faim, peur**

3 (âge, dimensions) to be; **il a 3 ans** he is 3
(years old); **le mur a 3 mètres de haut** the
wall is 3 metres high

4 (fam: duper) to do, have; **on vous a
eu!** you've been done ou had!; (fait une
plaisanterie) we ou they had you there

5: **en avoir contre qn** to have a grudge
against sb; **en avoir assez** to be fed up;
j'en ai pour une demi-heure it'll take me
half an hour

6 (obtenir, attraper) to get; **j'ai réussi à avoir
mon train** I managed to get ou catch my
train; **j'ai réussi à avoir le renseignement
qu'il me fallait** I managed to get (hold of)
the information I needed

▷ vb aux 1 to have; **avoir mangé/dormi** to
have eaten/slept

2 (avoir + à + infinitif): **avoir à faire qch**
to have to do sth; **vous n'avez qu'à lui
demander** you only have to ask him

▷ vb impers 1: **il y a** (+ singulier) there is;
(+ pluriel) there are; **il y avait du café/
des gâteaux** there was coffee/there were
cakes; **qu'y a-t-il?, qu'est-ce qu'il y a?**
what's the matter?, what is it?; **il doit y
avoir une explication** there must be an
explanation; **il n'y a qu'à ...** we (ou you etc)

will just have to ...; **il ne peut y en avoir
qu'un** there can only be one

2: **il y a** (temporel): **il y a 10 ans** 10 years ago;
il y a 10 ans/longtemps que je le connais
I've known him for 10 years/a long time;
il y a 10 ans qu'il est arrivé it's 10 years
since he arrived

▷ nm assets pl, resources pl; (Comm) credit

avortement [avɔʀtəmɑ̃] nm abortion

avouer [avwe] /1/ vt (crime, défaut) to
confess (to); **~ avoir fait/que** to admit ou
confess to having done/that

avril [avʀil] nm April

axe [aks] nm axis (pl axes); (de roue etc) axle;
(fig) main line; **~ routier** trunk road (BRIT),
main road, highway (US)

ayons etc [ɛjɔ̃] vb voir **avoir**

bâbord [babɔʀ] *nm*: **à** *ou* **par ~** to port, on the port side

baby-foot [babifut] *nm inv* table football

baby-sitting [babisitiŋ] *nm* baby-sitting; **faire du ~** to baby-sit

bac [bak] *nm* (*récipient*) tub

baccalauréat [bakalɔʀea] *nm* ≈ high school diploma

bâcler [bakle] /1/ *vt* to botch (up)

baffe [baf] *nf* (*fam*) slap, clout

bafouiller [bafuje] /1/ *vi, vt* to stammer

bagage [bagaʒ] *nm*: **~s** luggage *sg*; (*connaissances*) background, knowledge; **~s à main** hand-luggage

bagarre [bagaʀ] *nf* fight, brawl; **bagarrer** /1/: **se bagarrer** *vi* to (have a) fight

bagnole [baɲɔl] *nf* (*fam*) car

bague [bag] *nf* ring; **~ de fiançailles** engagement ring

baguette [baget] *nf* stick; (*cuisine chinoise*) chopstick; (*de chef d'orchestre*) baton; (*pain*) stick of (French) bread; **~ magique** magic wand

baie [bɛ] *nf* (*Géo*) bay; (*fruit*) berry; **~ (vitrée)** picture window

baignade [bɛɲad] *nf* bathing; **"~ interdite"** "no bathing"

baigner [bɛɲe] /1/ *vt* (*bébé*) to bath; **se baigner** *vi* to go swimming *ou* bathing; **baignoire** *nf* bath(tub)

bail (*pl* **baux**) [baj, bo] *nm* lease

bâiller [baje] /1/ *vi* to yawn; (*être ouvert*) to gape

bain [bɛ̃] *nm* bath; **prendre un ~** to have a bath; **se mettre dans le ~** (*fig*) to get into (the way of) it *ou* things; **~ de bouche** mouthwash; **~ moussant** bubble bath; **~ de soleil; prendre un ~ de soleil** to sunbathe; **bain-marie** *nm*: **faire chauffer au bain-marie** (*boîte etc*) to immerse in boiling water

baiser [beze] /1/ *nm* kiss ▷ *vt* (*main, front*) to kiss; (*fam!*) to screw (!)

baisse [bɛs] *nf* fall, drop; **en ~** falling

baisser [bese] /1/ *vt* to lower; (*radio, chauffage*) to turn down ▷ *vi* to fall, drop, go down; (*vue, santé*) to fail, dwindle; **se baisser** *vi* to bend down

bal [bal] *nm* dance; (*grande soirée*) ball; **~ costumé/masqué** fancy-dress/masked ball

balade [balad] (*fam*) *nf* (*à pied*) walk, stroll; (*en voiture*) drive; **balader** /1/ (*fam*): **se balader** *vi* to go for a walk *ou* stroll; to go for a drive; **baladeur** [baladœʀ] *nm* personal stereo, Walkman®

balai [balɛ] *nm* broom, brush

balance [balɑ̃s] *nf* scales *pl*; (*signe*): **la B~** Libra; **~ commerciale** balance of trade

balancer [balɑ̃se] /3/ *vt* to swing; (*lancer*) to fling, chuck; (*renvoyer, jeter*) to chuck out; **se balancer** *vi* to swing; to rock; **se ~ de qch** (*fam*) not to give a toss about sth; **balançoire** *nf* swing; (*sur pivot*) seesaw

balayer [baleje] /8/ *vt* (*feuilles etc*) to sweep up, brush up; (*pièce, cour*) to sweep; (*chasser*) to sweep away *ou* aside; (*radar*) to scan; **balayeur, -euse** [balɛjœʀ, -øz] *nm/f* road sweeper ▷ *nf* (*engin*) road sweeper

balbutier [balbysje] /7/ *vi, vt* to stammer

balcon [balkɔ̃] *nm* balcony; (*Théât*) dress circle

Bâle [bal] *n* Basle *ou* Basel

Baléares [baleaʀ] *nfpl*: **les ~** the Balearic Islands, the Balearics

baleine [balɛn] *nf* whale

balise [baliz] *nf* (*Navig*) beacon, (marker) buoy; (*Aviat*) runway light, beacon; (*Auto, Ski*) sign, marker; **baliser** /1/ *vt* to mark out (with beacons *ou* lights *etc*)

balle [bal] *nf* (*de fusil*) bullet; (*de sport*) ball; (*fam: franc*) franc

ballerine [bal(ə)ʀin] *nf* (*danseuse*) ballet dancer; (*chaussure*) pump, ballet shoe

ballet [balɛ] *nm* ballet

ballon [balɔ̃] *nm* (*de sport*) ball; (*jouet, Aviat*) balloon; **~ de football** football; **~ d'oxygène** oxygen bottle

balnéaire [balneɛʀ] *adj* seaside *cpd*; **station ~** seaside resort

balustrade [balystʀad] *nf* railings *pl*, handrail

bambin [bɑ̃bɛ̃] *nm* little child

bambou [bɑ̃bu] *nm* bamboo

banal, e [banal] *adj* banal, commonplace; (*péj*) trite; **banalité** *nf* banality

banane [banan] *nf* banana; (*sac*) waist-bag, bum-bag

banc [bɑ̃] *nm* seat, bench; (*de poissons*) shoal; **~ d'essai** (*fig*) testing ground

bancaire [bɑ̃kɛʀ] *adj* banking; (*chèque, carte*) bank *cpd*

bancal, e [bɑ̃kal] *adj* wobbly

bandage [bɑ̃daʒ] nm bandage

bande [bɑ̃d] nf (de tissu etc) strip; (Méd) bandage; (motif, dessin) stripe; (groupe) band; (péj): **une ~ de** a bunch ou crowd of; **faire ~ à part** to keep to o.s.; **~ dessinée (BD)** comic strip; **~ magnétique** magnetic tape; **~ sonore** sound track

bande-annonce [bɑ̃dɑnɔ̃s] nf trailer

bandeau, x [bɑ̃do] nm headband; (sur les yeux) blindfold

bander [bɑ̃de] /1/ vt (blessure) to bandage; **~ les yeux à qn** to blindfold sb

bandit [bɑ̃di] nm bandit

bandoulière [bɑ̃duljɛʀ] nf: **en ~** (slung ou worn) across the shoulder

Bangladesh [bɑ̃gladɛʃ] nm: **le ~** Bangladesh

banlieue [bɑ̃ljø] nf suburbs pl; **quartiers de ~** suburban areas; **trains de ~** commuter trains

bannir [baniʀ] /2/ vt to banish

banque [bɑ̃k] nf bank; (activités) banking; **~ de données** data bank

banquet [bɑ̃kɛ] nm dinner; (d'apparat) banquet

banquette [bɑ̃kɛt] nf seat

banquier [bɑ̃kje] nm banker

banquise [bɑ̃kiz] nf ice field

baptême [batɛm] nm christening; baptism; **~ de l'air** first flight

baptiser [batize] /1/ vt to christen; to baptize

bar [baʀ] nm bar

baraque [baʀak] nf shed; (fam) house; **~ foraine** fairground stand; **baraqué, e** (fam) adj well-built, hefty

barbant, e [baʀbɑ̃, -ɑ̃t] adj (fam) deadly (boring)

barbare [baʀbaʀ] adj barbaric

barbe [baʀb] nf beard; **(au nez et) à la ~ de qn** (fig) under sb's very nose; **la ~!** (fam) damn it!; **quelle ~!** (fam) what a drag ou bore!; **~ à papa** candy-floss (BRIT), cotton candy (US)

barbelé [baʀbəle] adj, nm: **(fil de fer) ~** barbed wire no pl

barbiturique [baʀbityʀik] nm barbiturate

barbouiller [baʀbuje] /1/ vt to daub; **avoir l'estomac barbouillé** to feel queasy ou sick

barbu, e [baʀby] adj bearded

barder [baʀde] /1/ vi (fam): **ça va ~** sparks will fly

barème [baʀɛm] nm (Scol) scale; (liste) table

baril [baʀi(l)] nm barrel; (de poudre) keg

bariolé, e [baʀjɔle] adj many-coloured, rainbow-coloured

baromètre [baʀɔmɛtʀ] nm barometer

baron [baʀɔ̃] nm baron

baronne [baʀɔn] nf baroness

baroque [baʀɔk] adj (Art) baroque; (fig) weird

barque [baʀk] nf small boat

barquette [baʀkɛt] nf small boat-shaped tart; (récipient: en aluminium) tub; (: en bois) basket; (pour repas) tray; (pour fruits) punnet

barrage [baʀaʒ] nm dam; (sur route) roadblock, barricade

barre [baʀ] nf (de fer etc) rod; (Navig) helm; (écrite) line, stroke

barreau, x [baʀo] nm bar; (Jur): **le ~** the Bar

barrer [baʀe] /1/ vt (route etc) to block; (mot) to cross out; (chèque) to cross (BRIT); (Navig) to steer; **se barrer** vi (fam) to clear off

barrette [baʀɛt] nf (pour cheveux) (hair) slide (BRIT) ou clip (US)

barricader [baʀikade] /1/: **se barricader** vi: **se ~ chez soi** to lock o.s. in

barrière [baʀjɛʀ] nf fence; (obstacle) barrier; (porte) gate

barrique [baʀik] nf barrel, cask

bar-tabac [baʀtaba] nm bar (which sells tobacco and stamps)

bas, basse [bɑ, bɑs] adj low ▷ nm (vêtement) stocking; (partie inférieure): **le ~ de** the lower part ou foot ou bottom of ▷ adv low; (parler) softly; **au ~ mot** at the lowest estimate; **enfant en ~ âge** young child; **en ~** down below; (d'une liste, d'un mur etc) at (ou to) the bottom; (dans une maison) downstairs; **en ~ de** at the bottom of; **à ~ la dictature!** down with dictatorship!

bas-côté [bɑkote] nm (de route) verge (BRIT), shoulder (US)

basculer [baskyle] /1/ vi to fall over, topple (over); (benne) to tip up ▷ vt (contenu) to tip out; (benne) tip up

base [bɑz] nf base; (fondement, principe) basis (pl bases); **la ~** (Pol) the rank and file; **de ~** basic; **à ~ de café** etc coffee etc -based; **~ de données** database; **baser** /1/ vt: **baser qch sur** to base sth on; **se baser sur** (données, preuves) to base one's argument on

bas-fond [bɑfɔ̃] nm (Navig) shallow; **bas-fonds** nmpl (fig) dregs

basilic [bazilik] nm (Culin) basil

basket [baskɛt] nm basketball

baskets [baskɛt] nfpl trainers (BRIT), sneakers (US)

basque [bask] adj Basque ▷ nm/f: **B~** Basque; **le Pays ~** the Basque country

basse [bɑs] adj voir **bas** ▷ nf (Mus) bass; **basse-cour** nf farmyard

bassin [basɛ̃] nm (pièce d'eau) pond, pool; (de fontaine, Géo) basin; (Anat) pelvis; (portuaire) dock

bassine [basin] nf basin; (contenu) bowl, bowlful

basson [basɔ̃] nm bassoon

bat [ba] vb voir **battre**

bataille [bataj] nf battle; (rixe) fight; **elle avait les cheveux en ~** her hair was a mess

bateau, x [bato] nm boat; ship; **bateau-mouche** nm (passenger) pleasure boat (on the Seine)

bâti, e [bɑti] adj (terrain) developed; **bien ~** well-built

bâtiment [bɑtimɑ̃] nm building; (Navig) ship, vessel; (industrie): **le ~** the building trade

bâtir [bɑtiʀ] /2/ vt to build

bâtisse [bɑtis] nf building

bâton [bɑtɔ̃] nm stick; **parler à ~s rompus** to chat about this and that

bats [ba] vb voir **battre**

battement [batmɑ̃] nm (de cœur) beat; (intervalle) interval (between classes, trains etc); **10 minutes de ~** 10 minutes to spare

batterie [batʀi] nf (Mil, Élec) battery; (Mus) drums pl, drum kit; **~ de cuisine** kitchen utensils pl; (casseroles etc) pots and pans pl

batteur [batœʀ] nm (Mus) drummer; (appareil) whisk

battre [batʀ] /41/ vt to beat; (blé) to thresh; (cartes) to shuffle; (passer au peigne fin) to scour ▷ vi (cœur) to beat; (volets etc) to bang, rattle; **se battre** vi to fight; **~ la mesure** to beat time; **~ son plein** to be at its height, be going full swing; **~ des mains** to clap one's hands

baume [bom] nm balm

bavard, e [bavaʀ, aʀd] adj (very) talkative; gossipy; **bavarder** /1/ vi to chatter; (indiscrètement) to gossip; (révéler un secret) to blab

baver [bave] /1/ vi to dribble; (chien) to slobber, slaver; **en ~** (fam) to have a hard time (of it)

bavoir [bavwaʀ] nm bib

bavure [bavyʀ] nf smudge; (fig) hitch; (policière etc) blunder

bazar [bazaʀ] nm general store; (fam) jumble; **bazarder** /1/ vt (fam) to chuck out

BCBG sigle adj (= bon chic bon genre) smart and trendy, ≈ preppy

BD sigle f = **bande dessinée**

bd abr = **boulevard**

béant, e [beɑ̃, -ɑ̃t] adj gaping

beau (bel), belle, beaux [bo, bɛl] adj beautiful, lovely; (homme) handsome ▷ adv: **il fait ~** the weather's fine ▷ nm: **un ~ jour** one (fine) day; **de plus belle** more than ever, even more; **bel et bien** well and truly; **le plus ~ c'est que …** the best of it is that …; **on a ~ essayer** however hard ou no matter how hard we try; **faire le ~** (chien) to sit up and beg

MOT-CLÉ

beaucoup [boku] adv **1** a lot; **il boit beaucoup** he drinks a lot; **il ne boit pas beaucoup** he doesn't drink much ou a lot **2** (suivi de plus, trop etc) much, a lot; **il est beaucoup plus grand** he is much ou a lot ou far taller; **c'est beaucoup plus cher** it's a lot ou much more expensive; **il a beaucoup**

plus de temps que moi he has much ou a lot more time than me; **il y a beaucoup plus de touristes ici** there are a lot ou many more tourists here; **beaucoup trop vite** much too fast; **il fume beaucoup trop** he smokes far too much

3: **beaucoup de** (nombre) many, a lot of; (quantité) a lot of; **beaucoup d'étudiants/ de touristes** a lot of ou many students/ tourists; **beaucoup de courage** a lot of courage; **il n'a pas beaucoup d'argent** he hasn't got much ou a lot of money

4: **de beaucoup** by far

beau: **beau-fils** nm son-in-law; (remariage) stepson; **beau-frère** nm brother-in-law; **beau-père** nm father-in-law; (remariage) stepfather

beauté [bote] nf beauty; **de toute ~** beautiful; **finir qch en ~** to complete sth brilliantly

beaux-arts [bozaʀ] nmpl fine arts

beaux-parents [bopaʀɑ̃] nmpl wife's/ husband's family, in-laws

bébé [bebe] nm baby

bec [bɛk] nm beak, bill; (de cafetière etc) spout; (de casserole etc) lip; (fam) mouth; **~ de gaz** (street) gaslamp

bêche [bɛʃ] nf spade; **bêcher** /1/ vt to dig

bedaine [bədɛn] nf paunch

bedonnant, e [bədɔnɑ̃, -ɑ̃t] adj potbellied

bée [be] adj: **bouche ~** gaping

bégayer [begeje] /8/ vt, vi to stammer

beige [bɛʒ] adj beige

beignet [bɛɲɛ] nm fritter

bel [bɛl] adj m voir **beau**

bêler [bele] /1/ vi to bleat

belette [bəlɛt] nf weasel

belge [bɛlʒ] adj Belgian ▷ nm/f: **B~** Belgian

Belgique [bɛlʒik] nf: **la ~** Belgium

bélier [belje] nm ram; (signe): **le B~** Aries

belle [bɛl] adj voir **beau** ▷ nf (Sport): **la ~** the decider; **belle-fille** nf daughter-in-law; (remariage) stepdaughter; **belle-mère** nf mother-in-law; (remariage) stepmother; **belle-sœur** nf sister-in-law

belvédère [bɛlvedeʀ] nm panoramic viewpoint (or small building there)

bémol [bemɔl] nm (Mus) flat

bénédiction [benediksjɔ̃] nf blessing

bénéfice [benefis] nm (Comm) profit; (avantage) benefit; **bénéficier** /7/ vi: **bénéficier de** to enjoy; (profiter) to benefit by ou from; **bénéfique** adj beneficial

Benelux [benelyks] nm: **le ~** Benelux, the Benelux countries

bénévole [benevɔl] adj voluntary, unpaid

bénin, -igne [benɛ̃, -iɲ] adj minor, mild; (tumeur) benign

bénir [beniʀ] /2/ vt to bless; **bénit, e** adj consecrated; **eau bénite** holy water

benne [bɛn] nf skip; (de téléphérique) (cable) car; **~ à ordures** (amovible) skip
béquille [bekij] nf crutch; (de bicyclette) stand
berceau, x [bɛʀso] nm cradle, crib
bercer [bɛʀse] /3/ vt to rock, cradle; (musique etc) to lull; **~ qn de** (promesses etc) to delude sb with; **berceuse** nf lullaby
béret [beʀɛ] nm (aussi: **~ basque**) beret
berge [bɛʀʒ] nf bank
berger, -ère [bɛʀʒe, -ɛʀ] nm/f shepherd/shepherdess; **~ allemand** alsatian (dog) (BRIT), German shepherd (dog) (US)
Berlin [bɛʀlɛ̃] n Berlin
Bermudes [bɛʀmyd] nfpl: **les (îles) ~** Bermuda
Berne [bɛʀn] n Bern
berner [bɛʀne] /1/ vt to fool
besogne [bəzɔɲ] nf work no pl, job
besoin [bəzwɛ̃] nm need; (pauvreté): **le ~** need, want; **faire ses ~s** to relieve o.s.; **avoir ~ de qch/faire qch** to need sth/to do sth; **au ~** if need be; **être dans le ~** to be in need ou want
bestiole [bɛstjɔl] nf (tiny) creature
bétail [betaj] nm livestock, cattle pl
bête [bɛt] nf animal; (bestiole) insect, creature ▷ adj stupid, silly; **chercher la petite ~** to nit-pick; **~ noire** pet hate; **~ sauvage** wild beast
bêtise [betiz] nf stupidity; (action, remarque) stupid thing (to say ou do)
béton [betɔ̃] nm concrete; **(en) ~** (fig: alibi, argument) cast iron; **~ armé** reinforced concrete
betterave [bɛtʀav] nf beetroot (BRIT), beet (US); **~ sucrière** sugar beet
Beur [bœʀ] nm/f see note **"Beur"**

beurre [bœʀ] nm butter; **beurrer** /1/ vt to butter; **beurrier** nm butter dish
biais [bjɛ] nm (moyen) device, expedient; (aspect) angle; **en ~, de ~** (obliquement) at an angle; **par le ~ de** by means of
bibelot [biblo] nm trinket, curio
biberon [bibʀɔ̃] nm (feeding) bottle; **nourrir au ~** to bottle-feed
bible [bibl] nf bible
bibliobus nm mobile library van
bibliothécaire [biblijotekɛʀ] nm/f librarian
bibliothèque nf library; (meuble) bookcase
bic® [bik] nm Biro®

bicarbonate [bikaʀbɔnat] nm: **~ (de soude)** bicarbonate of soda
biceps [bisɛps] nm biceps
biche [biʃ] nf doe
bicolore [bikɔlɔʀ] adj two-coloured
bicoque [bikɔk] nf (péj) shack
bicyclette [bisiklɛt] nf bicycle
bidet [bidɛ] nm bidet
bidon [bidɔ̃] nm can ▷ adj inv (fam) phoney
bidonville [bidɔ̃vil] nm shanty town
bidule [bidyl] nm (fam) thingamajig

⊙ **MOT-CLÉ**

bien [bjɛ̃] nm **1** (avantage, profit): **faire du bien à qn** to do sb good; **dire du bien de** to speak well of; **c'est pour son bien** it's for his own good
2 (possession, patrimoine) possession, property; **son bien le plus précieux** his most treasured possession; **avoir du bien** to have property; **biens (de consommation etc)** (consumer etc) goods
3 (moral): **le bien** good; **distinguer le bien du mal** to tell good from evil
▶ adv **1** (de façon satisfaisante) well; **elle travaille/mange bien** she works/eats well; **croyant bien faire, je/il ...** thinking I/he was doing the right thing, I/he ...; **tiens-toi bien!** (assieds-toi correctement) sit up straight!; (debout) stand up straight!; (sois sage) behave yourself!; (prépare-toi) wait for it!
2 (valeur intensive) quite; **bien jeune** quite young; **bien assez** quite enough; **bien mieux** (very) much better; **bien du temps/des gens** quite a time/a number of people; **j'espère bien y aller** I do hope to go; **je veux bien le faire** (concession) I'm quite willing to do it; **il faut bien le faire** it has to be done; **cela fait bien deux ans que je ne l'ai pas vu** I haven't seen him for at least ou a good two years; **Paul est bien venu, n'est-ce pas?** Paul HAS come, hasn't he?; **où peut-il bien être passé?** where on earth can he have got to?
▶ excl right!, OK!, fine!; **(c'est) bien fait!** it serves you (ou him etc) right!; **bien sûr!** certainly!
▶ adj inv **1** (en bonne forme, à l'aise): **je me sens bien** I feel fine; **je ne me sens pas bien** I don't feel well; **on est bien dans ce fauteuil** this chair is very comfortable
2 (joli, beau) good-looking; **tu es bien dans cette robe** you look good in that dress
3 (satisfaisant) good; **elle est bien, cette maison/secrétaire** it's a nice house/she's a good secretary; **c'est très bien (comme ça)** it's fine (like that); **c'est bien?** is that all right?
4 (moralement) right; (: personne) good, nice; (respectable) respectable; **ce n'est pas bien**

de ... it's not right to ...; **elle est bien, cette femme** she's a nice woman, she's a good sort; **des gens bien** respectable people **5** (*en bons termes*): **être bien avec qn** to be on good terms with sb; **bien-aimé, e** *adj, nm/f* beloved; **bien-être** *nm* well-being; **bienfaisance** *nf* charity; **bienfait** *nm* act of generosity, benefaction; (*de la science etc*) benefit; **bienfaiteur, -trice** *nm/f* benefactor/benefactress; **bien-fondé** *nm* soundness; **bien que** *conj* although

bientôt [bjɛ̃to] *adv* soon; **à ~** see you soon
bienveillant, e [bjɛ̃vɛjɑ̃, -ɑ̃t] *adj* kindly
bienvenu, e [bjɛ̃vny] *adj* welcome ▷ *nf*: **souhaiter la ~e à** to welcome; **~e à** welcome to
bière [bjɛʀ] *nf* (*boisson*) beer; (*cercueil*) bier; **~ blonde** lager; **~ brune** brown ale (*BRIT*), dark beer (*US*); **~ (à la) pression** draught beer
bifteck [biftɛk] *nm* steak
bigoudi [bigudi] *nm* curler
bijou, x [biʒu] *nm* jewel; **bijouterie** *nf* jeweller's (shop); **bijoutier, -ière** *nm/f* jeweller
bikini [bikini] *nm* bikini
bilan [bilɑ̃] *nm* (*Comm*) balance sheet(s); (*fig*) (*net*) outcome (: *de victimes*) toll; **faire le ~ de** to assess; to review; **déposer son ~** to file a bankruptcy statement; **~ de santé** check-up
bile [bil] *nf* bile; **se faire de la ~** (*fam*) to worry o.s. sick
bilieux, -euse [biljø, -øz] *adj* bilious; (*fig: colérique*) testy
bilingue [bilɛ̃g] *adj* bilingual
billard [bijaʀ] *nm* billiards *sg*; (*table*) billiard table
bille [bij] *nf* ball; (*du jeu de billes*) marble
billet [bijɛ] *nm* (*aussi*: **~ de banque**) (bank) note; (*de cinéma, de bus etc*) ticket; (*courte lettre*) note; **~ électronique** e-ticket; **billetterie** *nf* ticket office; (*distributeur*) ticket dispenser; (*Banque*) cash dispenser
billion [biljɔ̃] *nm* billion (*BRIT*), trillion (*US*)
bimensuel, le [bimɑ̃sɥɛl] *adj* bimonthly
bio [bjo] *adj* organic
bio... [bjo] *préfixe* bio...; **biocarburant** *nm* biofuel; **biochimie** *nf* biochemistry; **biodiesel** *nm* biodiesel; **biogazole** *nm* biodiesel; **biographie** *nf* biography; **biologie** *nf* biology; **biologique** *adj* biological; **biométrie** *nf* biometrics; **biotechnologie** *nf* biotechnology; **bioterrorisme** *nm* bioterrorism
bipolaire [bipolɛʀ] *adj* bipolar
Birmanie [birmani] *nf* Burma
bis¹, e [bi, biz] *adj* (*couleur*) greyish brown ▷ *nf* (*baiser*) kiss; (*vent*) North wind; **faire une** *ou* **la ~e à qn** to kiss sb; **grosses ~es (de)** (*sur lettre*) love and kisses (from)

bis² [bis] *adv*: **12 ~ 12a** *ou* A ▷ *excl, nm* encore
biscotte [biskɔt] *nf* toasted bread (*sold in packets*)
biscuit [biskɥi] *nm* biscuit (*BRIT*), cookie (*US*)
bise [biz] *nf voir* **bis²**
bisexuel, le [bisɛksɥɛl] *adj* bisexual
bisou [bizu] *nm* (*fam*) kiss
bissextile [bisɛkstil] *adj*: **année ~** leap year
bistro(t) [bistro] *nm* bistro, café
bitume [bitym] *nm* asphalt
bizarre [bizaʀ] *adj* strange, odd
blague [blag] *nf* (*propos*) joke; (*farce*) trick; **sans ~!** no kidding!; **blaguer** /1/ *vi* to joke
blaireau, x [blɛʀo] *nm* (*Zool*) badger; (*brosse*) shaving brush
blâme [blam] *nm* blame; (*sanction*) reprimand; **blâmer** /1/ *vt* to blame
blanc, blanche [blɑ̃, blɑ̃ʃ] *adj* white; (*non imprimé*) blank ▷ *nm/f* white, white man/woman ▷ *nm* (*couleur*) white; (*espace non écrit*) blank; (*aussi*: **~ d'œuf**) (egg-)white; (*aussi*: **~ de poulet**) breast, white meat; (*aussi*: **vin ~**) white wine ▷ *nf* (*Mus*) minim (*BRIT*), half-note (*US*); **chèque en ~** blank cheque; **à ~** (*chauffer*) white-hot; (*tirer, charger*) with blanks; **~ cassé** off-white; **blancheur** *nf* whiteness
blanchir [blɑ̃ʃiʀ] /2/ *vt* (*gén*) to whiten; (*linge*) to launder; (*Culin*) to blanch; (*fig: disculper*) to clear ▷ *vi* (*cheveux*) to go white; **blanchisserie** *nf* laundry
blason [blazɔ̃] *nm* coat of arms
blasphème [blasfɛm] *nm* blasphemy
blazer [blazɛʀ] *nm* blazer
blé [ble] *nm* wheat
bled [blɛd] *nm* (*péj*) hole
blême [blɛm] *adj* pale
blessé, e [blese] *adj* injured ▷ *nm/f* injured person, casualty
blesser [blese] /1/ *vt* to injure; (*délibérément*) to wound; (*offenser*) to hurt; **se blesser** to injure o.s.; **se ~ au pied** *etc* to injure one's foot *etc*; **blessure** *nf* (*accidentelle*) injury; (*intentionnelle*) wound
bleu, e [blø] *adj* blue; (*bifteck*) very rare ▷ *nm* (*couleur*) blue; (*contusion*) bruise; (*vêtement: aussi*: **~s**) overalls *pl*; **fromage ~** blue cheese; **~ marine/nuit/roi** navy/midnight/royal blue; **bleuet** *nm* cornflower
bloc [blɔk] *nm* (*de pierre etc*) block; (*de papier à lettres*) pad; (*ensemble*) group, block; **serré à ~** tightened right down; **en ~** as a whole; **~ opératoire** operating *ou* theatre block; **blocage** *nm* (*des prix*) freezing; (*Psych*) hang-up; **bloc-notes** *nm* note pad
blog [blɔg] *nm* blog; **blogosphère** *nf* blogosphere; **bloguer** /1/ *vi* to blog
blond, e [blɔ̃, -ɔ̃d] *adj* fair; blond; (*sable, blés*) golden
bloquer [blɔke] /1/ *vt* (*passage*) to block; (*pièce mobile*) to jam; (*crédits, compte*) to freeze

blottir [blɔtiʀ] /2/: **se blottir** vi to huddle up

blouse [bluz] nf overall

blouson [bluzõ] nm blouson (jacket); **~ noir** (fig) ≈ rocker

bluff [blœf] nm bluff

bobine [bɔbin] nf reel; (Élec) coil

bobo [bobo] sigle m/f (= bourgeois bohème) boho

bocal, -aux [bɔkal, -o] nm jar

bock [bɔk] nm glass of beer

bœuf (pl **bœufs**) [bœf, bø] nm ox; (Culin) beef

bof [bɔf] excl (fam: indifférence) don't care!; (pas terrible) nothing special

bohémien, ne [bɔemjɛ̃, -ɛn] nm/f gipsy

boire [bwaʀ] /53/ vt to drink; (s'imprégner de) to soak up; **~ un coup** to have a drink

bois [bwa] nm wood; **de ~, en ~** wooden; **boisé, e** adj woody, wooded

boisson [bwasõ] nf drink

boîte [bwat] nf box; (fam: entreprise) firm; **aliments en ~** canned ou tinned (BRIT) foods; **~ à gants** glove compartment; **~ à ordures** dustbin (BRIT), trash can (US); **~ aux lettres** letter box; **~ d'allumettes** box of matches; (vide) matchbox; **~ de conserves** can ou tin (BRIT) (of food); **~ de nuit** night club; **~ de vitesses** gear box; **~ postale (BP)** PO box; **~ vocale** voice mail

boiter [bwate] /1/ vi to limp; (fig: raisonnement) to be shaky

boîtier [bwatje] nm case

boive etc [bwav] vb voir **boire**

bol [bɔl] nm bowl; **un ~ d'air** a breath of fresh air; **en avoir ras le ~** (fam) to have had a bellyful; **avoir du ~** (fam) to be lucky

bombarder [bõbaʀde] /1/ vt to bomb; **~ qn de** (cailloux, lettres) to bombard sb with

bombe [bõb] nf bomb; (atomiseur) (aerosol) spray

⬤ **MOT-CLÉ**

bon, bonne [bõ, bɔn] adj **1** (agréable, satisfaisant) good; **un bon repas/ restaurant** a good meal/restaurant; **être bon en maths** to be good at maths

2 (charitable): **être bon (envers)** to be good (to)

3 (correct) right; **le bon numéro/moment** the right number/moment

4 (souhaits): **bon anniversaire!** happy birthday!; **bon courage!** good luck!; **bon séjour!** enjoy your stay!; **bon voyage!** have a good trip!; **bonne année!** happy New Year!; **bonne chance!** good luck!; **bonne fête!** happy holiday!; **bonne nuit!** good night!

5 (approprié): **bon à/pour** fit to/for; **à quoi bon (…)?** what's the point ou use (of …)?

6: **bon enfant** adj inv accommodating, easy-going; **bonne femme** (péj) woman;

de bonne heure early; **bon marché** cheap; **bon mot** witticism; **bon sens** common sense; **bon vivant** jovial chap; **bonnes œuvres** charitable works, charities

▶ nm **1** (billet) voucher; (aussi: **bon cadeau**) gift voucher; **bon d'essence** petrol coupon; **bon du Trésor** Treasury bond

2: **avoir du bon** to have its good points; **pour de bon** for good

▶ adv: **il fait bon** it's ou the weather is fine; **sentir bon** to smell good; **tenir bon** to stand firm

▶ excl good!; **ah bon?** really?; **bon, je reste** right, I'll stay; voir aussi **bonne**

bonbon [bõbõ] nm (boiled) sweet

bond [bõ] nm leap; **faire un ~** to leap in the air

bondé, e [bõde] adj packed (full)

bondir [bõdiʀ] /2/ vi to leap

bonheur [bɔnœʀ] nm happiness; **porter ~ (à qn)** to bring (sb) luck; **au petit ~** haphazardly; **par ~** fortunately

bonhomme [bɔnɔm] (pl **bonshommes**) nm fellow; **~ de neige** snowman

bonjour [bõʒuʀ] excl, nm hello; (selon l'heure) good morning (ou afternoon); **c'est simple comme ~** it's easy as pie!

bonne [bɔn] adj f voir **bon** ▷ nf (domestique) maid

bonnet [bɔnɛ] nm hat; (de soutien-gorge) cup; **~ de bain** bathing cap

bonsoir [bõswaʀ] excl good evening

bonté [bõte] nf kindness no pl

bonus [bɔnys] nm (Assurances) no-claims bonus; (de DVD) extras pl

bord [bɔʀ] nm (de table, verre, falaise) edge; (de rivière, lac) bank; (de route) side; **(monter) à ~** (to go) on board; **jeter par-dessus ~** to throw overboard; **le commandant de ~/les hommes du ~** the ship's master/crew; **au ~ de la mer/route** at the seaside/roadside; **être au ~ des larmes** to be on the verge of tears

bordeaux [bɔʀdo] nm Bordeaux ▷ adj inv maroon

bordel [bɔʀdɛl] nm brothel; (fam!) bloody (BRIT) ou goddamn (US) mess (!)

border [bɔʀde] /1/ vt (être le long de) to line, border; (qn dans son lit) to tuck up; **~ qch de** (garnir) to trim sth with

bordure [bɔʀdyʀ] nf border; **en ~ de** on the edge of

borne [bɔʀn] nf boundary stone; (aussi: **~ kilométrique**) kilometre-marker, ≈ milestone; **bornes** nfpl (fig) limits; **dépasser les ~s** to go too far

borné, e [bɔʀne] adj (personne) narrow-minded

borner [bɔʀne] /1/ vt: **se ~ à faire** (se contenter de) to content o.s. with doing; (se limiter à) to limit o.s. to doing

bosniaque [bɔznjak] *adj* Bosnian ▷ *nm/f*: **B~** Bosnian

Bosnie-Herzégovine [bɔsniɛʀzegɔvin] *nf* Bosnia-Herzegovina

bosquet [bɔskɛ] *nm* grove

bosse [bɔs] *nf (de terrain etc)* bump; *(enflure)* lump; *(du bossu, du chameau)* hump; **avoir la ~ des maths** *etc (fam)* to have a gift for maths *etc*; **il a roulé sa ~** *(fam)* he's been around

bosser [bɔse] /1/ *vi (fam)* to work; (: *dur*) to slave (away)

bossu, e [bɔsy] *nm/f* hunchback

botanique [bɔtanik] *nf* botany ▷ *adj* botanic(al)

botte [bɔt] *nf (soulier)* (high) boot; *(gerbe)*: **~ de paille** bundle of straw; **~ de radis/ d'asperges** bunch of radishes/asparagus; **~s de caoutchouc** wellington boots

bottine [bɔtin] *nf* ankle boot

bouc [buk] *nm* goat; *(barbe)* goatee; **~ émissaire** scapegoat

boucan [bukã] *nm* din, racket

bouche [buʃ] *nf* mouth; **faire du ~ à ~ à qn** to give sb the kiss of life (BRIT), give sb mouth-to-mouth resuscitation; **rester ~ bée** to stand open-mouthed; **~ d'égout** manhole; **~ d'incendie** fire hydrant; **~ de métro** métro entrance

bouché, e [buʃe] *adj (flacon etc)* stoppered; *(temps, ciel)* overcast; *(péj: personne)* thick; **avoir le nez ~** to have a blocked(-up) nose; **c'est un secteur ~** there's no future in that area; **l'évier est ~** the sink's blocked

bouchée [buʃe] *nf* mouthful; **~s à la reine** chicken vol-au-vents

boucher [buʃe] /1/ *vt (pour colmater)* to stop up; *(trou)* to fill up; *(obstruer)* to block (up); **se boucher** *vi (tuyau etc)* to block up, get blocked up; **j'ai le nez bouché** my nose is blocked; **se ~ le nez** to hold one's nose

bouchère [buʃɛʀ] *nf* butcher

boucherie *nf* butcher's (shop); *(fig)* slaughter

bouchon [buʃɔ̃] *nm (en liège)* cork; *(autre matière)* stopper; *(de tube)* top; *(fig: embouteillage)* holdup; *(Pêche)* float

boucle [bukl] *nf (forme, figure)* loop; *(objet)* buckle; **~ (de cheveux)** curl; **~ d'oreille** earring

bouclé, e [bukle] *adj (cheveux)* curly

boucler [bukle] /1/ *vt (fermer: ceinture etc)* to fasten; *(terminer)* to finish off; *(enfermer)* to shut away; *(quartier)* to seal off ▷ *vi* to curl

bouder [bude] /1/ *vi* to sulk ▷ *vt (personne)* to refuse to have anything to do with

boudin [budɛ̃] *nm*: **~ (noir)** black pudding; **~ blanc** white pudding

boue [bu] *nf* mud

bouée [bwe] *nf* buoy; **~ (de sauvetage)** lifebuoy

boueux, -euse [bwø, -øz] *adj* muddy

bouffe [buf] *nf (fam)* grub, food

bouffée [bufe] *nf (de cigarette)* puff; **une ~ d'air pur** a breath of fresh air; **~ de chaleur** hot flush (BRIT) ou flash (US)

bouffer [bufe] /1/ *vi (fam)* to eat

bouffi, e [bufi] *adj* swollen

bouger [buʒe] /3/ *vi* to move; *(dent etc)* to be loose; *(s'activer)* to get moving ▷ *vt* to move; **les prix/les couleurs n'ont pas bougé** prices/colours haven't changed

bougie [buʒi] *nf* candle; *(Auto)* spark(ing) plug

bouillabaisse [bujabɛs] *nf* type of fish soup

bouillant, e [bujã, -ãt] *adj (qui bout)* boiling; *(très chaud)* boiling (hot)

bouillie [buji] *nf (de bébé)* cereal; **en ~** *(fig)* crushed

bouillir [bujiʀ] /15/ *vi* to boil ▷ *vt* to boil; **~ de colère** *etc* to seethe with anger *etc*

bouilloire [bujwaʀ] *nf* kettle

bouillon [bujɔ̃] *nm (Culin)* stock *no pl*; **bouillonner** /1/ *vi* to bubble; *(fig: idées)* to bubble up

bouillotte [bujɔt] *nf* hot-water bottle

boulanger, -ère [bulãʒe, -ɛʀ] *nm/f* baker; **boulangerie** *nf* bakery

boule [bul] *nf (gén)* ball; *(de pétanque)* bowl; **~ de neige** snowball

boulette [bulɛt] *nf (de viande)* meatball

boulevard [bulvaʀ] *nm* boulevard

bouleversement [bulvɛʀsəmã] *nm* upheaval

bouleverser [bulvɛʀse] /1/ *vt (émouvoir)* to overwhelm; *(causer du chagrin à)* to distress; *(pays, vie)* to disrupt; *(papiers, objets)* to turn upside down

boulimie [bulimi] *nf* bulimia

boulimique [bulimik] *adj* bulimic

boulon [bulɔ̃] *nm* bolt

boulot¹ [bulo] *nm (fam: travail)* work

boulot², te [bulo, -ɔt] *adj* plump, tubby

boum [bum] *nm* bang ▷ *nf (fam)* party

bouquet [bukɛ] *nm (de fleurs)* bunch (of flowers), bouquet; *(de persil etc)* bunch; **c'est le ~!** that's the last straw!

bouquin [bukɛ̃] *nm (fam)* book; **bouquiner** /1/ *vi (fam)* to read

bourdon [buʀdɔ̃] *nm* bumblebee

bourg [buʀ] *nm* small market town *(ou* village)

bourgeois, e [buʀʒwa, -waz] *adj* ≈ (upper) middle class; **bourgeoisie** *nf* ≈ upper middle classes *pl*

bourgeon [buʀʒɔ̃] *nm* bud

Bourgogne [buʀgɔɲ] *nf*: **la ~** Burgundy ▷ *nm*: **b~** Burgundy (wine)

bourguignon, ne [buʀgiɲɔ̃, -ɔn] *adj* of *ou* from Burgundy, Burgundian

bourrasque [buʀask] *nf* squall

bourratif, -ive [buʀatif, -iv] *(fam) adj* filling, stodgy

bourré, e [buʀe] *adj* (*rempli*): ~ **de** crammed full of; (*fam: ivre*) pickled, plastered

bourrer [buʀe] /1/ *vt* (*pipe*) to fill; (*poêle*) to pack; (*valise*) to cram (full)

bourru, e [buʀy] *adj* surly, gruff

bourse [buʀs] *nf* (*subvention*) grant; (*porte-monnaie*) purse; **la B~** the Stock Exchange

bous [bu] *vb voir* **bouillir**

bousculade [buskylad] *nf* (*hâte*) rush; (*poussée*) crush; **bousculer** /1/ *vt* (*heurter*) to knock into; (*fig*) to push, rush

boussole [busɔl] *nf* compass

bout [bu] *vb voir* **bouillir** ▷ *nm* bit; (*d'un bâton etc*) tip; (*d'une ficelle, table, rue, période*) end; **au ~ de** at the end of, after; **pousser qn à ~** to push sb to the limit (of his patience); **venir.à ~ de** to manage to finish (off) *ou* overcome; **à ~ portant** at point-blank range

bouteille [butɛj] *nf* bottle; (*de gaz butane*) cylinder

boutique [butik] *nf* shop

bouton [butɔ̃] *nm* button; (*Bot*) bud; (*sur la peau*) spot; **boutonner** /1/ *vt* to button up; **boutonnière** *nf* buttonhole; **bouton-pression** *nm* press stud

bovin, e [bɔvɛ̃, -in] *adj* bovine ▷ *nm*: ~**s** cattle *pl*

bowling [bolin] *nm* (*tenpin*) bowling; (*salle*) bowling alley

boxe [bɔks] *nf* boxing

BP *sigle f* = **boîte postale**

bracelet [bʀaslɛ] *nm* bracelet

braconnier [bʀakɔnje] *nm* poacher

brader [bʀade] /1/ *vt* to sell off; **braderie** *nf* cut-price (BRIT) *ou* cut-rate (US) stall

braguette [bʀagɛt] *nf* fly, flies *pl* (BRIT), zipper (US)

braise [bʀɛz] *nf* embers *pl*

brancard [bʀɑ̃kaʀ] *nm* (*civière*) stretcher; **brancardier** *nm* stretcher-bearer

branche [bʀɑ̃ʃ] *nf* branch

branché, e [bʀɑ̃ʃe] *adj* (*fam*) trendy

brancher [bʀɑ̃ʃe] /1/ *vt* to connect (up); (*en mettant la prise*) to plug in

brandir [bʀɑ̃diʀ] /2/ *vt* to brandish

braquer [bʀake] /1/ *vi* (*Auto*) to turn (the wheel) ▷ *vt* (*revolver etc*): ~ **qch sur** to aim sth at, point sth at; (*mettre en colère*): ~ **qn** to antagonize sb

bras [bʀa] *nm* arm; ~ **dessus ~ dessous** arm in arm; **se retrouver avec qch sur les ~** (*fam*) to be landed with sth; ~ **droit** (*fig*) right hand man

brassard [bʀasaʀ] *nm* armband

brasse [bʀas] *nf* (*nage*) breast-stroke; ~ **papillon** butterfly(-stroke)

brassée [bʀase] *nf* armful

brasser [bʀase] /1/ *vt* to mix; ~ **l'argent/les affaires** to handle a lot of money/ business

brasserie [bʀasʀi] *nf* (*restaurant*) bar (*selling food*); (*usine*) brewery

brave [bʀav] *adj* (*courageux*) brave; (*bon, gentil*) good, kind

braver [bʀave] /1/ *vt* to defy

bravo [bʀavo] *excl* bravo! ▷ *nm* cheer

bravoure [bʀavuʀ] *nf* bravery

break [bʀɛk] *nm* (*Auto*) estate car

brebis [bʀəbi] *nf* ewe; ~ **galeuse** black sheep

bredouiller [bʀəduje] /1/ *vi, vt* to mumble, stammer

bref, brève [bʀɛf, bʀɛv] *adj* short, brief ▷ *adv* in short; **d'un ton ~** sharply, curtly; **en ~** in short, in brief

Brésil [bʀezil] *nm*: **le ~** Brazil

Bretagne [bʀətaɲ] *nf*: **la ~** Brittany

bretelle [bʀətɛl] *nf* (*de vêtement*) strap; (*d'autoroute*) slip road (BRIT), entrance *ou* exit ramp (US); **bretelles** *nfpl* (*pour pantalon*) braces (BRIT), suspenders (US)

breton, ne [bʀətɔ̃, -ɔn] *adj* Breton ▷ *nm/f*: **B~, ne** Breton

brève [bʀɛv] *adj f voir* **bref**

brevet [bʀəvɛ] *nm* diploma, certificate; ~ **(des collèges)** school certificate, taken at approx. 16 years; ~ **(d'invention)** patent; **breveté, e** *adj* patented

bricolage [bʀikɔlaʒ] *nm*: **le ~** do-it-yourself (jobs)

bricoler [bʀikɔle] /1/ *vi* (*en amateur*) to do DIY jobs; (*passe-temps*) to potter about ▷ *vt* (*réparer*) to fix up; **bricoleur, -euse** *nm/f* handyman/woman, DIY enthusiast

bridge [bʀidʒ] *nm* (*Cartes*) bridge

brièvement [bʀijevmɑ̃] *adv* briefly

brigade [bʀigad] *nf* (*Police*) squad; (*Mil*) brigade; **brigadier** *nm* = sergeant

brillamment [bʀijamɑ̃] *adv* brilliantly

brillant, e [bʀijɑ̃, ɑ̃t] *adj* (*remarquable*) bright; (*luisant*) shiny, shining

briller [bʀije] /1/ *vi* to shine

brin [bʀɛ̃] *nm* (*de laine, ficelle etc*) strand; (*fig*): **un ~ de** a bit of

brindille [bʀɛ̃dij] *nf* twig

brioche [bʀijɔʃ] *nf* brioche (bun); (*fam: ventre*) paunch

brique [bʀik] *nf* brick; (*de lait*) carton

briquet [bʀikɛ] *nm* (*cigarette*) lighter

brise [bʀiz] *nf* breeze

briser [bʀize] /1/ *vt* to break; **se briser** *vi* to break

britannique [bʀitanik] *adj* British ▷ *nm/f*: **B~** Briton, British person; **les B~s** the British

brocante [bʀɔkɑ̃t] *nf* (*objets*) secondhand goods *pl*, junk; **brocanteur, -euse** *nm/f* junk shop owner; junk dealer

broche [bʀɔʃ] *nf* brooch; (*Culin*) spit; (*Méd*) pin; **à la ~** spit-roasted

broché, e [bʀɔʃe] *adj* (*livre*) paper-backed

brochet [bʀɔʃɛ] *nm* pike *inv*

brochette [bʀɔʃɛt] *nf* (*ustensile*) skewer; (*plat*) kebab

brochure [bʀɔʃyʀ] nf pamphlet, brochure, booklet

broder [bʀɔde] /1/ vt to embroider ▷ vi: **~ (sur des faits** ou **une histoire)** to embroider the facts; **broderie** nf embroidery

bronches [bʀɔ̃ʃ] nfpl bronchial tubes; **bronchite** nf bronchitis

bronze [bʀɔ̃z] nm bronze

bronzer [bʀɔ̃ze] /1/ vi to get a tan; **se bronzer** to sunbathe

brosse [bʀɔs] nf brush; **coiffé en ~** with a crewcut; **~ à cheveux** hairbrush; **~ à dents** toothbrush; **~ à habits** clothesbrush; **brosser** /1/ vt (nettoyer) to brush; (fig: tableau etc) to paint; **se brosser les dents** to brush one's teeth

brouette [bʀuɛt] nf wheelbarrow

brouillard [bʀujaʀ] nm fog

brouiller [bʀuje] /1/ vt (œufs, message) to scramble; (idées) to mix up; (rendre trouble) to cloud; (désunir: amis) to set at odds; **se brouiller** vi (ciel, vue) to cloud over; **se ~ (avec)** to fall out (with)

brouillon, ne [bʀujɔ̃, -ɔn] adj (sans soin) untidy; (qui manque d'organisation) disorganized ▷ nm (first) draft; **(papier) ~** rough paper

broussailles [bʀusaj] nfpl undergrowth sg; **broussailleux, -euse** adj bushy

brousse [bʀus] nf: **la ~** the bush

brouter [bʀute] /1/ vi to graze

brugnon [bʀyɲɔ̃] nm nectarine

bruiner [bʀɥine] /1/ vb impers: **il bruine** it's drizzling, there's a drizzle

bruit [bʀɥi] nm: **un ~** a noise, a sound; (fig: rumeur) a rumour; **le ~** noise; **sans ~** without a sound, noiselessly; **~ de fond** background noise

brûlant, e [bʀylɑ̃, -ɑ̃t] adj burning (hot); (liquide) boiling (hot)

brûlé, e [bʀyle] adj (fig: démasqué) blown ▷ nm: **odeur de ~** smell of burning

brûler [bʀyle] /1/ vt to burn; (eau bouillante) to scald; (consommer: électricité, essence) to use; (: feu rouge, signal) to go through (without stopping) ▷ vi to burn; **se brûler** to burn o.s.; (s'ébouillanter) to scald o.s.; **tu brûles** (jeu) you're getting warm ou hot

brûlure [bʀylyʀ] nf (lésion) burn; **~s d'estomac** heartburn sg

brume [bʀym] nf mist

brumeux, -euse [bʀymø, -øz] adj misty

brun, e [bʀœ̃, -yn] adj (gén, bière) brown; (cheveux, personne, tabac) dark; **elle est ~e** she's got dark hair

brunch [bʀœ̃ntʃ] nm brunch

brushing [bʀœʃiŋ] nm blow-dry

brusque [bʀysk] adj abrupt

brut, e [bʀyt] adj (diamant) uncut; (soie, minéral) raw; (Comm) gross; **(pétrole) ~** crude (oil)

brutal, e, -aux [bʀytal, -o] adj brutal

Bruxelles [bʀysɛl] n Brussels

bruyamment [bʀɥijamɑ̃] adv noisily

bruyant, e [bʀɥijɑ̃, -ɑ̃t] adj noisy

bruyère [bʀyjɛʀ] nf heather

BTS sigle m (= Brevet de technicien supérieur) vocational training certificate taken at end of two-year higher education course

bu, e [by] pp de **boire**

buccal, e, -aux [bykal, -o] adj: **par voie ~e** orally

bûche [byʃ] nf log; **prendre une ~** (fig) to come a cropper (BRIT), fall flat on one's face; **~ de Noël** Yule log

bûcher [byʃe] /1/ nm (funéraire) pyre; (supplice) stake ▷ vt (fam) to swot, slave (away) ▷ vt to swot up at, slave away at

budget [bydʒɛ] nm budget

buée [bɥe] nf (sur une vitre) mist

buffet [byfɛ] nm (meuble) sideboard; (de réception) buffet; **~ (de gare)** (station) buffet, snack bar

buis [bɥi] nm box tree; (bois) box(wood)

buisson [bɥisɔ̃] nm bush

bulbe [bylb] nm (Bot, Anat) bulb

Bulgarie [bylgaʀi] nf: **la ~** Bulgaria

bulle [byl] nf bubble

bulletin [byltɛ̃] nm (communiqué, journal) bulletin; (Scol) report; **~ d'informations** news bulletin; **~ (de vote)** ballot paper; **~ météorologique** weather report

bureau, x [byʀo] nm (meuble) desk; (pièce, service) office; (Inform) desktop; **~ de change** (foreign) exchange office ou bureau; **~ de poste** post office; **~ de tabac** tobacconist's (shop); **bureaucratie** [byʀokʀasi] nf bureaucracy

bus¹ vb [by] voir **boire**

bus² nm [bys] (véhicule) bus

buste [byst] nm (Anat) chest (: de femme) bust

but [by] vb voir **boire** ▷ nm (cible) target; (fig) goal, aim; (Football etc) goal; **de ~ en blanc** point-blank; **avoir pour ~ de faire** to aim to do; **dans le ~ de** with the intention of

butane [bytan] nm butane; (domestique) calor gas® (BRIT), butane

butiner [bytine] /1/ vi (abeilles) to gather nectar

buvais etc [byvɛ] vb voir **boire**

buvard [byvaʀ] nm blotter

buvette [byvɛt] nf bar

C

c' [s] *pron voir* **ce**

ça [sa] *pron (pour désigner)* this (: *plus loin*) that; *(comme sujet indéfini)* it; **ça m'étonne que** it surprises me that; **ça va?** how are you?; how are things?; *(d'accord?)* OK?, all right?; **où ça?** where's that?; **pourquoi ça?** why's that?; **qui ça?** who's that?; **ça alors!** *(désapprobation)* well!, really!; **c'est ça** that's right; **ça y est** that's it

cabane [kaban] *nf* hut, cabin

cabaret [kabaʀɛ] *nm* night club

cabillaud [kabijo] *nm* cod *inv*

cabine [kabin] *nf (de bateau)* cabin; *(de piscine etc)* cubicle; *(de camion, train)* cab; *(d'avion)* cockpit; **~ d'essayage** fitting room; **~ (téléphonique)** call *ou* (tele)phone box

cabinet [kabinɛ] *nm (petite pièce)* closet; *(de médecin)* surgery (BRIT), office (US); *(de notaire etc)* office (: *clientèle*) practice; *(Pol)* cabinet; **cabinets** *nmpl (w.-c.)* toilet *sg*; **~ de toilette** toilet

câble [kɑbl] *nm* cable; **le ~** *(TV)* cable television, cablevision (US)

cacahuète [kakaɥɛt] *nf* peanut

cacao [kakao] *nm* cocoa

cache [kaʃ] *nm* mask, card *(for masking)*

cache-cache [kaʃkaʃ] *nm*: **jouer à ~** to play hide-and-seek

cachemire [kaʃmiʀ] *nm* cashmere

cacher [kaʃe] /1/ *vt* to hide, conceal; **~ qch à qn** to hide *ou* conceal sth from sb; **se cacher** *vi (volontairement)* to hide; *(être caché)* to be hidden *ou* concealed

cachet [kaʃɛ] *nm (comprimé)* tablet; *(de la poste)* postmark; *(rétribution)* fee; *(fig)* style, character

cachette [kaʃɛt] *nf* hiding place; **en ~** on the sly, secretly

cactus [kaktys] *nm* cactus

cadavre [kadɑvʀ] *nm* corpse, (dead) body

Caddie® [kadi] *nm (supermarket)* trolley (BRIT), (grocery) cart (US)

cadeau, x [kado] *nm* present, gift; **faire un ~ à qn** to give sb a present *ou* gift; **faire ~ de qch à qn** to make a present of sth to sb, give sb sth as a present

cadenas [kadnɑ] *nm* padlock

cadet, te [kadɛ, -ɛt] *adj* younger; *(le plus jeune)* youngest ▷ *nm/f* youngest child *ou* one

cadran [kadʀɑ̃] *nm* dial; **~ solaire** sundial

cadre [kɑdʀ] *nm* frame; *(environnement)* surroundings *pl* ▷ *nm/f (Admin)* managerial employee, executive; **dans le ~ de** *(fig)* within the framework *ou* context of

cafard [kafaʀ] *nm* cockroach; **avoir le ~** to be down in the dumps

café [kafe] *nm* coffee; *(bistro)* café ▷ *adj inv* coffee *cpd*; **~ au lait** white coffee; **~ noir** black coffee; **café-tabac** *nm* tobacconist's or newsagent's also serving coffee and spirits; **cafétéria** *nf* cafeteria; **cafetière** *nf (pot)* coffee-pot

cage [kaʒ] *nf* cage; **~ d'escalier** (stair)well; **~ thoracique** rib cage

cageot [kaʒo] *nm* crate

cagoule [kagul] *nf (passe-montagne)* balaclava

cahier [kaje] *nm* notebook; **~ de brouillons** rough book, jotter; **~ d'exercices** exercise book

caille [kaj] *nf* quail

caillou, x [kaju] *nm (little)* stone; **caillouteux, -euse** *adj* stony

Caire [kɛʀ] *nm*: **le ~** Cairo

caisse [kɛs] *nf* box; *(où l'on met la recette)* till; *(où l'on paye)* cash desk (BRIT), checkout counter; *(: au supermarché)* checkout; *(de banque)* cashier's desk; **~ enregistreuse** cash register; **~ d'épargne (CE)** savings bank; **~ de retraite** pension fund; **caissier, -ière** *nm/f* cashier

cake [kɛk] *nm* fruit cake

calandre [kalɑ̃dʀ] *nf* radiator grill

calcaire [kalkɛʀ] *nm* limestone ▷ *adj (eau)* hard; *(Géo)* limestone *cpd*

calcul [kalkyl] *nm* calculation; **le ~** *(Scol)* arithmetic; **~ (biliaire)** (gall)stone; **calculateur** *nm*, **calculatrice** *nf* calculator; **calculer** /1/ *vt* to calculate, work out; **calculette** *nf (pocket)* calculator

cale [kal] *nf (de bateau)* hold; *(en bois)* wedge

calé, e [kale] *adj (fam)* clever, bright

caleçon [kalsɔ̃] *nm (d'homme)* boxer shorts; *(de femme)* leggings

calendrier [kalɑ̃dʀije] *nm* calendar; *(fig)* timetable

calepin [kalpɛ̃] *nm* notebook

caler [kale] /1/ *vt* to wedge ▷ *vi (moteur, véhicule)* to stall

calibre [kalibʀ] *nm* calibre

câlin, e [kalɛ̃, -in] *adj* cuddly, cuddlesome; *(regard, voix)* tender

calmant [kalmã] nm tranquillizer, sedative; (contre la douleur) painkiller

calme [kalm] adj calm, quiet ▷ nm calm(ness), quietness; **sans perdre son ~** without losing one's cool ou calmness; **calmer** /1/ vt to calm (down); (douleur, inquiétude) to ease, soothe; **se calmer** vi to calm down

calorie [kalɔʀi] nf calorie

camarade [kamaʀad] nm/f friend, pal; (Pol) comrade

Cambodge [kãbɔdʒ] nm: **le ~** Cambodia

cambriolage [kãbʀijɔlaʒ] nm burglary; **cambrioler** /1/ vt to burgle (BRIT), burglarize (US); **cambrioleur, -euse** nm/f burglar

camelote [kamlɔt] (fam) nf rubbish, trash, junk

caméra [kameʀa] nf (Ciné, TV) camera; (d'amateur) cine-camera

Cameroun [kamʀun] nm: **le ~** Cameroon

caméscope® [kameskɔp] nm camcorder

camion [kamjõ] nm lorry (BRIT), truck; **~ de dépannage** breakdown (BRIT) ou tow (US) truck; **camionnette** nf (small) van; **camionneur** nm (entrepreneur) haulage contractor (BRIT), trucker (US); (chauffeur) lorry (BRIT) ou truck driver

camomille [kamɔmij] nf camomile; (boisson) camomile tea

camp [kã] nm camp; (fig) side

campagnard, e [kãpaɲaʀ, -aʀd] adj country cpd

campagne [kãpaɲ] nf country, countryside; (Mil, Pol, Comm) campaign; **à la ~** in/to the country

camper [kãpe] /1/ vi to camp ▷ vt to sketch; **se ~ devant** to plant o.s. in front of; **campeur, -euse** nm/f camper

camping [kãpiŋ] nm camping; (terrain de) ~ campsite, camping site; **faire du ~** to go camping; **camping-car** nm camper, motorhome (US); **camping-gaz®** nm inv camp(ing) stove

Canada [kanada] nm: **le ~** Canada; **canadien, ne** adj Canadian ▷ nm/f: **Canadien, ne** Canadian ▷ nf (veste) fur-lined jacket

canal, -aux [kanal, -o] nm canal; (naturel, TV) channel; **canalisation** nf (tuyau) pipe

canapé [kanape] nm settee, sofa

canard [kanaʀ] nm duck; (fam: journal) rag

cancer [kãseʀ] nm cancer; (signe): **le C~** Cancer

cancre [kãkʀ] nm dunce

candidat, e [kãdida, -at] nm/f candidate; (à un poste) applicant, candidate; **candidature** nf (Pol) candidature; (à poste) application; **poser sa candidature à un poste** to apply for a job

cane [kan] nf (female) duck

canette [kanɛt] nf (de bière) (flip-top) bottle

canevas [kanva] nm (Couture) canvas (for tapestry work)

caniche [kaniʃ] nm poodle

canicule [kanikyl] nf scorching heat

canif [kanif] nm penknife, pocket knife

canne [kan] nf (walking) stick; **~ à pêche** fishing rod; **~ à sucre** sugar cane

cannelle [kanɛl] nf cinnamon

canoë [kanɔe] nm canoe; (sport) canoeing; **~ (kayak)** kayak

canot [kano] nm ding(h)y; **~ pneumatique** rubber ou inflatable ding(h)y; **~ de sauvetage** lifeboat

cantatrice [kãtatʀis] nf (opera) singer

cantine [kãtin] nf canteen

canton [kãtõ] nm district (consisting of several communes); (en Suisse) canton

caoutchouc [kautʃu] nm rubber; **~ mousse** foam rubber; **en ~** rubber cpd

CAP sigle m (= Certificat d'aptitude professionnelle) vocational training certificate taken at secondary school

cap [kap] nm (Géo) cape; (promontoire) headland; (fig: tournant) watershed; (Navig): **changer de ~** to change course; **mettre le ~ sur** to head for

capable [kapabl] adj able, capable; **~ de qch/faire** capable of sth/doing

capacité [kapasite] nf ability; (Jur, Inform, d'un récipient) capacity

cape [kap] nf cape, cloak; **rire sous ~** to laugh up one's sleeve

CAPES [kapɛs] sigle m (= Certificat d'aptitude au professorat de l'enseignement du second degré) secondary teaching diploma

capitaine [kapitɛn] nm captain

capital, e, -aux [kapital, -o] adj (œuvre) major; (question, rôle) fundamental ▷ nm capital; (fig) stock ▷ nf (ville) capital; (lettre) capital (letter); **d'une importance ~e** of capital importance; **capitaux** nmpl (fonds) capital sg; **~ (social)** authorized capital; **~ d'exploitation** working capital; **capitalisme** nm capitalism; **capitaliste** adj, nm/f capitalist

caporal, -aux [kapɔʀal, -o] nm lance corporal

capot [kapo] nm (Auto) bonnet (BRIT), hood (US)

câpre [kɑpʀ] nf caper

caprice [kapʀis] nm whim, caprice; **faire des ~s** to be temperamental; **capricieux, -euse** adj (fantasque) capricious; whimsical; (enfant) temperamental

Capricorne [kapʀikɔʀn] nm: **le ~** Capricorn

capsule [kapsyl] nf (de bouteille) cap; cap; (Bot etc, spatiale) capsule

capter [kapte] /1/ vt (ondes radio) to pick up; (fig) to win, capture

captivant, e [kaptivã, -ãt] adj captivating

capture [kaptyʀ] nf (action) capture;
~ **d'écran** (Inform) screenshot
capturer [kaptyʀe] /1/ vt to capture
capuche [kapyʃ] nf hood
capuchon [kapyʃɔ̃] nm hood; (de stylo)
cap, top
car [kaʀ] nm coach (BRIT), bus ▷ conj
because, for
carabine [kaʀabin] nf rifle
caractère [kaʀaktɛʀ] nm (gén)
character; **en ~s gras** in bold type; **en
petits ~s** in small print; **en ~s
d'imprimerie** in block capitals; **avoir bon/
mauvais ~** to be good-/ill-natured ou
tempered
caractériser [kaʀakteʀize] /1/ vt to
characterize; **se ~ par** to be characterized
ou distinguished by
caractéristique [kaʀakteʀistik] adj, nf
characteristic
carafe [kaʀaf] nf decanter; (pour eau, vin
ordinaire) carafe
caraïbe [kaʀaib] adj Caribbean; **les
Caraïbes** nfpl the Caribbean (Islands)
carambolage [kaʀɑ̃bɔlaʒ] nm multiple
crash, pileup
caramel [kaʀamɛl] nm (bonbon) caramel,
toffee; (substance) caramel
caravane [kaʀavan] nf caravan;
caravaning nm caravanning
carbone [kaʀbɔn] nm carbon; (double)
carbon (copy)
carbonique [kaʀbɔnik] adj: **gaz ~** carbon
dioxide; **neige ~** dry ice
carbonisé, e [kaʀbɔnize] adj charred
carburant [kaʀbyʀɑ̃] nm (motor) fuel
carburateur [kaʀbyʀatœʀ] nm
carburettor
cardiaque [kaʀdjak] adj cardiac, heart cpd
▷ nm/f heart patient; **être ~** to have a heart
condition
cardigan [kaʀdigɑ̃] nm cardigan
cardiologue [kaʀdjɔlɔg] nm/f cardiologist,
heart specialist
Carême [kaʀɛm] nm: **le ~** Lent
carence [kaʀɑ̃s] nf (manque) deficiency
caresse [kaʀɛs] nf caress
caresser [kaʀese] /1/ vt to caress; (animal)
to stroke
cargaison [kaʀgɛzɔ̃] nf cargo, freight
cargo [kaʀgo] nm freighter
caricature [kaʀikatyʀ] nf caricature
carie [kaʀi] nf: **la ~ (dentaire)** tooth decay;
une ~ a bad tooth
carnaval [kaʀnaval] nm carnival
carnet [kaʀnɛ] nm (calepin) notebook; (de
tickets, timbres etc) book; **~ de chèques**
cheque book
carotte [kaʀɔt] nf carrot
carré, e [kaʀe] adj square; (fig: franc)
straightforward ▷ nm (Math) square;
kilomètre ~ square kilometre

carreau, x [kaʀo] nm (en faïence etc) (floor)
tile; (au mur) (wall) tile; (de fenêtre) (window)
pane; (motif) check, square; (Cartes: couleur)
diamonds pl; **tissu à ~x** checked fabric
carrefour [kaʀfuʀ] nm crossroads sg
carrelage [kaʀlaʒ] nm (sol) (tiled) floor
carrelet [kaʀlɛ] nm (poisson) plaice
carrément [kaʀemɑ̃] adv (franchement)
straight out, bluntly; (sans détours, sans
hésiter) straight; (intensif) completely; **c'est
~ impossible** it's completely impossible
carrière [kaʀjɛʀ] nf (de roches) quarry;
(métier) career; **militaire de ~** professional
soldier
carrosserie [kaʀɔsʀi] nf body, bodywork
no pl (BRIT)
carrure [kaʀyʀ] nf build; (fig) calibre
cartable [kaʀtabl] nm satchel, (school)bag
carte [kaʀt] nf (de géographie) map; (marine,
du ciel) chart; (de fichier, d'abonnement etc,
à jouer) card; (au restaurant) menu; (aussi:
~ **postale**) (post)card; (aussi: ~ **de visite**)
(visiting) card; **avoir/donner ~ blanche**
to have/give carte blanche ou a free hand;
à la ~ (au restaurant) à la carte; **~ à puce**
smartcard; **~ bancaire** cash card; **C~
Bleue**® debit card; **~ de crédit** credit card;
~ de fidélité loyalty card; **~ d'identité**
identity card; **la ~ grise** (Auto) ≈ the (car)
registration document; **~ mémoire**
(d'appareil photo numérique) memory card;
~ routière road map; **~ de séjour** residence
permit; **~ SIM** SIM card; **~ téléphonique**
phonecard
carter [kaʀtɛʀ] nm sump
carton [kaʀtɔ̃] nm (matériau) cardboard;
(boîte) (cardboard) box; **faire un ~** to score a
hit; **~ (à dessin)** portfolio
cartouche [kaʀtuʃ] nf cartridge; (de
cigarettes) carton
cas [kɑ] nm case; **ne faire aucun ~ de**
to take no notice of; **en aucun ~** on no
account; **au ~ où** in case; **en ~ de** in case of,
in the event of; **en ~ de besoin** if need be;
en tout ~ in any case, at any rate
cascade [kaskad] nf waterfall, cascade
case [kɑz] nf (hutte) hut; (compartiment)
compartment; (sur un formulaire, de mots
croisés) box
caser [kɑze] /1/ (fam) vt (mettre) to put;
(loger) to put up; **se caser** vi (se marier) to
settle down; (trouver un emploi) to find a
(steady) job
caserne [kazɛʀn] nf barracks
casier [kazje] nm (case) compartment;
(pour courrier) pigeonhole (: à clef) locker;
~ judiciaire police record
casino [kazino] nm casino
casque [kask] nm helmet; (chez le coiffeur)
(hair-)dryer; (pour audition) (head-)phones
pl, headset
casquette [kaskɛt] nf cap

casse-croûte nm inv snack
casse-noisettes, casse-noix nm inv
nutcrackers pl
casse-pieds nm/f inv (fam): **il est ~, c'est un
~** he's a pain (in the neck)
casser [kɑse] /1/ vt to break; (Jur) to quash;
se casser vi, vt to break; **~ les pieds à qn**
(fam: irriter) to get on sb's nerves; **se ~ la
tête** (fam) to go to a lot of trouble
casserole [kɑsʀɔl] nf saucepan
casse-tête [kɑstɛt] nm inv (difficultés)
headache (fig)
cassette [kaset] nf (bande magnétique)
cassette; (coffret) casket
cassis [kasis] nm blackcurrant
cassoulet [kasulɛ] nm sausage and bean
hotpot
catalogue [katalɔg] nm catalogue
catalytique [katalitik] adj: **pot ~** catalytic
converter
catastrophe [katastʀɔf] nf catastrophe,
disaster
catéchisme [katefism] nm catechism
catégorie [kategɔʀi] nf category;
catégorique adj categorical
cathédrale [katedʀal] nf cathedral
catholique [katɔlik] adj, nm/f (Roman)
Catholic; **pas très ~** a bit shady ou fishy
cauchemar [koʃmaʀ] nm nightmare
cause [koz] nf cause; (Jur) lawsuit, case;
à ~ de because of, owing to; **pour ~ de** on
account of; **(et) pour ~** and for (a very) good
reason; **être en ~** (intérêts) to be at stake;
remettre en ~ to challenge; **causer** /1/ vt to
cause ▷ vi to chat, talk
caution [kosjɔ̃] nf guarantee, security; (Jur)
bail (bond); (fig) backing, support; **libéré
sous ~** released on bail
cavalier, -ière [kavalje, -jɛʀ] adj
(désinvolte) offhand ▷ nm/f rider; (au bal)
partner ▷ nm (Échecs) knight
cave [kav] nf cellar
caverne [kavɛʀn] nf cave
CD sigle m (= compact disc) CD
CDD sigle m (= contrat à durée déterminée)
fixed-term contract
CDI sigle m (= centre de documentation et
d'information) school library; (= contrat à
durée indéterminée) permanent ou open-
ended contract
CD-ROM [sedeʀɔm] nm inv CD-ROM

⊙ **MOT-CLÉ**

ce, cette [sə, sɛt] (devant nm **cet** + voyelle ou
h aspiré; pl **ces**) adj dém (proximité) this; these
pl; (non-proximité) that; those pl; **cette
maison(-ci/là)** this/that house; **cette nuit**
(qui vient) tonight; (passée) last night
▶ pron **1**: **c'est** it's, it is; **c'est un peintre**
he's ou he is a painter; **ce sont des peintres**
they're ou they are painters; **c'est le facteur**

etc (à la porte) it's the postman etc; **qui est-
ce?** who is it?; (en désignant) who is he/she?;
qu'est-ce? what is it?; **c'est toi qui lui as
parlé** it was you who spoke to him
2: **c'est ça** (correct) that's right
3: **ce qui, ce que** what; **ce qui me plaît,
c'est sa franchise** what I like about him ou
her is his ou her frankness; **il est bête, ce qui
me chagrine** he's stupid, which saddens
me; **tout ce qui bouge** everything that ou
which moves; **tout ce que je sais** all I know;
ce dont j'ai parlé what I talked about; **ce
que c'est grand!** it's so big!; voir aussi **c'est-
à-dire; -ci; est-ce que; n'est-ce pas**

ceci [səsi] pron this
céder [sede] /6/ vt to give up ▷ vi (pont,
barrage) to give way; (personne) to give in;
~ à to yield to, give in to
cédérom [sedeʀɔm] nm CD-ROM
CEDEX [sedɛks] sigle m (= courrier d'entreprise
à distribution exceptionnelle) accelerated postal
service for bulk users
cédille [sedij] nf cedilla
ceinture [sɛ̃tyʀ] nf belt; (taille) waist; **~ de
sécurité** safety ou seat belt
cela [s(ə)la] pron that; (comme sujet indéfini)
it; **~ m'étonne** it surprises me that;
quand/où ~? when/where (was that)?
célèbre [selɛbʀ] adj famous; **célébrer** /6/
vt to celebrate
céleri [selʀi] nm: **~(-rave)** celeriac; **~ (en
branche)** celery
célibataire [selibatɛʀ] adj single,
unmarried ▷ nm/f bachelor/unmarried ou
single woman; **mère ~** single ou unmarried
mother
celle, celles [sɛl] pron voir **celui**
cellule [selyl] nf (gén) cell; **~ souche** stem
cell
cellulite [selylit] nf cellulite

⊙ **MOT-CLÉ**

celui, celle (mpl **ceux**, fpl **celles**) [səlɥi, sɛl]
pron **1**: **celui-ci/là, celle-ci/là** this one/that
one; **ceux-ci, celles-ci** these (ones); **ceux-là,
celles-là** those (ones); **celui de mon frère**
my brother's; **celui du salon/du dessous**
the one in (ou from) the lounge/below
2 (+ relatif): **celui qui bouge** the one which
ou that moves; (personne) the one who
moves; **celui que je vois** the one (which
ou that) I see; (personne) the one (whom) I
see; **celui dont je parle** the one I'm talking
about
3 (valeur indéfinie): **celui qui veut** whoever
wants

cendre [sɑ̃dʀ] nf ash; **~s** (d'un défunt) ashes;
sous la ~ (Culin) in (the) embers; **cendrier**
nm ashtray

censé, e [sɑ̃se] *adj*: **être ~ faire** to be supposed to do

censeur [sɑ̃sœʀ] *nm* (*Scol*) deputy head (*BRIT*), vice-principal (*US*)

censure [sɑ̃syʀ] *nf* censorship; **censurer** /1/ *vt* (*Ciné, Presse*) to censor; (*Pol*) to censure

cent [sɑ̃] *num* a hundred, one hundred ▷ *nm* (*US, Canada, partie de l'euro etc*) cent; **centaine** *nf*: **une centaine (de)** about a hundred, a hundred or so; **des centaines (de)** hundreds (of); **centenaire** *adj* hundred-year-old ▷ *nm* (*anniversaire*) centenary; (*monnaie*) cent; **centième** *num* hundredth; **centigrade** *nm* centigrade; **centilitre** *nm* centilitre; **centime** *nm* centime; **centime d'euro** euro cent; **centimètre** *nm* centimetre; (*ruban*) tape measure, measuring tape

central, e, -aux [sɑ̃tʀal, -o] *adj* central ▷ *nm*: **~ (téléphonique)** (telephone) exchange ▷ *nf* power station; **~e électrique/nucléaire** electric/nuclear power station

centre [sɑ̃tʀ] *nm* centre; **~ commercial/ sportif/culturel** shopping/sports/arts centre; **~ d'appels** call centre; **centre-ville** *nm* town centre (*BRIT*) center (*US*)

cèpe [sɛp] *nm* (edible) boletus

cependant [s(ə)pɑ̃dɑ̃] *adv* however, nevertheless

céramique [seʀamik] *nf* ceramics *sg*

cercle [sɛʀkl] *nm* circle; **~ vicieux** vicious circle

cercueil [sɛʀkœj] *nm* coffin

céréale [seʀeal] *nf* cereal

cérémonie [seʀemɔni] *nf* ceremony; **sans ~** (*inviter, manger*) informally

cerf [sɛʀ] *nm* stag

cerf-volant [sɛʀvɔlɑ̃] *nm* kite

cerise [səʀiz] *nf* cherry; **cerisier** *nm* cherry (tree)

cerner [sɛʀne] /1/ *vt* (*Mil etc*) to surround; (*fig: problème*) to delimit, define

certain, e [sɛʀtɛ̃, -ɛn] *adj* certain; **~ (de/ que)** certain *ou* sure (of/ that); **d'un ~ âge** past one's prime, not so young; **un ~ temps** (quite) some time; **sûr et ~** absolutely certain; **un ~ Georges** someone called Georges; **~s** *pron* some; **certainement** *adv* (*probablement*) most probably *ou* likely; (*bien sûr*) certainly, of course

certes [sɛʀt] *adv* (*sans doute*) admittedly; (*bien sûr*) of course; indeed (yes)

certificat [sɛʀtifika] *nm* certificate

certifier [sɛʀtifje] /7/ *vt*: **~ qch à qn** to guarantee sth to sb

certitude [sɛʀtityd] *nf* certainty

cerveau, x [sɛʀvo] *nm* brain

cervelas [sɛʀvəla] *nm* saveloy

cervelle [sɛʀvɛl] *nf* (*Anat*) brain; (*Culin*) brain(s)

CES *sigle m* (= *Collège d'enseignement secondaire*) ≈ (junior) secondary school

ces [se] *adj dém voir* **ce**

cesse [sɛs]: **sans ~** *adv* (*tout le temps*) continually, constantly; (*sans interruption*) continuously; **il n'avait de ~ que** he would not rest until; **cesser** /1/ *vt* to stop ▷ *vi* to stop, cease; **cesser de faire** to stop doing; **cessez-le-feu** *nm inv* ceasefire

c'est-à-dire [sɛtadiʀ] *adv* that is (to say)

cet [sɛt] *adj dém voir* **ce**

ceux [sø] *pron voir* **celui**

chacun, e [ʃakœ̃, -yn] *pron* each; (*indéfini*) everyone, everybody

chagrin, e [ʃagʀɛ̃, -in] *adj* morose ▷ *nm* grief, sorrow; **avoir du ~** to be grieved *ou* sorrowful

chahut [ʃay] *nm* uproar; **chahuter** /1/ *vt* to rag, bait ▷ *vi* to make an uproar

chaîne [ʃɛn] *nf* chain; (*Radio, TV: stations*) channel; **travail à la ~** production line work; **réactions en ~** chain reactions; **~ (haute-fidélité** *ou* **hi-fi)** hi-fi system; **~ (de montagnes)** (mountain) range

chair [ʃɛʀ] *nf* flesh; **avoir la ~ de poule** to have goose pimples *ou* goose flesh; **bien en ~** plump, well-padded; **en ~ et en os** in the flesh; **~ à saucisse** sausage meat

chaise [ʃɛz] *nf* chair; **~ longue** deckchair

châle [ʃal] *nm* shawl

chaleur [ʃalœʀ] *nf* heat; (*fig: d'accueil*) warmth; **chaleureux, -euse** *adj* warm

chamailler [ʃamaje] /1/: **se chamailler** *vi* to squabble, bicker

chambre [ʃɑ̃bʀ] *nf* bedroom; (*Pol*) chamber; (*Comm*) chamber; **faire ~ à part** to sleep in separate rooms; **~ à un lit/deux lits** single/twin-bedded room; **~ à air** (*de pneu*) (inner) tube; **~ d'amis** spare *ou* guest room; **~ à coucher** bedroom; **~ d'hôte** ≈ bed and breakfast (*in private home*); **~ meublée** bedsit(ter) (*BRIT*), furnished room; **~ noire** (*Photo*) dark room

chameau, x [ʃamo] *nm* camel

chamois [ʃamwa] *nm* chamois

champ [ʃɑ̃] *nm* field; **~ de bataille** battlefield; **~ de courses** racecourse

champagne [ʃɑ̃paɲ] *nm* champagne

champignon [ʃɑ̃piɲɔ̃] *nm* mushroom; (*terme générique*) fungus; **~ de couche** *ou* **de Paris** button mushroom

champion, ne [ʃɑ̃pjɔ̃, -ɔn] *adj, nm/f* champion; **championnat** *nm* championship

chance [ʃɑ̃s] *nf*: **la ~** luck; **chances** *nfpl* (*probabilités*) chances; **avoir de la ~** to be lucky; **il a des ~s de gagner** he has a chance of winning; **bonne ~!** good luck!

change [ʃɑ̃ʒ] *nm* (*Comm*) exchange

changement [ʃɑ̃ʒmɑ̃] *nm* change; **~ climatique** climate change; **~ de vitesse** gears *pl*; (*action*) gear change

changer [ʃãʒe] /3/ vt (modifier) to change, alter; (remplacer, Comm) to change ▷ vi to change, alter; **se changer** vi to change (o.s.); **~ de** (remplacer: adresse, nom, voiture etc) to change one's; **~ de train** to change trains; **~ d'avis, ~ d'idée** to change one's mind; **~ de vitesse** to change gear; **~ qn/ qch de place** to move sb/sth to another place

chanson [ʃãsɔ̃] nf song

chant [ʃã] nm song; (art vocal) singing; (d'église) hymn

chantage [ʃãtaʒ] nm blackmail; **faire du ~** to use blackmail

chanter [ʃãte] /1/ vt, vi to sing; **si cela lui chante** (fam) if he feels like it ou fancies it; **chanteur, -euse** nm/f singer

chantier [ʃãtje] nm (building) site; (sur une route) roadworks pl; **mettre en ~** to start work on; **~ naval** shipyard

chantilly [ʃãtiji] nf voir **crème**

chantonner [ʃãtɔne] /1/ vi, vt to sing to oneself, hum

chapeau, x [ʃapo] nm hat; **~!** well done!

chapelle [ʃapɛl] nf chapel

chapitre [ʃapitʀ] nm chapter

chaque [ʃak] adj each, every; (indéfini) every

char [ʃaʀ] nm: **~ (d'assaut)** tank; **~ à voile** sand yacht

charbon [ʃaʀbɔ̃] nm coal; **~ de bois** charcoal

charcuterie [ʃaʀkytʀi] nf (magasin) pork butcher's shop and delicatessen; (produits) cooked pork meats pl; **charcutier, -ière** nm/f pork butcher

chardon [ʃaʀdɔ̃] nm thistle

charge [ʃaʀʒ] nf (fardeau) load; (Élec, Mil, Jur) charge; (rôle, mission) responsibility; **charges** nfpl (du loyer) service charges; **à la ~ de** (dépendant de) dependent upon; (aux frais de) chargeable to; **prendre en ~** to take charge of; (véhicule) to take on; (dépenses) to take care of; **~s sociales** social security contributions

chargement [ʃaʀʒəmã] nm (objets) load

charger [ʃaʀʒe] /3/ vt (voiture, fusil, caméra) to load; (batterie) to charge ▷ vi (Mil etc) to charge; **se ~ de** to see to, take care of

chargeur [ʃaʀʒœʀ] nm (de batterie) charger

chariot [ʃaʀjo] nm trolley; (charrette) waggon

charité [ʃaʀite] nf charity; **faire la ~ à** to give (something) to

charmant, e [ʃaʀmã, -ãt] adj charming

charme [ʃaʀm] nm charm; **charmer** /1/ vt to charm

charpente [ʃaʀpãt] nf frame(work); **charpentier** nm carpenter

charrette [ʃaʀɛt] nf cart

charter [tʃaʀtœʀ] nm (vol) charter flight

chasse [ʃas] nf hunting; (au fusil) shooting; (poursuite) chase; (aussi: **~ d'eau**) flush;

prendre en ~ to give chase to; **tirer la ~ (d'eau)** to flush the toilet, pull the chain; **~ à courre** hunting; **chasse-neige** nm inv snowplough (BRIT), snowplow (US); **chasser** /1/ vt to hunt; (expulser) to chase away ou out, drive away ou out; **chasseur, -euse** nm/f hunter ▷ nm (avion) fighter

chat¹ [ʃa] nm cat

chat² [tʃat] nm (Internet: salon) chat room; (: conversation) chat

châtaigne [ʃatɛɲ] nf chestnut

châtain [ʃatɛ̃] adj inv chestnut (brown); (personne) chestnut-haired

château, x [ʃato] nm (forteresse) castle; (résidence royale) palace; (manoir) mansion; **~ d'eau** water tower; **~ fort** stronghold, fortified castle

châtiment [ʃatimã] nm punishment

chaton [ʃatɔ̃] nm (Zool) kitten

chatouiller [ʃatuje] /1/ vt to tickle; **chatouilleux, -euse** [ʃatujø, -øz] adj ticklish; (fig) touchy, over-sensitive

chatte [ʃat] nf (she-)cat

chatter [tʃate] /1/ vi (Internet) to chat

chaud, e [ʃo, -od] adj (gén) warm; (très chaud) hot ▷ nm: **il fait ~** it's warm; it's hot; **avoir ~** to be warm; to be hot; **ça me tient ~** it keeps me warm; **rester au ~** to stay in the warm

chaudière [ʃodjɛʀ] nf boiler

chauffage [ʃofaʒ] nm heating; **~ central** central heating

chauffe-eau [ʃofo] nm inv water heater

chauffer [ʃofe] /1/ vt to heat ▷ vi to heat up, warm up; (trop chauffer: moteur) to overheat; **se chauffer** vi (au soleil) to warm o.s.

chauffeur [ʃofœʀ] nm driver; (privé) chauffeur

chaumière [ʃomjɛʀ] nf (thatched) cottage

chaussée [ʃose] nf road(way)

chausser [ʃose] /1/ vt (bottes, skis) to put on; (enfant) to put shoes on; **~ du 38/42** to take size 38/42

chaussette [ʃosɛt] nf sock

chausson [ʃosɔ̃] nm slipper; (de bébé) bootee; **~ (aux pommes)** (apple) turnover

chaussure [ʃosyʀ] nf shoe; **~s basses** flat shoes; **~s montantes** ankle boots; **~s de ski** ski boots

chauve [ʃov] adj bald; **chauve-souris** nf bat

chauvin, e [ʃovɛ̃, -in] adj chauvinistic

chaux [ʃo] nf lime; **blanchi à la ~** whitewashed

chef [ʃɛf] nm head, leader; (de cuisine) chef; **général/commandant en ~** general-/ commander-in-chief; **~ d'accusation** charge; **~ d'entreprise** company head; **~ d'état** head of state; **~ de famille** head of the family; **~ de file** (de parti etc) leader; **~ de gare** station master; **~ d'orchestre**

conductor; **chef-d'œuvre** nm masterpiece; **chef-lieu** nm county town

chelou, e [ʃəlu] (fam) adj sketchy, dodgy

chemin [ʃəmɛ̃] nm path; (itinéraire, direction, trajet) way; **en ~** on the way; **~ de fer** railway (BRIT), railroad (US)

cheminée [ʃəmine] nf chimney; (à l'intérieur) chimney piece, fireplace; (de bateau) funnel

chemise [ʃəmiz] nf shirt; (dossier) folder; **~ de nuit** nightdress

chemisier [ʃəmizje] nm blouse

chêne [ʃɛn] nm oak (tree); (bois) oak

chenil [ʃənil] nm kennels pl

chenille [ʃənij] nf (Zool) caterpillar

chèque [ʃɛk] nm cheque (BRIT), check (US); **faire/toucher un ~** to write/cash a cheque; **par ~** by cheque; **~ barré/sans provision** crossed (BRIT)/bad cheque; **~ de voyage** traveller's cheque; **chéquier** [ʃekje] nm cheque book

cher, -ère [ʃɛʀ] adj (aimé) dear; (coûteux) expensive, dear ▷ adv: **cela coûte ~** it's expensive

chercher [ʃɛʀʃe] /1/ vt to look for; (gloire etc) to seek; **aller ~** to go for, go and fetch; **~ à faire** to try to do; **chercheur, -euse** nm/f researcher

chéri, e [ʃeʀi] adj beloved, dear; **(mon) ~** darling

cheval, -aux [ʃəval, -o] nm horse; (Auto): **~ (vapeur)** horsepower no pl; **faire du ~** to ride; **à ~** on horseback; **à ~ sur** astride; (fig) overlapping; **~ de course** race horse

chevalier [ʃəvalje] nm knight

chevaux [ʃəvo] nmpl voir **cheval**

chevet [ʃəvɛ] nm: **au ~ de qn** at sb's bedside; **lampe de ~** bedside lamp

cheveu, x [ʃəvø] nm hair ▷ nmpl (chevelure) hair sg; **avoir les ~x courts/en brosse** to have short hair/a crew cut

cheville [ʃəvij] nf (Anat) ankle; (de bois) peg; (pour enfoncer une vis) plug

chèvre [ʃɛvʀ] nf (she-)goat

chèvrefeuille [ʃɛvʀəfœj] nm honeysuckle

chevreuil [ʃəvʀœj] nm roe deer inv; (Culin) venison

○ **MOT-CLÉ**

chez [ʃe] prép **1** (à la demeure de) at; (: direction) to; **chez qn** at/to sb's house ou place; **je suis chez moi** I'm at home; **je rentre chez moi** I'm going home; **allons chez Nathalie** let's go to Nathalie's

2 (+profession) at; (: direction) to; **chez le boulanger/dentiste** at ou to the baker's/dentist's

3 (dans le caractère, l'œuvre de) in; **chez ce poète** in this poet's work; **c'est ce que je préfère chez lui** that's what I like best about him

chic [ʃik] adj inv chic, smart; (généreux) nice, decent ▷ nm stylishness; **avoir le ~ de ou pour** to have the knack of ou for; **~!** great!

chicorée [ʃikɔʀe] nf (café) chicory; (salade) endive

chien [ʃjɛ̃] nm dog; (de pistolet) hammer; **~ d'aveugle** guide dog; **~ de garde** guard dog

chienne [ʃjɛn] nf (she-)dog, bitch

chiffon [ʃifɔ̃] nm (piece of) rag; **chiffonner** /1/ vt to crumple; (tracasser) to concern

chiffre [ʃifʀ] nm (représentant un nombre) figure; numeral; (montant, total) total, sum; **en ~s ronds** in round figures; **~ d'affaires (CA)** turnover; **chiffrer** /1/ vt (dépense) to put a figure to, assess; (message) to (en)code, cipher ▷ vi: **chiffrer à, se chiffrer à** to add up to

chignon [ʃiɲɔ̃] nm chignon, bun

Chili [ʃili] nm: **le ~** Chile; **chilien, ne** adj Chilean ▷ nm/f: **Chilien, ne** Chilean

chimie [ʃimi] nf chemistry; **chimiothérapie** [ʃimjɔteʀapi] nf chemotherapy; **chimique** adj chemical; **produits chimiques** chemicals

chimpanzé [ʃɛ̃pɑ̃ze] nm chimpanzee

Chine [ʃin] nf: **la ~** China; **chinois, e** adj Chinese ▷ nm (Ling) Chinese ▷ nm/f: **Chinois, e** Chinese

chiot [ʃjo] nm pup(py)

chips [ʃips] nfpl crisps (BRIT), (potato) chips (US)

chirurgie [ʃiʀyʀʒi] nf surgery; **~ esthétique** cosmetic ou plastic surgery; **chirurgien, ne** nm/f surgeon

chlore [klɔʀ] nm chlorine

choc [ʃɔk] nm (heurt) impact; shock; (collision) crash; (moral) shock; (affrontement) clash

chocolat [ʃɔkɔla] nm chocolate; **~ au lait** milk chocolate

chœur [kœʀ] nm (chorale) choir; (Opéra, Théât) chorus; **en ~** in chorus

choisir [ʃwaziʀ] /2/ vt to choose, select

choix [ʃwa] nm choice; selection; **avoir le ~** to have the choice; **de premier ~** (Comm) class ou grade one; **de ~** choice cpd, selected; **au ~** as you wish ou prefer

chômage [ʃomaʒ] nm unemployment; **mettre au ~** to make redundant, put out of work; **être au ~** to be unemployed ou out of work; **chômeur, -euse** nm/f unemployed person

chope [ʃɔp] nf tankard

choquer [ʃɔke] /1/ vt (offenser) to shock; (commotionner) to shake (up)

chorale [kɔʀal] nf choir

chose [ʃoz] nf thing; **c'est peu de ~** it's nothing much

chou, x [ʃu] nm cabbage; **mon petit ~** (my) sweetheart; **~ à la crème** cream bun (made of choux pastry); **~ de Bruxelles** Brussels sprout; **choucroute** nf sauerkraut

chouette [ʃwɛt] nf owl ▷ adj (fam) great, smashing

chou-fleur [ʃuflœʀ] nm cauliflower

chrétien, ne [kʀetjɛ̃, -ɛn] adj, nm/f Christian

Christ [kʀist] nm: **le ~** Christ; **christianisme** nm Christianity

chronique [kʀɔnik] adj chronic ▷ nf (de journal) column, page; (historique) chronicle; (Radio, TV): **la ~ sportive/théâtrale** the sports/theatre review

chronologique [kʀɔnɔlɔʒik] adj chronological

chronomètre [kʀɔnɔmɛtʀ] nm stopwatch; **chronométrer** /6/ vt to time

chrysanthème [kʀizɑ̃tɛm] nm chrysanthemum

- **CHRYSANTHÈME**
- Chrysanthemums are strongly associated
- with funerals in France, and therefore
- should not be given as gifts.

chuchotement [ʃyʃɔtmɑ̃] nm whisper

chuchoter [ʃyʃɔte] /1/ vt, vi to whisper

chut [ʃyt] excl sh!

chute [ʃyt] nf fall; (déchet) scrap; **faire une ~ (de 10 m)** to fall (10 m); **~s de pluie/neige** rain/snowfalls; **~ (d'eau)** waterfall; **~ libre** free fall

Chypre [ʃipʀ] nm/f Cyprus

-ci [si] adv voir **par** ▷ adj dém: **ce garçon~/-là** this/that boy; **ces femmes~/-là** these/those women

cible [sibl] nf target

cicatrice [sikatʀis] nf scar; **cicatriser** /1/ vt to heal

ci-contre [sikɔ̃tʀ] adv opposite

ci-dessous [sidəsu] adv below

ci-dessus [sidəsy] adv above

cidre [sidʀ] nm cider

Cie abr (= compagnie) Co

ciel [sjɛl] nm sky; (Rel) heaven

cieux [sjø] nmpl voir **ciel**

cigale [sigal] nf cicada

cigare [sigaʀ] nm cigar

cigarette [sigaʀɛt] nf cigarette; **~ électronique** e-cigarette

ci-inclus, e [siɛ̃kly, -yz] adj, adv enclosed

ci-joint, e [siʒwɛ̃, -ɛ̃t] adj, adv enclosed

cil [sil] nm (eye)lash

cime [sim] nf top; (montagne) peak

ciment [simɑ̃] nm cement

cimetière [simtjɛʀ] nm cemetery; (d'église) churchyard

cinéaste [sineast] nm/f film-maker

cinéma [sinema] nm cinema

cinq [sɛ̃k] num five; **cinquantaine** nf: **une cinquantaine (de)** about fifty; **avoir la cinquantaine** (âge) to be around fifty; **cinquante** num fifty; **cinquantenaire** adj,

nm/f fifty-year-old; **cinquième** num fifth ▷ nf (Scol) year 8 (BRIT), seventh grade (US)

cintre [sɛ̃tʀ] nm coat-hanger

cintré, e [sɛ̃tʀe] adj (chemise) fitted

cirage [siʀaʒ] nm (shoe) polish

circonflexe [siʀkɔ̃flɛks] adj: **accent ~** circumflex accent

circonstance [siʀkɔ̃stɑ̃s] nf circumstance; (occasion) occasion; **~s atténuantes** mitigating circumstances

circuit [siʀkɥi] nm (trajet) tour, (round) trip; (Élec, Tech) circuit

circulaire [siʀkylɛʀ] adj, nf circular

circulation [siʀkylasjɔ̃] nf circulation; (Auto): **la ~** (the) traffic

circuler [siʀkyle] /1/ vi (véhicules) to drive (along); (passants) to walk along; (train etc) to run; (sang, devises) to circulate; **faire ~** (nouvelle) to spread (about), circulate; (badauds) to move on

cire [siʀ] nf wax; **ciré** nm oilskin; **cirer** /1/ vt to wax, polish

cirque [siʀk] nm circus; (fig) chaos, bedlam; **quel ~!** what a carry-on!

ciseau, x [sizo] nm: **~ (à bois)** chisel ▷ nmpl (paire de ciseaux) (pair of) scissors

citadin, e [sitadɛ̃, -in] nm/f city dweller

citation [sitasjɔ̃] nf (d'auteur) quotation; (Jur) summons sg

cité [site] nf town; (plus grande) city; **~ universitaire** students' residences pl

citer [site] /1/ vt (un auteur) to quote (from); (nommer) to name; (Jur) to summon

citoyen, ne [sitwajɛ̃, -ɛn] nm/f citizen

citron [sitʀɔ̃] nm lemon; **~ pressé** (fresh) lemon juice; **~ vert** lime; **citronnade** nf still lemonade

citrouille [sitʀuj] nf pumpkin

civet [sivɛ] nm: **~ de lapin** rabbit stew

civière [sivjɛʀ] nf stretcher

civil, e [sivil] adj (Jur, Admin, poli) civil; (non militaire) civilian; **en ~** in civilian clothes; **dans le ~** in civilian life

civilisation [sivilizasjɔ̃] nf civilization

clair, e [klɛʀ] adj light; (chambre) light, bright; (eau, son, fig) clear ▷ adv: **voir ~** to see clearly ▷ nm: **mettre au ~** (notes etc) to tidy up; **tirer qch au ~** to clear sth up, clarify sth; **~ de lune** moonlight; **clairement** adv clearly

clairière [klɛʀjɛʀ] nf clearing

clandestin, e [klɑ̃dɛstɛ̃, -in] adj clandestine, covert; (Pol) underground, clandestine; (travailleur, immigration) illegal; **passager ~** stowaway

claque [klak] nf (gifle) slap; **claquer** /1/ vi (porte) to bang, slam; (fam: mourir) to snuff it ▷ vt (porte) to slam, bang; (doigts) to snap; (fam: dépenser) to blow; **elle claquait des dents** her teeth were chattering; **être claqué** (fam) to be dead tired; **se claquer un muscle** to pull ou strain a muscle; **claquettes** *nfpl* tap-dancing *sg*; (*chaussures*) flip-flops

clarinette [klaʀinɛt] *nf* clarinet

classe [klɑs] *nf* class; (*Scol: local*) class(room); (: *leçon*) class; (: *élèves*) class; **aller en ~** to go to school; **classement** *nm* (*rang: Scol*) place; (: *Sport*) placing; (*liste: Scol*) class list (in order of merit); (: *Sport*) placings *pl*

classer [klɑse] /1/ *vt* (*idées, livres*) to classify; (*papiers*) to file; (*candidat, concurrent*) to grade; (*Jur: affaire*) to close; **se ~ premier/ dernier** to come first/last; (*Sport*) to finish first/last; **classeur** *nm* (*cahier*) file

classique [klasik] *adj* (*sobre, coupe etc*) classic(al), classical; (*habituel*) standard, classic

clavicule [klavikyl] *nf* collarbone

clavier [klavje] *nm* keyboard; (*de portable*) keypad

clé [kle] *nf* key; (*Mus*) clef; (*de mécanicien*) spanner (*BRIT*), wrench (*US*); **prix ~s en main** (*d'une voiture*) on-the-road price; **~ de contact** ignition key; **~ USB** USB key

clergé [klɛʀʒe] *nm* clergy

clic [klik] *nm* (*Inform*) click

cliché [kliʃe] *nm* (*fig*) cliché; (*Photo*) negative; print; (*Typo*) (printing) plate; (*Ling*) cliché

client, e [klijã, -ãt] *nm/f* (*acheteur*) customer, client; (*d'hôtel*) guest, patron; (*du docteur*) patient; (*de l'avocat*) client; **clientèle** *nf* (*du magasin*) customers *pl*, clientèle; (*du docteur, de l'avocat*) practice

cligner [kliɲe] /1/ *vi*: **~ des yeux** to blink (one's eyes); **~ de l'œil** to wink; **clignotant** *nm* (*Auto*) indicator; **clignoter** /1/ *vi* (*étoiles etc*) to twinkle; (*lumière*) to flicker

climat [klima] *nm* climate

climatisation [klimatizasjɔ̃] *nf* air conditioning; **climatisé, e** *adj* air-conditioned

clin d'œil [klɛ̃dœj] *nm* wink; **en un ~** in a flash

clinique [klinik] *nf* (*private*) clinic

clip [klip] *nm* (*pince*) clip; (*boucle d'oreille*) clip-on; **(vidéo) ~** pop (*ou* promotional) video

cliquer [klike] /1/ *vi* (*Inform*) to click; **~ deux fois** to double-click ▷ *vt* to click; **~ sur** to click on

clochard, e [klɔʃaʀ, -aʀd] *nm/f* tramp

cloche [klɔʃ] *nf* (*d'église*) bell; (*fam*) clot; **clocher** /1/ *nm* church tower; (*en pointe*) steeple ▷ *vi* (*fam*) to be *ou* go wrong; **de clocher** (*péj*) parochial

cloison [klwazɔ̃] *nf* partition (wall)

clonage [klɔnaʒ] *nm* cloning

cloner [klɔne] /1/ *vt* to clone

cloque [klɔk] *nf* blister

clore [klɔʀ] /45/ *vt* to close

clôture [klotyʀ] *nf* closure; (*barrière*) enclosure

clou [klu] *nm* nail; **clous** *nmpl* = **passage clouté**; **pneus à ~s** studded tyres; **le ~ du spectacle** the highlight of the show; **~ de girofle** clove

clown [klun] *nm* clown

club [klœb] *nm* club

CNRS *sigle m* (= *Centre national de la recherche scientifique*) ≈ SERC (*BRIT*), ≈ NSF (*US*)

coaguler [kɔagyle] /1/ *vi, vt*, **se coaguler** *vi* (*sang*) to coagulate

cobaye [kɔbaj] *nm* guinea-pig

coca® [kɔka] *nm* Coke®

cocaïne [kɔkain] *nf* cocaine

coccinelle [kɔksinɛl] *nf* ladybird (*BRIT*), ladybug (*US*)

cocher [kɔʃe] /1/ *vt* to tick off

cochon, ne [kɔʃɔ̃, -ɔn] *nm* pig ▷ *adj* (*fam*) dirty, smutty; **~ d'Inde** guinea pig, **cochonnerie** *nf* (*fam: saleté*) filth; (*marchandises*) rubbish, trash

cocktail [kɔktɛl] *nm* cocktail; (*réception*) cocktail party

cocorico [kɔkɔriko] *excl, nm* cock-a-doodle-do

cocotte [kɔkɔt] *nf* (*en fonte*) casserole; **ma ~** (*fam*) sweetie (pie); **~ (minute)®** pressure cooker

code [kɔd] *nm* code ▷ *adj*: **phares ~s** dipped lights, **se mettre en ~(s)** to dip (*BRIT*) *ou* dim (*US*) one's (head)lights; **~ à barres** bar code; **~ civil** Common Law; **~ pénal** penal code; **~ postal** (*numéro*) postcode (*BRIT*), zip code (*US*); **~ de la route** highway code; **~ secret** cipher

cœur [kœʀ] *nm* heart; (*Cartes: couleur*) hearts *pl*; (: *carte*) heart; **avoir bon ~** to be kind-hearted; **avoir mal au ~** to feel sick; **par ~** by heart; **de bon ~** willingly; **cela lui tient à ~** that's (very) close to his heart

coffre [kɔfʀ] *nm* (*meuble*) chest; (*d'auto*) boot (*BRIT*), trunk (*US*); **coffre-fort** *nm* safe; **coffret** *nm* casket

cognac [kɔɲak] *nm* brandy, cognac

cogner [kɔɲe] /1/ *vi* to knock; **se ~ contre** to knock *ou* bump into; **se ~ la tête** to bang one's head

cohérent, e [kɔeʀã, -ãt] *adj* coherent, consistent

coiffé, e [kwafe] *adj*: **bien/mal ~** with tidy/ untidy hair; **~ d'un béret** wearing a beret

coiffer [kwafe] /1/ *vt* (*fig: surmonter*) to cover, top; **~ qn** to do sb's hair; **se coiffer** *vi* to do one's hair; **coiffeur, -euse** *nm/f* hairdresser ▷ *nf* (*table*) dressing table; **coiffure** *nf* (*cheveux*) hairstyle, hairdo; (*art*): **la coiffure** hairdressing

coin [kwɛ̃] *nm* corner; (*pour coincer*) wedge; **l'épicerie du ~** the local grocer; **dans le ~** (*aux alentours*) in the area, around about; (*habiter*) locally; **je ne suis pas du ~** I'm not from here; **au ~ du feu** by the fireside; **regard en ~** side(ways) glance

coincé, e [kwɛse] *adj* stuck, jammed; (*fig: inhibé*) inhibited, with hang-ups

coïncidence [kɔɛ̃sidɑ̃s] *nf* coincidence

coing [kwɛ̃] *nm* quince

col [kɔl] *nm* (*de chemise*) collar; (*encolure, cou*) neck; (*de montagne*) pass; ~ **roulé** polo-neck; ~ **de l'utérus** cervix

colère [kɔlɛʀ] *nf* anger; **une ~** a fit of anger; **être en ~ (contre qn)** to be angry (with sb); **mettre qn en ~** to make sb angry; **se mettre en ~ contre qn** to get angry with sb; **se mettre en ~** to get angry; **coléreux, -euse, colérique** *adj* quick-tempered, irascible

colin [kɔlɛ̃] *nm* hake

colique [kɔlik] *nf* diarrhoea

colis [kɔli] *nm* parcel

collaborer [kɔ(l)labɔʀe] /1/ *vi* to collaborate; ~ **à** to collaborate on; (*revue*) to contribute to

collant, e [kɔlɑ̃, -ɑ̃t] *adj* sticky; (*robe etc*) clinging, skintight; (*péj*) clinging ▷ *nm* (*bas*) tights *pl*; (*de danseur*) leotard

colle [kɔl] *nf* glue; (*à papiers peints*) (wallpaper) paste; (*devinette*) teaser, riddle; (*Scol: fam*) detention

collecte [kɔlɛkt] *nf* collection; **collectif, -ive** *adj* collective; (*visite, billet etc*) group *cpd*

collection [kɔlɛksjɔ̃] *nf* collection; (*Édition*) series; **collectionner** /1/ *vt* (*tableaux, timbres*) to collect; **collectionneur, -euse** [kɔlɛksjɔnœʀ, -øz] *nm/f* collector

collectivité [kɔlɛktivite] *nf* group; **les ~s locales** local authorities

collège [kɔlɛʒ] *nm* (*école*) (secondary) school; (*assemblée*) body; **collégien, ne** *nm/f* secondary school pupil (BRIT), high school student (US)

collègue [kɔ(l)lɛg] *nm/f* colleague

coller [kɔle] /1/ *vt* (*papier, timbre*) to stick (on); (*affiche*) to stick up; (*enveloppe*) to stick down; (*morceaux*) to stick *ou* glue together; (*Inform*) to paste; (*fam: mettre, fourrer*) to stick, shove; (*Scol: fam*) to keep in ▷ *vi* (*être collant*) to be sticky; (*adhérer*) to stick; ~ **à** to stick to; **être collé à un examen** (*fam*) to fail an exam

collier [kɔlje] *nm* (*bijou*) necklace; (*de chien, Tech*) collar

colline [kɔlin] *nf* hill

collision [kɔlizjɔ̃] *nf* collision, crash; **entrer en ~ (avec)** to collide (with)

collyre [kɔliʀ] *nm* eye lotion

colombe [kɔlɔ̃b] *nf* dove

Colombie [kɔlɔ̃bi] *nf*: **la ~** Colombia

colonie [kɔlɔni] *nf* colony; ~ **(de vacances)** holiday camp (*for children*)

colonne [kɔlɔn] *nf* column; **se mettre en ~ par deux/quatre** to get into twos/fours; ~ **(vertébrale)** spine, spinal column

colorant [kɔlɔʀɑ̃] *nm* colouring

colorer [kɔlɔʀe] /1/ *vt* to colour

colorier [kɔlɔʀje] /7/ *vt* to colour (in)

coloris [kɔlɔʀi] *nm* colour, shade

colza [kɔlza] *nm* rape(seed)

coma [kɔma] *nm* coma; **être dans le ~** to be in a coma

combat [kɔ̃ba] *nm* fight; fighting *no pl*; ~ **de boxe** boxing match; **combattant** *nm*: **ancien combattant** war veteran; **combattre** /41/ *vt* to fight; (*épidémie, ignorance*) to combat, fight against

combien [kɔ̃bjɛ̃] *adv* (*quantité*) how much; (*nombre*) how many; ~ **de** how much; (*nombre*) how many; ~ **de temps** how long; ~ **coûte/pèse ceci?** how much does this cost/weigh?; **on est le ~ aujourd'hui?** (*fam*) what's the date today?

combinaison [kɔ̃binɛzɔ̃] *nf* combination; (*astuce*) scheme; (*de femme*) slip; (*de plongée*) wetsuit; (*bleu de travail*) boilersuit (BRIT), coveralls *pl* (US)

combiné [kɔ̃bine] *nm* (*aussi*: ~ **téléphonique**) receiver

comble [kɔ̃bl] *adj* (*salle*) packed (full) ▷ *nm* (*du bonheur, plaisir*) height; **combles** *nmpl* (*Constr*) attic *sg*, loft *sg*; **c'est le ~!** that beats everything!

combler [kɔ̃ble] /1/ *vt* (*trou*) to fill in; (*besoin, lacune*) to fill; (*déficit*) to make good; (*satisfaire*) fulfil

comédie [kɔmedi] *nf* comedy; (*fig*) playacting *no pl*; **faire une ~** (*fig*) to make a fuss; ~ **musicale** musical; **comédien, ne** *nm/f* actor/actress

comestible [kɔmɛstibl] *adj* edible

comique [kɔmik] *adj* (*drôle*) comical; (*Théât*) comic ▷ *nm* (*artiste*) comic, comedian

commandant [kɔmɑ̃dɑ̃] *nm* (*gén*) commander, commandant; (*Navig*) captain

commande [kɔmɑ̃d] *nf* (*Comm*) order; **commandes** *nfpl* (*Aviat etc*) controls; **sur ~** to order; **commander** /1/ *vt* (*Comm*) to order; (*diriger, ordonner*) to command; **commander à qn de faire** to command *ou* order sb to do

⬤ **MOT-CLÉ**

comme [kɔm] *prép* **1** (*comparaison*) like; **tout comme son père** just like his father; **fort comme un bœuf** as strong as an ox; **joli comme tout** ever so pretty

2 (*manière*) like; **faites-le comme ça** do it like this, do it this way; **comme ci, comme ça** so-so, middling

3 (*en tant que*) as a; **donner comme prix** to give as a prize; **travailler comme secrétaire** to work as a secretary

4: **comme il faut** *adv* properly

▶ *conj* **1** (*ainsi que*) as; **elle écrit comme elle parle** she writes as she talks; **comme si** as if

2 (*au moment où, alors que*) as; **il est parti**

comme j'arrivais he left as I arrived **3** (*parce que, puisque*) as; **comme il était en retard, il ...** as he was late, he ... ▶ *adv*: **comme il est fort/c'est bon!** he's so strong/it's so good!

commencement [kɔmɑ̃smɑ̃] *nm* beginning, start

commencer [kɔmɑ̃se] /3/ *vt, vi* to begin, start; **~ à** *ou* **de faire** to begin *ou* start doing

comment [kɔmɑ̃] *adv* how; **~?** (*que dites-vous*) (I beg your) pardon?; **et ~!** and how!

commentaire [kɔmɑ̃tɛʀ] *nm* comment; remark; **~ (de texte)** commentary

commerçant, e [kɔmɛʀsɑ̃, -ɑ̃t] *nm/f* shopkeeper, trader

commerce [kɔmɛʀs] *nm* (*activité*) trade, commerce; (*boutique*) business; **~ électronique** e-commerce; **~ équitable** fair trade, **commercial, e, -aux** *adj* commercial, trading; (*péj*) commercial; **commercialiser** /1/ *vt* to market

commettre [kɔmɛtʀ] /56/ *vt* to commit

commissaire [kɔmisɛʀ] *nm* (*de police*) ≈ (police) superintendent; **~ aux comptes** (*Admin*) auditor; **commissariat** *nm* police station

commission [kɔmisjɔ̃] *nf* (*comité, pourcentage*) commission; (*message*) message; (*course*) errand; **commissions** *nfpl* (*achats*) shopping *sg*

commode [kɔmɔd] *adj* (*pratique*) convenient, handy; (*facile*) easy; (*personne*): **pas ~** awkward (to deal with) ▷ *nf* chest of drawers

commun, e [kɔmœ̃, -yn] *adj* common; (*pièce*) communal, shared; (*réunion, effort*) joint ▷ *nf* (*Admin*) commune; ≈ district (: *urbaine*) ≈ borough, **communs** *nmpl* (*bâtiments*) outbuildings; **cela sort du ~** it's out of the ordinary; **le ~ des mortels** the common run of people; **en ~** (*faire*) jointly; **mettre en ~** to pool, share; **d'un ~ accord** of one accord

communauté [kɔmynote] *nf* community

commune [kɔmyn] *adj f, nf voir* **commun**

communication [kɔmynikasjɔ̃] *nf* communication

communier [kɔmynje] /7/ *vi* (*Rel*) to receive communion

communion [kɔmynjɔ̃] *nf* communion

communiquer [kɔmynike] /1/ *vt* (*nouvelle, dossier*) to pass on, convey; (*peur etc*) to communicate ▷ *vi* to communicate; **se ~ à** (*se propager*) to spread to

communisme [kɔmynism] *nm* communism; **communiste** *adj, nm/f* communist

commutateur [kɔmytatœʀ] *nm* (*Elec*) (change-over) switch, commutator

compact, e [kɔ̃pakt] *adj* (*dense*) dense; (*appareil*) compact

compagne [kɔ̃paɲ] *nf* companion

compagnie [kɔ̃paɲi] *nf* (*firme, Mil*) company; **tenir ~ à qn** to keep sb company; **fausser ~ à qn** to give sb the slip, slip *ou* sneak away from sb; **~ aérienne** airline (company)

compagnon [kɔ̃paɲɔ̃] *nm* companion

comparable [kɔ̃paʀabl] *adj*: **~ (à)** comparable (to)

comparaison [kɔ̃paʀɛzɔ̃] *nf* comparison

comparer [kɔ̃paʀe] /1/ *vt* to compare; **~ qch/qn à** *ou* **et** (*pour choisir*) to compare sth/sb with *ou* and; (*pour établir une similitude*) to compare sth/sb to *ou* and

compartiment [kɔ̃paʀtimɑ̃] *nm* compartment

compas [kɔ̃pɑ] *nm* (*Géom*) (pair of) compasses *pl*; (*Navig*) compass

compatible [kɔ̃patibl] *adj* compatible

compatriote [kɔ̃patʀijɔt] *nm/f* compatriot

compensation [kɔ̃pɑ̃sasjɔ̃] *nf* compensation

compenser [kɔ̃pɑ̃se] /1/ *vt* to compensate for, make up for

compétence [kɔ̃petɑ̃s] *nf* competence

compétent, e [kɔ̃petɑ̃, -ɑ̃t] *adj* (*apte*) competent, capable

compétition [kɔ̃petisjɔ̃] *nf* (*gén*) competition; (*Sport: épreuve*) event; **la ~ automobile** motor racing

complément [kɔ̃plemɑ̃] *nm* complement; (*reste*) remainder; **~ d'information** (*Admin*) supplementary *ou* further information; **complémentaire** *adj* complementary; (*additionnel*) supplementary

complet, -ète [kɔ̃plɛ, -ɛt] *adj* complete; (*plein: hôtel etc*) full ▷ *nm* (*aussi*: **~-veston**) suit; **pain ~** wholemeal bread, **complètement** *adv* completely; **compléter** /6/ *vt* (*porter à la quantité voulue*) to complete; (*augmenter: connaissances, études*) to complement, supplement; (: *garde-robe*) to add to

complexe [kɔ̃plɛks] *adj* complex ▷ *nm*: **~ hospitalier/industriel** hospital/industrial complex; **complexé, e** *adj* mixed-up, hung-up

complication [kɔ̃plikasjɔ̃] *nf* complexity, intricacy; (*difficulté, ennui*) complication; **complications** *nfpl* (*Méd*) complications

complice [kɔ̃plis] *nm* accomplice

compliment [kɔ̃plimɑ̃] *nm* (*louange*) compliment; **compliments** *nmpl* (*félicitations*) congratulations

compliqué, e [kɔ̃plike] *adj* complicated, complex; (*personne*) complicated

comportement [kɔ̃pɔʀtəmɑ̃] *nm* behaviour

comporter [kɔ̃pɔʀte] /1/ *vt* (*consister en*) to consist of, comprise; (*être équipé de*) to have; **se comporter** *vi* to behave

composer [kɔ̃poze] /1/ vt (musique, texte) to compose; (mélange, équipe) to make up; (faire partie de) to make up, form ▷ vi (transiger) to come to terms; **se ~ de** to be composed of, be made up of; **~ un numéro** (au téléphone) to dial a number; **compositeur, -trice** nm/f (Mus) composer; **composition** nf composition; (Scol) test

composter [kɔ̃pɔste] /1/ vt (billet) to punch

* **COMPOSTER**
*
* In France you have to punch your ticket on
* the platform to validate it before getting
* onto the train.

compote [kɔ̃pɔt] nf stewed fruit no pl; **~ de pommes** stewed apples

compréhensible [kɔ̃preãsibl] adj comprehensible; (attitude) understandable

compréhensif, -ive [kɔ̃preãsif, -iv] adj understanding

▌ Attention à ne pas traduire compréhensif par comprehensive.

comprendre [kɔ̃prãdr] /58/ vt to understand; (se composer de) to comprise, consist of

compresse [kɔ̃pres] nf compress

comprimé [kɔ̃prime] nm tablet

compris, e [kɔ̃pri, -iz] pp de **comprendre** ▷ adj (inclus) included; **~ entre** (situé) contained between; **la maison ~e/non ~e, y/non ~ la maison** including/excluding the house; **100 euros tout ~** 100 euros all inclusive ou all-in

comptabilité [kɔ̃tabilite] nf (activité, technique) accounting, accountancy; accounts pl, books pl; (service) accounts office ou department

comptable [kɔ̃tabl] nm/f accountant

comptant [kɔ̃tã] adv: **payer ~** to pay cash; **acheter ~** to buy for cash

compte [kɔ̃t] nm count; (total, montant) count, (right) number; (bancaire, facture) account; **comptes** nmpl accounts, books; (fig) explanation sg; **en fin de ~** all things considered; **s'en tirer à bon ~** to get off lightly; **pour le ~ de** on behalf of; **pour son propre ~** for one's own benefit; **travailler à son ~** to work for oneself; **régler un ~** (s'acquitter de qch) to settle an account; (se venger) to get one's own back; **rendre des ~s à qn** (fig) to be answerable to sb; **tenir ~ de qch** to take sth into account; **~ courant (CC)** current account; **~ à rebours** countdown; **~ rendu** account, report; (de film, livre) review; voir aussi **rendre; compte-gouttes** nm inv dropper

compter [kɔ̃te] /1/ vt to count; (facturer) to charge for; (avoir à son actif, comporter) to have; (prévoir) to allow, reckon; (penser, espérer): **~ réussir/revenir** to expect to succeed/return ▷ vi to count; (être économe) to economize; (figurer): **~ parmi** to be ou rank among; **~ sur** to count (up)on; **~ avec qch/qn** to reckon with ou take account of sth/sb; **sans ~ que** besides which

compteur [kɔ̃tœr] nm meter; **~ de vitesse** speedometer

comptine [kɔ̃tin] nf nursery rhyme

comptoir [kɔ̃twar] nm (de magasin) counter; (de café) counter, bar

con, ne [kɔ̃, kɔn] adj (fam!) bloody (BRIT !) ou damned stupid

concentrer [kɔ̃sãtre] /1/ vt to concentrate; **se concentrer** vi to concentrate

concerner [kɔ̃serne] /1/ vt to concern; **en ce qui me concerne** as far as I am concerned

concert [kɔ̃ser] nm concert; **de ~** (décider) unanimously

concessionnaire [kɔ̃sesjɔner] nm/f agent, dealer

concevoir [kɔ̃s(ə)vwar] /28/ vt (idée, projet) to conceive (of); (comprendre) to understand; (enfant) to conceive; **maison bien/mal conçue** well-/badly-designed ou -planned house

concierge [kɔ̃sjɛrʒ] nm/f caretaker

concis, e [kɔ̃si, -iz] adj concise

conclure [kɔ̃klyr] /35/ vt to conclude; **conclusion** nf conclusion

conçois [kɔ̃swa] vb voir **concevoir**

concombre [kɔ̃kɔ̃br] nm cucumber

concours [kɔ̃kur] nm competition; (Scol) competitive examination; (assistance) aid, help; **~ de circonstances** combination of circumstances; **~ hippique** horse show; voir **hors-concours**

concret, -ète [kɔ̃krɛ, -ɛt] adj concrete

conçu, e [kɔ̃sy] pp de **concevoir**

concubinage [kɔ̃kybinaʒ] nm (Jur) cohabitation

concurrence [kɔ̃kyrãs] nf competition; **jusqu'à ~ de** up to; **faire ~ à** to be in competition with

concurrent, e [kɔ̃kyrã, -ãt] nm/f (Sport, Écon etc) competitor; (Scol) candidate

condamner [kɔ̃dane] /1/ vt (blâmer) to condemn; (Jur) to sentence; (porte, ouverture) to fill in, block up; **~ qn à deux ans de prison** to sentence sb to two years' imprisonment

condensation [kɔ̃dãsasjɔ̃] nf condensation

condition [kɔ̃disjɔ̃] nf condition; **conditions** nfpl (tarif, prix) terms; (circonstances) conditions; **sans ~** unconditionally; **à ~ de ou que** provided that; **conditionnel, le** nm conditional (tense)

conditionnement [kɔ̃disjɔnmã] nm (emballage) packaging

condoléances [kɔ̃dɔleãs] nfpl condolences

conducteur, -trice [kɔ̃dyktœr, -tris] nm/f driver ▷ nm (Élec etc) conductor
conduire [kɔ̃dɥir] /38/ vt to drive; (délégation, troupeau) to lead; **se conduire** vi to behave; **~ vers/à** to lead towards/to; **~ qn quelque part** to take sb somewhere; to drive sb somewhere
conduite [kɔ̃dɥit] nf (comportement) behaviour; (d'eau, de gaz) pipe; **sous la ~ de** led by
confection [kɔ̃fɛksjɔ̃] nf (fabrication) making; (Couture): **la ~** the clothing industry
conférence [kɔ̃ferɑ̃s] nf (exposé) lecture; (pourparlers) conference; **~ de presse** press conference
confesser [kɔ̃fese] /1/ vt to confess; **confession** nf confession; (culte: catholique etc) denomination
confetti [kɔ̃feti] nm confetti no pl
confiance [kɔ̃fjɑ̃s] nf (en l'honnêteté de qn) confidence, trust; (en la valeur de qch) faith; **avoir ~ en** to have confidence ou faith in, trust; **faire ~ à** to trust; **mettre qn en ~** to win sb's trust; **~ en soi** self-confidence; voir **question**
confiant, e [kɔ̃fjɑ̃, -ɑ̃t] adj confident; trusting
confidence [kɔ̃fidɑ̃s] nf confidence, **confidentiel, le** adj confidential
confier [kɔ̃fje] /7/ vt: **~ à qn** (objet en dépot, travail etc) to entrust to sb; (secret, pensée) to confide to sb; **se ~ à qn** to confide in sb
confirmation [kɔ̃firmasjɔ̃] nf confirmation
confirmer [kɔ̃firme] /1/ vt to confirm
confiserie [kɔ̃fizri] nf (magasin) confectioner's ou sweet shop; **confiseries** nfpl (bonbons) confectionery sg
confisquer [kɔ̃fiske] /1/ vt to confiscate
confit, e [kɔ̃fi, -it] adj: **fruits ~s** crystallized fruits ▷ nm: **~ d'oie** potted goose
confiture [kɔ̃fityr] nf jam
conflit [kɔ̃fli] nm conflict
confondre [kɔ̃fɔ̃dr] /41/ vt (jumeaux, faits) to confuse, mix up; (témoin, menteur) to confound; **se confondre** vi to merge; **se ~ en excuses** to offer profuse apologies
conforme [kɔ̃fɔrm] adj: **~ à** (en accord avec: loi, règle) in accordance with; **conformément** adv: **conformément à** in accordance with; **conformer** /1/ vt: **se conformer à** to conform to
confort [kɔ̃fɔr] nm comfort; **tout ~** (Comm) with all mod cons (BRIT) ou modern conveniences; **confortable** adj comfortable
confronter [kɔ̃frɔ̃te] /1/ vt to confront
confus, e [kɔ̃fy, -yz] adj (vague) confused; (embarrassé) embarrassed; **confusion** nf (voir confus) confusion; embarrassment; (voir confondre) confusion; mixing up

congé [kɔ̃ʒe] nm (vacances) holiday; **en ~** on holiday; **semaine/jour de ~** week/day off; **prendre ~ de qn** to take one's leave of sb; **donner son ~ à** to hand ou give in one's notice to; **~ de maladie** sick leave; **~ de maternité** maternity leave; **~s payés** paid holiday ou leave
congédier [kɔ̃ʒedje] /7/ vt to dismiss
congélateur [kɔ̃ʒelatœr] nm freezer
congeler [kɔ̃ʒ(ə)le] /5/ vt to freeze; **les produits congelés** frozen foods; **se congeler** vi to freeze
congestion [kɔ̃ʒestjɔ̃] nf congestion
Congo [kɔ̃o] nm: **le ~** the Congo
congrès [kɔ̃grɛ] nm congress
conifère [kɔnifɛr] nm conifer
conjoint, e [kɔ̃ʒwɛ̃, -wɛ̃t] adj joint ▷ nm/f spouse
conjonctivite [kɔ̃ʒɔ̃ktivit] nf conjunctivitis
conjoncture [kɔ̃ʒɔ̃ktyr] nf circumstances pl; **la ~ (économique)** the economic climate ou situation
conjugaison [kɔ̃ʒygɛzɔ̃] nf (Ling) conjugation
connaissance [kɔnesɑ̃s] nf (savoir) knowledge no pl; (personne connue) acquaintance; **être sans ~** to be unconscious; **perdre/reprendre ~** to lose/ regain consciousness; **à ma/sa ~** to (the best of) my/his knowledge; **faire ~ avec qn** ou **la ~ de qn** to meet sb
connaisseur, -euse [kɔnesœr, -øz] nm/f connoisseur
connaître [kɔnɛtr] /57/ vt to know; (éprouver) to experience; (avoir: succès) to have; to enjoy; **~ de nom/vue** to know by name/sight; **ils se sont connus à Genève** they (first) met in Geneva; **s'y ~ en qch** to know about sth
connecter [kɔnɛkte] /1/ vt to connect; **se ~ à Internet** to log onto the Internet
connerie [kɔnri] nf (fam!) (bloody) stupid (BRIT) ou damn-fool (US) thing to do ou say
connexion [kɔnɛksjɔ̃] nf connection
connu, e [kɔny] adj (célèbre) well-known
conquérir [kɔ̃kerir] /21/ vt to conquer; **conquête** nf conquest
consacrer [kɔ̃sakre] /1/ vt (Rel) to consecrate; **~ qch à** (employer) to devote ou dedicate sth to; **se ~ à qch/faire** to dedicate ou devote o.s. to sth/to doing
conscience [kɔ̃sjɑ̃s] nf conscience; **avoir/prendre ~ de** to be/become aware of; **perdre/reprendre ~** to lose/regain consciousness; **avoir bonne/mauvaise ~** to have a clear/guilty conscience; **consciencieux, -euse** adj conscientious; **conscient, e** adj conscious
consécutif, -ive [kɔ̃sekytif, -iv] adj consecutive; **~ à** following upon

conseil [kɔ̃sɛj] *nm* (*avis*) piece of advice; (*assemblée*) council; **donner un ~ ou des ~s à qn** to give sb (a piece of) advice; **prendre ~ (auprès de qn)** to take advice (from sb); **~ d'administration (CA)** board (of directors); **~ général** regional council; **le ~ des ministres** ≈ the Cabinet; **~ municipal (CM)** town council

conseiller¹ [kɔ̃seje] *vt* (*personne*) to advise; (*méthode, action*) to recommend, advise; **~ à qn de faire qch** to advise sb to do sth

conseiller², -ière [kɔ̃seje, -ɛʀ] *nm/f* adviser; **~ d'orientation** (*Scol*) careers adviser (BRIT), (school) counselor (US)

consentement [kɔ̃sɑ̃tmɑ̃] *nm* consent

consentir [kɔ̃sɑ̃tiʀ] /16/ *vt*: **~ (à qch/faire)** to agree ou consent (to sth/to doing)

conséquence [kɔ̃sekɑ̃s] *nf* consequence; **en ~** (*donc*) consequently; (*de façon appropriée*) accordingly; **conséquent, e** *adj* logical, rational; (*fam: important*) substantial; **par conséquent** consequently

conservateur, -trice [kɔ̃sɛʀvatœʀ, -tʀis] *nm/f* (*Pol*) conservative; (*de musée*) curator ▷ *nm* (*pour aliments*) preservative

conservatoire [kɔ̃sɛʀvatwaʀ] *nm* academy

conserve [kɔ̃sɛʀv] *nf* (*gén pl*) canned ou tinned (BRIT) food; **en ~** canned, tinned (BRIT)

conserver [kɔ̃sɛʀve] /1/ *vt* (*faculté*) to retain, keep; (*amis, livres*) to keep; (*préserver, Culin*) to preserve

considérable [kɔ̃sideʀabl] *adj* considerable, significant, extensive

considération [kɔ̃sideʀasjɔ̃] *nf* consideration; (*estime*) esteem

considérer [kɔ̃sideʀe] /6/ *vt* to consider; **~ qch comme** to regard sth as

consigne [kɔ̃siɲ] *nf* (*de gare*) left luggage (office) (BRIT), checkroom (US); (*ordre, instruction*) instructions *pl*; **~ automatique** left-luggage locker

consister [kɔ̃siste] /1/ *vi*: **~ en/dans/à faire** to consist of/in/in doing

consoler [kɔ̃sɔle] /1/ *vt* to console

consommateur, -trice [kɔ̃sɔmatœʀ, -tʀis] *nm/f* (*Écon*) consumer; (*dans un café*) customer

consommation [kɔ̃sɔmasjɔ̃] *nf* (*Écon*) consumption; (*boisson*) drink; **de ~** (*biens, société*) consumer *cpd*

consommer [kɔ̃sɔme] /1/ *vt* (*personne*) to eat ou drink, consume; (*voiture, usine, poêle*) to use, consume; (*Jur: mariage*) to consummate ▷ *vi* (*dans un café*) to (have a) drink

consonne [kɔ̃sɔn] *nf* consonant

constamment [kɔ̃stamɑ̃] *adv* constantly

constant, e [kɔ̃stɑ̃, -ɑ̃t] *adj* constant; (*personne*) steadfast

constat [kɔ̃sta] *nm* (*de police*) report; **~ (à l'amiable)** (*jointly agreed*) statement for insurance purposes; **~ d'échec** acknowledgement of failure

constatation [kɔ̃statasjɔ̃] *nf* (*remarque*) observation

constater [kɔ̃state] /1/ *vt* (*remarquer*) to note; (*Admin, Jur: attester*) to certify

consterner [kɔ̃stɛʀne] /1/ *vt* to dismay

constipé, e [kɔ̃stipe] *adj* constipated

constitué, e [kɔ̃stitɥe] *adj*: **~ de** made up ou composed of

constituer [kɔ̃stitɥe] /1/ *vt* (*comité, équipe*) to set up; (*dossier, collection*) to put together; (*éléments, parties: composer*) to make up, constitute; (: *représenter, être*) to constitute; **se ~ prisonnier** to give o.s. up

constructeur [kɔ̃stʀyktœʀ] *nm/f* manufacturer, builder

constructif, -ive [kɔ̃stʀyktif, -iv] *adj* constructive

construction [kɔ̃stʀyksjɔ̃] *nf* construction, building

construire [kɔ̃stʀɥiʀ] /38/ *vt* to build, construct

consul [kɔ̃syl] *nm* consul; **consulat** *nm* consulate

consultant, e *adj, nm* consultant

consultation [kɔ̃syltasjɔ̃] *nf* consultation; **heures de ~** (*Méd*) surgery (BRIT) ou office (US) hours

consulter [kɔ̃sylte] /1/ *vt* to consult ▷ *vi* (*médecin*) to hold surgery (BRIT), be in (the office) (US)

contact [kɔ̃takt] *nm* contact; **au ~ de** (*air, peau*) on contact with; (*gens*) through contact with; **mettre/couper le ~** (*Auto*) to switch on/off the ignition; **entrer en ~** to come into contact; **prendre ~ avec** to get in touch ou contact with; **contacter** /1/ *vt* to contact, get in touch with

contagieux, -euse [kɔ̃taʒjø, -øz] *adj* infectious; (*par le contact*) contagious

contaminer [kɔ̃tamine] /1/ *vt* to contaminate

conte [kɔ̃t] *nm* tale; **~ de fées** fairy tale

contempler [kɔ̃tɑ̃ple] /1/ *vt* to contemplate, gaze at

contemporain, e [kɔ̃tɑ̃pɔʀɛ̃, -ɛn] *adj, nm/f* contemporary

contenir [kɔ̃t(ə)niʀ] /22/ *vt* to contain; (*avoir une capacité de*) to hold

content, e [kɔ̃tɑ̃, -ɑ̃t] *adj* pleased, glad; **~ de** pleased with; **contenter** /1/ *vt* to satisfy, please; **se contenter de** to content o.s. with

contenu, e [kɔ̃t(ə)ny] *nm* (*d'un bol*) contents *pl*; (*d'un texte*) content

conter [kɔ̃te] /1/ *vt* to recount, relate

conteste [kɔ̃tɛst]: **sans ~** *adv* unquestionably, indisputably; **contester** /1/ *vt* to question ▷ *vi* (*Pol, gén*) to rebel (against established authority)

contexte [kɔ̃tɛkst] *nm* context

continent [kɔ̃tinɑ̃] *nm* continent

continu, e [kɔ̃tiny] *adj* continuous; **faire la journée ~e** to work without taking a full lunch break; **(courant) ~** direct current, DC

continuel, le [kɔ̃tinɥɛl] *adj (qui se répète)* constant, continual; *(continu)* continuous

continuer [kɔ̃tinɥe] /1/ *vt (travail, voyage etc)* to continue (with), carry on (with), go on with; *(prolonger: alignement, rue)* to continue ▷ *vi (pluie, vie, bruit)* to continue, go on; **~ à** *ou* **de faire** to go on *ou* continue doing

contourner [kɔ̃turne] /1/ *vt* to bypass, walk *ou* drive round; *(difficulté)* to get round

contraceptif, -ive [kɔ̃trasɛptif, -iv] *adj, nm* contraceptive; **contraception** *nf* contraception

contracté, e [kɔ̃trakte] *adj* tense

contracter [kɔ̃trakte] /1/ *vt (muscle etc)* to tense, contract; *(maladie, dette, obligation)* to contract; *(assurance)* to take out; **se contracter** *vi (métal, muscles)* to contract

contractuel, le [kɔ̃traktɥɛl] *nm/f (agent)* traffic warden

contradiction [kɔ̃tradiksjɔ̃] *nf* contradiction; **contradictoire** *adj* contradictory, conflicting

contraignant, e [kɔ̃trɛɲɑ̃, -ɑ̃t] *adj* restricting

contraindre [kɔ̃trɛ̃dr] /52/ *vt*: **~ qn à faire** to force *ou* compel sb to do

contraint, e *pp de* **contraindre** ▷ *nf* constraint

contraire [kɔ̃trɛr] *adj, nm* opposite; **~ à** contrary to; **au ~** on the contrary

contrarier [kɔ̃trarje] /7/ *vt (personne)* to annoy; *(projets)* to thwart, frustrate; **contrariété** [kɔ̃trarjete] *nf* annoyance

contraste [kɔ̃trast] *nm* contrast

contrat [kɔ̃tra] *nm* contract

contravention [kɔ̃travɑ̃sjɔ̃] *nf* parking ticket

contre [kɔ̃tr] *prép* against; *(en échange)* (in exchange) for; **par ~** on the other hand

contrebande [kɔ̃trəbɑ̃d] *nf (trafic)* contraband, smuggling; *(marchandise)* contraband, smuggled goods *pl*; **faire la ~ de** to smuggle

contrebas [kɔ̃trəba]: **en ~** *adv* (down) below

contrebasse [kɔ̃trəbas] *nf* (double) bass

contre: contrecoup *nm* repercussions *pl*; **contredire** /37/ *vt (personne)* to contradict; *(témoignage, assertion, faits)* to refute

contrefaçon [kɔ̃trəfasɔ̃] *nf* forgery

contre: contre-indication *(pl* **contre-indications)** *nf (Méd)* contra-indication; **"contre-indication en cas d'eczéma"** "should not be used by people with eczema"; **contre-indiqué, e** *adj (Méd)* contraindicated; *(déconseillé)* unadvisable, ill-advised

contremaître [kɔ̃trəmɛtr] *nm* foreman

contre-plaqué [kɔ̃trəplake] *nm* plywood

contresens [kɔ̃trəsɑ̃s] *nm (erreur)* misinterpretation; *(mauvaise traduction)* mistranslation; **à ~** the wrong way

contretemps [kɔ̃trətɑ̃] *nm* hitch; **à ~** *(fig)* at an inopportune moment

contribuer [kɔ̃tribɥe] /1/: **~ à** *vt* to contribute towards; **contribution** *nf* contribution; **mettre à contribution** to call upon; **contributions directes/indirectes** direct/indirect taxation

contrôle [kɔ̃trol] *nm* checking *no pl*, check; monitoring; *(test)* test, examination; **perdre le ~ de son véhicule** to lose control of one's vehicle; **~ continu** *(Scol)* continuous assessment; **~ d'identité** identity check

contrôler [kɔ̃trole] /1/ *vt (vérifier)* to check; *(surveiller: opérations)* to supervise; *(: prix)* to monitor, control, *(maîtriser, Comm: firme)* to control; **contrôleur, -euse** *nm/f (de train)* (ticket) inspector; *(de bus)* (bus) conductor/ tress

controversé, e [kɔ̃trɔvɛrse] *adj (personnage, question)* controversial

contusion [kɔ̃tyzjɔ̃] *nf* bruise, contusion

convaincre [kɔ̃vɛ̃kr] /42/ *vt*: **~ qn (de qch)** to convince sb (of sth); **~ qn (de faire)** to persuade sb (to do)

convalescence [kɔ̃valesɑ̃s] *nf* convalescence

convenable [kɔ̃vnabl] *adj* suitable; *(assez bon)* decent

convenir [kɔ̃vnir] /22/ *vi* to be suitable; **~ à** to suit; **~ de** *(bien-fondé de qch)* to admit (to), acknowledge; *(date, somme etc)* to agree upon; **~ que** *(admettre)* to admit that; **~ de faire qch** to agree to do sth

convention [kɔ̃vɑ̃sjɔ̃] *nf* convention; **conventions** *nfpl (convenances)* convention *sg*; **~ collective** *(Écon)* collective agreement; **conventionné, e** *adj (Admin)* applying charges laid down by the state

convenu, e [kɔ̃vny] *pp de* **convenir** ▷ *adj* agreed

conversation [kɔ̃vɛrsasjɔ̃] *nf* conversation

convertir [kɔ̃vɛrtir] /2/ *vt*: **~ qn (à)** to convert sb (to); **~ qch en** to convert sth into; **se ~ (à)** to be converted (to)

conviction [kɔ̃viksjɔ̃] *nf* conviction

convienne *etc* [kɔ̃vjɛn] *vb voir* **convenir**

convivial, e [kɔ̃vivjal] *adj (Inform)* user-friendly

convocation [kɔ̃vɔkasjɔ̃] *nf (document)* notification to attend; *(Jur)* summons *sg*

convoquer [kɔ̃vɔke] /1/ *vt (assemblée)* to convene; *(subordonné, témoin)* to summon; *(candidat)* to ask to attend

coopération [kɔɔperasjɔ̃] *nf* co-operation; *(Admin)*: **la C~ ≈** Voluntary Service Overseas (*BRIT*) *ou* the Peace Corps (*US: done as alternative to military service)*

coopérer [kɔɔpeʀe] /6/ vi : ~ **(à)** to co-operate (in)

coordonné, e [kɔɔʀdɔne] adj coordinated; **coordonnées** nfpl (détails personnels) address, phone number, schedule etc

coordonner [kɔɔʀdɔne] /1/ vt to coordinate

copain, copine nm/f pal; (petit ami) boyfriend; (petite amie) girlfriend

copie [kɔpi] nf copy; (Scol) script, paper; **copier** /7/ vt, vi to copy; **copier coller** (Inform) copy and paste; **copier sur** to copy from; **copieur** nm (photo)copier

copieux, -euse [kɔpjø, -øz] adj copious

copine [kɔpin] nf voir **copain**

coq [kɔk] nm cockerel

coque [kɔk] nf (de noix, mollusque) shell; (de bateau) hull; **à la ~** (Culin) (soft-)boiled

coquelicot [kɔkliko] nm poppy

coqueluche [kɔklyʃ] nf whooping-cough

coquet, te [kɔkɛ, -ɛt] adj appearance-conscious; (logement) smart, charming

coquetier [kɔk(ə)tje] nm egg-cup

coquillage [kɔkijaʒ] nm (mollusque) shellfish inv; (coquille) shell

coquille [kɔkij] nf shell; (Typo) misprint; **~ St Jacques** scallop

coquin, e [kɔkɛ̃, -in] adj mischievous, roguish; (polisson) naughty

cor [kɔʀ] nm (Mus) horn; (Méd): ~ **(au pied)** corn

corail, -aux [kɔʀaj, -o] nm coral no pl

Coran [kɔʀɑ̃] nm: **le ~** the Koran

corbeau, x [kɔʀbo] nm crow

corbeille [kɔʀbɛj] nf basket; (Inform) recycle bin; **~ à papier** waste paper basket ou bin

corde [kɔʀd] nf rope; (de violon, raquette, d'arc) string; **usé jusqu'à la ~** threadbare; **~ à linge** washing ou clothes line; **~ à sauter** skipping rope; **~s vocales** vocal cords

cordée [kɔʀde] nf (d'alpinistes) rope, roped party

cordialement [kɔʀdjalmɑ̃] adv (formule épistolaire) (kind) regards

cordon [kɔʀdɔ̃] nm cord, string; **~ sanitaire/de police** sanitary/police cordon; **~ ombilical** umbilical cord

cordonnerie [kɔʀdɔnʀi] nf shoe repairer's ou mender's (shop); **cordonnier** nm shoe repairer ou mender

Corée [kɔʀe] nf: **la ~ du Sud/du Nord** South/North Korea

coriace [kɔʀjas] adj tough

corne [kɔʀn] nf horn; (de cerf) antler

cornée [kɔʀne] nf cornea

corneille [kɔʀnɛj] nf crow

cornemuse [kɔʀnəmyz] nf bagpipes pl

cornet [kɔʀnɛ] nm (paper) cone; (de glace) cornet, cone

corniche [kɔʀniʃ] nf (route) coast road

cornichon [kɔʀniʃɔ̃] nm gherkin

Cornouailles [kɔʀnwaj] fpl Cornwall

corporel, le [kɔʀpɔʀɛl] adj bodily; (punition) corporal

corps [kɔʀ] nm body; **à ~ perdu** headlong; **prendre ~** to take shape; **le ~ électoral** the electorate; **le ~ enseignant** the teaching profession

correct, e [kɔʀɛkt] adj correct; **correcteur, -trice** nm/f (Scol) examiner; **correction** nf (voir corriger) correction; (voir correct) correctness; (coups) thrashing

correspondance [kɔʀɛspɔ̃dɑ̃s] nf correspondence; (de train, d'avion) connection; **cours par ~** correspondence course; **vente par ~** mail-order business

correspondant, e [kɔʀɛspɔ̃dɑ̃, -ɑ̃t] nm/f correspondent; (Tél) person phoning (ou being phoned)

correspondre [kɔʀɛspɔ̃dʀ] /41/ vi to correspond, tally; **~ à** to correspond to; **~ avec qn** to correspond with sb

corrida [kɔʀida] nf bullfight

corridor [kɔʀidɔʀ] nm corridor

corrigé [kɔʀiʒe] nm (Scol: d'exercice) correct version

corriger [kɔʀiʒe] /3/ vt (devoir) to correct; (punir) to thrash; **~ qn de** (défaut) to cure sb of

corrompre [kɔʀɔ̃pʀ] /41/ vt to corrupt; (acheter: témoin etc) to bribe

corruption [kɔʀypsjɔ̃] nf corruption; (de témoins) bribery

corse [kɔʀs] adj Corsican ▷ nm/f: **C~** Corsican ▷ nf: **la C~** Corsica

corsé, e [kɔʀse] adj (café etc) full-flavoured (BRIT) ou -flavored (US); (sauce) spicy; (problème) tough

cortège [kɔʀtɛʒ] nm procession

cortisone [kɔʀtizɔn] nf cortisone

corvée [kɔʀve] nf chore, drudgery no pl

cosmétique [kɔsmetik] nm beauty care product

cosmopolite [kɔsmɔpɔlit] adj cosmopolitan

costaud, e [kɔsto, -od] adj strong, sturdy

costume [kɔstym] nm (d'homme) suit; (de théâtre) costume; **costumé, e** adj dressed up

cote [kɔt] nf (en Bourse etc) quotation; **~ d'alerte** danger ou flood level; **~ de popularité** popularity rating

côte [kot] nf (rivage) coast(line); (pente) hill; (Anat) rib; (d'un tricot, tissu) rib, ribbing no pl; **~ à ~** side by side; **la C~ (d'Azur)** the (French) Riviera

côté [kote] nm (gén) side; (direction) way, direction; **de chaque ~ (de)** on each side of; **de tous les ~s** from all directions; **de quel ~ est-il parti?** which way ou in which direction did he go?; **de ce/de l'autre ~** this/the other way; **du ~ de** (provenance) from; (direction) towards; **du ~ de Lyon**

(*proximité*) near Lyons; **de ~** (*regarder*) sideways; **mettre de ~** to put aside, put on one side; **mettre de l'argent de ~** to save some money; **à ~** (right) nearby; (*voisins*) next door; **à ~ de** beside; next to; (*fig*) in comparison to; **être aux ~s de** to be by the side of

Côte d'Ivoire [kotdivwaʀ] *nf*: **la ~** Côte d'Ivoire, the Ivory Coast

côtelette [kotlɛt] *nf* chop

côtier, -ière [kotje, -jɛʀ] *adj* coastal

cotisation [kotizasjɔ̃] *nf* subscription, dues *pl*; (*pour une pension*) contributions *pl*

cotiser [kotize] /1/ *vi*: **~ (à)** to pay contributions (to); **se cotiser** *vi* to club together

coton [kotɔ̃] *nm* cotton; **~ hydrophile** cotton wool (*BRIT*), absorbent cotton (*US*)

Coton-Tige® *nm* cotton bud

cou [ku] *nm* neck

couchant [kuʃɑ̃] *adj*: **soleil ~** setting sun

couche [kuʃ] *nf* layer; (*de peinture, vernis*) coat; (*de bébé*) nappy (*BRIT*), diaper (*US*); **~s sociales** social levels *ou* strata

couché, e [kuʃe] *adj* lying down; (*au lit*) in bed

coucher [kuʃe] /1/ *vt* (*personne*) to put to bed (: *loger*) to put up; (*objet*) to lay on its side ▷ *vi* to sleep; **~ avec qn** to sleep with sb; **se coucher** *vi* (*pour dormir*) to go to bed; (*pour se reposer*) to lie down; (*soleil*) to set; **~ de soleil** sunset

couchette [kuʃɛt] *nf* couchette; (*pour voyageur, sur bateau*) berth

coucou [kuku] *nm* cuckoo

coude [kud] *nm* (*ANAT*) elbow; (*de tuyau, de la route*) bend; **~ à ~** shoulder to shoulder, side by side

coudre [kudʀ] /48/ *vt* (*bouton*) to sew on ▷ *vi* to sew

couette [kwɛt] *nf* duvet; **couettes** *nfpl* (*cheveux*) bunches

couffin [kufɛ̃] *nm* Moses basket

couler [kule] /1/ *vi* to flow, run; (*fuir: stylo, récipient*) to leak; (: *nez*) to run; (*sombrer: bateau*) to sink ▷ *vt* (*cloche, sculpture*) to cast; (*bateau*) to sink; (*faire échouer: personne*) to bring down, ruin

couleur [kulœʀ] *nf* colour (*BRIT*), color (*US*); (*Cartes*) suit; **en ~s** (*film*) in colo(u)r; **télévision en ~s** colo(u)r television; **de ~** (*homme, femme: vieilli*) colo(u)red

couleuvre [kulœvʀ] *nf* grass snake

coulisse [kulis] *nf* (*Tech*) runner; **coulisses** *nfpl* (*Théât*) wings; (*fig*): **dans les ~s** behind the scenes

couloir [kulwaʀ] *nm* corridor, passage; (*d'avion*) aisle; (*de bus*) gangway; **~ aérien** air corridor *ou* lane; **~ de navigation** shipping lane

coup [ku] *nm* (*heurt, choc*) knock; (*affectif*) blow, shock; (*agressif*) blow; (*avec arme à feu*) shot; (*de l'horloge*) stroke; (*Sport: golf*) stroke; (: *tennis*) shot; (*fam: fois*) time; **~ de coude/genou** nudge (with the elbow)/with the knee; **donner un ~ de balai** to give the floor a sweep; **être dans le/hors du ~** to be/not to be in on it; (*à la page*) to be hip *ou* trendy; **du ~** as a result; **d'un seul ~** (*subitement*) suddenly; (*à la fois*) at one go; **du premier ~** first time *ou* go; **du même ~** at the same time; **à ~ sûr** definitely, without fail; **après ~** afterwards; **~ sur ~** in quick succession; **sur le ~** outright; **sous le ~ de** (*surprise etc*) under the influence of; **à tous les ~s** every time; **tenir le ~** to hold out; **~ de chance** stroke of luck; **~ de couteau** stab (of a knife); **~ d'envoi** kick-off; **~ d'essai** first attempt; **~ d'état** coup d'état; **~ de feu** shot; **~ de filet** (*Police*) haul; **~ de foudre** (*fig*) love at first sight; **~ franc** free kick; **~ de frein** (sharp) braking *no pl*; **~ de grâce** coup de grâce; **~ de main**: **donner un ~ de main à qn** to give sb a (helping) hand; **~ d'œil** glance; **~ de pied** kick; **~ de poing** punch; **~ de soleil** sunburn *no pl*; **~ de sonnette** ring of the bell; **~ de téléphone** phone call; **~ de tête** (*fig*) (sudden) impulse; **~ de théâtre** (*fig*) dramatic turn of events; **~ de tonnerre** clap of thunder; **~ de vent** gust of wind; **en ~ de vent** (*rapidement*) in a tearing hurry

coupable [kupabl] *adj* guilty ▷ *nm/f* (*gen*) culprit; (*Jur*) guilty party

coupe [kup] *nf* (*verre*) goblet; (*à fruits*) dish; (*Sport*) cup; (*de cheveux, de vêtement*) cut; (*graphique, plan*) (cross) section

couper [kupe] /1/ *vt* to cut; (*retrancher*) to cut (out), (*route, courant*) to cut off; (*appétit*) to take away; (*vin, cidre: à table*) to dilute (with water) ▷ *vi* to cut; (*prendre un raccourci*) to take a short-cut; **se couper** *vi* (*se blesser*) to cut o.s.; **~ la parole à qn** to cut sb short; **nous avons été coupés** we've been cut off

couple [kupl] *nm* couple

couplet [kuplɛ] *nm* verse

coupole [kupɔl] *nf* dome

coupon [kupɔ̃] *nm* (*ticket*) coupon; (*de tissu*) remnant

coupure [kupyʀ] *nf* cut; (*billet de banque*) note; (*de journal*) cutting; **~ de courant** power cut

cour [kuʀ] *nf* (*de ferme, jardin*) (court)yard; (*d'immeuble*) back yard; (*Jur, royale*) court; **faire la ~ à qn** to court sb; **~ d'assises** court of assizes; **~ de récréation** playground

courage [kuʀaʒ] *nm* courage, bravery; **courageux, -euse** *adj* brave, courageous

couramment [kuʀamɑ̃] *adv* commonly; (*parler*) fluently

courant, e [kuʀɑ̃, -ɑ̃t] *adj* (*fréquent*) common; (*Comm, gén: normal*) standard; (*en cours*) current ▷ *nm* current; (*fig*) movement; (: *d'opinion*) trend; **être au ~**

(de) (fait, nouvelle) to know (about); **mettre qn au ~ (de)** to tell sb (about); (nouveau travail etc) to teach sb the basics (of); **se tenir au ~ (de)** (techniques etc) to keep o.s. up-to-date (on); **dans le ~ (de)** (pendant) in the course of; **le 10 ~** (Comm) the 10th inst.; **~ d'air** draught; **~ électrique** (electric) current, power

courbature [kurbatyr] nf ache

courbe [kurb] adj curved ▷ nf curve

coureur, -euse [kurœr, -øz] nm/f (Sport) runner (ou driver); (péj) womanizer/manhunter

courge [kurʒ] nf (Culin) marrow; **courgette** nf courgette (BRIT), zucchini (US)

courir [kurir] /11/ vi to run ▷ vt (Sport: épreuve) to compete in; (risque) to run; (danger) to face; **~ les cafés/bals** to do the rounds of the cafés/dances; **le bruit court que** the rumour is going round that

couronne [kuron] nf crown; (de fleurs) wreath, circlet

courons [kurɔ̃] vb voir **courir**

courriel [kurjɛl] nm email

courrier [kurje] nm mail, post; (lettres à écrire) letters pl; **est-ce que j'ai du ~?** are there any letters for me?; **~ électronique** email

▌ Attention à ne pas traduire courrier par le mot anglais courier.

courroie [kurwa] nf strap; (Tech) belt

courrons etc [kurɔ̃] vb voir **courir**

cours [kur] nm (leçon) class (: particulier) lesson; (série de leçons) course; (écoulement) flow; (Comm: de devises) rate; (: de denrées) price; **donner libre ~ à** to give free expression to; **avoir ~** (Scol) to have a class ou lecture; **en ~** (année) current; (travaux) in progress; **en ~ de route** on the way; **au ~ de** in the course of, during; **le ~ du change** the exchange rate; **~ d'eau** waterway; **~ du soir** night school

course [kurs] nf running; (Sport: épreuve) race; (d'un taxi, autocar) journey, trip; (petite mission) errand; **courses** nfpl (achats) shopping sg; **faire les ou ses ~s** to go shopping

court, e [kur, kurt] adj short ▷ adv short ▷ nm: **~** (de tennis) (tennis) court; **à ~ de** short of; **prendre qn de ~** to catch sb unawares; **court-circuit** nm short-circuit

courtoisie [kurtwazi] nf courtesy

couru, e [kury] pp de **courir**

cousais etc [kuze] vb voir **coudre**

couscous [kuskus] nm couscous

cousin, e [kuzɛ̃, -in] nm/f cousin

coussin [kusɛ̃] nm cushion

cousu, e [kuzy] pp de **coudre**

coût [ku] nm cost; **le ~ de la vie** the cost of living

couteau, x [kuto] nm knife

coûter [kute] /1/ vt to cost ▷ vi to cost; **~ cher** to be expensive; **combien ça coûte?** how much is it?, what does it cost?; **coûte que coûte** at all costs; **coûteux, -euse** adj costly, expensive

coutume [kutym] nf custom

couture [kutyr] nf sewing; (profession) dress-making; (points) seam; **couturier** nm fashion designer; **couturière** nf dressmaker

couvent [kuvɑ̃] nm (de sœurs) convent; (de frères) monastery

couver [kuve] /1/ vt to hatch; (maladie) to be sickening for ▷ vi (feu) to smoulder; (révolte) to be brewing

couvercle [kuvɛrkl] nm lid; (de bombe aérosol etc, qui se visse) cap, top

couvert, e [kuvɛr, -ɛrt] pp de **couvrir** ▷ adj (ciel) overcast ▷ nm place setting; (place à table) place; **couverts** nmpl (ustensiles) cutlery sg; **~ de** covered with ou in; **mettre le ~** to lay the table

couverture [kuvɛrtyr] nf blanket; (de livre, fig, Assurances) cover; (Presse) coverage

couvre-lit [kuvrəli] nm bedspread

couvrir [kuvrir] /18/ vt to cover; **se couvrir** vi (ciel) to cloud over; (s'habiller) to cover up; (se coiffer) to put on one's hat

cow-boy [koboj] nm cowboy

crabe [krab] nm crab

cracher [kraʃe] /1/ vi to spit ▷ vt to spit out

crachin [kraʃɛ̃] nm drizzle

craie [krɛ] nf chalk

craindre [krɛ̃dr] /52/ vt to fear, be afraid of; (être sensible à: chaleur, froid) to be easily damaged by

crainte [krɛ̃t] nf fear; **de ~ de/que** for fear of/that; **craintif, -ive** adj timid

crampe [krɑ̃p] nf cramp; **j'ai une ~ à la jambe** I've got cramp in my leg

cramponner [krɑ̃pɔne] /1/: **se cramponner** vi: **se ~ (à)** to hang ou cling on (to)

cran [krɑ̃] nm (entaille) notch; (de courroie) hole; (courage) guts pl

crâne [krɑn] nm skull

crapaud [krapo] nm toad

craquement [krakmɑ̃] nm crack, snap; (du plancher) creak, creaking no pl

craquer [krake] /1/ vi (bois, plancher) to creak; (fil, branche) to snap; (couture) to come apart; (fig: accusé) to break down, fall apart ▷ vt: **~ une allumette** to strike a match; **j'ai craqué** (fam) I couldn't resist it

crasse [kras] nf grime, filth; **crasseux, -euse** adj filthy

cravache [kravaʃ] nf (riding) crop

cravate [kravat] nf tie

crawl [krol] nm crawl; **dos ~é** backstroke

crayon [krɛjɔ̃] nm pencil; **~ à bille** ball-point pen; **~ de couleur** crayon; **crayon-feutre** (pl **crayons-feutres**) nm felt(-tip) pen

création [kʁeasjɔ̃] nf creation

crèche [kʁɛʃ] nf (de Noël) crib; (garderie) crèche, day nursery

crédit [kʁedi] nm (gén) credit; **crédits** nmpl funds; **acheter à ~** to buy on credit ou on easy terms; **faire ~ à qn** to give sb credit; **créditer** /1/ vt: **créditer un compte (de)** to credit an account (with)

créer [kʁee] /1/ vt to create

crémaillère [kʁemajɛʁ] nf: **pendre la ~** to have a house-warming party

crème [kʁɛm] nf cream; (entremets) cream dessert ▷ adj inv cream; **un (café) ~ =** a white coffee; **~ anglaise** (egg) custard; **~ chantilly** whipped cream; **~ à raser** shaving cream; **~ solaire** sun cream

créneau, x [kʁeno] nm (de fortification) crenel(le); (fig, aussi Comm) gap, slot; (Auto): **faire un ~** to reverse into a parking space (between cars alongside the kerb)

crêpe [kʁɛp] nf (galette) pancake ▷ nm (tissu) crêpe; **crêperie** nf pancake shop ou restaurant

crépuscule [kʁepyskyl] nm twilight, dusk

cresson [kʁesɔ̃] nm watercress

creuser [kʁøze] /1/ vt (trou, tunnel) to dig; (sol) to dig a hole in; (fig) to go (deeply) into; **ça creuse** that gives you a real appetite; **se ~ (la cervelle)** to rack one's brains

creux, -euse [kʁø, -øz] adj hollow ▷ nm hollow; **heures creuses** slack periods; (électricité, téléphone) off-peak periods; **avoir un ~** (fam) to be hungry

crevaison [kʁəvɛzɔ̃] nf puncture

crevé, e [kʁəve] adj (fam: fatigué) shattered (BRIT), exhausted

crever [kʁəve] /5/ vt (tambour, ballon) to burst ▷ vi (pneu) to burst; (automobiliste) to have a puncture (BRIT) ou a flat (tire) (US); (fam) to die

crevette [kʁəvɛt] nf: **~ (rose)** prawn; **~ grise** shrimp

cri [kʁi] nm cry, shout; (d'animal: spécifique) cry, call; **c'est le dernier ~** (fig) it's the latest fashion

criard, e [kʁijaʁ, -aʁd] adj (couleur) garish, loud; (voix) yelling

cric [kʁik] nm (Auto) jack

crier [kʁije] /7/ vi (pour appeler) to shout, cry (out); (de peur, de douleur etc) to scream, yell ▷ vt (ordre, injure) to shout (out), yell (out)

crime [kʁim] nm crime; (meurtre) murder; **criminel, le** nm/f criminal; murderer

crin [kʁɛ̃] nm (de cheval) hair no pl

crinière [kʁinjɛʁ] nf mane

crique [kʁik] nf creek, inlet

criquet [kʁikɛ] nm grasshopper

crise [kʁiz] nf crisis (pl crises); (Méd) attack (: d'épilepsie) fit; **~ cardiaque** heart attack; **avoir une ~ de foie** to have really bad indigestion; **piquer une ~ de nerfs** to go hysterical

cristal, -aux [kʁistal, -o] nm crystal

critère [kʁitɛʁ] nm criterion (pl criteria)

critiquable [kʁitikabl] adj open to criticism

critique [kʁitik] adj critical ▷ nm/f (de théâtre, musique) critic ▷ nf criticism; (de théâtre, musique: article) review

critiquer [kʁitike] /1/ vt (dénigrer) to criticize; (évaluer, juger) to assess, examine (critically)

croate [kʁɔat] adj Croatian ▷ nm (Ling) Croat, Croatian ▷ nm/f: **C~** Croat, Croatian

Croatie [kʁɔasi] nf: **la ~** Croatia

crochet [kʁɔʃɛ] nm hook; (détour) detour; (Tricot: aiguille) crochet hook; (: technique) crochet; **vivre aux ~s de qn** to live ou sponge off sb

crocodile [kʁɔkɔdil] nm crocodile

croire [kʁwaʁ] vt to believe; **se ~ fort** to think one is strong; **~ que** to believe ou think that; **~ à, ~ en** to believe in

croisade [kʁwazad] nf crusade

croisement [kʁwazmɑ̃] nm (carrefour) crossroads sg; (Bio) crossing (: résultat) crossbreed

croiser [kʁwaze] /1/ vt (personne, voiture) to pass; (route) to cross, cut across; (Bio) to cross; **se croiser** vi (personnes, véhicules) to pass each other; (routes) to cross; (regards) to meet; **se ~ les bras** (fig) to fold one's arms, to twiddle one's thumbs

croisière [kʁwazjɛʁ] nf cruise

croissance [kʁwasɑ̃s] nf growth

croissant, e [kʁwasɑ̃, -ɑ̃t] adj growing ▷ nm (à manger) croissant; (motif) crescent

croître [kʁwatʁ] /55/ vi to grow

croix [kʁwa] nf cross, **la C~ Rouge** the Red Cross

croque-madame [kʁɔkmadam] nm inv toasted cheese sandwich with a fried egg on top

croque-monsieur [kʁɔkməsjø] nm inv toasted ham and cheese sandwich

croquer [kʁɔke] /1/ vt (manger) to crunch (: fruit) to munch; (dessiner) to sketch; **chocolat à ~** plain dessert chocolate

croquis [kʁɔki] nm sketch

crotte [kʁɔt] nf droppings pl; **crottin** [kʁɔtɛ̃] nm dung, manure; (fromage) (small round) cheese (made of goat's milk)

croustillant, e [kʁustijɑ̃, -ɑ̃t] adj crisp

croûte [kʁut] nf crust; (du fromage) rind; (Méd) scab; **en ~** (Culin) in pastry

croûton [kʁutɔ̃] nm (Culin) crouton; (bout du pain) crust, heel

croyant, e [kʁwajɑ̃, -ɑ̃t] nm/f believer

CRS sigle fpl (= Compagnies républicaines de sécurité) state security police force ▷ sigle m member of the CRS

cru, e [kʁy] pp de **croire** ▷ adj (non cuit) raw; (lumière, couleur) harsh; (paroles, langage) crude ▷ nm (vignoble) vineyard; (vin) wine; **un grand ~** a great vintage; **jambon ~** Parma ham

crû [kʀy] *pp de* **croître**
cruauté [kʀyote] *nf* cruelty
cruche [kʀyʃ] *nf* pitcher, (earthenware) jug
crucifix [kʀysifi] *nm* crucifix
crudité [kʀydite] *nf* crudeness *no pl*;
  crudités *nfpl* (*Culin*) selection of raw vegetables
crue [kʀy] *nf* (*inondation*) flood; *voir aussi* **cru**
cruel, le [kʀyɛl] *adj* cruel
crus, crûs *etc* [kʀy] *vb voir* **croire**; **croître**
crustacés [kʀystase] *nmpl* shellfish
Cuba [kyba] *nm* Cuba; **cubain, e** *adj* Cuban ▷ *nm/f*: **Cubain, e** Cuban
cube [kyb] *nm* cube; (*jouet*) brick; **mètre ~** cubic metre; **2 au ~ = 8** 2 cubed is 8
cueillette [kœjɛt] *nf* picking; (*quantité*) crop, harvest
cueillir [kœjiʀ] /12/ *vt* (*fruits, fleurs*) to pick, gather; (*fig*) to catch
cuiller, cuillère [kɥijɛʀ] *nf* spoon; **~ à café** coffee spoon; (*Culin*) ≈ teaspoonful; **~ à soupe** soup spoon; (*Culin*) ≈ tablespoonful; **cuillerée** *nf* spoonful
cuir [kɥiʀ] *nm* leather; (*avant tannage*) hide; **~ chevelu** scalp
cuire [kɥiʀ] /38/ *vt*: (*aliments*) to cook; (*au four*) to bake ▷ *vi* to cook; **bien cuit** (*viande*) well done; **trop cuit** overdone
cuisine [kɥizin] *nf* (*pièce*) kitchen; (*art culinaire*) cookery, cooking; (*nourriture*) cooking, food; **faire la ~** to cook; **cuisiné, e** *adj*: **plat cuisiné** ready-made meal *ou* dish; **cuisiner** /1/ *vt* to cook; (*fam*) to grill ▷ *vi* to cook; **cuisinier, -ière** *nm/f* cook ▷ *nf* (*poêle*) cooker
cuisse [kɥis] *nf* thigh; (*Culin*) leg
cuisson [kɥisɔ̃] *nf* cooking
cuit, e [kɥi, -it] *pp de* **cuire**
cuivre [kɥivʀ] *nm* copper; **les ~s** (*Mus*) the brass
cul [ky] *nm* (*fam!*) arse (!)
culminant, e [kylminɑ̃, -ɑ̃t] *adj*: **point ~** highest point
culot [kylo] (*fam*) *nm* (*effronterie*) cheek
culotte [kylɔt] *nf* (*de femme*) panties *pl*, knickers *pl* (BRIT)
culte [kylt] *nm* (*religion*) religion; (*hommage, vénération*) worship; (*protestant*) service
cultivateur, -trice [kyltivatœʀ, -tʀis] *nm/f* farmer
cultivé, e [kyltive] *adj* (*personne*) cultured, cultivated
cultiver [kyltive] /1/ *vt* to cultivate; (*légumes*) to grow, cultivate
culture [kyltyʀ] *nf* cultivation; (*connaissances etc*) culture; **les ~s intensives** intensive farming; **~ OGM** GM crop; **~ physique** physical training; **culturel, le** *adj* cultural
cumin [kymɛ̃] *nm* cumin

cure [kyʀ] *nf* (*Méd*) course of treatment; **~ d'amaigrissement** slimming course; **~ de repos** rest cure
curé [kyʀe] *nm* parish priest
cure-dent [kyʀdɑ̃] *nm* toothpick
curieux, -euse [kyʀjø, -øz] *adj* (*étrange*) strange, curious; (*indiscret*) curious, inquisitive ▷ *nmpl* (*badauds*) onlookers; **curiosité** *nf* curiosity; (*site*) unusual feature *ou* sight
curriculum vitae [kyʀikylɔmvite] *nm inv* curriculum vitae
curseur [kyʀsœʀ] *nm* (*Inform*) cursor; (*de règle*) slide; (*de fermeture-éclair*) slider
cutané, e [kytane] *adj* skin *cpd*
cuve [kyv] *nf* vat; (*à mazout etc*) tank
cuvée [kyve] *nf* vintage
cuvette [kyvɛt] *nf* (*récipient*) bowl, basin; (*Géo*) basin
CV *sigle m* (*Auto*) = **cheval (vapeur)**; (*Admin*) = **curriculum vitae**
cybercafé [sibɛʀkafe] *nm* Internet café
cyberespace [sibɛʀɛspas] *nm* cyberspace
cybernaute [sibɛʀnot] *nm/f* Internet user
cyclable [siklabl] *adj*: **piste ~** cycle track
cycle [sikl] *nm* cycle; **cyclisme** [siklism] *nm* cycling; **cycliste** [siklist] *nm/f* cyclist ▷ *adj* cycle *cpd*; **coureur cycliste** racing cyclist
cyclomoteur [siklomɔtœʀ] *nm* moped
cyclone [siklon] *nm* hurricane
cygne [siɲ] *nm* swan
cylindre [silɛ̃dʀ] *nm* cylinder; **cylindrée** *nf* (*Auto*) (*cubic*) capacity; **une (voiture de) grosse cylindrée** a big-engined car
cymbale [sɛ̃bal] *nf* cymbal
cynique [sinik] *adj* cynical
cystite [sistit] *nf* cystitis

d

d' prép, art voir **de**

dactylo [daktilo] nf (aussi: **~graphe**) typist; (aussi: **~graphie**) typing

dada [dada] nm hobby-horse

daim [dɛ̃] nm (fallow) deer inv; (cuir suédé) suede

daltonien, ne [daltɔnjɛ̃, -ɛn] adj colour-blind

dame [dam] nf lady; (Cartes, Échecs) queen; **dames** nfpl (jeu) draughts sg (BRIT), checkers sg (US)

Danemark [danmark] nm: **le ~** Denmark

danger [dɑ̃ʒe] nm danger; **mettre en ~** (personne) to put in danger; (projet, carrière) to jeopardize; **être en ~** (personne) to be in danger; **être en ~ de mort** to be in peril of one's life; **être hors de ~** to be out of danger; **dangereux, -euse** adj dangerous

danois, e [danwa, -waz] adj Danish ▷ nm (Ling) Danish ▷ nm/f: **D~, e** Dane

dans [dɑ̃] prép **1** (position) in; (: à l'intérieur de) inside; **c'est dans le tiroir/le salon** it's in the drawer/lounge; **dans la boîte** in ou inside the box; **marcher dans la ville/la rue** to walk about the town/along the street; **je l'ai lu dans le journal** I read it in the newspaper
2 (direction) into; **elle a couru dans le salon** she ran into the lounge; **monter dans une voiture/le bus** to get into a car/on to the bus
3 (provenance) out of, from; **je l'ai pris dans le tiroir/salon** I took it out of ou from the drawer/lounge; **boire dans un verre** to drink out of ou from a glass
4 (temps) in; **dans deux mois** in two months, in two months' time
5 (approximation) about; **dans les 20 euros** about 20 euros

---

danse [dɑ̃s] nf: **la ~** dancing; (classique) (ballet) dancing; **une ~** a dance; **danser** /1/ vi, vt to dance; **danseur, -euse** nm/f ballet dancer; (au bal etc) dancer (: cavalier) partner

date [dat] nf date; **de longue ~** longstanding; **~ de naissance** date of birth; **~ limite** deadline; **dater** /1/ vt, vi to date; **dater de** to date from; **à dater de** (as) from

datte [dat] nf date

dauphin [dofɛ̃] nm (Zool) dolphin

davantage [davɑ̃taʒ] adv more; (plus longtemps) longer; **~ de** more

 MOT-CLÉ

de, d' [də, d] (de + le = **du**, de + les = **des**) prép
1 (appartenance) of; **le toit de la maison** the roof of the house; **la voiture d'Elisabeth/de mes parents** Elizabeth's/my parents' car
2 (provenance) from; **il vient de Londres** he comes from London; **elle est sortie du cinéma** she came out of the cinema
3 (moyen) with; **je l'ai fait de mes propres mains** I did it with my own two hands
4 (caractérisation, mesure): **un mur de brique/bureau d'acajou** a brick wall/mahogany desk; **un billet de 10 euros** a 10 euro note; **une pièce de 2 m de large** ou **large de 2 m** a room 2 m wide, a 2m-wide room; **un bébé de 10 mois** a 10-month-old baby; **12 mois de crédit/travail** 12 months' credit/work; **elle est payée 20 euros de l'heure** she's paid 20 euros an hour ou per hour; **augmenter de 10 euros** to increase by 10 euros
5 (rapport) from; **de quatre à six** from four to six
6 (cause): **mourir de faim** to die of hunger; **rouge de colère** red with fury
7 (vb + de + infin) to; **il m'a dit de rester** he told me to stay
▶ art **1** (phrases affirmatives) some (souvent omis); **du vin, de l'eau, des pommes** (some) wine, (some) water, (some) apples; **des enfants sont venus** some children came; **pendant des mois** for months
2 (phrases interrogatives et négatives) any; **a-t-il du vin?** has he got any wine?; **il n'a pas de pommes/d'enfants** he hasn't (got) any apples/children, he has no apples/children

---

dé [de] nm (à jouer) die ou dice; (aussi: **dé à coudre**) thimble

déballer [debale] /1/ vt to unpack

débarcadère [debarkadɛr] nm wharf

débardeur [debardœr] nm (pour femme) vest top; (pour homme) sleeveless top

débarquer [debarke] /1/ vt to unload, land ▷ vi to disembark; (fig) to turn up

débarras [debara] nm (pièce) lumber room; (placard) junk cupboard; **bon ~!** good riddance!; **débarrasser** /1/ vt to clear ▷ vi (enlever le couvert) to clear away; **se débarrasser de** vt to get rid of; **débarrasser qn de** (vêtements, paquets) to relieve sb of

débat [deba] nm discussion, debate; **débattre** /41/ vt to discuss, debate; **se débattre** vi to struggle

débit [debi] nm (d'un liquide, fleuve) (rate of) flow; (d'un magasin) turnover (of goods); (élocution) delivery; (bancaire) debit; ~ **de boissons** drinking establishment; ~ **de tabac** tobacconist's (shop)

déblayer [debleje] /8/ vt to clear

débloquer [debloke] /1/ vt (frein, fonds) to release; (prix, crédits) to free ▷ vi (fam) to talk rubbish

déboîter [debwate] /1/ vt (Auto) to pull out; **se ~ le genou** etc to dislocate one's knee etc

débordé, e [deborde] adj: **être ~ de** (travail, demandes) to be snowed under with

déborder [deborde] /1/ vi to overflow; (lait etc) to boil over; ~ **(de) qch** (dépasser) to extend beyond sth; ~ **de** (joie, zèle) to be brimming over with ou bursting with

débouché [debuʃe] nm (pour vendre) outlet; (perspective d'emploi) opening

déboucher [debuʃe] /1/ vt (évier, tuyau etc) to unblock; (bouteille) to uncork ▷ vi: ~ **de** to emerge from; ~ **sur** (études) to lead on to

debout [dəbu] adv (personne) to be standing, stand; (levé, éveillé) to be up (and about); **se mettre ~** to get up (on one's feet); **se tenir ~** to stand; ~! stand up!; (du lit) get up!; **cette histoire ne tient pas ~** this story doesn't hold water

déboutonner [debutone] /1/ vt to undo, unbutton

débraillé, e [debraje] adj slovenly, untidy

débrancher [debrɑ̃ʃe] /1/ vt (appareil électrique) to unplug; (téléphone, courant électrique) to disconnect

débrayage [debrɛjaʒ] nm (Auto) clutch; **débrayer** /8/ vi (Auto) to declutch; (cesser le travail) to stop work

débris [debri] nm fragment ▷ nmpl: **des ~ de verre** bits of glass

débrouillard, e [debrujar, -ard] adj smart, resourceful

débrouiller [debruje] /1/ vt to disentangle, untangle; **se débrouiller** vi to manage; **débrouillez-vous** you'll have to sort things out yourself

début [deby] nm beginning, start; **débuts** nmpl (de carrière) début sg; ~ **juin** in early June; **débutant, e** nm/f beginner, novice; **débuter** /1/ vi to begin, start; (faire ses débuts) to start out

décaféiné, e [dekafeine] adj decaffeinated

décalage [dekalaʒ] nm gap; ~ **horaire** time difference (between time zones), time-lag

décaler [dekale] /1/ vt to shift forward ou back

décapotable [dekapotabl] adj convertible

décapsuleur [dekapsylœr] nm bottle-opener

décédé, e [desede] adj deceased

décéder [desede] /6/ vi to die

décembre [desɑ̃br] nm December

décennie [deseni] nf decade

décent, e [desɑ̃, -ɑ̃t] adj decent

déception [desɛpsjɔ̃] nf disappointment

décès [desɛ] nm death

décevoir [des(ə)vwar] /28/ vt to disappoint

décharge [deʃarʒ] nf (dépôt d'ordures) rubbish tip ou dump; (électrique) electrical discharge; **décharger** /3/ vt (marchandise, véhicule) to unload; (faire feu) to discharge, fire; **décharger qn de** (responsabilité) to relieve sb of, release sb from

déchausser [deʃose] /1/ vt (skis) to take off; **se déchausser** vi to take off one's shoes; (dent) to come ou work loose

déchet [deʃɛ] nm (de bois, tissu etc) scrap; **déchets** nmpl (ordures) refuse sg, rubbish sg; ~**s nucléaires** nuclear waste

déchiffrer [deʃifre] /1/ vt to decipher

déchirant, e [deʃirɑ̃, -ɑ̃t] adj heart-rending

déchirement [deʃirmɑ̃] nm (chagrin) wrench, heartbreak; (gén pl: conflit) rift, split

déchirer [deʃire] /1/ vt to tear; (mettre en morceaux) to tear up; (arracher) to tear out; (fig) to tear apart; **se déchirer** vi to tear, rip; **se ~ un muscle/tendon** to tear a muscle/tendon

déchirure [deʃiryr] nf (accroc) tear, rip; ~ **musculaire** torn muscle

décidé, e [deside] adj (personne, air) determined; **c'est ~** it's decided; **décidément** adv really

décider [deside] /1/ vt: ~ **qch** to decide on sth; ~ **de faire/que** to decide to do/that; ~ **qn (à faire qch)** to persuade ou induce sb (to do sth); **se ~ à faire** to decide ou make up one's mind to do; **se ~ pour qch** to decide on ou in favour of sth

décimal, e, -aux [desimal, -o] adj decimal

décimètre [desimɛtr] nm decimetre

décisif, -ive [desizif, -iv] adj decisive

décision [desizjɔ̃] nf decision

déclaration [deklarasjɔ̃] nf declaration; (discours: Pol etc) statement; ~ **(d'impôts)** ≈ tax return; ~ **de revenus** statement of income; **faire une ~ de vol** to report a theft

déclarer [deklare] /1/ vt to declare; (décès, naissance) to register; **se déclarer** vi (feu, maladie) to break out

déclencher [deklɑ̃ʃe] /1/ vt (mécanisme etc) to release; (sonnerie) to set off; (attaque, grève) to launch; (provoquer) to trigger off; **se déclencher** vi (sonnerie) to go off

décliner [dekline] /1/ vi to decline ▷ vt (invitation) to decline; (nom, adresse) to state

décoiffer [dekwafe] /1/ vt: ~ **qn** to mess up sb's hair; **je suis toute décoiffée** my hair is in a real mess

déçois etc [deswa] vb voir **décevoir**

décollage [dekɔlaʒ] nm (Aviat, Écon) takeoff

décoller [dekɔle] /1/ vt to unstick ▷ vi (avion) to take off; **se décoller** vi to come unstuck

décolleté, e [dekɔlte] adj low-cut ▷ nm low neck(line); (plongeant) cleavage

décolorer [dekɔlɔre] /1/: **se décolorer** vi to fade; **se faire ~ les cheveux** to have one's hair bleached

décommander [dekɔmɑ̃de] /1/ vt to cancel; **se décommander** vi to cancel

déconcerter [dekɔ̃sɛrte] /1/ vt to disconcert, confound

décongeler [dekɔ̃ʒ(ə)le] /5/ vt to thaw (out)

déconner [dekɔne] /1/ vi (fam!) to talk (a load of) rubbish (BRIT) ou garbage (US)

déconseiller [dekɔ̃seje] /1/ vt: ~ **qch (à qn)** to advise (sb) against sth; **c'est déconseillé** it's not advised ou advisable

décontracté, e [dekɔ̃trakte] adj relaxed, laid-back (fam)

décontracter [dekɔ̃trakte] /1/: **se décontracter** vi to relax

décor [dekɔr] nm décor; (paysage) scenery; **décorateur, -trice** nm/f (interior) decorator; **décoration** nf decoration; **décorer** /1/ vt to decorate

décortiquer [dekɔrtike] /1/ vt to shell; (fig: texte) to dissect

découdre /48/: **se découdre** vi to come unstitched

découper [dekupe] /1/ vt (papier, tissu etc) to cut up; (volaille, viande) to carve; (manche, article) to cut out

décourager [dekuraʒe] /3/ vt to discourage; **se décourager** vi to lose heart, become discouraged

décousu, e [dekuzy] adj unstitched; (fig) disjointed, disconnected

découvert, e [dekuvɛr, -ɛrt] adj (tête) bare, uncovered; (lieu) open, exposed ▷ nm (bancaire) overdraft ▷ nf discovery; **faire la ~e de** to discover

découvrir [dekuvrir] /18/ vt to discover; (enlever ce qui couvre ou protège) to uncover; (montrer, dévoiler) to reveal; **se découvrir** vi (chapeau) to take off one's hat; (se déshabiller) to take something off; (ciel) to clear

décrire [dekrir] /39/ vt to describe

décrocher [dekrɔʃe] /1/ vt (dépendre) to take down; (téléphone) to take off the hook; (: pour répondre): ~ **(le téléphone)** to pick up ou lift the receiver; (fig: contrat etc) to get, land ▷ vi (fam: abandonner) to drop out; (: cesser d'écouter) to switch off

déçu, e [desy] pp de **décevoir**

dédaigner [dedeɲe] /1/ vt to despise, scorn; (négliger) to disregard, spurn; **dédaigneux, -euse** adj scornful, disdainful; **dédain** nm scorn, disdain

dedans [dədɑ̃] adv inside; (pas en plein air) indoors, inside ▷ nm inside; **au ~** inside

dédicacer [dedikase] /3/ vt: ~ **(à qn)** to sign (for sb), autograph (for sb)

dédier [dedje] /7/ vt: ~ **à** to dedicate to

dédommagement [dedɔmaʒmɑ̃] nm compensation

dédommager [dedɔmaʒe] /3/ vt: ~ **qn (de)** to compensate sb (for)

dédouaner [dedwane] /1/ vt to clear through customs

déduire [dedɥir] /38/ vt: ~ **qch (de)** (ôter) to deduct sth (from); (conclure) to deduce ou infer sth (from)

défaillance [defajɑ̃s] nf (syncope) blackout; (fatigue) (sudden) weakness no pl; (technique) fault, failure; ~ **cardiaque** heart failure

défaire [defɛr] /60/ vt (installation, échafaudage) to take down, dismantle; (paquet etc, nœud, vêtement) to undo; **se défaire** vi to come undone; **se ~ de** to get rid of

défait, e [defɛ, ɛt] adj (visage) haggard, ravaged ▷ nf defeat

défaut [defo] nm (moral) fault, failing; (d'étoffe, métal) fault, flaw; (manque, carence): ~ **de** shortage of; **prendre qn en** ~ to catch sb out; **faire ~** (manquer) to be lacking; **à ~ de** for lack ou want of

défavorable [defavɔrabl] adj unfavourable (BRIT), unfavorable (US)

défavoriser [defavɔrize] /1/ vt to put at a disadvantage

défectueux, -euse [defɛktɥø, -øz] adj faulty, defective

défendre [defɑ̃dr] /41/ vt to defend; (interdire) to forbid; **se défendre** vi to defend o.s.; ~ **à qn qch/de faire** to forbid sb sth/ to do; **il se défend** (fig) he can hold his own; **se ~ de/contre** (se protéger) to protect o.s. from/against; **se ~ de** (se garder de) to refrain from

défense [defɑ̃s] nf defence; (d'éléphant etc) tusk; **ministre de la ~** Minister of Defence (BRIT), Defence Secretary; **"~ de fumer/cracher"** "no smoking/spitting"

défi [defi] nm challenge; **lancer un ~ à qn** to challenge sb; **sur un ton de ~** defiantly

déficit [defisit] nm (Comm) deficit

défier [defje] /7/ vt (provoquer) to challenge; (fig) to defy; ~ **qn de faire** to challenge ou defy sb to do

défigurer [defigyre] /1/ vt to disfigure

défilé [defile] nm (Géo) (narrow) gorge ou pass; (soldats) parade; (manifestants) procession, march

défiler [defile] /1/ vi (troupes) to march past; (sportifs) to parade; (manifestants) to march; (visiteurs) to pour, stream; **faire ~ un document** (Inform) to scroll a document; **se défiler** vi: **il s'est défilé** (fam) he wriggled out of it

définir [definiʀ] /2/ vt to define

définitif, -ive [definitif, -iv] adj (final) final, definitive; (pour longtemps) permanent, definitive; (sans appel) definite ▷ nf: **en définitive** eventually; (somme toute) when all is said and done; **définitivement** adv permanently

déformer [defɔʀme] /1/ vt to put out of shape; (pensée, fait) to distort; **se déformer** vi to lose its shape

défouler [defule] /1/: **se défouler** vi to unwind, let off steam

défunt, e [defœ̃, -œ̃t] adj: **son ~ père** his late father ▷ nm/f deceased

dégagé, e [degaʒe] adj (route, ciel) clear; **sur un ton ~** casually

dégager [degaʒe] /3/ vt (exhaler) to give off; (délivrer) to free, extricate; (désencombrer) to clear; (isoler, mettre en valeur) to bring out; **se dégager** vi (passage, ciel) to clear; **~ qn de** (engagement, parole etc) to release ou free sb from

dégâts [dega] nmpl damage sg; **faire des ~** to damage

dégel [deʒɛl] nm thaw; **dégeler** /5/ vt to thaw (out)

dégivrer [deʒivʀe] /1/ vt (frigo) to defrost; (vitres) to de-ice

dégonflé, e [degɔ̃fle] adj (pneu) flat

dégonfler [degɔ̃fle] /1/ vt (pneu, ballon) to let down, deflate; **se dégonfler** vi (fam) to chicken out

dégouliner [deguline] /1/ vi to trickle, drip

dégourdi, e [deguʀdi] adj smart, resourceful

dégourdir [deguʀdiʀ] /2/ vt: **se ~ (les jambes)** to stretch one's legs

dégoût [degu] nm disgust, distaste; **dégoûtant, e** adj disgusting; **dégoûté, e** adj disgusted; **dégoûté de** sick of; **dégoûter** /1/ vt to disgust; **dégoûter qn de qch** to put sb off sth

dégrader [degʀade] /1/ vt (Mil: officier) to degrade; (abîmer) to damage, deface; **se dégrader** vi (relations, situation) to deteriorate

degré [dəgʀe] nm degree

dégressif, -ive [degʀesif, -iv] adj on a decreasing scale

dégringoler [degʀɛ̃ɡɔle] /1/ vi to tumble (down)

déguisement [degizmɑ̃] nm (pour s'amuser) fancy dress

déguiser [degize] /1/: **se déguiser (en)** vi (se costumer) to dress up (as); (pour tromper) to disguise o.s. (as)

dégustation [degystasjɔ̃] nf (de fromages etc) sampling; **~ de vin(s)** wine-tasting

déguster [degyste] /1/ vt (vins) to taste; (fromages etc) to sample; (savourer) to enjoy

dehors [dəɔʀ] adv outside; (en plein air) outdoors ▷ nm outside ▷ nmpl (apparences) appearances; **mettre** ou **jeter ~** to throw out; **au ~** outside; **au ~ de** outside; **en ~ de** apart from

déjà [deʒa] adv already; (auparavant) before, already

déjeuner [deʒœne] /1/ vi to (have) lunch; (le matin) to have breakfast ▷ nm lunch

delà [dəla] adv: **en ~ (de), au ~ (de)** beyond

délacer [delase] /3/ vt (chaussures) to undo, unlace

délai [delɛ] nm (attente) waiting period; (sursis) extension (of time); (temps accordé) time limit; **sans ~** without delay; **dans les ~s** within the time limit

délaisser [delese] /1/ vt to abandon, desert

délasser [delase] /1/ vt to relax; **se délasser** vi to relax

délavé, e [delave] adj faded

délayer [deleje] /8/ vt (Culin) to mix (with water etc); (peinture) to thin down

delco® [dɛlko] nm (Auto) distributor

délégué, e [delege] nm/f representative

déléguer [delege] /6/ vt to delegate

délibéré, e [delibeʀe] adj (conscient) deliberate

délicat, e [delika, -at] adj delicate; (plein de tact) tactful; (attentionné) thoughtful; **délicatement** adv delicately; (avec douceur) gently

délice [delis] nm delight

délicieux, -euse [delisjø, -øz] adj (au goût) delicious; (sensation, impression) delightful

délimiter [delimite] /1/ vt (terrain) to delimit, demarcate

délinquant, e [delɛ̃kɑ̃, -ɑ̃t] adj, nm/f delinquent

délirer [deliʀe] /1/ vi to be delirious; **tu délires!** (fam) you're crazy!

délit [deli] nm (criminal) offence

délivrer [delivʀe] /1/ vt (prisonnier) to (set) free, release; (passeport, certificat) to issue

deltaplane® [dɛltaplan] nm hang-glider

déluge [delyʒ] nm (biblique) Flood; (grosse pluie) downpour

demain [d(ə)mɛ̃] adv tomorrow; **~ matin/ soir** tomorrow morning/evening

demande [d(ə)mɑ̃d] nf (requête) request; (revendication) demand; (formulaire) application; (Écon): **la ~** demand; **"~s d'emploi"** "situations wanted"

demandé, e [d(ə)mɑ̃de] adj (article etc): **très ~** (very) much in demand

demander [d(ə)mɑ̃de] /1/ vt to ask for; (date, heure, chemin) to ask; (requérir,

nécessiter) to require, demand; **~ qch à qn**
to ask sb for sth; **~ à qn de faire** to ask sb
to do; **se ~ si/pourquoi** *etc* to wonder if/
why *etc*; **je ne demande pas mieux** I'm
asking nothing more; **demandeur, -euse**
nm/f: **demandeur d'asile** asylum-seeker;
demandeur d'emploi job-seeker
démangeaison [demãʒɛzɔ̃] *nf* itching;
avoir des ~s to be itching
démanger [demãʒe] /3/ *vi* to itch
démaquillant [demakijã] *nm* make-up
remover
démaquiller [demakije] /1/ *vt*: **se**
démaquiller to remove one's make-up
démarche [demarʃ] *nf (allure)* gait,
walk; *(intervention)* step; *(fig: intellectuelle)*
thought processes *pl*; **faire les ~s**
nécessaires (pour obtenir qch) to take the
necessary steps (to obtain sth)
démarrage [demaraʒ] *nm* start
démarrer [demare] /1/ *vi (conducteur)* to
start (up); *(véhicule)* to move off; *(travaux,*
affaire) to get moving; **démarreur** *nm*
(Auto) starter
démêlant, e [demelã, -ãt] *adj*: **crème ~e**
(hair) conditioner ▷ *nm* conditioner
démêler [demele] /1/ *vt* to untangle;
démêlés *nmpl* problems
déménagement [demenaʒmã] *nm* move;
entreprise/camion de ~ removal (BRIT) *ou*
moving (US) firm/van
déménager [demenaʒe] /3/ *vt (meubles)*
to (re)move ▷ *vi* to move (house);
déménageur *nm* removal man
démerder [demɛrde] /1/: **se démerder** *vi*
(fam!) to bloody well manage for o.s.
démettre [demɛtr] /56/ *vt*: **~ qn de**
(fonction, poste) to dismiss sb from; **se ~**
l'épaule *etc* to dislocate one's shoulder *etc*
demeurer [d(ə)mœre] /1/ *vi (habiter)* to
live; *(rester)* to remain
demi, e [dəmi] *adj* half; **et ~: trois heures/**
bouteilles et ~es three and a half hours/
bottles ▷ *nm (bière: = 0.25 litre)* ≈ half-pint;
il est 2 heures et ~e it's half past 2; **il est**
midi et ~ it's half past 12; **à ~ half-**; **à la ~e**
(heure) on the half-hour; **demi-douzaine**
nf half-dozen, half a dozen; **demi-finale**
nf semifinal; **demi-frère** *nm* half-brother;
demi-heure *nf*: **une demi-heure** a
half-hour, half an hour; **demi-journée**
nf half-day, half a day; **demi-litre** *nm*
half-litre (BRIT), half-liter (US), half a litre
ou liter; **demi-livre** *nf* half-pound, half
a pound; **demi-pension** *nf* half-board;
demi-pensionnaire *nm/f*: **être demi-**
pensionnaire to take school lunches
démis, e *adj (épaule etc)* dislocated
demi-sœur [dəmisœr] *nf* half-sister
démission [demisjɔ̃] *nf* resignation;
donner sa ~ to give *ou* hand in one's notice;
démissionner /1/ *vi* to resign

demi-tarif [dəmitarif] *nm* half-price;
(Transports) half-fare; **voyager à ~** to travel
half-fare
demi-tour [dəmitur] *nm* about-turn;
faire ~ to turn (and go) back
démocratie [demokrasi] *nf* democracy;
démocratique *adj* democratic
démodé, e [demode] *adj* old-fashioned
demoiselle [d(ə)mwazɛl] *nf (jeune fille)*
young lady; *(célibataire)* single lady, maiden
lady; **~ d'honneur** bridesmaid
démolir [demolir] /2/ *vt* to demolish
démon [demɔ̃] *nm (enfant turbulent)* devil,
demon; **le D~** the Devil
démonstration [demɔ̃strasjɔ̃] *nf*
demonstration
démonter [demɔ̃te] /1/ *vt (machine etc)*
to take down, dismantle; **se démonter**
vi (meuble) to be dismantled, be taken to
pieces; *(personne)* to lose countenance
démontrer [demɔ̃tre] /1/ *vt* to
demonstrate
démouler [demule] /1/ *vt* to turn out
démuni, e [demyni] *adj (sans argent)*
impoverished; **~ de** without
dénicher [denife] /1/ *vt (fam: objet)* to
unearth; *(: restaurant etc)* to discover
dénier [denje] /7/ *vt* to deny
dénivellation [denivelasjɔ̃] *nf (pente)*
ramp
dénombrer [denɔ̃bre] /1/ *vt* to count
dénomination [denominasjɔ̃] *nf*
designation, appellation
dénoncer [denɔ̃se] /3/ *vt* to denounce; **se**
dénoncer to give o.s. up, come forward
dénouement [denumã] *nm* outcome
dénouer [denwe] /1/ *vt* to unknot, undo
denrée [dãre] *nf (aussi: ~ alimentaire)*
food(stuff)
dense [dãs] *adj* dense; **densité** *nf* density
dent [dã] *nf* tooth; **~ de lait/sagesse**
milk/wisdom tooth; **dentaire** *adj* dental;
cabinet dentaire dental surgery
dentelle [dãtɛl] *nf* lace *no pl*
dentier [dãtje] *nm* denture
dentifrice [dãtifris] *nm*: **(pâte) ~**
toothpaste
dentiste *nm/f* dentist
dentition [dãtisjɔ̃] *nf* teeth *pl*
dénué, e [denɥe] *adj*: **~ de** devoid of
déodorant [deodorã] *nm* deodorant
déontologie [deɔ̃tɔlɔʒi] *nf (professional)*
code of practice
dépannage [depanaʒ] *nm*: **service/**
camion de ~ *(Auto)* breakdown service/
truck
dépanner [depane] /1/ *vt (voiture,*
télévision) to fix, repair; *(fig)* to bail out,
help out; **dépanneuse** *nf* breakdown lorry
(BRIT), tow truck (US)
dépareillé, e [depareje] *adj (collection,*
service) incomplete; *(gant, volume, objet)* odd

départ [depaʀ] nm departure; (Sport) start;
au ~ at the start; **la veille de son ~** the day
before he leaves/left
département [depaʀtəmɑ̃] nm
department

● **DÉPARTEMENTS**

● France is divided into 96 administrative
● units called *départements*. These local
● government divisions are headed
● by a state-appointed 'préfet', and
● administered by an elected 'Conseil
● général'. *Départements* are usually named
● after prominent geographical features
● such as rivers or mountain ranges.

dépassé, e [depɑse] adj superseded,
outmoded; (fig) out of one's depth
dépasser [depɑse] /1/ vt (véhicule,
concurrent) to overtake; (endroit) to pass,
go past; (somme, limite) to exceed; (fig: en
beauté etc) to surpass, outshine ▷ vi (jupon)
to show; **se dépasser** to excel o.s.
dépaysé, e [depeize] adj disoriented
dépaysement [depeizmɑ̃] nm change of
scenery
dépêcher [depeʃe] /1/: **se dépêcher** vi to
hurry
dépendance [depɑ̃dɑ̃s] nf dependence no
pl; (bâtiment) outbuilding
dépendre [depɑ̃dʀ] /41/ vt: **~ de** vt to
depend on, to be dependent on; **ça dépend**
it depends
dépens [depɑ̃] nmpl: **aux ~** at the
expense of
dépense [depɑ̃s] nf spending no pl,
expense, expenditure no pl; **dépenser**
/1/ vt to spend; (fig) to expend, use up; **se
dépenser** vi to exert o.s.
dépeupler [depœple] /1/: **se dépeupler** vi
to become depopulated
dépilatoire [depilatwaʀ] adj: **crème ~**
hair-removing ou depilatory cream
dépister [depiste] /1/ vt to detect; (voleur)
to track down
dépit [depi] nm vexation, frustration; **en
~ de** in spite of; **en ~ du bon sens** contrary
to all good sense; **dépité, e** adj vexed,
frustrated
déplacé, e [deplase] adj (propos) out of
place, uncalled-for
déplacement [deplasmɑ̃] nm (voyage) trip,
travelling no pl; **en ~** away (on a trip)
déplacer [deplase] /3/ vt (table, voiture)
to move, shift; **se déplacer** vi to move;
(voyager) to travel; **se ~ une vertèbre** to
slip a disc
déplaire [deplɛʀ] /54/ vi: **ceci me déplaît**
I don't like this, I dislike this; **se ~ quelque
part** to dislike it ou be unhappy somewhere;
déplaisant, e adj disagreeable

dépliant [deplijɑ̃] nm leaflet
déplier [deplije] /7/ vt to unfold
déposer [depoze] /1/ vt (gén: mettre, poser)
to lay down, put down; (à la banque, à la
consigne) to deposit; (passager) to drop
(off), set down; (roi) to depose; (marque) to
register; (plainte) to lodge; **se déposer** vi
to settle; **dépositaire** nm/f (Comm) agent;
déposition nf statement
dépôt [depo] nm (à la banque, sédiment)
deposit; (entrepôt, réserve) warehouse, store
dépourvu, e [depuʀvy] adj: **~ de** lacking
in, without; **prendre qn au ~** to catch sb
unawares
dépression nf depression; **~ (nerveuse)**
(nervous) breakdown
déprimant, e [depʀimɑ̃, -ɑ̃t] adj
depressing
déprimer [depʀime] /1/ vt to depress

🔵 **MOT-CLÉ**

depuis [dəpɥi] prép **1** (point de départ dans
le temps) since; **il habite Paris depuis
1983/l'an dernier** he has been living in Paris
since 1983/last year; **depuis quand?** since
when?; **depuis quand le connaissez-vous?**
how long have you known him?
2 (temps écoulé) for; **il habite Paris depuis
cinq ans** he has been living in Paris for five
years; **je le connais depuis trois ans** I've
known him for three years
3 (lieu): **il a plu depuis Metz** it's been
raining since Metz; **elle a téléphoné
depuis Valence** she rang from Valence
4 (quantité, rang) from; **depuis les plus
petits jusqu'aux plus grands** from the
youngest to the oldest
▶ adv (temps) since (then); **je ne lui ai pas
parlé depuis** I haven't spoken to him since
(then); **depuis que** conj (ever) since; **depuis
qu'il m'a dit ça** (ever) since he said that
to me

député, e [depyte] nm/f (Pol) ≈ Member
of Parliament (BRIT), ≈ Congressman/
woman (us)
dérangement [deʀɑ̃ʒmɑ̃] nm (gêne,
déplacement) trouble; (gastrique etc)
disorder; **en ~** (téléphone) out of order
déranger [deʀɑ̃ʒe] /3/ vt (personne)
to trouble, bother; (projets) to disrupt,
upset; (objets, vêtements) to disarrange; **se
déranger** vi: **surtout ne vous dérangez
pas pour moi** please don't put yourself
out on my account; **est-ce que cela vous
dérange si ...?** do you mind if ...?
déraper [deʀape] /1/ vi (voiture) to skid;
(personne, semelles, couteau) to slip
dérégler [deʀegle] /6/ vt (mécanisme) to
put out of order; (estomac) to upset
dérisoire [deʀizwaʀ] adj derisory

dérive [deʀiv] *nf*: **aller à la ~** (*Navig, fig*) to drift

dérivé, e [deʀive] *nm* (*Tech*) by-product

dermatologue [dɛʀmatɔlɔg] *nm/f* dermatologist

dernier, -ière [dɛʀnje, -jɛʀ] *adj* last; (*le plus récent: gén avant n*) latest, last; **lundi/ le mois ~** last Monday/month; **le ~ cri** the last word (in fashion); **en ~** last; **ce ~, cette dernière** the latter; **dernièrement** *adv* recently

dérogation [deʀɔgasjɔ̃] *nf* (special) dispensation

dérouiller [deʀuje] /1/ *vt*: **se ~ les jambes** to stretch one's legs (*fig*)

déroulement [deʀulmɑ̃] *nm* (*d'une opération etc*) progress

dérouler [deʀule] /1/ *vt* (*ficelle*) to unwind; **se dérouler** *vi* (*avoir lieu*) to take place; (*se passer*) to go, **tout s'est déroulé comme prévu** everything went as planned

dérouter [deʀute] /1/ *vt* (*avion, train*) to reroute, divert; (*étonner*) to disconcert, throw (out)

derrière [dɛʀjɛʀ] *adv, prép* behind ▷ *nm* (*d'une maison*) back; (*postérieur*) behind, bottom; **les pattes de ~** the back legs, the hind legs; **par ~** from behind; (*fig*) behind one's back

des [de] *art voir* **de**

dès [dɛ] *prép* from; **que** as soon as; **~ son retour** as soon as he was (*ou* is) back

désaccord [dezakɔʀ] *nm* disagreement

désagréable [dezagʀeabl] *adj* unpleasant

désagrément [dezagʀemɑ̃] *nm* annoyance, trouble *no pl*

désaltérer [dezaltere] /6/ *vt*: **se désaltérer** to quench one's thirst

désapprobateur, -trice [dezapʀɔbatœʀ, -tʀis] *adj* disapproving

désapprouver [dezapʀuve] /1/ *vt* to disapprove of

désarmant, e [dezaʀmɑ̃, -ɑ̃t] *adj* disarming

désastre [dezastʀ] *nm* disaster; **désastreux, -euse** *adj* disastrous

désavantage [dezavɑ̃taʒ] *nm* disadvantage; **désavantager** /3/ *vt* to put at a disadvantage

descendre [desɑ̃dʀ] /41/ *vt* (*escalier, montagne*) to go (*ou* come) down; (*valise, paquet*) to take *ou* get down; (*étagère etc*) to lower; (*fam: abattre*) to shoot down ▷ *vi* to go (*ou* come) down; (*passager: s'arrêter*) to get out, alight; **~ à pied/en voiture** to walk/drive down; **~ de** (*famille*) to be descended from; **~ du train** to get out of *ou* off the train; **~ d'un arbre** to climb down from a tree; **~ de cheval** to dismount; **~ à l'hôtel** to stay at a hotel

descente [desɑ̃t] *nf* descent, going down; (*chemin*) way down; (*Ski*) downhill (race);

au milieu de la ~ halfway down; **~ de lit** bedside rug; **~ (de police)** (police) raid

description [dɛskʀipsjɔ̃] *nf* description

déséquilibre [dezekilibʀ] *nm* (*position*): **être en ~** to be unsteady; (*fig: des forces, du budget*) imbalance

désert, e [dezɛʀ, -ɛʀt] *adj* deserted ▷ *nm* desert; **désertique** *adj* desert *cpd*

désespéré, e [dezɛspeʀe] *adj* desperate

désespérer [dezɛspeʀe] /6/ *vi*: **~ de** to despair of; **désespoir** *nm* despair; **en désespoir de cause** in desperation

déshabiller [dezabije] /1/ *vt* to undress; **se déshabiller** *vi* to undress (o.s.)

déshydraté, e [dezidʀate] *adj* dehydrated

désigner [dezipe] /1/ *vt* (*montrer*) to point out, indicate; (*dénommer*) to denote; (*candidat etc*) to name

désinfectant, e [dezɛ̃fɛktɑ̃, -ɑ̃t] *adj, nm* disinfectant

désinfecter [dezɛ̃fɛkte] /1/ *vt* to disinfect

désintéressé, e [dezɛ̃teʀese] *adj* disinterested, unselfish

désintéresser [dezɛ̃teʀese] /1/ *vt*: **se désintéresser (de)** to lose interest (in)

désintoxication [dezɛ̃tɔksikasjɔ̃] *nf*: **faire une cure de ~** to have *ou* undergo treatment for alcoholism (*ou* drug addiction)

désinvolte [dezɛ̃vɔlt] *adj* casual, off-hand

désir [deziʀ] *nm* wish; (*fort, sensuel*) desire; **désirer** /1/ *vt* to want, wish for; (*sexuellement*) to desire, **je désire ...** (*formule de politesse*) I would like ...

désister [deziste] /1/: **se désister** *vi* to stand down, withdraw

désobéir [dezɔbeiʀ] /2/ *vi*: **~ (à qn/qch)** to disobey (sb/sth); **désobéissant, e** *adj* disobedient

désodorisant [dezɔdɔʀizɑ̃] *nm* air freshener, deodorizer

désolé, e [dezɔle] *adj* (*paysage*) desolate; **je suis ~** I'm sorry

désordonné, e [dezɔʀdɔne] *adj* untidy

désordre [dezɔʀdʀ] *nm* disorder(liness), untidiness; (*anarchie*) disorder; **en ~** in a mess, untidy

désormais [dezɔʀmɛ] *adv* from now on

desquels, desquelles [dekɛl] *voir* **lequel**

dessécher [deseʃe] /6/: **se dessécher** *vi* to dry out

desserrer [deseʀe] /1/ *vt* to loosen; (*frein*) to release

dessert [desɛʀ] *nm* dessert, pudding

desservir [desɛʀviʀ] /14/ *vt* (*ville, quartier*) to serve; (*débarrasser*): **~ (la table)** to clear the table

dessin [desɛ̃] *nm* (*œuvre, art*) drawing; (*motif*) pattern, design; **~ animé** cartoon (film); **~ humoristique** cartoon; **dessinateur, -trice** *nm/f* drawer; (*de bandes dessinées*) cartoonist; (*industriel*)

draughtsman (BRIT), draftsman (US);
dessiner /1/ vt to draw; (concevoir)
to design; **se dessiner** vi (forme) to be
outlined; (fig: solution) to emerge
dessous [d(ə)su] adv underneath, beneath
▷ nm underside; **les voisins du ~** the
downstairs neighbours ▷ nmpl (sous-
vêtements) underwear sg; **en ~** underneath;
below; **par ~** underneath; below; **avoir le ~**
to get the worst of it; **dessous-de-plat** nm
inv tablemat
dessus [d(ə)sy] adv on top; (collé, écrit) on
it ▷ nm top; **les voisins/l'appartement
du ~** the upstairs neighbours/flat; **en ~**
above; **par ~** adv over it; prép over; **au-**
above; **avoir/prendre le ~** to have/get the
upper hand; **sens ~ dessous** upside down;
dessus-de-lit nm inv bedspread
destin [dɛstɛ̃] nm fate; (avenir) destiny
destinataire [dɛstinatɛʀ] nm/f (Postes)
addressee; (d'un colis) consignee
destination [dɛstinasjɔ̃] nf (lieu)
destination; (usage) purpose; **à ~ de** bound
for; travelling to
destiner [dɛstine] /1/ vt: **~ qch à qn**
(envisager de donner) to intend sb to have
sth; (adresser) to intend sth for sb; **se ~
à l'enseignement** to intend to become
a teacher; **être destiné à** (usage) to be
intended ou meant for
détachant [detaʃɑ̃] nm stain remover
détacher [detaʃe] /1/ vt (enlever) to
detach, remove; (délier) to untie; (Admin):
~ qn (auprès de ou à) to post sb (to); **se
détacher** vi (se séparer) to come off; (page)
to come out; (se défaire) to come undone;
se ~ sur to stand out against; **se ~ de** (se
désintéresser) to grow away from
détail [detaj] nm detail; (Comm): **le ~**
retail; **au ~** (Comm) retail; **en ~** in detail;
détaillant, e nm/f retailer; **détaillé, e** adj
(récit, plan, explications) detailed; (facture)
itemized; **détailler** /1/ vt (expliquer) to
explain in detail
détecter [detɛkte] /1/ vt to detect
détective [detɛktiv] nm detective;
~ (privé) private detective ou investigator
déteindre [detɛ̃dʀ] /52/ vi to fade; (au
lavage) to run; **~ sur** (vêtement) to run into;
(fig) to rub off on
détendre [detɑ̃dʀ] /41/ vt (personne,
atmosphère, corps, esprit) to relax; **se
détendre** vi (ressort) to lose its tension;
(personne) to relax
détenir [det(ə)niʀ] /22/ vt (fortune, objet,
secret) to be in possession of; (prisonnier) to
detain; (record) to hold; **~ le pouvoir** to be
in power
détente [detɑ̃t] nf relaxation
détention [detɑ̃sjɔ̃] nf (de fortune, objet,
secret) possession; (captivité) detention;
~ préventive (pre-trial) custody

détenu, e [det(ə)ny] pp de **détenir** ▷ nm/f
prisoner
détergent [detɛʀʒɑ̃] nm detergent
détériorer [deteʀjɔʀe] /1/ vt to damage;
se détériorer vi to deteriorate
déterminé, e [detɛʀmine] adj (résolu)
determined; (précis) specific, definite
déterminer [detɛʀmine] /1/ vt (fixer) to
determine; **~ qn à faire** to decide sb to do;
se ~ à faire to make up one's mind to do
détester [detɛste] /1/ vt to hate, detest
détour [detuʀ] nm detour; (tournant) bend,
curve; **ça vaut le ~** it's worth the trip;
sans ~ (fig) plainly
détourné, e [detuʀne] adj (sentier, chemin,
moyen) roundabout
détourner [detuʀne] /1/ vt to divert; (par
la force) to hijack; (yeux, tête) to turn away;
(de l'argent) to embezzle; **se détourner** vi to
turn away
détraquer [detʀake] /1/ vt to put out of
order; (estomac) to upset; **se détraquer** vi
to go wrong
détriment [detʀimɑ̃] nm: **au ~ de** to the
detriment of
détroit [detʀwa] nm strait
détruire [detʀɥiʀ] /38/ vt to destroy
dette [dɛt] nf debt
DEUG [dœg] sigle m = **Diplôme d'études
universitaires générales**

deuil [dœj] nm (perte) bereavement;
(période) mourning; **prendre le/être en ~**
to go into/be in mourning
deux [dø] num two; **les ~** both; **ses ~ mains**
both his hands, his two hands; **~ fois** twice;
deuxième num second; **deuxièmement**
adv secondly; **deux-pièces** nm inv (tailleur)
two-piece (suit); (de bain) two-piece
(swimsuit); (appartement) two-roomed
flat (BRIT) ou apartment (US); **deux-points**
nm inv colon sg; **deux-roues** nm inv two-
wheeled vehicle
devais etc [d(ə)vɛ] vb voir **devoir**
dévaluation [devalɥasjɔ̃] nf devaluation
devancer [d(ə)vɑ̃se] /3/ vt to get ahead of;
(arriver avant) to arrive before; (prévenir) to
anticipate
devant [d(ə)vɑ̃] adv in front; (à distance: en
avant) ahead ▷ prép in front of; (en avant)
ahead of; (avec mouvement: passer) past; (fig)

before, in front of (: *vu*) in view of ▷ *nm* front;
prendre les ~s to make the first move; **les
pattes de ~** the front legs, the forelegs; **par ~**
(*boutonner*) at the front; (*entrer*) the front
way; **aller au-~ de qn** to go out to meet sb;
aller au-~ de (*désirs de qn*) to anticipate

devanture [d(ə)vãtyʀ] *nf* (*étalage*) display;
(*vitrine*) (shop) window

développement [dev(ə)lɔpmã] *nm*
development; **pays en voie de ~**
developing countries; **~ durable**
sustainable development

développer [dev(ə)lɔpe] /1/ *vt* to develop;
se développer *vi* to develop

devenir [dəv(ə)niʀ] /22/ *vi* to become;
que sont-ils devenus? what has become
of them?

devez [dəve] *vb voir* **devoir**

déviation [devjasjɔ̃] *nf* (*Auto*) diversion
(*BRIT*), detour (*US*)

devienne *etc* [dəvjɛn] *vb voir* **devenir**

deviner [d(ə)vine] /1/ *vt* to guess;
(*apercevoir*) to distinguish; **devinette** *nf*
riddle

devis [d(ə)vi] *nm* estimate, quotation

devise [dəviz] *nf* (*formule*) motto, watchword;
devises *nfpl* (*argent*) currency *sg*

dévisser [devise] /1/ *vt* to unscrew, undo;
se dévisser *vi* to come unscrewed

devoir [d(ə)vwaʀ] /28/ *nm* duty; (*Scol*)
homework *no pl* (: *en classe*) exercise ▷ *vt*
(*argent, respect*): **~ qch (à qn)** to owe (sb)
sth; **combien est-ce que je vous dois?**
how much do I owe you?; **il doit le faire**
(*obligation*) he has to do it, he must do it;
cela devait arriver un jour it was bound to
happen; **il doit partir demain** (*intention*) he
is due to leave tomorrow; **il doit être tard**
(*probabilité*) it must be late

dévorer [devɔʀe] /1/ *vt* to devour; (*feu,
soucis*) to consume; **~ qn/qch des yeux** *ou*
du regard (*convoitise*) to eye sb/sth greedily

dévoué, e [devwe] *adj* devoted

dévouer [devwe] /1/: **se dévouer** *vi* (*se
sacrifier*): **se ~ (pour)** to sacrifice o.s. (for);
(*se consacrer*): **se ~ à** to devote *ou* dedicate
o.s. to

devrai *etc* [dəvʀe] *vb voir* **devoir**

dézipper [dezipe] /1/ *vt* to unzip

diabète [djabɛt] *nm* diabetes *sg*;
diabétique *nm/f* diabetic

diable [djabl] *nm* devil

diabolo [djabɔlɔ] *nm* (*boisson*) lemonade
and fruit cordial

diagnostic [djagnɔstik] *nm* diagnosis *sg*;
diagnostiquer /1/ *vt* to diagnose

diagonal, e, -aux [djagɔnal, -o] *adj, nf*
diagonal; **en ~e** diagonally

diagramme [djagʀam] *nm* chart, graph

dialecte [djalɛkt] *nm* dialect

dialogue [djalɔg] *nm* dialogue

diamant [djamã] *nm* diamond

diamètre [djamɛtʀ] *nm* diameter

diapo [djapo], **diapositive** [djapozitiv] *nf*
transparency, slide

diarrhée [djaʀe] *nf* diarrhoea

dictateur [diktatœʀ] *nm* dictator;
dictature [diktatyʀ] *nf* dictatorship

dictée [dikte] *nf* dictation

dicter [dikte] /1/ *vt* to dictate

dictionnaire [diksjɔnɛʀ] *nm* dictionary

dièse [djɛz] *nm* sharp

diesel [djezɛl] *nm, adj inv* diesel

diète [djɛt] *nf* (*jeûne*) starvation diet;
(*régime*) diet; **diététique** *adj*: **magasin
diététique** health food shop (*BRIT*) *ou*
store (*US*)

dieu, x [djø] *nm* god; **D~** God; **mon D~!**
good heavens!

différemment [difeʀamã] *adv* differently

différence [difeʀãs] *nf* difference; **à la ~ de**
unlike; **différencier** /7/ *vt* to differentiate

différent, e [difeʀã, -ãt] *adj* (*dissemblable*)
different; **~ de** different from; **~s objets**
different *ou* various objects

différer [difeʀe] /6/ *vt* to postpone, put off
▷ *vi*: **~ (de)** to differ (from)

difficile [difisil] *adj* difficult; (*exigeant*) hard
to please; **difficilement** *adv* with difficulty

difficulté [difikylte] *nf* difficulty; **en ~**
(*bateau, alpiniste*) in trouble *ou* difficulties

diffuser [difyze] /1/ *vt* (*chaleur, bruit,
lumière*) to diffuse; (*émission, musique*) to
broadcast; (*nouvelle, idée*) to circulate;
(*Comm*) to distribute

digérer [diʒeʀe] /6/ *vt* to digest; (*fig:
accepter*) to stomach, put up with; **digestif**
nm (after-dinner) liqueur; **digestion** *nf*
digestion

digne [diɲ] *adj* dignified; **~ de** worthy of;
~ de foi trustworthy; **dignité** *nf* dignity

digue [dig] *nf* dike, dyke

dilemme [dilɛm] *nm* dilemma

diligence [diliʒãs] *nf* stagecoach

diluer [dilɥe] /1/ *vt* to dilute

dimanche [dimãʃ] *nm* Sunday

dimension [dimãsjɔ̃] *nf* (*grandeur*) size;
(*dimensions*) dimensions

diminuer [diminɥe] /1/ *vt* to reduce,
decrease; (*ardeur etc*) to lessen; (*dénigrer*)
to belittle ▷ *vi* to decrease, diminish;
diminutif *nm* (*surnom*) pet name

dinde [dɛ̃d] *nf* turkey

dindon [dɛ̃dɔ̃] *nm* turkey

dîner [dine] /1/ *nm* dinner ▷ *vi* to have
dinner

dingue [dɛ̃g] *adj* (*fam*) crazy

dinosaure [dinɔzɔʀ] *nm* dinosaur

diplomate [diplɔmat] *adj* diplomatic ▷ *nm*
diplomat, (*fig*) diplomatist; **diplomatie** *nf*
diplomacy

diplôme [diplom] *nm* diploma certificate;
avoir des ~s to have qualifications;
diplômé, e *adj* qualified

dire [diʀ] /37/ vt to say; (secret, mensonge) to tell; **se dire** (à soi-même) to say to oneself ▷ nm: **au ~ de** according to; **~ qch à qn** to tell sb sth; **~ à qn qu'il fasse** ou **de faire** to tell sb to do; **on dit que** they say that; **on dirait que** it looks (ou sounds etc) as though; **que dites-vous de** (penser) what do you think of; **si cela lui dit** if he fancies it; **dis donc!, dites donc!** (pour attirer l'attention) hey!; (au fait) by the way; **ceci** ou **cela dit** that being said; **ça ne se dit pas** (impoli) you shouldn't say that; (pas en usage) you don't say that

direct, e [diʀɛkt] adj direct ▷ nm: **en ~** (émission) live; **directement** adv directly

directeur, -trice [diʀɛktœʀ, -tʀis] nm/f (d'entreprise) director; (de service) manager/eress; (d'école) head(teacher) (BRIT), principal (US)

direction [diʀɛksjɔ̃] nf (d'entreprise) management; (Auto) steering; (sens) direction; **"toutes ~s"** "all routes"

dirent [diʀ] vb voir **dire**

dirigeant, e [diʀiʒɑ̃, -ɑ̃t] adj (classes) ruling ▷ nm/f (d'un parti etc) leader

diriger [diʀiʒe] /3/ vt (entreprise) to manage, run; (véhicule) to steer; (orchestre) to conduct; (recherches, travaux) to supervise; (arme): **~ sur** to point ou level ou aim at; **se diriger** vi (s'orienter) to find one's way; **~ son regard sur** to look in the direction of; **se ~ vers** ou **sur** to make ou head for

dis [di] vb voir **dire**

discerner [disɛʀne] /1/ vt to discern, make out

discipline [disiplin] nf discipline; **discipliner** /1/ vt to discipline

discontinu, e [diskɔ̃tiny] adj intermittent

discontinuer [diskɔ̃tinɥe] /1/ vi: **sans ~** without stopping, without a break

discothèque [diskɔtɛk] nf (boîte de nuit) disco(thèque)

discours [diskuʀ] nm speech

discret, -ète [diskʀɛ, -ɛt] adj discreet; (fig: musique, style, maquillage) unobtrusive; **discrétion** nf discretion; **à discrétion** as much as one wants

discrimination nf discrimination; **sans ~** indiscriminately

discussion [diskysjɔ̃] nf discussion

discutable [diskytabl] adj debatable

discuter [diskyte] /1/ vt (contester) to question, dispute; (débattre: prix) to discuss ▷ vi to talk; (protester) to argue; **~ de** to discuss

dise etc [diz] vb voir **dire**

disjoncteur [disʒɔ̃ktœʀ] nm (Élec) circuit breaker

disloquer [dislɔke] /1/: **se disloquer** vi (parti, empire) to break up; (meuble) to come apart; **se ~ l'épaule** to dislocate one's shoulder

disons etc [dizɔ̃] vb voir **dire**

disparaître [dispaʀɛtʀ] /57/ vi to disappear; (se perdre: traditions etc) to die out; (personne: mourir) to die; **faire ~** (objet, tache, trace) to remove; (personne, douleur) to get rid of

disparition [dispaʀisjɔ̃] nf disappearance; **espèce en voie de ~** endangered species

disparu, e [dispaʀy] nm/f missing person; **être porté ~** to be reported missing

dispensaire [dispɑ̃sɛʀ] nm community clinic

dispenser [dispɑ̃se] /1/ vt: **~ qn de** to exempt sb from

disperser [dispɛʀse] /1/ vt to scatter; **se disperser** vi to scatter

disponible [dispɔnibl] adj available

disposé, e [dispoze] adj: **bien/mal ~** (humeur) in a good/bad mood; **~ à** (prêt à) willing ou prepared to

disposer [dispoze] /1/ vt to arrange ▷ vi: **vous pouvez ~** you may leave; **~ de** to have (at one's disposal); **se ~ à faire** to prepare to do, be about to do

dispositif [dispozitif] nm device; (fig) system, plan of action

disposition [dispozisjɔ̃] nf (arrangement) arrangement, layout; (humeur) mood; **prendre ses ~s** to make arrangements; **avoir des ~s pour la musique** etc to have a special aptitude for music etc; **à la ~ de qn** at sb's disposal; **je suis à votre ~** I am at your service

disproportionné, e [dispʀɔpɔʀsjɔne] adj disproportionate, out of all proportion

dispute [dispyt] nf quarrel, argument; **disputer** /1/ vt (match) to play; (combat) to fight; **se disputer** vi to quarrel

disqualifier [diskalifje] /7/ vt to disqualify

disque [disk] nm (Mus) record; (forme, pièce) disc; (Sport) discus; **~ compact** compact disc; **~ dur** hard disk; **disquette** nf floppy (disk), diskette

dissertation [disɛʀtasjɔ̃] nf (Scol) essay

dissimuler [disimyle] /1/ vt to conceal

dissipé, e [disipe] adj (indiscipliné) unruly

dissolvant [disɔlvɑ̃] nm nail polish remover

dissuader [disɥade] /1/ vt: **~ qn de faire/de qch** to dissuade sb from doing/from sth

distance [distɑ̃s] nf distance; (fig: écart) gap; **à ~** at ou from a distance; **distancer** /3/ vt to outdistance

distant, e [distɑ̃, -ɑ̃t] adj (réservé) distant; **~ de** (lieu) far away ou a long way from

distillerie [distilʀi] nf distillery

distinct, e [distɛ̃(kt), distɛ̃kt] adj distinct; **distinctement** [distɛ̃ktəmɑ̃] adv distinctly; **distinctif, -ive** adj distinctive

distingué, e [distɛ̃ge] adj distinguished

distinguer [distɛ̃ge] /1/ vt to distinguish; **se distinguer** vi: **se ~ (de)** to distinguish o.s. ou be distinguished (from)

distraction [distraksjɔ̃] nf (*manque d'attention*) absent-mindedness; (*passe-temps*) distraction, entertainment

distraire [distrɛʀ] /50/ vt (*déranger*) to distract; (*divertir*) to entertain, divert; **se distraire** vi to amuse ou enjoy o.s.; **distrait, e** [distrɛ, -ɛt] pp de **distraire** ▷ adj absent-minded

distrayant, e [distrɛjɑ̃, -ɑ̃t] adj entertaining

distribuer [distribɥe] /1/ vt to distribute; to hand out; (*Cartes*) to deal (out); (*courrier*) to deliver; **distributeur** nm (*Auto, Comm*) distributor; (*automatique*) (vending) machine; **distributeur de billets** cash dispenser

dit, e [di, dit] pp de **dire** ▷ adj (*fixé*): **le jour ~** the arranged day; (*surnommé*): **X, ~ Pierrot X**, known as ou called Pierrot

dîtes [dit] vb voir **dire**

divan [divɑ̃] nm divan

divers, e [divɛʀ, -ɛʀs] adj (*varié*) diverse, varied; (*différent*) different, various; **~es personnes** various ou several people

diversité [divɛʀsite] nf diversity, variety

divertir [divɛʀtiʀ] /2/: **se divertir** vi to amuse ou enjoy o.s.; **divertissement** nm entertainment

diviser [divize] /1/ vt to divide; **division** nf division

divorce [divɔʀs] nm divorce; **divorcé, e** nm/f divorcee; **divorcer** /3/ vi to get a divorce, get divorced; **divorcer de** ou **d'avec qn** to divorce sb

divulguer [divylge] /1/ vt to disclose

dix [di, dis, diz] num ten; **dix-huit** num eighteen; **dix-huitième** num eighteenth; **dixième** num tenth; **dix-neuf** num nineteen; **dix-neuvième** num nineteenth; **dix-sept** num seventeen; **dix-septième** num seventeenth

dizaine [dizɛn] nf: **une ~ (de)** about ten, ten or so

do [do] nm (*note*) C; (*en chantant la gamme*) do(h)

docile [dɔsil] adj docile

dock [dɔk] nm dock; **docker** nm docker

docteur, e [dɔktœʀ] nm/f doctor; **doctorat** nm: **doctorat (d'Université)** ≈ doctorate

doctrine [dɔktʀin] nf doctrine

document [dɔkymɑ̃] nm document; **documentaire** adj, nm documentary; **documentation** nf documentation, literature; **documenter** /1/ vt: **se documenter (sur)** to gather information ou material (on ou about)

dodo [dodo] nm: **aller faire ~** to go to beddy-byes

dogue [dɔg] nm mastiff

doigt [dwa] nm finger; **à deux ~s de** within an ace (*BRIT*) ou an inch of; **un ~ de lait/** whisky a drop of milk/whisky; **~ de pied** toe

doit etc [dwa] vb voir **devoir**

dollar [dɔlaʀ] nm dollar

domaine [dɔmɛn] nm estate, property; (*fig*) domain, field

domestique [dɔmɛstik] adj domestic ▷ nm/f servant, domestic

domicile [dɔmisil] nm home, place of residence; **à ~** at home; **livrer à ~** to deliver; **domicilié, e** adj: **être domicilié à** to have one's home in ou at

dominant, e [dɔminɑ̃, -ɑ̃t] adj (*opinion*) predominant

dominer [dɔmine] /1/ vt to dominate; (*sujet*) to master; (*surpasser*) to outclass, surpass; (*surplomber*) to tower above, dominate ▷ vi to be in the dominant position; **se dominer** vi to control o.s.

domino [dɔmino] nm domino; **dominos** nmpl (*jeu*) dominoes sg

dommage [dɔmaʒ] nm: **~s** (*dégâts, pertes*) damage no pl; **c'est ~ de faire/que** it's a shame ou pity to do/that; **quel ~!, c'est ~!** what a pity ou shame!

dompter [dɔ̃(p)te] /1/ vt to tame; **dompteur, -euse** nm/f trainer

DOM-ROM [dɔmʀɔm] sigle m (pl) (= *Département(s) et Régions/Territoire(s) d'outre-mer*) French overseas departments and regions

don [dɔ̃] nm gift; (*charité*) donation; **avoir des ~s pour** to have a gift ou talent for; **elle a le ~ de m'énerver** she's got a knack of getting on my nerves

donc [dɔ̃k] conj therefore, so; (*après une digression*) so, then

dongle [dɔ̃gl] nm dongle

donné, e [dɔne] adj (*convenu: lieu, heure*) given; (*pas cher*) very cheap; **données** nfpl data; **c'est ~** it's a gift; **étant ~ que ...** given that ...

donner [dɔne] /1/ vt to give; (*vieux habits etc*) to give away; (*spectacle*) to put on; **~ qch à qn** to give sb sth, give sth to sb; **~ sur** (*fenêtre, chambre*) to look (out) onto; **ça donne soif/faim** it makes you (feel) thirsty/hungry; **se ~ à fond (à son travail)** to give one's all (to one's work); **se ~ du mal** ou **de la peine (pour faire qch)** to go to a lot of trouble (to do sth); **s'en ~ à cœur joie** (*fam*) to have a great time (of it)

🅞 **MOT-CLÉ**

dont [dɔ̃] pron relatif **1** (*appartenance: objets*) whose, of which; (: *êtres animés*) whose; **la maison dont le toit est rouge** the house the roof of which is red, the house whose roof is red; **l'homme dont je connais la sœur** the man whose sister I know
2 (*parmi lesquel(le)s*): **deux livres, dont l'un**

est ... two books, one of which is ...; **il y avait plusieurs personnes, dont Gabrielle** there were several people, among them Gabrielle; **10 blessés, dont 2 grièvement** 10 injured, 2 of them seriously **3** (*complément d'adjectif, de verbe*): **le fils dont il est si fier** the son he's so proud of; **le pays dont il est originaire** the country he's from; **ce dont je parle** what I'm talking about; **la façon dont il l'a fait** the way (in which) he did it

dopage [dɔpaʒ] *nm* (*Sport*) drug use; (*de cheval*) doping
doré, e [dɔʀe] *adj* golden; (*avec dorure*) gilt, gilded
dorénavant [dɔʀenavã] *adv* henceforth
dorer [dɔʀe] /1/ *vt* to gild; **(faire) ~** (*Culin*) to brown
dorloter [dɔʀlɔte] /1/ *vt* to pamper
dormir [dɔʀmiʀ] *vi* to sleep; (*être endormi*) to be asleep
dortoir [dɔʀtwaʀ] *nm* dormitory
dos [do] *nm* back; (*de livre*) spine; **"voir au ~"** "see over"; **de ~** from the back
dosage [dozaʒ] *nm* mixture
dose [doz] *nf* dose; **doser** /1/ *vt* to measure out; **il faut savoir doser ses efforts** you have to be able to pace yourself
dossier [dosje] *nm* (*renseignements, fichier*) file; (*de chaise*) back; (*Presse*) feature; (*Inform*) folder; **un ~ scolaire** a school report
douane [dwan] *nf* customs *pl*; **douanier, -ière** *adj* customs *cpd* ▷ *nm* customs officer
double [dubl] *adj, adv* double ▷ *nm* (*autre exemplaire*) duplicate, copy; (*sosie*) double; (*Tennis*) doubles *sg*; (*2 fois plus*): **le ~ (de)** twice as much (*ou* many) (as); **en ~ (exemplaire)** in duplicate; **faire ~ emploi** to be redundant; **double-cliquer** /1/ *vi* (*Inform*) to double-click
doubler [duble] /1/ *vt* (*multiplier par 2*) to double; (*vêtement*) to line; (*dépasser*) to overtake, pass; (*film*) to dub; (*acteur*) to stand in for ▷ *vi* to double
doublure [dublyʀ] *nf* lining; (*Ciné*) stand-in
douce [dus] *adj f voir* **doux; douceâtre** *adj* sickly sweet; **doucement** *adv* gently; (*lentement*) slowly; **douceur** *nf* softness; (*de climat*) mildness; (*de quelqu'un*) gentleness
douche [duʃ] *nf* shower; **prendre une ~** to have *ou* take a shower; **doucher** /1/: **se doucher** *vi* to have *ou* take a shower
doué, e [dwe] *adj* gifted, talented; **être ~ pour** to have a gift for
douille [duj] *nf* (*Élec*) socket
douillet, te [dujɛ, -ɛt] *adj* cosy; (*péj: à la douleur*) soft
douleur [dulœʀ] *nf* pain; (*chagrin*) grief, distress; **douloureux, -euse** *adj* painful
doute [dut] *nm* doubt; **sans ~** no doubt; (*probablement*) probably; **sans nul** *ou*

aucun ~ without (a) doubt; **douter** /1/ *vt* to doubt; **douter de** (*allié, sincérité de qn*) to have (one's) doubts about, doubt; (*résultat, réussite*) to be doubtful of; **douter que** to doubt whether *ou* if; **se douter de qch/que** to suspect sth/that; **je m'en doutais** I suspected as much; **douteux, -euse** *adj* (*incertain*) doubtful; (*péj*) dubious-looking
Douvres [duvʀ] *n* Dover
doux, douce [du, dus] *adj* soft; (*sucré, agréable*) sweet; (*peu fort: moutarde etc, clément: climat*) mild; (*pas brusque*) gentle
douzaine [duzɛn] *nf* (*12*) dozen; (*environ 12*): **une ~ (de)** a dozen *or* so
douze [duz] *num* twelve; **douzième** *num* twelfth
dragée [dʀaʒe] *nf* sugared almond
draguer [dʀage] /1/ *vt* (*rivière*) to dredge; (*fam*) to try and pick up
dramatique [dʀamatik] *adj* dramatic; (*tragique*) tragic ▷ *nf* (*TV*) (television) drama
drame [dʀam] *nm* drama
drap [dʀa] *nm* (*de lit*) sheet; (*tissu*) woollen fabric
drapeau, x [dʀapo] *nm* flag
drap-housse [dʀaus] *nm* fitted sheet
dresser [dʀese] /1/ *vt* (*mettre vertical, monter*) to put up, erect; (*liste, bilan, contrat*) to draw up; (*animal*) to train; **se dresser** *vi* (*falaise, obstacle*) to stand; (*personne*) to draw o.s. up; **~ l'oreille** to prick up one's ears; **~ qn contre qn d'autre** to set sb against sb else
drogue [dʀɔg] *nf* drug; **la ~** drugs *pl*; **drogué, e** *nm/f* drug addict; **droguer** /1/ *vt* (*victime*) to drug; **se droguer** *vi* (*aux stupéfiants*) to take drugs; (*péj: de médicaments*) to dose o.s. up; **droguerie** *nf* ≈ hardware shop (*BRIT*) *ou* store (*US*); **droguiste** *nm* ≈ keeper (*ou* owner) of a hardware shop *ou* store
droit, e [dʀwa, dʀwat] *adj* (*non courbe*) straight; (*vertical*) upright, straight; (*fig: loyal, franc*) upright, straight(forward); (*opposé à gauche*) right, right-hand ▷ *adv* straight ▷ *nm* (*prérogative*) right; (*taxe*) duty, tax; (: *d'inscription*) fee; (*lois, branche*): **le ~** law ▷ *nf* (*Pol*) right (wing); **avoir le ~ de** to be allowed to; **avoir ~ à** to be entitled to; **être dans son ~** to be within one's rights; **à ~e** on the right; (*direction*) (to the) right; **~s d'auteur** royalties; **~s d'inscription** enrolment *ou* registration fees; **droitier, -ière** *adj* right-handed
drôle [dʀol] *adj* (*amusant*) funny, amusing; (*bizarre*) funny, peculiar; **un ~ de ...** (*bizarre*) a strange *ou* funny ...; (*intensif*) an incredible ..., a terrific ...
dromadaire [dʀɔmadɛʀ] *nm* dromedary
du [dy] *art voir* **de**
dû, due [dy] *pp de* **devoir** ▷ *adj* (*somme*) owing, owed; (*causé par*): **dû à** due to ▷ *nm* due

dune [dyn] *nf* dune

duplex [dyplɛks] *nm* (*appartement*) split-level apartment, duplex

duquel [dykɛl] *voir* **lequel**

dur, e [dyʀ] *adj* (*pierre, siège, travail, problème*) hard; (*lumière, voix, climat*) harsh; (*sévère*) hard, harsh; (*cruel*) hard(-hearted); (*porte, col*) stiff; (*viande*) tough ▷ *adv* hard ▷ *nm* (*fam: meneur*) tough nut; **~ d'oreille** hard of hearing

durant [dyʀɑ̃] *prép* (*au cours de*) during; (*pendant*) for; **des mois ~** for months

durcir [dyʀsiʀ] /2/ *vt, vi* to harden; **se durcir** *vi* to harden

durée [dyʀe] *nf* length; (*d'une pile etc*) life; **de courte ~** (*séjour, répit*) brief

durement [dyʀmɑ̃] *adv* harshly

durer [dyʀe] /1/ *vi* to last

dureté [dyʀte] *nf* hardness; harshness; stiffness; toughness

durit® [dyʀit] *nf* (*car radiator*) hose

duvet [dyvɛ] *nm* down

DVD *sigle m* (= *digital versatile disc*) DVD

dynamique [dinamik] *adj* dynamic; **dynamisme** *nm* dynamism

dynamo [dinamo] *nf* dynamo

dyslexie [dislɛksi] *nf* dyslexia, word blindness

eau, x [o] *nf* water ▷ *nfpl* (*Méd*) waters; **prendre l'~** to leak, let in water; **tomber à l'~** (*fig*) to fall through; **~ de Cologne** eau de Cologne; **~ courante** running water; **~ douce** fresh water; **~ gazeuse** sparkling (mineral) water; **~ de Javel** bleach; **~ minérale** mineral water; **~ plate** still water; **~ salée** salt water; **~ de toilette** toilet water; **eau-de-vie** *nf* brandy

ébène [eben] *nf* ebony; **ébéniste** *nm* cabinetmaker

éblouir [ebluiʀ] /2/ *vt* to dazzle

éboueur [ebwœʀ] *nm* dustman (*BRIT*), garbage man (*US*)

ébouillanter [ebujɑ̃te] /1/ *vt* to scald; (*Culin*) to blanch

éboulement [ebulmɑ̃] *nm* rock fall

ébranler [ebʀɑ̃le] /1/ *vt* to shake; (*rendre instable*) to weaken; **s'ébranler** *vi* (*partir*) to move off

ébullition [ebylisjɔ̃] *nf* boiling point; **en ~** boiling

écaille [ekaj] *nf* (*de poisson*) scale; (*matière*) tortoiseshell; **écailler** /1/ *vt* (*poisson*) to scale; **s'écailler** *vi* to flake *ou* peel (off)

écart [ekaʀ] *nm* gap; **à l'~** out of the way; **à l'~ de** away from; **faire un ~** (*voiture*) to swerve

écarté, e [ekaʀte] *adj* (*lieu*) out-of-the-way, remote; (*ouvert*): **les jambes ~es** legs apart; **les bras ~s** arms outstretched

écarter [ekaʀte] /1/ *vt* (*séparer*) to move apart, separate; (*éloigner*) to push back, move away; (*ouvrir: bras, jambes*) to spread, open; (: *rideau*) to draw (back); (*éliminer: candidat, possibilité*) to dismiss; **s'écarter** *vi* to part; (*personne*) to move away; **s'~ de** to wander from

échafaudage [eʃafodaʒ] *nm* scaffolding

échalote [eʃalɔt] *nf* shallot

échange [eʃɑ̃ʒ] *nm* exchange; **en ~ de** in exchange *ou* return for; **échanger** /3/ *vt*:

échanger qch (contre) to exchange sth (for)

échantillon [eʃɑ̃tijɔ̃] *nm* sample

échapper [eʃape] /1/: ~ **à** *vt* (*gardien*) to escape (from); (*punition, péril*) to escape; ~ **à qn** (*détail, sens*) to escape sb; (*objet qu'on tient*) to slip out of sb's hands; **laisser ~** (*cri etc*) to let out; **l'~ belle** to have a narrow escape

écharde [eʃaʀd] *nf* splinter (of wood)

écharpe [eʃaʀp] *nf* scarf; **avoir le bras en ~** to have one's arm in a sling

échauffer [eʃofe] /1/ *vt* (*métal, moteur*) to overheat; **s'échauffer** *vi* (*Sport*) to warm up; (*discussion*) to become heated

échéance [eʃeɑ̃s] *nf* (*d'un paiement: date*) settlement date; (*fig*) deadline; **à brève/longue ~** in the short/long term

échéant [eʃeɑ̃]: **le cas ~** *adv* if the case arises

échec [eʃɛk] *nm* failure; (*Échecs*): ~ **et mat/au roi** checkmate/check; **échecs** *nmpl* (*jeu*) chess *sg*; **tenir en ~** to hold in check

échelle [eʃɛl] *nf* ladder; (*fig, d'une carte*) scale

échelon [eʃ(ə)lɔ̃] *nm* (*d'échelle*) rung; (*Admin*) grade; **échelonner** /1/ *vt* to space out, spread out

échiquier [eʃikje] *nm* chessboard

écho [eko] *nm* echo; **échographie** *nf*: **passer une échographie** to have a scan

échouer [eʃwe] /1/ *vi* to fail; **s'échouer** *vi* to run aground

éclabousser [eklabuse] /1/ *vt* to splash

éclair [eklɛʀ] *nm* (*d'orage*) flash of lightning, lightning *no pl*; (*gâteau*) éclair

éclairage [eklɛʀaʒ] *nm* lighting

éclaircie [eklɛʀsi] *nf* bright *ou* sunny interval

éclaircir [eklɛʀsiʀ] /2/ *vt* to lighten; (*fig: mystère*) to clear up; (*point*) to clarify; **s'éclaircir** *vi* (*ciel*) to brighten up; **s'~ la voix** to clear one's throat; **éclaircissement** *nm* clarification

éclairer [eklɛʀe] /1/ *vt* (*lieu*) to light (up); (*personne: avec une lampe de poche etc*) to light the way for; (*fig: rendre compréhensible*) to shed light on ▷ *vi*: ~ **mal/bien** to give a poor/good light; **s'~ à la bougie/l'électricité** to use candlelight/have electric lighting

éclat [ekla] *nm* (*de bombe, de verre*) fragment; (*du soleil, d'une couleur etc*) brightness, brilliance; (*d'une cérémonie*) splendour; (*scandale*): **faire un ~** to cause a commotion; ~ **de rire** burst *ou* roar of laughter; ~ **de voix** shout

éclatant, e [eklatɑ̃, -ɑ̃t] *adj* brilliant

éclater [eklate] /1/ *vi* (*pneu*) to burst; (*bombe*) to explode; (*guerre, épidémie*) to break out; (*groupe, parti*) to break up; ~ **de rire/en sanglots** to burst out laughing/sobbing

écluse [eklyz] *nf* lock

écœurant, e [ekœʀɑ̃, -ɑ̃t] *adj* sickening; (*gâteau etc*) sickly

écœurer [ekœʀe] *vt*: ~ **qn** (*nourriture*) to make sb feel sick; (*fig: conduite, personne*) to disgust sb

école [ekɔl] *nf* school; **aller à l'~** to go to school; ~ **maternelle** nursery school; ~ **primaire** primary (*BRIT*) *ou* grade (*US*) school; ~ **secondaire** secondary (*BRIT*) *ou* high (*US*) school; **écolier, -ière** *nm/f* schoolboy/girl

écologie [ekɔlɔʒi] *nf* ecology; **écologique** *adj* environment-friendly; **écologiste** *nm/f* ecologist

économe [ekɔnɔm] *adj* thrifty ▷ *nm/f* (*de lycée etc*) bursar (*BRIT*), treasurer (*US*)

économie [ekɔnɔmi] *nf* economy; (*gain: d'argent, de temps etc*) saving; (*science*) economics *sg*; **économies** *nfpl* (*pécule*) savings; **économique** *adj* (*avantageux*) economical; (*Écon*) economic; **économiser** /1/ *vt, vi* to save

écorce [ekɔʀs] *nf* bark; (*de fruit*) peel

écorcher [ekɔʀʃe] /1/ *vt*: **s'~ le genou** *etc* to scrape *ou* graze one's knee *etc*; **écorchure** *nf* graze

écossais, e [ekɔsɛ, -ɛz] *adj* Scottish ▷ *nm/f*: **É~, e** Scot

Écosse [ekɔs] *nf*: **l'~** Scotland

écotaxe [ekotaks] *nf* green tax

écouter [ekute] /1/ *vt* to listen to; **s'écouter** *vi* (*malade*) to be a bit of a hypochondriac; **si je m'écoutais** if I followed my instincts; **écouteur** *nm* (*Tél*) receiver; **écouteurs** *nmpl* (*casque*) headphones, headset *sg*

écran [ekʀɑ̃] *nm* screen; **le petit ~** television; ~ **tactile** touchscreen; ~ **total** sunblock

écrasant, e [ekʀazɑ̃, -ɑ̃t] *adj* overwhelming

écraser [ekʀaze] /1/ *vt* to crush; (*piéton*) to run over; **s'~ (au sol)** *vi* to crash; **s'~ contre** to crash into

écrémé, e [ekʀeme] *adj* (*lait*) skimmed

écrevisse [ekʀəvis] *nf* crayfish *inv*

écrire [ekʀiʀ] /39/ *vt, vi* to write; **s'écrire** *vi* to write to one another; **ça s'écrit comment?** how is it spelt?; **écrit** *nm* (*examen*) written paper; **par écrit** in writing

écriteau, x [ekʀito] *nm* notice, sign

écriture [ekʀityʀ] *nf* writing; **écritures** *nfpl* (*Comm*) accounts, books; **l'É~ (sainte), les É~s** the Scriptures

écrivain [ekʀivɛ̃] *nm* writer

écrou [ekʀu] *nm* nut

écrouler [ekʀule] /1/: **s'écrouler** *vi* to collapse

écru, e [ekʀy] *adj* off-white, écru

écume [ekym] *nf* foam

écureuil [ekyʀœj] *nm* squirrel

écurie [ekyʀi] *nf* stable

eczéma [ɛgzema] nm eczema

EDF sigle f (= Électricité de France) national electricity company

Édimbourg [edɛ̃buʀ] n Edinburgh

éditer [edite] /1/ vt (publier) to publish; (annoter) to edit; **éditeur, -trice** nm/f publisher; **édition** nf edition; **l'édition** publishing

édredon [edʀədɔ̃] nm eiderdown

éducateur, -trice [edykatœʀ, -tʀis] nm/f teacher; (en école spécialisée) instructor

éducatif, -ive [edykatif, -iv] adj educational

éducation [edykasjɔ̃] nf education; (familiale) upbringing; (manières) (good) manners pl

édulcorant [edylkɔʀɑ̃] nm sweetener

éduquer [edyke] /1/ vt to educate; (élever) to bring up

effacer [efase] /3/ vt to erase, rub out; **s'effacer** vi (inscription etc) to wear off; (pour laisser passer) to step aside

effarant, e [efaʀɑ̃, -ɑ̃t] adj alarming

effectif, -ive [efɛktif, -iv] adj real ⊳ nm (Scol) total number of pupils; (Comm) manpower sg; **effectivement** adv (réellement) actually, really; (en effet) indeed

effectuer [efɛktɥe] /1/ vt (opération, mission) to carry out; (déplacement, trajet) to make

effervescent, e [efɛʀvesɑ̃, ɑ̃t] adj effervescent

effet [efɛ] nm effect; (impression) impression; **effets** nmpl (vêtements etc) things; **faire ~** (médicament) to take effect; **faire de l'~** (impressionner) to make an impression; **faire bon/mauvais ~ sur qn** to make a good/bad impression on sb; **en ~** indeed; **~ de serre** greenhouse effect

efficace [efikas] adj (personne) efficient; (action, médicament) effective; **efficacité** nf efficiency; effectiveness

effondrer [efɔ̃dʀe] /1/: **s'effondrer** vi to collapse

efforcer [efɔʀse] /3/: **s'efforcer de** vt: **s'~ de faire** to try hard to do

effort [efɔʀ] nm effort

effrayant, e [efʀɛjɑ̃, -ɑ̃t] adj frightening

effrayer [efʀeje] /8/ vt to frighten, scare; **s'effrayer (de)** to be frightened ou scared (by)

effréné, e [efʀene] adj wild

effronté, e [efʀɔ̃te] adj insolent

effroyable [efʀwajabl] adj horrifying, appalling

égal, e, -aux [egal, -o] adj equal; (constant: vitesse) steady ⊳ nm/f equal; **être ~ à** (prix, nombre) to be equal to; **ça m'est ~** it's all the same to me, I don't mind; **sans ~** matchless, unequalled; **d'~ à ~** as equals; **également** adv equally; (aussi) too, as well; **égaler** /1/ vt to equal; **égaliser** /1/ vt (sol, salaires) to level

(out); (chances) to equalize ⊳ vi (Sport) to equalize; **égalité** nf equality; **être à égalité (de points)** to be level

égard [egaʀ] nm: **égards** nmpl consideration sg; **à cet ~** in this respect; **par ~ pour** out of consideration for; **à l'~ de** towards

égarer [egaʀe] /1/ vt to mislay; **s'égarer** vi to get lost, lose one's way; (objet) to go astray

églefin [egləfɛ̃] nm haddock

église [egliz] nf church; **aller à l'~** to go to church

égoïsme [egɔism] nm selfishness; **égoïste** adj selfish

égout [egu] nm sewer

égoutter [egute] /1/ vi to drip; **s'égoutter** vi to drip; **égouttoir** nm draining board; (mobile) draining rack

égratignure [egʀatiɲyʀ] nf scratch

Égypte [eʒipt] nf: **l'~** Egypt; **égyptien, ne** adj Egyptian ⊳ nm/f: **Égyptien, ne** Egyptian

eh [e] excl hey!; **eh bien** well

élaborer [elabɔʀe] /1/ vt to elaborate; (projet, stratégie) to work out; (rapport) to draft

élan [elɑ̃] nm (Zool) elk, moose; (Sport) run up; (fig: de tendresse etc) surge; **prendre son ~/de l'~** to take a run up/gather speed

élancer [elɑ̃se] /3/: **s'élancer** vi to dash, hurl o.s.

élargir [elaʀʒiʀ] /2/ vt to widen; **s'élargir** vi to widen; (vêtement) to stretch

élastique [elastik] adj elastic ⊳ nm (de bureau) rubber band; (pour la couture) elastic no pl

élection [elɛksjɔ̃] nf election

électricien, ne [elɛktʀisjɛ̃, -ɛn] nm/f electrician

électricité [elɛktʀisite] nf electricity; **allumer/éteindre l'~** to put on/off the light

électrique [elɛktʀik] adj electric(al)

électrocuter [elɛktʀɔkyte] /1/ vt to electrocute

électroménager [elɛktʀɔmenaʒe] adj: **appareils ~s** domestic (electrical) appliances ⊳ nm: **l'~** household appliances

électronique [elɛktʀɔnik] adj electronic ⊳ nf electronics sg

élégance [elegɑ̃s] nf elegance

élégant, e [elegɑ̃, -ɑ̃t] adj elegant

élément [elemɑ̃] nm element; (pièce) component, part; **élémentaire** adj elementary

éléphant [elefɑ̃] nm elephant

élevage [el(ə)vaʒ] nm breeding; (de bovins) cattle breeding ou rearing; **truite d'~** farmed trout

élevé, e [el(ə)ve] adj high; **bien/mal ~** well-/ill-mannered

élève [elɛv] nm/f pupil

élever [el(ə)ve] /5/ vt (enfant) to bring up, raise; (bétail, volaille) to breed; (hausser: taux, niveau) to raise; (édifier: monument) to put up, erect; **s'élever** vi (avion, alpiniste) to go up; (niveau, température, aussi) to rise; **s'~ à** (frais, dégâts) to amount to, add up to; **s'~ contre** to rise up against; **~ la voix** to raise one's voice; **éleveur, -euse** nm/f stock breeder

éliminatoire [eliminatwaʀ] nf (Sport) heat

éliminer [elimine] /1/ vt to eliminate

élire [eliʀ] /43/ vt to elect

elle [ɛl] pron (sujet) she; (: chose) it; (complément) her; it; **~s** (sujet) they; (complément) them; **~-même** herself; itself; **~s-mêmes** themselves; voir **il**

éloigné, e [elwaɲe] adj distant, far-off; (parent) distant

éloigner [elwaɲe] /1/ vt (échéance) to put off, postpone; (soupçons, danger) to ward off; **~ qch (de)** to move ou take sth away (from); **s'éloigner (de)** (personne) to go away (from); (véhicule) to move away (from); (affectivement) to become estranged (from); **~ qn (de)** to take sb away ou remove sb (from)

élu, e [ely] pp de **élire** ▷ nm/f (Pol) elected representative

Élysée [elize] nm: **(le palais de) l'~** the Élysée palace

émail, -aux [emaj, -o] nm enamel

e-mail [imɛl] nm email; **envoyer qch par ~** to email sth

émanciper [emãsipe] /1/: **s'émanciper** vi (fig) to become emancipated ou liberated

emballage [ãbalaʒ] nm (papier) wrapping; (carton) packaging

emballer [ãbale] /1/ vt to wrap (up); (dans un carton) to pack (up); (fig: fam) to thrill (to bits); **s'emballer** vi (moteur) to race; (cheval) to bolt; (fig: personne) to get carried away

embarcadère [ãbaʀkadɛʀ] nm landing stage (BRIT), pier

embarquement [ãbaʀkəmã] nm embarkation; (de marchandises) loading; (de passagers) boarding

embarquer [ãbaʀke] /1/ vt (personne) to embark; (marchandise) to load; (fam) to cart off ▷ vi (passager) to board; **s'embarquer** vi to board; **s'~ dans** (affaire, aventure) to embark upon

embarras [ãbaʀa] nm (confusion) embarrassment; **être dans l'~** to be in a predicament ou an awkward position; **vous n'avez que l'~ du choix** the only problem is choosing

embarrassant, e [ãbaʀasã, -ãt] adj embarrassing

embarrasser [ãbaʀase] /1/ vt (encombrer) to clutter (up); (gêner) to hinder, hamper; to put in an awkward position;

s'embarrasser de to burden o.s. with

embaucher [ãboʃe] /1/ vt to take on, hire

embêtant, e [ãbetã, -ãt] adj annoying

embêter [ãbete] /1/ vt to bother; **s'embêter** vi (s'ennuyer) to be bored

emblée [ãble]: **d'~** adv straightaway

embouchure [ãbuʃyʀ] nf (Géo) mouth

embourber [ãbuʀbe] /1/: **s'embourber** vi to get stuck in the mud

embouteillage [ãbutɛjaʒ] nm traffic jam, (traffic) holdup (BRIT)

embranchement [ãbʀãʃmã] nm (routier) junction

embrasser [ãbʀase] /1/ vt to kiss; (sujet, période) to embrace, encompass

embrayage [ãbʀɛjaʒ] nm clutch

embrouiller [ãbʀuje] /1/ vt (fils) to tangle (up); (fiches, idées, personne) to muddle up; **s'embrouiller** vi to get in a muddle

embruns [ãbʀœ̃] nmpl sea spray sg

embué, e [ãbɥe] adj misted up

émeraude [em(ə)ʀod] nf emerald

émerger [emɛʀʒe] /3/ vi to emerge; (faire saillie, aussi fig) to stand out

émeri [em(ə)ʀi] nm: **toile** ou **papier ~** emery paper

émerveiller [emɛʀveje] /1/ vt to fill with wonder; **s'émerveiller de** to marvel at

émettre [emɛtʀ] /56/ vt (son, lumière) to give out, emit; (message etc: Radio) to transmit; (billet, timbre, emprunt, chèque) to issue; (hypothèse, avis) to voice, put forward ▷ vi to broadcast

émeus etc [emø] vb voir **émouvoir**

émeute [emøt] nf riot

émigrer [emigʀe] /1/ vi to emigrate

émincer [emɛ̃se] /3/ vt to slice thinly

émission [emisjɔ̃] nf (voir émettre) emission; (d'un message) transmission; (de billet, timbre, emprunt, chèque) issue; (Radio, TV) programme, broadcast

emmêler [ãmele] /1/ vt to tangle (up); (fig) to muddle up; **s'emmêler** vi to get into a tangle

emménager [ãmenaʒe] /3/ vi to move in; **~ dans** to move into

emmener [ãm(ə)ne] /5/ vt to take (with one); (comme otage, capture) to take away; **~ qn au cinéma** to take sb to the cinema

emmerder [ãmɛʀde] /1/ (!) vt to bug, bother; **s'emmerder** vi to be bored stiff

émoticone [emɔtikɔn] nm smiley

émotif, -ive [emɔtif, -iv] adj emotional

émotion [emosjɔ̃] nf emotion

émouvoir [emuvwaʀ] /27/ vt to move; **s'émouvoir** vi to be moved; to be roused

empaqueter [ãpakte] /4/ vt to pack up

emparer [ãpaʀe] /1/: **s'emparer de** vt (objet) to seize, grab; (comme otage, Mil) to seize; (peur etc) to take hold of

empêchement [ãpɛʃmã] nm (unexpected) obstacle, hitch

empêcher [ɑ̃peʃe] /1/ *vt* to prevent; ~ **qn de
faire** to prevent *ou* stop sb (from) doing; **il
n'empêche que** nevertheless; **il n'a pas pu
s'~ de rire** he couldn't help laughing
empereur [ɑ̃pʀœʀ] *nm* emperor
empiffrer [ɑ̃pifʀe] /1/: **s'empiffrer** *vi* (*péj*)
to stuff o.s.
empiler [ɑ̃pile] /1/ *vt* to pile (up)
empire [ɑ̃piʀ] *nm* empire; (*fig*) influence
empirer [ɑ̃piʀe] /1/ *vi* to worsen,
deteriorate
emplacement [ɑ̃plasmɑ̃] *nm* site
emploi [ɑ̃plwa] *nm* use; (*poste*) job,
situation; (*Comm, Écon*) employment;
mode d'~ directions for use; ~ **du temps**
timetable, schedule
employé, e [ɑ̃plwaje] *nm/f* employee;
~ **de bureau/banque** office/bank
employee *ou* clerk
employer [ɑ̃plwaje] /8/ *vt* to use; (*ouvrier,
main-d'œuvre*) to employ; **s'~ à qch/à faire**
to apply *ou* devote o.s. to sth/to doing;
employeur, -euse *nm/f* employer
empoigner [ɑ̃pwaɲe] /1/ *vt* to grab
empoisonner [ɑ̃pwazɔne] /1/ *vt* to poison;
(*empester: air, pièce*) to stink out; (*fam*): ~ **qn**
to drive sb mad
emporter [ɑ̃pɔʀte] /1/ *vt* to take (with
one); (*en dérobant ou enlevant, emmener:
blessés, voyageurs*) to take away; (*entraîner*)
to carry away *ou* along; (*rivière, vent*) to carry
away; **s'emporter** *vi* (*de colère*) to fly into a
rage; **l'~ (sur)** to get the upper hand (of);
plats à ~ take-away meals
empreint, e [ɑ̃pʀɛ̃, -ɛ̃t] *adj*: ~ **de** marked
with ▷ *nf* (*de pied, main*) print; ~**e (digitale)**
fingerprint; ~**e écologique** carbon
footprint
empressé, e [ɑ̃pʀese] *adj* attentive
empresser [ɑ̃pʀese] /1/: **s'empresser**
vi: **s'~ auprès de qn** to surround sb with
attentions; **s'~ de faire** to hasten to do
emprisonner [ɑ̃pʀizɔne] /1/ *vt* to imprison
emprunt [ɑ̃pʀœ̃] *nm* loan (*from debtor's
point of view*)
emprunter [ɑ̃pʀœ̃te] /1/ *vt* to borrow;
(*itinéraire*) to take, follow
ému, e [emy] *pp de* **émouvoir** ▷ *adj*
(*gratitude*) touched; (*compassion*) moved

 MOT-CLÉ

en [ɑ̃] *prép* **1** (*endroit, pays*) in; (: *direction*) to;
habiter en France/ville to live in France/
town; **aller en France/ville** to go to
France/town
2 (*moment, temps*) in; **en été/juin** in
summer/June; **en 3 jours/20 ans** in 3 days/
20 years
3 (*moyen*) by; **en avion/taxi** by plane/taxi
4 (*composition*) made of; **c'est en verre/
coton/laine** it's (made of) glass/cotton/

wool; **un collier en argent** a silver necklace
5 (*description, état*): **une femme (habillée)
en rouge** a woman (dressed) in red;
peindre qch en rouge to paint sth red; **en
T/étoile** T-/star-shaped; **en chemise/
chaussettes** in one's shirt sleeves/socks;
en soldat as a soldier; **cassé en plusieurs
morceaux** broken into several pieces; **en
réparation** being repaired, under repair; **en
vacances** on holiday; **en deuil** in mourning;
le même en plus grand the same but *ou*
only bigger
6 (*avec gérondif*) while; on; **en dormant**
while sleeping, as one sleeps; **en sortant**
on going out, as he *etc* went out; **sortir en
courant** to run out
7: **en tant que** as; **je te parle en ami** I'm
talking to you as a friend
▶ *pron* **1** (*indéfini*): **j'en ai/veux** I have/want
some; **en as-tu?** have you got any?; **je n'en
veux pas** I don't want any; **j'en ai deux** I've
got two; **combien y en a-t-il?** how many
(of them) are there?; **j'en ai assez** I've got
enough (of it *ou* them); (*j'en ai marre*) I've had
enough
2 (*provenance*) from there; **j'en viens** I've
come from there
3 (*cause*): **il en est malade/perd le sommeil**
he is ill/can't sleep because of it
4 (*complément de nom, d'adjectif, de verbe*):
j'en connais les dangers I know its *ou* the
dangers; **j'en suis fier/ai besoin** I am proud
of it/need it

encadrer [ɑ̃kadʀe] /1/ *vt* (*tableau, image*) to
frame; (*fig: entourer*) to surround; (*personnel,
soldats etc*) to train
encaisser [ɑ̃kese] /1/ *vt* (*chèque*) to cash;
(*argent*) to collect; (*fig: coup, défaite*) to take
en-cas [ɑ̃kɑ] *nm inv* snack
enceinte [ɑ̃sɛ̃t] *adj f*: ~ **(de six mois)** (six
months) pregnant ▷ *nf* (*mur*) wall; (*espace*)
enclosure; ~ **(acoustique)** speaker
encens [ɑ̃sɑ̃] *nm* incense
encercler [ɑ̃seʀkle] /1/ *vt* to surround
enchaîner [ɑ̃ʃene] /1/ *vt* to chain up;
(*mouvements, séquences*) to link (together)
▷ *vi* to carry on
enchanté, e [ɑ̃ʃɑ̃te] *adj* (*ravi*) delighted;
(*ensorcelé*) enchanted; ~ **(de faire votre
connaissance)** pleased to meet you
enchère [ɑ̃ʃeʀ] *nf* bid; **mettre/vendre aux
~s** to put up for (sale by)/sell by auction
enclencher [ɑ̃klɑ̃ʃe] /1/ *vt* (*mécanisme*) to
engage; **s'enclencher** *vi* to engage
encombrant, e [ɑ̃kɔ̃bʀɑ̃, -ɑ̃t] *adj*
cumbersome, bulky
encombrement [ɑ̃kɔ̃bʀəmɑ̃] *nm*: **être
pris dans un ~** to be stuck in a traffic jam
encombrer [ɑ̃kɔ̃bʀe] /1/ *vt* to clutter
(up); (*gêner*) to hamper; **s'encombrer de**
(*bagages etc*) to load *ou* burden o.s. with

MOT-CLÉ

encore [ākɔʀ] adv 1 (continuation) still; **il y travaille encore** he's still working on it; **pas encore** not yet
2 (de nouveau) again; **j'irai encore demain** I'll go again tomorrow; **encore une fois** (once) again
3 (en plus) more; **encore un peu de viande?** a little more meat?; **encore deux jours** two more days
4 (intensif) even, still; **encore plus fort/ mieux** even louder/better, louder/better still; **quoi encore?** what now?
5 (restriction) even so ou then, only; **encore pourrais-je le faire si …** even so, I might be able to do it if …; **si encore** if only

encourager [ākuʀaʒe] /3/ vt to encourage; **~ qn à faire qch** to encourage sb to do sth
encourir [ākuʀiʀ] /11/ vt to incur
encre [ākʀ] nf ink; **~ de Chine** Indian ink
encyclopédie [āsiklɔpedi] nf encyclopaedia
endetter [ādete] /1/: **s'endetter** vi to get into debt
endive [ādiv] nf chicory no pl
endormi, e [ādɔʀmi] adj asleep
endormir [ādɔʀmiʀ] /16/ vt to put to sleep; (chaleur etc) to send to sleep; (Méd: dent, nerf) to anaesthetize; (fig: soupçons) to allay; **s'endormir** vi to fall asleep, go to sleep
endroit [ādʀwa] nm place; (opposé à l'envers) right side; **à l'~** (vêtement) the right way out; (objet posé) the right way round
endurance [ādyʀās] nf endurance
endurant, e [ādyʀā, -āt] adj tough, hardy
endurcir [ādyʀsiʀ] /2/: **s'endurcir** vi (physiquement) to become tougher; (moralement) to become hardened
endurer [ādyʀe] /1/ vt to endure, bear
énergétique [enɛʀʒetik] adj (aliment) energizing
énergie [enɛʀʒi] nf (Physique) energy; (Tech) power; (morale) vigour, spirit; **énergique** adj energetic; vigorous; (mesures) drastic, stringent
énervant, e [enɛʀvā, -āt] adj irritating, annoying
énerver [enɛʀve] /1/ vt to irritate, annoy; **s'énerver** vi to get excited, get worked up
enfance [āfās] nf childhood
enfant [āfā] nm/f child; **enfantin, e** adj childlike; (langage) children's cpd
enfer [āfɛʀ] nm hell
enfermer [āfɛʀme] /1/ vt to shut up; (à clef, interner) to lock up; **s'enfermer** to shut o.s. away
enfiler [āfile] /1/ vt (vêtement) to slip on; (perles) to string; (aiguille) to thread; **~ un tee-shirt** to slip into a T-shirt

enfin [āfɛ̃] adv at last; (en énumérant) lastly; (de restriction, résignation) still; (pour conclure) in a word; (somme toute) after all
enflammer [āflame] /1/: **s'enflammer** vi to catch fire; (Méd) to become inflamed
enflé, e [āfle] adj swollen
enfler [āfle] /1/ vi to swell (up)
enfoncer [āfɔ̃se] /3/ vt (clou) to drive in; (faire pénétrer): **~ qch dans** to push (ou drive) sth into; (forcer: porte) to break open; **s'enfoncer** vi to sink; **s'~ dans** to sink into; (forêt, ville) to disappear into
enfouir [āfwiʀ] /2/ vt (dans le sol) to bury; (dans un tiroir etc) to tuck away
enfuir [āfɥiʀ] /17/: **s'enfuir** vi to run away ou off
engagement [āɡaʒmā] nm commitment; **sans ~** without obligation
engager [āɡaʒe] /3/ vt (embaucher) to take on; (: artiste) to engage; (commencer) to start; (lier) to bind, commit; (impliquer, entraîner) to involve; (investir) to invest, lay out; (introduire, clé) to insert; (inciter): **~ qn à faire** to urge sb to do; **s'engager** vi (Mil) to enlist; (promettre) to commit o.s.; (débuter: conversation etc) to start (up); **s'~ à faire** to undertake to do; **s'~ dans** (rue, passage) to turn into; (fig: affaire, discussion) to enter into, embark on
engelures [āʒlyʀ] nfpl chilblains
engin [āʒɛ̃] nm machine; (outil) instrument; (Auto) vehicle; (Aviat) aircraft inv
▌ Attention à ne pas traduire engin par le mot anglais engine.
engloutir [āɡlutiʀ] /2/ vt to swallow up
engouement [āɡumā] nm (sudden) passion
engouffrer [āɡufʀe] /1/ vt to swallow up, devour; **s'engouffrer dans** to rush into
engourdir [āɡuʀdiʀ] /2/ vt to numb; (fig) to dull, blunt; **s'engourdir** vi to go numb
engrais [āɡʀɛ] nm manure; **~ (chimique)** (chemical) fertilizer
engraisser [āɡʀese] /1/ vt to fatten (up)
engrenage [āɡʀənaʒ] nm gears pl, gearing; (fig) chain
engueuler [āɡœle] /1/ vt (fam) to bawl at ou out
enhardir [āaʀdiʀ] /2/: **s'enhardir** vi to grow bolder
énigme [enigm] nf riddle
enivrer [ānivʀe] /1/ vt: **s'enivrer** to get drunk
enjamber [āʒābe] /1/ vt to stride over
enjeu, x [āʒø] nm stakes pl
enjoué, e [āʒwe] adj playful
enlaidir [ālediʀ] /2/ vt to make ugly ▷ vi to become ugly
enlèvement [ālɛvmā] nm (rapt) abduction, kidnapping
enlever [āl(ə)ve] /5/ vt (ôter: gén) to remove; (: vêtement, lunettes) to take off;

(*emporter: ordures etc*) to collect; (*kidnapper*) to abduct, kidnap; (*obtenir: prix, contrat*) to win; (*prendre*): **~ qch à qn** to take sth (away) from sb

enliser [ɑ̃lize] /1/: **s'enliser** *vi* to sink, get stuck

enneigé, e [ɑ̃neʒe] *adj* snowy

ennemi, e [ɛnmi] *adj* hostile; (*Mil*) enemy *cpd* ▷ *nm/f* enemy

ennui [ɑ̃nɥi] *nm* (*lassitude*) boredom; (*difficulté*) trouble *no pl*; **avoir des ~s** to have problems; **ennuyer** /8/ *vt* to bother; (*lasser*) to bore; **s'ennuyer** *vi* to be bored; **si cela ne vous ennuie pas** if it's no trouble to you; **ennuyeux, -euse** *adj* boring, tedious; (*agaçant*) annoying

énorme [enɔrm] *adj* enormous, huge; **énormément** *adv* enormously; **énormément de neige/gens** an enormous amount of snow/number of people

enquête [ɑ̃kɛt] *nf* (*de journaliste, de police*) investigation; (*judiciaire, administrative*) inquiry; (*sondage d'opinion*) survey; **enquêter** /1/ *vi* to investigate; **enquêter (sur)** to do a survey (on)

enragé, e [ɑ̃raʒe] *adj* (*Méd*) rabid, with rabies; (*fig*) fanatical

enrageant, e [ɑ̃raʒɑ̃, -ɑ̃t] *adj* infuriating

enrager [ɑ̃raʒe] /3/ *vi* to be furious

enregistrement [ɑ̃r(ə)ʒistrəmɑ̃] *nm* recording; **~ des bagages** baggage check-in

enregistrer [ɑ̃r(ə)ʒistre] /1/ *vt* (*Mus*) to record; (*fig: mémoriser*) to make a mental note of; (*bagages: à l'aéroport*) to check in

enrhumer [ɑ̃ryme] /1/: **s'enrhumer** *vi* to catch a cold

enrichir [ɑ̃riʃir] /2/ *vt* to make rich(er); (*fig*) to enrich; **s'enrichir** *vi* to get rich(er)

enrouer [ɑ̃rwe] /1/: **s'enrouer** *vi* to go hoarse

enrouler [ɑ̃rule] /1/ *vt* (*fil, corde*) to wind (up); **s'enrouler** to coil up; **~ qch autour de** to wind sth (a)round

enseignant, e [ɑ̃sɛɲɑ̃, -ɑ̃t] *nm/f* teacher

enseignement [ɑ̃sɛɲ(ə)mɑ̃] *nm* teaching; (*Admin*) education

enseigner [ɑ̃seɲe] /1/ *vt, vi* to teach; **~ qch à qn/à qn que** to teach sb sth/sb that

ensemble [ɑ̃sɑ̃bl] *adv* together ▷ *nm* (*assemblage*) set; (*vêtements*) outfit; (*unité, harmonie*) unity; **l'~ du/de la** (*totalité*) the whole *ou* entire; **impression/idée d'~** overall *ou* general impression/idea; **dans l'~** (*en gros*) on the whole

ensoleillé, e [ɑ̃sɔleje] *adj* sunny

ensuite [ɑ̃sɥit] *adv* then, next; (*plus tard*) afterwards, later

entamer [ɑ̃tame] /1/ *vt* (*pain, bouteille*) to start; (*hostilités, pourparlers*) to open

entasser [ɑ̃tase] /1/ *vt* (*empiler*) to pile up, heap up; **s'entasser** *vi* (*s'amonceler*) to pile up; **s'~ dans** to cram into

entendre [ɑ̃tɑ̃dr] /41/ *vt* to hear; (*comprendre*) to understand; (*vouloir dire*) to mean; **s'entendre** *vi* (*sympathiser*) to get on; (*se mettre d'accord*) to agree; **j'ai entendu dire que** I've heard (it said) that; **~ parler de** to hear of

entendu, e [ɑ̃tɑ̃dy] *adj* (*réglé*) agreed; (*au courant: air*) knowing; **(c'est) ~** all right, agreed; **bien ~** of course

entente [ɑ̃tɑ̃t] *nf* understanding; (*accord, traité*) agreement; **à double ~** (*sens*) with a double meaning

enterrement [ɑ̃tɛrmɑ̃] *nm* (*cérémonie*) funeral, burial

enterrer [ɑ̃tere] /1/ *vt* to bury

entêtant, e [ɑ̃tɛtɑ̃, -ɑ̃t] *adj* heady

en-tête [ɑ̃tɛt] *nm* heading; **papier à ~** headed notepaper

entêté, e [ɑ̃tete] *adj* stubborn

entêter [ɑ̃tete] /1/: **s'entêter** *vi*: **s'~ (à faire)** to persist (in doing)

enthousiasme [ɑ̃tuzjasm] *nm* enthusiasm; **enthousiasmer** /1/ *vt* to fill with enthusiasm; **s'enthousiasmer (pour qch)** to get enthusiastic (about sth); **enthousiaste** *adj* enthusiastic

entier, -ière [ɑ̃tje, -jɛr] *adj* whole; (*total, complet: satisfaction etc*) complete; (*fig: caractère*) unbending ▷ *nm* (*Math*) whole; **en ~** totally; **lait ~** full-cream milk; **entièrement** *adv* entirely, wholly

entonnoir [ɑ̃tɔnwar] *nm* funnel

entorse [ɑ̃tɔrs] *nf* (*Méd*) sprain; (*fig*): **~ à la loi/au règlement** infringement of the law/rule

entourage [ɑ̃turaʒ] *nm* circle; (*famille*) family (circle); (*ce qui enclôt*) surround

entourer [ɑ̃ture] /1/ *vt* to surround; (*apporter son soutien à*) to rally round; **~ de** to surround with; **s'entourer de** to surround o.s. with

entracte [ɑ̃trakt] *nm* interval

entraide [ɑ̃trɛd] *nf* mutual aid *ou* assistance

entrain [ɑ̃trɛ̃] *nm* spirit; **avec ~** energetically; **faire qch sans ~** to do sth half-heartedly *ou* without enthusiasm

entraînement [ɑ̃trɛnmɑ̃] *nm* training

entraîner [ɑ̃trene] /1/ *vt* (*charrier*) to carry *ou* drag along; (*Tech*) to drive; (*emmener: personne*) to take (off); (*mener à l'assaut, influencer*) to lead; (*Sport*) to train; (*impliquer*) to entail; **~ qn à faire** (*inciter*) to lead sb to do; **s'entraîner** *vi* (*Sport*) to train; **s'~ à qch/à faire** to train o.s. for sth/to do; **entraîneur** *nm/f* (*Sport*) coach, trainer ▷ *nm* (*Hippisme*) trainer

entre [ɑ̃tr] *prép* between; (*parmi*) among(st); **l'un d'~ eux/nous** one of them/ us; **~ autres (choses)** among other things; **ils se battent ~ eux** they are fighting among(st) themselves; **entrecôte** *nf* entrecôte *ou* rib steak

entrée [ɑ̃tʀe] nf entrance; (accès: au cinéma etc) admission; (billet) (admission) ticket; (Culin) first course

entre: entrefilet nm (article) paragraph, short report; **entremets** nm (cream) dessert

entrepôt [ɑ̃tʀəpo] nm warehouse

entreprendre [ɑ̃tʀəpʀɑ̃dʀ] /58/ vt (se lancer dans) to undertake; (commencer) to begin ou start (upon)

entrepreneur, -euse [ɑ̃tʀəpʀənœʀ, -øz] nm/f: ~ **(en bâtiment)** (building) contractor

entrepris, e [ɑ̃tʀəpʀi, -iz] pp de **entreprendre** ▷ nf (société) firm, business; (action) undertaking, venture

entrer [ɑ̃tʀe] /1/ vi to go (ou come) in, enter ▷ vt (Inform) to input, enter; ~ **dans** (gén) to enter; (pièce) to go (ou come) into, enter; (club) to join; (heurter) to run into; **(faire)** ~ **qch dans** to get sth into; ~ **à l'hôpital** to go into hospital; **faire** ~ (visiteur) to show in

entre-temps [ɑ̃tʀətɑ̃] adv meanwhile

entretenir [ɑ̃tʀət(ə)niʀ] /22/ vt to maintain; (famille, maîtresse) to support, keep; ~ **qn (de)** to speak to sb (about)

entretien [ɑ̃tʀətjɛ̃] nm maintenance; (discussion) discussion, talk; (pour un emploi) interview

entrevoir [ɑ̃tʀəvwaʀ] /30/ vt (à peine) to make out; (brièvement) to catch a glimpse of

entrevu, e [ɑ̃tʀəvy] pp de **entrevoir** ▷ nf (audience) interview

entrouvert, e [ɑ̃tʀuvɛʀ, -ɛʀt] adj half-open

énumérer [enymeʀe] /6/ vt to list

envahir [ɑ̃vaiʀ] /2/ vt to invade; (inquiétude, peur) to come over; **envahissant, e** adj (péj: personne) intrusive

enveloppe [ɑ̃v(ə)lɔp] nf (de lettre) envelope; (crédits) budget; **envelopper** /1/ vt to wrap; (fig) to envelop, shroud

enverrai etc [ɑ̃veʀe] vb voir **envoyer**

envers [ɑ̃vɛʀ] prép towards, to ▷ nm other side; (d'une étoffe) wrong side; **à l'~** (verticalement) upside down; (pull) back to front; (vêtement) inside out

envie [ɑ̃vi] nf (sentiment) envy; (souhait) desire, wish; **avoir ~ de** to feel like; (désir plus fort) to want; **avoir ~ de faire** to feel like doing; to want to do; **avoir ~ que** to wish that; **cette glace me fait ~** I fancy some of that ice cream; **envier** /7/ vt to envy; **envieux, -euse** adj envious

environ [ɑ̃viʀɔ̃] adv: ~ **3 h/2 km** (around) about 3 o'clock/2 km; voir aussi **environs**

environnant, e [ɑ̃viʀɔnɑ̃, -ɑ̃t] adj surrounding

environnement [ɑ̃viʀɔnmɑ̃] nm environment

environs [ɑ̃viʀɔ̃] nmpl surroundings; **aux ~ de** around

envisager [ɑ̃vizaʒe] /3/ vt to contemplate; (avoir en vue) to envisage; ~ **de faire** to consider doing

envoler [ɑ̃vɔle] /1/: **s'envoler** vi (oiseau) to fly away ou off; (avion) to take off; (papier, feuille) to blow away; (fig) to vanish (into thin air)

envoyé, e [ɑ̃vwaje] nm/f (Pol) envoy; (Presse) correspondent; ~ **spécial** special correspondent

envoyer [ɑ̃vwaje] /8/ vt to send; (lancer) to hurl, throw; ~ **chercher** to send for; ~ **promener qn** (fam) to send sb packing

éolien, ne [eɔljɛ̃, -ɛn] adj wind ▷ nf wind turbine

épagneul, e [epaɲœl] nm/f spaniel

épais, se [epɛ, -ɛs] adj thick; **épaisseur** nf thickness

épanouir [epanwiʀ] /2/: **s'épanouir** vi (fleur) to bloom, open out; (visage) to light up; (se développer) to blossom (out)

épargne [epaʀɲ] nf saving

épargner [epaʀɲe] /1/ vt to save; (ne pas tuer ou endommager) to spare ▷ vi to save; ~ **qch à qn** to spare sb sth

éparpiller [epaʀpije] /1/ vt to scatter; **s'éparpiller** vi to scatter; (fig) to dissipate one's efforts

épatant, e [epatɑ̃, -ɑ̃t] adj (fam) super

épater [epate] /1/ vt (fam) to amaze; (: impressionner) to impress

épaule [epol] nf shoulder

épave [epav] nf wreck

épée [epe] nf sword

épeler [ep(ə)le] /4/ vt to spell

éperon [epʀɔ̃] nm spur

épervier [epɛʀvje] nm sparrowhawk

épi [epi] nm (de blé, d'orge) ear; (de maïs) cob

épice [epis] nf spice

épicé, e [epise] adj spicy

épicer [epise] /3/ vt to spice

épicerie [episʀi] nf grocer's shop; (denrées) groceries pl; ~ **fine** delicatessen (shop); **épicier, -ière** nm/f grocer

épidémie [epidemi] nf epidemic

épiderme [epidɛʀm] nm skin

épier [epje] /7/ vt to spy on, watch closely

épilepsie [epilɛpsi] nf epilepsy

épiler [epile] /1/ vt (jambes) to remove the hair from; (sourcils) to pluck

épinards [epinaʀ] nmpl spinach sg

épine [epin] nf thorn, prickle; (d'oursin etc) spine

épingle [epɛ̃gl] nf pin; ~ **de nourrice** ou **de sûreté** ou **double** safety pin

épisode [epizɔd] nm episode; **film/roman à ~s** serial; **épisodique** adj occasional

épluche-légumes [eplyʃlegym] nm inv potato peeler

éplucher [eplyʃe] /1/ vt (fruit, légumes) to peel; (comptes, dossier) to go over with a fine-tooth comb; **épluchures** nfpl peelings

éponge [epɔ̃ʒ] nf sponge; **éponger** /3/ vt (liquide) to mop ou sponge up; (surface) to sponge; (fig: déficit) to soak up

époque [epɔk] nf (de l'histoire) age, era; (de l'année, la vie) time; (de ~ (meuble) period cpd

épouse [epuz] nf wife; **épouser** /1/ vt to marry

épousseter [epuste] /4/ vt to dust

épouvantable [epuvɑ̃tabl] adj appalling, dreadful

épouvantail [epuvɑ̃taj] nm scarecrow

épouvante [epuvɑ̃t] nf terror; **film d'~** horror film; **épouvanter** /1/ vt to terrify

époux [epu] nm husband ▷ nmpl: **les ~** the (married) couple

épreuve [eprœv] nf (d'examen) test; (malheur, difficulté) trial, ordeal; (Photo) print; (Typo) proof; (Sport) event; **à toute ~** unfailing; **mettre à l'~** to put to the test

éprouver [epruve] /1/ vt (tester) to test; to afflict, distress; (ressentir) to experience

EPS sigle f (= Éducation physique et sportive) ≈ PE

épuisé, e [epɥize] adj exhausted; (livre) out of print; **épuisement** nm exhaustion

épuiser [epɥize] /1/ vt (fatiguer) to exhaust, wear ou tire out; (stock, sujet) to exhaust; **s'épuiser** vi to wear ou tire o.s. out, exhaust o.s.

épuisette [epɥizɛt] nf shrimping net

équateur [ekwatœr] nm equator; **(la république de) l'É~** Ecuador

équation [ekwasjɔ̃] nf equation

équerre [ekɛr] nf (à dessin) (set) square

équilibre [ekilibr] nm balance; **garder/ perdre l'~** to keep/lose one's balance; **être en ~** to be balanced; **équilibré, e** adj well-balanced; **équilibrer** /1/ vt to balance; **s'équilibrer** vi to balance

équipage [ekipaʒ] nm crew

équipe [ekip] nf team; **travailler en ~** to work as a team

équipé, e [ekipe] adj: **bien/mal ~** well-/ poorly-equipped

équipement [ekipmɑ̃] nm equipment

équiper [ekipe] /1/ vt to equip; **~ qn/qch de** to equip sb/sth with

équipier, -ière [ekipje, -jɛr] nm/f team member

équitation [ekitasjɔ̃] nf (horse-)riding; **faire de l'~** to go (horse-)riding

équivalent, e [ekivalɑ̃, -ɑ̃t] adj, nm equivalent

équivaloir [ekivalwar] /29/: **~ à** vt to be equivalent to

érable [erabl] nm maple

érafler [erafle] /1/ vt to scratch; **éraflure** nf scratch

ère [ɛr] nf era; **en l'an 1050 de notre ~** in the year 1050 A.D.

érection [erɛksjɔ̃] nf erection

éroder [erɔde] /1/ vt to erode

érotique [erɔtik] adj erotic

errer [ere] /1/ vi to wander

erreur [erœr] nf mistake, error; **par ~** by mistake; **faire ~** to be mistaken

éruption [erypsjɔ̃] nf eruption; (boutons) rash

es [ɛ] vb voir **être**

ès [ɛs] prép: **licencié ès lettres/sciences** ≈ Bachelor of Arts/Science

ESB sigle f (= encéphalopathie spongiforme bovine) BSE

escabeau, x [ɛskabo] nm (tabouret) stool; (échelle) stepladder

escalade [ɛskalad] nf climbing no pl; (Pol etc) escalation; **escalader** /1/ vt to climb

escale [ɛskal] nf (Navig: durée) call; (: port) port of call; (Aviat) stop(over); **faire ~ à** (Navig) to put in at; (Aviat) to stop over at; **vol sans ~** nonstop flight

escalier [ɛskalje] nm stairs pl; **dans l'~** ou **les ~s** on the stairs; **~ mécanique** ou **roulant** escalator

escapade [ɛskapad] nf: **faire une ~** to go on a jaunt; (s'enfuir) to run away ou off

escargot [ɛskargo] nm snail

escarpé, e [ɛskarpe] adj steep

esclavage [ɛsklavaʒ] nm slavery

esclave [ɛsklav] nm/f slave

escompte [ɛskɔ̃t] nm discount

escrime [ɛskrim] nf fencing

escroc [ɛskro] nm swindler, con-man; **escroquer** /1/ vt: **escroquer qn (de qch)/ qch à qn** to swindle sb (out of sth)/sth out of sb; **escroquerie** [ɛskrɔkri] nf swindle

espace [ɛspas] nm space; **espacer** /3/ vt to space out; **s'espacer** vi (visites etc) to become less frequent

espadon [ɛspadɔ̃] nm swordfish inv

espadrille [ɛspadrij] nf rope-soled sandal

Espagne [ɛspaɲ] nf: **l'~** Spain; **espagnol, e** adj Spanish ▷ nm (Ling) Spanish ▷ nm/f: **Espagnol, e** Spaniard

espèce [ɛspɛs] nf (Bio, Bot, Zool) species inv; (gén: sorte) sort, kind, type, (péj): **~ de maladroit/de brute!** you clumsy oaf/you brute!; **espèces** nfpl (Comm) cash sg; **payer en ~s** to pay (in) cash

espérance [ɛsperɑ̃s] nf hope; **~ de vie** life expectancy

espérer [ɛspere] /6/ vt to hope for; **j'espère (bien)** I hope so; **~ que/faire** to hope that/to do

espiègle [ɛspjɛgl] adj mischievous

espion, ne [ɛspjɔ̃, -ɔn] nm/f spy; **espionnage** nm espionage, spying; **espionner** /1/ vt to spy (up)on

espoir [ɛspwar] nm hope; **dans l'~ de/ que** in the hope of/that; **reprendre ~** not to lose hope

esprit [ɛspri] nm (pensée, intellect) mind; (humour, ironie) wit; (mentalité, d'une loi etc, fantôme etc) spirit; **faire de l'~** to try to be witty; **reprendre ses ~s** to come to; **perdre l'~** to lose one's mind

esquimau, de, x [ɛskimo, -od] *adj* Inuit ▷ *nm*: **E~®** ice lolly (BRIT), popsicle (US) ▷ *nm/f*: **E~, de** Inuit

essai [esɛ] *nm* (*tentative*) attempt, try; (*de produit*) testing; (*Rugby*) try; (*Littérature*) essay; **à l'~** on a trial basis; **mettre à l'~** to put to the test

essaim [esɛ̃] *nm* swarm

essayer [eseje] /8/ *vt* to try; (*vêtement, chaussures*) to try (on); (*restaurant, méthode, voiture*) to try (out) ▷ *vi* to try; **~ de faire** to try *ou* attempt to do

essence [esɑ̃s] *nf* (*de voiture*) petrol (BRIT), gas(oline) (US); (*extrait de plante*) essence; (*espèce: d'arbre*) species *inv*

essentiel, le [esɑ̃sjɛl] *adj* essential; **c'est l'~** (*ce qui importe*) that's the main thing; **l'~ de** the main part of

essieu, x [esjø] *nm* axle

essor [esɔʀ] *nm* (*de l'économie etc*) rapid expansion

essorer [esɔʀe] /1/ *vt* (*en tordant*) to wring (out); (*par la force centrifuge*) to spin-dry; **essoreuse** *nf* spin-dryer

essouffler [esufle] /1/: **s'essouffler** *vi* to get out of breath

essuie-glace [esɥiglas] *nm* windscreen (BRIT) *ou* windshield (US) wiper

essuyer [esɥije] /8/ *vt* to wipe; (*fig: subir*) to suffer; **s'essuyer** (*après le bain*) to dry o.s.; **~ la vaisselle** to dry up

est *vb* [ɛ] *voir* **être** ▷ *nm* [ɛst]: **l'~** the east ▷ *adj inv* [ɛst] east; (*région*) east(ern); **à l'~** in the east; (*direction*) to the east, east(wards); **à l'~ de** (to the) east of

est-ce que [ɛskə] *adv*: **~ c'est cher/c'était bon?** is it expensive/was it good?; **quand est-ce qu'il part?** when does he leave?, when is he leaving?; *voir aussi* **que**

esthéticienne [ɛstetisjɛn] *nf* beautician

esthétique [ɛstetik] *adj* attractive

estimation [ɛstimasjɔ̃] *nf* valuation; (*chiffre*) estimate

estime [ɛstim] *nf* esteem, regard; **estimer** /1/ *vt* (*respecter*) to esteem; (*expertiser: bijou*) to value; (*évaluer: coût etc*) to assess, estimate; (*penser*): **estimer que/être** to consider that/o.s. to be

estival, e, -aux [ɛstival, -o] *adj* summer *cpd*

estivant, e [ɛstivɑ̃, -ɑ̃t] *nm/f* (summer) holiday-maker

estomac [ɛstɔma] *nm* stomach

estragon [ɛstʀagɔ̃] *nm* tarragon

estuaire [ɛstɥɛʀ] *nm* estuary

et [e] *conj* and; **et lui?** what about him?; **et alors?** so what?

étable [etabl] *nf* cowshed

établi, e [etabli] *nm* (work)bench

établir [etabliʀ] /2/ *vt* (*papiers d'identité, facture*) to make out; (*liste, programme*)

to draw up; (*gouvernement, artisan etc*) to set up; (*réputation, usage, fait, culpabilité, relations*) to establish; **s'établir** *vi* to be established; **s'~ (à son compte)** to set up in business; **s'~ à/près de** to settle in/near

établissement [etablismɑ̃] *nm* (*entreprise, institution*) establishment; **~ scolaire** school, educational establishment

étage [etaʒ] *nm* (*d'immeuble*) storey, floor; **au 2ème ~** on the 2nd (BRIT) *ou* 3rd (US) floor; **à l'~** upstairs; **c'est à quel ~?** what floor is it on?

étagère [etaʒɛʀ] *nf* (*rayon*) shelf; (*meuble*) shelves *pl*

étai [etɛ] *nm* stay, prop

étain [etɛ̃] *nm* pewter *no pl*

étais *etc* [etɛ] *vb voir* **être**

étaler [etale] /1/ *vt* (*carte, nappe*) to spread (out); (*peinture, liquide*) to spread; (*échelonner: paiements, dates, vacances*) to spread, stagger; (*marchandises*) to display; (*richesses, connaissances*) to parade; **s'étaler** *vi* (*liquide*) to spread out; (*fam*) to fall flat on one's face; **s'~ sur** (*paiements etc*) to be spread over

étalon [etalɔ̃] *nm* (*cheval*) stallion

étanche [etɑ̃ʃ] *adj* (*récipient*) watertight; (*montre, vêtement*) waterproof

étang [etɑ̃] *nm* pond

étant [etɑ̃] *vb voir* **être**; **donné**

étape [etap] *nf* stage; (*lieu d'arrivée*) stopping place; (: *Cyclisme*) staging point

état [eta] *nm* (*Pol, condition*) state; **en bon/ mauvais ~** in good/poor condition; **en ~ (de marche)** in (working) order; **remettre en ~** to repair; **hors d'~** out of order; **être en ~/hors d'~ de faire** to be in a state/in no fit state to do; **être dans tous ses ~s** to be in a state; **faire ~ de** (*alléguer*) to put forward; **l'É~** the State; **~ civil** civil status; **~ des lieux** inventory of fixtures; **États-Unis** *nmpl*: **les États-Unis (d'Amérique)** the United States (of America)

et cætera, et cetera, etc. [ɛtsetera] *adv* etc

été [ete] *pp de* **être** ▷ *nm* summer

éteindre [etɛ̃dʀ] /52/ *vt* (*lampe, lumière, radio, chauffage*) to turn *ou* switch off; (*cigarette, incendie, bougie*) to put out, extinguish; **s'éteindre** *vi* (*feu, lumière*) to go out; (*mourir*) to pass away; **éteint, e** *adj* (*fig*) lacklustre, dull; (*volcan*) extinct

étendre [etɑ̃dʀ] /41/ *vt* (*pâte, liquide*) to spread; (*carte etc*) to spread out; (*lessive, linge*) to hang up *ou* out; (*bras, jambes*) to stretch out; (*fig: agrandir*) to extend; **s'étendre** *vi* (*augmenter, se propager*) to spread; (*terrain, forêt etc*): **s'~ jusqu'à/de ... à** to stretch as far as/from ... to; **s'~ sur** (*se coucher*) to lie down (on); (*fig: expliquer*) to elaborate *ou* enlarge (upon)

étendu, e [etɑ̃dy] *adj* extensive

éternel, le [etɛʀnɛl] *adj* eternal

éternité [etɛʀnite] nf eternity; **ça a duré une ~** it lasted for ages
éternuement [etɛʀnymã] nm sneeze
éternuer [etɛʀnɥe] /1/ vi to sneeze
êtes [ɛt(z)] vb voir **être**
Éthiopie [etjɔpi] nf: **l'~** Ethiopia
étiez [etje] vb voir **être**
étinceler [etɛ̃sle] /4/ vi to sparkle
étincelle [etɛ̃sɛl] nf spark
étiquette [etikɛt] nf label; (protocole): **l'~** etiquette
étirer [etiʀe] /1/ vt to stretch out; **s'étirer** vi (personne) to stretch; (convoi, route): **s'~ sur** to stretch out over
étoile [etwal] nf star; **à la belle ~** (out) in the open; **~ filante** shooting star; **~ de mer** starfish; **étoilé, e** adj starry
étonnant, e [etɔnɑ̃, -ɑ̃t] adj surprising
étonnement [etɔnmɑ̃] nm surprise, amazing
étonner [etɔne] /1/ vt to surprise, amaze; **s'étonner que/de** to be surprised that/at; **cela m'~ait (que)** (j'en doute) I'd be (very) surprised (if)
étouffer [etufe] /1/ vt to suffocate; (bruit) to muffle; (scandale) to hush up ▷ vi to suffocate; **s'étouffer** vi (en mangeant etc) to choke; **on étouffe** it's stifling
étourderie [etuʀdəʀi] nf (caractère) absent-mindedness no pl; (faute) thoughtless blunder
étourdi, e [etuʀdi] adj (distrait) scatterbrained, heedless
étourdir [etuʀdiʀ] /2/ vt (assommer) to stun, daze; (griser) to make dizzy ou giddy; **étourdissement** nm dizzy spell
étrange [etʀɑ̃ʒ] adj strange
étranger, ère [etʀɑ̃ʒe, -ɛʀ] adj foreign; (pas de la famille, non familier) strange ▷ nm/f foreigner; stranger ▷ nm: **à l'~** abroad
étrangler [etʀɑ̃gle] /1/ vt to strangle; **s'étrangler** vi (en mangeant etc) to choke

⊙ **MOT-CLÉ**

être [ɛtʀ] /61/ nm being; **être humain** human being
▶ vb copule **1** (état, description) to be; **il est instituteur** he is ou he's a teacher; **vous êtes grand/intelligent/fatigué** you are ou you're tall/clever/tired
2 (+à: appartenir) to be; **le livre est à Paul** the book is Paul's ou belongs to Paul; **c'est à moi/eux** it is ou it's mine/theirs
3 (+de: provenance): **il est de Paris** he is from Paris; (: appartenance): **il est des nôtres** he is one of us
4 (date): **nous sommes le 10 janvier** it's the 10th of January (today)
▶ vi to be; **je ne serai pas ici demain** I won't be here tomorrow
▶ vb aux **1** to have; to be; **être arrivé/allé** to have arrived/gone; **il est parti** he has left, he has gone
2 (forme passive) to be; **être fait par** to be made by; **il a été promu** he has been promoted
3 (+à +inf: obligation, but): **c'est à réparer** it needs repairing; **c'est à essayer** it should be tried; **il est à espérer que ...** it is ou it's to be hoped that ...
▶ vb impers **1**: **il est** (+ adj) it is; **il est impossible de le faire** it's impossible to do it
2: **il est** (heure, date): **il est 10 heures** it is ou it's 10 o'clock
3 (emphatique): **c'est moi** it's me; **c'est à lui de le faire** it's up to him to do it

étrennes [etʀɛn] nfpl ≈ Christmas box sg
étrier [etʀije] nm stirrup
étroit, e [etʀwa, -wat] adj narrow; (vêtement) tight; (fig: liens, collaboration) close; **à l'~** cramped; **~ d'esprit** narrow-minded
étude [etyd] nf studying; (ouvrage, rapport) study; (Scol: salle de travail) study room; **études** nfpl (Scol) studies; **être à l'~** (projet etc) to be under consideration; **faire des ~s (de droit/médecine)** to study (law/medicine)
étudiant, e [etydjã, -ãt] nm/f student
étudier [etydje] /7/ vt, vi to study
étui [etɥi] nm case
eu, eue [y] pp de **avoir**
euh [ø] excl er
euro [øʀo] nm euro
Europe [øʀɔp] nf: **l'~** Europe; **européen, ne** adj European ▷ nm/f: **Européen, ne** European
eus etc [y] vb voir **avoir**
eux [ø] pron (sujet) they; (objet) them
évacuer [evakɥe] /1/ vt to evacuate
évader [evade] /1/: **s'évader** vi to escape
évaluer [evalɥe] /1/ vt (expertiser) to assess, evaluate; (juger approximativement) to estimate
évangile [evɑ̃ʒil] nm gospel; **É~** Gospel
évanouir [evanwiʀ] /2/: **s'évanouir** vi to faint; (disparaître) to vanish, disappear; **évanouissement** nm (syncope) fainting fit
évaporer [evapɔʀe] /1/: **s'évaporer** vi to evaporate
évasion [evazjɔ̃] nf escape
éveillé, e [eveje] adj awake; (vif) alert, sharp; **éveiller** /1/ vt to (a)waken; (soupçons etc) to arouse; **s'éveiller** vi to (a)waken; (fig) to be aroused
événement [evɛnmɑ̃] nm event
éventail [evɑ̃taj] nm fan; (choix) range
éventualité [evɑ̃tɥalite] nf eventuality; possibility; **dans l'~ de** in the event of
éventuel, le [evɑ̃tɥɛl] adj possible
▌ Attention à ne pas traduire *éventuel* par *eventual*.

éventuellement [evãtɥɛlmã] *adv* possibly

> ▌Attention à ne pas traduire *éventuellement* par *eventually*.

évêque [evɛk] *nm* bishop

évidemment [evidamã] *adv* (*bien sûr*) of course; (*certainement*) obviously

évidence [evidãs] *nf* obviousness; (*fait*) obvious fact; **de toute ~** quite obviously *ou* evidently; **être en ~** to be clearly visible; **mettre en ~** (*fait*) to highlight; **évident, e** *adj* obvious, evident; **ce n'est pas évident** it's not as simple as all that

évier [evje] *nm* (kitchen) sink

éviter [evite] /1/ *vt* to avoid; **~ de faire/ que qch ne se passe** to avoid doing/sth happening; **~ qch à qn** to spare sb sth

évoluer [evɔlɥe] /1/ *vi* (*enfant, maladie*) to develop; (*situation, moralement*) to evolve, develop; (*aller et venir*) to move about; **évolution** *nf* development; evolution

évoquer [evɔke] /1/ *vt* to call to mind, evoke; (*mentionner*) to mention

ex- [ɛks] *préfixe* ex-; **son ~mari** her ex-husband; **son ~femme** his ex-wife

exact, e [ɛgza(kt), ɛgzakt] *adj* exact; (*correct*) correct; (*ponctuel*) punctual; **l'heure ~e** the right *ou* exact time, **exactement** *adv* exactly

ex aequo [ɛgzeko] *adj* equally placed; **arriver ~** to finish neck and neck

exagéré, e [ɛgzaʒere] *adj* (*prix etc*) excessive

exagérer [ɛgzaʒere] /6/ *vt* to exaggerate ▷ *vi* (*abuser*) to go too far; (*déformer les faits*) to exaggerate

examen [ɛgzamɛ̃] *nm* examination; (*Scol*) exam, examination; **à l'~** under consideration; **~ médical** (medical) examination; (*analyse*) test

examinateur, -trice [ɛgzaminatœʀ, -tʀis] *nm/f* examiner

examiner [ɛgzamine] /1/ *vt* to examine

exaspérant, e [ɛgzasperã, -ãt] *adj* exasperating

exaspérer [ɛgzaspere] /6/ *vt* to exasperate

exaucer [ɛgzose] /3/ *vt* (*vœu*) to grant

excéder [ɛksede] /6/ *vt* (*dépasser*) to exceed; (*agacer*) to exasperate

excellent, e [ɛkselã, -ãt] *adj* excellent

excentrique [ɛksãtʀik] *adj* eccentric

excepté, e [ɛksɛpte] *adj, prép*: **les élèves ~s, ~ les élèves** except for *ou* apart from the pupils

exception [ɛksɛpsjɔ̃] *nf* exception; **à l'~ de** except for, with the exception of; **d'~** (*mesure, loi*) special, exceptional; **exceptionnel, le** *adj* exceptional; **exceptionnellement** *adv* exceptionally

excès [ɛksɛ] *nm* surplus ▷ *nmpl* excesses; **faire des ~** to overindulge; **~ de vitesse** speeding *no pl*; **excessif, -ive** *adj* excessive

excitant, e [ɛksitã, -ãt] *adj* exciting ▷ *nm* stimulant; **excitation** *nf* (*état*) excitement

exciter [ɛksite] /1/ *vt* to excite; (*café etc*) to stimulate; **s'exciter** *vi* to get excited

exclamer [ɛksklame] /1/: **s'exclamer** *vi* to exclaim

exclu, e [ɛkskly] *adj*: **il est/n'est pas ~ que ...** it's out of the question/not impossible that ...

exclure [ɛksklyʀ] /35/ *vt* (*faire sortir*) to expel; (*ne pas compter*) to exclude, leave out; (*rendre impossible*) to exclude, rule out; **exclusif, -ive** *adj* exclusive; **exclusion** *nf* expulsion; **à l'exclusion de** with the exclusion *ou* exception of; **exclusivité** *nf* (*Comm*) exclusive rights *pl*; **film passant en exclusivité à** film showing only at

excursion [ɛkskyʀsjɔ̃] *nf* (*en autocar*) excursion, trip; (*à pied*) walk, hike

excuse [ɛkskyz] *nf* excuse; **excuses** *nfpl* (*regret*) apology *sg*, apologies; **excuser** /1/ *vt* to excuse; **s'excuser (de)** to apologize (for); **"excusez-moi"** "I'm sorry"; (*pour attirer l'attention*) "excuse me"

exécuter [ɛgzekyte] /1/ *vt* (*prisonnier*) to execute; (*tâche etc*) to execute, carry out; (*Mus: jouer*) to perform, execute; **s'exécuter** *vi* to comply

exemplaire [ɛgzãplɛʀ] *nm* copy

exemple [ɛgzãpl] *nm* example; **par ~** for instance, for example; **donner l'~** to set an example

exercer [ɛgzɛʀse] /3/ *vt* (*pratiquer*) to exercise, practise; (*influence, contrôle, pression*) to exert; (*former*) to exercise, train; **s'exercer** *vi* (*médecin*) to be in practice; (*sportif, musicien*) to practise

exercice [ɛgzɛʀsis] *nm* exercise

exhiber [ɛgzibe] /1/ *vt* (*montrer: papiers, certificat*) to present, produce; (*péj*) to display, flaunt; **s'exhiber** *vi* to parade; (*exhibitionniste*) to expose o.s.; **exhibitionniste** *nm/f* exhibitionist

exigeant, e [ɛgziʒã, -ãt] *adj* demanding; (*péj*) hard to please

exiger [ɛgziʒe] /3/ *vt* to demand, require

exil [ɛgzil] *nm* exile; **exiler** /1/ *vt* to exile; **s'exiler** *vi* to go into exile

existence [ɛgzistãs] *nf* existence

exister [ɛgziste] /1/ *vi* to exist; **il existe un/ des** there is a/are (some)

exorbitant, e [ɛgzɔʀbitã, -ãt] *adj* exorbitant

exotique [ɛgzɔtik] *adj* exotic; **yaourt aux fruits ~s** tropical fruit yoghurt

expédier [ɛkspedje] /7/ *vt* (*lettre, paquet*) to send; (*troupes, renfort*) to dispatch; (*péj: travail etc*) to dispose of, dispatch; **expéditeur, -trice** *nm/f* sender; **expédition** *nf* sending; (*scientifique, sportive, Mil*) expedition

expérience [ɛkspeʀjɑ̃s] *nf* (*de la vie, des choses*) experience; (*scientifique*) experiment

expérimenté, e [ɛkspeʀimɑ̃te] *adj* experienced

expérimenter [ɛkspeʀimɑ̃te] /1/ *vt* to test out, experiment with

expert, e [ɛkspɛʀ, -ɛʀt] *adj* ▷ *nm* expert; ~ **en assurances** insurance valuer; **expert-comptable** *nm* ≈ chartered (BRIT) *ou* certified public (US) accountant

expirer [ɛkspiʀe] /1/ *vi* (*prendre fin, lit: mourir*) to expire; (*respirer*) to breathe out

explication [ɛksplikasjɔ̃] *nf* explanation; (*discussion*) discussion; (*dispute*) argument

explicite [ɛksplisit] *adj* explicit

expliquer [ɛksplike] /1/ *vt* to explain; **s'expliquer** to explain o.s.; **s'~ avec qn** (*discuter*) to explain o.s. to sb

exploit [ɛksplwa] *nm* exploit, feat; **exploitant** *nm/f:* **exploitant (agricole)** farmer; **exploitation** *nf* exploitation; (*d'une entreprise*) running; **exploitation agricole** farming concern; **exploiter** /1/ *vt* (*personne, don*) to exploit; (*entreprise, ferme*) to run, operate; (*mine*) to exploit, work

explorer [ɛksplɔʀe] /1/ *vt* to explore

exploser [ɛksploze] /1/ *vi* to explode, blow up; (*engin explosif*) to go off; (*personne: de colère*) to explode; **explosif, -ive** *adj, nm* explosive; **explosion** *nf* explosion; **explosion de joie/colère** outburst of joy/rage

exportateur, -trice [ɛkspɔʀtatœʀ, -tʀis] *adj* export *cpd*, exporting ▷ *nm* exporter

exportation [ɛkspɔʀtasjɔ̃] *nf* (*action*) exportation; (*produit*) export

exporter [ɛkspɔʀte] /1/ *vt* to export

exposant [ɛkspozɑ̃] *nm* exhibitor

exposé, e [ɛkspoze] *nm* talk ▷ *adj:* ~ **au sud** facing south

exposer [ɛkspoze] /1/ *vt* (*marchandise*) to display; (*peinture*) to exhibit, show; (*parler de*) to explain, set out; (*mettre en danger, orienter, Photo*) to expose; **s'exposer à** (*soleil, danger*) to expose o.s. to; **exposition** *nf* (*manifestation*) exhibition; (*Photo*) exposure

exprès¹ [ɛkspʀɛ] *adv* (*délibérément*) on purpose; (*spécialement*) specially; **faire ~ de faire qch** to do sth on purpose

exprès², -esse [ɛkspʀɛs] *adj inv* (*Postes: lettre, colis*) express

express [ɛkspʀɛs] *adj, nm:* **(café) ~** espresso; **(train) ~** fast train

expressif, -ive [ɛkspʀɛsif, -iv] *adj* expressive

expression [ɛkspʀɛsjɔ̃] *nf* expression

exprimer [ɛkspʀime] /1/ *vt* (*sentiment, idée*) to express; (*jus, liquide*) to press out; **s'exprimer** *vi* (*personne*) to express o.s.

expulser [ɛkspylse] /1/ *vt* to expel; (*locataire*) to evict; (*Football*) to send off

exquis, e [ɛkski, -iz] *adj* exquisite

extasier [ɛkstazje] /7/: **s'extasier** *vi:* **s'~ sur** to go into raptures over

exténuer [ɛkstenɥe] /1/ *vt* to exhaust

extérieur, e [ɛksteʀjœʀ] *adj* (*porte, mur etc*) outer, outside; (*commerce, politique*) foreign; (*influences, pressions*) external; (*apparent: calme, gaieté etc*) outer ▷ *nm* (*d'une maison, d'un récipient etc*) outside, exterior; (*apparence*) exterior; **à l'~** outside; (*à l'étranger*) abroad

externat [ɛkstɛʀna] *nm* day school

externe [ɛkstɛʀn] *adj* external, outer ▷ *nm/f* (*Méd*) non-resident medical student, extern (US); (*Scol*) day pupil

extincteur [ɛkstɛ̃ktœʀ] *nm* (fire) extinguisher

extinction [ɛkstɛ̃ksjɔ̃] *nf:* ~ **de voix** loss of voice

extra [ɛkstʀa] *adj inv* first-rate; (*fam*) fantastic ▷ *nm inv* extra help

extraire [ɛkstʀɛʀ] /50/ *vt* to extract; ~ **qch de** to extract sth from; **extrait** *nm* extract; **extrait de naissance** birth certificate

extraordinaire [ɛkstʀaɔʀdinɛʀ] *adj* extraordinary; (*Pol, Admin: mesures etc*) special

extravagant, e [ɛkstʀavagɑ̃, -ɑ̃t] *adj* extravagant

extraverti, e [ɛkstʀavɛʀti] *adj* extrovert

extrême [ɛkstʀɛm] *adj, nm* extreme; **d'un ~ à l'autre** from one extreme to another; **extrêmement** *adv* extremely; **Extrême-Orient** *nm:* **l'Extrême-Orient** the Far East

extrémité [ɛkstʀemite] *nf* end; (*situation*) straits *pl*, plight; (*geste désespéré*) extreme action; **extrémités** *nfpl* (*pieds et mains*) extremities

exubérant, e [ɛgzybeʀɑ̃, -ɑ̃t] *adj* exuberant

F _abr_ (= _franc_) fr.; (_appartement_): **un F2/F3** a 2-/3-roomed flat (BRIT) _ou_ apartment (US)

fa [fa] _nm inv_ (_Mus_) F; (_en chantant la gamme_) fa

fabricant, e [fabʀikɑ̃, -ɑ̃t] _nm/f_ manufacturer

fabrication [fabʀikasjɔ̃] _nf_ manufacture

fabrique [fabʀik] _nf_ factory; **fabriquer** [fabʀike] /1/ _vt_ to make; (_industriellement_) to manufacture; (_fam_): **qu'est-ce qu'il fabrique?** what is he up to?

fac [fak] _nf_ (_fam: Scol_) (= _faculté_) Uni (BRIT _fam_), ≈ college (US)

façade [fasad] _nf_ front, façade

face [fas] _nf_ face; (_fig: aspect_) side ▷ _adj_: **le côté ~** heads; **en ~ de** opposite; (_fig_) in front of; **de ~** face on; (_fig_) faced with, in the face of; **faire ~ à** to face; **~ à ~** _adv_ facing each other; **face-à-face** _nm inv_ encounter

fâché, e [fɑʃe] _adj_ angry; (_désolé_) sorry

fâcher [fɑʃe] /1/ _vt_ to anger; **se fâcher** _vi_ to get angry; **se ~ avec** (_se brouiller_) to fall out with

facile [fasil] _adj_ easy; (_caractère_) easy-going; **facilement** _adv_ easily; **facilité** _nf_ easiness; (_disposition, don_) aptitude; **facilités** _nfpl_ (_possibilités_) facilities; (_Comm_) terms; **faciliter** /1/ _vt_ to make easier

façon [fasɔ̃] _nf_ (_manière_) way; (_d'une robe etc_) making-up; cut; **façons** _nfpl_ (_péj_) fuss _sg_; **sans ~** _adv_ without fuss; **non merci, sans ~** no thanks, honestly; **de ~ à** so as to; **de ~ à ce que** so that; **de toute ~** anyway, in any case

facteur, -trice [faktœʀ, -tʀis] _nm/f_ postman/woman (BRIT), mailman/woman (US) ▷ _nm_ (_Math, gén_): **élément**) factor

facture [faktyʀ] _nf_ (_à payer: gén_) bill; (: _Comm_) invoice

facultatif, -ive [fakyltatif, -iv] _adj_ optional

faculté [fakylte] _nf_ (_intellectuelle, d'université_) faculty; (_pouvoir, possibilité_) power

fade [fad] _adj_ insipid

faible [fɛbl] _adj_ weak; (_voix, lumière, vent_) faint; (_rendement, intensité, revenu etc_) low ▷ _nm_ (_pour quelqu'un_) weakness, soft spot; **faiblesse** _nf_ weakness; **faiblir** [feblir] /2/ _vi_ to weaken; (_lumière_) to dim; (_vent_) to drop

faïence [fajɑ̃s] _nf_ earthenware _no pl_

faillir [fajiʀ] /2/ _vi_: **j'ai failli tomber/lui dire** I almost _ou_ nearly fell/told him

faillite [fajit] _nf_ bankruptcy; **faire ~** to go bankrupt

faim [fɛ̃] _nf_ hunger; **avoir ~** to be hungry; **rester sur sa ~** (_aussi fig_) to be left wanting more

fainéant, e [fɛneɑ̃, -ɑ̃t] _nm/f_ idler, loafer

MOT-CLÉ

faire [fɛʀ] /60/ _vt_ **1** (_fabriquer, être l'auteur de_) to make; **faire du vin/une offre/un film** to make wine/an offer/a film; **faire du bruit** to make a noise

2 (_effectuer: travail, opération_) to do; **que faites-vous?** (_quel métier etc_) what do you do?; (_quelle activité: au moment de la question_) what are you doing?; **faire la lessive/le ménage** to do the washing/the housework

3 (_études_) to do; (_sport, musique_) to play; **faire du droit/du français** to do law/French; **faire du rugby/piano** to play rugby/the piano

4 (_visiter_): **faire les magasins** to go shopping; **faire l'Europe** to tour _ou_ do Europe

5 (_distance_): **faire du 50 (à l'heure)** to do 50 (km an hour); **nous avons fait 1000 km en 2 jours** we did _ou_ covered 1000 km in 2 days

6 (_simuler_): **faire le malade/l'ignorant** to act the invalid/the fool

7 (_transformer, avoir un effet sur_): **faire de qn un frustré/avocat** to make sb frustrated/a lawyer; **ça ne me fait rien** (_m'est égal_) I don't care _ou_ mind; (_me laisse froid_) it has no effect on me; **ça ne fait rien** it doesn't matter; **faire que** (_impliquer_) to mean that

8 (_calculs, prix, mesures_): **deux et deux font quatre** two and two are _ou_ make four; **ça fait 10 m/15 euros** it's 10 m/15 euros; **je vous le fais 10 euros** I'll let you have it for 10 euros; **je fais du 40** I take a size 40

9: **qu'a-t-il fait de sa valise/de sa sœur?** what has he done with his case/his sister?

10: **ne faire que**: **il ne fait que critiquer** (_sans cesse_) all he (ever) does is criticize; (_seulement_) he's only criticizing

11 (*dire*) to say; **vraiment? fit-il** really? he said

12 (*maladie*) to have; **faire du diabète/de la tension** to have diabetes *sg*/high blood pressure

▶ *vi* **1** (*agir, s'y prendre*) to act, do; **il faut faire vite** we (*ou* you *etc*) must act quickly; **comment a-t-il fait pour?** how did he manage to?; **faites comme chez vous** make yourself at home

2 (*paraître*) to look; **faire vieux/démodé** to look old/old-fashioned; **ça fait bien** it looks good

3 (*remplaçant un autre verbe*) to do; **ne le casse pas comme je l'ai fait** don't break it as I did; **je peux le voir? — faites!** can I see it? — please do!

▶ *vb impers* **1**: **il fait beau** *etc* the weather is fine *etc*; *voir aussi* **froid; jour** *etc*

2 (*temps écoulé, durée*). **ça fait deux ans qu'il est parti** it's two years since he left; **ça fait deux ans qu'il y est** he's been there for two years

▶ *vb aux* **1**: **faire** (+*infinitif: action directe*) to make; **faire tomber/bouger qch** to make sth fall/move; **faire démarrer un moteur/chauffer de l'eau** to start up an engine/heat some water; **faire dormir** it makes you sleep; **faire travailler les enfants** to make the children work *ou* get the children to work; **il m'a fait traverser la rue** he helped me to cross the road

2: **faire** (+*infinitif: indirectement, par un intermédiaire*): **faire réparer qch** to get *ou* have sth repaired; **faire punir les enfants** to have the children punished **se faire** *vr* **1** (*vin, fromage*) to mature

2 (*être convenable*): **cela se fait beaucoup/ne se fait pas** it's done a lot/not done

3 (+*nom ou pron*): **se faire une jupe** to make o.s. a skirt; **se faire des amis** to make friends; **se faire du souci** to worry; **il ne s'en fait pas** he doesn't worry

4 (+*adj: devenir*): **se faire vieux** to be getting old; (: *délibérément*): **se faire beau** to do o.s. up

5: **se faire à** (*s'habituer*) to get used to; **je n'arrive pas à me faire à la nourriture/au climat** I can't get used to the food/climate

6 (+*infinitif*): **se faire examiner la vue/opérer** to have one's eyes tested/have an operation; **se faire couper les cheveux** to get one's hair cut; **il va se faire tuer/punir** he's going to get himself killed/get (himself) punished; **il s'est fait aider** he got somebody to help him; **il s'est fait aider par Simon** he got Simon to help him; **se faire faire un vêtement** to get a garment made for o.s.

7 (*impersonnel*): **comment se fait-il/faisait-il que?** how is it/was it that?

faire-part [fɛʀpaʀ] *nm inv* announcement (*of birth, marriage etc*)

faisan, e [fəzɑ̃, -an] *nm/f* pheasant

faisons *etc* [fəzɔ̃] *vb voir* **faire**

fait¹ [fɛ] *nm* (*événement*) event, occurrence; (*réalité, donnée*) fact; **être au ~ (de)** to be informed (of); **au ~** (*à propos*) by the way; **en venir au ~** to get to the point; **du ~ de ceci/qu'il a menti** because of *ou* on account of this/his having lied; **de ce ~** for this reason; **en ~** in fact; **prendre qn sur le ~** to catch sb in the act; **~ divers** (short) news item

fait², e [fɛ, fɛt] *adj* (*mûr: fromage, melon*) ripe; **c'est bien ~ (pour lui ou eux etc)** it serves him (*ou* them *etc*) right

faites [fɛt] *vb voir* **faire**

falaise [falɛz] *nf* cliff

falloir [falwaʀ] /29/ *vb impers*: **il faut faire les lits** we (*ou* you *etc*) have to *ou* must make the beds; **il faut que je fasse les lits** I have to *ou* must make the beds; **il a fallu qu'il parte** he had to leave; **il faudrait qu'elle rentre** she should come *ou* go back, she ought to come *ou* go back; **il faut faire attention** you have to be careful; **il me faudrait 100 euros** I would need 100 euros; **il vous faut tourner à gauche après l'église** you have to turn left past the church; **nous avons ce qu'il (nous) faut** we have what we need; **il ne fallait pas** you shouldn't have (done); **s'en falloir** *vi*: **il s'en est fallu de 10 euros/5 minutes** we (*ou* they *etc*) were 10 euros short/5 minutes late (*ou* early); **il s'en faut de beaucoup qu'il soit ...** he is far from being ...; **il s'en est fallu de peu que cela n'arrive** it very nearly happened; **comme il faut** *adj* proper; *adv* properly

famé, e [fame] *adj*: **mal ~** disreputable, of ill repute

fameux, -euse [famø, -øz] *adj* (*illustre*) famous; (*bon: repas, plat etc*) first-rate, first-class; (*intensif*): **un ~ problème** *etc* a real problem *etc*

familial, e, -aux [familjal, -o] *adj* family *cpd*

familiarité [familjaʀite] *nf* familiarity

familier, -ière [familje, -jɛʀ] *adj* (*connu, impertinent*) familiar; (*atmosphère*) informal, friendly; (*Ling*) informal, colloquial ▷ *nm* regular (visitor)

famille [famij] *nf* family; **il a de la ~ à Paris** he has relatives in Paris

famine [famin] *nf* famine

fana [fana] *adj, nm/f* (*fam*) = **fanatique**

fanatique [fanatik] *adj*: **~ (de)** fanatical (about) ▷ *nm/f* fanatic

faner [fane] /1/: **se faner** *vi* to fade

fanfare [fɑ̃faʀ] *nf* (*orchestre*) brass band; (*musique*) fanfare

fantaisie [fɑ̃tezi] nf (spontanéité) fancy, imagination; (caprice) whim ▷ adj: **bijou (de) ~** (piece of) costume jewellery (BRIT) ou jewelry (US)

fantasme [fɑ̃tasm] nm fantasy

fantastique [fɑ̃tastik] adj fantastic

fantôme [fɑ̃tom] nm ghost, phantom

faon [fɑ̃] nm fawn (deer)

FAQ sigle f (= foire aux questions) FAQ pl

farce [faʀs] nf (viande) stuffing; (blague) (practical) joke; (Théât) farce; **farcir** /2/ vt (viande) to stuff

farder [faʀde] /1/: **se farder** vi to make o.s. up

farine [faʀin] nf flour

farouche [faʀuʃ] adj shy, timid

fart [faʀt] nm (ski) wax

fascination [fasinasjɔ̃] nf fascination

fasciner [fasine] /1/ vt to fascinate

fascisme [faʃism] nm fascism

fasse etc [fas] vb voir **faire**

fastidieux, -euse [fastidjø, -øz] adj tedious, tiresome

fatal, e [fatal] adj fatal; (inévitable) inevitable; **fatalité** nf (destin) fate; (coïncidence) fateful coincidence

fatidique [fatidik] adj fateful

fatigant, e [fatigɑ̃, -ɑ̃t] adj tiring; (agaçant) tiresome

fatigue [fatig] nf tiredness, fatigue; **fatigué, e** adj tired; **fatiguer** /1/ vt to tire, make tired; (fig: agacer) to annoy ▷ vi (moteur) to labour, strain; **se fatiguer** to get tired

fauché, e [foʃe] adj (fam) broke

faucher [foʃe] /1/ vt (herbe) to cut; (champs, blés) to reap; (véhicule) to mow down; (fam: voler) to pinch

faucon [fokɔ̃] nm falcon, hawk

faudra etc [fodʀa] vb voir **falloir**

faufiler [fofile] /1/: **se faufiler** vi: **se ~ dans** to edge one's way into; **se ~ parmi/entre** to thread one's way among/between

faune [fon] nf (Zool) wildlife, fauna

fausse [fos] adj f voir **faux²**; **faussement** adv (accuser) wrongly, wrongfully; (croire) falsely

fausser [fose] /1/ vt (objet) to bend, buckle; (fig) to distort; **~ compagnie à qn** to give sb the slip

faut [fo] vb voir **falloir**

faute [fot] nf (erreur) mistake, error; (péché, manquement) misdemeanour; (Football etc) offence; (Tennis) fault; **c'est de sa/ma ~** it's his/my fault; **être en ~** to be in the wrong; **~ de** (temps, argent) for ou through lack of; **sans ~** without fail; **~ de frappe** typing error; **~ professionnelle** professional misconduct no pl

fauteuil [fotœj] nm armchair; **~ d'orchestre** seat in the front stalls (BRIT) ou the orchestra (US); **~ roulant** wheelchair

fautif, -ive [fotif, -iv] adj (incorrect) incorrect, inaccurate; (responsable) at fault, in the wrong; **il se sentait ~** he felt guilty

fauve [fov] nm wildcat ▷ adj (couleur) fawn

faux¹ [fo] nf scythe

faux², fausse [fo, fos] adj (inexact) wrong; (piano, voix) out of tune; (billet) fake, forged; (sournois, postiche) false ▷ adv (Mus) out of tune ▷ nm (copie) fake, forgery; **faire ~ bond à qn** to let sb down; **~ frais** nm pl extras, incidental expenses; **~ mouvement** awkward movement; **faire un ~ pas** to trip; (fig) to make a faux pas; **~ témoignage** (délit) perjury; **fausse alerte** false alarm; **fausse couche** miscarriage; **fausse note** wrong note; **faux-filet** nm sirloin

faveur [favœʀ] nf favour (BRIT), favor (US); **traitement de ~** preferential treatment; **en ~ de** in favo(u)r of

favorable [favɔʀabl] adj favourable

favori, te [favɔʀi, -it] adj, nm/f favourite

favoriser [favɔʀize] /1/ vt to favour

fax [faks] nm fax

fécond, e [fekɔ̃, -ɔ̃d] adj fertile; **féconder** /1/ vt to fertilize

féculent [fekylɑ̃] nm starchy food

fédéral, e, -aux [federal, -o] adj federal

fée [fe] nf fairy

feignant, e [fɛɲɑ̃, -ɑ̃t] nm/f = **fainéant**

feindre [fɛ̃dʀ] /52/ vt to feign; **~ de faire** to pretend to do

fêler [fele] /1/ vt to crack

félicitations [felisitasjɔ̃] nfpl congratulations

féliciter [felisite] /1/ vt: **~ qn (de)** to congratulate sb (on)

félin, e [felɛ̃, -in] nm (big) cat

femelle [fəmɛl] adj, nf female

féminin, e [feminɛ̃, -in] adj feminine; (sexe) female; (équipe, vêtements etc) women's ▷ nm (Ling) feminine; **féministe** adj feminist

femme [fam] nf woman; (épouse) wife; **~ de chambre** chambermaid; **~ au foyer** housewife; **~ de ménage** cleaning lady

fémur [femyʀ] nm femur, thighbone

fendre [fɑ̃dʀ] /41/ vt (couper en deux) to split; (fissurer) to crack; (traverser) to cut through; **se fendre** vi to crack

fenêtre [f(ə)nɛtʀ] nf window

fenouil [fənuj] nm fennel

fente [fɑ̃t] nf (fissure) crack; (de boîte à lettres etc) slit

fer [fɛʀ] nm iron; **~ à cheval** horseshoe; **~ forgé** wrought iron; **~ à friser** curling tongs; **~ (à repasser)** iron

ferai etc [fəʀe] vb voir **faire**

fer-blanc [fɛʀblɑ̃] nm tin(plate)

férié, e [feʀje] adj: **jour ~** public holiday

ferions etc [fəʀjɔ̃] vb voir **faire**

ferme [fɛʀm] adj firm ▷ adv (travailler etc) hard ▷ nf (exploitation) farm; (maison) farmhouse

fermé, e [fɛrme] *adj* closed, shut; (*gaz, eau etc*) off; (*fig: milieu*) exclusive

fermenter [fɛrmɑ̃te] /1/ *vi* to ferment

fermer [fɛrme] /1/ *vt* to close, shut; (*cesser l'exploitation de*) to close down, shut down; (*eau, lumière, électricité, robinet*) to turn off; (*aéroport, route*) to close ▷ *vi* to close, shut; (*magasin: définitivement*) to close down, shut down; **se fermer** *vi* to close, shut; **~ à clef** to lock

fermeté [fɛrməte] *nf* firmness

fermeture [fɛrmətyr] *nf* closing; (*dispositif*) catch; **heure de ~** closing time; **~ éclair® ou à glissière** zip (fastener) (BRIT), zipper (US)

fermier, -ière [fɛrmje, -jɛr] *nm/f* farmer

féroce [feros] *adj* ferocious, fierce

ferons *etc* [fərɔ̃] *vb voir* **faire**

ferrer [fɛre] /1/ *vt* (*cheval*) to shoe

ferroviaire [fɛrɔvjɛr] *adj* rail *cpd*, railway *cpd* (BRIT), railroad *cpd* (US)

ferry(-boat) [fɛre(bot)] *nm* ferry

fertile [fɛrtil] *adj* fertile; **~ en incidents** eventful, packed with incidents

fervent, e [fɛrvɑ̃, -ɑ̃t] *adj* fervent

fesse [fɛs] *nf* buttock; **fessée** *nf* spanking

festin [fɛstɛ̃] *nm* feast

festival [fɛstival] *nm* festival

festivités [fɛstivite] *nfpl* festivities

fêtard, e [fɛtar, -ard] (*fam*) *nm/f* (*péj*) high liver, merrymaker

fête [fɛt] *nf* (*religieuse*) feast; (*publique*) holiday; (*réception*) party; (*kermesse*) fête, fair; (*du nom*) feast day, name day; **faire la ~** to live it up; **faire ~ à qn** to give sb a warm welcome; **les ~s (de fin d'année)** the festive season; **la salle/le comité des ~s** the village hall/festival committee; **la ~ des Mères/Pères** Mother's/Father's Day; **~ foraine** (fun)fair; **la ~ de la musique**, *see note* **"fête de la musique"**; **fêter** /1/ *vt* to celebrate; (*personne*) to have a celebration for

FÊTE DE LA MUSIQUE

- The *Fête de la Musique* is a music festival
- which has taken place every year since
- 1981. On 21 June throughout France local
- musicians perform free of charge in parks,
- streets and squares.

feu, x [fø] *nm* (*gén*) fire; (*signal lumineux*) light; (*de cuisinière*) ring; **feux** *nmpl* (*Auto*) (traffic) lights; **au ~!** (*incendie*) fire!; **à ~ doux/vif** over a slow/brisk heat; **à petit ~** (*Culin*) over a gentle heat; (*fig*) slowly; **faire ~** to fire; **ne pas faire long ~** not to last long; **prendre ~** to catch fire; **mettre le ~ à** to set fire to; **faire du ~** to make a fire; **avez-vous du ~?** (*pour cigarette*) have you (got) a light?; **~ rouge/vert/orange** red/

green/amber (BRIT) *ou* yellow (US) light; **~ arrière** rear light; **~ d'artifice** firework; (*spectacle*) fireworks *pl*; **~ de joie** bonfire; **~x de brouillard** fog lights *ou* lamps; **~x de croisement** dipped (BRIT) *ou* dimmed (US) headlights; **~x de position** sidelights; **~x de route** (*Auto*) headlights (on full (BRIT) *ou* high (US) beam)

feuillage [fœjaʒ] *nm* foliage, leaves *pl*

feuille [fœj] *nf* (*d'arbre*) leaf; **~ (de papier)** sheet (of paper); **~ de calcul** spreadsheet; **~ d'impôts** tax form; **~ de maladie** medical expenses claim form; **~ de paye** pay slip

feuillet [fœjɛ] *nm* leaf

feuilleté, e [fœjte] *adj*: **pâte ~** flaky pastry

feuilleter [fœjte] /4/ *vt* (*livre*) to leaf through

feuilleton [fœjtɔ̃] *nm* serial

feutre [føtr] *nm* felt; (*chapeau*) felt hat; (*stylo*) felt-tip(ped pen); **feutré, e** *adj* (*pas, voix, atmosphère*) muffled

fève [fɛv] *nf* broad bean

février [fevrije] *nm* February

fiable [fjabl] *adj* reliable

fiançailles [fjɑ̃saj] *nfpl* engagement *sg*

fiancé, e [fjɑ̃se] *nm/f* fiancé (fiancée) ▷ *adj*: **être ~ (à)** to be engaged (to)

fibre [fibr] *nf* fibre; **~ de verre** fibreglass

ficeler [fis(ə)le] /4/ *vt* to tie up

ficelle [fisɛl] *nf* string *no pl*; (*morceau*) piece *ou* length of string

fiche [fiʃ] *nf* (*carte*) (index) card; (*formulaire*) form; (*Élec*) plug; **~ de paye** pay slip

ficher [fiʃe] /1/ *vt* (*dans un fichier*) to file; (: *Police*) to put on file; (*fam: faire*) to do; (: *donner*) to give; (: *mettre*) to stick *ou* shove; **fiche(-moi) le camp** (*fam*) clear off; **fiche-moi la paix** (*fam*) leave me alone; **se ~ de** (*fam: rire de*) to make fun of; (: *être indifférent à*) not to care about

fichier [fiʃje] *nm* file; **~ joint** (*Inform*) attachment

fichu, e [fiʃy] *pp de* **ficher** ▷ *adj* (*fam: fini, inutilisable*) bust, done for; (: *intensif*) wretched, darned ▷ *nm* (*foulard*) (head) scarf; **mal ~** feeling lousy

fictif, -ive [fiktif, -iv] *adj* fictitious

fiction [fiksjɔ̃] *nf* fiction; (*fait imaginé*) invention

fidèle [fidɛl] *adj*: **~ (à)** faithful (to) ▷ *nm/f* (*Rel*): **les ~s** (*à l'église*) the congregation; **fidélité** *nf* (*d'un conjoint*) fidelity, faithfulness; (*d'un ami, client*) loyalty

fier¹ [fje]: **se ~ à** *vt* to trust

fier², fière [fjɛr] *adj* proud; **~ de** proud of; **fierté** *nf* pride

fièvre [fjɛvr] *nf* fever; **avoir de la ~/39 de ~** to have a high temperature/a temperature of 39° C; **fiévreux, -euse** *adj* feverish

figer [fiʒe] /3/: **se figer** *vi* to congeal; (*personne*) to freeze

fignoler [fiɲɔle] /1/ vt to put the finishing touches to

figue [fig] nf fig; **figuier** nm fig tree

figurant, e [figyʀɑ̃, -ɑ̃t] nm/f (Théât) walk-on; (Ciné) extra

figure [figyʀ] nf (visage) face; (image, tracé, forme, personnage) figure; (illustration) picture, diagram

figuré, e [figyʀe] adj (sens) figurative

figurer [figyʀe] /1/ vi to appear ▷ vt to represent; **se ~ que** to imagine that

fil [fil] nm (brin, fig: d'une histoire) thread; (d'un couteau) edge; **au ~ des années** with the passing of the years; **au ~ de l'eau** with the stream ou current; **coup de ~** (fam) phone call; **donner/recevoir un coup de ~** to make/get a phone call; **~ électrique** electric wire; **~ de fer** wire; **~ de fer barbelé** barbed wire

file [fil] nf line; (Auto) lane; **~ (d'attente)** queue (BRIT), line (US); **à la ~ (d'affilée)** in succession; **à la** ou **en ~ indienne** in single file

filer [file] /1/ vt (tissu, toile, verre) to spin; (prendre en filature) to shadow, tail; (fam: donner): **~ qch à qn** to slip sb sth ▷ vi (bas, maille, liquide, pâte) to run; (aller vite) to fly past ou by; (fam: partir) to make off; **~ doux** to behave o.s.

filet [filɛ] nm net; (Culin) fillet; (d'eau, de sang) trickle; **~ (à provisions)** string bag

filial, e, -aux [filjal, -o] adj filial ▷ nf (Comm) subsidiary

filière [filjɛʀ] nf (carrière) path; **suivre la ~** to work one's way up (through the hierarchy)

fille [fij] nf girl; (opposé à fils) daughter; **vieille ~** old maid; **fillette** nf (little) girl

filleul, e [fijœl] nm/f godchild, godson (goddaughter)

film [film] nm (pour photo) (roll of) film; (œuvre) film, picture, movie

fils [fis] nm son; **~ à papa** (péj) daddy's boy

filtre [filtʀ] nm filter; **filtrer** /1/ vt to filter; (fig: candidats, visiteurs) to screen

fin¹ [fɛ̃] nf end; **fins** nfpl (but) ends; **~ mai** at the end of May; **prendre ~** to come to an end; **mettre ~ à** to put an end to; **à la ~** in the end, eventually; **en ~ de compte** in the end; **sans ~** endless

fin², e [fɛ̃, fin] adj (papier, couche, fil) thin; (cheveux, poudre, pointe, visage) fine; (taille) neat, slim; (esprit, remarque) subtle ▷ adv (moudre, couper) finely; **~ prêt/soûl** quite ready/drunk; **avoir la vue/l'ouïe ~e** to have keen eyesight/hearing; **or/linge/vin ~** fine gold/linen/wine; **~es herbes** mixed herbs

final, e [final] adj, nf final ▷ nm (Mus) finale; **quarts de ~e** quarter finals; **finalement** adv finally, in the end; (après tout) after all

finance [finɑ̃s] nf finance; **finances** nfpl (situation financière) finances; (activités financières) finance sg; **moyennant ~** for a fee ou consideration; **financer** /3/ vt to finance; **financier, -ière** adj financial

finesse [fines] nf thinness; (raffinement) fineness; (subtilité) subtlety

fini, e [fini] adj finished; (Math) finite ▷ nm (d'un objet manufacturé) finish

finir [finiʀ] /2/ vt to finish ▷ vi to finish, end; **~ de faire** to finish doing; (cesser) to stop doing; **~ par faire** to end ou finish up doing; **il finit par m'agacer** he's beginning to get on my nerves; **en ~ avec** to be ou have done with; **il va mal ~** he will come to a bad end

finition [finisjɔ̃] nf (résultat) finish

finlandais, e [fɛ̃lɑ̃dɛ, -ɛz] adj Finnish ▷ nm/f: **F~, e** Finn

Finlande [fɛ̃lɑ̃d] nf: **la ~** Finland

finnois, e [finwa, -waz] adj Finnish ▷ nm (Ling) Finnish

fioul [fjul] nm fuel oil

firme [fiʀm] nf firm

fis [fi] vb voir **faire**

fisc [fisk] nm tax authorities pl; **fiscal, e, -aux** adj tax cpd, fiscal; **fiscalité** nf tax system

fissure [fisyʀ] nf crack; **fissurer** /1/ vt to crack; **se fissurer** vi to crack

fit [fi] vb voir **faire**

fixation [fiksasjɔ̃] nf (attache) fastening; (Psych) fixation

fixe [fiks] adj fixed; (emploi) steady, regular ▷ nm (salaire) basic salary; (téléphone) landline; **à heure ~** at a set time; **menu à prix ~** set menu

fixé, e [fikse] adj: **être ~ (sur)** (savoir à quoi s'en tenir) to have made up one's mind (about)

fixer [fikse] /1/ vt (attacher): **~ qch (à/sur)** to fix ou fasten sth (to/onto); (déterminer) to fix, set; (poser son regard sur) to stare at; **se fixer** (s'établir) to settle down; **se ~ sur** (attention) to focus on

flacon [flakɔ̃] nm bottle

flageolet [flaʒɔlɛ] nm (Culin) dwarf kidney bean

flagrant, e [flagʀɑ̃, -ɑ̃t] adj flagrant, blatant; **en ~ délit** in the act

flair [flɛʀ] nm sense of smell; (fig) intuition; **flairer** /1/ vt (humer) to sniff (at); (détecter) to scent

flamand, e [flamɑ̃, -ɑ̃d] adj Flemish ▷ nm (Ling) Flemish ▷ nm/f: **F~, e** Fleming

flamant [flamɑ̃] nm flamingo

flambant [flɑ̃bɑ̃] adv: **~ neuf** brand new

flambé, e [flɑ̃be] adj (Culin) flambé

flambée [flɑ̃be] nf blaze; **~ des prix** (sudden) shooting up of prices

flamber [flɑ̃be] /1/ vi to blaze (up)

flamboyer [flɑ̃bwaje] /8/ vi to blaze (up)

flamme [flɑm] nf flame; (fig) fire, fervour; **en ~s** on fire, ablaze

flan [flɑ̃] nm (Culin) custard tart ou pie

flanc [flɑ̃] nm side; (Mil) flank

flancher [flɑ̃ʃe] /1/ vi to fail, pack up

flanelle [flanɛl] nf flannel

flâner [flɑne] /1/ vi to stroll

flanquer [flɑ̃ke] /1/ vt to flank; (fam: mettre) to chuck, shove; **~ par terre/à la porte** (jeter) to fling to the ground/chuck out

flaque [flak] nf (d'eau) puddle; (d'huile, de sang etc) pool

flash [flaʃ] (pl **flashes**) nm (Photo) flash; **~ (d'information)** newsflash

flatter [flate] /1/ vt to flatter; **se ~ de qch** to pride o.s. on sth; **flatteur, -euse** adj flattering

flèche [flɛʃ] nf arrow; (de clocher) spire; **monter en ~** (fig) to soar, rocket; **partir en ~** to be off like a shot; **fléchette** nf dart

flétrir [fletʀiʀ] /2/: **se flétrir** vi to wither

fleur [flœʀ] nf flower; (d'un arbre) blossom; **être en ~** (arbre) to be in blossom; **tissu à ~s** flowered ou flowery fabric

fleuri, e [flœʀi] adj (jardin) in flower ou bloom; (style, tissu, papier) flowery; (teint) glowing

fleurir [flœʀiʀ] /2/ vi (rose) to flower; (arbre) to blossom, (fig) to flourish ▷ vt (tombe) to put flowers on; (chambre) to decorate with flowers

fleuriste [flœʀist] nm/f florist

fleuve [flœv] nm river

flexible [flɛksibl] adj flexible

flic [flik] nm (fam: péj) cop

flipper [flipœʀ] nm pinball (machine)

flirter [flœʀte] /1/ vi to flirt

flocon [flɔkɔ̃] nm flake

flore [flɔʀ] nf flora

florissant, e [flɔʀisɑ̃, -ɑ̃t] adj (économie) flourishing

flot [flo] nm flood, stream; **flots** nmpl (de la mer) waves; **être à ~** (Navig) to be afloat; **entrer à ~s** to stream ou pour in

flottant, e [flɔtɑ̃, -ɑ̃t] adj (vêtement) loose(-fitting)

flotte [flɔt] nf (Navig) fleet; (fam: eau) water; (: pluie) rain

flotter [flɔte] /1/ vi to float; (nuage, odeur) to drift; (drapeau) to fly; (vêtements) to hang loose ▷ vb impers (fam: pleuvoir): **il flotte** it's raining; **faire ~** to float; **flotteur** nm float

flou, e [flu] adj fuzzy, blurred; (fig) woolly (BRIT), vague

fluide [flɥid] adj fluid; (circulation etc) flowing freely ▷ nm fluid

fluor [flyɔʀ] nm: **dentifrice au ~** fluoride toothpaste

fluorescent, e [flyɔʀesɑ̃, -ɑ̃t] adj fluorescent

flûte [flyt] nf (aussi: **~ traversière**) flute; (verre) flute glass; (pain) (thin) baguette; **~!** drat it!; **~ (à bec)** recorder

flux [fly] nm incoming tide; (écoulement) flow; **le ~ et le re~** the ebb and flow

foc [fɔk] nm jib

foi [fwa] nf faith; **digne de ~** reliable; **être de bonne/mauvaise ~** to be in good faith/ not to be in good faith

foie [fwa] nm liver; **crise de ~** stomach upset

foin [fwɛ̃] nm hay; **faire du ~** (fam) to kick up a row

foire [fwaʀ] nf fair; (fête foraine) (fun)fair; **~ aux questions** (Internet) frequently asked questions; **faire la ~** to whoop it up; **~ (exposition)** trade fair

fois [fwa] nf time; **une/deux ~** once/twice; **deux ~ deux** twice two; **une ~** (passé) once; (futur) sometime; **une (bonne) ~ pour toutes** once and for all; **une ~ que c'est fait** once it's done; **des ~** (parfois) sometimes; **à la ~ (ensemble)** (all) at once

fol [fɔl] adj m voir **fou**

folie [fɔli] nf (d'une décision, d'un acte) madness, folly; (état) madness, insanity; **la ~ des grandeurs** delusions of grandeur; **faire des ~s** (en dépenses) to be extravagant

folklorique [fɔlklɔʀik] adj folk cpd; (fam) weird

folle [fɔl] adj f, nf voir **fou**; **follement** adv (très) madly, wildly

foncé, e [fɔ̃se] adj dark

foncer [fɔ̃se] /3/ vi to go darker; (fam: aller vite) to tear ou belt along; **~ sur** to charge at

fonction [fɔ̃ksjɔ̃] nf function; (emploi, poste) post, position; **fonctions** nfpl (professionnelles) duties; **voiture de ~** company car; **en ~ de** (par rapport à) according to; **faire ~ de** to serve as; **la ~ publique** the state ou civil (BRIT) service; **fonctionnaire** nm/f state employee ou official; (dans l'administration) ≈ civil servant; **fonctionner** /1/ vi to work, function

fond [fɔ̃] nm voir aussi **fonds**; (d'un récipient, trou) bottom; (d'une salle, scène) back; (d'un tableau, décor) background; (opposé à la forme) content; (Sport): **le ~** long distance (running); **au ~ de** at the bottom of; at the back of; **à ~** (connaître, soutenir) thoroughly; (appuyer, visser) right down ou home; **à ~ (de train)** (fam) full tilt; **dans le ~, au ~** (en somme) basically, really; **de ~ en comble** from top to bottom; **~ de teint** foundation

fondamental, e, -aux [fɔ̃damɑ̃tal, -o] adj fundamental

fondant, e [fɔ̃dɑ̃, -ɑ̃t] adj (neige) melting; (poire) that melts in the mouth

fondation [fɔ̃dasjɔ̃] nf founding; (établissement) foundation; **fondations** nfpl (d'une maison) foundations

fondé, e [fɔ̃de] *adj (accusation etc)* well-founded; **être ~ à croire** to have grounds for believing *ou* good reason to believe

fondement [fɔ̃dmɑ̃] *nm*: **sans ~** *(rumeur etc)* groundless, unfounded

fonder [fɔ̃de] /1/ *vt* to found; *(fig)*: **~ qch sur** to base sth on; **se ~ sur** *(personne)* to base o.s. on

fonderie [fɔ̃dʀi] *nf* smelting works *sg*

fondre [fɔ̃dʀ] /41/ *vt (aussi:* **faire ~**) to melt; *(dans l'eau)* to dissolve; *(fig: mélanger)* to merge, blend ▷ *vi (à la chaleur)* to melt; to dissolve; *(fig)* to melt away; *(se précipiter)*: **~ sur** to swoop down on; **~ en larmes** to dissolve into tears

fonds [fɔ̃] *nm (Comm)*: **~ (de commerce)** business ▷ *nmpl (argent)* funds

fondu, e [fɔ̃dy] *adj (beurre, neige)* melted; *(métal)* molten ▷ *nf (Culin)* fondue

font [fɔ̃] *vb voir* **faire**

fontaine [fɔ̃tɛn] *nf* fountain; *(source)* spring

fonte [fɔ̃t] *nf* melting; *(métal)* cast iron; **la ~ des neiges** the (spring) thaw

foot [fut], **football** [futbol] *nm* football, soccer; **footballeur, -euse** *nm/f* footballer (BRIT), football *ou* soccer player

footing [futiŋ] *nm* jogging; **faire du ~** to go jogging

forain, e [fɔʀɛ̃, -ɛn] *adj* fairground *cpd* ▷ *nm (marchand)* stallholder; *(acteur etc)* fairground entertainer

forçat [fɔʀsa] *nm* convict

force [fɔʀs] *nf* strength; *(Physique, Mécanique)* force; **forces** *nfpl (physiques)* strength *sg*; *(Mil)* forces; **à ~ de faire** by dint of doing; **de ~** forcibly, by force; **dans la ~ de l'âge** in the prime of life; **les ~s de l'ordre** the police

forcé, e [fɔʀse] *adj* forced; **c'est ~!** it's inevitable!; **forcément** *adv* inevitably; **pas forcément** not necessarily

forcer [fɔʀse] /3/ *vt* to force; *(moteur, voix)* to strain ▷ *vi (Sport)* to overtax o.s.; **se ~ à faire qch** to force o.s. to do sth; **~ la dose/l'allure** to overdo it/increase the pace

forestier, -ière [fɔʀɛstje, -jɛʀ] *adj* forest *cpd*

forêt [fɔʀɛ] *nf* forest

forfait [fɔʀfɛ] *nm (Comm)* all-in deal *ou* price; **déclarer ~** to withdraw; **forfaitaire** *adj* inclusive

forge [fɔʀʒ] *nf* forge, smithy; **forgeron** *nm* (black)smith

formaliser [fɔʀmalize] /1/: **se formaliser** *vi*: **se ~ (de)** to take offence (at)

formalité [fɔʀmalite] *nf* formality; **simple ~** mere formality

format [fɔʀma] *nm* size; **formater** /1/ *vt (disque)* to format

formation [fɔʀmasjɔ̃] *nf* forming; training; **la ~ permanente** *ou* **continue** continuing education; **la ~ professionnelle** vocational training

forme [fɔʀm] *nf (gén)* form; *(d'un objet)* shape, form; **formes** *nfpl (bonnes manières)* proprieties; *(d'une femme)* figure *sg*; **en ~ de poire** pear-shaped, in the shape of a pear; **être en (bonne** *ou* **pleine) ~** *(Sport etc)* to be on form; **en bonne et due ~** in due form

formel, le [fɔʀmɛl] *adj (preuve, décision)* definite, positive; **formellement** *adv (interdit)* strictly; *(absolument)* positively

former [fɔʀme] /1/ *vt* to form; *(éduquer)* to train; **se former** *vi* to form

formidable [fɔʀmidabl] *adj* tremendous

formulaire [fɔʀmylɛʀ] *nm* form

formule [fɔʀmyl] *nf (gén)* formula; *(expression)* phrase; **~ de politesse** polite phrase; *(en fin de lettre)* letter ending

fort, e [fɔʀ, fɔʀt] *adj* strong; *(intensité, rendement)* high, great; *(corpulent)* large; *(doué)*: **être ~ (en)** to be good (at) ▷ *adv (serrer, frapper)* hard; *(sonner)* loud(ly); *(beaucoup)* greatly, very much; *(très)* very ▷ *nm (édifice)* fort; *(point fort)* strong point, forte; **~ e tête** rebel; **forteresse** *nf* fortress

fortifiant [fɔʀtifjɑ̃] *nm* tonic

fortune [fɔʀtyn] *nf* fortune; **faire ~** to make one's fortune; **de ~** makeshift; **fortuné, e** *adj* wealthy

forum [fɔʀɔm] *nm* forum; **~ de discussion** *(Internet)* message board

fosse [fos] *nf (grand trou)* pit; *(tombe)* grave

fossé [fose] *nm* ditch; *(fig)* gulf, gap

fossette [fosɛt] *nf* dimple

fossile [fosil] *nm* fossil ▷ *adj* fossilized, fossil *cpd*

fou (fol), folle [fu, fɔl] *adj* mad; *(déréglé etc)* wild, erratic; *(fam: extrême, très grand)* terrific, tremendous ▷ *nm/f* madman/woman ▷ *nm (du roi)* jester; **être ~ de** to be mad *ou* crazy about; **avoir le ~ rire** to have the giggles

foudre [fudʀ] *nf*: **la ~** lightning

foudroyant, e [fudʀwajɑ̃, -ɑ̃t] *adj (progrès)* lightning *cpd*; *(succès)* stunning; *(maladie, poison)* violent

fouet [fwɛ] *nm* whip; *(Culin)* whisk; **de plein ~** *adv (se heurter)* head on; **fouetter** /1/ *vt* to whip; *(crème)* to whisk

fougère [fuʒɛʀ] *nf* fern

fougue [fug] *nf* ardour, spirit; **fougueux, -euse** *adj* fiery

fouille [fuj] *nf* search; **fouilles** *nfpl (archéologiques)* excavations; **fouiller** /1/ *vt* to search; *(creuser)* to dig ▷ *vi*: **fouiller dans/parmi** to rummage in/among; **fouillis** *nm* jumble, muddle

foulard [fulaʀ] *nm* scarf

foule [ful] *nf* crowd; **la ~** crowds *pl*; **une ~ de** masses of

foulée [fule] *nf* stride

fouler [fule] /1/ vt to press; (sol) to tread
upon; **se ~ la cheville** to sprain one's ankle;
ne pas se ~ not to overexert o.s.; **il ne
se foule pas** he doesn't put himself out;
foulure nf sprain

four [fuʀ] nm oven; (de potier) kiln; (Théât:
échec) flop

fourche [fuʀʃ] nf pitchfork

fourchette [fuʀʃɛt] nf fork; (Statistique)
bracket, margin

fourgon [fuʀgɔ̃] nm van; (Rail) wag(g)on;
fourgonnette nf (delivery) van

fourmi [fuʀmi] nf ant; **avoir des ~s dans
les jambes/mains** to have pins and needles
in one's legs/hands; **fourmilière** nf ant-hill;
fourmiller /1/ vi to swarm

fourneau, x [fuʀno] nm stove

fourni, e [fuʀni] adj (barbe, cheveux) thick;
(magasin): **bien ~ (en)** well stocked (with)

fournir [fuʀniʀ] /2/ vt to supply; (preuve,
exemple) to provide, supply; (effort) to put
in; **~ qch à qn** to supply sth to sb, supply
ou provide sb with sth; **fournisseur, -euse**
nm/f supplier; **fournisseur d'accès à
Internet** (Internet) service provider, ISP;
fourniture nf supply(ing); **fournitures
scolaires** school stationery

fourrage [fuʀaʒ] nm fodder

fourré, e [fuʀe] adj (bonbon, chocolat) filled;
(manteau, botte) fur lined ▷ nm thicket

fourrer [fuʀe] /1/ vt (fam) to stick, shove;
se ~ dans/sous to get into/under

fourrière [fuʀjɛʀ] nf pound

fourrure [fuʀyʀ] nf fur; (pelage) coat

foutre [futʀ] vt (fam!) = **ficher**; **foutu, e** adj
(fam!) = **fichu**

foyer [fwaje] nm (de cheminée) hearth;
(famille) family; (domicile) home; (local de
réunion) (social) club; (résidence) hostel;
(salon) foyer; **lunettes à double ~** bi-focal
glasses

fracassant, e [fʀakasɑ̃, -ɑ̃t] adj (succès)
staggering

fraction [fʀaksjɔ̃] nf fraction

fracturation [fʀaktyʀasjɔ̃] nf:
~ hydraulique fracking

fracture [fʀaktyʀ] nf fracture; **fracturer** /1/ vt (coffre,
serrure) to break open; (os, membre) to
fracture; **se fracturer le crâne** to fracture
one's skull

fragile [fʀaʒil] adj fragile, delicate; (fig)
frail; **fragilité** nf fragility

fragment [fʀagmɑ̃] nm (d'un objet)
fragment, piece

fraîche [fʀɛʃ] adj f voir **frais**; **fraîcheur** nf
coolness; (d'un aliment) freshness; voir
frais; **fraîchir** /2/ vi to get cooler; (vent) to
freshen

frais, fraîche [fʀɛ, fʀɛʃ] adj (air, eau, accueil)
cool; (petit pois, œufs, nouvelles, couleur,
troupes) fresh ▷ adv (récemment) newly,

fresh(ly) ▷ nm: **mettre au ~** to put in a cool
place; **prendre le ~** to take a breath of cool
air ▷ nmpl (débours) expenses; (Comm) costs;
il fait ~ it's cool; **servir ~** serve chilled; **faire
des ~** to go to a lot of expense; **~ généraux**
overheads; **~ de scolarité** school fees
(BRIT), tuition (US)

fraise [fʀɛz] nf strawberry; **~ des bois** wild
strawberry

framboise [fʀɑ̃bwaz] nf raspberry

franc, franche [fʀɑ̃, fʀɑ̃ʃ] adj (personne)
frank, straightforward; (visage) open;
(net: refus, couleur) clear; (: coupure) clean;
(intensif) downright ▷ nm franc

français, e [fʀɑ̃sɛ, -ɛz] adj French ▷ nm
(Ling) French ▷ nm/f: **F~, e** Frenchman/
woman

France [fʀɑ̃s] nf: **la ~** France; **~2, ~3** public-
sector television channels

franche [fʀɑ̃ʃ] adj f voir **franc**;
franchement adv frankly; clearly;
(nettement) definitely; (tout à fait) downright

franchir [fʀɑ̃ʃiʀ] /2/ vt (obstacle) to clear,
get over; (seuil, ligne, rivière) to cross;
(distance) to cover

franchise [fʀɑ̃ʃiz] nf frankness; (douanière)
exemption; (Assurances) excess

franc-maçon [fʀɑ̃masɔ̃] nm Freemason

franco [fʀɑ̃ko] adv (Comm): **~ (de port)**
postage paid

francophone [fʀɑ̃kɔfɔn] adj French-
speaking

franc-parler [fʀɑ̃paʀle] nm inv
outspokenness; **avoir son ~** to speak one's
mind

frange [fʀɑ̃ʒ] nf fringe

frangipane [fʀɑ̃ʒipan] nf almond paste

frappant, e [fʀapɑ̃, -ɑ̃t] adj striking

frappé, e [fʀape] adj iced

frapper [fʀape] /1/ vt to hit, strike; (étonner)
to strike; **~ dans ses mains** to clap one's
hands; **frappé de stupeur** dumbfounded

fraternel, le [fʀatɛʀnɛl] adj brotherly,
fraternal; **fraternité** nf brotherhood

fraude [fʀod] nf fraud; (Scol) cheating;
passer qch en ~ to smuggle sth in (ou out);
~ fiscale tax evasion

frayeur [fʀɛjœʀ] nf fright

fredonner [fʀədɔne] /1/ vt to hum

freezer [fʀizœʀ] nm freezing compartment

frein [fʀɛ̃] nm brake; **mettre un ~ à** (fig) to
put a brake on, check; **~ à main** handbrake;

freiner /1/ vi to brake ▷ vt (progrès etc) to check

frêle [fʀɛl] adj frail, fragile

frelon [fʀəlɔ̃] nm hornet

frémir [fʀemiʀ] /2/ vi (de froid, de peur) to shudder; (de colère) to shake; (de joie, feuillage) to quiver

frêne [fʀɛn] nm ash (tree)

fréquemment [fʀekamɑ̃] adv frequently

fréquent, e [fʀekɑ̃, -ɑ̃t] adj frequent

fréquentation [fʀekɑ̃tasjɔ̃] nf frequenting; **fréquentations** nfpl (relations) company sg; **avoir de mauvaises ~s** to be in with the wrong crowd, keep bad company

fréquenté, e [fʀekɑ̃te] adj: **très ~** (very) busy; **mal ~** patronized by disreputable elements

fréquenter [fʀekɑ̃te] /1/ vt (lieu) to frequent; (personne) to see; **se fréquenter** to see a lot of each other

frère [fʀɛʀ] nm brother

fresque [fʀɛsk] nf (Art) fresco

fret [fʀɛ(t)] nm freight

friand, e [fʀijɑ̃, -ɑ̃d] adj: **~ de** very fond of ▷ nm: **~ au fromage** cheese puff

friandise [fʀijɑ̃diz] nf sweet

fric [fʀik] nm (fam) cash, bread

friche [fʀiʃ]: **en ~** adj, adv (lying) fallow

friction [fʀiksjɔ̃] nf (massage) rub, rub-down; (Tech, fig) friction

frigidaire® [fʀiʒidɛʀ] nm refrigerator

frigo [fʀigo] nm fridge

frigorifique [fʀigɔʀifik] adj refrigerating

frileux, -euse [fʀilø, -øz] adj sensitive to (the) cold

frimer [fʀime] /1/ vi (fam) to show off

fringale [fʀɛ̃gal] nf (fam): **avoir la ~** to be ravenous

fringues [fʀɛ̃g] nfpl (fam) clothes

fripé, e [fʀipe] adj crumpled

frire [fʀiʀ] vt to fry ▷ vi to fry

frisé, e [fʀize] adj (cheveux) curly; (personne) curly-haired

frisson [fʀisɔ̃] nm (de froid) shiver; (de peur) shudder; **frissonner** /1/ vi (de fièvre, froid) to shiver; (d'horreur) to shudder

frit, e [fʀi, fʀit] pp de **frire** ▷ nf: (pommes) **~es** chips (BRIT), French fries; **friteuse** nf deep fryer, chip pan (BRIT); **friture** nf (huile) (deep) fat; (plat): **friture (de poissons)** fried fish

froid, e [fʀwa, fʀwad] adj ▷ nm cold; **il fait ~** it's cold; **avoir ~** to be cold; **prendre ~** to catch a chill ou cold; **être en ~ avec** to be on bad terms with; **froidement** adv (accueillir) coldly; (décider) coolly

froisser [fʀwase] /1/ vt to crumple (up), crease; (fig) to hurt, offend; **se froisser** vi to crumple, crease; (personne) to take offence (BRIT) ou offense (US); **se ~ un muscle** to strain a muscle

frôler [fʀole] /1/ vt to brush against; (projectile) to skim past; (fig) to come very close to, come within a hair's breadth of

fromage [fʀomaʒ] nm cheese; **~ blanc** soft white cheese

froment [fʀomɑ̃] nm wheat

froncer [fʀɔ̃se] /3/ vt to gather; **~ les sourcils** to frown

front [fʀɔ̃] nm forehead, brow; (Mil, Météorologie, Pol) front; **de ~** (se heurter) head-on; (rouler) together (2 or 3 abreast); (simultanément) at once; **faire ~ à** to face up to

frontalier, -ière [fʀɔ̃talje, -jɛʀ] adj border cpd, frontier cpd ▷ **(travailleurs) ~s** commuters from across the border

frontière [fʀɔ̃tjɛʀ] nf frontier, border

frotter [fʀote] /1/ vi to rub, scrape ▷ vt to rub; (pommes de terre, plancher) to scrub; **~ une allumette** to strike a match

fruit [fʀɥi] nm fruit no pl; **~s de mer** seafood(s); **~s secs** dried fruit sg; **fruité, e** [fʀɥite] adj fruity; **fruitier, -ière** adj: **arbre fruitier** fruit tree

frustrer [fʀystʀe] /1/ vt to frustrate

fuel(-oil) [fjul(ɔjl)] nm fuel oil; (pour chauffer) heating oil

fugace [fygas] adj fleeting

fugitif, -ive [fyʒitif, -iv] adj (lueur, amour) fleeting ▷ nm/f fugitive

fugue [fyg] nf: **faire une ~** to run away, abscond

fuir [fɥiʀ] /17/ vt to flee from; (éviter) to shun ▷ vi to run away; (gaz, robinet) to leak

fuite [fɥit] nf flight; (divulgation) leak; **être en ~** to be on the run; **mettre en ~** to put to flight

fulgurant, e [fylgyʀɑ̃, -ɑ̃t] adj lightning cpd, dazzling

fumé, e [fyme] adj (Culin) smoked; (verre) tinted ▷ nf smoke

fumer [fyme] /1/ vi to smoke; (liquide) to steam ▷ vt to smoke

fûmes [fym] vb voir **être**

fumeur, -euse [fymœʀ, -øz] nm/f smoker

fumier [fymje] nm manure

funérailles [fyneʀaj] nfpl funeral sg

fur [fyʀ]: **au ~ et à mesure** adv as one goes along; **au ~ et à mesure que** as

furet [fyʀɛ] nm ferret

fureter [fyʀ(ə)te] /5/ vi (péj) to nose about

fureur [fyʀœʀ] nf fury; **être en ~** to be infuriated; **faire ~** to be all the rage

furie [fyʀi] nf fury; (femme) shrew, vixen; **en ~** (mer) raging; **furieux, -euse** adj furious

furoncle [fyʀɔ̃kl] nm boil

furtif, -ive [fyʀtif, -iv] adj furtive

fus [fy] vb voir **être**

fusain [fyzɛ̃] nm (Art) charcoal

fuseau, x [fyzo] nm (pantalon) (ski-)pants pl; (pour filer) spindle; **~ horaire** time zone

fusée [fyze] nf rocket

fusible [fyzibl] nm (Élec: fil) fuse wire;
(: fiche) fuse

fusil [fyzi] nm (de guerre, à canon rayé) rifle,
gun; (de chasse, à canon lisse) shotgun, gun;
fusillade nf gunfire no pl, shooting no pl;
fusiller /1/ vt to shoot; **fusiller qn du
regard** to look daggers at sb

fusionner [fyzjɔne] /1/ vi to merge

fût [fy] vb voir **être** ▷ nm (tonneau) barrel,
cask

futé, e [fyte] adj crafty; **Bison ~**® TV and
radio traffic monitoring service

futile [fytil] adj futile; (frivole) frivolous

futur, e [fytyʀ] adj, nm future

fuyard, e [fɥijaʀ, -aʀd] nm/f runaway

Gabon [gabɔ̃] nm: **le ~** Gabon

gâcher [gɑʃe] /1/ vt (gâter) to spoil;
(gaspiller) to waste; **gâchis** nm waste no pl

gaffe [gaf] nf blunder; **faire ~** (fam) to watch out

gage [gaʒ] nm (dans un jeu) forfeit; (fig: de
fidélité) token; **gages** nmpl (salaire) wages;
mettre en ~ to pawn

gagnant, e [gaɲɑ̃, -ɑ̃t] adj: **billet/numéro
~** winning ticket/number ▷ nm/f winner

gagne-pain [gaɲpɛ̃] nm inv job

gagner [gaɲe] /1/ vt to win; (somme d'argent,
revenu) to earn; (aller vers, atteindre) to reach;
(s'emparer de) to overcome; (envahir) to
spread to ▷ vi to win; (fig) to gain; **~ du
temps/de la place** to gain time/save
space; **~ sa vie** to earn one's living

gai, e [ge] adj cheerful; (un peu ivre) merry;
gaiement adv cheerfully; **gaieté** nf
cheerfulness; **de gaieté de cœur** with a
light heart

gain [gɛ̃] nm (revenu) earnings pl; (bénéfice:
gén pl) profits pl

gala [gala] nm official reception; **soirée de
~** gala evening

galant, e [galɑ̃, -ɑ̃t] adj (courtois) courteous,
gentlemanly; (entreprenant) flirtatious,
gallant; (scène, rendez-vous) romantic

galerie [galʀi] nf gallery; (Théât) circle; (de
voiture) roof rack; (fig: spectateurs) audience;
~ marchande shopping mall; **~ de peinture**
(private) art gallery

galet [galɛ] nm pebble

galette [galɛt] nf flat pastry cake; **la ~ des
Rois** cake traditionally eaten on Twelfth Night

- **GALETTE DES ROIS**
-
- A galette des Rois is a cake eaten on Twelfth
- Night containing a figurine. The person
- who finds it is the king (or queen) and
- gets a paper crown. They then choose
- someone else to be their queen (or king).

galipette [galipɛt] *nf* somersault

Galles [gal] *nfpl*: **le pays de ~** Wales; **gallois, e** *adj* Welsh ▷ *nm* (Ling) Welsh ▷ *nm/f*: **Gallois, e** Welshman(-woman)

galocher [galɔʃe] *(fam)* *vt* to French kiss

galon [galɔ̃] *nm* (Mil) stripe; (décoratif) piece of braid

galop [galo] *nm* gallop; **galoper** /1/ *vi* to gallop

gambader [gɑ̃bade] /1/ *vi* (animal, enfant) to leap about

gamin, e [gamɛ̃, -in] *nm/f* kid ▷ *adj* mischievous

gamme [gam] *nf* (Mus) scale; (fig) range

gang [gɑ̃g] *nm* (de criminels) gang

gant [gɑ̃] *nm* glove; **~ de toilette** (face) flannel (BRIT), face cloth

garage [garaʒ] *nm* garage; **garagiste** *nm/f* garage owner; (mécanicien) garage mechanic

garantie [garɑ̃ti] *nf* guarantee; **(bon de) ~** guarantee *ou* warranty slip

garantir [garɑ̃tir] /2/ *vt* to guarantee; **je vous garantis que** I can assure you that

garçon [garsɔ̃] *nm* boy; (aussi: **~ de café**) waiter; **vieux ~** (célibataire) bachelor; **~ de courses** messenger

garde [gard] *nm* (de prisonnier) guard; (de domaine etc) warden; (soldat, sentinelle) guardsman ▷ *nf* (soldats) guard; **de ~** on duty; **monter la ~** to stand guard; **mettre en ~** to warn; **prendre ~ (à)** to be careful (of); **~ champêtre** rural police officer; **~ du corps** *nm* bodyguard; **~ à vue** *nf* (Jur) ≈ police custody; **garde-boue** *nm inv* mudguard; **garde-chasse** *nm* gamekeeper

garder [garde] /1/ *vt* (conserver) to keep; (surveiller: enfants) to look after; (: immeuble, lieu, prisonnier) to guard; **se garder** *vi* (aliment: se conserver) to keep; **se ~ de faire** to be careful not to do; **~ le lit/la chambre** to stay in bed/indoors; **pêche/chasse gardée** private fishing/hunting (ground)

garderie [gardəri] *nf* day nursery, crèche

garde-robe [gardərɔb] *nf* wardrobe

gardien, ne [gardjɛ̃, -ɛn] *nm/f* (garde) guard; (de prison) warder; (de domaine, réserve) warden; (de musée etc) attendant; (de phare, cimetière) keeper; (d'immeuble) caretaker; (fig) guardian; **~ de but** goalkeeper; **~ de nuit** night watchman; **~ de la paix** police officer

gare [gar] *nf* (railway) station ▷ *excl*: **~ à ... mind ...!; ~ à toi!** watch out!; **~ routière** bus station

garer [gare] /1/ *vt* to park; **se garer** *vi* to park

garni, e [garni] *adj* (plat) served with vegetables (and chips, pasta or rice)

garniture [garnityr] *nf* (Culin) vegetables *pl*; **~ de frein** brake lining

gars [ga] *nm* guy

Gascogne [gaskɔɲ] *nf*: **la ~** Gascony; **le golfe de ~** the Bay of Biscay

gas-oil [gazɔjl] *nm* diesel oil

gaspiller [gaspije] /1/ *vt* to waste

gastronome [gastrɔnɔm] *nm/f* gourmet; **gastronomique** *adj* gastronomic

gâteau, x [gɑto] *nm* cake; **~ sec** biscuit

gâter [gɑte] /1/ *vt* to spoil; **se gâter** *vi* (dent, fruit) to go bad; (temps, situation) to change for the worse

gâteux, -euse [gɑtø, -øz] *adj* senile

gauche [goʃ] *adj* left, left-hand; (maladroit) awkward, clumsy ▷ *nf* (Pol) left (wing); **le bras ~** the left arm; **le côté ~** the left-hand side; **à ~** on the left; (direction) (to the) left; **gaucher, -ère** *adj* left-handed; **gauchiste** *nm/f* leftist

gaufre [gofr] *nf* waffle

gaufrette [gofrɛt] *nf* wafer

gaulois, e [golwa, -waz] *adj* Gallic ▷ *nm/f*: **G~, e** Gaul

gaz [gaz] *nm inv* gas; **ça sent le ~** I can smell gas, there's a smell of gas

gaze [gaz] *nf* gauze

gazette [gazɛt] *nf* news sheet

gazeux, -euse [gazø, -øz] *adj* (eau) sparkling; (boisson) fizzy

gazoduc [gazɔdyk] *nm* gas pipeline

gazon [gazɔ̃] *nm* (herbe) grass; (pelouse) lawn

géant, e [ʒeɑ̃, -ɑ̃t] *adj* gigantic; (Comm) giant-size ▷ *nm/f* giant

geindre [ʒɛ̃dr] /52/ *vi* to groan, moan

gel [ʒɛl] *nm* frost; **~ douche** shower gel

gélatine [ʒelatin] *nf* gelatine

gelé, e [ʒəle] *adj* frozen ▷ *nf* jelly; (gel) frost

geler [ʒ(ə)le] /5/ *vt*, *vi* to freeze; **il gèle** it's freezing

gélule [ʒelyl] *nf* (Méd) capsule

Gémeaux [ʒemo] *nmpl*: **les ~** Gemini

gémir [ʒemir] /2/ *vi* to groan, moan

gênant, e [ʒenɑ̃, -ɑ̃t] *adj* (objet) in the way; (histoire, personne) embarrassing

gencive [ʒɑ̃siv] *nf* gum

gendarme [ʒɑ̃darm] *nm* gendarme; **gendarmerie** *nf* military police force in countryside and small towns; their police station or barracks

gendre [ʒɑ̃dr] *nm* son-in-law

gêné, e [ʒene] *adj* embarrassed

gêner [ʒene] /1/ *vt* (incommoder) to bother; (encombrer) to be in the way of; (embarrasser): **~ qn** to make sb feel ill-at-ease; **se gêner** to put o.s. out; **ne vous gênez pas!** don't mind me!

général, e, -aux [ʒeneral, -o] *adj*, *nm* general; **en ~** usually, in general; **généralement** *adv* generally; **généraliser** /1/ *vt* to generalize; **se généraliser** *vi* to become widespread; **généraliste** *nm/f* general practitioner, GP

génération [ʒeneʀasjɔ̃] nf generation

généreux, -euse [ʒeneʀø, -øz] adj generous

générique [ʒeneʀik] nm (Ciné, TV) credits pl

générosité [ʒeneʀozite] nf generosity

genêt [ʒ(ə)nɛ] nm (Bot) broom no pl

génétique [ʒenetik] adj genetic

Genève [ʒ(ə)nɛv] n Geneva

génial, e, -aux [ʒenjal, -o] adj of genius; (fam: formidable) fantastic, brilliant

génie [ʒeni] nm genius; (Mil): **le ~** ≈ the Engineers pl; **~ civil** civil engineering

genièvre [ʒənjɛvʀ] nm juniper (tree)

génisse [ʒenis] nf heifer

génital, e, -aux [ʒenital, -o] adj genital; **les parties ~es** the genitals

génois, e [ʒenwa, -waz] adj Genoese ▷ nf (gâteau) ≈ sponge cake

génome [ʒenom] nm genome

genou, x [ʒ(ə)nu] nm knee; **à ~x** on one's knees; **se mettre à ~x** to kneel down

genre [ʒɑ̃ʀ] nm kind, type, sort; (Ling) gender; **avoir bon ~** to look a nice sort; **avoir mauvais ~** to be coarse-looking; **ce n'est pas son ~** it's not like him

gens [ʒɑ̃] nmpl (in some phrases) people pl

gentil, le [ʒɑ̃ti, -ij] adj kind; (enfant: sage) good; (sympathique: endroit etc) nice; **gentillesse** nf kindness; **gentiment** adv kindly

géographie [ʒeɔgʀafi] nf geography

géologie [ʒeɔlɔʒi] nf geology

géomètre [ʒeɔmɛtʀ] nm: **(arpenteur-)~** (land) surveyor

géométrie [ʒeɔmetʀi] nf geometry; **géométrique** adj geometric

géranium [ʒeʀanjɔm] nm geranium

gérant, e [ʒeʀɑ̃, -ɑ̃t] nm/f manager/manageress; **~ d'immeuble** managing agent

gerbe [ʒɛʀb] nf (de fleurs, d'eau) spray; (de blé) sheaf

gercé, e [ʒɛʀse] adj chapped

gerçure [ʒɛʀsyʀ] nf crack

gérer [ʒeʀe] /6/ vt to manage

germain, e [ʒɛʀmɛ̃, -ɛn] adj: **cousin ~** first cousin

germe [ʒɛʀm] nm germ; **germer** /1/ vi to sprout; (semence) to germinate

geste [ʒɛst] nm gesture

gestion [ʒɛstjɔ̃] nf management

Ghana [gana] nm: **le ~** Ghana

gibier [ʒibje] nm (animaux) game

gicler [ʒikle] /1/ vi to spurt, squirt

gifle [ʒifl] nf slap (in the face); **gifler** /1/ vt to slap (in the face)

gigantesque [ʒigɑ̃tɛsk] adj gigantic

gigot [ʒigo] nm leg (of mutton ou lamb)

gigoter [ʒigɔte] /1/ vi to wriggle (about)

gilet [ʒilɛ] nm waistcoat; (pull) cardigan; **~ de sauvetage** life jacket

gin [dʒin] nm gin; **~-tonic** gin and tonic

gingembre [ʒɛ̃ʒɑ̃bʀ] nm ginger

girafe [ʒiʀaf] nf giraffe

giratoire [ʒiʀatwaʀ] adj: **sens ~** roundabout

girofle [ʒiʀɔfl] nm: **clou de ~** clove

girouette [ʒiʀwɛt] nf weather vane ou cock

gitan, e [ʒitɑ̃, -an] nm/f gipsy

gîte [ʒit] nm (maison) home; (abri) shelter; **~ (rural)** (country) holiday cottage ou apartment, gîte (self-catering accommodation in the country)

givre [ʒivʀ] nm (hoar) frost; **givré, e** adj covered in frost; (fam: fou) nuts; **citron givré/orange givrée** lemon/orange sorbet (served in fruit skin)

glace [glas] nf ice; (crème glacée) ice cream; (miroir) mirror; (de voiture) window

glacé, e [glase] adj (mains, vent, pluie) freezing; (lac) frozen; (boisson) iced

glacer [glase] /3/ vt to freeze; (gâteau) to ice; **~ qn** (intimider) to chill sb; (fig) to make sb's blood run cold

glacial, e [glasjal] adj icy

glacier [glasje] nm (Géo) glacier; (marchand) ice-cream maker

glacière [glasjɛʀ] nf icebox

glaçon [glasɔ̃] nm icicle; (pour boisson) ice cube

glaïeul [glajœl] nm gladiola

glaise [glɛz] nf clay

gland [glɑ̃] nm acorn; (décoration) tassel

glande [glɑ̃d] nf gland

glissade [glisad] nf (par jeu) slide; (chute) slip; **faire des ~s** to slide

glissant, e [glisɑ̃, -ɑ̃t] adj slippery

glissement [glismɑ̃] nm: **~ de terrain** landslide

glisser [glise] /1/ vi (avancer) to glide ou slide along; (coulisser, tomber) to slide; (déraper) to slip; (être glissant) to be slippery ▷ vt to slip; **se ~ dans/entre** to slip into/between

global, e, -aux [glɔbal, -o] adj overall

globe [glɔb] nm globe

globule [glɔbyl] nm (du sang): **~ blanc/rouge** white/red corpuscle

gloire [glwaʀ] nf glory

glousser [gluse] /1/ vi to cluck; (rire) to chuckle

glouton, ne [glutɔ̃, -ɔn] adj gluttonous

gluant, e [glyɑ̃, -ɑ̃t] adj sticky, gummy

glucose [glykoz] nm glucose

glycine [glisin] nf wisteria

GO sigle fpl (= grandes ondes) LW

goal [gol] nm goalkeeper

gobelet [gɔblɛ] nm (en métal) tumbler; (en plastique) beaker; (à dés) cup

goéland [gɔelɑ̃] nm (sea)gull

goélette [gɔelɛt] nf schooner

goinfre [gwɛ̃fʀ] nm glutton

golf [gɔlf] *nm* golf; (*terrain*) golf course; ~ **miniature** crazy *ou* miniature golf

golfe [gɔlf] *nm* gulf; (*petit*) bay

gomme [gɔm] *nf* (*à effacer*) rubber (BRIT), eraser; **gommer** /1/ *vt* to rub out (BRIT), erase

gonflé, e [gɔ̃fle] *adj* swollen; **il est ~** (*fam: courageux*) he's got some nerve; (: *impertinent*) he's got a nerve

gonfler [gɔ̃fle] /1/ *vt* (*pneu, ballon*) to inflate, blow up; (*nombre, importance*) to inflate ▷ *vi* to swell (up); (*Culin: pâte*) to rise

gonzesse [gɔ̃zɛs] *nf* (*fam*) chick, bird (BRIT)

googler [gugle] /1/ *vt* to google

gorge [gɔʀʒ] *nf* (*Anat*) throat; (*Géo*) gorge

gorgé, e [gɔʀʒe] *adj*: ~ **de** filled with ▷ *nf* (*petite*) sip; (*grande*) gulp

gorille [gɔʀij] *nm* gorilla; (*fam*) bodyguard

gosse [gɔs] *nm/f* kid

goudron [gudʀɔ̃] *nm* tar; **goudronner** /1/ *vt* to tar(mac) (BRIT), asphalt (US)

gouffre [gufʀ] *nm* abyss, gulf

goulot [gulo] *nm* neck; **boire au ~** to drink from the bottle

goulu, e [guly] *adj* greedy

gourde [guʀd] *nf* (*récipient*) flask; (*fam*) (*clumsy*) clot *ou* oaf ▷ *adj* oafish

gourdin [guʀdɛ̃] *nm* club, bludgeon

gourmand, e [guʀmɑ̃, -ɑ̃d] *adj* greedy; **gourmandise** *nf* greed; (*bonbon*) sweet

gousse [gus] *nf*: ~ **d'ail** clove of garlic

goût [gu] *nm* taste; **de bon ~** tasteful; **de mauvais ~** tasteless; **avoir bon/mauvais ~** to taste nice/ nasty; **prendre ~ à** to develop a taste *ou* a liking for

goûter [gute] /1/ *vt* (*essayer*) to taste; (*apprécier*) to enjoy ▷ *vi* to have (afternoon) tea ▷ *nm* (afternoon) tea; **je peux ~?** can I have a taste?

goutte [gut] *nf* drop; (*Méd*) gout; (*alcool*) nip (BRIT), drop (US); **tomber à ~** to drip; **goutte-à-goutte** *nm inv* (*Méd*) drip

gouttière [gutjɛʀ] *nf* gutter

gouvernail [guvɛʀnaj] *nm* rudder; (*barre*) helm, tiller

gouvernement [guvɛʀnəmɑ̃] *nm* government

gouverner [guvɛʀne] /1/ *vt* to govern

grâce [gʀɑs] *nf* (*charme, Rel*) grace; (*faveur*) favour; (*Jur*) pardon; **faire ~ à qn de qch** to spare sb sth; **demander ~** to beg for mercy; ~ **à** thanks to; **gracieux, -euse** *adj* graceful

grade [gʀad] *nm* rank; **monter en ~** to be promoted

gradin [gʀadɛ̃] *nm* tier; (*de stade*) step; **gradins** *nmpl* (*de stade*) terracing *no pl*

gradué, e [gʀadɥe] *adj*: **verre ~** measuring jug

graduel, le [gʀadɥɛl] *adj* gradual

graduer [gʀadɥe] /1/ *vt* (*effort etc*) to increase gradually; (*règle, verre*) to graduate

graffiti [gʀafiti] *nmpl* graffiti

grain [gʀɛ̃] *nm* (*gén*) grain; (*Navig*) squall; ~ **de beauté** beauty spot; ~ **de café** coffee bean; ~ **de poivre** peppercorn

graine [gʀɛn] *nf* seed

graissage [gʀɛsaʒ] *nm* lubrication, greasing

graisse [gʀɛs] *nf* fat; (*lubrifiant*) grease; **graisser** /1/ *vt* to lubricate, grease; (*tacher*) to make greasy; **graisseux, -euse** *adj* greasy

grammaire [gʀamɛʀ] *nf* grammar

gramme [gʀam] *nm* gramme

grand, e [gʀɑ̃, gʀɑ̃d] *adj* (*haut*) tall; (*gros, vaste, large*) big, large; (*long*) long; (*plus âgé*) big; (*adulte*) grown-up; (*important, brillant*) great ▷ *adv*: ~ **ouvert** wide open; **au ~ air** in the open (air); **les ~s blessés/brûlés** the severely injured/burned; ~ **ensemble** housing scheme; ~ **magasin** department store; **~e personne** grown-up; **~e surface** hypermarket; **~es écoles** *prestige university-level colleges with competitive entrance examinations*; **~es lignes** (*Rail*) main lines; **~es vacances** summer holidays (BRIT) *ou* vacation (US); **grand-chose** *nm/f inv*: **pas grand-chose** not much; **Grande-Bretagne** *nf*: **la Grande-Bretagne** (Great) Britain; **grandeur** *nf* (*dimension*) size; **grandeur nature** life-size; **grandiose** *adj* imposing; **grandir** /2/ *vi* to grow; grow ▷ *vt*: **grandir qn** (*vêtement, chaussure*) to make sb look taller; **grand-mère** *nf* grandmother; **grand-peine**: **à grand-peine** *adv* with (great) difficulty; **grand-père** *nm* grandfather; **grands-parents** *nmpl* grandparents

grange [gʀɑ̃ʒ] *nf* barn

granit [gʀanit] *nm* granite

graphique [gʀafik] *adj* graphic ▷ *nm* graph

grappe [gʀap] *nf* cluster; ~ **de raisin** bunch of grapes

gras, se [gʀɑ, gʀɑs] *adj* (*viande, soupe*) fatty; (*personne*) fat; (*main, cheveux*) greasy; (*plaisanterie*) coarse; (*Typo*) bold ▷ *nm* (*Culin*) fat; **faire la ~se matinée** to have a lie-in (BRIT), sleep late; **grassement** *adv*: **grassement payé** handsomely paid

gratifiant, e [gʀatifjɑ̃, -ɑ̃t] *adj* gratifying, rewarding

gratin [gʀatɛ̃] *nm* (*Culin*) cheese- (*ou* crumb-)topped dish (: *croûte*) topping; **tout le ~ parisien** all the best people of Paris; **gratiné** *adj* (*Culin*) au gratin

gratis [gʀatis] *adv* free

gratitude [gʀatityd] *nf* gratitude

gratte-ciel [gʀatsjɛl] *nm inv* skyscraper

gratter [gʀate] /1/ *vt* (*frotter*) to scrape; (*avec un ongle*) to scratch; (*enlever: avec un outil*) to scrape off; (: *avec un ongle*) to scratch off ▷ *vi* (*irriter*) to be scratchy; (*démanger*) to itch; **se gratter** to scratch o.s.

gratuit, e [gratɥi, -ɥit] *adj* (*entrée*) free;
(*fig*) gratuitous

grave [gʀav] *adj* (*maladie, accident*)
serious, bad; (*sujet, problème*) serious,
grave; (*personne, air*) grave, solemn; (*voix,
son*) deep, low-pitched; **gravement** *adv*
seriously; (*parler, regarder*) gravely

graver [gʀave] /1/ *vt* (*plaque, nom*) to
engrave; (*CD, DVD*) to burn

graveur [gʀavœʀ] *nm* engraver; **~ de CD/
DVD** CD/DVD burner *or* writer

gravier [gʀavje] *nm* (loose) gravel *no pl*;
gravillons *nmpl* gravel *sg*

gravir [gʀaviʀ] /2/ *vt* to climb (up)

gravité [gʀavite] *nf* (*de maladie, d'accident*)
seriousness; (*de sujet, problème*) gravity

graviter [gʀavite] /1/ *vi* to revolve

gravure [gʀavyʀ] *nf* engraving;
(*reproduction*) print

gré [gʀe] *nm*: **à son ~** to his liking; **contre
le ~ de qn** against sb's will; **de son** (plein)
~ of one's own free will; **de ~ ou de force**
whether one likes it or not; **de bon ~**
willingly; **bon ~ mal ~** like it or not; **savoir
(bien) ~ à qn de qch** to be (most) grateful
to sb for sth

grec, grecque [gʀɛk] *adj* Greek; (*classique:
vase etc*) Grecian ▷ *nm* (*Ling*) Greek ▷ *nm/f*:
Grec, Grecque Greek

Grèce [gʀɛs] *nf*: **la ~** Greece

greffe [gʀɛf] *nf* (*Bot, Méd: de tissu*) graft;
(*Méd: d'organe*) transplant; **greffer** /1/ *vt*
(*Bot, Méd: tissu*) to graft; (*Méd: organe*) to
transplant

grêle [gʀɛl] *adj* (very) thin ▷ *nf* hail; **grêler**
/1/ *vb impers*: **il grêle** it's hailing; **grêlon** *nm*
hailstone

grelot [gʀəlo] *nm* little bell

grelotter [gʀəlɔte] /1/ *vi* to shiver

grenade [gʀənad] *nf* (*explosive*) grenade;
(*Bot*) pomegranate; **grenadine** *nf*
grenadine

grenier [gʀənje] *nm* attic; (*de ferme*) loft

grenouille [gʀənuj] *nf* frog

grès [gʀɛ] *nm* sandstone; (*poterie*)
stoneware

grève [gʀɛv] *nf* (*d'ouvriers*) strike; (*plage*)
shore; **se mettre en/faire ~** to go on/be on
strike; **~ de la faim** hunger strike;
~ sauvage wildcat strike

gréviste [gʀevist] *nm/f* striker

grièvement [gʀijɛvmɑ̃] *adv* seriously

griffe [gʀif] *nf* claw; (*d'un couturier,
parfumeur*) label; **griffer** /1/ *vt* to scratch

grignoter [gʀiɲɔte] /1/ *vt* (*personne*) to
nibble at; (*souris*) to gnaw at ▷ *vi* to nibble

gril [gʀil] *nm* steak *ou* grill pan; **grillade** *nf*
grill

grillage [gʀijaʒ] *nm* (*treillis*) wire netting;
(*clôture*) wire fencing

grille [gʀij] *nf* (*portail*) (metal) gate; (*clôture*)
railings *pl*; (*d'égout*) (metal) grate; grid

grille-pain [gʀijpɛ̃] *nm inv* toaster

griller [gʀije] /1/ *vt* (*aussi*: **faire ~**) (*pain*)
to toast; (*viande*) to grill; (*châtaignes*) to
roast; (*fig: ampoule etc*) to burn out; **~ un feu
rouge** to jump the lights

grillon [gʀijɔ̃] *nm* cricket

grimace [gʀimas] *nf* grimace; (*pour faire
rire*): **faire des ~s** to pull *ou* make faces

grimper [gʀɛ̃pe] /1/ *vi, vt* to climb

grincer [gʀɛ̃se] /3/ *vi* (*porte, roue*) to grate;
(*plancher*) to creak; **~ des dents** to grind
one's teeth

grincheux, -euse [gʀɛ̃ʃø, -øz] *adj*
grumpy

grippe [gʀip] *nf* flu, influenza; **~ A** swine flu;
~ aviaire bird flu; **grippé, e** *adj*: **être grippé**
to have (the) flu

gris, e [gʀi, gʀiz] *adj* grey; (*ivre*) tipsy

grisaille [gʀizaj] *nf* greyness, dullness

griser [gʀize] /1/ *vt* to intoxicate

grive [gʀiv] *nf* thrush

Groenland [gʀɔɛnlɑ̃d] *nm*: **le ~** Greenland

grogner [gʀɔɲe] /1/ *vi* to growl; (*fig*) to
grumble; **grognon, ne** *adj* grumpy

grommeler [gʀɔmle] /4/ *vi* to mutter
to o.s.

gronder [gʀɔ̃de] /1/ *vi* to rumble; (*fig:
révolte*) to be brewing ▷ *vt* to scold; **se faire
~** to get a telling-off

gros, se [gʀo, gʀos] *adj* big, large; (*obèse*)
fat; (*travaux, dégâts*) extensive; (*large*)
thick; (*rhume, averse*) heavy ▷ *adv*: **risquer/
gagner ~** to risk/win a lot ▷ *nm/f* fat man/
woman ▷ *nm* (*Comm*): **le ~** the wholesale
business; **prix de ~** wholesale price; **par ~
temps/~se mer** in rough weather/heavy
seas; **le ~ de** the bulk of; **en ~** roughly;
(*Comm*) wholesale; **~ lot** jackpot; **~ mot**
swearword; **~ plan** (*Photo*) close-up; **~ sel**
cooking salt; **~ titre** headline; **~se caisse**
big drum

groseille [gʀozɛj] *nf*: **~ (rouge)/(blanche)**
red/white currant; **~ à maquereau**
gooseberry

grosse [gʀos] *adj* f *voir* **gros**; **grossesse** *nf*
pregnancy; **grosseur** *nf* size; (*tumeur*)
lump

grossier, -ière [gʀosje, -jɛʀ] *adj* coarse;
(*insolent*) rude; (*dessin*) rough; (*travail*)
roughly done; (*imitation, instrument*) crude;
(*évident: erreur*) gross; **grossièrement** *adv*
(*vulgairement*) coarsely; (*sommairement*)
roughly; crudely; (*en gros*) roughly;
grossièreté *nf* rudeness; (*mot*): **dire des
grossièretés** to use coarse language

grossir [gʀosiʀ] /2/ *vi* (*personne*) to put on
weight ▷ *vt* (*exagérer*) to exaggerate; (*au
microscope*) to magnify; (*vêtement*): **~ qn** to
make sb look fatter

grossiste [gʀosist] *nm/f* wholesaler

grotesque [gʀɔtɛsk] *adj* (*extravagant*)
grotesque; (*ridicule*) ludicrous

grotte [grɔt] nf cave
groupe [grup] nm group; ~ **de parole** support group; ~ **sanguin** blood group; ~ **scolaire** school complex; **grouper** /1/ vt to group; **se grouper** vi to get together
grue [gry] nf crane
GSM [ʒeɛsɛm] nm, adj GSM
guenon [gənɔ̃] nf female monkey
guépard [gepar] nm cheetah
guêpe [gɛp] nf wasp
guère [gɛr] adv (avec adjectif, adverbe): **ne ... ~** hardly; (avec verbe: pas beaucoup): **ne ... ~** (tournure négative) much; (pas souvent) hardly ever; (tournure négative) (very) long; **il n'y a ~ que/de** there's hardly anybody (ou anything) but/hardly any; **ce n'est ~ difficile** it's hardly difficult; **nous n'avons ~ de temps** we have hardly any time
guérilla [gerija] nf guerrilla warfare
guérillero [gerijero] nm guerrilla
guérir [gerir] /2/ vt (personne, maladie) to cure; (membre, plaie) to heal ▷ vi (personne, malade) to recover, be cured; (maladie) to be cured; (plaie, chagrin, blessure) to heal; **guérison** nf (de maladie) curing; (de membre, plaie) healing; (de malade) recovery; **guérisseur, -euse** nm/f healer
guerre [gɛr] nf war; **en ~** at war; **faire la ~ à** to wage war against; ~ **civile/mondiale** civil/world war; **guerrier, -ière** adj warlike ▷ nm/f warrior
guet [gɛ] nm: **faire le ~** to be on the watch ou look-out; **guet-apens** [gɛtapɑ̃] nm ambush; **guetter** /1/ vt (épier) to watch (intently); (attendre) to watch (out) for; (: pour surprendre) to be lying in wait for
gueule [gœl] nf (d'animal) mouth; (fam: visage) mug; (: bouche) gob (!), mouth; **ta ~!** (fam) shut up!; **avoir la ~ de bois** (fam) to have a hangover, be hung over; **gueuler** /1/ vi to bawl
gui [gi] nm mistletoe
guichet [giʃɛ] nm (de bureau, banque) counter; **les ~s** (à la gare, au théâtre) the ticket office
guide [gid] nm (personne) guide; (livre) guide(book) ▷ nf (fille scout) (girl) guide; **guider** /1/ vt to guide
guidon [gidɔ̃] nm handlebars pl
guignol [giɲɔl] nm ≈ Punch and Judy show; (fig) clown
guillemets [gijmɛ] nmpl: **entre ~** in inverted commas ou quotation marks
guindé, e [gɛ̃de] adj (personne, air) stiff, starchy; (style) stilted
Guinée [gine] nf: **la (République de) ~** (the Republic of) Guinea
guirlande [girlɑ̃d] nf (fleurs) garland; ~ **de Noël** tinsel no pl
guise [giz] nf: **à votre ~** as you wish ou please; **en ~ de** by way of

guitare [gitar] nf guitar
Guyane [gɥijan] nf: **la ~ (française)** (French) Guiana
gym [ʒim] nf (exercices) gym; **gymnase** nm gym(nasium); **gymnaste** nm/f gymnast; **gymnastique** nf gymnastics sg; (au réveil etc) keep-fit exercises pl
gynécologie [ʒinekɔlɔʒi] nf gynaecology; **gynécologique** adj gynaecological; **gynécologue** nm/f gynaecologist

h

habile [abil] *adj* skilful; (*malin*) clever; **habileté** [abilte] *nf* skill, skilfulness; cleverness

habillé, e [abije] *adj* dressed; (*chic*) dressy

habiller [abije] /1/ *vt* to dress; (*fournir en vêtements*) to clothe; (*couvrir*) to cover; **s'habiller** *vi* to dress (o.s.); (*se déguiser, mettre des vêtements chic*) to dress up

habit [abi] *nm* outfit; **habits** *nmpl* (*vêtements*) clothes; **~ (de soirée)** evening dress; (*pour homme*) tails *pl*

habitant, e [abitɑ̃, -ɑ̃t] *nm/f* inhabitant; (*d'une maison*) occupant; **loger chez l'~** to stay with the locals

habitation [abitasjɔ̃] *nf* house; **~s à loyer modéré (HLM)** ≈ council flats

habiter [abite] /1/ *vt* to live in ▷ *vi*: **~ à/ dans** to live in *ou* at/in

habitude [abityd] *nf* habit; **avoir l'~ de faire** to be in the habit of doing; (*expérience*) to be used to doing; **avoir l'~ des enfants** to be used to children; **d'~** usually; **comme d'~** as usual

habitué, e [abitɥe] *nm/f* (*de maison*) regular visitor; (*client*) regular (customer)

habituel, le [abitɥɛl] *adj* usual

habituer [abitɥe] /1/ *vt*: **~ qn à** to get sb used to; **s'habituer à** to get used to

hache ['aʃ] *nf* axe

hacher ['aʃe] /1/ *vt* (*viande*) to mince; (*persil*) to chop; **hachis** *nm* mince *no pl*; **hachis Parmentier** ≈ shepherd's pie

haie ['ɛ] *nf* hedge; (*Sport*) hurdle

haillons ['ajɔ̃] *nmpl* rags

haine ['ɛn] *nf* hatred

haïr ['aiʀ] /10/ *vt* to detest, hate

hâlé, e ['ɑle] *adj* (sun)tanned, sunburnt

haleine [alɛn] *nf* breath; **hors d'~** out of breath; **tenir en ~** (*attention*) to hold spellbound; (*en attente*) to keep in suspense; **de longue ~** long-term

haleter ['alte] /5/ *vi* to pant

hall ['ol] *nm* hall

halle ['al] *nf* (covered) market; **halles** *nfpl* (*d'une grande ville*) central food market *sg*

hallucination [alysinasjɔ̃] *nf* hallucination

halte ['alt] *nf* stop, break; (*escale*) stopping place ▷ *excl* stop!; **faire ~** to stop

haltère [altɛʀ] *nm* dumbbell, barbell; **(poids et) ~s** (*activité*) weightlifting *sg*; **haltérophilie** *nf* weightlifting

hamac ['amak] *nm* hammock

hamburger ['ɑ̃buʀgœʀ] *nm* hamburger

hameau, x ['amo] *nm* hamlet

hameçon [amsɔ̃] *nm* (fish) hook

hamster ['amstɛʀ] *nm* hamster

hanche ['ɑ̃ʃ] *nf* hip

hand-ball ['ɑ̃dbal] *nm* handball

handicapé, e ['ɑ̃dikape] *adj* disabled ▷ *nm/f* person with a disability; **~ mental/ physique** person with a mental/physical disability; **~ moteur** person with a movement disorder

hangar ['ɑ̃gaʀ] *nm* shed; (*Aviat*) hangar

hanneton ['antɔ̃] *nm* cockchafer

hanter ['ɑ̃te] /1/ *vt* to haunt

hantise ['ɑ̃tiz] *nf* obsessive fear

harceler ['aʀsəle] /5/ *vt* to harass; **~ qn de questions** to plague sb with questions

hardi, e ['aʀdi] *adj* bold, daring

hareng ['aʀɑ̃] *nm* herring; **~ saur** kipper, smoked herring

hargne ['aʀɲ] *nf* aggressivity, aggressiveness; **hargneux, -euse** *adj* aggressive

haricot ['aʀiko] *nm* bean; **~ blanc/rouge** haricot/kidney bean; **~ vert** French (*BRIT*) *ou* green bean

harmonica [aʀmɔnika] *nm* mouth organ

harmonie [aʀmɔni] *nf* harmony; **harmonieux, -euse** *adj* harmonious; (*couleurs, couple*) well-matched

harpe ['aʀp] *nf* harp

hasard ['azaʀ] *nm*: **le ~** chance, fate; **un ~** a coincidence; **au ~** (*sans but*) aimlessly; (*à l'aveuglette*) at random; **par ~** by chance; **à tout ~** (*en espérant trouver ce qu'on cherche*) on the off chance; (*en cas de besoin*) just in case

hâte ['ɑt] *nf* haste; **à la ~** hurriedly, hastily; **en ~** posthaste, with all possible speed; **avoir ~ de** to be eager *ou* anxious to; **hâter** /1/ *vt* to hasten; **se hâter** to hurry; **hâtif, -ive** *adj* (*travail*) hurried; (*décision*) hasty

hausse ['os] *nf* rise, increase; **être en ~** to be going up; **hausser** /1/ *vt* to raise; **hausser les épaules** to shrug (one's shoulders)

haut, e ['o, 'ot] *adj* high; (*grand*) tall ▷ *adv* high ▷ *nm* top (part); **de 3 m de ~** 3 m high, 3 m in height; **en ~ lieu** in high places; **à ~e voix, (tout) ~** aloud, out loud; **des ~s et des**

bas ups and downs; **du ~ de** from the top of; **de ~ en bas** from top to bottom; **plus ~** higher up, further up; (*dans un texte*) above; (*parler*) louder; **en ~ (être/aller)** at (*ou* to) the top; (*dans une maison*) upstairs; **en ~ de** at the top of; **~ débit** broadband

'**hautain, e** [otɛ̃, -ɛn] *adj* haughty

'**hautbois** ['obwa] *nm* oboe

'**hauteur** ['otœʀ] *nf* height; **à la ~ de** (*sur la même ligne*) level with; (*fig: tâche, situation*) equal to; **à la ~** (*fig*) up to it

'**haut-parleur** ['oparlœʀ] *nm* (loud) speaker

Hawaï [awai] *n* Hawaii; **les îles ~** the Hawaiian Islands

'**Haye** ['ɛ] *n*: **la ~** the Hague

hebdomadaire [ɛbdɔmadɛʀ] *adj, nm* weekly

hébergement [ebɛʀʒəmɑ̃] *nm* accommodation

héberger [ebɛʀʒe] /3/ *vt* (*touristes*) to accommodate, lodge; (*amis*) to put up; (*réfugiés*) to take in

hébergeur [ebɛʀʒœʀ] *nm* (*Internet*) host

hébreu, x [ebʀø] *adj m, nm* Hebrew

Hébrides [ebʀid] *nf*: **les ~** the Hebrides

hectare [ɛktaʀ] *nm* hectare

'**hein** ['ɛ̃] *excl* eh?

'**hélas** ['elɑs] *excl* alas! ▷ *adv* unfortunately

'**héler** ['ele] /6/ *vt* to hail

hélice [elis] *nf* propeller

hélicoptère [elikɔptɛʀ] *nm* helicopter

helvétique [ɛlvetik] *adj* Swiss

hématome [ematom] *nm* haematoma

hémisphère [emisfɛʀ] *nm*: **~ nord/sud** northern/southern hemisphere

hémorragie [emɔʀaʒi] *nf* bleeding *no pl*, haemorrhage

hémorroïdes [emɔʀɔid] *nfpl* piles, haemorrhoids

'**hennir** ['enir] /2/ *vi* to neigh, whinny

hépatite [epatit] *nf* hepatitis

herbe [ɛʀb] *nf* grass; (*Culin, Méd*) herb; **~s de Provence** mixed herbs; **en ~** unripe; (*fig*) budding; **herbicide** *nm* weed-killer; **herboriste** *nm/f* herbalist

héréditaire [eʀeditɛʀ] *adj* hereditary

'**hérisson** ['eʀisɔ̃] *nm* hedgehog

héritage [eʀitaʒ] *nm* inheritance; (*coutumes, système*) heritage; legacy

hériter [eʀite] /1/ *vi*: **~ de qch (de qn)** to inherit sth (from sb); **héritier, -ière** *nm/f* heir/heiress

hermétique [ɛʀmetik] *adj* airtight; (*à l'eau*) watertight; (*fig: écrivain, style*) abstruse; (: *visage*) impenetrable

hermine [ɛʀmin] *nf* ermine

'**hernie** ['ɛʀni] *nf* hernia

héroïne [eʀɔin] *nf* heroine; (*drogue*) heroin

héroïque [eʀɔik] *adj* heroic

'**héron** ['eʀɔ̃] *nm* heron

'**héros** ['eʀo] *nm* hero

hésitant, e [ezitɑ̃, -ɑ̃t] *adj* hesitant

hésitation [ezitasjɔ̃] *nf* hesitation

hésiter [ezite] /1/ *vi*: **~ (à faire)** to hesitate (to do)

hétérosexuel, le [eteʀɔsɛkɥɛl] *adj* heterosexual

'**hêtre** ['ɛtʀ] *nm* beech

heure [œʀ] *nf* hour; (*Scol*) period; (*moment, moment fixé*) time; **c'est l'~** it's time; **quelle ~ est-il?** what time is it?; **2 ~s (du matin)** 2 o'clock (in the morning); **être à l'~** to be on time; (*montre*) to be right; **mettre à l'~** to set right; **à toute ~** at any time; **24 ~s sur 24** round the clock, 24 hours a day; **à l'~ qu'il est** at this time (of day), (*fig*) now; **à l'~ actuelle** at the present time; **sur l'~** at once; **à une ~ avancée (de la nuit)** at a late hour (of the night); **de bonne ~** early; **~ de pointe** rush hour; (*téléphone*) peak period; **~s de bureau** office hours; **~s supplémentaires** overtime *sg*

heureusement [œʀøzmɑ̃] *adv* (*par bonheur*) fortunately, luckily

heureux, -euse [œʀø, -øz] *adj* happy; (*chanceux*) lucky, fortunate

'**heurt** ['œʀ] *nm* (*choc*) collision

'**heurter** ['œʀte] /1/ *vt* (*mur*) to strike, hit; (*personne*) to collide with

hexagone [ɛgzagɔn] *nm* hexagon; **l'H~** (*la France*) France (*because of its roughly hexagonal shape*)

hiberner [ibɛʀne] /1/ *vi* to hibernate

'**hibou, x** ['ibu] *nm* owl

'**hideux, -euse** ['idø, -øz] *adj* hideous

'**hier** [jɛʀ] *adv* yesterday; **~ matin/soir/midi** yesterday morning/evening/lunchtime; **toute la journée d'~** all day yesterday; **toute la matinée d'~** all yesterday morning

'**hiérarchie** ['jeʀaʀʃi] *nf* hierarchy

hindou, e [ɛ̃du] *adj* Hindu ▷ *nm/f*: **H~, e** Hindu; (*Indien*) Indian

hippique [ipik] *adj* equestrian, horse *cpd*; **un club ~** a riding centre; **un concours ~** a horse show; **hippisme** [ipism] *nm* (horse-) riding

hippodrome [ipodʀom] *nm* racecourse

hippopotame [ipopotam] *nm* hippopotamus

hirondelle [iʀɔ̃dɛl] *nf* swallow

'**hisser** ['ise] /1/ *vt* to hoist, haul up

histoire [istwaʀ] *nf* (*science, événements*) history; (*anecdote, récit, mensonge*) story; (*affaire*) business *no pl*; (*chichis: gén pl*) fuss *no pl*; **histoires** *nfpl* (*ennuis*) trouble *sg*; **~ géo** humanities *pl*; **historique** *adj* historical; (*important*) historic ▷ *nm*: **faire l'historique de** to give the background to

'**hit-parade** ['itpaʀad] *nm*: **le ~** the charts

hiver [ivɛʀ] nm winter; **hivernal, e, -aux**
adj winter cpd; (comme en hiver) wintry;
hiverner /1/ vi to winter

HLM sigle m ou f (= habitations à loyer modéré)
low-rent, state-owned housing; **un(e) ~** ≈ a
council flat (ou house)

'hobby ['ɔbi] nm hobby

'hocher ['ɔʃe] /1/ vt: **~ la tête** to nod; (signe
négatif ou dubitatif) to shake one's head

'hockey ['ɔkɛ] nm: **~ (sur glace/gazon)**
(ice/field) hockey

'hold-up ['ɔldœp] nm inv hold-up

'hollandais, e ['ɔlɑ̃dɛ, -ɛz] adj Dutch ▷ nm
(Ling) Dutch ▷ nm/f: **H~, e** Dutchman/
woman

'Hollande ['ɔlɑ̃d] nf: **la ~** Holland

'homard ['ɔmaʀ] nm lobster

homéopathique [ɔmeɔpatik] adj
homoeopathic

homicide [ɔmisid] nm murder;
~ involontaire manslaughter

hommage [ɔmaʒ] nm tribute; **rendre ~ à**
to pay tribute to

homme [ɔm] nm man; **~ d'affaires**
businessman; **~ d'État** statesman; **~ de
main** hired man; **~ de paille** stooge; **~
politique** politician; **l'~ de la rue** the man
in the street

homogène adj homogeneous

homologue nm/f counterpart

homologué, e adj (Sport) ratified; (tarif)
authorized

homonyme nm (Ling) homonym; (d'une
personne) namesake

homoparental, e, -aux [ɔmɔpaʀɑ̃tal, o]
adj (famille) same-sex

homosexuel, le adj homosexual

'Hong-Kong ['ɔ̃gkɔ̃g] n Hong Kong

'Hongrie ['ɔ̃gʀi] nf: **la ~** Hungary;
'hongrois, e adj Hungarian ▷ nm (Ling)
Hungarian ▷ nm/f: **Hongrois, e** Hungarian

honnête [ɔnɛt] adj (intègre) honest; (juste,
satisfaisant) fair; **honnêtement** adv
honestly; **honnêteté** nf honesty

honneur [ɔnœʀ] nm honour; (mérite): **l'~ lui
revient** the credit is his; **en l'~ de** (personne)
in honour of; (événement) on the occasion of;
faire ~ à (engagements) to honour; (famille,
professeur) to be a credit to; (fig: repas etc) to
do justice to

honorable [ɔnɔʀabl] adj worthy,
honourable; (suffisant) decent

honoraire [ɔnɔʀɛʀ] adj honorary;
honoraires nmpl fees; **professeur ~**
professor emeritus

honorer [ɔnɔʀe] /1/ vt to honour; (estimer)
to hold in high regard; (faire honneur à) to
do credit to

'honte ['ɔ̃t] nf shame; **avoir ~ de** to be
ashamed of; **faire ~ à qn** to make sb (feel)
ashamed; **'honteux, -euse** adj ashamed;
(conduite, acte) shameful, disgraceful

hôpital, -aux [ɔpital, -o] nm hospital; **où
est l'~ le plus proche?** where is the nearest
hospital?

'hoquet ['ɔkɛ] nm: **avoir le ~** to have (the)
hiccups

horaire [ɔʀɛʀ] adj hourly ▷ nm timetable,
schedule; **horaires** nmpl (heures de travail)
hours; **~ flexible ou mobile ou à la carte ou
souple** flex(i)time

horizon [ɔʀizɔ̃] nm horizon

horizontal, e, -aux adj horizontal

horloge [ɔʀlɔʒ] nf clock; **l'~ parlante**
the speaking clock; **horloger, -ère** nm/f
watchmaker; clockmaker

'hormis ['ɔʀmi] prép save

horoscope [ɔʀɔskɔp] nm horoscope

horreur [ɔʀœʀ] nf horror; **quelle ~!** how
awful!; **avoir ~ de** to loathe ou detest;
horrible adj horrible; **horrifier** /7/ vt to
horrify

'hors ['ɔʀ] prép: **~ de** out of; **~ pair**
outstanding; **~ de propos** inopportune;
~ service (HS), ~ d'usage out of service;
être ~ de soi to be beside o.s.; **'hors-bord**
nm inv speedboat (with outboard motor);
'hors-d'œuvre nm inv hors d'œuvre;
'hors-la-loi nm inv outlaw; **'hors-taxe** adj
duty-free

hortensia [ɔʀtɑ̃sja] nm hydrangea

hospice [ɔspis] nm (de vieillards) home

hospitalier, -ière [ɔspitalje, -jɛʀ] adj
(accueillant) hospitable; (Méd: service, centre)
hospital cpd

hospitaliser [ɔspitalize] /1/ vt to take (ou
send) to hospital, hospitalize

hospitalité [ɔspitalite] nf hospitality

hostie [ɔsti] nf host

hostile [ɔstil] adj hostile; **hostilité** nf
hostility

hôte [ot] nm (maître de maison) host ▷ nm/f
(invité) guest

hôtel [otɛl] nm hotel; **aller à l'~** to stay in
a hotel; **~ (particulier)** (private) mansion;
~ de ville town hall; see note **"hôtels"**;
hôtellerie [otɛlʀi] nf hotel business

HÔTELS

There are six categories of hotel in
France, from zero ('non classé') to four
stars and luxury four stars ('quatre étoiles
luxe'). Prices include VAT but not
breakfast. In some towns, guests pay a
small additional tourist tax, the 'taxe de
séjour'.

hôtesse [otɛs] nf hostess; **~ de l'air** flight
attendant

'houblon ['ublɔ̃] nm (Bot) hop; (pour la bière)
hops pl

'houille ['uj] nf coal; **~ blanche**
hydroelectric power

'houle ['ul] *nf* swell; **'houleux, -euse** *adj* stormy
'hourra ['uʀa] *excl* hurrah!
'housse ['us] *nf* cover
'houx ['u] *nm* holly
hovercraft [ovœʀkʀaft] *nm* hovercraft
'hublot ['yblo] *nm* porthole
'huche ['yʃ] *nf*: **huche à pain** bread bin
'huer ['ɥe] /1/ *vt* to boo
huile [ɥil] *nf* oil
huissier [ɥisje] *nm* usher; (*Jur*) ≈ bailiff
'huit ['ɥi(t)] *num* eight; **samedi en ~** a week on Saturday; **dans ~ jours** in a week('s time); **'huitaine** *nf*: **une huitaine de jours** a week or so; **'huitième** *num* eighth
huître [ɥitʀ] *nf* oyster
humain, e [ymɛ̃, -ɛn] *adj* human; (*compatissant*) humane ▷ *nm* human (being); **humanitaire** *adj* humanitarian; **humanité** *nf* humanity
humble [œ̃bl] *adj* humble
'humer ['yme] /1/ *vt* (*parfum*) to inhale; (*pour sentir*) to smell
humeur [ymœʀ] *nf* mood; **de bonne/ mauvaise ~** in a good/bad mood
humide [ymid] *adj* damp; (*main, yeux*) moist; (*climat, chaleur*) humid; (*saison, route*) wet
humilier [ymilje] /7/ *vt* to humiliate
humilité [ymilite] *nf* humility, humbleness
humoristique [ymɔʀistik] *adj* humorous
humour [ymuʀ] *nm* humour; **avoir de l'~** to have a sense of humour; **~ noir** sick humour
'huppé, e ['ype] *adj* (*fam*) posh
'hurlement ['yʀləmɑ̃] *nm* howling *no pl*, howl; yelling *no pl*, yell
'hurler ['yʀle] /1/ *vi* to howl, yell
'hutte ['yt] *nf* hut
hydratant, e [idʀatɑ̃, -ɑ̃t] *adj* (*crème*) moisturizing
hydraulique [idʀolik] *adj* hydraulic
hydravion [idʀavjɔ̃] *nm* seaplane
hydrogène [idʀɔʒɛn] *nm* hydrogen
hydroglisseur [idʀɔglisœʀ] *nm* hydroplane
hyène [jɛn] *nf* hyena
hygiène [iʒjɛn] *nf* hygiene
hygiénique [iʒenik] *adj* hygienic
hymne [imn] *nm* hymn
hyperlien [ipɛʀljɛ̃] *nm* hyperlink
hypermarché [ipɛʀmaʀʃe] *nm* hypermarket
hypermétrope [ipɛʀmetʀɔp] *adj* long-sighted
hypertension [ipɛʀtɑ̃sjɔ̃] *nf* high blood pressure
hypnose [ipnoz] *nf* hypnosis; **hypnotiser** /1/ *vt* to hypnotize

hypocrisie [ipɔkʀizi] *nf* hypocrisy; **hypocrite** *adj* hypocritical
hypothèque [ipɔtɛk] *nf* mortgage
hypothèse [ipɔtɛz] *nf* hypothesis
hystérique [isteʀik] *adj* hysterical

I

iceberg [isbɛʀg] *nm* iceberg
ici [isi] *adv* here; **jusqu'~** as far as this; (*temporel*) until now; **d'~ là** by then; **d'~ demain** by tomorrow; in the meantime; **d'~ peu** before long
icône [ikon] *nf* icon
idéal, e, -aux [ideal, -o] *adj* ideal ▷ *nm* ideal; **idéaliste** *adj* idealistic ▷ *nm/f* idealist
idée [ide] *nf* idea; **se faire des ~s** to imagine things, get ideas into one's head; **avoir dans l'~ que** to have an idea that; **~s noires** black *ou* dark thoughts; **~s reçues** accepted ideas *ou* wisdom
identifier [idãtifje] /7/ *vt* to identify; **s'identifier** *vi*; **s'~ avec** *ou* **à qn/qch** (*héros etc*) to identify with sb/sth
identique [idãtik] *adj*: **~ (à)** identical (to)
identité [idãtite] *nf* identity
idiot, e [idjo, idjɔt] *adj* idiotic ▷ *nm/f* idiot
idole [idɔl] *nf* idol
if [if] *nm* yew
ignoble [iɲɔbl] *adj* vile
ignorant, e [iɲɔʀã, -ãt] *adj* ignorant; **~ de** ignorant of, not aware of
ignorer [iɲɔʀe] /1/ *vt* not to know; (*personne*) to ignore
il [il] *pron* he; (*animal, chose, en tournure impersonnelle*) it; **il neige** it's snowing; **Pierre est-il arrivé?** has Pierre arrived?; **il a gagné** he won; *voir aussi* **avoir**
île [il] *nf* island; **l'~ Maurice** Mauritius; **les ~s anglo-normandes** the Channel Islands; **les ~s Britanniques** the British Isles
illégal, e, -aux [ilegal, -o] *adj* illegal
illimité, e [ilimite] *adj* unlimited
illisible [ilizibl] *adj* illegible; (*roman*) unreadable
illogique [ilɔʒik] *adj* illogical
illuminer [ilymine] /1/ *vt* to light up; (*monument, rue: pour une fête*) to illuminate; (*: au moyen de projecteurs*) floodlight

illusion [ilyzjɔ̃] *nf* illusion; **se faire des ~s** to delude o.s.; **faire ~** to delude *ou* fool people
illustration [ilystʀasjɔ̃] *nf* illustration
illustré, e [ilystʀe] *adj* illustrated ▷ *nm* comic
illustrer [ilystʀe] /1/ *vt* to illustrate; **s'illustrer** to become famous, win fame
ils [il] *pron* they
image [imaʒ] *nf* (*gén*) picture; (*comparaison, ressemblance*) image; **~ de marque** brand image; (*d'une personne*) (*public*) image; **imagé, e** *adj* (*texte*) full of imagery; (*language*) colourful
imaginaire [imaʒinɛʀ] *adj* imaginary
imagination [imaʒinasjɔ̃] *nf* imagination; **avoir de l'~** to be imaginative
imaginer [imaʒine] /1/ *vt* to imagine; (*inventer: expédient, mesure*) to devise, think up; **s'imaginer** *vt* (*se figurer: scène etc*) to imagine, picture; **s'~ que** to imagine that
imam [imam] *nm* imam
imbécile [ɛ̃besil] *adj* idiotic ▷ *nm/f* idiot
imbu, e [ɛ̃by] *adj*: **~ de** full of
imitateur, -trice [imitatœʀ, -tʀis] *nm/f* (*gén*) imitator; (*Music-Hall*) impersonator
imitation [imitasjɔ̃] *nf* imitation, (*de personnalité*) impersonation
imiter [imite] /1/ *vt* to imitate; (*contrefaire*) to forge; (*ressembler à*) to look like
immangeable [ɛ̃mãʒabl] *adj* inedible
immatriculation [imatʀikylasjɔ̃] *nf* registration

IMMATRICULATION

- The last two numbers on vehicle licence
- plates used to show which 'département'
- of France the vehicle was registered in.
- For example, a car registered in Paris had
- the number 75 on its licence plates. In
- 2009, a new alphanumeric system was
- introduced, in which the 'département'
- number no longer features. Displaying
- this number to the right of the plate is
- now optional.

---

immatriculer [imatʀikyle] /1/ *vt* to register; **faire/se faire ~** to register
immédiat, e [imedja, -at] *adj* immediate ▷ *nm*: **dans l'~** for the time being; **immédiatement** *adv* immediately
immense [imãs] *adj* immense
immerger [imɛʀʒe] /3/ *vt* to immerse, submerge
immeuble [imœbl] *nm* building; **~ locatif** block of rented flats
immigration [imigʀasjɔ̃] *nf* immigration
immigré, e [imigʀe] *nm/f* immigrant
imminent, e [iminã, -ãt] *adj* imminent
immobile [imɔbil] *adj* still, motionless

immobilier, -ière [imɔbilje, -jɛʀ] adj
property cpd ▷ nm: l'~ the property ou the
real estate business

immobiliser [imɔbilize] /1/ vt (gén) to
immobilize; (circulation, véhicule, affaires)
to bring to a standstill; **s'immobiliser**
(personne) to stand still; (machine, véhicule)
to come to a halt ou a standstill

immoral, e, -aux [imɔʀal, -o] adj immoral

immortel, le [imɔʀtɛl] adj immortal

immunisé, e [im(m)ynize] adj: ~ contre
immune to

immunité [imynite] nf immunity

impact [ɛ̃pakt] nm impact

impair [ɛ̃pɛʀ] adj odd ▷ nm faux pas,
blunder

impardonnable [ɛ̃paʀdɔnabl] adj
unpardonable, unforgivable

imparfait, e [ɛ̃paʀfɛ, -ɛt] adj imperfect

impartial, e, -aux [ɛ̃paʀsjal, -o] adj
impartial, unbiased

impasse [ɛ̃pɑs] nf dead-end, cul-de-sac;
(fig) deadlock

impassible [ɛ̃pasibl] adj impassive

impatience [ɛ̃pasjɑ̃s] nf impatience

impatient, e [ɛ̃pasjɑ̃, -ɑ̃t] adj impatient;
impatienter /1/: **s'impatienter** vi to get
impatient

impeccable [ɛ̃pekabl] adj faultless; (propre)
spotlessly clean; (fam) smashing

impensable [ɛ̃pɑ̃sabl] adj (événement
hypothétique) unthinkable; (événement qui a
eu lieu) unbelievable

impératif, -ive [ɛ̃peʀatif, -iv] adj
imperative ▷ nm (Ling) imperative;
impératifs nmpl (exigences: d'une fonction,
d'une charge) requirements; (: de la mode)
demands

impératrice [ɛ̃peʀatʀis] nf empress

imperceptible [ɛ̃pɛʀsɛptibl] adj
imperceptible

impérial, e, -aux [ɛ̃peʀjal, -o] adj
imperial

impérieux, -euse [ɛ̃peʀjø, -øz] adj
(caractère, ton) imperious; (obligation, besoin)
pressing, urgent

impérissable [ɛ̃peʀisabl] adj undying

imperméable [ɛ̃pɛʀmeabl] adj
waterproof; (fig): ~ à impervious to ▷ nm
raincoat

impertinent, e [ɛ̃pɛʀtinɑ̃, -ɑ̃t] adj
impertinent

impitoyable [ɛ̃pitwajabl] adj pitiless,
merciless

implanter [ɛ̃plɑ̃te] /1/: **s'implanter dans**
vi to be established in

impliquer [ɛ̃plike] /1/ vt to imply; ~ qn
(dans) to implicate sb (in)

impoli, e [ɛ̃pɔli] adj impolite, rude

impopulaire [ɛ̃pɔpylɛʀ] adj unpopular

importance [ɛ̃pɔʀtɑ̃s] nf importance;
(de somme) size; **sans ~** unimportant

important, e [ɛ̃pɔʀtɑ̃, -ɑ̃t] adj important;
(en quantité: somme, retard) considerable,
sizeable; (: gamme, dégâts) extensive; (péj:
airs, ton) self-important ▷ nm: l'~ the
important thing

importateur, -trice [ɛ̃pɔʀtatœʀ, -tʀis]
nm/f importer

importation [ɛ̃pɔʀtasjɔ̃] nf (produit)
import

importer [ɛ̃pɔʀte] /1/ vt (Comm) to import;
(maladies, plantes) to introduce ▷ vi (être
important) to matter; **il importe qu'il fasse**
it is important that he should do; **peu
m'importe** (je n'ai pas de préférence) I don't
mind; (je m'en moque) I don't care; **peu
importe (que)** it doesn't matter (if); voir
aussi **n'importe**

importun, e [ɛ̃pɔʀtœ̃, -yn] adj irksome,
importunate; (arrivée, visite) inopportune,
ill-timed ▷ nm intruder; **importuner** /1/ vt
to bother

imposant, e [ɛ̃pozɑ̃, -ɑ̃t] adj imposing

imposer [ɛ̃poze] /1/ vt (taxer) to tax;
~ **qch à qn** to impose sth on sb; **s'imposer**
(être nécessaire) to be imperative; **en ~ à**
to impress; **s'~ comme** to emerge as; **s'~
par** to win recognition through

impossible [ɛ̃pɔsibl] adj impossible; **il
m'est ~ de le faire** it is impossible for
me to do it, I can't possibly do it; **faire l'~
(pour que)** to do one's utmost (so that)

imposteur [ɛ̃pɔstœʀ] nm impostor

impôt [ɛ̃po] nm tax; ~ **sur le chiffre
d'affaires** corporation (BRIT) ou corporate
(US) tax; ~ **foncier** land tax; ~ **sur le revenu**
income tax; ~**s locaux** rates, local taxes
(US), ≈ council tax (BRIT)

impotent, e [ɛ̃pɔtɑ̃, -ɑ̃t] adj disabled

impraticable [ɛ̃pʀatikabl] adj (projet)
impracticable, unworkable; (piste)
impassable

imprécis, e [ɛ̃pʀesi, -iz] adj imprecise

imprégner [ɛ̃pʀeɲe] /6/ vt: ~ (de) (tissu,
tampon) to soak ou impregnate (with); (lieu,
air) to fill (with); **s'imprégner de** (fig) to
absorb

imprenable [ɛ̃pʀənabl] adj (forteresse)
impregnable; **vue ~** unimpeded outlook

impression [ɛ̃pʀesjɔ̃] nf impression;
(d'un ouvrage, tissu) printing; **faire
bonne/mauvaise ~** to make a good/
bad impression; **impressionnant, e** adj
(imposant) impressive; (bouleversant)
upsetting; **impressionner** /1/ vt (frapper) to
impress; (troubler) to upset

imprévisible [ɛ̃pʀevizibl] adj unforeseeable

imprévu, e [ɛ̃pʀevy] adj unforeseen,
unexpected ▷ nm (incident) unexpected
incident; **des vacances pleines d'~**
holidays full of surprises; **en cas d'~** if
anything unexpected happens; **sauf ~**
unless anything unexpected crops up

imprimante [ɛ̃pʀimɑ̃t] nf printer; **~ à laser** laser printer

imprimé [ɛ̃pʀime] nm (formulaire) printed form; (Postes) printed matter no pl; (tissu) printed fabric; **un ~ à fleurs/pois** (tissu) a floral/polka-dot print

imprimer [ɛ̃pʀime] /1/ vt to print; (publier) to publish; **imprimerie** nf printing; (établissement) printing works sg; **imprimeur** nm printer

impropre [ɛ̃pʀɔpʀ] adj inappropriate; **~ à** unsuitable for

improviser [ɛ̃pʀɔvize] /1/ vt, vi to improvize

improviste [ɛ̃pʀɔvist]: **à l'~** adv unexpectedly, without warning

imprudence [ɛ̃pʀydɑ̃s] nf (d'une personne, d'une action) carelessness no pl; (d'une remarque) imprudence no pl; **commettre une ~** to do something foolish

imprudent, e [ɛ̃pʀydɑ̃, -ɑ̃t] adj (conducteur, geste, action) careless; (remarque) unwise, imprudent; (projet) foolhardy

impuissant, e [ɛ̃pɥisɑ̃, -ɑ̃t] adj helpless; (sans effet) ineffectual; (sexuellement) impotent

impulsif, -ive [ɛ̃pylsif, -iv] adj impulsive

impulsion [ɛ̃pylsjɔ̃] nf (Élec, instinct) impulse; (élan, influence) impetus

inabordable [inabɔʀdabl] adj (cher) prohibitive

inacceptable [inaksɛptabl] adj unacceptable

inaccessible [inaksesibl] adj inaccessible; **~ à** impervious to

inachevé, e [inaʃve] adj unfinished

inactif, -ive [inaktif, -iv] adj inactive; (remède) ineffective; (Bourse: marché) slack

inadapté, e [inadapte] adj (Psych) maladjusted; **~ à** not adapted to, unsuited to

inadéquat, e [inadekwa, -wat] adj inadequate

inadmissible [inadmisibl] adj inadmissible

inadvertance [inadvɛʀtɑ̃s]: **par ~** adv inadvertently

inanimé, e [inanime] adj (matière) inanimate; (évanoui) unconscious; (sans vie) lifeless

inanition [inanisjɔ̃] nf: **tomber d'~** to faint with hunger (and exhaustion)

inaperçu, e [inapɛʀsy] adj: **passer ~** to go unnoticed

inapte [inapt] adj: **~ à** incapable of; (Mil) unfit for

inattendu, e [inatɑ̃dy] adj unexpected

inattentif, -ive [inatɑ̃tif, -iv] adj inattentive; **~ à** (dangers, détails) heedless of; **inattention** nf inattention; **faute d'inattention** careless mistake

inaugurer [inɔɡyʀe] /1/ vt (monument) to unveil; (exposition, usine) to open; (fig) to inaugurate

inavouable [inavwabl] adj (bénéfices) undisclosable; (honteux) shameful

incalculable [ɛ̃kalkylabl] adj incalculable

incapable [ɛ̃kapabl] adj incapable; **~ de faire** incapable of doing; (empêché) unable to do

incapacité [ɛ̃kapasite] nf (incompétence) incapability; (impossibilité) incapacity; **être dans l'~ de faire** to be unable to do

incarcérer [ɛ̃kaʀseʀe] /6/ vt to incarcerate, imprison

incassable [ɛ̃kasabl] adj unbreakable

incendie [ɛ̃sɑ̃di] nm fire; **~ criminel** arson no pl; **~ de forêt** forest fire; **incendier** /7/ vt (mettre le feu à) to set fire to, set alight; (brûler complètement) to burn down

incertain, e [ɛ̃sɛʀtɛ̃, -ɛn] adj uncertain; (temps) unsettled; (imprécis: contours) indistinct, blurred; **incertitude** nf uncertainty

incessamment [ɛ̃sesamɑ̃] adv very shortly

incident [ɛ̃sidɑ̃] nm incident; **~ de parcours** minor hitch ou setback; **~ technique** technical difficulties pl

incinérer [ɛ̃sineʀe] /6/ vt (ordures) to incinerate; (mort) to cremate

incisif, -ive [ɛ̃sizif, -iv] adj incisive ▷ nf incisor

inciter [ɛ̃site] /1/ vt: **~ qn à (faire) qch** to prompt ou encourage sb to do sth; (à la révolte etc) to incite sb to do sth

incivilité [ɛ̃sivilite] nf (grossièreté) incivility; **incivilités** nfpl antisocial behaviour sg

inclinable [ɛ̃klinabl] adj: **siège à dossier ~** reclining seat

inclination [ɛ̃klinasjɔ̃] nf (penchant) inclination

incliner [ɛ̃kline] /1/ vt (bouteille) to tilt ▷ vi. **~ à qch/à faire** to incline towards sth/ doing; **s'incliner** vi (route) to slope; **s'~ (devant)** to bow (before)

inclure [ɛ̃klyʀ] /35/ vt to include, (joindre à un envoi) to enclose

inclus, e [ɛ̃kly, -yz] pp de **inclure** ▷ adj included; (joint à un envoi) enclosed; (compris: frais, dépense) included; **jusqu'au 10 mars ~** until 10th March inclusive

incognito [ɛ̃kɔɲito] adv incognito ▷ nm: **garder l'~** to remain incognito

incohérent, e [ɛ̃kɔeʀɑ̃, -ɑ̃t] adj (comportement) inconsistent; (geste, langage, texte) incoherent

incollable [ɛ̃kɔlabl] adj (riz) that does not stick; (fam) **il est ~** he's got all the answers

incolore [ɛ̃kɔlɔʀ] adj colourless

incommoder [ɛ̃kɔmɔde] /1/ vt: **~ qn** (chaleur, odeur) to bother ou inconvenience sb

incomparable [ɛ̃kɔ̃paʀabl] adj incomparable

incompatible [ɛ̃kɔ̃patibl] *adj*
incompatible

incompétent, e [ɛ̃kɔ̃petã, -ãt] *adj*
incompetent

incomplet, -ète [ɛ̃kɔ̃plɛ, -ɛt] *adj*
incomplete

incompréhensible [ɛ̃kɔ̃pʀeãsibl] *adj*
incomprehensible

incompris, e [ɛ̃kɔ̃pʀi, -iz] *adj*
misunderstood

inconcevable [ɛ̃kɔ̃svabl] *adj* inconceivable

inconfortable [ɛ̃kɔ̃fɔʀtabl] *adj*
uncomfortable

incongru, e [ɛ̃kɔ̃gʀy] *adj* unseemly

inconnu, e [ɛ̃kɔny] *adj* unknown ▷ *nm/f*
stranger ▷ *nm:* l'~ the unknown ▷ *nf*
unknown factor

inconsciemment [ɛ̃kɔ̃sjamã] *adv*
unconsciously

inconscient, e [ɛ̃kɔ̃sjã, -ãt] *adj*
unconscious; (*irréfléchi*) thoughtless,
reckless; (*sentiment*) subconscious ▷ *nm*
(*Psych*): l'~ the unconscious; ~ **de**
unaware of

inconsidéré, e [ɛ̃kɔ̃sideʀe] *adj* ill-
considered

inconsistant, e [ɛ̃kɔ̃sistã, ãt] *adj* flimsy,
weak

inconsolable [ɛ̃kɔ̃sɔlabl] *adj* inconsolable

incontestable [ɛ̃kɔ̃testabl] *adj*
indisputable

incontinent, e [ɛ̃kɔ̃tinã, -ãt] *adj*
incontinent

incontournable [ɛ̃kɔ̃tuʀnabl] *adj*
unavoidable

incontrôlable [ɛ̃kɔ̃tʀolabl] *adj*
unverifiable; (*irrépressible*) uncontrollable

inconvénient [ɛ̃kɔ̃venjã] *nm*
disadvantage, drawback; **si vous n'y voyez
pas d'~** if you have no objections

incorporer [ɛ̃kɔʀpɔʀe] /1/ *vt:* ~ **(à)** to
mix in (with); ~ **(dans)** (*paragraphe etc*) to
incorporate (in); (*Mil: appeler*) to recruit
(into); **il a très bien su s'~ à notre groupe**
he was very easily incorporated into our
group

incorrect, e [ɛ̃kɔʀɛkt] *adj* (*impropre,
inconvenant*) improper; (*défectueux*) faulty;
(*inexact*) incorrect; (*impoli*) impolite;
(*déloyal*) underhand

incorrigible [ɛ̃kɔʀiʒibl] *adj* incorrigible

incrédule [ɛ̃kʀedyl] *adj* incredulous; (*Rel*)
unbelieving

incroyable [ɛ̃kʀwajabl] *adj* incredible

incruster [ɛ̃kʀyste] /1/ *vt,* **s'incruster** *vi*
(*invité*) to take root; ~ **qch dans/qch de**
(*Art*) to inlay sth into/sth with

inculpé, e [ɛ̃kylpe] *nm/f* accused

inculper [ɛ̃kylpe] /1/ *vt:* ~ **(de)** to charge
(with)

inculquer [ɛ̃kylke] /1/ *vt:* ~ **qch à** to
inculcate sth in, instil sth into

Inde [ɛ̃d] *nf:* l'~ India

indécent, e [ɛ̃desã, -ãt] *adj* indecent

indécis, e [ɛ̃desi, -iz] *adj* (*par nature*)
indecisive; (*perplexe*) undecided

indéfendable [ɛ̃defãdabl] *adj* indefensible

indéfini, e [ɛ̃defini] *adj* (*imprécis,
incertain*) undefined; (*illimité, Ling*)
indefinite; **indéfiniment** *adv* indefinitely;
indéfinissable *adj* indefinable

indélébile [ɛ̃delebil] *adj* indelible

indélicat, e [ɛ̃delika, -at] *adj* tactless

indemne [ɛ̃dɛmn] *adj* unharmed;
indemniser /1/ *vt:* **indemniser qn (de)** to
compensate sb (for)

indemnité [ɛ̃dɛmnite] *nf* (*dédommagement*)
compensation *no pl;* (*allocation*) allowance;
~ **de licenciement** redundancy payment

indépendamment [ɛ̃depãdamã] *adv*
independently; ~ **de** (*abstraction faite de*)
irrespective of; (*en plus de*) over and above

indépendance [ɛ̃depãdãs] *nf*
independence

indépendant, e [ɛ̃depãdã, -ãt] *adj*
independent; ~ **de** independent of;
travailleur ~ self-employed worker

indescriptible [ɛ̃deskʀiptibl] *adj*
indescribable

indésirable [ɛ̃deziʀabl] *adj* undesirable

indestructible [ɛ̃destʀyktibl] *adj*
indestructible

indéterminé, e [ɛ̃detɛʀmine] *adj* (*date,
cause, nature*) unspecified; (*forme, longueur,
quantité*) indeterminate

index [ɛ̃dɛks] *nm* (*doigt*) index finger; (*d'un
livre etc*) index; **mettre à l'~** to blacklist

indicateur [ɛ̃dikatœʀ] *nm* (*Police*)
informer; (*Tech*) gauge; indicator ▷ *adj:*
poteau ~ signpost; ~ **des chemins de
fer** railway timetable; ~ **de rues** street
directory

indicatif, -ive [ɛ̃dikatif, -iv] *adj:* **à
titre** ~ for (your) information ▷ *nm* (*Ling*)
indicative; (*d'une émission*) theme *ou*
signature tune; (*Tél*) dialling code (BRIT),
area code (US); **quel est l'~ de …** what's the
code for …?

indication [ɛ̃dikasjɔ̃] *nf* indication;
(*renseignement*) information *no pl;*
indications *nfpl* (*directives*) instructions

indice [ɛ̃dis] *nm* (*marque, signe*) indication,
sign; (*Police: lors d'une enquête*) clue; (*Jur:
présomption*) piece of evidence; (*Science,
Écon, Tech*) index; ~ **de protection** (sun
protection) factor

indicible [ɛ̃disibl] *adj* inexpressible

indien, ne [ɛ̃djɛ̃, -ɛn] *adj* Indian ▷ *nm/f:*
l'~, ne Indian

indifféremment [ɛ̃difeʀamã] *adv* (*sans
distinction*) equally

indifférence [ɛ̃difeʀãs] *nf* indifference

indifférent, e [ɛ̃difeʀã, -ãt] *adj* (*peu
intéressé*) indifferent; **ça m'est** ~ **(que …)**

it doesn't matter to me (whether ...); **elle m'est ~e** I am indifferent to her

indigène [ɛ̃diʒɛn] *adj* native, indigenous; *(de la région)* local ▷ *nm/f* native

indigeste [ɛ̃diʒɛst] *adj* indigestible

indigestion [ɛ̃diʒɛstjɔ̃] *nf* indigestion *no pl*; **avoir une ~** to have indigestion

indigne [ɛ̃diɲ] *adj*: **~ (de)** unworthy (of)

indigner [ɛ̃diɲe] /1/ *vt*: **s'indigner (de/ contre)** to be (*ou* become) indignant (at)

indiqué, e [ɛ̃dike] *adj* (*date, lieu*) given; (*adéquat*) appropriate; (*conseillé*) advisable

indiquer [ɛ̃dike] /1/ *vt*: **~ qch/qn à qn** to point sth/sb out to sb; (*faire connaître*: *médecin, lieu, restaurant*) to tell sb of sth/sb; (*pendule, aiguille*) to show; (*étiquette, plan*) to show, indicate; (*renseigner sur*) to point out, tell; (*déterminer*: *date, lieu*) to give, state; (*dénoter*) to indicate, point to; **pourriez-vous m'~ les toilettes/l'heure?** could you direct me to the toilets/tell me the time?

indiscipliné, e [ɛ̃disipline] *adj* undisciplined

indiscret, -ète [ɛ̃diskʀɛ, -ɛt] *adj* indiscreet

indiscutable [ɛ̃diskytabl] *adj* indisputable

indispensable [ɛ̃dispɑ̃sabl] *adj* indispensable, essential

indisposé, e [ɛ̃dispoze] *adj* indisposed

indistinct, e [ɛ̃distɛ̃, -ɛkt] *adj* indistinct; **indistinctement** *adv* (*voir, prononcer*) indistinctly; (*sans distinction*) indiscriminately

individu [ɛ̃dividy] *nm* individual; **individuel, le** *adj* (*gén*) individual; (*opinion, livret, contrôle, avantages*) personal; **chambre individuelle** single room; **maison individuelle** detached house, **propriété individuelle** personal *ou* private property

indolore [ɛ̃dɔlɔʀ] *adj* painless

Indonésie [ɛ̃dɔnezi] *nf*: **l'~** Indonesia

indu, e [ɛ̃dy] *adj*: **à une heure ~e** at some ungodly hour

indulgent, e [ɛ̃dylʒɑ̃, -ɑ̃t] *adj* (*parent, regard*) indulgent; (*juge, examinateur*) lenient

industrialisé, e [ɛ̃dystʀijalize] *adj* industrialized

industrie [ɛ̃dystʀi] *nf* industry; **industriel, le** *adj* industrial ▷ *nm* industrialist

inébranlable [inebʀɑ̃labl] *adj* (*masse, colonne*) solid; (*personne, certitude, foi*) unwavering

inédit, e [inedi, -it] *adj* (*correspondance etc*) (hitherto) unpublished; (*spectacle, moyen*) novel, original; (*film*) unreleased

inefficace [inefikas] *adj* (*remède, moyen*) ineffective; (*machine, employé*) inefficient

inégal, e, -aux [inegal, -o] *adj* unequal; (*irrégulier*) uneven; **inégalable** *adj* matchless; **inégalé, e** *adj* (*record*) unequalled; (*beauté*) unrivalled; **inégalité** *nf* inequality

inépuisable [inepɥizabl] *adj* inexhaustible

inerte [inɛʀt] *adj* (*immobile*) lifeless; (*apathique*) passive

inespéré, e [inɛspeʀe] *adj* unhoped-for, unexpected

inestimable [inɛstimabl] *adj* priceless; (*fig: bienfait*) invaluable

inévitable [inevitabl] *adj* unavoidable; (*fatal, habituel*) inevitable

inexact, e [inɛgzakt] *adj* inaccurate

inexcusable [inɛkskyzabl] *adj* unforgivable

inexplicable [inɛksplikabl] *adj* inexplicable

in extremis [inɛkstʀemis] *adv* at the last minute ▷ *adj* last-minute

infaillible [ɛ̃fajibl] *adj* infallible

infarctus [ɛ̃faʀktys] *nm*: **~ (du myocarde)** coronary (thrombosis)

infatigable [ɛ̃fatigabl] *adj* tireless

infect, e [ɛ̃fɛkt] *adj* revolting; (*repas, vin*) revolting, foul; (*personne*) obnoxious; (*temps*) foul

infecter [ɛ̃fɛkte] /1/ *vt* (*atmosphère, eau*) to contaminate; (*Méd*) to infect; **s'infecter** to become infected *ou* septic; **infection** *nf* infection; (*puanteur*) stench

inférieur, e [ɛ̃feʀjœʀ] *adj* lower; (*en qualité, intelligence*) inferior ▷ *nm/f* inferior; **~ à** (*somme, quantité*) less *ou* smaller than; (*moins bon que*) inferior to

infernal, e, -aux [ɛ̃fɛʀnal, -o] *adj* (*insupportable: chaleur, rythme*) infernal; (*: enfant*) horrid; (*méchanceté, complot*) diabolical

infidèle [ɛ̃fidɛl] *adj* unfaithful

infiltrer [ɛ̃filtʀe] /1/: **s'infiltrer** *vi*: **s'~ dans** to penetrate into; (*liquide*) to seep into; (*fig: noyauter*) to infiltrate

infime [ɛ̃fim] *adj* minute, tiny

infini, e [ɛ̃fini] *adj* infinite ▷ *nm* infinity, **à l'~** endlessly; **infiniment** *adv* infinitely; **infinité** *nf*: **une infinité de** an infinite number of

infinitif, -ive [ɛ̃finitif, -iv] *nm* infinitive

infirme [ɛ̃fiʀm] *adj* disabled ▷ *nm/f* person with a disability

infirmerie [ɛ̃fiʀməʀi] *nf* sick bay

infirmier, -ière [ɛ̃fiʀmje, -jɛʀ] *nm/f* nurse; **infirmière chef** sister

infirmité [ɛ̃fiʀmite] *nf* disability

inflammable [ɛ̃flamabl] *adj* (in)flammable

inflation [ɛ̃flasjɔ̃] *nf* inflation

influençable [ɛ̃flyɑ̃sabl] *adj* easily influenced

influence [ɛ̃flyɑ̃s] *nf* influence; **influencer** /3/ *vt* to influence; **influent, e** *adj* influential

informaticien, ne [ɛ̃fɔʀmatisjɛ̃, -ɛn] *nm/f* computer scientist

information [ɛ̃fɔʀmasjɔ̃] *nf* (*renseignement*) piece of information;

(*Presse, TV: nouvelle*) item of news; (*diffusion de renseignements, Inform*) information; (*Jur*) inquiry, investigation; **informations** *nfpl* (*TV*) news *sg*

informatique [ɛ̃fɔʀmatik] *nf* (*technique*) data processing; (*science*) computer science ▷ *adj* computer *cpd*; **informatiser** /1/ *vt* to computerize

informer [ɛ̃fɔʀme] /1/ *vt*: ~ **qn (de)** to inform sb (of); **s'informer (sur)** to inform o.s. (about); **s'~ (de qch/si)** to inquire *ou* find out (about sth/whether *ou* if)

infos [ɛ̃fo] *nfpl* (= *informations*) news

infraction [ɛ̃fʀaksjɔ̃] *nf* offence; ~ **à** violation *ou* breach of; **être en ~** to be in breach of the law

infranchissable [ɛ̃fʀɑ̃ʃisabl] *adj* impassable; (*fig*) insuperable

infrarouge [ɛ̃fʀaʀuʒ] *adj* infrared

infrastructure [ɛ̃fʀastʀyktyʀ] *nf* (*Aviat, Mil*) ground installations *pl*; (*Écon: touristique etc*) facilities *pl*

infuser [ɛ̃fyze] /1/ *vt* (*thé*) to brew; (*tisane*) to infuse ▷ *vi* to brew; to infuse; **infusion** *nf* (*tisane*) herb tea

ingénier [ɛ̃ʒenje] /7/: **s'ingénier** *vi*: **s'~ à faire** to strive to do

ingénierie [ɛ̃ʒeniʀi] *nf* engineering

ingénieur [ɛ̃ʒenjœʀ] *nm* engineer; ~ **du son** sound engineer

ingénieux, -euse [ɛ̃ʒenjø, -øz] *adj* ingenious, clever

ingrat, e [ɛ̃gʀa, -at] *adj* (*personne*) ungrateful; (*travail, sujet*) thankless; (*visage*) unprepossessing

ingrédient [ɛ̃gʀedjɑ̃] *nm* ingredient

inhabité, e [inabite] *adj* uninhabited

inhabituel, le [inabitɥɛl] *adj* unusual

inhibition [inibisjɔ̃] *nf* inhibition

inhumain, e [inymɛ̃, -ɛn] *adj* inhuman

inimaginable [inimaʒinabl] *adj* unimaginable

ininterrompu, e [inɛ̃teʀɔ̃py] *adj* (*file, série*) unbroken; (*flot, vacarme*) uninterrupted, non-stop; (*effort*) unremitting, continuous; (*suite, ligne*) unbroken

initial, e, -aux [inisjal, -o] *adj* initial; **initiales** *nfpl* initials

initiation [inisjasjɔ̃] *nf*: ~ **à** introduction to

initiative [inisjativ] *nf* initiative

initier [inisje] /7/ *vt*: ~ **qn à** to initiate sb into; (*faire découvrir: art, jeu*) to introduce sb to

injecter [ɛ̃ʒɛkte] /1/ *vt* to inject; **injection** *nf* injection; **à injection** (*Auto*) fuel injection *cpd*

injure [ɛ̃ʒyʀ] *nf* insult, abuse *no pl*; **injurier** /7/ *vt* to insult, abuse; **injurieux, -euse** *adj* abusive, insulting

injuste [ɛ̃ʒyst] *adj* unjust, unfair; **injustice** [ɛ̃ʒystis] *nf* injustice

inlassable [ɛ̃lasabl] *adj* tireless

inné, e [ine] *adj* innate, inborn

innocent, e [inɔsɑ̃, -ɑ̃t] *adj* innocent; **innocenter** /1/ *vt* to clear, prove innocent

innombrable [inɔ̃bʀabl] *adj* innumerable

innover [inɔve] /1/ *vi*: ~ **en matière d'art** to break new ground in the field of art

inoccupé, e [inɔkype] *adj* unoccupied

inodore [inɔdɔʀ] *adj* (*gaz*) odourless; (*fleur*) scentless

inoffensif, -ive [inɔfɑ̃sif, -iv] *adj* harmless, innocuous

inondation [inɔ̃dasjɔ̃] *nf* flood

inonder [inɔ̃de] /1/ *vt* to flood; ~ **de** to flood *ou* swamp with

inopportun, e [inɔpɔʀtœ̃, -yn] *adj* ill-timed, untimely

inoubliable [inublijabl] *adj* unforgettable

inouï, e [inwi] *adj* unheard-of, extraordinary

inox [inɔks] *nm* stainless (steel)

inquiet, -ète [ɛ̃kjɛ, -ɛt] *adj* anxious; **inquiétant, e** *adj* worrying, disturbing; **inquiéter** /6/ *vt* to worry; **s'inquiéter** to worry; **s'inquiéter de** to worry about; (*s'enquérir de*) to inquire about; **inquiétude** *nf* anxiety

insaisissable [ɛ̃sezisabl] *adj* (*fugitif, ennemi*) elusive; (*différence, nuance*) imperceptible

insalubre [ɛ̃salybʀ] *adj* insalubrious

insatisfait, e [ɛ̃satisfɛ, -ɛt] *adj* (*non comblé*) unsatisfied; (*mécontent*) dissatisfied

inscription [ɛ̃skʀipsjɔ̃] *nf* inscription; (*à une institution*) enrolment

inscrire [ɛ̃skʀiʀ] /39/ *vt* (*marquer: sur son calepin etc*) to note *ou* write down; (: *sur un mur, une affiche etc*) to write; (: *dans la pierre, le métal*) to inscribe; (*mettre: sur une liste, un budget etc*) to put down; ~ **qn à** (*club, école etc*) to enrol sb at; **s'inscrire** (*pour une excursion etc*) to put one's name down; **s'~ (à)** (*club, parti*) to join; (*université*) to register *ou* enrol (at); (*examen, concours*) to register *ou* enter (for)

insecte [ɛ̃sɛkt] *nm* insect; **insecticide** *nm* insecticide

insensé, e [ɛ̃sɑ̃se] *adj* mad

insensible [ɛ̃sɑ̃sibl] *adj* (*nerf, membre*) numb; (*dur, indifférent*) insensitive

inséparable [ɛ̃sepaʀabl] *adj*: ~ **(de)** inseparable (from) ▷ *nmpl*: ~**s** (*oiseaux*) lovebirds

insigne [ɛ̃siɲ] *nm* (*d'un parti, club*) badge ▷ *adj* distinguished; **insignes** *nmpl* (*d'une fonction*) insignia *pl*

insignifiant, e [ɛ̃siɲifjɑ̃, -ɑ̃t] *adj* insignificant; trivial

insinuer [ɛ̃sinɥe] /1/ *vt* to insinuate; **s'insinuer dans** (*fig*) to worm one's way into

insipide [ɛ̃sipid] *adj* insipid

insister [ɛ̃siste] /1/ *vi* to insist; (*s'obstiner*) to keep on; ~ **sur** (*détail, note*) to stress

insolation [ɛ̃sɔlasjɔ̃] nf (Méd) sunstroke
no pl
insolent, e [ɛ̃sɔlɑ̃, -ɑ̃t] adj insolent
insolite [ɛ̃sɔlit] adj strange, unusual
insomnie [ɛ̃sɔmni] nf insomnia no pl; **avoir
des ~s** to sleep badly
insouciant, e [ɛ̃susjɑ̃, -ɑ̃t] adj carefree;
~ du danger heedless of (the) danger
insoupçonnable [ɛ̃supsɔnabl] adj
unsuspected; (personne) above suspicion
insoupçonné, e [ɛ̃supsɔne] adj
unsuspected
insoutenable [ɛ̃sutnabl] adj (argument)
untenable; (chaleur) unbearable
inspecter [ɛ̃spɛkte] /1/ vt to inspect;
inspecteur, -trice nm/f inspector;
inspecteur d'Académie (regional) director
of education; **inspecteur des finances**
≈ tax inspector (BRIT), ≈ Internal Revenue
Service agent (US); **inspecteur (de police)**
(police) inspector; **inspection** nf inspection
inspirer [ɛ̃spiRe] /1/ vt (gén) to inspire ▷ vi
(aspirer) to breathe in; **s'inspirer de** to be
inspired by
instable [ɛ̃stabl] adj (meuble, équilibre)
unsteady; (population, temps) unsettled;
(paix, régime, caractère) unstable
installation [ɛ̃stalasjɔ̃] nf (mise en
place) installation; **installations** nfpl
installations; (industrielles) plant sg;
(de sport, dans un camping) facilities; **l'~
électrique** wiring
installer [ɛ̃stale] /1/ vt to put; (meuble)
to put in; (rideau, étagère, tente) to put
up; (appartement) to fit out; **s'installer**
(s'établir: artisan, dentiste etc) to set o.s.
up; (emménager) to settle in; (sur un siège,
à un emplacement) to settle (down); (fig:
maladie, grève) to take a firm hold ou grip;
s'~ à l'hôtel/chez qn to move into a hotel/
in with sb
instance [ɛ̃stɑ̃s] nf (Admin: autorité)
authority; **affaire en ~** matter pending;
être en ~ de divorce to be awaiting a
divorce
instant [ɛ̃stɑ̃] nm moment, instant; **dans
un ~** in a moment; **à l'~** this instant; **je
l'ai vu à l'~** I've just this minute seen him,
I saw him a moment ago; **pour l'~** for the
moment, for the time being
instantané, e [ɛ̃stɑ̃tane] adj (lait, café)
instant; (explosion, mort) instantaneous
▷ nm snapshot
instar [ɛ̃staR]: **à l'~ de** prép following the
example of, like
instaurer [ɛ̃stɔRe] /1/ vt to institute;
(couvre-feu) to impose; **s'instaurer** vi
(collaboration, paix etc) to be established;
(doute) to set in
instinct [ɛ̃stɛ̃] nm instinct;
instinctivement adv instinctively
instituer [ɛ̃stitɥe] /1/ vt to establish

institut [ɛ̃stity] nm institute; **~ de
beauté** beauty salon; **I~ universitaire de
technologie (IUT)** ≈ Institute of technology
instituteur, -trice [ɛ̃stitytœR, -tRis]
nm/f (primary (BRIT) ou grade (US) school)
teacher
institution [ɛ̃stitysjɔ̃] nf institution;
(collège) private school; **institutions** nfpl
(structures politiques et sociales) institutions
instructif, -ive [ɛ̃stRyktif, -iv] adj
instructive
instruction [ɛ̃stRyksjɔ̃] nf (enseignement,
savoir) education; (Jur) (preliminary)
investigation and hearing; **instructions**
nfpl (mode d'emploi) instructions; **~ civique**
civics sg
instruire [ɛ̃stRɥiR] /38/ vt (élèves) to teach;
(recrues) to train; (Jur: affaire) to conduct the
investigation for; **s'instruire** to educate
o.s.; **instruit, e** adj educated
instrument [ɛ̃stRymɑ̃] nm instrument;
~ à cordes/vent stringed/wind
instrument; **~ de mesure** measuring
instrument; **~ de musique** musical
instrument; **~ de travail** (working) tool
insu [ɛ̃sy] nm: **à l'~ de qn** without sb
knowing
insuffisant, e [ɛ̃syfizɑ̃, -ɑ̃t] adj (en quantité)
insufficient; (en qualité) inadequate; (sur une
copie) poor
insulaire [ɛ̃sylɛR] adj island cpd; (attitude)
insular
insuline [ɛ̃sylin] nf insulin
insulte [ɛ̃sylt] nf insult; **insulter** /1/ vt to
insult
insupportable [ɛ̃sypɔRtabl] adj
unbearable
insurmontable [ɛ̃syRmɔ̃tabl] adj
(difficulté) insuperable; (aversion)
unconquerable
intact, e [ɛ̃takt] adj intact
intarissable [ɛ̃taRisabl] adj inexhaustible
intégral, e, -aux [ɛ̃tegRal, -o] adj complete;
texte ~ unabridged version; **bronzage ~**
all-over suntan; **intégralement** adv in full;
intégralité nf whole (ou full) amount; **dans
son intégralité** in its entirety; **intégrant,
e** adj: **faire partie intégrante de** to be an
integral part of
intègre [ɛ̃tegR] adj upright
intégrer [ɛ̃tegRe] /6/: **s'intégrer** vr: **s'~ à
ou dans** to become integrated into; **bien
s'~** to fit in
intégrisme [ɛ̃tegRism] nm
fundamentalism
intellectuel, le [ɛ̃telɛktɥɛl] adj, nm/f
intellectual; (péj) highbrow
intelligence [ɛ̃teliʒɑ̃s] nf intelligence;
(compréhension): **l'~ de** the understanding
of; (complicité): **regard d'~** glance of
complicity; (accord): **vivre en bonne ~ avec
qn** to be on good terms with sb

intelligent, e [ɛ̃teliʒã, -ãt] *adj* intelligent
intelligible [ɛ̃teliʒibl] *adj* intelligible
intempéries [ɛ̃tãperi] *nfpl* bad weather *sg*
intenable [ɛ̃tnabl] *adj* unbearable
intendant, e [ɛ̃tãdã, -ãt] *nm/f* (*Mil*)
quartermaster; (*Scol*) bursar
intense [ɛ̃tãs] *adj* intense; **intensif, -ive** *adj*
intensive; **cours intensif** crash course
intenter [ɛ̃tãte] /1/ *vt*: ~ **un procès contre**
ou **à qn** to start proceedings against sb
intention [ɛ̃tãsjõ] *nf* intention; (*Jur*) intent;
avoir l'~ de faire to intend to do; **à l'~**
de for; (*renseignement*) for the benefit *ou*
information of; (*film, ouvrage*) aimed at;
à cette ~ with this aim in view;
intentionné, e *adj*: **bien intentionné**
well-meaning *ou* -intentioned; **mal**
intentionné ill-intentioned
interactif, -ive [ɛ̃teraktif, -iv] *adj* (*aussi*
Inform) interactive
intercepter [ɛ̃tersepte] /1/ *vt* to intercept;
(*lumière, chaleur*) to cut off
interchangeable [ɛ̃terʃãʒabl] *adj*
interchangeable
interdiction [ɛ̃terdiksjõ] *nf* ban; ~ **de**
fumer no smoking
interdire [ɛ̃terdir] /37/ *vt* to forbid; (*Admin*)
to ban, prohibit; (: *journal, livre*) to ban; ~ **à**
qn de faire to forbid sb to do; (*empêchement*)
to prevent *ou* preclude sb from doing
interdit, e [ɛ̃terdi, -it] *pp de* **interdire**
▷ *adj* (*stupéfait*) taken aback; **film ~ aux**
moins de 18/12 ans ≈ 18-/12A-rated film;
stationnement ~ no parking
intéressant, e [ɛ̃teresã, -ãt] *adj*
interesting; (*avantageux*) attractive
intéressé, e [ɛ̃terese] *adj* (*parties*) involved,
concerned; (*amitié, motifs*) self-interested
intéresser [ɛ̃terese] /1/ *vt* (*captiver*) to
interest; (*toucher*) to be of interest *ou*
concern to; (*Admin: concerner*) to affect,
concern; **s'intéresser à** *vi* to take an
interest in
intérêt [ɛ̃tere] *nm* interest; (*égoïsme*) self-
interest; **tu as ~ à accepter** it's in your
interest to accept; **tu as ~ à te dépêcher**
you'd better hurry
intérieur, e [ɛ̃terjœr] *adj* (*mur, escalier,*
poche) inside; (*commerce, politique*)
domestic; (*cour, calme, vie*) inner; (*navigation*)
inland ▷ *nm* (*d'une maison, d'un récipient*
etc) inside; (*d'un pays, aussi décor, mobilier*)
interior; **l'I~** (the Department of) the
Interior, ≈ the Home Office (*BRIT*); **à l'~ (de)**
inside; **intérieurement** *adv* inwardly
intérim [ɛ̃terim] *nm* interim period;
assurer l'~ (de) to deputize (for); **président**
par ~ interim president; **faire de l'~** to temp
intérimaire [ɛ̃terimɛr] *adj* (*directeur,*
ministre) acting; (*secrétaire, personnel*)
temporary ▷ *nm/f* (*secrétaire etc*) temporary,
temp (*BRIT*)

interlocuteur, -trice [ɛ̃terlɔkytœr, -tris]
nm/f speaker; **son ~** the person he *ou* she
was speaking to
intermédiaire [ɛ̃termedjɛr] *adj*
intermediate; (*solution*) temporary ▷ *nm/f*
intermediary; (*Comm*) middleman; **sans ~**
directly; **par l'~ de** through
interminable [ɛ̃terminabl] *adj* never-
ending
intermittence [ɛ̃termitãs] *nf*: **par ~**
intermittently, sporadically
internat [ɛ̃terna] *nm* boarding school
international, e, -aux [ɛ̃ternasjɔnal, -o]
adj, nm/f international
internaute [ɛ̃ternot] *nm/f* Internet user
interne [ɛ̃tern] *adj* internal ▷ *nm/f* (*Scol*)
boarder; (*Méd*) houseman
Internet [ɛ̃ternɛt] *nm*: **l'~** the Internet
interpeller [ɛ̃terpele] /1/ *vt* (*appeler*) to call
out to; (*apostropher*) to shout at; (*Police*) to
take in for questioning; (*Pol*) to question;
(*concerner*) to concern
interphone [ɛ̃terfɔn] *nm* intercom;
(*d'immeuble*) entry phone
interposer [ɛ̃terpoze] /1/ *vt*: **s'interposer**
to intervene; **par personnes interposées**
through a third party
interprète [ɛ̃terprɛt] *nm/f* interpreter;
(*porte-parole*) spokesman
interpréter [ɛ̃terprete] /6/ *vt* to interpret;
(*jouer*) to play; (*chanter*) to sing
interrogatif, -ive [ɛ̃terɔgatif, -iv] *adj*
(*Ling*) interrogative
interrogation [ɛ̃terɔgasjõ] *nf* question;
(*Scol*) (written *ou* oral) test
interrogatoire [ɛ̃terɔgatwar] *nm* (*Police*)
questioning *no pl*; (*Jur, aussi fig*) cross-
examination
interroger [ɛ̃terɔʒe] /3/ *vt* to question;
(*Inform*) to search; (*Scol*) to test
interrompre [ɛ̃terõpr] /41/ *vt* (*gén*)
to interrupt; (*négociations*) to break
off; (*match*) to stop; **s'interrompre** to
break off; **interrupteur** *nm* switch;
interruption *nf* interruption; (*pause*)
break; **sans interruption** without a break;
interruption volontaire de grossesse
abortion
intersection [ɛ̃tersɛksjõ] *nf*
intersection
intervalle [ɛ̃terval] *nm* (*espace*) space; (*de*
temps) interval; **dans l'~** in the meantime;
à deux jours d'~ two days apart
intervenir [ɛ̃tervənir] /22/ *vi* (*gén*) to
intervene; ~ **auprès de/en faveur de**
qn to intervene with/on behalf of sb;
intervention *nf* intervention; (*discours*)
speech; **intervention (chirurgicale)**
operation
interview [ɛ̃tervju] *nf* interview
intestin, e [ɛ̃testɛ̃, -in] *adj* internal ▷ *nm*
intestine

intime [ɛ̃tim] *adj* intimate; (*vie, journal*) private; (*convictions*) inmost; (*dîner, cérémonie*) quiet ▷ *nm/f* close friend; **un journal ~** a diary

intimider [ɛ̃timide] /1/ *vt* to intimidate

intimité [ɛ̃timite] *nf*: **dans l'~** in private; (*sans formalités*) with only a few friends, quietly

intolérable [ɛ̃tɔlɛʀabl] *adj* intolerable

intox [ɛtɔks] (*fam*) *nf* brainwashing

intoxication [ɛ̃tɔksikasjɔ̃] *nf*: **~ alimentaire** food poisoning

intoxiquer [ɛ̃tɔksike] /1/ *vt* to poison; (*fig*) to brainwash

intraitable [ɛ̃tʀɛtabl] *adj* inflexible, uncompromising

intransigeant, e [ɛ̃tʀɑ̃ziʒɑ̃, -ɑ̃t] *adj* intransigent

intrépide [ɛ̃tʀepid] *adj* dauntless

intrigue [ɛ̃tʀig] *nf* (*scénario*) plot; **intriguer** /1/ *vt* to puzzle, intrigue

introduction [ɛ̃tʀɔdyksjɔ̃] *nf* introduction

introduire [ɛ̃tʀɔdɥiʀ] /38/ *vt* to introduce; (*visiteur*) to show in; (*aiguille, clef*) to insert *ou* introduce sth into; **qch dans** to insert *ou* introduce sth into; **s'introduire** *vi* (*techniques, usages*) to be introduced; **s'~ dans** to gain entry into; (*dans un groupe*) to get o.s. accepted into

introuvable [ɛ̃tʀuvabl] *adj* which cannot be found; (*Comm*) unobtainable

intrus, e [ɛ̃tʀy, -yz] *nm/f* intruder

intuition [ɛ̃tɥisjɔ̃] *nf* intuition

inusable [inyzabl] *adj* hard-wearing

inutile [inytil] *adj* useless; (*superflu*) unnecessary; **inutilement** *adv* needlessly; **inutilisable** *adj* unusable

invalide [ɛ̃valid] *adj* disabled ▷ *nm/f*: **~ de guerre** disabled ex-serviceman

invariable [ɛ̃vaʀjabl] *adj* invariable

invasion [ɛ̃vazjɔ̃] *nf* invasion

inventaire [ɛ̃vɑ̃tɛʀ] *nm* inventory; (*Comm: liste*) stocklist; (: *opération*) stocktaking *no pl*

inventer [ɛ̃vɑ̃te] /1/ *vt* to invent; (*subterfuge*) to devise, invent; (*histoire, excuse*) to make up, invent; **inventeur, -trice** *nm/f* inventor; **inventif, -ive** *adj* inventive; **invention** *nf* invention

inverse [ɛ̃vɛʀs] *adj* opposite ▷ *nm* inverse; **l'~** the opposite; **dans l'ordre ~** in the reverse order; **dans le sens ~ des aiguilles d'une montre** anti-clockwise; **en sens ~** in (*ou* from) the opposite direction; **inversement** *adv* conversely; **inverser** /1/ *vt* to reverse, invert; (*Élec*) to reverse

investir [ɛ̃vɛstiʀ] /2/ *vt* to invest; **~ qn de** (*d'une fonction, d'un pouvoir*) to vest *ou* invest sb with; **s'investir** *vi* (*Psych*) to involve o.s.; **s'~ dans** to put a lot into; **investissement** *nm* investment

invisible [ɛ̃vizibl] *adj* invisible

invitation [ɛ̃vitasjɔ̃] *nf* invitation

invité, e [ɛ̃vite] *nm/f* guest

inviter [ɛ̃vite] /1/ *vt* to invite; **~ qn à faire qch** to invite sb to do sth

invivable [ɛ̃vivabl] *adj* unbearable

involontaire [ɛ̃vɔlɔ̃tɛʀ] *adj* (*mouvement*) involuntary; (*insulte*) unintentional; (*complice*) unwitting

invoquer [ɛ̃vɔke] /1/ *vt* (*Dieu, muse*) to call upon, invoke; (*prétexte*) to put forward (as an excuse); (*loi, texte*) to refer to

invraisemblable [ɛ̃vʀɛsɑ̃blabl] *adj* (*fait, nouvelle*) unlikely, improbable; (*bizarre*) incredible

iode [jɔd] *nm* iodine

irai *etc* [iʀe] *vb voir* **aller**

Irak [iʀak] *nm*: **l'~** Iraq *ou* Irak; **irakien, ne** *adj* Iraqi ▷ *nm/f*: **Irakien, ne** Iraqi

Iran [iʀɑ̃] *nm*: **l'~** Iran; **iranien, ne** *adj* Iranian ▷ *nm/f*: **Iranien, ne** Iranian

irions *etc* [iʀjɔ̃] *vb voir* **aller**

iris [iʀis] *nm* iris

irlandais, e [iʀlɑ̃dɛ, -ɛz] *adj* Irish ▷ *nm/f*: **I~, e** Irishman/woman

Irlande [iʀlɑ̃d] *nf*: **l'~** Ireland; **la République d'~** the Irish Republic; **~ du Nord** Northern Ireland; **la mer d'~** the Irish Sea

ironie [iʀɔni] *nf* irony; **ironique** *adj* ironical; **ironiser** /1/ *vi* to be ironical

irons *etc* [iʀɔ̃] *vb voir* **aller**

irradier [iʀadje] /7/ *vt* to irradiate

irraisonné, e [iʀezɔne] *adj* irrational

irrationnel, le [iʀasjɔnɛl] *adj* irrational

irréalisable [iʀealizabl] *adj* unrealizable; (*projet*) impracticable

irrécupérable [iʀekypeʀabl] *adj* beyond repair; (*personne*) beyond redemption *ou* recall

irréel, le [iʀeɛl] *adj* unreal

irréfléchi, e [iʀefleʃi] *adj* thoughtless

irrégularité [iʀegylaʀite] *nf* irregularity; (*de travail, d'effort, de qualité*) unevenness *no pl*

irrégulier, -ière [iʀegylje, -jɛʀ] *adj* irregular; (*travail, effort, qualité*) uneven; (*élève, athlète*) erratic

irrémédiable [iʀemedjabl] *adj* irreparable

irremplaçable [iʀɑ̃plasabl] *adj* irreplaceable

irréparable [iʀepaʀabl] *adj* beyond repair; (*fig*) irreparable

irréprochable [iʀepʀɔʃabl] *adj* irreproachable, beyond reproach; (*tenue, toilette*) impeccable

irrésistible [iʀezistibl] *adj* irresistible; (*preuve, logique*) compelling; (*amusant*) hilarious

irrésolu, e [iʀezɔly] *adj* irresolute

irrespectueux, -euse [iʀɛspɛktɥø, -øz] *adj* disrespectful

irresponsable [iʀɛspɔ̃sabl] *adj* irresponsible

irriguer [iʀige] /1/ *vt* to irrigate

irritable [iʀitabl] *adj* irritable
irriter [iʀite] /1/ *vt* to irritate
irruption [iʀypsjɔ̃] *nf*: **faire ~ chez qn** to burst in on sb
Islam [islam] *nm*: **l'~** Islam; **islamique** *adj* Islamic; **islamophobie** *nf* Islamophobia
Islande [islɑ̃d] *nf*: **l'~** Iceland
isolant, e [izɔlɑ̃, -ɑ̃t] *adj* insulating; (*insonorisant*) soundproofing
isolation [izɔlasjɔ̃] *nf* insulation; **~ acoustique** soundproofing
isolé, e [izɔle] *adj* isolated; (*contre le froid*) insulated
isoler [izɔle] /1/ *vt* to isolate; (*prisonnier*) to put in solitary confinement; (*ville*) to cut off, isolate; (*contre le froid*) to insulate; **s'isoler** *vi* to isolate o.s.
Israël [isʀaɛl] *nm*: **l'~** Israel; **israélien, ne** *adj* Israeli ▷ *nm/f*: **Israélien, ne** Israeli; **israélite** *adj* Jewish ▷ *nm/f*: **Israélite** Jew/Jewess
issu, e [isy] *adj*: **~ de** (*né de*) descended from; (*résultant de*) stemming from ▷ *nf* (*ouverture, sortie*) exit; (*solution*) way out, solution; (*dénouement*) outcome; **à l'~e de** at the conclusion *ou* close of; **voie sans ~e** dead end; **~e de secours** emergency exit
Italie [itali] *nf*: **l'~** Italy; **italien, ne** *adj* Italian ▷ *nm* (*Ling*) Italian ▷ *nm/f*: **Italien, ne** Italian
italique [italik] *nm*: **en ~(s)** in italics
itinéraire [itineʀɛʀ] *nm* itinerary, route; **~ bis** alternative route
IUT *sigle m* = **Institut universitaire de technologie**
IVG *sigle f* (= *interruption volontaire de grossesse*) abortion
ivoire [ivwaʀ] *nm* ivory
ivre [ivʀ] *adj* drunk; **~ de** (*colère*) wild with; **ivrogne** *nm/f* drunkard

J

j' [ʒ] *pron voir* **je**
jacinthe [ʒasɛ̃t] *nf* hyacinth
jadis [ʒadis] *adv* formerly
jaillir [ʒajiʀ] /2/ *vi* (*liquide*) to spurt out; (*cris, réponses*) to burst out
jais [ʒɛ] *nm* jet; (**d'un noir**) **de ~** jet-black
jalousie [ʒaluzi] *nf* jealousy; (*store*) (venetian) blind
jaloux, -ouse [ʒalu, -uz] *adj* jealous; **être ~ de qn/qch** to be jealous of sb/sth
jamaïquain, e [ʒamaikɛ̃, -ɛn] *adj* Jamaican ▷ *nm/f*: **J~, e** Jamaican
Jamaïque [ʒamaik] *nf*: **la ~** Jamaica
jamais [ʒamɛ] *adv* never; (*sans négation*) ever; **ne ... ~** never; **si ... ~** if ever ...; **je ne suis ~ allé en Espagne** I've never been to Spain
jambe [ʒɑ̃b] *nf* leg
jambon [ʒɑ̃bɔ̃] *nm* ham
jante [ʒɑ̃t] *nf* (*wheel*) rim
janvier [ʒɑ̃vje] *nm* January
Japon [ʒapɔ̃] *nm*: **le ~** Japan; **japonais, e** *adj* Japanese ▷ *nm* (*Ling*) Japanese ▷ *nm/f*: **Japonais, e** Japanese
jardin [ʒaʀdɛ̃] *nm* garden; **~ d'enfants** nursery school; **jardinage** *nm* gardening; **jardiner** /1/ *vi* to garden; **jardinier, -ière** *nm/f* gardener ▷ *nf* (*de fenêtre*) window box; **jardinière (de légumes)** (*Culin*) mixed vegetables
jargon [ʒaʀgɔ̃] *nm* (*charabia*) gibberish; (*publicitaire, scientifique etc*) jargon
jarret [ʒaʀɛ] *nm* back of knee; (*Culin*) knuckle, shin
jauge [ʒoʒ] *nf* (*instrument*) gauge; **~ (de niveau) d'huile** (*Auto*) dipstick
jaune [ʒon] *adj, nm* yellow ▷ *adv* (*fam*): **rire ~** to laugh on the other side of one's face; **~ d'œuf** (*egg*) yolk; **jaunir** /2/ *vi, vt* to turn yellow; **jaunisse** *nf* jaundice
Javel [ʒavɛl] *nf voir* **eau**
javelot [ʒavlo] *nm* javelin

J.-C. *sigle m* = **Jésus-Christ**

je, j' [ʒə, ʒ] *pron* I

jean [dʒin] *nm* jeans *pl*

Jésus-Christ [ʒezykRi(st)] *n* Jesus Christ; **600 avant/après ~** 600 B.C./A.D.

jet [ʒɛ] *nm* (*lancer: action*) throwing *no pl*; (: *résultat*) throw; (*jaillissement: d'eaux*) jet; (: *de sang*) spurt; **~ d'eau** spray

jetable [ʒətabl] *adj* disposable

jetée [ʒəte] *nf* jetty; (*grande*) pier

jeter [ʒəte] /4/ *vt* (*gén*) to throw; (*se défaire de*) to throw away *ou* out; **~ qch à qn** to throw sth to sb; (*de façon agressive*) to throw sth at sb; **~ un coup d'œil (à)** to take a look (at); **~ un sort à qn** to cast a spell on sb; **se ~ sur** to throw o.s. onto; **se ~ dans** (*fleuve*) to flow into

jeton [ʒətɔ̃] *nm* (*au jeu*) counter

jette *etc* [ʒɛt] *vb voir* **jeter**

jeu, x [ʒø] *nm* (*divertissement, Tech: d'une pièce*) play; (*Tennis: partie, Football etc: façon de jouer*) game; (*Théât etc*) acting; (*série d'objets, jouet*) set; (*Cartes*) hand; (*au casino*): **le ~** gambling; **en ~** at stake; **remettre en ~** to throw in; **entrer/mettre en ~** to come/bring into play; **~ de cartes** pack of cards; **~ d'échecs** chess set; **~ de hasard** game of chance; **~ de société** board game; **~ télévisé** television quiz; **~ vidéo** video game

jeudi [ʒødi] *nm* Thursday

jeun [ʒœ̃]: **à ~** *adv* on an empty stomach; **être à ~** to have eaten nothing; **rester à ~** not to eat anything

jeune [ʒœn] *adj* young; **les ~s** young people; **~ fille** girl; **~ homme** young man; **~s gens** young people

jeûne [ʒøn] *nm* fast

jeunesse [ʒœnɛs] *nf* youth; (*aspect*) youthfulness

joaillier, -ière [ʒɔaje, -jɛR] *nm/f* jeweller

jogging [dʒɔgiŋ] *nm* jogging; (*survêtement*) tracksuit; **faire du ~** to go jogging

joie [ʒwa] *nf* joy

joindre [ʒwɛ̃dR] /49/ *vt* to join; (*contacter*) to contact, get in touch with; **~ qch à** (*à une lettre*) to enclose sth with; **~ un fichier à un mail** (*Inform*) to attach a file to an email; **se ~ à qn** to join sb; **se ~ à qch** to join in sth

joint, e [ʒwɛ̃, -ɛ̃t] *adj*: **~ (à)** (*lettre, paquet*) attached (to), enclosed (with) ▷ *nm* joint; (*ligne*) join; **pièce ~e** (*de lettre*) enclosure; (*de mail*) attachment; **~ de culasse** cylinder head gasket

joli, e [ʒɔli] *adj* pretty, attractive; **une ~e somme/situation** a nice little sum/situation; **c'est du ~!** (*ironique*) that's very nice!; **tout ça, c'est bien ~ mais ...** that's all very well but ...

jonc [ʒɔ̃] *nm* (bul)rush

jonction [ʒɔ̃ksjɔ̃] *nf* junction

jongleur, -euse [ʒɔ̃glœR, -øz] *nm/f* juggler

jonquille [ʒɔ̃kij] *nf* daffodil

Jordanie [ʒɔRdani] *nf*: **la ~** Jordan

joue [ʒu] *nf* cheek

jouer [ʒwe] /1/ *vt* to play; (*somme d'argent, réputation*) to stake, wager; (*simuler: sentiment*) to affect, feign ▷ *vi* to play; (*Théât, Ciné*) to act; (*au casino*) to gamble; (*bois, porte: se voiler*) to warp; (*clef, pièce: avoir du jeu*) to be loose; **~ sur** (*miser*) to gamble on; **~ de** (*Mus*) to play; **~ à** (*jeu, sport, roulette*) to play; **~ un tour à qn** to play a trick on sb; **~ la comédie** to put on an act; **~ serré** to play a close game; **à toi/nous de ~** it's your/our go *ou* turn; **bien joué!** well done!; **on joue Hamlet au théâtre X** Hamlet is on at the X theatre

jouet [ʒwɛ] *nm* toy; **être le ~ de** (*illusion etc*) to be the victim of

joueur, -euse [ʒwœR, -øz] *nm/f* player; **être beau/mauvais ~** to be a good/bad loser

jouir [ʒwiR] /2/ *vi* (*sexe: fam*) to come ▷ *vt*: **~ de** to enjoy

jour [ʒuR] *nm* day; (*opposé à la nuit*) day, daytime; (*clarté*) daylight; (*fig: aspect, ouverture*) opening; **sous un ~ favorable/nouveau** in a favourable/new light; **de ~** (*crème, service*) day *cpd*; **travailler de ~** to work during the day; **voyager de ~** to travel by day; **au ~ le ~** from day to day, **de nos ~s** these days; **du ~ au lendemain** overnight; **il fait ~** it's daylight; **au grand ~** (*fig*) in the open; **mettre au ~** to disclose; **mettre à ~** to bring up to date; **donner le ~ à** to give birth to; **voir le ~** to be born; **~ férié** public holiday; **le ~ J** D-day; **~ ouvrable** working day

journal, -aux [ʒuRnal, o] *nm* (*news*) paper; (*personnel*) journal; (*intime*) diary; **~ de bord** log; **~ parlé/télévisé** radio/television news *sg*

journalier, -ière [ʒuRnalje, -jɛR] *adj* daily; (*banal*) everyday

journalisme [ʒuRnalism] *nm* journalism; **journaliste** *nm/f* journalist

journée [ʒuRne] *nf* day; **la ~ continue** the 9 to 5 working day (*with short lunch break*)

joyau, x [ʒwajo] *nm* gem, jewel

joyeux, -euse [ʒwajø, -øz] *adj* joyful, merry; **~ Noël!** Merry *ou* Happy Christmas!; **~ anniversaire!** many happy returns!

jubiler [ʒybile] /1/ *vi* to be jubilant, exult

judas [ʒyda] *nm* (*trou*) spy-hole

judiciaire [ʒydisjɛR] *adj* judicial

judicieux, -euse [ʒydisjø, -øz] *adj* judicious

judo [ʒydo] *nm* judo

juge [ʒyʒ] *nm* judge; **~ d'instruction** examining (BRIT) *ou* committing (US) magistrate; **~ de paix** justice of the peace

jugé [ʒyʒe]: **au ~** *adv* by guesswork

jugement [ʒyʒmã] *nm* judgment; (*Jur: au pénal*) sentence; (: *au civil*) decision

juger [ʒyʒe] /3/ vt to judge; (*estimer*) to consider; ~ **qn/qch satisfaisant** to consider sb/sth (to be) satisfactory; ~ **bon de faire** to consider it a good idea to do
juif, -ive [ʒɥif, -iv] *adj* Jewish ▷ *nm/f*: J~,-ive Jewish man/woman *ou* Jew
juillet [ʒɥijɛ] *nm* July

* **LE 14 JUILLET**
*
* *Le 14 juillet* is a national holiday in France
* and commemorates the storming of the
* Bastille during the French Revolution.
* Throughout the country there are
* celebrations, which feature parades,
* music, dancing and firework displays.
* In Paris a military parade along the
* Champs-Élysées is attended by the
* President.

juin [ʒɥɛ̃] *nm* June
jumeau, -elle, x [ʒymo, -ɛl] *adj, nm/f* twin
jumeler [ʒymle] /4/ *vt* to twin
jumelle [ʒymɛl] *adj f, nf voir* **jumeau**
jument [ʒymɑ̃] *nf* mare
jungle [ʒɔ̃gl] *nf* jungle
jupe [ʒyp] *nf* skirt
jupon [ʒypɔ̃] *nm* waist slip *ou* petticoat
juré, e [ʒyʀe] *nm/f* juror ▷ *adj*: **ennemi ~** sworn *ou* avowed enemy
jurer [ʒyʀe] /1/ *vt* (*obéissance etc*) to swear, vow ▷ *vi* (*dire des jurons*) to swear, curse; (*dissoner*): ~ **(avec)** to clash (with); ~ **de faire/que** to swear *ou* vow to do/that; ~ **de qch** (*s'en porter garant*) to swear to sth
juridique [ʒyʀidik] *adj* legal
juron [ʒyʀɔ̃] *nm* curse, swearword
jury [ʒyʀi] *nm* jury; (*Art, Sport*) panel of judges; (*Scol*) board (of examiners), jury
jus [ʒy] *nm* juice; (*de viande*) gravy, (meat) juice; ~ **de fruits** fruit juice
jusque [ʒysk]: **jusqu'à** *prép* (*endroit*) as far as, (up) to; (*moment*) until, till; (*limite*) up to; ~ **sur/dans** up to; (*y compris*) even on/in; **jusqu'à ce que** until; **jusqu'à présent** *ou* **maintenant** so far; **jusqu'où?** how far?
justaucorps [ʒystokɔʀ] *nm inv* leotard
juste [ʒyst] *adj* (*équitable*) just, fair; (*légitime*) just; (*exact, vrai*) right; (*pertinent*) apt; (*étroit*) tight; (*insuffisant*) on the short side ▷ *adv* right; (*chanter*) in tune; (*seulement*) just; ~ **assez/au-dessus** just enough/above; **pouvoir tout ~ faire** to be only just able to do; **au ~** exactly; **le ~ milieu** the happy medium; **c'était ~** it was a close thing; **justement** *adv* justly; (*précisément*) just, precisely; **justesse** *nf* (*précision*) accuracy; (*d'une remarque*) aptness; (*d'une opinion*) soundness; **de justesse** only just
justice [ʒystis] *nf* (*équité*) fairness, justice; (*Admin*) justice; **rendre ~ à qn** to do sb justice

justificatif, -ive [ʒystifikatif, -iv] *adj* (*document etc*) supporting; **pièce justificative** written proof
justifier [ʒystifje] /7/ *vt* to justify; ~ **de** to prove
juteux, -euse [ʒytø, -øz] *adj* juicy
juvénile [ʒyvenil] *adj* youthful

K l

K [kɑ] *nm inv* K

kaki [kaki] *adj inv* khaki

kangourou [kɑ̃guʀu] *nm* kangaroo

karaté [kaʀate] *nm* karate

kascher [kaʃɛʀ] *adj inv* kosher

kayak [kajak] *nm* kayak; **faire du ~** to go
kayaking

képi [kepi] *nm* kepi

kermesse [kɛʀmɛs] *nf* bazaar, (charity)
fête; village fair

kidnapper [kidnape] /1/ *vt* to kidnap

kilo [kilo] *nm* kilo; **kilogramme** *nm*
kilogramme; **kilométrage** *nm* number of
kilometres travelled, ≈ mileage; **kilomètre**
nm kilometre; **kilométrique** *adj* (*distance*)
in kilometres

kinésithérapeute [kineziteʀapøt] *nm/f*
physiotherapist

kiosque [kjɔsk] *nm* kiosk, stall

kir [kiʀ] *nm* kir (*white wine with blackcurrant
liqueur*)

kit [kit] *nm* kit; **~ piéton** *ou* **mains libres**
hands-free kit; **en ~** in kit form

kiwi [kiwi] *nm* kiwi

klaxon [klaksɔn] *nm* horn; **klaxonner** /1/
vi, vt to hoot (*BRIT*), honk (one's horn) (*US*)

km *abr* (= *kilomètre*) km

km/h *abr* (= *kilomètres/heure*) km/h, kph

K.-O. *adj inv* shattered, knackered

Kosovo [kɔsɔvo] *nm*: **le ~** Kosovo

Koweit, Kuweit [kɔwɛt] *nm*: **le ~** Kuwait

k-way® [kawɛ] *nm* (*lightweight nylon*)
cagoule

kyste [kist] *nm* cyst

l' [l] *art déf voir* **le**

la [la] *art déf voir* **le** ▷ *nm* (*Mus*) A; (*en chantant
la gamme*) la

là [la] *adv* there; (*ici*) here; (*dans le temps*)
then; **elle n'est pas là** she isn't here; **c'est
là que** this is where; **là où** where; **de là** (*fig*)
hence; **par là** (*fig*) by that; *voir aussi* **-ci;
celui; là-bas** *adv* there

labo [labo] *nm* (= *laboratoire*) lab

laboratoire [labɔʀatwaʀ] *nm* laboratory;
~ de langues/d'analyses language/
(medical) analysis laboratory

laborieux, -euse [labɔʀjø, -øz] *adj* (*tâche*)
laborious

labourer /1/ *vt* to plough

labyrinthe [labiʀɛ̃t] *nm* labyrinth, maze

lac [lak] *nm* lake

lacet [lasɛ] *nm* (*de chaussure*) lace; (*de route*)
sharp bend; (*piège*) snare

lâche [lɑʃ] *adj* (*poltron*) cowardly; (*desserré*)
loose, slack ▷ *nm/f* coward

lâcher [lɑʃe] /1/ *vt* to let go of; (*ce qui tombe,
abandonner*) to drop; (*oiseau, animal: libérer*)
to release, set free; (*fig: mot, remarque*) to let
slip, come out with ▷ *vi* (*freins*) to fail; **~ les
amarres** (*Navig*) to cast off (the moorings);
~ prise to let go

lacrymogène [lakʀimɔʒɛn] *adj*:
grenade/gaz ~ tear gas grenade/tear gas

lacune [lakyn] *nf* gap

là-dedans [ladədɑ̃] *adv* inside (there), in it;
(*fig*) in that

là-dessous [ladsu] *adv* underneath, under
there; (*fig*) behind that

là-dessus [ladsy] *adv* on there; (*fig: sur
ces mots*) at that point; (: *à ce sujet*) about
that

ladite [ladit] *adj f voir* **ledit**

lagune [lagyn] *nf* lagoon

là-haut [lao] *adv* up there

laid, e [lɛ, lɛd] *adj* ugly; **laideur** *nf* ugliness
no pl

lainage [lɛnaʒ] nm (vêtement) woollen garment; (étoffe) woollen material

laine [lɛn] nf wool

laïque [laik] adj lay, civil; (Scol) state cpd (as opposed to private and Roman Catholic) ▷ nm/f layman(-woman)

laisse [lɛs] nf (de chien) lead, leash; **tenir en ~** to keep on a lead ou leash

laisser [lese] /1/ vt to leave ▷ vb aux: **~ qn faire** to let sb do; **se ~ aller** to let o.s. go; **laisse-toi faire** let me (ou him) do it; **laisser-aller** nm carelessness, slovenliness; **laissez-passer** nm inv pass

lait [lɛ] nm milk; **frère/sœur de ~** foster brother/sister; **~ écrémé/entier/ concentré/condensé** skimmed/full-fat/ condensed/evaporated milk; **laitage** nm dairy product; **laiterie** nf dairy; **laitier, -ière** adj dairy cpd ▷ nm/f milkman (dairywoman)

laiton [lɛtɔ̃] nm brass

laitue [lety] nf lettuce

lambeau, x [lɑ̃bo] nm scrap; **en ~x** in tatters, tattered

lame [lam] nf blade; (vague) wave; (lamelle) strip; **~ de fond** ground swell no pl; **~ de rasoir** razor blade; **lamelle** nf small blade

lamentable [lamɑ̃tabl] adj appalling

lamenter [lamɑ̃te] /1/: **se lamenter** vi: **se ~ (sur)** to moan (over)

lampadaire [lɑ̃padɛʀ] nm (de salon) standard lamp; (dans la rue) street lamp

lampe [lɑ̃p] nf lamp; (Tech) valve; **~ à pétrole** oil lamp; **~ à bronzer** sunlamp; **~ de poche** torch (BRIT), flashlight (US); **~ halogène** halogen lamp

lance [lɑ̃s] nf spear; **~ d'incendie** fire hose

lancée [lɑ̃se] nf: **être/continuer sur sa ~** to be under way/keep going

lancement [lɑ̃smɑ̃] nm launching no pl

lance-pierres [lɑ̃spjɛʀ] nm inv catapult

lancer [lɑ̃se] /3/ nm (Sport) throwing no pl, throw ▷ vt to throw; (émettre, projeter) to throw out, send out; (produit, fusée, bateau, artiste) to launch; (injure) to hurl, fling; **se lancer** vi (prendre de l'élan) to build up speed; (se précipiter): **se ~ sur** ou **contre** to rush at; **~ du poids** putting the shot; **~ qch à qn** to throw sth to sb; (de façon agressive) to throw sth at sb; **~ un cri** ou **un appel** to shout ou call out; **se ~ dans** (discussion) to launch into; (aventure) to embark on

landau [lɑ̃do] nm pram (BRIT), baby carriage (US)

lande [lɑ̃d] nf moor

langage [lɑ̃gaʒ] nm language

langouste [lɑ̃gust] nf crayfish inv; **langoustine** nf Dublin Bay prawn

langue [lɑ̃g] nf (Anat, Culin) tongue; (Ling) language; **tirer la ~ (à)** to stick out one's tongue (at); **de ~ française** French-speaking; **~ maternelle** native language,

mother tongue; **~s vivantes** modern languages

langueur [lɑ̃gœʀ] nf languidness

languir [lɑ̃giʀ] /2/ vi to languish; (conversation) to flag; **faire ~ qn** to keep sb waiting

lanière [lanjɛʀ] nf (de fouet) lash; (de valise, bretelle) strap

lanterne [lɑ̃tɛʀn] nf (portable) lantern; (électrique) light, lamp; (de voiture) (side)light

laper [lape] /1/ vt to lap up

lapidaire [lapidɛʀ] adj (fig) terse

lapin [lapɛ̃] nm rabbit; (peau) rabbitskin; (fourrure) cony; **poser un ~ à qn** to stand sb up

Laponie [laponi] nf: **la ~** Lapland

laps [laps] nm: **~ de temps** space of time, time no pl

laque [lak] nf (vernis) lacquer; (pour cheveux) hair spray

laquelle [lakɛl] pron voir **lequel**

larcin [laʀsɛ̃] nm theft

lard [laʀ] nm (graisse) fat; (bacon) (streaky) bacon

lardon [laʀdɔ̃] nm piece of chopped bacon

large [laʀʒ] adj wide; broad; (fig) generous ▷ adv: **calculer/voir ~** to allow extra/think big ▷ nm (largeur): **5 m de ~** 5 m wide ou in width; (mer): **le ~** the open sea; **au ~ de** off; **~ d'esprit** broad-minded; **largement** adv widely; (de loin) greatly; (amplement, au minimum) easily; (donner etc) generously; **c'est largement suffisant** that's ample; **largesse** nf generosity; **largesses** nfpl (dons) liberalities; **largeur** nf (qu'on mesure) width; (impression visuelle) wideness, width; (d'esprit) broadness

larguer [laʀge] /1/ vt to drop; **~ les amarres** to cast off (the moorings)

larme [laʀm] nf tear; (fig): **une ~ de** a drop of; **en ~s** in tears; **larmoyer** /8/ vi (yeux) to water; (se plaindre) to whimper

larvé, e [laʀve] adj (fig) latent

laryngite [laʀɛ̃ʒit] nf laryngitis

las, lasse [lɑ, lɑs] adj weary

laser [lazɛʀ] nm: **(rayon) ~** laser (beam); **chaîne** ou **platine ~** compact disc (player); **disque ~** compact disc

lasse [lɑs] adj f voir **las**

lasser [lɑse] /1/ vt to weary, tire

latéral, e, -aux [lateʀal, -o] adj side cpd, lateral

latin, e [latɛ̃, -in] adj Latin ▷ nm (Ling) Latin ▷ nm/f: **L~, e** Latin

latitude [latityd] nf latitude

lauréat, e [loʀea, -at] nm/f winner

laurier [loʀje] nm (Bot) laurel; (Culin) bay leaves pl

lavable [lavabl] adj washable

lavabo [lavabo] nm washbasin; **lavabos** nmpl toilet sg

lavage [lavaʒ] nm washing no pl, wash; ~ **de cerveau** brainwashing no pl

lavande [lavɑ̃d] nf lavender

lave [lav] nf lava no pl

lave-linge [lavlɛ̃ʒ] nm inv washing machine

laver [lave] /1/ vt to wash; (tache) to wash off; **se laver** vi to have a wash, wash; **se ~ les mains/dents** to wash one's hands/clean one's teeth; **~ la vaisselle/le linge** to wash the dishes/clothes; **~ qn de** (accusation) to clear sb of; **laverie** nf: **laverie (automatique)** Launderette® (BRIT), Laundromat® (US); **lavette** nf dish cloth; (fam) drip; **laveur, -euse** nm/f cleaner; **lave-vaisselle** nm inv dishwasher; **lavoir** nm wash house; (évier) sink

laxatif, -ive [laksatif, -iv] adj, nm laxative

layette [lɛjɛt] nf layette

MOT-CLÉ

le, la, l' [lə, la, l] (pl **les**) art déf **1** the; **le livre/la pomme/l'arbre** the book/the apple/the tree; **les étudiants** the students **2** (noms abstraits): **le courage/l'amour/la jeunesse** courage/love/youth **3** (indiquant la possession): **se casser la jambe** etc to break one's leg etc; **levez la main** put your hand up; **avoir les yeux gris/le nez rouge** to have grey eyes/a red nose **4** (temps): **le matin/soir** in the morning/evening; mornings/evenings; **le jeudi** etc (d'habitude) on Thursdays etc; (ce jeudi-là etc) on (the) Thursday **5** (distribution, évaluation) a, an; **trois euros le mètre/kilo** three euros a ou per metre/kilo; **le tiers/quart de** a third/quarter of
▶ pron **1** (personne: mâle) him; (: femelle) her; (: pluriel) them; **je le/la/les vois** I can see him/her/them **2** (animal, chose: singulier) it; (: pluriel) them; **je le (ou la) vois** I can see it; **je les vois** I can see them **3** (remplaçant une phrase): **je ne le savais pas** I didn't know (about it); **il était riche et ne l'est plus** he was once rich but no longer is

lécher [leʃe] /6/ vt to lick; (laper: lait, eau) to lick ou lap up; **se ~ les doigts/lèvres** to lick one's fingers/lips; **lèche-vitrines** nm inv: **faire du lèche-vitrines** to go window-shopping

leçon [ləsɔ̃] nf lesson; **faire la ~ à** (fig) to give a lecture to; **~s de conduite** driving lessons; **~s particulières** private lessons ou tuition sg (BRIT)

lecteur, -trice [lɛktœʀ, -tʀis] nm/f reader; (d'université) (foreign language) assistant ▷ nm (Tech): **~ de cassettes** cassette player; **~ de disquette(s)** disk drive; **~ de CD/DVD** CD/DVD player; **~ MP3** MP3 player

lecture [lɛktyʀ] nf reading.

Attention à ne pas traduire *lecture* par le mot anglais *lecture*.

ledit, ladite [lədi, ladit] (mpl **lesdits**, fpl **lesdites**) adj the aforesaid

légal, e, -aux [legal, -o] adj legal; **légaliser** /1/ vt to legalize; **légalité** nf legality

légendaire [leʒɑ̃dɛʀ] adj legendary

légende [leʒɑ̃d] nf (mythe) legend; (de carte, plan) key; (de dessin) caption

léger, -ère [leʒe, -ɛʀ] adj light; (bruit, retard) slight; (superficiel) thoughtless; (volage) free and easy; **à la légère** (parler, agir) rashly, thoughtlessly; **légèrement** adv (s'habiller, bouger) lightly; **légèrement plus grand** slightly bigger; **manger légèrement** to eat a light meal; **légèreté** nf lightness; (d'une remarque) flippancy

législatif, -ive [leʒislatif, -iv] adj legislative; **législatives** nfpl general election sg

légitime [leʒitim] adj (Jur) lawful, legitimate; (fig) rightful, legitimate; **en état de ~ défense** in self-defence

legs [lɛg] nm legacy

léguer [lege] /6/ vt: **~ qch à qn** (Jur) to bequeath sth to sb

légume [legym] nm vegetable; **~s verts** green vegetables; **~s secs** pulses

lendemain [lɑ̃dmɛ̃] nm: **le ~** the next ou following day; **le ~ matin/soir** the next ou following morning/evening; **le ~ de** the day after

lent, e [lɑ̃, lɑ̃t] adj slow; **lentement** adv slowly; **lenteur** nf slowness no pl

lentille [lɑ̃tij] nf (Optique) lens sg; (Bot) lentil; **~s de contact** contact lenses

léopard [leɔpaʀ] nm leopard

lèpre [lɛpʀ] nf leprosy

MOT-CLÉ

lequel, laquelle [ləkɛl, lakɛl] (mpl **lesquels**, fpl **lesquelles**) (à + **lequel** = **auquel**, de + **lequel** = **duquel** etc) pron **1** (interrogatif) which, which one; **lequel des deux?** which one? **2** (relatif: personne: sujet) who; (: objet, après préposition) whom; (: chose) which ▶ adj: **auquel cas** in which case

les [le] art déf, pron voir **le**

lesbienne [lɛsbjɛn] nf lesbian

lesdits, lesdites [ledi, ledit] adj pl voir **ledit**

léser [leze] /6/ vt to wrong

lésiner [lezine] /1/ vi: **ne pas ~ sur les moyens** (pour mariage etc) to push the boat out

lésion [lezjɔ̃] nf lesion, damage no pl

lessive [lesiv] *nf* (*poudre*) washing powder; (*linge*) washing *no pl*, wash; **lessiver** /1/ *vt* to wash; (*fam: fatiguer*) to tire out, exhaust
lest [lɛst] *nm* ballast
leste [lɛst] *adj* sprightly, nimble
lettre [lɛtʀ] *nf* letter; **lettres** *nfpl* (*étude, culture*) literature *sg*; (*Scol*) arts (subjects); **à la ~** literally; **en toutes ~s** in full; **~ piégée** letter bomb
leucémie [løsemi] *nf* leukaemia

MOT-CLÉ

leur [lœʀ] *adj poss* their; **leur maison** their house; **leurs amis** their friends
▶ *pron* **1** (*objet indirect*) (to) them; **je leur ai dit la vérité** I told them the truth; **je le leur ai donné** I gave it to them, I gave them it
2 (*possessif*): **le (la) leur, les leurs** theirs

levain [ləvɛ̃] *nm* leaven
levé, e [ləve] *adj*: **être ~** to be up; **levée** *nf* (*Postes*) collection
lever [ləve] /5/ *vt* (*vitre, bras etc*) to raise; (*soulever de terre, supprimer: interdiction, siège*) to lift; (*impôts, armée*) to levy ▷ *vi* to rise ▷ *nm*: **au ~** on getting up; **se lever** *vi* to get up, (*soleil*) to rise; (*jour*) to break; (*brouillard*) to lift; **ça va se ~** (*temps*) it's going to clear up; **~ du jour** daybreak; **~ de soleil** sunrise
levier [ləvje] *nm* lever
lèvre [lɛvʀ] *nf* lip
lévrier [levʀije] *nm* greyhound
levure [ləvyʀ] *nf* yeast; **~ chimique** baking powder
lexique [lɛksik] *nm* vocabulary, lexicon; (*glossaire*) vocabulary
lézard [lezaʀ] *nm* lizard
lézarde [lezaʀd] *nf* crack
liaison [ljɛzɔ̃] *nf* (*rapport*) connection; (*Rail, Aviat etc*) link; (*amoureuse*) affair; (*Culin, Phonétique*) liaison; **entrer/être en ~ avec** to get/be in contact with
liane [ljan] *nf* creeper
liasse [ljas] *nf* wad, bundle
Liban [libɑ̃] *nm*: **le ~** (the) Lebanon
libeller [libele] /1/ *vt* (*chèque, mandat*): **~ (au nom de)** to make out (to); (*lettre*) to word
libellule [libelyl] *nf* dragonfly
libéral, e, -aux [libeʀal, -o] *adj, nm/f* liberal; **les professions ~es** liberal professions
libérer [libeʀe] /6/ *vt* (*délivrer*) to free, liberate (*Psych*) to liberate; (*relâcher: prisonnier*) to discharge, release; (*gaz, cran d'arrêt*) to release; **se libérer** *vi* (*de rendez-vous*) to get out of previous engagements
liberté [libɛʀte] *nf* freedom; (*loisir*) free time; **libertés** *nfpl* (*privautés*) liberties; **mettre/être en ~** to set/be free; **en ~ provisoire/surveillée/conditionnelle** on bail/probation/parole

libraire [libʀɛʀ] *nm/f* bookseller
librairie [libʀeʀi] *nf* bookshop

▌ Attention à ne pas traduire *librairie* par *library*.

libre [libʀ] *adj* free; (*route*) clear; (*place etc*) free; (*ligne*) not engaged; (*Scol*) non-state; **~ de qch/de faire** free from sth/to do; **~ arbitre** free will; **libre-échange** *nm* free trade; **libre-service** *nm inv* self-service store
Libye [libi] *nf*: **la ~** Libya
licence [lisɑ̃s] *nf* (*permis*) permit; (*diplôme*) (first) degree; (*liberté*) liberty; **licencié, e** *nm/f* (*Scol*): **licencié ès lettres/en droit** ≈ Bachelor of Arts/Law
licenciement [lisɑ̃simɑ̃] *nm* redundancy
licencier [lisɑ̃sje] /7/ *vt* (*renvoyer*) to dismiss; (*débaucher*) to make redundant
licite [lisit] *adj* lawful
lie [li] *nf* dregs *pl*, sediment
lié, e [lje] *adj*: **très ~ avec** very friendly with *ou* close to
Liechtenstein [liʃtɛnʃtajn] *nm*: **le ~** Liechtenstein
liège [ljɛʒ] *nm* cork
lien [ljɛ̃] *nm* (*corde, fig: affectif, culturel*) bond; (*rapport*) link, connection; **~ de parenté** family tie; **~ hypertexte** hyperlink
lier [lje] /7/ *vt* (*attacher*) to tie up; (*joindre*) to link up; (*fig: unir, engager*) to bind; **~ conversation (avec)** to strike up a conversation (with); **~ connaissance avec** to get to know
lierre [ljɛʀ] *nm* ivy
lieu, x [ljø] *nm* place; **lieux** *nmpl* (*locaux*) premises; (*endroit: d'un accident etc*) scene *sg*; **arriver/être sur les ~x** to arrive/be on the scene; **en premier ~** in the first place; **en dernier ~** lastly; **avoir ~** to take place; **tenir ~ de** to serve as; **donner ~ à** to give rise to; **au ~ de** instead of; **~ commun** commonplace; **lieu-dit** (*pl* **lieux-dits**) *nm* locality
lieutenant [ljøtnɑ̃] *nm* lieutenant
lièvre [ljɛvʀ] *nm* hare
ligament [ligamɑ̃] *nm* ligament
ligne [liɲ] *nf* (*gén*) line; (*Transports: liaison*) service; (*: trajet*) route; (*silhouette*) figure; **garder la ~** to keep one's figure; **en ~** (*Inform*) online; **entrer en ~ de compte** to be taken into account; **~ fixe** (*Tél*) landline
ligné, e [liɲe] *adj*: **papier ~** ruled paper ▷ *nf* line, lineage
ligoter [ligɔte] /1/ *vt* to tie up
ligue [lig] *nf* league
lilas [lila] *nm* lilac
limace [limas] *nf* slug
limande [limɑ̃d] *nf* dab
lime [lim] *nf* file; **~ à ongles** nail file; **limer** /1/ *vt* to file
limitation [limitasjɔ̃] *nf*: **~ de vitesse** speed limit

limite [limit] *nf* (*de terrain*) boundary;
(*partie ou point extrême*) limit; **à la ~** (*au pire*)
if the worst comes (*ou* came) to the worst;
vitesse/charge ~ maximum speed/load;
cas ~ borderline case; **date ~** deadline;
date ~ de vente/consommation sell-by/
best-before date; **limiter** /1/ *vt* (*restreindre*)
to limit, restrict; (*délimiter*) to border;
limitrophe *adj* border *cpd*
limoger [limɔʒe] /3/ *vt* to dismiss
limon [limɔ̃] *nm* silt
limonade [limɔnad] *nf* lemonade
lin [lɛ̃] *nm* (*tissu, toile*) linen
linceul [lɛ̃sœl] *nm* shroud
linge [lɛ̃ʒ] *nm* (*serviettes etc*) linen; (*aussi:*
~ de corps) underwear; (*lessive*) washing;
lingerie *nf* lingerie, underwear
lingot [lɛ̃go] *nm* ingot
linguistique [lɛ̃gɥistik] *adj* linguistic ⊳ *nf*
linguistics *sg*
lion, ne [ljɔ̃, ljɔn] *nm/f* lion (lioness);
(*signe*): **le L~** Leo; **lionceau, x** *nm* lion cub
liqueur [likœr] *nf* liqueur
liquidation [likidasjɔ̃] *nf* (*vente*) sale,
liquidation; (*Comm*) clearance (sale)
liquide [likid] *adj* liquid ⊳ *nm* liquid;
(*Comm*): **en ~** in ready money *ou* cash; **je
n'ai pas de ~** I haven't got any cash; **liquider**
/1/ *vt* to liquidate; (*Comm: articles*) to clear,
sell off
lire [liʀ] /43/ *nf* (*monnaie*) lira ⊳ *vt, vi* to read
lis *vb* [li] *voir* **lire** ⊳ *nm* [lis] = **lys**
Lisbonne [lizbɔn] *n* Lisbon
liseuse [lizøz] *nf* e-reader
lisible [lizibl] *adj* legible
lisière [lizjɛʀ] *nf* (*de forêt*) edge
lisons [lizɔ̃] *vb voir* **lire**
lisse [lis] *adj* smooth
lisseur [lisœʀ] *nm* straighteners
liste [list] *nf* list; **faire la ~ de** to list;
~ électorale electoral roll; **~ de mariage**
wedding (present) list; **listing** *nm* (*Inform*)
printout
lit [li] *nm* bed; **petit ~, ~ à une place** single
bed; **grand ~, ~ à deux places** double
bed; **faire son ~** to make one's bed; **aller/
se mettre au ~** to go to/get into bed; **~ de
camp** camp bed; **~ d'enfant** cot (*BRIT*),
crib (*US*)
literie [litʀi] *nf* bedding, bedclothes *pl*
litige [litiʒ] *nm* dispute
litre [litʀ] *nm* litre
littéraire [liteʀɛʀ] *adj* literary ⊳ *nm/f* arts
student; **elle est très ~** she's very literary
littéral, e, -aux [liteʀal, -o] *adj* literal
littérature [liteʀatyʀ] *nf* literature
littoral, e, -aux [litɔʀal, -o] *nm* coast
livide [livid] *adj* livid, pallid
livraison [livʀɛzɔ̃] *nf* delivery
livre [livʀ] *nm* book ⊳ *nf* (*poids, monnaie*)
pound; **~ numérique** e-book; **~ de poche**
paperback

livré, e [livʀe] *adj*: **~ à soi-même** left to
oneself *ou* one's own devices
livrer [livʀe] /1/ *vt* (*Comm*) to deliver; (*otage,
coupable*) to hand over; (*secret, information*)
to give away; **se ~ à** (*se rendre*) to give o.s.
up to; (*faire: pratiques, actes*) to indulge in;
(*enquête*) to carry out
livret [livʀɛ] *nm* booklet; (*d'opéra*) libretto;
~ de caisse d'épargne (savings) bank-book;
~ de famille (official) family record book;
~ scolaire (school) report book
livreur, -euse [livʀœʀ, -øz] *nm/f* delivery
boy *ou* man/girl *ou* woman
local, e, -aux [lɔkal, -o] *adj* local ⊳ *nm*
(*salle*) premises *pl* ⊳ *nmpl* premises; **localité**
nf locality
locataire [lɔkatɛʀ] *nm/f* tenant; (*de
chambre*) lodger
location [lɔkasjɔ̃] *nf* (*par le locataire*)
renting; (*par le propriétaire*) renting out,
letting; (*bureau*) booking office; **~ de
voitures** "car hire (*BRIT*) *ou* rental (*US*)";
habiter en ~ to live in rented
accommodation; **prendre une ~ (pour les
vacances)** to rent a house *etc* (for the
holidays)
▌ Attention à ne pas traduire *location* par
le mot anglais *location*.
locomotive [lɔkɔmɔtiv] *nf* locomotive,
engine
locution [lɔkysjɔ̃] *nf* phrase
loge [lɔʒ] *nf* (*Théât: d'artiste*) dressing room;
(: *de spectateurs*) box; (*de concierge, franc-
maçon*) lodge
logement [lɔʒmɑ̃] *nm* flat (*BRIT*),
apartment (*US*); accommodation *no pl*
(*BRIT*), accommodations *pl* (*US*); (*Pol,
Admin*): **le ~** housing
loger [lɔʒe] /3/ *vt* to accommodate ⊳ *vi*
to live; **se loger** *vr*: **trouver à se ~** to find
accommodation; **se ~ dans** (*balle, flèche*)
to lodge itself in; **être logé, nourri** to have
board and lodging; **logeur, -euse** *nm/f*
landlord (landlady)
logiciel [lɔʒisjɛl] *nm* piece of software
logique [lɔʒik] *adj* logical ⊳ *nf* logic
logo [lɔgo] *nm* logo
loi [lwa] *nf* law; **faire la ~** to lay down the
law
loin [lwɛ̃] *adv* far; (*dans le temps: futur*) a
long way off; (: *passé*) a long time ago;
plus ~ further; **~ de** far from; **~ d'ici** a long
way from here; **au ~** far off; **de ~** from a
distance; (*fig: de beaucoup*) by far
lointain, e [lwɛ̃tɛ̃, -ɛn] *adj* faraway,
distant; (*dans le futur, passé*) distant; (*cause,
parent*) remote, distant ⊳ *nm*: **dans le ~** in
the distance
loir [lwaʀ] *nm* dormouse
Loire [lwaʀ] *nf*: **la ~** the Loire
loisir [lwaziʀ] *nm*: **heures de ~** spare time;
loisirs *nmpl* (*temps libre*) leisure *sg*; (*activités*)

leisure activities; **avoir le ~ de faire** to have the time ou opportunity to do; **(tout) à ~** at leisure

londonien, ne [lɔ̃dɔnjɛ̃, -ɛn] adj London cpd, of London ▷ nm/f: **L~, ne** Londoner

Londres [lɔ̃dʀ] n London

long, longue [lɔ̃, lɔ̃g] adj long ▷ adv: **en savoir ~** to know a great deal ▷ nm: **de 3 m de ~** 3 m long, 3 m in length; **ne pas faire ~ feu** not to last long; **(tout) le ~ de** (all) along; **tout au ~ de** (année, vie) throughout; **de ~ en large** (marcher) to and fro, up and down

longer [lɔ̃ʒe] /3/ vt to go (ou walk ou drive) along(side); (mur, route) to border

longiligne [lɔ̃ʒiliɲ] adj long-limbed

longitude [lɔ̃ʒityd] nf longitude

longtemps [lɔ̃tɑ̃] adv (for) a long time, (for) long; **avant ~** before long; **pour/pendant ~** for a long time; **mettre ~ à faire** to take a long time to do; **il en a pour ~** he'll be a long time

longue [lɔ̃g] adj f voir **long** ▷ nf: **à la ~** in the end; **longuement** adv (longtemps) for a long time; (en détail) at length

longueur [lɔ̃gœʀ] nf length; **longueurs** nfpl (fig: d'un film etc) tedious parts; **en ~** lengthwise; **tirer en ~** to drag on; **à ~ de journée** all day long

loquet [lɔkɛ] nm latch

lorgner [lɔʀɲe] /1/ vt to eye; (fig) to have one's eye on

lors [lɔʀ]: **~ de** prép (au moment de) at the time of; (pendant) during; **~ même que** even though

lorsque [lɔʀsk] conj when, as

losange [lozɑ̃ʒ] nm diamond

lot [lo] nm (part) share; (de loterie) prize; (fig: destin) fate, lot; (Comm, Inform) batch; **le gros ~** the jackpot

loterie [lɔtʀi] nf lottery

lotion [losjɔ̃] nf lotion; **~ après rasage** after-shave (lotion)

lotissement [lɔtismɑ̃] nm housing development; (parcelle) (building) plot, lot

loto [lɔto] nm lotto

lotte [lɔt] nf monkfish

louange [lwɑ̃ʒ] nf: **à la ~ de** in praise of; **louanges** nfpl praise sg

loubar(d) [lubaʀ] nm (fam) lout

louche [luʃ] adj shady, fishy, dubious ▷ nf ladle; **loucher** /1/ vi to squint

louer [lwe] /1/ vt (maison: propriétaire) to let, rent (out); (: locataire) to rent; (voiture etc: entreprise) to hire out (BRIT), rent (out); (: locataire) to hire (BRIT), rent; (réserver) to book; (faire l'éloge de) to praise; **"à ~"** "to let" (BRIT), "for rent" (US)

loup [lu] nm wolf; **jeune ~** young go-getter

loupe [lup] nf magnifying glass; **à la ~** in minute detail

louper [lupe] /1/ vt (fam: manquer) to miss; (examen) to flunk

lourd, e [luʀ, luʀd] adj heavy; (chaleur, temps) sultry; **~ de** (menaces) charged with; (conséquences) fraught with; **lourdaud, e** adj clumsy; **lourdement** adv heavily

loutre [lutʀ] nf otter

louveteau, x [luvto] nm wolf-cub; (scout) cub (scout)

louvoyer [luvwaje] /8/ vi (fig) to hedge, evade the issue

loyal, e, -aux [lwajal, -o] adj (fidèle) loyal, faithful; (fair-play) fair; **loyauté** nf loyalty, faithfulness; fairness

loyer [lwaje] nm rent

lu, e [ly] pp de **lire**

lubie [lybi] nf whim, craze

lubrifiant [lybʀifjɑ̃] nm lubricant

lubrifier [lybʀifje] /7/ vt to lubricate

lubrique [lybʀik] adj lecherous

lucarne [lykaʀn] nf skylight

lucide [lysid] adj lucid; (accidenté) conscious

lucratif, -ive [lykʀatif, -iv] adj lucrative; profitable; **à but non ~** non profit-making

lueur [lɥœʀ] nf (chatoyante) glimmer no pl; (pâle) (faint) light; (fig) glimmer, gleam

luge [lyʒ] nf sledge (BRIT), sled (US)

lugubre [lygybʀ] adj gloomy; dismal

⊙ MOT-CLÉ

lui [lɥi] pron **1** (objet indirect: mâle) (to) him; (: femelle) (to) her; (: chose, animal) (to) it; **je lui ai parlé** I have spoken to him (ou to her); **il lui a offert un cadeau** he gave him (ou her) a present

2 (après préposition, comparatif: personne) him; (: chose, animal) it; **elle est contente de lui** she is pleased with him; **je la connais mieux que lui** I know her better than he does; I know her better than him; **cette voiture est à lui** this car belongs to him, this is HIS car; **c'est à lui de jouer** it's his turn ou go

3 (sujet, forme emphatique) he; **lui, il est à Paris** HE is in Paris; **c'est lui qui l'a fait** HE did it

4 (objet, forme emphatique) him; **c'est lui que j'attends** I'm waiting for HIM

5: **lui-même** himself; itself

luire [lɥiʀ] /38/ vi to shine; (reflets chauds, cuivrés) to glow

lumière [lymjɛʀ] nf light; **mettre en ~** (fig) to highlight; **~ du jour/soleil** day/sunlight

luminaire [lyminɛʀ] nm lamp, light

lumineux, -euse [lyminø, -øz] adj luminous; (éclairé) illuminated; (ciel, journée, couleur) bright; (rayon etc) of light, light cpd; (fig: regard) radiant

lunatique [lynatik] adj whimsical, temperamental

lundi [lœdi] *nm* Monday; **on est ~** it's Monday; **le(s) ~(s)** on Mondays; **à ~!** see you (on) Monday!; **~ de Pâques** Easter Monday

lune [lyn] *nf* moon; **~ de miel** honeymoon

lunette [lynɛt] *nf*: **~s** glasses, spectacles; (*protectrices*) goggles; **~ arrière** (*Auto*) rear window; **~s noires** dark glasses; **~s de soleil** sunglasses

lustre [lystʀ] *nm* (*de plafond*) chandelier; (*fig: éclat*) lustre; **lustrer** /1/ *vt*: **lustrer qch** to make sth shine

luth [lyt] *nm* lute

lutin [lytɛ̃] *nm* imp, goblin

lutte [lyt] *nf* (*conflit*) struggle; (*Sport*): **la ~** wrestling; **lutter** /1/ *vi* to fight, struggle

luxe [lyks] *nm* luxury; **de ~** luxury *cpd*

Luxembourg [lyksãbuʀ] *nm*: **le ~** Luxembourg

luxer [lykse] /1/ *vt*: **se ~ l'épaule** to dislocate one's shoulder

luxueux, -euse [lyksɥø, -øz] *adj* luxurious

lycée [lise] *nm* (state) secondary (BRIT) *ou* high (US) school; **lycéen, ne** *nm/f* secondary school pupil

Lyon [ljɔ̃] *n* Lyons

lyophilisé, e [ljofilize] *adj* (*café*) freeze-dried

lyrique [liʀik] *adj* lyrical; (*Opéra*) lyric; **artiste ~** opera singer

lys [lis] *nm* lily

M *abr* = **Monsieur**

m' [m] *pron voir* **me**

ma [ma] *adj poss voir* **mon**

macaron [makaʀɔ̃] *nm* (*gâteau*) macaroon; (*insigne*) (round) badge

macaroni(s) [makaʀɔni] *nm(pl)* macaroni *sg*; **~ au gratin** macaroni cheese (BRIT), macaroni and cheese (US)

Macédoine [masedwan] *nf* Macedonia

macédoine [masedwan] *nf*: **~ de fruits** fruit salad; **~ de légumes** mixed vegetables *pl*

macérer [masere] /6/ *vi, vt* to macerate; (*dans du vinaigre*) to pickle

mâcher [maʃe] /1/ *vt* to chew; **ne pas ~ ses mots** not to mince one's words

machin [maʃɛ̃] *nm* (*fam*) thingamajig; (*personne*): **M~(e)** what's-his(*ou* her)-name

machinal, e, -aux [maʃinal, -o] *adj* mechanical, automatic

machination [maʃinasjɔ̃] *nf* frame-up

machine [maʃin] *nf* machine; (*locomotive*) engine; **~ à laver/coudre/tricoter** washing/sewing/knitting machine; **~ à sous** fruit machine

mâchoire [maʃwaʀ] *nf* jaw

mâchonner [maʃɔne] /1/ *vt* to chew (at)

maçon [masɔ̃] *nm* bricklayer; (*constructeur*) builder; **maçonnerie** *nf* (*murs*) brickwork; (: *de pierre*) masonry, stonework

Madagascar [madagaskaʀ] *nf* Madagascar

Madame [madam] (*pl* **Mesdames**) *nf*: **~ X** Mrs X; **occupez-vous de ~/Monsieur/ Mademoiselle** please serve this lady/ gentleman/(young) lady; **bonjour ~/ Monsieur/Mademoiselle** good morning; (*ton déférent*) good morning Madam/Sir/ Madam; (*le nom est connu*) good morning Mrs X/Mr X/Miss X; **~/Monsieur/ Mademoiselle!** (*pour appeler*) excuse me!; **~/Monsieur/Mademoiselle** (*sur lettre*)

Dear Madam/Sir/Madam; **chère ~/cher Monsieur/chère Mademoiselle** Dear Mrs X/Mr X/Miss X; **Mesdames** Ladies; **mesdames, mesdemoiselles, messieurs** ladies and gentlemen

madeleine [madlɛn] *nf* madeleine, ≈ sponge finger cake

Mademoiselle [madmwazɛl] (*pl* **Mesdemoiselles**) *nf* Miss; *voir aussi* **Madame**

Madère [madɛʀ] *nf* Madeira ▷ *nm*: **madère** Madeira (wine)

Madrid [madʀid] *n* Madrid

magasin [magazɛ̃] *nm* (*boutique*) shop; (*entrepôt*) warehouse; **en ~** (*Comm*) in stock

magazine [magazin] *nm* magazine

Maghreb [magʀɛb] *nm*: **le ~** North(-West) Africa; **maghrébin, e** *adj* North African ▷ *nm/f*: **Maghrébin, e** North African

magicien, ne [maʒisjɛ̃, -ɛn] *nm/f* magician

magie [maʒi] *nf* magic; **magique** *adj* magic; (*fig*) magical

magistral, e, -aux [maʒistʀal, -o] *adj* (*œuvre, adresse*) masterly; (*ton*) authoritative; **cours ~** lecture

magistrat [maʒistʀa] *nm* magistrate

magnétique [maɲetik] *adj* magnetic

magnétophone [maɲetɔfɔn] *nm* tape recorder; **~ à cassettes** cassette recorder

magnétoscope [maɲetɔskɔp] *nm*: **~ (à cassette)** video (recorder)

magnifique [maɲifik] *adj* magnificent

magret [magʀɛ] *nm*: **~ de canard** duck breast

mai [mɛ] *nm* May; *voir aussi* **juillet**

maigre [mɛgʀ] *adj* (very) thin, skinny; (*viande*) lean; (*fromage*) low-fat; (*végétation*) thin, sparse; (*fig*) poor, meagre, skimpy; **jours ~s** days of abstinence, fish days; **maigreur** *nf* thinness; **maigrir** /2/ *vi* to get thinner, lose weight; **maigrir de 2 kilos** to lose 2 kilos

mail [mɛl] *nm* email

maille [maj] *nf* stitch; **~ à l'endroit/à l'envers** plain/purl stitch

maillet [majɛ] *nm* mallet

maillon [majɔ̃] *nm* link

maillot [majo] *nm* (*aussi*: **~ de corps**) vest; (*de sportif*) jersey; **~ de bain** swimming *ou* bathing (BRIT) costume, swimsuit; (*d'homme*) (swimming *ou* bathing (BRIT)) trunks *pl*

main [mɛ̃] *nf* hand; **à la ~** (*tenir, avoir*) in one's hand; (*faire, tricoter etc*) by hand; **se donner la ~** to hold hands; **donner** *ou* **tendre la ~ à qn** to hold out one's hand to sb; **se serrer la ~** to shake hands; **serrer la ~ à qn** to shake hands with sb; **sous la ~** to *ou* at hand; **haut les ~s!** hands up!; **attaque à ~ armée** armed attack; **à remettre en ~s propres** to be delivered personally; **mettre la dernière ~ à** to put the finishing touches to; **se faire/perdre la ~** to get one's hand in/lose one's touch; **avoir qch bien en ~** to have got the hang of sth; **main-d'œuvre** *nf* manpower, labour; **mainmise** *nf* (*fig*): **avoir la mainmise sur** to have a grip *ou* stranglehold on

mains-libres [mɛ̃libʀ] *adj inv* (*téléphone, kit*) hands-free

maint, e [mɛ̃, mɛ̃t] *adj* many a; **~s** many; **à ~es reprises** time and (time) again

maintenant [mɛ̃tnɑ̃] *adv* now; (*actuellement*) nowadays

maintenir [mɛ̃tniʀ] /22/ *vt* (*retenir, soutenir*) to support; (*contenir: foule etc*) to keep in check; (*conserver*) to maintain; **se maintenir** *vi* (*prix*) to keep steady; (*préjugé*) to persist

maintien [mɛ̃tjɛ̃] *nm* maintaining; (*attitude*) bearing

maire [mɛʀ] *nm* mayor; **mairie** *nf* (*bâtiment*) town hall; (*administration*) town council

mais [mɛ] *conj* but; **~ non!** of course not!; **~ enfin** but after all; (*indignation*) look here!

maïs [mais] *nm* maize (BRIT), corn (US)

maison [mɛzɔ̃] *nf* house; (*chez-soi*) home; (*Comm*) firm ▷ *adj inv* (*Culin*) home-made; (*Comm*) in-house, own; **à la ~** at home;

(*direction*) home; **~ close** brothel; **~ des
jeunes** ≈ youth club; **~ mère** parent
company; **~ de passe** = **maison close**; **~ de
repos** convalescent home; **~ de retraite** old
people's home; **~ de santé** psychiatric unit

maître, -esse [mɛtʀ, mɛtʀɛs] *nm/f* master
(mistress); (*Scol*) teacher, schoolmaster/-
mistress ▷ *nm* (*peintre etc*) master; (*titre*):
M~ (Mᵉ) Maître (*term of address for lawyers
etc*) ▷ *adj* (*principal, essentiel*) main; **être ~
de** (*soi-même, situation*) to be in control of;
une maîtresse femme a forceful woman;
~ chanteur blackmailer; **~/maîtresse
d'école** schoolmaster/-mistress; **~ d'hôtel**
(*domestique*) butler; (*d'hôtel*) head waiter;
~ nageur lifeguard; **maîtresse de maison**
hostess; (*ménagère*) housewife

maîtrise [mɛtʀiz] *nf* (*aussi*: **~ de soi**)
self-control, self-possession; (*habileté*) skill,
mastery; (*suprématie*) mastery, command;
(*diplôme*) ≈ master's degree; **maîtriser** /1/
vt (*cheval, incendie*) to (bring under) control;
(*sujet*) to master; (*émotion*) to control,
master; **se maîtriser** to control o.s.

majestueux, -euse [maʒɛstɥø, -øz] *adj*
majestic

majeur, e [maʒœʀ] *adj* (*important*) major;
(*Jur*) of age ▷ *nm* (*doigt*) middle finger; **en
~e partie** for the most part; **la ~e partie
de** most of

majorer [maʒɔʀe] /1/ *vt* to increase

majoritaire [maʒɔʀitɛʀ] *adj* majority *cpd*

majorité [maʒɔʀite] *nf* (*gén*) majority;
(*parti*) party in power; **en ~** (*composé etc*)
mainly; **avoir la ~** to have the majority

majuscule [maʒyskyl] *adj, nf*: (**lettre**) **~**
capital (letter)

mal (*pl* **maux**) [mal, mo] *nm* (*opposé au bien*)
evil; (*tort, dommage*) harm; (*douleur physique*)
pain, ache; (*maladie*) illness, sickness *no
pl* ▷ *adv* badly ▷ *adj*: **être ~ (à l'aise)** to
be uncomfortable; **être ~ avec qn** to be
on bad terms with sb; **il a ~ compris** he
misunderstood; **se sentir** *ou* **se trouver ~**
to feel ill *ou* unwell; **dire/penser du ~ de**
to speak/think ill of; **avoir du ~ à faire qch**
to have trouble doing sth; **se donner du ~
pour faire qch** to go to a lot of trouble to
do sth; **ne voir aucun ~ à** to see no harm
in, see nothing wrong in; **faire du ~ à qn** to
hurt sb; **se faire ~** to hurt o.s.; **ça fait ~** it
hurts; **j'ai ~ au dos** my back aches; **avoir ~
à la tête/à la gorge** to have a headache/a
sore throat; **avoir ~ aux dents/à l'oreille**
to have toothache/earache; **avoir le ~ du
pays** to be homesick; **~ de mer** seasickness;
~ en point in a bad state; *voir aussi* **cœur**

malade [malad] *adj* ill, sick; (*poitrine, jambe*)
bad; (*plante*) diseased ▷ *nm/f* invalid, sick
person; (*à l'hôpital etc*) patient; **tomber
~** to fall ill; **être ~ du cœur** to have heart
trouble *ou* a bad heart; **~ mental** mentally

ill person; **maladie** *nf* (*spécifique*) disease,
illness; (*mauvaise santé*) illness, sickness;
maladif, -ive *adj* sickly; (*curiosité, besoin*)
pathological

maladresse [maladʀɛs] *nf* clumsiness *no
pl*; (*gaffe*) blunder

maladroit, e [maladʀwa, -wat] *adj* clumsy

malaise [malɛz] *nm* (*Méd*) feeling of
faintness; (*fig*) uneasiness, malaise; **avoir
un ~** to feel faint *ou* dizzy

Malaisie [malɛzi] *nf*: **la ~** Malaysia

malaria [malaʀja] *nf* malaria

malaxer [malakse] /1/ *vt* (*pétrir*) to knead;
(*mêler*) to mix

malbouffe [malbuf] *nf* (*fam*): **la ~** junk food

malchance [malʃɑ̃s] *nf* misfortune, ill luck
no pl; **par ~** unfortunately; **malchanceux,
-euse** *adj* unlucky

mâle [mɑl] *adj* (*Élec, Tech*) male; (*viril: voix,
traits*) manly ▷ *nm* male

malédiction [malediksjɔ̃] *nf* curse

mal: malentendant, e *nm/f*: **les
malentendants** the hard of hearing;
malentendu *nm* misunderstanding; **il
y a eu un malentendu** there's been a
misunderstanding; **malfaçon** *nf* fault;
malfaisant, e *adj* evil, harmful; **malfaiteur**
nm lawbreaker, criminal; (*voleur*) burglar,
thief; **malfamé, e** *adj* disreputable

malgache [malgaʃ] *adj* Malagasy,
Madagascan ▷ *nm* (*Ling*) Malagasy ▷ *nm/f*:
M~ Malagasy, Madagascan

malgré [malgʀe] *prép* in spite of, despite;
~ tout in spite of everything

malheur [malœʀ] *nm* (*situation*) adversity,
misfortune; (*événement*) misfortune; (*: plus
fort*) disaster, tragedy; **faire un ~** to be
a smash hit; **malheureusement** *adv*
unfortunately; **malheureux, -euse** *adj*
(*triste*) unhappy, miserable; (*infortuné,
regrettable*) unfortunate; (*malchanceux*)
unlucky; (*insignifiant*) wretched ▷ *nm/f*
poor soul

malhonnête [malɔnɛt] *adj* dishonest;
malhonnêteté *nf* dishonesty

malice [malis] *nf* mischievousness;
(*méchanceté*): **par ~** out of malice *ou* spite;
sans ~ guileless; **malicieux, -euse** *adj*
mischievous

Attention à ne pas traduire *malicieux* par
malicious.

malin, -igne [malɛ̃, -iɲ] *adj* (*futé*) (*f gén*
maline) smart, shrewd; (*Méd*) malignant

malingre [malɛ̃gʀ] *adj* puny

malle [mal] *nf* trunk; **mallette** *nf* (*small*)
suitcase; (*pour documents*) attaché case

malmener [malməne] /5/ *vt* to
manhandle; (*fig*) to give a rough ride to

malodorant, e [malɔdɔʀɑ̃, -ɑ̃t] *adj* foul-
smelling

malpoli, e [malpɔli] *adj* impolite

malsain, e [malsɛ̃, -ɛn] *adj* unhealthy

malt [malt] *nm* malt
Malte [malt] *nf* Malta
maltraiter [maltrete] /1/ *vt* to manhandle, ill-treat
malveillance [malvɛjɑ̃s] *nf* (*animosité*) ill will; (*intention de nuire*) malevolence
malversation [malvɛrsasjɔ̃] *nf* embezzlement
maman [mamɑ̃] *nf* mum(my)
mamelle [mamɛl] *nf* teat
mamelon [mamlɔ̃] *nm* (*Anat*) nipple
mamie [mami] *nf* (*fam*) granny
mammifère [mamifɛr] *nm* mammal
mammouth [mamut] *nm* mammoth
manche [mɑ̃ʃ] *nf* (*de vêtement*) sleeve; (*d'un jeu, tournoi*) round; (*Géo*): **la M~** the (English) Channel ▷ *nm* (*d'outil, casserole*) handle; (*de pelle, pioche etc*) shaft; **à ~s courtes/longues** short-/long-sleeved; **~ à balai** broomstick; (*Aviat, Inform*) joystick *nm inv*
manchette [mɑ̃ʃɛt] *nf* (*de chemise*) cuff; (*coup*) forearm blow; (*titre*) headline
manchot [mɑ̃ʃo] *nm* one-armed man; armless man; (*Zool*) penguin
mandarine [mɑ̃darin] *nf* mandarin (orange), tangerine
mandat [mɑ̃da] *nm* (*postal*) postal *ou* money order; (*d'un député etc*) mandate; (*procuration*) power of attorney, proxy; (*Police*) warrant; **~ d'arrêt** warrant for arrest; **~ de perquisition** search warrant; **mandataire** *nm/f* (*représentant, délégué*) representative; (*Jur*) proxy
manège [manɛʒ] *nm* riding school; (*à la foire*) roundabout (BRIT), merry-go-round; (*fig*) game, ploy
manette [manɛt] *nf* lever, tap; **~ de jeu** joystick
mangeable [mɑ̃ʒabl] *adj* edible, eatable
mangeoire [mɑ̃ʒwar] *nf* trough, manger
manger [mɑ̃ʒe] /3/ *vt* to eat; (*ronger: rouille etc*) to eat into *ou* away ▷ *vi* to eat; **donner à ~ à** (*enfant*) to feed
mangue [mɑ̃g] *nf* mango
maniable [manjabl] *adj* (*outil*) handy; (*voiture, voilier*) easy to handle
maniaque [manjak] *adj* finicky, fussy ▷ *nm/f* (*méticuleux*) fusspot; (*fou*) maniac
manie [mani] *nf* mania; (*tic*) odd habit; **avoir la ~ de** to be obsessive about
manier [manje] /7/ *vt* to handle
maniéré, e [manjere] *adj* affected
manière [manjɛr] *nf* (*façon*) way, manner; **manières** *nfpl* (*attitude*) manners; (*chichis*) fuss *sg*; **de ~ à** so as to; **de cette ~** in this way *ou* manner; **d'une ~ générale** generally speaking, as a general rule; **de toute ~** in any case; **d'une certaine ~** in a (certain) way
manifestant, e [manifɛstɑ̃, -ɑ̃t] *nm/f* demonstrator

manifestation [manifɛstasjɔ̃] *nf* (*de joie, mécontentement*) expression, demonstration; (*symptôme*) outward sign; (*fête etc*) event; (*Pol*) demonstration
manifeste [manifɛst] *adj* obvious, evident ▷ *nm* manifesto; **manifester** /1/ *vt* (*volonté, intentions*) to show, indicate; (*joie, peur*) to express, show ▷ *vi* to demonstrate; **se manifester** *vi* (*émotion*) to show *ou* express itself; (*difficultés*) to arise; (*symptômes*) to appear
manigancer [manigɑ̃se] /3/ *vt* to plot
manipulation [manipylasjɔ̃] *nf* handling; (*Pol, génétique*) manipulation
manipuler [manipyle] /1/ *vt* to handle; (*fig*) to manipulate
manivelle [manivɛl] *nf* crank
mannequin [mankɛ̃] *nm* (*Couture*) dummy; (*Mode*) model
manœuvre [manœvr] *nf* (*gén*) manoeuvre (BRIT), maneuver (US) ▷ *nm* labourer; **manœuvrer** /1/ *vt* to manoeuvre (BRIT), maneuver (US); (*levier, machine*) to operate ▷ *vi* to manoeuvre *ou* maneuver
manoir [manwar] *nm* manor *ou* country house
manque [mɑ̃k] *nm* (*insuffisance, vide*) emptiness, gap; (*Méd*) withdrawal; **~ de** lack of; **être en état de ~** to suffer withdrawal symptoms
manqué [mɑ̃ke] *adj* failed; **garçon ~** tomboy
manquer [mɑ̃ke] /1/ *vi* (*faire défaut*) to be lacking; (*être absent*) to be missing; (*échouer*) to fail ▷ *vt* to miss ▷ *vb impers*: **il (nous) manque encore 10 euros** we are still 10 euros short; **il manque des pages (au livre)** there are some pages missing *ou* some pages are missing (from the book); **~ à qn** (*absent etc*): **il/cela me manque** I miss him/that; **~ à** (*règles etc*) to be in breach of, fail to observe; **~ de** to lack; **ne pas ~ de faire**: **je ne manquerai pas de le lui dire** I'll be sure to tell him; **il a manqué (de) se tuer** he very nearly got killed
mansarde [mɑ̃sard] *nf* attic; **mansardé, e** *adj*: **chambre mansardée** attic room
manteau, x [mɑ̃to] *nm* coat
manucure [manykyr] *nf* manicurist
manuel, le [manɥɛl] *adj* manual ▷ *nm* (*ouvrage*) manual, handbook
manufacture [manyfaktyr] *nf* factory; **manufacturé, e** *adj* manufactured
manuscrit, e [manyskri, -it] *adj* handwritten ▷ *nm* manuscript
manutention [manytɑ̃sjɔ̃] *nf* (*Comm*) handling
mappemonde [mapmɔ̃d] *nf* (*plane*) map of the world; (*sphère*) globe
maquereau, x [makro] *nm* (*Zool*) mackerel *inv*; (*fam*) pimp

maquette [makɛt] nf (d'un décor, bâtiment, véhicule) (scale) model

maquillage [makijaʒ] nm making up; (produits) make-up

maquiller [makije] /1/ vt (personne, visage) to make up; (truquer: passeport, statistique) to fake; (: voiture volée) to do over (respray etc); **se maquiller** vi to make o.s. up

maquis [maki] nm (Géo) scrub; (Mil) maquis, underground fighting no pl

maraîcher, -ère [maʁeʃe, maʁeʃɛʁ] adj: **cultures maraîchères** market gardening sg ▷ nm/f market gardener

marais [maʁɛ] nm marsh, swamp

marasme [maʁasm] nm stagnation, sluggishness

marathon [maʁatɔ̃] nm marathon

marbre [maʁbʁ] nm marble

marc [maʁ] nm (de raisin, pommes) marc

marchand, e [maʁʃɑ̃, -ɑ̃d] nm/f shopkeeper, tradesman/-woman; (au marché) stallholder; **~ de charbon/vins** coal/wine merchant ▷ adj: **prix/valeur ~(e)** market price/value; **~ de fruits** fruiterer (BRIT), fruit seller (US); **~ de journaux** newsagent; **~ de légumes** greengrocer (BRIT), produce dealer (US); **~ de poisson** fishmonger (BRIT), fish seller (US); **marchander** /1/ vi to bargain, haggle; **marchandise** nf goods pl, merchandise no pl

marche [maʁʃ] nf (d'escalier) step; (activité) walking; (promenade, trajet, allure) walk; (démarche) walk, gait; (Mil, Mus) march; (fonctionnement) running, (des événements) course; **dans le sens de la ~** (Rail) facing the engine; **en ~** (monter etc) while the vehicle is moving ou in motion; **mettre en ~** to start; **se mettre en ~** (personne) to get moving; (machine) to start; **être en état de ~** to be in working order; **arrière** reverse (gear); **faire ~ arrière** to reverse; (fig) to backtrack, back-pedal; **~ à suivre** (correct) procedure

marché [maʁʃe] nm market; (transaction) bargain, deal; **faire du ~ noir** to buy and sell on the black market; **~ aux puces** flea market

marcher [maʁʃe] /1/ vi to walk; (Mil) to march; (aller: voiture, train, affaires) to go; (prospérer) to go well; (fonctionner) to work, run; (fam: consentir) to go along, agree; (: croire naïvement) to be taken in; **faire ~ qn** (pour rire) to pull sb's leg; (pour tromper) to lead sb up the garden path; **marcheur, -euse** nm/f walker

mardi [maʁdi] nm Tuesday; **M~ gras** Shrove Tuesday

mare [maʁ] nf pond; (flaque) pool

marécage [maʁekaʒ] nm marsh, swamp; **marécageux, -euse** adj marshy

maréchal, -aux [maʁeʃal, -o] nm marshal

marée [maʁe] nf tide; (poissons) fresh (sea) fish; **~ haute/basse** high/low tide; **~ noire** oil slick

marelle [maʁɛl] nf: **(jouer à) la ~** (to play) hopscotch

margarine [maʁgaʁin] nf margarine

marge [maʁʒ] nf margin; **en ~ de** (fig) on the fringe of; **~ bénéficiaire** profit margin

marginal, e, -aux [maʁʒinal, -o] nm/f (original) eccentric; (déshérité) dropout

marguerite [maʁgəʁit] nf marguerite, (oxeye) daisy; (d'imprimante) daisy-wheel

mari [maʁi] nm husband

mariage [maʁjaʒ] nm marriage; (noce) wedding; **~ civil/religieux** registry office (BRIT) ou civil/church wedding

marié, e [maʁje] adj married ▷ nm/f (bride) groom/bride; **les ~s** the bride and groom; **les (jeunes) ~s** the newly-weds

marier [maʁje] /7/ vt to marry; (fig) to blend; **se ~ (avec)** to marry, get married (to)

marin, e [maʁɛ̃, -in] adj sea cpd, marine ▷ nm sailor ▷ nf navy; **~e marchande** merchant navy

marine [maʁin] adj f voir **marin** ▷ adj inv navy (blue) ▷ nm (Mil) marine

mariner [maʁine] /1/ vt to marinate

marionnette [maʁjɔnɛt] nf puppet

maritalement [maʁitalmɑ̃] adv: **vivre ~** to live together (as husband and wife)

maritime [maʁitim] adj sea cpd, maritime

mark [maʁk] nm mark

marmelade [maʁməlad] nf stewed fruit, compote; **~ d'oranges** (orange) marmalade

marmite [maʁmit] nf (cooking-)pot

marmonner [maʁmɔne] /1/ vt, vi to mumble, mutter

marmotter [maʁmɔte] /1/ vt to mumble

Maroc [maʁɔk] nm: **le ~** Morocco; **marocain, e** [maʁɔkɛ̃, -ɛn] adj Moroccan ▷ nm/f: **Marocain, e** Moroccan

maroquinerie [maʁɔkinʁi] nf (commerce) leather shop; (articles) fine leather goods pl

marquant, e [maʁkɑ̃, -ɑ̃t] adj outstanding

marque [maʁk] nf mark; (Comm: de nourriture) brand; (: de voiture, produits manufacturés) make; (: de disques) label; **de ~** high-class; (personnage, hôte) distinguished; **~ déposée** registered trademark; **~ de fabrique** trademark; **une grande ~ de vin** a well-known brand of wine

marquer [maʁke] /1/ vt to mark; (inscrire) to write down; (bétail) to brand; (Sport: but etc) to score; (: joueur) to mark; (accentuer: taille etc) to emphasize; (manifester: refus, intérêt) to show ▷ vi (événement, personnalité) to stand out, be outstanding; (Sport) to score; **~ les points** to keep the score

marqueterie [maʁkɛtʁi] nf inlaid work, marquetry

marquis, e [maʁki, -iz] nm/f marquis ou marquess (marchioness)

marraine [maʀɛn] nf godmother
marrant, e [maʀɑ̃, -ɑ̃t] adj (fam) funny
marre [maʀ] adv (fam): **en avoir ~ de** to be fed up with
marrer [maʀe] /1/: **se marrer** vi (fam) to have a (good) laugh
marron, ne [maʀɔ̃, -ɔn] nm (fruit) chestnut ▷ adj inv brown ▷ adj (péj) crooked; **~s glacés** marrons glacés; **marronnier** nm chestnut (tree)
mars [maʀs] nm March
Marseille [maʀsɛj] n Marseilles
marteau, x [maʀto] nm hammer; **être ~** (fam) to be nuts; **marteau-piqueur** nm pneumatic drill
marteler [maʀtəle] /5/ vt to hammer
martien, ne [maʀsjɛ̃, -ɛn] adj Martian, of ou from Mars
martyr, e [maʀtiʀ] nm/f martyr ▷ adj martyred; **enfants ~s** battered children; **martyre** nm martyrdom; (fig: sens affaibli) agony, torture; **martyriser** /1/ vt (Rel) to martyr; (fig) to bully (: enfant) to batter
marxiste [maʀksist] adj, nm/f Marxist
mascara [maskaʀa] nm mascara
masculin, e [maskylɛ̃, -in] adj masculine; (sexe, population) male; (équipe, vêtements) men's; (viril) manly ▷ nm masculine
masochiste [mazɔʃist] adj masochistic
masque [mask] nm mask; **~ de beauté** face pack; **~ de plongée** diving mask; **masquer** /1/ vt (cacher: porte, goût) to hide, conceal; (dissimuler: vérité, projet) to mask, obscure
massacre [masakʀ] nm massacre, slaughter; **massacrer** /1/ vt to massacre, slaughter; (texte etc) to murder
massage [masaʒ] nm massage
masse [mas] nf mass; (Élec) earth; (maillet) sledgehammer; **une ~ de** (fam) masses ou loads of; **la ~** (péj) the masses pl: **en ~** (adv: en bloc) in bulk; (en foule) en masse; adj: exécutions, production) mass cpd
masser [mase] /1/ vt (assembler: gens) to gather; (pétrir) to massage; **se masser** vi (foule) to gather; **masseur, -euse** nm/f masseur(-euse)
massif, -ive [masif, -iv] adj (porte) solid, massive; (visage) heavy, large; (bois, or) solid; (dose) massive; (déportations etc) mass cpd ▷ nm (montagneux) massif; (de fleurs) clump, bank; **le M~ Central** the Massif Central
massue [masy] nf club, bludgeon
mastic [mastik] nm (pour vitres) putty; (pour fentes) filler
mastiquer [mastike] /1/ vt (aliment) to chew, masticate
mat, e [mat] adj (couleur, métal) mat(t); (bruit, son) dull ▷ adj inv (Échecs): **être ~** to be checkmate
mât [mɑ] nm (Navig) mast; (poteau) pole, post

match [matʃ] nm match; **faire ~ nul** to draw; **~ aller** first leg; **~ retour** second leg, return match
matelas [matla] nm mattress; **~ pneumatique** air bed ou mattress
matelot [matlo] nm sailor, seaman
mater [mate] /1/ vt (personne) to bring to heel, subdue; (révolte) to put down
matérialiser [mateʀjalize] /1/: **se matérialiser** vi to materialize
matérialiste [mateʀjalist] adj materialistic
matériau, x [mateʀjo] nm material; **matériaux** nmpl material(s)
matériel, le [mateʀjɛl] adj material ▷ nm equipment no pl; (de camping etc) gear no pl; (Inform) hardware
maternel, le [mateʀnɛl] adj (amour, geste) motherly, maternal; (grand-père, oncle) maternal ▷ nf (aussi: **école maternelle**) (state) nursery school
maternité [mateʀnite] nf (établissement) maternity hospital; (état de mère) motherhood, maternity; (grossesse) pregnancy; **congé de ~** maternity leave
mathématique [matematik] adj mathematical; **mathématiques** nfpl mathematics sg
maths [mat] nfpl maths
matière [matjɛʀ] nf matter; (Comm, Tech) material; matter no pl; (fig: d'un livre etc) subject matter, material; (Scol) subject; **en ~ de** as regards; **~s grasses** fat (content) sg; **~s premières** raw materials
Matignon [matiɲɔ̃] nm: (**l'hôtel**) **~** the French Prime Minister's residence
matin [matɛ̃] nm, adv morning; **le ~** (pendant le matin) in the morning; **demain/hier/dimanche ~** tomorrow/yesterday/Sunday morning; **tous les ~s** every morning; **du ~ au soir** from morning till night; **une heure du ~** one o'clock in the morning; **de grand** ou **bon ~** early in the morning; **matinal, e, -aux** [matinal, -o] adj (toilette, gymnastique) morning cpd; **être matinal** (personne) to be up early; (habituellement) to be an early riser; **matinée** nf morning; (spectacle) matinée
matou [matu] nm tom(cat)
matraque [matʀak] nf (de policier) truncheon (BRIT), billy (US)
matricule [matʀikyl] nm (Mil) regimental number; (Admin) reference number
matrimonial, e, -aux [matʀimɔnjal, -o] adj marital, marriage cpd
maudit, e [modi, -it] adj (fam: satané) blasted, confounded
maugréer [mogʀee] /1/ vi to grumble
maussade [mosad] adj sullen; (ciel, temps) gloomy
mauvais, e [mɔvɛ, -ɛz] adj bad; (méchant, malveillant) malicious, spiteful; (faux): **le ~**

numéro the wrong number ▷ adv: **il fait ~** the weather is bad; **sentir ~** to have a nasty smell, smell bad ou nasty; **la mer est ~e** the sea is rough; **~e plaisanterie** nasty trick; **~ joueur** bad loser; **~e herbe** weed; **~e langue** gossip, scandalmonger (BRIT)

mauve [mov] adj mauve

maux [mo] nmpl voir **mal**

maximum [maksimɔm] adj, nm maximum; **au ~** (le plus possible) as much as one can; (tout au plus) at the (very) most ou maximum; **faire le** to do one's level best

mayonnaise [majɔnɛz] nf mayonnaise

mazout [mazut] nm (fuel) oil

me, m' [mə, m] pron (direct: téléphoner, attendre etc) me; (indirect: parler, donner etc) (to) me; (réfléchi) myself

mec [mɛk] nm (fam) guy, bloke (BRIT)

mécanicien, ne [mekanisjɛ̃, -ɛn] nm/f mechanic; (Rail) (train ou engine) driver

mécanique [mekanik] adj mechanical ▷ nf (science) mechanics sg; (mécanisme) mechanism; **ennui ~** engine trouble no pl

mécanisme [mekanism] nm mechanism

méchamment [meʃamɑ̃] adv nastily, maliciously; spitefully

méchanceté [meʃɑ̃ste] nf nastiness, maliciousness; **dire des ~s à qn** to say spiteful things to sb

méchant, e [meʃɑ̃, -ɑ̃t] adj nasty, malicious, spiteful; (enfant: pas sage) naughty; (animal) vicious

mèche [mɛʃ] nf (de lampe, bougie) wick; (d'un explosif) fuse, (de cheveux) lock; **se faire faire des ~s** to have highlights put in one's hair; **de ~ avec** in league with

méchoui [meʃwi] nm whole sheep barbecue

méconnaissable [mekɔnɛsabl] adj unrecognizable

méconnaître [mekɔnɛtʀ] /57/ vt (ignorer) to be unaware of; (mésestimer) to misjudge

mécontent, e [mekɔ̃tɑ̃, -ɑ̃t] adj: **~ (de)** discontented ou dissatisfied ou displeased (with); (contrarié) annoyed (at); **mécontentement** nm dissatisfaction, discontent, displeasure; (irritation) annoyance

Mecque [mɛk] nf: **la ~** Mecca

médaille [medaj] nf medal

médaillon [medajɔ̃] nm (bijou) locket

médecin [medsɛ̃] nm doctor

médecine [medsin] nf medicine

média [medja] nmpl: **les ~** the media; **médiatique** adj media cpd

médical, e, -aux [medikal, -o] adj medical; **passer une visite ~e** to have a medical

médicament [medikamɑ̃] nm medicine, drug

médiéval, e, -aux [medjeval, -o] adj medieval

médiocre [medjɔkʀ] adj mediocre, poor

méditer [medite] /1/ vi to meditate

Méditerranée [mediteʀane] nf: **la (mer) ~** the Mediterranean (Sea); **méditerranéen, ne** adj Mediterranean ▷ nm/f: **Méditerranéen, ne** Mediterranean

méduse [medyz] nf jellyfish

méfait [mefɛ] nm (faute) misdemeanour, wrongdoing; **méfaits** nmpl (ravages) ravages, damage sg

méfiance [mefjɑ̃s] nf mistrust, distrust

méfiant, e [mefjɑ̃, -ɑ̃t] adj mistrustful, distrustful

méfier [mefje] /7/: **se méfier** vi to be wary; (faire attention) to be careful; **se ~ de** to mistrust, distrust, be wary of

méga-octet [megaɔktɛ] nm megabyte

mégarde [megaʀd] nf: **par ~** (accidentellement) accidentally; (par erreur) by mistake

mégère [meʒɛʀ] nf shrew

mégot [mego] nm cigarette end ou butt

meilleur, e [mejœʀ] adj, adv better ▷ nm: **le ~** the best; **le ~ des deux** the better of the two; **il fait ~ qu'hier** it's better weather than yesterday; **~ marché** cheaper

mél [mɛl] nm email

mélancolie [melɑ̃kɔli] nf melancholy, gloom, **mélancolique** adj melancholy

mélange [melɑ̃ʒ] nm mixture; **mélanger** /3/ vt to mix; (vins, couleurs) to blend; (mettre en désordre, confondre) to mix up, muddle (up)

mêlée [mele] nf mêlée, scramble; (Rugby) scrum(mage)

mêler [mele] /1/ vt (substances, odeurs, races) to mix; (embrouiller) to muddle (up), mix up; **se mêler** vi to mix; **se ~ à** (personne) to join; (s'associer à) to mix with; **se ~ de** (personne) to meddle with, interfere in; **mêle-toi de tes affaires!** mind your own business!

mélodie [melɔdi] nf melody; **mélodieux, -euse** adj melodious

melon [məlɔ̃] nm (Bot) (honeydew) melon; (aussi: **chapeau ~**) bowler (hat)

membre [mɑ̃bʀ] nm (Anat) limb; (personne, pays, élément) member ▷ adj member cpd

mémé [meme] nf (fam) granny

 MOT-CLÉ

même [mɛm] adj **1** (avant le nom) same; **en même temps** at the same time; **ils ont les mêmes goûts** they have the same ou similar tastes

2 (après le nom, renforcement): **il est la loyauté même** he is loyalty itself; **ce sont ses paroles/celles-là même** they are his very words/the very ones
▷ pron: **le (la) même** the same one
▷ adv **1** (renforcement): **il n'a même pas pleuré** he didn't even cry; **même lui l'a dit**

even HE said it; **ici même** at this very place; **même si** even if

2: **à même**: **à même la bouteille** straight from the bottle; **à même la peau** next to the skin; **être à même de faire** to be in a position to do, be able to do

3: **de même** likewise; **faire de même** to do likewise *ou* the same; **lui de même** so does (*ou* did *ou* is) he; **de même que** just as; **il en va de même pour** the same goes for

mémoire [memwaʀ] *nf* memory ▷ *nm* (*Scol*) dissertation, paper; **à la ~ de** to the *ou* in memory of; **de ~** from memory; **~ morte** read-only memory, ROM; **~ vive** random access memory, RAM

mémoires [memwaʀ] *nmpl* memoirs

mémorable [memɔʀabl] *adj* memorable

menace [mənas] *nf* threat; **menacer** /3/ *vt* to threaten

ménage [menaʒ] *nm* (*travail*) housework; (*couple*) (married) couple; (*famille, Admin*) household; **faire le ~** to do the housework; **ménagement** *nm* care and attention

ménager¹ [menaʒe] *vt* (*traiter avec mesure*) to handle with tact; (*utiliser*) to use sparingly; (*prendre soin de*) to take (great) care of, look after; (*organiser*) to arrange

ménager², -ère *adj* household *cpd*, domestic ▷ *nf* housewife

mendiant, e [mãdjã, -ãt] *nm/f* beggar

mendier [mãdje] /7/ *vi* to beg ▷ *vt* to beg (for)

mener [məne] /5/ *vt* to lead; (*enquête*) to conduct; (*affaires*) to manage ▷ *vi*: **~ à/dans** (*emmener*) to take to/into; **~ qch à bonne fin** *ou* **à terme** *ou* **à bien** to see sth through (to a successful conclusion), complete sth successfully

meneur, -euse [mənœʀ, -øz] *nm/f* leader; (*péj*) ringleader

méningite [menēʒit] *nf* meningitis *no pl*

ménopause [menopoz] *nf* menopause

menotte [mənɔt] *nf* (*langage enfantin*) handie; **menottes** *nfpl* handcuffs

mensonge [mãsɔ̃ʒ] *nm*: **le ~** lying *no pl*; **un ~** a lie; **mensonger, -ère** *adj* false

mensualité [mãsɥalite] *nf* (*somme payée*) monthly payment

mensuel, le [mãsɥɛl] *adj* monthly

mensurations [mãsyʀasjɔ̃] *nfpl* measurements

mental, e, -aux [mãtal, -o] *adj* mental; **mentalité** *nf* mentality

menteur, -euse [mãtœʀ, -øz] *nm/f* liar

menthe [mãt] *nf* mint

mention [mãsjɔ̃] *nf* (*note*) note, comment; (*Scol*): **~ (très) bien/passable** (*very*) good/ satisfactory pass; **"rayer la ~ inutile"** "delete as appropriate"; **mentionner** /1/ *vt* to mention

mentir [mãtiʀ] /16/ *vi* to lie

menton [mãtɔ̃] *nm* chin

menu, e [məny] *adj* (*mince*) slim, slight; (*frais, difficulté*) minor ▷ *adv* (*couper, hacher*) very fine ▷ *nm* menu; **~ touristique** popular *ou* tourist menu

menuiserie [mənɥizʀi] *nf* (*travail*) joinery, carpentry; (*d'amateur*) woodwork; **menuisier** *nm* joiner, carpenter

méprendre [mepʀãdʀ] /58/: **se méprendre** *vi*: **se ~ sur** to be mistaken about

mépris, e [mepʀi, -iz] *pp de* **méprendre** ▷ *nm* (*dédain*) contempt, scorn; **au ~ de** regardless of, in defiance of; **méprisable** *adj* contemptible, despicable; **méprisant, e** *adj* scornful; **méprise** *nf* mistake, error; **mépriser** /1/ *vt* to scorn, despise; (*gloire, danger*) to scorn, spurn

mer [mɛʀ] *nf* sea; (*marée*) tide; **en ~** at sea; **en haute** *ou* **pleine ~** off shore, on the open sea; **la ~ Morte** the Dead Sea; **la ~ Noire** the Black Sea; **la ~ du Nord** the North Sea; **la ~ Rouge** the Red Sea

mercenaire [mɛʀsənɛʀ] *nm* mercenary, hired soldier

mercerie [mɛʀsəʀi] *nf* (*boutique*) haberdasher's (shop) (BRIT), notions store (US)

merci [mɛʀsi] *excl* thank you ▷ *nf*: **à la ~ de qn/qch** at sb's mercy/the mercy of sth; **~ beaucoup** thank you very much; **~ de** *ou* **pour** thank you for; **sans ~** merciless; mercilessly

mercredi [mɛʀkʀədi] *nm* Wednesday; **~ des Cendres** Ash Wednesday; *voir aussi* **lundi**

mercure [mɛʀkyʀ] *nm* mercury

merde [mɛʀd] (!) *nf* shit (!) ▷ *excl* (bloody) hell (!)

mère [mɛʀ] *nf* mother ▷ *adj inv* mother *cpd*; **~ célibataire** single parent, unmarried mother; **~ de famille** housewife, mother

merguez [mɛʀgɛz] *nf* spicy North African sausage

méridional, e, -aux [meʀidjɔnal, -o] *adj* southern ▷ *nm/f* Southerner

meringue [məʀɛ̃g] *nf* meringue

mérite [meʀit] *nm* merit; **avoir du ~ (à faire qch)** to deserve credit (for doing sth); **mériter** /1/ *vt* to deserve

merle [mɛʀl] *nm* blackbird

merveille [mɛʀvɛj] *nf* marvel, wonder; **faire ~** *ou* **des ~s** to work wonders; **à ~** perfectly, wonderfully; **merveilleux, -euse** *adj* marvellous, wonderful

mes [me] *adj poss voir* **mon**

mésange [mezãʒ] *nf* tit(mouse)

mésaventure [mezavãtyʀ] *nf* misadventure, misfortune

Mesdames [medam] *nfpl voir* **Madame**

Mesdemoiselles [medmwazɛl] *nfpl voir* **Mademoiselle**

mesquin, e [mɛskɛ̃, -in] adj mean, petty; **mesquinerie** nf meanness no pl; (procédé) mean trick

message [mesaʒ] nm message; **~ SMS** text message; **messager, -ère** nm/f messenger; **messagerie** nf (Internet): **messagerie électronique** email; **messagerie instantanée** instant messenger; **messagerie vocale** voice mail

messe [mɛs] nf mass; **aller à la ~** to go to mass

Messieurs [mesjø] nmpl voir **Monsieur**

mesure [məzyr] nf (évaluation, dimension) measurement; (étalon, récipient, contenu) measure; (Mus: cadence) time, tempo; (: division) bar; (retenue) moderation; (disposition) measure, step; **sur ~** (costume) made-to-measure; **dans la ~ où** insofar as, inasmuch as; **dans une certaine ~** to some ou a certain extent; **à ~ que** as; **être en ~ de** to be in a position to

mesurer [məzyre] /1/ vt to measure; (juger) to weigh up, assess; (modérer: ses paroles etc) to moderate

métal, -aux [metal, -o] nm metal; **métallique** adj metallic

météo [meteo] nf (bulletin) (weather) forecast

météorologie [meteɔrɔlɔʒi] nf meteorology

méthode [metɔd] nf method; (livre, ouvrage) manual, tutor

méticuleux, -euse [metikylø, -øz] adj meticulous

métier [metje] nm (profession: gén) job; (: manuel) trade; (: artisanal) craft; (technique, expérience) (acquired) skill ou technique; (aussi: **à tisser**) (weaving) loom

métrage [metraʒ] nm: **long/moyen/court ~** feature ou full-length/medium-length/short film

mètre [mɛtr] nm metre; (règle) metre rule; (ruban) tape measure; **métrique** adj metric

métro [metro] nm underground (BRIT), subway (US)

métropole [metrɔpɔl] nf (capitale) metropolis; (pays) home country

mets [mɛ] nm dish

metteur [mɛtœr] nm: **~ en scène** (Théât) producer; (Ciné) director

⊙ **MOT-CLÉ**

mettre [mɛtr] /56/ vt **1** (placer) to put; **mettre en bouteille/en sac** to bottle/put in bags ou sacks

2 (vêtements: revêtir) to put on; (: porter) to wear; **mets ton gilet** put your cardigan on; **je ne mets plus mon manteau** I no longer wear my coat

3 (faire fonctionner: chauffage, électricité) to put on; (: réveil, minuteur) to set; (: installer: gaz, eau) to put in, lay on; **mettre en marche** to start up

4 (consacrer): **mettre du temps/deux heures à faire qch** to take time/two hours to do sth; **y mettre du sien** to pull one's weight

5 (noter, écrire) to say, put (down); **qu'est-ce qu'il a mis sur la carte?** what did he say ou write on the card?; **mettez au pluriel ...** put ... into the plural

6 (supposer): **mettons que ...** let's suppose ou say that ...

se mettre vr **1** (se placer): **vous pouvez vous mettre là** you can sit (ou stand) there; **où ça se met?** where does it go?; **se mettre au lit** to get into bed; **se mettre au piano** to sit down at the piano; **se mettre de l'encre sur les doigts** to get ink on one's fingers

2 (s'habiller): **se mettre en maillot de bain** to get into ou put on a swimsuit; **n'avoir rien à se mettre** to have nothing to wear

3: **se mettre à** to begin, start; **se mettre à faire** to begin ou start doing ou to do; **se mettre au piano** to start learning the piano; **se mettre au régime** to go on a diet; **se mettre au travail/à l'étude** to get down to work/one's studies

meuble [mœbl] nm piece of furniture; (ameublement) furniture no pl, **meublé** nm furnished flat (BRIT) ou apartment (US); **meubler** /1/ vt to furnish; **se meubler** to furnish one's house

meuf [mœf] nf (fam) woman

meugler [møgle] /1/ vi to low, moo

meule [møl] nf (à broyer) millstone; (de foin, blé) stack; (de fromage) round

meunier, -ière [mønje, -jɛr] nm miller ▷ nf miller's wife

meurs etc [mœr] vb voir **mourir**

meurtre [mœrtr] nm murder; **meurtrier, -ière** adj (arme, épidémie, combat) deadly; (fureur, instincts) murderous ▷ nm/f murderer(-ess)

meurtrir [mœrtrir] /2/ vt to bruise; (fig) to wound

meus etc [mœ] vb voir **mouvoir**

meute [møt] nf pack

mexicain, e [mɛksikɛ̃, -ɛn] adj Mexican ▷ nm/f: **M~, e** Mexican

Mexico [mɛksiko] n Mexico City

Mexique [mɛksik] nm: **le ~** Mexico

mi [mi] nm (Mus) E; (en chantant la gamme) mi

mi... [mi] préfixe half(-), mid-; **à la mi-janvier** in mid-January; **à mi-jambes/-corps** (up ou down) to the knees/waist; **à mi-hauteur/-pente** halfway up (ou down)/up (ou down) the hill

miauler [mjole] /1/ vi to miaow

miche [miʃ] nf round ou cob loaf

mi-chemin [miʃmɛ̃]: **à ~** adv halfway, midway

mi-clos, e [miklo, -kloz] *adj* half-closed
micro [mikʀo] *nm* mike, microphone;
(*Inform*) micro
microbe [mikʀɔb] *nm* germ, microbe
micro: micro-onde *nf*: **four à micro-ondes**
microwave oven; **micro-ordinateur**
nm microcomputer; **microscope** *nm*
microscope; **microscopique** *adj*
microscopic
midi [midi] *nm* midday, noon; (*moment
du déjeuner*) lunchtime; (*sud*) south; **le M~**
the South (of France), the Midi; **à ~** at 12
(o'clock) *ou* midday *ou* noon
mie [mi] *nf* inside of the loaf
miel [mjɛl] *nm* honey; **mielleux, -euse** *adj*
(*personne*) sugary, syrupy
mien, ne [mjɛ̃, mjɛn] *pron*: **le (la) ~(ne)**,
les ~s mine; **les ~s** my family
miette [mjɛt] *nf* (*de pain, gâteau*) crumb;
(*fig: de la conversation etc*) scrap; **en ~s** in
pieces *ou* bits

🔘 **MOT-CLÉ**

mieux [mjø] *adv* **1** (*d'une meilleure façon*):
mieux (que) better (than); **elle travaille/
mange mieux** she works/eats better;
aimer mieux to prefer; **elle va mieux** she
is better; **de mieux en mieux** better and
better
2 (*de la meilleure façon*) best; **ce que je sais
le mieux** what I know best; **les livres les
mieux faits** the best made books
▶ *adj inv* **1** (*plus à l'aise, en meilleure forme*)
better; **se sentir mieux** to feel better
2 (*plus satisfaisant*) better; **c'est mieux
ainsi** it's better like this; **c'est le mieux des
deux** it's the better of the two; **le/la mieux,
les mieux** the best; **demandez-lui, c'est le
mieux** ask him, it's the best thing
3 (*plus joli*) better-looking; **il est mieux que
son frère** (*plus beau*) he's better-looking
than his brother; (*plus gentil*) he's nicer than
his brother; **il est mieux sans moustache**
he looks better without a moustache
4: **au mieux** at best; **au mieux avec** on
the best of terms with; **pour le mieux** for
the best
▶ *nm* **1** (*progrès*) improvement
2: **de mon/ton mieux** as best I/you can (*ou*
could); **faire de son mieux** to do one's best

mignon, ne [miɲɔ̃, -ɔn] *adj* sweet, cute
migraine [migʀɛn] *nf* headache; (*Méd*)
migraine
mijoter [miʒɔte] /1/ *vt* to simmer; (*préparer
avec soin*) to cook lovingly; (*affaire, projet*) to
plot, cook up ▷ *vi* to simmer
milieu, x [miljø] *nm* (*centre*) middle;
(*aussi*: **juste ~**) happy medium; (*Bio, Géo*)
environment; (*entourage social*) milieu;
(*familial*) background; (*pègre*): **le ~** the

underworld; **au ~ de** in the middle of; **au
beau ou en plein ~ (de)** right in the middle
(of)
militaire [militɛʀ] *adj* military, army *cpd*
▷ *nm* serviceman
militant, e [militɑ̃, -ɑ̃t] *adj, nm/f* militant
militer [milite] /1/ *vi* to be a militant
mille [mil] *num* a *ou* one thousand ▶ *nm*
(*mesure*): **~ (marin)** nautical mile; **mettre
dans le ~** (*fig*) to be bang on (target);
millefeuille *nm* cream *ou* vanilla slice;
millénaire *nm* millennium ▷ *adj* thousand-
year-old; (*fig*) ancient; **mille-pattes** *nm inv*
centipede
millet [mijɛ] *nm* millet
milliard [miljaʀ] *nm* milliard, thousand
million (BRIT), billion (US); **milliardaire**
nm/f multimillionaire (BRIT), billionaire (US)
millier [milje] *nm* thousand; **un ~ (de)** a
thousand or so, about a thousand; **par ~s** in
(their) thousands, by the thousand
milligramme [miligʀam] *nm*
milligramme
millimètre [milimɛtʀ] *nm* millimetre
million [miljɔ̃] *nm* million; **deux ~s de** two
million; **millionnaire** *nm/f* millionaire
mime [mim] *nm/f* (*acteur*) mime(r) ▷ *nm*
(*art*) mime, miming; **mimer** /1/ *vt* to mime;
(*singer*) to mimic, take off
minable [minabl] *adj* (*personne*) shabby(-
looking); (*travail*) pathetic
mince [mɛ̃s] *adj* thin; (*personne, taille*) slim,
slender; (*fig: profit, connaissances*) slight,
small; (: *prétexte*) weak ▷ *excl*: ~ **(alors)**!
darn it!; **minceur** *nf* thinness; (*d'une
personne*) slimness, slenderness; **mincir** /2/
vi to get slimmer *ou* thinner
mine [min] *nf* (*physionomie*) expression,
look; (*extérieur*) exterior, appearance; (*de
crayon*) lead; (*gisement, exploitation, explosif*)
mine; **avoir bonne ~** (*personne*) to look
well; (*ironique*) to look an utter idiot; **avoir
mauvaise ~** to look unwell; **faire ~ de faire**
to make a pretence of doing; **~ de rien**
although you wouldn't think so
miner [mine] /1/ *vt* (*saper*) to undermine,
erode; (*Mil*) to mine
minerai [minʀɛ] *nm* ore
minéral, e, -aux [mineʀal, -o] *adj* mineral
minéralogique [mineʀalɔʒik] *adj*:
plaque ~ number (BRIT) *ou* license (US)
plate; **numéro ~** registration (BRIT) *ou*
license (US) number
minet, te [minɛ, -ɛt] *nm/f* (*chat*) pussy-cat;
(*péj*) young trendy
mineur, e [minœʀ] *adj* minor ▷ *nm/f* (*Jur*)
minor ▷ *nm* (*travailleur*) miner
miniature [minjatyʀ] *adj, nf* miniature
minibus [minibys] *nm* minibus
minier, -ière [minje, -jɛʀ] *adj* mining
mini-jupe [miniʒyp] *nf* mini-skirt
minime [minim] *adj* minor, minimal

, e [mɔtɔʀize] adj (personne)
ne's own transport
mɔtʀis] adj f voir **moteur**
tɔt] nf: **~ de terre** lump of earth,
arth); **~ de beurre** lump of butter
), molle [mu, mɔl] adj soft;
sluggish; (résistance, protestations)
m: **avoir du ~** to be slack
muʃ] nf fly
[muʃe] /1/: **se moucher** vi to
s nose
on [muʃʀɔ̃] nm midge
[muʃwaʀ] nm handkerchief,
en papier tissue, paper hanky
udʀ] /47/ vt to grind
] nf pout; **faire la ~** to pout; (fig)
ce
mwɛt] nf (sea)gull
uʃl] nf (gant) mitt(en)
[muje] adj wet
uje] /1/ vt (humecter) to wet,
tʀemper); **~ qn/qch** to make sb/
i (Navig) to lie ou be at anchor;
r to get wet; (fam: prendre des
ommit o.s.
e [mulɑ̃, -ɑ̃t] adj figure-hugging
l] nf mussel ▷ nm (Culin) mould;
nm cake tin (BRIT) ou pan (US)
ule] /1/ vt (vêtement) to hug, fit
nd
ulɛ̃] nm mill; **~ à café** coffee mill;
ermill; **~ à légumes** (vegetable)
à paroles (fig) chatterbox; **~ à**
er mill; **~ à vent** windmill
ulinɛ] nm (de canne à pêche)
ment): **faire des ~s avec qch** to
ound
® [mulinɛt] nf (vegetable)

uly] pp de **moudre**
[muʀɑ̃, -ɑ̃t] adj dying
ʀiʀ] /1/ vi to die; (civilisation)
de froid/faim/vieillesse
sure/hunger/old age; **~ de**
i (fig) to be starving/be bored
'envie de faire to be dying to do
s] nf (Bot) moss; (de savon)
e: sur eau, bière) froth, foam;
e ▷ nm (Navig) ship's boy; **~ à**
foam
muslin] nf muslin; **pommes**
tatoes
se] /1/ vi (bière, détergent) to
to lather; **mousseux, -euse**
: **(vin) mousseux** sparkling

usɔ̃] nf monsoon
mustaʃ] nf moustache
nfpl (d'animal) whiskers pl;
e adj with a moustache
[mustikɛʀ] nf mosquito net
ustik] nm mosquito

moutarde [mutaʀd] nf mustard
mouton [mutɔ̃] nm sheep inv; (peau)
sheepskin; (Culin) mutton
mouvement [muvmɑ̃] nm movement;
(geste) gesture; **avoir un bon ~** to make
a nice gesture; **en ~** in motion; on the
move; **mouvementé, e** adj (vie, poursuite)
eventful; (réunion) turbulent
mouvoir [muvwaʀ] /27/: **se mouvoir** vi
to move
moyen, ne [mwajɛ̃, -ɛn] adj average;
(tailles, prix) medium; (de grandeur moyenne)
medium-sized ▷ nm (façon) means sg,
way ▷ nf average; (Statistique) mean;
(Scol: à l'examen) pass mark; **moyens** nmpl
(capacités) means; **très ~** (résultats) pretty
poor; **je n'en ai pas les ~s** I can't afford it;
au ~ de by means of; **par tous les ~s** by
every possible means, every possible
way; **par ses propres ~s** all by oneself;
~ âge Middle Ages; **~ de transport** means
of transport; **~ne d'âge** average age; **~ne
entreprise** (Comm) medium-sized firm
moyennant [mwajɛnɑ̃] prép (somme) for;
(service, conditions) in return for; (travail,
effort) with
Moyen-Orient [mwajɛnɔʀjɑ̃] nm: **le ~** the
Middle East
moyeu, x [mwajø] nm hub
MST sigle f (= maladie sexuellement
transmissible) STD
mû, mue [my] pp de **mouvoir**
muer [mɥe] /1/ vi (oiseau, mammifère) to
moult, (serpent) to slough (its skin); (jeune
garçon): **il mue** his voice is breaking
muet, te [mɥɛ, -ɛt] adj (fig): **~ d'admiration**
etc speechless with admiration etc; (Ciné)
silent
mufle [myfl] nm muzzle; (goujat) boor
mugir [myʒiʀ] /2/ vi (bœuf) to bellow;
(vache) to low; (fig) to howl
muguet [mygɛ] nm (Bot) lily of the valley
mule [myl] nf (Zool) (she-)mule
mulet [mylɛ] nm (Zool) (he-)mule; (poisson)
mullet
multinational, e, -aux [myltinasjɔnal,
-o] adj, nf multinational
multiple [myltipl] adj multiple, numerous;
(varié) many, manifold; **multiplication**
nf multiplication; **multiplier** /7/ vt to
multiply; **se multiplier** vi to multiply
municipal, e, -aux [mynisipal, -o] adj
(élections, stade) municipal; (conseil) town
cpd; piscine/bibliothèque **~e** public
swimming pool/library; **municipalité** nf
(corps municipal) town council; (commune)
municipality
munir [myniʀ] /2/ vt: **~ qn/qch de** to equip
sb/sth with; **se ~ de** to provide o.s. with
munitions [mynisjɔ̃] nfpl ammunition sg
mur [myʀ] nm wall; **~ (payant)** (Inform)
paywall; **~ du son** sound barrier

---

minimiser [minimize] /1/ vt to minimize;
(fig) to play down
minimum [minimɔm] adj, nm minimum;
au ~ at the very least
ministère [ministɛʀ] nm (cabinet)
government; (département) ministry; (Rel)
ministry
ministre [ministʀ] nm minister (BRIT),
secretary; (Rel) minister; **~ d'État** senior
minister ou secretary
Minitel® [minitɛl] nm (former) videotext
terminal and service
minoritaire [minɔʀitɛʀ] adj minority cpd
minorité [minɔʀite] nf minority; **être en ~**
to be in the ou a minority
minuit [minɥi] nm midnight
minuscule [minyskyl] adj minute, tiny
▷ nf: (lettre) **~** small letter
minute [minyt] nf minute; **à la ~** (just) this
instant; (passé) there and then; **minuter** /1/
vt to time; **minuterie** nf time switch
minutieux, -euse [minysjø, -øz] adj
(personne) meticulous; (travail) requiring
painstaking attention to detail
mirabelle [miʀabɛl] nf (cherry) plum
miracle [miʀakl] nm miracle
mirage [miʀaʒ] nm mirage
mire [miʀ] nf: **point de ~** (fig) focal point
miroir [miʀwaʀ] nm mirror
miroiter [miʀwate] /1/ vi to sparkle,
shimmer; **faire ~ qch à qn** to paint sth in
glowing colours for sb; dangle sth in front
of sb's eyes
mis, e [mi, miz] pp de **mettre** ▷ adj:
bien ~ well dressed ▷ nf (argent: au jeu)
stake; (tenue) clothing; attire; **être de ~e**
to be acceptable ou in season; **~e de fonds**
capital outlay; **~e à jour** update; **~e en plis**
set; **~e au point** (fig) clarification; **~e en
scène** production
miser [mize] /1/ vt (enjeu) to stake, bet;
~ sur (cheval, numéro) to bet on; (fig) to
bank ou count on
misérable [mizeʀabl] adj (lamentable,
malheureux) pitiful, wretched; (pauvre)
poverty-stricken; (insignifiant, mesquin)
miserable ▷ nm/f wretch
misère [mizɛʀ] nf (extreme) poverty,
destitution; **misères** nfpl (malheurs) woes,
miseries; (ennuis) little troubles; **salaire
de ~** starvation wage
missile [misil] nm missile
mission [misjɔ̃] nf mission; **partir en ~**
(Admin, Pol) to go on an assignment;
missionnaire nm/f missionary
mité, e [mite] adj moth-eaten
mi-temps [mitɑ̃] nf inv (Sport: période) half;
(: pause) half-time; **à ~** part-time
miteux, -euse [mitø, -øz] adj seedy
mitigé, e [mitiʒe] adj (sentiments) mixed
mitoyen, ne [mitwajɛ̃, -ɛn] adj (mur)
common, party cpd; **maisons ~nes** semi-

detached houses; (plus de deux) terraced
(BRIT) ou row (US) houses
mitrailler [mitʀaje] /1/ vt to machine-gun;
(fig: photographier) to snap away at; **~ qn de**
to pelt ou bombard sb with; **mitraillette** nf
submachine gun; **mitrailleuse** nf machine
gun
mi-voix [mivwa]: **à ~** adv in a low ou hushed
voice
mixage [miksaʒ] nm (Ciné) (sound) mixing
mixer [miksœʀ] nm (food) mixer
mixte [mikst] adj (gén) mixed; (Scol) mixed,
coeducational; **cuisinière ~** combined gas
and electric cooker
mixture [mikstyʀ] nf mixture; (fig)
concoction
Mlle (pl **Mlles**) abr = **Mademoiselle**
MM abr = **Messieurs**
Mme (pl **Mmes**) abr = **Madame**
mobile [mɔbil] adj mobile; (pièce de
machine) moving ▷ nm (motif) motive;
(œuvre d'art) mobile; **(téléphone) ~** mobile
(phone)
mobilier, -ière [mɔbilje, -jɛʀ] nm furniture
mobiliser [mɔbilize] /1/ vt to mobilize
mobylette® [mɔbilɛt] nf moped
mocassin [mɔkasɛ̃] nm moccasin
moche [mɔʃ] adj (fam: laid) ugly; (mauvais,
méprisable) rotten
modalité [mɔdalite] nf form, mode
mode [mɔd] nf fashion ▷ nm (manière) form,
mode; (Ling) mood; (Inform, Mus) mode;
à la ~ fashionable, in fashion; **~ d'emploi**
directions pl (for use); **~ de paiement**
method of payment; **~ de vie** way of life
modèle [mɔdɛl] adj ▷ nm model; (qui
pose: de peintre) sitter; **~ déposé** registered
design; **~ réduit** small-scale model;
modeler /5/ vt to model
modem [mɔdɛm] nm modem
modéré, e [mɔdeʀe] adj, nm/f moderate
modérer [mɔdeʀe] /6/ vt to moderate;
se modérer vi to restrain o.s.
moderne [mɔdɛʀn] adj modern ▷ nm
(Art) modern style; (ameublement) modern
furniture; **moderniser** /1/ vt to modernize
modeste [mɔdɛst] adj modest; **modestie**
nf modesty
modifier [mɔdifje] /7/ vt to modify, alter;
se modifier vi to alter
modique [mɔdik] adj modest
module [mɔdyl] nm module
moelle [mwal] nf marrow
moelleux, -euse [mwalø, -øz] adj soft;
(gâteau) light and moist
mœurs [mœʀ] nfpl (conduite) morals;
(manières) manners; (pratiques sociales)
habits
moi [mwa] pron me; (emphatique): **~, je ...**
for my part, I ..., I myself ...; **c'est ~ qui l'ai
fait** I did it, it was me who did it;
apporte-le-~ bring it to me; **à ~-mine**; (dans

un jeu) my turn; **moi-même** *pron* myself; *(emphatique)* I myself
moindre [mwɛ̃dʀ] *adj* lesser; lower; **le (la) ~, les ~s** the least; the slightest; **c'est la ~ des choses** it's nothing at all
moine [mwan] *nm* monk, friar
moineau, x [mwano] *nm* sparrow

◯ **MOT-CLÉ**

moins [mwɛ̃] *adv* **1** *(comparatif)*: **moins (que)** less (than); **moins grand que** less tall than, not as tall as; **il a trois ans de moins que moi** he's three years younger than me; **moins je travaille, mieux je me porte** the less I work, the better I feel
2 *(superlatif)*: **le moins** (the) least; **c'est ce que j'aime le moins** it's what I like (the) least; **le (la) moins doué(e)** the least gifted; **au moins, du moins** at least; **pour le moins** at the very least
3: **moins de** *(quantité)* less (than); *(nombre)* fewer (than); **moins de sable/d'eau** less sand/water; **moins de livres/gens** fewer books/people; **moins de deux ans** less than two years; **moins de midi** not yet midday
4: **de moins, en moins**: **100 euros/3 jours de moins** 100 euros/3 days less; **trois livres en moins** three books fewer; three books too few; **de l'argent en moins** less money; **le soleil en moins** but for the sun, minus the sun; **de moins en moins** less and less
5: **à moins de, à moins que** unless; **à moins de faire** unless we do *(ou* he does *etc)*; **à moins que tu ne fasses** unless you do; **à moins d'un accident** barring any accident ▸ *prép*: **quatre moins deux** four minus two; **dix heures moins cinq** five to ten; **il fait moins cinq** it's five (degrees) below (freezing), it's minus five; **il est moins cinq** it's five to

mois [mwa] *nm* month
moisi [mwazi] *nm* mould, mildew; **odeur de ~** musty smell; **moisir** /2/ *vi* to go mouldy; **moisissure** *nf* mould *no pl*
moisson [mwasɔ̃] *nf* harvest; **moissonner** /1/ *vt* to harvest, reap; **moissonneuse** *nf (machine)* harvester
moite [mwat] *adj* sweaty, sticky
moitié [mwatje] *nf* half; **la ~** half; **la ~ de** half (of); **la ~ du temps/des gens** half the time/the people; **à la ~ de** halfway through; **à ~** half *(avant le verbe)*, half- *(avant l'adjectif)*; **à ~ prix** (at) half price
molaire [mɔlɛʀ] *nf* molar
molester [mɔlɛste] /1/ *vt* to manhandle, maul (about)
molle [mɔl] *adj f voir* **mou**; **mollement** *adv (péj: travailler)* sluggishly; *(protester)* feebly
mollet [mɔlɛ] *nm* calf ▸ *adj m*: **œuf ~** soft-boiled egg

molletonné, e [mɔltɔne] *adj* fleece-lined
mollir [mɔliʀ] /2/ *vi (personne)* to relent; *(substance)* to go soft
mollusque [mɔlysk] *nm* mollusc
môme [mom] *nm/f (fam: enfant)* brat
moment [mɔmɑ̃] *nm* moment; **ce n'est pas le ~** this is not the right time; **au même ~** at the same time; *(instant)* at the same moment; **pour un bon ~** for a good while; **pour le ~** for the moment, for the time being; **au ~ de** at the time of; **au ~ où** as; **à tout ~** at any time *ou* moment; *(continuellement)* constantly, continually; **en ce ~** at the moment; *(aujourd'hui)* at present; **sur le ~** at the time; **par ~s** now and then, at times; **d'un ~ à l'autre** any time (now); **du ~ où** *ou* **que** seeing that, since; **momentané, e** *adj* temporary, momentary; **momentanément** *adv* for a while
momie [mɔmi] *nf* mummy
mon, ma *(pl* **mes)** [mɔ̃, ma, me] *adj poss* my
Monaco [mɔnako] *nm*: **le ~** Monaco
monarchie [mɔnaʀʃi] *nf* monarchy
monastère [mɔnastɛʀ] *nm* monastery
mondain, e [mɔ̃dɛ̃, -ɛn] *adj (soirée, vie)* society *cpd*
monde [mɔ̃d] *nm* world; **le ~** *(personnes mondaines)* (high) society; **il y a du ~** *(beaucoup de gens)* there are a lot of people; *(quelques personnes)* there are some people; **beaucoup/peu de ~** many/few people; **mettre au ~** to bring into the world; **pas le moins du ~** not in the least; **mondial, e, -aux** *(population)* world *cpd*; *(influence)* world-wide; **mondialement** *adv* throughout the world; **mondialisation** *nf* globalization
monégasque [mɔnegask] *adj* Monegasque, of *ou* from Monaco ▸ *nm/f*: **M~** Monegasque
monétaire [mɔnetɛʀ] *adj* monetary
moniteur, -trice [mɔnitœʀ, -tʀis] *nm/f (Sport)* instructor (instructress); *(de colonie de vacances)* supervisor ▸ *nm (écran)* monitor
monnaie [mɔnɛ] *nf (Écon: moyen d'échange)* currency; *(petites pièces)*: **avoir de la ~** to have (some) change; **faire de la ~** to get (some) change; **avoir/faire la ~ de 20 euros** to have change of/get change for 20 euros; **rendre à qn la ~ (sur 20 euros)** to give sb the change (from *ou* out of 20 euros)
monologue [mɔnɔlɔg] *nm* monologue, soliloquy; **monologuer** /1/ *vi* to soliloquize
monopole [mɔnɔpɔl] *nm* monopoly
monotone [mɔnɔtɔn] *adj* monotonous
Monsieur *(pl* **Messieurs)** [məsjø, mesjø] *nm (titre)* Mr; **un/le monsieur** *(homme quelconque)* a/the gentleman; **~, ...** *(en tête de lettre)* Dear Sir, ...; *voir aussi* **Madame**
monstre [mɔ̃stʀ] *nm* monster ▸ *adj (fam: effet, publicité)* massive; **un travail ~** a

fantastic amount of work; **monstrueux, -euse** *adj* monstrous
mont [mɔ̃] *nm*: **par ~s et par vaux** up hill and down dale; **le M~ Blanc** Mont Blanc
montage [mɔ̃taʒ] *nm (d'une machine etc)* assembly; *(Photo)* photomontage; *(Ciné)* editing
montagnard, e [mɔ̃taɲaʀ, -aʀd] *adj* mountain *cpd* ▸ *nm/f* mountain-dweller
montagne [mɔ̃taɲ] *nf (cime)* mountain; *(région)*: **la ~** the mountains *pl*; **~s russes** big dipper *sg*, switchback *sg*; **montagneux, -euse** *adj* mountainous; *(basse montagne)* hilly
montant, e [mɔ̃tɑ̃, -ɑ̃t] *adj* rising; *(robe, corsage)* high-necked ▸ *nm (somme, total)* (sum) total, (total) amount; *(de fenêtre)* upright; *(de lit)* post
monte-charge [mɔ̃tʃaʀʒ] *nm inv* goods lift, hoist
montée [mɔ̃te] *nf* rise; *(escalade)* climb; *(côte)* hill; **au milieu de la ~** halfway up
monter [mɔ̃te] /1/ *vt (escalier, côte)* to go (*ou* come) up; *(valise, paquet)* to take (*ou* bring) up; *(étagère)* to raise; *(tente, échafaudage)* to put up; *(machine)* to assemble; *(Ciné)* to edit; *(Théât)* to put on, stage; *(société, coup etc)* to set up ▸ *vi* to go (*ou* come) up; *(chemin, niveau, température, voix, prix)* to go up, rise; *(passager)* to get on; **~ à cheval** *(faire du cheval)* to ride (a horse); **~ sur** to climb up onto; **~ sur** *ou* **à un arbre/une échelle** to climb (up) a tree/ladder; **se ~ à** *(frais etc)* to add up to, come to
montgolfière [mɔ̃gɔlfjɛʀ] *nf* hot-air balloon
montre [mɔ̃tʀ] *nf* watch; **contre la ~** *(Sport)* against the clock
Montréal [mɔ̃ʀeal] *n* Montreal
montrer [mɔ̃tʀe] /1/ *vt* to show; **~ qch à qn** to show sb sth
monture [mɔ̃tyʀ] *nf (bête)* mount; *(d'une bague)* setting; *(de lunettes)* frame
monument [mɔnymɑ̃] *nm* monument; **~ aux morts** war memorial
moquer [mɔke] /1/: **se ~ de** *vt* to make fun of, laugh at; *(fam: se désintéresser de)* not to care about; *(tromper)*: **se ~ de qn** to take sb for a ride
moquette [mɔkɛt] *nf* fitted carpet
moqueur, -euse [mɔkœʀ, -øz] *adj* mocking
moral, e, -aux [mɔʀal, -o] *adj* moral ▸ *nm* morale ▸ *nf (conduite)* morals *pl (règles)*; *(valeurs)* moral standards *pl*, morality; *(d'une fable etc)* moral; **faire la ~e à** to lecture, preach at; **moralité** *nf* morality; *(conclusion, enseignement)* moral
morceau, x [mɔʀso] *nm* piece, bit; *(d'une œuvre)* passage, extract; *(Mus)* piece; *(Culin: de viande)* cut; *(: de sucre)* lump; **mettre en ~x** to pull to pieces *ou* bits; **manger un ~** to have a bite (to eat)

morceler [mɔʀs...] divide up
mordant, e [m...] scathing, cutting; *(fougue)* bite, pu...
mordiller [mɔʀ...] chew at
mordre [mɔʀd...] to bite; **~ sur** *(...* into; **~ à l'ham...**
mordu, e [mɔʀ...] du jazz/de la [...] *ou* buff
morfondre [...] *vi* to mope
morgue [mɔʀ...] *(lieu: de la poli...* mortuary
morne [mɔʀn...]
morose [mɔ...]
mors [mɔʀ] [...]
morse [mɔʀs...] (code)
morsure [m...]
mort[1] [mɔʀ...] risques?)
mort[2], e [m...] dead ▸ *nm/...* *(victime)*: il y... people wer... frightened...
mortalité [...] rate
mortel, le [...] lethal; *(acc...* ennemi)* m... mortal; *(e...*
mort-né, [...]
mortuaire [...] announce...
morue [m...]
mosaïque [...]
Moscou [...]
mosquée [...]
mot [mo...] **~ à ~** wo... **~s croisé...**
motard [...] motorcy...
mot-diè [...]
motel [...]
moteur [...] *Physiol)* m... **roues m...** motor... reche...
motif [...] design...
motiva [...]
motiv [...] accou...
moto [...] *nm/f...*

motoris [...] having...
motrice [...]
motte [...] clod (of...
mou (mo [...] *(personne...* feeble ▸ [...]
mouche [...]
moucher [...] blow on...
moucher [...]
mouchoi [...] hanky; [...]
moudre [...]
moue [m...] to pull a f...
mouette [...]
moufle [n...]
mouillé, [...]
mouiller [...] moisten; [...] sth wet ▸ [...] **se mouil...** risques) ▸ [...]
moulant, [...]
moule [m...] **~ à gâteau...**
mouler [...] closely rou...
moulin [...] **~ à eau w...** shredder; [...] poivre pep...
moulinet [...] reel; *(mouve...* whirl sth ar...
moulinett [...] shredder
moulu, e [...]
mourant, e [...]
mourir [mu...] to die out; [...] to die of exp... **faim/d'enn...** to death; **~ ...**
mousse [...] lather; *(écum...* *(Culin)* mous... raser shavin...
mousseline [...] **~ creamed p...**
mousser [m...] foam; *(savon...* *adj* frothy ▸ [...] wine
mousson [...]
moustache [...]
moustache... [...]
moustachu, [...]
moustiquai... [...]
moustique [...]

mûr, e [myʀ] *adj* ripe; *(personne)* mature

muraille [myʀɑj] *nf* (high) wall

mural, e, -aux [myʀal, -o] *adj* wall *cpd*
▷ *nm* (Art) mural

mûre [myʀ] *nf* blackberry

muret [myʀɛ] *nm* low wall

mûrir [myʀiʀ] /2/ *vi (fruit, blé)* to ripen;
(abcès, furoncle) to come to a head; *(fig:
idée, personne)* to mature ▷ *vt (personne)* to
(make) mature; *(pensée, projet)* to nurture

murmure [myʀmyʀ] *nm* murmur;
murmurer /1/ *vi* to murmur

muscade [myskad] *nf (aussi:* **noix (de) ~**)
nutmeg

muscat [myska] *nm (raisin)* muscat grape;
(vin) muscatel (wine)

muscle [myskl] *nm* muscle; **musclé, e** *adj*
muscular; *(fig)* strong-arm *cpd*

museau, x [myzo] *nm* muzzle; *(Culin)*
brawn

musée [myze] *nm* museum; *(de peinture)*
art gallery

museler [myzle] /4/ *vt* to muzzle;
muselière *nf* muzzle

musette [myzɛt] *nf (sac)* lunch bag

musical, e, -aux [myzikal, -o] *adj* musical

music-hall [myzikol] *nm (salle)* variety
theatre; *(genre)* variety

musicien, ne [myzisjɛ̃, -ɛn] *adj* musical
▷ *nm/f* musician

musique [myzik] *nf* music

musulman, e [myzylmɑ̃, -an] *adj, nm/f*
Moslem, Muslim

mutation [mytasjɔ̃] *nf (Admin)* transfer

muter [myte] /1/ *vt* to transfer, move

mutilé, e [mytile] *nm/f* person with a
disability *(through loss of limbs)*

mutiler [mytile] /1/ *vt* to mutilate, maim

mutin, e [mytɛ̃, -in] *adj (enfant, air, ton)*
mischievous, impish ▷ *nm/f* (Mil, Navig)
mutineer; **mutinerie** *nf* mutiny

mutisme [mytism] *nm* silence

mutuel, le [mytɥɛl] *adj* mutual ▷ *nf*
mutual benefit society

myope [mjɔp] *adj* short-sighted

myosotis [mjɔzɔtis] *nm* forget-me-not

myrtille [miʀtij] *nf* blueberry

mystère [mistɛʀ] *nm* mystery;
mystérieux, -euse *adj* mysterious

mystifier [mistifje] /7/ *vt* to fool

mythe [mit] *nm* myth

mythologie [mitɔlɔʒi] *nf* mythology

n

n' [n] *adv voir* **ne**

nacre [nakʀ] *nf* mother-of-pearl

nage [naʒ] *nf* swimming; *(manière)* style of
swimming, stroke; **traverser/s'éloigner
à la ~** to swim across/away; **en ~** bathed
in sweat; **nageoire** *nf* fin; **nager** /3/ *vi* to
swim; **nageur, -euse** *nm/f* swimmer

naïf, -ïve [naif, naiv] *adj* naïve

nain, e [nɛ̃, nɛn] *nm/f (péj)* dwarf (!)

naissance [nɛsɑ̃s] *nf* birth; **donner ~ à** to
give birth to; *(fig)* to give rise to; **lieu de ~**
place of birth

naître [nɛtʀ] /59/ *vi* to be born; *(conflit,
complications)*: **~ de** to arise from, be born
out of; **je suis né en 1960** I was born in
1960; **faire ~** *(fig)* to give rise to, arouse

naïveté [naivte] *nf* naivety

nana [nana] *nf (fam: fille)* bird (BRIT), chick

nappe [nap] *nf* tablecloth; *(de pétrole, gaz)*
layer; **napperon** *nm* table-mat

narguer [naʀge] /1/ *vt* to taunt

narine [naʀin] *nf* nostril

natal, e [natal] *adj* native; **natalité** *nf*
birth rate

natation [natasjɔ̃] *nf* swimming

natif, -ive [natif, -iv] *adj* native

nation [nasjɔ̃] *nf* nation; **national, e,
-aux** *adj* national ▷ *nf:* **(route) nationale**
≈ A road (BRIT), ≈ state highway (US);
nationaliser /1/ *vt* to nationalize;
nationalisme *nm* nationalism;
nationalité *nf* nationality

natte [nat] *nf (tapis)* mat; *(cheveux)* plait

naturaliser [natyʀalize] /1/ *vt* to naturalize

nature [natyʀ] *nf* nature ▷ *adj, adv* (Culin)
plain, without seasoning or sweetening;
(café, thé) black; without sugar; *(yaourt)*
natural; **payer en ~** to pay in kind; **~ morte**
still-life; **naturel, le** *adj* natural ▷ *nm*
naturalness; *(caractère)* disposition,
nature; **naturellement** *adv* naturally;
(bien sûr) of course

naufrage [nofʀaʒ] nm (ship)wreck; **faire ~** to be shipwrecked

nausée [noze] nf nausea; **avoir la ~** to feel sick

nautique [notik] adj nautical, water cpd; **sports ~s** water sports

naval, e [naval] adj naval; (industrie) shipbuilding

navet [navɛ] nm turnip; (péj: film) third-rate film

navette [navɛt] nf shuttle; **faire la ~ (entre)** to go to and fro (between)

navigateur [navigatœʀ] nm (Navig) seafarer; (Inform) browser

navigation [navigasjɔ̃] nf navigation, sailing

naviguer [navige] /1/ vi to navigate, sail; **~ sur Internet** to browse the Internet

navire [naviʀ] nm ship

navrer [navʀe] /1/ vt to upset, distress; **je suis navré (de/de faire/que)** I'm so sorry (for/for doing/that)

né, e [ne] pp de **naître**; **né en 1960** born in 1960; **née Scott** née Scott

néanmoins [neɑ̃mwɛ̃] adv nevertheless

néant [neɑ̃] nm nothingness; **réduire à ~** to bring to nought; (espoir) to dash

nécessaire [nesesɛʀ] adj necessary ▷ nm necessary; (sac) kit; **faire le ~** to do the necessary; **~ de couture** sewing kit; **~ de toilette** toilet bag; **nécessité** nf necessity; **nécessiter** /1/ vt to require

nectar [nɛktaʀ] nm nectar

néerlandais, e [neɛʀlɑ̃dɛ, -ɛz] adj Dutch

nef [nɛf] nf (d'église) nave

néfaste [nefast] adj (nuisible) harmful; (funeste) ill-fated

négatif, -ive [negatif, -iv] adj negative ▷ nm (Photo) negative

négligé, e [negliʒe] adj (en désordre) slovenly ▷ nm (tenue) negligee

négligeable [negliʒabl] adj negligible

négligent, e [negliʒɑ̃, -ɑ̃t] adj careless; negligent

négliger [negliʒe] /3/ vt (épouse, jardin) to neglect; (tenue) to be careless about; (avis, précautions) to disregard; **~ de faire** to fail to do, not bother to do

négociant, e [negɔsjɑ̃, -jɑ̃t] nm/f merchant

négociation [negɔsjasjɔ̃] nf negotiation

négocier [negɔsje] /7/ vi, vt to negotiate

nègre [nɛgʀ] nm (péj) Negro (!); (écrivain) ghost writer

neige [nɛʒ] nf snow; **neiger** /3/ vi to snow

nénuphar [nenyfaʀ] nm water-lily

néon [neɔ̃] nm neon

néo-zélandais, e [neozelɑ̃dɛ, -ɛz] adj New Zealand cpd ▷ nm/f: **N~, e** New Zealander

Népal [nepal] nm: **le ~** Nepal

nerf [nɛʀ] nm nerve; **être** ou **vivre sur les ~s** to live on one's nerves; **nerveux, -euse** adj nervous; (irritable) touchy, nervy; (voiture) nippy, responsive; **nervosité** nf excitability, tenseness

n'est-ce pas [nɛspɑ] adv isn't it?, won't you? etc (selon le verbe qui précède)

net, nette [nɛt] adj (sans équivoque, distinct) clear; (amélioration, différence) marked, distinct; (propre) neat, clean; (Comm: prix, salaire, poids) net ▷ adv (refuser) flatly ▷ nm: **mettre au ~** to copy out; **s'arrêter ~** to stop dead; **nettement** adv clearly; (incontestablement) decidedly; **netteté** nf clearness

nettoyage [netwajaʒ] nm cleaning; **~ à sec** dry cleaning

nettoyer [netwaje] /8/ vt to clean

neuf¹ [nœf] num nine

neuf², neuve [nœf, nœv] adj new; **remettre à ~** to do up (as good as new), refurbish; **quoi de ~?** what's new?

neutre [nøtʀ] adj (Ling) neuter

neuve [nœv] adj f voir **neuf²**

neuvième [nœvjɛm] num ninth

neveu, x [nəvø] nm nephew

New York [njujɔʀk] n New York

nez [ne] nm nose; **avoir du ~** to have flair; **~ à ~ avec** face to face with

ni [ni] conj: **ni … ni** neither … nor; **je n'aime ni les lentilles ni les épinards** I like neither lentils nor spinach; **il n'a dit ni oui ni non** he didn't say either yes or no; **elles ne sont venues ni l'une ni l'autre** neither of them came; **il n'a rien vu ni entendu** he didn't see or hear anything

niche [niʃ] nf (du chien) kennel; (de mur) recess, niche; **nicher** /1/ vi to nest

nid [ni] nm nest; **~ de poule** pothole

nièce [njɛs] nf niece

nier [nje] /7/ vt to deny

Nil [nil] nm: **le ~** the Nile

n'importe [nɛ̃pɔʀt] adv: **~ qui/quoi/où** anybody/anything/anywhere; **~ quand** any time; **~ quel/quelle** any; **~ lequel/laquelle** any (one); **~ comment** (sans soin) carelessly

niveau, x [nivo] nm level; (des élèves, études) standard; **~ de vie** standard of living

niveler [nivle] /4/ vt to level

noble [nɔbl] adj noble; **noblesse** nf nobility; (d'une action etc) nobleness

noce [nɔs] nf wedding; (gens) wedding party (ou guests pl); **faire la ~** (fam) to go on a binge; **~s d'or/d'argent/de diamant** golden/silver/diamond wedding

nocif, -ive [nɔsif, -iv] adj harmful

nocturne [nɔktyʀn] adj nocturnal ▷ nf late opening

Noël [nɔɛl] nm Christmas

nœud [nø] nm knot; (ruban) bow; **~ papillon** bow tie

noir, e [nwaʀ] *adj* black; (*obscur, sombre*) dark ▷ *nm/f* black man/woman ▷ *nm:* **dans le ~** in the dark ▷ *nf* (*Mus*) crotchet (*BRIT*), quarter note (*US*); **travailler au ~** to work on the side; **noircir** /2/ *vt, vi* to blacken

noisette [nwazɛt] *nf* hazelnut

noix [nwa] *nf* walnut; (*Culin*): **une ~ de beurre** a knob of butter; **à la ~** (*fam*) worthless; **~ de cajou** cashew nut; **~ de coco** coconut; **~ muscade** nutmeg

nom [nɔ̃] *nm* name; (*Ling*) **~ de famille** surname; **~ de jeune fille** maiden name; **~ d'utilisateur** username

nomade [nɔmad] *nm/f* nomad

nombre [nɔ̃bʀ] *nm* number; **venir en ~** to come in large numbers; **depuis ~ d'années** for many years; **au ~ de mes amis** among my friends; **nombreux, -euse** *adj* many, numerous; (*avec nom sg: foule etc*) large; **peu nombreux** few; **de nombreux cas** many cases

nombril [nɔ̃bʀi(l)] *nm* navel

nommer [nɔme] /1/ *vt* to name; (*élire*) to appoint, nominate; **se nommer** *vr:* **il se nomme Pascal** his name's Pascal, he's called Pascal

non [nɔ̃] *adv* (*réponse*) no; (*suivi d'un adjectif, adverbe*) not; **Paul est venu, ~?** Paul came, didn't he?; **~ pas que** not that; **moi ~ plus** neither do I, I don't either; **je pense que ~** I don't think so; **~ alcoolisé** non-alcoholic

nonchalant, e [nɔ̃ʃalɑ̃, -ɑ̃t] *adj* nonchalant

non-fumeur, -euse [nɔ̃fymœʀ, -øz] *nm/f* non smoker

non-sens [nɔ̃sɑ̃s] *nm* absurdity

nord [nɔʀ] *nm* north ▷ *adj* northern; north; **au ~** (*situation*) in the north; (*direction*) to the north; **au ~ de** to the north of; **nord-africain, e** *adj* North-African ▷ *nm/f:* **Nord-Africain, e** North African; **nord-est** *nm* north-east; **nord-ouest** *nm* north-west

normal, e, -aux [nɔʀmal, -o] *adj* normal ▷ *nf:* **la ~e** the norm, the average; **c'est tout à fait ~** it's perfectly natural; **vous trouvez ça ~?** does it seem right to you?; **normalement** *adv* (*en général*) normally

normand, e [nɔʀmɑ̃, -ɑ̃d] *adj* Norman ▷ *nm/f:* **N~, e** (*de Normandie*) Norman

Normandie [nɔʀmɑ̃di] *nf:* **la ~** Normandy

norme [nɔʀm] *nf* norm; (*Tech*) standard

Norvège [nɔʀvɛʒ] *nf:* **la ~** Norway; **norvégien, ne** *adj* Norwegian ▷ *nm* (*Ling*) Norwegian ▷ *nm/f:* **Norvégien, ne** Norwegian

nos [no] *adj poss voir* **notre**

nostalgie [nɔstalʒi] *nf* nostalgia; **nostalgique** *adj* nostalgic

notable [nɔtabl] *adj* notable, noteworthy; (*marqué*) noticeable, marked ▷ *nm* prominent citizen

notaire [nɔtɛʀ] *nm* solicitor

notamment [nɔtamɑ̃] *adv* in particular, among others

note [nɔt] *nf* (*écrite, Mus*) note; (*Scol*) mark (*BRIT*), grade; (*facture*) bill; **~ de service** memorandum

noter [nɔte] /1/ *vt* (*écrire*) to write down; (*remarquer*) to note, notice; (*devoir*) to mark, give a grade to

notice [nɔtis] *nf* summary, short article; (*brochure*): **~ explicative** explanatory leaflet, instruction booklet

notifier [nɔtifje] /7/ *vt:* **~ qch à qn** to notify sb of sth, notify sth to sb

notion [nɔsjɔ̃] *nf* notion, idea

notoire [nɔtwaʀ] *adj* widely known; (*en mal*) notorious

notre (*pl* **nos**) [nɔtʀ(ə), no] *adj poss* our

nôtre [notʀ] *adj* ours ▷ *pron:* **le/la ~** ours; **les ~s** ours; (*alliés etc*) our own people; **soyez des ~s** join us

nouer [nwe] /1/ *vt* to tie, knot; (*fig: alliance etc*) to strike up

noueux, -euse [nwø, -øz] *adj* gnarled

nourrice [nuʀis] *nf* ≈ child-minder

nourrir [nuʀiʀ] /2/ *vt* to feed; (*fig: espoir*) to harbour, nurse; **nourrissant, e** *adj* nutritious; **nourrisson** *nm* (*unweaned*) infant; **nourriture** *nf* food

nous [nu] *pron* (*sujet*) we; (*objet*) us; **nous-mêmes** *pron* ourselves

nouveau (nouvel), -elle, x [nuvo, -ɛl] *adj* new ▷ *nm/f* new pupil (*ou* employee) ▷ *nm:* **il y a du ~** there's something new ▷ *nf* (*pièce of*) news *sg;* (*Littérature*) short story; **nouvelles** *nfpl* (*Presse, TV*) news; **de ~à ~** again; **je suis sans nouvelles de lui** I haven't heard from him; **Nouvel An** New Year; **~ venu, nouvelle venue** newcomer; **~x mariés** newly-weds; **nouveau-né, e** *nm/f* newborn (baby); **nouveauté** *nf* novelty; (*chose nouvelle*) something new

nouvelle: Nouvelle-Calédonie [nuvɛlkaledɔni] *nf:* **la Nouvelle-Calédonie** New Caledonia; **Nouvelle-Zélande** [nuvɛlzelɑ̃d] *nf:* **la Nouvelle-Zélande** New Zealand

novembre [nɔvɑ̃bʀ] *nm* November; *voir aussi* **juillet**

● **LE 11 NOVEMBRE**

● *Le 11 novembre* is a public holiday in France
● and commemorates the signing of the
● armistice, near Compiègne, at the end of
● the First World War.

noyade [nwajad] *nf* drowning *no pl*

noyau, x [nwajo] *nm* (*de fruit*) stone; (*Bio, Physique*) nucleus; (*fig: centre*) core

noyer [nwaje] /8/ *nm* walnut (tree); (*bois*) walnut ▷ *vt* to drown; (*moteur*) to flood;

se noyer to be drowned, drown; (*suicide*) to drown o.s.

nu, e [ny] *adj* naked; (*membres*) naked, bare; (*chambre, fil, plaine*) bare ▷ *nm* (*Art*) nude; **tout nu** stark naked; **se mettre nu** to strip

nuage [nɥaʒ] *nm* (*aussi Inform*) cloud; **informatique en ~** cloud computing; **nuageux, -euse** *adj* cloudy

nuance [nɥɑ̃s] *nf* (*de couleur, sens*) shade; **il y a une ~ (entre)** there's a slight difference (between); **nuancer** /3/ *vt* (*pensée, opinion*) to qualify

nucléaire [nykleɛʀ] *adj* nuclear ▷ *nm*: **le ~** nuclear power

nudiste [nydist] *nm/f* nudist

nuée [nɥe] *nf*: **une ~ de** a cloud *ou* host *ou* swarm of

nuire [nɥiʀ] /38/ *vi* to be harmful; **~ à** to harm, do damage to; **nuisible** [nɥizibl] *adj* harmful; (*animal*) **nuisible** pest

nuit [nɥi] *nf* night; **il fait ~** it's dark; **cette ~** (*hier*) last night; (*aujourd'hui*) tonight; **de ~** (*vol, service*) night *cpd*; **~ blanche** sleepless night

nul, nulle [nyl] *adj* (*aucun*) no; (*minime*) nil, non-existent; (*non valable*) null; (*péj*) useless, hopeless ▷ *pron* none, no one; **résultat ~, match ~** draw; **nulle part** nowhere; **nullement** *adv* by no means

numérique [nymeʀik] *adj* numerical; (*affichage, son, télévision*) digital

numéro [nymeʀo] *nm* number; (*spectacle*) act, turn; (*Presse*) issue, number; **~ de téléphone** (tele)phone number; **~ vert** ≈ Freefone® number (BRIT), ≈ toll-free number (US); **numéroter** /1/ *vt* to number

nuque [nyk] *nf* nape of the neck

nu-tête [nytɛt] *adj inv* bareheaded

nutritif, -ive [nytʀitif, -iv] *adj* (*besoins, valeur*) nutritional; (*aliment*) nutritious, nourishing

nylon [nilɔ̃] *nm* nylon

oasis [ɔazis] *nm ou f* oasis

obéir [ɔbeiʀ] /2/ *vi* to obey; **~ à** to obey; **obéissance** *nf* obedience; **obéissant, e** *adj* obedient

obèse [ɔbɛz] *adj* obese; **obésité** *nf* obesity

objecter [ɔbʒɛkte] /1/ *vt*: **~ (à qn) que** to object (to sb) that; **objecteur** *nm*: **objecteur de conscience** conscientious objector

objectif, -ive [ɔbʒɛktif, -iv] *adj* objective ▷ *nm* (*Optique, Photo*) lens *sg*; (*Mil, fig*) objective

objection [ɔbʒɛksjɔ̃] *nf* objection

objectivité [ɔbʒɛktivite] *nf* objectivity

objet [ɔbʒɛ] *nm* object; (*d'une discussion, recherche*) subject; **être** *ou* **faire l'~ de** (*discussion*) to be the subject of; (*soins*) to be given *ou* shown; **sans ~** purposeless; (*sans fondement*) groundless; **~ d'art** objet d'art; **~s personnels** personal items; **~s trouvés** lost property *sg* (BRIT), lost-and-found *sg* (US); **~s de valeur** valuables

obligation [ɔbligasjɔ̃] *nf* obligation; (*Comm*) bond, debenture; **obligatoire** *adj* compulsory, obligatory; **obligatoirement** *adv* necessarily; (*fam: sans aucun doute*) inevitably

obliger [ɔbliʒe] /3/ *vt* (*contraindre*): **~ qn à faire** to force *ou* oblige sb to do; **je suis bien obligé (de le faire)** I have to (do it)

oblique [ɔblik] *adj* oblique; **en ~** diagonally

oblitérer [ɔblitere] /6/ *vt* (*timbre-poste*) to cancel

obnubiler [ɔbnybile] /1/ *vt* to obsess

obscène [ɔpsɛn] *adj* obscene

obscur, e [ɔpskyʀ] *adj* dark; (*raisons*) obscure; **obscurcir** /2/ *vt* to darken; (*fig*) to obscure; **s'obscurcir** *vi* to grow dark; **obscurité** *nf* darkness; **dans l'obscurité** in the dark, in darkness

obsédé, e [ɔpsede] *nm/f* fanatic; **~(e) sexuel(le)** sex maniac

obséder [ɔpsede] /6/ vt to obsess, haunt

obsèques [ɔpsɛk] nfpl funeral sg

observateur, -trice [ɔpsɛʀvatœʀ, -tʀis] adj observant, perceptive ▷ nm/f observer

observation [ɔpsɛʀvasjɔ̃] nf observation; (d'un règlement etc) observance; (reproche) reproof; **en ~** (Méd) under observation

observatoire [ɔpsɛʀvatwaʀ] nm observatory

observer [ɔpsɛʀve] /1/ vt (regarder) to observe, watch; (scientifique, aussi: règlement, jeûne etc) to observe; (surveiller) to watch; (remarquer) to observe, notice; **faire ~ qch à qn** (dire) to point out sth to sb

obsession [ɔpsesjɔ̃] nf obsession

obstacle [ɔpstakl] nm obstacle; (Équitation) jump, hurdle; **faire ~ à** (projet) to hinder, put obstacles in the path of

obstiné, e [ɔpstine] adj obstinate

obstiner [ɔpstine] /1/: **s'obstiner** vi to insist, dig one's heels in; **s'~ à faire** to persist (obstinately) in doing

obstruer [ɔpstʀye] /1/ vt to block, obstruct

obtenir [ɔptəniʀ] /22/ vt to obtain, get; (résultat) to achieve, obtain; **~ de pouvoir faire** to obtain permission to do

obturateur [ɔptyʀatœʀ] nm (Photo) shutter

obus [ɔby] nm shell

occasion [ɔkazjɔ̃] nf (aubaine, possibilité) opportunity; (circonstance) occasion; (Comm: article non neuf) secondhand buy; (: acquisition avantageuse) bargain; **à plusieurs ~s** on several occasions; **à l'~** sometimes, on occasions; **d'~** secondhand; **occasionnel, le** adj occasional

occasionner [ɔkazjɔne] /1/ vt to cause

occident [ɔksidɑ̃] nm: **l'O~** the West; **occidental, e, -aux** adj western; (Pol) Western ▷ nm/f Westerner

occupation [ɔkypasjɔ̃] nf occupation

occupé, e [ɔkype] adj (Mil, Pol) occupied; (personne) busy; (place, sièges) taken; (toilettes) engaged; **la ligne est ~e** the line's engaged (BRIT) ou busy (US)

occuper [ɔkype] /1/ vt to occupy; (poste, fonction) to hold; **s'~ (à qch)** to occupy o.s. ou keep o.s. busy (with sth); **s'~ de** (être responsable de) to be in charge of; (se charger de: affaire) to take charge of, deal with; (: clients etc) to attend to

occurrence [ɔkyʀɑ̃s] nf: **en l'~** in this case

océan [ɔseɑ̃] nm ocean

octet [ɔktɛ] nm byte

octobre [ɔktɔbʀ] nm October

oculiste [ɔkylist] nm/f eye specialist

odeur [ɔdœʀ] nf smell

odieux, -euse [ɔdjø, -øz] adj hateful

odorant, e [ɔdɔʀɑ̃, -ɑ̃t] adj sweet-smelling, fragrant

odorat [ɔdɔʀa] nm (sense of) smell

œil [œj] (pl **yeux**) nm eye; **avoir un ~ poché ou au beurre noir** to have a black eye; **à l'~** (fam) for free; **à l'~ nu** with the naked eye; **fermer les yeux (sur)** (fig) to turn a blind eye (to); **les yeux fermés** (aussi fig) with one's eyes shut; **ouvrir l'~** (fig) to keep one's eyes open ou an eye out

œillères [œjɛʀ] nfpl blinkers (BRIT), blinders (US)

œillet [œjɛ] nm (Bot) carnation

œuf [œf] nm egg; **~ à la coque/dur/mollet** boiled/hard-boiled/soft-boiled egg; **~ au plat/poché** fried/poached egg; **~s brouillés** scrambled eggs; **~ de Pâques** Easter egg

œuvre [œvʀ] nf (tâche) task, undertaking; (ouvrage achevé, livre, tableau etc) work; (ensemble de la production artistique) works pl ▷ nm (Constr): **le gros ~** the shell; **mettre en ~** (moyens) to make use of; **~ d'art** work of art; **~s de bienfaisance** charitable works

offense [ɔfɑ̃s] nf insult; **offenser** /1/ vt to offend, hurt; **s'offenser de** vi to take offence (BRIT) ou offense (US) at

offert, e [ɔfɛʀ, -ɛʀt] pp de **offrir**

office [ɔfis] nm (agence) bureau, agency; (Rel) service ▷ nm ou f (pièce) pantry; **faire ~ de** to act as; **d'~** automatically; **~ du tourisme** tourist office

officiel, le [ɔfisjɛl] adj, nm/f official

officier [ɔfisje] /7/ nm officer

officieux, -euse [ɔfisjø, -øz] adj unofficial

offrande [ɔfʀɑ̃d] nf offering

offre [ɔfʀ] nf offer; (aux enchères) bid; (Admin: soumission) tender; (Écon): **l'~ et la demande** supply and demand; **~ d'emploi** job advertised; **"~s d'emploi"** "situations vacant"; **~ publique d'achat (OPA)** takeover bid

offrir [ɔfʀiʀ] /18/ vt: **~ (à qn)** to offer (to sb); (faire cadeau) to give to (sb); **s'offrir**, vt (vacances, voiture) to treat o.s. to; **~ (à qn) de faire qch** to offer to do sth (for sb); **~ à boire à qn** (chez soi) to offer sb a drink; **je vous offre un verre** I'll buy you a drink

OGM sigle m (= organisme génétiquement modifié) GMO

oie [wa] nf (Zool) goose

oignon [ɔɲɔ̃] nm onion; (de tulipe etc) bulb

oiseau, x [wazo] nm bird; **~ de proie** bird of prey

oisif, -ive [wazif, -iv] adj idle

oléoduc [ɔleɔdyk] nm (oil) pipeline

olive [ɔliv] nf (Bot) olive; **olivier** nm olive (tree)

OLP sigle f (= Organisation de libération de la Palestine) PLO

olympique [ɔlɛ̃pik] adj Olympic®

ombragé, e [ɔ̃bʀaʒe] adj shaded, shady

ombre [ɔ̃bʀ] nf (espace non ensoleillé) shade; (ombre portée, tache) shadow; **à l'~** in the shade; **dans l'~** (fig) in the dark; **~ à paupières** eye shadow

omelette [ɔmlɛt] *nf* omelette;
~ **norvégienne** baked Alaska
omettre [ɔmɛtʀ] /56/ *vt* to omit, leave out
omoplate [ɔmɔplat] *nf* shoulder blade

🔵 **MOT-CLÉ**

on [ɔ̃] *pron* **1** (*indéterminé*) you, one; **on peut
le faire ainsi** you *ou* one can do it like this, it
can be done like this
2 (*quelqu'un*): **on les a attaqués** they were
attacked; **on vous demande au téléphone**
there's a phone call for you, you're wanted
on the phone
3 (*nous*) we; **on va y aller demain** we're
going tomorrow
4 (*les gens*) they; **autrefois, on croyait ...**
they used to believe ...
5: **on ne peut plus** *adv*: **on ne peut plus
stupide** as stupid as can be

oncle [ɔ̃kl] *nm* uncle
onctueux, -euse [ɔ̃ktɥø, -øz] *adj* creamy;
smooth
onde [ɔ̃d] *nf* wave; ~**s courtes (OC)** short
wave *sg*; ~**s moyennes (OM)** medium wave
sg; **grandes** ~**s (GO),** ~**s longues (OL)** long
wave *sg*
ondée [ɔ̃de] *nf* shower
on-dit [ɔ̃di] *nm inv* rumour
onduler [ɔ̃dyle] /1/ *vi* to undulate; (*cheveux*)
to wave
onéreux, -euse [ɔneʀø, -øz] *adj* costly
ongle [ɔ̃gl] *nm* nail
ont [ɔ̃] *vb voir* **avoir**
ONU *sigle f* (= *Organisation des Nations unies*)
UN(O)
onze [ˈɔ̃z] *num* eleven; **onzième** *num*
eleventh
OPA *sigle f* = **offre publique d'achat**
opaque [ɔpak] *adj* opaque
opéra [ɔpeʀa] *nm* opera; (*édifice*) opera
house
opérateur, -trice [ɔpeʀatœʀ, -tʀis] *nm/f*
operator; ~ **(de prise de vues)**
cameraman
opération [ɔpeʀasjɔ̃] *nf* operation; (*Comm*)
dealing
opératoire [ɔpeʀatwaʀ] *adj* (*choc etc*)
post-operative
opérer [ɔpeʀe] /6/ *vt* (*Méd*) to operate
on; (*faire, exécuter*) to carry out, make ▷ *vi*
(*remède: faire effet*) to act, work; (*Méd*) to
operate; **s'opérer** *vi* (*avoir lieu*) to occur,
take place; **se faire** ~ to have an operation
opérette [ɔpeʀɛt] *nf* operetta, light opera
opinion [ɔpinjɔ̃] *nf* opinion; **l'**~ **(publique)**
public opinion
opportun, e [ɔpɔʀtœ̃, -yn] *adj* timely,
opportune; **opportuniste** [ɔpɔʀtynist]
nm/f opportunist
opposant, e [ɔpozɑ̃, -ɑ̃t] *nm/f* opponent

opposé, e [ɔpoze] *adj* (*direction, rive*)
opposite; (*faction*) opposing; (*opinions,
intérêts*) conflicting; (*contre*): ~ **à** opposed
to, against ▷ *nm*: **l'**~ the other *ou* opposite
side (*ou* direction); (*contraire*) the opposite;
à l'~ (*fig*) on the other hand; **à l'**~ **de** (*fig*)
contrary to, unlike
opposer [ɔpoze] /1/ *vt* (*personnes, armées,
équipes*) to oppose; (*couleurs, termes, tons*) to
contrast; ~ **qch à** (*comme obstacle, défense*) to
set sth against; (*comme objection*) to put sth
forward against; **s'opposer** *vi* (*équipes*) to
confront each other; (*opinions*) to conflict;
(*couleurs, styles*) to contrast; **s'**~ **à** (*interdire,
empêcher*) to oppose
opposition [ɔpozisjɔ̃] *nf* opposition; **par** ~
à as opposed to; **entrer en** ~ **avec** to come
into conflict with; **faire** ~ **à un chèque** to
stop a cheque
oppressant, e [ɔpʀesɑ̃, -ɑ̃t] *adj* oppressive
oppresser [ɔpʀese] /1/ *vt* to oppress;
oppression *nf* oppression
opprimer [ɔpʀime] /1/ *vt* to oppress
opter [ɔpte] /1/ *vi*: ~ **pour** to opt for;
~ **entre** to choose between
opticien, ne [ɔptisjɛ̃, -ɛn] *nm/f* optician
optimisme [ɔptimism] *nm* optimism;
optimiste [ɔptimist] *adj* optimistic ▷ *nm/f*
optimist
option [ɔpsjɔ̃] *nf* option; **matière à** ~ (*Scol*)
optional subject
optique [ɔptik] *adj* (*nerf*) optic; (*verres*)
optical ▷ *nf* (*fig: manière de voir*) perspective
or [ɔʀ] *nm* gold ▷ *conj* now, but; **en** *ou* gold
cpd; **une affaire en or** a real bargain; **il
croyait gagner or il a perdu** he was sure he
would win and yet he lost
orage [ɔʀaʒ] *nm* (thunder)storm; **orageux,
-euse** *adj* stormy
oral, e, -aux [ɔʀal, -o] *adj* oral; (*Méd*): **par
voie** ~**e** orally ▷ *nm* oral
orange [ɔʀɑ̃ʒ] *adj inv, nf* orange; **orangé, e**
adj orangey, orange-coloured; **orangeade**
nf orangeade; **oranger** *nm* orange tree
orateur [ɔʀatœʀ] *nm* speaker
orbite [ɔʀbit] *nf* (*Anat*) (eye-)socket;
(*Physique*) orbit
Orcades [ɔʀkad] *nfpl*: **les** ~ the Orkneys,
the Orkney Islands
orchestre [ɔʀkɛstʀ] *nm* orchestra; (*de
jazz, danse*) band; (*places*) stalls *pl* (*BRIT*),
orchestra (*US*)
orchidée [ɔʀkide] *nf* orchid
ordinaire [ɔʀdinɛʀ] *adj* ordinary; (*modèle,
qualité*) standard; (*péj: commun*) common
▷ *nm* ordinary; (*menus*) everyday fare ▷ *nf*
(*essence*) ≈ two-star (petrol) (*BRIT*), ≈ regular
(gas) (*US*); **d'**~ usually, normally; **comme
à l'**~ as usual
ordinateur [ɔʀdinatœʀ] *nm* computer;
~ **individuel** *ou* **personnel** personal
computer; ~ **portable** laptop (computer)

ordonnance [ɔʀdɔnɑ̃s] nf (Méd)
prescription; (Mil) orderly, batman (BRIT)
ordonné, e [ɔʀdɔne] adj tidy, orderly
ordonner [ɔʀdɔne] /1/ vt (agencer) to
organize, arrange; (donner un ordre): **~ à qn
de faire** to order sb to do; (Rel) to ordain;
(Méd) to prescribe
ordre [ɔʀdʀ] nm order; (propreté et soin)
orderliness, tidiness; **à l'~ de** payable
to; (nature): **d'~ pratique** of a practical
nature; **ordres** nmpl (Rel) holy orders;
mettre en ~ to tidy (up), put in order;
par ~ alphabétique/d'importance in
alphabetical order/in order of importance;
être aux ~s de qn/sous les ~s de qn to be at
sb's disposal/under sb's command; **jusqu'à
nouvel ~** until further notice; **de premier ~**
first-rate; **~ du jour** (d'une réunion) agenda;
à l'~ du jour (fig) topical; **~ public** law and
order
ordure [ɔʀdyʀ] nf filth no pl; **ordures** nfpl
(balayures, déchets) rubbish sg, refuse sg;
~s ménagères household refuse
oreille [ɔʀɛj] nf ear; **avoir de l'~** to have a
good ear (for music)
oreiller [ɔʀeje] nm pillow
oreillons [ɔʀejɔ̃] nmpl mumps sg
ores [ɔʀ]: **d'~ et déjà** adv already
orfèvrerie [ɔʀfɛvʀəʀi] nf goldsmith's (ou
silversmith's) trade; (ouvrage) (silver ou
gold) plate
organe [ɔʀgan] nm organ; (porte-parole)
representative, mouthpiece
organigramme [ɔʀganigʀam] nm
(hiérarchique, structure) organization chart;
(des opérations) flow chart
organique [ɔʀganik] adj organic
organisateur, -trice [ɔʀganizatœʀ, -tʀis]
nm/f organizer
organisation [ɔʀganizasjɔ̃] nf
organization; **O~ des Nations unies (ONU)**
United Nations (Organization) (UN(O))
organiser [ɔʀganize] /1/ vt to organize,
(mettre sur pied: service etc) to set up;
s'organiser to get organized
organisme [ɔʀganism] nm (Bio) organism;
(corps humain) body; (Admin, Pol etc) body
organiste [ɔʀganist] nm/f organist
orgasme [ɔʀgasm] nm orgasm, climax
orge [ɔʀʒ] nf barley
orgue [ɔʀg] nm organ
orgueil [ɔʀgœj] nm pride; **orgueilleux,
-euse** adj proud
oriental, e, -aux [ɔʀjɑ̃tal, -o] adj (langue,
produit) oriental; (frontière) eastern
orientation [ɔʀjɑ̃tasjɔ̃] nf (de recherches)
orientation; (d'une maison etc) aspect;
(d'un journal) leanings pl; **avoir le sens de
l'~** to have a (good) sense of direction; **~
professionnelle** careers advisory service
orienté, e [ɔʀjɑ̃te] adj (fig: article, journal)
slanted; **bien/mal ~** (appartement) well/

badly positioned; **~ au sud** facing south,
with a southern aspect
orienter [ɔʀjɑ̃te] /1/ vt (tourner: antenne) to
direct, turn; (: voyageur, touriste, recherches)
to direct; (fig: élève) to orientate; **s'orienter**
(se repérer) to find one's bearings; **s'~ vers**
(fig) to turn towards
origan [ɔʀigɑ̃] nm oregano
originaire [ɔʀiʒinɛʀ] adj: **être ~ de** to be
a native of
original, e, -aux [ɔʀiʒinal, -o] adj original;
(bizarre) eccentric ▷ nm/f eccentric ▷ nm
(document etc, Art) original
origine [ɔʀiʒin] nf origin; **origines** nfpl
(d'une personne) origins; **d'~** (pays) of origin;
(pneus etc) original; **d'~ française** of French
origin; **à l'~** originally; **originel, le** adj
original
orme [ɔʀm] nm elm
ornement [ɔʀnəmɑ̃] nm ornament
orner [ɔʀne] /1/ vt to decorate, adorn
ornière [ɔʀnjɛʀ] nf rut
orphelin, e [ɔʀfəlɛ̃, -in] adj orphan(ed)
▷ nm/f orphan; **~ de père/mère** fatherless/
motherless; **orphelinat** nm orphanage
orteil [ɔʀtɛj] nm toe; **gros ~** big toe
orthographe [ɔʀtɔgʀaf] nf spelling
ortie [ɔʀti] nf (stinging) nettle
os [ɔs] nm bone; **os à moelle** marrowbone
osciller [ɔsile] /1/ vi (au vent etc) to rock;
(fly). **~ entre** to waver ou fluctuate between
osé, e [oze] adj daring, bold
oseille [ozɛj] nf sorrel
oser [oze] /1/ vi, vt to dare; **~ faire** to dare
(to) do
osier [ozje] nm willow; **d'~, en ~**
wicker(work) cpd
osseux, -euse [ɔsø, -øz] adj bony; (tissu,
maladie, greffe) bone cpd
otage [ɔtaʒ] nm hostage; **prendre qn
comme ~** to take sb hostage
OTAN sigle f (= Organisation du traité de
l'Atlantique Nord) NATO
otarie [ɔtaʀi] nf sea-lion
ôter [ote] /1/ vt to remove; (soustraire) to
take away; **~ qch à qn** to take sth (away)
from sb; **~ qch de** to remove sth from
otite [ɔtit] nf ear infection
ou [u] conj or; **ou ... ou** either ... or; **ou bien**
or (else)

⊙ **MOT-CLÉ**

où [u] pron relatif **1** (position, situation)
where, that (souvent omis); **la chambre où
il était** the room (that) he was in, the room
where he was; **la ville où je l'ai rencontré**
the town where I met him; **la pièce d'où
il est sorti** the room he came out of; **le
village d'où je viens** the village I come
from; **les villes par où il est passé** the
towns he went through

2 (*temps, état*) that (*souvent omis*); **le jour où il est parti** the day (that) he left; **au prix où c'est** at the price it is
▶ *adv* **1** (*interrogation*) where; **où est-il/va-t-il?** where is he/is he going?; **par où?** which way?; **d'où vient que ...?** how come ...?
2 (*position*) where; **je sais où il est** I know where he is; **où que l'on aille** wherever you go

ouate [wat] *nf* cotton wool (BRIT), cotton (US)
oubli [ubli] *nm* (*acte*): **l'~ de** forgetting; (*trou de mémoire*) lapse of memory; (*négligence*) omission, oversight; **tomber dans l'~** to sink into oblivion
oublier [ublije] /7/ *vt* to forget; (*ne pas voir: erreurs etc*) to miss; (*laisser quelque part: chapeau etc*) to leave behind
ouest [wɛst] *nm* west ▷ *adj inv* west; (*région*) western; **à l'~** in the west; (*direction*) (to the) west, westwards; **à l'~ de** (to the) west of
ouf [uf] *excl* phew!
oui [wi] *adv* yes
ouï-dire ['widiʀ]: **par ~** *adv* by hearsay
ouïe [wi] *nf* hearing; **ouïes** *nfpl* (*de poisson*) gills
ouragan [uʀagɑ̃] *nm* hurricane
ourlet [uʀlɛ] *nm* hem
ours [uʀs] *nm* bear; **~ brun/blanc** brown/polar bear; **~ (en peluche)** teddy (bear)
oursin [uʀsɛ̃] *nm* sea urchin
ourson [uʀsɔ̃] *nm* (bear-)cub
ouste [ust] *excl* hop it!
outil [uti] *nm* tool; **outiller** /1/ *vt* to equip
outrage [utʀaʒ] *nm* insult; **~ à la pudeur** indecent behaviour *no pl*
outrance [utʀɑ̃s]: **à ~** *adv* excessively, to excess
outre [utʀ] *prép* besides ▷ *adv*: **passer ~ à** to disregard, take no notice of; **en ~** besides, moreover; **~ mesure** to excess; (*manger, boire*) immoderately; **outre-Atlantique** *adv* across the Atlantic; **outre-mer** *adv* overseas
ouvert, e [uvɛʀ, -ɛʀt] *pp de* **ouvrir** ▷ *adj* open; (*robinet, gaz etc*) on; **ouvertement** *adv* openly; **ouverture** *nf* opening; (*Mus*) overture; **ouverture d'esprit** open-mindedness; **heures d'ouverture** (*Comm*) opening hours
ouvrable [uvʀabl] *adj*: **jour ~** working day, weekday
ouvrage [uvʀaʒ] *nm* (*tâche, de tricot etc*) work *no pl*; (*texte, livre*) work
ouvre-boîte(s) [uvʀəbwat] *nm inv* tin (BRIT) *ou* can opener
ouvre-bouteille(s) [uvʀəbutɛj] *nm inv* bottle-opener
ouvreuse [uvʀøz] *nf* usherette
ouvrier, -ière [uvʀije, -jɛʀ] *nm/f* worker ▷ *adj* working-class; (*problèmes, conflit*) industrial; (*mouvement*) labour *cpd*; **classe ouvrière** working class
ouvrir [uvʀiʀ] /18/ *vt* (*gén*) to open; (*brèche, passage*) to open up; (*commencer l'exploitation de, créer*) to open (up); (*eau, électricité, chauffage, robinet*) to turn on; (*Méd: abcès*) to open up, cut open ▷ *vi* to open; to open up; **s'ouvrir** *vi* to open; **s'~ à qn (de qch)** to open one's heart to sb (about sth); **~ l'appétit à qn** to whet sb's appetite
ovaire [ɔvɛʀ] *nm* ovary
ovale [ɔval] *adj* oval
OVNI [ɔvni] *sigle m* (= *objet volant non identifié*) UFO
oxyder [ɔkside] /1/: **s'oxyder** *vi* to become oxidized
oxygéné, e [ɔksiʒene] *adj*: **eau ~e** hydrogen peroxide
oxygène [ɔksiʒɛn] *nm* oxygen
ozone [ozon] *nm* ozone; **trou dans la couche d'~** hole in the ozone layer

P

pacifique [pasifik] *adj* peaceful ▷ *nm*: le P~, l'océan P~ the Pacific (Ocean)

pack [pak] *nm* pack

pacotille [pakɔtij] *nf* cheap junk *pl*

PACS *sigle m* (= pacte civil de solidarité) ≈ civil partnership; **pacser** /1/; **se pacser** *vi* ≈ to form a civil partnership

pacte [pakt] *nm* pact, treaty

pagaille [pagaj] *nf* mess, shambles *sg*

page [paʒ] *nf* page ▷ *nm* page (boy); **à la ~** (fig) up-to-date; **~ d'accueil** (Inform) home page; **~ Web** (Inform) web page

païen, ne [pajɛ̃, -ɛn] *adj*, *nm/f* pagan, heathen

paillasson [pajasɔ̃] *nm* doormat

paille [paj] *nf* straw

pain [pɛ̃] *nm* (substance) bread; (unité) loaf (of bread); (morceau) **~ de cire** etc bar of wax etc; **~ bis/complet** brown/wholemeal (BRIT) ou wholewheat (US) bread; **~ d'épice** ≈ gingerbread; **~ grillé** toast; **~ de mie** sandwich loaf; **~ au chocolat** pain au chocolat; **~ aux raisins** currant pastry

pair, e [pɛʀ] *adj* (nombre) even ▷ *nm* peer; **aller de ~ (avec)** to go hand in hand ou together (with); **jeune fille au ~** au pair; **paire** *nf* pair

paisible [pezibl] *adj* peaceful, quiet

paix [pɛ] *nf* peace; **faire la ~ avec** to make peace with; **fiche-lui la ~!** (fam) leave him alone!

Pakistan [pakistɑ̃] *nm*: **le ~** Pakistan

palais [palɛ] *nm* palace; (Anat) palate

pâle [pɑl] *adj* pale; **bleu ~** pale blue

Palestine [palɛstin] *nf*: **la ~** Palestine

palette [palɛt] *nf* (de peintre) palette; (de produits) range

pâleur [pɑlœʀ] *nf* paleness

palier [palje] *nm* (d'escalier) landing; (fig) level, plateau; **par ~s** in stages

pâlir [pɑliʀ] /2/ *vi* to turn ou go pale; (couleur) to fade

pallier [palje] /7/ *vt*: **~ à** to offset, make up for

palme [palm] *nf* (de plongeur) flipper; **palmé, e** [palme] *adj* (pattes) webbed

palmier [palmje] *nm* palm tree; (gâteau) heart-shaped biscuit made of flaky pastry

pâlot, te [pɑlo, -ɔt] *adj* pale, peaky

palourde [paluʀd] *nf* clam

palper [palpe] /1/ *vt* to feel, finger

palpitant, e [palpitɑ̃, -ɑ̃t] *adj* thrilling

palpiter [palpite] /1/ *vi* (cœur, pouls) to beat (: plus fort) to pound, throb

paludisme [palydism] *nm* malaria

pamphlet [pɑ̃flɛ] *nm* lampoon, satirical tract

pamplemousse [pɑ̃pləmus] *nm* grapefruit

pan [pɑ̃] *nm* section, piece ▷ *excl* bang!

panache [panaʃ] *nm* plume; (fig) spirit, panache

panaché, e [panaʃe] *nm* (bière) shandy; **glace ~e** mixed ice cream

pancarte [pɑ̃kaʀt] *nf* sign, notice

pancréas [pɑ̃kʀeas] *nm* pancreas

pandémie [pɑ̃demi] *nf* pandemic

pané, e [pane] *adj* fried in breadcrumbs

panier [panje] *nm* basket; **mettre au ~** to chuck away; **~ à provisions** shopping basket; **panier-repas** *nm* packed lunch

panique [panik] *adj* panicky ▷ *nf* panic; **paniquer** /1/ *vi* to panic

panne [pan] *nf* breakdown; **être/tomber en ~** to have broken down/break down; **être en ~ d'essence** ou **en ~ sèche** to have run out of petrol (BRIT) ou gas (US); **~ d'électricité** ou **de courant** power ou electrical failure

panneau, x [pano] *nm* (écriteau) sign, notice; **~ d'affichage** notice (BRIT) ou bulletin (US) board; **~ indicateur** signpost; **~ de signalisation** roadsign

panoplie [panɔpli] *nf* (jouet) outfit; (d'armes) display; (fig) array

panorama [panɔʀama] *nm* panorama

panse [pɑ̃s] *nf* paunch

pansement [pɑ̃smɑ̃] *nm* dressing, bandage; **~ adhésif** sticking plaster

pantacourt [pɑ̃takuʀ] *nm* cropped trousers *pl*

pantalon [pɑ̃talɔ̃] *nm* trousers *pl* (BRIT), pants *pl* (US), pair of trousers ou pants; **~ de ski** ski pants *pl*

panthère [pɑ̃tɛʀ] *nf* panther

pantin [pɑ̃tɛ̃] *nm* puppet

pantoufle [pɑ̃tufl] *nf* slipper

paon [pɑ̃] *nm* peacock

papa [papa] *nm* dad(dy)

pape [pap] *nm* pope

paperasse [papʀas] *nf* (péj) bumf *no pl*, papers *pl*; **paperasserie** *nf* (péj) red tape *no pl*; paperwork *no pl*

papeterie [papɛtʀi] *nf* (magasin) stationer's (shop) (BRIT)

papi [papi] *nm (fam)* granddad

papier [papje] *nm* paper; *(article)* article; **papiers** *nmpl (aussi:* **~s d'identité)** (identity) papers; **~ (d')aluminium** aluminium *(BRIT) ou* aluminum *(US)* foil, tinfoil; **~ calque** tracing paper; **~ hygiénique** *ou* **(de) toilette** toilet paper; **~journal** newspaper; **~ à lettres** writing paper, notepaper; **~ peint** wallpaper; **~ de verre** sandpaper

papillon [papijɔ̃] *nm* butterfly; *(fam: contravention)* (parking) ticket; **~ de nuit** moth

papillote [papijɔt] *nf:* **en ~** cooked in tinfoil

papoter [papɔte] /1/ *vi* to chatter

paquebot [pakbo] *nm* liner

pâquerette [pɑkʀɛt] *nf* daisy

Pâques [pɑk] *nm, nfpl* Easter

paquet [pakɛ] *nm* packet; *(colis)* parcel; *(fig: tas):* **~ de** pile *ou* heap of; **paquet-cadeau** *nm* gift-wrapped parcel

par [paʀ] *prép* by; **finir** *etc* **~** to end *etc* with; **~ amour** out of love; **passer ~ Lyon/la côte** to go via *ou* through Lyons/along by the coast; **~ la fenêtre** *(jeter, regarder)* out of the window; **trois ~ jour/personne** three a *ou* per day/head; **deux ~ deux** in twos; **~ ici** this way; *(dans le coin)* round here; **~-ci, ~-là** here and there; **~ temps de pluie** in wet weather

parabolique [paʀabɔlik] *adj:* **antenne ~** satellite dish

parachute [paʀaʃyt] *nm* parachute; **parachutiste** [paʀaʃytist] *nm/f* parachutist; *(Mil)* paratrooper

parade [paʀad] *nf (spectacle, défilé)* parade; *(Escrime, Boxe)* parry

paradis [paʀadi] *nm* heaven, paradise

paradoxe [paʀadɔks] *nm* paradox

paraffine [paʀafin] *nf* paraffin

parages [paʀaʒ] *nmpl:* **dans les ~ (de)** in the area *ou* vicinity (of)

paragraphe [paʀagʀaf] *nm* paragraph

paraître [paʀɛtʀ] /57/ *vb copule* to seem, look, appear ▷ *vi* to appear; *(être visible)* to show; *(Presse, Édition)* to be published, come out, appear ▷ *vb impers:* **il paraît que** it seems *ou* appears that

parallèle [paʀalɛl] *adj* parallel; *(police, marché)* unofficial ▷ *nm (comparaison):* **faire un ~ entre** to draw a parallel between ▷ *nf* parallel (line)

paralyser [paʀalize] /1/ *vt* to paralyze

paramédical, e, -aux [paʀamedikal, -o] *adj:* **personnel ~** paramedics *pl,* paramedical workers *pl*

paraphrase [paʀafʀɑz] *nf* paraphrase

parapluie [paʀaplɥi] *nm* umbrella

parasite [paʀazit] *nm* parasite; **parasites** *nmpl (Tél)* interference *sg*

parasol [paʀasɔl] *nm* parasol, sunshade

paratonnerre [paʀatɔnɛʀ] *nm* lightning conductor

parc [paʀk] *nm (public)* park, gardens *pl;* *(de château etc)* grounds *pl; (d'enfant)* playpen; **~ d'attractions** amusement park; **~ éolien** wind farm; **~ de stationnement** car park; **~ à thème** theme park

parcelle [paʀsɛl] *nf* fragment, scrap; *(de terrain)* plot, parcel

parce que [paʀskə] *conj* because

parchemin [paʀʃəmɛ̃] *nm* parchment

parc(o)mètre [paʀk(ɔ)mɛtʀ] *nm* parking meter

parcourir [paʀkuʀiʀ] /11/ *vt (trajet, distance)* to cover; *(article, livre)* to skim *ou* glance through; *(lieu)* to go all over, travel up and down; *(frisson, vibration)* to run through

parcours [paʀkuʀ] *nm (trajet)* journey; *(itinéraire)* route

par-dessous [paʀdəsu] *prép, adv* under(neath)

pardessus [paʀdəsy] *nm* overcoat

par-dessus [paʀdəsy] *prép* over (the top of) ▷ *adv* over (the top); **~ le marché** on top of it all; **~ tout** above all; **en avoir ~ la tête** to have had enough

par-devant [paʀdəvɑ̃] *adv (passer)* round the front

pardon [paʀdɔ̃] *nm* forgiveness *no pl* ▷ *excl* (I'm) sorry; *(pour interpeller etc)* excuse me; **demander ~ à qn (de)** to apologize to sb (for); **je vous demande ~** I'm sorry; *(pour interpeller)* excuse me; **pardonner** /1/ *vt* to forgive; **pardonner qch à qn** to forgive sb for sth

pare: **pare-brise** *nm inv* windscreen *(BRIT),* windshield *(US);* **pare-chocs** *nm inv* bumper; **pare-feu** *nm inv (de foyer)* fireguard; *(Inform)* firewall ▷ *adj inv*

pareil, le [paʀɛj] *adj (identique)* the same, alike; *(similaire)* similar; *(tel):* **un courage/ livre ~** such courage/a book, courage/a book like this; **de ~s livres** such books; **faire ~** to do the same (thing); **~ à** the same as; similar to; **sans ~** unparalleled, unequalled

parent, e [paʀɑ̃, -ɑ̃t] *nm/f:* **un/une ~/e** a relative *ou* relation; **parents** *nmpl (père et mère)* parents; **parenté** *nf (lien)* relationship

parenthèse [paʀɑ̃tɛz] *nf (ponctuation)* bracket, parenthesis; *(digression)* parenthesis, digression; **entre ~s** in brackets; *(fig)* incidentally

paresse [paʀɛs] nf laziness; **paresseux, -euse** adj lazy

parfait, e [paʀfɛ, -ɛt] adj perfect ▷ nm (Ling) perfect (tense); **parfaitement** adv perfectly ▷ excl (most) certainly

parfois [paʀfwa] adv sometimes

parfum [paʀfœ̃] nm (produit) perfume, scent; (odeur: de fleur) scent, fragrance; (goût) flavour; **parfumé, e** adj (fleur, fruit) fragrant; (femme) perfumed; **parfumé au café** coffee-flavoured (BRIT) ou -flavored (US); **parfumer** /1/ vt (odeur, bouquet) to perfume; (crème, gâteau) to flavour; **parfumerie** nf (produits) perfumes; (boutique) perfume shop (BRIT) ou store (US)

pari [paʀi] nm bet; **parier** /7/ vt to bet

Paris [paʀi] n Paris; **parisien, ne** adj Parisian; (Géo, Admin) Paris cpd ▷ nm/f: **Parisien, ne** Parisian

parité [paʀite] nf: ~ **hommes-femmes** (Pol) balanced representation of men and women

parjure [paʀʒyʀ] nm perjury

parking [paʀkiŋ] nm (lieu) car park (BRIT), parking lot (US)

⚠ Attention à ne pas traduire parking par le mot anglais parking.

parlant, e [paʀlɑ̃, -ɑ̃t] adj (comparaison, preuve) eloquent; (Ciné) talking

parlement [paʀləmɑ̃] nm parliament; **parlementaire** adj parliamentary ▷ nm/f ≈ Member of Parliament (BRIT) ou Congress (US)

parler [paʀle] /1/ vi to speak, talk; (avouer) to talk; ~ **(à qn) de** to talk ou speak (to sb) about; ~ **le/en français** to speak French/ in French; ~ **affaires** to talk business; **sans ~ de** (fig) not to mention, to say nothing of; **tu parles!** (bien sûr) you bet!

parloir [paʀlwaʀ] nm (d'une prison, d'un hôpital) visiting room

parmi [paʀmi] prép among(st)

paroi [paʀwa] nf wall; (cloison) partition

paroisse [paʀwas] nf parish

parole [paʀɔl] nf (mot, promesse) word; (faculté): **la** ~ speech; **paroles** nfpl (Mus) words, lyrics; **tenir** ~ to keep one's word; **prendre la** ~ to speak; **demander la** ~ to ask for permission to speak; **je le crois sur** ~ I'll take his word for it

parquet [paʀkɛ] nm (parquet) floor; (Jur) public prosecutor's office; **le** ~ **(général)** ≈ the Bench

parrain [paʀɛ̃] nm godfather; **parrainer** /1/ vt (nouvel adhérent) to sponsor

pars [paʀ] vb voir **partir**

parsemer [paʀsəme] /5/ vt (feuilles, papiers) to be scattered over; ~ **qch de** to scatter sth with

part [paʀ] nf (qui revient à qn) share; (fraction, partie) part; **prendre** ~ **à** (débat etc) to take part in; (soucis, douleur de qn) to share in;

faire ~ **de qch à qn** to announce sth to sb, inform sb of sth; **pour ma** ~ as for me, as far as I'm concerned; **à** ~ **entière** full; **de la** ~ **de** (au nom de) on behalf of; (donné par) from; **de toute(s) la** ~**(s)** from all sides ou quarters; **de** ~ **et d'autre** on both sides, on either side; **d'une** ~ ... **d'autre** ~ on the one hand ... on the other hand; **d'autre** ~ (de plus) moreover; **à** ~ adv separately; (de côté) aside; prép apart from, except for; **faire la** ~ **des choses** to make allowances

partage [paʀtaʒ] nm sharing (out) no pl, share-out; dividing up

partager [paʀtaʒe] /3/ vt to share; (distribuer, répartir) to share (out); (morceler, diviser) to divide (up); **se partager** vt (héritage etc) to share between themselves (ou ourselves etc)

partenaire [paʀtənɛʀ] nm/f partner

parterre [paʀtɛʀ] nm (de fleurs) (flower) bed; (Théât) stalls pl

parti [paʀti] nm (Pol) party; (décision) course of action; (personne à marier) match; **tirer** ~ **de** to take advantage of, turn to good account; **prendre** ~ **(pour/contre)** to take sides ou a stand (for/against); ~ **pris** bias

partial, e, -aux [paʀsjal, -o] adj biased, partial

participant, e [paʀtisipɑ̃, -ɑ̃t] nm/f participant; (à un concours) entrant

participation [paʀtisipasjɔ̃] nf participation; (financière) contribution

participer [paʀtisipe] /1/: ~ **à** vt (course, réunion) to take part in; (frais etc) to contribute to; (chagrin, succès de qn) to share (in)

particularité [paʀtikylaʀite] nf (distinctive) characteristic

particulier, -ière [paʀtikylje, -jɛʀ] adj (personnel, privé) private; (étrange) peculiar, odd; (spécial) special, particular; (spécifique) particular ▷ nm (individu: Admin) private individual; ~ **à** peculiar to; **en** ~ (surtout) in particular, particularly; (en privé) in private; **particulièrement** adv particularly

partie [paʀti] nf (gén) part; (Jur etc: protagonistes) party; (de cartes, tennis etc) game; **une** ~ **de campagne/de pêche** an outing in the country/a fishing party ou trip; **en** ~ partly, in part; **faire** ~ **de** (chose) to be part of; **prendre qn à** ~ to take sb to task; **en grande** ~ largely, in the main; ~ **civile** (Jur) party claiming damages in a criminal case

partiel, le [paʀsjɛl] adj partial ▷ nm (Scol) class exam

partir [paʀtiʀ] /16/ vi (gén) to go; (quitter) to go, leave; (tache) to go, come out; ~ **de** (lieu: quitter) to leave; (: commencer à) to start from; ~ **pour/à** (lieu, pays etc) to leave for/go off to; **à** ~ **de** from

partisan, e [paʀtizɑ̃, -an] nm/f partisan, **être** ~ **de qch/faire** to be in favour (BRIT) ou favor (US) of sth/doing

partition [paʀtisjɔ̃] nf (Mus) score
partout [paʀtu] adv everywhere; ~ **où il
allait** everywhere ou wherever he went
paru [paʀy] pp de **paraître**
parution [paʀysjɔ̃] nf publication
parvenir [paʀvəniʀ] /22/: ~ **à** vt (atteindre)
to reach; (réussir): ~ **à faire** to manage to
do, succeed in doing; **faire ~ qch à qn** to
have sth sent to sb

MOT-CLÉ

pas¹ [pɑ] adv **1** (en corrélation avec ne, non
etc) not; **il ne pleure pas** (habituellement)
he does not ou doesn't cry; (maintenant)
he's not ou isn't crying; **il n'a pas pleuré/ne
pleurera pas** he did not ou didn't/will not
ou won't cry; **ils n'ont pas de voiture/
d'enfants** they haven't got a car/any
children; **il m'a dit de ne pas le faire** he told
me not to do it; **non pas que ...** not that ...
2 (employé sans ne etc): **pas moi** not me, I
don't (ou can't etc); **elle travaille, (mais) lui
pas** ou **pas lui** she works but he doesn't ou
does not; **une pomme pas mûre** an apple
which isn't ripe; **pas du tout** not at all; **pas
de sucre, merci** no sugar, thanks; **ceci est
à vous ou pas?** is this yours or not?, is this
yours or isn't it?
3: **pas mal** (joli: personne, maison) not bad;
pas mal fait not badly done ou made;
comment ça va? — pas mal how are
things? — not bad; **pas mal de** quite a lot of

pas² [pɑ] nm (enjambée, Danse) step; (bruit)
(foot)step; (trace) footprint; (allure, mesure)
pace; ~ **à ~** step by step; **au ~** at a walking
pace; **marcher à grands ~** to stride along;
à ~ de loup stealthily; **faire les cent ~** to
pace up and down; **faire les premiers ~** to
make the first move; **sur le ~ de la porte** on
the doorstep
passage [pasaʒ] nm (fait de passer); voir
passer; (lieu, prix de la traversée, extrait de livre
etc) passage; (chemin) way; **de ~** (touristes)
passing through; **~ clouté** pedestrian
crossing; **"~ interdit"** "no entry"; **~ à
niveau** level (BRIT) ou grade (US) crossing;
~ souterrain subway (BRIT), underpass
passager, -ère [pasaʒe, -ɛʀ] adj passing
▷ nm/f passenger
passant, e [pasɑ̃, -ɑ̃t] adj (rue, endroit) busy
▷ nm/f passer-by; **remarquer qch en ~** to
notice sth in passing
passe [pas] nf (Sport) pass; (Navig) channel;
être en ~ de faire to be on the way to doing;
être dans une mauvaise ~ to be going
through a bad patch
passé, e [pase] adj (événement, temps)
past; (dernier: semaine etc) last; (couleur,
tapisserie) faded ▷ prép after ▷ nm past;
(Ling) past (tense); **~ de mode** out of

fashion; **~ composé** perfect (tense);
~ simple past historic
passe-partout [paspaʀtu] nm inv master
ou skeleton key ▷ adj inv all-purpose
passeport [paspɔʀ] nm passport
passer [pase] /1/ vi (se rendre, aller) to go;
(voiture, piétons: défiler) to pass (by), go by;
(facteur, laitier etc) to come, call; (pour rendre
visite) to call ou drop in; (film, émission) to be
on; (temps, jours) to pass, go by; (couleur,
papier) to fade; (mode) to die out; (douleur) to
pass, go away; (Scol): **~ dans la classe
supérieure** to go up (to the next class) ▷ vt
(frontière, rivière etc) to cross; (douane) to go
through; (examen) to sit, take; (visite
médicale etc) to have; (journée, temps) to
spend; **~ qch à qn** (sel etc) to pass sth to sb;
(prêter) to lend sb sth; (lettre, message) to
pass sth on to sb; (tolérer) to let sb get away
with sth; (enfiler: vêtement) to slip on; (film,
pièce) to show, put on; (disque) to play, put
on; (commande) to place; (marché, accord) to
agree on; **se passer** vi (avoir lieu: scène,
action) to take place; (se dérouler: entretien
etc) to go; (arriver): **que s'est-il passé?** what
happened?; (s'écouler: semaine etc) to pass,
go by; **se ~ de** to go ou do without;
~ par to go through; **~ avant qch/qn** (fig) to
come before sth/sb; **~ un coup de fil à qn**
(fam) to give sb a ring; **laisser ~** (air, lumière,
personne) to let through; (occasion) to let
slip, miss; (erreur) to overlook; **~ à la radio/
télévision** to be on the radio/on television;
~ à table to sit down to eat; **~ au salon** to
go through to ou into the sitting room;
~ son tour to miss one's turn; **~ la seconde**
(Auto) to change into second; **~ le balai/
l'aspirateur** to sweep up/hoover; **je vous
passe M. Dupont** (je vous mets en
communication avec lui) I'm putting you
through to Mr Dupont; (je lui passe l'appareil)
here is Mr Dupont, I'll hand you over to Mr
Dupont
passerelle [pasʀɛl] nf footbridge; (de
navire, avion) gangway
passe-temps [pastɑ̃] nm inv pastime
passif, -ive [pasif, -iv] adj passive
passion [pasjɔ̃] nf passion; **passionnant, e**
adj fascinating; **passionné, e** adj (personne,
tempérament) passionate; (description, récit)
impassioned; **être passionné de** ou **pour
qch** to have a passion for sth; **passionner**
/1/ vt (personne) to fascinate, grip
passoire [paswaʀ] nf sieve; (à légumes)
colander; (à thé) strainer
pastèque [pastɛk] nf watermelon
pasteur [pastœʀ] nm (protestant) minister,
pastor
pastille [pastij] nf (à sucer) lozenge, pastille
patate [patat] nf spud; **~ douce** sweet
potato
patauger [patoʒe] /3/ vi to splash about

pâte [pɑt] *nf (à tarte)* pastry; *(à pain)* dough; *(à frire)* batter; **pâtes** *nfpl (macaroni etc)* pasta *sg*; **~ d'amandes** almond paste, marzipan; **~ brisée** shortcrust *(BRIT) ou* pie crust *(US)* pastry; **~ à choux/feuilletée** choux/puff *ou* flaky *(BRIT)* pastry; **~ de fruits** crystallized fruit *no pl*; **~ à modeler** modelling clay, Plasticine® *(BRIT)*

pâté [pɑte] *nm (charcuterie)* pâté; *(tache)* ink blot; *(de sable)* sandpie; **~ (en croûte)** ≈ meat pie; **~ de maisons** block (of houses)

pâtée [pɑte] *nf* mash, feed

patente [patɑ̃t] *nf (Comm)* trading licence *(BRIT) ou* license *(US)*

paternel, le [patɛʀnɛl] *adj (amour, soins)* fatherly; *(ligne, autorité)* paternal

pâteux, -euse [pɑtø, -øz] *adj* pasty; **avoir la bouche** *ou* **langue pâteuse** to have a furred *(BRIT) ou* coated tongue

pathétique [patetik] *adj* moving

patience [pasjɑ̃s] *nf* patience

patient, e [pasjɑ̃, -ɑ̃t] *adj, nm/f* patient; **patienter** /1/ *vi* to wait

patin [patɛ̃] *nm* skate; *(sport)* skating; **~s (à glace)** (ice) skates; **~s à roulettes** roller skates

patinage [patinaʒ] *nm* skating

patiner [patine] /1/ *vi* to skate; *(roue, voiture)* to spin; **se patiner** *vi (meuble, cuir)* to acquire a sheen; **patineur, -euse** *nm/f* skater; **patinoire** *nf* skating rink, (ice) rink

pâtir [pɑtiʀ] /2/: **~ de** *vt* to suffer because of

pâtisserie [pɑtisʀi] *nf (boutique)* cake shop; *(à la maison)* pastry- *ou* cake-making, baking; **pâtisseries** *nfpl (gâteaux)* pastries, cakes; **pâtissier, -ière** *nm/f* pastrycook

patois [patwa] *nm* dialect, patois

patrie [patʀi] *nf* homeland

patrimoine [patʀimwan] *nm (culture)* heritage

● **JOURNÉES DU PATRIMOINE**

● Once a year, important public buildings
● are open to the public for a weekend.
● During these *Journées du Patrimoine*, there
● are guided visits and talks based on a
● particular theme.

patriotique [patʀijɔtik] *adj* patriotic

patron, ne [patʀɔ̃, -ɔn] *nm/f* boss; *(Rel)* patron saint ▷ *nm (Couture)* pattern; **patronat** *nm* employers *pl*; **patronner** /1/ *vt* to sponsor, support

patrouille [patʀuj] *nf* patrol

patte [pat] *nf (jambe)* leg; *(pied: de chien, chat)* paw; *(: d'oiseau)* foot

pâturage [pɑtyʀaʒ] *nm* pasture

paume [pom] *nf* palm

paumé, e [pome] *nm/f (fam)* drop-out

paupière [popjɛʀ] *nf* eyelid

pause [poz] *nf (arrêt)* break; *(en parlant, Mus)* pause; **~ de midi** lunch break

pauvre [povʀ] *adj* poor; **les ~s** the poor; **pauvreté** *nf (état)* poverty

pavé, e [pave] *adj (cour)* paved; *(rue)* cobbled ▷ *nm (bloc)* paving stone; cobblestone; **~ numérique** keypad

pavillon [pavijɔ̃] *nm (de banlieue)* small (detached) house; pavilion; *(Navig)* flag

payant, e [pɛjɑ̃, -ɑ̃t] *adj (spectateurs etc)* paying; *(fig: entreprise)* profitable; *(effort)* which pays off; **c'est ~** you have to pay, there is a charge

paye [pɛj] *nf* pay, wages *pl*

payer [peje] *nf* pay, wages *pl*

payer [peje] /8/ *vt (créancier, employé, loyer)* to pay; *(achat, réparations, faute)* to pay for ▷ *vi* to pay; *(métier)* to be well-paid; *(effort, tactique etc)* to pay off; **il me l'a fait ~ 10 euros** he charged me 10 euros for it; **~ qch à qn** to buy sth for sb, buy sb sth; **se ~ la tête de qn** to take the mickey out of sb *(BRIT)*

pays [pei] *nm* country; *(région)* region; **du ~** local

paysage [peizaʒ] *nm* landscape

paysan, ne [peizɑ̃, -an] *nm/f* farmer; *(péj)* peasant ▷ *adj (rural)* country *cpd*; *(agricole)* farming

Pays-Bas [peiba] *nmpl*: **les ~** the Netherlands

PC *sigle m (Inform: = personal computer)* PC; **= permis de construire**; *(= prêt conventionné)* type of loan for house purchase

PDA *sigle m (= personal digital assistant)* PDA

PDG *sigle m* **= président directeur général**

péage [peaʒ] *nm* toll; *(endroit)* tollgate

peau, x [po] *nf* skin; **gants de ~** leather gloves; **être bien/mal dans sa ~** to be at ease/ill-at-ease; **~ de chamois** *(chiffon)* chamois leather, shammy

péché [peʃe] *nm* sin

pêche [pɛʃ] *nf (sport, activité)* fishing; *(poissons pêchés)* catch; *(fruit)* peach; **~ à la ligne** *(en rivière)* angling

pécher [peʃe] /6/ *vi (Rel)* to sin

pêcher [peʃe] /1/ *vi* to go fishing ▷ *vt (attraper)* to catch; *(chercher)* to fish for ▷ *nm* peach tree

pécheur, -eresse [peʃœʀ, peʃʀɛs] *nm/f* sinner

pêcheur [peʃœʀ] *nm voir* **pêcher** fisherman; *(à la ligne)* angler

pédagogie [pedagɔʒi] *nf* educational methods *pl*, pedagogy; **pédagogique** *adj* educational

pédale [pedal] *nf* pedal

pédalo [pedalo] *nm* pedal-boat

pédant, e [pedɑ̃, -ɑ̃t] *adj (péj)* pedantic ▷ *nm/f* pedant

pédestre [pedɛstʀ] *adj*: **randonnée ~** ramble; **sentier ~** pedestrian footpath

pédiatre [pedjatʀ] *nm/f* paediatrician, child specialist

pédicure [pedikyR] nm/f chiropodist

pègre [pɛgR] nf underworld

peigne [pɛɲ] nm comb; **peigner** /1/ vt to comb (the hair of); **se peigner** vi to comb one's hair; **peignoir** nm dressing gown; **peignoir de bain** bathrobe

peindre [pɛ̃dR] /52/ vt to paint; (fig) to portray, depict

peine [pɛn] nf (affliction) sorrow, sadness no pl; (mal, effort) trouble no pl, effort; (difficulté) difficulty; (Jur) sentence; **faire de la ~ à qn** to distress ou upset sb; **prendre la ~ de faire** to go to the trouble of doing; **se donner de la ~** to make an effort; **ce n'est pas la ~ de faire** there's no point in doing, it's not worth doing; **avoir de la ~** to be sad; **à ~** scarcely, barely; **à ~ ... que** hardly ... than, no sooner ... than; **~ capitale** capital punishment; **~ de mort** death sentence ou penalty; **peiner** [pene] /1/ vi to work hard; to struggle; (moteur, voiture) to labour (BRIT), labor (US) ▷ vt to grieve, sadden

peintre [pɛ̃tR] nm painter; **~ en bâtiment** painter and decorator

peinture [pɛ̃tyR] nf painting; (couche de couleur, couleur) paint; (surfaces peintes: aussi: **~s**) paintwork; **"~ fraîche"** "wet paint"

péjoratif, -ive [peʒɔRatif, -iv] adj pejorative, derogatory

Pékin [pekɛ̃] n Beijing

pêle-mêle [pɛlmɛl] adv higgledy-piggledy

peler [pəle] /5/ vt, vi to peel

pèlerin [pɛlRɛ̃] nm pilgrim

pèlerinage [pɛlRinaʒ] nm pilgrimage

pelle [pɛl] nf shovel; (d'enfant, de terrassier) spade

pellicule [pelikyl] nf film; **pellicules** nfpl (Méd) dandruff sg

pelote [pəlɔt] nf (de fil, laine) ball; **~ basque** pelota

peloton [pəlɔtɔ̃] nm group; squad; (Sport) pack

pelotonner [pəlɔtɔne] /1/: **se pelotonner** vi to curl (o.s.) up

pelouse [pəluz] nf lawn

peluche [pəlyʃ] nf: **animal en ~** soft toy, fluffy animal; **chien/lapin en ~** fluffy dog/rabbit

pelure [pəlyR] nf peeling, peel no pl

pénal, e, -aux [penal, -o] adj penal; **pénalité** nf penalty

penchant [pɑ̃ʃɑ̃] nm: **un ~ à faire/à qch** a tendency to do/to sth; **un ~ pour qch** a liking ou fondness for sth

pencher [pɑ̃ʃe] /1/ vi to tilt, lean over ▷ vt to tilt; **se pencher** vi to lean over; (se baisser) to bend down; **se ~ sur** (fig: problème) to look into; **~ pour** to be inclined to favour (BRIT) ou favor (US)

pendant, e [pɑ̃dɑ̃, -ɑ̃t] adj hanging (out) ▷ prép (au cours de) during; (indiquant la durée) for; **~ que** while

pendentif [pɑ̃datif] nm pendant

penderie [pɑ̃dRi] nf wardrobe

pendre [pɑ̃dR] /41/ vt, vi to hang; **se ~ (à)** (se suicider) to hang o.s. (on); **~ qch à (mur)** to hang sth (up) on; (plafond) to hang sth (up) from

pendule [pɑ̃dyl] nf clock ▷ nm pendulum

pénétrer [penetRe] /6/ vi to come ou get in ▷ vt to penetrate; **~ dans** to enter

pénible [penibl] adj (astreignant) hard; (affligeant) painful; (personne, caractère) tiresome; **péniblement** adv with difficulty

péniche [peniʃ] nf barge

pénicilline [penisilin] nf penicillin

péninsule [penɛ̃syl] nf peninsula

pénis [penis] nm penis

pénitence [penitɑ̃s] nf (repentir) penitence; (peine) penance; **pénitencier** nm penitentiary (US)

pénombre [penɔ̃bR] nf (faible clarté) half-light; (obscurité) darkness

pensée [pɑ̃se] nf thought; (démarche, doctrine) thinking no pl; (Bot) pansy; **en ~** in one's mind

penser [pɑ̃se] /1/ vi to think ▷ vt to think; **~ à** (prévoir) to think of; (ami, vacances) to think of ou about; **~ faire qch** to be thinking of doing sth, intend to do sth; **faire ~ à** to remind one of; **pensif, -ive** adj pensive, thoughtful

pension [pɑ̃sjɔ̃] nf (allocation) pension; (prix du logement) board and lodging, bed and board; (école) boarding school; **~ alimentaire** (de divorcée) maintenance allowance; alimony; **~ complète** full board; **~ de famille** boarding house, guesthouse; **pensionnaire** nm/f (Scol) boarder; **pensionnat** nm boarding school

pente [pɑ̃t] nf slope; **en ~** sloping

Pentecôte [pɑ̃tkot] nf: **la ~** Whitsun (BRIT), Pentecost

pénurie [penyRi] nf shortage

pépé [pepe] nm (fam) grandad

pépin [pepɛ̃] nm (Bot: graine) pip; (fam: ennui) snag, hitch

pépinière [pepinjɛR] nf nursery

perçant, e [pɛRsɑ̃, -ɑ̃t] adj (vue, regard, yeux) sharp; (cri, voix) piercing, shrill

perce-neige [pɛRsənɛʒ] nm ou f inv snowdrop

percepteur, -trice [pɛRsɛptœR, -tRis] nm/f tax collector

perception [pɛRsɛpsjɔ̃] nf perception; (bureau) tax (collector's) office

percer [pɛRse] /3/ vt to pierce; (ouverture etc) to make; (mystère, énigme) to penetrate ▷ vi to break through; **perceuse** nf drill

percevoir [pɛRsəvwaR] /28/ vt (distinguer) to perceive, detect; (taxe, impôt) to collect; (revenu, indemnité) to receive

perche [pɛRʃ] nf (bâton) pole

percher [pɛʀʃe] /1/ vt to perch; **se percher** vi to perch; **perchoir** nm perch

perçois etc [pɛʀswa] vb voir **percevoir**

perçu, e [pɛʀsy] pp de **percevoir**

percussion [pɛʀkysjɔ̃] nf percussion

percuter [pɛʀkyte] /1/ vt to strike; (véhicule) to crash into

perdant, e [pɛʀdɑ̃, -ɑ̃t] nm/f loser

perdre [pɛʀdʀ] /41/ vt to lose; (gaspiller: temps, argent) to waste; (personne: moralement etc) to ruin ▷ vi to lose; (sur une vente etc) to lose out; **se perdre** vi (s'égarer) to get lost, lose one's way; (se gâter) to go to waste; **je me suis perdu** (et je le suis encore) I'm lost; (et je ne le suis plus) I got lost

perdrix [pɛʀdʀi] nf partridge

perdu, e [pɛʀdy] pp de **perdre** ▷ adj (isolé) out-of-the-way; (Comm: emballage) non-returnable; (malade): **il est ~** there's no hope left for him; **à vos moments ~s** in your spare time

père [pɛʀ] nm father; **~ de famille** father; **le ~ Noël** Father Christmas

perfection [pɛʀfɛksjɔ̃] nf perfection; **à la ~** to perfection; **perfectionné, e** adj sophisticated; **perfectionner** /1/ vt to improve, perfect; **se perfectionner en anglais** to improve one's English

perforer [pɛʀfɔʀe] /1/ vt (ticket, bande, carte) to punch

performant, e [pɛʀfɔʀmɑ̃, -ɑ̃t] adj: **très ~** high-performance cpd

perfusion [pɛʀfyzjɔ̃] nf: **faire une ~ à qn** to put sb on a drip

péril [peʀil] nm peril

périmé, e [peʀime] adj (Admin) out-of-date, expired

périmètre [peʀimɛtʀ] nm perimeter

période [peʀjɔd] nf period; **périodique** adj periodic ▷ nm periodical; **garniture** ou **serviette périodique** sanitary towel (BRIT) ou napkin (US)

périphérique [peʀifeʀik] adj (quartiers) outlying ▷ nm (Auto): **(boulevard) ~** ring road (BRIT), beltway (US)

périr [peʀiʀ] /2/ vi to die, perish

périssable [peʀisabl] adj perishable

perle [pɛʀl] nf pearl; (de plastique, métal, sueur) bead

permanence [pɛʀmanɑ̃s] nf permanence; (local) (duty) office; **assurer une ~** (service public, bureaux) to operate ou maintain a basic service; **être de ~** to be on call ou duty; **en ~** continuously

permanent, e [pɛʀmanɑ̃, -ɑ̃t] adj permanent; (spectacle) continuous ▷ nf perm

perméable [pɛʀmeabl] adj (terrain) permeable; **~ à** (fig) receptive ou open to

permettre [pɛʀmɛtʀ] /56/ vt to allow, permit; **~ à qn de faire/qch** to allow sb to

do/sth; **se ~ de faire qch** to take the liberty of doing sth

permis [pɛʀmi] nm permit, licence; **~ (de conduire)** (driving) licence (BRIT), (driver's) license (US); **~ de construire** planning permission (BRIT), building permit (US); **~ de séjour** residence permit; **~ de travail** work permit

permission [pɛʀmisjɔ̃] nf permission; (Mil) leave; **en ~** on leave; **avoir la ~ de faire** to have permission to do

Pérou [peʀu] nm: **le ~** Peru

perpétuel, le [pɛʀpetɥɛl] adj perpetual; **perpétuité** nf: **à perpétuité** for life; **être condamné à perpétuité** to be sentenced to life imprisonment

perplexe [pɛʀplɛks] adj perplexed, puzzled

perquisitionner [pɛʀkizisjɔne] /1/ vi to carry out a search

perron [peʀɔ̃] nm steps pl (in front of mansion etc)

perroquet [peʀɔke] nm parrot

perruche [peʀyʃ] nf budgerigar (BRIT), budgie (BRIT), parakeet (US)

perruque [peʀyk] nf wig

persécuter [pɛʀsekyte] /1/ vt to persecute

persévérer [pɛʀsevere] /6/ vi to persevere

persil [pɛʀsi] nm parsley

Persique [pɛʀsik] adj: **le golfe ~** the (Persian) Gulf

persistant, e [pɛʀsistɑ̃, -ɑ̃t] adj persistent

persister [pɛʀsiste] /1/ vi to persist; **~ à faire qch** to persist in doing sth

personnage [pɛʀsɔnaʒ] nm (notable) personality; (individu) character, individual; (de roman, film) character; (Peinture) figure

personnalité [pɛʀsɔnalite] nf personality; (personnage) prominent figure

personne [pɛʀsɔn] nf person ▷ pron nobody, no one; (avec négation en anglais) anybody, anyone; **~ âgée** elderly person; **personnel, le** adj personal; (égoïste) selfish ▷ nm personnel; **personnellement** adv personally

perspective [pɛʀspɛktiv] nf (Art) perspective; (vue, coup d'œil) view; (point de vue) viewpoint, angle; (chose escomptée, envisagée) prospect; **en ~** in prospect

perspicace [pɛʀspikas] adj clear-sighted, gifted with (ou showing) insight; **perspicacité** nf insight

persuader [pɛʀsɥade] /1/ vt: **~ qn (de/de faire)** to persuade sb (of/to do); **persuasif, -ive** adj persuasive

perte [pɛʀt] nf loss; (de temps) waste; (fig: morale) ruin; **à ~ de vue** as far as the eye can (ou could) see; **~s blanches** (vaginal) discharge sg

pertinent, e [pɛʀtinɑ̃, -ɑ̃t] adj apt, relevant

perturbation [pɛʀtyʀbasjɔ̃] nf: **~ (atmosphérique)** atmospheric disturbance

perturber [pɛʀtyʀbe] /1/ vt to disrupt; (Psych) to perturb, disturb

pervers, e [pɛʀvɛʀ, -ɛʀs] adj perverted

pervertir [pɛʀvɛʀtiʀ] /2/ vt to pervert

pesant, e [pəzɑ̃, -ɑ̃t] adj heavy; (fig: présence) burdensome

pèse-personne [pɛzpɛʀsɔn] nm (bathroom) scales pl

peser [pəze] /5/ vt to weigh ▷ vi to be heavy; (fig: avoir de l'importance) to carry weight

pessimiste [pesimist] adj pessimistic ▷ nm/f pessimist

peste [pɛst] nf plague

pétale [petal] nm petal

pétanque [petɑ̃k] nf type of bowls

- **PÉTANQUE**
-
- Pétanque is a version of the game of
- 'boules', played on a variety of hard
- surfaces. Standing with their feet
- together, players throw steel bowls at a
- wooden jack. Pétanque originated in the
- South of France and is still very much
- associated with that area.

pétard [petaʀ] nm banger (BRIT), firecracker

péter [pete] /6/ vi (fam: casser, sauter) to bust; (fam!) to fart (!)

pétillant, e [petijɑ̃, -ɑ̃t] adj (eau) sparkling

pétiller [petije] /1/ vi (flamme, bois) to crackle; (mousse, champagne) to bubble; (yeux) to sparkle

petit, e [pəti, -it] adj small; (avec nuance affective) little; (voyage) short, little; (bruit etc) faint, slight ▷ nm/f (petit enfant) little one, child; **petits** nmpl (d'un animal) young pl; **faire des ~s** to have kittens (ou puppies etc); **la classe des ~s** the infant class; **les tout-~s** toddlers; **~ à ~** bit by bit, gradually; **~(e) ami(e)** boyfriend/girlfriend; **les ~es annonces** the small ads; **~ déjeuner** breakfast; **~ four** petit four; **~ pain** (bread) roll; **~s pois** garden peas; **petite-fille** nf granddaughter; **petit-fils** nm grandson

pétition [petisjɔ̃] nf petition

petits-enfants [pətizɑ̃fɑ̃] nmpl grandchildren

pétrin [petʀɛ̃] nm (fig): **dans le ~** in a jam ou fix

pétrir [petʀiʀ] /2/ vt to knead

pétrole [petʀɔl] nm oil; (pour lampe, réchaud etc) paraffin; **pétrolier, -ière** nm oil tanker
  ▮ Attention à ne pas traduire pétrole par le mot anglais petrol.

○ MOT-CLÉ

peu [pø] adv **1** (modifiant verbe, adjectif, adverbe): **il boit peu** he doesn't drink (very) much; **il est peu bavard** he's not very

talkative; **peu avant/après** shortly before/ afterwards

2 (modifiant nom): **peu de: peu de gens/ d'arbres** few ou not (very) many people/ trees; **il a peu d'espoir** he hasn't (got) much hope, he has little hope; **pour peu de temps** for (only) a short while

3: **peu à peu** little by little; **à peu près** just about, more or less; **à peu près 10 kg/10 euros** approximately 10 kg/10 euros
  ▶ nm **1**: **le peu de gens qui** the few people who; **le peu de sable qui** what little sand, the little sand which

2: **un peu** a little; **un petit peu** a little bit; **un peu d'espoir** a little hope; **elle est un peu bavarde** she's rather talkative; **un peu plus de** slightly more than; **un peu moins de** slightly less than; (avec pluriel) slightly fewer than
  ▶ pron: **peu le savent** few know (it); **de peu** (only) just

peuple [pœpl] nm people; **peupler** /1/ vt (pays, région) to populate; (étang) to stock; (hommes, poissons) to inhabit

peuplier [pøplije] nm poplar (tree)

peur [pœʀ] nf fear; **avoir ~ (de/de faire/ que)** to be frightened ou afraid (of/of doing/ that); **faire ~ à** to frighten; **de ~ de/que** for fear of/that; **peureux, -euse** adj fearful, timorous

peut [pø] vb voir **pouvoir**

peut-être [pøtɛtʀ] adv perhaps, maybe; **~ que** perhaps, maybe; **~ bien qu'il fera/est** he may well do/be

phare [faʀ] nm (en mer) lighthouse; (de véhicule) headlight

pharmacie [faʀmasi] nf (magasin) chemist's (BRIT), pharmacy; (armoire) medicine chest ou cupboard; **pharmacien, ne** nm/f pharmacist, chemist (BRIT)

phénomène [fenɔmɛn] nm phenomenon

philosophe [filɔzɔf] nm/f philosopher ▷ adj philosophical

philosophie [filɔzɔfi] nf philosophy

phobie [fɔbi] nf phobia

phoque [fɔk] nm seal

phosphorescent, e [fɔsfɔʀesɑ̃, -ɑ̃t] adj luminous

photo [fɔto] nf photo; **prendre en ~** to take a photo of; **aimer la/faire de la ~** to like taking/take photos; **~ d'identité** passport photo; **photocopie** nf photocopy; **photocopier** /7/ vt to photocopy

photocopieur [fɔtɔkɔpjœʀ] nm, **photocopieuse** [fɔtɔkɔpjøz] nf (photo) copier

photo: photographe nm/f photographer; **photographie** nf (procédé, technique) photography; (cliché) photograph; **photographier** /7/ vt to photograph

phrase [fʀɑz] nf sentence

physicien, ne [fizisjɛ̃, -ɛn] nm/f physicist
physique [fizik] adj physical ▷ nm
physique ▷ nf physics sg; **au ~** physically;
physiquement adv physically
pianiste [pjanist] nm/f pianist
piano [pjano] nm piano; **pianoter** /1/ vi to
tinkle away (at the piano)
pic [pik] nm (instrument) pick(axe);
(montagne) peak; (Zool) woodpecker; **à ~**
vertically; (fig: tomber, arriver) just at the
right time
pichet [piʃɛ] nm jug
picorer [pikɔʀe] /1/ vt to peck
pie [pi] nf magpie
pièce [pjɛs] nf (d'un logement) room; (Théât)
play; (de mécanisme, machine) part; (de
monnaie) coin; (document) document; (de
drap, fragment, d'une collection) piece; **deux
euros ~** two euros each; **vendre à la ~** to
sell separately ou individually; **travailler/
payer à la ~** to do piecework/pay piece rate;
un maillot une ~ a one-piece swimsuit; **un
deux-~s cuisine** a two-room(ed) flat (BRIT)
ou apartment (US) with kitchen; **~ à
conviction** exhibit; **~ d'eau** ornamental
lake ou pond; **~ d'identité: avez-vous une
~ d'identité?** have you got any (means of)
identification?; **~ jointe** (Inform)
attachment; **~ montée** tiered cake; **~ de
rechange** spare (part); **~s détachées**
spares, (spare) parts; **~s justificatives**
supporting documents
pied [pje] nm foot; (de table) leg; (de lampe)
base; **~s nus** barefoot; **à ~** on foot; **au ~
de la lettre** literally; **avoir ~** to be able to
touch the bottom, not to be out of one's
depth; **avoir le ~ marin** to be a good sailor;
sur ~ (debout, rétabli) up and about; **mettre
sur ~** (entreprise) to set up; **c'est le ~!** (fam)
it's brilliant!; **mettre les ~s dans le plat**
(fam) to put one's foot in it; **il se débrouille
comme un ~** (fam) he's completely useless;
pied-noir nm Algerian-born Frenchman
piège [pjɛʒ] nm trap; **prendre au ~** to
trap; **piéger** /3, 6/ vt (avec une bombe) to
booby-trap; **lettre/voiture piégée** letter-/
car-bomb
piercing [pjɛʀsiŋ] nm piercing
pierre [pjɛʀ] nf stone; **~ tombale**
tombstone; **pierreries** nfpl gems, precious
stones
piétiner [pjetine] /1/ vi (trépigner) to stamp
(one's foot); (fig) to be at a standstill ▷ vt to
trample on
piéton, ne [pjetɔ̃, -ɔn] nm/f pedestrian;
piétonnier, -ière adj pedestrian cpd
pieu, x [pjø] nm post; (pointu) stake
pieuvre [pjœvʀ] nf octopus
pieux, -euse [pjø, -øz] adj pious
pigeon [piʒɔ̃] nm pigeon
piger [piʒe] /3/ vi (fam) to get it ▷ vt (fam)
to get

pigiste [piʒist] nm/f freelance journalist
(paid by the line)
pignon [piɲɔ̃] nm (de mur) gable
pile [pil] nf (tas, pilier) pile; (Élec) battery
▷ adv (net, brusquement) dead; **à deux
heures ~** at two on the dot; **jouer à ~ ou
face** to toss up (for it); **~ ou face?** heads
or tails?
piler [pile] /1/ vt to crush, pound
pilier [pilje] nm pillar
piller [pije] /1/ vt to pillage, plunder, loot
pilote [pilɔt] nm pilot; (de char, voiture)
driver ▷ adj pilot cpd; **~ de chasse/d'essai/
de ligne** fighter/test/airline pilot; **~ de
course** racing driver; **piloter** /1/ vt (navire)
to pilot; (avion) to fly; (automobile) to drive
pilule [pilyl] nf pill; **prendre la ~** to be on
the pill
piment [pimɑ̃] nm (Bot) pepper, capsicum;
(fig) spice, piquancy; **~ rouge** (Culin) chilli;
pimenté, e adj (plat) hot and spicy
pin [pɛ̃] nm pine (tree)
pinard [pinaʀ] nm (fam) (cheap) wine,
plonk (BRIT)
pince [pɛ̃s] nf (outil) pliers pl; (de homard,
crabe) pincer, claw; (Couture: pli) dart; **~ à
épiler** tweezers pl; **~ à linge** clothes peg
(BRIT) nm pin (US)
pincé, e [pɛ̃se] adj (air) stiff
pinceau, x [pɛ̃so] nm (paint)brush
pincer [pɛ̃se] /3/ vt to pinch; (fam) to nab
pinède [pinɛd] nf pinewood, pine forest
pingouin [pɛ̃gwɛ̃] nm penguin
ping-pong [piŋpɔ̃g] nm table tennis
pinson [pɛ̃sɔ̃] nm chaffinch
pintade [pɛ̃tad] nf guinea-fowl
pion, ne [pjɔ̃, pjɔn] nm/f (Scol: péj) student
paid to supervise schoolchildren ▷ nm (Échecs)
pawn; (Dames) piece
pionnier [pjɔnje] nm pioneer
pipe [pip] nf pipe; **fumer la** ou **une ~** to
smoke a pipe
piquant, e [pikɑ̃, -ɑ̃t] adj (barbe, rosier etc)
prickly; (saveur, sauce) hot, pungent; (fig:
détail) titillating; (: mordant, caustique) biting
▷ nm (épine) thorn, prickle; (fig) spiciness,
spice
pique [pik] nf pike; (fig): **envoyer** ou **lancer
des ~s à qn** to make cutting remarks to sb
▷ nm (Cartes) spades pl
pique-nique [piknik] nm picnic; **pique-
niquer** /1/ vi to (have a) picnic
piquer [pike] /1/ vt (percer) to prick; (Méd)
to give an injection to; (: animal blessé etc) to
put to sleep; (insecte, fumée, ortie) to sting;
(moustique) to bite; (froid) to bite; (intérêt etc)
to arouse; (fam: voler) to pinch ▷ vi (oiseau,
avion) to go into a dive
piquet [pikɛ] nm (pieu) post, stake; (de
tente) peg
piqûre [pikyʀ] nf (d'épingle) prick; (d'ortie)
sting; (de moustique) bite; (Méd) injection,

shot (us); **faire une ~ à qn** to give sb an injection

pirate [piʀat] adj ▷ nm pirate; **~ de l'air** hijacker

pire [piʀ] adj worse; (superlatif): **le (la) ~ ...** the worst ... ▷ nm: **le ~ (de)** the worst (of); **au ~** at (the very) worst

pis [pi] nm (de vache) udder ▷ adj, adv worse; **de mal en ~** from bad to worse

piscine [pisin] nf (swimming) pool; **~ couverte** indoor (swimming) pool

pissenlit [pisāli] nm dandelion

pistache [pistaʃ] nf pistachio (nut)

piste [pist] nf (d'un animal, sentier) track, trail; (indice) lead; (de stade, de magnétophone) track; (de cirque) ring; (de danse) floor; (de patinage) rink; (de ski) run; (Aviat) runway; **~ cyclable** cycle track

pistolet [pistɔlɛ] nm (arme) pistol, gun; (à peinture) spray gun; **pistolet-mitrailleur** nm submachine gun

piston [pistɔ̃] nm (Tech) piston; **avoir du ~** (fam) to have friends in the right places; **pistonner** /1/ vt (candidat) to pull strings for

piteux, -euse [pitø, -øz] adj pitiful, sorry (avant le nom); **en ~ état** in a sorry state

pitié [pitje] nf pity; **il me fait ~** I feel sorry for him; **avoir ~ de** (compassion) to pity, feel sorry for; (merci) to have pity ou mercy on

pitoyable [pitwajabl] adj pitiful

pittoresque [pitɔʀɛsk] adj picturesque

pizza [pidza] nf pizza

PJ sigle f (= police judiciaire) ≈ CID (BRIT), ≈ FBI (us)

placard [plakaʀ] nm (armoire) cupboard; (affiche) poster, notice

place [plas] nf (emplacement, situation, classement) place; (de ville, village) square; (espace libre) room, space; (de parking) space; (siège: de train, cinéma, voiture) seat; (emploi) job; **en ~** (mettre) in its place; **sur ~** on the spot; **faire ~ à** to give way to; **ça prend de la ~** it takes up a lot of room ou space; **à la ~ de** in place of, instead of; **à votre ~ ...** if I were you ...; **se mettre à la ~ de qn** to put o.s. in sb's place ou in sb's shoes

placé, e [plase] adj: **haut ~** (fig) high-ranking; **être bien/mal ~** to be well/badly placed; (spectateur) to have a good/bad seat; **il est bien ~ pour le savoir** he is in a position to know

placement [plasmã] nm (Finance) investment; **agence** ou **bureau de ~** employment agency

placer [plase] /3/ vt to place; (convive, spectateur) to seat; (capital, argent) to place, invest; **se ~ au premier rang** to go and stand (ou sit) in the first row

plafond [plafɔ̃] nm ceiling

plage [plaʒ] nf beach; **~ arrière** (Auto) parcel ou back shelf

plaider [plede] /1/ vi (avocat) to plead ▷ vt to plead; **~ pour** (fig) to speak for; **plaidoyer** nm (Jur) speech for the defence (BRIT) ou defense (us); (fig) plea

plaie [plɛ] nf wound

plaignant, e [plɛɲã, -ãt] nm/f plaintiff

plaindre [plɛ̃dʀ] /52/ vt to pity, feel sorry for; **se plaindre** vi (gémir) to moan; (protester, rouspéter): **se ~ (à qn) (de)** to complain (to sb) (about); **se ~ de** (souffrir) to complain of

plaine [plɛn] nf plain

plain-pied [plɛ̃pje] adv: **de ~ (avec)** on the same level (as)

plaint, e [plɛ̃, -ɛ̃t] pp de plaindre ▷ nf (gémissement) moan, groan; (doléance) complaint; **porter ~e** to lodge a complaint

plaire [plɛʀ] /54/ vi to be a success, be successful; **cela me plaît** I like it; **ça plaît beaucoup aux jeunes** it's very popular with young people; **se ~ quelque part** to like being somewhere; **s'il vous plaît, s'il te plaît** please

plaisance [plɛzãs] nf (aussi: **navigation de ~**) (pleasure) sailing, yachting

plaisant, e [plɛzã, -ãt] adj pleasant; (histoire, anecdote) amusing

plaisanter [plɛzãte] /1/ vi to joke; **plaisanterie** nf joke

plaisir [pleziʀ] nm pleasure; **faire ~ à qn** (délibérément) to be nice to sb, please sb; **ça me fait ~** I'm delighted ou very pleased with this; **j'espère que ça te fera ~** I hope you'll like it; **pour le** ou **pour son** ou **par ~** for pleasure

plaît [plɛ] vb voir **plaire**

plan, e [plã, -an] adj flat ▷ nm plan; (fig) level, plane; (Ciné) shot; **au premier/second ~** in the foreground/middle distance; **à l'arrière ~** in the background; **~ d'eau** lake

planche [plãʃ] nf (pièce de bois) plank, (wooden) board; (illustration) plate; **~ à repasser** ironing board; **~ (à roulettes)** skateboard; **~ à voile** (sport) windsurfing

plancher [plãʃe] /1/ nm floor; (planches) floorboards pl ▷ vi to work hard

planer [plane] /1/ vi to glide; (fam: rêveur) to have one's head in the clouds; **~ sur** (danger) to hang over

planète [planɛt] nf planet

planeur [planœʀ] nm glider

planifier [planifje] /7/ vt to plan

planning [planiŋ] nm programme, schedule; **~ familial** family planning

plant [plã] nm seedling, young plant

plante [plãt] nf plant; **~ d'appartement** house ou pot plant; **~ du pied** sole (of the foot); **~ verte** house plant

planter [plãte] /1/ vt (plante) to plant; (enfoncer) to hammer ou drive in; (tente) to put up, pitch; (fam: mettre) to dump;

se planter vi (fam: se tromper) to get it wrong; (': ordinateur) to crash

plaque [plak] nf plate; (de verglas, d'eczéma) patch; (avec inscription) plaque; **~ chauffante** hotplate; **~ de chocolat** bar of chocolate; **~ tournante** (fig) centre

plaqué, e [plake] adj: **~ or/argent** gold-/silver-plated

plaquer [plake] /1/ vt (Rugby) to bring down; (fam: laisser tomber) to drop

plaquette [plakɛt] nf (de chocolat) bar; (de beurre) packet; **~ de frein** brake pad

plastique [plastik] adj ▷ nm plastic ▷ nf plastic arts pl; (d'une statue) modelling; **plastiquer** /1/ vt to blow up

plat, e [pla, -at] adj flat; (style) flat, dull ▷ nm (récipient, Culin) dish; (d'un repas) course; **à ~ ventre** face down; **à ~** (pneu, batterie) flat; (fam: fatigué) dead beat; **~ cuisiné** pre-cooked meal (ou dish); **~ du jour** dish of the day; **~ principal** ou **de résistance** main course

platane [platan] nm plane tree

plateau, x [plato] nm (support) tray; (Géo) plateau; (Ciné) set; **~ à fromages** cheeseboard

plate-bande [platbɑ̃d] nf flower bed

plate-forme [platfɔʀm] nf platform; **~ de forage/pétrolière** drilling/oil rig

platine [platin] nm platinum ▷ nf (d'un tourne-disque) turntable; **~ laser** ou **compact-disc** compact disc (player)

plâtre [platʀ] nm (matériau) plaster; (statue) plaster statue; (Méd) (plaster) cast; **avoir un bras dans le ~** to have an arm in plaster

plein, e [plɛ̃, -ɛn] adj full ▷ nm: **faire le ~ (d'essence)** to fill up (with petrol (BRIT) ou gas (US)); **à ~es mains** (ramasser) in handfuls; **à ~ temps** full-time; **en ~ air** in the open air; **en ~ soleil** in direct sunlight; **en ~ nuit/rue** in the middle of the night/street; **en ~ jour** in broad daylight

pleurer [plœʀe] /1/ vi to cry; (yeux) to water ▷ vt to mourn (for); **~ sur** to lament (over), bemoan

pleurnicher [plœʀniʃe] /1/ vi to snivel, whine

pleurs [plœʀ] nmpl: **en ~** in tears

pleut [plø] vb voir **pleuvoir**

pleuvoir [pløvwaʀ] /23/ vb impers to rain ▷ vi (coups) to rain down; (critiques, invitations) to shower down; **il pleut** it's raining; **il pleut des cordes** ou **à verse** ou **à torrents** it's pouring (down), it's raining cats and dogs

pli [pli] nm fold; (de jupe) pleat; (de pantalon) crease

pliant, e [plijɑ̃, -ɑ̃t] adj folding

plier [plije] /7/ vt to fold; (pour ranger) to fold up; (genou, bras) to bend ▷ vi to bend; (fig) to yield; **se ~ à** to submit to

plisser [plise] /1/ vt (yeux) to screw up; (front) to furrow; (jupe) to put pleats in

plomb [plɔ̃] nm (métal) lead; (d'une cartouche) (lead) shot; (Pêche) sinker; (Élec) fuse; **sans ~** (essence) unleaded

plomberie [plɔ̃bʀi] nf plumbing

plombier [plɔ̃bje] nm plumber

plonge [plɔ̃ʒ] nf: **faire la ~** to be a washer-up (BRIT) ou dishwasher (person)

plongeant, e [plɔ̃ʒɑ̃, -ɑ̃t] adj (vue) from above; (tir, décolleté) plunging

plongée [plɔ̃ʒe] nf (Sport) diving no pl; (': sans scaphandre) skin diving; **~ sous-marine** diving

plongeoir [plɔ̃ʒwaʀ] nm diving board

plongeon [plɔ̃ʒɔ̃] nm dive

plonger [plɔ̃ʒe] /3/ vi to dive ▷ vt: **~ qch dans** to plunge sth into; **se ~ dans** (études, lecture) to bury ou immerse o.s. in; **plongeur, -euse** [plɔ̃ʒœʀ, -øz] nm/f diver

plu [ply] pp de **plaire**; **pleuvoir**

pluie [plɥi] nf rain

plume [plym] nf feather; (pour écrire) (pen) nib; (fig) pen

plupart [plypaʀ]: **la ~** pron the majority, most (of them); **la ~ des** most, the majority of; **la ~ du temps/d'entre nous** most of the time/of us; **pour la ~** for the most part, mostly

pluriel [plyʀjɛl] nm plural

plus¹ [ply] vb voir **plaire**

 MOT-CLÉ

plus² [ply] adv **1** (forme négative): **ne … plus** no more, no longer; **je n'ai plus d'argent** I've got no more money ou no money left; **il ne travaille plus** he's no longer working, he doesn't work any more

2 [ply, plyz + voyelle] (comparatif) more, …+er; (superlatif): **le plus** the most, the …+est; **plus grand/intelligent (que)** bigger/more intelligent (than); **le plus grand/intelligent** the biggest/most intelligent; **tout au plus** at the very most

3 [plys, plyz + voyelle] (davantage) more; **il travaille plus (que)** he works more (than); **plus il travaille, plus il est heureux** the more he works, the happier he is; **plus de 10 personnes/trois heures/quatre kilos** more than ou over 10 people/three hours/four kilos; **trois heures de plus que** three hours more than; **de plus** what's more, moreover; **il a trois ans de plus que moi** he's three years older than me; **trois kilos en plus** three kilos more; **en plus de** in addition to; **de plus en plus** more and more; **plus ou moins** more or less; **ni plus ni moins** no more, no less

▷ prép [plys]: **quatre plus deux** four plus two

plusieurs [plyzjœʀ] adj, pron several; **ils sont ~** there are several of them

plus-value [plyvaly] nf (bénéfice) capital gain

plutôt [plyto] adv rather; **je ferais ~ ceci** I'd rather ou sooner do this; **~ que (de) faire** rather than ou instead of doing

pluvieux, -euse [plyvjø, -øz] adj rainy, wet

PME sigle fpl (= petites et moyennes entreprises) small businesses

PMU sigle m (= pari mutuel urbain) (dans un café) betting agency

PNB sigle m (= produit national brut) GNP

pneu [pnø] nm tyre (BRIT), tire (US)

pneumonie [pnømɔni] nf pneumonia

poche [pɔʃ] nf pocket; (sous les yeux) bag, pouch; **argent de ~** pocket money

pochette [pɔʃɛt] nf (d'aiguilles etc) case; (de femme) clutch bag; (mouchoir) breast pocket handkerchief; **~ de disque** record sleeve

podcast [pɔdkast] nm podcast; **podcaster** /1/ vi to podcast

poêle [pwal] nm stove ▷ nf: **~ (à frire)** frying pan

poème [pɔɛm] nm poem

poésie [pɔezi] nf (poème) poem; (art): **la ~** poetry

poète [pɔɛt] nm poet

poids [pwa] nm weight; (Sport) shot; **vendre au ~** to sell by weight; **perdre/ prendre du ~** to lose/put on weight; **~ lourd** (camion) (big) lorry (BRIT), truck (US)

poignant, e [pwaɲɑ̃, -ɑ̃t] adj poignant

poignard [pwaɲaʀ] nm dagger; **poignarder** /1/ vt to stab, knife

poigne [pwaɲ] nf grip; **avoir de la ~** (fig) to rule with a firm hand

poignée [pwaɲe] nf (de sel etc, fig) handful; (de couvercle, porte) handle; **~ de main** handshake

poignet [pwaɲɛ] nm (Anat) wrist; (de chemise) cuff

poil [pwal] nm (Anat) hair; (de pinceau, brosse) bristle; (de tapis, tissu) strand; (pelage) coat; **à ~** (fam) starkers; **au ~** (fam) hunky-dory; **poilu, e** adj hairy

poinçonner [pwɛ̃sɔne] /1/ vt (bijou etc) to hallmark; (billet, ticket) to punch

poing [pwɛ̃] nm fist; **coup de ~** punch

point [pwɛ̃] nm dot; (de ponctuation) full stop, period (US); (Couture, Tricot) stitch ▷ adv = **pas¹**; **faire le ~** (fig) to take stock (of the situation); **sur le ~ de faire** (just) about to do; **à tel ~ que** so much so that; **mettre au ~** (mécanisme, procédé) to develop; (affaire) to settle; **à ~** (Culin: viande) medium; **à ~ (nommé)** just at the right time; **deux ~s** colon; **~ (de côté)** stitch (pain); **~ d'exclamation** exclamation mark; **~ faible** weak spot; **~ final** full stop, period (US); **~ d'interrogation** question mark; **~ mort**; **au ~ mort** (Auto) in neutral; **~ de repère** landmark; (dans le temps) point of reference; **~ de vente** retail outlet; **~**

de vue viewpoint; (fig: opinion) point of view; **~s cardinaux** cardinal points; **~s de suspension** suspension points

pointe [pwɛ̃t] nf point; (clou) tack; **une ~ d'ail/d'accent** a touch ou hint of garlic/of an accent; **être à la ~ de** (fig) to be in the forefront of; **sur la ~ des pieds** on tiptoe; **en ~** pointed, tapered; **de ~** (technique etc) leading; **heures/jours de ~** peak hours/days

pointer [pwɛ̃te] /1/ vt (diriger: canon, longue-vue, doigt): **~ vers qch, ~ sur qch** to point at sth ▷ vi (employé) to clock in ou on

pointeur, -euse [pwɛ̃tœʀ, -øz] nf timeclock ▷ nm (Inform) cursor

pointillé [pwɛ̃tije] nm (trait) dotted line

pointilleux, -euse [pwɛ̃tijø, -øz] adj particular, pernickety

pointu, e [pwɛ̃ty] adj pointed; (voix) shrill; (analyse) precise

pointure [pwɛ̃tyʀ] nf size

point-virgule [pwɛ̃viʀgyl] nm semi-colon

poire [pwaʀ] nf pear; (fam, péj) mug

poireau, x [pwaʀo] nm leek

poirier [pwaʀje] nm pear tree

pois [pwa] nm (Bot) pea; (sur une étoffe) dot, spot; **à ~** (cravate etc) spotted, polka-dot cpd; **~ chiche** chickpea

poison [pwazɔ̃] nm poison

poisseux, -euse [pwasø, -øz] adj sticky

poisson [pwasɔ̃] nm fish gén inv; **les P~s** (Astrologie: signe) Pisces; **~ d'avril** April fool; (blague) April fools' day trick; see note **"poisson d'avril"**; **~ rouge** goldfish; **poissonnerie** nf fishmonger's; **poissonnier, -ière** nm/f fishmonger (BRIT), fish merchant (US)

⬤ POISSON D'AVRIL

⬤

⬤ The traditional April Fools' Day prank in
⬤ France involves attaching a cut-out paper
⬤ fish, known as a 'poisson d'avril', to the
⬤ back of one's victim, without being caught.

---

poitrine [pwatʀin] nf chest; (seins) bust, bosom; (Culin) breast

poivre [pwavʀ] nm pepper

poivron [pwavʀɔ̃] nm pepper, capsicum

polaire [pɔlɛʀ] adj polar

pôle [pol] nm (Géo, Élec) pole; **le ~ Nord/Sud** the North/South Pole

poli, e [pɔli] adj polite; (lisse) smooth

police [pɔlis] nf police; **~ judiciaire (PJ)** ≈ Criminal Investigation Department (CID) (BRIT), ≈ Federal Bureau of Investigation (FBI) (US); **~ secours** ≈ emergency services pl (BRIT), ≈ paramedics pl (US); **policier, -ière** adj police cpd ▷ nm police officer; (aussi: **roman policier**) detective novel

polir [pɔliʀ] /2/ vt to polish

politesse [pɔlitɛs] nf politeness

politicien, ne [pɔlitisjɛ̃, -ɛn] nm/f (péj) politician

politique [pɔlitik] adj political ▷ nf politics sg; (principes, tactique) policies pl

politiquement [pɔlitikmɑ̃] adv politically; **~ correct** politically correct

pollen [pɔlɛn] nm pollen

polluant, e [pɔlɥɑ̃, -ɑ̃t] adj polluting ▷ nm pollutant; **non~** non-polluting

polluer [pɔlɥe] /1/ vt to pollute; **pollution** nf pollution

polo [pɔlo] nm (tricot) polo shirt

Pologne [pɔlɔɲ] nf: **la ~** Poland; **polonais, e** adj Polish ▷ nm (Ling) Polish ▷ nm/f: **Polonais, e** Pole

poltron, ne [pɔltrɔ̃, ɔn] adj cowardly

polycopier [pɔlikɔpje] /7/ vt to duplicate

Polynésie [pɔlinezi] nf: **la ~** Polynesia; **la ~ française** French Polynesia

polyvalent, e [pɔlivalɑ̃, -ɑ̃t] adj (rôle) varied; (salle) multi-purpose

pommade [pɔmad] nf ointment, cream

pomme [pɔm] nf apple; **tomber dans les ~s** (fam) to pass out; **~ d'Adam** Adam's apple; **~ de pin** fir cone; **~ de terre** potato; **~s vapeur** boiled potatoes

pommette [pɔmɛt] nf cheekbone

pommier [pɔmje] nm apple tree

pompe [pɔ̃p] nf pump; (faste) pomp (and ceremony); **~ à eau/essence** water/petrol pump; **~s funèbres** undertaker's sg, funeral parlour sg; **pomper** /1/ vt to pump; (aspirer) to pump up; (absorber) to soak up

pompeux, -euse [pɔ̃pø, -øz] adj pompous

pompier [pɔ̃pje] nm firefighter

pompiste [pɔ̃pist] nm/f petrol (BRIT) ou gas (US) pump attendant

poncer [pɔ̃se] /3/ vt to sand (down)

ponctuation [pɔ̃ktɥasjɔ̃] nf punctuation

ponctuel, le [pɔ̃ktɥɛl] adj punctual

pondéré, e [pɔ̃dere] adj level-headed, composed

pondre [pɔ̃dr] /41/ vt to lay

poney [pɔnɛ] nm pony

pont [pɔ̃] nm bridge; (Navig) deck; **faire le ~** to take the extra day off; see note **"faire le pont"**; **~ suspendu** suspension bridge; **pont-levis** nm drawbridge

● **FAIRE LE PONT**

● The expression 'faire le pont' refers to the practice of taking a Monday or Friday off to make a long weekend if a public holiday falls on a Tuesday or Thursday. The French commonly take an extra day off work to give four consecutive days' holiday at 'l'Ascension', 'le 14 juillet' and 'le 15 août'.

pop [pɔp] adj inv pop

populaire [pɔpylɛr] adj popular; (manifestation) mass cpd; (milieux, clientèle)

working-class; (mot etc) used by the lower classes (of society)

popularité [pɔpylarite] nf popularity

population [pɔpylasjɔ̃] nf population

populeux, -euse [pɔpylø, -øz] adj densely populated

porc [pɔr] nm pig; (Culin) pork

porcelaine [pɔrsəlɛn] nf porcelain, china; (objet) piece of china(ware)

porc-épic [pɔrkepik] nm porcupine

porche [pɔrʃ] nm porch

porcherie [pɔrʃəri] nf pigsty

pore [pɔr] nm pore

porno [pɔrno] adj porno ▷ nm porn

port [pɔr] nm harbour, port; (ville) port; (de l'uniforme etc) wearing; (pour lettre) postage; (pour colis, aussi: posture) carriage; **~ d'arme** (Jur) carrying of a firearm; **~ payé** postage paid

portable [pɔrtabl] adj (portatif) portable; (téléphone) mobile ▷ nm (Inform) laptop (computer); (téléphone) mobile (phone)

portail [pɔrtaj] nm gate

portant, e [pɔrtɑ̃, -ɑ̃t] adj: **bien/mal ~** in good/poor health

portatif, -ive [pɔrtatif, -iv] adj portable

porte [pɔrt] nf door; (de ville, forteresse) gate; **mettre à la ~** to throw out; **~ d'entrée** front door

porté, e [pɔrte] adj: **être ~ à faire qch** to be apt ou to do sth; **être ~ sur qch** to be partial to sth

porte: porte-avions nm inv aircraft carrier; **porte-bagages** nm inv luggage rack (ou basket etc); **porte-bonheur** nm inv lucky charm; **porte-clefs** nm inv key ring; **porte-documents** nm inv attaché ou document case

portée [pɔrte] nf (d'une arme) range; (fig: importance) impact, import; (: capacités) scope, capability; (de chatte etc) litter; (Mus) stave, staff; **à/hors de ~ (de)** within/out of reach (of); **à ~ de (la) main** within (arm's) reach; **à la ~ de qn** (fig) at sb's level, within sb's capabilities

porte: portefeuille nm wallet; **portemanteau, x** nm coat rack; (cintre) coat hanger; **porte-monnaie** nm inv purse; **porte-parole** nm inv spokesperson

porter [pɔrte] /1/ vt to carry; (sur soi: vêtement, barbe, bague) to wear; (fig: responsabilité etc) to bear, carry; (inscription, marque, titre, patronyme, fruits, fleurs) to bear; (coup) to deal; (attention) to turn; (apporter): **~ qch quelque part/à qn** to take sth somewhere/to sb ▷ vi to carry; (coup, argument) to hit home; **se porter** vi (se sentir): **se ~ bien/mal** to be well/unwell; **~ sur** (conférence etc) to concern; **se faire ~ malade** to report sick

porteur, -euse [pɔrtœr, -øz] nm/f ▷ nm (de bagages) porter; (de chèque) bearer

porte-voix [pɔʀtəvwa] *nm inv* megaphone

portier [pɔʀtje] *nm* doorman

portière [pɔʀtjɛʀ] *nf* door

portion [pɔʀsjɔ̃] *nf* (*part*) portion, share; (*partie*) portion, section

porto [pɔʀto] *nm* port (wine)

portrait [pɔʀtʀɛ] *nm* portrait; (*photographie*) photograph; **portrait-robot** *nm* Identikit® *ou* Photo-fit® (BRIT) picture

portuaire [pɔʀtɥɛʀ] *adj* port *cpd*, harbour *cpd*

portugais, e [pɔʀtygɛ, -ɛz] *adj* Portuguese ▷ *nm* (*Ling*) Portuguese ▷ *nm/f*: **P~, e** Portuguese

Portugal [pɔʀtygal] *nm*: **le ~** Portugal

pose [poz] *nf* (*de moquette*) laying; (*attitude, d'un modèle*) pose; (*Photo*) exposure

posé, e [poze] *adj* calm

poser [poze] /1/ *vt* (*place*) to put down, to put; (*déposer, installer: moquette, carrelage*) to lay; (*rideaux, papier peint*) to hang; (*question*) to ask; (*principe, conditions*) to lay *ou* set down; (*problème*) to formulate; (*difficulté*) to pose ▷ *vi* (*modèle*) to pose; **se poser** *vi* (*oiseau, avion*) to land; (*question*) to arise; **~ qch (sur)** to put sth down (on); **~ qn à** to drop sb at; **~ qch sur qch/quelque part** to put sth on sth/somewhere; **~ sa candidature à un poste** to apply for a post

positif, -ive [pozitif, -iv] *adj* positive

position [pozisjɔ̃] *nf* position; **prendre ~** (*fig*) to take a stand

posologie [pozɔlɔʒi] *nf* dosage

posséder [posede] /6/ *vt* to own, possess; (*qualité, talent*) to have, possess; (*sexuellement*) to possess; **possession** *nf* ownership *no pl*; possession; **être en possession de qch** to be in possession of sth; **prendre possession de qch** to take possession of sth

possibilité [pɔsibilite] *nf* possibility; **possibilités** *nfpl* potential *sg*

possible [pɔsibl] *adj* possible; (*projet, entreprise*) feasible ▷ *nm*: **faire son ~** to do all one can, do one's utmost; **le plus/moins de livres ~** as many/few books as possible; **le plus vite ~** as quickly as possible; **dès que ~** as soon as possible

postal, e, -aux [pɔstal, -o] *adj* postal

poste¹ [pɔst] *nf* (*service*) post, postal service; (*administration, bureau*) post office; **mettre à la ~** to post; **~ restante** (PR) poste restante (BRIT), general delivery (US)

poste² [pɔst] *nm* (*fonction, Mil*) post; (*Tél*) extension; (*de radio etc*) set; **~ d'essence** filling station; **~ d'incendie** fire point; **~ de pilotage** cockpit, flight deck; **~ (de police)** police station; **~ de secours** first-aid post

poster /1/ *vt* [pɔste] to post ▷ *nm* [pɔstɛʀ] poster

postérieur, e [pɔsteʀjœʀ] *adj* (*date*) later; (*partie*) back ▷ *nm* (*fam*) behind

postuler [pɔstyle] /1/ *vi*: **~ à** *ou* **pour un emploi** to apply for a job

pot [po] *nm* (*en verre*) jar; (*en terre*) pot; (*en plastique, carton*) carton; (*en métal*) tin; (*fam: chance*) luck; **avoir du ~** to be lucky; **boire** *ou* **prendre un ~** (*fam*) to have a drink; **petit ~ (pour bébé)** (jar of) baby food; **~ catalytique** catalytic converter; **~ d'échappement** exhaust pipe

potable [pɔtabl] *adj*: **eau (non) ~** (not) drinking water

potage [pɔtaʒ] *nm* soup; **potager, -ère** *adj*: **(jardin) potager** kitchen *ou* vegetable garden

pot-au-feu [pɔtofø] *nm inv* (beef) stew

pot-de-vin [pɔdvɛ̃] *nm* bribe

pote [pɔt] *nm* (*fam*) pal

poteau, x [pɔto] *nm* post; **~ indicateur** signpost

potelé, e [pɔtle] *adj* plump, chubby

potentiel, le [pɔtɑ̃sjɛl] *adj, nm* potential

poterie [pɔtʀi] *nf* pottery; (*objet*) piece of pottery

potier, -ière [pɔtje, -jɛʀ] *nm/f* potter

potiron [pɔtiʀɔ̃] *nm* pumpkin

pou, x [pu] *nm* louse

poubelle [pubɛl] *nf* (dust)bin

pouce [pus] *nm* thumb

poudre [pudʀ] *nf* powder; (*fard*) (face) powder; (*explosif*) gunpowder; **en ~**: **café en ~** instant coffee; **lait en ~** dried *ou* powdered milk

poudreux, -euse [pudʀø, -øz] *adj* dusty; (*neige*) powder *cpd*

poudrier [pudʀije] *nm* (powder) compact

pouffer [pufe] /1/ *vi*: **~ (de rire)** to burst out laughing

poulailler [pulaje] *nm* henhouse

poulain [pulɛ̃] *nm* foal; (*fig*) protégé

poule [pul] *nf* hen; (*Culin*) (boiling) fowl; **~ mouillée** coward

poulet [pulɛ] *nm* chicken; (*fam*) cop

poulie [puli] *nf* pulley

pouls [pu] *nm* pulse; **prendre le ~ de qn** to take sb's pulse

poumon [pumɔ̃] *nm* lung

poupée [pupe] *nf* doll

pour [puʀ] *prép* for ▷ *nm*: **le ~ et le contre** the pros and cons; **~ faire** (so as) to do, in order to do; **~ avoir fait** for having done; **~ que** so that, in order that; **fermé ~ (cause de) travaux** closed for refurbishment *ou* alterations; **c'est ~ ça que** ... that's why ...; **~ quoi faire?** what for?; **~ 20 euros d'essence** 20 euros' worth of petrol; **~ cent** per cent; **~ ce qui est de** as for

pourboire [puʀbwaʀ] *nm* tip

pourcentage [puʀsɑ̃taʒ] *nm* percentage

pourchasser [puʀʃase] /1/ *vt* to pursue

pourparlers [puʀpaʀle] *nmpl* talks, negotiations

pourpre [puʀpʀ] *adj* crimson
pourquoi [puʀkwa] *adv, conj* why ▷ *nm inv:*
  le ~ (de) the reason (for)
pourrai *etc* [puʀe] *vb voir* **pouvoir**
pourri, e [puʀi] *adj* rotten
pourrir [puʀiʀ] /2/ *vi* to rot; (*fruit*) to
  go rotten *ou* bad ▷ *vt* to rot; (*fig*) to spoil
  thoroughly; **pourriture** *nf* rot
poursuite [puʀsɥit] *nf* pursuit, chase;
  poursuites *nfpl* (*Jur*) legal proceedings
poursuivre [puʀsɥivʀ] /40/ *vt* to pursue,
  chase (after); (*obséder*) to haunt; (*Jur*) to
  bring proceedings against, prosecute (: *au
  civil*) to sue; (*but*) to strive towards; (*voyage,
  études*) to carry on with, continue; **se
  poursuivre** *vi* to go on, continue
pourtant [puʀtã] *adv* yet; **c'est ~ facile**
  (and) yet it's easy
pourtour [puʀtuʀ] *nm* perimeter
pourvoir [puʀvwaʀ] /25/ *vt:* **~ qch/qn de**
  to equip sth/sb with ▷ *vi:* **~ à** to provide for;
  pourvu, e *adj:* **pourvu de** equipped with;
  pourvu que (*si*) provided that, so long as;
  (*espérons que*) let's hope (that)
pousse [pus] *nf* growth; (*bourgeon*) shoot
poussée [puse] *nf* thrust; (*d'acné*) eruption;
  (*fig: prix*) upsurge
pousser [puse] /1/ *vt* to push; (*émettre:
  cri etc*) to give; (*stimuler: élève*) to urge on;
  (*poursuivre: études, discussion*) to carry on
  ▷ *vi* to push; (*croître*) to grow; **se pousser**
  vi to move over; **~ qn à faire qch** (*inciter*) to
  urge *ou* press sb to do sth; **faire ~** (*plante*)
  to grow
poussette [puset] *nf* pushchair (BRIT),
  stroller (US)
poussière [pusjɛʀ] *nf* dust; **poussiéreux,
  -euse** *adj* dusty
poussin [pusɛ̃] *nm* chick
poutre [putʀ] *nf* beam

🔘 **MOT-CLÉ**

pouvoir [puvwaʀ] /33/ *nm* power;
  (*dirigeants*): **le pouvoir** those in power; **les
  pouvoirs publics** the authorities; **pouvoir
  d'achat** purchasing power
  ▷ *vb aux* **1** (*être en état de*) can, be able to; **je
  ne peux pas le réparer** I can't *ou* I am not
  able to repair it; **déçu de ne pas pouvoir le
  faire** disappointed not to be able to do it
  2 (*avoir la permission*) can, may, be allowed
  to; **vous pouvez aller au cinéma** you can
  ou may go to the pictures
  3 (*probabilité, hypothèse*) may, might, could;
  il a pu avoir un accident he may *ou* might
  ou could have had an accident; **il aurait pu
  le dire!** he might *ou* could have said (so)!
  ▷ *vb impers* may, might, could; **il peut
  arriver que** it may *ou* might *ou* could
  happen that; **il pourrait pleuvoir** it might
  rain

  ▷ *vt* can, be able to; **j'ai fait tout ce que
  j'ai pu** I did all I could; **je n'en peux plus**
  (*épuisé*) I'm exhausted; (*à bout*) I can't take
  any more
  se pouvoir *vi:* **il se peut que** it may *ou*
  might be that; **cela se pourrait** that's quite
  possible

prairie [pʀeʀi] *nf* meadow
praline [pʀalin] *nf* sugared almond
praticable [pʀatikabl] *adj* passable;
  practicable
pratiquant, e [pʀatikã, -ãt] *nm/f* (*regular*)
  churchgoer
pratique [pʀatik] *nf* practice ▷ *adj*
  practical; **pratiquement** *adv* (*pour ainsi
  dire*) practically, virtually; **pratiquer** /1/ *vt*
  to practise; (*l'équitation, la pêche*) to go in
  for; (*le golf, football*) to play; (*intervention,
  opération*) to carry out
pré [pʀe] *nm* meadow
préalable [pʀealabl] *adj* preliminary; **au ~**
  beforehand
préambule [pʀeãbyl] *nm* preamble; (*fig*)
  prelude; **sans ~** straight away
préau, x [pʀeo] *nm* (*d'une cour d'école*)
  covered playground
préavis [pʀeavi] *nm* notice
précaution [pʀekosjɔ̃] *nf* precaution;
  avec ~ cautiously; **par ~** as a precaution
précédemment [pʀesedamã] *adv* before,
  previously
précédent, e [pʀesedã, -ãt] *adj* previous
  ▷ *nm* precedent; **sans ~** unprecedented;
  le jour ~ the day before, the previous day
précéder [pʀesede] /6/ *vt* to precede
prêcher [pʀeʃe] /1/ *vt* to preach
précieux, -euse [pʀesjø, -øz] *adj* precious;
  (*collaborateur, conseils*) invaluable
précipice [pʀesipis] *nm* drop, chasm
précipitamment [pʀesipitamã] *adv*
  hurriedly, hastily
précipitation [pʀesipitasjɔ̃] *nf* (*hâte*)
  haste
précipité, e [pʀesipite] *adj* hurried; hasty
précipiter [pʀesipite] /1/ *vt* (*hâter: départ*)
  to hasten; **se précipiter** *vi* to speed up; **~
  qn/qch du haut de** (*faire tomber*) to throw
  ou hurl sb/sth off *ou* from; **se ~ sur/vers** to
  rush at/towards
précis, e [pʀesi, -iz] *adj* precise; (*tir,
  mesures*) accurate, precise; **à 4 heures ~es** at
  4 o'clock sharp; **précisément** *adv* precisely;
  préciser /1/ *vt* (*expliquer*) to be more specific
  about, clarify; (*spécifier*) to state, specify; **se
  préciser** *vi* to become clear(er); **précision**
  nf precision; (*détail*) point *ou* detail (*made
  clear or to be clarified*)
précoce [pʀekɔs] *adj* early; (*enfant*)
  precocious
préconçu, e [pʀekɔ̃sy] *adj* preconceived
préconiser [pʀekɔnize] /1/ *vt* to advocate

prédécesseur [pʀedesesœʀ] nm
predecessor
prédilection [pʀedilɛksjɔ̃] nf: **avoir une ~
pour** to be partial to
prédire [pʀediʀ] /37/ vt to predict
prédominer [pʀedɔmine] /1/ vi to
predominate
préface [pʀefas] nf preface
préfecture [pʀefɛktyʀ] nf prefecture; **~ de
police** police headquarters
préférable [pʀefeʀabl] adj preferable
préféré, e [pʀefeʀe] adj, nm/f favourite
préférence [pʀefeʀɑ̃s] nf preference; **de ~**
preferably
préférer [pʀefeʀe] /6/ vt: **~ qn/qch (à)** to
prefer sb/sth (to), like sb/sth better (than);
~ faire to prefer to do; **je préférerais du thé**
I would rather have tea, I'd prefer tea
préfet [pʀefɛ] nm prefect
préhistorique [pʀeistɔʀik] adj
prehistoric
préjudice [pʀeʒydis] nm (matériel) loss;
(moral) harm no pl; **porter ~ à** to harm, be
detrimental to; **au ~ de** at the expense of
préjugé [pʀeʒyʒe] nm prejudice; **avoir un ~
contre** to be prejudiced against
prélasser [pʀelase] /1/: **se prélasser** vi to
lounge
prélèvement [pʀelɛvmɑ̃] nm (montant)
deduction; **faire un ~ de sang** to take a
blood sample
prélever [pʀelve] /5/ vt (échantillon) to
take; **~ (sur)** (argent) to deduct (from); (sur
son compte) to withdraw (from)
prématuré, e [pʀematyʀe] adj premature
▷ nm premature baby
premier, -ière [pʀəmje, -jɛʀ] adj first;
(rang) front; (fig: fondamental) basic ▷ nf
(Rail, Aviat etc) first class; (Scol) year 12
(BRIT), eleventh grade (US); **de ~ ordre**
first-rate; **le ~ venu** the first person to
come along; **P~ Ministre** Prime Minister;
premièrement adv firstly
prémonition [pʀemɔnisjɔ̃] nf
premonition
prenant, e [pʀənɑ̃, -ɑ̃t] adj absorbing,
engrossing
prénatal, e [pʀenatal] adj (Méd) antenatal
prendre [pʀɑ̃dʀ] /58/ vt to take; (repas)
to have; (aller chercher) to get; (malfaiteur,
poisson) to catch; (passager) to pick up;
(personnel) to take on; (traiter: enfant,
problème) to handle; (voix, ton) to put on;
(ôter): **~ qch à** to take sth from; (coincer):
se ~ les doigts dans to get one's fingers
caught in ▷ vi (liquide, ciment) to set; (greffe,
vaccin) to take; (feu: foyer) to go; (se diriger):
~ à gauche to turn (to the) left; **~ froid** to
catch cold; **se ~ pour** to think one is; **s'en ~
à** to attack; **se ~ d'amitié/d'affection pour**
to befriend/become fond of; **s'y ~** (procéder)
to set about it

preneur [pʀənœʀ] nm: **être ~** to be willing
to buy; **trouver ~** to find a buyer
prénom [pʀenɔ̃] nm first name
préoccupation [pʀeɔkypasjɔ̃] nf (souci)
concern; (idée fixe) preoccupation
préoccuper [pʀeɔkype] /1/ vt (tourmenter,
tracasser) to concern; (absorber, obséder) to
preoccupy; **se ~ de qch** to be concerned
about sth
préparatifs [pʀepaʀatif] nmpl
preparations
préparation [pʀepaʀasjɔ̃] nf preparation
préparer [pʀepaʀe] /1/ vt to prepare; (café,
repas) to make; (examen) to prepare for;
(voyage, entreprise) to plan; **se préparer** vi
(orage, tragédie) to brew, be in the air; **se ~
(à qch/à faire)** to prepare (o.s.) ou get ready
(for sth/to do); **~ qch à qn** (surprise etc) to
have sth in store for sb
prépondérant, e [pʀepɔ̃deʀɑ̃, -ɑ̃t] adj
major, dominating
préposé, e [pʀepoze] nm/f employee;
(facteur) postman/woman
préposition [pʀepozisjɔ̃] nf preposition
près [pʀɛ] adv near, close; **~ de** near (to),
close to; (environ) nearly, almost; **de ~**
closely; **à cinq kg ~** to within about five kg;
il n'est pas à 10 minutes ~ he can spare 10
minutes
présage [pʀezaʒ] nm omen
presbyte [pʀɛsbit] adj long-sighted
presbytère [pʀɛsbiteʀ] nm presbytery
prescription [pʀɛskʀipsjɔ̃] nf prescription
prescrire [pʀɛskʀiʀ] /39/ vt to prescribe
présence [pʀezɑ̃s] nf presence; (au bureau
etc) attendance
présent, e [pʀezɑ̃, -ɑ̃t] adj, nm present; **à ~
que** now that
présentation [pʀezɑ̃tasjɔ̃] nf
presentation; (de nouveau venu)
introduction; (allure) appearance; **faire les
~s** to do the introductions
présenter [pʀezɑ̃te] /1/ vt to present;
(invité, candidat) to introduce; (félicitations,
condoléances) to offer; **~ qn à** to introduce
sb to ▷ vi: **~ mal/bien** to have an
unattractive/a pleasing appearance;
se présenter vi (à une élection) to stand;
(occasion) to arise; **se ~ à un examen** to sit
an exam; **je vous présente Nadine** this is
Nadine
préservatif [pʀezɛʀvatif] nm condom,
sheath
préserver [pʀezɛʀve] /1/ vt: **~ de** (protéger)
to protect from
président [pʀezidɑ̃] nm (Pol) president;
(d'une assemblée, Comm) chairman;
~ directeur général chairman and
managing director
présidentiel, le [pʀezidɑ̃sjɛl] adj
presidential; **présidentielles** nfpl
presidential election(s)

présider [prezide] /1/ vt to preside over; (dîner) to be the guest of honour (BRIT) ou honor (US) at

presque [prɛsk] adv almost, nearly; ~ rien hardly anything; ~ pas hardly (at all); ~ pas de hardly any; personne, ou ~ next to nobody, hardly anyone

presqu'île [prɛskil] nf peninsula

pressant, e [prɛsɑ̃, -ɑ̃t] adj urgent

presse [prɛs] nf press; (affluence): heures de ~ busy times

pressé, e [prese] adj in a hurry; (besogne) urgent; orange ~e freshly squeezed orange juice

pressentiment [prɛsɑ̃timɑ̃] nm foreboding, premonition

pressentir [prɛsɑ̃tir] /16/ vt to sense

presse-papiers [prɛspapje] nm inv paperweight

presser [prese] /1/ vt (fruit, éponge) to squeeze; (interrupteur, bouton) to press; (allure, affaire) to speed up; (inciter): ~ qn de faire to urge ou press sb to do ▷ vi to be urgent; se presser vi (se hâter) to hurry (up); rien ne presse there's no hurry; se ~ contre qn to squeeze up against sb; le temps presse there's not much time

pressing [prɛsiŋ] nm (magasin) dry cleaner's

pression [prɛsjɔ̃] nf pressure; (bouton) press stud (BRIT), snap fastener (US); (fam: bière) draught beer; faire ~ sur to put pressure on; sous ~ pressurized, under pressure; (fig) keyed up; ~ artérielle blood pressure

prestataire [prɛstatɛr] nm/f person receiving benefits; ~ de services provider of services

prestation [prɛstasjɔ̃] nf (allocation) benefit; (d'une entreprise) service provided; (d'un joueur, artiste) performance

prestidigitateur, -trice [prɛstidiʒitatœr, -tris] nm/f conjurer

prestige [prɛstiʒ] nm prestige; **prestigieux, -euse** adj prestigious

présumer [prezyme] /1/ vt: ~ que to presume ou assume that

prêt, e [prɛ, prɛt] adj ready ▷ nm (somme prêtée) loan; **prêt-à-porter** nm ready-to-wear ou off-the-peg (BRIT) clothes pl

prétendre [pretɑ̃dr] /41/ vt (affirmer): ~ que to claim that; ~ faire qch (avoir l'intention de) to mean ou intend to do sth; **prétendu, e** adj (supposé) so-called

■ Attention à ne pas traduire prétendre par to pretend.

prétentieux, -euse [pretɑ̃sjø, -øz] adj pretentious

prétention [pretɑ̃sjɔ̃] nf pretentiousness; (exigence, ambition) claim

prêter [prete] /1/ vt: ~ qch à qn (livres, argent) to lend sth to sb; (caractère, propos) to attribute sth to sb

prétexte [pretɛkst] nm pretext, excuse; sous aucun ~ on no account; **prétexter** /1/ vt to give as a pretext ou an excuse

prêtre [prɛtr] nm priest

preuve [prœv] nf proof; (indice) proof, evidence no pl; faire ~ de to show; faire ses ~s to prove o.s. (ou itself)

prévaloir [prevalwar] /29/ vi to prevail

prévenant, e [prevnɑ̃, -ɑ̃t] adj thoughtful, kind

prévenir [prevnir] /22/ vt (éviter: catastrophe etc) to avoid, prevent; (anticiper: désirs, besoins) to anticipate; ~ qn (de) (avertir) to warn sb (about); (informer) to tell ou inform sb (about)

préventif, -ive [prevɑ̃tif, -iv] adj preventive

prévention [prevɑ̃sjɔ̃] nf prevention; ~ routière road safety

prévenu, e [prevny] nm/f (Jur) defendant, accused

prévision [previzjɔ̃] nf: ~s predictions; (météorologiques, économiques) forecast sg; en ~ de in anticipation of; ~s météorologiques ou du temps weather forecast sg

prévoir [prevwar] /24/ vt (deviner) to foresee; (s'attendre à) to expect, reckon on; (organiser: voyage etc) to plan; (préparer, réserver) to allow; comme prévu as planned; **prévoyant, e** adj gifted with (ou showing) foresight; **prévu, e** pp de prévoir

prier [prije] /7/ vi to pray ▷ vt (Dieu) to pray to; (implorer) to beg; (demander): ~ qn de faire to ask sb to do; se faire ~ to need coaxing ou persuading; je vous en prie (allez-y) please do; (de rien) don't mention it; **prière** nf prayer; "prière de faire ..." "please do ..."

primaire [primɛr] adj primary ▷ nm (Scol) primary education

prime [prim] nf (bonification) bonus; (subside) allowance; (Comm: cadeau) free gift; (Assurances, Bourse) premium ▷ adj: de ~ abord at first glance; **primer** /1/ vt (récompenser) to award a prize to ▷ vi to dominate

primevère [primvɛr] nf primrose

primitif, -ive [primitif, -iv] adj primitive; (originel) original

prince [prɛ̃s] nm prince; **princesse** nf princess

principal, e, -aux [prɛ̃sipal, -o] adj principal, main ▷ nm (Scol) head (teacher) (BRIT), principal (US); (essentiel) main thing

principe [prɛ̃sip] nm principle; par ~ on principle; en ~ (habituellement) as a rule; (théoriquement) in principle

printemps [prɛ̃tɑ̃] nm spring

priorité [prijɔrite] nf priority; (Auto) ~ à droite right of way to vehicles coming from the right

pris, e [pʀi, pʀiz] *pp de* **prendre** ▷ *adj* (*place*) taken; (*journée, mains*) full; (*personne*) busy; **avoir le nez/la gorge ~(e)** to have a stuffy nose/a bad throat; **être ~ de peur/ de fatigue/de panique** to be stricken with fear/overcome with fatigue/panic-stricken

prise [pʀiz] *nf* (*d'une ville*) capture; (*Pêche, Chasse*) catch; (*point d'appui ou pour empoigner*) hold; (*Élec: fiche*) plug; (: *femelle*) socket; **être aux ~s avec** to be grappling with; **~ de courant** power point; **~ multiple** adaptor; **~ de sang** blood test

priser [pʀize] /1/ *vt* (*estimer*) to prize, value

prison [pʀizɔ̃] *nf* prison; **aller/être en ~** to go to/be in prison *ou* jail; **prisonnier, -ière** *nm/f* prisoner ▷ *adj* captive

privé, e [pʀive] *adj* private; (*en punition*): **tu es ~ de télé!** no TV for you! ▷ *nm* (*Comm*) private sector; **en ~** in private

priver [pʀive] /1/ *vt*: **~ qn de** to deprive sb of; **se ~ de** to go *ou* do without

privilège [pʀivilɛʒ] *nm* privilege

prix [pʀi] *nm* price; (*récompense, Scol*) prize; **hors de ~** exorbitantly priced; **à aucun ~** not at any price; **à tout ~** at all costs

probable [pʀɔbabl] *adj* likely, probable; **probablement** *adv* probably

problème [pʀɔblɛm] *nm* problem

procédé [pʀɔsede] *nm* (*méthode*) process; (*comportement*) behaviour *no pl*

procéder [pʀɔsede] /6/ *vi* to proceed; (*moralement*) to behave; **~ à** to carry out

procès [pʀɔsɛ] *nm* trial (*poursuites*) proceedings *pl*; **être en ~ avec** to be involved in a lawsuit with

processus [pʀɔsesys] *nm* process

procès-verbal, -aux [pʀɔsɛvɛʀbal, -o] *nm* (*de réunion*) minutes *pl*; (*aussi*: **PV**): **avoir un ~** to get a parking ticket

prochain, e [pʀɔʃɛ̃, -ɛn] *adj* next; (*proche: départ, arrivée*) impending ▷ *nm* fellow man; **la ~e fois/semaine ~e** next time/week; **prochainement** *adv* soon, shortly

proche [pʀɔʃ] *adj* nearby; (*dans le temps*) imminent; (*parent, ami*) close; **proches** *nmpl* (*parents*) close relatives; **être ~ (de)** to be near, be close (to)

proclamer [pʀɔklame] /1/ *vt* to proclaim

procuration [pʀɔkyʀasjɔ̃] *nf* proxy

procurer [pʀɔkyʀe] /1/ *vt* (*fournir*): **~ qch à qn** (*obtenir*) to get *ou* obtain sth for sb; (*plaisir etc*) to bring *ou* give sb sth; **se procurer** *vt* to get; **procureur** *nm* public prosecutor

prodige [pʀɔdiʒ] *nm* marvel, wonder; (*personne*) prodigy; **prodiguer** /1/ *vt* (*soins, attentions*): **prodiguer qch à qn** to lavish sth on sb

producteur, -trice [pʀɔdyktœʀ, -tʀis] *nm/f* producer

productif, -ive [pʀɔdyktif, -iv] *adj* productive

production [pʀɔdyksjɔ̃] *nf* production; (*rendement*) output

productivité [pʀɔdyktivite] *nf* productivity

produire [pʀɔdɥiʀ] /38/ *vt* to produce; **se produire** *vi* (*acteur*) to perform, appear; (*événement*) to happen, occur

produit, e [pʀɔdɥi, -it] *nm* product; **~ chimique** chemical; **~ d'entretien** cleaning product; **~s agricoles** farm produce *sg*; **~s de beauté** beauty products, cosmetics

prof [pʀɔf] *nm* (*fam*) teacher

proférer [pʀɔfeʀe] /6/ *vt* to utter

professeur, e [pʀɔfesœʀ] *nm/f* teacher; (*titulaire d'une chaire*) professor; **~ (de faculté)** (university) lecturer

profession [pʀɔfesjɔ̃] *nf* (*libérale*) profession; (*gén*) occupation; **"sans ~"** "unemployed"; **professionnel, le** *adj, nm/f* professional

profil [pʀɔfil] *nm* profile; **de ~** in profile

profit [pʀɔfi] *nm* (*avantage*) benefit, advantage; (*Comm, Finance*) profit; **au ~ de** in aid of; **tirer ou retirer ~ de** to profit from; **profitable** *adj* (*utile*) beneficial; (*lucratif*) profitable; **profiter** /1/ *vi*: **profiter de** (*situation, occasion*) to take advantage of; (*vacances, jeunesse etc*) to make the most of

profond, e [pʀɔfɔ̃, -ɔ̃d] *adj* deep; (*méditation, mépris*) profound; **profondément** *adv* deeply; **il dort profondément** he is sound asleep; **profondeur** *nf* depth; **l'eau à quelle profondeur?** how deep is the water?

programme [pʀɔgʀam] *nm* programme; (*Scol*) syllabus, curriculum; (*Inform*) program; **programmer** /1/ *vt* (*organiser, prévoir: émission*) to schedule; (*Inform*) to program; **programmeur, -euse** *nm/f* (computer) programmer

progrès [pʀɔgʀɛ] *nm* progress *no pl*; **faire des/être en ~** to make/be making progress; **progresser** /1/ *vi* to progress; **progressif, -ive** *adj* progressive

proie [pʀwa] *nf* prey *no pl*

projecteur [pʀɔʒɛktœʀ] *nm* projector; (*de théâtre, cirque*) spotlight

projectile [pʀɔʒɛktil] *nm* missile

projection [pʀɔʒɛksjɔ̃] *nf* projection; (*séance*) showing

projet [pʀɔʒɛ] *nm* plan; (*ébauche*) draft; **~ de loi** bill; **projeter** /4/ *vt* (*envisager*) to plan; (*film, photos*) to project; (*ombre, lueur*) to throw, cast; (*jeter*) to throw up (*ou* off *ou* out)

prolétaire [pʀɔletɛʀ] *adj, nm/f* proletarian

prolongement [pʀɔlɔ̃ʒmɑ̃] *nm* extension; **dans le ~ de** running on from

prolonger [pʀɔlɔ̃ʒe] /3/ *vt* (*débat, séjour*) to prolong; (*délai, billet, rue*) to extend; **se prolonger** *vi* to go on

promenade [pʀɔmnad] *nf* walk (*ou* drive *ou* ride); **faire une ~** to go for a walk; **une ~ (à pied)/en voiture/à vélo** a walk/drive/ (bicycle) ride

promener [pʀɔmne] /5/ *vt* (*personne, chien*) to take out for a walk; (*doigts, regard*): **~ qch sur** to run sth over; **se promener** *vi* to go for (*ou* be out for) a walk

promesse [pʀɔmɛs] *nf* promise

promettre [pʀɔmɛtʀ] /56/ *vt* to promise ▷ *vi* to look promising; **~ à qn de faire** to promise sb that one will do

promiscuité [pʀɔmiskɥite] *nf* lack of privacy

promontoire [pʀɔmɔ̃twaʀ] *nm* headland

promoteur, -trice [pʀɔmɔtœʀ, -tʀis] *nm/f*: **~ (immobilier)** property developer (ʙʀɪᴛ), real estate promoter (ᴜꜱ)

promotion [pʀɔmosjɔ̃] *nf* promotion; **en ~** on (special) offer

promouvoir [pʀɔmuvwaʀ] /27/ *vt* to promote

prompt, e [pʀɔ̃, pʀɔ̃t] *adj* swift, rapid

prôner [pʀone] /1/ *vt* (*préconiser*) to advocate

pronom [pʀɔnɔ̃] *nm* pronoun

prononcer [pʀɔnɔ̃se] /3/ *vt* to pronounce; (*dire*) to utter; (*discours*) to deliver; **se prononcer** *vi* to be pronounced; **se ~ (sur)** (*se décider*) to reach a decision (on *ou* about); give a verdict (on); **ça se prononce comment?** how do you pronounce this?; **prononciation** *nf* pronunciation

pronostic [pʀɔnɔstik] *nm* (*Méd*) prognosis; (*fig: aussi:* **~s**) forecast

propagande [pʀɔpagɑ̃d] *nf* propaganda

propager [pʀɔpaʒe] /3/ *vt* to spread; **se propager** *vi* to spread

prophète, prophétesse [pʀɔfɛt, pʀɔfetɛs] *nm/f* prophet(ess)

prophétie [pʀɔfesi] *nf* prophecy

propice [pʀɔpis] *adj* favourable

proportion [pʀɔpɔʀsjɔ̃] *nf* proportion; **toute(s) ~(s) gardée(s)** making due allowance(s)

propos [pʀɔpo] *nm* (*paroles*) talk *no pl*, remark; (*intention, but*) intention, aim; (*sujet*): **à quel ~?** what about?; **à ~ de** about, regarding; **à tout ~** for no reason at all; **à ~** by the way; (*opportunément*) (just) at the right moment

proposer [pʀɔpoze] /1/ *vt* to propose; **~ qch (à qn)/de faire** (*suggérer*) to suggest sth (to sb)/doing, propose sth (to sb)/ (to) do; (*offrir*) to offer (sb) sth/to do; **se ~ (pour faire)** to offer one's services (to do); **proposition** *nf* suggestion; proposal; (*Ling*) clause

propre [pʀɔpʀ] *adj* clean; (*net*) neat, tidy; (*possessif*) own; (*sens*) literal; (*particulier*): **~ à** peculiar to; (*approprié*): **~ à** suitable *ou* appropriate for ▷ *nm*: **recopier au ~ to**

make a fair copy of; **proprement** *adv* (*avec propreté*) cleanly; **à proprement parler** strictly speaking; **le village proprement dit** the village itself; **propreté** *nf* cleanliness

propriétaire [pʀɔpʀijetɛʀ] *nm/f* owner; (*pour le locataire*) landlord(-lady)

propriété [pʀɔpʀijete] *nf* (*droit*) ownership; (*objet, immeuble etc*) property

propulser [pʀɔpylse] /1/ *vt* to propel

prose [pʀoz] *nf* prose (*style*)

prospecter [pʀɔspɛkte] /1/ *vt* to prospect; (*Comm*) to canvass

prospectus [pʀɔspɛktys] *nm* leaflet

prospère [pʀɔspɛʀ] *adj* prosperous; **prospérer** /6/ *vi* to thrive

prosterner [pʀɔstɛʀne] /1/: **se prosterner** *vi* to bow low, prostrate o.s.

prostituée [pʀɔstitɥe] *nf* prostitute

prostitution [pʀɔstitysjɔ̃] *nf* prostitution

protecteur, -trice [pʀɔtɛktœʀ, -tʀis] *adj* protective; (*air, ton: péj*) patronizing ▷ *nm/f* protector

protection [pʀɔtɛksjɔ̃] *nf* protection; (*d'un personnage influent: aide*) patronage

protéger [pʀɔteʒe] /6, 3/ *vt* to protect; **se ~ de/contre** to protect o.s. from

protège-slip [pʀɔtɛʒslip] *nm* panty liner

protéine [pʀɔtein] *nf* protein

protestant, e [pʀɔtɛstɑ̃, -ɑ̃t] *adj, nm/f* Protestant

protestation [pʀɔtɛstasjɔ̃] *nf* (*plainte*) protest

protester [pʀɔtɛste] /1/ *vi*: **~ (contre)** to protest (against *ou* about); **~ de** (*son innocence, sa loyauté*) to protest

prothèse [pʀɔtɛz] *nf*: **~ dentaire** denture

protocole [pʀɔtɔkɔl] *nm* (*fig*) etiquette

proue [pʀu] *nf* bow(s *pl*), prow

prouesse [pʀuɛs] *nf* feat

prouver [pʀuve] /1/ *vt* to prove

provenance [pʀɔvnɑ̃s] *nf* origin; **avion en ~ de** plane (arriving) from

provenir [pʀɔvniʀ] /22/: **~ de** *vt* to come from

proverbe [pʀɔvɛʀb] *nm* proverb

province [pʀɔvɛ̃s] *nf* province

proviseur [pʀɔvizœʀ] *nm* ≈ head (teacher) (ʙʀɪᴛ), ≈ principal (ᴜꜱ)

provision [pʀɔvizjɔ̃] *nf* (*réserve*) stock, supply; **provisions** *nfpl* (*vivres*) provisions, food *no pl*

provisoire [pʀɔvizwaʀ] *adj* temporary; **provisoirement** *adv* temporarily

provocant, e [pʀɔvɔkɑ̃, -ɑ̃t] *adj* provocative

provoquer [pʀɔvɔke] /1/ *vt* (*défier*) to provoke; (*causer*) to cause, bring about; (*inciter*): **~ qn à** to incite sb to

proxénète [pʀɔksenɛt] *nm* procurer

proximité [pʀɔksimite] *nf* nearness, closeness; (*dans le temps*) imminence, closeness; **à ~** near *ou* close by; **à ~ de** near (to), close to

prudemment [pʀydamɑ̃] *adv* carefully; wisely, sensibly

prudence [pʀydɑ̃s] *nf* carefulness; **avec ~** carefully; **par (mesure de) ~** as a precaution

prudent, e [pʀydɑ̃, -ɑ̃t] *adj* (*pas téméraire*) careful (: *en général*) safety-conscious; (*sage, conseillé*) wise, sensible; **c'est plus ~** it's wiser

prune [pʀyn] *nf* plum

pruneau, x [pʀyno] *nm* prune

prunier [pʀynje] *nm* plum tree

PS *sigle m* = **parti socialiste**; (= *post-scriptum*) PS

pseudonyme [psødɔnim] *nm* (*gén*) fictitious name; (*d'écrivain*) pseudonym, pen name

psychanalyse [psikanaliz] *nf* psychoanalysis

psychiatre [psikjatʀ] *nm/f* psychiatrist; **psychiatrique** *adj* psychiatric

psychique [psiʃik] *adj* psychological

psychologie [psikɔlɔʒi] *nf* psychology; **psychologique** *adj* psychological; **psychologue** *nm/f* psychologist

pu [py] *pp de* **pouvoir**

puanteur [pɥɑ̃tœʀ] *nf* stink, stench

pub [pyb] *nf* (*fam*) = **publicité**; **la ~** advertising

public, -ique [pyblik] *adj* public; (*école, instruction*) state *cpd* ▷ *nm* public; (*assistance*) audience; **en ~** in public

publicitaire [pyblisitɛʀ] *adj* advertising *cpd*; (*film, voiture*) publicity *cpd*

publicité [pyblisite] *nf* (*méthode, profession*) advertising; (*annonce*) advertisement; (*révélations*) publicity

publier [pyblije] /7/ *vt* to publish

publipostage [pyblipɔstaʒ] *nm* (*mass*) mailing

publique [pyblik] *adj f voir* **public**

puce [pys] *nf* flea; (*Inform*) chip; **carte à ~** smart card; **(marché aux) ~s** flea market *sg*

pudeur [pydœʀ] *nf* modesty; **pudique** *adj* (*chaste*) modest; (*discret*) discreet

puer [pɥe] /1/ (*péj*) *vi* to stink

puéricultrice [pɥeʀikyltʀis] *nf* ≈ paediatric nurse

puéril, e [pɥeʀil] *adj* childish

puis [pɥi] *vb voir* **pouvoir** ▷ *adv* then

puiser [pɥize] /1/ *vt*: **~ (dans)** to draw (from)

puisque [pɥisk] *conj* since

puissance [pɥisɑ̃s] *nf* power; **en ~** *adj* potential

puissant, e [pɥisɑ̃, -ɑ̃t] *adj* powerful

puits [pɥi] *nm* well

pull(-over) [pyl(ɔvœʀ)] *nm* sweater

pulluler [pylyle] /1/ *vi* to swarm

pulpe [pylp] *nf* pulp

pulvériser [pylveʀize] /1/ *vt* to pulverize; (*liquide*) to spray

punaise [pynɛz] *nf* (*Zool*) bug; (*clou*) drawing pin (*BRIT*), thumb tack (*US*)

punch [pɔ̃ʃ] *nm* (*boisson*) punch

punir [pyniʀ] /2/ *vt* to punish; **punition** *nf* punishment

pupille [pypij] *nf* (*Anat*) pupil ▷ *nm/f* (*enfant*) ward

pupitre [pypitʀ] *nm* (*Scol*) desk

pur, e [pyʀ] *adj* pure; (*vin*) undiluted; (*whisky*) neat; **en ~e perte** to no avail; **c'est de la folie ~e** it's sheer madness

purée [pyʀe] *nf*: **~ (de pommes de terre)** ≈ mashed potatoes *pl*; **~ de marrons** chestnut purée

purement [pyʀmɑ̃] *adv* purely

purgatoire [pyʀgatwaʀ] *nm* purgatory

purger [pyʀʒe] /3/ *vt* (*Méd, Pol*) to purge; (*Jur: peine*) to serve

pur-sang [pyʀsɑ̃] *nm inv* thoroughbred

pus [py] *nm* pus

putain [pytɛ̃] *nf* (!) whore (!)

puzzle [pœzl] *nm* jigsaw (puzzle)

PV *sigle m* = **procès-verbal**

pyjama [piʒama] *nm* pyjamas *pl* (*BRIT*), pajamas *pl* (*US*)

pyramide [piʀamid] *nf* pyramid

Pyrénées [piʀene] *nfpl*: **les ~** the Pyrenees

q

QI *sigle m* (= *quotient intellectuel*) IQ

quadragénaire [kadʀaʒenɛʀ] *nm/f* man/
woman in his/her forties

quadruple [k(w)adʀypl] *nm*: **le ~ de** four
times as much as

quai [ke] *nm* (*de port*) quay; (*de gare*)
platform; **être à ~** (*navire*) to be alongside

qualification [kalifikasjɔ̃] *nf* qualification

qualifier [kalifje] /7/ *vt* to qualify; **~ qch/**
qn de to describe sth/sb as; **se qualifier** *vi*
to qualify

qualité [kalite] *nf* quality

quand [kɑ̃] *conj, adv* when; **~ je serai riche**
when I'm rich; **~ même** all the same,
il exagère! really, he overdoes it!; **~ bien**
même even though

quant [kɑ̃]: **~ à** *prép* (*pour ce qui est de*) as for,
as to; (*au sujet de*) regarding

quantité [kɑ̃tite] *nf* quantity, amount; **une**
ou des ~(s) de (*grand nombre*) a great deal of

quarantaine [kaʀɑ̃tɛn] *nf* (*isolement*)
quarantine; **une ~ (de)** forty or so, about
forty; **avoir la ~** (*âge*) to be around forty

quarante [kaʀɑ̃t] *num* forty

quart [kaʀ] *nm* (*fraction*) quarter;
(*surveillance*) watch; **un ~ de vin** a quarter
litre of wine; **le ~ de** a quarter of; **~ d'heure**
quarter of an hour; **~s de finale** quarter
finals

quartier [kaʀtje] *nm* (*de ville*) district, area;
(*de bœuf, de la lune*) piece; (*de fruit, fromage*)
piece; **cinéma/salle de ~** local cinema/
hall; **avoir ~ libre** to be free; **~ général (QG)**
headquarters (HQ)

quartz [kwaʀts] *nm* quartz

quasi [kazi] *adv* almost, nearly; **quasiment**
adv almost, (very) nearly; **quasiment**
jamais hardly ever

quatorze [katɔʀz] *num* fourteen

quatorzième [katɔʀzjɛm] *num* fourteenth

quatre [katʀ] *num* four; **à ~ pattes** on all
fours; **se mettre en ~ pour qn** to go out of
one's way for sb; **~ à ~** (*monter, descendre*)
four at a time; **quatre-vingt-dix** *num*
ninety; **quatre-vingts** *num* eighty;
quatrième *num* fourth ▷ *nf* (*Scol*) year 9
(*BRIT*), eighth grade (*US*)

quatuor [kwatɥɔʀ] *nm* quartet(te)

 MOT-CLÉ

que [kə] *conj* **1** (*introduisant complétive*) that;
il sait que tu es là he knows (that) you're
here; **je veux que tu acceptes** I want you
to accept; **il a dit que oui** he said he would
(*ou it was etc*)

2 (*reprise d'autres conjonctions*): **quand il**
rentrera et qu'il aura mangé when he gets
back and (when) he has eaten; **si vous y**
allez ou que vous ... if you go there or if
you ...

3 (*en tête de phrase, hypothèse, souhait etc*):
qu'il le veuille ou non whether he likes it or
not; **qu'il fasse ce qu'il voudra!** let him do
as he pleases!

4 (*but*): **tenez-le qu'il ne tombe pas** hold it
so (that) it doesn't fall

5 (*après comparatif*) than, as; *voir aussi* **plus²,**
aussi, autant *etc*

6 (*seulement*): **ne ... que** only; **il ne boit que**
de l'eau he only drinks water

7 (*temps*): **il y a quatre ans qu'il est parti** it
is four years since he left, he left four years
ago

▶ *adv* (*exclamation*): **qu'il ou qu'est-ce qu'il**
est bête/court vite! he's so silly!/he runs so
fast!; **que de livres!** what a lot of books!

▶ *pron* **1** (*relatif: personne*) whom; (*chose*)
that, which; **l'homme que je vois** the man
(whom) I see; **le livre que tu vois** the book
(that *ou* which) you see; **un jour que**
j'étais ... a day when I was ...

2 (*interrogatif*) what; **que fais-tu?, qu'est-**
ce que tu fais? what are you doing?; **qu'est-**
ce que c'est? what is it?, what's that?; **que**
faire? what can one do?

Québec [kebɛk] *nm*: **le ~** Quebec
(Province)

québécois, e *adj* Quebec *cpd* ▷ *nm* (*Ling*)
Quebec French ▷ *nm/f*: **Q~, e** Quebecois,
Quebec(k)er

 MOT-CLÉ

quel, quelle [kɛl] *adj* **1** (*interrogatif:*
personne) who; (*chose*) what; **quel est**
cet homme? who is this man?; **quel est**
ce livre? what is this book?; **quel livre/**
homme? what book/man?; (*parmi un*
certain choix) which book/man?; **quels**
acteurs préférez-vous? which actors do
you prefer?; **dans quels pays êtes-vous**
allé? which *ou* what countries did you go to?

2 (exclamatif): **quelle surprise/coïncidence!** what a surprise/coincidence! **3**: **quel que soit le coupable** whoever is guilty; **quel que soit votre avis** whatever your opinion (may be)

quelconque [kɛlkɔ̃k] adj (médiocre: repas) indifferent, poor; (sans attrait) ordinary, plain; (indéfini): **un ami/prétexte ~** some friend/pretext or other

MOT-CLÉ

quelque [kɛlk] adj **1** (au singulier) some; (au pluriel) a few, some; (tournure interrogative) any; **quelque espoir** some hope; **il a quelques amis** he has a few ou some friends; **a-t-il quelques amis?** does he have any friends?; **les quelques livres qui** the few books which; **20 kg et quelque(s)** a bit over 20 kg **2**: **quelque … que: quelque livre qu'il choisisse** whatever (ou whichever) book he chooses **3**: **quelque chose** something; (tournure interrogative) anything; **quelque chose d'autre** something else; anything else; **quelque part** somewhere; anywhere; **en quelque sorte** as it were
▶ adv **1** (environ): **quelque 100 mètres** some 100 metres **2**: **quelque peu** rather, somewhat

quelquefois [kɛlkəfwa] adv sometimes
quelques-uns, -unes [kɛlkəzœ̃, -yn] pron some, a few
quelqu'un [kɛlkœ̃] pron someone, somebody; (+ tournure interrogative ou négative) anyone, anybody; **~ d'autre** someone ou somebody else; anybody else
qu'en dira-t-on [kɑ̃diratɔ̃] nm inv: **le ~** gossip, what people say
querelle [kərɛl] nf quarrel; **quereller** /1/: **se quereller** vi to quarrel
qu'est-ce que [kɛskə] voir **que**
qu'est-ce qui [kɛski] voir **qui**
question [kɛstjɔ̃] nf question; (fig) matter; issue; **il a été ~ de** we (ou they) spoke about; **de quoi est-il ~?** what is it about?; **il n'en est pas ~** there's no question of it; **en ~** in question; **hors de ~** out of the question; **(re)mettre en ~** to question; **questionnaire** nm questionnaire; **questionner** /1/ vt to question
quête [kɛt] nf collection; (recherche) quest, search; **faire la ~** (à l'église) to take the collection; (artiste) to pass the hat round
quetsche [kwɛtʃ] nf damson
queue [kø] nf tail; (fig: du classement) bottom; (: de poêle) handle; (: de fruit, feuille) stalk; (: de train, colonne, file) rear; **faire la ~** to queue (up) (BRIT), line up (US); **~ de** cheval ponytail; **~ de poisson: faire une ~ de poisson à qn** (Auto) to cut in front of sb

MOT-CLÉ

qui [ki] pron **1** (interrogatif: personne) who; (: chose): **qu'est-ce qui est sur la table?** what is on the table?; **qui est-ce qui?** who?; **qui est-ce que?** who?; **à qui est ce sac?** whose bag is this?; **à qui parlais-tu?** who were you talking to?, to whom were you talking?; **chez qui allez-vous?** whose house are you going to?
2 (relatif: personne) who; (+prép) whom; **l'ami de qui je vous ai parlé** the friend I told you about; **la dame chez qui je suis allé** the lady whose house I went to
3 (sans antécédent): **amenez qui vous voulez** bring who you like; **qui que ce soit** whoever it may be

quiche [kiʃ] nf quiche
quiconque [kikɔ̃k] pron (celui qui) whoever, anyone who; (n'importe qui, personne) anyone, anybody
quille [kij] nf: **(jeu de) ~s** skittles sg (BRIT), bowling (US)
quincaillerie [kɛ̃kajʀi] nf (ustensiles) hardware; (magasin) hardware shop ou store (US)
quinquagénaire [kɛ̃kaʒenɛʀ] nm/f man/woman in his/her fifties
quinquennat [kɛ̃kena] nm five year term of office (of French President)
quinte [kɛ̃t] nf: **~ (de toux)** coughing fit
quintuple [kɛ̃typl] nm: **le ~ de** five times as much as
quinzaine [kɛ̃zɛn] nf: **une ~ (de)** about fifteen, fifteen or so; **une ~ (de jours)** a fortnight (BRIT), two weeks
quinze [kɛ̃z] num fifteen; **dans ~ jours** in a fortnight('s time) (BRIT), in two weeks(' time)
quinzième [kɛ̃zjɛm] num fifteenth
quittance [kitɑ̃s] nf (reçu) receipt
quitte [kit] adj: **être ~ envers qn** to be no longer in sb's debt; (fig) to be quits with sb; **~ à faire** even if it means doing
quitter [kite] /1/ vt to leave; (vêtement) to take off; **se quitter** vi (couples, interlocuteurs) to part; **ne quittez pas** (au téléphone) hold the line
qui-vive [kiviv] nm inv: **être sur le ~** to be on the alert

MOT-CLÉ

quoi [kwa] pron interrog **1** what; **~ de neuf?** what's new?; **~?** (qu'est-ce que tu dis?) what? **2** (avec prép): **à ~ penses-tu?** what are you thinking about?; **de ~ parlez-vous?** what are you talking about?; **à ~ bon?** what's the use?

▶ *pron relatif*: **as-tu de ~ écrire?** do you have anything to write with?; **il n'y a pas de ~** (please) don't mention it; **il n'y a pas de ~ rire** there's nothing to laugh about
▶ *pron (locutions)*: **~ qu'il arrive** whatever happens; **~ qu'il en soit** be that as it may; **~ que ce soit** anything at all
▶ *excl* what!

quoique [kwak] *conj* (al)though
quotidien, ne [kɔtidjɛ̃, -ɛn] *adj* daily, (*banal*) everyday ▷ *nm* (*journal*) daily (paper); **quotidiennement** *adv* daily, every day

r

R, r *abr* = **route**; **rue**
rab [ʀab] *nm* (*fam: nourriture*) extra; **est-ce qu'il y a du ~?** are there any seconds?
rabâcher [ʀabaʃe] /1/ *vt* to keep on repeating
rabais [ʀabɛ] *nm* reduction, discount; **rabaisser** /1/ *vt* (*rabattre: prix*) to reduce; (*dénigrer*) to belittle
Rabat [ʀaba(t)] *n* Rabat
rabattre [ʀabatʀ] /41/ *vt* (*couvercle, siège*) to pull down; (*déduire*) to reduce; **se rabattre** *vi* (*bords, couvercle*) to fall shut; (*véhicule, coureur*) to cut in; **se ~ sur** to fall back on
rabbin [ʀabɛ̃] *nm* rabbi
rabougri, e [ʀabugʀi] *adj* stunted
raccommoder [ʀakɔmɔde] /1/ *vt* to mend, repair
raccompagner [ʀakɔ̃paɲe] /1/ *vt* to take *ou* see back
raccord [ʀakɔʀ] *nm* link; (*retouche*) touch-up; **raccorder** /1/ *vt* to join (up), link up; (*pont etc*) to connect, link
raccourci [ʀakuʀsi] *nm* short cut
raccourcir [ʀakuʀsiʀ] /2/ *vt* to shorten ▷ *vi* (*jours*) to grow shorter, draw in
raccrocher [ʀakʀɔʃe] /1/ *vt* (*tableau, vêtement*) to hang back up; (*récepteur*) to put down ▷ *vi* (*Tél*) to hang up, ring off
race [ʀas] *nf* race; (*d'animaux, fig*) breed; **de ~** purebred, pedigree
rachat [ʀaʃa] *nm* buying; (*du même objet*) buying back
racheter [ʀaʃte] /5/ *vt* (*article perdu*) to buy another; (*davantage*) to buy more; (*après avoir vendu*) to buy back; (*d'occasion*) to buy; (*Comm: part, firme*) to buy up; **se racheter** (*gén*) to make amends; **~ du lait/ trois œufs** to buy more milk/another three eggs
racial, e, -aux [ʀasjal, -o] *adj* racial
racine [ʀasin] *nf* root; **~ carrée/cubique** square/cube root

racisme [ʀasism] nm racism

raciste [ʀasist] adj, nm/f racist

racket [ʀakɛt] nm racketeering no pl

raclée [ʀɑkle] nf (fam) hiding, thrashing

racler [ʀɑkle] /1/ vt (os, plat) to scrape; **se ~ la gorge** to clear one's throat

racontars [ʀakɔ̃taʀ] nmpl stories, gossip sg

raconter [ʀakɔ̃te] /1/ vt: **~ (à qn)** (décrire) to relate (to sb), tell (sb) about; (dire) to tell (sb); **~ une histoire** to tell a story

radar [ʀadaʀ] nm radar; **~ (automatique)** (Auto) speed camera

rade [ʀad] nf (natural) harbour; **rester en ~** (fig) to be left stranded

radeau, x [ʀado] nm raft

radiateur [ʀadjatœʀ] nm radiator, heater; (Auto) radiator; **~ électrique/à gaz** electric/gas heater ou fire

radiation [ʀadjasjɔ̃] nf (Physique) radiation

radical, e, -aux [ʀadikal, -o] adj radical

radieux, -euse [ʀadjø, -øz] adj radiant

radin, e [ʀadɛ̃, -in] adj (fam) stingy

radio [ʀadjo] nf radio; (Méd) X-ray ▷ nm radio operator; **à la ~** on the radio; **radioactif, -ive** adj radioactive; **radiocassette** nf cassette radio; **radiographie** nf radiography; (photo) X-ray photograph; **radiophonique** adj radio cpd; **radio-réveil** (pl **radios-réveils**) nm radio alarm (clock)

radis [ʀadi] nm radish

radoter [ʀadote] /1/ vi to ramble on

radoucir [ʀadusiʀ] /2/: **se radoucir** vi (se réchauffer) to become milder; (se calmer) to calm down

rafale [ʀafal] nf (vent) gust (of wind); (de balles, d'applaudissements) burst

raffermir [ʀafɛʀmiʀ] /2/ vt, **se raffermir** vi to firm up

raffiner [ʀafine] /1/ vt to refine; **raffinerie** nf refinery

raffoler [ʀafole] /1/: **~ de** vt to be very keen on

rafle [ʀafl] nf (de police) raid; **rafler** /1/ vt (fam) to swipe, nick

rafraîchir [ʀafʀeʃiʀ] /2/ vt (atmosphère, température) to cool (down); (boisson) to chill; (fig: rénover) to brighten up; **se rafraîchir** vi to grow cooler; (en se lavant) to freshen up; (en buvant etc) to refresh o.s.; **rafraîchissant, e** adj refreshing; **rafraîchissement** nm (boisson) cool drink; **rafraîchissements** nmpl (boissons, fruits etc) refreshments

rage [ʀaʒ] nf (Méd): **la ~** rabies; (fureur) rage, fury; **faire ~** to rage; **~ de dents** (raging) toothache

ragot [ʀago] nm (fam) malicious gossip no pl

ragoût [ʀagu] nm stew

raide [ʀɛd] adj (tendu) taut, tight; (escarpé) steep; (droit: cheveux) straight; (ankylosé, dur, guindé) stiff; (fam: sans argent) flat broke; (osé, licencieux) daring ▷ adv (en pente) steeply; **~ mort** stone dead; **raideur** nf (rigidité) stiffness; **avec raideur** (répondre) stiffly, abruptly; **raidir** /2/ vt (muscles) to stiffen; **se raidir** vi to stiffen; (personne) to tense up; (: se préparer moralement) to brace o.s.; (fig: devenir intransigeant) to harden

raie [ʀɛ] nf (Zool) skate, ray; (rayure) stripe; (des cheveux) parting

raifort [ʀefɔʀ] nm horseradish

rail [ʀaj] nm rail; (chemins de fer) railways pl; **par ~** by rail

railler [ʀaje] /1/ vt to scoff at, jeer at

rainure [ʀenyʀ] nf groove

raisin [ʀezɛ̃] nm (aussi: **~s**) grapes pl; **~s secs** raisins

raison [ʀezɔ̃] nf reason; **avoir ~** to be right; **donner ~ à qn** to agree with sb; (fait) to prove sb right; **se faire une ~** to learn to live with it; **perdre la ~** to become insane; **~ de plus** all the more reason; **à plus forte ~** all the more so; **sans ~** for no reason; **en ~ de** because of; **à ~ de** at the rate of; **~ sociale** corporate name; **raisonnable** adj reasonable, sensible

raisonnement [ʀezɔnmɑ̃] nm reasoning; argument

raisonner [ʀezone] /1/ vi (penser) to reason; (argumenter, discuter) to argue ▷ vt (personne) to reason with

rajeunir [ʀaʒœniʀ] /2/ vt (en recrutant) to inject new blood into ▷ vi to become (ou look) younger; **~ qn** (coiffure, robe) to make sb look younger

rajouter [ʀaʒute] /1/ vt to add

rajuster [ʀaʒyste] /1/ vt (vêtement) to straighten, tidy; (salaires) to adjust

ralenti [ʀalɑ̃ti] nm: **au ~** (fig) at a slower pace; **tourner au ~** (Auto) to tick over, idle

ralentir [ʀalɑ̃tiʀ] /2/ vt, vi, **se ralentir** vi to slow down

râler [ʀɑle] /1/ vi to groan; (fam) to grouse, moan (and groan)

rallier [ʀalje] /7/ vt (rejoindre) to rejoin; (gagner à sa cause) to win over

rallonge [ʀalɔ̃ʒ] nf (de table) (extra) leaf

rallonger [ʀalɔ̃ʒe] /3/ vt to lengthen

rallye [ʀali] nm rally; (Pol) march

ramassage [ʀamasaʒ] nm: **~ scolaire** school bus service

ramasser [ʀamase] /1/ vt (objet tombé ou par terre) to pick up; (recueillir: copies, ordures) to collect; (récolter) to gather; **ramassis** nm (péj: de voyous) bunch; (de choses) jumble

rambarde [ʀɑ̃baʀd] nf guardrail

rame [ʀam] nf (aviron) oar; (de métro) train; (de papier) ream

rameau, x [ʀamo] *nm* (small) branch; **les R~x** (*Rel*) Palm Sunday *sg*

ramener [ʀamne] /5/ *vt* to bring back; (*reconduire*) to take back; **~ qch à** (*réduire à*) to reduce sth to

ramer [ʀame] /1/ *vi* to row

ramollir [ʀamɔliʀ] /2/ *vt* to soften; **se ramollir** *vi* to get (*ou* go) soft

rampe [ʀɑ̃p] *nf* (*d'escalier*) banister(s *pl*); (*dans un garage, d'un terrain*) ramp; **la ~** (*Théât*) the footlights *pl*; **~ de lancement** launching pad

ramper [ʀɑ̃pe] /1/ *vi* to crawl

rancard [ʀɑ̃kaʀ] *nm* (*fam*) date

rancart [ʀɑ̃kaʀ] *nm*: **mettre au ~** to scrap

rance [ʀɑ̃s] *adj* rancid

rancœur [ʀɑ̃kœʀ] *nf* rancour

rançon [ʀɑ̃sɔ̃] *nf* ransom

rancune [ʀɑ̃kyn] *nf* grudge, rancour; **garder ~ à qn (de qch)** to bear sb a grudge (for sth); **sans ~!** no hard feelings!; **rancunier, -ière** *adj* vindictive, spiteful

randonnée [ʀɑ̃dɔne] *nf* ride; (*à pied*) walk, ramble; (*en montagne*) hike, hiking *no pl*; **la ~** (*activité*) hiking, walking; **une ~ à cheval** a pony trek

rang [ʀɑ̃] *nm* (*rangée*) row; (*grade, condition sociale, classement*) rank; **rangs** *nmpl* (*Mil*) ranks, **se mettre en ~s/sur un ~** to get into *ou* form rows/a line; **au premier ~** in the first row; (*fig*) ranking first

rangé, e [ʀɑ̃ʒe] *adj* (*vie*) well-ordered; (*sérieux: personne*) steady

rangée [ʀɑ̃ʒe] *nf* row

ranger [ʀɑ̃ʒe] /3/ *vt* (*classer, grouper*) to order, arrange; (*mettre à sa place*) to put away; (*mettre de l'ordre dans*) to tidy up; (*fig: classer*): **~ qn/qch parmi** to rank sb/sth among; **se ranger** *vi* (*véhicule, conducteur*) to pull over or in; (*piéton*) to step aside; (*s'assagir*) to settle down; **se ~ à** (*avis*) to come round to

ranimer [ʀanime] /1/ *vt* (*personne évanouie*) to bring round; (*douleur, souvenir*) to revive; (*feu*) to rekindle

rapace [ʀapas] *nm* bird of prey

râpe [ʀɑp] *nf* (*Culin*) grater; **râper** /1/ *vt* (*Culin*) to grate

rapide [ʀapid] *adj* fast; (*prompt: intelligence, coup d'œil, mouvement*) quick ▷ *nm* express (train); (*de cours d'eau*) rapid; **rapidement** *adv* fast; quickly

rapiécer [ʀapjese] /3, 6/ *vt* to patch

rappel [ʀapɛl] *nm* (*Théât*) curtain call; (*Méd: vaccination*) booster; (*d'une aventure, d'un nom*) reminder; **rappeler** /4/ *vt* to call back; (*ambassadeur, Mil*) to recall; (*faire se souvenir*): **rappeler qch à qn** to remind sb of sth; **se rappeler** *vt* (*se souvenir de*) to remember, recall

rapport [ʀapɔʀ] *nm* (*compte rendu*) report; (*profit*) yield, return; (*lien, analogie*) relationship; (*corrélation*) connection; **rapports** *nmpl* (*entre personnes, pays*) relations; **avoir ~ à** to have something to do with; **être/se mettre en ~ avec qn** to be/ get in touch with sb; **par ~ à** in relation to; **~s (sexuels)** (sexual) intercourse *sg*; **~ qualité-prix** value (for money)

rapporter [ʀapɔʀte] /1/ *vt* (*rendre, ramener*) to bring back; (*investissement*) to yield; (*relater*) to report ▷ *vi* (*investissement*) to give a good return *ou* yield; (*activité*) to be very profitable; **se ~ à** to relate to

rapprochement [ʀapʀɔʃmɑ̃] *nm* (*de nations, familles*) reconciliation; (*analogie, rapport*) parallel

rapprocher [ʀapʀɔʃe] /1/ *vt* (*deux objets*) to bring closer together; (*ennemis, partis etc*) to bring together; (*comparer*) to establish a parallel between; (*chaise d'une table*): **~ qch (de)** to bring sth closer (to); **se rapprocher** *vi* to draw closer *ou* nearer; **se ~ de** to come closer to; (*présenter une analogie avec*) to be close to

raquette [ʀakɛt] *nf* (*de tennis*) racket; (*de ping-pong*) bat

rare [ʀɑʀ] *adj* rare; **se faire ~** to become scarce; **rarement** *adv* rarely, seldom

ras, e [ʀɑ, ʀɑz] *adj* (*tête, cheveux*) close-cropped; (*poil, herbe*) short ▷ *adv* short; **en ~e campagne** in open country; **à ~ bords** to the brim; **en avoir ~ le bol** (*fam*) to be fed up

raser [ʀɑze] /1/ *vt* (*barbe, cheveux*) to shave off; (*menton, personne*) to shave; (*fam: ennuyer*) to bore; (*démolir*) to raze (to the ground); (*frôler*) to graze, skim; **se raser** *vi* to shave; (*fam*) to be bored (to tears); **rasoir** *nm* razor

rassasier [ʀasazje] /7/ *vt*: **être rassasié** to be sated

rassemblement [ʀasɑ̃bləmɑ̃] *nm* (*groupe*) gathering; (*Pol*) union

rassembler [ʀasɑ̃ble] /1/ *vt* (*réunir*) to assemble, gather; (*documents, notes*) to gather together, collect; **se rassembler** *vi* to gather

rassurer [ʀasyʀe] /1/ *vt* to reassure; **se rassurer** *vi* to be reassured; **rassure-toi** don't worry

rat [ʀa] *nm* rat

rate [ʀat] *nf* spleen

raté, e [ʀate] *adj* (*tentative*) unsuccessful, failed ▷ *nm/f* (*fam: personne*) failure

râteau, x [ʀɑto] *nm* rake

rater [ʀate] /1/ *vi* (*affaire, projet etc*) to go wrong, fail ▷ *vt* (*cible, train, occasion*) to miss; (*démonstration, plat*) to spoil; (*examen*) to fail

ration [ʀasjɔ̃] *nf* ration

RATP *sigle f* (= *Régie autonome des transports parisiens*) Paris transport authority

rattacher [Rataʃe] /1/ vt (animal, cheveux) to tie up again; **~ qch à** (relier) to link sth with

rattraper [RatRape] /1/ vt (fugitif) to recapture; (retenir, empêcher de tomber) to catch (hold of); (atteindre, rejoindre) to catch up with; (réparer: erreur) to make up for; **se rattraper** vi to make up for it; **se ~ (à)** (se raccrocher) to stop o.s. falling (by catching hold of)

rature [RatyR] nf deletion, erasure

rauque [Rok] adj (voix) hoarse

ravages [Rava3] nmpl: **faire des ~** to wreak havoc

ravi, e [Ravi] adj: **être ~ de/que** to be delighted with/that

ravin [Ravɛ̃] nm gully, ravine

ravir [RaviR] /2/ vt (enchanter) to delight; **à ~** adv beautifully

raviser [Ravize] /1/: **se raviser** vi to change one's mind

ravissant, e [Ravisã, -ãt] adj delightful

ravisseur, -euse [RavisœR, -øz] nm/f abductor, kidnapper

ravitailler [Ravitaje] /1/ vt (en vivres, munitions) to provide with fresh supplies; (véhicule) to refuel; **se ravitailler** vi to get fresh supplies

raviver [Ravive] /1/ vt (feu) to rekindle; (douleur) to revive; (couleurs) to brighten up

rayé, e [Reje] adj (à rayures) striped

rayer [Reje] /8/ vt (érafler) to scratch; (barrer) to cross ou score out; (d'une liste) to cross ou strike off

rayon [Rejɔ̃] nm (de soleil etc) ray; (Géom) radius; (de roue) spoke; (étagère) shelf; (de grand magasin) department; **dans un ~ de** within a radius of; **~ de soleil** sunbeam; **~s X** X-rays

rayonnement [Rejɔnmã] nm (d'une culture) influence

rayonner [Rejɔne] /1/ vi (fig) to shine forth; (: visage, personne) to be radiant; (touriste) to go touring (from one base)

rayure [RejyR] nf (motif) stripe; (éraflure) scratch; **à ~s** striped

raz-de-marée [RɑdmaRe] nm inv tidal wave

ré [Re] nm (Mus) D; (en chantant la gamme) re

réaction [Reaksjɔ̃] nf reaction

réadapter [Readapte] /1/: **se ~ (à)** vi to readjust (to)

réagir [Rea3iR] /2/ vi to react

réalisateur, -trice [RealizatœR, -tRis] nm/f (TV, Ciné) director

réalisation [Realizasjɔ̃] nf realization; (Ciné) production; **en cours de ~** under way

réaliser [Realize] /1/ vt (projet, opération) to carry out, realize; (rêve, souhait) to realize, fulfil; (exploit) to achieve; (film) to produce; (se rendre compte de) to realize; **se réaliser** vi to be realized

réaliste [Realist] adj realistic

réalité [Realite] nf reality; **en ~** in (actual) fact; **dans la ~** in reality

réanimation [Reanimasjɔ̃] nf resuscitation; **service de ~** intensive care unit

rébarbatif, -ive [RebaRbatif, -iv] adj forbidding

rebattu, e [Rəbaty] adj hackneyed

rebelle [Rəbɛl] nm/f rebel ▷ adj (troupes) rebel; (enfant) rebellious; (mèche etc) unruly

rebeller [Rəbele] /1/: **se rebeller** vi to rebel

rebondir [Rəbɔ̃diR] /2/ vi (ballon: au sol) to bounce; (: contre un mur) to rebound; (fig) to get moving again

rebord [RəbɔR] nm edge; **le ~ de la fenêtre** the windowsill

rebours [RəbuR]: **à ~** adv the wrong way

rebrousser [RəbRuse] /1/ vt: **~ chemin** to turn back

rebuter [Rəbyte] /1/ vt to put off

récalcitrant, e [Rekalsitrã, -ãt] adj refractory

récapituler [Rekapityle] /1/ vt to recapitulate; to sum up

receler [Rəsəle] /5/ vt (produit d'un vol) to receive; (fig) to conceal; **receleur, -euse** nm/f receiver

récemment [Resamã] adv recently

recensement [Rəsãsmã] nm census

recenser [Rəsãse] /1/ vt (population) to take a census of; (dénombrer) to list

récent, e [Resã, -ãt] adj recent

récépissé [Resepise] nm receipt

récepteur, -trice [ReseptœR, -tRis] adj receiving ▷ nm receiver

réception [Resepsjɔ̃] nf receiving no pl; (accueil) reception, welcome; (bureau) reception (desk); (réunion mondaine) reception, party; **réceptionniste** nm/f receptionist

recette [Rəsɛt] nf recipe; (Comm) takings pl; **recettes** nfpl (Comm: rentrées) receipts; **faire ~** (spectacle, exposition) to be a winner

recevoir [RəsvwaR] /28/ vt to receive; (client, patient, représentant) to see; **être reçu (à un examen)** to pass

rechange [Rəʃã3]: **de ~** adj (pièces, roue) spare; (fig: solution) alternative; **des vêtements de ~** a change of clothes

recharge [RəʃaR3] nf refill; **rechargeable** adj (stylo etc) refillable; **recharger** /3/ vt (briquet, stylo) to refill; (batterie) to recharge

réchaud [Reʃo] nm (portable) stove

réchauffement [Reʃofmã] nm warming (up); **le ~ de la planète** global warming

réchauffer [Reʃofe] /1/ vt (plat) to reheat; (mains, personne) to warm; **se réchauffer** vi (*température*) to get warmer; (*personne*) to warm o.s. (up)

rêche [ʀɛʃ] *adj* rough

recherche [ʀəʃɛʀʃ] *nf* (*action*): **la ~ de** the search for; (*raffinement*) studied elegance; (*scientifique etc*): **la ~** research; **recherches** *nfpl* (*de la police*) investigations; (*scientifiques*) research *sg*; **être/se mettre à la ~ de** to be/go in search of

recherché, e [ʀəʃɛʀʃe] *adj* (*rare, demandé*) much sought-after; (*raffiné*) affected, (*tenue*) elegant

rechercher [ʀəʃɛʀʃe] /1/ *vt* (*objet égaré, personne*) to look for; (*causes d'un phénomène, nouveau procédé*) to try to find; (*bonheur etc, l'amitié de qn*) to seek

rechute [ʀəʃyt] *nf* (*Méd*) relapse

récidiver [ʀesidive] /1/ *vi* to commit a second (*ou* subsequent) offence; (*fig*) to do it again

récif [ʀesif] *nm* reef

récipient [ʀesipjɑ̃] *nm* container

réciproque [ʀesipʀɔk] *adj* reciprocal

récit [ʀesi] *nm* story; **récital** *nm* recital; **réciter** /1/ *vt* to recite

réclamation [ʀeklamasjɔ̃] *nf* complaint, **réclamations** *nfpl* complaints department *sg*

réclame [ʀeklam] *nf*: **une ~** an ad(vertisement), an advert (*BRIT*); **article en ~** special offer; **réclamer** /1/ *vt* to ask for; (*revendiquer*) to claim, demand ▷ *vi* to complain

réclusion [ʀeklyzjɔ̃] *nf* imprisonment

recoin [ʀəkwɛ̃] *nm* nook, corner

reçois *etc* [ʀəswa] *vb voir* **recevoir**

récolte [ʀekɔlt] *nf* harvesting, gathering; (*produits*) harvest, crop; **récolter** /1/ *vt* to harvest, gather (in); (*fig*) to get

recommandé [ʀəkɔmɑ̃de] *nm* (*Postes*): **en ~** by registered mail

recommander [ʀəkɔmɑ̃de] /1/ *vt* to recommend; (*Postes*) to register

recommencer [ʀəkɔmɑ̃se] /3/ *vt* (*reprendre: lutte, séance*) to resume, start again; (*refaire: travail, explications*) to start afresh, start (over) again ▷ *vi* to start again; (*récidiver*) to do it again

récompense [ʀekɔ̃pɑ̃s] *nf* reward; (*prix*) award; **récompenser** /1/ *vt*: **récompenser qn (de *ou* pour)** to reward sb (for)

réconcilier [ʀekɔ̃silje] /7/ *vt* to reconcile; **se réconcilier (avec)** to be reconciled (with)

reconduire [ʀəkɔ̃dɥiʀ] /38/ *vt* (*raccompagner*) to take *ou* see back; (*renouveler*) to renew

réconfort [ʀekɔ̃fɔʀ] *nm* comfort; **réconforter** /1/ *vt* (*consoler*) to comfort

reconnaissance [ʀəkɔnɛsɑ̃s] *nf* (*action de reconnaître*) recognition; (*gratitude*) gratitude, gratefulness; (*Mil*)

reconnaissance, recce; **reconnaissant, e** *adj* grateful; **je vous serais reconnaissant de bien vouloir** I should be most grateful if you would (kindly)

reconnaître [ʀəkɔnɛtʀ] /57/ *vt* to recognize; (*Mil: lieu*) to reconnoitre; (*Jur: enfant, dette, droit*) to acknowledge; **~ que** to admit *ou* acknowledge that; **~ qn/qch à** (*l'identifier grâce à*) to recognize sb/sth by; **reconnu, e** *adj* (*indiscuté, connu*) recognized

reconstituer [ʀəkɔ̃stitɥe] /1/ *vt* (*fresque, vase brisé*) to piece together, reconstitute; (*événement, accident*) to reconstruct

reconstruire [ʀəkɔ̃stʀɥiʀ] /38/ *vt* to rebuild

reconvertir [ʀəkɔ̃vɛʀtiʀ] /2/ *vt* to reconvert; **se ~ dans** (*un métier, une branche*) to move into

record [ʀəkɔʀ] *nm, adj* record

recoupement [ʀəkupmɑ̃] *nm*: **par ~** by cross-checking

recouper [ʀəkupe] /1/: **se recouper** *vi* (*témoignages*) to tie *ou* match up

recourber [ʀəkuʀbe] /1/: **se recourber** *vi* to curve (up), bend (up)

recourir [ʀəkuʀiʀ] /11/: **~ à** *vt* (*ami, agence*) to turn *ou* appeal to; (*force, ruse, emprunt*) to resort to

recours [ʀəkuʀ] *nm*: **avoir ~ à** = **recourir à**; **en dernier ~** as a last resort

recouvrer [ʀəkuvʀe] /1/ *vt* (*vue, santé etc*) to recover, regain

recouvrir [ʀəkuvʀiʀ] /18/ *vt* (*couvrir à nouveau*) to re-cover; (*couvrir entièrement, aussi fig*) to cover

récréation [ʀekʀeasjɔ̃] *nf* (*Scol*) break

recroqueviller [ʀəkʀɔkvije] /1/: **se recroqueviller** *vi* (*personne*) to huddle up

recrudescence [ʀəkʀydesɑ̃s] *nf* fresh outbreak

recruter [ʀəkʀyte] /1/ *vt* to recruit

rectangle [ʀɛktɑ̃gl] *nm* rectangle; **rectangulaire** *adj* rectangular

rectificatif, -ive [ʀɛktifikatif, -iv] *adj* corrected ▷ *nm* correction

rectifier [ʀɛktifje] /7/ *vt* (*calcul, adresse*) to correct; (*erreur, faute*) to rectify

rectiligne [ʀɛktiliɲ] *adj* straight

recto [ʀɛkto] *nm* front (*of a sheet of paper*); **~ verso** on both sides (*of the page*)

reçu, e [ʀəsy] *pp de* **recevoir** ▷ *adj* (*candidat*) successful; (*admis, consacré*) accepted ▷ *nm* (*Comm*) receipt

recueil [ʀəkœj] *nm* collection; **recueillir** /12/ *vt* to collect; (*voix, suffrages*) to win; (*accueillir: réfugiés, chat*) to take in; **se recueillir** *vi* to gather one's thoughts; to meditate

recul [ʀəkyl] *nm* (*déclin*) decline; (*éloignement*) distance; **avoir un mouvement de ~** to recoil; **prendre du ~**

to stand back; **être en ~** to be on the decline; **avec le ~ in** retrospect; **reculé, e** adj remote; **reculer** /1/ vi to move back, back away; (*Auto*) to reverse, back (up); (*fig*) to (be on the) decline ▷ vt to move back; (*véhicule*) to reverse, back (up); (*date, décision*) to postpone; **reculer devant** (*danger, difficulté*) to shrink from; **reculons**: **à reculons** adv backwards

récupérer [Rekypere] /6/ vt to recover, get back; (*déchets etc*) to salvage (for reprocessing); (*journée, heures de travail*) to make up ▷ vi to recover

récurer [RekyRe] /1/ vt to scour; **poudre à ~** scouring powder

reçus etc [Rəsy] vb voir **recevoir**

recycler [Rəsikle] /1/ vt (*matériau*) to recycle; **se recycler** vi to retrain

rédacteur, -trice [Redaktœr, -tRis] nm/f (*journaliste*) writer; subeditor; (*d'ouvrage de référence*) editor, compiler

rédaction [Redaksjɔ̃] nf writing; (*rédacteurs*) editorial staff; (*Scol: devoir*) essay, composition

redescendre [Rədesɑ̃dR] /41/ vi to go back down ▷ vt (*pente etc*) to go down

rédiger [Redize] /3/ vt to write; (*contrat*) to draw up

redire [RədiR] /37/ vt to repeat; **trouver à ~ à** to find fault with

redoubler [Rəduble] /1/ vi (*tempête, violence*) to intensify; (*Scol*) to repeat a year; **~ de patience/prudence** to be doubly patient/careful

redoutable [Rədutabl] adj formidable, fearsome

redouter [Rədute] /1/ vt to dread

redressement [Rədɛɛsmɑ̃] nm (*économique*) recovery

redresser [Rədrese] /1/ vt (*arbre, mât*) to set upright; (*pièce tordue*) to straighten out; (*situation, économie*) to put right; **se redresser** vi (*personne*) to sit (ou stand) up; (*pays, situation*) to recover

réduction [Redyksjɔ̃] nf reduction

réduire [RedɥiR] /38/ vt to reduce; (*prix, dépenses*) to cut; reduce; **réduit** nm tiny room

rééducation [Reedykasjɔ̃] nf (*d'un membre*) re-education; (*de délinquants, d'un blessé*) rehabilitation

réel, le [Reɛl] adj real; **réellement** adv really

réexpédier [Reɛkspedje] /7/ vt (*à l'envoyeur*) to return, send back; (*au destinataire*) to send on, forward

refaire [RəfɛR] /60/ vt to do again; (*sport*) to take up again; (*réparer, restaurer*) to do up

réfectoire [RefɛktwaR] nm refectory

référence [Referɑ̃s] nf reference; **références** nfpl (*recommandations*) reference sg

référer [Refere] /6/: **se ~ à** vt to refer to

refermer [Rəfɛrme] /1/ vt to close again, shut again; **se refermer** vi (*porte*) to close ou shut (again)

refiler [Rəfile] /1/ vt (*fam*): **~ qch à qn** to palm (*brit*) ou fob sth off on sb

réfléchi, e [Refleʃi] adj (*caractère*) thoughtful; (*action*) well-thought-out; (*Ling*) reflexive; **c'est tout ~** my mind's made up

réfléchir [RefleʃiR] /2/ vt to reflect ▷ vi to think; **~ à** ou **sur** to think about

reflet [Rəflɛ] nm reflection; (*sur l'eau etc*) sheen no pl, glint; **refléter** /6/ vt to reflect; **se refléter** vi to be reflected

réflexe [Reflɛks] adj, nm reflex

réflexion [Reflɛksjɔ̃] nf (*de la lumière etc*) reflection; (*fait de penser*) thought; (*remarque*) remark; **~ faite, à la ~** on reflection; **délai de ~** cooling-off period; **groupe de ~** think tank

réflexologie [Reflɛksɔlɔʒi] nf reflexology

réforme [RefɔRm] nf reform; (*Rel*): **la R~** the Reformation; **réformer** /1/ vt to reform; (*Mil*) to declare unfit for service

refouler [Rəfule] /1/ vt (*envahisseurs*) to drive back; (*liquide, larmes*) to force back; (*désir, colère*) to repress

refrain [RəfRɛ̃] nm refrain, chorus

refréner /6/, **réfréner** [Rəfrene, Refrene] vt to curb, check

réfrigérateur [RefRizeRatœR] nm refrigerator

refroidir [RəfRwadiR] /2/ vt to cool; (*personne*) to put off ▷ vi to cool (down); **se refroidir** vi (*temps*) to get cooler ou colder; (*fig: ardeur*) to cool (off); **refroidissement** nm (*grippe etc*) chill

refuge [Rəfyʒ] nm refuge; **réfugié, e** adj, nm/f refugee; **réfugier** /7/: **se réfugier** vi to take refuge

refus [Rəfy] nm refusal; **ce n'est pas de ~** I won't say no, it's very welcome; **refuser** /1/ vt to refuse; (*Scol: candidat*) to fail; **refuser qch à qn/de faire** to refuse sb sth/ to do; **refuser du monde** to have to turn people away; **se refuser à qch** ou **à faire qch** to refuse to do sth

regagner [Rəɡaɲe] /1/ vt (*argent, faveur*) to win back; (*lieu*) to get back to

régal [Reɡal] nm treat; **régaler** /1/ vt: **régaler qn de** to treat sb to; **se régaler** vi to have a delicious meal; (*fig*) to enjoy o.s.

regard [RəɡaR] nm (*coup d'œil*) look, glance; (*expression*) look (in one's eye); **au ~ de** (*loi, morale*) from the point of view of; **en ~ de** in comparison with

regardant, e [Rəɡaɛdɑ̃, -ɑ̃t] adj: **très/ peu ~ (sur)** quite fussy/very free (about); (*économe*) very tight-fisted/quite generous (with)

regarder [RəgaRde] /1/ vt to look at; (film, télévision, match) to watch; (concerner) to concern ▷ vi to look; **ne pas ~ à la dépense** to spare no expense; **~ qn/qch comme** to regard sb/sth as

régie [Reʒi] nf (Comm, Industrie) state-owned company; (Théât, Ciné) production; (Radio, TV) control room

régime [Reʒim] nm (Pol) régime; (Admin: carcéral, fiscal etc) system; (Méd) diet; (de bananes, dattes) bunch; **se mettre au/suivre un ~** to go on/be on a diet

régiment [Reʒimã] nm regiment

région [Reʒjõ] nf region; **régional, e, -aux** adj regional

régir [Reʒiʀ] /2/ vt to govern

régisseur [Reʒisœʀ] nm (d'un domaine) steward; (Ciné, TV) assistant director; (Théât) stage manager

registre [Reʒistʀ] nm register

réglage [Regla3] nm adjustment

réglé, e [Regle] adj well-ordered; (arrangé) settled

règle [Regl] nf (instrument) ruler; (loi, prescription) rule; **règles** nfpl (Physiol) period sg, **en ~** (papiers d'identité) in order; **en ~ générale** as a (general) rule

règlement [Regləmã] nm (paiement) settlement; (arrêté) regulation; (règles, statuts) regulations pl, rules pl; **réglementaire** adj conforming to the regulations; (tenue, uniforme) regulation cpd; **réglementation** nf (règlements) regulations pl; **réglementer** /1/ vt to regulate

régler [Regle] /6/ vt (mécanisme, machine) to regulate, adjust; (thermostat etc) to set, adjust; (question, conflit, facture, dette) to settle; (fournisseur) to settle up with

réglisse [Reglis] nm ou nf liquorice

règne [Reɲ] nm (d'un roi etc, fig) reign; **le ~ végétal/animal** the vegetable/animal kingdom; **régner** /6/ vi (roi) to rule, reign; (fig) to reign

regorger [RəgɔRʒe] /3/ vi: **~ de** to overflow with, be bursting with

regret [RəgRɛ] nm regret; **à ~** with regret; **sans ~** with no regrets; **regrettable** adj regrettable; **regretter** /1/ vt to regret; (personne) to miss; **non, je regrette** no, I'm sorry

regrouper [RəgRupe] /1/ vt (grouper) to group together; (contenir) to include, comprise; **se regrouper** vi to gather (together)

régulier, -ière [Regylje, -jɛR] adj (gén) regular; (vitesse, qualité) steady; (répartition, pression) even; (Transports: ligne, service) scheduled, regular; (légal, réglementaire) lawful, in order; (fam: correct) straight, on the level; **régulièrement** adv regularly; evenly

rehausser [Rəose] /1/ vt (relever) to heighten, raise; (fig: souligner) to set off, enhance

rein [Rɛ̃] nm kidney; **reins** nmpl (dos) back sg

reine [Rɛn] nf queen

reine-claude [Rɛnklod] nf greengage

réinscriptible [Reɛ̃skʀiptibl] adj (CD, DVD) rewritable

réinsertion [Reɛ̃sɛRsjõ] nf (de délinquant) reintegration, rehabilitation

réintégrer [Reɛ̃tegRe] /6/ vt (lieu) to return to; (fonctionnaire) to reinstate

rejaillir [RəʒajiR] /2/ vi to splash up; **~ sur** (fig: scandale) to rebound on; (: gloire) to be reflected on

rejet [Rəʒɛ] nm rejection; **rejeter** /4/ vt (relancer) to throw back; (vomir) to bring ou throw up; (écarter) to reject; (déverser) to throw out, discharge; **rejeter la responsabilité de qch sur qn** to lay the responsibility for sth at sb's door

rejoindre [RəʒwɛdR] /49/ vt (famille, régiment) to rejoin, return to; (lieu) to get (back) to; (route etc) to meet, join; (rattraper) to catch up (with); **se rejoindre** vi to meet; **je te rejoins au café** I'll see ou meet you at the café

réjouir [Reʒwiʀ] /2/ vt to delight; **se ~ de qch/de faire** to be delighted about sth/to do; **réjouissances** nfpl (fête) festivities

relâche [Rəlɑʃ]: **sans ~** adv without respite ou a break; **relâché, e** adj loose, lax; **relâcher** /1/ vt (ressort, prisonnier) to release; (étreinte, cordes) to loosen; **se relâcher** vi (discipline) to become slack ou lax; (élève etc) to slacken off

relais [Rəlɛ] nm (Sport): **(course de) ~** relay (race); **prendre le ~ (de)** to take over (from); **~ routier** ≈ transport café (BRIT), ≈ truck stop (US)

relancer [Rəlãse] /3/ vt (balle) to throw back (again); (moteur) to restart; (fig) to boost, revive; (personne): **~ qn** to pester sb

relatif, -ive [Rəlatif, -iv] adj relative

relation [Rəlasjõ] nf (rapport) relation(ship); (connaissance) acquaintance; **relations** nfpl (rapports) relations; (connaissances) connections; **être/entrer en ~(s) avec** to be in contact ou be dealing/get in contact with

relaxer [Rəlakse] /1/: **se relaxer** vi to relax

relayer [Rəleje] /8/ vt (collaborateur, coureur etc) to relieve; **se relayer** vi (dans une activité) to take it in turns

reléguer [Rəlege] /6/ vt to relegate

relevé, e [Rəlve] adj (manches) rolled-up; (sauce) highly-seasoned ▷ nm (lecture) reading; **~ bancaire** ou **de compte** bank statement

relève [Rəlɛv] nf (personne) relief; **prendre la ~** to take over

relever [Rəlve] /5/ vt (statue, meuble) to
stand up again; (personne tombée) to help
up; (vitre, plafond, niveau de vie) to raise; (col)
to turn up; (style, conversation) to elevate;
(plat, sauce) to season; (sentinelle, équipe) to
relieve; (fautes, points) to pick out; (défi) to
accept, take up; (noter: adresse etc) to take
down, note; (: plan) to sketch; (compteur)
to read; (ramasser: cahiers, copies) to collect,
take in ▷ vi: ~ **de** (maladie) to be recovering
from; (être du ressort de) to be a matter for;
(fig) to pertain to; **se relever** vi (se remettre
debout) to get up; ~ **qn de** (fonctions) to
relieve sb of; ~ **la tête** to look up

relief [Rəljɛf] nm relief; **mettre en ~** (fig) to
bring out, highlight

relier [Rəlje] /7/ vt to link up; (livre) to bind;
~ **qch à** to link sth to

religieux, -euse [Rəliʒjø, -øz] adj religious
▷ nm monk

religion [Rəliʒjɔ̃] nf religion

relire [RəliR] /43/ vt (à nouveau) to reread,
read again; (vérifier) to read over

reluire [RəlɥiR] /38/ vi to gleam

remanier [Rəmanje] /7/ vt to reshape,
recast; (Pol) to reshuffle

remarquable [RəmaRkabl] adj remarkable

remarque [RəmaRk] nf remark; (écrite)
note

remarquer [RəmaRke] /1/ vt (voir) to
notice; **se remarquer** vi to be noticeable;
se faire ~ to draw attention to o.s.; **faire
~ (à qn) que** to point out (to sb) that;
faire ~ qch (à qn) to point sth out (to sb);
remarquez, ... mind you, ...

rembourrer [RãbuRe] /1/ vt to stuff

remboursement [RãbuRsəmã] nm
(de dette, d'emprunt) repayment; (de frais)
refund; **rembourser** /1/ vt to pay back,
repay; (frais, billet etc) to refund; **se faire
rembourser** to get a refund

remède [Rəmɛd] nm (médicament)
medicine; (traitement, fig) remedy, cure

remémorer [RəmemɔRe] /1/: **se
remémorer** vt to recall, recollect

remerciements [RəmɛRsimã] nmpl
thanks; **(avec) tous mes ~** (with) grateful
ou many thanks

remercier [RəmɛRsje] /7/ vt to thank;
(congédier) to dismiss; ~ **qn de/d'avoir fait**
to thank sb for/for having done

remettre [RəmɛtR] /56/ vt (vêtement):
~ **qch** to put sth back on; (replacer): ~ **qch
quelque part** to put sth back somewhere;
(ajouter): ~ **du sel/un sucre** to add more
salt/another lump of sugar; (ajourner):
~ **qch (à)** to postpone sth ou put sth off
(until); **se remettre** vi to get better; ~ **qch
à qn** (donner) to hand over sth to sb; (prix,
décoration) to present sb with sth; (recover from): **s'en ~ à** to leave it (up) to; **se
~ à faire/qch** to start doing/sth again

remis, e [Rəmi, -iz] pp de **remettre** ▷ nf
(rabais) discount; (local) shed; ~**e en
cause/question** calling into question/
challenging; ~**e en jeu** (Football) throw-in;
~**e de peine** remission of sentence; ~**e des
prix** prize-giving

remontant [Rəmɔ̃tã] nm tonic,
pick-me-up

remonte-pente [Rəmɔ̃tpãt] nm ski lift

remonter [Rəmɔ̃te] /1/ vi to go back up;
(prix, température) to go up again; (en voiture)
to get back in ▷ vt (pente) to go up; (fleuve)
to sail (ou swim etc) up; (manches, pantalon)
to roll up; (fam) to turn up; (niveau, limite)
to raise; (fig: personne) to buck up; (moteur,
meuble) to put back together, reassemble;
(montre, mécanisme) to wind up; ~ **le moral
à qn** to raise sb's spirits; ~ **à** (dater de) to date
ou go back to

remords [RəmɔR] nm remorse no pl; **avoir
des ~** to feel remorse

remorque [RəmɔRk] nf trailer; **remorquer**
/1/ vt to tow; **remorqueur** nm tug (boat)

remous [Rəmu] nm (d'un navire) (back)wash
no pl; (de rivière) swirl, eddy pl; (fig) stir sg

remparts [Rãpar] nmpl walls, ramparts

remplaçant, e [Rãplasã, -ãt] nm/f
replacement, stand-in; (Scol) supply (BRIT)
ou substitute (US) teacher

remplacement [Rãplasmã] nm
replacement; **faire des ~s** (professeur) to do
supply ou substitute teaching; (secrétaire)
to temp

remplacer [Rãplase] /3/ vt to replace;
~ **qch/qn par** to replace sth/sb with

rempli, e [Rãpli] adj (emploi du temps) full,
busy; ~ **de** full of, filled with

remplir [RãpliR] /2/ vt to fill (up);
(questionnaire) to fill out ou up; (obligations,
fonction, condition) to fulfil; **se remplir** vi
to fill up

remporter [RãpɔRte] /1/ vt (marchandise)
to take away; (fig) to win, achieve

remuant, e [Rəmɥã, -ãt] adj restless

remue-ménage [Rəmymenaʒ] nm inv
commotion

remuer [Rəmɥe] /1/ vt to move; (café, sauce)
to stir ▷ vi to move; **se remuer** vi to move;
(fam: s'activer) to get a move on

rémunérer [RemyneRe] /6/ vt to
remunerate

renard [Rənar] nm fox

renchérir [RãʃeRiR] /2/ vi (fig): ~ **(sur)** (en
paroles) to add something (to)

rencontre [Rãkɔ̃tR] nf meeting; (imprévue)
encounter; **aller à la ~ de qn** to go and
meet sb; **rencontrer** /1/ vt to meet; (mot,
expression) to come across; (difficultés) to
meet with; **se rencontrer** vi to meet

rendement [Rãdmã] nm (d'un travailleur,
d'une machine) output; (d'une culture, d'un
champ) yield

rendez-vous [ʀɑ̃devu] *nm* appointment; (*d'amoureux*) date; (*lieu*) meeting place; **donner ~ à qn** to arrange to meet sb; **avoir/prendre ~ (avec)** to have/make an appointment (with)

rendre [ʀɑ̃dʀ] /41/ *vt* (*livre, argent etc*) to give back, return; (*otages, visite, politesse, invitation*) to return; (*sang, aliments*) to bring up; (*exprimer, traduire*) to render; (*faire devenir*): **~ qn célèbre/qch possible** to make sb famous/sth possible; **se rendre** *vi* (*capituler*) to surrender, give o.s. up; (*aller*): **se ~ quelque part** to go somewhere; **se ~ compte de qch** to realize sth; **~ la monnaie** to give change

rênes [ʀɛn] *nfpl* reins

renfermé, e [ʀɑ̃fɛʀme] *adj* (*fig*) withdrawn ▷ *nm*: **sentir le ~** to smell stuffy

renfermer [ʀɑ̃fɛʀme] /1/ *vt* to contain

renforcer [ʀɑ̃fɔʀse] /3/ *vt* to reinforce; **renfort** *nm*: **renforts** *nmpl* reinforcements; **à grand renfort de** with a great deal of

renfrogné, e [ʀɑ̃fʀɔɲe] *adj* sullen, scowling

renier [ʀənje] /7/ *vt* (*parents*) to disown, repudiate; (*foi*) to renounce

renifler [ʀənifle] /1/ *vi* to sniff ▷ *vt* (*odeur*) to sniff

renne [ʀɛn] *nm* reindeer *inv*

renom [ʀənɔ̃] *nm* reputation; (*célébrité*) renown; **renommé, e** *adj* celebrated, renowned ▷ *nf* fame

renoncer [ʀənɔ̃se] /3/: **~ à** *vt* to give up; **~ à faire** to give up the idea of doing

renouer [ʀənwe] /1/ *vt*: **~ avec** (*habitude*) to take up again

renouvelable [ʀ(ə)nuvlabl] *adj* (*contrat, bail, énergie*) renewable

renouveler [ʀənuvle] /4/ *vt* to renew; (*exploit, méfait*) to repeat; **se renouveler** *vi* (*incident*) to recur, happen again; **renouvellement** *nm* renewal

rénover [ʀenɔve] /1/ *vt* (*immeuble*) to renovate, do up; (*quartier*) to redevelop

renseignement [ʀɑ̃sɛɲmɑ̃] *nm* information *no pl*, piece of information; (**guichet des**) **~s** information desk; (**service des**) **~s** (*Tél*) directory inquiries (BRIT), information (US)

renseigner [ʀɑ̃seɲe] /1/ *vt*: **~ qn (sur)** to give information to sb (about); **se renseigner** *vi* to ask for information, make inquiries

rentabilité [ʀɑ̃tabilite] *nf* profitability

rentable [ʀɑ̃tabl] *adj* profitable

rente [ʀɑ̃t] *nf* income; (*pension*) pension

rentrée [ʀɑ̃tʀe] *nf*: **~ (d'argent)** cash *no pl* coming in; **la ~ (des classes** *ou* **scolaire)** the start of the new school year

rentrer [ʀɑ̃tʀe] /1/ *vi* (*entrer de nouveau*) to go (*ou* come) back in; (*entrer*) to go (*ou* come) in; (*revenir chez soi*) to go (*ou* come) (back) home; (*air, clou: pénétrer*) to go in; (*revenu, argent*) to come in ▷ *vt* to bring in; (*véhicule*) to put away; (*chemise dans pantalon etc*) to tuck in; (*griffes*) to draw in; **~ le ventre** to pull in one's stomach; **~ dans** (*heurter*) to crash into; **~ dans l'ordre** to get back to normal; **~ dans ses frais** to recover one's expenses (*ou* initial outlay)

renverse [ʀɑ̃vɛʀs]: **à la ~** *adv* backwards

renverser [ʀɑ̃vɛʀse] /1/ *vt* (*faire tomber: chaise, verre*) to knock over, overturn; (: *piéton*) to knock down; (: *liquide, contenu*) to spill, upset; (*retourner*) to turn upside down; (: *ordre des mots etc*) to reverse; (*fig: gouvernement etc*) to overthrow; (*stupéfier*) to bowl over; **se renverser** *vi* (*verre, vase*) to fall over; (*contenu*) to spill

renvoi [ʀɑ̃vwa] *nm* (*d'employé*) dismissal; (*d'élève*) expulsion; (*référence*) cross-reference; (*éructation*) belch; **renvoyer** /8/ *vt* to send back; (*congédier*) to dismiss; (*élève: définitivement*) to expel; (*lumière*) to reflect; (*ajourner*): **renvoyer qch (à)** to postpone sth (until)

repaire [ʀəpɛʀ] *nm* den

répandre [ʀepɑ̃dʀ] /41/ *vt* (*renverser*) to spill; (*étaler, diffuser*) to spread; (*chaleur, odeur*) to give off; **se répandre** *vi* to spill; to spread; **répandu, e** *adj* (*opinion, usage*) widespread

réparateur, -trice [ʀepaʀatœʀ, -tʀis] *nm/f* repairer

réparation [ʀepaʀasjɔ̃] *nf* repair

réparer [ʀepaʀe] /1/ *vt* to repair; (*fig: offense*) to make up for, atone for; (: *oubli, erreur*) to put right

repartie [ʀepaʀti] *nf* retort; **avoir de la ~** to be quick at repartee

repartir [ʀəpaʀtiʀ] /16/ *vi* to set off again; (*voyageur*) to leave again; (*fig*) to get going again; **~ à zéro** to start from scratch (again)

répartir [ʀepaʀtiʀ] /2/ *vt* (*pour attribuer*) to share out; (*pour disperser, disposer*) to divide up; (*poids, chaleur*) to distribute; **se répartir** *vt* (*travail, rôles*) to share out between themselves; **répartition** *nf* (*des richesses etc*) distribution

repas [ʀəpɑ] *nm* meal

repassage [ʀəpɑsaʒ] *nm* ironing

repasser [ʀəpɑse] /1/ *vi* to come (*ou* go) back ▷ *vt* (*vêtement, tissu*) to iron; (*examen*) to retake, resit; (*film*) to show again; (*leçon, rôle: revoir*) to go over (again)

repentir [ʀəpɑ̃tiʀ] /16/ *nm* repentance; **se repentir** *vi* to repent; **se ~ d'avoir fait qch** (*regretter*) to regret having done sth

répercussions [ʀepɛʀkysjɔ̃] *nfpl* repercussions

répercuter [ʀepɛʀkyte] /1/: **se répercuter** *vi* (*bruit*) to reverberate; (*fig*): **se ~ sur** to have repercussions on

repère [ʀəpɛʀ] *nm* mark; (*monument etc*) landmark

repérer [ʀəpeʀe] /6/ *vt* (*erreur, connaissance*) to spot; (*abri, ennemi*) to locate; **se repérer** *vi* to get one's bearings

répertoire [ʀepɛʀtwaʀ] *nm* (*liste*) (alphabetical) list; (*carnet*) index notebook; (*Inform*) directory; (*d'un théâtre, artiste*) repertoire

répéter [ʀepete] /6/ *vt* to repeat; (*préparer: leçon*) to learn, go over; (*Théât*) to rehearse; **se répéter** (*redire*) to repeat o.s.; (*se reproduire*) to be repeated, recur

répétition [ʀepetisjɔ̃] *nf* repetition; (*Théât*) rehearsal; **~ générale** final dress rehearsal

répit [ʀepi] *nm* respite; **sans ~** without letting up

replier [ʀəplije] /7/ *vt* (*rabattre*) to fold down *ou* over; **se replier** *vi* (*armée*) to withdraw, fall back; **se ~ sur soi-même** to withdraw into oneself

réplique [ʀeplik] *nf* (*repartie, fig*) reply; (*Théât*) line; (*copie*) replica; **répliquer** /1/ *vi* to reply; (*riposter*) to retaliate

répondeur [ʀepɔ̃dœʀ] *nm*: **~ (automatique)** (*Tél*) answering machine

répondre [ʀepɔ̃dʀ] /41/ *vi* to answer, reply; (*freins, mécanisme*) to respond; **~ à** to reply to, answer; (*affection, salut*) to return; (*provocation*) to respond to; (*correspondre à*) to answer; (*conditions*) to meet; (*description*) to match; **~ à qn** (*avec impertinence*) to answer sb back; **~ de** to answer for

réponse [ʀepɔ̃s] *nf* answer, reply; **en ~ à** in reply to

reportage [ʀəpɔʀtaʒ] *nm* report

reporter¹ [ʀəpɔʀtɛʀ] *nm* reporter

reporter² [ʀəpɔʀte] *vt* (*ajourner*): **~ qch (à)** to postpone sth (until); (*transférer*): **~ qch sur** to transfer sth to; **se ~ à** (*époque*) to think back to; (*document*) to refer to

repos [ʀəpo] *nm* rest; (*fig*) peace (and quiet); (*Mil*): **~!** (stand) at ease!; **ce n'est pas de tout ~!** it's no picnic!

reposant, e [ʀ(ə)pozɑ̃, -ɑ̃t] *adj* restful

reposer [ʀəpoze] /1/ *vt* (*verre, livre*) to put down; (*délasser*) to rest ▷ *vi*: **laisser ~** (*pâte*) to leave to stand

repoussant, e [ʀəpusɑ̃, -ɑ̃t] *adj* repulsive

repousser [ʀəpuse] /1/ *vi* to grow again ▷ *vt* to repel, repulse; (*offre*) to turn down, reject; (*tiroir, personne*) to push back; (*différer*) to put back

reprendre [ʀəpʀɑ̃dʀ] /58/ *vt* (*prisonnier, ville*) to recapture; (*firme, entreprise*) to take over; (*emprunter: argument, idée*) to take up, use; (*refaire: article etc*) to go over again; (*jupe etc*) to alter; (*réprimander*) to tell off; (*corriger*) to correct; (*travail, promenade*) to resume; (*chercher*): **je viendrai te ~ à 4 h** I'll come and fetch you *ou* I'll come back for you

at 4; (*se resservir de*): **~ du pain/un œuf** to take (*ou* eat) more bread/another egg ▷ *vi* (*classes, pluie*) to start (up) again; (*activités, travaux, combats*) to resume, start (up) again; (*affaires, industrie*) to pick up; (*dire*): **reprit-il** he went on; **~ des forces** to recover one's strength; **~ courage** to take new heart; **~ la route** to resume one's journey, set off again; **~ haleine** *ou* **son souffle** to get one's breath back

représentant, e [ʀəpʀezɑ̃tɑ̃, -ɑ̃t] *nm/f* representative

représentation [ʀəpʀezɑ̃tasjɔ̃] *nf* representation; (*spectacle*) performance

représenter [ʀəpʀezɑ̃te] /1/ *vt* to represent; (*donner: pièce, opéra*) to perform; **se représenter** *vt* (*se figurer*) to imagine

répression [ʀepʀesjɔ̃] *nf* repression

réprimer [ʀepʀime] /1/ *vt* (*émotions*) to suppress; (*peuple etc*) repress

repris, e [ʀəpʀi, -iz] *pp de* **reprendre** ▷ *nm*: **~ de justice** ex-prisoner, ex-convict

reprise [ʀəpʀiz] *nf* (*recommencement*) resumption; (*économique*) recovery; (*TV*) repeat; (*Comm*) trade-in, part exchange; (*raccommodage*) mend; **à plusieurs ~s** on several occasions

repriser [ʀəpʀize] /1/ *vt* (*chaussette, lainage*) to darn; (*tissu*) to mend

reproche [ʀəpʀɔʃ] *nm* (*remontrance*) reproach; **faire des ~s à qn** to reproach sb; **sans ~(s)** beyond *ou* above reproach; **reprocher** /1/ *vt*: **reprocher qch à qn** to reproach *ou* blame sb for sth; **reprocher qch à** (*machine, théorie*) to have sth against

reproduction [ʀəpʀɔdyksjɔ̃] *nf* reproduction

reproduire [ʀəpʀɔdɥiʀ] /38/ *vt* to reproduce; **se reproduire** *vi* (*Bio*) to reproduce; (*recommencer*) to recur, re-occur

reptile [ʀɛptil] *nm* reptile

république [ʀepyblik] *nf* republic

répugnant, e [ʀepyɲɑ̃, -ɑ̃t] *adj* repulsive

répugner [ʀepyɲe] /1/: **~ à** *vt*: **~ à qn** to repel *ou* disgust sb; **~ à faire** to be loath *ou* reluctant to do

réputation [ʀepytasjɔ̃] *nf* reputation; **réputé, e** *adj* renowned

requérir [ʀəkeʀiʀ] /21/ *vt* (*nécessiter*) to require, call for

requête [ʀəkɛt] *nf* request

requin [ʀəkɛ̃] *nm* shark

requis, e [ʀəki, -iz] *adj* required

RER *sigle m* (= *Réseau express régional*) *Greater Paris high-speed train service*

rescapé, e [ʀɛskape] *nm/f* survivor

rescousse [ʀɛskus] *nf*: **aller à la ~ de qn** to go to sb's aid *ou* rescue

réseau, x [ʀezo] *nm* network; **~ social** social network

réseautage [ʀezotaʒ] *nm* social networking

réservation [RezɛRvasjõ] *nf* reservation; booking

réserve [RezɛRv] *nf* (*retenue*) reserve; (*entrepôt*) storeroom; (*restriction, aussi: d'Indiens*) reservation; (*de pêche, chasse*) preserve; **de ~** (*provisions etc*) in reserve

réservé, e [RezɛRve] *adj* reserved; (*chasse, pêche*) private

réserver [RezɛRve] /1/ *vt* to reserve; (*chambre, billet etc*) to book, reserve; (*mettre de côté, garder*): **~ qch pour** *ou* **à** to keep *ou* save sth for

réservoir [RezɛRvwaR] *nm* tank

résidence [Rezidãs] *nf* residence; **~ principale/secondaire** main/second home; **~ universitaire** hall of residence (BRIT), dormitory (US); **résidentiel, le** *adj* residential; **résider** /1/ *vi*: **résider à** *ou* **dans** *ou* **en** to reside in; **résider dans** (*fig*) to lie in

résidu [Rezidy] *nm* residue *no pl*

résigner [Reziɲe] /1/: **se résigner** *vi*: **se ~ (à qch/à faire)** to resign o.s. (to sth/to doing)

résilier [Rezilje] /7/ *vt* to terminate

résistance [Rezistãs] *nf* resistance; (*de réchaud, bouilloire: fil*) element

résistant, e [Rezistã, -ãt] *adj* (*personne*) robust, tough; (*matériau*) strong, hard-wearing

résister [Reziste] /1/ *vi* to resist; **~ à** (*assaut, tentation*) to resist; (*matériau, plante*) to withstand; (*désobéir à*) to stand up to, oppose

résolu, e [Rezɔly] *pp de* **résoudre** ▷ *adj*: **être ~ à qch/faire** to be set upon sth/doing

résolution [Rezɔlysjõ] *nf* (*fermeté, décision*) resolution; (*d'un problème*) solution

résolvais *etc* [Rezɔlvɛ] *vb voir* **résoudre**

résonner [Rezɔne] /1/ *vi* (*cloche, pas*) to reverberate, resound; (*salle*) to be resonant

résorber [RezɔRbe] /1/: **se résorber** *vi* (*Méd*) to be resorbed; (*fig*) to be absorbed

résoudre [RezudR] /51/ *vt* to solve; **se ~ à faire** to bring o.s. to do

respect [Rɛspɛ] *nm* respect; **tenir en ~** to keep at bay; **présenter ses ~s à qn** to pay one's respects to sb; **respecter** /1/ *vt* to respect; **respectueux, -euse** *adj* respectful

respiration [RɛspiRasjõ] *nf* breathing *no pl*

respirer [RɛspiRe] /1/ *vi* to breathe; (*fig: se reposer*) to get one's breath; (: *être soulagé*) to breathe again ▷ *vt* to breathe (in), inhale; (*manifester: santé, calme etc*) to exude

resplendir [Rɛsplɑ̃diR] /2/ *vi* to shine; (*fig*): **~ (de)** to be radiant (with)

responsabilité [Rɛspõsabilite] *nf* responsibility; (*légale*) liability

responsable [Rɛspõsabl] *adj* responsible ▷ *nm/f* (*personne coupable*) person responsible; (*du ravitaillement etc*) person in charge; (*de parti, syndicat*) official; **~ de** responsible for

ressaisir [RəseziR] /2/: **se ressaisir** *vi* to regain one's self-control

ressasser [Rəsase] /1/ *vt* to keep turning over

ressemblance [Rəsãblãs] *nf* resemblance, similarity, likeness

ressemblant, e [Rəsãblã, -ãt] *adj* (*portrait*) lifelike, true to life

ressembler [Rəsãble] /1/: **~ à** *vt* to be like, resemble; (*visuellement*) to look like; **se ressembler** *vi* to be (*ou* look) alike

ressentiment [Rəsãtimã] *nm* resentment

ressentir [RəsãtiR] /16/ *vt* to feel; **se ~ de** to feel (*ou* show) the effects of

resserrer [RəseRe] /1/ *vt* (*nœud, boulon*) to tighten (up); (*fig: liens*) to strengthen

resservir [RəseRviR] /14/ *vi* to do *ou* serve again; **~ qn (d'un plat)** to give sb a second helping (of a dish); **se ~ de** (*plat*) to take a second helping of; (*outil etc*) to use again

ressort [RəsɔR] *nm* (*pièce*) spring; (*force morale*) spirit; **en dernier ~** as a last resort; **être du ~ de** to fall within the competence of

ressortir [RəsɔRtiR] /16/ *vi* to go (*ou* come) out (again); (*contraster*) to stand out; **~ de**: **il ressort de ceci que** it emerges from this that; **faire ~** (*fig: souligner*) to bring out

ressortissant, e [RəsɔRtisã, -ãt] *nm/f* national

ressources [RəsuRs] *nfpl* resources

ressusciter [Resysite] /1/ *vt* (*fig*) to revive, bring back ▷ *vi* to rise (from the dead)

restant, e [Rɛstã, -ãt] *adj* remaining ▷ *nm*: **le ~ (de)** the remainder (of); **un ~ de** (*de trop*) some leftover

restaurant [RɛstɔRɑ̃] *nm* restaurant

restauration [RɛstɔRasjõ] *nf* restoration; (*hôtellerie*) catering; **~ rapide** fast food

restaurer [RɛstɔRe] /1/ *vt* to restore; **se restaurer** *vi* to have something to eat

reste [Rɛst] *nm* (*restant*): **le ~ (de)** the rest (of); (*de trop*): **un ~ (de)** some leftover; **restes** *nmpl* leftovers; (*d'une cité etc, dépouille mortelle*) remains; **du ~, au ~** besides, moreover

rester [Rɛste] /1/ *vi* to stay, remain; (*subsister*) to remain, be left; (*durer*) to last, live on ▷ *vb impers*: **il reste du pain/deux œufs** there's some bread/there are two eggs left (over); **il me reste assez de temps** I have enough time left; **il ne me reste plus qu'à ...** I've just got to ...; **restons-en là** let's leave it at that

restituer [Rɛstitɥe] /1/ *vt* (*objet, somme*): **~ qch (à qn)** to return *ou* restore sth (to sb)

restreindre [RɛstRɛ̃dR] /52/ *vt* to restrict, limit

restriction [RɛstRiksjõ] *nf* restriction

résultat [Rezylta] *nm* result; (*d'élection etc*) results *pl*; **résultats** *nmpl* (*d'une enquête*) findings

résulter [Rezylte] /1/: **~ de** vt to result from, be the result of

résumé [Rezyme] nm summary, résumé; **en ~** in brief; (pour conclure) to sum up

résumer [Rezyme] /1/ vt (texte) to summarize; (récapituler) to sum up

> ▌ Attention à ne pas traduire résumer par to resume.

résurrection [RezyRɛksjɔ̃] nf resurrection

rétablir [Retablir] /2/ vt to restore, re-establish; **se rétablir** vi (guérir) to recover; (silence, calme) to return, be restored; **rétablissement** nm restoring; (guérison) recovery

retaper [Rətape] /1/ vt (maison, voiture etc) to do up; (fam: revigorer) to buck up

retard [RətaR] nm (d'une personne attendue) lateness no pl; (sur l'horaire, un programme, une échéance) delay; (fig: scolaire, mental etc) backwardness; **en ~ (de deux heures)** (two hours) late; **avoir du ~** to be late; (sur un programme) to be behind (schedule); **prendre du ~** (train, avion) to be delayed; **sans ~** without delay

retardataire [RətaRdatɛR] nm/f latecomer

retardement [RətaRdəmɑ̃]: **à ~** adj delayed action cpd; **bombe à ~** time bomb

retarder [RətaRde] /1/ vt to delay; (horloge) to put back; **~ qn (d'une heure)** to delay sb (an hour); **~ qch (de deux jours)** to put sth back (two days) ▷ vi (montre) to be slow

retenir [Rətnir] /22/ vt (garder, retarder) to keep, detain; (maintenir: objet qui glisse, colère, larmes, rire) to hold back; (se rappeler) to retain; (accepter) to accept; (fig: empêcher d'agir): **~ qn (de faire)** to hold sb back (from doing); (prélever): **~ qch (sur)** to deduct sth (from); **se retenir** vi (se raccrocher): **se ~ à** to hold onto; (se contenir): **se ~ de faire** to restrain o.s. from doing; **~ son souffle** ou **haleine** to hold one's breath

retentir [Rətɑ̃tiR] /2/ vi to ring out; **retentissant, e** adj resounding

retenu, e [Rətny] adj (place) reserved ▷ nf (prélèvement) deduction; (Scol) detention; (modération) (self-)restraint

réticence [Retisɑ̃s] nf reticence no pl, reluctance no pl; **réticent, e** adj reticent, reluctant

rétine [Retin] nf retina

retiré, e [RətiRe] adj (solitaire) secluded; (éloigné) remote

retirer [RətiRe] /1/ vt (argent, plainte) to withdraw; (vêtement) to take off, remove; (reprendre: billets) to collect, pick up; **~ qn/qch de** to take sb away from/sth out of, remove sb/sth from

retomber [Rətɔ̃be] /1/ vi (à nouveau) to fall again; (atterrir: après un saut etc) to land; (échoir): **~ sur qn** to fall on sb

rétorquer [Retɔʀke] /1/ vt: **~ (à qn) que** to retort (to sb) that

retouche [Rətuʃ] nf (sur vêtement) alteration; **retoucher** /1/ vt (photographie, tableau) to touch up; (texte, vêtement) to alter

retour [RətuR] nm return; **au ~** (en route) on the way back; **à mon/ton ~** on my/your return; **être de ~ (de)** to be back (from); **quand serons-nous de ~?** when do we get back?; **par ~ du courrier** by return of post

retourner [RətuRne] /1/ vt (dans l'autre sens: matelas, crêpe) to turn (over); (: sac, vêtement) to turn inside out; (émouvoir) to shake; (renvoyer, restituer): **~ qch à qn** to return sth to sb ▷ vi (aller, revenir): **~ quelque part/à** to go back ou return somewhere/to; **~ à** (état, activité) to return to, go back to; **se retourner** vi (tourner la tête) to turn round; **se ~ contre** (fig) to turn against

retrait [RətRɛ] nm (d'argent) withdrawal; **en ~** set back; **~ du permis (de conduire)** disqualification from driving (BRIT), revocation of driver's license (US)

retraite [RətRɛt] nf (d'une armée, Rel) retreat; (d'un employé) retirement; (revenu) (retirement) pension; **prendre sa ~** to retire; **~ anticipée** early retirement; **retraité, e** adj retired ▷ nm/f (old age) pensioner

retrancher [RətRɑ̃ʃe] /1/ vt: **~ qch de** (nombre, somme) to take ou deduct sth from; **se ~ derrière/dans** to take refuge behind/in

rétrécir [RetResiR] /2/ vt (vêtement) to take in ▷ vi to shrink; **se rétrécir** (route, vallée) to narrow

rétro [RetRo] adj inv: **la mode ~** the nostalgia vogue

rétrospectif, -ive [RetRɔspɛktif, -iv] adj retrospective ▷ nf (Art) retrospective; (Ciné) season, retrospective; **rétrospectivement** adv in retrospect

retrousser [RətRuse] /1/ vt to roll up

retrouvailles [RətRuvaj] nfpl reunion sg

retrouver [RətRuve] /1/ vt (fugitif, objet perdu) to find; (calme, santé) to regain; (revoir) to see again; (rejoindre) to meet (again), join; **se retrouver** vi to meet; (s'orienter) to find one's way; **se ~ quelque part** to find o.s. somewhere; **s'y ~** (y voir clair) to make sense of it; (rentrer dans ses frais) to break even

rétroviseur [RetRɔvizœR] nm (rear-view) mirror

retweeter [Rətwite] /1/ vt (Inform: Twitter) to retweet

réunion [Reynjɔ̃] nf (séance) meeting

réunir [ReyniR] /2/ vt (rassembler) to gather together; (inviter: amis, famille) to have round, have in; (cumuler: qualités etc) to combine; (rapprocher: ennemis) to bring together (again), reunite; (*rattacher: parties*) to join (together); **se réunir** vi (*se rencontrer*) to meet

réussi, e [Reysi] *adj* successful

réussir [Reysir] /2/ vi to succeed, be successful; (*à un examen*) to pass ▷ vt to make a success of; **~ à faire** to succeed in doing; **~ à qn** (*être bénéfique à*) to agree with sb; **réussite** nf success; (*Cartes*) patience

revaloir [Rəvalwar] /29/ vt: **je vous revaudrai cela** I'll repay you some day; (*en mal*) I'll pay you back for this

revanche [Rəvɑ̃ʃ] nf revenge; (*sport*) revenge match; **en ~** on the other hand

rêve [Rɛv] nm dream; **de ~** dream cpd; **faire un ~** to have a dream

réveil [Revɛj] nm waking up no pl; (*fig*) awakening; (*pendule*) alarm (clock); **au ~** on waking (up); **réveiller** /1/ vt (*personne*) to wake up; (*fig*) to awaken, revive; **se réveiller** vi to wake up

réveillon [Revɛjɔ̃] nm Christmas Eve; (*de la Saint-Sylvestre*) New Year's Eve; **réveillonner** /1/ vi to celebrate Christmas Eve (*ou* New Year's Eve)

révélateur, -trice [Revelatœr, -tris] *adj*: **~ (de qch)** revealing (sth)

révéler [Revele] /6/ vt to reveal; **se révéler** vi to be revealed, reveal itself; **se ~ facile/faux** to prove (to be) easy/false

revenant, e [Rəvnɑ̃, -ɑ̃t] nm/f ghost

revendeur, -euse [Rəvɑ̃dœr, -øz] nm/f (*détaillant*) retailer; (*de drogue*) (drug-)dealer

revendication [Rəvɑ̃dikasjɔ̃] nf claim, demand

revendiquer [Rəvɑ̃dike] /1/ vt to claim, demand; (*responsabilité*) to claim

revendre [Rəvɑ̃dr] /41/ vt (*d'occasion*) to resell; (*détailler*) to sell; **à ~** (*en abondance*) to spare

revenir [Rəvnir] /22/ vi to come back; **faire ~** (*Culin*) to brown; **~ cher/à 100 euros** (*à qn*) to cost (sb) a lot/100 euros; **~ à** (*reprendre: études, projet*) to return to, go back to; (*équivaloir à*) to amount to; **~ à qn** (*part, honneur*) to go to sb, be sb's; (*souvenir, nom*) to come back to sb; **~ sur** (*question, sujet*) to go back over; (*engagement*) to go back on; **~ à soi** to come round; **je n'en reviens pas** I can't get over it; **~ sur ses pas** to retrace one's steps; **cela revient à dire que/au même** it amounts to saying that/to the same thing

revenu [Rəvny] nm income; **revenus** nmpl income sg

rêver [Reve] /1/ vi, vt to dream; **~ de qch/de faire** to dream of sth/of doing; **~ à** to dream of

réverbère [Reverber] nm street lamp *ou* light; **réverbérer** /6/ vt to reflect

revers [Rəver] nm (*de feuille, main*) back; (*d'étoffe*) wrong side; (*de pièce, médaille*) back,

reverse; (*Tennis, Ping-Pong*) backhand; (*de veston*) lapel; (*fig: échec*) setback

revêtement [Rəvɛtmɑ̃] nm (*des sols*) flooring; (*de chaussée*) surface

revêtir [Rəvetir] /20/ vt (*habit*) to don, put on; (*prendre: importance, apparence*) to take on; **~ qch de** to cover sth with

rêveur, -euse [Revœr, -øz] *adj* dreamy ▷ nm/f dreamer

revient [Rəvjɛ̃] vb voir **revenir**

revigorer [Rəvigore] /1/ vt (*air frais*) to invigorate, brace up; (*repas, boisson*) to revive, buck up

revirement [Rəvirmɑ̃] nm change of mind; (*d'une situation*) reversal

réviser [Revize] /1/ vt to revise; (*machine, installation, moteur*) to overhaul, service

révision [Revizjɔ̃] nf revision; (*de voiture*) servicing no pl

revivre [Rəvivr] /46/ vi (*reprendre des forces*) to come alive again ▷ vt (*épreuve, moment*) to relive

revoir [Rəvwar] /30/ vt to see again ▷ nm: **au ~** goodbye

révoltant, e [Revoltɑ̃, -ɑ̃t] *adj* revolting, appalling

révolte [Revolt] nf rebellion, revolt

révolter [Revolte] /1/ vt to revolt; **se révolter** vi; **se ~ (contre)** to rebel (against)

révolu, e [Revoly] *adj* past; (*Admin*): **âgé de 18 ans ~s** over 18 years of age

révolution [Revolysjɔ̃] nf revolution; **révolutionnaire** adj, nm/f revolutionary

revolver [Revolver] nm gun; (*à barillet*) revolver

révoquer [Revoke] /1/ vt (*fonctionnaire*) to dismiss; (*arrêt, contrat*) to revoke

revu, e [Rəvy] pp de **revoir** ▷ nf review; (*périodique*) review, magazine; (*de music-hall*) variety show; **passer en ~** (*mentalement*) to go through

rez-de-chaussée [Redʃose] nm inv ground floor

RF sigle f = **République française**

Rhin [Rɛ̃] nm: **le ~** the Rhine

rhinocéros [Rinoseros] nm rhinoceros

Rhône [Ron] nm: **le ~** the Rhone

rhubarbe [Rybarb] nf rhubarb

rhum [Rom] nm rum

rhumatisme [Rymatism] nm rheumatism no pl

rhume [Rym] nm cold; **~ de cerveau** head cold; **le ~ des foins** hay fever

ricaner [Rikane] /1/ vi (*avec méchanceté*) to snigger; (*bêtement, avec gêne*) to giggle

riche [Riʃ] *adj* rich; (*personne, pays*) rich, wealthy; **~ en** rich in; **richesse** nf wealth; (*fig: de sol, musée etc*) richness; **richesses** nfpl (*ressources, argent*) wealth sg; (*fig: trésors*) treasures

ricochet [Rikoʃe] nm: **faire des ~s** to skip stones

ride [ʀid] nf wrinkle
rideau, x [ʀido] nm curtain; **~ de fer** (lit) metal shutter
rider [ʀide] /1/ vt to wrinkle; **se rider** vi to become wrinkled
ridicule [ʀidikyl] adj ridiculous ▷ nm: **le ~** ridicule; **ridiculiser** /1/ vt to ridicule; **se ridiculiser** vi to make a fool of o.s.

○ **MOT-CLÉ**

rien [ʀjɛ̃] pron **1** : (ne) ... **rien** nothing; (tournure négative) anything; **qu'est-ce que vous avez? — rien** what have you got? — nothing; **il n'a rien dit/fait** he said/did nothing, he hasn't said/done anything; **n'avoir peur de rien** to be afraid ou frightened of nothing, not to be afraid ou frightened of anything; **il n'a rien** (n'est pas blessé) he's all right; **ça ne fait rien** it doesn't matter
2 (quelque chose): **a-t-il jamais rien fait pour nous?** has he ever done anything for us?
3 : **rien de** : **rien d'intéressant** nothing interesting; **rien d'autre** nothing else; **rien du tout** nothing at all
4 : **rien que** just, only; nothing but; **rien que pour lui faire plaisir** only ou just to please him; **rien que la vérité** nothing but the truth; **rien que cela** that alone
▶ excl: **de rien!** not at all!
▶ nm: **un petit rien** (cadeau) a little something; **des riens** trivia pl; **un rien de** a hint of; **en un rien de temps** in no time at all

rieur, -euse [ʀjœʀ, -øz] adj cheerful
rigide [ʀiʒid] adj stiff; (fig) rigid; (moralement) strict
rigoler [ʀiɡɔle] /1/ vi (rire) to laugh; (s'amuser) to have (some) fun; (plaisanter) to be joking ou kidding; **rigolo, rigolote** adj funny ▷ nm/f (péj) comic, phoney
rigoureusement [ʀiɡuʀøzmɑ̃] adv rigorously
rigoureux, -euse [ʀiɡuʀø, -øz] adj rigorous; (climat, châtiment) harsh, severe
rigueur [ʀiɡœʀ] nf rigour; **"tenue de soirée de ~"** "evening dress (to be worn)"; **à la ~** at a pinch; **tenir ~ à qn de qch** to hold sth against sb
rillettes [ʀijɛt] nfpl ≈ potted meat sg (made from pork or goose)
rime [ʀim] nf rhyme
rinçage [ʀɛ̃saʒ] nm rinsing (out); (opération) rinse
rincer [ʀɛ̃se] /3/ vt to rinse; (récipient) to rinse out
ringard, e [ʀɛ̃ɡaʀ, -aʀd] adj old-fashioned
riposter [ʀipɔste] /1/ vi to retaliate ▷ vt: **~ que** to retort that

rire [ʀiʀ] /36/ vi to laugh; (se divertir) to have fun ▷ nm laugh; **le ~** laughter; **~ de** to laugh at; **pour ~** (pas sérieusement) for a joke ou a laugh
risible [ʀizibl] adj laughable
risque [ʀisk] nm risk; **le ~** danger; **à ses ~s et périls** at his own risk; **risqué, e** adj risky; (plaisanterie) risqué, daring; **risquer** /1/ vt to risk; (allusion, question) to venture, hazard; **se risquer** vi: **ça ne risque rien** it's quite safe; **il risque de se tuer** he could get ou risks getting himself killed; **ce qui risque de se produire** what might ou could well happen; **il ne risque pas de recommencer** there's no chance of him doing that again; **se risquer à faire** (tenter) to dare to do
rissoler [ʀisɔle] /1/ vi, vt: **(faire) ~** to brown
ristourne [ʀistuʀn] nf discount
rite [ʀit] nm rite; (fig) ritual
rivage [ʀivaʒ] nm shore
rival, e, -aux [ʀival, -o] adj, nm/f rival; **rivaliser** /1/ vi: **rivaliser avec** to rival, vie with; **rivalité** nf rivalry
rive [ʀiv] nf shore; (de fleuve) bank; **riverain, e** nm/f riverside (ou lakeside) resident; (d'une route) local ou roadside resident
rivière [ʀivjɛʀ] nf river
riz [ʀi] nm rice; **rizière** nf paddy field
RMI sigle m (= revenu minimum d'insertion) ≈ income support (BRIT), ≈ welfare (US)
RN sigle f = **route nationale**
robe [ʀɔb] nf dress; (de juge, d'ecclésiastique) robe; (pelage) coat; **~ de soirée/de mariée** evening/wedding dress; **~ de chambre** dressing gown
robinet [ʀɔbinɛ] nm tap (BRIT), faucet (US)
robot [ʀɔbo] nm robot; **~ de cuisine** food processor
robuste [ʀɔbyst] adj robust, sturdy; **robustesse** nf robustness, sturdiness
roc [ʀɔk] nm rock
rocade [ʀɔkad] nf bypass
rocaille [ʀɔkaj] nf loose stones pl; (jardin) rockery, rock garden
roche [ʀɔʃ] nf rock
rocher [ʀɔʃe] nm rock
rocheux, -euse [ʀɔʃø, -øz] adj rocky
rodage [ʀɔdaʒ] nm: **en ~** running ou breaking in
rôder [ʀode] /1/ vi to roam ou wander about; (de façon suspecte) to lurk (about ou around); **rôdeur, -euse** nm/f prowler
rogne [ʀɔɲ] nf: **être en ~** to be mad ou in a temper
rogner [ʀɔɲe] /1/ vt to trim; **~ sur** (fig) to cut down ou back on
rognons [ʀɔɲɔ̃] nmpl kidneys
roi [ʀwa] nm king; **le jour** ou **la fête des R~s** Twelfth Night
rôle [ʀol] nm role; part
rollers [ʀɔlœʀ] nmpl Rollerblades®

romain, e [ʀɔmɛ̃, -ɛn] *adj* Roman ▷ *nm/f*:
R~, e Roman

roman, e [ʀɔmã, -an] *adj* (*Archit*)
Romanesque ▷ *nm* novel; **~ policier**
detective novel

romancer [ʀɔmãse] /3/ *vt* to romanticize;
romancier, -ière *nm/f* novelist;
romanesque *adj* (*amours, aventures*)
storybook *cpd*; (*sentimental: personne*)
romantic

roman-feuilleton [ʀɔmãfœjtɔ̃] *nm*
serialized novel

romanichel, le [ʀɔmaniʃɛl] *nm/f* gipsy

romantique [ʀɔmãtik] *adj* romantic

romarin [ʀɔmaʀɛ̃] *nm* rosemary

Rome [ʀɔm] *n* Rome

rompre [ʀɔ̃pʀ] /41/ *vt* to break; (*entretien,
fiançailles*) to break off ▷ *vi* (*fiancés*) to break
it off; **se rompre** *vi* to break; **rompu, e** *adj*
(*fourbu*) exhausted

ronce [ʀɔ̃s] *nf* bramble branch; **ronces** *nfpl*
brambles

ronchonner [ʀɔ̃ʃɔne] /1/ *vi* (*fam*) to grouse,
grouch

rond, e [ʀɔ̃, ʀɔ̃d] *adj* round; (*joues, mollets*)
well-rounded; (*fam: ivre*) tight ▷ *nm* (*cercle*)
ring; (*fam: sou*): **je n'ai plus un ~** I haven't a
penny left ▷ *nf* (*gén: de surveillance*) rounds
pl, patrol; (*danse*) round (*dance*); (*Mus*)
semibreve (*BRIT*), whole note (*US*); **en ~**
(*s'asseoir, danser*) in a ring; **à la ~e** (*alentour*):
à 10 km à la ~e for 10 km round; **rondelet,
te** *adj* plump

rondelle [ʀɔ̃dɛl] *nf* (*Tech*) washer; (*tranche*)
slice, round

rond-point [ʀɔ̃pwɛ̃] *nm* roundabout

ronflement [ʀɔ̃fləmã] *nm* snore

ronfler [ʀɔ̃fle] /1/ *vi* to snore; (*moteur, poêle*)
to hum

ronger [ʀɔ̃ʒe] /3/ *vt* to gnaw (at); (*vers,
rouille*) to eat into; **se ~ les sangs** to worry
o.s. sick; **se ~ les ongles** to bite one's
nails; **rongeur, -euse** *nm/f* rodent

ronronner [ʀɔ̃ʀɔne] /1/ *vi* to purr

rosbif [ʀɔsbif] *nm*: **du ~** roasting beef; (*cuit*)
roast beef

rose [ʀoz] *nf* rose ▷ *adj* pink; **~ bonbon** *adj
inv* candy pink

rosé, e [ʀoze] *adj* pinkish; (*vin*) **~** rosé
(wine)

roseau, x [ʀozo] *nm* reed

rosée [ʀoze] *nf* dew

rosier [ʀozje] *nm* rosebush, rose tree

rossignol [ʀɔsiɲɔl] *nm* (*Zool*) nightingale

rotation [ʀɔtasjɔ̃] *nf* rotation

roter [ʀɔte] /1/ *vi* (*fam*) to burp, belch

rôti [ʀoti] *nm*: **du ~** roasting meat; (*cuit*)
roast meat; **un ~ de bœuf/porc** a joint of
beef/pork

rotin [ʀɔtɛ̃] *nm* rattan (cane); **fauteuil en ~**
cane (arm)chair

rôtir [ʀotiʀ] /2/ *vt* (*aussi*: **faire ~**) to roast
▷ *vi* to roast; **rôtisserie** *nf* (*restaurant*)
steakhouse; (*traiteur*) roast meat shop;
rôtissoire *nf* (roasting) spit

rotule [ʀɔtyl] *nf* kneecap

rouage [ʀwaʒ] *nm* cog(wheel), gearwheel;
les ~s de l'État the wheels of State

roue [ʀu] *nf* wheel; **~ de secours** spare
wheel

rouer [ʀwe] /1/ *vt*: **~ qn de coups** to give sb
a thrashing

rouge [ʀuʒ] *adj, nm/f* red ▷ *nm* red; (*vin*) **~**
red wine; **passer au ~** (*signal*) to go red;
(*automobiliste*) to go through a red light;
sur la liste ~ ex-directory (*BRIT*), unlisted
(*US*); **~ à joue** blusher; **~ (à lèvres)** lipstick;
rouge-gorge *nm* robin (redbreast)

rougeole [ʀuʒɔl] *nf* measles *sg*

rougeoyer [ʀuʒwaje] /8/ *vi* to glow red

rouget [ʀuʒɛ] *nm* mullet

rougeur [ʀuʒœʀ] *nf* redness; **rougeurs** *nfpl*
(*Méd*) red blotches

rougir [ʀuʒiʀ] /2/ *vi* to turn red; (*de honte,
timidité*) to blush, flush; (*de plaisir, colère*)
to flush

rouille [ʀuj] *nf* rust; **rouillé, e** *adj* rusty;
rouiller /1/ *vt* to rust ▷ *vi* to rust, go rusty

roulant, e [ʀulã, -ãt] *adj* (*meuble*) on
wheels; (*surface, trottoir, tapis*) moving;
escalier ~ escalator

rouleau, x [ʀulo] *nm* roll; (*à mise en plis,
à peinture, vague*) roller; **~ à pâtisserie**
rolling pin

roulement [ʀulmã] *nm* (*bruit*) rumbling
no pl, rumble; (*rotation*) rotation; **par ~**
on a rota (*BRIT*) *ou* rotation (*US*) basis;
~ (à billes) ball bearings *pl*; **~ de tambour**
drum roll

rouler [ʀule] /1/ *vt* to roll; (*papier, tapis*)
to roll up; (*Culin: pâte*) to roll out; (*fam:
duper*) to do, con ▷ *vi* (*bille, boule*) to roll;
(*voiture, train*) to go, run; (*automobiliste*) to
drive; (*cycliste*) to ride; (*bateau*) to roll; **se
~ dans** (*boue*) to roll in; (*couverture*) to roll
o.s. (up) in

roulette [ʀulɛt] *nf* (*de table, fauteuil*) castor;
(*de dentiste*) drill; (*jeu*): **la ~** roulette; **à ~s** on
castors; **ça a marché comme sur des ~s**
(*fam*) it went off very smoothly

roulotte [ʀulɔt] *nf* caravan

roumain, e [ʀumɛ̃, -ɛn] *adj* Rumanian
▷ *nm/f*: R~, e Rumanian

Roumanie [ʀumani] *nf*: **la ~** Rumania

rouquin, e [ʀukɛ̃, -in] *nm/f* (*péj*) redhead

rouspéter [ʀuspete] /6/ *vi* (*fam*) to moan

rousse [ʀus] *adj f voir* **roux**

roussir [ʀusiʀ] /2/ *vt* to scorch ▷ *vi* (*Culin*):
faire ~ to brown

route [ʀut] *nf* road; (*fig: chemin*) way,
(*itinéraire, parcours*) route; (*fig: voie*) road,
path; **il y a trois heures de ~** it's a three-
hour ride *ou* journey; **en ~** on the way; **en ~!**

let's go!; **mettre en ~** to start up; **se mettre en ~** to set off; **~ nationale** ≈ A-road (BRIT), ≈ state highway (US)

routeur [ʀutœʀ] nm (Inform) router

routier, -ière [ʀutje, -jɛʀ] adj road cpd ▷ nm (camionneur) (long-distance) lorry (BRIT) ou truck (US) driver; (restaurant) ≈ transport café (BRIT), ≈ truck stop (US)

routine [ʀutin] nf routine; **routinier, -ière** [ʀutinje, -jɛʀ] adj (péj: travail) humdrum; (: personne) addicted to routine

rouvrir [ʀuvʀiʀ] /18/ vt, vi to reopen, open again; **se rouvrir** vi to open up again

roux, rousse [ʀu, ʀus] adj red; (personne) red-haired ▷ nm/f redhead

royal, e, -aux [ʀwajal, -o] adj royal; (fig) fit for a king

royaume [ʀwajom] nm kingdom; (fig) realm

Royaume-Uni [ʀwajomyni] nm: **le ~** the United Kingdom

royauté [ʀwajote] nf (régime) monarchy

ruban [ʀybɑ̃] nm ribbon; **~ adhésif** adhesive tape

rubéole [ʀybeɔl] nf German measles sg, rubella

rubis [ʀybi] nm ruby

rubrique [ʀybʀik] nf (titre, catégorie) heading; (Presse: article) column

ruche [ʀyʃ] nf hive

rude [ʀyd] adj (barbe, toile) rough; (métier, tâche) hard, tough; (climat) severe, harsh; (bourru) harsh, rough; (fruste: manières) rugged, tough; (fam: fameux) jolly good; **rudement** adv (très) terribly

rudimentaire [ʀydimɑ̃tɛʀ] adj rudimentary, basic

rudiments [ʀydimɑ̃] nmpl: **avoir des ~ d'anglais** to have a smattering of English

rue [ʀy] nf street

ruée [ʀɥe] nf rush

ruelle [ʀɥɛl] nf alley(way)

ruer [ʀɥe] /1/ vi (cheval) to kick out; **se ruer** vi: **se ~ sur** to pounce on; **se ~ vers/dans/ hors de** to rush ou dash towards/into/ out of

rugby [ʀygbi] nm rugby (football)

rugir [ʀyʒiʀ] /2/ vi to roar

rugueux, -euse [ʀygø, -øz] adj rough

ruine [ʀɥin] nf ruin; **ruiner** /1/ vt to ruin; **ruineux, -euse** adj ruinous

ruisseau, x [ʀɥiso] nm stream, brook

ruisseler [ʀɥisle] /4/ vi to stream

rumeur [ʀymœʀ] nf (bruit confus) rumbling; (nouvelle) rumour

ruminer [ʀymine] /1/ vt (herbe) to ruminate; (fig) to ruminate on ou over, chew over

rupture [ʀyptyʀ] nf (de négociations etc) breakdown; (de contrat) breach; (dans continuité) break; (séparation, désunion) break-up, split

rural, e, -aux [ʀyʀal, -o] adj rural, country cpd

ruse [ʀyz] nf: **la ~** cunning, craftiness; (pour tromper) trickery; **une ~** a trick, a ruse; **rusé, e** adj cunning, crafty

russe [ʀys] adj Russian ▷ nm (Ling) Russian ▷ nm/f: **R~** Russian

Russie [ʀysi] nf: **la ~** Russia

rustine [ʀystin] nf repair patch (for bicycle inner tube)

rustique [ʀystik] adj rustic

rythme [ʀitm] nm rhythm; (vitesse) rate (: de la vie) pace, tempo; **rythmé, e** adj rhythmic(al)

S

s' [s] pron voir **se**

sa [sa] adj poss voir **son¹**

sable [sablə] nm sand

sablé [sable] nm shortbread biscuit

sabler [sable] /1/ vt (contre le verglas) to grit; **~ le champagne** to drink champagne

sabot [sabo] nm clog; (de cheval, bœuf) hoof; **~ de frein** brake shoe

saboter [sabote] /1/ vt (travail, morceau de musique) to botch, make a mess of; (machine, installation, négociation etc) to sabotage

sac [sak] nm bag; (à charbon etc) sack; **mettre à ~** to sack; **~ à provisions/de voyage** shopping/travelling bag; **~ de couchage** sleeping bag; **~ à dos** rucksack; **~ à main** handbag

saccadé, e [sakade] adj jerky; (respiration) spasmodic

saccager [sakaʒe] /3/ vt (piller) to sack; (dévaster) to create havoc in

saccharine [sakarin] nf saccharin(e)

sachet [saʃɛ] nm (small) bag; (de lavande, poudre, shampo(o)ing) sachet; **~ de thé** tea bag; **du potage en ~** packet soup

sacoche [sakɔʃ] nf (gén) bag; (de bicyclette) saddlebag

sacré, e [sakre] adj sacred; (fam: satané) blasted; (: fameux): **un ~ ...** a heck of a ...

sacrement [sakrəmã] nm sacrament

sacrifice [sakrifis] nm sacrifice; **sacrifier** /7/ vt to sacrifice

sacristie [sakristi] nf sacristy; (culte protestant) vestry

sadique [sadik] adj sadistic

safran [safrã] nm saffron

sage [saʒ] adj wise; (enfant) good

sage-femme [saʒfam] nf midwife

sagesse [saʒɛs] nf wisdom

Sagittaire [saʒitɛr] nm: **le ~** Sagittarius

Sahara [saara] nm: **le ~** the Sahara (Desert)

saignant, e [sɛɲɑ̃, -ɑ̃t] adj (viande) rare

saigner [seɲe] /1/ vi to bleed ▷ vt to bleed; (animal) to bleed to death; **~ du nez** to have a nosebleed

saillir [sajir] /13/ vi to project, stick out; (veine, muscle) to bulge

sain, e [sɛ̃, sɛn] adj healthy; **~ et sauf** safe and sound, unharmed; **~ d'esprit** sound in mind, sane

saindoux [sɛ̃du] nm lard

saint, e [sɛ̃, sɛ̃t] adj holy ▷ nm/f saint; **la S~e Vierge** the Blessed Virgin

Saint-Esprit [sɛ̃tɛspri] nm: **le ~** the Holy Spirit ou Ghost

sainteté [sɛ̃tate] nf holiness

Saint-Sylvestre [sɛ̃silvɛstr] nf: **la ~** New Year's Eve

sais etc [sɛ] vb voir **savoir**

saisie [sezi] nf seizure; **~ (de données)** (data) capture

saisir [sezir] /2/ vt to take hold of, grab; (fig: occasion) to seize; (comprendre) to grasp; (entendre) to get, catch; (Inform) to capture; (Culin) to fry quickly; (Jur: biens, publication) to seize; **saisissant, e** adj startling, striking

saison [sɛzɔ̃] nf season; **haute/basse/morte ~** high/low/slack season; **saisonnier, -ière** adj seasonal

salade [salad] nf (Bot) lettuce etc (generic term), (Culin: green) salad; (fam: confusion) tangle, muddle; **~ composée** mixed salad; **~ de fruits** fruit salad; **~ verte** green salad; **saladier** nm (salad) bowl

salaire [salɛr] nm (annuel, mensuel) salary; (hebdomadaire, journalier) pay, wages pl; **~ minimum interprofessionnel de croissance** index-linked guaranteed minimum wage

salarié, e [salarje] nm/f salaried employee, wage-earner

salaud [salo] nm (fam!) sod (!), bastard (!)

sale [sal] adj dirty, filthy; (fig: mauvais) nasty

salé, e [sale] adj (liquide, saveur, mer, goût) salty; (Culin: amandes, beurre etc) salted; (: gâteaux) savoury; (fig: grivois) spicy; (: note, facture) steep

saler [sale] /1/ vt to salt

saleté [salte] nf (état) dirtiness; (crasse) dirt, filth; (tache etc) dirt no pl; (fig: tour) filthy trick; (: chose sans valeur) rubbish no pl; (: obscénité) filth no pl

salière [saljɛr] nf saltcellar

salir [salir] /2/ vt to (make) dirty; (fig) to soil the reputation of; **se salir** vi to get dirty; **salissant, e** adj (tissu) which shows the dirt; (métier) dirty, messy

salle [sal] nf room; (d'hôpital) ward; (de restaurant) dining room; (d'un cinéma) auditorium (: public) audience; **~ d'attente** waiting room; **~ de bain(s)** bathroom; **~ de**

classe classroom; **~ de concert** concert hall; **~ d'eau** shower-room; **~ d'embarquement** (à l'aéroport) departure lounge; **~ de jeux** (pour enfants) playroom; **~ à manger** dining room; **~ des professeurs** staffroom; **~ de séjour** living room; **~ des ventes** saleroom

salon [salɔ̃] nm lounge, sitting room; (mobilier) lounge suite; (exposition) exhibition, show; **~ de coiffure** hairdressing salon; **~ de thé** tearoom

salope [salɔp] nf (fam!) bitch (!); **saloperie** nf (fam!: action) dirty trick; (: chose sans valeur) rubbish no pl

salopette [salɔpɛt] nf dungarees pl; (d'ouvrier) overall(s)

salsifis [salsifi] nm salsify

salubre [salybʀ] adj healthy, salubrious

saluer [salɥe] /1/ vt (pour dire bonjour, fig) to greet; (pour dire au revoir) to take one's leave; (Mil) to salute

salut [saly] nm (sauvegarde) safety; (Rel) salvation; (geste) wave; (parole) greeting; (Mil) salute ▷ excl (fam: pour dire bonjour) hi (there); (: pour dire au revoir) see you!, bye!

salutations [salytasjɔ̃] nfpl greetings; **recevez mes ~ distinguées** ou **respectueuses** yours faithfully

samedi [samdi] nm Saturday

SAMU [samy] sigle m (= service d'assistance médicale d'urgence) ≈ ambulance (service) (BRIT), ≈ paramedics (US)

sanction [sɑ̃ksjɔ̃] nf sanction; **sanctionner** /1/ vt (loi, usage) to sanction; (punir) to punish

sandale [sɑ̃dal] nf sandal

sandwich [sɑ̃dwitʃ] nm sandwich

sang [sɑ̃] nm blood; **en ~** covered in blood; **se faire du mauvais ~** to fret, get in a state; **sang-froid** nm calm, sangfroid; **de sang-froid** in cold blood; **sanglant, e** adj bloody

sangle [sɑ̃gl] nf strap

sanglier [sɑ̃glije] nm (wild) boar

sanglot [sɑ̃glo] nm sob; **sangloter** /1/ vi to sob

sangsue [sɑ̃sy] nf leech

sanguin, e [sɑ̃gɛ̃, -in] adj blood cpd

sanitaire [sanitɛʀ] adj health cpd; **sanitaires** nmpl (salle de bain et w.-c.) bathroom sg

sans [sɑ̃] prép without; **~ qu'il s'en aperçoive** without him ou his noticing; **un pull ~ manches** a sleeveless jumper; **~ faute** without fail; **~ arrêt** without a break; **~ ça** (fam) otherwise; **sans-abri** nmpl homeless; **sans-emploi** nm/f inv unemployed person; **les sans-emploi** the unemployed; **sans-gêne** adj inv inconsiderate

santé [sɑ̃te] nf health; **être en bonne ~** to be in good health; **boire à la ~ de qn**

to drink (to) sb's health; **à ta** ou **votre ~!** cheers!

saoudien, ne [saudjɛ̃, -ɛn] adj Saudi (Arabian) ▷ nm/f: **S~, ne** Saudi (Arabian)

saoul, e [su, sul] adj = **soûl**

saper [sape] /1/ vt to undermine, sap

sapeur-pompier [sapœʀpɔ̃pje] nm firefighter

saphir [safiʀ] nm sapphire

sapin [sapɛ̃] nm fir (tree); (bois) fir; **~ de Noël** Christmas tree

sarcastique [saʀkastik] adj sarcastic

Sardaigne [saʀdɛɲ] nf: **la ~** Sardinia

sardine [saʀdin] nf sardine

SARL [saʀl] sigle f (= société à responsabilité limitée) ≈ plc (BRIT), ≈ Inc. (US)

sarrasin [saʀazɛ̃] nm buckwheat

satané, e [satane] adj (fam) confounded

satellite [satelit] nm satellite

satin [satɛ̃] nm satin

satire [satiʀ] nf satire; **satirique** adj satirical

satisfaction [satisfaksjɔ̃] nf satisfaction

satisfaire [satisfɛʀ] /60/ vt to satisfy; **~ à** (revendications, conditions) to meet; **satisfaisant, e** adj (acceptable) satisfactory; **satisfait, e** adj satisfied; **satisfait de** happy ou satisfied with

saturer [satyʀe] /1/ vt to saturate

sauce [sos] nf sauce; (avec un rôti) gravy; **~ tomate** tomato sauce; **saucière** nf sauceboat

saucisse [sosis] nf sausage

saucisson [sosisɔ̃] nm (slicing) sausage

sauf¹ [sof] prép except; **~ si** (à moins que) unless; **~ avis contraire** unless you hear to the contrary; **~ erreur** if I'm not mistaken

sauf², sauve [sof, sov] adj unharmed, unhurt; (fig: honneur) intact, saved; **laisser la vie sauve à qn** to spare sb's life

sauge [soʒ] nf sage

saugrenu, e [sogʀəny] adj preposterous

saule [sol] nm willow (tree)

saumon [somɔ̃] nm salmon inv

saupoudrer [sopudʀe] /1/ vt: **~ qch de** to sprinkle sth with

saur [sɔʀ] adj m: **hareng ~** smoked ou red herring, kipper

saut [so] nm jump; (discipline sportive) jumping; **faire un ~ chez qn** to pop over to sb's (place); **~ en hauteur/longueur** high/ long jump; **~ à la perche** pole vaulting; **~ à l'élastique** bungee jumping; **~ périlleux** somersault

sauter [sote] /1/ vi to jump, leap; (exploser) to blow up, explode; (: fusibles) to blow; (se détacher) to pop out (ou off) ▷ vt to jump (over), leap (over); (fig: omettre) to skip, miss (out); **faire ~** (Culin) to sauté; **~ à la corde** to skip; **~ au cou de qn** to fly into sb's arms; **~ sur une occasion** to jump

at an opportunity; **~ aux yeux** to be quite
obvious

sauterelle [sotʀɛl] *nf* grasshopper

sautiller [sotije] /1/ *vi (oiseau)* to hop;
(enfant) to skip

sauvage [sovaʒ] *adj (gén)* wild; *(peuplade)*
savage; *(farouche)* unsociable; *(barbare)*
wild, savage; *(non officiel)* unauthorized,
unofficial; **faire du camping ~** to camp in
the wild ▷ *nm/f* savage; *(timide)* unsociable
type

sauve [sov] *adj f* voir **sauf²**

sauvegarde [sovgaʀd] *nf* safeguard;
(Inform) backup; **sauvegarder** /1/ *vt* to
safeguard; *(Inform: enregistrer)* to save;
(: copier) to back up

sauve-qui-peut [sovkipø] *excl* run for
your life!

sauver [sove] /1/ *vt* to save; *(porter secours à)*
to rescue; *(récupérer)* to salvage, rescue; **se
sauver** *vi (s'enfuir)* to run away; *(fam: partir)*
to be off; **sauvetage** *nm* rescue; **sauveteur**
nm rescuer; **sauvette: à la sauvette** *adv (se
marier etc)* hastily, hurriedly; **sauveur** *nm*
saviour (BRIT), savior (US)

savant, e [savɑ̃, -ɑ̃t] *adj* scholarly, learned
▷ *nm* scientist

saveur [savœʀ] *nf* flavour; *(fig)* savour

savoir [savwaʀ] /32/ *vt* to know, *(être
capable de)*: **il sait nager** he can swim ▷ *nm*
knowledge; **se savoir** *vi (être connu)* to be
known; **je n'en sais rien** I (really) don't
know; **à ~ (que)** that is, namely; **faire ~ qch
à qn** to let sb know sth; **pas que je sache**
not as far as I know

savon [savɔ̃] *nm (produit)* soap; *(morceau)*
bar *ou* tablet of soap; *(fam)*: **passer un ~
à qn** to give sb a good dressing-down;
savonner /1/ *vt* to soap; **savonnette** *nf*
bar of soap

savourer [savuʀe] /1/ *vt* to savour;
savoureux, -euse *adj* tasty; *(fig: anecdote)*
spicy, juicy

saxo(phone) [saksɔ(fɔn)] *nm*
sax(ophone)

scabreux, -euse [skabʀø, -øz] *adj* risky;
(indécent) improper, shocking

scandale [skɑ̃dal] *nm* scandal; **faire un
~ (scène)** to make a scene; *(Jur)* create a
disturbance; **faire ~** to scandalize people;
scandaleux, -euse *adj* scandalous,
outrageous

scandinave [skɑ̃dinav] *adj* Scandinavian
▷ *nm/f*: **S~** Scandinavian

Scandinavie [skɑ̃dinavi] *nf*: **la ~**
Scandinavia

scarabée [skaʀabe] *nm* beetle

scarlatine [skaʀlatin] *nf* scarlet fever

scarole [skaʀɔl] *nf* endive

sceau, x [so] *nm* seal

sceller [sele] /1/ *vt* to seal

scénario [senaʀjo] *nm* scenario

scène [sɛn] *nf (gén)* scene; *(estrade, fig:
théâtre)* stage; **entrer en ~** to come on
stage; **mettre en ~** *(Théât)* to stage; *(Ciné)*
to direct; **faire une ~ (à qn)** to make a scene
(with sb); **~ de ménage** domestic fight *ou*
scene

sceptique [sɛptik] *adj* sceptical

schéma [ʃema] *nm (diagramme)*
diagram, sketch; **schématique** *adj*
diagrammatic(al), schematic; *(fig)*
oversimplified

sciatique [sjatik] *nf* sciatica

scie [si] *nf* saw

sciemment [sjamɑ̃] *adv* knowingly

science [sjɑ̃s] *nf* science; *(savoir)*
knowledge; **~s humaines/sociales** social
sciences; **~s naturelles** *(Scol)* natural
science *sg*, biology *sg*; **~s po** political
science *ou* studies *pl*; **science-fiction** *nf*
science fiction; **scientifique** *adj*
scientific ▷ *nm/f* scientist; *(étudiant)* science
student

scier [sje] /7/ *vt* to saw; *(retrancher)* to saw
off; **scierie** *nf* sawmill

scintiller [sɛ̃tije] /1/ *vi* to sparkle; *(étoile)*
to twinkle

sciure [sjyʀ] *nf*: **~ (de bois)** sawdust

sclérose [skleʀoz] *nf*: **~ en plaques (SEP)**
multiple sclerosis (MS)

scolaire [skɔlɛʀ] *adj* school *cpd*; **scolariser**
/1/ *vt* to provide with schooling *(ou*
schools)*; **scolarité** *nf* schooling

scooter [skutœʀ] *nm* (motor) scooter

score [skɔʀ] *nm* score

scorpion [skɔʀpjɔ̃] *nm (signe)*: **le S~**
Scorpio

scotch [skɔtʃ] *nm (whisky)* scotch, whisky;
Scotch® *(adhésif)* Sellotape® (BRIT), Scotch
tape® (US)

scout, e [skut] *adj, nm* scout

script [skʀipt] *nm (écriture)* printing; *(Ciné)*
(shooting) script

scrupule [skʀypyl] *nm* scruple

scruter [skʀyte] /1/ *vt* to scrutinize;
(l'obscurité) to peer into

scrutin [skʀytɛ̃] *nm (vote)* ballot; *(ensemble
des opérations)* poll

sculpter [skylte] /1/ *vt* to sculpt; *(érosion)*
to carve; **sculpteur** *nm* sculptor; **sculpture**
nf sculpture

SDF *sigle m* (= *sans domicile fixe*) homeless
person; **les ~** the homeless

⃝ MOT-CLÉ

se, s' [sə, s] *pron* **1** *(emploi réfléchi)* oneself;
(: masc) himself; *(: fém)* herself; *(: sujet
non humain)* itself; *(: pl)* themselves; **se
savonner** to soap o.s.
2 *(réciproque)* one another, each other; **ils
s'aiment** they love one another *ou* each
other

3 (*passif*): **cela se répare facilement** it is easily repaired
4 (*possessif*): **se casser la jambe/se laver les mains** to break one's leg/wash one's hands

séance [seɑ̃s] *nf* (*d'assemblée*) meeting, session; (*de tribunal*) sitting, session; (*musicale, Ciné, Théât*) performance
seau, x [so] *nm* bucket, pail
sec, sèche [sɛk, sɛʃ] *adj* dry; (*raisins, figues*) dried; (*insensible: cœur, personne*) hard, cold ▷ *nm*: **tenir au ~** to keep in a dry place ▷ *adv* hard; **je le bois ~** I drink it straight *ou* neat; **à ~** (*puits*) dried up
sécateur [sekatœʀ] *nm* secateurs *pl* (BRIT), shears *pl*
sèche [sɛʃ] *adj f voir* **sec**; **sèche-cheveux** *nm inv* hair-drier; **sèche-linge** *nm inv* tumble dryer; **sèchement** *adv* (*répliquer etc*) drily
sécher [seʃe] /6/ *vt* to dry; (*dessécher: peau, blé*) to dry (out); (: *étang*) to dry up; (*fam: classe, cours*) to skip ▷ *vi* to dry; to dry out; to dry up; (*fam: candidat*) to be stumped; **se sécher** *vi* (*après le bain*) to dry o.s.; **sécheresse** *nf* dryness; (*absence de pluie*) drought; **séchoir** *nm* drier
second, e [səɡɔ̃, -ɔ̃d] *adj* second ▷ *nm* (*assistant*) second in command; (*Navig*) first mate ▷ *nf* second; (*Scol*) ≈ year 11 (BRIT), ≈ tenth grade (US); (*Aviat, Rail etc*) second class; **voyager en ~e** to travel second-class; **secondaire** *adj* secondary; **seconder** /1/ *vt* to assist
secouer [səkwe] /1/ *vt* to shake; (*passagers*) to rock; (*traumatiser*) to shake (up)
secourir [səkuʀiʀ] /11/ *vt* (*venir en aide à*) to assist, aid; **secourisme** *nm* first aid; **secouriste** *nm/f* first-aid worker
secours *nm* help, aid, assistance ▷ *nmpl* aid *sg*; **au ~!** help!; **appeler au ~** to shout *ou* call for help; **porter ~ à qn** to give sb assistance, help sb; **les premiers ~** first aid *sg*

● **ÉQUIPES DE SECOURS**
●
● Emergency phone numbers can be dialled
● free from public phones. For the police
● ('la police') dial 17; for medical services
● ('le SAMU') dial 15; for the fire brigade
● ('les sapeurs-pompiers') dial 18.

secousse [səkus] *nf* jolt, jerk; (*électrique*) shock; (*fig: psychologique*) jolt, shock
secret, -ète [səkʀɛ, -ɛt] *adj* secret; (*fig: renfermé*) reticent, reserved ▷ *nm* secret; (*discrétion absolue*): **le ~** secrecy; **en ~** in secret, secretly; **~ professionnel** professional secrecy
secrétaire [səkʀetɛʀ] *nm/f* secretary ▷ *nm* (*meuble*) writing desk; **~ de direction** private *ou* personal secretary; **~ d'État** ≈ junior minister; **secrétariat** *nm* (*profession*) secretarial work; (*bureau*) (secretary's) office; (: *d'organisation internationale*) secretariat
secteur [sɛktœʀ] *nm* sector; (*Admin*) district; (*Élec*): **branché sur le ~** plugged into the mains (supply)
section [sɛksjɔ̃] *nf* section; (*de parcours d'autobus*) fare stage; (*Mil: unité*) platoon; **sectionner** /1/ *vt* to sever
sécu [seky] *nf* = **sécurité sociale**
sécurité [sekyʀite] *nf* (*absence de troubles*) security; (*absence de danger*) safety; **système de ~** security (*ou* safety) system; **être en ~** to be safe; **la ~ routière** road safety; **la ~ sociale** ≈ (the) Social Security (BRIT), ≈ (the) Welfare (US)
sédentaire [sedɑ̃tɛʀ] *adj* sedentary
séduction [sedyksjɔ̃] *nf* seduction; (*charme, attrait*) appeal, charm
séduire [seduiʀ] /38/ *vt* to charm; (*femme: abuser de*) to seduce; **séduisant, e** *adj* (*femme*) seductive; (*homme, offre*) very attractive
ségrégation [seɡʀeɡasjɔ̃] *nf* segregation
seigle [sɛɡl] *nm* rye
seigneur [sɛɲœʀ] *nm* lord
sein [sɛ̃] *nm* breast; (*entrailles*) womb; **au ~ de** (*équipe, institution*) within
séisme [seism] *nm* earthquake
seize [sɛz] *num* sixteen; **seizième** *num* sixteenth
séjour [seʒuʀ] *nm* stay; (*pièce*) living room; **séjourner** /1/ *vi* to stay
sel [sɛl] *nm* salt; (*fig: piquant*) spice
sélection [selɛksjɔ̃] *nf* selection; **sélectionner** /1/ *vt* to select
self [sɛlf] *nm* (*fam*) self-service
selfie [sɛlfi] *nm* selfie
self-service [sɛlfsɛʀvis] *adj* self-service ▷ *nm* self-service (restaurant)
selle [sɛl] *nf* saddle; **selles** *nfpl* (*Méd*) stools; **seller** /1/ *vt* to saddle
selon [səlɔ̃] *prép* according to; (*en se conformant à*) in accordance with; **~ moi** as I see it; **~ que** according to
semaine [səmɛn] *nf* week; **en ~** during the week, on weekdays
semblable [sɑ̃blabl] *adj* similar; (*de ce genre*): **de ~s mésaventures** such mishaps ▷ *nm* fellow creature *ou* man; **~ à** similar to, like
semblant [sɑ̃blɑ̃] *nm*: **un ~ de vérité** a semblance of truth; **faire ~ (de faire)** to pretend (to do)
sembler [sɑ̃ble] /1/ *vb copule* to seem ▷ *vb impers*: **il semble (bien) que/inutile de** it (really) seems *ou* appears that/useless to; **il me semble (bien) que** it (really) seems to me that; **comme bon lui semble** as he sees fit

semelle [səmɛl] *nf* sole; (*intérieure*) insole, inner sole

semer [səme] /5/ *vt* to sow; (*fig: éparpiller*) to scatter; (: *confusion*) to spread; (*fam: poursuivants*) to lose, shake off; **semé de** (*difficultés*) riddled with

semestre [səmɛstʁ] *nm* half-year; (*Scol*) semester

séminaire [seminɛʁ] *nm* seminar; **~ en ligne** webinar

semi-remorque [səmiʁəmɔʁk] *nm* articulated lorry (BRIT), semi(trailer) (US)

semoule [səmul] *nf* semolina

sénat [sena] *nm* senate; **sénateur** *nm* senator

Sénégal [senegal] *nm*: **le ~** Senegal

sens [sɑ̃s] *nm* (*Physiol*) sense; (*signification*) meaning, sense; (*direction*) direction; **à mon ~** to my mind; **dans le ~ des aiguilles d'une montre** clockwise; **dans le ~ contraire des aiguilles d'une montre** anticlockwise; **dans le mauvais ~** (*aller*) the wrong way; in the wrong direction; **bon ~** good sense; **~ dessus dessous** upside down; **~ interdit, ~ unique** one-way street

sensation [sɑ̃sasjɔ̃] *nf* sensation; **faire ~** to cause a sensation, create a stir; **à ~** (*péj*) sensational; **sensationnel, le** *adj* sensational, fantastic

sensé, e [sɑ̃se] *adj* sensible

sensibiliser [sɑ̃sibilize] /1/ *vt*: **~ qn (à)** to make sb sensitive (to)

sensibilité [sɑ̃sibilite] *nf* sensitivity

sensible [sɑ̃sibl] *adj* sensitive; (*aux sens*) perceptible; (*appréciable: différence, progrès*) appreciable, noticeable; **~ à** sensitive to; **sensiblement** *adv* (*à peu près*): **ils ont sensiblement le même poids** they weigh approximately the same; **sensiblerie** *nf* sentimentality

> Attention à ne pas traduire *sensible* par le mot anglais *sensible*.

sensuel, le [sɑ̃sɥɛl] *adj* (*personne*) sensual; (*musique*) sensuous

sentence [sɑ̃tɑ̃s] *nf* (*Jur*) sentence

sentier [sɑ̃tje] *nm* path

sentiment [sɑ̃timɑ̃] *nm* feeling; **recevez mes ~s respectueux** (*personne nommée*) yours sincerely; (*personne non nommée*) yours faithfully; **sentimental, e, -aux** *adj* sentimental; (*vie, aventure*) love *cpd*

sentinelle [sɑ̃tinɛl] *nf* sentry

sentir [sɑ̃tiʁ] /16/ *vt* (*par l'odorat*) to smell; (*par le goût*) to taste; (*au toucher, fig*) to feel; (*répandre une odeur de*) to smell of; (: *ressemblance*) to smell like ▷ *vi* to smell; **~ mauvais** to smell bad; **se ~ bien** to feel good; **se ~ mal** (*être indisposé*) to feel unwell ou ill; **se ~ le courage/la force de faire** to feel brave/strong enough to do; **il ne peut pas le ~** (*fam*) he can't stand him; **je ne me sens pas bien** I don't feel well

séparation [separasjɔ̃] *nf* separation; (*cloison*) division, partition

séparé, e [separe] *adj* (*appartements, pouvoirs*) separate; (*époux*) separated; **séparément** *adv* separately

séparer [separe] /1/ *vt* to separate; (*désunir*) to drive apart; (*détacher*): **~ qch de** to pull sth (off) from; **se séparer** *vi* (*époux*) to separate; (*prendre congé: amis etc*) to part; (*se diviser: route, tige etc*) to divide; **se ~ de** (*époux*) to separate ou part from; (*employé, objet personnel*) to part with

sept [sɛt] *num* seven; **septante** *num* (BELGIQUE, SUISSE) seventy

septembre [sɛptɑ̃bʁ] *nm* September

septicémie [sɛptisemi] *nf* blood poisoning, septicaemia

septième [sɛtjɛm] *num* seventh

séquelles [sekɛl] *nfpl* after-effects; (*fig*) aftermath *sg*

serbe [sɛʁb] *adj* Serbian

Serbie [sɛʁbi] *nf*: **la ~** Serbia

serein, e [səʁɛ̃, -ɛn] *adj* serene

sergent [sɛʁʒɑ̃] *nm* sergeant

série [seʁi] *nf* series *inv*; (*de clés, casseroles, outils*) set; (*catégorie: Sport*) rank; **en ~** in quick succession; (*Comm*) mass *cpd*; **de ~** (*voiture*) standard; **hors ~** (*Comm*) custom-built; **~ noire** (*crime*) thriller

sérieusement [seʁjøzmɑ̃] *adv* seriously

sérieux, -euse [seʁjø, -øz] *adj* serious; (*élève, employé*) reliable, responsible; (*client, maison*) reliable, dependable ▷ *nm* seriousness; (*d'une entreprise etc*) reliability; **garder son ~** to keep a straight face; **prendre qch/qn au ~** to take sth/sb seriously

serin [səʁɛ̃] *nm* canary

seringue [səʁɛ̃g] *nf* syringe

serment [sɛʁmɑ̃] *nm* (*juré*) oath; (*promesse*) pledge, vow

sermon [sɛʁmɔ̃] *nm* sermon

séropositif, -ive [seʁopozitif, -iv] *adj* HIV positive

serpent [sɛʁpɑ̃] *nm* snake; **serpenter** /1/ *vi* to wind

serpillière [sɛʁpijɛʁ] *nf* floorcloth

serre [sɛʁ] *nf* (*Agr*) greenhouse; **serres** *nfpl* (*griffes*) claws, talons

serré, e [seʁe] *adj* (*réseau*) dense; (*habits*) tight; (*fig: lutte, match*) tight, close-fought; (*passagers etc*) (tightly) packed; **avoir le cœur ~** to have a heavy heart

serrer [seʁe] /1/ *vt* (*tenir*) to grip ou hold tight; (*comprimer, presser*) to squeeze; (*poings, mâchoires*) to clench; (*vêtement*) to be too tight for; (*ceinture, nœud, frein, vis*) to tighten ▷ *vi*: **~ à droite** to keep to the right

serrure [seʀyʀ] nf lock; **serrurier** nm locksmith

sers, sert [seʀ] vb voir **servir**

servante [seʀvɑ̃t] nf (maid)servant

serveur, -euse [seʀvœʀ, -øz] nm/f waiter (waitress)

serviable [seʀvjabl] adj obliging, willing to help

service [seʀvis] nm service; (série de repas): **premier ~** first sitting; (assortiment de vaisselle) set, service; (bureau: de la vente etc) department, section; **faire le ~** to serve; **rendre ~ à qn** to help sb; **rendre un ~ à qn** to do sb a favour; **être de ~** to be on duty; **être/mettre en ~** to be in/put into service ou operation; **~ compris/non compris** service included/not included; **hors ~** out of order; **~ après-vente** after-sales service; **~ militaire** military service; see note **"service militaire"**; **~ d'ordre** police (ou stewards) in charge of maintaining order; **~s secrets** secret service sg

serviette [seʀvjɛt] nf (de table) (table) napkin, serviette; (de toilette) towel; (porte-documents) briefcase; **~ hygiénique** sanitary towel

servir [seʀviʀ] /14/ vt to serve; (au restaurant) to wait on; (au magasin) to serve, attend to ▷ vi (Tennis) to serve; (Cartes) to deal; **se servir** vi (prendre d'un plat) to help o.s.; **vous êtes servi?** are you being served?; **sers-toi!** help yourself!; **se ~ de** (plat) to help o.s. to; (voiture, outil, relations) to use; **~ à qn** (diplôme, livre) to be of use to sb; **~ à qch/à faire** (outil etc) to be used for sth/for doing; **ça ne sert à rien** it's no use; **~ (à qn) de ...** to serve as ... (for sb)

serviteur [seʀvitœʀ] nm servant

ses [se] adj poss voir **son¹**

seuil [sœj] nm doorstep; (fig) threshold

seul, e [sœl] adj (sans compagnie) alone; (unique): **un ~ livre** only one book, a single book; **le ~ livre** the only book ▷ adv (vivre) alone, on one's own; **faire qch (tout) ~** to do sth (all) on one's own ou (all) by oneself ▷ nm/f: **il en reste un(e) ~(e)** there's only one left; **à lui (tout) ~** single-handed, on his own; **se sentir ~** to feel lonely; **parler tout ~** to talk to oneself; **seulement** adv only; **non seulement ... mais aussi** ou **encore** not only ... but also

sève [sɛv] nf sap

sévère [sevɛʀ] adj severe

sexe [sɛks] nm sex; (organe mâle) member; **sexuel, le** adj sexual

shampo(o)ing [ʃɑ̃pwɛ̃] nm shampoo

Shetland [ʃɛtlɑ̃d] n: **les îles ~** the Shetland Islands, Shetland

shopping [ʃɔpiŋ] nm: **faire du ~** to go shopping

short [ʃɔʀt] nm (pair of) shorts pl

🔘 **MOT-CLÉ**

si [si] adv **1** (oui) yes; **"Paul n'est pas venu"** — **"si!"** "Paul hasn't come" — "Yes he has!"; **je vous assure que si** I assure you he did/ she is etc
2 (tellement) so; **si gentil/rapidement** so kind/fast; **(tant et) si bien que** so much so that; **si rapide qu'il soit** however fast he may be
▶ conj if; **si tu veux** if you want; **je me demande si** I wonder if ou whether; **si seulement** if only
▶ nm (Mus) B; (: en chantant la gamme) ti

Sicile [sisil] nf: **la ~** Sicily

sida [sida] nm (= syndrome immuno-déficitaire acquis) AIDS sg

sidéré, e [sideʀe] adj staggered

sidérurgie [sideʀyʀʒi] nf steel industry

siècle [sjɛkl] nm century

siège [sjɛʒ] nm seat; (d'entreprise) head office; (d'organisation) headquarters pl; (Mil) siege; **~ social** registered office; **siéger** /3, 6/ vi to sit

sien, ne [sjɛ̃, sjɛn] pron: **le (la) ~(ne), les ~(ne)s** (d'un homme) his; (d'une femme) hers; (d'une chose) its

sieste [sjɛst] nf (afternoon) snooze ou nap; **faire la ~** to have a snooze ou nap

sifflement [sifləmɑ̃] nm whistle

siffler [sifle] /1/ vi (gén) to whistle; (en respirant) to wheeze; (serpent, vapeur) to hiss ▷ vt (chanson) to whistle; (chien etc) to whistle for; (fille) to whistle at; (pièce, orateur) to hiss, boo; (fin du match, départ) to blow one's whistle for; (fam: verre, bouteille) to guzzle

sifflet [siflɛ] nm whistle; **coup de ~** whistle

siffloter [siflɔte] /1/ vi, vt to whistle

sigle [sigl] nm acronym

signal, -aux [siɲal, -o] nm signal; (indice, écriteau) sign; **donner le ~ de** to give the signal for; **~ d'alarme** alarm signal; **signalement** nm description, particulars pl

signaler [siɲale] /1/ vt to indicate; (vol, perte) to report; (personne, faire un signe) to signal; **~ qch à qn/à qn que** to point out sth to sb/to sb that

signature [siɲatyʀ] nf signature; (action) signing

signe [siɲ] nm sign; (Typo) mark; **faire un ~ de la main/tête** to give a sign with one's hand/shake one's head; **faire ~ à qn** (fig: contacter) to get in touch with sb; **faire ~ à qn d'entrer** to motion (to) sb to come in; **signer** /1/ vt to sign; **se signer** vi to cross o.s.

significatif, -ive [siɲifikatif, -iv] adj significant

signification [siɲifikasjɔ̃] nf meaning

signifier [siɲifje] /7/ vt (vouloir dire) to mean; (faire connaître): **~ qch (à qn)** to make sth known (to sb)

silence [silɑ̃s] nm silence; (Mus) rest; **garder le ~ (sur qch)** to keep silent (about sth), say nothing (about sth); **silencieux, -euse** adj quiet, silent ▷ nm silencer

silhouette [silwɛt] nf outline, silhouette; (figure) figure

sillage [sijaʒ] nm wake

sillon [sijɔ̃] nm furrow; (de disque) groove; **sillonner** /1/ vt to criss-cross

simagrées [simagʀe] nfpl fuss sg

similaire [similɛʀ] adj similar; **similicuir** nm imitation leather; **similitude** nf similarity

simple [sɛ̃pl] adj simple; (non multiple) single; **~ messieurs/dames** nm (Tennis) men's/ladies' singles sg; **~ d'esprit** nm/f simpleton; **~ soldat** private

simplicité [sɛ̃plisite] nf simplicity; **en toute ~** quite simply

simplifier [sɛ̃plifje] /7/ vt to simplify

simuler [simyle] /1/ vt to sham, simulate

simultané, e [simyltane] adj simultaneous

sincère [sɛ̃sɛʀ] adj sincere; **sincèrement** adv sincerely; genuinely; **sincérité** nf sincerity

Singapour [sɛ̃gapuʀ] nm: Singapore

singe [sɛ̃ʒ] nm monkey; (de grande taille) ape; **singer** /3/ vt to ape, mimic; **singeries** nfpl antics

singulariser [sɛ̃gylaʀize] /1/: **se singulariser** vi to call attention to o.s.

singularité [sɛ̃gylaʀite] nf peculiarity

singulier, -ière [sɛ̃gylje, -jɛʀ] adj remarkable, singular ▷ nm singular

sinistre [sinistʀ] adj sinister ▷ nm (incendie) blaze; (catastrophe) disaster; (Assurances) damage (giving rise to a claim); **sinistré, e** adj disaster-stricken ▷ nm/f disaster victim

sinon [sinɔ̃] conj (autrement, sans quoi) otherwise, or else; (sauf) except, other than; (si ce n'est) if not

sinueux, -euse [sinɥø, -øz] adj winding

sinus [sinys] nm (Anat) sinus; (Géom) sine; **sinusite** nf sinusitis

sirène [siʀɛn] nf siren; **~ d'alarme** fire alarm; (pendant la guerre) air-raid siren

sirop [siʀo] nm (à diluer: de fruit etc) syrup, (pharmaceutique) syrup, mixture; **contre la toux** cough syrup ou mixture

siroter [siʀɔte] /1/ vt to sip

sismique [sismik] adj seismic

site [sit] nm (paysage, environnement) setting; (d'une ville etc: emplacement) site; **~ (pittoresque)** beauty spot; **~s touristiques** places of interest; **~ web** (Inform) website

sitôt [sito] adv: **~ parti** as soon as he etc had left; **pas de ~** not for a long time; **~ (après) que** as soon as

situation [sitɥasjɔ̃] nf situation; (d'un édifice, d'une ville) position; location; **~ de famille** marital status

situé, e [sitɥe] adj: **bien ~** well situated

situer [sitɥe] /1/ vt to site, situate; (en pensée) to set, place; **se situer** vi: **se ~ à/ près de** to be situated at/near

six [sis] num six; **sixième** num sixth ▷ nf (Scol) year 7

skaï® [skaj] nm ≈ Leatherette®

skate [sket], **skate-board** [sketbɔʀd] nm (sport) skateboarding; (planche) skateboard

ski [ski] nm (objet) ski; (sport) skiing; **faire du ~** to ski; **~ de fond** cross-country skiing; **~ nautique** water-skiing; **~ de piste** downhill skiing; **~ de randonnée** cross-country skiing; **skier** /7/ vi to ski; **skieur, -euse** nm/f skier

slip [slip] nm (sous-vêtement) pants pl (BRIT), briefs pl; (de bain: d'homme) trunks pl; (: du bikini) (bikini) briefs pl

slogan [slɔgɑ̃] nm slogan

Slovaquie [slɔvaki] nf: **la ~** Slovakia

SMIC [smik] sigle m = **salaire minimum interprofessionnel de croissance**

smoking [smɔkiŋ] nm dinner ou evening suit

SMS sigle m (= short message service) (service) SMS; (message) text (message)

SNCF sigle f (= Société nationale des chemins de fer français) French railways

snob [snɔb] adj snobbish ▷ nm/f snob; **snobisme** nm snobbery, snobbishness

sobre [sɔbʀ] adj (personne) temperate, abstemious; (élégance, style) sober

sobriquet [sɔbʀikɛ] nm nickname

social, e, -aux [sɔsjal, -o] adj social

socialisme [sɔsjalism] nm socialism; **socialiste** nm/f socialist

société [sɔsjete] nf society; (sportive) club; (Comm) company; **la ~ d'abondance/de consommation** the affluent/consumer society; **~ anonyme** ≈ limited company (BRIT), ≈ incorporated company (US)

sociologie [sɔsjɔlɔʒi] nf sociology

socle [sɔkl] nm (de colonne, statue) plinth, pedestal; (de lampe) base

socquette [sɔkɛt] nf ankle sock

sœur [sœʀ] nf sister; (religieuse) nun, sister

soi [swa] pron oneself; **en ~** (intrinsèquement) in itself; **cela va de ~** that ou it goes without saying; **soi-disant** adj inv so-called ▷ adv supposedly

soie [swa] nf silk; **soierie** nf (tissu) silk

soif [swaf] nf thirst; **avoir ~** to be thirsty; **donner ~ à qn** to make sb thirsty

soigné, e [swaɲe] adj (tenue) well-groomed, neat; (travail) careful, meticulous

soigner [swaɲe] /1/ vt (malade, maladie: docteur) to treat; (: infirmière, mère) to nurse, look after; (travail, détails) to take care over; (jardin, chevelure, invités) to look after; **soigneux, -euse** adj tidy, neat; (méticuleux) painstaking, careful

soi-même [swamɛm] pron oneself

soin [swɛ̃] nm (application) care; (propreté, ordre) tidiness, neatness; **soins** nmpl (à un malade, blessé) treatment sg, medical attention sg; (hygiène) care sg; **avoir** ou **prendre ~ de** to take care of, look after; **avoir** ou **prendre ~ de faire** to take care to do; **les premiers ~s** first aid sg

soir [swaʀ] nm evening; **ce ~** this evening, tonight; **à ce ~!** see you this evening (ou tonight)!; **sept/dix heures du ~** seven in the evening/ten at night; **~ demain** tomorrow evening, tomorrow night; **soirée** nf evening; (réception) party

soit [swa] vb voir **être** ▷ conj (à savoir) namely; (ou): **~ ... ~ ...** either ... or ▷ adv so be it, very well; **~ que ... ~ que** ou **ou que** whether ... or whether

soixantaine [swasɑ̃tɛn] nf: **une ~ (de)** sixty or so, about sixty; **avoir la ~ (âge)** to be around sixty

soixante [swasɑ̃t] num sixty; **soixante-dix** num seventy

soja [sɔʒa] nm soya; (graines) soya beans pl; **germes de ~** beansprouts

sol [sɔl] nm ground; (de logement) floor; (Agr, Géo) soil; (Mus) G; (: en chantant la gamme) so(h)

solaire [sɔlɛʀ] adj (énergie etc) solar; (crème etc) sun cpd

soldat [sɔlda] nm soldier

solde [sɔld] nf pay ▷ nm (Comm) balance; **soldes** nmpl ou nfpl (Comm) sales; **en ~** at sale price; **solder** /1/ vt (marchandise) to sell at sale price, sell off

sole [sɔl] nf sole inv (fish)

soleil [sɔlɛj] nm sun; (lumière) sun(light); (temps ensoleillé) sun(shine); **il y a** ou **il fait du ~** it's sunny; **au ~** in the sun

solennel, le [sɔlanɛl] adj solemn

solfège [sɔlfɛʒ] nm rudiments pl of music

solidaire [sɔlidɛʀ] adj: **être ~s** (personnes) to show solidarity, stand ou stick together; **être ~ de** (collègues) to stand by; **solidarité** nf solidarity; **par solidarité (avec)** in sympathy (with)

solide [sɔlid] adj solid; (mur, maison, meuble) solid, sturdy; (connaissances, argument) sound; (personne) robust, sturdy ▷ nm solid

soliste [sɔlist] nm/f soloist

solitaire [sɔlitɛʀ] adj (sans compagnie) solitary, lonely; (lieu) lonely ▷ nm/f (ermite) recluse; (fig: ours) loner

solitude [sɔlityd] nf loneliness; (paix) solitude

solliciter [sɔlisite] /1/ vt (personne) to appeal to; (emploi, faveur) to seek

sollicitude [sɔlisityd] nf concern

soluble [sɔlybl] adj soluble

solution [sɔlysjɔ̃] nf solution; **~ de facilité** easy way out

solvable [sɔlvabl] adj solvent

sombre [sɔ̃bʀ] adj dark; (fig) gloomy; **sombrer** /1/ vi (bateau) to sink; **sombrer dans** (misère, désespoir) to sink into

sommaire [sɔmɛʀ] adj (simple) basic; (expéditif) summary ▷ nm summary

somme [sɔm] nf (Math) sum; (fig) amount; (argent) sum, amount ▷ nm: **faire un ~** to have a (short) nap; **en ~, ~ toute** all in all

sommeil [sɔmɛj] nm sleep; **avoir ~** to be sleepy; **sommeiller** /1/ vi to doze

sommet [sɔmɛ] nm top; (d'une montagne) summit, top; (fig: de la perfection, gloire) height

sommier [sɔmje] nm bed base

somnambule [sɔmnɑ̃byl] nm/f sleepwalker

somnifère [sɔmnifɛʀ] nm sleeping drug; sleeping pill ou tablet

somnoler [sɔmnɔle] /1/ vi to doze

somptueux, -euse [sɔ̃ptɥø, -øz] adj sumptuous

son¹, sa (pl **ses**) [sɔ̃, sa, se] adj poss (antécédent humain: mâle) his; (: femelle) her; (: valeur indéfinie) one's, his (her); (: non humain) its

son² [sɔ̃] nm sound; (de blé etc) bran

sondage [sɔ̃daʒ] nm: **~ (d'opinion)** (opinion) poll

sonde [sɔ̃d] nf (Navig) lead ou sounding line; (Méd) probe; (Tech: de forage, sondage) drill

sonder [sɔ̃de] /1/ vt (Navig) to sound; (Tech) to bore, drill; (fig: personne) to sound out; **~ le terrain** (fig) to see how the land lies

songe [sɔ̃ʒ] nm dream; **songer** /3/ vi: **songer à** (rêver à) to think over; (envisager) to contemplate, think of; **songer que** to think that; **songeur, -euse** adj pensive

sonnant, e [sɔnɑ̃, -ɑ̃t] adj: **à huit heures ~es** on the stroke of eight

sonné, e [sɔne] adj (fam) cracked; **il est midi ~** it's gone twelve

sonner [sɔne] /1/ vi to ring ▷ vt (cloche) to ring; (glas, tocsin) to sound; (portier, infirmière) to ring for; **~ faux** (instrument) to sound out of tune, (rire) to ring false

sonnerie [sɔnʀi] nf (son) ringing; (sonnette) bell; (de portable) ringtone; **~ d'alarme** alarm bell

sonnette [sɔnɛt] nf bell; **~ d'alarme** alarm bell

sonore [sɔnɔʀ] adj (voix) sonorous, ringing; (salle, métal) resonant; (ondes, film, signal) sound cpd; **sonorisation** nf (équipement: de salle de conférences) public address system, P.A. system; (: de discothèque) sound system; **sonorité** nf (de piano, violon) tone; (d'une salle) acoustics pl

sophistiqué, e [sɔfistike] adj sophisticated

sorbet [sɔʀbɛ] nm water ice, sorbet

sorcier, -ière [sɔʀsje, -jɛʀ] nm/f sorcerer (witch ou sorceress)

sordide [sɔʀdid] adj (lieu) squalid; (action) sordid

sort [sɔʀ] nm (fortune, destinée) fate; (condition, situation) lot; (magique): **jeter un ~** to cast a spell; **tirer au ~** to draw lots

sorte [sɔʀt] nf sort, kind; **de la ~** in that way; **en quelque ~** in a way; **de (telle) ~ que** so that; **faire en ~ que** to see to it that

sortie [sɔʀti] nf (issue) way out, exit; (verbale) sally; (promenade) outing; (le soir, au restaurant etc) night out; (Comm: d'un disque) release; (: d'un livre) publication; (: d'un modèle) launching; **~ de bain** (vêtement) bathrobe; **~ de secours** emergency exit

sortilège [sɔʀtilɛʒ] nm (magic) spell

sortir [sɔʀtiʀ] /16/ vi (gén) to come out; (partir, se promener, aller au spectacle etc) to go out; (bourgeon, plante, numéro gagnant) to come up ▷ vt (gén) to take out; (produit, ouvrage, modèle) to bring out; (fam: dire) to come out with; **~ avec qn** to be going out with sb; **~ de** (endroit) to go (ou come) out of, leave; (cadre, compétence) to be outside; (provenir de) to come from; **s'en ~** (malade) to pull through; (d'une difficulté etc) to get through

sosie [sɔzi] nm double

sot, sotte [so, sɔt] adj silly, foolish ▷ nm/f fool; **sottise** nf silliness no pl, foolishness no pl; (propos, acte) silly ou foolish thing (to do ou say)

sou [su] nm: **près de ses ~s** tight-fisted; **sans le ~** penniless

soubresaut [subʀəso] nm start; (cahot) jolt

souche [suʃ] nf (d'arbre) stump; (de carnet) counterfoil (BRIT), stub

souci [susi] nm (inquiétude) worry; (préoccupation) concern; (Bot) marigold; **se faire du ~** to worry; **soucier** /7/: **se soucier de** vt to care about; **soucieux, -euse** adj concerned, worried

soucoupe [sukup] nf saucer; **~ volante** flying saucer

soudain, e [sudɛ̃, -ɛn] adj (douleur, mort) sudden ▷ adv suddenly, all of a sudden

Soudan [sudɑ̃] nm: **le ~** Sudan

soude [sud] nf soda

souder [sude] /1/ vt (avec fil à souder) to solder; (par soudure autogène) to weld; (fig) to bind ou knit together

soudure [sudyʀ] nf soldering; welding; (joint) soldered joint; weld

souffle [sufl] nm (en expirant) breath; (en soufflant) puff, blow; (respiration) breathing; (d'explosion, de ventilateur) blast; (du vent) blowing; **être à bout de ~** to be out of breath; **un ~ d'air** ou **de vent** a breath of air

soufflé, e [sufle] adj (fam: ahuri, stupéfié) staggered ▷ nm (Culin) soufflé

souffler [sufle] /1/ vi (gén) to blow; (haleter) to puff (and blow) ▷ vt (feu, bougie) to blow out; (chasser: poussière etc) to blow away; (Tech: verre) to blow; (dire): **~ qch à qn** to whisper sth to sb

souffrance [sufʀɑ̃s] nf suffering; **en ~** (affaire) pending

souffrant, e [sufʀɑ̃, -ɑ̃t] adj unwell

souffre-douleur [sufʀədulœʀ] nm inv butt, underdog

souffrir [sufʀiʀ] /18/ vi to suffer; (éprouver des douleurs) to be in pain ▷ vt to suffer, endure; (supporter) to bear, stand; **~ de** (maladie, froid) to suffer from; **elle ne peut pas le ~** she can't stand ou bear him

soufre [sufʀ] nm sulphur

souhait [swɛ] nm wish; **tous nos ~s pour la nouvelle année** (our) best wishes for the New Year; **souhaitable** adj desirable

souhaiter [swete] /1/ vt to wish for; **~ la bonne année à qn** to wish sb a happy New Year; **~ que** to hope that

soûl, e [su, sul] adj drunk ▷ nm: **tout son ~** to one's heart's content

soulagement [sulaʒmɑ̃] nm relief

soulager [sulaʒe] /3/ vt to relieve

soûler [sule] /1/ vt: **~ qn** to get sb drunk; (boisson) to make sb drunk; (fig) to make sb's head spin ou reel; **se soûler** vi to get drunk

soulever [sulve] /5/ vt to lift; (vagues, poussière) to send up; (enthousiasme) to arouse; (question, débat, protestations, difficultés) to raise; **se soulever** vi (peuple) to rise up; (personne couchée) to lift o.s. up

soulier [sulje] nm shoe

souligner [suliɲe] /1/ vt to underline; (fig) to emphasize, stress

soumettre [sumɛtʀ] /56/ vt (pays) to subject, subjugate; (rebelles) to put down, subdue; ~ **qch à qn** (projet etc) to submit sth to sb; **se ~ (à)** to submit (to)

soumis, e [sumi, -iz] adj submissive; **soumission** nf submission

soupçon [supsɔ̃] nm suspicion; (petite quantité): **un ~ de** a hint ou touch of; **soupçonner** /1/ vt to suspect; **soupçonneux, -euse** adj suspicious

soupe [sup] nf soup

souper [supe] /1/ vi to have supper ▷ nm supper

soupeser [supəze] /5/ vt to weigh in one's hand(s); (fig) to weigh up

soupière [supjɛʀ] nf (soup) tureen

soupir [supiʀ] nm sigh; **pousser un ~ de soulagement** to heave a sigh of relief

soupirer [supiʀe] /1/ vi to sigh

souple [supl] adj supple; (fig: règlement, caractère) flexible; (: démarche, taille) lithe, supple; **souplesse** nf suppleness; (de caractère) flexibility

source [suʀs] nf (point d'eau) spring; (d'un cours d'eau, fig) source; **tenir qch de bonne ~/de ~ sûre** to have sth on good authority/ from a reliable source

sourcil [suʀsij] nm (eye)brow; **sourciller** /1/ vi: **sans sourciller** without turning a hair ou batting an eyelid

sourd, e [suʀ, suʀd] adj deaf; (bruit, voix) muffled; (douleur) dull ▷ nm/f deaf person; **faire la ~e oreille** to turn a deaf ear; **sourdine** nf (Mus) mute; **en sourdine** softly, quietly; **sourd-muet, sourde-muette** adj with a speech and hearing impairment

souriant, e [suʀjɑ̃, -ɑ̃t] adj cheerful

sourire [suʀiʀ] /36/ nm smile ▷ vi to smile; **~ à qn** to smile at sb; (fig: plaire à) to appeal to sb; (chance) to smile on sb; **garder le ~** to keep smiling

souris [suʀi] nf mouse

sournois, e [suʀnwa, -waz] adj deceitful, underhand

sous [su] prép under; **~ la pluie/le soleil** in the rain/sunshine; **~ terre** underground; **~ peu** shortly, before long; **sous-bois** nm inv undergrowth

souscrire [suskʀiʀ] /39/: **~ à** vt to subscribe to

sous: sous-directeur, -trice nm/f assistant manager/manageress; **sous-entendre** /41/ vt to imply, infer; **sous-entendu, e** adj implied ▷ nm innuendo, insinuation; **sous-estimer** /1/ vt to underestimate; **sous-jacent, e** adj underlying; **sous-louer** /1/ vt to sublet; **sous-marin, e** adj (flore, volcan) submarine; (navigation, pêche, explosif) underwater ▷ nm submarine; **sous-pull** nm thin poloneck sweater; **soussigné, e** adj: **je soussigné** I the

undersigned; **sous-sol** nm basement; **sous-titre** [sutitʀ] nm subtitle

soustraction [sustʀaksjɔ̃] nf subtraction

soustraire [sustʀɛʀ] /50/ vt to subtract, take away; (dérober): **~ qch à qn** to remove sth from sb; **se ~ à** (autorité, obligation, devoir) to elude, escape from

sous: sous-traitant nm subcontractor; **sous-traiter** /1/ vt, vi to subcontract; **sous-vêtement** nm item of underwear; **sous-vêtements** nmpl underwear sg

soutane [sutan] nf cassock, soutane

soute [sut] nf hold

soutenir [sutniʀ] /22/ vt to support; (assaut, choc, regard) to stand up to, withstand; (intérêt, effort) to keep up; (assurer): **~ que** to maintain that; **soutenu, e** adj (efforts) sustained, unflagging; (style) elevated

souterrain, e [suteʀɛ̃, -ɛn] adj underground ▷ nm underground passage

soutien [sutjɛ̃] nm support; **soutien-gorge** nm bra

soutirer [sutiʀe] /1/ vt: **~ qch à qn** to squeeze ou get sth out of sb

souvenir [suvniʀ] /22/ nm (réminiscence) memory; (cadeau) souvenir ▷ vb: **se ~ de** to remember; **se ~ que** to remember that; **en ~ de** in memory ou remembrance of; **avec mes affectueux/meilleurs ~s, ...** with love from, .../regards, ...

souvent [suvɑ̃] adv often; **peu ~** seldom, infrequently

souverain, e [suvʀɛ̃, -ɛn] nm/f sovereign, monarch

soyeux, -euse [swajø, -øz] adj silky

spacieux, -euse [spasjø, -øz] adj spacious; roomy

spaghettis [spageti] nmpl spaghetti sg

sparadrap [spaʀadʀa] nm adhesive ou sticking (BRIT) plaster, bandaid® (US)

spatial, e, -aux [spasjal, -o] adj (Aviat) space cpd

speaker, ine [spikœʀ, -kʀin] nm/f announcer

spécial, e, -aux [spesjal, -o] adj special; (bizarre) peculiar; **spécialement** adv especially, particularly; (tout exprès) specially; **spécialiser** /1/: **se spécialiser** vi to specialize; **spécialiste** nm/f specialist; **spécialité** nf speciality; (Scol) special field

spécifier [spesifje] /7/ vt to specify, state

spécimen [spesimɛn] nm specimen

spectacle [spɛktakl] nm (tableau, scène) sight; (représentation) show; (industrie) show business; **spectaculaire** adj spectacular

spectateur, -trice [spɛktatœʀ, -tʀis] nm/f (Ciné etc) member of the audience; (Sport) spectator; (d'un événement) onlooker, witness

spéculer [spekyle] /1/ vi to speculate

spéléologie [speleɔlɔʒi] nf potholing

sperme [spɛʀm] *nm* semen, sperm

sphère [sfɛʀ] *nf* sphere

spirale [spiʀal] *nf* spiral

spirituel, le [spiʀituɛl] *adj* spiritual; (*fin, piquant*) witty

splendide [splɑ̃did] *adj* splendid

spontané, e [spɔ̃tane] *adj* spontaneous; **spontanéité** *nf* spontaneity

sport [spɔʀ] *nm* sport ▷ *adj inv* (*vêtement*) casual; **faire du ~** to do sport; **~s d'hiver** winter sports; **sportif, -ive** *adj* (*journal, association, épreuve*) sports *cpd*; (*allure, démarche*) athletic; (*attitude, esprit*) sporting

spot [spɔt] *nm* (*lampe*) spot(light); (*annonce*): **~ (publicitaire)** commercial (break)

square [skwaʀ] *nm* public garden(s)

squelette [skəlɛt] *nm* skeleton; **squelettique** *adj* scrawny

SRAS [sʀas] *sigle m* (= *syndrome respiratoire aigu sévère*) SARS

Sri Lanka [sʀilɑ̃ka] *nm*: **le ~** Sri Lanka

stabiliser [stabilize] /1/ *vt* to stabilize

stable [stabl] *adj* stable, steady

stade [stad] *nm* (*Sport*) stadium; (*phase, niveau*) stage

stage [staʒ] *nm* (*cours*) training course; **~ de formation (professionnelle)** vocational (training) course; **~ de perfectionnement** advanced training course; **stagiaire** [staʒjɛʀ] *nm/f, adj* trainee

▮ Attention à ne pas traduire *stage* par le mot anglais *stage*.

stagner [stagne] /1/ *vi* to stagnate

stand [stɑ̃d] *nm* (*d'exposition*) stand; (*de foire*) stall; **~ de tir** (*à la foire, Sport*) shooting range

standard [stɑ̃daʀ] *adj inv* standard ▷ *nm* switchboard; **standardiste** *nm/f* switchboard operator

standing [stɑ̃diŋ] *nm* standing; **de grand ~** luxury

starter [staʀtɛʀ] *nm* (*Auto*) choke

station [stasjɔ̃] *nf* station; (*de bus*) stop; (*de villégiature*) resort; **~ de ski** ski resort; **~ de taxis** taxi rank (BRIT) *ou* stand (US); **stationnement** *nm* parking; **stationner** /1/ *vi* to park; **station-service** *nf* service station

statistique [statistik] *nf* (*science*) statistics *sg*; (*rapport, étude*) statistic ▷ *adj* statistical

statue [staty] *nf* statue

statu quo [statykwo] *nm* status quo

statut [staty] *nm* status; **statuts** *nmpl* (*Jur, Admin*) statutes; **statutaire** *adj* statutory

Sté *abr* (= *société*) soc

steak [stɛk] *nm* steak; **~ haché** hamburger

sténo [stenɔ] *nf* (*aussi*: **~graphie**) shorthand

stérile [steʀil] *adj* sterile

stérilet [steʀilɛ] *nm* coil, loop

stériliser [steʀilize] /1/ *vt* to sterilize

stimulant, e [stimylɑ̃, -ɑ̃t] *adj* stimulating ▷ *nm* (*Méd*) stimulant; (*fig*) stimulus, incentive

stimuler [stimyle] /1/ *vt* to stimulate

stipuler [stipyle] /1/ *vt* to stipulate

stock [stɔk] *nm* stock; **stocker** /1/ *vt* to stock

stop [stɔp] *nm* (*Auto: écriteau*) stop sign; (*: signal*) brake-light; **faire du ~** (*fam*) to hitch(hike); **stopper** /1/ *vt* to stop ▷ *vi* to stop, halt

store [stɔʀ] *nm* blind; (*de magasin*) shade, awning

strabisme [stʀabism] *nm* squint(ing)

strapontin [stʀapɔ̃tɛ̃] *nm* jump *ou* foldaway seat

stratégie [stʀateʒi] *nf* strategy; **stratégique** *adj* strategic

stress [stʀɛs] *nm inv* stress; **stressant, e** *adj* stressful; **stresser** /1/ *vt*: **stresser qn** to make sb (feel) tense

strict, e [stʀikt] *adj* strict; (*tenue, décor*) severe, plain; **le ~ nécessaire/minimum** the bare essentials/minimum

strident, e [stʀidɑ̃, -ɑ̃t] *adj* shrill, strident

strophe [stʀɔf] *nf* verse, stanza

structure [stʀyktyʀ] *nf* structure; **~s d'accueil/touristiques** reception/tourist facilities

studieux, -euse [stydjø, -øz] *adj* studious

studio [stydjo] *nm* (*logement*) studio flat (BRIT) *ou* apartment (US); (*d'artiste, TV etc*) studio

stupéfait, e [stypefɛ, -ɛt] *adj* astonished

stupéfiant, e [stypefjɑ̃, -ɑ̃t] *adj* (*étonnant*) stunning, astonishing ▷ *nm* (*Méd*) drug, narcotic

stupéfier [stypefje] /7/ *vt* (*étonner*) to stun, astonish

stupeur [stypœʀ] *nf* astonishment

stupide [stypid] *adj* stupid; **stupidité** *nf* stupidity *no pl*; (*parole, acte*) stupid thing (to say *ou* do)

style [stil] *nm* style

stylé, e [stile] *adj* well-trained

styliste [stilist] *nm/f* designer

stylo [stilo] *nm*: **~ (à encre)** (fountain) pen; **~ (à) bille** ballpoint pen

su, e [sy] *pp de* **savoir** ▷ *nm*: **au su de** with the knowledge of

suave [suav] *adj* sweet

subalterne [sybaltɛʀn] *adj* (*employé, officier*) junior; (*rôle*) subordinate, subsidiary ▷ *nm/f* subordinate

subconscient [sypkɔ̃sjɑ̃] *nm* subconscious

subir [sybiʀ] /2/ *vt* (*affront, dégâts, mauvais traitements*) to suffer; (*traitement, opération, châtiment*) to undergo

subit, e [sybi, -it] *adj* sudden; **subitement** *adv* suddenly, all of a sudden

subjectif, -ive [sybʒɛktif, -iv] *adj* subjective

subjonctif [sybʒɔ̃ktif] *nm* subjunctive
subjuguer [sybʒyge] /1/ *vt* to subjugate
submerger [sybmɛrʒe] /3/ *vt* to submerge; *(fig)* to overwhelm
subordonné, e [sybɔrdɔne] *adj, nm/f* subordinate
subrepticement [sybrɛptismɑ̃] *adv* surreptitiously
subside [sypsid] *nm* grant
subsidiaire [sypsidjɛr] *adj*: **question ~** deciding question
subsister [sybziste] /1/ *vi (rester)* to remain, subsist; *(survivre)* to live on
substance [sypstɑ̃s] *nf* substance
substituer [sypstitɥe] /1/ *vt*: **~ qn/qch à** to substitute sb/sth for; **se ~ à qn** *(évincer)* to substitute o.s. for sb
substitut [sypstity] *nm (succédané)* substitute
subterfuge [syptɛrfyʒ] *nm* subterfuge
subtil, e [syptil] *adj* subtle
subvenir [sybvənir] /22/: **~ à** *vt* to meet
subvention [sybvɑ̃sjɔ̃] *nf* subsidy, grant; **subventionner** /1/ *vt* to subsidize
suc [syk] *nm (Bot)* sap; *(de viande, fruit)* juice
succéder [syksede] /6/: **~ à** *vt* to succeed; **se succéder** *vi (accidents, années)* to follow one another
succès [syksɛ] *nm* success; **avoir du ~** to be a success, be successful; **à ~** successful; **~ de librairie** bestseller
successeur [syksesœr] *nm* successor
successif, -ive [syksesif, -iv] *adj* successive
succession [syksesjɔ̃] *nf (série, Pol)* succession; *(Jur: patrimoine)* estate, inheritance
succomber [sykɔ̃be] /1/ *vi* to die, succumb; *(fig)*: **~ à** to succumb to
succulent, e [sykylɑ̃, -ɑ̃t] *adj* delicious
succursale [sykyrsal] *nf* branch
sucer [syse] /3/ *vt* to suck; **sucette** *nf (bonbon)* lollipop; *(de bébé)* dummy (BRIT), pacifier (US)
sucre [sykr] *nm (substance)* sugar; *(morceau)* lump of sugar, sugar lump *ou* cube; **~ en morceaux/cristallisé/en poudre** lump *ou* cube/granulated/caster sugar; **~ glace** icing sugar (BRIT), confectioner's sugar (US); **~ d'orge** barley sugar; **sucré, e** *adj (produit alimentaire)* sweetened; *(au goût)* sweet; **sucrer** /1/ *vt (thé, café)* to sweeten, put sugar in; **sucrerie** *nf* sugar refinery; **sucreries** *nfpl (bonbons)* sweets, sweet things; **sucrier** *nm (récipient)* sugar bowl *ou* basin
sud [syd] *nm*: **le ~** the south ▷ *adj inv* south; *(côte)* south, southern; **au ~** *(situation)* in the south; *(direction)* to the south; **au ~ de** (to the) south of; **sud-africain, e** *adj* South African ▷ *nm/f*: **Sud-Africain, e** South African; **sud-américain, e** *adj* South

American ▷ *nm/f*: **Sud-Américain, e** South American; **sud-est** *nm, adj inv* south-east; **sud-ouest** *nm, adj inv* south-west
Suède [sɥɛd] *nf*: **la ~** Sweden; **suédois, e** *adj* Swedish ▷ *nm (Ling)* Swedish ▷ *nm/f*: **Suédois, e** Swede
suer [sɥe] /1/ *vi* to sweat; *(suinter)* to ooze; **sueur** *nf* sweat; **en sueur** sweating, in a sweat; **avoir des sueurs froides** to be in a cold sweat
suffire [syfir] /37/ *vi (être assez)*: **~ (à qn/ pour qch/pour faire)** to be enough *ou* sufficient (for sb/for sth/to do); **il suffit d'une négligence/qu'on oublie pour que** ... it only takes one act of carelessness/one only needs to forget for ...; **ça suffit!** that's enough!
suffisamment [syfizamɑ̃] *adv* sufficiently, enough; **~ de** sufficient, enough
suffisant, e [syfizɑ̃, -ɑ̃t] *adj* sufficient; *(résultats)* satisfactory; *(vaniteux)* self-important, bumptious
suffixe [syfiks] *nm* suffix
suffoquer [syfɔke] /1/ *vt* to choke, suffocate; *(stupéfier)* to stagger, astound ▷ *vi* to choke, suffocate
suffrage [syfraʒ] *nm (Pol: voix)* vote
suggérer [sygʒere] /6/ *vt* to suggest; **suggestion** *nf* suggestion
suicide [sɥisid] *nm* suicide; **suicider** /1/: **se suicider** *vi* to commit suicide
suie [sɥi] *nf* soot
suisse [sɥis] *adj* Swiss ▷ *nm/f*: **S~** Swiss *inv* ▷ *nf*: **la S~** Switzerland; **la S~ romande/ allemande** French-speaking/German-speaking Switzerland
suite [sɥit] *nf (continuation: d'énumération etc)* rest, remainder; (: *de feuilleton)* continuation; (: *second film etc sur le même thème)* sequel; *(série)* series, succession; *(conséquence)* result; *(ordre, liaison logique)* coherence; *(appartement, Mus)* suite; *(escorte)* retinue, suite; **suites** *nfpl (d'une maladie etc)* effects; **une ~ de** a series *ou* succession of; **prendre la ~ de** *(directeur etc)* to succeed, take over from; **donner ~ à** *(requête, projet)* to follow up; **faire ~ à** to follow; **(faisant) ~ à votre lettre du** further to your letter of; **de ~** *(d'affilée)* in succession; *(immédiatement)* at once; **par la ~** afterwards, subsequently; **à la ~** one after the other; **à la ~ de** *(derrière)* behind; *(en conséquence de)* following
suivant, e [sɥivɑ̃, -ɑ̃t] *adj* next, following ▷ *prép (selon)* according to; **au ~!** next!
suivi, e [sɥivi] *adj (effort, qualité)* consistent; *(cohérent)* coherent; **très/peu ~** *(cours)* well-/poorly-attended
suivre [sɥivr] /40/ *vt (gén)* to follow; *(Scol: cours)* to attend; (: *programme)* to keep up with; *(Comm: article)* to continue to stock ▷ *vi* to follow; *(élève: assimiler le programme)*

to keep up; **se suivre** vi (accidents, personnes, voitures etc) to follow one after the other; **faire ~** (lettre) to forward; **"à ~"** "to be continued"

sujet, te [syʒɛ, -ɛt] adj: **être ~ à** (vertige etc) to be liable ou subject to ▷ nm/f (d'un souverain) subject ▷ nm subject; **au ~ de** about; **~ de conversation** topic ou subject of conversation; **~ d'examen** (Scol) examination question

super [sypɛʀ] adj inv great, fantastic

superbe [sypɛʀb] adj magnificent, superb

superficie [sypɛʀfisi] nf (surface) area

superficiel, le [sypɛʀfisjɛl] adj superficial

superflu, e [sypɛʀfly] adj superfluous

supérieur, e [sypeʀjœʀ] adj (lèvre, étages, classes) upper; **~ (à)** (plus élevé: température, niveau) higher (than); (meilleur: qualité, produit) superior (to); (excellent, hautain) superior ▷ nm/f superior; **supériorité** nf superiority

supermarché [sypɛʀmaʀʃe] nm supermarket

superposer [sypɛʀpoze] /1/ vt (faire chevaucher) to superimpose; **lits superposés** bunk beds

superpuissance [sypɛʀpɥisɑ̃s] nf superpower

superstitieux, -euse [sypɛʀstisjø, øz] adj superstitious

superviser [sypɛʀvize] /1/ vt to supervise

supplanter [syplɑ̃te] /1/ vt to supplant

suppléant, e [sypleɑ̃, -ɑ̃t] adj (juge, fonctionnaire) deputy cpd; (professeur) supply cpd (BRIT), substitute cpd (US) ▷ nm/f (professeur) supply ou substitute teacher

suppléer [syplee] /1/ vt (ajouter: mot manquant etc) to supply, provide; (compenser: lacune) to fill in; **~ à** to make up for

supplément [syplemɑ̃] nm supplement; **un ~ de travail** extra ou additional work; **un ~ de frites** etc an extra portion of chips etc; **le vin est en ~** wine is extra; **payer un ~** to pay an additional charge; **supplémentaire** adj additional, further; (train, bus) relief cpd, extra

supplication [syplikasjɔ̃] nf supplication; **supplications** nfpl pleas, entreaties

supplice [syplis] nm torture no pl

supplier [syplije] /7/ vt to implore, beseech

support [sypɔʀ] nm support; **~ audio-visuel** audio-visual aid; **~ publicitaire** advertising medium

supportable [sypɔʀtabl] adj (douleur, température) bearable

supporter[1] [sypɔʀtɛʀ] nm supporter, fan

supporter[2] [sypɔʀte] vt (conséquences, épreuve) to bear, endure; (défauts, personne) to tolerate, put up with; (chose, chaleur etc) to withstand; (personne, chaleur, vin) to take

▌ Attention à ne pas traduire supporter par to support.

supposer [sypoze] /1/ vt to suppose; (impliquer) to presuppose; **en supposant** ou **à ~ que** supposing (that)

suppositoire [sypozitwaʀ] nm suppository

suppression [sypʀesjɔ̃] nf (voir supprimer) removal; deletion; cancellation

supprimer [sypʀime] /1/ vt (cloison, cause, anxiété) to remove; (clause, mot) to delete; (congés, service d'autobus etc) to cancel; (emplois, privilèges, témoin gênant) to do away with

suprême [sypʀɛm] adj supreme

MOT-CLÉ

sur [syʀ] prép **1** (position) on; (: par-dessus) over; (: au-dessus) above; **pose-le sur la table** put it on the table; **je n'ai pas d'argent sur moi** I haven't any money on me

2 (direction) towards; **en allant sur Paris** going towards Paris; **sur votre droite** on ou to your right

3 (à propos de) on, about; **un livre/une conférence sur Balzac** a book/lecture on ou about Balzac

4 (proportion, mesures) out of; **un sur 10** one in 10; (Scol) one out of 10; **4 m sur 2** 4 m by 2; **avoir accident sur accident** to have one accident after another

sûr, e [syʀ] adj sure, certain; (digne de confiance) reliable; (sans danger) safe; **~ de soi** self-assured, self-confident; **le plus ~ est de** the safest thing is to

surcharge [syʀʃaʀʒ] nf (de passagers, marchandises) excess load; **surcharger** /3/ vt to overload; (décoration) to overdo

surcroît [syʀkʀwa] nm: **~ de qch** additional sth; **par** ou **de ~** moreover; **en ~** in addition

surdité [syʀdite] nf deafness

sûrement [syʀmɑ̃] adv (sans risques) safely; (certainement) certainly

surenchère [syʀɑ̃ʃɛʀ] nf (aux enchères) higher bid; **surenchérir** /2/ vi to bid higher; (fig) to try and outbid each other

surestimer [syʀɛstime] /1/ vt to overestimate

sûreté [syʀte] nf (exactitude: de renseignements etc) reliability; (sécurité) safety; (d'un geste) steadiness; **mettre en ~** to put in a safe place; **pour plus de ~** as an extra precaution; **être en ~** to be on the safe side

surf [sœʀf] nm surfing

surface [syʀfas] nf surface; (superficie) surface area; **une grande ~** a supermarket; **faire ~** to surface; **en ~** near the surface; (fig) superficially

surfait, e [syʀfɛ, -ɛt] adj overrated

surfer [sœʀfe] /1/ vi to surf; **~ sur Internet** to surf ou browse the Internet

surgelé, e [syrʒəle] adj (deep-)frozen ▷ nm: **les ~s** (deep-)frozen food

surgir [syrʒir] /2/ vi to appear suddenly; (fig: problème, conflit) to arise

sur: surhumain, e adj superhuman; **sur-le-champ** adv immediately; **surlendemain** nm: **le surlendemain (soir)** two days later (in the evening); **le surlendemain de** two days after; **surmenage** nm overwork; **surmener** /5/: **se surmener** vi to overwork

surmonter [syrmɔ̃te] /1/ vt (vaincre) to overcome; (être au-dessus de) to top

surnaturel, le [syrnatyrɛl] adj, nm supernatural

surnom [syrnɔ̃] nm nickname

surnombre [syrnɔ̃br] nm: **être en ~** to be too many (ou one too many)

surpeuplé, e [syrpœple] adj overpopulated

surplace [syrplas] nm: **faire du ~** to mark time

surplomber [syrplɔ̃be] /1/ vi to be overhanging ▷ vt to overhang

surplus [syrply] nm (Comm) surplus; (reste): **~ de bois** wood left over

surprenant, e [syrprənɑ̃, -ɑ̃t] adj amazing

surprendre [syrprɑ̃dr] /58/ vt (étonner, prendre à l'improviste) to amaze; (tomber sur: intrus etc) to catch; (conversation) to overhear

surpris, e [syrpri, -iz] adj: **~ (de/que)** amazed ou surprised (at/that); **surprise** nf surprise; **faire une surprise à qn** to give sb a surprise; **surprise-partie** nf party

sursaut [syrso] nm start, jump; **~ de** (énergie, indignation) sudden fit ou burst of; **en ~** with a start; **sursauter** /1/ vi to (give a) start, jump

sursis [syrsi] nm (Jur: gén) suspended sentence; (aussi fig) reprieve

surtout [syrtu] adv (avant tout, d'abord) above all; (spécialement, particulièrement) especially; **~, ne dites rien!** whatever you do, don't say anything!; **~ pas!** certainly ou definitely not!; **~ que ...** especially as ...

surveillance [syrvɛjɑ̃s] nf watch; (Police, Mil) surveillance; **sous ~ médicale** under medical supervision

surveillant, e [syrvɛjɑ̃, -ɑ̃t] nm/f (de prison) warder; (Scol) monitor

surveiller [syrveje] /1/ vt (enfant, élèves, bagages) to watch, keep an eye on; (prisonnier, suspect) to keep (a) watch on; (territoire, bâtiment) to (keep) watch over; (travaux, cuisson) to supervise; (Scol: examen) to invigilate; **~ son langage/sa ligne** to watch one's language/figure

survenir [syrvənir] /22/ vi (incident, retards) to occur, arise; (événement) to take place

survêt [syrvɛt], **survêtement** [syrvɛtmɑ̃] nm tracksuit

survie [syrvi] nf survival; **survivant, e** nm/f survivor; **survivre** /46/ vi to survive; **survivre à** (accident etc) to survive

survoler [syrvɔle] /1/ vt to fly over; (fig: livre) to skim through

survolté, e [syrvɔlte] adj (fig) worked up

sus [sy(s)]: **en ~ de** prép in addition to, over and above; **en ~** in addition

susceptible [sysɛptibl] adj touchy, sensitive; **~ de faire** (probabilité) liable to do

susciter [sysite] /1/ vt (admiration) to arouse; (obstacles, ennuis): **~ (à qn)** to create (for sb)

suspect, e [syspɛ(kt), -ɛkt] adj suspicious; (témoignage, opinions, vin etc) suspect ▷ nm/f suspect; **suspecter** /1/ vt to suspect; (honnêteté de qn) to question, have one's suspicions about

suspendre [syspɑ̃dr] /41/ vt (interrompre, démettre) to suspend; (accrocher: vêtement): **~ qch (à)** to hang sth up (on)

suspendu, e [syspɑ̃dy] adj (accroché): **~ à** hanging on (ou from); (perché): **~ au-dessus de** suspended over

suspens [syspɑ̃]: **en ~** adv (affaire) in abeyance; **tenir en ~** to keep in suspense

suspense [syspɑ̃s] nm suspense

suspension [syspɑ̃sjɔ̃] nf suspension; (lustre) pendant light fitting

suture [sytyr] nf: **point de ~** stitch

svelte [svɛlt] adj slender, svelte

SVP abr (= s'il vous plaît) please

sweat [swit] nm (fam) sweatshirt

sweat-shirt (pl **sweat-shirts**) [switʃœrt] nm sweatshirt

syllabe [silab] nf syllable

symbole [sɛ̃bɔl] nm symbol; **symbolique** adj symbolic; (geste, offrande) token cpd; **symboliser** /1/ vt to symbolize

symétrique [simetrik] adj symmetrical

sympa [sɛ̃pa] adj inv (fam) nice; **sois ~, prête-le moi** be a pal and lend it to me

sympathie [sɛ̃pati] nf (inclination) liking; (affinité) fellow feeling; (condoléances) sympathy; **avoir de la ~ pour qn** to like sb; **sympathique** adj nice, friendly

  █ Attention à ne pas traduire sympathique par sympathetic.

sympathisant, e [sɛ̃patizɑ̃, -ɑ̃t] nm/f sympathizer

sympathiser [sɛ̃patize] /1/ vi (voisins etc): **s'entendre** to get on (BRIT) ou along (US) (well)

symphonie [sɛ̃fɔni] nf symphony

symptôme [sɛ̃ptom] nm symptom

synagogue [sinagɔg] nf synagogue

syncope [sɛ̃kɔp] nf (Méd) blackout; **tomber en ~** to faint, pass out

syndic [sɛ̃dik] nm managing agent

syndical, e, -aux [sẽdikal, -o] *adj* (trade-)union *cpd*; **syndicaliste** *nm/f* trade unionist
syndicat [sẽdika] *nm* (*d'ouvriers, employés*) (trade(s)) union; **~ d'initiative** tourist office *ou* bureau; **syndiqué, e** *adj* belonging to a (trade) union; **syndiquer** /1/: **se syndiquer** *vi* to form a trade union; (*adhérer*) to join a trade union
synonyme [sinɔnim] *adj* synonymous ▷ *nm* synonym; **~ de** synonymous with
syntaxe [sẽtaks] *nf* syntax
synthèse [sẽtez] *nf* synthesis
synthétique [sẽtetik] *adj* synthetic
Syrie [siʀi] *nf*: **la ~** Syria
systématique [sistematik] *adj* systematic
système [sistɛm] *nm* system; **le ~ D** resourcefulness

t

t' [t] *pron voir* **te**
ta [ta] *adj poss voir* **ton**[1]
tabac [taba] *nm* tobacco; (*aussi*: **débit** *ou* **bureau de ~**) tobacconist's (shop)
tabagisme [tabaʒism] *nm*: **~ passif** passive smoking
table [tabl] *nf* table; **à ~!** dinner *etc* is ready!; **se mettre à ~** to sit down to eat; **mettre** *ou* **dresser/desservir la ~** to lay *ou* set/clear the table; **~ à repasser** ironing board; **~ de cuisson** hob; **~ des matières** (table of) contents *pl*; **~ de nuit** *ou* **de chevet** bedside table; **~ d'orientation** viewpoint indicator; **~ roulante** (tea) trolley (BRIT), tea wagon (US)
tableau, x [tablo] *nm* (*Art*) painting; (*reproduction, fig*) picture; (*panneau*) board; (*schéma*) table, chart; **~ d'affichage** notice board; **~ de bord** dashboard; (*Aviat*) instrument panel; **~ noir** blackboard
tablette [tablɛt] *nf* (*planche*) shelf; **~ de chocolat** bar of chocolate; **~ tactile** (*Inform*) tablet
tablier [tablije] *nm* apron
tabou [tabu] *nm* taboo
tabouret [tabuʀɛ] *nm* stool
tac [tak] *nm*: **du ~ au ~** tit for tat
tache [taʃ] *nf* (*saleté*) stain, mark; (*Art, de couleur, lumière*) spot; **~ de rousseur** *ou* **de son** freckle
tâche [taʃ] *nf* task
tacher [taʃe] /1/ *vt* to stain, mark
tâcher [taʃe] /1/ *vi*: **~ de faire** to try to do, endeavour (BRIT) *ou* endeavor (US) to do
tacheté, e [taʃte] *adj*: **~ de** speckled *ou* spotted with
tact [takt] *nm* tact; **avoir du ~** to be tactful
tactique [taktik] *adj* tactical ▷ *nf* (*technique*) tactics *sg*; (*plan*) tactic
taie [te] *nf*: **~ (d'oreiller)** pillowslip, pillowcase
taille [taj] *nf* cutting; (*d'arbre*) pruning; (*milieu du corps*) waist; (*hauteur*) height;

(*grandeur*) size; **de ~ à faire** capable of doing; **de ~** sizeable

taille-crayon [tɑjkʀɛjɔ̃] *nm inv* pencil sharpener

tailler [tɑje] /1/ *vt* (*pierre, diamant*) to cut; (*arbre, plante*) to prune; (*vêtement*) to cut out; (*crayon*) to sharpen

tailleur [tɑjœʀ] *nm* (*couturier*) tailor; (*vêtement*) suit; **en ~** (*assis*) cross-legged

taillis [tɑji] *nm* copse

taire [tɛʀ] /54/ *vi*: **faire ~ qn** to make sb be quiet; **se taire** *vi* to be silent *ou* quiet; **taisez-vous!** be quiet!

Taiwan [tajwan] *nf* Taiwan

talc [talk] *nm* talc, talcum powder

talent [talɑ̃] *nm* talent

talkie-walkie [tɔkiwɔki] *nm* walkie-talkie

talon [talɔ̃] *nm* heel; (*de chèque, billet*) stub, counterfoil (*BRIT*); **~s plats/aiguilles** flat/ stiletto heels

talus [taly] *nm* embankment

tambour [tɑ̃buʀ] *nm* (*Mus, Tech*) drum; (*musicien*) drummer; (*porte*) revolving door(s *pl*); **tambourin** *nm* tambourine

Tamise [tamiz] *nf*: **la ~** the Thames

tamisé, e [tamize] *adj* (*fig*) subdued, soft

tampon [tɑ̃pɔ̃] *nm* (*de coton, d'ouate*) pad; (*aussi*: **~ hygiénique** *ou* **périodique**) tampon; (*amortisseur, Inform*: *aussi*: **mémoire ~**) buffer; (*bouchon*) plug, stopper; (*cachet, timbre*) stamp; **tamponner** /1/ *vt* (*timbres*) to stamp; (*heurter*) to crash *ou* ram into; **tamponneuse** *adj f*: **autos tamponneuses** dodgems

tandem [tɑ̃dɛm] *nm* tandem

tandis [tɑ̃di]: **~ que** *conj* while

tanguer [tɑ̃ge] /1/ *vi* to pitch (and toss)

tant [tɑ̃] *adv* so much; **~ de** (*sable, eau*) so much; (*gens, livres*) so many; **~ que** as long as; **~ que** as much as; **~ mieux** that's great; (*avec une certaine réserve*) so much the better; **~ pis** too bad; (*conciliant*) never mind; **~ bien que mal** as well as can be expected

tante [tɑ̃t] *nf* aunt

tantôt [tɑ̃to] *adv* (*parfois*): **tantôt … tantôt** now … now; (*cet après-midi*) this afternoon

taon [tɑ̃] *nm* horsefly

tapage [tapaʒ] *nm* uproar, din

tapageur, -euse [tapaʒœʀ, -øz] *adj* noisy; (*voyant*) loud, flashy

tape [tap] *nf* slap

tape-à-l'œil [tapalœj] *adj inv* flashy, showy

taper [tape] /1/ *vt* (*porte*) to bang, slam; (*enfant*) to slap; (*dactylographier*) to type (out); (*fam: emprunter*): **~ qn de 10 euros** to touch sb for 10 euros ▷ *vi* (*soleil*) to beat down; **se taper** *vt* (*fam: travail*) to get landed with; (: *boire, manger*) to down; **~ sur qn** to thump sb; (*fig*) to run sb down; **~ sur qch** (*clou etc*) to hit sth; (*table etc*) to bang on sth; **~ à** (*porte etc*) to knock on; **~ dans**

(*se servir*) to dig into; **~ des mains/pieds** to clap one's hands/stamp one's feet; **~ (à la machine)** to type

tapi, e [tapi] *adj*: **~ dans/derrière** (*caché*) hidden away in/behind

tapis [tapi] *nm* carpet; (*petit*) rug; **~ roulant** (*pour piétons*) moving walkway; (*pour bagages*) carousel; **~ de sol** (*de tente*) groundsheet; **~ de souris** (*Inform*) mouse mat

tapisser [tapise] /1/ *vt* (*avec du papier peint*) to paper; (*recouvrir*): **~ qch (de)** to cover sth (with); **tapisserie** *nf* (*tenture, broderie*) tapestry; (*papier peint*) wallpaper

tapissier, -ière [tapisje, -jɛʀ] *nm/f*: **~-décorateur** interior decorator

tapoter [tapɔte] /1/ *vt* (*joue, main*) to pat; (*objet*) to tap

taquiner [takine] /1/ *vt* to tease

tard [taʀ] *adv* late ▷ *nm*: **sur le ~** late in life; **plus ~** later (on); **au plus ~** at the latest; **il est trop ~** it's too late

tarder [taʀde] /1/ *vi* (*chose*) to be a long time coming; (*personne*): **~ à faire** to delay doing; **il me tarde d'être** I am longing to be; **sans (plus) ~** without (further) delay

tardif, -ive [taʀdif, -iv] *adj* late

tarif [taʀif] *nm*: **~ des consommations** price list; **~s postaux/douaniers** postal/ customs rates; **~ des taxis** taxi fares; **~ plein/réduit** (*train*) full/reduced fare; (*téléphone*) peak/off-peak rate

tarir [taʀiʀ] /2/ *vi* to dry up, run dry

tarte [taʀt] *nf* tart; **~ aux pommes/à la crème** apple/custard tart; **~ Tatin** ≈ apple upside-down tart

tartine [taʀtin] *nf* slice of bread (and butter (*ou* jam)); **~ de miel** slice of bread and honey; **tartiner** /1/ *vt* to spread; **fromage à tartiner** cheese spread

tartre [taʀtʀ] *nm* (*des dents*) tartar; (*de chaudière*) fur, scale

tas [tɑ] *nm* heap, pile; **un ~ de** (*fig*) heaps of, lots of; **en ~** in a heap *ou* pile; **formé sur le ~** trained on the job

tasse [tɑs] *nf* cup; **~ à café/thé** coffee/ teacup

tassé, e [tɑse] *adj*: **bien ~** (*café etc*) strong

tasser [tɑse] /1/ *vt* (*terre, neige*) to pack down; (*entasser*): **~ qch dans** to cram sth into; **se tasser** *vi* (*se serrer*) to squeeze up; (*s'affaisser*) to settle; (*personne: avec l'âge*) to shrink; (*fig*) to sort itself out, settle down

tâter [tɑte] /1/ *vt* to feel; (*fig*) to try out; **~ de** (*prison etc*) to have a taste of; **se tâter** (*hésiter*) to be in two minds

tatillon, ne [tatijɔ̃, -ɔn] *adj* pernickety

tâtonnement [tɑtɔnmɑ̃] *nm*: **par ~s** (*fig*) by trial and error

tâtonner [tɑtɔne] /1/ *vi* to grope one's way along

tâtons [tɑtɔ̃]: **à ~** *adv*: **chercher/avancer à ~** to grope around for/grope one's way forward

tatouage [tatwaʒ] *nm* tattoo
tatouer [tatwe] /1/ *vt* to tattoo
taudis [todi] *nm* hovel, slum
taule [tol] *nf (fam)* nick (BRIT), jail
taupe [top] *nf* mole
taureau, x [tɔʀo] *nm* bull; *(signe):* **le T~** Taurus
taux [to] *nm* rate; *(d'alcool)* level; **~ d'intérêt** interest rate
taxe [taks] *nf* tax; *(douanière)* duty; **toutes ~s comprises** inclusive of tax; **la boutique hors ~s** the duty-free shop; **~ de séjour** tourist tax; **~ à ou sur la valeur ajoutée** value added tax
taxer [takse] /1/ *vt (personne)* to tax; *(produit)* to put a tax on, tax
taxi [taksi] *nm* taxi; *(chauffeur: fam)* taxi driver
Tchécoslovaquie [tʃekɔslɔvaki] *nf:* **la ~** Czechoslovakia; **tchèque** *adj* Czech ▷ *nm* *(Ling)* Czech ▷ *nm/f:* **Tchèque** Czech; **la République tchèque** the Czech Republic
Tchétchénie [tʃetʃeni] *nf:* **la ~** Chechnya
te, t' [tə] *pron* you; *(réfléchi)* yourself
technicien, ne [tɛknisjɛ̃, -ɛn] *nm/f* technician
technico-commercial, e, -aux [tɛknikɔmɔmɛʀsjal, o] *adj:* **agent ~** sales technician
technique [tɛknik] *adj* technical ▷ *nf* technique; **techniquement** *adv* technically
techno [tɛkno] *nf:* **la (musique) ~** techno (music)
technologie [tɛknɔlɔʒi] *nf* technology; **technologique** *adj* technological
teck [tɛk] *nm* teak
tee-shirt [tiʃœʀt] *nm* T-shirt, tee-shirt
teindre [tɛ̃dʀ] /52/ *vt* to dye; **se ~ (les cheveux)** to dye one's hair; **teint, e** *adj* dyed ▷ *nm (du visage)* complexion; (: *momentané)* colour ▷ *nf* shade; **grand teint** colourfast
teinté, e [tɛ̃te] *adj:* **~ de** *(fig)* tinged with
teinter [tɛ̃te] /1/ *vt (verre)* to tint; *(bois)* to stain
teinture [tɛ̃tyʀ] *nf* dye; **~ d'iode** tincture of iodine; **teinturerie** *nf* dry cleaner's; **teinturier, -ière** *nm/f* dry cleaner
tel, telle [tɛl] *adj (pareil)* such; *(comme):* **~ un/des ...** like a/like ...; *(indéfini)* such-and-such a; *(intensif):* **un ~/de ~s ...** such (a)/such ...; **venez ~ jour** come on such-and-such a day; **rien de ~** nothing like it; **~ que** like, such as; **~ quel** as it is *ou* stands (*ou* was *etc*)
télé [tele] *nf (fam)* TV; **à la ~** on TV *ou* telly; **télécabine** *nf (benne)* cable car; **télécarte** *nf* phonecard; **téléchargeable** *adj* downloadable; **téléchargement** *nm (action)* downloading; *(fichier)* download; **télécharger** /3/ *vt (recevoir)* to download; *(transmettre)* to upload; **télécommande** *nf* remote control; **télécopieur** *nm* fax

(machine); **télédistribution** *nf* cable TV; **télégramme** *nm* telegram; **télégraphier** /7/ *vt* to telegraph, cable; **téléguider** /1/ *vt* to operate by remote control; **télématique** *nf* telematics *sg;* **téléobjectif** *nm* telephoto lens *sg;* **télépathie** *nf* telepathy; **téléphérique** *nm* cable-car
téléphone [telefɔn] *nm* telephone; **avoir le ~** to be on the (tele)phone; **au ~** on the phone; **~ sans fil** cordless (tele)phone; **téléphoner** /1/ *vi* to make a phone call; **téléphoner à** to phone, call up; **téléphonique** *adj* (tele)phone *cpd*
téléréalité [telereralite] *nf* reality TV
télescope [teleskɔp] *nm* telescope
télescoper [teleskɔpe] /1/ *vt* to smash up; **se télescoper** *(véhicules)* to concertina
télé: téléscripteur *nm* teleprinter; **télésiège** *nm* chairlift; **téléski** *nm* ski-tow; **téléspectateur, -trice** *nm/f* (television) viewer; **télétravail** *nm* telecommuting; **télévente** *nf* telesales; **téléviseur** *nm* television set; **télévision** *nf* television; **à la télévision** on television; **télévision numérique** digital TV; **télévision par câble/satellite** cable/satellite television
télex [tɛlɛks] *nm* telex
telle [tɛl] *adj f voir* **tel; tellement** *adv (tant)* so much; *(si)* so; **tellement de** *(sable, eau)* so much; *(gens, livres)* so many; **il s'est endormi tellement il était fatigué** he was so tired (that) he fell asleep; **pas tellement** not really; **pas tellement fort/lentement** not (all) that strong/slowly; **il ne mange pas tellement** he doesn't eat (all that) much
téméraire [temeʀɛʀ] *adj* reckless, rash
témoignage [temwaɲaʒ] *nm (Jur: déclaration)* testimony *no pl,* evidence *no pl;* *(rapport, récit)* account; *(fig: d'affection etc)* token, mark; *(geste)* expression
témoigner [temwaɲe] /1/ *vt (intérêt, gratitude)* to show ▷ *vi (Jur)* to testify, give evidence; **~ de** to bear witness to, testify to
témoin [temwɛ̃] *nm* witness ▷ *adj:* **appartement-~** show flat; **être ~ de** to witness; **~ oculaire** eyewitness
tempe [tɑ̃p] *nf* temple
tempérament [tɑ̃peʀamɑ̃] *nm* temperament, disposition; **à ~** *(vente)* on deferred (payment) terms; *(achat)* by instalments, hire purchase *cpd*
température [tɑ̃peʀatyʀ] *nf* temperature; **avoir** *ou* **faire de la ~** to be running *ou* have a temperature
tempête [tɑ̃pɛt] *nf* storm; **~ de sable/ neige** sand/snowstorm
temple [tɑ̃pl] *nm* temple; *(protestant)* church
temporaire [tɑ̃pɔʀɛʀ] *adj* temporary
temps [tɑ̃] *nm (atmosphérique)* weather; *(durée)* time; *(époque)* time, times *pl;* *(Ling)*

tense; (*Mus*) beat; (*Tech*) stroke; **un ~ de chien** (*fam*) rotten weather; **quel ~ fait-il?** what's the weather like?; **il fait beau/ mauvais ~** the weather is fine/bad; **avoir le ~/tout le ~/juste le ~** to have time/ plenty of time/just enough time; **en ~ de paix/guerre** in peacetime/wartime; **en ~ utile** *ou* **voulu** in due time *ou* course; **ces derniers ~** lately; **dans quelque ~** in a (little) while; **de ~ en ~, de ~ à autre** from time to time; **à ~** (*partir, arriver*) in time; **à ~ complet, à plein ~** *adv, adj* full-time; **à ~ partiel, à mi~** *adv, adj* part-time; **dans le ~** at one time; **~ d'arrêt** pause, halt; **~ libre** free *ou* spare time; **~ mort** (*Comm*) slack period

tenable [tənabl] *adj* bearable

tenace [tənas] *adj* persistent

tenant, e [tənɑ̃, -ɑ̃t] *nm/f* (*Sport*): **~ du titre** title-holder

tendance [tɑ̃dɑ̃s] *nf* (*opinions*) leanings *pl*, sympathies *pl*; (*inclination*) tendency; (*évolution*) trend ▷ *adj inv* trendy; **avoir ~ à** to have a tendency to, tend to

tendeur [tɑ̃dœʀ] *nm* (*attache*) elastic strap

tendre [tɑ̃dʀ] /41/ *adj* tender; (*bois, roche, couleur*) soft ▷ *vt* (*élastique, peau*) to stretch; (*corde*) to tighten; (*muscle*) to tense; (*fig: piège*) to set, lay; (*donner*): **~ qch à qn** to hold sth out to sb; (*offrir*) to offer sb sth; **se tendre** *vi* (*corde*) to tighten; (*relations*) to become strained; **~ à qch/à faire** to tend towards sth/to do; **~ l'oreille** to prick up one's ears; **~ la main/le bras** to hold out one's hand/stretch out one's arm; **tendrement** *adv* tenderly; **tendresse** *nf* tenderness

tendu, e [tɑ̃dy] *pp de* **tendre** ▷ *adj* (*corde*) tight; (*muscles*) tensed; (*relations*) strained

ténèbres [tenɛbʀ] *nfpl* darkness *sg*

teneur [tənœʀ] *nf* content; (*d'une lettre*) terms *pl*, content

tenir [təniʀ] /22/ *vt* to hold; (*magasin, hôtel*) to run; (*promesse*) to keep ▷ *vi* to hold; (*neige, gel*) to last; **se tenir** *vi* (*avoir lieu*) to be held, take place; (*être: personne*) to stand; **se ~ droit** to stand up (*ou* sit up) straight; **bien se ~** to behave well; **se ~ à qch** to hold on to sth; **s'en ~ à qch** to confine o.s. to sth; **~ à** (*personne, objet*) to be attached to, care about (*ou* for); (*réputation*) to care about; **~ à faire** to want to do; **~ de** (*ressembler à*) to take after; **ça ne tient qu'à lui** it is entirely up to him; **~ qn pour** to take sb for; **~ qch de qn** (*histoire*) to have heard *ou* learnt sth from sb; (*qualité, défaut*) to have inherited *ou* got sth from sb; **~ dans** to fit into; **~ compte de qch** to take sth into account; **~ les comptes** to keep the books; **~ le coup** to hold out; **~ bon** to stand *ou* hold fast; **~ au chaud/à l'abri** to keep hot/under shelter *ou* cover; **un manteau qui tient**

chaud a warm coat; **tiens** (*ou* **tenez**), **voilà le stylo** there's the pen!; **tiens, voilà Alain!** look, here's Alain!; **tiens?** (*surprise*) really?

tennis [tenis] *nm* tennis; (*aussi:* **court de ~**) tennis court ▷ *nmpl, nfpl* (*aussi:* **chaussures de ~**) tennis *ou* gym shoes; **~ de table** table tennis; **tennisman** *nm* tennis player

tension [tɑ̃sjɔ̃] *nf* tension; (*Méd*) blood pressure; **faire** *ou* **avoir de la ~** to have high blood pressure

tentation [tɑ̃tɑsjɔ̃] *nf* temptation

tentative [tɑ̃tativ] *nf* attempt

tente [tɑ̃t] *nf* tent

tenter [tɑ̃te] /1/ *vt* (*éprouver, attirer*) to tempt; (*essayer*): **~ qch/de faire** to attempt *ou* try sth/to do; **~ sa chance** to try one's luck

tenture [tɑ̃tyʀ] *nf* hanging

tenu, e [təny] *pp de* **tenir** ▷ *adj*: **bien ~** (*maison, comptes*) well-kept; **~ de faire** (*obligé*) under an obligation to do ▷ *nf* (*vêtements*) clothes *pl*; (*comportement*) manners *pl*, behaviour; (*d'une maison*) upkeep; **en petite ~e** scantily dressed *ou* clad

ter [tɛʀ] *adj*: **16 ~** 16b *ou* B

terme [tɛʀm] *nm* term; (*fin*) end; **être en bons/mauvais ~s avec qn** to be on good/bad terms with sb; **à court/long ~** *adj* short-/long-term *ou* -range; *adv* in the short/long term; **avant ~** (*Méd*) prematurely; **mettre un ~ à** to put an end *ou* a stop to

terminaison [tɛʀminɛzɔ̃] *nf* (*Ling*) ending

terminal, e, -aux [tɛʀminal, -o] *nm* terminal ▷ *nf* (*Scol*) ≈ year 13 (*BRIT*), ≈ twelfth grade (*US*)

terminer [tɛʀmine] /1/ *vt* to finish; **se terminer** *vi* to end

terne [tɛʀn] *adj* dull

ternir [tɛʀniʀ] /2/ *vt* to dull; (*fig*) to sully, tarnish; **se ternir** *vi* to become dull

terrain [teʀɛ̃] *nm* (*sol, fig*) ground; (*Comm: étendue de terre*) land *no pl*; (: *parcelle*) plot (of land); (: *à bâtir*) site; **sur le ~** (*fig*) on the field; **~ de football/rugby** football/rugby pitch (*BRIT*), field (*US*); **~ d'aviation** airfield; **~ de camping** campsite; **~ de golf** golf course; **~ de jeu** (*pour les petits*) playground; (*Sport*) games field; **~ de sport** sports ground; **~ vague** waste ground *no pl*

terrasse [teʀas] *nf* terrace; **à la ~** (*café*) outside; **terrasser** /1/ *vt* (*adversaire*) to floor; (*maladie etc*) to lay low

terre [tɛʀ] *nf* (*gén, aussi Élec*) earth; (*substance*) soil, earth; (*opposé à mer*) land *no pl*; (*contrée*) land; **terres** *nfpl* (*terrains*) lands, land *sg*; **en ~** (*pipe, poterie*) clay *cpd*; **à** *ou* **par ~** (*mettre, être, s'asseoir*) on the ground (*ou* floor); (*jeter, tomber*) to the ground, down; **~ à ~** *adj inv* down-to-earth; **~ cuite** terracotta; **la ~ ferme** dry land; **~ glaise** clay

terreau [teʀo] nm compost

terre-plein [teʀplɛ̃] nm platform; (sur chaussée) central reservation

terrestre [teʀɛstʀ] adj (surface) earth's, of the earth; (Bot, Zool, Mil) land cpd; (Rel) earthly

terreur [teʀœʀ] nf terror no pl

terrible [teʀibl] adj terrible, dreadful; (fam) terrific; **pas ~** nothing special

terrien, ne [teʀjɛ̃, ɛn] adj: **propriétaire ~** landowner ▷ nm/f (non martien etc) earthling

terrier [teʀje] nm burrow, hole; (chien) terrier

terrifier [teʀifje] /7/ vt to terrify

terrine [teʀin] nf (récipient) terrine; (Culin) pâté

territoire [teʀitwaʀ] nm territory

terroriser [teʀɔʀize] /1/ vt to terrorize

terrorisme [teʀɔʀism] nm terrorism; **terroriste** [teʀɔʀist] nm/f terrorist

tertiaire [teʀsjɛʀ] adj tertiary ▷ nm (Écon) service industries pl

tes [te] adj poss voir **ton¹**

test [tɛst] nm test

testament [tɛstamɑ̃] nm (Jur) will; (fig) legacy; (Rel): **T~** Testament

tester [tɛste] /1/ vt to test

testicule [tɛstikyl] nm testicle

tétanos [tetanos] nm tetanus

têtard [tɛtaʀ] nm tadpole

tête [tɛt] nf head; (cheveux) hair no pl; (visage) face; **de ~** adj (wagon etc) front cpd ▷ adv (calculer) in one's head, mentally; **perdre la ~** (fig: s'affoler) to lose one's head; (: devenir fou) to go off one's head; **tenir ~ à qn** to stand up to ou defy sb; **la ~ en bas** with one's head down; **la ~ la première** (tomber) head-first; **faire une ~** (Football) to head the ball; **faire la ~** (fig) to sulk; **en ~** (Sport) in the lead; **à la ~ de** at the head of; **à ~ reposée** in a more leisurely moment; **n'en faire qu'à sa ~** to do as one pleases; **en avoir par-dessus la ~** to be fed up; **en ~ à ~** in private, alone together; **de la ~ aux pieds** from head to toe; **~ de lecture** (playback) head; **~ de liste** (Pol) chief candidate; **~ de mort** skull and crossbones; **~ de série** (Tennis) seeded player, seed; **~ de Turc** (fig) whipping boy (BRIT), butt; **tête-à-queue** nm inv: **faire un tête-à-queue** to spin round; **tête-à-tête** nm inv: **en tête-à-tête** in private, alone together

téter [tete] /6/ vt: **~ (sa mère)** to suck at one's mother's breast, feed

tétine [tetin] nf teat; (sucette) dummy (BRIT), pacifier (US)

têtu, e [tety] adj stubborn, pigheaded

texte [tɛkst] nm text; (morceau choisi) passage

texter [tɛkste] /1/ vi, vt to text

textile [tɛkstil] adj textile cpd ▷ nm textile; (industrie) textile industry

Texto [tɛksto] nm text (message)

textoter [tɛkstɔte] /1/ vi, vt to text

texture [tɛkstyʀ] nf texture

TGV sigle m = **train à grande vitesse**

thaïlandais, e [tailɑ̃dɛ, -ɛz] adj Thai ▷ nm/f: **T~, e** Thai

Thaïlande [tailɑ̃d] nf: **la ~** Thailand

thé [te] nm tea; **prendre le ~** to have tea; **~ au lait/citron** tea with milk/lemon; **faire le ~** to make the tea

théâtral, e, -aux [teatʀal, -o] adj theatrical

théâtre [teatʀ] nm theatre; (péj) playacting; (fig: lieu): **le ~ de** the scene of; **faire du ~** to act

théière [tejɛʀ] nf teapot

thème [tɛm] nm theme; (Scol: traduction) prose (composition)

théologie [teɔlɔʒi] nf theology

théorie [teɔʀi] nf theory; **théorique** adj theoretical

thérapie [teʀapi] nf therapy

thermal, e, -aux [tɛʀmal, -o] adj: **station ~e** spa; **cure ~e** water cure

thermomètre [tɛʀmɔmɛtʀ] nm thermometer

thermos® [tɛʀmos] nm ou f: **(bouteille) ~** vacuum ou Thermos® flask (BRIT) ou bottle (US)

thermostat [tɛʀmɔsta] nm thermostat

thèse [tɛz] nf thesis

thon [tɔ̃] nm tuna (fish)

thym [tɛ̃] nm thyme

Tibet [tibɛ] nm: **le ~** Tibet

tibia [tibja] nm shin; shinbone, tibia

TIC sigle fpl (= technologies de l'information et de la communication) ICT sg

tic [tik] nm tic, (nervous) twitch; (de langage etc) mannerism

ticket [tikɛ] nm ticket; **~ de caisse** till receipt

tiède [tjɛd] adj lukewarm; (vent, air) mild, warm; **tiédir** /2/ vi (se réchauffer) to grow warmer; (refroidir) to cool

tien, tienne [tjɛ̃, tjɛn] pron: **le (la) ~(ne)** yours; **les ~(ne)s** yours; **à la ~ne!** cheers!

tiens [tjɛ̃] vb, excl voir **tenir**

tiercé [tjɛʀse] nm system of forecast betting giving first three horses

tiers, tierce [tjɛʀ, tjɛʀs] adj third ▷ nm (Jur) third party; (fraction) third; **le ~ monde** the third world

tige [tiʒ] nf stem; (baguette) rod

tignasse [tiɲas] nf (péj) shock ou mop of hair

tigre [tigʀ] nm tiger; **tigré, e** adj (rayé) striped; (tacheté) spotted; (chat) tabby; **tigresse** nf tigress

tilleul [tijœl] nm lime (tree), linden (tree); (boisson) lime(-blossom) tea

timbre [tɛ̃bʀ] nm (tampon) stamp; (aussi: **~-poste**) (postage) stamp; (Mus: de voix, instrument) timbre, tone

timbré, e [tɛ̃bʀe] adj (fam) cracked

timide [timid] adj shy; (timoré) timid; **timidement** adv shyly; timidly; **timidité** nf shyness; timidity

tintamarre [tɛ̃tamaʀ] nm din, uproar

tinter [tɛ̃te] /1/ vi to ring, chime; (argent, clés) to jingle

tique [tik] nf tick (insect)

tir [tiʀ] nm (sport) shooting; (fait ou manière de tirer) firing no pl; (rafale) fire; (stand) shooting gallery; **~ à l'arc** archery

tirage [tiʀaʒ] nm (action) printing; (Photo) print; (de journal) circulation; (de livre) (print-)run; edition; (de loterie) draw; **~ au sort** drawing lots

tire [tiʀ] nf: **vol à la ~** pickpocketing

tiré, e [tiʀe] adj (visage, traits) drawn; **~ par les cheveux** far-fetched

tire-bouchon [tiʀbuʃɔ̃] nm corkscrew

tirelire [tiʀliʀ] nf moneybox

tirer [tiʀe] /1/ vt (gén) to pull; (ligne, trait) to draw; (rideau) to draw; (carte, conclusion, chèque) to draw; (en faisant feu: balle, coup) to fire; (: animal) to shoot; (journal, livre, photo) to print; (Football: corner etc) to take ▷ vi (faire feu) to fire; (faire du tir, Football) to shoot; **se tirer** vi (fam) to push off; (aussi: **s'en ~**) (éviter le pire) to get off; (survivre) to pull through; (se débrouiller) to manage; (extraire): **~ qch de** to take ou pull sth out of; **~ sur** (corde, poignée) to pull on ou at; (faire feu sur) to shoot ou fire at; (pipe) to draw on; (fig: avoisiner) to verge ou border on; **~ qn de** (embarras etc) to help ou get sb out of; **~ à l'arc/la carabine** to shoot with a bow and arrow/with a rifle; **~ à sa fin** to be drawing to an end; **~ qch au clair** to clear sth up; **~ au sort** to draw lots; **~ parti de** to take advantage of; **~ profit de** to profit from; **~ les cartes** to read ou tell the cards

tiret [tiʀe] nm dash

tireur [tiʀœʀ] nm gunman; **~ d'élite** marksman

tiroir [tiʀwaʀ] nm drawer; **tiroir-caisse** nm till

tisane [tizan] nf herb tea

tisser [tise] /1/ vt to weave

tissu [tisy] nm fabric, material, cloth no pl; (Anat, Bio) tissue; **tissu-éponge** nm (terry) towelling no pl

titre [titʀ] nm (gén) title; (de journal) headline; (diplôme) qualification; (Comm) security; **en ~** (champion, responsable) official; **à juste ~** rightly; **à quel ~?** on what grounds?; **à aucun ~** on no account; **au même ~ (que)** in the same way (as); **à ~ d'information** for (your) information; **à ~ gracieux** free of charge; **à ~ d'essai** on a trial basis; **à ~ privé** in a private capacity;

~ de propriété title deed; **~ de transport** ticket

tituber [titybe] /1/ vi to stagger ou reel (along)

titulaire [titylɛʀ] adj (Admin) with tenure ▷ nm/f (de permis) holder; **être ~ de** (diplôme, permis) to hold

toast [tost] nm slice ou piece of toast; (de bienvenue) (welcoming) toast; **porter un ~ à qn** to propose ou drink a toast to sb

toboggan [tɔbɔgɑ̃] nm slide; (Auto) flyover

toc [tɔk] nm: **en toc** imitation cpd ▷ excl: **toc, toc** knock knock

tocsin [tɔksɛ̃] nm alarm (bell)

tohu-bohu [tɔybɔy] nm commotion

toi [twa] pron you

toile [twal] nf (tableau) canvas; **de** ou **en ~** (pantalon) cotton; (sac) canvas; **~ d'araignée** cobweb; **la T~** (Internet) the Web; **~ cirée** oilcloth; **~ de fond** (fig) backdrop

toilette [twalɛt] nf (habits) outfit; **toilettes** nfpl toilet sg; **faire sa ~** to have a wash, get washed; **articles de ~** toiletries

toi-même [twamɛm] pron yourself

toit [twa] nm roof; **~ ouvrant** sun roof

toiture [twatyʀ] nf roof

Tokyo [tɔkjo] n Tokyo

tôle [tol] nf (plaque) steel (ou iron) sheet; **~ ondulée** corrugated iron

tolérable [tɔleʀabl] adj tolerable

tolérant, e [tɔleʀɑ̃, -ɑ̃t] adj tolerant

tolérer [tɔleʀe] /6/ vt to tolerate; (Admin: hors taxe etc) to allow

tollé [tɔle] nm: **un ~ (de protestations)** a general outcry

tomate [tɔmat] nf tomato; **~s farcies** stuffed tomatoes

tombe [tɔ̃b] nf (sépulture) grave; (avec monument) tomb

tombeau, x [tɔ̃bo] nm tomb

tombée [tɔ̃be] nf: **à la ~ du jour** ou **de la nuit** at nightfall

tomber [tɔ̃be] /1/ vi to fall; (fièvre, vent) to drop ▷ vt: **laisser ~** (objet) to drop; (personne) to let down; (activité) to give up; **laisse ~!** forget it!; **faire ~** to knock over; **~ sur** (rencontrer) to come across; **~ de fatigue/sommeil** to drop from exhaustion/be falling asleep on one's feet; **~ à l'eau** (projet etc) to fall through; **~ en panne** to break down; **~ en ruine** to fall into ruins; **ça tombe bien/mal** (fig) that's come at the right/wrong time; **il est bien/mal tombé** (fig) he's been lucky/unlucky

tombola [tɔ̃bɔla] nf raffle

tome [tɔm] nm volume

ton¹, ta (pl **tes**) [tɔ̃, ta, te] adj poss your

ton² [tɔ̃] nm (gén) tone; (couleur) shade, tone; **de bon ~** in good taste

tonalité [tɔnalite] nf (au téléphone) dialling tone

tondeuse [tɔ̃døz] nf (à gazon) (lawn) mower; (du coiffeur) clippers pl; (pour la tonte) shears pl

tondre [tɔ̃dʀ] /41/ vt (pelouse, herbe) to mow; (haie) to cut, clip; (mouton, toison) to shear; (cheveux) to crop

tongs [tɔ̃g] nfpl flip-flops

tonifier [tɔnifje] /7/ vt (peau, organisme) to tone up

tonique [tɔnik] adj fortifying ▷ nm tonic

tonne [tɔn] nf metric ton, tonne

tonneau, x [tɔno] nm (à vin, cidre) barrel; **faire des ~x** (voiture, avion) to roll over

tonnelle [tɔnɛl] nf bower, arbour

tonner [tɔne] /1/ vi to thunder; **il tonne** it is thundering, there's some thunder

tonnerre [tɔnɛʀ] nm thunder

tonus [tɔnys] nm energy

top [tɔp] nm: **au troisième ~** at the third stroke ▷ adj: **~ secret** top secret

topinambour [tɔpinɑ̃buʀ] nm Jerusalem artichoke

torche [tɔʀʃ] nf torch

torchon [tɔʀʃɔ̃] nm cloth; (à vaisselle) tea towel ou cloth

tordre [tɔʀdʀ] /41/ vt (chiffon) to wring; (barre, fig: visage) to twist; **se tordre** vi; **se ~ le poignet/la cheville** to twist one's wrist/ ankle, **se ~ de douleur/rire** to writhe in pain/be doubled up with laughter; **tordu, e** adj (fig) twisted, crazy

tornade [tɔʀnad] nf tornado

torrent [tɔʀɑ̃] nm mountain stream

torsade [tɔʀsad] nf: **un pull à ~s** a cable sweater

torse [tɔʀs] nm chest; (Anat. Sculpture) torso; **~ nu** stripped to the waist

tort [tɔʀ] nm (défaut) fault; **torts** nmpl (Jur) fault sg; **avoir ~** to be wrong; **être dans son ~** to be in the wrong; **donner ~ à qn** to lay the blame on sb; **causer du ~ à** to harm; **à ~** wrongly; **à ~ et à travers** wildly

torticolis [tɔʀtikɔli] nm stiff neck

tortiller [tɔʀtije] /1/ vt to twist; (moustache) to twirl; **se tortiller** vi to wriggle; (en dansant) to wiggle

tortionnaire [tɔʀsjɔnɛʀ] nm torturer

tortue [tɔʀty] nf tortoise; (d'eau douce) terrapin; (d'eau de mer) turtle

tortueux, -euse [tɔʀtɥø, -øz] adj (rue) twisting; (fig) tortuous

torture [tɔʀtyʀ] nf torture; **torturer** /1/ vt to torture; (fig) to torment

tôt [to] adv early; **~ ou tard** sooner or later; **si ~** so early; (déjà) so soon; **au plus ~** at the earliest; **plus ~** earlier

total, e, -aux [tɔtal, -o] adj, nm total; **au ~** in total ou all; (fig) on the whole; **faire le ~** to work out the total; **totalement** adv totally; **totaliser** /1/ vt to total (up); **totalitaire** adj totalitarian; **totalité** nf: **la totalité de:** **la totalité des élèves** all (of) the pupils; **la**

totalité de la population/classe the whole population/class; **en totalité** entirely

toubib [tubib] nm (fam) doctor

touchant, e [tuʃɑ̃, -ɑ̃t] adj touching

touche [tuʃ] nf (de piano, de machine à écrire) key; (de téléphone) button; (Peinture etc) stroke, touch; (fig: de couleur, nostalgie) touch; (Football: aussi: **remise en ~**) throw-in; (aussi: **ligne de ~**) touch-line; (Escrime) hit; **~ dièse** (de téléphone, clavier) hash key

toucher [tuʃe] /1/ nm touch ▷ vt to touch; (palper) to feel; (atteindre: d'un coup de feu etc) to hit; (concerner) to concern, affect; (contacter) to reach, contact; (recevoir: récompense) to receive, get; (: salaire) to draw, get; (chèque) to cash; (aborder: problème, sujet) to touch on; **au ~** to the touch; **~ à** to touch; (traiter de, concerner) to have to do with, concern; **je vais lui en ~ un mot** I'll have a word with him about it; **~ au but** (fig) to near one's goal; **~ à sa fin** to be drawing to a close

touffe [tuf] nf tuft

touffu, e [tufy] adj thick, dense

toujours [tuʒuʀ] adv always; (encore) still; (constamment) forever; **essaie ~** (you can) try anyway; **pour ~** forever; **~ est-il que** the fact remains that; **~ plus** more and more

toupie [tupi] nf (spinning) top

tour [tuʀ] nf tower; (immeuble) high-rise block (BRIT) ou building (US); (Échecs) castle, rook ▷ nm (excursion: à pied) stroll, walk; (: en voiture etc) run, ride; (: plus long) trip; (Sport: aussi: **~ de piste**) lap; (d'être servi ou de jouer etc) turn; (de roue etc) revolution; (Pol: aussi: **~ de scrutin**) ballot; (ruse, de prestidigitation, de cartes) trick; (de potier) wheel; (à bois, métaux) lathe; (circonférence): **de 3 m de ~** 3 m round, with a circumference ou girth of 3 m; **faire le ~ de** to go (a)round; (à pied) to walk (a)round; **faire un ~** to go for a walk; **c'est au ~ de Renée** it's Renée's turn; **à ~ de rôle, ~ à ~** in turn; **~ de taille/tête** nm waist/head measurement; **~ de chant** nm song recital; **~ de contrôle** nf control tower; **la ~ Eiffel** the Eiffel Tower; **le T~ de France** the Tour de France; **~ de force** nm tour de force; **~ de garde** nm spell of duty; **un 33 ~s** an LP; **un 45 ~s** a single; **~ d'horizon** nm (fig) general survey

tourbe [tuʀb] nf peat

tourbillon [tuʀbijɔ̃] nm whirlwind; (d'eau) whirlpool; (fig) whirl, swirl; **tourbillonner** /1/ vi to whirl ou twirl round

tourelle [tuʀɛl] nf turret

tourisme [tuʀism] nm tourism; **agence de ~** tourist agency; **faire du ~** to go touring; (en ville) to go sightseeing; **touriste** nm/f tourist; **touristique** adj tourist cpd; (région) touristy (péj)

tourment [tuʀmɑ̃] nm torment; **tourmenter** /1/ vt to torment; **se tourmenter** to fret, worry o.s.

tournage [tuʀnaʒ] nm (d'un film) shooting

tournant, e [tuʀnɑ̃, -ɑ̃t] adj (feu, scène) revolving ▷ nm (de route) bend; (fig) turning point

tournée [tuʀne] nf (du facteur etc) round; (d'artiste, politicien) tour; (au café) round (of drinks)

tourner [tuʀne] /1/ vt to turn; (sauce, mélange) to stir; (Ciné: faire les prises de vues) to shoot; (: produire) to make ▷ vi to turn; (moteur) to run; (compteur) to tick away; (lait etc) to turn (sour); **se tourner** vi to turn (a)round; **se ~ vers** to turn to; to turn towards; **mal ~** to go wrong; **~ autour de** to go (a)round; (péj) to hang (a)round; **~ à/en** to turn into; **~ en ridicule** to ridicule; **~ le dos à** (mouvement) to turn one's back on; (position) to have one's back to; **se ~ les pouces** to twiddle one's thumbs; **~ de l'œil** to pass out

tournesol [tuʀnəsɔl] nm sunflower

tournevis [tuʀnəvis] nm screwdriver

tournoi [tuʀnwa] nm tournament

tournure [tuʀnyʀ] nf (Ling) turn of phrase; **la ~ de qch** (évolution) the way sth is developing; **~ d'esprit** turn ou cast of mind

tourte [tuʀt] nf pie

tourterelle [tuʀtəʀɛl] nf turtledove

tous [tu, tus] adj, pron voir **tout**

Toussaint [tusɛ̃] nf: **la ~** All Saints' Day

tousser [tuse] /1/ vi to cough

MOT-CLÉ

tout, e (mpl **tous**, fpl **toutes**) [tu, tut, tus, tut] adj **1** (avec article singulier) all; **tout le lait** all the milk; **toute la nuit** all night, the whole night; **tout le livre** the whole book; **tout un pain** a whole loaf; **tout le temps** all the time, the whole time; **c'est tout le contraire** it's quite the opposite

2 (avec article pluriel) every; all; **tous les livres** all the books; **toutes les nuits** every night; **toutes les fois** every time; **toutes les trois/deux semaines** every third/other ou second week, every three/two weeks; **tous les deux** both ou each of us (ou them ou you); **toutes les trois** all three of us (ou them ou you)

3 (sans article): **à tout âge** at any age; **pour toute nourriture, il avait ...** his only food was ...

▶ pron everything, all; **il a tout fait** he's done everything; **je les vois tous** I can see them all ou all of them; **nous y sommes tous allés** all of us went, we all went; **c'est tout** that's all; **en tout** in all; **tout ce qu'il sait** all he knows

▶ nm whole; **le tout** all of it (ou them); **le tout est de ...** the main thing is to ...; **pas du tout** not at all

▶ adv **1** (très, complètement) very; **tout près** ou **à côté** very near; **le tout premier** the very first; **tout seul** all alone; **le livre tout entier** the whole book; **tout en haut** right at the top; **tout droit** straight ahead

2: **tout en** while; **tout en travaillant** while working, as he etc works

3: **tout d'abord** first of all; **tout à coup** suddenly; **tout à fait** absolutely; **tout à l'heure** a short while ago; (futur) in a short while, shortly; **à tout à l'heure!** see you later!; **tout de même** all the same; **tout le monde** everybody; **tout simplement** quite simply; **tout de suite** immediately, straight away

toutefois [tutfwa] adv however

toutes [tut] adj, pron voir **tout**

tout-terrain [tuteʀɛ̃] adj: **vélo ~** mountain bike; **véhicule ~** four-wheel drive

toux [tu] nf cough

toxicomane [tɔksikɔman] nm/f drug addict

toxique [tɔksik] adj toxic

trac [tʀak] nm (aux examens) nerves pl; (Théât) stage fright; **avoir le ~** (aux examens) to get an attack of nerves; (Théât) to have stage fright

tracasser [tʀakase] /1/ vt to worry, bother; **se tracasser** to worry (o.s.)

trace [tʀas] nf (empreintes) tracks pl; (marques, fig) mark; (restes, vestige) trace; **~s de pas** footprints

tracer [tʀase] /3/ vt to draw; (piste) to open up

tract [tʀakt] nm tract, pamphlet

tracteur [tʀaktœʀ] nm tractor

traction [tʀaksjɔ̃] nf: **~ avant/arrière** front-wheel/rear-wheel drive

tradition [tʀadisjɔ̃] nf tradition; **traditionnel, le** adj traditional

traducteur, -trice [tʀadyktœʀ, -tʀis] nm/f translator

traduction [tʀadyksjɔ̃] nf translation

traduire [tʀadɥiʀ] /38/ vt to translate; (exprimer) to convey; **~ en français** to translate into French; **~ en justice** to bring before the courts

trafic [tʀafik] nm traffic; **~ d'armes** arms dealing; **trafiquant, e** nm/f trafficker; (d'armes) dealer; **trafiquer** /1/ vt (péj: vin) to doctor; (: moteur, document) to tamper with

tragédie [tʀaʒedi] nf tragedy; **tragique** adj tragic

trahir [tʀaiʀ] /2/ vt to betray; **trahison** nf
betrayal; (Jur) treason

train [tʀɛ̃] nm (Rail) train; (allure) pace;
être en ~ de faire qch to be doing sth;
~ à grande vitesse high-speed train;
~ d'atterrissage undercarriage; ~ électrique
(jouet) (electric) train set; ~ de vie style of
living

traîne [tʀɛn] nf (de robe) train; être à la ~ to
lag behind

traîneau, x [tʀɛno] nm sleigh, sledge

traîner [tʀɛne] /1/ vt (remorque) to pull;
(enfant, chien) to drag ou trail along ▷ vi
(robe, manteau) to trail; (être en désordre) to
lie around; (marcher lentement) to dawdle
(along); (vagabonder) to hang about; (durer)
to drag on; **se traîner** vi: **se ~ par terre** to
crawl (on the ground), **~ les pieds** to drag
one's feet

train-train [tʀɛ̃tʀɛ̃] nm humdrum routine

traire [tʀɛʀ] /50/ vt to milk

trait, e [tʀɛ, -ɛt] nm (ligne) line; (de dessin)
stroke; (caractéristique) feature, trait; **traits**
nmpl (du visage) features; **d'un ~** (boire) in
one gulp; **de ~** (animal) draught; **avoir ~ à**
to concern; **~ d'union** hyphen

traitant, e [tʀɛtɑ̃, -ɑ̃t] adj: **votre**
médecin ~ your usual ou family doctor;
shampo(o)ing ~ medicated shampoo

traite [tʀɛt] nf (Comm) draft; (Agr) milking;
d'une (seule) ~ without stopping (once)

traité [tʀɛte] nm treaty

traitement [tʀɛtmɑ̃] nm treatment;
(salaire) salary; **~ de données** ou **de**
l'information data processing; **~ de texte**
word processing; (logiciel) word processing
package

traiter [tʀɛte] /1/ vt to treat; (qualifier):
~ qn d'idiot to call sb a fool ▷ vi to deal;
~ de to deal with

traiteur [tʀɛtœʀ] nm caterer

traître, -esse [tʀɛtʀ, -tʀɛs] adj (dangereux)
treacherous ▷ nm/f traitor (traitress)

trajectoire [tʀaʒɛktwaʀ] nf path

trajet [tʀaʒɛ] nm (parcours, voyage) journey;
(itinéraire) route; (distance à parcourir)
distance; **il y a une heure de ~** the journey
takes one hour

trampoline [tʀɑ̃polin] nm trampoline

tramway [tʀamwɛ] nm tram(way);
(voiture) tram(car) (BRIT), streetcar (US)

tranchant, e [tʀɑ̃ʃɑ̃, -ɑ̃t] adj sharp; (fig)
peremptory ▷ nm (d'un couteau) cutting
edge; (de la main) edge; **à double ~** double-
edged

tranche [tʀɑ̃ʃ] nf (morceau) slice; (arête)
edge; **~ d'âge/de salaires** age/wage
bracket

tranché, e [tʀɑ̃ʃe] adj (couleurs) distinct;
(opinions) clear-cut

trancher [tʀɑ̃ʃe] /1/ vt to cut, sever ▷ vi to
be decisive; **~ avec** to contrast sharply with

tranquille [tʀɑ̃kil] adj quiet; (rassuré)
easy in one's mind, with one's mind at rest;
se tenir ~ (enfant) to be quiet; **avoir la**
conscience ~ to have an easy conscience;
laisse-moi/laisse-ça ~ leave me/it
alone; **tranquillisant** nm tranquillizer;
tranquillité nf peace (and quiet);
tranquillité d'esprit peace of mind

transférer [tʀɑ̃sfeʀe] /6/ vt to transfer;
transfert nm transfer

transformation [tʀɑ̃sfɔʀmasjɔ̃]
nf change, alteration; (radicale)
transformation; (Rugby) conversion;
transformations nfpl (travaux) alterations

transformer [tʀɑ̃sfɔʀme] /1/ vt to change;
(radicalement) to transform; (vêtement) alter;
(matière première, appartement, Rugby) to
convert; **~ en** to turn into

transfusion [tʀɑ̃sfyzjɔ̃] nf: **~ sanguine**
blood transfusion

transgénique [tʀɑ̃sʒenik] adj transgenic

transgresser [tʀɑ̃sgʀese] /1/ vt to
contravene

transi, e [tʀɑ̃zi] adj numb (with cold),
chilled to the bone

transiger [tʀɑ̃ziʒe] /3/ vi to compromise

transit [tʀɑ̃zit] nm transit; **transiter** /1/ vi
to pass in transit

transition [tʀɑ̃zisjɔ̃] nf transition;
transitoire adj transitional

transmettre [tʀɑ̃smɛtʀ] /56/ vt (passer):
~ qch à qn to pass sth on to sb; (Tech, Tél, Méd)
to transmit; (TV, Radio: retransmettre) to
broadcast, **transmission** nf transmission

transparent, e [tʀɑ̃spaʀɑ̃, -ɑ̃t] adj
transparent

transpercer [tʀɑ̃spɛʀse] /3/ vt (froid, pluie)
to go through, pierce; (balle) to go through

transpiration [tʀɑ̃spiʀasjɔ̃] nf
perspiration

transpirer [tʀɑ̃spiʀe] /1/ vi to perspire

transplanter [tʀɑ̃splɑ̃te] /1/ vt (Méd, Bot)
to transplant

transport [tʀɑ̃spɔʀ] nm transport; **~s en**
commun public transport sg; **transporter**
/1/ vt to carry, move; (Comm) to transport,
convey; **transporteur** nm haulage
contractor (BRIT), trucker (US)

transvaser [tʀɑ̃svaze] /1/ vt to decant

transversal, e, -aux [tʀɑ̃svɛʀsal, -o] adj
(mur, chemin, rue) running at right angles;
coupe ~e cross section

trapèze [tʀapɛz] nm (au cirque) trapeze

trappe [tʀap] nf trap door

trapu, e [tʀapy] adj squat, stocky

traquenard [tʀaknaʀ] nm trap

traquer [tʀake] /1/ vt to track down;
(harceler) to hound

traumatiser [tʀomatize] /1/ vt to
traumatize

travail, -aux [tʀavaj, -o] nm (gén) work;
(tâche, métier) work no pl, job; (Écon, Méd)

labour; **travaux** nmpl (de réparation, agricoles etc) work sg; (sur route) roadworks; (de construction) building (work) sg; **être sans ~** (employé) to be out of work; **~ (au) noir** moonlighting; **travaux des champs** farmwork sg; **travaux dirigés** (Scol) supervised practical work sg; **travaux forcés** hard labour sg; **travaux manuels** (Scol) handicrafts; **travaux ménagers** housework sg; **travaux pratiques** (gén) practical work sg; (en laboratoire) lab work sg

travailler [tʀavaje] /1/ vi to work; (bois) to warp ▷ vt (bois, métal) to work; (objet d'art, discipline) to work; **cela le travaille** it is on his mind; **travailleur, -euse** adj hard-working ▷ nm/f worker; **travailleur social** social worker; **travailliste** adj ≈ Labour cpd

travaux [tʀavo] nmpl voir **travail**

travers [tʀavɛʀ] nm fault, failing; **en ~ (de)** across; **au ~ (de)** through; **de ~** (nez, bouche) crooked; (chapeau) askew; **à ~** through; **regarder de ~** (fig) to look askance at; **comprendre de ~** to misunderstand

traverse [tʀavɛʀs] nf (de voie ferrée) sleeper; **chemin de ~** shortcut

traversée [tʀavɛʀse] nf crossing

traverser [tʀavɛʀse] /1/ vt (gén) to cross; (ville, tunnel, aussi percer, fig) to go through; (ligne, trait) to run across

traversin [tʀavɛʀsɛ̃] nm bolster

travesti [tʀavɛsti] nm transvestite

trébucher [tʀebyʃe] /1/ vi: **~ (sur)** to stumble (over), trip (over)

trèfle [tʀɛfl] nm (Bot) clover; (Cartes: couleur) clubs pl; (: carte) club; **~ à quatre feuilles** four-leaf clover

treize [tʀɛz] num thirteen; **treizième** num thirteenth

tréma [tʀema] nm diaeresis

tremblement [tʀɑ̃bləmɑ̃] nm: **~ de terre** earthquake

trembler [tʀɑ̃ble] /1/ vi to tremble, shake; **~ de** (froid, fièvre) to shiver ou tremble with; (peur) to shake ou tremble with; **~ pour qn** to fear for sb

trémousser [tʀemuse] /1/: **se trémousser** vi to jig about, wriggle about

trempé, e [tʀɑ̃pe] adj soaking (wet), drenched; (Tech): **acier ~** tempered steel

tremper [tʀɑ̃pe] /1/ vt to soak, drench; (aussi: **faire ~, mettre à ~**) to soak ▷ vi to soak; (fig): **~ dans** to be involved ou have a hand in; **se tremper** vi to have a quick dip

tremplin [tʀɑ̃plɛ̃] nm springboard; (Ski) ski jump

trentaine [tʀɑ̃tɛn] nf (âge): **avoir la ~** to be around thirty; **une ~ (de)** thirty or so, about thirty

trente [tʀɑ̃t] num thirty; **être/se mettre sur son ~ et un** to be wearing/put on one's Sunday best; **trentième** num thirtieth

trépidant, e [tʀepidɑ̃, -ɑ̃t] adj (fig: rythme) pulsating; (: vie) hectic

trépigner [tʀepiɲe] /1/ vi to stamp (one's feet)

très [tʀɛ] adv very; **~ beau/bien** very beautiful/well; **~ critiqué** much criticized; **~ industrialisé** highly industrialized

trésor [tʀezɔʀ] nm treasure; **~ (public)** public revenue; **trésorerie** nf (gestion) accounts pl; (bureaux) accounts department; **difficultés de trésorerie** cash problems, shortage of cash ou funds; **trésorier, -ière** nm/f treasurer

tressaillir [tʀesajiʀ] /13/ vi to shiver, shudder

tressauter [tʀesote] /1/ vi to start, jump

tresse [tʀɛs] nf braid, plait; **tresser** /1/ vt (cheveux) to braid, plait; (fil, jonc) to plait; (corbeille) to weave; (corde) to twist

trêve [tʀɛv] nf (Mil, Pol) truce; (fig) respite; **~ de ...** enough of this ...

tri [tʀi] nm: **faire le ~ (de)** to sort out; **le (bureau de) ~** (Postes) the sorting office

triangle [tʀijɑ̃gl] nm triangle; **triangulaire** adj triangular

tribord [tʀibɔʀ] nm: **à ~** to starboard, on the starboard side

tribu [tʀiby] nf tribe

tribunal, -aux [tʀibynal, -o] nm (Jur) court; (Mil) tribunal

tribune [tʀibyn] nf (estrade) platform, rostrum; (débat) forum; (d'église, de tribunal) gallery; (de stade) stand

tribut [tʀiby] nm tribute

tributaire [tʀibytɛʀ] adj: **être ~ de** to be dependent on

tricher [tʀiʃe] /1/ vi to cheat; **tricheur, -euse** nm/f cheat

tricolore [tʀikɔlɔʀ] adj three-coloured; (français) red, white and blue

tricot [tʀiko] nm (technique, ouvrage) knitting no pl; (vêtement) jersey, sweater; **~ de corps, ~ de peau** vest; **tricoter** /1/ vt to knit

tricycle [tʀisikl] nm tricycle

trier [tʀije] /7/ vt to sort (out); (Postes, Inform, fruits) to sort

trimestre [tʀimɛstʀ] nm (Scol) term; (Comm) quarter; **trimestriel, le** adj quarterly; (Scol) end-of-term

trinquer [tʀɛ̃ke] /1/ vi to clink glasses

triomphe [tʀijɔ̃f] nm triumph; **triompher** /1/ vi to triumph, win; **triompher de** to triumph over, overcome

tripes [tʀip] nfpl (Culin) tripe sg

triple [tʀipl] adj triple ▷ nm: **le ~ (de)** (comparaison) three times as much (as); **en ~ exemplaire** in triplicate; **tripler** /1/ vi, vt to triple, treble

triplés, -ées [tʀiple] nm/f pl triplets

tripoter [tʀipɔte] /1/ vt to fiddle with

triste [tʀist] *adj* sad; (*couleur, temps, journée*) dreary; (*péj*): ~ **personnage/affaire** sorry individual/affair; **tristesse** *nf* sadness

trivial, e, -aux [tʀivjal, -o] *adj* coarse, crude; (*commun*) mundane

troc [tʀɔk] *nm* barter

trognon [tʀɔɲɔ̃] *nm* (*de fruit*) core; (*de légume*) stalk

trois [tʀwɑ] *num* three; **troisième** *num* third ▷ *nf* (*Scol*) year 10 (*BRIT*), ninth grade (*US*); **le troisième âge** (*période de vie*) one's retirement years; (*personnes âgées*) senior citizens *pl*

troll [tʀɔl] *nm*, **trolleur, -euse** [tʀɔlœʀ, -øz] *nm/f* (*Inform*) troll

trombe [tʀɔ̃b] *nf*: **des ~s d'eau** a downpour; **en ~** like a whirlwind

trombone [tʀɔ̃bɔn] *nm* (*Mus*) trombone; (*de bureau*) paper clip

trompe [tʀɔ̃p] *nf* (*d'éléphant*) trunk; (*Mus*) trumpet, horn

tromper [tʀɔ̃pe] /1/ *vt* to deceive; (*vigilance, poursuivants*) to elude; **se tromper** *vi* to make a mistake, be mistaken; **se ~ de voiture/jour** to take the wrong car/get the day wrong; **se ~ de 3 cm/20 euros** to be out by 3 cm/20 euros

trompette [tʀɔ̃pɛt] *nf* trumpet; **en ~** (*nez*) turned-up

trompeur, -euse [tʀɔ̃pœʀ, -øz] *adj* deceptive

tronc [tʀɔ̃] *nm* (*Bot, Anat*) trunk; (*d'église*) collection box

tronçon [tʀɔ̃sɔ̃] *nm* section, **tronçonner** /1/ *vt* to saw up; **tronçonneuse** *nf* chainsaw

trône [tʀon] *nm* throne

trop [tʀo] *adv* too; (*avec verbe*) too much; (*aussi*: ~ **nombreux**) too many; (*aussi*: ~ **souvent**) too often; ~ **peu (nombreux)** too few; ~ **longtemps** (for) too long; ~ **de** (*nombre*) too many; (*quantité*) too much; **de ~, en ~: des livres en ~** a few books too many; **du lait en ~** too much milk; **trois livres/cinq euros de ~** three books too many/five euros too much; **ça coûte ~ cher** it's too expensive

tropical, e, -aux [tʀɔpikal, -o] *adj* tropical

tropique [tʀɔpik] *nm* tropic

trop-plein [tʀoplɛ̃] *nm* (*tuyau*) overflow *ou* outlet (*pipe*); (*liquide*) overflow

troquer [tʀɔke] /1/ *vt*: ~ **qch contre** to barter *ou* trade sth for; (*fig*) to swap sth for

trot [tʀo] *nm* trot; **trotter** /1/ *vi* to trot

trottinette [tʀɔtinet] *nf* (*child's*) scooter

trottoir [tʀɔtwaʀ] *nm* pavement (*BRIT*), sidewalk (*US*); **faire le ~** (*péj*) to walk the streets; ~ **roulant** moving walkway, travelator

trou [tʀu] *nm* hole; (*fig*) gap; (*Comm*) deficit; ~ **d'air** air pocket; ~ **de mémoire** blank, lapse of memory

troublant, e [tʀublɑ̃, -ɑ̃t] *adj* disturbing

trouble [tʀubl] *adj* (*liquide*) cloudy; (*image, photo*) blurred; (*affaire*) shady, murky ▷ *adv*: **voir ~** to have blurred vision ▷ *nm* agitation; **troubles** *nmpl* (*Pol*) disturbances, troubles, unrest *sg*; (*Méd*) trouble *sg*, disorders; **trouble-fête** *nm/f inv* spoilsport

troubler [tʀuble] /1/ *vt* to disturb; (*liquide*) to make cloudy; (*intriguer*) to bother; **se troubler** *vi* (*personne*) to become flustered *ou* confused

trouer [tʀue] /1/ *vt* to make a hole (*ou* holes) in

trouille [tʀuj] *nf* (*fam*): **avoir la ~** to be scared stiff

troupe [tʀup] *nf* troop; ~ **(de théâtre)** (theatrical) company

troupeau, x [tʀupo] *nm* (*de moutons*) flock; (*de vaches*) herd

trousse [tʀus] *nf* case, kit; (*d'écolier*) pencil case; **aux ~s de** (*fig*) on the heels *ou* tail of; ~ **à outils** toolkit; ~ **de toilette** toilet bag

trousseau, x [tʀuso] *nm* (*de mariée*) trousseau; ~ **de clefs** bunch of keys

trouvaille [tʀuvaj] *nf* find

trouver [tʀuve] /1/ *vt* to find; (*rendre visite*): **aller/venir ~ qn** to go/come and see sb; **se trouver** *vi* (*être*) to be; **je trouve que** I find *ou* think that; ~ **à boire/critiquer** to find something to drink/criticize; **se ~ mal** to pass out

truand [tʀyɑ̃] *nm* villain; **truander** /1/ *vt*: **se faire truander** to be swindled

truc [tʀyk] *nm* (*astuce*) way; (*de cinéma, prestidigitateur*) trick effect; (*chose*) thing; thingumajig; **avoir le ~** to have the knack; **c'est pas son** (*ou* **mon** *etc*) ~ (*fam*) it's not really his (*ou* my *etc*) thing

truffe [tʀyf] *nf* truffle; (*nez*) nose

truffé, e [tʀyfe] *adj* (*Culin*) garnished with truffles

truie [tʀɥi] *nf* sow

truite [tʀɥit] *nf* trout *inv*

truquage [tʀykaʒ] *nm* special effects *pl*

truquer [tʀyke] /1/ *vt* (*élections, serrure, dés*) to fix

TSVP *abr* (= *tournez s'il vous plaît*) PTO

TTC *abr* (= *toutes taxes comprises*) inclusive of tax

tu¹ [ty] *pron* you ▷ *nm*: **employer le tu** to use the "tu" form

tu², e [ty] *pp de* **taire**

tuba [tyba] *nm* (*Mus*) tuba; (*Sport*) snorkel

tube [tyb] *nm* tube; (*chanson, disque*) hit song *ou* record

tuberculose [tybɛʀkyloz] *nf* tuberculosis

tuer [tɥe] /1/ *vt* to kill; **se tuer** (*se suicider*) to kill o.s.; (*dans un accident*) to be killed; **se ~ au travail** (*fig*) to work o.s. to death, **tuerie** *nf* slaughter *no pl*

tue-tête [tytɛt]: **à ~** *adv* at the top of one's voice

tueur [tɥœʀ] *nm* killer; **~ à gages** hired killer

tuile [tɥil] *nf* tile; (*fam*) spot of bad luck, blow

tulipe [tylip] *nf* tulip

tuméfié, e [tymefje] *adj* puffy, swollen

tumeur [tymœʀ] *nf* growth, tumour

tumulte [tymylt] *nm* commotion; **tumultueux, -euse** *adj* stormy, turbulent

tunique [tynik] *nf* tunic

Tunis [tynis] *n* Tunis

Tunisie [tynizi] *nf*: **la ~** Tunisia; **tunisien, ne** *adj* Tunisian ▷ *nm/f*: **Tunisien, ne** Tunisian

tunnel [tynɛl] *nm* tunnel; **le ~ sous la Manche** the Channel Tunnel

turbulent, e [tyʀbylɑ̃, -ɑ̃t] *adj* boisterous, unruly

turc, turque [tyʀk] *adj* Turkish ▷ *nm* (*Ling*) Turkish ▷ *nm/f*: **Turc, Turque** Turk/Turkish woman

turf [tyʀf] *nm* racing; **turfiste** *nm/f* racegoer

Turquie [tyʀki] *nf*: **la ~** Turkey

turquoise [tyʀkwaz] *nf, adj inv* turquoise

tutelle [tytɛl] *nf* (*Jur*) guardianship; (*Pol*) trusteeship; **sous la ~ de** (*fig*) under the supervision of

tuteur, -trice [tytœʀ, -tʀis] *nm/f* (*Jur*) guardian; (*de plante*) stake, support

tutoyer [tytwaje] /8/ *vt*: **~ qn** to address sb as "tu"

tuyau, x [tɥijo] *nm* pipe; (*flexible*) tube; (*fam*) tip; **~ d'arrosage** hosepipe; **~ d'échappement** exhaust pipe; **tuyauterie** *nf* piping *no pl*

TVA *sigle f* (= *taxe à ou sur la valeur ajoutée*) VAT

tweet [twit] *nm* (*aussi Internet*: *Twitter*) tweet; **tweeter** /1/ *vi* (*Internet*: *Twitter*) to tweet

tympan [tɛ̃pɑ̃] *nm* (*Anat*) eardrum

type [tip] *nm* type; (*fam*) chap, guy ▷ *adj* typical, standard

typé, e [tipe] *adj* ethnic (*euphémisme*)

typique [tipik] *adj* typical

tyran [tiʀɑ̃] *nm* tyrant; **tyrannique** *adj* tyrannical

tzigane [dzigan] *adj* gipsy, tzigane

u

ulcère [ylsɛʀ] *nm* ulcer

ultérieur, e [ylteʀjœʀ] *adj* later, subsequent; **remis à une date ~e** postponed to a later date; **ultérieurement** *adv* later, subsequently

ultime [yltim] *adj* final

 MOT-CLÉ

un, une [œ̃, yn] *art indéf* a; (*devant voyelle*) an; **un garçon/vieillard** a boy/an old man; **une fille** a girl
▶ *pron* one; **l'un des meilleurs** one of the best; **l'un ..., l'autre** (the) one ..., the other; **les uns ..., les autres** some ..., others; **l'un et l'autre** both (of them); **l'un ou l'autre** either (of them); **l'un l'autre, les uns les autres** each other, one another; **pas un seul** not a single one; **un par un** one by one
▶ *num* one; **une pomme seulement** one apple only, just one apple
▶ *nf*: **la une** (*Presse*) the front page

unanime [ynanim] *adj* unanimous; **unanimité** *nf*: **à l'unanimité** unanimously

uni, e [yni] *adj* (*ton, tissu*) plain; (*surface*) smooth, even; (*famille*) close(-knit); (*pays*) united

unifier [ynifje] /7/ *vt* to unite, unify

uniforme [ynifɔʀm] *adj* uniform; (*surface, ton*) even ▷ *nm* uniform; **uniformiser** /1/ *vt* (*systèmes*) to standardize

union [ynjɔ̃] *nf* union; **~ de consommateurs** consumers' association; **~ libre: vivre en ~ libre** (*en concubinage*) to cohabit; **l'U~ européenne** the European Union; **l'U~ soviétique** the Soviet Union

unique [ynik] *adj* (*seul*) only; (*exceptionnel*) unique; **un prix/système ~** a single price/system; **fils/fille ~** only son/daughter, only child; **sens ~** one-way street; **uniquement** *adv* only, solely; (*juste*) only, merely

unir [ynir] /2/ vt (nations) to unite; (en mariage) to unite, join together; **s'unir** vi to unite; (en mariage) to be joined together

unitaire [yniter] adj: **prix ~** unit price

unité [ynite] nf (harmonie, cohésion) unity; (Math) unit

univers [yniver] nm universe; **universel, le** adj universal

universitaire [yniversiter] adj university cpd; (diplôme, études) academic, university cpd ▷ nm/f academic

université [yniversite] nf university

urbain, e [yrbɛ̃, -ɛn] adj urban, city cpd, town cpd; **urbanisme** nm town planning

urgence [yrʒɑ̃s] nf urgency; (Méd etc) emergency; **d'~** adj emergency cpd ▷ adv as a matter of urgency; **service des ~s** emergency service

urgent, e [yrʒɑ̃, -ɑ̃t] adj urgent

urine [yrin] nf urine; **urinoir** nm (public) urinal

urne [yrn] nf (électorale) ballot box; (vase) urn

urticaire [yrtiker] nf nettle rash

us [ys] nmpl: **us et coutumes** (habits and) customs

usage [yzaʒ] nm (emploi, utilisation) use; (coutume) custom; **à l'~** with use; **à l'~ de** (pour) for (use of); **en ~** in use; **hors d'~** out of service; **à ~ interne** (Méd) to be taken (internally); **à ~ externe** (Méd) for external use only; **usagé, e** adj (usé) worn; **usager, -ère** nm/f user

usé, e [yze] adj worn (down ou out ou away); (banal: argument etc) hackneyed

user [yze] /1/ vt (outil) to wear down; (vêtement) to wear out; (matière) to wear away; (consommer: charbon etc) to use; **s'user** vi (tissu, vêtement) to wear out; **~ de** (moyen, procédé) to use, employ; (droit) to exercise

usine [yzin] nf factory

usité, e [yzite] adj common

ustensile [ystɑ̃sil] nm implement; **~ de cuisine** kitchen utensil

usuel, le [yzɥɛl] adj everyday, common

usure [yzyr] nf wear

utérus [yterys] nm uterus, womb

utile [ytil] adj useful

utilisation [ytilizasjɔ̃] nf use

utiliser [ytilize] /1/ vt to use

utilitaire [ytiliter] adj utilitarian

utilité [ytilite] nf usefulness no pl; **de peu d'~** of little use ou help

utopie [ytɔpi] nf utopia

va [va] vb voir **aller**

vacance [vakɑ̃s] nf (Admin) vacancy; **vacances** nfpl holiday(s) pl (BRIT), vacation sg (US); **les grandes ~s** the summer holidays ou vacation; **prendre des/ses ~s** to take a holiday ou vacation/one's holiday(s) ou vacation; **aller en ~s** to go on holiday ou vacation; **vacancier, -ière** nm/f holidaymaker

vacant, e [vakɑ̃, -ɑ̃t] adj vacant

vacarme [vakarm] nm row, din

vaccin [vaksɛ̃] nm vaccine; (opération) vaccination; **vaccination** nf vaccination; **vacciner** /1/ vt to vaccinate; **être vacciné** (fig) to be immune

vache [vaʃ] nf (Zool) cow; (cuir) cowhide ▷ adj (fam) rotten, mean; **vachement** adv (fam) really; **vacherie** nf (action) dirty trick; (propos) nasty remark

vaciller [vasije] /1/ vi to sway, wobble; (bougie, lumière) to flicker; (fig) to be failing, falter

VAE sigle m (= vélo (à assistance) électrique) e-bike

va-et-vient [vaevjɛ̃] nm inv comings and goings pl

vagabond, e [vagabɔ̃, -ɔ̃d] adj wandering ▷ nm (rôdeur) tramp, vagrant; (voyageur) wanderer; **vagabonder** /1/ vi to roam, wander

vagin [vaʒɛ̃] nm vagina

vague [vag] nf wave ▷ adj vague; (regard) faraway; (manteau, robe) loose(-fitting); (quelconque): **un ~ bureau/cousin** some office/cousin or other; **~ de fond** ground swell; **~ de froid** cold spell

vaillant, e [vajɑ̃, -ɑ̃t] adj (courageux) gallant; (robuste) hale and hearty

vain, e [vɛ̃, vɛn] adj vain; **en ~** in vain

vaincre [vɛ̃kr] /42/ vt to defeat; (fig) to conquer, overcome; **vaincu, e** nm/f defeated party; **vainqueur** nm victor; (Sport) winner

vaisseau, x [vɛso] nm (Anat) vessel; (Navig) ship, vessel; **~ spatial** spaceship

vaisselier [vɛsəlje] nm dresser

vaisselle [vɛsɛl] nf (service) crockery; (plats etc à laver) (dirty) dishes pl; **faire la ~** to do the dishes

valable [valabl] adj valid; (acceptable) decent, worthwhile

valet [valɛ] nm valet; (Cartes) jack

valeur [valœʀ] nf (gén) value; (mérite) worth, merit; (Comm: titre) security; **valeurs** nfpl (morales) values; **mettre en ~** (fig) to highlight; to show off to advantage; **avoir de la ~** to be valuable; **prendre de la ~** to go up ou gain in value; **sans ~** worthless

valide [valid] adj (en bonne santé) fit; (valable) valid; **valider** /1/ vt to validate

valise [valiz] nf (suit)case; **faire sa ~** to pack one's (suit)case

vallée [vale] nf valley

vallon [valɔ̃] nm small valley

valoir [valwaʀ] /29/ vi (être valable) to hold, apply ▷ vt (prix, valeur, effort) to be worth; (causer): **~ qch à qn** to earn sb sth; **se valoir** to be of equal merit; (péj) to be two of a kind; **faire ~** (droits, prérogatives) to assert; **se faire ~** to make the most of o.s.; **à ~ sur** to be deducted from; **vaille que vaille** somehow or other; **cela ne me dit rien qui vaille** I don't like the look of it at all; **ce climat ne me vaut rien** this climate doesn't suit me; **~ la peine** to be worth the trouble, be worth it; **~ mieux: il vaut mieux se taire** it's better to say nothing; **ça ne vaut rien** it's worthless; **que vaut ce candidat?** how good is this applicant?

valse [vals] nf waltz

vandalisme [vɑ̃dalism] nm vandalism

vanille [vanij] nf vanilla

vanité [vanite] nf vanity; **vaniteux, -euse** adj vain, conceited

vanne [van] nf gate; (fam) dig

vantard, e [vɑ̃taʀ, -aʀd] adj boastful

vanter [vɑ̃te] /1/ vt to speak highly of, praise; **se vanter** vi to boast, brag; **se ~ de** to pride o.s. on; (péj) to boast of

vapeur [vapœʀ] nf steam; (émanation) vapour, fumes pl; **vapeurs** nfpl (bouffées) vapours; **à ~** steam-powered, steam cpd; **cuit à la ~** steamed; **vaporeux, -euse** adj (flou) hazy, misty; (léger) filmy; **vaporisateur** nm spray; **vaporiser** /1/ vt (parfum etc) to spray

vapoter [vapɔte] /1/ vi to smoke an e-cigarette

varappe [vaʀap] nf rock climbing

vareuse [vaʀøz] nf (blouson) pea jacket; (d'uniforme) tunic

variable [vaʀjabl] adj variable; (temps, humeur) changeable; (divers: résultats) varied, various

varice [vaʀis] nf varicose vein

varicelle [vaʀisɛl] nf chickenpox

varié, e [vaʀje] adj varied; (divers) various; **hors-d'œuvre ~s** selection of hors d'œuvres

varier [vaʀje] /7/ vi to vary; (temps, humeur) to change ▷ vt to vary; **variété** nf variety; **spectacle de variétés** variety show

variole [vaʀjɔl] nf smallpox

Varsovie [vaʀsɔvi] n Warsaw

vas [va] vb voir **aller**; **~-y!** go on!

vase [vaz] nm vase ▷ nf silt, mud; **vaseux, -euse** adj silty, muddy; (fig: confus) woolly, hazy; (: fatigué) peaky

vasistas [vazistɑs] nm fanlight

vaste [vast] adj vast, immense

vautour [votuʀ] nm vulture

vautrer [votʀe] /1/: **se vautrer** vi: **se ~ dans** to wallow in; **se ~ sur** to sprawl on

va-vite [vavit]: **à la ~** adv in a rush

VDQS sigle m (= vin délimité de qualité supérieure) label guaranteeing quality of wine

veau, x [vo] nm (Zool) calf; (Culin) veal; (peau) calfskin

vécu, e [veky] pp de **vivre**

vedette [vədɛt] nf (artiste etc) star; (canot) patrol boat; (police) launch

végétal, e, -aux [veʒetal, -o] adj vegetable ▷ nm vegetable, plant; **végétalien, ne** adj, nm/f vegan

végétarien, ne [veʒetaʀjɛ̃, -ɛn] adj, nm/f vegetarian

végétation [veʒetasjɔ̃] nf vegetation; **végétations** nfpl (Méd) adenoids

véhicule [veikyl] nm vehicle; **~ utilitaire** commercial vehicle

veille [vɛj] nf (Psych) wakefulness; (jour): **la ~** the day before; **la ~ au soir** the previous evening; **la ~ de** the day before; **la ~ de Noël** Christmas Eve; **la ~ du jour de l'An** New Year's Eve; **à la ~ de** on the eve of

veillée [veje] nf (soirée) evening; (réunion) evening gathering; **~ (funèbre)** wake

veiller [veje] /1/ vi to stay ou sit up ▷ vt (malade, mort) to watch over, sit up with; **~ à** to attend to, see to; **~ à ce que** to make sure that; **~ sur** to keep a watch ou an eye on; **veilleur** nm: **veilleur de nuit** night watchman; **veilleuse** nf (lampe) night light; (Auto) sidelight; (flamme) pilot light

veinard, e [vɛnaʀ, -aʀd] nm/f lucky devil

veine [vɛn] nf (Anat, du bois etc) vein; (filon) vein, seam; **avoir de la ~** (fam) (chance) to be lucky

véliplanchiste [veliplɑ̃ʃist] nm/f windsurfer

vélo [velo] nm bike, cycle; **faire du ~** to go cycling; **vélomoteur** nm moped

velours [v(ə)luʀ] nm velvet; **~ côtelé** corduroy; **velouté, e** adj velvety ▷ nm: **velouté d'asperges/de tomates** cream of asparagus/tomato soup

velu, e [vəly] *adj* hairy

vendange [vɑ̃dɑ̃ʒ] *nf* (*aussi:* **~s**) grape harvest; **vendanger** /3/ *vi* to harvest the grapes

vendeur, -euse [vɑ̃dœʀ, -øz] *nm/f* shop *ou* sales assistant ▷ *nm* (*Jur*) vendor, seller

vendre [vɑ̃dʀ] /41/ *vt* to sell; **~ qch à qn** to sell sb sth; **"à ~"** "for sale"

vendredi [vɑ̃dʀədi] *nm* Friday; **V~ saint** Good Friday

vénéneux, -euse [venenø, -øz] *adj* poisonous

vénérien, ne [veneʀjɛ̃, -ɛn] *adj* venereal

vengeance [vɑ̃ʒɑ̃s] *nf* vengeance *no pl*, revenge *no pl*

venger [vɑ̃ʒe] /3/ *vt* to avenge; **se venger** *vi* to avenge o.s.; **se ~ de qch** to avenge o.s. for sth; to take one's revenge for sth; **se ~ de qn** to take revenge on sb; **se ~ sur** to take revenge on

venimeux, -euse [vənimø, -øz] *adj* poisonous, venomous; (*fig*: *haineux*) venomous, vicious

venin [vənɛ̃] *nm* venom, poison

venir [v(ə)niʀ] /22/ *vi* to come; **~ de** to come from; **~ de faire: je viens d'y aller/ de le voir** I've just been there/seen him; **s'il vient à pleuvoir** if it should rain; **où veux-tu en ~?** what are you getting at?; **faire ~** (*docteur, plombier*) to call (out)

vent [vɑ̃] *nm* wind; **il y a du ~** it's windy; **c'est du ~** it's all hot air; **dans le ~** (*fam*) trendy

vente [vɑ̃t] *nf* sale; **la ~** (*activité*) selling; (*secteur*) sales *pl*; **mettre en ~** to put on sale; (*objets personnels*) to put up for sale; **~ aux enchères** auction sale; **~ de charité** jumble (*BRIT*) *ou* rummage (*US*) sale

venteux, -euse [vɑ̃tø, -øz] *adj* windy

ventilateur [vɑ̃tilatœʀ] *nm* fan

ventiler [vɑ̃tile] /1/ *vt* to ventilate

ventouse [vɑ̃tuz] *nf* (*de caoutchouc*) suction pad

ventre [vɑ̃tʀ] *nm* (*Anat*) stomach; (*fig*) belly; **avoir mal au ~** to have (a) stomach ache

venu, e [v(ə)ny] *pp de* **venir** ▷ *adj*: **être mal ~ à** *ou* **de faire** to have no grounds for doing, be in no position to do; **mal ~** ill-timed; **bien ~** timely

ver [vɛʀ] *nm* worm; (*des fruits etc*) maggot; (*du bois*) woodworm *no pl*; **~ luisant** glow-worm; **~ à soie** silkworm; **~ solitaire** tapeworm; **~ de terre** earthworm

verbe [vɛʀb] *nm* verb

verdâtre [vɛʀdɑtʀ] *adj* greenish

verdict [vɛʀdik(t)] *nm* verdict

verdir [vɛʀdiʀ] /2/ *vi*, *vt* to turn green; **verdure** *nf* greenery

véreux, -euse [veʀø, -øz] *adj* worm-eaten; (*malhonnête*) shady, corrupt

verge [vɛʀʒ] *nf* (*Anat*) penis

verger [vɛʀʒe] *nm* orchard

verglacé, e [vɛʀglase] *adj* icy, iced-over

verglas [vɛʀglɑ] *nm* (black) ice

véridique [veʀidik] *adj* truthful

vérification [veʀifikɑsjɔ̃] *nf* checking *no pl*, check

vérifier [veʀifje] /7/ *vt* to check; (*corroborer*) to confirm, bear out

véritable [veʀitabl] *adj* real; (*ami, amour*) true; **un ~ désastre** an absolute disaster

vérité [veʀite] *nf* truth; **en ~** to tell the truth

verlan [vɛʀlɑ̃] *nm* (back) slang

vermeil, le [vɛʀmɛj] *adj* ruby red

vermine [vɛʀmin] *nf* vermin *pl*

vermoulu, e [vɛʀmuly] *adj* worm-eaten

verni, e [vɛʀni] *adj* (*fam*) lucky; **cuir ~** patent leather

vernir [vɛʀniʀ] /2/ *vt* (*bois, tableau, ongles*) to varnish; (*poterie*) to glaze; **vernis** *nm* (*enduit*) varnish; glaze; (*fig*) veneer; **vernis à ongles** nail varnish (*BRIT*) *ou* polish; **vernissage** *nm* (*d'une exposition*) preview

vérole [veʀɔl] *nf* (*variole*) smallpox

verre [vɛʀ] *nm* glass; (*de lunettes*) lens *sg*; **boire** *ou* **prendre un ~** to have a drink; **~s de contact** contact lenses; **verrière** *nf* (*grand vitrage*) window; (*toit vitré*) glass roof

verrou [veʀu] *nm* (*targette*) bolt; **mettre qn sous les ~s** to put sb behind bars; **verrouillage** *nm* locking mechanism; **verrouillage central** *ou* **centralisé** central locking; **verrouiller** /1/ *vt* to bolt; to lock

verrue [veʀy] *nf* wart

vers [vɛʀ] *nm* line ▷ *nmpl* (*poésie*) verse *sg* ▷ *prép* (*en direction de*) toward(s), (*près de*) around (about); (*temporel*) about, around

versant [vɛʀsɑ̃] *nm* slopes *pl*, side

versatile [vɛʀsatil] *adj* fickle, changeable

verse [vɛʀs]: **à ~** *adv*: **il pleut à ~** it's pouring (with rain)

Verseau [vɛʀso] *nm*: **le ~** Aquarius

versement [vɛʀsəmɑ̃] *nm* payment; **en trois ~s** in three instalments

verser [vɛʀse] /1/ *vt* (*liquide, grains*) to pour; (*larmes, sang*) to shed; (*argent*) to pay; **~ sur un compte** to pay into an account

version [vɛʀsjɔ̃] *nf* version; (*Scol*) translation (*into the mother tongue*); **film en ~ originale** film in the original language

verso [vɛʀso] *nm* back; **voir au ~** see over(leaf)

vert, e [vɛʀ, vɛʀt] *adj* green; (*vin*) young; (*vigoureux*) sprightly ▷ *nm* green; **les V~s** (*Pol*) the Greens

vertèbre [vɛʀtɛbʀ] *nf* vertebra

vertement [vɛʀtəmɑ̃] *adv* (*réprimander*) sharply

vertical, e, -aux [vɛʀtikal, -o] *adj* vertical; **verticale** *nf* vertical; **à la verticale** vertically; **verticalement** *adv* vertically

vertige [vɛʀtiʒ] *nm (peur du vide)* vertigo; *(étourdissement)* dizzy spell; *(fig)* fever; **vertigineux, -euse** *adj* breathtaking

vertu [vɛʀty] *nf* virtue; **en ~ de** in accordance with; **vertueux, -euse** *adj* virtuous

verve [vɛʀv] *nf* witty eloquence; **être en ~** to be in brilliant form

verveine [vɛʀvɛn] *nf (Bot)* verbena, vervain; *(infusion)* verbena tea

vésicule [vezikyl] *nf* vesicle; **~ biliaire** gall-bladder

vessie [vesi] *nf* bladder

veste [vɛst] *nf* jacket; **~ droite/croisée** single-/double-breasted jacket

vestiaire [vɛstjɛʀ] *nm (au théâtre etc)* cloakroom; *(de stade etc)* changing-room *(BRIT)*, locker-room *(US)*

vestibule [vɛstibyl] *nm* hall

vestige [vɛstiʒ] *nm* relic; *(fig)* vestige; **vestiges** *nmpl (d'une ville)* remains

vestimentaire [vɛstimɑ̃tɛʀ] *adj (détail)* of dress; *(élégance)* sartorial; **dépenses ~s** clothing expenditure

veston [vɛstɔ̃] *nm* jacket

vêtement [vɛtmɑ̃] *nm* garment, item of clothing; **vêtements** *nmpl* clothes

vétérinaire [veteʀinɛʀ] *nm/f* vet, veterinary surgeon

vêtir [vetiʀ] /20/ *vt* to clothe, dress

vêtu, e [vety] *pp de* **vêtir** ▷ *adj*: **~ de** dressed in, wearing

vétuste [vetyst] *adj* ancient, timeworn

veuf, veuve [vœf, vœv] *adj* widowed ▷ *nm* widower ▷ *nf* widow

vexant, e [vɛksɑ̃, -ɑ̃t] *adj (contrariant)* annoying; *(blessant)* upsetting

vexation [vɛksasjɔ̃] *nf* humiliation

vexer [vɛkse] /1/ *vt* to hurt; **se vexer** *vi* to be offended

viable [vjabl] *adj* viable; *(économie, industrie etc)* sustainable

viande [vjɑ̃d] *nf* meat; **je ne mange pas de ~** I don't eat meat

vibrer [vibʀe] /1/ *vi* to vibrate; *(son, voix)* to be vibrant; *(fig)* to be stirred; **faire ~** to (cause to) vibrate; to stir, thrill

vice [vis] *nm* vice; *(défaut)* fault; **~ de forme** legal flaw *ou* irregularity

vicié, e [visje] *adj (air)* polluted, tainted; *(Jur)* invalidated

vicieux, -euse [visjø, -øz] *adj (pervers)* dirty(-minded); *(méchant)* nasty ▷ *nm/f* lecher

vicinal, e, -aux [visinal, -o] *adj*: **chemin ~** byroad, byway

victime [viktim] *nf* victim; *(d'accident)* casualty

victoire [viktwaʀ] *nf* victory

victuailles [viktɥaj] *nfpl* provisions

vidange [vidɑ̃ʒ] *nf (d'un fossé, réservoir)* emptying; *(Auto)* oil change; *(de lavabo: bonde)* waste outlet; **vidanges** *nfpl (matières)* sewage *sg*; **vidanger** /3/ *vt* to empty

vide [vid] *adj* empty ▷ *nm (Physique)* vacuum; *(espace)* (empty) space, gap; *(futilité, néant)* void; **emballé sous ~** vacuum-packed; **avoir peur du ~** to be afraid of heights; **à ~** *(sans occupants)* empty; *(sans charge)* unladen

vidéo [video] *nf* video; **cassette ~** video cassette; **vidéoclip** *nm* music video; **vidéoconférence** *nf* videoconference

vide-ordures [vidɔʀdyʀ] *nm inv* (rubbish) chute

vider [vide] /1/ *vt* to empty; *(Culin: volaille, poisson)* to gut, clean out; **se vider** *vi* to empty; **~ les lieux** to quit *ou* vacate the premises; **videur** *nm (de boîte de nuit)* bouncer

vie [vi] *nf* life; **être en ~** to be alive; **sans ~** lifeless; **à ~** for life; **que faites-vous dans la ~?** what do you do?

vieil [vjɛj] *adj m voir* **vieux**; **vieillard** *nm* old man; **vieille** *adj f, nf voir* **vieux**; **vieilleries** *nfpl* old things *ou* stuff *sg*; **vieillesse** *nf* old age; **vieillir** /2/ *vi (prendre de l'âge)* to grow old; *(population, vin)* to age; *(doctrine, auteur)* to become dated ▷ *vt* to age; **se vieillir** to make o.s. older; **vieillissement** *nm* growing old; ageing

Vienne [vjɛn] *n* Vienna

viens [vjɛ̃] *vb voir* **venir**

vierge [vjɛʀʒ] *adj* virgin; *(page)* clean, blank ▷ *nf* virgin; *(signe)*: **la V~** Virgo

Viêtnam, Vietnam [vjɛtnam] *nm*: **le ~** Vietnam; **vietnamien, ne** *adj* Vietnamese ▷ *nm/f*: **Vietnamien, ne** Vietnamese

vieux (vieil), vieille [vjø, vjɛj] *adj* old ▷ *nm/f* old man/woman ▷ *nmpl*: **les ~** *(pej)* old people; **un petit ~** a little old man; **mon ~/ma vieille** *(fam)* old man/girl; **prendre un coup de ~** to put years on; **~ garçon** bachelor; **~ jeu** *adj inv* old-fashioned

vif, vive [vif, viv] *adj (animé)* lively; *(alerte)* sharp; *(lumière, couleur)* brilliant; *(air)* crisp; *(vent, émotion)* keen; *(fort: regret, déception)* great, deep; *(vivant)*: **brûlé ~** burnt alive; **de vive voix** personally; **avoir l'esprit ~** to be quick-witted; **piquer qn au ~** to cut sb to the quick; **à ~** *(plaie)* open; **avoir les nerfs à ~** to be on edge

vigne [viɲ] *nf (plante)* vine; *(plantation)* vineyard; **vigneron** *nm* wine grower

vignette [viɲɛt] *nf (pour voiture)* ≈ (road) tax disc *(BRIT)*, ≈ license plate sticker *(US)*; *(sur médicament)* price label *(on medicines for reimbursement by Social Security)*

vignoble [viɲɔbl] *nm (plantation)* vineyard; *(vignes d'une région)* vineyards *pl*

vigoureux, -euse [viguʀø, -øz] *adj* vigorous, robust

vigueur [vigœʀ] nf vigour; **être/entrer en ~** to be in/come into force; **en ~** current

vilain, e [vilɛ̃, -ɛn] adj (laid) ugly; (affaire, blessure) nasty; (pas sage: enfant) naughty; **~ mot** bad word

villa [vila] nf (detached) house; **~ en multipropriété** time-share villa

village [vilaʒ] nm village; **villageois, e** adj village cpd ▷ nm/f villager

ville [vil] nf town; (importante) city; (administration): **la ~ ≈** the (town) council; **~ d'eaux** spa; **~ nouvelle** new town

vin [vɛ̃] nm wine; **avoir le ~ gai/triste** to get happy/miserable after a few drinks; **~ d'honneur** reception (with wine and snacks); **~ ordinaire** ou **de table** table wine; **~ de pays** local wine

vinaigre [vinɛgʀ] nm vinegar; **vinaigrette** nf vinaigrette, French dressing

vindicatif, -ive [vɛ̃dikatif, -iv] adj vindictive

vingt [vɛ̃, vɛ̃t] (2nd pron used when followed by a vowel) num twenty; **~-quatre heures sur ~-quatre** twenty-four hours a day, round the clock; **vingtaine** nf: **une vingtaine (de)** around twenty, twenty or so; **vingtième** num twentieth

vinicole [vinikɔl] adj wine cpd; wine-growing

vinyle [vinil] nm vinyl

viol [vjɔl] nm (d'une femme) rape; (d'un lieu sacré) violation

violacé, e [vjɔlase] adj purplish, mauvish

violemment [vjɔlamɑ̃] adv violently

violence [vjɔlɑ̃s] nf violence

violent, e [vjɔlɑ̃, -ɑ̃t] adj violent; (remède) drastic

violer [vjɔle] /1/ vt (femme) to rape; (sépulture) to desecrate; (loi, traité) to violate

violet, te [vjɔlɛ, -ɛt] adj, nm purple, mauve ▷ nf (fleur) violet

violon [vjɔlɔ̃] nm violin; (fam: prison) lock-up; **~ d'Ingres** (artistic) hobby; **violoncelle** nm cello; **violoniste** nm/f violinist

virage [viʀaʒ] nm (d'un véhicule) turn; (d'une route, piste) bend

viral, e, -aux [viʀal, -o] adj (aussi Inform) viral

virée [viʀe] nf run; (à pied) walk; (longue) hike

virement [viʀmɑ̃] nm (Comm) transfer

virer [viʀe] /1/ vt (Comm) to transfer; (fam: renvoyer) to sack ▷ vi to turn; (Chimie) to change colour (BRIT) ou color (US); **~ au bleu** to turn blue; **~ de bord** to tack

virevolter [viʀvɔlte] /1/ vi to twirl around

virgule [viʀgyl] nf comma; (Math) point

viril, e [viʀil] adj (propre à l'homme) masculine; (énergique, courageux) manly, virile

virtuel, le [viʀtɥɛl] adj potential; (théorique) virtual

virtuose [viʀtɥoz] nm/f (Mus) virtuoso; (gén) master

virus [viʀys] nm virus

vis vb [vi] voir **voir, vivre** ▷ nf [vis] screw

visa [viza] nm (sceau) stamp; (validation de passeport) visa

visage [vizaʒ] nm face

vis-à-vis [vizavi]: **~ de** prép towards; **en ~** facing ou opposite each other

visée [vize] nf aiming; **visées** nfpl (intentions) designs

viser [vize] /1/ vi to aim ▷ vt to aim at; (concerner) to be aimed ou directed at; (apposer un visa sur) to stamp, visa; **~ à qch/faire** to aim at sth/at doing ou to do

visibilité [vizibilite] nf visibility

visible [vizibl] adj visible; (disponible): **est-il ~?** can he see me?, will he see visitors?

visière [vizjɛʀ] nf (de casquette) peak; (qui s'attache) eyeshade

vision [vizjɔ̃] nf vision; (sens) (eye)sight, vision; (fait de voir): **la ~ de** the sight of; **visionneuse** nf viewer

visiophone [vizjɔfɔn] nm videophone

visite [vizit] nf visit; **~ médicale** medical examination; **~ accompagnée** ou **guidée** guided tour; **faire une ~ à qn** to call on sb, pay sb a visit; **rendre ~ à qn** to visit sb, pay sb a visit; **être en ~ (chez qn)** to be visiting (sb); **avoir de la ~** to have visitors; **heures de ~** (hôpital, prison) visiting hours

visiter [vizite] /1/ vt to visit; **visiteur, -euse** nm/f visitor

vison [vizɔ̃] nm mink

visser [vise] /1/ vt: **~ qch** (fixer, serrer) to screw sth on

visuel, le [vizɥɛl] adj visual

vital, e, -aux [vital, -o] adj vital

vitamine [vitamin] nf vitamin

vite [vit] adv (rapidement) quickly, fast; (sans délai) quickly; soon; **~!** quick!; **faire ~** to be quick

vitesse [vitɛs] nf speed; (Auto: dispositif) gear; **prendre de la ~** to pick up ou gather speed; **à toute ~** at full ou top speed; **en ~** quickly

● **LIMITE DE VITESSE**
●
● The speed limit in France is 50 km/h in
● built-up areas, 90 km/h on main roads,
● and 130 km/h on motorways (110 km/h
● when it is raining).

viticulteur [vitikyltœʀ] nm wine grower

vitrage [vitʀaʒ] nm: **double ~** double glazing

vitrail, -aux [vitʀaj, -o] nm stained-glass window

vitre [vitʀ] nf (window) pane; (de portière, voiture) window; **vitré, e** adj glass cpd

vitrine [vitʀin] *nf* (shop) window; (*petite armoire*) display cabinet; **en ~** in the window

vivable [vivabl] *adj* (*personne*) livable-with; (*maison*) fit to live in

vivace [vivas] *adj* (*arbre, plante*) hardy; (*fig*) enduring

vivacité [vivasite] *nf* liveliness, vivacity

vivant, e [vivɑ̃, -ɑ̃t] *adj* (*qui vit*) living, alive; (*animé*) lively; (*preuve, exemple*) living ▷ *nm*: **du ~ de qn** in sb's lifetime; **les ~s et les morts** the living and the dead

vive [viv] *adj f voir* **vif** ▷ *vb voir* **vivre** ▷ *excl*: **~ le roi!** long live the king!; **vivement** *adv* sharply ▷ *excl*: **vivement les vacances!** roll on the holidays!

vivier [vivje] *nm* (*au restaurant etc*) fish tank; (*étang*) fishpond

vivifiant, e [vivifjɑ̃, -ɑ̃t] *adj* invigorating

vivoter [vivɔte] /1/ *vi* (*personne*) to scrape a living, get by; (*fig: affaire etc*) to struggle along

vivre [vivʀ] /46/ *vi, vt* to live; **vivres** *nmpl* provisions, food supplies; **il vit encore** he is still alive; **se laisser ~** to take life as it comes; **ne plus ~** (*être anxieux*) to live on one's nerves; **il a vécu** (*eu une vie aventureuse*) he has seen life; **être facile à ~** to be easy to get on with; **faire ~ qn** (*pourvoir à sa subsistance*) to provide (a living) for sb; **~ de** to live on

vlan [vlɑ̃] *excl* wham!, bang!

VO *sigle f* = **version originale**; **voir un film en VO** to see a film in its original language

vocabulaire [vɔkabylɛʀ] *nm* vocabulary

vocation [vɔkasjɔ̃] *nf* vocation, calling

vœu, x [vø] *nm* wish; (*à Dieu*) vow; **faire ~ de** to take a vow of; **avec tous nos ~x** with every good wish *ou* our best wishes

vogue [vɔg] *nf* fashion, vogue; **en ~** in fashion, in vogue

voici [vwasi] *prép* (*pour introduire, désigner*) here is (+ *sg*); here are (+ *pl*); **et ~ que ...** and now it (*ou* he) ...; *voir aussi* **voilà**

voie [vwa] *nf* way; (*Rail*) track, line; (*Auto*) lane; **par ~ buccale** *ou* **orale** orally; **être en bonne ~** to be shaping *ou* going well; **mettre qn sur la ~** to put sb on the right track; **être en ~ d'achèvement/de rénovation** to be nearing completion/in the process of renovation; **à ~ unique** single-track; **route à deux/trois ~s** two-/three-lane road; **~ express** expressway; **~ ferrée** track; railway line (BRIT), railroad (US); **~ de garage** (*Rail*) siding; **la ~ lactée** the Milky Way; **la ~ publique** the public highway

voilà [vwala] *prép* (*en désignant*) there is (+ *sg*); there are (+ *pl*); **les ~** *ou* **voici** here *ou* there they are; **en ~** *ou* **voici un** here's one, there's one; **voici mon frère et ~ ma sœur** this is my brother and that's my sister; **~ ou voici deux ans** two years ago; **~ ou voici**

deux ans que it's two years since; **et ~!** there we are!; **~ tout** that's all; **"~ ou voici"** (*en offrant etc*) "there *ou* here you are"; **tiens! ~ Paul** look! there's Paul

voile [vwal] *nm* veil; (*tissu léger*) net ▷ *nf* sail; (*sport*) sailing; **voiler** /1/ *vt* to veil; (*fausser: roue*) to buckle; (*: bois*) to warp; **se voiler** *vi* (*lune, regard*) to mist over; (*voix*) to become husky; (*roue, disque*) to buckle; (*planche*) to warp; **voilier** *nm* sailing ship; (*de plaisance*) sailing boat; **voilure** *nf* (*de voilier*) sails *pl*

voir [vwaʀ] /30/ *vi, vt* to see; **se voir: cela se voit** (*c'est visible*) that's obvious, it shows; **faire ~ qch à qn** to show sb sth; **en faire ~ à qn** (*fig*) to give sb a hard time; **ne pas pouvoir ~ qn** not to be able to stand sb; **voyons!** let's see now; (*indignation etc*) come (along) now!; **ça n'a rien à ~ avec lui** that has nothing to do with him

voire [vwaʀ] *adv* or even

voisin, e [vwazɛ̃, -in] *adj* (*proche*) neighbouring; next; (*ressemblant*) connected ▷ *nm/f* neighbour; **voisinage** *nm* (*proximité*) proximity; (*environs*) vicinity; (*quartier, voisins*) neighbourhood

voiture [vwatyʀ] *nf* car; (*wagon*) coach, carriage; **~ de course** racing car; **~ de sport** sports car

voix [vwa] *nf* voice; (*Pol*) vote; **à haute ~** aloud; **à ~ basse** in a low voice; **à deux/quatre ~** (*Mus*) in two/four parts; **avoir ~ au chapitre** to have a say in the matter

vol [vɔl] *nm* (*trajet, voyage, groupe d'oiseaux*) flight; (*mode d'appropriation*) theft, stealing; (*larcin*) theft; **à ~ d'oiseau** as the crow flies; **au ~: attraper qch au ~** to catch sth as it flies past; **en ~** in flight; **~ libre** hang-gliding; **~ à main armée** armed robbery; **~ régulier** scheduled flight; **~ à voile** gliding

volage [vɔlaʒ] *adj* fickle

volaille [vɔlaj] *nf* (*oiseaux*) poultry *pl*; (*viande*) poultry *no pl*; (*oiseau*) fowl

volant, e [vɔlɑ̃, -ɑ̃t] *adj* flying ▷ *nm* (*d'automobile*) (steering) wheel; (*de commande*) wheel; (*objet lancé*) shuttlecock; (*bande de tissu*) flounce

volcan [vɔlkɑ̃] *nm* volcano

volée [vɔle] *nf* (*Tennis*) volley; **à la ~: rattraper à la ~** to catch in midair; **à toute ~** (*sonner les cloches*) vigorously; (*lancer un projectile*) with full force

voler [vɔle] /1/ *vi* (*avion, oiseau, fig*) to fly; (*voleur*) to steal ▷ *vt* (*objet*) to steal; (*personne*) to rob; **~ qch à qn** to steal sth from sb; **on m'a volé mon portefeuille** my wallet *ou* billfold (US) has been stolen; **il ne l'a pas volé!** he asked for it!

volet [vɔlɛ] *nm* (*de fenêtre*) shutter; (*Aviat*) flap; (*de feuillet, document*) section; (*fig: d'un plan*) facet

voleur, -euse [vɔlœʀ, -øz] *nm/f* thief ▷ *adj* thieving; **"au ~!"** "stop thief!"

volley [vɔlɛ], **volley-ball** [vɔlɛbol] *nm* volleyball

volontaire [vɔlɔ̃tɛʀ] *adj* (*acte, activité*) voluntary; (*délibéré*) deliberate; (*caractère, personne: décidé*) self-willed ▷ *nm/f* volunteer

volonté [vɔlɔ̃te] *nf* (*faculté de vouloir*) will; (*énergie, fermeté*) will(power); (*souhait, désir*) wish; **se servir/boire à ~** to take/drink as much as one likes; **bonne ~** goodwill, willingness, **mauvaise ~** lack of goodwill, unwillingness

volontiers [vɔlɔ̃tje] *adv* (*avec plaisir*) willingly, gladly; (*habituellement, souvent*) readily, willingly; **"~"** "with pleasure"

volt [vɔlt] *nm* volt

volte-face [vɔltəfas] *nf inv*: **faire ~** to do an about-turn

voltige [vɔltiʒ] *nf* (*Équitation*) trick riding; (*au cirque*) acrobatics *sg*; **voltiger** [vɔltiʒe] /3/ *vi* to flutter (about)

volubile [vɔlybil] *adj* voluble

volume [vɔlym] *nm* volume; (*Géom: solide*) solid; **volumineux, -euse** *adj* voluminous, bulky

volupté [vɔlypte] *nf* sensual delight *ou* pleasure

vomi [vɔmi] *nm* vomit; **vomir** /2/ *vi* to vomit, be sick ▷ *vt* to vomit, bring up; (*fig*) to belch out, spew out; (*exécrer*) to loathe, abhor

vorace [vɔʀas] *adj* voracious

vos [vo] *adj poss voir* **votre**

vote [vɔt] *nm* vote; **~ par correspondance/ procuration** postal/proxy vote; **voter** [vɔte] /1/ *vi* to vote ▷ *vt* (*loi, décision*) to vote for

votre [vɔtʀ] (*pl* **vos**) *adj poss* your

vôtre [vɔtʀ] *pron*: **le ~, la ~, les ~s** yours; **les ~s** (*fig*) your family *ou* folks; **à la ~** (*toast*) your (good) health!

vouer [vwe] /1/ *vt*: **~ sa vie/son temps à** (*étude, cause etc*) to devote one's life/time to; **~ une haine/amitié éternelle à qn** to vow undying hatred/friendship to sb

⬤ **MOT-CLÉ**

vouloir [vulwaʀ] /31/ *vt* **1** (*exiger, désirer*) want; **vouloir faire/que qn fasse** to want to do/sb to do; **voulez-vous du thé?** would you like *ou* do you want some tea?; **que me veut-il?** what does he want with me?; **sans le vouloir** (*involontairement*) without meaning to, unintentionally; **je voudrais ceci/faire** I would *ou* I'd like this/to do; **le hasard a voulu que …** as fate would have it, …; **la tradition veut que …** tradition demands that …

2 (*consentir*): **je veux bien** (*bonne volonté*) I'll be happy to; (*concession*) fair enough, that's fine; **oui, si on veut** (*en quelque sorte*) yes,

if you like; **veuillez attendre** please wait; **veuillez agréer …** (*formule épistolaire*) yours faithfully

3: **en vouloir à qn** to bear sb a grudge; **s'en vouloir (de)** to be annoyed with o.s. (for); **il en veut à mon argent** he's after my money

4: **vouloir de: l'entreprise ne veut plus de lui** the firm doesn't want him any more; **elle ne veut pas de son aide** she doesn't want his help

5: **vouloir dire** to mean

▷ *nm*: **le bon vouloir de qn** sb's goodwill, sb's pleasure

voulu, e [vuly] *pp de* **vouloir** ▷ *adj* (*requis*) required, requisite; (*délibéré*) deliberate, intentional

vous [vu] *pron* you; (*objet indirect*) (to) you; (*réfléchi: sg*) yourself; (: *pl*) yourselves; (*réciproque*) each other ▷ *nm*: **employer le ~** (*vouvoyer*) to use the "vous" form; **~-même** yourself; **~-mêmes** yourselves

vouvoyer [vuvwaje] /8/ *vt*: **~ qn** to address sb as "vous"

voyage [vwajaʒ] *nm* journey, trip; (*fait de voyager*): **le ~** travel(ling); **partir/être en ~** to go off/be away on a journey *ou* trip; **faire bon ~** to have a good journey; **~ d'agrément/d'affaires** pleasure/ business trip; **~ de noces** honeymoon; **~ organisé** package tour

voyager [vwajaʒe] /3/ *vi* to travel; **voyageur, -euse** *nm/f* traveller; (*passager*) passenger; **voyageur (de commerce)** commercial traveller

voyant, e [vwajã, -ãt] *adj* (*couleur*) loud, gaudy ▷ *nm* (*signal*) (warning) light

voyelle [vwajɛl] *nf* vowel

voyou [vwaju] *nm* hoodlum

vrac [vʀak]: **en ~** *adv* loose; (*Comm*) in bulk

vrai, e [vʀɛ] *adj* (*véridique: récit, faits*) true; (*non factice, authentique*) real; **à ~ dire** to tell the truth; **vraiment** *adv* really; **vraisemblable** *adj* likely; (*excuse*) plausible; **vraisemblablement** *adv* in all likelihood, very likely; **vraisemblance** *nf* likelihood; (*romanesque*) verisimilitude

vrombir [vʀɔ̃biʀ] /2/ *vi* to hum

VRP *sigle m* (= *voyageur, représentant, placier*) (sales) rep (*fam*)

VTT *sigle m* (= *vélo tout-terrain*) mountain bike

vu¹ [vy] *prép* (*en raison de*) in view of; **vu que** in view of the fact that

vu², e [vy] *pp de* **voir** ▷ *adj*: **bien/mal vu** (*personne*) well/poorly thought of

vue [vy] *nf* (*sens, faculté*) (eye)sight; (*panorama, image, photo*) view; **la ~ de** (*spectacle*) the sight of; **vues** *nfpl* (*idées*) views; (*dessein*) designs; **perdre la ~** to lose one's (eye)sight; **perdre de ~** to lose sight of; **hors de ~** out of sight; **à première ~** at first sight; **tirer à ~** to shoot on sight;

à ~ d'œil visibly; **avoir ~ sur** to have a view of; **en ~** (*visible*) in sight; (*célèbre*) in the public eye; **en ~ de faire** with a view to doing; **~ d'ensemble** overall view

vulgaire [vylgɛʀ] *adj* (*grossier*) vulgar, coarse; (*trivial*) commonplace, mundane; (*péj: quelconque*): **de ~s touristes/chaises de cuisine** common tourists/kitchen chairs; (*Bot, Zool: non latin*) common;

vulgariser /1/ *vt* to popularize

vulnérable [vylneʀabl] *adj* vulnerable

W

wagon [vagɔ̃] *nm* (*de voyageurs*) carriage; (*de marchandises*) truck, wagon; **wagon-lit** *nm* sleeper, sleeping car; **wagon-restaurant** *nm* restaurant *ou* dining car

wallon, ne [walɔ̃, -ɔn] *adj* Walloon ▷ *nm* (*Ling*) Walloon ▷ *nm/f*: **W~, ne** Walloon

watt [wat] *nm* watt

WC [vese] *nmpl* toilet *sg*

Web [wɛb] *nm inv*: **le ~** the (World Wide) Web; **webcam** *nf* webcam; **webmaster, webmestre** *nm/f* webmaster

week-end [wikɛnd] *nm* weekend

western [wɛstɛʀn] *nm* western

whisky [wiski] (*pl* **whiskies**) *nm* whisky

wifi [wifi] *nm inv* wifi

WWW *sigle m* (= *World Wide Web*) WWW

xénophobe [gzenɔfɔb] *adj* xenophobic
  ▷ *nm/f* xenophobe
xérès [gzerɛs] *nm* sherry
xylophone [gzilɔfɔn] *nm* xylophone

y [i] *adv* (*à cet endroit*) there; (*dessus*) on it
  (*ou* them); (*dedans*) in it (*ou* them) ▷ *pron*
  (about *ou* on *ou* of) it (*vérifier la syntaxe du
  verbe employé*); **j'y pense** I'm thinking about
  it; **ça y est!** that's it!; *voir aussi* **aller, avoir**
yacht [jɔt] *nm* yacht
yaourt [jauʀt] *nm* yogurt; **~ nature/aux
  fruits** plain/fruit yogurt
yeux [jø] *nmpl de* **œil**
yoga [jɔga] *nm* yoga
yoghourt [jɔguʀt] *nm* = **yaourt**
yougoslave [jugɔslav] *adj* Yugoslav(ian)
  ▷ *nm/f*: **Y~** Yugoslav(ian)
Yougoslavie [jugɔslavi] *nf*: **la ~**
  Yugoslavia; **l'ex-~** the former Yugoslavia

Z

zapper [zape] /1/ *vi* to zap
zapping [zapiŋ] *nm*: **faire du ~** to flick
through the channels
zèbre [zɛbʀ] *nm* (*Zool*) zebra; **zébré, e** *adj*
striped, streaked
zèle [zɛl] *nm* zeal; **faire du ~** (*péj*) to be over-
zealous; **zélé, e** *adj* zealous
zéro [zeʀo] *nm* zero, nought (*BRIT*); **au-
dessous de ~** below zero (Centigrade),
below freezing; **partir de ~** to start from
scratch; **trois (buts) à ~** three (goals to) nil
zeste [zɛst] *nm* peel, zest
zézayer [zezeje] /8/ *vi* to have a lisp
zigzag [zigzag] *nm* zigzag; **zigzaguer** /1/ *vi*
to zigzag (along)
Zimbabwe [zimbabwe] *nm*: **le ~**
Zimbabwe
zinc [zɛ̃g] *nm* (*Chimie*) zinc
zipper [zipe] /1/ *vt* (*Inform*) to zip
zizi [zizi] *nm* (*fam*) willy
zodiaque [zɔdjak] *nm* zodiac
zona [zona] *nm* shingles *sg*
zone [zon] *nf* zone, area; (*quartiers pauvres*):
la ~ the slums; **~ bleue** ≈ restricted parking
area; **~ industrielle (ZI)** industrial estate
zoo [zoo] *nm* zoo
zoologie [zɔɔlɔʒi] *nf* zoology; **zoologique**
adj zoological
zut [zyt] *excl* dash (it)! (*BRIT*), nuts! (*US*)

French Grammar

1 Nouns

1.1 Gender of nouns

In French, all nouns are either masculine or feminine. This is called their gender. Even words for things have a gender.

Whenever you are using a noun, you need to know whether it is masculine or feminine as this affects the form of other words used with it, such as:

- adjectives that describe it
- articles (such as **le** or **une**) that go before it
- pronouns (such as **il** or **elle**) that replace it

le or **un** before a noun tells you it is masculine. **la** or **une** before a noun tells you it is feminine.

A few words have different meanings depending on whether they are masculine or feminine.

un livre	*a book*
une livre	*a pound*

Most nouns referring to men, boys and male animals are masculine; most nouns referring to women, girls and female animals are feminine.

Generally, words ending in **-e** are feminine and words ending in a consonant are masculine, though there are many exceptions to this rule.

These endings are often found on masculine nouns: **-age**, **-ment**, **-oir**, **-sme**, **-eau**, **-eu**, **-ou**, **-ier**, **-in** and **-on**.

These endings are often found on feminine nouns: **-ance**, **-anse**, **-ence**, **-ense**, **-ion**, **-té**, **-tié**.

Days of the week, months and seasons of the year are masculine.

1.2 Forming plurals

Most French nouns form their plural by adding an **-s** to their singular form. If the singular noun ends in **-s**, **-x** or **-z**, no further **-s** is added.

Most nouns ending in **-eau** or **-eu** add an **-x** in the plural.

Most nouns ending in **-ou** take an **-s** in the plural, with a few exceptions.

If the singular noun ends in **-al** or **-ail**, the plural usually ends in **-aux**.

A few common words are plural in English but not in French, and vice versa.

un short	*shorts*
un pantalon	*trousers*

2 Articles

2.1 The definite article

The word you choose for *the* depends on whether the noun it is used with is masculine or feminine, singular or plural.

le is used in front of masculine singular nouns.

le roi	*the king*
le chien	*the dog*

la is used in front of feminine singular nouns.

la reine	*the queen*
la souris	*the mouse*

l' is used in front of singular nouns that start with a vowel, whether they are masculine or feminine.

l'ami *(masculine)*	*the friend*
l'eau *(feminine)*	*the water*

l' is also used in front of most (but not all) words starting with **h**.

l'hôpital	*the hospital*
le hamster	*the hamster*

les is used in front of plural nouns, whether they are masculine or feminine and whatever letter they start with.

les chiens	*the dogs*
les portes	*the doors*

When the definite article is used with certain prepositions, the two words are combined to make a new word:

• When **à** is followed by **le**, the two words become **au**.

au cinéma	*to/at the cinema*

• When **à** is followed by **la** or **l'**, the words do not change.

à l'hôtel	*to/at the hotel*

• When **à** is followed by **les**, the two words become **aux**.

aux maisons	*to the houses*

• When **de** is followed by **le**, the two words become **du**.

du cinéma	*from/of the cinema*

• When **de** is followed by **les**, the two words become **des**.

des maisons	*from/of the houses*

• When **de** is followed by **la** or **l'**, the words do not change.

de la bibliothèque	*from/of the library*

2.2 The indefinite article

With masculine singular nouns, use **un**.

un chien	*a dog*

With feminine singular nouns, use **une**.

une fille	*a girl*

There are some cases in French where the indefinite article is not used, including when you say what jobs people do.

Quel dommage!	*What a shame!*
Il est professeur.	*He's a teacher.*

3 Adjectives

3.1 Adjective forms and position

Most French adjectives change their form, according to whether the person or thing they are describing is masculine or feminine, singular or plural.

To make an adjective feminine, usually add **-e** to the masculine form. To make it plural, add **-s** for masculine plural, and **-es** for feminine plural.

un mot anglais	*an English word*
une chanson anglaise	*an English song*
des traditions anglaises	*English traditions*

Some very common adjectives have irregular feminine forms.

Masculine form	Feminine form	Meaning
blanc	**blanche**	*white, blank*
doux	**douce**	*soft, sweet, mild, gentle*
faux	**fausse**	*untrue*

A very small group of French adjectives have an extra masculine singular form that is used in front of words that begin with a vowel and most words beginning with **h**. These adjectives also have an irregular feminine form.

Masculine form		Feminine form	Meaning
beau	**bel**	**belle**	*lovely, beautiful, good-looking, handsome*
fou	**fol**	**folle**	*mad*
nouveau	**nouvel**	**nouvelle**	*new*
vieux	**vieil**	**vieille**	*old*

When an adjective describes a masculine and a feminine noun or pronoun, use the masculine plural form of the adjective.

La maison et le jardin sont beaux.
The house and garden are beautiful.

If the masculine singular form ends in **-eau** or **-al**, the masculine plural is usually **-eaux** or **-aux**.

le nouveau professeur	*the new teacher*
les nouveaux professeurs	*the new teachers*

A small number of adjectives (mostly relating to colours) do not change in the feminine or plural. They are called invariable because their form never changes, no matter what they are describing.

des chaussures marron *brown shoes*

In French, adjectives usually go after the noun they describe.

un chat noir	*a black cat*
l'heure exacte	*the right time*

However, there are some very common French adjectives that usually come before the noun.

beau	*lovely, beautiful, handsome*
bon	*good, right*
une belle journée	*a lovely day*

3.2 Comparatives of adjectives

In French, to say that something is *easier, more expensive* and so on, you use **plus** (meaning *more*) before the adjective.

Cette question est plus facile. *This question is easier.*

To say something is *less expensive, less complicated* and so on, you use **moins** (meaning *less*) before the adjective.

Cette veste est moins chère. *This jacket is less expensive.*

To introduce the person or thing you are making the comparison with, use **que** (meaning *than*).

Elle est plus petite que moi. *She's smaller than me.*

Some adjectives in French have irregular comparative forms.

J'ai une meilleur idée. *I've got a better idea.*

3.3 Possessive adjectives

Here are the French possessive adjectives. Like all French adjectives, these agree with the noun they refer to.

With masculine singular noun	With feminine singular noun	With plural noun (masculine or feminine)	Meaning
mon	ma (mon)	mes	*my*
ton	ta (ton)	tes	*your*
son	sa (son)	ses	*his* *her* *its* *one's*
notre	notre	nos	*our*
votre	votre	vos	*your*
leur	leur	leurs	*their*

You use **mon**, **ton** and **son** with feminine singular nouns in front of words that begin with a vowel and most words beginning with **h**.

| **mon assiette** | *my plate* |
| **ton histoire** | *your story* |

Possessive adjectives agree with what they describe, not with the person who owns that thing.

| **Paul cherche sa montre.** | *Paul's looking for his watch.* |
| **Paul cherche ses lunettes.** | *Paul's looking for his glasses.* |

4 Pronouns

4.1 Subject pronouns

Here are the French subject pronouns:

Singular	Meaning	Plural	Meaning
je (j')	*I*	**nous**	*we*
tu or **vous**	*you*	**vous**	*you*
il	*he* *it*	**ils**	*they (masculine)*
elle	*she* *it*	**elles**	*they (feminine)*
on	*one*		

je changes to **j'** in front of words beginning with a vowel, most words beginning with **h**, and the French word **y**.

J'arrive!   *I'm just coming!*

In English, we have only one way of saying *you*. In French, there are two words: **tu** and **vous**.

If you are talking to one person you know well, such as a friend, a young person or a relative, use **tu**.

Tu me prêtes ce CD?   *Will you lend me this CD?*

If you are talking to one person you do not know so well, such as your teacher, your boss or a stranger, use **vous**.

Vous pouvez entrer.   *You may come in.*

If you are in doubt as to which form of *you* to use, it is safest to use **vous** and you will not offend anybody.

4.2 Direct object pronouns

Here are the French direct object pronouns:

Singular	Meaning	Plural	Meaning
me (m')	me	**nous**	*us*
te (t')	you	**vous**	*you*
le (l')	him it	**les**	*them (masculine and feminine)*
la (l')	her it		

me changes to **m'**, **te** to **t'**, and **le/la** to **l'** in front of words beginning with a vowel, most words beginning with **h**, and the French word **y**.

Tu m'entends?   *Can you hear me?*

In orders and instructions telling someone to do something, **moi** is used instead of **me**, and **toi** is used instead of **te**.

Aidez-moi!   *Help me!*
Assieds-toi.   *Sit down.*

4.3 Indirect object pronouns

Here are the French indirect object pronouns:

Singular	Meaning	Plural	Meaning
me (m')	*me, to me, for me*	**nous**	*us, to us, for us*
te (t')	*you, to you, for you*	**vous**	*you, to you, for you*
lui	*him, to him, for him her, to her, for her it, to it, for it*	**les**	*them, to them, for them (masculine and feminine)*

me changes to **m'** and **te** to **t'** in front of words beginning with a vowel, most words beginning with **h**, and the French word **y**.

> **Il m'a donné un livre.** *He gave me a book.*
> **Tu m'apportes une serviette?**
> *Can you get me a towel?*

The indirect object pronoun usually comes before the verb.

> **Dominique vous écrit une lettre.**
> *Dominique's writing you a letter.*

> **Il ne nous parle pas.** *He doesn't speak to us.*
> **Il ne veut pas me répondre.** *He won't answer me.*

5 Verbs

5.1 The three conjugations

French verbs have an infinitive, which ends in **-er**, **-ir** or **-re**, for example:

- **donner** (meaning *to give*) – first conjugation verb
- **finir** (meaning *to finish*) – second conjugation verb
- **attendre** (meaning *to wait*) – third conjugation verb.

Regular French verbs belong to one of these three verb groups, which are called conjugations. Each conjugation has a set of endings which are added to the stem of the verb, depending on the person doing the verb.

5.2 The present tense

The present tense endings for first conjugation **-er** verbs are shown in the table below:

Pronoun	Ending	Add to stem, e.g. donn-	Meaning
je (j')	-e	je donn**e**	*I give* *I am giving*
tu	-es	tu donn**es**	*you give* *you are giving*
il elle on	-e	il donn**e** elle donn**e** on donn**e**	*he/she/it/one gives* *he/she/it/one is* *giving*
nous	-ons	nous donn**ons**	*we give* *we are giving*
vous	-ez	vous donn**ez**	*you give* *you are giving*
ils elles	-ent	ils donn**ent** elles donn**ent**	*they give* *they are giving*

The present tense endings for second conjugation **-ir** verbs are shown in the table below:

Pronoun	Ending	Add to stem, e.g. fin-	Meaning
je (j')	-is	je fin<u>is</u>	*I finish* *I am finishing*
tu	-is	tu fin<u>is</u>	*you finish* *you are finishing*
il elle on	-it	il fin<u>it</u> elle fin<u>it</u> on fin<u>it</u>	*he/she/it/one finishes* *he/she/it/one is* *finishing*
nous	-issons	nous fin<u>issons</u>	*we finish* *we are finishing*
vous	-issez	vous fin<u>issez</u>	*you finish* *you are finishing*
ils elles	-issent	ils fin<u>issent</u> elles fin<u>issent</u>	*they finish* *they are finishing*

The present tense endings for third conjugation **-re** verbs are shown in the table below:

Pronoun	Ending	Add to stem, e.g. attend-	Meaning
je (j')	-s	j'attend<u>s</u>	*I wait* *I am waiting*
tu	-s	tu attend<u>s</u>	*you wait* *you are waiting*
il elle on	-	il attend elle attend on attend	*he/she/it/one waits* *he/she/it/one is* *waiting*
nous	-ons	nous attend<u>ons</u>	*we wait* *we are waiting*
vous	-ez	vous attend<u>ez</u>	*you wait* *you are waiting*
ils elles	-ent	ils attend<u>ent</u> elles attend<u>ent</u>	*they wait* *they are waiting*

5.3 Irregular verbs

Some verbs in French do not follow the normal rules. These verbs include some very common and important verbs like **avoir** (meaning *to have*), **être** (meaning *to be*), **faire** (meaning *to do, to make*), and **aller** (meaning *to go*).

The present tense for these irregular verbs is shown in the tables below:

Pronoun	avoir	Meaning
j'	ai	*I have*
tu	as	*you have*
il elle on	a	*he/she/it/one has*
nous	avons	*we have*
vous	avez	*you have*
ils elles	ont	*they have*

Pronoun	être	Meaning
je	suis	*I am*
tu	es	*you are*
il elle on	est	*he/she/it/one is*
nous	sommes	*we are*
vous	êtes	*you are*
ils elles	sont	*they are*

Pronoun	faire	Meaning
je	fais	*I do/make* *I am doing/making*
tu	fais	*you do/make* *you are doing/making*
il elle on	fait	*he/she/it/one does/makes* *he/she/it/one is doing/ making*
nous	faisons	*we do/make* *we are doing/making*
vous	faites	*you do/make* *you are doing/making*
ils elles	sont	*they do/make* *they are doing/making*

Pronoun	aller	Meaning
je	vais	*I go* *I am going*
tu	vas	*you go* *you are going*
il elle on	va	*he/she/it/one goes* *he/she/it/one is going*
nous	allons	*we go* *we are going*
vous	allez	*you go* *you are going*
ils elles	vont	*they go* *they are going*

5.4 Reflexive verbs

Reflexive verbs are shown as **se** plus the infinitive. **se** is called a reflexive pronoun. The present tense forms of a reflexive verb work in just the same way as an ordinary verb, except that the reflexive pronoun is used as well. The reflexive pronouns in French are shown in the table below:

Subject pronoun	Reflexive pronoun	Meaning
je	me (m')	*myself*
tu	te (t')	*yourself*
il elle on	se (s')	*himself* *herself* *itself* *oneself*
nous	nous	*ourselves*
vous	vous	*yourself (singular)* *yourself (plural)*
ils elles	se (s')	*themselves*

Note that **se** changes to **s'** in front of a word starting with a vowel, most words starting with **h**, and the French word **y**.

Some common French reflexive verbs are listed here:

s'appeler	*to be called*
se dépêcher	*to hurry*
s'habiller	*to get dressed*
se lever	*to get up, to rise, to stand up*
se passer	*to take place, to happen, to go*

11

5.5 The imperfect tense

To form the imperfect tense of **-er** verbs, you use the same stem of the verb as for the present tense.

The imperfect tense endings for **-er** verbs are:

Pronoun	Ending	Add to stem, e.g. donn-	Meaning
je (j')	-ais	je donn<u>ais</u>	*I gave* *I was giving*
tu	-ais	tu donn<u>ais</u>	*you gave* *you were giving*
il elle on	-ait	il donn<u>ait</u> elle donn<u>ait</u> on donn<u>ait</u>	*he/she/it/one gave* *he/she/it/one was giving*
nous	-ions	nous donn<u>ions</u>	*we gave* *we were giving*
vous	-iez	vous donn<u>iez</u>	*you gave* *you were giving*
ils elles	-aient	ils donn<u>aient</u> elles donn<u>aient</u>	*they gave* *they were giving*

To form the imperfect tense of **-ir** verbs, you use the same stem of the verb as for the present tense.

The imperfect tense endings for **-ir** verbs are:

Pronoun	Ending	Add to stem, e.g. fin-	Meaning
je (j')	-issais	je fin<u>issais</u>	*I finished* *I was finishing*
tu	-issais	tu fin<u>issais</u>	*you finished* *you were finishing*
il elle on	-issait	il fin<u>issait</u> elle fin<u>issait</u> on fin<u>issait</u>	*he/she/it/one finished* *he/she/it/one was finishing*
nous	-issions	nous fin<u>issions</u>	*we finished* *we were finishing*
vous	-issiez	vous fin<u>issiez</u>	*you finished* *you were finishing*
ils elles	-issaient	ils fin<u>issaient</u> elles fin<u>issaient</u>	*they finished* *they were finishing*

To form the imperfect tense of **-re** verbs, you use the same stem of the verb as for the present tense.

The imperfect tense endings for **-re** verbs are:

Pronoun	Ending	Add to stem, e.g. attend-	Meaning
je (j')	-ais	**je attend<u>ais</u>**	*I waited* *I was waiting*
tu	-ais	**tu attend<u>ais</u>**	*you waited* *you were waiting*
il **elle** **on**	-ait	**il attend<u>ait</u>** **elle attend<u>ait</u>** **on attend<u>ait</u>**	*he/she/it/one waited* *he/she/it/one was waiting*
nous	-ions	**nous attend<u>ions</u>**	*we waited* *we were waiting*
vous	-iez	**vous attend<u>iez</u>**	*you waited* *you were waiting*
ils **elles**	-aient	**ils attend<u>aient</u>** **elles attend<u>aient</u>**	*they waited* *they were waiting*

The only verb that is irregular in the imperfect tense is **être**.

Pronoun	être	Meaning
j'	étais	*I was*
tu	étais	*you were*
il **elle** **on**	était	*he/she/it/one was*
nous	étions	*we were*
vous	étiez	*you were*
ils **elles**	étaient	*they were*

5.6 The future tense

To form the future tense in French, you use:

• the infinitive of **-er** and **-ir** verbs, for example, **donner**, **finir**

• the infinitive without the final **e** of **-re** verbs: for example, **attendr-**

Then add the correct ending to the stem depending on the person doing the verb.

The future tense endings are the same for **-er**, **-ir** and **-re** verbs – these are shown in the table below:

Pronoun	Ending	Add to stem, e.g. donner-, finir, attendr-	Meaning
je (j')	-ai	**je donnerai** **je finirai** **j'attendrai**	*I will give* *I will finish* *I will wait*
tu	-as	**tu donneras** **tu finiras** **tu attendras**	*you will give* *you will finish* *you will wait*
il **elle** **on**	-a	**il/elle/on donnera** **il/elle/on finira** **il/elle/on attendra**	*he/she/it/one will give* *he/she/it/one will finish* *he/she/it/one will wait*
nous	-ons	**nous donnerons** **nous finirons** **nous attendrons**	*we will give* *we will finish* *we will wait*
vous	-ez	**vous donnerez** **vous finirez** **vous attendrez**	*you will give* *you will finish* *you will wait*
ils **elles**	-ent	**ils/elles donneront** **ils/elles finiront** **ils/elles attendront**	*they will give* *they will finish* *they will wait*

There are some verbs that do not use their infinitives as the stem for the future tense, including **avoir**, **être**, **faire** and **aller**. The future tenses of **avoir** and **être** are shown in the tables below:

Pronoun	avoir	Meaning
j'	**aurai**	*I will have*
tu	**auras**	*you will have*
il **elle** **on**	**aura**	*he/she/it/one will have*
nous	**aurons**	*we will have*
vous	**aurez**	*you will have*
ils **elles**	**auront**	*they will have*

Pronoun	être	Meaning
je	serai	I will be
tu	seras	you will be
il elle on	sera	he/she/it/one will be
nous	serons	we will be
vous	serez	you will be
ils elles	seront	they will be

5.7 The perfect tense

The perfect tense in French has two parts to it:

- the present tense of the verb **avoir** (meaning *to have*) or **être** (meaning *to be*).

- a part of the main verb called the past participle, like *given*, *finished* and *done* in English. To form the past participle, take the stem of the verb and add **-é** for **-er** verbs, in **-i** for **-ir** verbs, and in **-u** for **-re** verbs.

Most verbs take **avoir** in the perfect tense. All reflexive verbs and a small group of verbs referring to movement or change take **être** – these include verbs used mainly to talk about movement or a change of some kind, for example, **aller**, **venir**, **arriver**, **entrer**, **sortir**, **rester** and **tomber**.

When a verb takes **avoir**, the past participle usually stays in the masculine singular form, and does not change for the feminine or plural forms.

> **Il a fini sa dissertation.**   *He's finished his essay.*
> **Elles ont fini leur dissertation.**   *They've finished their essay.*

When a verb takes **être**, the past participle always agrees with the subject of the verb; that is, the endings change in the feminine and plural forms.

> **Est-ce ton frère est allé à l'étranger?**
> *Did your brother go abroad?*

> **Elle est venue avec nous.**   *She came with us.*

6 Negatives

Negative expressions in French 'sandwich' the verb in the present tense and in other tenses that consist of just one word. **ne** goes before the verb and the other half of the expression comes after the verb. **ne** changes to **n'** in front of a word that starts with a vowel, most words beginning with **h** and the French word **y**.

> **Il ne pleuvait pas.** *It wasn't raining.*
> **Elle n'arrive jamais à l'heure.** *She never arrives on time.*

After these negative expressions, **un**, **une** and **des** and **du**, **de la**, **de l'** and **des** change to **de**.

> **Il ne reste plus de biscuits.** *There aren't any biscuits left.*

7 Questions

7.1 Asking a question by using est-ce que

The phrase **est-ce que** is used to ask a question. Word order stays just the same as it would in an ordinary sentence. **Est-ce que** comes before the subject, and the verb comes after the subject. So to turn the sentence **Tu connais Marie** (meaning *You know Marie*) into a question, all you need to do is to add **est-ce que** before the rest of sentence.

> **Est-ce que tu** *(subject)* **connais** *(verb)* **Marie?**
> *Do you know Marie?*

7.2 Asking a question by changing the word order

In ordinary sentences, the verb comes after its subject. When you ask a question by changing the word order, the verb is put before the subject. This change to normal word order is called inversion. You can do this when the subject is a pronoun such as **vous** or **il**. When you change the word order (or invert) in this way, you add a hyphen (-) between the verb and the pronoun.

> **Vous** *(subject)* **aimez** *(verb)* **la France.**
> *You like France.*

> **Aimez** *(verb)*-**vous** *(subject)* **la France?**
> *Do you like France?*

Grammaire anglaise

1 Les verbes

1.1 Le présent simple

Le présent simple est utilisé :

• pour les vérités générales.

> **February is the shortest month.**
> *Février est le mois le plus court.*

• pour parler du présent en général, de quelque chose d'habituel, qui arrive régulièrement.

> **I take the bus every morning.**
> *Je prends le bus tous les matins.*

> **George lives in Birmingham.**
> *George vit à Birmingham.*

Affirmations	Négations	Questions
I work	I don't work	Do I work?
You work	You don't work	Do you work?
He/she/it works	He/she/it doesn't work	Does he/she/it work?
We work	We don't work	Do we work?
You work	You don't work	Do you work
They work	They don't work	Do they work?

Remarques :

• Le verbe garde la même forme à toutes les personnes, sauf à la troisième personne du singulier (**he/she/it**) où il se termine par un **-s**.

• Si le verbe se termine en **-o/-os/-ch/-sh/-ss/-x**, on rajoute **-es** à la troisième personne du singulier :

> **watch → watches**
> **go → goes**

• Si le verbe se termine par une consonne suivie de **-y**, le **-y** se transforme en **-ies** à la troisième personne du singulier :

> **study → studies**
> **cry → cries**

• **Have** à la troisième personne devient **has**.

> **She has a computer in her room.**
> *Elle a un ordinateur dans sa chambre.*

- On utilise l'auxiliaire **do** (**does** à la troisième personne du singulier) pour les questions et les négations. La forme contractée au négatif (**don't/doesn't**) est la plus souvent utilisée par rapport à la forme pleine (**do not/does not**).

> **Do you know Peter? No, I don't know him.**
> *Est-ce que tu connais Peter ? Non, je ne le connais pas.*

> **Does she go to university?**
> *Est-ce qu'elle va à l'université ?*

> **He doesn't eat meat.**
> *Il ne mange pas de viande.*

Le verbe *be*

Le verbe **be** est l'équivalent du verbe *être*. Au présent simple, il se conjugue ainsi :

Positives			
Dans les phrases positives		**Français**	**Questions**
Forme Pleine	**Forme Contractée**	**Forme Pleine**	**Contractée**
I am late.	**I'm** late.	*Je suis en retard.*	**Am I** late?
You are next.	**You're** next.	*Tu es le prochain.*	**Are you** next?
He is blond.	**He's** blond.	*Il est blond.*	**Is he** blond?
She is at home.	**She's** at home.	*Elle est à la maison.*	**Is she** at home?
It is on the table.	**It's** on the table.	*Il/Elle [objet] est sur la table.*	**Is it** on the table?
We are British.	**We're** British.	*Nous sommes Britanniques.*	**Are we** British?
You are here.	**You're** here.	*Vous êtes ici.*	**Are you** here?
They are happy.	**They're** happy.	*Ils/Elles sont heureux/ heureuses.*	**Are they** happy?

Négatives			
Dans les phrases négatives		**Français**	**Questions**
Forme Pleine	**Forme Contractée**	**Forme Pleine**	**Contractée**
I am not late.	**I'm not** late.	*Je ne suis pas en retard.*	**Aren't I** late?
You are not next.	**You're not/ aren't** next.	*Tu n'es pas le prochain.*	**Aren't you** next?
He is not blond.	**He's not/isn't** blond.	*Il n'est pas blond.*	**Isn't he** blond?
She is not at home.	**She's not/isn't** at home.	*Elle n'est pas à la maison.*	**Isn't she** at home?
It is not on the table.	**It's not/isn't** on the table.	*Il/Elle n'est pas sur la table.*	**Isn't it** on the table?
We are not British.	**We're not/ aren't** British.	*Nous ne sommes pas Britanniques.*	**Aren't we** British?
You are not here.	**You're not/ aren't** here.	*Vous n'êtes pas ici.*	**Aren't you** here?
They are not happy.	**They're not/ aren't** happy.	*Ils/Elles ne sont pas heureux/ heureuses.*	**Aren't they** happy?

1.2 Le présent progressif

Le présent progressif est utilisé :

• pour parler d'une action en cours (*être en train de*).

> **They're talking to the teacher.**
> *Ils sont en train de parler au professeur.*

• pour parler d'une situation temporaire.

> **I'm living with my friends at the moment.**
> *Je vis avec des amis en ce moment.*

Le présent progressif se compose ainsi :

be au présent + verbe **-ing**

Affirmations	Négations	Questions
I am playing	I'm not playing	Am I playing?
You are playing	You're not playing	Are you playing?
He/She/It is playing	He/She/It's not playing	Is he/she/it playing?
We are playing	We're not playing	Are we playing?
You are playing	You're not playing	Are you playing?
They are playing	They're not playing	Are they playing?

Remarques :

- La forme contractée au négatif (**I'm not ...**) est la plus souvent utilisée par rapport à la forme pleine (**I am not ...**).

1.3 Le « *present perfect* »

Le « *present perfect* » s'emploie :

- pour évoquer les effets présents d'une action ou d'un événement passés.

   I'm afraid I have forgotten my book.
   Je suis désolé, mais j'ai oublié mon livre.

- pour une action qui vient de se produire (avec **just**).

   Karen has just finished her homework.
   Karen vient de finir ses devoirs.

- lorsqu'on parle d'une période qui a débuté dans le passé et qui se prolonge dans le présent.

   I've lived in London for three years.
   Je vis à Londres depuis trois ans.

- pour faire le bilan des expériences passées.

   Have you ever been to the US?
   Es-tu déjà allé aux États-Unis ?

Le « *present perfect* » se compose ainsi :

Have au présent + participe passé

Le participe passé se forme en ajoutant **-ed** à la fin du verbe, sauf pour les verbes irréguliers.

Affirmations	Négations	Questions
I have visited	I haven't visited	Have I visited?
You have visited	You haven't visited	Have you visited?
He/She/It has visited	He/She/It hasn't visited	Has he/she/it visited?
We have eaten	We haven't eaten	Have we eaten?
You have eaten	You haven't eaten	Have you eaten?
They have eaten	They haven't eaten	Have they eaten?

Remarques :

- La forme contractée au négatif (**haven't/hasn't**) est la plus souvent utilisée par rapport à la forme pleine (**have not/has not**). Dans un language plus familier, on peut également utiliser des formes contractées à l'affirmatif en remplaçant **have** par **'ve** et **has** par **'s**.

- Le « *present perfect* » ne s'utilise pas avec une indication de temps précise.

   I've read that book (before). I read it last week.
   J'ai (déjà) lu ce livre. Je l'ai lu la semaine dernière.

- Le « *present perfect* » est souvent traduit en français par le passé composé, mais ces deux temps ne sont pas toujours équivalents et la traduction par le passé composé ne doit pas être automatique.

   They've known each other for ten years.
   Ils se connaissent depuis dix ans.

   I've been to Canada twice.
   Je suis allée au Canada deux fois.

1.4 Le passé simple ou prétérit

Le passé simple s'emploie pour évoquer une action ou une habitude du passé qui est complétement révolue.

   He went home last night.
   Il est rentré chez lui hier soir.

   I often watched TV when I was a child.
   Je regardais souvent la télévision quand j'étais enfant.

Le passé se forme en ajoutant **-ed** à la fin du verbe, sauf pour les verbes irréguliers.

Affirmations	Négations	Questions
I walked	I didn't walk	Did I walk?
You walked	You didn't walk	Did you walk?
He/She/It walked	He/She/It didn't walk	Did he/she/it walk?
We left	We didn't leave	Did we leave?
You left	You didn't leave	Did you leave?
They left	They didn't leave	Did they leave?

Remarques :

• Le verbe garde la même forme à toutes les personnes, sauf pour **be** (**was** à la première et troisième personne du singulier, **were** pour toutes les autres personnes).

• On utilise l'auxiliaire **do** au passé (**did**) pour les questions et les négations. La forme contractée au négatif (**didn't**) est la plus souvent utilisée par rapport à la forme pleine (**did not**).

• Le prétérit peut se traduire en français par le passé simple, l'imparfait ou le passé composé.

> **The prince killed the dragon with his sword.**
> *Le prince tua le dragon avec son épée.*

> **I was so tired yesterday.**
> *J'étais super fatiguée hier.*

> **Where did you go last night?**
> *Où es-tu allé hier soir ?*

1.5 L'expression du futur

En anglais, il n'y a pas de temps verbal propre au futur. Le futur peut être exprimé de différentes manières :

• en utilisant le modal **will**

• en utilisant **be going to**

• en utilisant les temps du présent

Will

Le modal **will** s'emploie :

• pour prédire le futur.

> **The weather tomorrow will be warm and sunny.**
> *Il fera beau et chaud demain.*

- pour faire une promesse ou une offre.

> **I'll come next week.**
> *Je viendrai la semaine prochaine.*

- pour parler d'un futur lointain.

> **In ten years' time, we'll be retired.**
> *Dans dix ans, nous serons à la retraite.*

La construction avec **will** est la suivante :

Will + verbe

Affirmations	Négations	Questions
I will come	I won't come	Will I come?
You will come	You won't come	Will you come?
He/She/It will come	He/She/It won't come	Will he/she/it come?
We will come	We won't come	Will we come?
You will come	You won't come	Will you come?
They will come	They won't come	Will they come?

Remarque : la forme contractée de **will** est **'ll** et celle de **will not** est **won't**.

Be going to

Be going to s'emploie :

- pour le futur proche.

> **They're going to sleep.**
> *Elles vont dormir.*

- quand on prédit le futur.

> **I think he's going to leave.**
> *Je pense qu'il va partir.*

- quand des éléments du présent laissent penser qu'une action va se produire dans le futur.

> **It's cloudy today: it's going to rain.**
> *Le temps est nuageux aujourd'hui : il va pleuvoir.*

La construction avec **be going to** est la suivante :

Be au présent + **going to** + verbe

Affirmations	Négations	Questions
I am going to stay	I am not going to stay	Am I going to stay?
You are going to stay	You are not going to stay	Are you going to stay?
He/She/It is going to stay	He/She/It is not going to stay	Is he/she/it going to stay?
We are going to stay	We are not going to stay	Are we going to stay?
You are going to stay	You are not going to stay	Are you going to stay?
They are going to stay	They are not going to stay	Are they going to stay?

Remarques :

• La forme contractée du verbe **be** peut être utilisée.

You aren't going to stay. / You're not going to stay.
Vous n'allez pas rester.

• **Be going to** est souvent traduit par le futur proche en français (aller + verbe).

She's going to write you a letter.
Elle va t'écrire une lettre.

Le présent

Les temps du présent, et en particulier le présent progressif, peuvent servir à exprimer le futur :

• pour un fait planifié ou prévisible dans le futur.

The train arrives at 9:00 am.
Le train arrive à 9h.

We're having a party next week.
Nous organisons une fête la semaine prochaine.

• pour parler d'un avenir proche.

What are you doing on Sunday?
Qu'est-ce que tu fais dimanche ?

1.6 *There is / There are*

There + be est l'équivalent de *il y a* en français. La forme verbale employée varie selon que le nom qui suit est singulier ou pluriel. **There** peut être suivi de **be** au présent, au passé ou au futur (avec **will**).

> **There is a spider in my room.**
> *Il y a une araignée dans ma chambre.*

> **There were many people at this party.**
> *Il y avait beaucoup de monde à cette fête.*

> **There will be a meeting tomorrow.**
> *Il va y avoir une réunion demain.*

Pour poser une question, on place **there** après le verbe **be**.

> **Is there anyone at home?**
> *Il y a quelqu'un à la maison ?*

1.7 Les verbes à particule

Les phrasal verbs (verbes à particule) sont composés d'un verbe suivi d'un adverbe ou d'une préposition (**in/on/out/up/off**...). Le sens habituel du verbe seul peut parfois changer radicalement après adjonction de la préposition.

> **Turn right at the next corner.**
> *Tourne à droite au prochain croisement.*

> **She turned off the radio.**
> *Elle a éteint la radio.*

Il y a plusieurs types de structures possibles :

• verbe + particule

> **We grew up in Dublin.**
> *Nous avons grandi à Dublin.*

• verbe + particule + objet

> **Can you look after the children?**
> *Peux-tu t'occuper des enfants ?*

• verbe + objet + particule

> **She'll call me back later.**
> *Elle me rappellera plus tard.*

Avec certains verbes à particule, l'objet peut se placer indifféremment avant ou après la particule.

> **He took his coat off. / He took off his coat.**
> *Il a enlevé son manteau.*

Dans d'autres cas, lorsque l'objet est un pronom, il se place impérativement avant la particule.

> **He threw it away.**
> *Il l'a jeté (à la poubelle).*

26

1.8 Les modaux

Les modaux n'ont qu'une seule forme et se placent devant le verbe à l'infinitif (sans **to**). Il n'est pas possible d'associer deux modaux ou un modal et un auxiliaire.

Can (présent) et **could** (passé ou conditionnel) peuvent exprimer la capacité, la possibilité ou la permission. Ils se traduisent souvent par *pouvoir*. **Can't** est la forme contractée du négatif **can not** et **couldn't** celle de **could not**.

> **She can run very fast.**
> *Elle court très vite.*

> **He could be at his grandma's house.**
> *Il se peut qu'il soit chez sa grand-mère.*

> **Can I go out tonight? No, you can't.**
> *Est-ce que je peux sortir ce soir ? Non, tu ne peux pas.*

May (présent) et **might** (passé ou conditionnel) expriment la probabilité. Dans un style soutenu, **may** peut également servir à demander ou accorder la permission. **Might** est surtout utilisé quand la probabilité que quelque chose se produise n'est pas très grande. Ces deux modaux n'ont pas de formes contractées au négatif.

> **He might come.**
> *Il va peut-être venir.*

> **I may go to London next month.**
> *Je vais peut-être aller à Londres le mois prochain.*

> **May I open the window? No, you may not.**
> *Puis-je ouvrir la fenêtre ? Non, vous ne pouvez pas.*

Le modal **must** exprime l'obligation. On peut le traduire par *devoir* ou *il faut que* en français. **Mustn't** est la forme contractée du négatif **must not**.

> **I must see her.**
> *Je dois la voir.*

Should signifie *il faudrait que* ou *devrait*. On l'utilise pour donner un conseil ou parler de ce qui devrait être fait. **Shouldn't** est la forme contractée du négatif **should not**.

> **We should send her a postcard.**
> *Il faudrait qu'on lui envoie une carte postale.*

> **You shouldn't drink and drive.**
> *Tu ne devrais pas conduire après avoir bu.*

Would est la marque du conditionnel. **Wouldn't** est la forme contractée du négatif **would not**.

> **I would like to come with you.**
> *J'aimerais venir avec toi.*

2 Les noms

2.1 Les noms dénombrables

Certaines choses sont des éléments individuels pouvant être comptés un par un. Les noms qui servent à les décrire sont des **noms dénombrables** qui possèdent une forme au singulier, ainsi qu'une forme au pluriel avec la terminaison **-s** :

> **book → books**
>
> **holiday → holidays**

Pour mettre au pluriel les noms se terminant en **-ss/-s/-ch/-sh/-x/-o**, on ajoute **-es** à la fin :

> **boss → bosses**
>
> **ditch → ditches**
>
> **domino → dominoes**

Pour les noms qui se terminent par une consonne suivie de **-y**, on remplace le **-y** final par **-ies** :

> **baby → babies**

Certains noms possèdent des pluriels irréguliers :

Singulier	Pluriel	Français
child	children	*enfant(s)*
foot	feet	*pied(s)*
mouse	mice	*souris*
fish	fish	*poisson(s)*
man	men	*homme(s)*
woman	women	*femme(s)*
person	people	*personne(s)*
tooth	teeth	*dent(s)*

2.2 Les noms singuliers, pluriels et collectifs

Certains noms sont utilisés uniquement au singulier. Parfois, c'est parce que le nom désigne une chose qui n'existe qu'en un seul exemplaire (**the air** *l'air*, **the sun** *le soleil*, **the past** *le passé*) ; on utilise souvent ce type de nom avec l'article **the**.

Certains noms n'ont pas de forme au singulier (**your clothes** *tes vêtements*). Ils sont utilisés avec **the** ou un possessif, et avec un verbe au pluriel. Certains outils ou vêtements qui possèdent deux parties identiques sont également des noms pluriels (**jeans** *un jean*, **glasses** *des lunettes*, **pyjamas** *un pyjama*, **scissors** *des ciseaux*).

Les noms collectifs sont des noms qui désignent un groupe de personnes ou de choses (**family** *famille*, **team** *équipe*, **army** *armée*). Ils peuvent être utilisés avec un verbe au singulier ou au pluriel, selon que le groupe est considéré comme un seul ensemble ou une série de plusieurs individus.

> **My family is in Brazil.**
> *Ma famille est au Brésil.*

> **His family are all strange.**
> *Les membres de sa famille sont tous bizarres.*

2.3 Les noms indénombrables

Il existe également des choses qui ne peuvent pas se compter une par une ; elles sont désignées par des noms indénombrables. Souvent, il s'agit de substances, de qualités humaines, de sentiments, d'activités ou d'abstractions.

Attention, dans certains cas, l'anglais utilise un indénombrable pour désigner une chose qui en français est dénombrable : **advice** (*conseil*), **luggage** (*bagages*), **furniture** (*meubles*).

> **My luggage is too heavy.**
> *Mes bagages sont trop lourds.*

Les noms indénombrables n'ont pas de forme plurielle et s'utilisent avec un verbe au singulier. Ils ne peuvent pas être accompagnés des articles **a/an** mais peuvent l'être de **the/this/that** ou d'un possessif. On peut également les associer à des mots ou expressions comme **some**, **much**, **any**, **a piece of**, etc.

> **We sold this old piece of furniture.**
> *Nous avons vendu ce vieux meuble.*

3 Les déterminants

3.1 Les articles indéfinis et définis

A/an s'utilisent comme leurs équivalents français, les articles indéfinis *un*, *une* (**a week** *une semaine*, **a book** *un livre*, **a person** *une personne*). **An** s'utilise devant un nom commençant par une voyelle (**an elephant** *un éléphant*, **an aunt** *une tante*, **an apple** *une pomme*).

En anglais, pour parler d'un type de chose, d'animal ou de personne de manière générale, on utilise le pluriel du nom seul, sans déterminant.

> **Adults often don't listen to children.**
> *Souvent, les adultes n'écoutent pas les enfants.*

The s'utilise généralement comme les articles définis français correspondants, *le*, *la*, *les* (**the person** *la personne*, **the people** *les gens*, **the chair** *la chaise*, **the chairs** *les chaises*).

3.2 Les déterminants possessifs

Anglais	Français
my	mon/ma/mes
your	ton/ta/tes
his	son/sa/ses (pour un homme)
her	son/sa/ses (pour une femme)
its	son/sa/ses (pour un objet)
our	notre/nos
your	votre/vos
their	leur/leurs

En anglais, contrairement au français, les déterminants possessifs s'accordent avec le possesseur et non avec la chose possédée.

She's eating her sandwich.
Elle mange son sandwich.

Pour exprimer la possession, on peut également utiliser la construction suivante :

Possesseur + **'s** + possession

Mark is Jane's brother.
Mark est le frère de Jane.

It's my uncle's birthday next week.
C'est l'anniversaire de mon oncle la semaine prochaine.

Si le possesseur est au pluriel et se termine par **-s**, on ajoute juste une apostrophe.

My parents' new car is great.
La nouvelle voiture de mes parents est géniale.

3.3 Les adjectifs démonstratifs

This signifie *ce, cet, cette* et **these** est sa forme plurielle (*ces*). **That** signifie aussi *ce, cet, cette* et s'emploie à la place de **this** dans certains contextes, par exemple lorsqu'on veut indiquer l'éloignement. **Those** est sa forme plurielle.

This book is a present from my mother.
Ce livre est un cadeau de ma mère.

When did you buy that hat?
Quand as-tu acheté ce chapeau ?

Ces déterminants s'utilisent aussi comme pronoms démonstratifs :

This is a list of rules.
Ceci est une liste de règles.

Those are mine.
Celles-là sont les miennes.

4 Les pronoms

4.1 Les pronoms personnels (sujets et objets) et les pronoms possessifs

Pronom sujet	Pronom objet	Pronom possessif
I	me	mine
you	you	yours
he	him	his
she	her	hers
it	it	its
we	us	ours
you	you	yours
they	them	theirs

Remarques :

• Le pronom possessif **its** existe, mais s'emploie très rarement.

• L'emploi des pronoms anglais est comparable au français.

Have you seen him?
Est-ce que tu l'as vu ?

Is that coffee yours or mine?
Ce café est à toi ou à moi ?

Can you help us?
Pouvez-vous nous aider ?

Whose house is this? This is ours.
À qui est cette maison ? C'est la nôtre.

4.2 Les pronoms interrogatifs

Les pronoms interrogatifs sont : **what** (*quoi, qu'est-ce que*), **when** (*quand*), **where** (*où*), **why** (*pourquoi*), **who** (*qui*), **how** (*comment*), **how many/how much** (*combien*) et **which** (*lequel*). Ils servent à poser une question ouverte, à laquelle on peut répondre autrement que par *oui* ou *non*. Avec les pronoms interrogatifs, l'ordre de l'auxiliaire et du sujet s'inverse comme dans n'importe quelle question.

Which do you like best?
Lequel préfères-tu ?

Where do you live?
Où habites-tu ?

When did she arrive?
Quand est-elle arrivée ?

Why did you do it?
Pourquoi as-tu fait ça ?

La seule exception à cette construction intervient quand le sujet de l'interrogative est aussi celui du verbe. Dans ce cas, l'ordre des mots ne change pas et on utilise une forme verbale simple (sans l'auxiliaire).

Who is this person?
Qui est cette personne ?

What happened?
Qu'est-ce qui s'est passé ?

Anglais – Français

English – French

a

A [eɪ] n (Mus) la m

○ KEYWORD

a [eɪ, ə] (before vowel and silent h **an**) indef art **1** un(e); **a book** un livre; **an apple** une pomme; **she's a doctor** elle est médecin
2 (instead of the number "one") un(e); **a year ago** il y a un an; **a hundred/thousand** etc **pounds** cent/mille etc livres
3 (in expressing ratios, prices etc): **three a day/week** trois par jour/semaine; **10 km an hour** 10 km à l'heure; **£5 a person** 5£ par personne; **30p a kilo** 30p le kilo

A2 n (BRIT Scol) deuxième partie de l'examen équivalent au baccalauréat
A.A. n abbr (BRIT: = Automobile Association) ≈ ACF m; (= Alcoholics Anonymous) AA
A.A.A. n abbr (= American Automobile Association) ≈ ACF m
aback [ə'bæk] adv: **to be taken ~** être décontenancé(e)
abandon [ə'bændən] vt abandonner
abattoir ['æbətwɑː'] n (BRIT) abattoir m
abbey ['æbɪ] n abbaye f
abbreviation [əbriːvɪ'eɪʃən] n abréviation f
abdomen ['æbdəmən] n abdomen m
abduct [æb'dʌkt] vt enlever
abide [ə'baɪd] vt souffrir, supporter; **I can't ~ it/him** je ne le supporte pas; **abide by** vt fus observer, respecter
ability [ə'bɪlɪtɪ] n compétence f; capacité f; (skill) talent m
able ['eɪbl] adj compétent(e); **to be ~ to do sth** pouvoir faire qch, être capable de faire qch
abnormal [æb'nɔːməl] adj anormal(e)
aboard [ə'bɔːd] adv à bord ▷ prep à bord de; (train) dans
abolish [ə'bɔlɪʃ] vt abolir

abolition [æbə'lɪʃən] n abolition f
abort [ə'bɔːt] vt (Med) faire avorter; (Comput, fig) abandonner; **abortion** [ə'bɔːʃən] n avortement m; **to have an abortion** se faire avorter

○ KEYWORD

about [ə'baut] adv **1** (approximately) environ, à peu près; **about a hundred/thousand** etc environ cent/mille etc, une centaine (de)/un millier (de) etc; **it takes about 10 hours** ça prend environ or à peu près 10 heures; **at about 2 o'clock** vers 2 heures; **I've just about finished** j'ai presque fini
2 (referring to place) çà et là, de-ci de-là; **to run about** courir çà et là; **to walk about** se promener, aller et venir; **they left all their things lying about** ils ont laissé traîner toutes leurs affaires
3: **to be about to do sth** être sur le point de faire qch
▶ prep **1** (relating to) au sujet de, à propos de; **a book about London** un livre sur Londres, **what is it about?** de quoi s'agit-il?; **we talked about it** nous en avons parlé; **what** or **how about doing this?** et si nous faisions ceci?
2 (referring to place) dans; **to walk about the town** se promener dans la ville

above [ə'bʌv] adv au-dessus ▷ prep au-dessus de; (more than) plus de; **mentioned ~** mentionné ci-dessus; **~ all** par-dessus tout, surtout
abroad [ə'brɔːd] adv à l'étranger
abrupt [ə'brʌpt] adj (steep, blunt) abrupt(e); (sudden, gruff) brusque
abscess ['æbsɪs] n abcès m
absence ['æbsəns] n absence f
absent ['æbsənt] adj absent(e); **absent-minded** adj distrait(e)
absolute ['æbsəluːt] adj absolu(e), **absolutely** [æbsə'luːtlɪ] adv absolument
absorb [əb'zɔːb] vt absorber; **to be ~ed in a book** être plongé(e) dans un livre; **absorbent cotton** n (US) coton m hydrophile; **absorbing** adj absorbant(e); (book, film etc) captivant(e)
abstain [əb'steɪn] vi: **to ~ (from)** s'abstenir (de)
abstract ['æbstrækt] adj abstrait(e)
absurd [əb'səːd] adj absurde
abundance [ə'bʌndəns] n abondance f
abundant [ə'bʌndənt] adj abondant(e)
abuse n [ə'bjuːs] (insults) insultes fpl, injures fpl; (ill-treatment) mauvais traitements mpl; (of power etc) abus m ▷ vt [ə'bjuːz] (insult) insulter; (ill-treat) malmener; (power etc) abuser de; **abusive** adj grossier(-ière), injurieux(-euse)

abysmal [ə'bɪzməl] *adj* exécrable;
(*ignorance etc*) sans bornes
academic [ækə'dɛmɪk] *adj* universitaire;
(*person: scholarly*) intellectuel(le); (*pej:
issue*) oiseux(-euse), purement théorique
▷ *n* universitaire *m/f*; **academic year** *n*
(*University*) année *f* universitaire; (*Scol*)
année scolaire
academy [ə'kædəmɪ] *n* (*learned body*)
académie *f*; (*school*) collège *m*; **~ of music**
conservatoire *m*
accelerate [æk'sɛləreɪt] *vt*, *vi* accélérer;
acceleration [æksɛlə'reɪʃən] *n*
accélération *f*; **accelerator** *n* (*BRIT*)
accélérateur *m*
accent ['æksɛnt] *n* accent *m*
accept [ək'sɛpt] *vt* accepter; **acceptable**
adj acceptable; **acceptance** *n*
acceptation *f*
access ['æksɛs] *n* accès *m*; **to have ~
to** (*information, library etc*) avoir accès à,
pouvoir utiliser or consulter; (*person*) avoir
accès auprès de; **accessible** [æk'sɛsəbl] *adj*
accessible
accessory [æk'sɛsərɪ] *n* accessoire *m*; **~ to**
(*Law*) accessoire à
accident ['æksɪdənt] *n* accident *m*; (*chance*)
hasard *m*; **I've had an ~** j'ai eu un accident;
by ~ (*by chance*) par hasard; (*not deliberately*)
accidentellement; **accidental** [æksɪ'dɛntl]
adj accidentel(le); **accidentally**
[æksɪ'dɛntəlɪ] *adv* accidentellement;
Accident and Emergency Department
n (*BRIT*) service *m* des urgences; **accident
insurance** *n* assurance *f* accident
acclaim [ə'kleɪm] *vt* acclamer ▷ *n*
acclamations *fpl*
accommodate [ə'kɔmədeɪt] *vt* loger,
recevoir; (*oblige, help*) obliger; (*car etc*)
contenir
accommodation, (*US*) **accommodations**
[əkɔmə'deɪʃən(z)] *n*, *npl* logement *m*
accompaniment [ə'kʌmpənɪmənt] *n*
accompagnement *m*
accompany [ə'kʌmpənɪ] *vt* accompagner
accomplice [ə'kʌmplɪs] *n* complice *m/f*
accomplish [ə'kʌmplɪʃ] *vt* accomplir;
accomplishment *n* (*skill: gen pl*) talent
m; (*completion*) accomplissement *m*;
(*achievement*) réussite *f*
accord [ə'kɔːd] *n* accord *m* ▷ *vt* accorder;
of his own ~ de son plein gré; **accordance**
n: **in accordance with** conformément
à; **according: according to** *prep* selon;
accordingly *adv* (*appropriately*) en
conséquence; (*as a result*) par conséquent
account [ə'kaunt] *n* (*Comm*) compte *m*;
(*report*) compte rendu, récit *m*; **accounts**
npl (*Comm: records*) comptabilité *f*, comptes;
of no ~ sans importance; **on ~** en acompte;
to buy sth on ~ acheter qch à crédit; **on no
~** en aucun cas; **on ~ of** à cause de; **to take**

into ~, take ~ of tenir compte de; **account
for** *vt fus* (*explain*) expliquer, rendre compte
de; (*represent*) représenter; **accountable**
adj: **accountable (for/to)** responsable (de/
devant); **accountant** *n* comptable *m/f*;
account number *n* numéro *m* de compte
accumulate [ə'kjuːmjuleɪt] *vt* accumuler,
amasser ▷ *vi* s'accumuler, s'amasser
accuracy ['ækjurəsɪ] *n* exactitude *f*,
précision *f*
accurate ['ækjurɪt] *adj* exact(e), précis(e);
(*device*) précis; **accurately** *adv* avec
précision
accusation [ækju'zeɪʃən] *n* accusation *f*
accuse [ə'kjuːz] *vt*: **to ~ sb (of sth)** accuser
qn (de qch); **accused** *n* (*Law*) accusé(e)
accustomed [ə'kʌstəmd] *adj*: **~ to**
habitué(e) or accoutumé(e) à
ace [eɪs] *n* as *m*
ache [eɪk] *n* mal *m*, douleur *f* ▷ *vi* (*be sore*)
faire mal, être douloureux(-euse); **my head
~s** j'ai mal à la tête
achieve [ə'tʃiːv] *vt* (*aim*) atteindre;
(*victory, success*) remporter, obtenir;
achievement *n* exploit *m*, réussite *f*; (*of
aims*) réalisation *f*
acid ['æsɪd] *adj*, *n* acide (*m*)
acknowledge [ək'nɔlɪdʒ] *vt* (*also:
~ receipt of*) accuser réception de; (*fact*)
reconnaître; **acknowledgement** *n* (*of
letter*) accusé *m* de réception
acne ['æknɪ] *n* acné *m*
acorn ['eɪkɔːn] *n* gland *m*
acoustic [ə'kuːstɪk] *adj* acoustique
acquaintance [ə'kweɪntəns] *n*
connaissance *f*
acquire [ə'kwaɪə'] *vt* acquérir; **acquisition**
[ækwɪ'zɪʃən] *n* acquisition *f*
acquit [ə'kwɪt] *vt* acquitter; **to ~ o.s. well**
s'en tirer très honorablement
acre ['eɪkə'] *n* acre *f* (= 4047 m²)
acronym ['ækrənɪm] *n* acronyme *m*
across [ə'krɔs] *prep* (*on the other side*) de
l'autre côté de; (*crosswise*) en travers de
▷ *adv* de l'autre côté; en travers; **to run/
swim ~** traverser en courant/à la nage;
~ from en face de
acrylic [ə'krɪlɪk] *adj*, *n* acrylique (*m*)
act [ækt] *n* acte *m*, action *f*; (*Theat: part
of play*) acte; (*: of performer*) numéro *m*;
(*Law*) loi *f* ▷ *vi* agir; (*Theat*) jouer; (*pretend*)
jouer la comédie ▷ *vt* (*role*) jouer, tenir;
to catch sb in the ~ prendre qn sur le fait
or en flagrant délit; **to ~ as** servir de; **act
up** (*inf*) *vi* (*person*) se conduire mal; (*knee,
back, injury*) jouer des tours; (*machine*) être
capricieux(-euse); **acting** *adj* suppléant(e),
par intérim ▷ *n* (*activity*): **to do some acting**
faire du théâtre (*or* du cinéma)
action ['ækʃən] *n* action *f*; (*Mil*) combat(s)
m(*pl*); (*Law*) procès *m*, action en justice;
out of ~ hors de combat; (*machine etc*)

hors d'usage; **to take ~** agir, prendre des mesures; **action replay** n (BRIT TV) ralenti m

activate ['æktɪveɪt] vt (mechanism) actionner, faire fonctionner

active ['æktɪv] adj actif(-ive); (volcano) en activité; **actively** adv activement; (discourage) vivement

activist ['æktɪvɪst] n activiste m/f

activity [æk'tɪvɪtɪ] n activité f; **activity holiday** n vacances actives

actor ['æktə'] n acteur m

actress ['æktrɪs] n actrice f

actual ['æktjuəl] adj réel(le), véritable; (emphatic use) lui-même (elle-même)
▌ Be careful not to translate actual by the French word actuel.

actually ['æktjuəlɪ] adv réellement, véritablement; (in fact) en fait
▌ Be careful not to translate actually by the French word actuellement.

acupuncture ['ækjupʌŋktʃə'] n acupuncture f

acute [ə'kjuːt] adj aigu(ë); (mind, observer) pénétrant(e)

ad [æd] n abbr = **advertisement**

A.D. adv abbr (= Anno Domini) ap. J.-C.

adamant ['ædəmənt] adj inflexible

adapt [ə'dæpt] vt adapter ▷ vi: **to ~ (to)** s'adapter (à); **adapter, adaptor** n (Elec) adaptateur m; (for several plugs) prise f multiple

add [æd] vt ajouter; (figures: also: **to ~ up**) additionner; **it doesn't ~ up** (fig) cela ne rime à rien; **add up to** vt fus (Math) s'élever à; (fig: mean) signifier

addict ['ædɪkt] n toxicomane m/f; (fig) fanatique m/f; **addicted** [ə'dɪktɪd] adj: **to be addicted to** (drink, drugs) être adonné(e) à; (fig: football etc) être un(e) fanatique de; **addiction** [ə'dɪkʃən] n (Med) dépendance f; **addictive** [ə'dɪktɪv] adj qui crée une dépendance

addition [ə'dɪʃən] n (adding up) addition f; (thing added) ajout m; **in ~** de plus, de surcroît; **in ~ to** en plus de; **additional** adj supplémentaire

additive ['ædɪtɪv] n additif m

address [ə'drɛs] n adresse f; (talk) discours m, allocution f ▷ vt adresser; (speak to) s'adresser à; **my ~ is, c'est ...;** **address book** n carnet m d'adresses

adequate ['ædɪkwɪt] adj (enough) suffisant(e); (satisfactory) satisfaisant(e)

adhere [əd'hɪə'] vi: **to ~ to** adhérer à; (fig: rule, decision) se tenir à

adhesive [əd'hiːzɪv] n adhésif m; **adhesive tape** n (BRIT) ruban m adhésif; (US Med) sparadrap m

adjacent [ə'dʒeɪsənt] adj adjacent(e), contigu(ë); **~ to** adjacent à

adjective ['ædʒɛktɪv] n adjectif m

adjoining [ə'dʒɔɪnɪŋ] adj voisin(e), adjacent(e), attenant(e)

adjourn [ə'dʒəːn] vt ajourner ▷ vi suspendre la séance; lever la séance; clore la session

adjust [ə'dʒʌst] vt (machine) ajuster, régler; (prices, wages) rajuster ▷ vi: **to ~ (to)** s'adapter (à); **adjustable** adj réglable; **adjustment** n (of machine) ajustage m, réglage m; (of prices, wages) rajustement m; (of person) adaptation f

administer [əd'mɪnɪstə'] vt administrer; **administration** [ədmɪnɪs'treɪʃən] n (management) administration f; (government) gouvernement m; **administrative** [əd'mɪnɪstrətɪv] adj administratif(-ive); **administrator** [əd'mɪnɪstreɪtə'] n administrateur(-trice)

admiral ['ædmərəl] n amiral m

admiration [ædmə'reɪʃən] n admiration f

admire [əd'maɪə'] vt admirer; **admirer** n (fan) admirateur(-trice)

admission [əd'mɪʃən] n admission f; (to exhibition, night club etc) entrée f; (confession) aveu m

admit [əd'mɪt] vt laisser entrer; admettre; (agree) reconnaître, admettre; (crime) reconnaître avoir commis; **"children not ~ted"** "entrée interdite aux enfants", **admit to** vt fus reconnaître, avouer; **admittance** n admission f, (droit m d')entrée f; **admittedly** adv il faut en convenir

adolescent [ædəu'lɛsnt] adj, n adolescent(e)

adopt [ə'dɔpt] vt adopter; **adopted** adj adoptif(-ive), adopté(e); **adoption** [ə'dɔpʃən] n adoption f

adore [ə'dɔː'] vt adorer

adorn [ə'dɔːn] vt orner

Adriatic (Sea) [eɪdrɪ'ætɪk-] n: **the Adriatic (Sea)** la mer Adriatique, l'Adriatique f

adrift [ə'drɪft] adv à la dérive

ADSL n abbr (= asymmetric digital subscriber line) ADSL m

adult ['ædʌlt] n adulte m/f ▷ adj (grown-up) adulte; (for adults) pour adultes; **adult education** n éducation f des adultes

adultery [ə'dʌltərɪ] n adultère m

advance [əd'vɑːns] n avance f ▷ vt avancer ▷ vi s'avancer; **in ~** en avance, d'avance; **to make ~s to sb** (amorously) faire des avances à qn; **~ booking** location f; **~ notice, ~ warning** préavis m; (verbal) avertissement m; **do I need to book in ~?** est-ce qu'il faut réserver à l'avance?; **advanced** adj avancé(e); (Scol: studies) supérieur(e)

advantage [əd'vɑːntɪdʒ] n (also Tennis) avantage m; **to take ~ of** (person) exploiter; (opportunity) profiter de

advent ['ædvənt] n avènement m, venue f; **A~** (Rel) avent m

adventure [əd'vɛntʃəʳ] n aventure f; **adventurous** [əd'vɛntʃərəs] adj aventureux(-euse)

adverb ['ædvə:b] n adverbe m

adversary ['ædvəsərɪ] n adversaire m/f

adverse ['ædvə:s] adj adverse; (effect) négatif(-ive); (weather, publicity) mauvais(e); (wind) contraire

advert ['ædvə:t] n abbr (BRIT) = advertisement

advertise ['ædvətaɪz] vi faire de la publicité or de la réclame; (in classified ads etc) mettre une annonce ▷ vt faire de la publicité or de la réclame pour; (in classified ads etc) mettre une annonce pour vendre; **to ~ for** (staff) recruter par (voie d')annonce; **advertisement** [əd'və:tɪsmənt] n publicité f, réclame f; (in classified ads etc) annonce f; **advertiser** n annonceur m; **advertising** n publicité f

advice [əd'vaɪs] n conseils mpl; (notification) avis m; **a piece of ~** un conseil; **to take legal ~** consulter un avocat

advisable [əd'vaɪzəbl] adj recommandable, indiqué(e)

advise [əd'vaɪz] vt conseiller; **to ~ sb of sth** aviser or informer qn de qch; **to ~ against sth/doing sth** déconseiller qch/conseiller de ne pas faire qch; **adviser**, **advisor** n conseiller(-ère); **advisory** adj consultatif(-ive)

advocate n ['ædvəkɪt] (lawyer) avocat (plaidant); (upholder) défenseur m, avocat(e) ▷ vt ['ædvəkeɪt] recommander, prôner; **to be an ~ of** être partisan(e) de

Aegean [i:'dʒi:ən] n, adj: **the ~ (Sea)** la mer Égée, l'Égée f

aerial ['ɛərɪəl] n antenne f ▷ adj aérien(ne)

aerobics [ɛə'rəubɪks] n aérobic m

aeroplane ['ɛərəpleɪn] n (BRIT) avion m

aerosol ['ɛərəsɔl] n aérosol m

affair [ə'fɛəʳ] n affaire f; (also: **love ~**) liaison f; aventure f

affect [ə'fɛkt] vt affecter; (subj: disease) atteindre; **affected** adj affecté(e); **affection** n affection f; **affectionate** adj affectueux(-euse)

afflict [ə'flɪkt] vt affliger

affluent ['æfluənt] adj aisé(e), riche; **the ~ society** la société d'abondance

afford [ə'fɔ:d] vt (behaviour) se permettre; (provide) fournir, procurer; **can we ~ a car?** avons-nous de quoi acheter or les moyens d'acheter une voiture?; **affordable** adj abordable

Afghanistan [æf'gænɪstæn] n Afghanistan m

afraid [ə'freɪd] adj effrayé(e); **to be ~ of** or **to** avoir peur de; **I am ~ that** je crains que + sub; **I'm ~ so/not** oui/non, malheureusement

Africa ['æfrɪkə] n Afrique f; **African** adj africain(e) ▷ n Africain(e); **African-American** adj afro-américain(e) ▷ n Afro-Américain(e)

after ['ɑ:ftəʳ] prep, adv après ▷ conj après que; **it's quarter ~ two** (US) il est deux heures et quart; **~ having done/~ he left** après avoir fait/après son départ; **to name sb ~ sb** donner à qn le nom de qn; **to ask ~ sb** demander des nouvelles de qn; **what/who are you ~?** que/qui cherchez-vous?; **~ you!** après vous!; **~ all** après tout; **after-effects** npl (of disaster, radiation, drink etc) répercussions fpl; (of illness) séquelles fpl, suites fpl; **aftermath** n conséquences fpl; **afternoon** n après-midi m/f; **after-shave (lotion)** n lotion f après-rasage; **aftersun (cream/lotion)** n après-soleil m inv; **afterwards**, (US) **afterward** ['ɑ:ftəwəd(z)] adv après

again [ə'gɛn] adv de nouveau, encore (une fois); **to do sth ~** refaire qch; **~ and ~** à plusieurs reprises

against [ə'gɛnst] prep contre; (compared to) par rapport à

age [eɪdʒ] n âge m ▷ vt, vi vieillir; **he is 20 years of ~** il a 20 ans; **to come of ~** atteindre sa majorité; **it's been ~s since I saw you** ça fait une éternité que je ne t'ai pas vu

aged adj âgé(e); **~ 10** âgé de 10 ans

age: **age group** n tranche f d'âge; **age limit** n limite f d'âge

agency ['eɪdʒənsɪ] n agence f

agenda [ə'dʒɛndə] n ordre m du jour

■ Be careful not to translate agenda by the French word agenda.

agent ['eɪdʒənt] n agent m; (firm) concessionnaire m

aggravate ['ægrəveɪt] vt (situation) aggraver; (annoy) exaspérer, agacer

aggression [ə'grɛʃən] n agression f

aggressive [ə'grɛsɪv] adj agressif(-ive)

agile ['ædʒaɪl] adj agile

AGM n abbr (= annual general meeting) AG f

ago [ə'gəu] adv: **two days ~** il y a deux jours; **not long ~** il n'y a pas longtemps; **how long ~?** il y a combien de temps (de cela)?

agony ['ægənɪ] n (pain) douleur f atroce; (distress) angoisse f; **to be in ~** souffrir le martyre

agree [ə'gri:] vt (price) convenir de ▷ vi: **to ~ with** (person) être d'accord avec; (statements etc) concorder avec; (Ling) s'accorder avec; **to ~ to do** accepter de or consentir à faire; **to ~ to sth** consentir à qch; **to ~ that** (admit) convenir or reconnaître que; **garlic doesn't ~ with me** je ne supporte pas l'ail; **agreeable** adj (pleasant) agréable; (willing) consentant(e), d'accord; **agreed** adj (time, place) convenu(e); **agreement** n accord m; **in agreement** d'accord

agricultural [ægrɪ'kʌltʃərəl] adj agricole

agriculture ['ægrɪkʌltʃəʳ] n agriculture f

ahead [əˈhɛd] adv en avant; devant; **go right** or **straight ~** (direction) allez tout droit; **go ~!** (permission) allez-y!; **~ of** devant; (fig: schedule etc) en avance sur; **~ of time** en avance

aid [eɪd] n aide f; (device) appareil m ▷ vt aider; **in ~ of** en faveur de

aide [eɪd] n (person) assistant(e)

AIDS [eɪdz] n abbr (= acquired immune (or immuno-)deficiency syndrome) SIDA m

ailing [ˈeɪlɪŋ] adj (person) souffreteux(euse); (economy) malade

ailment [ˈeɪlmənt] n affection f

aim [eɪm] n (objective) but m; (skill): **his ~ is bad** il vise mal ▷ vi (also: **to take ~**) viser ▷ vt: **to ~ sth (at)** (gun, camera) braquer or pointer qch (sur); (missile) lancer qch (à or contre or en direction de); (remark, blow) destiner or adresser qch (à); **to ~ at** viser; (fig) viser (à); **to ~ to do** avoir l'intention de faire

ain't [eɪnt] (inf) = **am not; aren't; isn't**

air [ɛəʳ] n air m ▷ vt aérer; (idea, grievance, views) mettre sur le tapis ▷ cpd (currents, attack etc) aérien(ne); **to throw sth into the ~** (ball etc) jeter qch en l'air; **by ~** par avion; **to be on the ~** (Radio, TV: programme) être diffusé(e); (: station) émettre; **airbag** n airbag m; **airbed** n (BRIT) matelas m pneumatique; **airborne** adj (plane) en vol; **as soon as the plane was airborne** dès que l'avion eut décollé; **air-conditioned** adj climatisé(e), à air conditionné; **air conditioning** n climatisation f; **aircraft** n inv avion m; **airfield** n terrain m d'aviation; **Air Force** n Armée f de l'air; **air hostess** n (BRIT) hôtesse f de l'air; **airing cupboard** n (BRIT) placard qui contient la chaudière et dans lequel on met le linge à sécher; **airlift** n pont aérien; **airline** n ligne aérienne, compagnie aérienne; **airliner** n avion m de ligne; **airmail** n: **by airmail** par avion; **airplane** n (US) avion m; **airport** n aéroport m; **air raid** n attaque aérienne; **airsick** adj: **to be airsick** avoir le mal de l'air; **airspace** n espace m aérien; **airstrip** n terrain m d'atterrissage; **air terminal** n aérogare f; **airtight** adj hermétique; **air-traffic controller** n aiguilleur m du ciel; **airy** adj bien aéré(e); (manners) dégagé(e)

aisle [aɪl] n (of church: central) allée f centrale; (: side) nef f latérale, bas-côté m; (in theatre, supermarket) allée; (on plane) couloir m; **aisle seat** n place f côté couloir

ajar [əˈdʒɑːʳ] adj entrouvert(e)

à la carte [ælæˈkɑːt] adv à la carte

alarm [əˈlɑːm] n alarme f ▷ vt alarmer; **alarm call** n coup m de fil pour réveiller; **could I have an alarm call at 7 am, please?** pouvez-vous me réveiller à 7 heures, s'il vous plaît?; **alarm clock** n réveille-matin m inv, réveil m; **alarmed** adj (frightened)

alarmé(e); (protected by an alarm) protégé(e) par un système d'alarme; **alarming** adj alarmant(e)

Albania [ælˈbeɪnɪə] n Albanie f

albeit [ɔːlˈbiːɪt] conj bien que + sub, encore que + sub

album [ˈælbəm] n album m

alcohol [ˈælkəhɔl] n alcool m; **alcohol-free** adj sans alcool; **alcoholic** [ælkəˈhɔlɪk] adj, n alcoolique (m/f)

alcove [ˈælkəuv] n alcôve f

ale [eɪl] n bière f

alert [əˈləːt] adj alerte, vif (vive); (watchful) vigilant(e) ▷ n alerte f ▷ vt alerter; **on the ~** sur le qui-vive; (Mil) en état d'alerte

algebra [ˈældʒɪbrə] n algèbre m

Algeria [ælˈdʒɪərɪə] n Algérie f

Algerian [ælˈdʒɪərɪən] adj algérien(ne) ▷ n Algérien(ne)

Algiers [ælˈdʒɪəz] n Alger

alias [ˈeɪlɪəs] adv alias ▷ n faux nom, nom d'emprunt

alibi [ˈælɪbaɪ] n alibi m

alien [ˈeɪlɪən] n (from abroad) étranger(-ère); (from outer space) extraterrestre ▷ adj: **~ (to)** étranger(-ère) (à); **alienate** vt aliéner; (subj: person) s'aliéner

alight [əˈlaɪt] adj en feu ▷ vi mettre pied à terre; (passenger) descendre; (bird) se poser

align [əˈlaɪn] vt aligner

alike [əˈlaɪk] adj semblable, pareil(le) ▷ adv de même; **to look ~** se ressembler

alive [əˈlaɪv] adj vivant(e); (active) plein(e) de vie

⊙ **KEYWORD**

all [ɔːl] adj (singular) tout(e); (plural) tous (toutes); **all day** toute la journée; **all night** toute la nuit, **all men** tous les hommes; **all five** tous les cinq; **all the books** tous les livres; **all his life** toute sa vie

▶ pron 1 tout; **I ate it all, I ate all of it** j'ai tout mangé; **all of us went** nous y sommes tous allés; **all of the boys went** tous les garçons y sont allés; **is that all?** c'est tout?; (in shop) ce sera tout?

2 (in phrases): **above all** surtout, par-dessus tout; **after all** après tout; **at all: not at all** (in answer to question) pas du tout; (in answer to thanks) je vous en prie!; **I'm not at all tired** je ne suis pas du tout fatigué(e); **anything at all will do** n'importe quoi fera l'affaire; **all in all** tout bien considéré, en fin de compte

▶ adv: **all alone** tout(e) seul(e); **it's not as hard as all that** ce n'est pas si difficile que ça; **all the more/the better** d'autant plus/ mieux; **all but** presque, pratiquement; **the score is 2 all** le score est de 2 partout

Allah [ˈælə] n Allah m

allegation [ˌælɪ'geɪʃən] n allégation f
alleged [ə'lɛdʒd] adj prétendu(e); **allegedly**
adv à ce que l'on prétend, paraît-il
allegiance [ə'liːdʒəns] n fidélité f,
obéissance f
allergic [ə'lɜːdʒɪk] adj: ~ **to** allergique à;
I'm ~ to penicillin je suis allergique à la
pénicilline
allergy ['ælədʒɪ] n allergie f
alleviate [ə'liːvɪeɪt] vt soulager, adoucir
alley ['ælɪ] n ruelle f
alliance [ə'laɪəns] n alliance f
allied ['ælaɪd] adj allié(e)
alligator ['ælɪgeɪtə'] n alligator m
all-in ['ɔːlɪn] adj, adv (BRIT: charge) tout
compris
allocate ['æləkeɪt] vt (share out) répartir,
distribuer; **to ~ sth to** (duties) assigner or
attribuer qch à; (sum, time) allouer qch à
allot [ə'lɔt] vt (share out) répartir, distribuer;
to ~ sth to (time) allouer qch à; (duties)
assigner qch à
all-out ['ɔːlaut] adj (effort etc) total(e)
allow [ə'lau] vt (practice, behaviour)
permettre, autoriser; (sum to spend etc)
accorder, allouer; (sum, time estimated)
compter, prévoir; (claim, goal) admettre;
(concede): **to ~ that** convenir que; **to ~ sb
to do** permettre à qn de faire, autoriser qn
à faire; **he is ~ed to ...** on lui permet de ...;
allow for vt fus tenir compte de; **allowance**
n (money received) allocation f (: from parent
etc) subside m; (: for expenses) indemnité f;
(US: pocket money) argent m de poche; (Tax)
somme f déductible du revenu imposable,
abattement m; **to make allowances for**
(person) essayer de comprendre; (thing) tenir
compte de
all right adv (feel, work) bien; (as answer)
d'accord
ally n ['ælaɪ] allié m ▷ vt [ə'laɪ]: **to ~ o.s.
with** s'allier avec
almighty [ɔːl'maɪtɪ] adj tout(e)-
puissant(e); (tremendous) énorme
almond ['ɑːmənd] n amande f
almost ['ɔːlməust] adv presque
alone [ə'ləun] adj, adv seul(e); **to leave sb ~**
laisser qn tranquille; **to leave sth ~** ne pas
toucher à qch; **let ~ ...** sans parler de ...;
encore moins ...
along [ə'lɔŋ] prep le long de ▷ adv: **is he
coming ~ with us?** vient-il avec nous?;
he was hopping/limping ~ il venait or
avançait en sautillant/boitant; **~ with**
avec, en plus de; (person) en compagnie de;
all ~ (all the time) depuis le début; **alongside**
prep (along) le long de; (beside) à côté de
▷ adv bord à bord; côte à côte
aloof [ə'luːf] adj distant(e) ▷ adv: **to stand ~**
se tenir à l'écart or à distance
aloud [ə'laud] adv à haute voix
alphabet ['ælfəbɛt] n alphabet m

Alps [ælps] npl: **the ~** les Alpes fpl
already [ɔːl'rɛdɪ] adv déjà
alright ['ɔːl'raɪt] adv (BRIT) = **all right**
also ['ɔːlsəu] adv aussi
altar ['ɔltə'] n autel m
alter ['ɔltə'] vt, vi changer; **alteration**
[ɔltə'reɪʃən] n changement m, modification
f; **alterations** npl (Sewing) retouches fpl;
(Archit) modifications fpl
alternate adj [ɔl'tə:nɪt] alterné(e),
alternant(e), alternatif(-ive); (US)
= **alternative** ▷ vi ['ɔltə:neɪt] alterner; **to
~ with** alterner avec; **on ~ days** un jour sur
deux, tous les deux jours
alternative [ɔl'tə:nətɪv] adj (solution, plan)
autre, de remplacement; (lifestyle) parallèle
▷ n (choice) alternative f; (other possibility)
autre possibilité f; **~ medicine** médecine
alternative, médecine douce; **alternatively**
adv: **alternatively one could ...** une autre
or l'autre solution serait de ...
although [ɔːl'ðəu] conj bien que + sub
altitude ['æltɪtjuːd] n altitude f
altogether [ɔːltə'gɛðə'] adv entièrement,
tout à fait; (on the whole) tout compte fait;
(in all) en tout
aluminium [ælju'mɪnɪəm], (US)
aluminum [ə'luːmɪnəm] n aluminium m
always ['ɔːlweɪz] adv toujours
Alzheimer's (disease) ['æltshaɪməz-] n
maladie f d'Alzheimer
am [æm] vb see **be**
a.m. adv abbr (= ante meridiem) du matin
amalgamate [ə'mælgəmeɪt] vt, vi
fusionner
amass [ə'mæs] vt amasser
amateur ['æmətə'] n amateur m
amaze [ə'meɪz] vt stupéfier; **to be ~d
(at)** être stupéfait(e) (de); **amazed** adj
stupéfait(e); **amazement** n surprise f,
étonnement m; **amazing** adj étonnant(e),
incroyable; (bargain, offer) exceptionnel(le)
Amazon ['æməzən] n (Geo) Amazone f
ambassador [æm'bæsədə'] n
ambassadeur m
amber ['æmbə'] n ambre m; **at ~** (BRIT Aut)
à l'orange
ambiguous [æm'bɪgjuəs] adj ambigu(ë)
ambition [æm'bɪʃən] n ambition
f; **ambitious** [æm'bɪʃəs] adj
ambitieux(-euse)
ambulance ['æmbjuləns] n ambulance f;
call an ~! appelez une ambulance!
ambush ['æmbuʃ] n embuscade f ▷ vt
tendre une embuscade à
amen ['ɑː'mɛn] excl amen
amend [ə'mɛnd] vt (law) amender; (text)
corriger; **to make ~s** réparer ses torts, faire
amende honorable; **amendment** n (to law)
amendement m; (to text) correction f
amenities [ə'miːnɪtɪz] npl aménagements
mpl, équipements mpl

America [əˈmɛrɪkə] n Amérique f; **American** adj américain(e) ▷ n Américain(e); **American football** n (BRIT) football m américain

amicable [ˈæmɪkəbl] adj amical(e); (Law) à l'amiable

amid(st) [əˈmɪd(st)] prep parmi, au milieu de

ammunition [æmjuˈnɪʃən] n munitions fpl

amnesty [ˈæmnɪstɪ] n amnistie f

among(st) [əˈmʌŋ(st)] prep parmi, entre

amount [əˈmaunt] n (sum of money) somme f; (total) montant m; (quantity) quantité f; nombre m ▷ vi: **to ~ to** (total) s'élever à; (be same as) équivaloir à, revenir à

amp(ère) [ˈæmp(ɛəʳ)] n ampère m

ample [ˈæmpl] adj ample, spacieux(-euse); (enough): **this is ~** c'est largement suffisant; **to have ~ time/room** avoir bien assez de temps/place

amplifier [ˈæmplɪfaɪəʳ] n amplificateur m

amputate [ˈæmpjuteɪt] vt amputer

Amtrak [ˈæmtræk] (US) n société mixte de transports ferroviaires interurbains pour voyageurs

amuse [əˈmjuːz] vt amuser; **amusement** n amusement m; (pastime) distraction f; **amusement arcade** n salle f de jeu; **amusement park** n parc m d'attractions

amusing [əˈmjuːzɪŋ] adj amusant(e), divertissant(e)

an [æn, ən, n] indef art see **a**

anaemia, (US) **anemia** [əˈniːmɪə] n anémie f

anaemic, (US) **anemic** [əˈniːmɪk] adj anémique

anaesthetic, (US) **anesthetic** [ænɪsˈθɛtɪk] n anesthésique m

analog(ue) [ˈænəlɔg] adj (watch, computer) analogique

analogy [əˈnælədʒɪ] n analogie f

analyse, (US) **analyze** [ˈænəlaɪz] vt analyser; **analysis** (pl **analyses**) [əˈnæləsɪs, -siːz] n analyse f; **analyst** [ˈænəlɪst] n (political analyst etc) analyste m/f; (US) psychanalyste m/f

analyze [ˈænəlaɪz] vt (US) = **analyse**

anarchy [ˈænəkɪ] n anarchie f

anatomy [əˈnætəmɪ] n anatomie f

ancestor [ˈænsɪstəʳ] n ancêtre m, aïeul m

anchor [ˈæŋkəʳ] n ancre f ▷ vi (also: **to drop ~**) jeter l'ancre, mouiller ▷ vt mettre à l'ancre; (fig): **to ~ sth to** fixer qch à

anchovy [ˈæntʃəvɪ] n anchois m

ancient [ˈeɪnʃənt] adj ancien(ne), antique; (person) d'un âge vénérable; (car) antédiluvien(ne)

and [ænd] conj et; **~ so on** et ainsi de suite; **try ~ come** tâchez de venir; **come ~ sit here** venez vous asseoir ici; **he talked ~ talked** il a parlé pendant des heures; **better ~ better** de mieux en mieux; **more ~ more** de plus en plus

Andorra [ænˈdɔːrə] n (principauté f d')Andorre f

anemia etc [əˈniːmɪə] n (US) = **anaemia** etc

anesthetic [ænɪsˈθɛtɪk] n, adj (US) = **anaesthetic**

angel [ˈeɪndʒəl] n ange m

anger [ˈæŋgəʳ] n colère f

angina [ænˈdʒaɪnə] n angine f de poitrine

angle [ˈæŋgl] n angle m; **from their ~** de leur point de vue

angler [ˈæŋgləʳ] n pêcheur(-euse) à la ligne

Anglican [ˈæŋglɪkən] adj, n anglican(e)

angling [ˈæŋglɪŋ] n pêche f à la ligne

angrily [ˈæŋgrɪlɪ] adv avec colère

angry [ˈæŋgrɪ] adj en colère, furieux(-euse); (wound) enflammé(e); **to be ~ with sb/at sth** être furieux contre qn/de qch; **to get ~** se fâcher, se mettre en colère

anguish [ˈæŋgwɪʃ] n angoisse f

animal [ˈænɪməl] n animal m ▷ adj animal(e)

animated [ˈænɪmeɪtɪd] adj animé(e)

animation [ænɪˈmeɪʃən] n (of person) entrain m; (of street, Cine) animation f

aniseed [ˈænɪsiːd] n anis m

ankle [ˈæŋkl] n cheville f

annex n [ˈænɛks] (BRIT: also: **~e**) annexe f ▷ vt [əˈnɛks] annexer

anniversary [ænɪˈvɔːsərɪ] n anniversaire m

announce [əˈnauns] vt annoncer; (birth, death) faire part de; **announcement** n annonce f; (for births etc: in newspaper) avis m de faire-part; (: letter, card) faire-part m; **announcer** n (Radio, TV: between programmes) speaker(ine); (: in a programme) présentateur(-trice)

annoy [əˈnɔɪ] vt agacer, ennuyer, contrarier; **don't get ~ed!** ne vous fâchez pas!; **annoying** adj agaçant(e), contrariant(e)

annual [ˈænjuəl] adj annuel(le) ▷ n (Bot) plante annuelle; (book) album m; **annually** adv annuellement

annum [ˈænəm] n see **per**

anonymous [əˈnɔnɪməs] adj anonyme

anorak [ˈænəræk] n anorak m

anorexia [ænəˈrɛksɪə] n (also: **~ nervosa**) anorexie f

anorexic [ænəˈrɛksɪk] adj, n anorexique (m/f)

another [əˈnʌðəʳ] adj: **~ book** (one more) un autre livre, encore un livre, un livre de plus; (a different one) un autre livre ▷ pron un(e) autre, encore un(e), un(e) de plus; see also **one**

answer [ˈɑːnsəʳ] n réponse f; (to problem) solution f ▷ vi répondre ▷ vt (reply to) répondre à; (problem) résoudre; (prayer) exaucer; **in ~ to your letter** suite à or en réponse à votre lettre; **to ~ the phone** répondre (au téléphone); **to ~ the bell** or **the door** aller or venir ouvrir (la porte);

answer back vi répondre, répliquer;
answerphone n (esp BRIT) répondeur m
(téléphonique)
ant [ænt] n fourmi f
Antarctic [ænt'ɑːktɪk] n: **the ~**
l'Antarctique m
antelope ['æntɪləʊp] n antilope f
antenatal ['æntɪ'neɪtl] adj prénatal(e)
antenna (pl **antennae**) [æn'tɛnə, -niː] n
antenne f
anthem ['ænθəm] n: **national ~** hymne
national
anthology [æn'θɔlədʒɪ] n anthologie f
anthropology [ænθrə'pɔlədʒɪ] n
anthropologie f
anti ['æntɪ] prefix anti-; **antibiotic**
['æntɪbaɪ'ɔtɪk] n antibiotique m; **antibody**
['æntɪbɔdɪ] n anticorps m
anticipate [æn'tɪsɪpeɪt] vt s'attendre à,
prévoir; (wishes, request) aller au devant de,
devancer; **anticipation** [æntɪsɪ'peɪʃən] n
attente f
anticlimax ['æntɪ'klaɪmæks] n
déception f
anticlockwise ['æntɪ'klɔkwaɪz] (BRIT)
adv dans le sens inverse des aiguilles d'une
montre
antics ['æntɪks] npl singeries fpl
anti: antidote ['æntɪdəʊt] n antidote m,
contrepoison m; **antifreeze** ['æntɪfriːz]
n antigel m; **anti-globalization** n
antimondialisation f; **antihistamine**
[æntɪ'hɪstəmɪn] n antihistaminique
m; **antiperspirant** [æntɪ'pəːspɪrənt] n
déodorant m
antique [æn'tiːk] n (ornament) objet m
d'art ancien; (furniture) meuble ancien ▷ adj
ancien(ne); **antique shop** n magasin m
d'antiquités
antiseptic [æntɪ'sɛptɪk] adj, n
antiseptique (m)
antisocial ['æntɪ'səʊʃəl] adj (unfriendly)
insociable; (against society) antisocial(e)
antivirus [æntɪ'vaɪrəs] adj (Comput)
antivirus inv; **~ software** (logiciel m)
antivirus
antlers ['æntləz] npl bois mpl, ramure f
anxiety [æŋ'zaɪətɪ] n anxiété f; (keenness):
~ to do grand désir or impatience f de faire
anxious ['æŋkʃəs] adj (très) inquiet(-ète);
(always worried) anxieux(-euse); (worrying)
angoissant(e); **~ to do/that** (keen) qui
tient beaucoup à faire/à ce que + sub;
impatient(e) de faire/que + sub

⬤ **KEYWORD**

any ['ɛnɪ] adj **1** (in questions etc: singular) du,
de l', de la; (: plural) des; **do you have any
butter/children/ink?** avez-vous du beurre/
des enfants/de l'encre?
2 (with negative) de, d'; **I don't have any**

money/books je n'ai pas d'argent/de livres
3 (no matter which) n'importe quel(le); (each
and every) tout(e), chaque; **choose any
book you like** vous pouvez choisir
n'importe quel livre; **any teacher you ask
will tell you** n'importe quel professeur vous
le dira
4 (in phrases): **in any case** de toute façon;
any day now d'un jour à l'autre; **at any
moment** à tout moment, d'un instant à
l'autre; **at any rate** en tout cas; **any time**
n'importe quand; **he might come (at) any
time** il pourrait venir n'importe quand;
come (at) any time venez quand vous
voulez
▶ pron **1** (in questions etc) en; **have you got
any?** est-ce que vous en avez?; **can any of
you sing?** est-ce que parmi vous il y en a qui
savent chanter?
2 (with negative) en; **I don't have any (of
them)** je n'en ai pas, je n'en ai aucun
3 (no matter which one(s)) n'importe lequel
(or laquelle); (anybody) n'importe qui; **take
any of those books (you like)** vous pouvez
prendre n'importe lequel de ces livres
▶ adv **1** (in questions etc): **do you want any
more soup/sandwiches?** voulez-vous
encore de la soupe/des sandwichs?; **are
you feeling any better?** est-ce que vous
vous sentez mieux?
2 (with negative): **I can't hear him any more**
je ne l'entends plus; **don't wait any longer**
n'attendez pas plus longtemps; **anybody**
pron n'importe qui; (in interrogative sentences)
quelqu'un; (in negative sentences): **I don't see
anybody** je ne vois personne; **if anybody
should phone ...** si quelqu'un téléphone ...;
anyhow adv quoi qu'il en soit; (haphazardly)
n'importe comment; **do it anyhow you
like** faites-le comme vous voulez; **she
leaves things just anyhow** elle laisse tout
traîner; **I shall go anyhow** j'irai de toute
façon; **anyone** pron = **anybody**; **anything**
pron (no matter what) n'importe quoi; (in
questions) quelque chose; (with negative) ne
... rien; **can you see anything?** tu vois
quelque chose?; **if anything happens to
me ...** s'il m'arrive quoi que ce soit ...; **you
can say anything you like** vous pouvez dire
ce que vous voulez; **anything will do**
n'importe quoi fera l'affaire; **he'll eat
anything** il mange de tout; **anytime** adv (at
any moment) d'un moment à l'autre;
(whenever) n'importe quand; **anyway** adv
de toute façon; **anyway, I couldn't come
even if I wanted to** de toute façon, je ne
pouvais pas venir même si je le voulais;
I shall go anyway j'irai quand même; **why
are you phoning, anyway?** au fait,
pourquoi tu me téléphones?; **anywhere**
adv n'importe où; (in interrogative sentences)
quelque part; (in negative sentences): **I can't**

see him anywhere je ne le vois nulle part; **can you see him anywhere?** tu le vois quelque part?; **put the books down anywhere** pose les livres n'importe où; **anywhere in the world** (no matter where) n'importe où dans le monde

apart [ə'pɑːt] adv (to one side) à part; de côté; à l'écart; (separately) séparément; **to take/pull ~** démonter; **10 miles/a long way ~** à 10 miles/très éloignés l'un de l'autre; **~ from** prep à part, excepté

apartment [ə'pɑːtmənt] n (us) appartement m, logement m; (room) chambre f; **apartment building** n (us) immeuble m; maison divisée en appartements

apathy ['æpəθɪ] n apathie f, indifférence f

ape [eɪp] n (grand) singe ▷ vt singer

aperitif [ə'pɛrɪtɪf] n apéritif m

aperture ['æpətʃuə'] n orifice m, ouverture f; (Phot) ouverture (du diaphragme)

APEX ['eɪpɛks] n abbr (Aviat: = advance purchase excursion) APEX m

apologize [ə'pɔlədʒaɪz] vi: **to ~ (for sth to sb)** s'excuser (de qch auprès de qn), présenter des excuses (à qn pour qch)

apology [ə'pɔlədʒɪ] n excuses fpl

apostrophe [ə'pɔstrəfɪ] n apostrophe f

app n abbr (inf: Comput: = application) appli f

appal, (us) **appall** [ə'pɔːl] vt consterner, atterrer; horrifier; **appalling** adj épouvantable; (stupidity) consternant(e)

apparatus [æpə'reɪtəs] n appareil m, dispositif m; (in gymnasium) agrès mpl

apparent [ə'pærənt] adj apparent(e); **apparently** adv apparemment

appeal [ə'piːl] vi (Law) faire or interjeter appel ▷ n (Law) appel m, (request) appel; prière f; (charm) attrait m, charme m; **to ~ for** demander (instamment); implorer; **to ~ to** (beg) faire appel à; (be attractive) plaire à; **it doesn't ~ to me** cela ne m'attire pas; **appealing** adj (attractive) attrayant(e)

appear [ə'pɪə'] vi apparaître, se montrer; (Law) comparaître; (publication) paraître, sortir, être publié(e); (seem) paraître, sembler; **it would ~ that** il semble que; **to ~ in Hamlet** jouer dans Hamlet; **to ~ on TV** passer à la télé; **appearance** n apparition f; parution f; (look, aspect) apparence f, aspect m

appendices [ə'pɛndɪsiːz] npl of **appendix**

appendicitis [əpɛndɪ'saɪtɪs] n appendicite f

appendix (pl **appendices**) [ə'pɛndɪks, -siːz] n appendice m

appetite ['æpɪtaɪt] n appétit m

appetizer ['æpɪtaɪzə'] n (food) amuse-gueule m; (drink) apéritif m

applaud [ə'plɔːd] vt, vi applaudir

applause [ə'plɔːz] n applaudissements mpl

apple ['æpl] n pomme f; **apple pie** n tarte f aux pommes

appliance [ə'plaɪəns] n appareil m

applicable [ə'plɪkəbl] adj applicable; **to be ~ to** (relevant) valoir pour

applicant ['æplɪkənt] n: **~ (for)** candidat(e) (à)

application [æplɪ'keɪʃən] n (also Comput) application f; (for a job, a grant etc) demande f; candidature f; **application form** n formulaire m de demande

apply [ə'plaɪ] vt: **to ~ (to)** (paint, ointment) appliquer (sur); (law, etc) appliquer (à) ▷ vi: **to ~ to** (ask) s'adresser à; (be suitable for, relevant to) s'appliquer à; **to ~ (for)** (permit, grant) faire une demande (en vue d'obtenir); (job) poser sa candidature (pour), faire une demande d'emploi (concernant); **to ~ o.s. to** s'appliquer à

appoint [ə'pɔɪnt] vt (to post) nommer, engager; (date, place) fixer, désigner; **appointment** n (to post) nomination f; (job) poste m; (arrangement to meet) rendez-vous m; **to have an appointment** avoir un rendez-vous; **to make an appointment (with)** prendre rendez-vous (avec); **I'd like to make an appointment** je voudrais prendre rendez-vous

appraisal [ə'preɪzl] n évaluation f

appreciate [ə'priːʃɪeɪt] vt (like) apprécier, faire cas de; (be grateful for) être reconnaissant(e) de; (be aware of) comprendre, se rendre compte de ▷ vi (Finance) prendre de la valeur; **appreciation** [əpriːʃɪ'eɪʃən] n appréciation f; (gratitude) reconnaissance f; (Finance) hausse f, valorisation f

apprehension [æprɪ'hɛnʃən] n appréhension f, inquiétude f

apprehensive [æprɪ'hɛnsɪv] adj inquiet(-ète), appréhensif(-ive)

apprentice [ə'prɛntɪs] n apprenti m

approach [ə'prəutʃ] vi approcher ▷ vt (come near) approcher de; (ask, apply to) s'adresser à; (subject, passer-by) aborder ▷ n approche f; accès m, abord m; (intellectual) démarche f

appropriate adj [ə'prəuprɪɪt] (tool etc) qui convient, approprié(e); (moment, remark) opportun(e) ▷ vt [ə'prəuprɪeɪt] (take) s'approprier

approval [ə'pruːvəl] n approbation f; **on ~** (Comm) à l'examen

approve [ə'pruːv] vt approuver; **approve of** vt fus (thing) approuver; (person): **they don't ~ of her** ils n'ont pas bonne opinion d'elle

approximate [ə'prɔksɪmɪt] adj approximatif(-ive); **approximately** adv approximativement

Apr. abbr = **April**

apricot ['eɪprɪkɔt] n abricot m

April ['eɪprəl] *n* avril *m*; **April Fools' Day** *n* le premier avril

apron ['eɪprən] *n* tablier *m*

apt [æpt] *adj* (*suitable*) approprié(e); ~ **to do** (*likely*) susceptible de faire; ayant tendance à faire

aquarium [ə'kwεərɪəm] *n* aquarium *m*

Aquarius [ə'kwεərɪəs] *n* le Verseau

Arab ['ærəb] *n* Arabe *m/f* ▷ *adj* arabe

Arabia [ə'reɪbɪə] *n* Arabie *f*; **Arabian** *adj* arabe; **Arabic** ['ærəbɪk] *adj*, *n* arabe (*m*)

arbitrary ['ɑːbɪtrərɪ] *adj* arbitraire

arbitration [ɑːbɪ'treɪʃən] *n* arbitrage *m*

arc [ɑːk] *n* arc *m*

arcade [ɑː'keɪd] *n* arcade *f*, (*passage with shops*) passage *m*, galerie *f*; (*with games*) salle *f* de jeu

arch [ɑːtʃ] *n* arche *f*, (*of foot*) cambrure *f*, voûte *f* plantaire ▷ *vt* arquer, cambrer

archaeology, (*US*) **archeology** [ɑːkɪ'ɒlədʒɪ] *n* archéologie *f*

archbishop [ɑːtʃ'bɪʃəp] *n* archevêque *m*

archeology [ɑːkɪ'ɒlədʒɪ] (*US*) *n* = **archaeology**

architect ['ɑːkɪtεkt] *n* architecte *m*; **architectural** [ɑːkɪ'tεktʃərəl] *adj* architectural(e); **architecture** *n* architecture *f*

archive ['ɑːkaɪv] *n* (*often pl*) archives *fpl*

Arctic ['ɑːktɪk] *adj* arctique ▷ *n*: **the ~** l'Arctique *m*

are [ɑːʳ] *vb see* **be**

area ['εərɪə] *n* (*Geom*) superficie *f*; (*zone*) région *f* (: *smaller*) secteur *m*; (*in room*) coin *m*; (*knowledge, research*) domaine *m*; **area code** (*US*) *n* (*Tel*) indicatif *m* de zone

arena [ə'riːnə] *n* arène *f*

aren't [ɑːnt] = **are not**

Argentina [ɑːdʒən'tiːnə] *n* Argentine *f*; **Argentinian** [ɑːdʒən'tɪnɪən] *adj* argentin(e) ▷ *n* Argentin(e)

arguably ['ɑːgjuəblɪ] *adv*: **it is ~ ...** on peut soutenir que c'est ...

argue ['ɑːgjuː] *vi* (*quarrel*) se disputer; (*reason*) argumenter; **to ~ that** objecter *or* alléguer que, donner comme argument que

argument ['ɑːgjumənt] *n* (*quarrel*) dispute *f*, discussion *f*; (*reasons*) argument *m*

Aries ['εərɪz] *n* le Bélier

arise (*pt* **arose**, *pp* **arisen**) [ə'raɪz, ə'rəuz, ə'rɪzn] *vi* survenir, se présenter

arithmetic [ə'rɪθmətɪk] *n* arithmétique *f*

arm [ɑːm] *n* bras *m* ▷ *vt* armer; **arms** *npl* (*weapons, Heraldry*) armes *fpl*; ~ **in ~** bras dessus bras dessous; **armchair** ['ɑːmtʃεəʳ] *n* fauteuil *m*

armed [ɑːmd] *adj* armé(e); **armed forces** *npl*: **the armed forces** les forces armées; **armed robbery** *n* vol *m* à main armée

armour, (*US*) **armor** ['ɑːməʳ] *n* armure *f*; (*Mil: tanks*) blindés *mpl*

armpit ['ɑːmpɪt] *n* aisselle *f*

armrest ['ɑːmrεst] *n* accoudoir *m*

army ['ɑːmɪ] *n* armée *f*

A road *n* (*BRIT*) ≈ route nationale

aroma [ə'rəumə] *n* arôme *m*; **aromatherapy** *n* aromathérapie *f*

arose [ə'rəuz] *pt of* **arise**

around [ə'raund] *adv* (tout) autour; (*nearby*) dans les parages ▷ *prep* autour de; (*near*) près de; (*fig: about*) environ; (: *date, time*) vers; **is he ~?** est-il dans les parages *or* là?

arouse [ə'rauz] *vt* (*sleeper*) éveiller; (*curiosity, passions*) éveiller, susciter; (*anger*) exciter

arrange [ə'reɪndʒ] *vt* arranger; **to ~ to do sth** prévoir de faire qch; **arrangement** *n* arrangement *m*; **arrangements** *npl* (*plans etc*) arrangements *mpl*, dispositions *fpl*

array [ə'reɪ] *n* (*of objects*) déploiement *m*, étalage *m*

arrears [ə'rɪəz] *npl* arriéré *m*; **to be in ~ with one's rent** devoir un arriéré de loyer

arrest [ə'rεst] *vt* arrêter; (*sb's attention*) retenir, attirer ▷ *n* arrestation *f*; **under ~** en état d'arrestation

arrival [ə'raɪvl] *n* arrivée *f*; **new ~** nouveau venu/nouvelle venue; (*baby*) nouveau-né(e)

arrive [ə'raɪv] *vi* arriver; **arrive at** *vt fus* (*decision, solution*) parvenir à

arrogance ['ærəgəns] *n* arrogance *f*

arrogant ['ærəgənt] *adj* arrogant(e)

arrow ['ærəu] *n* flèche *f*

arse [ɑːs] *n* (*BRIT infl*) cul *m* (!)

arson ['ɑːsn] *n* incendie criminel

art [ɑːt] *n* art *m*; **Arts** *npl* (*Scol*) les lettres *fpl*; **art college** *n* école *f* des beaux-arts

artery ['ɑːtərɪ] *n* artère *f*

art gallery *n* musée *m* d'art; (*saleroom*) galerie *f* de peinture

arthritis [ɑː'θraɪtɪs] *n* arthrite *f*

artichoke ['ɑːtɪtʃəuk] *n* artichaut *m*; **Jerusalem ~** topinambour *m*

article ['ɑːtɪkl] *n* article *m*

articulate *adj* [ɑː'tɪkjulɪt] (*person*) qui s'exprime clairement et aisément; (*speech*) bien articulé(e), prononcé(e) clairement ▷ *vi* [ɑː'tɪkjuleɪt] articuler, parler distinctement ▷ *vt* articuler

artificial [ɑːtɪ'fɪʃəl] *adj* artificiel(le)

artist ['ɑːtɪst] *n* artiste *m/f*; **artistic** [ɑː'tɪstɪk] *adj* artistique

art school *n* ≈ école *f* des beaux-arts

○ **KEYWORD**

as [æz] conj **1** (time: moment) comme, alors que; à mesure que; **he came in as I was leaving** il est arrivé comme je partais; **as the years went by** à mesure que les années passaient; **as from tomorrow** à partir de demain

2 (because) comme, puisque; **he left early as he had to be home by 10** comme il or puisqu'il devait être de retour avant 10h, il est parti de bonne heure

3 (referring to manner, way) comme; **do as you wish** faites comme vous voudrez; **as she said** comme elle disait

▸ adv **1** (in comparisons): **as big as** aussi grand que; **twice as big as** deux fois plus grand que; **as much** or **many as** autant que; **as much money/many books as** autant d'argent/de livres que; **as soon as** dès que

2 (concerning): **as for** or **to that** quant à cela, pour ce qui est de cela

3: **as if** or **though** comme si; **he looked as if he was ill** il avait l'air d'être malade; see also **long; such; well**

▸ prep (in the capacity of) en tant que, en qualité de; **he works as a driver** il travaille comme chauffeur; **as chairman of the company, he ...** en tant que président de la société, il ...; **he gave me it as a present** il me l'a offert, il m'en a fait cadeau

a.s.a.p. abbr = **as soon as possible**

asbestos [æz'bestəs] n asbeste m, amiante m

ascent [ə'sɛnt] n (climb) ascension f

ash [æʃ] n (dust) cendre f; (also: ~ **tree**) frêne m

ashamed [ə'ʃeɪmd] adj honteux(-euse), confus(e); **to be ~ of** avoir honte de

ashore [ə'ʃɔː] adv à terre

ashtray ['æʃtreɪ] n cendrier m

Ash Wednesday n mercredi m des Cendres

Asia ['eɪʃə] n Asie f; **Asian** n (from Asia) Asiatique m/f; (BRIT: from Indian subcontinent) Indo-Pakistanais(e) ▸ adj asiatique; indo-pakistanais(e)

aside [ə'saɪd] adv de côté; à l'écart ▸ n aparté m

ask [ɑːsk] vt demander; (invite) inviter; **to ~ sb sth/to do sth** demander à qn qch/de faire qch; **to ~ sb about sth** questionner qn au sujet de qch; se renseigner auprès de qn au sujet de qch; **to ~ (sb) a question** poser une question (à qn); **to ~ sb out to dinner** inviter qn au restaurant; **ask for** vt fus demander; **it's just ~ing for trouble** or **for it** ce serait chercher des ennuis

asleep [ə'sliːp] adj endormi(e); **to fall ~** s'endormir

AS level n abbr (= Advanced Subsidiary level) première partie de l'examen équivalent au baccalauréat

asparagus [əs'pærəgəs] n asperges fpl

aspect ['æspɛkt] n aspect m; (direction in which a building etc faces) orientation f, exposition f

aspire [əs'paɪə] vi: **to ~ to** aspirer à

aspirin ['æsprɪn] n aspirine f

ass [æs] n âne m; (inf) imbécile m/f; (US inf!) cul m (!)

assassin [ə'sæsɪn] n assassin m; **assassinate** vt assassiner

assault [ə'sɔːlt] n (Mil) assaut m; (gen: attack) agression f ▸ vt attaquer; (sexually) violenter

assemble [ə'sɛmbl] vt assembler ▸ vi s'assembler, se rassembler

assembly [ə'sɛmblɪ] n (meeting) rassemblement m; (parliament) assemblée f; (construction) assemblage m

assert [ə'səːt] vt affirmer, déclarer; (authority) faire valoir; (innocence) protester de; **assertion** [ə'səːʃən] n assertion f, affirmation f

assess [ə'sɛs] vt évaluer, estimer; (tax, damages) établir or fixer le montant de; (person) juger la valeur de; **assessment** n évaluation f, estimation f; (of tax) fixation f

asset ['æsɛt] n avantage m, atout m; (person) atout, **assets** npl (Comm) capital m; avoir(s) m(pl); actif m

assign [ə'saɪn] vt (date) fixer, arrêter; **to ~ sth to** (task) assigner qch à; (resources) affecter qch à; **assignment** n (task) mission f; (homework) devoir m

assist [ə'sɪst] vt aider, assister; **assistance** n aide f, assistance f; **assistant** n assistant(e), adjoint(e); (BRIT: also: **shop assistant**) vendeur(-euse)

associate adj, n [ə'səʊʃɪɪt] associé(e) ▸ vt [ə'səʊʃɪeɪt] associer ▸ vi [ə'səʊʃɪeɪt]: **to ~ with sb** fréquenter qn

association [əsəʊsɪ'eɪʃən] n association f

assorted [ə'sɔːtɪd] adj assorti(e)

assortment [ə'sɔːtmənt] n assortiment m; (of people) mélange m

assume [ə'sjuːm] vt supposer; (responsibilities etc) assumer; (attitude, name) prendre, adopter

assumption [ə'sʌmpʃən] n supposition f, hypothèse f; (of power) assomption f, prise f

assurance [ə'ʃʊərəns] n assurance f

assure [ə'ʃʊə] vt assurer

asterisk ['æstərɪsk] n astérisque m

asthma ['æsmə] n asthme m

astonish [ə'stɒnɪʃ] vt étonner, stupéfier; **astonished** adj étonné(e); **to be astonished at** être étonné(e) de; **astonishing** adj étonnant(e), stupéfiant(e); **I find it astonishing that ...** je trouve incroyable que ... + sub; **astonishment** n (grand) étonnement, stupéfaction f

astound [ə'staʊnd] vt stupéfier, sidérer

astray [ə'streɪ] *adv*: **to go ~** s'égarer; *(fig)* quitter le droit chemin; **to lead ~** *(morally)* détourner du droit chemin

astrology [əs'trɒlədʒɪ] *n* astrologie *f*

astronaut ['æstrənɔːt] *n* astronaute *m/f*

astronomer [əs'trɒnəmə^r] *n* astronome *m*

astronomical [æstrə'nɒmɪkl] *adj* astronomique

astronomy [əs'trɒnəmɪ] *n* astronomie *f*

astute [əs'tjuːt] *adj* astucieux(-euse), malin(-igne)

asylum [ə'saɪləm] *n* asile *m*; **asylum seeker** [-siːkə^r] *n* demandeur(-euse) d'asile

⭕ **KEYWORD**

at [æt] *prep* **1** *(referring to position, direction)* à; **at the top** au sommet; **at home/school** à la maison *or* chez soi/à l'école; **at the baker's** à la boulangerie, chez le boulanger; **to look at sth** regarder qch
2 *(referring to time)*: **at 4 o'clock** à 4 heures; **at Christmas** à Noël; **at night** la nuit; **at times** par moments, parfois
3 *(referring to rates, speed etc)* à; **at £1 a kilo** une livre le kilo; **two at a time** deux à la fois; **at 50 km/h** à 50 km/h
4 *(referring to manner)*: **at a stroke** d'un seul coup; **at peace** en paix
5 *(referring to activity)*: **to be at work** *(in the office etc)* être au travail; *(working)* travailler; **to play at cowboys** jouer aux cowboys; **to be good at sth** être bon en qch
6 *(referring to cause)*: **shocked/surprised/annoyed at sth** choqué par/étonné de/agacé par qch; **I went at his suggestion** j'y suis allé sur son conseil
▶ *n* (@ *symbol*) arobase *f*

ate [eɪt] *pt of* **eat**

atheist ['eɪθɪɪst] *n* athée *m/f*

Athens ['æθɪnz] *n* Athènes

athlete ['æθliːt] *n* athlète *m/f*

athletic [æθ'lɛtɪk] *adj* athlétique; **athletics** *n* athlétisme *m*

Atlantic [ət'læntɪk] *adj* atlantique ▷ *n*: **the ~ (Ocean)** l'(océan *m*) Atlantique *m*

atlas ['ætləs] *n* atlas *m*

A.T.M. *n abbr* (= *Automated Teller Machine*) guichet *m* automatique

atmosphere ['ætməsfɪə^r] *n* (*air*) atmosphère *f*; *(fig: of place etc)* atmosphère, ambiance *f*

atom ['ætəm] *n* atome *m*; **atomic** [ə'tɒmɪk] *adj* atomique; **atom(ic) bomb** *n* bombe *f* atomique

atrocity [ə'trɒsɪtɪ] *n* atrocité *f*

attach [ə'tætʃ] *vt* *(gen)* attacher; *(document, letter)* joindre; **to be ~ed to sb/sth** *(to like)* être attaché à qn/qch; **to ~ a file to an email** joindre un fichier à un e-mail; **attachment** *n* *(tool)* accessoire *m*; *(Comput)*

fichier *m* joint; *(love)*: **attachment (to)** affection *f* (pour), attachement *m* (à)

attack [ə'tæk] *vt* attaquer; *(task etc)* s'attaquer à ▷ *n* attaque *f*; **heart ~** crise *f* cardiaque; **attacker** *n* attaquant *m*; agresseur *m*

attain [ə'teɪn] *vt* (*also*: **to ~ to**) parvenir à, atteindre; *(knowledge)* acquérir

attempt [ə'tɛmpt] *n* tentative *f* ▷ *vt* essayer, tenter

attend [ə'tɛnd] *vt* *(course)* suivre; *(meeting, talk)* assister à; *(school, church)* aller à, fréquenter; *(patient)* soigner, s'occuper de; **attend to** *vt fus* *(needs, affairs etc)* s'occuper de; *(customer)* s'occuper de, servir; **attendance** *n* *(being present)* présence *f*; *(people present)* assistance *f*; **attendant** *n* employé(e); gardien(ne) ▷ *adj* concomitant(e), qui accompagne *or* s'ensuit

🔲 Be careful not to translate *attend* by the French word *attendre*.

attention [ə'tɛnʃən] *n* attention *f* ▷ *excl* *(Mil)* garde-à-vous!; **for the ~ of** *(Admin)* à l'attention de

attic ['ætɪk] *n* grenier *m*, combles *mpl*

attitude ['ætɪtjuːd] *n* attitude *f*

attorney [ə'tɜːnɪ] *n* *(US: lawyer)* avocat *m*; **Attorney General** *n* *(BRIT)* ≈ procureur général; *(US)* ≈ garde *m* des Sceaux, ministre *m* de la Justice

attract [ə'trækt] *vt* attirer; **attraction** [ə'trækʃən] *n* *(gen pl: pleasant things)* attraction *f*, attrait *m*; *(Physics)* attraction; *(fig: towards sb, sth)* attirance *f*; **attractive** *adj* séduisant(e), attrayant(e)

attribute *n* ['ætrɪbjuːt] attribut *m* ▷ *vt* [ə'trɪbjuːt]: **to ~ sth to** attribuer qch à

aubergine ['əʊbəʒiːn] *n* aubergine *f*

auburn ['ɔːbən] *adj* auburn *inv*, châtain roux *inv*

auction ['ɔːkʃən] *n* (*also*: **sale by ~**) vente *f* aux enchères ▷ *vt* (*also*: **to sell by ~**) vendre aux enchères

audible ['ɔːdɪbl] *adj* audible

audience ['ɔːdɪəns] *n* *(people)* assistance *f*, public *m*; *(on radio)* auditeurs *mpl*; *(at theatre)* spectateurs *mpl*; *(interview)* audience *f*

audit ['ɔːdɪt] *vt* vérifier

audition [ɔː'dɪʃən] *n* audition *f*

auditor ['ɔːdɪtə^r] *n* vérificateur *m* des comptes

auditorium [ɔːdɪ'tɔːrɪəm] *n* auditorium *m*, salle *f* de concert *or* de spectacle

Aug. *abbr* = **August**

August ['ɔːgəst] *n* août *m*

aunt [ɑːnt] *n* tante *f*; **auntie, aunty** *n* diminutive *of* **aunt**

au pair ['əʊ'pɛə^r] *n* (*also*: **~ girl**) jeune fille *f* au pair

aura ['ɔːrə] *n* atmosphère *f*; *(of person)* aura *f*

austerity [ɒs'tɛrɪtɪ] *n* austérité *f*

Australia [ɔs'treɪlɪə] n Australie f;
  Australian adj australien(ne) ▷ n
  Australien(ne)
Austria ['ɒstrɪə] n Autriche f; **Austrian** adj
  autrichien(ne) ▷ n Autrichien(ne)
authentic [ɔ:'θɛntɪk] adj authentique
author ['ɔ:θə'] n auteur m
authority [ɔ:'θɒrɪtɪ] n autorité f;
  (permission) autorisation (formelle);
  the authorities les autorités fpl,
  l'administration f
authorize ['ɔ:θəraɪz] vt autoriser
auto ['ɔ:təʊ] n (US) auto f, voiture f;
  autobiography [ɔ:təbaɪ'ɒgrəfɪ] n
  autobiographie f; **autograph** ['ɔ:təgrɑ:f]
  n autographe m ▷ vt signer, dédicacer;
  automatic [ɔ:tə'mætɪk] adj automatique
  ▷ n (gun) automatique m; (car) voiture f à
  transmission automatique; **automatically**
  adv automatiquement; **automobile**
  ['ɔ:təməbi:l] n (US) automobile f;
  autonomous [ɔ:'tɒnəməs] adj autonome;
  autonomy [ɔ:'tɒnəmɪ] n autonomie f
autumn ['ɔ:təm] n automne m
auxiliary [ɔ:g'zɪlɪərɪ] adj, n auxiliaire (m/f)
avail [ə'veɪl] vt: **to ~ o.s. of** user de; profiter
  de ▷ n: **to no ~** sans résultat, en vain, en
  pure perte
availability [əveɪlə'bɪlɪtɪ] n disponibilité f
available [ə'veɪləbl] adj disponible
avalanche ['ævəlɑ:nʃ] n avalanche f
Ave. abbr = **avenue**
avenue ['ævənju:] n avenue f; (fig) moyen m
average ['ævərɪdʒ] n moyenne f ▷ adj
  moyen(ne) ▷ vt (a certain figure) atteindre or
  faire etc en moyenne; **on ~** en moyenne
avert [ə'vɜ:t] vt (danger) prévenir, écarter;
  (one's eyes) détourner
avid ['ævɪd] adj avide
avocado [ævə'kɑ:dəʊ] n (BRIT: also: **~ pear**)
  avocat m
avoid [ə'vɔɪd] vt éviter
await [ə'weɪt] vt attendre
awake [ə'weɪk] (pt **awoke**, pp **awoken**) adj
  éveillé(e) ▷ vt éveiller ▷ vi s'éveiller; **to be ~**
  être réveillé(e)
award [ə'wɔ:d] n (for bravery) récompense
  f; (prize) prix m; (Law: damages) dommages-
  intérêts mpl ▷ vt (prize) décerner; (Law:
  damages) accorder
aware [ə'wɛə'] adj: **~ of** (conscious)
  conscient(e) de; (informed) au courant de;
  to become ~ of/that prendre conscience
  de/que; se rendre compte de/que;
  awareness n conscience f, connaissance f
away [ə'weɪ] adv (au) loin; (movement): **she
  went ~** elle est partie ▷ adj (not in, not here)
  absent(e); **far ~** (au) loin; **two kilometres ~**
  à (une distance de) deux kilomètres, à deux
  kilomètres de distance; **two hours ~ by car**
  à deux heures de voiture or de route; **the
  holiday was two weeks ~** il restait deux

semaines jusqu'aux vacances; **he's ~ for
  a week** il est parti (pour) une semaine; **to
  take sth ~ from sb** prendre qch à qn; **to
  take sth ~ from sth** (subtract) ôter qch de
  qch; **to work/pedal ~** travailler/pédaler
  à cœur joie; **to fade ~** (colour) s'estomper;
  (sound) s'affaiblir
awe [ɔ:] n respect mêlé de crainte, effroi
  mêlé d'admiration; **awesome** ['ɔ:səm] (US)
  adj (inf: excellent) génial(e)
awful ['ɔ:fəl] adj affreux(-euse); **an ~ lot
  of** énormément de; **awfully** adv (very)
  terriblement, vraiment
awkward ['ɔ:kwəd] adj (clumsy) gauche,
  maladroit(e); (inconvenient) peu pratique;
  (embarrassing) gênant
awoke [ə'wəʊk] pt of **awake**
awoken [ə'wəʊkən] pp of **awake**
axe, (US) **ax** [æks] n hache f ▷ vt (project etc)
  abandonner, (jobs) supprimer
axle ['æksl] n essieu m
ay(e) [aɪ] excl (yes) oui
azalea [ə'zeɪlɪə] n azalée f

b

B [biː] n (Mus) si m

B.A. abbr (Scol) = **Bachelor of Arts**

baby ['beɪbɪ] n bébé m; **baby carriage** n (US) voiture f de bébé; **baby-sit** vi garder les enfants; **baby-sitter** n baby-sitter m/f; **baby wipe** n lingette f (pour bébé)

bachelor ['bætʃələʳ] n célibataire m; **B~ of Arts/Science (BA/BSc)** ≈ licencié(e) ès or en lettres/sciences

back [bæk] n (of person, horse) dos m; (of hand, revers m; (of house) derrière m; (of car, train) arrière m; (of chair) dossier m; (of page) verso m; (Football) arrière m ▷ vt (financially) soutenir (financièrement); (candidate: also: ~ **up**) soutenir, appuyer; (horse: at races) parier or miser sur; (car) (faire) reculer ▷ vi reculer; (car etc) faire marche arrière ▷ adj (in compounds) de derrière, à l'arrière ▷ adv (not forward) en arrière; (returned): **he's ~** il est rentré, il est de retour; **can the people at the ~ hear me properly?** est-ce que les gens du fond m'entendent?; **~ to front** à l'envers; **~ seat/wheel** (Aut) siège m/roue f arrière inv; **~ payments/rent** arriéré m de paiements/loyer; **~ garden/room** jardin/pièce sur l'arrière; **he ran ~** il est revenu en courant; **throw the ball ~** renvoie la balle; **can I have it ~?** puis-je le ravoir?, peux-tu me le rendre?; **he called ~** (again) il a rappelé; **back down** vi rabattre de ses prétentions; **back out** vi (of promise) se dédire; **back up** vt (person) soutenir; (Comput) faire une copie de sauvegarde de; **backache** n mal m au dos; **backbencher** n (BRIT) membre du parlement sans portefeuille; **backbone** n colonne vertébrale, épine dorsale; **back door** n porte f de derrière; **backfire** vi (Aut) pétarader; (plans) mal tourner; **backgammon** n trictrac m; **background** n arrière-plan m; (of events) situation f, conjoncture f; (basic knowledge) éléments mpl de base; (experience) formation f; **family background** milieu familial; **backing** n (fig) soutien m, appui m; **backlog** n: **backlog of work** travail m en retard; **backpack** n sac m à dos; **backpacker** n randonneur(-euse); **backslash** n barre oblique inversée; **backstage** adv dans les coulisses; **backstroke** n dos crawlé; **backup** adj (train, plane) supplémentaire, de réserve; (Comput) de sauvegarde ▷ n (support) appui m, soutien m; (Comput: also: **backup file**) sauvegarde f; **backward** adj (movement) en arrière; (person, country) arriéré(e), attardé(e); **backwards** adv (move, go) en arrière; (read a list) à l'envers, à rebours; (fall) à la renverse; (walk) à reculons; **backyard** n arrière-cour f

bacon ['beɪkən] n bacon m, lard m

bacteria [bæk'tɪərɪə] npl bactéries fpl

bad [bæd] adj mauvais(e); (child) vilain(e); (mistake, accident) grave; (meat, food) gâté(e), avarié(e); **his ~ leg** sa jambe malade; **to go ~** (meat, food) se gâter; (milk) tourner

bade [bæd] pt of **bid**

badge [bædʒ] n insigne m; (of police officer) plaque f; (stick-on, sew-on) badge m

badger ['bædʒəʳ] n blaireau m

badly ['bædlɪ] adv (work, dress etc) mal; **to reflect ~ on sb** donner une mauvaise image de qn; **~ wounded** grièvement blessé; **he needs it ~** il en a absolument besoin; **~ off** adj, adv dans la gêne

bad-mannered ['bæd'mænəd] adj mal élevé(e)

badminton ['bædmɪntən] n badminton m

bad-tempered ['bæd'tempəd] adj (by nature) ayant mauvais caractère; (on one occasion) de mauvaise humeur

bag [bæg] n sac m; **~s of** (inf: lots of) des tas de; **baggage** n bagages mpl; **baggage allowance** n franchise f de bagages; **baggage reclaim** n (at airport) livraison f des bagages; **baggy** adj avachi(e), qui fait des poches; **bagpipes** npl cornemuse f

bail [beɪl] n caution f ▷ vt (prisoner: also: **grant ~ to**) mettre en liberté sous caution; (boat: also: **~ out**) écoper; **to be released on ~** être libéré(e) sous caution; **bail out** vt (prisoner) payer la caution de

bait [beɪt] n appât m ▷ vt appâter; (fig: tease) tourmenter

bake [beɪk] vt (faire) cuire au four ▷ vi (bread etc) cuire (au four); (make cakes etc) faire de la pâtisserie; **baked beans** npl haricots blancs à la sauce tomate; **baked potato** n pomme f de terre en robe des champs; **baker** n boulanger m; **bakery** n boulangerie f; **baking** n (process) cuisson f; **baking powder** n levure f (chimique)

balance ['bæləns] n équilibre m; (Comm: sum) solde m; (remainder) reste m; (scales)

balance f ▷ vt mettre or faire tenir en
équilibre; (pros and cons) peser; (budget)
équilibrer; (account) balancer; (compensate)
compenser, contrebalancer; **~ of trade/
payments** balance commerciale/des
comptes or paiements; **balanced** adj
(personality, diet) équilibré(e); (report)
objectif(-ive); **balance sheet** n bilan m
balcony ['bælkənɪ] n balcon m; **do you
have a room with a ~?** avez-vous une
chambre avec balcon?
bald [bɔːld] adj chauve; (tyre) lisse
ball [bɔːl] n boule f; (football) ballon m; (for
tennis, golf) balle f; (dance) bal m; **to play ~**
jouer au ballon (or à la balle); (fig) coopérer
ballerina [bælə'riːnə] n ballerine f
ballet ['bæleɪ] n ballet m; (art) danse f
(classique); **ballet dancer** n danseur(-euse)
de ballet
balloon [bə'luːn] n ballon m
ballot ['bælət] n scrutin m
ballpoint (pen) ['bɔːlpɔɪnt-] n stylo m à
bille
ballroom ['bɔːlrum] n salle f de bal
Baltic [bɔːltɪk] n: **the ~ (Sea)** la (mer)
Baltique
bamboo [bæm'buː] n bambou m
ban [bæn] n interdiction f ▷ vt interdire
banana [bə'nɑːnə] n banane f
band [bænd] n bande f; (at a dance)
orchestre m; (Mil) musique f, fanfare f
bandage ['bændɪdʒ] n bandage m,
pansement m ▷ vt (wound, leg) mettre un
pansement or un bandage sur
Band-Aid® ['bændeɪd] n (US) pansement
adhésif
B. & B. n abbr = **bed and breakfast**
bandit ['bændɪt] n bandit m
bang [bæŋ] n détonation f; (of door)
claquement m; (blow) coup (violent) ▷ vt
frapper (violemment); (door) claquer ▷ vi
détoner; claquer
Bangladesh [bæŋglə'deʃ] n Bangladesh m
Bangladeshi [bæŋglə'deʃɪ] adj du
Bangladesh ▷ n habitant(e) du
Bangladesh
bangle ['bæŋgl] n bracelet m
bangs [bæŋz] npl (US: fringe) frange f
banish ['bænɪʃ] vt bannir
banister(s) ['bænɪstə(z)] n(pl) rampe f
(d'escalier)
banjo ['bændʒəu] (pl **banjoes** or **banjos**) n
banjo m
bank [bæŋk] n banque f; (of river, lake) bord
m, rive f; (of earth) talus m, remblai m ▷ vi
(Aviat) virer sur l'aile; **bank on** vt fus miser
or tabler sur; **bank account** n compte m en
banque; **bank balance** n solde m bancaire;
bank card (BRIT) n carte f d'identité
bancaire; **bank charges** npl (BRIT) frais mpl
de banque; **bank holiday** n banquier m; **bank
holiday** n (BRIT) jour férié (où les banques
sont fermées); voir article **"bank holiday"**;

banking n opérations fpl bancaires;
profession f de banquier; **bank manager** n
directeur m d'agence (bancaire); **banknote**
n billet m de banque

● **BANK HOLIDAY**
●
● Le terme **bank holiday** s'applique au
● Royaume-Uni aux jours fériés pendant
● lesquels banques et commerces sont
● fermés. Les principaux **bank holidays** à part
● Noël et Pâques se situent au mois de mai
● et fin août, et contrairement aux pays de
● tradition catholique, ne coïncident pas
● nécessairement avec une fête religieuse.

bankrupt ['bæŋkrʌpt] adj en faillite; **to go
~** faire faillite; **bankruptcy** n faillite f
bank statement n relevé m de compte
banner ['bænər] n bannière f
bannister(s) ['bænɪstə(z)] n(pl)
= **banister(s)**
banquet ['bæŋkwɪt] n banquet m, festin m
baptism ['bæptɪzəm] n baptême m
baptize [bæp'taɪz] vt baptiser
bar [bɑːr] n (pub) bar m; (counter) comptoir
m, bar; (rod: of metal etc) barre f; (: of window
etc) barreau m; (of chocolate) tablette
f, plaque f; (fig: obstacle) obstacle m;
(prohibition) mesure f d'exclusion; (Mus)
mesure f ▷ vt (road) barrer; (person) exclure;
(activity) interdire; **~ of soap** savonnette f;
behind ~s (prisoner) derrière les barreaux;
the B~ (Law) le barreau; **~ none** sans
exception
barbaric [bɑː'bærɪk] adj barbare
barbecue ['bɑːbɪkjuː] n barbecue m
barbed wire ['bɑːbd-] n fil m de fer barbelé
barber ['bɑːbər] n coiffeur m (pour
hommes); **barber's (shop)**, (US) **barber
shop** n salon m de coiffure (pour hommes)
bar code n code m à barres, code-barre m
bare [bɛər] adj nu(e) ▷ vt mettre à nu,
dénuder; (teeth) découvrir; **barefoot** adj, adv
nu-pieds, (les) pieds nus; **barely** adv à peine
bargain ['bɑːgɪn] n (transaction) marché m;
(good buy) affaire f, occasion f ▷ vi (haggle)
marchander; (negotiate) négocier, traiter;
into the ~ par-dessus le marché; **bargain
for** vt fus (inf): **he got more than he ~ed
for!** il en a eu pour son argent!
barge [bɑːdʒ] n péniche f; **barge in** vi (walk
in) faire irruption; (interrupt talk) intervenir
mal à propos
bark [bɑːk] n (of tree) écorce f; (of dog)
aboiement m ▷ vi aboyer
barley ['bɑːlɪ] n orge f
barmaid ['bɑːmeɪd] n serveuse f (de bar),
barmaid f
barman ['bɑːmən] (irreg) n serveur m (de
bar), barman m
barn [bɑːn] n grange f

barometer [bəˈrɒmɪtəʳ] n baromètre m
baron [ˈbærən] n baron m; **baroness** n
baronne f
barracks [ˈbærəks] npl caserne f
barrage [ˈbærɑːʒ] n (Mil) tir m de barrage;
(dam) barrage m; (of criticism) feu m
barrel [ˈbærəl] n tonneau m; (of gun)
canon m
barren [ˈbærən] adj stérile
barrette [bəˈrɛt] (US) n barrette f
barricade [bærɪˈkeɪd] n barricade f
barrier [ˈbærɪəʳ] n barrière f
barring [ˈbɑːrɪŋ] prep sauf
barrister [ˈbærɪstəʳ] n (BRIT) avocat (plaidant)
barrow [ˈbærəʊ] n (cart) charrette f à bras
bartender [ˈbɑːtɛndəʳ] n (US) serveur m (de
bar), barman m
base [beɪs] n base f ⊳ vt (opinion, belief): to
~ sth on baser or fonder qch sur ⊳ adj vil(e),
bas(se)
baseball [ˈbeɪsbɔːl] n base-ball m; **baseball
cap** n casquette f de base-ball
Basel [bɑːl] n = **Basle**
basement [ˈbeɪsmənt] n sous-sol m
bases [ˈbeɪsiːz] npl of **basis**
bash [bæʃ] vt (inf) frapper, cogner
basic [ˈbeɪsɪk] adj (precautions, rules)
élémentaire; (principles, research)
fondamental(e); (vocabulary, salary) de
base; (minimal) réduit(e) au minimum,
rudimentaire; **basically** adv (in fact) en fait;
(essentially) fondamentalement; **basics** npl:
the basics l'essentiel m
basil [ˈbæzl] n basilic m
basin [ˈbeɪsn] n (vessel, also Geo) cuvette f,
bassin m; (BRIT: for food) bol m; (also: **wash~**)
lavabo m
basis (pl **bases**) [ˈbeɪsɪs, -siːz] n base f; **on a
part-time/trial ~** à temps partiel/à l'essai
basket [ˈbɑːskɪt] n corbeille f; (with handle)
panier m; **basketball** n basket-ball m
Basle [bɑːl] n Bâle
Basque [bæsk] adj basque ⊳ n Basque m/f;
the ~ Country le Pays basque
bass [beɪs] n (Mus) basse f
bastard [ˈbɑːstəd] n enfant naturel(le),
bâtard(e); (inf!) salaud m (!)
bat [bæt] n chauve-souris f; (for baseball etc)
batte f; (BRIT: for table tennis) raquette f ⊳ vt:
he didn't ~ an eyelid il n'a pas sourcillé or
bronché
batch [bætʃ] n (of bread) fournée f; (of papers)
liasse f; (of applicants, letters) paquet m
bath (pl **baths**) [bɑːθ, bɑːðz] n bain m;
(bathtub) baignoire f ⊳ vt baigner, donner
un bain à; **to have a ~** prendre un bain; see
also **baths**
bathe [beɪð] vi se baigner ⊳ vt baigner;
(wound etc) laver
bathing [ˈbeɪðɪŋ] n baignade f; **bathing
costume**, (US) **bathing suit** n maillot m
(de bain)

bath: bathrobe n peignoir m de bain;
bathroom n salle f de bains; **baths** [bɑːðz]
npl (BRIT: also: **swimming baths**) piscine f;
bath towel n serviette f de bain; **bathtub**
n baignoire f
baton [ˈbætən] n bâton m; (Mus) baguette f;
(club) matraque f
batter [ˈbætəʳ] vt battre ⊳ n pâte f à
frire; **battered** adj (hat, pan) cabossé(e);
battered wife/child épouse/enfant
maltraité(e) or martyr(e)
battery [ˈbætərɪ] n (for torch, radio) pile f;
(Aut, Mil) batterie f; **battery farming** n
élevage m en batterie
battle [ˈbætl] n bataille f, combat m ⊳ vi se
battre, lutter; **battlefield** n champ m de
bataille
bay [beɪ] n (of sea) baie f; (BRIT: for parking)
place f de stationnement; (: for loading)
aire f de chargement; **B~ of Biscay** golfe
m de Gascogne; **to hold sb at ~** tenir qn à
distance or en échec
bay leaf n laurier m
bazaar [bəˈzɑːʳ] n (shop, market) bazar m;
(sale) vente f de charité
BBC n abbr (= British Broadcasting Corporation)
office de la radiodiffusion et télévision
britannique
B.C. adv abbr (= before Christ) av. J.-C.

KEYWORD

be [biː] (pt **was**, **were**, pp **been**) aux vb
1 (with present participle, forming continuous
tenses): **what are you doing?** que faites-
vous?; **they're coming tomorrow** ils
viennent demain; **I've been waiting for
you for 2 hours** je t'attends depuis
2 heures
2 (with pp, forming passives) être; **to be
killed** être tué(e); **the box had been
opened** la boîte avait été ouverte; **he was
nowhere to be seen** on ne le voyait nulle
part
3 (in tag questions): **it was fun, wasn't it?**
c'était drôle, n'est-ce pas?; **he's good-
looking, isn't he?** il est beau, n'est-ce pas?;
she's back, is she? elle est rentrée, n'est-ce
pas or alors?
4 (+to +infinitive): **the house is to be sold**
(necessity) la maison doit être vendue;
(future) la maison va être vendue; **he's not
to open it** il ne doit pas l'ouvrir
▶ vb + complement **1** (gen) être; **I'm English** je
suis anglais(e); **I'm tired** je suis fatigué(e);
I'm hot/cold j'ai chaud/froid; **he's a doctor**
il est médecin; **be careful/good/quiet!**
faites attention/soyez sages/taisez-vous!;
2 and 2 are 4 2 et 2 font 4
2 (of health) aller; **how are you?** comment
allez-vous?; **I'm better now** je vais mieux
maintenant; **he's very ill** il est très malade

3 (*of age*) avoir; **how old are you?** quel âge avez-vous?; **I'm sixteen (years old)** j'ai seize ans

4 (*cost*) coûter; **how much was the meal?** combien a coûté le repas?; **that'll be £5, please** ça fera 5 livres, s'il vous plaît; **this shirt is £17** cette chemise coûte 17 livres

▶ *vi* **1** (*exist, occur etc*) être, exister; **the prettiest girl that ever was** la fille la plus jolie qui ait jamais existé; **is there a God?** y a-t-il un dieu?; **be that as it may** quoi qu'il en soit; **so be it** soit

2 (*referring to place*) être, se trouver; **I won't be here tomorrow** je ne serai pas là demain **3** (*referring to movement*) aller; **where have you been?** où êtes-vous allé(s)?

▶ *impers vb* **1** (*referring to time*) être; **it's 5 o'clock** il est 5 heures; **it's the 28th of April** c'est le 28 avril

2 (*referring to distance*): **it's 10 km to the village** le village est à 10 km

3 (*referring to the weather*) faire; **it's too hot/cold** il fait trop chaud/froid; **it's windy today** il y a du vent aujourd'hui

4 (*emphatic*): **it's me/the postman** c'est moi/le facteur; **it was Maria who paid the bill** c'est Maria qui a payé la note

beauté; **beauty spot** *n* (*on skin*) grain *m* de beauté; (BRIT Tourism) site naturel (d'une grande beauté)

beaver ['biːvə^r] *n* castor *m*

became [bɪ'keɪm] *pt of* **become**

because [bɪ'kɔz] *conj* parce que; **~ of** *prep* à cause de

beckon ['bɛkən] *vt* (*also:* **~ to**) faire signe (de venir) à

become [bɪ'kʌm] *vi* devenir; **to ~ fat/thin** grossir/maigrir; **to ~ angry** se mettre en colère

bed [bɛd] *n* lit *m*; (*of flowers*) parterre *m*, (*of coal, clay*) couche *f*; (*of sea, lake*) fond *m*; **to go to ~** aller se coucher; **bed and breakfast** *n* (*terms*) chambre et petit déjeuner; (*place*) ≈ chambre *f* d'hôte; *voir article* **"bed and breakfast"**; **bedclothes** *npl* couvertures *fpl* et draps *mpl*; **bedding** *n* literie *f*; **bed linen** *n* draps *mpl* de lit (et taies *fpl* d'oreillers), literie *f*; **bedroom** *n* chambre *f* (à coucher); **bedside** *n*: **at sb's bedside** au chevet de qn; **bedside lamp** *n* lampe *f* de chevet; **bedside table** *n* table *f* de chevet; **bedsit(ter)** *n* (BRIT) chambre meublée, studio *m*; **bedspread** *n* couvre-lit *m*, dessus-de-lit *m*; **bedtime** *n*: **it's bedtime** c'est l'heure de se coucher

---

beach [biːtʃ] *n* plage *f* ▷ *vt* échouer

beacon ['biːkən] *n* (*lighthouse*) fanal *m*; (*marker*) balise *f*

bead [biːd] *n* perle *f*; (*of dew, sweat*) goutte *f*; **beads** *npl* (*necklace*) collier *m*

beak [biːk] *n* bec *m*

beam [biːm] *n* (Archit) poutre *f*, (*of light*) rayon *m* ▷ *vi* rayonner

bean [biːn] *n* haricot *m*; (*of coffee*) grain *m*; **beansprouts** *npl* pousses *fpl* or germes *mpl* de soja

bear [bɛə^r] *n* ours *m* ▷ *vt* (*pt* **bore**, *pp* **borne**) porter; (*endure*) supporter; (*interest*) rapporter ▷ *vi*: **to ~ right/left** obliquer à droite/gauche, se diriger vers la droite/gauche

beard [bɪəd] *n* barbe *f*

bearer ['bɛərə^r] *n* porteur *m*; (*of passport etc*) titulaire *m/f*

bearing ['bɛərɪŋ] *n* maintien *m*, allure *f*; (*connection*) rapport *m*; **(ball) bearings** *npl* (Tech) roulement *m* (à billes)

beast [biːst] *n* bête *f*; (*inf: person*) brute *f*

beat [biːt] *n* battement *m*; (Mus) temps *m*, mesure *f*; (*of police officer*) ronde *f* ▷ *vt*, *vi* (*pt* **beat**, *pp* **beaten**) battre; **off the ~en track** hors des chemins or sentiers battus; **to ~ it** (*inf*) ficher le camp; **beat up** *vt* (*inf: person*) tabasser; **beating** *n* raclée *f*

beautiful ['bjuːtɪful] *adj* beau (belle); **beautifully** *adv* admirablement

beauty ['bjuːtɪ] *n* beauté *f*; **beauty parlour**, (*us*) **beauty parlor** *n* institut *m* de beauté; **beauty salon** *n* institut *m* de

---

BED AND BREAKFAST

Un *bed and breakfast* est une petite pension dans une maison particulière ou une ferme où l'on peut louer une chambre avec petit déjeuner compris pour un prix modique par rapport à ce que l'on paierait dans un hôtel. Ces établissements sont communément appelés "B & B", et sont signalés par une pancarte dans le jardin ou au-dessus de la porte.

bee [biː] *n* abeille *f*

beech [biːtʃ] *n* hêtre *m*

beef [biːf] *n* bœuf *m*; **roast ~** rosbif *m*; **beefburger** *n* hamburger *m*

been [biːn] *pp of* **be**

beer [bɪə^r] *n* bière *f*; **beer garden** *n* (BRIT) jardin *m* d'un pub (*où l'on peut emmener ses consommations*)

beet [biːt] *n* (*vegetable*) betterave *f*; (*us: also:* **red ~**) betterave (potagère)

beetle ['biːtl] *n* scarabée *m*, coléoptère *m*

beetroot ['biːtruːt] *n* (BRIT) betterave *f*

before [bɪ'fɔː^r] *prep* (*of time*) avant; (*of space*) devant ▷ *conj* avant que + *sub*; avant de ▷ *adv* avant; **~ going** avant de partir; **~ she goes** avant qu'elle (ne) parte; **the week ~** la semaine précédente or d'avant; **I've never seen it ~** c'est la première fois que je le vois; **beforehand** *adv* au préalable, à l'avance

beg [bɛg] *vi* mendier ▷ *vt* mendier; (*forgiveness, mercy etc*) demander; (*entreat*) supplier; **to ~ sb to do sth** supplier qn de faire qch; *see also* **pardon**

began [bɪ'gæn] *pt of* **begin**

beggar ['bɛgər] *n* mendiant(e)

begin [bɪ'gɪn] (*pt* **began**, *pp* **begun**) *vt, vi* commencer; **to ~ doing** *or* **to do sth** commencer à faire qch; **beginner** *n* débutant(e); **beginning** *n* commencement *m*, début *m*

begun [bɪ'gʌn] *pp of* **begin**

behalf [bɪ'hɑːf] *n* **on ~ of**, *(us)* **in ~ of** *(representing)* de la part de; *(for benefit of)* pour le compte de; **on my/his ~** de ma/sa part

behave [bɪ'heɪv] *vi* se conduire, se comporter; *(well: also: ~ o.s.)* se conduire bien *or* comme il faut; **behaviour**, *(us)* **behavior** *n* comportement *m*, conduite *f*

behind [bɪ'haɪnd] *prep* derrière; *(time)* en retard sur; *(supporting)*: **to be ~ sb** soutenir qn ▷ *adv* derrière; en retard ▷ *n* derrière *m*; **~ the scenes** dans les coulisses; **to be ~ (schedule) with sth** être en retard dans qch

beige [beɪʒ] *adj* beige

Beijing ['beɪ'dʒɪŋ] *n* Pékin

being ['biːɪŋ] *n* être *m*; **to come into ~** prendre naissance

belated [bɪ'leɪtɪd] *adj* tardif(-ive)

belch [bɛltʃ] *vi* avoir un renvoi, roter ▷ *vt* *(smoke etc: also: ~ out)* vomir, cracher

Belgian ['bɛldʒən] *adj* belge, de Belgique ▷ *n* Belge *m/f*

Belgium ['bɛldʒəm] *n* Belgique *f*

belief [bɪ'liːf] *n (opinion)* conviction *f*; *(trust, faith)* foi *f*

believe [bɪ'liːv] *vt, vi* croire, estimer; **to ~ in** *(God)* croire en; *(ghosts, method)* croire à; **believer** *n (in idea, activity)* partisan(e); *(Rel)* croyant(e)

bell [bɛl] *n* cloche *f*; *(small)* clochette *f*, grelot *m*; *(on door)* sonnette *f*; *(electric)* sonnerie *f*

bellboy ['bɛlbɔɪ], *(us)* **bellhop** ['bɛlhɔp] *n* groom *m*, chasseur *m*

bellow ['bɛləu] *vi (bull)* meugler; *(person)* brailler

bell pepper *n (esp us)* poivron *m*

belly ['bɛlɪ] *n* ventre *m*; **belly button** *(inf)* *n* nombril *m*

belong [bɪ'lɔŋ] *vi*: **to ~ to** appartenir à; *(club etc)* faire partie de; **this book ~s here** ce livre va ici, la place de ce livre est ici; **belongings** *npl* affaires *fpl*, possessions *fpl*

beloved [bɪ'lʌvɪd] *adj* (bien-)aimé(e), chéri(e)

below [bɪ'ləu] *prep* sous, au-dessous de ▷ *adv* en dessous; en contre-bas; **see ~** voir plus bas *or* plus loin *or* ci-dessous

belt [bɛlt] *n* ceinture *f*; *(Tech)* courroie *f* ▷ *vt* *(thrash)* donner une raclée à; **beltway** *n (us Aut)* route *f* de ceinture; *(: motorway)* périphérique *m*

bemused [bɪ'mjuːzd] *adj* médusé(e)

bench [bɛntʃ] *n* banc *m*; *(in workshop)* établi *m*; **the B~** *(Law: judges)* la magistrature, la Cour

bend [bɛnd] *(pt, pp* **bent**) *vt* courber; *(leg, arm)* plier ▷ *vi* se courber ▷ *n (in road)* virage *m*, tournant *m*; *(in pipe, river)* coude *m*; **bend down** *vi* se baisser; **bend over** *vi* se pencher

beneath [bɪ'niːθ] *prep* sous, au-dessous de; *(unworthy of)* indigne de ▷ *adv* dessous, au-dessous, en bas

beneficial [bɛnɪ'fɪʃəl] *adj*: **~ (to)** salutaire (pour), bénéfique (à)

benefit ['bɛnɪfɪt] *n* avantage *m*, profit *m*; *(allowance of money)* allocation *f* ▷ *vt* faire du bien à, profiter à ▷ *vi*: **he'll ~ from it** cela lui fera du bien, il y gagnera *or* s'en trouvera bien

Benelux ['bɛnɪlʌks] *n* Bénélux *m*

benign [bɪ'naɪn] *adj (person, smile)* bienveillant(e), affable; *(Med)* bénin(-igne)

bent [bɛnt] *pt, pp of* **bend** ▷ *n* inclination *f*, penchant *m* ▷ *adj*: **to be ~ on** être résolu(e) à

bereaved [bɪ'riːvd] *n*: **the ~** la famille du disparu

beret ['bɛreɪ] *n* béret *m*

Berlin [bə:'lɪn] *n* Berlin

Bermuda [bə:'mjuːdə] *n* Bermudes *fpl*

Bern [bə:n] *n* Berne

berry ['bɛrɪ] *n* baie *f*

berth [bə:θ] *n (bed)* couchette *f*; *(for ship)* poste *m* d'amarrage, mouillage *m* ▷ *vi (in harbour)* venir à quai; *(at anchor)* mouiller

beside [bɪ'saɪd] *prep* à côté de; *(compared with)* par rapport à; **that's ~ the point** ça n'a rien à voir; **to be ~ o.s. (with anger)** être hors de soi; **besides** *adv* en outre, de plus ▷ *prep* en plus de; *(except)* excepté

best [bɛst] *adj* meilleur(e) ▷ *adv* le mieux; **the ~ part of** *(quantity)* le plus clair de, la plus grande partie de; **at ~** au mieux; **to make the ~ of sth** s'accommoder de qch (du mieux que l'on peut); **to do one's ~** faire de son mieux; **to the ~ of my knowledge** pour autant que je sache; **to the ~ of my ability** du mieux que je pourrai; **best-before date** *n* date *f* de limite d'utilisation *or* de consommation; **best man** *(irreg)* *n* garçon *m* d'honneur; **bestseller** *n* best-seller *m*, succès *m* de librairie

bet [bɛt] *n* pari *m* ▷ *vt, vi (pt* **bet**, *pp* **betted**) parier; **to ~ sb sth** parier qch à qn

betray [bɪ'treɪ] *vt* trahir

better ['bɛtər] *adj* meilleur(e) ▷ *adv* mieux ▷ *vt* améliorer ▷ *n*: **to get the ~ of** triompher de, l'emporter sur; **you had ~ do it** vous feriez mieux de le faire; **he thought ~ of it** il s'est ravisé; **to get ~** *(Med)* aller mieux; *(improve)* s'améliorer

betting ['bɛtɪŋ] n paris mpl; **betting shop** n (BRIT) bureau m de paris

between [bɪ'twiːn] prep entre ▷ adv au milieu, dans l'intervalle

beverage ['bɛvərɪdʒ] n boisson f (gén sans alcool)

beware [bɪ'wɛəʳ] vi: **to ~ (of)** prendre garde (à); **"~ of the dog"** "(attention) chien méchant"

bewildered [bɪ'wɪldəd] adj déróuté(e), ahuri(e)

beyond [bɪ'jɔnd] prep (in space, time) au-delà de; (exceeding) au-dessus de ▷ adv au-delà; **~ doubt** hors de doute; **~ repair** irréparable

bias ['baɪəs] n (prejudice) préjugé m, parti pris; (preference) prévention f; **bias(s)ed** adj partial(e), montrant un parti pris

bib [bɪb] n bavoir m

Bible ['baɪbl] n Bible f

bicarbonate of soda [baɪ'kɑːbənɪt-] n bicarbonate m de soude

biceps ['baɪsɛps] n biceps m

bicycle ['baɪsɪkl] n bicyclette f; **bicycle pump** n pompe f à vélo

bid [bɪd] n offre f; (at auction) enchère f; (attempt) tentative f ▷ vi (pt, pp **bid**) faire une enchère or offre ▷ vt (pt **bade**, pp **bidden**) faire une enchère or offre de; **to ~ sb good day** souhaiter le bonjour à qn; **bidder** n: **the highest bidder** le plus offrant

bidet ['biːdeɪ] n bidet m

big [bɪg] adj (in height: person, building, tree) grand(e); (in bulk, amount: person, parcel, book) gros(se); **Big Apple** n voir article **"Big Apple"**; **bigheaded** adj prétentieux(-euse); **big toe** n gros orteil

● BIG APPLE

● Si l'on sait que "The Big Apple" désigne la
● ville de New York ("apple" est en réalité un
● terme d'argot signifiant "grande ville"),
● on connaît moins les surnoms donnés
● aux autres grandes villes américaines.
● Chicago est surnommée "Windy City"
● à cause des rafales soufflant du lac
● Michigan, La Nouvelle-Orléans doit son
● sobriquet de "Big Easy" à son style de vie
● décontracté, et l'industrie automobile a
● donné à Detroit son surnom de "Motown".

bike [baɪk] n vélo m; **bike lane** n piste f cyclable

bikini [bɪ'kiːnɪ] n bikini m

bilateral [baɪ'lætərl] adj bilatéral(e)

bilingual [baɪ'lɪŋgwəl] adj bilingue

bill [bɪl] n note f, facture f; (in restaurant) addition f, note f; (Pol) projet m de loi; (US: banknote) billet m (de banque); (notice) affiche f; (of bird) bec m; **put it on my ~**

mettez-le sur mon compte; **"post no ~s"** "défense d'afficher"; **to fit** or **fill the ~** (fig) faire l'affaire; **billboard** n (US) panneau m d'affichage; **billfold** ['bɪlfəuld] n (US) portefeuille m

billiards ['bɪljədz] n billard m

billion ['bɪljən] n (BRIT) billion m (million de millions); (US) milliard m

bin [bɪn] n boîte f; (BRIT: also: **dust~, litter ~**) poubelle f; (for coal) coffre m

bind (pt, pp **bound**) [baɪnd, baund] vt attacher; (book) relier; (oblige) obliger, contraindre ▷ n (inf: nuisance) scie f

binge [bɪndʒ] n (inf): **to go on a ~** faire la bringue

bingo ['bɪŋgəu] n sorte de jeu de loto pratiqué dans des établissements publics

binoculars [bɪ'nɔkjuləz] npl jumelles fpl

bio...: biochemistry [baɪə'kɛmɪstrɪ] n biochimie f; **biodegradable** ['baɪəudɪ'greɪdəbl] adj biodégradable; **biodiesel** ['baɪəudiːzl] n biogazole m, biodiesel m; **biofuel** ['baɪəufjuəl] n biocarburant; **biography** [baɪ'ɔgrəfɪ] n biographie f; **biological** adj biologique; **biology** [baɪ'ɔlədʒɪ] n biologie f; **biometric** [baɪə'mɛtrɪk] adj biométrique

bipolar [baɪ'pəulɑʳ] adj bipolaire

birch [bəːtʃ] n bouleau m

bird [bəːd] n oiseau m; (BRIT inf: girl) nana f; **bird flu** n grippe f aviaire; **bird of prey** n oiseau m de proie; **birdwatching** n ornithologie f (d'amateur)

Biro® ['baɪərəu] n stylo m à bille

birth [bəːθ] n naissance f; **to give ~ to** donner naissance à, mettre au monde; (animal) mettre bas; **birth certificate** n acte m de naissance; **birth control** n (policy) limitation f des naissances; (methods) méthode(s) contraceptive(s); **birthday** n anniversaire m ▷ cpd (cake, card etc) d'anniversaire; **birthmark** n envie f, tache f de vin; **birthplace** n lieu m de naissance

biscuit ['bɪskɪt] n (BRIT) biscuit m; (US) petit pain au lait

bishop ['bɪʃəp] n évêque m; (Chess) fou m

bistro ['biːstrəu] n petit restaurant m, bistrot m

bit [bɪt] pt of **bite** ▷ n morceau m; (Comput) bit m, élément m binaire; (of tool) mèche f; (of horse) mors m; **a ~ of** un peu de; **a ~ mad/dangerous** un peu fou/risqué; **~ by ~** petit à petit

bitch [bɪtʃ] n (dog) chienne f; (offensive) salope f (!), garce f

bite [baɪt] vt, vi (pt **bit**, pp **bitten**) mordre; (insect) piquer ▷ n morsure f; (insect bite) piqûre f; (mouthful) bouchée f; **let's have a ~ (to eat)** mangeons un morceau; **to ~ one's nails** se ronger les ongles

bitten ['bɪtn] pp of **bite**

bitter ['bɪtər] adj amer(-ère); (criticism)
cinglant(e); (icy: weather, wind) glacial(e)
▷ n (BRIT: beer) bière f (à forte teneur en
houblon)

bizarre [bɪ'zɑːr] adj bizarre

black [blæk] adj noir(e) ▷ n (colour) noir m
▷ vt (BRIT Industry) boycotter; **to give sb a ~
eye** pocher l'œil à qn, faire un œil au beurre
noir à qn; **to be in the ~** (in credit) avoir un
compte créditeur; **~ and blue** (bruised)
couvert(e) de bleus; **black out** vi (faint)
s'évanouir; **blackberry** n mûre f; **blackbird**
n merle m; **blackboard** n tableau noir;
black coffee n café noir; **blackcurrant** n
cassis m; **black ice** n verglas m; **blackmail**
n chantage m ▷ vt faire chanter, soumettre
au chantage; **black market** n marché
noir; **blackout** n panne f d'électricité; (in
wartime) black-out m; (TV) interruption
f d'émission; (fainting) syncope f; **black
pepper** n poivre noir; **black pudding** n
boudin (noir); **Black Sea** n: **the Black Sea**
la mer Noire

bladder ['blædər] n vessie f

blade [bleɪd] n lame f; (of propeller) pale f;
a ~ of grass un brin d'herbe

blame [bleɪm] n faute f, blâme m ▷ vt:
to ~ sb/sth for sth attribuer à qn/qch la
responsabilité de qch; reprocher qch à qn/
qch; **I'm not to ~** ce n'est pas ma faute

bland [blænd] adj (taste, food) doux (douce),
fade

blank [blæŋk] adj blanc (blanche); (look)
sans expression, dénué(e) d'expression
▷ n espace m vide, blanc m; (cartridge)
cartouche f à blanc; **his mind was a ~** il
avait la tête vide

blanket ['blæŋkɪt] n couverture f; (of snow,
cloud) couche f

blast [blɑːst] n explosion f; (shock wave)
souffle m; (of air, steam) bouffée f ▷ vt faire
sauter or exploser

blatant ['bleɪtənt] adj flagrant(e),
criant(e)

blaze [bleɪz] n (fire) incendie m; (fig)
flamboiement m ▷ vi (fire) flamber; (fig)
flamboyer, resplendir ▷ vt: **to ~ a trail** (fig)
montrer la voie; **in a ~ of publicity** à grand
renfort de publicité

blazer ['bleɪzər] n blazer m

bleach [bliːtʃ] n (also: **household ~**) eau f de
Javel ▷ vt (linen) blanchir; **bleachers** npl (US
Sport) gradins mpl (en plein soleil)

bleak [bliːk] adj morne, désolé(e); (weather)
triste, maussade; (smile) lugubre; (prospect,
future) morose

bled [bled] pt, pp of **bleed**

bleed (pt, pp **bled**) [bliːd, bled] vt saigner;
(brakes, radiator) purger ▷ vi saigner; **my
nose is ~ing** je saigne du nez

blemish ['blemɪʃ] n défaut m; (on reputation)
tache f

blend [blend] n mélange m ▷ vt mélanger
▷ vi (colours etc: also: **~ in**) se mélanger, se
fondre, s'allier; **blender** n (Culin) mixeur m

bless (pt, pp **blessed** or **blest**) [bles, blest] vt
bénir; **~ you!** (after sneeze) à tes souhaits!;
blessing n bénédiction f; (godsend)
bienfait m

blew [bluː] pt of **blow**

blight [blaɪt] vt (hopes etc) anéantir, briser

blind [blaɪnd] adj aveugle ▷ n (for window)
store m ▷ vt aveugler; **~ people** les aveugles
mpl; **blind alley** n impasse f; **blindfold** n
bandeau m ▷ adj, adv les yeux bandés ▷ vt
bander les yeux à

blink [blɪŋk] vi cligner des yeux; (light)
clignoter

bliss [blɪs] n félicité f, bonheur m sans
mélange

blister ['blɪstər] n (on skin) ampoule f, cloque
f; (on paintwork) boursouflure f ▷ vi (paint) se
boursoufler, se cloquer

blizzard ['blɪzəd] n blizzard m, tempête f
de neige

bloated ['bləʊtɪd] adj (face) bouffi(e);
(stomach, person) gonflé(e)

blob [blɔb] n (drop) goutte f; (stain, spot)
tache f

block [blɔk] n bloc m; (in pipes) obstruction
f; (toy) cube m; (of buildings) pâté m (de
maisons) ▷ vt bloquer; (fig) faire obstacle
à; **the sink is ~ed** l'évier est bouché; **~ of
flats** (BRIT) immeuble (locatif); **mental ~**
blocage m; **block up** vt boucher; **blockade**
[blɔ'keɪd] n blocus m ▷ vt faire le blocus de;
blockage n obstruction f; **blockbuster** n
(film, book) grand succès m; **block capitals** npl
majuscules fpl d'imprimerie; **block letters**
npl majuscules fpl

blog [blɔg] n blog m ▷ vi bloguer

blogger ['blɔgər] n blogueur(-euse)

blogosphere ['blɔgəsfɪər] n blogosphère f

bloke [bləʊk] n (BRIT inf) type m

blond(e) [blɔnd] adj, n blond(e)

blood [blʌd] n sang m; **blood donor** n
donneur(-euse) de sang; **blood group**
n groupe sanguin; **blood poisoning** n
empoisonnement m du sang; **blood
pressure** n tension (artérielle);
bloodshed n effusion f de sang, carnage
m; **bloodshot** adj: **bloodshot eyes** yeux
injectés de sang; **bloodstream** n sang m,
système sanguin; **blood test** n analyse f
de sang; **blood transfusion** n transfusion
f de sang; **blood type** n groupe sanguin;
blood vessel n vaisseau sanguin; **bloody**
adj sanglant(e); (BRIT inf!): **this bloody ...** ce
foutu ..., ce putain de ... (!) ▷ adv: **bloody
strong/good** (BRIT inf!) vachement or
sacrément fort/bon

bloom [bluːm] n fleur f ▷ vi être en fleur

blossom ['blɔsəm] n fleur(s) f(pl) ▷ vi être
en fleurs; (fig) s'épanouir

blot [blɒt] n tache f ▷ vt tacher; (ink) sécher

blouse [blauz] n (feminine garment) chemisier m, corsage m

blow [bləu] (pt **blew**, pp **blown**) n coup m ▷ vi souffler ▷ vt (instrument) jouer de; (fuse) faire sauter; **to ~ one's nose** se moucher; **blow away** vi s'envoler ▷ vt chasser, faire s'envoler; **blow out** vi (fire, flame) s'éteindre; (tyre) éclater; (fuse) sauter; **blow up** vi exploser, sauter ▷ vt faire sauter; (tyre) gonfler; (Phot) agrandir; **blow-dry** n (hairstyle) brushing m

blue [blu:] adj bleu(e); (depressed) triste; ~ **film/joke** film m/histoire f pornographique; **out of the ~** (fig) à l'improviste, sans qu'on s'y attende; **bluebell** n jacinthe f des bois; **blueberry** n myrtille f, airelle f; **blue cheese** n (fromage) bleu m; **blues** npl: **the blues** (Mus) le blues; **to have the blues** (inf: feeling) avoir le cafard

bluff [blʌf] vi bluffer ▷ n bluff m; **to call sb's ~** mettre qn au défi d'exécuter ses menaces

blunder ['blʌndə'] n gaffe f, bévue f ▷ vi faire une gaffe or une bévue

blunt [blʌnt] adj (knife) émoussé(e), peu tranchant(e); (pencil) mal taillé(e); (person) brusque, ne mâchant pas ses mots

blur [blə:'] n (shape): **to become a** ~ devenir flou ▷ vt brouiller, rendre flou(e); **blurred** adj flou(e)

blush [blʌʃ] vi rougir ▷ n rougeur f; **blusher** n rouge m à joues

board [bɔ:d] n (wooden) planche f; (on wall) panneau m; (for chess etc) plateau m; (cardboard) carton m; (committee) conseil m, comité m; (in firm) conseil d'administration; (Naut, Aviat): **on ~** à bord ▷ vt (ship) monter à bord de; (train) monter dans; **full ~** (BRIT) pension complète; **half ~** (BRIT) demi-pension f; ~ **and lodging** n chambre f avec pension; **to go by the ~** (hopes, principles) être abandonné(e); **board game** n jeu m de société; **boarding card** n (Aviat, Naut) carte f d'embarquement; **boarding pass** n (BRIT) = **boarding card**; **boarding school** n internat m, pensionnat m; **board room** n salle f du conseil d'administration

boast [bəust] vi: **to ~ (about or of)** se vanter (de)

boat [bəut] n bateau m; (small) canot m; barque f

bob [bɔb] vi (boat, cork on water: also: ~ **up and down**) danser, se balancer

bobby pin ['bɔbi-] n (US) pince f à cheveux

body ['bɔdi] n corps m; (of car) carrosserie f; (fig: society) organe m, organisme m; **body-building** n body-building m, culturisme m; **bodyguard** n garde m du corps; **bodywork** n carrosserie f

bog [bɔg] n tourbière f ▷ vt: **to get ~ged down (in)** (fig) s'enliser (dans)

bogus ['bəugəs] adj bidon inv; fantôme

boil [bɔil] vt (faire) bouillir ▷ vi bouillir ▷ n (Med) furoncle m; **to come to the** or (US) **a** ~ bouillir; **boil down** vi (fig): **to ~ down to** se réduire or ramener à; **boil over** vi déborder; **boiled egg** n œuf m à la coque; **boiler** n chaudière f; **boiling** ['bɔilɪŋ] adj: **I'm boiling (hot)** (inf) je crève de chaud; **boiling point** n point m d'ébullition

bold [bəuld] adj hardi(e), audacieux(-euse); (pej) effronté(e); (outline, colour) franc (franche), tranché(e), marqué(e)

bollard ['bɔləd] n (BRIT Aut) borne lumineuse or de signalisation

bolt [bəult] n verrou m; (with nut) boulon m ▷ adv: ~ **upright** droit(e) comme un piquet ▷ vt (door) verrouiller; (food) engloutir ▷ vi se sauver, filer (comme une flèche); (horse) s'emballer

bomb [bɔm] n bombe f ▷ vt bombarder; **bombard** [bɔm'bɑ:d] vt bombarder; **bomber** n (Aviat) bombardier m; (terrorist) poseur m de bombes; **bomb scare** n alerte f à la bombe

bond [bɔnd] n lien m; (binding promise) engagement m, obligation f; (Finance) obligation; **bonds** npl (chains) chaînes fpl; **in ~** (of goods) en entrepôt

bone [bəun] n os m; (of fish) arête f ▷ vt désosser, ôter les arêtes de

bonfire ['bɔnfaɪə'] n feu m (de joie), (for rubbish) feu

bonnet ['bɔnit] n bonnet m; (BRIT: of car) capot m

bonus ['bəunəs] n (money) prime f; (advantage) avantage m

boo [bu:] excl hou!, peuh! ▷ vt huer

book [buk] n livre m; (of stamps, tickets etc) carnet m ▷ vt (ticket) prendre; (seat, room) réserver; (football player) prendre le nom de, donner un carton à; **books** npl (Comm) comptes mpl, comptabilité f; **I ~ed a table in the name of ...** j'ai réservé une table au nom de ...; **book in** vi (BRIT: at hotel) prendre sa chambre; **book up** vt réserver; **the hotel is ~ed up** l'hôtel est complet; **bookcase** n bibliothèque f (meuble); **booking** n (BRIT) réservation f; **I confirmed my booking by fax/email** j'ai confirmé ma réservation par fax/e-mail; **booking office** n (BRIT) bureau m de location; **book-keeping** n comptabilité f; **booklet** n brochure f; **bookmaker** n bookmaker m; **bookmark** n (for book) marque-page m; (Comput) signet m; **bookseller** n libraire m/f; **bookshelf** n (single) étagère f (à livres); (bookcase) bibliothèque f; **bookshop**, **bookstore** n librairie f

boom [bu:m] n (noise) grondement m; (in prices, population) forte augmentation; (busy period) boom m, vague f de prospérité ▷ vi gronder; prospérer

boost [buːst] n stimulant m, remontant m
▷ vt stimuler

boot [buːt] n botte f; (for hiking) chaussure
f (de marche); (ankle boot) bottine f; (BRIT:
of car) coffre m ▷ vt (Comput) lancer, mettre
en route; **to ~** (in addition) par-dessus le
marché, en plus

booth [buːð] n (at fair) baraque (foraine);
(of telephone etc) cabine f; (also: **voting ~**)
isoloir m

booze [buːz] (inf) n boissons fpl alcoolisées,
alcool m

border [ˈbɔːdəʳ] n bordure f; bord m; (of a
country) frontière f; **borderline** n (fig) ligne f
de démarcation

bore [bɔːʳ] pt of **bear** ▷ vt (person) ennuyer,
raser; (hole) percer; (well, tunnel) creuser ▷ n
(person) raseur(-euse); (boring thing) barbe
f; (of gun) calibre m; **bored** adj: **to be bored**
s'ennuyer; **boredom** n ennui m

boring [ˈbɔːrɪŋ] adj ennuyeux(-euse)

born [bɔːn] adj: **to be ~** naître; **I was ~ in
1960** je suis né en 1960

borne [bɔːn] pp of **bear**

borough [ˈbʌrə] n municipalité f

borrow [ˈbɔrəu] vt: **to ~ sth (from sb)**
emprunter qch (à qn)

Bosnian [ˈbɔznɪən] adj bosniaque,
bosnien(ne) ▷ n Bosniaque m/f, Bosnien(ne)

bosom [ˈbuzəm] n poitrine f; (fig) sein m

boss [bɔs] n patron(ne) ▷ vt (also: **~ about,
~ around**) mener à la baguette; **bossy** adj
autoritaire

both [bəuθ] adj les deux, l'un(e) et l'autre
▷ pron: **~ (of them)** les deux, tous (toutes)
(les) deux, l'un(e) et l'autre; **~ of us went,
we ~ went** nous y sommes allés tous les
deux ▷ adv: **~ A and B** A et B

bother [ˈbɔðəʳ] vt (worry) tracasser; (needle,
bait) importuner, ennuyer; (disturb)
déranger ▷ vi (also: **~ o.s.**) se tracasser, se
faire du souci ▷ n (trouble) ennuis mpl; **to ~
doing** prendre la peine de faire; **don't ~** ce
n'est pas la peine; **it's no ~** aucun problème

bottle [ˈbɔtl] n bouteille f; (baby's) biberon
m; (of perfume, medicine) flacon m ▷ vt mettre
en bouteille(s); **bottle bank** n conteneur
m (de bouteilles); **bottle-opener** n ouvre-
bouteille m

bottom [ˈbɔtəm] n (of container, sea etc) fond
m; (buttocks) derrière m; (of page, list) bas
m; (of mountain, tree, hill) pied m ▷ adj (shelf,
step) du bas

bought [bɔːt] pt, pp of **buy**

boulder [ˈbəuldəʳ] n gros rocher (gén lisse,
arrondi)

bounce [bauns] vi (ball) rebondir; (cheque)
être refusé (étant sans provision) ▷ vt faire
rebondir ▷ n (rebound) rebond m; **bouncer** n
(inf: at dance, club) videur m

bound [baund] pt, pp of **bind** ▷ n (gen pl)
limite f; (leap) bond m ▷ vi (leap) bondir

▷ vt (limit) borner ▷ adj: **to be ~ to do sth**
(obliged) être obligé(e) ou avoir obligation
de faire qch; **he's ~ to fail** (likely) il est
sûr d'échouer, son échec est inévitable ou
assuré; **~ by** (law, regulation) engagé(e) par;
~ for à destination de; **out of ~s** dont l'accès
est interdit

boundary [ˈbaundrɪ] n frontière f

bouquet [ˈbukeɪ] n bouquet m

bourbon [ˈbuəbən] n (US: also: **~ whiskey**)
bourbon m

bout [baut] n période f; (of malaria etc) accès
m, crise f, attaque f; (Boxing etc) combat m,
match m

boutique [buːˈtiːk] n boutique f

bow[1] [bəu] n nœud m; (weapon) arc m; (Mus)
archet m

bow[2] [bau] n (with body) révérence f,
inclination f (du buste or corps); (Naut: also:
~s) proue f ▷ vi faire une révérence, s'incliner

bowels [bauəlz] npl intestins mpl; (fig)
entrailles fpl

bowl [bəul] n (for eating) bol m; (for washing)
cuvette f; (ball) boule f ▷ vt (Cricket) lancer
(la balle); **bowler** n (Cricket) lanceur m (de
la balle); (BRIT: also: **bowler hat**) (chapeau
m) melon m; **bowling** n (game) jeu m de
boules, jeu de quilles; **bowling alley** n
bowling m; **bowling green** n terrain m de
boules (gazonné et carré); **bowls** n (jeu m de)
boules fpl

bow tie [bəu-] n nœud m papillon

box [bɔks] n boîte f; (also: **cardboard ~**)
carton m; (Theat) loge f ▷ vt mettre en boîte
▷ vi boxer, faire de la boxe; **boxer** [ˈbɔksəʳ]
n (person) boxeur m; **boxer shorts** npl
caleçon m; **boxing** [ˈbɔksɪŋ] n (sport) boxe
f; **Boxing Day** n (BRIT) le lendemain de Noël;
voir article **"Boxing Day"**; **boxing gloves**
npl gants mpl de boxe; **boxing ring** n ring m;
box office n bureau m de location

● BOXING DAY

● Boxing Day est le lendemain de Noël, férié
● en Grande-Bretagne. Ce nom vient d'une
● coutume du XIXe siècle qui consistait à
● donner des cadeaux de Noël (dans des
● boîtes) à ses employés etc le 26 décembre.

boy [bɔɪ] n garçon m; **boy band** n boys
band m

boycott [ˈbɔɪkɔt] n boycottage m ▷ vt
boycotter

boyfriend [ˈbɔɪfrɛnd] n (petit) ami

bra [brɑː] n soutien-gorge m

brace [breɪs] n (support) attache f, agrafe
f; (BRIT: also: **~s**: on teeth) appareil m
(dentaire); (tool) vilebrequin m ▷ vt (support)
consolider, soutenir; **braces** npl (BRIT:
for trousers) bretelles fpl; **to ~ o.s.** (fig) se
préparer mentalement

bracelet ['breɪslɪt] n bracelet m
bracket ['brækɪt] n (Tech) tasseau m,
support m; (group) classe f, tranche f;
(also: **brace ~**) accolade f; (also: **round ~**)
parenthèse f; (also: **square ~**) crochet m
▷ vt mettre entre parenthèses; **in ~s** entre
parenthèses or crochets
brag [bræg] vi se vanter
braid [breɪd] n (trimming) galon m; (of hair)
tresse f, natte f
brain [breɪn] n cerveau m; **brains** npl
(intellect, food) cervelle f
braise [breɪz] vt braiser
brake [breɪk] n frein m ▷ vt, vi freiner; **brake
light** n feu m de stop
bran [bræn] n son m
branch [brɑːntʃ] n branche f; (Comm)
succursale f; (: of bank) agence f; **branch off**
vi (road) bifurquer; **branch out** vi diversifier
ses activités
brand [brænd] n marque (commerciale)
▷ vt (cattle) marquer (au fer rouge); **brand
name** n nom m de marque; **brand-new** adj
tout(e) neuf (neuve), flambant neuf (neuve)
brandy ['brændɪ] n cognac m
brash [bræʃ] adj effronté(e)
brass [brɑːs] n cuivre m (jaune), laiton m; **the ~**
(Mus) les cuivres; **brass band** n fanfare f
brat [bræt] n (pej) mioche m/f, môme m/f
brave [breɪv] adj courageux(-euse), brave
▷ vt braver, affronter; **bravery** n bravoure
f, courage m
brawl [brɔːl] n rixe f, bagarre f
Brazil [brə'zɪl] n Brésil m; **Brazilian** adj
brésilien(ne) ▷ n Brésilien(ne)
breach [briːtʃ] vt ouvrir une brèche dans
▷ n (gap) brèche f; (breaking): **~ of contract**
rupture f de contrat; **~ of the peace**
attentat m à l'ordre public
bread [bred] n pain m; **breadbin** n (BRIT)
boîte f or huche f à pain; **breadbox** n (US)
boîte f or huche f à pain; **breadcrumbs**
npl miettes fpl de pain; (Culin) chapelure f,
panure f
breadth [bretθ] n largeur f
break [breɪk] (pt broke, pp broken) vt
casser, briser; (promise) rompre; (law)
violer ▷ vi se casser, se briser; (weather)
tourner; (storm) éclater; (day) se lever ▷ n
(gap) brèche f; (fracture) cassure f; (rest)
interruption f, arrêt m (: short) pause f;
(: at school) récréation f; (chance) chance f,
occasion f favorable; **to ~ one's leg** etc se
casser la jambe etc; **to ~ a record** battre
un record; **to ~ the news to sb** annoncer
la nouvelle à qn; **break down** vt (door
etc) enfoncer; (figures, data) décomposer,
analyser ▷ vi s'effondrer; (Med) faire une
dépression (nerveuse); (Aut) tomber en
panne; **my car has broken down** ma
voiture est en panne; **break in** vt (horse etc)
dresser ▷ vi (burglar) entrer par effraction;

(interrupt) interrompre; **break into** vt
fus (house) s'introduire or pénétrer par
effraction dans; **break off** vi (speaker)
s'interrompre; (branch) se rompre ▷ vt (talks,
engagement) rompre; **break out** vi éclater,
se déclarer; (prisoner) s'évader; **to ~ out in
spots** se couvrir de boutons; **break up** vi
(partnership) cesser, prendre fin; (marriage)
se briser; (crowd, meeting) se séparer; (ship)
se disloquer; (Scol: pupils) être en vacances;
(line) couper ▷ vt fracasser, casser; (fight
etc) interrompre, faire cesser; (marriage)
désunir; **the line** or **you're ~ing up** ça
coupe; **breakdown** n (Aut) panne f; (in
communications, marriage) rupture f; (Med:
also: **nervous breakdown**) dépression
(nerveuse); (of figures) ventilation f,
répartition f; **breakdown van** n (US)
breakdown truck n dépanneuse f
breakfast ['brekfəst] n petit déjeuner m;
what time is ~? le petit déjeuner est à quelle
heure?
break: break-in n cambriolage m;
breakthrough n percée f
breast [brest] n (of woman) sein m; (chest)
poitrine f; (of chicken, turkey) blanc m;
breast-feed vt, vi (irreg: like **feed**) allaiter;
breast-stroke n brasse f
breath [breθ] n haleine f, souffle m; **to take
a deep ~** respirer à fond; **out of ~** à bout de
souffle, essoufflé(e)
Breathalyser® ['breθəlaɪzə'] (BRIT) n
alcootest m
breathe [briːð] vt, vi respirer; **breathe in**
vi inspirer ▷ vt aspirer; **breathe out** vt, vi
expirer; **breathing** n respiration f
breath: breathless adj essoufflé(e),
haletant(e); **breathtaking** adj
stupéfiant(e), à vous couper le souffle;
breath test n alcootest m
bred [bred] pt, pp of **breed**
breed [briːd] (pt, pp **bred**) vt élever, faire
l'élevage de ▷ vi se reproduire ▷ n race f,
variété f
breeze [briːz] n brise f
breezy ['briːzɪ] adj (day, weather)
venteux(-euse); (manner) désinvolte;
(person) jovial(e)
brew [bruː] vt (tea) faire infuser; (beer)
brasser ▷ vi (fig) se préparer, couver;
brewery n brasserie f (fabrique)
bribe [braɪb] n pot-de-vin m ▷ vt acheter;
soudoyer; **bribery** n corruption f
bric-a-brac ['brɪkəbræk] n bric-à-brac m
brick [brɪk] n brique f; **bricklayer** n
maçon m
bride [braɪd] n mariée f, épouse f;
bridegroom n marié m, époux m;
bridesmaid n demoiselle f d'honneur
bridge [brɪdʒ] n pont m; (Naut) passerelle
f (de commandement); (of nose) arête f;
(Cards, Dentistry) bridge m ▷ vt (gap) combler

bridle ['braɪdl] n bride f
brief [briːf] adj bref (brève) ▷ n (Law)
dossier m, cause f; (gen) tâche f ▷ vt mettre
au courant; **briefs** npl slip m; **briefcase**
n serviette f; porte-documents m inv;
briefing n instructions fpl; (Press) briefing
m; **briefly** adv brièvement
brigadier [brɪgə'dɪəʳ] n brigadier général
bright [braɪt] adj brillant(e); (room, weather)
clair(e); (person: clever) intelligent(e),
doué(e); (: cheerful) gai(e); (idea) génial(e);
(colour) vif (vive)
brilliant ['brɪljənt] adj brillant(e); (light,
sunshine) éclatant(e); (inf: great) super
brim [brɪm] n bord m
brine [braɪn] n (Culin) saumure f
bring (pt, pp brought) [brɪŋ, brɔːt] vt (thing)
apporter; (person) amener; **bring about**
vt provoquer, entraîner; **bring back** vt
rapporter; (person) ramener; **bring down**
vt (lower) abaisser; (shoot down) abattre;
(government) faire s'effondrer; **bring in** vt
(person) faire entrer; (object) rentrer; (Pol:
legislation) introduire; (produce: income)
rapporter; **bring on** vt (illness, attack)
provoquer; (player, substitute) amener;
bring out vt sortir; (meaning) faire ressortir,
mettre en relief; **bring up** vt élever; (carry
up) monter; (question) soulever; (food: vomit)
vomir, rendre
brink [brɪŋk] n bord m
brisk [brɪsk] adj vif (vive); (abrupt) brusque;
(trade etc) actif(-ive)
bristle ['brɪsl] n poil m ▷ vi se hérisser
Brit [brɪt] n abbr (inf: = British person)
Britannique m/f
Britain ['brɪtən] n (also: **Great ~**) la Grande-
Bretagne
British ['brɪtɪʃ] adj britannique ▷ npl: **the ~**
les Britanniques mpl; **British Isles** npl: **the**
British Isles les îles fpl Britanniques
Briton ['brɪtən] n Britannique m/f
Brittany ['brɪtəni] n Bretagne f
brittle ['brɪtl] adj cassant(e), fragile
broad [brɔːd] adj large; (distinction)
général(e); (accent) prononcé(e); **in ~**
daylight en plein jour
B road n (BRIT) ≈ route départementale
broad: broadband n transmission f à haut
débit; **broad bean** n fève f; **broadcast** (pt,
pp **broadcast**) n émission f ▷ vt (Radio)
radiodiffuser; (TV) téléviser ▷ vi émettre;
broaden vt élargir; **to broaden one's mind**
élargir ses horizons ▷ vi s'élargir; **broadly**
adv en gros, généralement; **broad-minded**
adj large d'esprit
broccoli ['brɔkəli] n brocoli m
brochure ['brəuʃjuəʳ] n prospectus m,
dépliant m
broil [brɔɪl] vt (US) rôtir
broke [brəuk] pt of **break** ▷ adj (inf)
fauché(e)

broken ['brəukn] pp of **break** ▷ adj (stick,
leg etc) cassé(e); (machine: also: **~ down**)
fichu(e); **in ~ French/English** dans un
français/anglais approximatif or hésitant
broker ['brəukəʳ] n courtier m
bronchitis [brɔŋ'kaɪtɪs] n bronchite f
bronze [brɔnz] n bronze m
brooch [brəutʃ] n broche f
brood [bruːd] n couvée f ▷ vi (person)
méditer (sombrement), ruminer
broom [brum] n balai m; (Bot) genêt m
Bros. abbr (Comm: = brothers) Frères
broth [brɔθ] n bouillon m de viande et de
légumes
brothel ['brɔθl] n maison close, bordel m
brother ['brʌðəʳ] n frère m; **brother-in-law**
n beau-frère m
brought [brɔːt] pt, pp of **bring**
brow [brau] n front m; (eyebrow) sourcil m;
(of hill) sommet m
brown [braun] adj brun(e), marron inv;
(hair) châtain inv; (tanned) bronzé(e) ▷ n
(colour) brun m, marron m ▷ vt brunir; (Culin)
faire dorer, faire roussir; **brown bread** n
pain m bis
Brownie ['brauni] n jeannette f éclaireuse
(cadette)
brown rice n riz m complet
brown sugar n cassonade f
browse [brauz] vi (in shop) regarder (sans
acheter); **to ~ through a book** feuilleter un
livre; **browser** n (Comput) navigateur m
bruise [bruːz] n bleu m, ecchymose f,
contusion f ▷ vt contusionner, meurtrir
brunette [bruː'nɛt] n (femme) brune
brush [brʌʃ] n brosse f; (for painting)
pinceau m; (for shaving) blaireau m; (quarrel)
accrochage m, prise f de bec ▷ vt brosser;
(also: **~ past, ~ against**) effleurer, frôler
Brussels ['brʌslz] n Bruxelles
Brussels sprout n chou m de Bruxelles
brutal ['bruːtl] adj brutal(e)
B.Sc. n abbr = **Bachelor of Science**
BSE n abbr (= bovine spongiform
encephalopathy) ESB f, BSE f
bubble ['bʌbl] n bulle f ▷ vi bouillonner,
faire des bulles; (sparkle, fig) pétiller;
bubble bath n bain moussant; **bubble**
gum n chewing-gum m; **bubblejet**
printer ['bʌbldʒɛt-] n imprimante f à bulle
d'encre
buck [bʌk] n mâle m (d'un lapin, lièvre, daim
etc); (US inf) dollar m ▷ vi ruer, lancer une
ruade; **to pass the ~ (to sb)** se décharger de
la responsabilité (sur qn)
bucket ['bʌkɪt] n seau m; **bucket list** n liste f
de choses à faire avant de mourir
buckle ['bʌkl] n boucle f ▷ vt (belt etc)
boucler, attacher ▷ vi (warp) tordre, gauchir
(: wheel) se voiler
bud [bʌd] n bourgeon m; (of flower) bouton
m ▷ vi bourgeonner; (flower) éclore

Buddhism ['budɪzəm] n bouddhisme m
Buddhist ['budɪst] adj bouddhiste ▷ n
Bouddhiste m/f
buddy ['bʌdɪ] n (US) copain m
budge [bʌdʒ] vt faire bouger ▷ vi bouger
budgerigar ['bʌdʒərɪgɑːʳ] n perruche f
budget ['bʌdʒɪt] n budget m ▷ vi: **to ~ for**
sth inscrire qch au budget
budgie ['bʌdʒɪ] n = **budgerigar**
buff [bʌf] adj (couleur f) chamois m ▷ n (inf:
enthusiast) mordu(e)
buffalo ['bʌfələu] (pl **buffalo** or **buffaloes**)
n (BRIT) buffle m; (US) bison m
buffer ['bʌfəʳ] n tampon m; (Comput)
mémoire f tampon
buffet n ['bufeɪ] (food, BRIT: bar) buffet m
▷ vt ['bʌfɪt] secouer, ébranler; **buffet car** n
(BRIT Rail) voiture-bar f
bug [bʌg] n (bedbug etc) punaise f; (esp US:
any insect) insecte m, bestiole f; (fig: germ)
virus m, microbe m; (spy device) dispositif m
d'écoute (électronique), micro clandestin;
(Comput: of program) erreur f ▷ vt (room)
poser des micros dans; (inf: annoy)
embêter
buggy ['bʌgɪ] n poussette f
build [bɪld] n (of person) carrure f,
charpente f ▷ vt (pt, pp **built**) construire,
bâtir; **build up** vt accumuler, amasser;
(business) développer; (reputation) bâtir;
builder n entrepreneur m; **building** n
(trade) construction f; (structure) bâtiment
m, construction (: residential, offices)
immeuble m; **building site** n chantier m (de
construction); **building society** n (BRIT)
société f de crédit immobilier
built [bɪlt] pt, pp of **build**; **built-in** adj
(cupboard) encastré(e); (device) incorporé(e);
intégré(e); **built-up** adj: **built-up area** zone
urbanisée
bulb [bʌlb] n (Bot) bulbe m, oignon m; (Elec)
ampoule f
Bulgaria [bʌl'gɛərɪə] n Bulgarie f;
Bulgarian adj bulgare ▷ n Bulgare m/f
bulge [bʌldʒ] n renflement m, gonflement
m ▷ vi faire saillie; présenter un renflement;
(pocket, file): **to be bulging with** être
plein(e) à craquer de
bulimia [bə'lɪmɪə] n boulimie f
bulimic [bju:'lɪmɪk] adj, n boulimique m/f
bulk [bʌlk] n masse f, volume m; **in ~**
(Comm) en gros, en vrac; **the ~ of** la plus
grande or grosse partie de; **bulky** adj
volumineux(-euse), encombrant(e)
bull [bul] n taureau m; (male elephant, whale)
mâle m
bulldozer ['buldəuzəʳ] n bulldozer m
bullet ['bulɪt] n balle f (de fusil etc)
bulletin ['bulɪtɪn] n bulletin m,
communiqué m; (also: **news ~**) (bulletin d')
informations fpl; **bulletin board** n (Comput)
messagerie f (électronique)

bullfight ['bulfaɪt] n corrida f, course
f de taureaux; **bullfighter** n torero m;
bullfighting n tauromachie f
bully ['bulɪ] n brute f, tyran m ▷ vt
tyranniser, rudoyer
bum [bʌm] n (inf: BRIT: backside) derrière m;
(esp US: tramp) vagabond(e), traîne-savates
m/f inv; (idler) glandeur m
bumblebee ['bʌmblbiː] n bourdon m
bump [bʌmp] n (blow) coup m, choc m;
(jolt) cahot m, (on road etc, on head) bosse f
▷ vt heurter, cogner; (car) emboutir;
bump into vt fus rentrer dans, tamponner;
(inf: meet) tomber sur; **bumper** n
pare-chocs m inv ▷ adj: **bumper crop/
harvest** récolte/moisson exceptionnelle;
bumpy adj (road) cahoteux(-euse); **it was
a bumpy flight/ride** on a été secoués dans
l'avion/la voiture
bun [bʌn] n (cake) petit gâteau; (bread) petit
pain au lait; (of hair) chignon m
bunch [bʌntʃ] n (of flowers) bouquet m;
(of keys) trousseau m; (of bananas)
régime m; (of people) groupe m; **bunches** npl
(in hair) couettes fpl; **~ of grapes** grappe f
de raisin
bundle ['bʌndl] n paquet m ▷ vt (also: **~ up**)
faire un paquet de; (put): **to ~ sth/sb into**
fourrer or enfourner qch/qn dans
bungalow ['bʌngələu] n bungalow m
bungee jumping ['bʌndʒiː'dʒʌmpɪŋ] n
saut m à l'élastique
bunion ['bʌnjən] n oignon m (au pied)
bunk [bʌŋk] n couchette f; **bunk beds** npl
lits superposés
bunker ['bʌŋkəʳ] n (coal store) soute f à
charbon; (Mil, Golf) bunker m
bunny ['bʌnɪ] n (also: **~ rabbit**) lapin m
buoy [bɔɪ] n bouée f; **buoyant** adj (ship)
flottable; (carefree) gai(e), plein(e) d'entrain;
(Comm: market, economy) actif(-ive)
burden ['bəːdn] n fardeau m, charge f ▷ vt
charger; (oppress) accabler, surcharger
bureau (pl **bureaux**) ['bjuərəu, -z] n (BRIT:
writing desk) bureau m, secrétaire m; (US:
chest of drawers) commode f; (office) bureau,
office m
bureaucracy [bjuə'rɔkrəsɪ] n
bureaucratie f
bureaucrat ['bjuərəkræt] n bureaucrate
m/f, rond-de-cuir m
bureau de change [-də'ʃɑ̃ʒ] (pl **bureaux
de change**) n bureau m de change
bureaux ['bjuərəuz] npl of **bureau**
burger ['bəːgəʳ] n hamburger m
burglar ['bəːgləʳ] n cambrioleur m; **burglar
alarm** n sonnerie f d'alarme; **burglary** n
cambriolage m
Burgundy ['bəːgəndɪ] n Bourgogne f
burial ['bɛrɪəl] n enterrement m
burn [bəːn] vt, vi (pt **burned**, pp **burnt**)
brûler ▷ n brûlure f; **burn down** vt

incendier, détruire par le feu; **burn out** vt (writer etc): **to ~ o.s.** s'user (à force de travailler); **burning** adj (building, forest) en flammes; (issue, question) brûlant(e); (ambition) dévorant(e)

Burns Night [bə:nz-] n fête écossaise à la mémoire du poète Robert Burns

BURNS NIGHT

Burns Night est une fête qui a lieu le 25 janvier, à la mémoire du poète écossais Robert Burns (1759–1796), à l'occasion de laquelle les Écossais partout dans le monde organisent un souper, en général arrosé de whisky. Le plat principal est toujours le haggis, servi avec de la purée de pommes de terre et de la purée de rutabagas. On apporte le haggis au son des cornemuses et au cours du repas on lit des poèmes de Burns et on chante ses chansons.

burnt [bə:nt] pt, pp of **burn**

burp [bə:p] (inf) n rot m ▷ vi roter

burrow ['bʌrəʊ] n terrier m ▷ vi (rabbit) creuser un terrier; (rummage) fouiller

burst [bə:st] (pt, pp **burst**) vt faire éclater; (river: banks etc) rompre ▷ vi éclater; (tyre) crever ▷ n explosion f; (also: **~ pipe**) fuite f (due à une rupture); **a ~ of enthusiasm/ energy** un accès d'enthousiasme/ d'énergie; **to ~ into flames** s'enflammer soudainement; **to ~ out laughing** éclater de rire; **to ~ into tears** fondre en larmes; **to ~ open** vi s'ouvrir violemment or soudainement; **to be ~ing with** (container) être plein(e) (à craquer) de, regorger de; (fig) être débordant(e) de; **burst into** vt fus (room etc) faire irruption dans

bury ['bɛrɪ] vt enterrer

bus (pl **buses**) [bʌs, 'bʌsɪz] n (auto)bus m; **bus conductor** n receveur(-euse) m/f de bus

bush [bʊʃ] n buisson m; (scrub land) brousse f; **to beat about the ~** tourner autour du pot

business ['bɪznɪs] n (matter, firm) affaire f; (trading) affaires fpl; (job, duty) travail m; **to be away on ~** être en déplacement d'affaires; **it's none of my ~** cela ne me regarde pas, ce ne sont pas mes affaires; **he means ~** il ne plaisante pas, il est sérieux; **business class** n (on plane) classe f affaires; **businesslike** adj sérieux(-euse), efficace; **businessman** (irreg) n homme m d'affaires; **business trip** n voyage m d'affaires; **businesswoman** (irreg) n femme f d'affaires

busker ['bʌskə'] n (BRIT) artiste ambulant(e)

bus: bus pass n carte f de bus; **bus shelter** n abribus m; **bus station** n gare routière; **bus stop** n arrêt m d'autobus

bust [bʌst] n buste m; (measurement) tour m de poitrine ▷ adj (inf: broken) fichu(e), fini(e); **to go ~** (inf) faire faillite

bustling ['bʌslɪŋ] adj (town) très animé(e)

busy ['bɪzɪ] adj occupé(e); (shop, street) très fréquenté(e); (us: telephone, line) occupé ▷ vt: **to ~ o.s.** s'occuper; **busy signal** n (us) tonalité f occupé inv

KEYWORD

but [bʌt] conj mais; **I'd love to come, but I'm busy** j'aimerais venir mais je suis occupé; **he's not English but French** il n'est pas anglais mais français; **but that's far too expensive!** mais c'est bien trop cher! ▷ prep (apart from, except) sauf, excepté; **nothing but** rien d'autre que; **we've had nothing but trouble** nous n'avons eu que des ennuis; **no-one but him can do it** lui seul peut le faire; **who but a lunatic would do such a thing?** qui sinon un fou ferait une chose pareille?; **but for you/your help** sans toi/ton aide; **anything but that** tout sauf or excepté ça, tout mais pas ça ▷ adv (just, only) ne ... que; **she's but a child** elle n'est qu'une enfant; **had I but known** si seulement j'avais su; **I can but try** je peux toujours essayer; **all but finished** pratiquement terminé

butcher ['bʊtʃə'] n boucher m ▷ vt massacrer; (cattle etc for meat) tuer; **butcher's (shop)** n boucherie f

butler ['bʌtlə'] n maître m d'hôtel

butt [bʌt] n (cask) gros tonneau; (of gun) crosse f; (of cigarette) mégot m; (BRIT fig: target) cible f ▷ vt donner un coup de tête à

butter ['bʌtə'] n beurre m ▷ vt beurrer; **buttercup** n bouton m d'or

butterfly ['bʌtəflaɪ] n papillon m; (Swimming: also: **~ stroke**) brasse f papillon

buttocks ['bʌtəks] npl fesses fpl

button ['bʌtn] n bouton m; (us: badge) pin m ▷ vt (also: **~ up**) boutonner ▷ vi se boutonner

buy [baɪ] (pt, pp **bought**) vt acheter ▷ n achat m; **to ~ sb sth/sth from sb** acheter qch à qn; **to ~ sb a drink** offrir un verre or à boire à qn; **can I ~ you a drink?** je vous offre un verre?; **where can I ~ some postcards?** où est-ce que je peux acheter des cartes postales?; **buy out** vt (partner) désintéresser; **buy up** vt acheter en bloc, rafler; **buyer** n acheteur(-euse) m/f

buzz [bʌz] n bourdonnement m; (inf: phone call): **to give sb a ~** passer un coup de fil à qn ▷ vi bourdonner; **buzzer** n timbre m électrique

by [baɪ] prep **1** (referring to cause, agent) par,
de; **killed by lightning** tué par la foudre;
surrounded by a fence entouré d'une
barrière; **a painting by Picasso** un tableau
de Picasso
2 (referring to method, manner, means): **by
bus/car** en autobus/voiture; **by train** par
le or en train; **to pay by cheque** payer par
chèque; **by moonlight/candlelight** à la
lueur de la lune/d'une bougie; **by saving
hard, he …** à force d'économiser, il …
3 (via, through) par; **we came by Dover**
nous sommes venus par Douvres
4 (close to, past) à côté de; **the house by
the school** la maison à côté de l'école; **a
holiday by the sea** des vacances au bord
de la mer, **she went by me** elle est passée à
côté de moi; **I go by the post office every
day** je passe devant la poste tous les jours
5 (with time: not later than) avant; (: during):
by daylight à la lumière du jour; **by night**
la nuit, de nuit; **by 4 o'clock** avant 4 heures;
by this time tomorrow d'ici demain à la
même heure; **by the time I got here it was
too late** lorsque je suis arrivé il était déjà
trop tard
6 (amount) à; **by the kilo/metre** au kilo/au
mètre; **paid by the hour** payé à l'heure
7 (Math: measure): **to divide/multiply by 3**
diviser/multiplier par 3; **a room 3 metres
by 4** une pièce de 3 mètres sur 4; **it's
broader by a metre** c'est plus large d'un
mètre
8 (according to) d'après, selon; **it's 3 o'clock
by my watch** il est 3 heures à ma montre;
it's all right by me je n'ai rien contre
9: **(all) by oneself** etc tout(e) seul(e)
▷ adv **1** see **go**; **pass** etc
2: **by and by** un peu plus tard, bientôt; **by
and large** dans l'ensemble

bye(-bye) ['baɪ-] excl au revoir!, salut!
by-election ['baɪɪlɛkʃən] n (BRIT) élection
(législative) partielle
bypass ['baɪpɑːs] n rocade f; (Med) pontage
m ▷ vt éviter
byte [baɪt] n (Comput) octet m

C

C [siː] n (Mus) do m
cab [kæb] n taxi m; (of train, truck) cabine f
cabaret ['kæbəreɪ] n (show) spectacle m de
cabaret
cabbage ['kæbɪdʒ] n chou m
cabin ['kæbɪn] n (house) cabane f, hutte f;
(on ship) cabine f; (on plane) compartiment
m; **cabin crew** n (Aviat) équipage m
cabinet ['kæbɪnɪt] n (Pol) cabinet m;
(furniture) petit meuble à tiroirs et rayons,
(also: **display ~**) vitrine f, petite armoire
vitrée; **cabinet minister** n ministre m
(membre du cabinet)
cable ['keɪbl] n câble m ▷ vt câbler,
télégraphier; **cable car** n téléphérique m;
cable television n télévision f par câble
cactus (pl **cacti**) ['kæktəs, -taɪ] n
cactus m
café ['kæfeɪ] n ≈ café(-restaurant) m (sans
alcool)
cafeteria [kæfɪ'tɪərɪə] n cafétéria f
caffeine ['kæfiːn] n caféine f
cage [keɪdʒ] n cage f
cagoule [kə'guːl] n K-way® m
Cairo ['kaɪərəu] n Le Caire
cake [keɪk] n gâteau m; **~ of soap**
savonnette f
calcium ['kælsɪəm] n calcium m
calculate ['kælkjuleɪt] vt calculer;
(estimate: chances, effect) évaluer;
calculation [kælkju'leɪʃən] n calcul m;
calculator n calculatrice f
calendar ['kæləndər] n calendrier m
calf (pl **calves**) [kɑːf, kɑːvz] n (of cow) veau
m; (of other animals) petit m, (also: **~skin**)
veau m, vachette f; (Anat) mollet m
calibre, (US) **caliber** ['kælɪbər] n calibre m
call [kɔːl] vt appeler; (meeting) convoquer
▷ vi appeler; (visit: also: **~ in**, **~ round**)
passer ▷ n (shout) appel m, cri m; (also:
telephone ~) coup m de téléphone; **to
be on ~** être de permanence; **to be ~ed**

s'appeler; **can I make a ~ from here?** est-ce que je peux téléphoner d'ici?; **call back** vi (return) repasser; (Tel) rappeler ▷ vt (Tel) rappeler; **can you ~ back later?** pouvez-vous rappeler plus tard?; **call for** vt fus (demand) demander; (fetch) passer prendre; **call in** vt (doctor, expert, police) appeler, faire venir; **call off** vt fus (visit) rendre visite à, passer voir; (request): **to ~ on sb to do** inviter qn à faire; **call out** vi pousser un cri or des cris; **call up** vt (Mil) appeler, mobiliser; (Tel) appeler; **call box** n (BRIT) cabine f téléphonique; **call centre**, (US) **call center** n centre m d'appels; **caller** n (Tel) personne f qui appelle; (visitor) visiteur m

callous ['kæləs] adj dur(e), insensible

calm [kɑːm] adj calme ▷ n calme m ▷ vt calmer, apaiser; **calm down** vi se calmer, s'apaiser ▷ vt calmer, apaiser; **calmly** ['kɑːmlɪ] adv calmement, avec calme

Calor gas® ['kælər-] n (BRIT) butane m, butagaz® m

calorie ['kælərɪ] n calorie f

calves [kɑːvz] npl of **calf**

Cambodia [kæm'bəʊdɪə] n Cambodge m

camcorder ['kæmkɔːdər] n caméscope m

came [keɪm] pt of **come**

camel ['kæməl] n chameau m

camera ['kæmərə] n appareil photo m; (Cine, TV) caméra f; **in ~** à huis clos, en privé; **cameraman** (irreg) n caméraman m; **camera phone** n téléphone m avec appareil photo

camouflage ['kæməflɑːʒ] n camouflage m ▷ vt camoufler

camp [kæmp] n camp m ▷ vi camper ▷ adj (man) efféminé(e)

campaign [kæm'peɪn] n (Mil, Pol) campagne f ▷ vi (also fig) faire campagne; **campaigner** n: campaigner for partisan(e) de; **campaigner against** opposant(e) à

camp: camp bed n (BRIT) lit m de camp; **camper** n campeur(-euse); (vehicle) camping-car m; **camping** n camping m; **to go camping** faire du camping; **campsite** n (terrain m de) camping m

campus ['kæmpəs] n campus m

can¹ [kæn] n (of milk, oil, water) bidon m; (tin) boîte f (de conserve) ▷ vt mettre en conserve

○ **KEYWORD**

can² [kæn] (negative **cannot** or **can't**, conditional, pt **could**) aux vb **1** (be able to) pouvoir; **you can do it if you try** vous pouvez le faire si vous essayez; **I can't hear you** je ne t'entends pas
2 (know how to) savoir; **I can swim/play tennis/drive** je sais nager/jouer au tennis/

conduire; **can you speak French?** parlez-vous français?
3 (may) pouvoir; **can I use your phone?** puis-je me servir de votre téléphone?
4 (expressing disbelief, puzzlement etc): **it can't be true!** ce n'est pas possible!; **what can he want?** qu'est-ce qu'il peut bien vouloir?
5 (expressing possibility, suggestion etc): **he could be in the library** il est peut-être dans la bibliothèque; **she could have been delayed** il se peut qu'elle ait été retardée

Canada ['kænədə] n Canada m; **Canadian** [kə'neɪdɪən] adj canadien(ne) ▷ n Canadien(ne)

canal [kə'næl] n canal m

canary [kə'nɛərɪ] n canari m, serin m

cancel ['kænsəl] vt annuler; (train) supprimer; (party, appointment) décommander; (cross out) barrer, rayer; (cheque) faire opposition à; **I would like to ~ my booking** je voudrais annuler ma réservation; **cancellation** [kænsə'leɪʃən] n annulation f; suppression f

Cancer ['kænsər] n (Astrology) le Cancer

cancer ['kænsər] n cancer m

candidate ['kændɪdeɪt] n candidat(e)

candle ['kændl] n bougie f; (in church) cierge m; **candlestick** n (also: **candle holder**) bougeoir m; (bigger, ornate) chandelier m

candy ['kændɪ] n sucre candi; (US) bonbon m; **candy bar** (US) n barre f chocolatée; **candyfloss** n (BRIT) barbe f à papa

cane [keɪn] n canne f; (for baskets, chairs etc) rotin m ▷ vt (BRIT Scol) administrer des coups de bâton à

canister ['kænɪstər] n boîte f (gén en métal); (of gas) bombe f

cannabis ['kænəbɪs] n (drug) cannabis m

canned ['kænd] adj (food) en boîte, en conserve; (inf: music) enregistré(e); (BRIT inf: drunk) bourré(e); (US inf: worker) mis(e) à la porte

cannon ['kænən] (pl **cannon** or **cannons**) n (gun) canon m

cannot ['kænɔt] = **can not**

canoe [kə'nuː] n pirogue f; (Sport) canoë m; **canoeing** n (sport) canoë m

canon ['kænən] n (clergyman) chanoine m; (standard) canon m

can-opener [-'əupnər] n ouvre-boîte m

can't [kɑːnt] = **can not**

canteen [kæn'tiːn] n (eating place) cantine f; (BRIT: of cutlery) ménagère f

canter ['kæntər] vi aller au petit galop

canvas ['kænvəs] n toile f

canvass ['kænvəs] vi (Pol): **to ~ for** faire campagne pour ▷ vt sonder

canyon ['kænjən] n cañon m, gorge f (profonde)

cap [kæp] n casquette f; (for swimming) bonnet m de bain; (of pen) capuchon m; (of bottle) capsule f; (BRIT: contraceptive: also: **Dutch ~**) diaphragme m ▷ vt (outdo) surpasser; (put limit on) plafonner

capability [keɪpə'bɪlɪtɪ] n aptitude f, capacité f

capable ['keɪpəbl] adj capable

capacity [kə'pæsɪtɪ] n (of container) capacité f, contenance f; (ability) aptitude f

cape [keɪp] n (garment) cape f; (Geo) cap m

caper ['keɪpə'] n (Culin: gen pl) câpre f; (prank) farce f

capital ['kæpɪtl] n (also: **~ city**) capitale f; (money) capital m; (also: **~ letter**) majuscule f; **capitalism** n capitalisme m; **capitalist** adj, n capitaliste m/f; **capital punishment** n peine capitale

Capitol ['kæpɪtl] n: **the ~** le Capitole

Capricorn ['kæprɪkɔːn] n le Capricorne

capsize [kæp'saɪz] vt faire chavirer ▷ vi chavirer

capsule ['kæpsjuːl] n capsule f

captain ['kæptɪn] n capitaine m

caption ['kæpʃən] n légende f

captivity [kæp'tɪvɪtɪ] n captivité f

capture ['kæptʃə'] vt (prisoner, animal) capturer; (town) prendre; (attention) capter; (Comput) saisir ▷ n capture f; (of data) saisie f de données

car [kɑː'] n voiture f, auto f; (us Rail) wagon m, voiture

caramel ['kærəməl] n caramel m

carat ['kærət] n carat m

caravan ['kærəvæn] n caravane f; **caravan site** n (BRIT) camping m pour caravanes

carbohydrate [kɑːbəu'haɪdreɪt] n hydrate m de carbone; (food) féculent m

carbon ['kɑːbən] n carbone m; **carbon dioxide** [-daɪ'ɒksaɪd] n gaz m carbonique, dioxyde m de carbone; **carbon footprint** n empreinte f carbone; **carbon monoxide** [-mɒ'nɒksaɪd] n oxyde m de carbone; **carbon-neutral** adj neutre en carbone

car boot sale n voir article **"car boot sale"**

● **CAR BOOT SALE**

●
● Type de brocante très populaire, où chacun
● vide sa cave ou son grenier. Les articles
● sont présentés dans des coffres de voitures
● et la vente a souvent lieu sur un parking
● ou dans un champ. Les brocanteurs d'un
● jour doivent s'acquitter d'une petite
● contribution pour participer à la vente.

carburettor, (us) carburetor [kɑːbju'rɛtə'] n carburateur m

card [kɑːd] n carte f; (material) carton m; **cardboard** n carton m; **card game** n jeu m de cartes

cardigan ['kɑːdɪgən] n cardigan m

cardinal ['kɑːdɪnl] adj cardinal(e); (importance) capital(e) ▷ n cardinal m

cardphone ['kɑːdfəun] n téléphone m à carte (magnétique)

care [kɛə'] n soin m, attention f; (worry) souci m ▷ vi: **to ~ about** (feel interest for) se soucier de, s'intéresser à; (person: love) être attaché(e) à; **in sb's ~** à la garde de qn, confié à qn; **~ of** (on letter) chez; **to take ~ (to do)** faire attention (à faire); **to take ~ of** vt s'occuper de; **I don't ~** ça m'est bien égal, peu m'importe; **I couldn't ~ less** cela m'est complètement égal, je m'en fiche complètement; **care for** vt fus s'occuper de; (like) aimer

career [kə'rɪə'] n carrière f ▷ vi (also: **~ along**) aller à toute allure

care: carefree adj sans souci, insouciant(e); **careful** adj soigneux(-euse); (cautious) prudent(e); **(be) careful!** (fais) attention!; **carefully** adv avec soin, soigneusement; prudemment; **caregiver** n (us) (professional) travailleur social; (unpaid) personne qui s'occupe d'un proche qui est malade; **careless** adj négligent(e); (heedless) insouciant(e); **carelessness** n manque m de soin, négligence f; insouciance f; **carer** ['kɛərə'] n (professional) travailleur social; (unpaid) personne qui s'occupe d'un proche qui est malade; **caretaker** n gardien(ne), concierge m/f

car-ferry ['kɑːfɛrɪ] n (on sea) ferry(-boat) m; (on river) bac m

cargo ['kɑːgəu] (pl **cargoes**) n cargaison f, chargement m

car hire n (BRIT) location f de voitures

Caribbean [kærɪ'biːən] adj, n: **the ~ (Sea)** la mer des Antilles or des Caraïbes

caring ['kɛərɪŋ] adj (person) bienveillant(e); (society, organization) humanitaire

carnation [kɑː'neɪʃən] n œillet m

carnival ['kɑːnɪvl] n (public celebration) carnaval m; (us: funfair) fête foraine

carol ['kærəl] n: **(Christmas) ~** chant m de Noël

carousel [kærə'sɛl] n (for luggage) carrousel m; (us) manège m

car park (BRIT) n parking m, parc m de stationnement

carpenter ['kɑːpɪntə'] n charpentier m; (joiner) menuisier m

carpet ['kɑːpɪt] n tapis m ▷ vt recouvrir (d'un tapis); **fitted ~** (BRIT) moquette f

car rental n (us) location f de voitures

carriage ['kærɪdʒ] n (BRIT Rail) wagon m; (horse-drawn) voiture f; (of goods) transport m; (: cost) port m; **carriageway** n (BRIT: part of road) chaussée f

carrier ['kærɪə'] n transporteur m, camionneur m; (company) entreprise f de transport; (Med) porteur(-euse); **carrier bag** n (BRIT) sac m en papier or en plastique

carrot ['kærət] n carotte f
carry ['kærɪ] vt (subj: person) porter;
(: vehicle) transporter; (involve:
responsibilities etc) comporter, impliquer;
(Med: disease) être porteur de ▷ vi (sound)
porter; **to get carried away** (fig) s'emballer,
s'enthousiasmer; **carry on** vi (continue)
continuer ▷ vt (conduct: business) diriger;
(: conversation) entretenir; (continue:
business, conversation) continuer; **to ~
on with sth/doing** continuer qch/à
faire; **carry out** vt (orders) exécuter;
(investigation) effectuer
cart [kɑ:t] n charrette f ▷ vt (inf) transporter
carton ['kɑ:tən] n (box) carton m; (of yogurt)
pot m (en carton)
cartoon [kɑ:'tu:n] n (Press) dessin m
(humoristique); (satirical) caricature f;
(comic strip) bande dessinée; (Cine) dessin
animé
cartridge ['kɑ:trɪdʒ] n (for gun, pen)
cartouche f
carve [kɑ:v] vt (meat: also: ~ up) découper;
(wood, stone) tailler, sculpter; **carving** n
(in wood etc) sculpture f
car wash n station f de lavage (de voitures)
case [keɪs] n cas m; (Law) affaire f, procès
m; (box) boîte f; (for glasses) étui m;
(BRIT: also: **suit~**) valise f; **in ~ of** en cas de;
in ~ he au cas où il; **just in ~** à tout hasard;
in any ~ en tout cas, de toute façon
cash [kæʃ] n argent m; (Comm) (argent m)
liquide m ▷ vt encaisser; **to pay (in) ~** payer
(en argent) comptant or en espèces; **~ with
order/on delivery** (Comm) payable or
paiement à la commande/livraison;
I haven't got any ~ je n'ai pas de liquide;
cashback n (discount) remise f; (at
supermarket etc) retrait m (à la caisse); **cash
card** n carte f de retrait; **cash desk** n (BRIT)
caisse f; **cash dispenser** n distributeur m
automatique de billets
cashew [kæ'ʃu:] n (also: ~ **nut**) noix f de
cajou
cashier [kæ'ʃɪər] n caissier(-ère)
cashmere ['kæʃmɪər] n cachemire m
cash point n distributeur m automatique
de billets
cash register n caisse enregistreuse
casino [kə'si:nəu] n casino m
casket ['kɑ:skɪt] n coffret m; (US: coffin)
cercueil m
casserole ['kæsərəul] n (pot) cocotte f;
(food) ragoût m (en cocotte)
cassette [kæ'sɛt] n cassette f; **cassette
player** n lecteur m de cassettes
cast [kɑ:st] (vb: pt, pp **cast**) vt (throw) jeter;
(shadow: lit) projeter; (: fig) jeter; (glance)
jeter ▷ n (Theat) distribution f; (also:
plaster ~) plâtre m; **to ~ sb as Hamlet**
attribuer à qn le rôle d'Hamlet; **to ~ one's
vote** voter, exprimer son suffrage; **to ~**

doubt on jeter un doute sur; **cast off** vi
(Naut) larguer les amarres; (Knitting) arrêter
les mailles
castanets [kæstə'nɛts] npl castagnettes
fpl
caster sugar ['kɑ:stə-] n (BRIT) sucre m
semoule
cast-iron ['kɑ:staɪən] adj (lit) de or en fonte;
(fig: will) de fer; (alibi) en béton
castle ['kɑ:sl] n château m; (fortress)
château-fort m; (Chess) tour f
casual ['kæʒjul] adj (by chance) de hasard,
fait(e) au hasard, fortuit(e); (irregular: work
etc) temporaire; (unconcerned) désinvolte;
~ wear vêtements mpl sport inv
casualty ['kæʒjultɪ] n accidenté(e),
blessé(e); (dead) victime f, mort(e); (BRIT
Med: department) urgences fpl
cat [kæt] n chat m
Catalan ['kætəlæn] adj catalan(e)
catalogue, (US) **catalog** ['kætəlɔg] n
catalogue m ▷ vt cataloguer
catalytic converter
[kætə'lɪtɪkkən'və:tər] n pot m catalytique
cataract ['kætərækt] n (also Med)
cataracte f
catarrh [kə'tɑ:r] n rhume m chronique,
catarrhe f
catastrophe [kə'tæstrəfɪ] n catastrophe f
catch [kætʃ] (pt, pp **caught**) vt attraper;
(person: by surprise) prendre, surprendre;
(understand) saisir; (get entangled) accrocher
▷ vi (fire) prendre; (get entangled) s'accrocher
▷ n (fish etc) prise f; (hidden problem) attrape
f; (Tech) loquet m; cliquet m; **to ~ sb's
attention** or **eye** attirer l'attention de qn;
to ~ fire prendre feu; **to ~ sight of**
apercevoir; **catch up** vi (with work) se
rattraper, combler son retard ▷ vt (also: **~ up
with**) rattraper; **catching** ['kætʃɪŋ] adj
(Med) contagieux(-euse)
category ['kætɪgərɪ] n catégorie f
cater ['keɪtər] vi: **to ~ for** (BRIT: needs)
satisfaire, pourvoir à; (readers, consumers)
s'adresser à, pourvoir aux besoins de;
(Comm: parties etc) préparer des repas pour
caterpillar ['kætəpɪlər] n chenille f
cathedral [kə'θi:drəl] n cathédrale f
Catholic ['kæθəlɪk] (Rel) adj catholique ▷ n
catholique m/f
cattle ['kætl] npl bétail m, bestiaux mpl
catwalk ['kætwɔ:k] n passerelle f; (for
models) podium m (de défilé de mode)
caught [kɔ:t] pt, pp of **catch**
cauliflower ['kɔlɪflauər] n chou-fleur m
cause [kɔ:z] n cause f ▷ vt causer
caution ['kɔ:ʃən] n prudence f; (warning)
avertissement m ▷ vt avertir, donner un
avertissement à; **cautious** adj prudent(e)
cave [keɪv] n caverne f, grotte f; **cave in** vi
(roof etc) s'effondrer
caviar(e) ['kævɪɑ:r] n caviar m

cavity ['kævɪtɪ] n cavité f; (Med) carie f
cc abbr (= cubic centimetre) cm³; (on letter etc = carbon copy) cc
CCTV n abbr = **closed-circuit television**
CD n abbr (= compact disc) CD m; **CD burner** n graveur m de CD; **CD player** n platine f laser; **CD-ROM** [si:di:'rɔm] n abbr (= compact disc read-only memory) CD-ROM m inv; **CD writer** n graveur m de CD
cease [si:s] vt, vi cesser; **ceasefire** n cessez-le-feu m
cedar ['si:dər] n cèdre m
ceilidh ['keɪlɪ] n bal m folklorique écossais or irlandais
ceiling ['si:lɪŋ] n (also fig) plafond m
celebrate ['sɛlɪbreɪt] vt, vi célébrer; **celebration** [sɛlɪ'breɪʃən] n célébration f
celebrity [sɪ'lɛbrɪtɪ] n célébrité f
celery ['sɛlərɪ] n céleri m (en branches)
cell [sɛl] n (gen) cellule f; (Elec) élément m (de pile)
cellar ['sɛlər] n cave f
cello ['tʃɛləu] n violoncelle m
Cellophane® ['sɛləfeɪn] n cellophane® f
cellphone ['sɛlfəun] n (téléphone m) portable m, mobile m
Celsius ['sɛlsɪəs] adj Celsius inv
Celtic ['kɛltɪk, 'sɛltɪk] adj celte, celtique
cement [sə'mɛnt] n ciment m
cemetery ['sɛmɪtrɪ] n cimetière m
censor ['sɛnsər] n censeur m ▷ vt censurer; **censorship** n censure f
census ['sɛnsəs] n recensement m
cent [sɛnt] n (unit of dollar, euro) cent m (= un centième du dollar, de l'euro); see also **per cent**
centenary [sɛn'ti:nərɪ], (US) **centennial** [sɛn'tɛnɪəl] n centenaire m
center ['sɛntər] (US) = **centre**
centi... ['sɛntɪ] **centigrade** adj centigrade; **centimetre**, (US) **centimeter** n centimètre m; **centipede** ['sɛntɪpi:d] n mille-pattes m inv
central ['sɛntrəl] adj central(e); **Central America** n Amérique centrale; **central heating** n chauffage central; **central reservation** n (BRIT Aut) terre-plein central
centre, (US) **center** ['sɛntər] n centre m ▷ vt centrer; **centre-forward** n (Sport) avant-centre m; **centre-half** n (Sport) demi-centre m
century ['sɛntjurɪ] n siècle m; **in the twentieth ~** au vingtième siècle
CEO n abbr (US) = **chief executive officer**
ceramic [sɪ'ræmɪk] adj céramique
cereal ['si:rɪəl] n céréale f
ceremony ['sɛrɪmənɪ] n cérémonie f; **to stand on ~** faire des façons
certain ['sə:tən] adj certain(e); **to make ~ of** s'assurer de; **for ~** certainement, sûrement; **certainly** adv certainement; **certainty** n certitude f
certificate [sə'tɪfɪkɪt] n certificat m

certify ['sə:tɪfaɪ] vt certifier; (award diploma to) conférer un diplôme etc à; (declare insane) déclarer malade mental(e)
cf. abbr (= compare) cf., voir
CFC n abbr (= chlorofluorocarbon) CFC m
chain [tʃeɪn] n (gen) chaîne f ▷ vt (also: ~ **up**) enchaîner, attacher (avec une chaîne); **chain-smoke** vi fumer cigarette sur cigarette
chair [tʃɛər] n chaise f; (armchair) fauteuil m; (of university) chaire f; (of meeting) présidence f ▷ vt (meeting) présider; **chairlift** n télésiège m; **chairman** (irreg) n président m; **chairperson** (irreg) n président(e); **chairwoman** (irreg) n présidente f
chalet ['ʃæleɪ] n chalet m
chalk [tʃɔ:k] n craie f
challenge ['tʃælɪndʒ] n défi m ▷ vt défier; (statement, right) mettre en question, contester; **to ~ sb to do** mettre qn au défi de faire; **challenging** adj (task, career) qui représente un défi or une gageure; (tone, look) de défi, provocateur(-trice)
chamber ['tʃeɪmbər] n chambre f; (BRIT Law: gen pl) cabinet m; **~ of commerce** chambre de commerce; **chambermaid** n femme f de chambre
champagne [ʃæm'peɪn] n champagne m
champion ['tʃæmpɪən] n (also of cause) champion(ne); **championship** n championnat m
chance [tʃɑ:ns] n (luck) hasard m; (opportunity) occasion f, possibilité f; (hope, likelihood) chance f; (risk) risque m ▷ vt (risk) risquer ▷ adj fortuit(e), de hasard; **to take a ~** prendre un risque; **by ~** par hasard; **to ~ it** risquer le coup, essayer
chancellor ['tʃɑ:nsələr] n chancelier m; **Chancellor of the Exchequer** [-ɪks'tʃɛkər] (BRIT) n chancelier m de l'Échiquier
chandelier [ʃændə'lɪər] n lustre m
change [tʃeɪndʒ] vt (alter, replace: Comm: money) changer; (switch, substitute: hands, trains, places, one's name etc) changer de ▷ vi (gen) changer; (change clothes) se changer; (be transformed): **to ~ into** se changer or transformer en ▷ n changement m; (money) monnaie f; **to ~ gear** (Aut) changer de vitesse; **to ~ one's mind** changer d'avis; **a ~ of clothes** des vêtements de rechange; **for a ~** pour changer; **do you have ~ for £10?** vous avez la monnaie de 10 livres?; **where can I ~ some money?** où est-ce que je peux changer de l'argent?; **keep the ~!** gardez la monnaie!; **change over** vi (swap) échanger; (change: drivers etc) changer; (change sides: players etc) changer de côté; **to ~ over from sth to sth** passer de qch à qch; **changeable** adj (weather) variable; **change machine** n distributeur m de monnaie; **changing room** n (BRIT: in shop) salon m d'essayage (: Sport) vestiaire m

channel ['tʃænl] n (TV) chaîne f; (waveband, groove, fig: medium) canal m; (of river, sea) chenal m ▷ vt canaliser; **the (English) C~** la Manche; **Channel Islands** npl: **the Channel Islands** les îles fpl Anglo-Normandes; **Channel Tunnel** n: the **Channel Tunnel** le tunnel sous la Manche

chant [tʃɑːnt] n chant m; (Rel) psalmodie f ▷ vt chanter, scander

chaos ['keɪɔs] n chaos m

chaotic [keɪ'ɔtɪk] adj chaotique

chap [tʃæp] n (BRIT inf: man) type m

chapel ['tʃæpl] n chapelle f

chapped [tʃæpt] adj (skin, lips) gercé(e)

chapter ['tʃæptə'] n chapitre m

character ['kærɪktə'] n caractère m; (in novel, film) personnage m; (eccentric person) numéro m, phénomène m; **characteristic** ['kærɪktə'rɪstɪk] adj, n caractéristique (f); **characterize** ['kærɪktəraɪz] vt caractériser

charcoal ['tʃɑːkəul] n charbon m de bois; (Art) charbon

charge [tʃɑːdʒ] n (accusation) accusation f; (Law) inculpation f; (cost) prix (demandé) ▷ vt (gun, battery, Mil: enemy) charger; (customer, sum) faire payer ▷ vi foncer; **charges** npl (costs) frais mpl; **to reverse the ~s** (BRIT Tel) téléphoner en PCV; **to take ~ of** se charger de; **to be in ~ of** être responsable de, s'occuper de; **to ~ sb (with)** (Law) inculper qn (de); **charge card** n carte f de client (émise par un grand magasin); **charger** n (also: **battery charger**) chargeur m

charismatic [kærɪz'mætɪk] adj charismatique

charity ['tʃærɪtɪ] n charité f; (organization) institution f charitable or de bienfaisance, œuvre f (de charité); **charity shop** n (BRIT) boutique vendant des articles d'occasion au profit d'une organisation caritative

charm [tʃɑːm] n charme m; (on bracelet) breloque f ▷ vt charmer, enchanter; **charming** adj charmant(e)

chart [tʃɑːt] n tableau m, diagramme m; graphique m; (map) carte marine ▷ vt dresser or établir la carte de; (sales, progress) établir la courbe de; **charts** npl (Mus) hit-parade m; **to be in the ~s** (record, pop group) figurer au hit-parade

charter ['tʃɑːtə'] vt (plane) affréter ▷ n (document) charte f; **chartered accountant** n (BRIT) expert-comptable m; **charter flight** n charter m

chase [tʃeɪs] vt poursuivre, pourchasser; (also: **~ away**) chasser ▷ n poursuite f, chasse f

chat [tʃæt] vi (also: **have a ~**) bavarder, causer; (on Internet) chatter ▷ n conversation f; (on Internet) chat m; **chat up** vt (BRIT inf: girl) baratiner; **chat room** n (Internet) salon m de discussion; **chat show** n (BRIT) talk-show m

chatter ['tʃætə'] vi (person) bavarder, papoter ▷ n bavardage m, papotage m; **my teeth are ~ing** je claque des dents

chauffeur ['ʃəufə'] n chauffeur m (de maître)

chauvinist ['ʃəuvɪnɪst] n (also: **male ~**) phallocrate m, macho m; (nationalist) chauvin(e)

cheap [tʃiːp] adj bon marché inv, pas cher (chère); (reduced: ticket) à prix réduit; (: fare) réduit(e); (joke) facile, d'un goût douteux; (poor quality) à bon marché, de qualité médiocre ▷ adv à bon marché, pour pas cher; **can you recommend a ~ hotel/ restaurant, please?** pourriez-vous m'indiquer un hôtel/restaurant bon marché?; **cheap day return** n billet m d'aller et retour réduit (valable pour la journée); **cheaply** adv à bon marché, à bon compte

cheat [tʃiːt] vi tricher; (in exam) copier ▷ vt tromper, duper; **to ~ sb out of sth** escroquer qch à qn ▷ n tricheur(-euse) m/f; escroc m; **cheat on** vt fus tromper

Chechnya [tʃɪtʃ'njɑː] n Tchétchénie f

check [tʃek] vt vérifier; (passport, ticket) contrôler; (halt) enrayer; (restrain) maîtriser ▷ vi (official etc) se renseigner ▷ n vérification f; contrôle m; (curb) frein m; (BRIT: bill) addition f; (US) = **cheque**; (pattern: gen pl) carreaux mpl; **to ~ with sb** demander à qn; **check in** vi (in hotel) remplir sa fiche (d'hôtel); (at airport) se présenter à l'enregistrement ▷ vt (luggage) (faire) enregistrer; **check off** vt (tick off) cocher; **check out** vi (in hotel) régler sa note ▷ vt (investigate: story) vérifier; **check up** vi: **to ~ up (on sth)** vérifier (qch); **to ~ up on sb** se renseigner sur le compte de qn; **checkbook** n (US) = **chequebook**; **checked** adj (pattern, cloth) à carreaux; **checkers** n (US) jeu m de dames; **check-in** n (at airport: also: **check-in desk**) enregistrement m; **checking account** n (US) compte courant; **checklist** n liste f de contrôle; **checkmate** n échec et mat m; **checkout** n (in supermarket) caisse f; **checkpoint** n contrôle m; **checkroom** (US) n consigne f; **checkup** n (Med) examen médical, check-up m

cheddar ['tʃedə'] n (also: **~ cheese**) cheddar m

cheek [tʃiːk] n joue f; (impudence) toupet m, culot m; **what a ~!** quel toupet!; **cheekbone** n pommette f; **cheeky** adj effronté(e), culotté(e)

cheer [tʃɪə'] vt acclamer, applaudir; (gladden) réjouir, réconforter ▷ vi applaudir ▷ n (gen pl) acclamations fpl, applaudissements mpl; bravos mpl, hourras mpl; **~s!** à la vôtre!; **cheer up** vi se dérider, reprendre courage ▷ vt remonter le moral à or de, dérider, égayer; **cheerful** adj gai(e), joyeux(-euse)

cheerio [tʃɪərɪ'əu] *excl* (BRIT) salut!, au revoir!

cheerleader ['tʃɪəli:də'] *n* membre d'un groupe de majorettes qui chantent et dansent pour soutenir leur équipe pendant les matchs de football américain

cheese [tʃi:z] *n* fromage *m*; **cheeseburger** *n* cheeseburger *m*; **cheesecake** *n* tarte *f* au fromage

chef [ʃɛf] *n* chef (cuisinier)

chemical ['kɛmɪkl] *adj* chimique ▷ *n* produit *m* chimique

chemist ['kemɪst] *n* (BRIT: pharmacist) pharmacien(ne); (scientist) chimiste *m/f*; **chemistry** *n* chimie *f*; **chemist's (shop)** *n* (BRIT) pharmacie *f*

cheque, (US) **check** [tʃɛk] *n* chèque *m*; **chequebook**, (US) **checkbook** *n* chéquier *m*, carnet *m* de chèques; **cheque card** *n* (BRIT) carte *f* (d'identité) bancaire

cherry ['tʃɛrɪ] *n* cerise *f*; (also: **~ tree**) cerisier *m*

chess [tʃɛs] *n* échecs *mpl*

chest [tʃɛst] *n* poitrine *f*; (box) coffre *m*, caisse *f*

chestnut ['tʃɛsnʌt] *n* châtaigne *f*; (also: **~ tree**) châtaignier *m*

chest of drawers *n* commode *f*

chew [tʃu:] *vt* mâcher; **chewing gum** *n* chewing-gum *m*

chic [ʃi:k] *adj* chic *inv*, élégant(e)

chick [tʃɪk] *n* poussin *m*; (inf) fille *f*

chicken ['tʃɪkɪn] *n* poulet *m*; (inf: coward) poule mouillée; **chicken out** *vi* (inf) se dégonfler; **chickenpox** *n* varicelle *f*

chickpea ['tʃɪkpi:] *n* pois *m* chiche

chief [tʃi:f] *n* chef *m* ▷ *adj* principal(e); **chief executive**, (US) **chief executive officer** *n* directeur(-trice) général(e); **chiefly** *adv* principalement, surtout

child (pl **children**) [tʃaɪld, 'tʃɪldrən] *n* enfant *m/f*; **child abuse** *n* maltraitance *f* d'enfants; (sexual) abus *mpl* sexuels sur des enfants; **child benefit** *n* (BRIT) ≈ allocations familiales; **childbirth** *n* accouchement *m*; **childcare** *n* (for working parents) garde *f* des enfants (pour les parents qui travaillent); **childhood** *n* enfance *f*; **childish** *adj* puéril(e), enfantin(e); **child minder** *n* (BRIT) garde *f* d'enfants; **children** ['tʃɪldrən] *npl* of **child**

Chile ['tʃɪlɪ] *n* Chili *m*

chill [tʃɪl] *n* (of water) froid *m*; (of air) fraîcheur *f*; (Med) refroidissement *m*, coup *m* de froid ▷ *vt* (person) faire frissonner; (Culin) mettre au frais, rafraîchir; **chill out** *vi* (inf: esp US) se relaxer

chil(l)i ['tʃɪlɪ] *n* piment *m* (rouge)

chilly ['tʃɪlɪ] *adj* froid(e), glacé(e); (sensitive to cold) frileux(-euse)

chimney ['tʃɪmnɪ] *n* cheminée *f*

chimpanzee [tʃɪmpæn'zi:] *n* chimpanzé *m*

chin [tʃɪn] *n* menton *m*

China ['tʃaɪnə] *n* Chine *f*

china ['tʃaɪnə] *n* (material) porcelaine *f*; (crockery) (vaisselle *f* en) porcelaine

Chinese [tʃaɪ'ni:z] *adj* chinois(e) ▷ *n* (pl inv) Chinois(e); (Ling) chinois *m*

chip [tʃɪp] *n* (gen pl: Culin: BRIT) frite *f*; (: US: also: **potato ~**) chip *m*; (of wood) copeau *m*; (of glass, stone) éclat *m*; (also: **micro~**) puce *f*; (in gambling) fiche *f* ▷ *vt* (cup, plate) ébrécher; **chip shop** *n* (BRIT) friterie *f*

● **CHIP SHOP**
●
● Un chip shop, que l'on appelle également
● un "fish-and-chip shop", est un magasin
● où l'on vend des plats à emporter. Les
● chip shops sont d'ailleurs à l'origine des
● "takeaways". On y achète en particulier
● du poisson frit et des frites, mais on y
● trouve également des plats traditionnels
● britanniques ("steak pies", saucisses, etc).
● Tous les plats étaient à l'origine emballés
● dans du papier journal. Dans certains
● de ces magasins, on peut s'asseoir pour
● consommer sur place.

chiropodist [kɪ'rɔpədɪst] *n* (BRIT) pédicure *m/f*

chisel ['tʃɪzl] *n* ciseau *m*

chives [tʃaɪvz] *npl* ciboulette *f*, civette *f*

chlorine ['klɔ:ri:n] *n* chlore *m*

choc-ice ['tʃɔkaɪs] *n* (BRIT) esquimau® *m*

chocolate ['tʃɔklɪt] *n* chocolat *m*

choice [tʃɔɪs] *n* choix *m* ▷ *adj* de choix

choir ['kwaɪə'] *n* chœur *m*, chorale *f*

choke [tʃəuk] *vi* étouffer ▷ *vt* étrangler; étouffer; (block) boucher, obstruer ▷ *n* (Aut) starter *m*

cholesterol [kə'lɛstərɔl] *n* cholestérol *m*

chook [tʃuk] *n* (AUST, NZ inf) poule *f*

choose (pt **chose**, pp **chosen**) [tʃu:z, tʃəuz, 'tʃəuzn] *vt* choisir; **to ~ to do** décider de faire, juger bon de faire

chop [tʃɔp] *vt* (wood) couper (à la hache); (Culin: also: **~ up**) couper (fin), émincer, hacher (en morceaux) ▷ *n* (Culin) côtelette *f*; **chop down** *vt* (tree) abattre; **chop off** *vt* trancher; **chopsticks** ['tʃɔpstɪks] *npl* baguettes *fpl*

chord [kɔ:d] *n* (Mus) accord *m*

chore [tʃɔ:'] *n* travail *m* de routine; **household ~s** travaux *mpl* du ménage

chorus ['kɔ:rəs] *n* chœur *m*; (repeated part of song, also fig) refrain *m*

chose [tʃəuz] *pt* of **choose**

chosen ['tʃəuzn] *pp* of **choose**

Christ [kraɪst] *n* Christ *m*

christen ['krɪsn] *vt* baptiser; **christening** *n* baptême *m*

Christian ['krɪstɪən] *adj, n* chrétien(ne); **Christianity** [krɪstɪ'ænɪtɪ] *n* christianisme *m*; **Christian name** *n* prénom *m*

Christmas ['krɪsməs] n Noël m or f; **happy**
or **merry ~!** joyeux Noël!; **Christmas card** n
carte f de Noël; **Christmas carol** n chant m
de Noël; **Christmas Day** n le jour de Noël;
Christmas Eve n la veille de Noël; la nuit
de Noël; **Christmas pudding** n (esp BRIT)
Christmas pudding m; **Christmas tree** n
arbre m de Noël

chrome [krəum] n chrome m

chronic ['krɒnɪk] adj chronique

chrysanthemum [krɪ'sænθəməm] n
chrysanthème m

chubby ['tʃʌbɪ] adj potelé(e), rondelet(te)

chuck [tʃʌk] vt (inf) lancer, jeter; (job) lâcher;
chuck out vt (inf: person) flanquer dehors or
à la porte; (: rubbish etc) jeter

chuckle ['tʃʌkl] vi glousser

chum [tʃʌm] n copain (copine)

chunk [tʃʌŋk] n gros morceau

church [tʃəːtʃ] n église f; **churchyard** n
cimetière m

churn [tʃəːn] n (for butter) baratte f; (also:
milk ~) (grand) bidon à lait

chute [ʃuːt] n goulotte f; (also: **rubbish ~**)
vide-ordures m inv; (BRIT: children's slide)
toboggan m

chutney ['tʃʌtnɪ] n chutney m

CIA n abbr (= Central Intelligence Agency) CIA f

CID n abbr (= Criminal Investigation
Department) ≈ P.J. f

cider ['saɪdə] n cidre m

cigar [sɪ'gɑː] n cigare m

cigarette [sɪgə'rɛt] n cigarette f; **cigarette
lighter** n briquet m

cinema ['sɪnəmə] n cinéma m

cinnamon ['sɪnəmən] n cannelle f

circle ['səːkl] n cercle m; (in cinema) balcon m
▷ vi faire or décrire des cercles ▷ vt (surround)
entourer, encercler; (move round) faire le
tour de, tourner autour de

circuit ['səːkɪt] n circuit m; (lap) tour m

circular ['səːkjulə] adj circulaire ▷ n
circulaire f; (as advertisement) prospectus m

circulate ['səːkjuleɪt] vi circuler ▷ vt faire
circuler; **circulation** [səːkju'leɪʃən] n
circulation f; (of newspaper) tirage m

circumstances ['səːkəmstənsɪz] npl
circonstances fpl; (financial condition)
moyens mpl, situation financière

circus ['səːkəs] n cirque m

cite [saɪt] vt citer

citizen ['sɪtɪzn] n (Pol) citoyen(ne);
(resident): **the ~s of this town** les habitants
de cette ville; **citizenship** n citoyenneté f;
(BRIT Scol) ≈ éducation f civique

citrus fruits ['sɪtrəs-] npl agrumes mpl

city ['sɪtɪ] n (grande) ville f; **the C~** la Cité
de Londres (centre des affaires); **city centre**
n centre ville m; **city technology college**
n (BRIT) établissement m d'enseignement
technologique (situé dans un quartier
défavorisé)

civic ['sɪvɪk] adj civique; (authorities)
municipal(e)

civil ['sɪvɪl] adj civil(e); (polite) poli(e),
civil(e); **civilian** [sɪ'vɪlɪən] adj, n civil(e)

civilization [sɪvɪlaɪ'zeɪʃən] n civilisation f

civilized ['sɪvɪlaɪzd] adj civilisé(e); (fig) où
règnent les bonnes manières

civil: civil law n code civil; (study) droit civil;
civil rights npl droits mpl civiques; **civil
servant** n fonctionnaire m/f; **Civil Service**
n fonction publique, administration f; **civil
war** n guerre civile

CJD n abbr (= Creutzfeldt-Jakob disease) MCJ f

claim [kleɪm] vt (rights etc) revendiquer;
(compensation) réclamer; (assert) déclarer,
prétendre ▷ vi (for insurance) faire une
déclaration de sinistre ▷ n revendication f;
prétention f; (right) droit m; (insurance) ~
demande f d'indemnisation, déclaration f
de sinistre; **claim form** n (gen) formulaire m
de demande

clam [klæm] n palourde f

clamp [klæmp] n crampon m; (on
workbench) valet m; (on car) sabot m de
Denver ▷ vt attacher; (car) mettre un
sabot à; **clamp down on** vt fus sévir
contre, prendre des mesures draconiennes
à l'égard de

clan [klæn] n clan m

clap [klæp] vi applaudir

claret ['klærət] n (vin m de) bordeaux m
(rouge)

clarify ['klærɪfaɪ] vt clarifier

clarinet [klærɪ'nɛt] n clarinette f

clarity ['klærɪtɪ] n clarté f

clash [klæʃ] n (sound) choc m, fracas m; (with
police) affrontement m; (fig) conflit m ▷ vi se
heurter; être or entrer en conflit; (colours)
jurer; (dates, events) tomber en même temps

clasp [klɑːsp] n (of necklace, bag) fermoir m
▷ vt serrer, étreindre

class [klɑːs] n (gen) classe f; (group, category)
catégorie f ▷ vt classer, classifier

classic ['klæsɪk] adj classique ▷ n (author,
work) classique m; **classical** adj classique

classification [klæsɪfɪ'keɪʃən] n
classification f

classify ['klæsɪfaɪ] vt classifier, classer

classmate ['klɑːsmeɪt] n camarade m/f
de classe

classroom ['klɑːsrum] n (salle f de) classe
f; **classroom assistant** n assistant(e)
d'éducation

classy ['klɑːsɪ] (inf) adj classe (inf)

clatter ['klætə] n cliquetis m ▷ vi cliqueter

clause [klɔːz] n clause f; (Ling) proposition f

claustrophobic [klɔːstrə'fəubɪk] adj
(person) claustrophobe; (place) où l'on se
sent claustrophobe

claw [klɔː] n griffe f; (of bird of prey) serre f; (of
lobster) pince f

clay [kleɪ] n argile f

clean [kli:n] *adj* propre; (*clear, smooth*) net(te); (*record, reputation*) sans tache; (*joke, story*) correct(e) ▷ *vt* nettoyer; **clean up** *vt* nettoyer; (*fig*) remettre de l'ordre dans; **cleaner** *n* (*person*) nettoyeur(-euse), femme *f* de ménage; (*product*) détachant *m*; **cleaner's** *n* (*also:* **dry cleaner's**) teinturier *m*; **cleaning** *n* nettoyage *m*

cleanser ['klɛnzəʳ] *n* (*for face*) démaquillant *m*

clear [klɪəʳ] *adj* clair(e); (*glass, plastic*) transparent(e); (*road, way*) libre, dégagé(e); (*profit, majority*) net(te); (*conscience*) tranquille; (*skin*) frais (fraîche); (*sky*) dégagé(e) ▷ *vt* (*road*) dégager, déblayer; (*table*) débarrasser; (*room etc: of people*) faire évacuer; (*cheque*) compenser; (*Law: suspect*) innocenter; (*obstacle*) franchir or sauter sans heurter ▷ *vi* (*weather*) s'éclaircir; (*fog*) se dissiper ▷ *adv*. ~ **of** à distance de, à l'écart de; **to ~ the table** débarrasser la table, desservir; **clear away** *vt* (*things, clothes etc*) enlever, retirer; **to ~ away the dishes** débarrasser la table; **clear up** *vt* ranger, mettre en ordre; (*mystery*) éclaircir, résoudre; **clearance** *n* (*removal*) déblayage *m*; (*permission*) autorisation *f*; **clear-cut** *adj* précis(e), nettement défini(e); **clearing** *n* (*in forest*) clairière *f*, **clearly** *adv* clairement; (*obviously*) de toute évidence; **clearway** *n* (*BRIT*) route *f* à stationnement interdit

clench [klɛntʃ] *vt* serrer

clergy ['klɜːdʒɪ] *n* clergé *m*

clerk [klɑːk, *US* klɜːrk] *n* (*BRIT*) employé(e) de bureau; (*US: salesman/woman*) vendeur(-euse)

clever ['klɛvəʳ] *adj* (*intelligent*) intelligent(e); (*skilful*) habile, adroit(e); (*device, arrangement*) ingénieux(-euse), astucieux(-euse)

cliché ['kliːʃeɪ] *n* cliché *m*

click [klɪk] *n* (*Comput*) clic *m* ▷ *vi* (*Comput*) cliquer ▷ *vt*: **to ~ one's tongue** faire claquer sa langue; **to ~ one's heels** claquer des talons; **to ~ on an icon** cliquer sur une icône

client ['klaɪənt] *n* client(e)

cliff [klɪf] *n* falaise *f*

climate ['klaɪmɪt] *n* climat *m*; **climate change** *n* changement *m* climatique

climax ['klaɪmæks] *n* apogée *m*, point culminant; (*sexual*) orgasme *m*

climb [klaɪm] *vi* grimper, monter; (*plane*) prendre de l'altitude ▷ *vt* (*stairs*) monter; (*mountain*) escalader; (*tree*) grimper à ▷ *n* montée *f*, escalade *f*; **to ~ over a wall** passer par dessus un mur; **climb down** *vi* (re)descendre; (*BRIT fig*) rabattre de ses prétentions; **climber** *n* (*also*: **rock climber**) grimpeur(-euse), varappeur(-euse); (*plant*) plante grimpante; **climbing** *n* (*also*: **rock climbing**) escalade *f*, varappe *f*

clinch [klɪntʃ] *vt* (*deal*) conclure, sceller

cling (*pt, pp* **clung**) [klɪŋ, klʌŋ] *vi*: **to ~ (to)** se cramponner (à), s'accrocher (à); (*clothes*) coller (à); **clingfilm** *n* film *m* alimentaire

clinic ['klɪnɪk] *n* clinique *f*; centre médical

clip [klɪp] *n* (*for hair*) barrette *f*; (*also*: **paper ~**) trombone *m*; (*TV, Cine*) clip *m* ▷ *vt* (*also*: **~ together**: *papers*) attacher; (*hair, nails*) couper; (*hedge*) tailler; **clipping** *n* (*from newspaper*) coupure *f* de journal

cloak [kləuk] *n* grande cape ▷ *vt* (*fig*) masquer, cacher; **cloakroom** *n* (*for coats etc*) vestiaire *m*; (*BRIT: W.C.*) toilettes *fpl*

clock [klɔk] *n* (*large*) horloge *f*; (*small*) pendule *f*; **clock in, clock on** (*BRIT*) *vi* (*with card*) pointer (en arrivant); (*start work*) commencer à travailler; **clock off, clock out** (*BRIT*) *vi* (*with card*) pointer (en partant); (*leave work*) quitter le travail; **clockwise** *adv* dans le sens des aiguilles d'une montre; **clockwork** *n* rouages *mpl*, mécanisme *m*; (*of clock*) mouvement *m* (d'horlogerie) ▷ *adj* (*toy, train*) mécanique

clog [klɔg] *n* sabot *m* ▷ *vt* boucher, encrasser ▷ *vi* (*also*: **~ up**) se boucher, s'encrasser

clone [kləun] *n* clone *m* ▷ *vt* cloner

close¹ [kləus] *adj* (*contact, link, watch*) étroit(e); (*examination*) attentif(-ive), minutieux(-euse); (*contest*) très serré(e); (*weather*) lourd(e), étouffant(e), (*near*): ~ **(to)** près (de), proche (de) ▷ *adv* près, à proximité; ~ **to** *prep* près de; ~ **by**, ~ **at hand** *adj*, *adv* tout(e) près; **a ~ friend** un ami intime; **to have a ~ shave** (*fig*) l'échapper belle

close² [kləuz] *vt* fermer ▷ *vi* (*shop etc*) fermer; (*lid, door etc*) se fermer; (*end*) se terminer, se conclure ▷ *n* (*end*) conclusion *f*; **what time do you ~?** à quelle heure fermez-vous?; **close down** *vi* fermer (définitivement); **closed** *adj* (*shop etc*) fermé(e)

closely ['kləuslɪ] *adv* (*examine, watch*) de près

closet ['klɔzɪt] *n* (*cupboard*) placard *m*, réduit *m*

close-up ['kləusʌp] *n* gros plan

closing time *n* heure *f* de fermeture

closure ['kləuʒəʳ] *n* fermeture *f*

clot [klɔt] *n* (*of blood, milk*) caillot *m*; (*inf: person*) ballot *m* ▷ *vi* (*external bleeding*) coaguler

cloth [klɔθ] *n* (*material*) tissu *m*, étoffe *f*; (*BRIT: also*. **tea ~**) torchon *m*; lavette *f*; (*also*: **table~**) nappe *f*

clothes [kləuðz] *npl* vêtements *mpl*, habits *mpl*; **clothes line** *n* corde *f* (à linge); **clothes peg**, (*US*) **clothes pin** *n* pince *f* à linge

clothing ['kləuðɪŋ] *n* = **clothes**

cloud [klaud] *n* (*also Comput*) nuage *m*; **cloud computing** *n* (*Comput*) informatique *f* en nuage; **cloud over** *vi* se couvrir; (*fig*) s'assombrir; **cloudy** adj nuageux(-euse), couvert(e); (liquid) trouble

clove [kləuv] n clou m de girofle; **a ~ of garlic** une gousse d'ail

clown [klaun] n clown m ▷ vi (also: **~ about, ~ around**) faire le clown

club [klʌb] n (society) club m; (weapon) massue f, matraque f; (also: **golf ~**) club ▷ vt matraquer ▷ vi: **to ~ together** s'associer; **clubs** npl (Cards) trèfle m; **club class** n (Aviat) classe f club

clue [kluː] n indice m; (in crosswords) définition f; **I haven't a ~** je n'en ai pas la moindre idée

clump [klʌmp] n: **~ of trees** bouquet m d'arbres

clumsy ['klʌmzɪ] adj (person) gauche, maladroit(e); (object) malcommode, peu maniable

clung [klʌŋ] pt, pp of **cling**

cluster ['klʌstəʳ] n (petit) groupe m; (of flowers) grappe f ▷ vi se rassembler

clutch [klʌtʃ] n (Aut) embrayage m; (grasp): **~es** étreinte f, prise f ▷ vt (grasp) agripper; (hold tightly) serrer fort; (hold on to) se cramponner à

cm abbr (= centimetre) cm

Co. abbr = **company, county**

c/o abbr (= care of) c/o, aux bons soins de

coach [kəutʃ] n (bus) autocar m; (horse-drawn) diligence f; (of train) voiture f, wagon m; (Sport: trainer) entraîneur(-euse); (school: tutor) répétiteur(-trice) ▷ vt (Sport) entraîner; (student) donner des leçons particulières à; **coach station** (BRIT) n gare routière; **coach trip** n excursion f en car

coal [kəul] n charbon m

coalition [kəuə'lɪʃən] n coalition f

coarse [kɔːs] adj grossier(-ère), rude; (vulgar) vulgaire

coast [kəust] n côte f ▷ vi (car, cycle) descendre en roue libre; **coastal** adj côtier(-ère); **coastguard** n garde-côte m; **coastline** n côte f, littoral m

coat [kəut] n manteau m; (of animal) pelage m, poil m; (of paint) couche f ▷ vt couvrir, enduire; **coat hanger** n cintre m; **coating** n couche f, enduit m

coax [kəuks] vt persuader par des cajoleries

cob [kɔb] n see **corn**

cobbled ['kɔbld] adj pavé(e)

cobweb ['kɔbwɛb] n toile f d'araignée

cocaine [kə'keɪn] n cocaïne f

cock [kɔk] n (rooster) coq m; (male bird) mâle m ▷ vt (gun) armer; **cockerel** n jeune coq m

cockney ['kɔknɪ] n cockney m/f (habitant des quartiers populaires de l'East End de Londres), ≈ faubourien(ne)

cockpit ['kɔkpɪt] n (in aircraft) poste m de pilotage, cockpit m

cockroach ['kɔkrəutʃ] n cafard m, cancrelat m

cocktail ['kɔkteɪl] n cocktail m

cocoa ['kəukəu] n cacao m

coconut ['kəukənʌt] n noix f de coco

cod [kɔd] n morue fraîche, cabillaud m

C.O.D. abbr = **cash on delivery**

code [kəud] n code m; (Tel: area code) indicatif m

coeducational ['kəuɛdju'keɪʃənl] adj mixte

coffee ['kɔfɪ] n café m; **coffee bar** n (BRIT) café m; **coffee bean** n grain m de café; **coffee break** n pause-café f; **coffee maker** n cafetière f; **coffeepot** n cafetière f; **coffee shop** n café m; **coffee table** n (petite) table basse

coffin ['kɔfɪn] n cercueil m

cog [kɔg] n (wheel) roue dentée; (tooth) dent f (d'engrenage)

cognac ['kɔnjæk] n cognac m

coherent [kəu'hɪərənt] adj cohérent(e)

coil [kɔɪl] n rouleau m, bobine f; (contraceptive) stérilet m ▷ vt enrouler

coin [kɔɪn] n pièce f (de monnaie) ▷ vt (word) inventer

coincide [kəuɪn'saɪd] vi coïncider; **coincidence** [kəu'ɪnsɪdəns] n coïncidence f

Coke® [kəuk] n coca m

coke [kəuk] n (coal) coke m

colander ['kɔləndəʳ] n passoire f (à légumes)

cold [kəuld] adj froid(e) ▷ n froid m; (Med) rhume m; **it's ~** il fait froid; **to be ~** (person) avoir froid; **to catch a ~** s'enrhumer, attraper un rhume; **in ~ blood** de sang-froid; **cold sore** n bouton m de fièvre

coleslaw ['kəulslɔː] n sorte de salade de chou cru

colic ['kɔlɪk] n colique(s) f(pl)

collaborate [kə'læbəreɪt] vi collaborer

collapse [kə'læps] vi s'effondrer, s'écrouler; (Med) avoir un malaise ▷ n effondrement m, écroulement m; (of government) chute f

collar ['kɔləʳ] n (of coat, shirt) col m; (for dog) collier m; **collarbone** n clavicule f

colleague ['kɔliːg] n collègue m/f

collect [kə'lɛkt] vt rassembler; (pick up) ramasser; (as a hobby) collectionner; (BRIT: call for) (passer) prendre; (mail) faire la levée de, ramasser; (money owed) encaisser; (donations, subscriptions) recueillir ▷ vi (people) se rassembler; (dust, dirt) s'amasser; **to call ~** (us Tel) téléphoner en PCV; **collection** [kə'lɛkʃən] n collection f; (of mail) levée f; (for money) collecte f, quête f; **collective** [kə'lɛktɪv] adj collectif(-ive); **collector** n collectionneur m

college ['kɔlɪdʒ] n collège m; (of technology, agriculture etc) institut m

collide [kə'laɪd] vi: **to ~ (with)** entrer en collision (avec)

collision [kə'lɪʒən] n collision f, heurt m
cologne [kə'ləun] n (also: **eau de ~**) eau f
de cologne
colon ['kəulən] n (sign) deux-points mpl;
(Med) côlon m
colonel ['kə:nl] n colonel m
colonial [kə'ləunɪəl] adj colonial(e)
colony ['kɔlənɪ] n colonie f
colour, (US) **color** ['kʌlə'] n couleur f ▷ vt
colorer; (dye) teindre; (paint) peindre; (with
crayons) colorier; (news) fausser, exagérer
▷ vi (blush) rougir; **I'd like a different ~** je
le voudrais dans un autre coloris; **colour
in** vt colorier; **colour-blind**, (US) **color-
blind** adj daltonien(ne); **coloured**, (US)
colored adj coloré(e); (photo) en couleur;
colour film, (US) **color film** n (for camera)
pellicule f (en) couleur; **colourful**, (US)
colorful adj coloré(e), vif (vive); (personality)
pittoresque, haut(e) en couleurs;
colouring, (US) **coloring** n colorant m;
(complexion) teint m; **colour television**, (US)
color television n télévision f (en) couleur
column ['kɔləm] n colonne f;
(fashion column, sports column etc) rubrique f
coma ['kəumə] n coma m
comb [kəum] n peigne m ▷ vt (hair) peigner;
(area) ratisser, passer au peigne fin
combat ['kɔmbæt] n combat m ▷ vt
combattre, lutter contre
combination [kɔmbɪ'neɪʃən] n (gen)
combinaison f
combine [kəm'baɪn] vt combiner
▷ vi s'associer; (Chem) se combiner
▷ n ['kɔmbaɪn] (Econ) trust m;
(also: **~ harvester**) moissonneuse-
batteuse(-lieuse) f; **to ~ sth with sth** (one
quality with another) joindre ou allier qch
à qch

○ **KEYWORD**

come (pt came, pp come) [kʌm, keɪm] vi
1 (movement towards) venir; **to come
running** arriver en courant; **he's come
here to work** il est venu ici pour travailler;
come with me suivez-moi
2 (arrive) arriver; **to come home** rentrer
(chez soi or à la maison); **we've just come
from Paris** nous arrivons de Paris
3 (reach): **to come to** (decision etc) parvenir
à, arriver à; **the bill came to £40** la note
s'est élevée à 40 livres
4 (occur): **an idea came to me** il m'est venu
une idée
5 (be, become): **to come loose/undone** se
défaire/desserrer; **I've come to like him** j'ai
fini par bien l'aimer
come across vt fus rencontrer par hasard,
tomber sur
come along vi (BRIT: pupil, work) faire des
progrès, avancer

come back vi revenir
come down vi descendre; (prices) baisser;
(buildings) s'écrouler; (: be demolished) être
démoli(e)
come from vt fus (source) venir de; (place)
venir de, être originaire de
come in vi entrer; (train) arriver; (fashion)
entrer en vogue; (on deal etc) participer
come off vi (button) se détacher; (attempt)
réussir
come on vi (lights, electricity) s'allumer;
(central heating) se mettre en marche; (pupil,
work, project) faire des progrès, avancer;
come on! viens!; allons!, allez!
come out vi sortir; (sun) se montrer; (book)
paraître; (stain) s'enlever; (strike) cesser le
travail, se mettre en grève
come round vi (after faint, operation) revenir
à soi, reprendre connaissance
come to vi revenir à soi
come up vi monter; (sun) se lever; (problem)
se poser; (event) survenir; (in conversation)
être soulevé
come up with vt fus (money) fournir; **he
came up with an idea** il a eu une idée, il a
proposé quelque chose
comeback ['kʌmbæk] n (Theat) rentrée f
comedian [kə'mi:dɪən] n (comic) comique
m; (Theat) comédien m
comedy ['kɔmɪdɪ] n comédie f; (humour)
comique m
comet ['kɔmɪt] n comète f
comfort ['kʌmfət] n confort m, bien-être
m, (solace) consolation f, réconfort m ▷ vt
consoler, réconforter; **comfortable** adj
confortable; (person) à l'aise; (financially)
aisé(e); (patient) dont l'état est stationnaire;
comfort station n (US) toilettes fpl
comic ['kɔmɪk] adj (also: **~al**) comique ▷ n
(person) comique m; (BRIT: magazine: for
children) magazine m de bandes dessinées
or de BD; (: for adults) illustré m; **comic book**
n (US: for children) magazine m de bandes
dessinées or de BD; (: for adults) illustré m;
comic strip n bande dessinée
comma ['kɔmə] n virgule f
command [kə'mɑ:nd] n ordre m,
commandement m; (Mil: authority)
commandement; (mastery) maîtrise f
▷ vt (troops) commander; **to ~ sb to do**
donner l'ordre or commander à qn de faire;
commander n (Mil) commandant m
commemorate [kə'mɛməreɪt] vt
commémorer
commence [kə'mɛns] vt, vi commencer
commend [kə'mɛnd] vt louer; (recommend)
recommander
comment ['kɔmɛnt] n commentaire m
▷ vi: **to ~ on** faire des remarques sur;
"no ~" "je n'ai rien à déclarer"; **commentary**
['kɔməntərɪ] n commentaire m; (Sport)

reportage *m* (en direct); **commentator** ['kɔmənteɪtəʳ] *n* commentateur *m*; (*Sport*) reporter *m*

commerce ['kɔmə:s] *n* commerce *m*

commercial [kə'mə:ʃəl] *adj* commercial(e) ▷ *n* (*Radio, TV*) annonce *f* publicitaire, spot *m* (publicitaire); **commercial break** *n* (*Radio, TV*) spot *m* (publicitaire)

commission [kə'mɪʃən] *n* (*committee, fee*) commission *f* ▷ *vt* (*work of art*) commander, charger un artiste de l'exécution de; **out of ~** (*machine*) hors service; **commissioner** *n* (*Police*) préfet *m* (de police)

commit [kə'mɪt] *vt* (*act*) commettre; (*resources*) consacrer; (*to sb's care*) confier (à); **to ~ o.s. (to do)** s'engager (à faire); **to ~ suicide** se suicider; **commitment** *n* engagement *m*; (*obligation*) responsabilité(s) *f(pl)*

committee [kə'mɪtɪ] *n* comité *m*; commission *f*

commodity [kə'mɔdɪtɪ] *n* produit *m*, marchandise *f*, article *m*

common ['kɔmən] *adj* (*gen*) commun(e); (*usual*) courant(e) ▷ *n* terrain communal; **commonly** *adv* communément, généralement; couramment; **commonplace** *adj* banal(e), ordinaire; **Commons** *npl* (*BRIT Pol*): **the (House of) Commons** la chambre des Communes; **common sense** *n* bon sens; **Commonwealth** *n*: **the Commonwealth** le Commonwealth

communal ['kɔmju:nl] *adj* (*life*) communautaire; (*for common use*) commun(e)

commune *n* ['kɔmju:n] (*group*) communauté *f* ▷ *vi* [kə'mju:n]: **to ~ with** (*nature*) communier avec

communicate [kə'mju:nɪkeɪt] *vt* communiquer, transmettre ▷ *vi*: **to ~ (with)** communiquer (avec)

communication [kəmju:nɪ'keɪʃən] *n* communication *f*

communion [kə'mju:nɪən] *n* (*also*: **Holy C~**) communion *f*

communism ['kɔmjunɪzəm] *n* communisme *m*; **communist** *adj, n* communiste *m/f*

community [kə'mju:nɪtɪ] *n* communauté *f*; **community centre**, (*US*) **community center** *n* foyer socio-éducatif, centre *m* de loisirs; **community service** *n* ≈ travail *m* d'intérêt général, TIG *m*

commute [kə'mju:t] *vi* faire le trajet journalier (*de son domicile à un lieu de travail assez éloigné*) ▷ *vt* (*Law*) commuer; **commuter** *n* banlieusard(e) (*qui fait un trajet journalier pour se rendre à son travail*)

compact *adj* [kəm'pækt] compact(e) ▷ *n* ['kɔmpækt] (*also*: **powder ~**) poudrier *m*; **compact disc** *n* disque compact; **compact disc player** *n* lecteur *m* de disques compacts

companion [kəm'pænjən] *n* compagnon (compagne)

company ['kʌmpənɪ] *n* compagnie *f*; **to keep sb ~** tenir compagnie à qn; **company car** *n* voiture *f* de fonction; **company director** *n* administrateur(-trice)

comparable ['kɔmpərəbl] *adj* comparable

comparative [kəm'pærətɪv] *adj* (*study*) comparatif(-ive); (*relative*) relatif(-ive); **comparatively** *adv* (*relatively*) relativement

compare [kəm'pɛəʳ] *vt*: **to ~ sth/sb with** *or* **to** comparer qch/qn avec *or* à ▷ *vi*: **to ~ (with)** se comparer (à); être comparable (à); **comparison** [kəm'pærɪsn] *n* comparaison *f*

compartment [kəm'pɑ:tmənt] *n* (*also Rail*) compartiment *m*; **a non-smoking ~** un compartiment non-fumeurs

compass ['kʌmpəs] *n* boussole *f*; **compasses** *npl* (*Math*) compas *m*

compassion [kəm'pæʃən] *n* compassion *f*, humanité *f*

compatible [kəm'pætɪbl] *adj* compatible

compel [kəm'pɛl] *vt* contraindre, obliger; **compelling** *adj* (*fig: argument*) irrésistible

compensate ['kɔmpənseɪt] *vt* indemniser, dédommager ▷ *vi*: **to ~ for** compenser; **compensation** [kɔmpən'seɪʃən] *n* compensation *f*; (*money*) dédommagement *m*, indemnité *f*

compete [kəm'pi:t] *vi* (*take part*) concourir; (*vie*) rivaliser (avec), faire concurrence (à)

competent ['kɔmpɪtənt] *adj* compétent(e), capable

competition [kɔmpɪ'tɪʃən] *n* (*contest*) compétition *f*, concours *m*; (*Econ*) concurrence *f*

competitive [kəm'pɛtɪtɪv] *adj* (*Econ*) concurrentiel(le); (*sports*) de compétition; (*person*) qui a l'esprit de compétition

competitor [kəm'pɛtɪtəʳ] *n* concurrent(e)

complacent [kəm'pleɪsnt] *adj* (*trop*) content(e) de soi

complain [kəm'pleɪn] *vi*: **to ~ (about)** se plaindre (de); (*in shop etc*) réclamer (au sujet de); **complaint** *n* plainte *f*; (*in shop etc*) réclamation *f*; (*Med*) affection *f*

complement *n* ['kɔmplɪmənt] *n* complément *m*; (*esp of ship's crew etc*) effectif complet ▷ *vt* (*enhance*) compléter; **complementary** [kɔmplɪ'mɛntərɪ] *adj* complémentaire

complete [kəm'pli:t] *adj* complet(-ète); (*finished*) achevé(e) ▷ *vt* achever, parachever; (*set, group*) compléter; (*a form*) remplir; **completely** *adv* complètement; **completion** [kəm'pli:ʃən] *n* achèvement *m*; (*of contract*) exécution *f*

complex ['kɒmplɛks] *adj* complexe ▷ *n* (*Psych, buildings etc*) complexe *m*

complexion [kəm'plɛkʃən] *n* (*of face*) teint *m*

compliance [kəm'plaɪəns] *n* (*submission*) docilité *f*; (*agreement*): **~ with** le fait de se conformer à; **in ~ with** en conformité avec, conformément à

complicate ['kɒmplɪkeɪt] *vt* compliquer; **complicated** *adj* compliqué(e); **complication** [kɒmplɪ'keɪʃən] *n* complication *f*

compliment *n* ['kɒmplɪmənt] compliment *m* ▷ *vt* ['kɒmplɪmɛnt] complimenter; **complimentary** [kɒmplɪ'mɛntərɪ] *adj* flatteur(-euse); (*free*) à titre gracieux

comply [kəm'plaɪ] *vi*: **to ~ with** se soumettre à, se conformer à

component [kəm'pəunənt] *adj* composant(e), constituant(e) ▷ *n* composant *m*, élément *m*

compose [kəm'pəuz] *vt* composer; (*form*): **to be ~d of** se composer de; **to ~ o.s.** se calmer, se maîtriser; **composer** *n* (*Mus*) compositeur *m*; **composition** [kɒmpə'zɪʃən] *n* composition *f*

composure [kəm'pəuʒə*r*] *n* calme *m*, maîtrise *f* de soi

compound ['kɒmpaund] *n* (*Chem, Ling*) composé *m*; (*enclosure*) enclos *m*, enceinte *f* ▷ *adj* composé(e); (*fracture*) compliqué(e)

comprehension [kɒmprɪ'hɛnʃən] *n* compréhension *f*

comprehensive [kɒmprɪ'hɛnsɪv] *adj* (*très*) complet(-ète); **~ policy** (*Insurance*) assurance *f* tous risques; **comprehensive (school)** *n* (BRIT) école secondaire non sélective avec libre circulation d'une section à l'autre, ≈ CES *m*

> Be careful not to translate *comprehensive* by the French word *compréhensif*.

compress *vt* [kəm'prɛs] comprimer; (*text, information*) condenser ▷ *n* ['kɒmprɛs] (*Med*) compresse *f*

comprise [kəm'praɪz] *vt* (*also*: **be ~d of**) comprendre; (*constitute*) constituer, représenter

compromise ['kɒmprəmaɪz] *n* compromis *m* ▷ *vt* compromettre ▷ *vi* transiger, accepter un compromis

compulsive [kəm'pʌlsɪv] *adj* (*Psych*) compulsif(-ive); (*book, film etc*) captivant(e)

compulsory [kəm'pʌlsərɪ] *adj* obligatoire

computer [kəm'pju:tə*r*] *n* ordinateur *m*; **computer game** *n* jeu *m* vidéo; **computer-generated** *adj* de synthèse; **computerize** *vt* (*data*) traiter par ordinateur; (*system, office*) informatiser; **computer programmer** *n* programmeur(-euse); **computer programming** *n* programmation *f*; **computer science** *n* informatique *f*; **computer studies** *npl*

informatique *f*; **computing** [kəm'pju:tɪŋ] *n* informatique *f*

con [kɒn] *vt* duper; (*cheat*) escroquer ▷ *n* escroquerie *f*

conceal [kən'si:l] *vt* cacher, dissimuler

concede [kən'si:d] *vt* concéder ▷ *vi* céder

conceited [kən'si:tɪd] *adj* vaniteux(-euse), suffisant(e)

conceive [kən'si:v] *vt, vi* concevoir

concentrate ['kɒnsəntreɪt] *vi* se concentrer ▷ *vt* concentrer

concentration [kɒnsən'treɪʃən] *n* concentration *f*

concept ['kɒnsɛpt] *n* concept *m*

concern [kən'sə:n] *n* affaire *f*; (*Comm*) entreprise *f*, firme *f*; (*anxiety*) inquiétude *f*, souci *m* ▷ *vt* (*worry*) inquiéter; (*involve*) concerner; (*relate to*) se rapporter à; **to be ~ed (about)** s'inquiéter (de), être inquiet(-ète) (au sujet de); **concerning** *prep* en ce qui concerne, à propos de

concert ['kɒnsət] *n* concert *m*; **concert hall** *n* salle *f* de concert

concerto [kən'tʃə:təu] *n* concerto *m*

concession [kən'sɛʃən] *n* (*compromise*) concession *f*; (*reduced price*) réduction *f*; **tax ~** dégrèvement fiscal; **"~s"** tarif réduit

concise [kən'saɪs] *adj* concis(e)

conclude [kən'klu:d] *vt* conclure; **conclusion** [kən'klu:ʒən] *n* conclusion *f*

concrete ['kɒnkri:t] *n* béton *m* ▷ *adj* concret(-ète); (*Constr*) en béton

concussion [kən'kʌʃən] *n* (*Med*) commotion (cérébrale)

condemn [kən'dɛm] *vt* condamner

condensation [kɒndɛn'seɪʃən] *n* condensation *f*

condense [kən'dɛns] *vi* se condenser ▷ *vt* condenser

condition [kən'dɪʃən] *n* condition *f*; (*disease*) maladie *f* ▷ *vt* déterminer, conditionner; **on ~ that** à condition que + *sub*, à condition de; **conditional** [kən'dɪʃənl] *adj* conditionnel(le); **conditioner** *n* (*for hair*) baume démêlant; (*for fabrics*) assouplissant *m*

condo ['kɒndəu] *n* (US *inf*) = **condominium**

condom ['kɒndəm] *n* préservatif *m*

condominium [kɒndə'mɪnɪəm] *n* (US: *building*) immeuble *m* (en copropriété); (: *rooms*) appartement *m* (dans un immeuble en copropriété)

condone [kən'dəun] *vt* fermer les yeux sur, approuver (tacitement)

conduct *n* ['kɒndʌkt] conduite *f* ▷ *vt* [kən'dʌkt] conduire; (*manage*) mener, diriger; (*Mus*) diriger; **to ~ o.s.** se conduire, se comporter; **conductor** *n* (*of orchestra*) chef *m* d'orchestre; (*on bus*) receveur *m*; (US: *on train*) chef *m* de train; (*Elec*) conducteur *m*

cone [kəun] *n* cône *m*; (*for ice-cream*) cornet *m*; (*Bot*) pomme *f* de pin, cône

confectionery [kənˈfɛkʃənrɪ] n (sweets)
confiserie f

confer [kənˈfəːʳ] vt: **to ~ sth on** conférer
qch à ▷ vi conférer, s'entretenir

conference [ˈkɒnfərns] n conférence f

confess [kənˈfɛs] vt confesser, avouer
▷ vi (admit sth) avouer; (Rel) se confesser;
confession [kənˈfɛʃən] n confession f

confide [kənˈfaɪd] vi: **to ~ in** s'ouvrir à, se
confier à

confidence [ˈkɒnfɪdns] n confiance
f; (also: **self-~**) assurance f, confiance
en soi; (secret) confidence f; **in ~** (speak,
write) en confidence, confidentiellement;
confident adj (self-assured) sûr(e) de soi;
(sure) sûr; **confidential** [kɒnfɪˈdɛnʃəl] adj
confidentiel(le)

confine [kənˈfaɪn] vt limiter, borner; (shut
up) confiner, enfermer; **confined** adj (space)
restreint(e), réduit(e)

confirm [kənˈfəːm] vt (report, Rel)
confirmer; (appointment) ratifier;
confirmation [kɒnfəˈmeɪʃən] n
confirmation f; ratification f

confiscate [ˈkɒnfɪskeɪt] vt confisquer

conflict n [ˈkɒnflɪkt] conflit m, lutte f ▷ vi
[kənˈflɪkt] (opinions) s'opposer, se heurter

conform [kənˈfɔːm] vi: **to ~ (to)** se
conformer (à)

confront [kənˈfrʌnt] vt (two people)
confronter; (enemy, danger) affronter, faire
face à; (problem) faire face à; **confrontation**
[kɒnfrənˈteɪʃən] n confrontation f

confuse [kənˈfjuːz] vt (person) troubler;
(situation) embrouiller; (one thing with
another) confondre; **confused** adj (person)
dérouté(e), désorienté(e); (situation)
embrouillé(e); **confusing** adj peu clair(e),
déroutant(e); **confusion** [kənˈfjuːʒən] n
confusion f

congestion [kənˈdʒɛstʃən] n (Med)
congestion f; (fig: traffic) encombrement m

congratulate [kənˈgrætjuleɪt] vt: **to ~
sb (on)** féliciter qn (de); **congratulations**
[kəngrætjuˈleɪʃənz] npl: **congratulations
(on)** félicitations fpl (pour) ▷ excl:
congratulations! (toutes mes)
félicitations!

congregation [kɒŋgrɪˈgeɪʃən] n
assemblée f (des fidèles)

congress [ˈkɒŋgrɛs] n congrès m; (Pol): **C~**
Congrès m; **congressman** (irreg) n membre
m du Congrès; **congresswoman** (irreg) n
membre m du Congrès

conifer [ˈkɒnɪfəʳ] n conifère m

conjugate [ˈkɒndʒugeɪt] vt conjuguer

conjugation [kɒndʒəˈgeɪʃən] n
conjugaison f

conjunction [kənˈdʒʌŋkʃən] n conjonction
f; **in ~ with** (conjointement) avec

conjure [ˈkʌndʒəʳ] vi faire des tours de
passe-passe

connect [kəˈnɛkt] vt joindre, relier;
(Elec) connecter; (Tel: caller) mettre
en connexion; (: subscriber) brancher;
(fig) établir un rapport entre, faire un
rapprochement entre ▷ vi (train): **to ~
with** assurer la correspondance avec; **to
be ~ed with** avoir un rapport avec; (have
dealings with) avoir des rapports avec, être
en relation avec; **connecting flight** n
(vol m de) correspondance f; **connection**
[kəˈnɛkʃən] n relation f, lien m; (Elec)
connexion f; (Tel) communication f; (train
etc) correspondance f

conquer [ˈkɒŋkəʳ] vt conquérir; (feelings)
vaincre, surmonter

conquest [ˈkɒŋkwɛst] n conquête f

cons [kɒnz] npl see **convenience; pro**

conscience [ˈkɒnʃəns] n conscience f

conscientious [kɒnʃɪˈɛnʃəs] adj
consciencieux(-euse)

conscious [ˈkɒnʃəs] adj conscient(e);
(deliberate: insult, error) délibéré(e);
consciousness n conscience f; (Med)
connaissance f

consecutive [kənˈsɛkjutɪv] adj
consécutif(-ive); **on three ~ occasions** trois
fois de suite

consensus [kənˈsɛnsəs] n consensus m

consent [kənˈsɛnt] n consentement m ▷ vi:
to ~ (to) consentir (à)

consequence [ˈkɒnsɪkwəns] n suites fpl,
conséquence f; (significance) importance f

consequently [ˈkɒnsɪkwəntlɪ] adv par
conséquent, donc

conservation [kɒnsəˈveɪʃən] n
préservation f, protection f; (also: **nature ~**)
défense f de l'environnement

Conservative [kənˈsəːvətɪv] adj, n (BRIT
Pol) conservateur(-trice)

conservative adj conservateur(-trice);
(cautious) prudent(e)

conservatory [kənˈsəːvətrɪ] n (room)
jardin m d'hiver; (Mus) conservatoire m

consider [kənˈsɪdəʳ] vt (study) considérer,
réfléchir à; (take into account) penser à,
prendre en considération; (regard, judge)
considérer, estimer; **to ~ doing sth**
envisager de faire qch; **considerable**
adj considérable; **considerably** adv
nettement; **considerate** adj prévenant(e),
plein(e) d'égards; **consideration**
[kənsɪdəˈreɪʃən] n considération f; (reward)
rétribution f, rémunération f; **considering**
prep: **considering (that)** étant donné (que)

consignment [kənˈsaɪnmənt] n arrivage
m, envoi m

consist [kənˈsɪst] vi: **to ~ of** consister en, se
composer de

consistency [kənˈsɪstənsɪ] n (thickness)
consistance f; (fig) cohérence f

consistent [kənˈsɪstənt] adj logique,
cohérent(e)

consolation [kɔnsə'leɪʃən] n consolation f
console¹ [kən'səul] vt consoler
console² ['kɔnsəul] n console f
consonant ['kɔnsənənt] n consonne f
conspicuous [kən'spɪkjuəs] adj voyant(e), qui attire l'attention
conspiracy [kən'spɪrəsɪ] n conspiration f, complot m
constable ['kʌnstəbl] n (BRIT) ≈ agent de police, gendarme m; **chief ~** ≈ préfet m de police
constant ['kɔnstənt] adj constant(e); incessant(e); **constantly** adv constamment, sans cesse
constipated ['kɔnstɪpeɪtɪd] adj constipé(e); **constipation** [kɔnstɪ'peɪʃən] n constipation f
constituency [kən'stɪtjuənsɪ] n (Pol: area) circonscription électorale; (: electors) électorat m
constitute ['kɔnstɪtjuːt] vt constituer
constitution [kɔnstɪ'tjuːʃən] n constitution f
constraint [kən'streɪnt] n contrainte f
construct [kən'strʌkt] vt construire; **construction** [kən'strʌkʃən] n construction f; **constructive** adj constructif(-ive)
consul ['kɔnsl] n consul m; **consulate** ['kɔnsjulɪt] n consulat m
consult [kən'sʌlt] vt consulter; **consultant** n (Med) médecin consultant; (other specialist) consultant m, (expert-)conseil m; **consultation** [kɔnsəl'teɪʃən] n consultation f; **consulting room** n (BRIT) cabinet m de consultation
consume [kən'sjuːm] vt consommer; (subj: flames, hatred, desire) consumer; **consumer** n consommateur(-trice)
consumption [kən'sʌmpʃən] n consommation f
cont. abbr (= continued) suite
contact ['kɔntækt] n contact m; (person) connaissance f, relation f ▷ vt se mettre en contact or en rapport avec; **~ number** numéro m de téléphone; **contact lenses** npl verres mpl de contact
contagious [kən'teɪdʒəs] adj contagieux(-euse)
contain [kən'teɪn] vt contenir; **to ~ o.s.** se contenir, se maîtriser; **container** n récipient m; (for shipping etc) conteneur m
contaminate [kən'tæmɪneɪt] vt contaminer
cont'd abbr (= continued) suite
contemplate ['kɔntəmpleɪt] vt contempler; (consider) envisager
contemporary [kən'tempərərɪ] adj contemporain(e); (design, wallpaper) moderne ▷ n contemporain(e)
contempt [kən'tempt] n mépris m, dédain m; **~ of court** (Law) outrage m à l'autorité de la justice

contend [kən'tend] vt: **to ~ that** soutenir or prétendre que ▷ vi: **to ~ with** (compete) rivaliser avec; (struggle) lutter avec
content adj [kən'tent] content(e), satisfait(e) ▷ vt contenter, satisfaire ▷ n ['kɔntent] contenu m; (of fat, moisture) teneur f; **contents** npl (of container etc) contenu m; **(table of) ~s** table f des matières; **contented** adj content(e), satisfait(e)
contest n ['kɔntest] combat m, lutte f; (competition) concours m ▷ vt [kən'test] contester, disputer; (compete for) disputer; (Law) attaquer; **contestant** [kən'testənt] n concurrent(e); (in fight) adversaire m/f
context ['kɔntekst] n contexte m
continent ['kɔntɪnənt] n continent m; **the C~** (BRIT) l'Europe continentale; **continental** [kɔntɪ'nentl] adj continental(e); **continental breakfast** n café (or thé) complet; **continental quilt** n (BRIT) couette f
continual [kən'tɪnjuəl] adj continuel(le); **continually** adv continuellement, sans cesse
continue [kən'tɪnjuː] vi continuer ▷ vt continuer; (start again) reprendre
continuity [kɔntɪ'njuːɪtɪ] n continuité f; (TV) enchaînement m
continuous [kən'tɪnjuəs] adj continu(e), permanent(e); (Ling) progressif(-ive); **continuous assessment** (BRIT) n contrôle continu; **continuously** adv (repeatedly) continuellement; (uninterruptedly) sans interruption
contour ['kɔntuər] n contour m, profil m; (also: **~ line**) courbe f de niveau
contraception [kɔntrə'sepʃən] n contraception f
contraceptive [kɔntrə'septɪv] adj contraceptif(-ive), anticonceptionnel(le) ▷ n contraceptif m
contract n ['kɔntrækt] contrat m ▷ vi [kən'trækt] (become smaller) se contracter, se resserrer ▷ vt [kən'trækt] contracter; (Comm): **to ~ to do sth** s'engager (par contrat) à faire qch; **contractor** n entrepreneur m
contradict [kɔntrə'dɪkt] vt contredire; **contradiction** [kɔntrə'dɪkʃən] n contradiction f
contrary¹ ['kɔntrərɪ] adj contraire, opposé(e) ▷ n contraire m; **on the ~** au contraire; **unless you hear to the ~** sauf avis contraire
contrary² [kən'treərɪ] adj (perverse) contrariant(e), entêté(e)
contrast n ['kɔntrɑːst] contraste m ▷ vt [kən'trɑːst] mettre en contraste, contraster; **in ~ to** or **with** contrairement à, par opposition à
contribute [kən'trɪbjuːt] vi contribuer ▷ vt: **to ~ £10/an article to** donner

10 livres/un article à; **to ~ to** (*gen*)
contribuer à; (*newspaper*) collaborer à;
(*discussion*) prendre part à; **contribution**
[kɔntrɪˈbjuːʃən] *n* contribution *f*; (BRIT: *for
social security*) cotisation *f*; (*to publication*)
article *m*; **contributor** *n* (*to newspaper*)
collaborateur(-trice); (*of money, goods*)
donateur(-trice)

control [kənˈtrəul] *vt* (*process, machinery*)
commander; (*temper*) maîtriser; (*disease*)
enrayer ▷ *n* maîtrise *f*; (*power*) autorité *f*;
controls *npl* (*of machine etc*) commandes
fpl; (*on radio*) boutons *mpl* de réglage; **to be
in ~ of** être maître de, maîtriser; (*in charge
of*) être responsable de; **everything is
under ~** j'ai (*or il a etc*) la situation en main;
the car went out of ~ j'ai (*or il a etc*) perdu
le contrôle du véhicule; **control tower** *n*
(*Aviat*) tour *f* de contrôle

controversial [kɔntrəˈvəːʃl] *adj* discutable,
controversé(e)

controversy [ˈkɔntrəvəːsɪ] *n* controverse
f, polémique *f*

convenience [kənˈviːnɪəns] *n* commodité
f; **at your ~** quand *or* comme cela vous
convient; **all modern ~s, all mod cons**
(BRIT) avec tout le confort moderne, tout
confort

convenient [kənˈviːnɪənt] *adj* commode

convent [ˈkɔnvənt] *n* couvent *m*

convention [kənˈvɛnʃən] *n* convention
f; (*custom*) usage *m*; **conventional** *adj*
conventionnel(le)

conversation [kɔnvəˈseɪʃən] *n*
conversation *f*

conversely [kɔnˈvəːslɪ] *adv* inversement,
réciproquement

conversion [kənˈvəːʃən] *n* conversion
f; (BRIT: *of house*) transformation *f*,
aménagement *m*; (*Rugby*) transformation *f*

convert *vt* [kənˈvəːt] (*Rel, Comm*) convertir;
(*alter*) transformer; (*house*) aménager ▷ *n*
[ˈkɔnvəːt] converti(e); **convertible** *adj*
convertible ▷ *n* (*voiture f*) décapotable *f*

convey [kənˈveɪ] *vt* transporter; (*thanks*)
transmettre; (*idea*) communiquer;
conveyor belt *n* convoyeur *m* tapis
roulant

convict *vt* [kənˈvɪkt] déclarer (*or
reconnaître*) coupable ▷ *n* [ˈkɔnvɪkt] forçat
m, convict *m*; **conviction** [kənˈvɪkʃən] *n*
(*Law*) condamnation *f*; (*belief*) conviction *f*

convince [kənˈvɪns] *vt* convaincre,
persuader; **convinced** *adj*: **convinced of/
that** convaincu(e) de/que; **convincing** *adj*
persuasif(-ive), convaincant(e)

convoy [ˈkɔnvɔɪ] *n* convoi *m*

cook [kuk] *vt* (*faire*) cuire ▷ *vi* cuire;
(*person*) faire la cuisine ▷ *n* cuisinier(-ière);
cookbook *n* livre *m* de cuisine; **cooker** *n*
cuisinière *f*; **cookery** *n* cuisine *f*; **cookery
book** *n* (BRIT) = **cookbook**; **cookie** *n* (US)

biscuit *m*, petit gâteau sec; **cooking** *n*
cuisine *f*

cool [kuːl] *adj* frais (fraîche); (*not afraid*)
calme; (*unfriendly*) froid(e); (*inf: trendy*)
cool *inv* (*inf*); (*: great*) super *inv* (*inf*) ▷ *vt, vi*
rafraîchir, refroidir; **cool down** *vi* refroidir;
(*fig: person, situation*) se calmer; **cool off** *vi*
(*become calmer*) se calmer; (*lose enthusiasm*)
perdre son enthousiasme

cop [kɔp] *n* (*inf*) flic *m*

cope [kəup] *vi* s'en sortir, tenir le coup; **to ~
with** (*problem*) faire face à

copper [ˈkɔpər] *n* cuivre *m*; (BRIT *inf: police
officer*) flic *m*

copy [ˈkɔpɪ] *n* copie *f*; (*book etc*) exemplaire
m ▷ *vt* copier; (*imitate*) imiter; **copyright** *n*
droit *m* d'auteur, copyright *m*

coral [ˈkɔrəl] *n* corail *m*

cord [kɔːd] *n* corde *f*; (*fabric*) velours côtelé;
(*Elec*) cordon *m* (d'alimentation), fil *m*
(électrique); **cords** *npl* (*trousers*) pantalon *m*
de velours côtelé; **cordless** *adj* sans fil

corduroy [ˈkɔːdərɔɪ] *n* velours côtelé

core [kɔːr] *n* (*of fruit*) trognon *m*, cœur *m*; (*fig:
of problem etc*) cœur ▷ *vt* enlever le trognon
or le cœur de

coriander [kɔrɪˈændər] *n* coriandre *f*

cork [kɔːk] *n* (*material*) liège *m*; (*of bottle*)
bouchon *m*; **corkscrew** *n* tire-bouchon *m*

corn [kɔːn] *n* (BRIT: *wheat*) blé *m*; (US: *maize*)
maïs *m*; (*on foot*) cor *m*; **~ on the cob** (*Culin*)
épi *m* de maïs au naturel

corned beef [ˈkɔːnd-] *n* corned-beef *m*

corner [ˈkɔːnər] *n* coin *m*; (*in road*) tournant
m, virage *m*; (*Football*) corner *m* ▷ *vt* (*trap:
prey*) acculer; (*fig*) coincer; (*Comm: market*)
accaparer ▷ *vi* prendre un virage; **corner
shop** (BRIT) *n* magasin *m* du coin

cornflakes [ˈkɔːnfleɪks] *npl* cornflakes *mpl*

cornflour [ˈkɔːnflauər] *n* (BRIT) farine *f* de
maïs, maïzena® *f*

cornstarch [ˈkɔːnstɑːtʃ] *n* (US) farine *f* de
maïs, maïzena® *f*

Cornwall [ˈkɔːnwəl] *n* Cornouailles *f*

coronary [ˈkɔrənərɪ] *n*: **~ (thrombosis)**
infarctus *m* (du myocarde), thrombose *f*
coronaire

coronation [kɔrəˈneɪʃən] *n*
couronnement *m*

coroner [ˈkɔrənər] *n* coroner *m*, *officier de
police judiciaire chargé de déterminer les causes
d'un décès*

corporal [ˈkɔːpərl] *n* caporal *m*, brigadier *m*
▷ *adj*: **~ punishment** châtiment corporel

corporate [ˈkɔːpərɪt] *adj* (*action, ownership*)
en commun; (*Comm*) de la société

corporation [kɔːpəˈreɪʃən] *n* (*of town*)
municipalité *f*, conseil municipal; (*Comm*)
société *f*

corps (*pl* **corps**) [kɔːr, kɔːz] *n* corps *m*; **the
diplomatic ~** le corps diplomatique; **the
press ~** la presse

corpse [kɔːps] n cadavre m
correct [kə'rɛkt] adj (accurate) correct(e),
exact(e); (proper) correct, convenable
▷ vt corriger; **correction** [kə'rɛkʃən] n
correction f
correspond [kɔrɪs'pɔnd] vi correspondre;
to ~ to sth (be equivalent to) correspondre à
qch; **correspondence** n correspondance
f; **correspondent** n correspondant(e);
corresponding adj correspondant(e)
corridor ['kɔrɪdɔː'] n couloir m, corridor m
corrode [kə'rəud] vt corroder, ronger ▷ vi
se corroder
corrupt [kə'rʌpt] adj corrompu(e); (Comput)
altéré(e) ▷ vt corrompre; (Comput) altérer;
corruption n corruption f; (Comput)
altération f (de données)
Corsica ['kɔːsɪkə] n Corse f
cosmetic [kɔz'mɛtɪk] n produit m de
beauté, cosmétique m ▷ adj (fig: reforms)
symbolique, superficiel(le); **cosmetic
surgery** n chirurgie f esthétique
cosmopolitan [kɔzmə'pɔlɪtn] adj
cosmopolite
cost [kɔst] n (pt, pp **cost**) n coût m ▷ vi coûter
▷ vt établir or calculer le prix de revient de;
costs npl (Comm) frais mpl; (Law) dépens
mpl; **how much does it ~?** combien ça
coûte?; **to ~ sb time/effort** demander du
temps/un effort à qn; **it ~ him his life/job**
ça lui a coûté la vie/son emploi; **at all ~s**
coûte que coûte, à tout prix
co-star ['kəustɑː'] n partenaire m/f
costly ['kɔstlɪ] adj coûteux(-euse)
cost of living n coût m de la vie
costume ['kɔstjuːm] n costume m; (Brit:
also: **swimming ~**) maillot m (de bain)
cosy, (US) **cozy** ['kəuzɪ] adj (room, bed)
douillet(te); **to be ~** (person) être bien (au
chaud)
cot [kɔt] n (Brit: child's) lit m d'enfant, petit
lit; (US: campbed) lit de camp
cottage ['kɔtɪdʒ] n petite maison (à la
campagne), cottage m; **cottage cheese** n
fromage blanc (maigre)
cotton ['kɔtn] n coton m; (thread) fil m (de
coton); **cotton on** vi (inf): **to ~ on (to sth)**
piger (qch); **cotton bud** (Brit) n coton-
tige® m; **cotton candy** (US) n barbe f à
papa; **cotton wool** n (Brit) ouate f, coton
m hydrophile
couch [kautʃ] n canapé m; divan m
cough [kɔf] vi tousser ▷ n toux f; **I've got
a ~** j'ai la toux; **cough mixture, cough
syrup** n sirop m pour la toux
could [kud] pt of **can²**; **couldn't** = **could
not**
council ['kaunsl] n conseil m; **city** or **town
~** conseil municipal; **council estate** n (Brit)
(quartier m or zone f de) logements loués
à/par la municipalité; **council house** n
(Brit) maison f (à loyer modéré) louée par la

municipalité; **councillor**, (US) **councilor** n
conseiller(-ère); **council tax** n (Brit) impôts
locaux
counsel ['kaunsl] n conseil m; (lawyer)
avocat(e) ▷ vt: **to ~ (sb to do sth)** conseiller
(à qn de faire qch); **counselling**, (US)
counseling n (Psych) aide psychosociale;
counsellor, (US) **counselor** n
conseiller(-ère); (US Law) avocat m
count [kaunt] vt, vi compter ▷ n compte m;
(nobleman) comte m; **count in** vt (inf): **to ~
sb in on sth** inclure qn dans qch; **count on**
vt fus compter sur; **countdown** n compte
m à rebours
counter ['kauntə'] n comptoir m; (in post
office, bank) guichet m; (in game) jeton m
▷ vt aller à l'encontre de, opposer ▷ adv:
~ to à l'encontre de; contrairement à;
counterclockwise (US) adv en sens inverse
des aiguilles d'une montre
counterfeit ['kauntəfɪt] n faux m,
contrefaçon f ▷ vt contrefaire ▷ adj faux
(fausse)
counterpart ['kauntəpɑːt] n (of person)
homologue m/f
countess ['kauntɪs] n comtesse f
countless ['kauntlɪs] adj innombrable
country ['kʌntrɪ] n pays m; (native land)
patrie f; (as opposed to town) campagne
f; (region) région f, pays, **country and
western (music)** n musique f country;
country house n manoir m, (petit)
château; **countryside** n campagne f
county ['kauntɪ] n comté m
coup (pl **coups**) [kuː, kuːz] n (achievement)
beau coup, (also: **~ d'état**) coup d'État
couple ['kʌpl] n couple m; **a ~ of** (two) deux;
(a few) deux ou trois
coupon ['kuːpɔn] n (voucher) bon m de
réduction; (detachable form) coupon m
détachable, coupon-réponse m
courage ['kʌrɪdʒ] n courage m;
courageous [kə'reɪdʒəs] adj
courageux(-euse)
courgette [kuə'ʒɛt] n (Brit) courgette f
courier ['kurɪə'] n messager m, courrier m;
(for tourists) accompagnateur(-trice)
course [kɔːs] n cours m; (of ship) route f; (for
golf) terrain m; (part of meal) plat m; **of ~** adv
bien sûr; **(no,) of ~ not!** bien sûr que non!,
évidemment que non!; **~ of treatment**
(Med) traitement m
court [kɔːt] n cour f; (Law) cour, tribunal
m; (Tennis) court m ▷ vt (woman) courtiser,
faire la cour à; **to take to ~** actionner or
poursuivre en justice
courtesy ['kɔːtəsɪ] n courtoisie f, politesse
f; **(by) ~ of** avec l'aimable autorisation de;
courtesy bus, courtesy coach n navette
gratuite
court: court-house ['kɔːthaus] n (US)
palais m de justice; **courtroom** ['kɔːtrum]

n salle *f* de tribunal; **courtyard** ['kɔ:tjɑ:d] *n* cour *f*

cousin ['kʌzn] *n* cousin(e); **first ~** cousin(e) germain(e)

cover ['kʌvə^r] *vt* couvrir; (*Press: report on*) faire un reportage sur; (*feelings, mistake*) cacher; (*include*) englober; (*discuss*) traiter ▷ *n* (*of book, Comm*) couverture *f*; (*of pan*) couvercle *m*; (*over furniture*) housse *f*; (*shelter*) abri *m*; **covers** *npl* (*on bed*) couvertures; **to take ~** se mettre à l'abri; **under ~** à l'abri; **under ~ of darkness** à la faveur de la nuit; **under separate ~** (*Comm*) sous pli séparé; **cover up** *vi*: **to ~ up for sb** (*fig*) couvrir qn; **coverage** *n* (*in media*) reportage *m*; **cover charge** *n* couvert *m* (*supplément à payer*); **cover-up** *n* tentative *f* pour étouffer une affaire

cow [kau] *n* vache *f* ▷ *vt* effrayer, intimider

coward ['kauəd] *n* lâche *m/f*; **cowardly** *adj* lâche

cowboy ['kaubɔı] *n* cow-boy *m*

cozy ['kəuzı] *adj* (*us*) = **cosy**

crab [kræb] *n* crabe *m*

crack [kræk] *n* (*split*) fente *f*, fissure *f*; (*in cup, bone*) fêlure *f*; (*in wall*) lézarde *f*; (*noise*) craquement *m*, coup (sec); (*Drugs*) crack *m* ▷ *vt* fendre, fissurer; fêler; lézarder; (*whip*) faire claquer; (*nut*) casser; (*problem*) résoudre; (*code*) déchiffrer ▷ *cpd* (*athlete*) de première classe, d'élite; **crack down on** *vt fus* (*crime*) sévir contre, réprimer; **cracked** *adj* (*cup, bone*) fêlé(e); (*broken*) cassé(e); (*wall*) lézardé(e); (*surface*) craquelé(e); (*inf*) toqué(e), timbré(e); **cracker** *n* (*also*: **Christmas cracker**) pétard *m*; (*biscuit*) biscuit (salé), craquelin *m*

crackle ['krækl] *vi* crépiter, grésiller

cradle ['kreıdl] *n* berceau *m*

craft [krɑ:ft] *n* métier (artisanal); (*cunning*) ruse *f*, astuce *f*; (*boat: pl inv*) embarcation *f*, barque *f*; (*plane: pl inv*) appareil *m*; **craftsman** (*irreg*) *n* artisan *m* ouvrier (qualifié); **craftsmanship** *n* métier *m*, habileté *f*

cram [kræm] *vt*: **to ~ sth with** (*fill*) bourrer qch de; **to ~ sth into** (*put*) fourrer qch dans ▷ *vi* (*for exams*) bachoter

cramp [kræmp] *n* crampe *f*; **I've got ~ in my leg** j'ai une crampe à la jambe; **cramped** *adj* à l'étroit, très serré(e)

cranberry ['krænbərı] *n* canneberge *f*

crane [kreın] *n* grue *f*

crap [kræp] *n* (*inf!: nonsense*) conneries *fpl* (!); (: *excrement*) merde *f* (!)

crash [kræʃ] *n* (*noise*) fracas *m*; (*of car, plane*) collision *f*; (*of business*) faillite *f* ▷ *vt* (*plane*) écraser ▷ *vi* (*plane*) s'écraser; (*two cars*) se percuter, s'emboutir; (*business*) s'effondrer; **to ~ into** se jeter *or* se fracasser contre; **crash course** *n* cours intensif; **crash helmet** *n* casque (protecteur)

crate [kreıt] *n* cageot *m*; (*for bottles*) caisse *f*

crave [kreıv] *vt, vi*: **to ~ (for)** avoir une envie irrésistible de

crawl [krɔ:l] *vi* ramper; (*vehicle*) avancer au pas ▷ *n* (*Swimming*) crawl *m*

crayfish ['kreıfıʃ] *n* (*pl inv: freshwater*) écrevisse *f*; (: *saltwater*) langoustine *f*

crayon ['kreıən] *n* crayon *m* (de couleur)

craze [kreız] *n* engouement *m*

crazy ['kreızı] *adj* fou (folle); **to be ~ about sb/sth** (*inf*) être fou de qn/qch

creak [kri:k] *vi* (*hinge*) grincer; (*floor, shoes*) craquer

cream [kri:m] *n* crème *f* ▷ *adj* (*colour*) crème *inv*; **cream cheese** *n* fromage *m* à la crème, fromage blanc; **creamy** *adj* crémeux(-euse)

crease [kri:s] *n* pli *m* ▷ *vt* froisser, chiffonner ▷ *vi* se froisser, se chiffonner

create [kri:'eıt] *vt* créer; **creation** [kri:'eıʃən] *n* création *f*; **creative** *adj* créatif(-ive); **creator** *n* créateur(-trice)

creature ['kri:tʃə^r] *n* créature *f*

crèche [kreʃ] *n* garderie *f*, crèche *f*

credentials [krı'denʃlz] *npl* (*references*) références *fpl*; (*identity papers*) pièce *f* d'identité

credibility [kredı'bılıtı] *n* crédibilité *f*

credible ['kredıbl] *adj* digne de foi, crédible

credit ['kredıt] *n* crédit *m*; (*recognition*) honneur *m*; (*Scol*) unité *f* de valeur *f* ▷ *vt* (*Comm*) créditer; (*believe: also*: **give ~ to**) ajouter foi à, croire; **credits** *npl* (*Cine*) générique *m*; **to be in ~** (*person, bank account*) être créditeur(-trice); **to ~ sb with** (*fig*) prêter *or* attribuer à qn; **credit card** *n* carte *f* de crédit; **do you take credit cards?** acceptez-vous les cartes de crédit?; **credit crunch** *n* crise *f* du crédit

creek [kri:k] *n* (*inlet*) crique *f*, anse *f*; (*us: stream*) ruisseau *m*, petit cours d'eau

creep (*pt, pp* **crept**) [kri:p, krept] *vi* ramper

cremate [krı'meıt] *vt* incinérer

crematorium (*pl* **crematoria**) [kremə'tɔ:rıəm, -'tɔ:rıə] *n* four *m* crématoire

crept [krept] *pt, pp of* **creep**

crescent ['kresnt] *n* croissant *m*; (*street*) rue *f* (en arc de cercle)

cress [kres] *n* cresson *m*

crest [krest] *n* crête *f*; (*of coat of arms*) timbre *m*

crew [kru:] *n* équipage *m*; (*Cine*) équipe *f* (de tournage); **crew-neck** *n* col ras

crib [krıb] *n* lit *m* d'enfant; (*for baby*) berceau *m* ▷ *vt* (*inf*) copier

cricket ['krıkıt] *n* (*insect*) grillon *m*, cri-cri *m inv*; (*game*) cricket *m*; **cricketer** *n* joueur *m* de cricket

crime [kraım] *n* crime *m*; **criminal** ['krımınl] *adj, n* criminel(le)

crimson ['krımzn] *adj* cramoisi(e)

cringe [krɪndʒ] *vi* avoir un mouvement de recul

cripple ['krɪpl] *n* (*pej*) boiteux(-euse), infirme *m/f* ▷ *vt* (*person*) estropier, paralyser; (*ship, plane*) immobiliser; (*production, exports*) paralyser

crisis (*pl* **crises**) ['kraɪsɪs, -siːz] *n* crise *f*

crisp [krɪsp] *adj* croquant(e); (*weather*) vif (vive); (*manner etc*) brusque; **crisps** (BRIT) *npl* (pommes *fpl*) chips *fpl*; **crispy** *adj* croustillant(e)

criterion (*pl* **criteria**) [kraɪ'tɪərɪən, -'tɪərɪə] *n* critère *m*

critic ['krɪtɪk] *n* critique *m/f*; **critical** *adj* critique; **criticism** ['krɪtɪsɪzəm] *n* critique *f*; **criticize** ['krɪtɪsaɪz] *vt* critiquer

Croat ['krəʊæt] *adj, n* = **Croatian**

Croatia [krəʊ'eɪʃə] *n* Croatie *f*; **Croatian** *adj* croate ▷ *n* Croate *m/f*; (*Ling*) croate *m*

crockery ['krɒkərɪ] *n* vaisselle *f*

crocodile ['krɒkədaɪl] *n* crocodile *m*

crocus ['krəʊkəs] *n* crocus *m*

croissant ['krwɑsɑ̃] *n* croissant *m*

crook [krʊk] *n* (*inf*) escroc *m*; (*of shepherd*) houlette *f*; **crooked** ['krʊkɪd] *adj* courbé(e), tordu(e); (*action*) malhonnête

crop [krɒp] *n* (*produce*) culture *f*; (*amount produced*) récolte *f*; (*riding crop*) cravache *f* ▷ *vt* (*hair*) tondre; **crop up** *vi* surgir, se présenter, survenir

cross [krɒs] *n* croix *f*; (*Biol*) croisement *m* ▷ *vt* (*street etc*) traverser; (*arms, legs, Biol*) croiser; (*cheque*) barrer ▷ *adj* en colère, fâché(e); **cross off, cross out** *vt* barrer, rayer; **cross over** *vi* traverser; **cross-Channel ferry** ['krɒs'tʃænl-] *n* ferry *m* qui fait la traversée de la Manche; **cross-country (race)** *n* cross(-country) *m*; **crossing** *n* (*sea passage*) traversée *f*; (*also:* **pedestrian crossing**) passage clouté; **how long does the crossing take?** combien de temps dure la traversée?; **crossing guard** *n* (US) contractuel qui fait traverser la rue aux enfants; **crossroads** *n* carrefour *m*; **crosswalk** *n* (US) passage clouté; **crossword** *n* mots *mpl* croisés

crotch [krɒtʃ] *n* (*of garment*) entrejambe *m*; (*Anat*) entrecuisse *m*

crouch [krautʃ] *vi* s'accroupir; (*hide*) se tapir; (*before springing*) se ramasser

crouton ['kruːtɒn] *n* croûton *m*

crow [krəʊ] *n* (*bird*) corneille *f*; (*of cock*) chant *m* du coq, cocorico *m* ▷ *vi* (*cock*) chanter

crowd [kraud] *n* foule *f* ▷ *vt* bourrer, remplir ▷ *vi* affluer, s'attrouper, s'entasser; **crowded** *adj* bondé(e)

crown [kraun] *n* couronne *f*; (*of head*) sommet *m* de la tête; (*of hill*) sommet *m* ▷ *vt* (*also tooth*) couronner; **crown jewels** *npl* joyaux *mpl* de la Couronne

crucial ['kruːʃl] *adj* crucial(e), décisif(-ive)

crucifix ['kruːsɪfɪks] *n* crucifix *m*

crude [kruːd] *adj* (*materials*) brut(e); non raffiné(e); (*basic*) rudimentaire, sommaire; (*vulgar*) cru(e), grossier(-ière) ▷ *n* (*also:* **~ oil**) (pétrole *m*) brut *m*

cruel ['kruəl] *adj* cruel(le); **cruelty** *n* cruauté *f*

cruise [kruːz] *n* croisière *f* ▷ *vi* (*ship*) croiser; (*car*) rouler; (*aircraft*) voler

crumb [krʌm] *n* miette *f*

crumble ['krʌmbl] *vt* émietter ▷ *vi* (*plaster etc*) s'effriter; (*land, earth*) s'ébouler; (*building*) s'écrouler, crouler; (*fig*) s'effondrer

crumpet ['krʌmpɪt] *n* petite crêpe (épaisse)

crumple ['krʌmpl] *vt* froisser, friper

crunch [krʌntʃ] *vt* croquer; (*underfoot*) faire craquer, écraser; faire crisser ▷ *n* (*fig*) instant *m* or moment *m* critique, moment de vérité; **crunchy** *adj* croquant(e), croustillant(e)

crush [krʌʃ] *n* (*crowd*) foule *f*, cohue *f*; (*love*): **to have a ~ on sb** avoir le béguin pour qn; (*drink*): **lemon ~** citron pressé ▷ *vt* écraser; (*crumple*) froisser; (*grind, break up: garlic, ice*) piler; (: *grapes*) presser; (*hopes*) anéantir

crust [krʌst] *n* croûte *f*; **crusty** *adj* (*bread*) croustillant(e); (*inf: person*) revêche, bourru(e)

crutch [krʌtʃ] *n* béquille *f*; (*of garment*) entrejambe *m*; (*Anat*) entrecuisse *m*

cry [kraɪ] *vi* pleurer; (*shout: also:* **~ out**) crier ▷ *n* cri *m*; **cry out** *vi* (*call out, shout*) pousser un cri ▷ *vt* crier

crystal ['krɪstl] *n* cristal *m*

cub [kʌb] *n* petit *m* (*d'un animal*); (*also:* **~ scout**) louveteau *m*

Cuba ['kjuːbə] *n* Cuba *m*

cube [kjuːb] *n* cube *m* ▷ *vt* (*Math*) élever au cube

cubicle ['kjuːbɪkl] *n* (*in hospital*) box *m*; (*at pool*) cabine *f*

cuckoo ['kʊkuː] *n* coucou *m*

cucumber ['kjuːkʌmbər] *n* concombre *m*

cuddle ['kʌdl] *vt* câliner, caresser ▷ *vi* se blottir l'un contre l'autre

cue [kjuː] *n* queue *f* de billard; (*Theat etc*) signal *m*

cuff [kʌf] *n* (BRIT: *of shirt, coat etc*) poignet *m*, manchette *f*; (US: *on trousers*) revers *m*; (*blow*) gifle *f*; **off the ~** *adv* à l'improviste; **cufflinks** *n* boutons *m* de manchette

cuisine [kwɪ'ziːn] *n* cuisine *f*

cul-de-sac ['kʌldəsæk] *n* cul-de-sac *m*, impasse *f*

cull [kʌl] *vt* sélectionner ▷ *n* (*of animals*) abattage sélectif

culminate ['kʌlmɪneɪt] *vi*: **to ~ in** finir or se terminer par; (*lead to*) mener à

culprit ['kʌlprɪt] *n* coupable *m/f*

cult [kʌlt] *n* culte *m*

cultivate ['kʌltɪveɪt] *vt* cultiver

cultural ['kʌltʃərəl] *adj* culturel(le)

culture [ˈkʌltʃəʳ] n culture f
cumin [ˈkʌmɪn] n (spice) cumin m
cunning [ˈkʌnɪŋ] n ruse f, astuce f ▷ adj
rusé(e), malin(-igne); (clever: device, idea)
astucieux(-euse)
cup [kʌp] n tasse f; (prize, event) coupe f; (of
bra) bonnet m
cupboard [ˈkʌbəd] n placard m
cup final n (BRIT Football) finale f de la
coupe
curator [kjuəˈreɪtəʳ] n conservateur m (d'un
musée etc)
curb [kəːb] vt refréner, mettre un frein à ▷ n
(fig) frein m; (US) bord m du trottoir
curdle [ˈkəːdl] vi (se) cailler
cure [kjuəʳ] vt guérir; (Culin: salt) saler;
(: smoke) fumer; (: dry) sécher ▷ n remède m
curfew [ˈkəːfjuː] n couvre-feu m
curiosity [kjuərɪˈɔsɪtɪ] n curiosité f
curious [ˈkjuərɪəs] adj curieux(-euse);
I'm ~ about him il m'intrigue
curl [kəːl] n boucle f (de cheveux) ▷ vt, vi
boucler; (tightly) friser; **curl up** vi s'enrouler;
(person) se pelotonner; **curler** n bigoudi
m, rouleau m; **curly** adj bouclé(e); (tightly
curled) frisé(e)
currant [ˈkʌrnt] n raisin m de Corinthe,
raisin sec; (fruit) groseille f
currency [ˈkʌrnsɪ] n monnaie f; **to gain ~**
(fig) s'accréditer
current [ˈkʌrnt] n courant m ▷ adj (common)
courant(e); (tendency, price, event) actuel(le);
current account n (BRIT) compte courant;
current affairs npl (questions fpl d')
actualité f; **currently** adv actuellement
curriculum (pl **curriculums** or **curricula**)
[kəˈrɪkjuləm, -lə] n programme m d'études;
curriculum vitae [-ˈviːtaɪ] n curriculum
vitae (CV) m
curry [ˈkʌrɪ] n curry m ▷ vt: **to ~ favour
with** chercher à gagner la faveur or à
s'attirer les bonnes grâces de; **curry
powder** n poudre f de curry
curse [kəːs] vi jurer, blasphémer ▷ vt
maudire ▷ n (spell) malédiction f; (problem,
scourge) fléau m; (swearword) juron m
cursor [ˈkəːsəʳ] n (Comput) curseur m
curt [kəːt] adj brusque, sec (sèche)
curtain [ˈkəːtn] n rideau m
curve [kəːv] n courbe f; (in the road)
tournant m, virage m ▷ vi se courber; (road)
faire une courbe; **curved** adj courbe
cushion [ˈkuʃən] n coussin m ▷ vt (fall,
shock) amortir
custard [ˈkʌstəd] n (for pouring) crème
anglaise
custody [ˈkʌstədɪ] n (of child) garde f; (for
offenders): **to take sb into ~** placer qn en
détention préventive
custom [ˈkʌstəm] n coutume f, usage m;
(Comm) clientèle f
customer [ˈkʌstəməʳ] n client(e)

customized [ˈkʌstəmaɪzd] adj
personnalisé(e); (car etc) construit(e) sur
commande
customs [ˈkʌstəmz] npl douane f; **customs
officer** n douanier m
cut [kʌt] (pt, pp **cut**) vt couper; (meat)
découper; (reduce) réduire ▷ vi couper ▷ n
(gen) coupure f; (of clothes) coupe f; (in salary
etc) réduction f; (of meat) morceau m; **to ~
a tooth** percer une dent; **to ~ one's finger**
se couper le doigt; **to get one's hair ~** se
faire couper les cheveux; **I've ~ myself** je
me suis coupé; **cut back** vt (plants) tailler;
(production, expenditure) réduire; **cut down**
vt (tree) abattre; (reduce) réduire; **cut off** vt
couper; (fig) isoler; **cut out** vt (picture etc)
découper; (remove) supprimer; **cut up** vt
découper; **cutback** n réduction f
cute [kjuːt] adj mignon(ne), adorable
cutlery [ˈkʌtlərɪ] n couverts mpl
cutlet [ˈkʌtlɪt] n côtelette f
cut-price [ˈkʌtˈpraɪs], (US) **cut-rate**
[ˈkʌtˈreɪt] adj au rabais, à prix réduit
cutting [ˈkʌtɪŋ] adj (fig) cinglant(e) ▷ n
(BRIT: from newspaper) coupure f (de journal);
(from plant) bouture f
CV n abbr = **curriculum vitae**
cyberbullying [ˈsaɪbəbulɪɪŋ] n
harcèlement m virtuel
cyberspace [ˈsaɪbəspeɪs] n cyberespace m
cycle [ˈsaɪkl] n cycle m; (bicycle) bicyclette f,
vélo m ▷ vi faire de la bicyclette; **cycle hire**
n location f de vélos; **cycle lane, cycle path**
n piste f cyclable; **cycling** n cyclisme m;
cyclist n cycliste m/f
cyclone [ˈsaɪkləun] n cyclone m
cylinder [ˈsɪlɪndəʳ] n cylindre m
cymbals [ˈsɪmblz] npl cymbales fpl
cynical [ˈsɪnɪkl] adj cynique
Cypriot [ˈsɪprɪət] adj cypriote, chypriote ▷ n
Cypriote m/f, Chypriote m/f
Cyprus [ˈsaɪprəs] n Chypre f
cyst [sɪst] n kyste m; **cystitis** [sɪsˈtaɪtɪs] n
cystite f
czar [zɑːʳ] n tsar m
Czech [tʃɛk] adj tchèque ▷ n Tchèque m/f;
(Ling) tchèque m; **Czech Republic** n: **the
Czech Republic** la République tchèque

d

D [di:] n (Mus) ré m
dab [dæb] vt (eyes, wound) tamponner; (paint, cream) appliquer (par petites touches or rapidement)
dad, daddy [dæd, 'dædɪ] n papa m
daffodil ['dæfədɪl] n jonquille f
daft [dɑːft] adj (inf) idiot(e), stupide
dagger ['dægəʳ] n poignard m
daily ['deɪlɪ] adj quotidien(ne), journalier(-ière) ▷ adv tous les jours
dairy ['dɛərɪ] n (shop) crémerie f, laiterie f; (on farm) laiterie; **dairy produce** n produits laitiers
daisy ['deɪzɪ] n pâquerette f
dam [dæm] n (wall) barrage m, (water) réservoir m, lac m de retenue ▷ vt endiguer
damage ['dæmɪdʒ] n dégâts mpl, dommages mpl; (fig) tort m ▷ vt endommager, abîmer; (fig) faire du tort à; **damages** npl (Law) dommages-intérêts mpl
damn [dæm] vt condamner; (curse) maudire ▷ n (inf): **I don't give a ~** je m'en fous ▷ adj (inf: also: **~ed**): **this ~ ...** ce sacré or foutu ...; **~ (it)!** zut!
damp [dæmp] adj humide ▷ n humidité f ▷ vt (also: **~en**: cloth, rag) humecter; (: enthusiasm etc) refroidir
dance [dɑːns] n danse f; (ball) bal m ▷ vi danser; **dance floor** n piste f de danse; **dancer** n danseur(-euse); **dancing** n danse f
dandelion ['dændɪlaɪən] n pissenlit m
dandruff ['dændrəf] n pellicules fpl
D & T n abbr (BRIT Scol) = **design and technology**
Dane [deɪn] n Danois(e)
danger ['deɪndʒəʳ] n danger m; **~!** (on sign) danger!; **in ~** en danger; **he was in ~ of falling** il risquait de tomber; **dangerous** adj dangereux(-euse)
dangle ['dæŋgl] vt balancer ▷ vi pendre, se balancer

Danish ['deɪnɪʃ] adj danois(e) ▷ n (Ling) danois m
dare [dɛəʳ] vt: **to ~ sb to do** défier qn or mettre qn au défi de faire ▷ vi: **to ~ (to) do sth** oser faire qch; **I ~ say he'll turn up** il est probable qu'il viendra; **daring** adj hardi(e), audacieux(-euse) ▷ n audace f, hardiesse f
dark [dɑːk] adj (night, room) obscur(e), sombre; (colour, complexion) foncé(e), sombre ▷ n: **in the ~** dans le noir; **to be in the ~ about** (fig) ignorer tout de; **after ~** après la tombée de la nuit; **darken** vt obscurcir, assombrir ▷ vi s'obscurcir, s'assombrir; **darkness** n obscurité f; **darkroom** n chambre noire
darling ['dɑːlɪŋ] adj, n chéri(e)
dart [dɑːt] n fléchette f; (in sewing) pince f ▷ vi: **to ~ towards** se précipiter or s'élancer vers; **dartboard** n cible f (de jeu de fléchettes); **darts** n jeu m de fléchettes
dash [dæʃ] n (sign) tiret m; (small quantity) goutte f, larme f ▷ vt (throw) jeter or lancer violemment; (hopes) anéantir ▷ vi: **to ~ towards** se précipiter or se ruer vers
dashboard ['dæʃbɔːd] n (Aut) tableau m de bord
data ['deɪtə] npl données fpl; **database** n base f de données; **data processing** n traitement m des données
date [deɪt] n date f; (with sb) rendez-vous m; (fruit) datte f ▷ vt dater; (person) sortir avec; **~ of birth** date de naissance; **to ~** adv à ce jour; **out of ~** périmé(e); **up to ~** à la page, mis(e) à jour, moderne; **dated** adj démodé(e)
daughter ['dɔːtəʳ] n fille f; **daughter-in-law** n belle-fille f, bru f
daunting ['dɔːntɪŋ] adj décourageant(e), intimidant(e)
dawn [dɔːn] n aube f, aurore f ▷ vi (day) se lever, poindre; **it ~ed on him that ...** il lui vint à l'esprit que ...
day [deɪ] n jour m; (as duration) journée f; (period of time, age) époque f, temps m; **the ~ before** la veille, le jour précédent; **the ~ after, the following ~** le lendemain, le jour suivant; **the ~ before yesterday** avant-hier; **the ~ after tomorrow** après-demain; **by ~** de jour; **day-care centre** ['deɪkɛə-] n (for elderly etc) centre m d'accueil de jour; (for children) garderie f; **daydream** vi rêver (tout éveillé); **daylight** n (lumière f du) jour m; **day return** n (BRIT) billet m d'aller-retour (valable pour la journée); **daytime** n jour m, journée f; **day-to-day** adj (routine, expenses) journalier(-ière); **day trip** n excursion f (d'une journée)
dazed [deɪzd] adj abruti(e)
dazzle ['dæzl] vt éblouir, aveugler; **dazzling** adj (light) aveuglant(e), éblouissant(e); (fig) éblouissant(e)
DC abbr (Elec) = **direct current**

dead [dɛd] *adj* mort(e); (*numb*) engourdi(e),
insensible; (*battery*) à plat ▷ *adv* (*completely*)
absolument, complètement; (*exactly*) juste;
he was shot ~ il a été tué d'un coup de
revolver; **~ tired** éreinté(e), complètement
fourbu(e); **to stop ~** s'arrêter pile *or* net;
the line is ~ (*Tel*) la ligne est coupée; **dead
end** *n* impasse *f*; **deadline** *n* date *f or* heure
f limite; **deadly** *adj* mortel(le); (*weapon*)
meurtrier(-ière); **Dead Sea** *n*: **the Dead
Sea** la mer Morte
deaf [dɛf] *adj* sourd(e); **deafen** *vt* rendre
sourd(e); **deafening** *adj* assourdissant(e)
deal [di:l] *n* affaire *f*, marché *m* ▷ *vt* (*pt,
pp* **dealt**) (*blow*) porter; (*cards*) donner,
distribuer; **a great ~ of** beaucoup de;
deal with *vt fus* (*handle*) s'occuper *or* se
charger de; (*be about*) traiter de; **dealer** *n*
(*Comm*) marchand *m*; (*Cards*) donneur *m*;
dealings *npl* (*in goods, shares*) opérations
fpl, transactions *fpl*; (*relations*) relations *fpl*,
rapports *mpl*
dealt [dɛlt] *pt, pp of* **deal**
dean [di:n] *n* (*Rel*, BRIT *Scol*) doyen *m*;
(*US Scol*) conseiller principal (conseillère
principale) d'éducation
dear [dɪər] *adj* cher (chère); (*expensive*) cher,
coûteux(-euse) ▷ *n*: **my ~** mon cher (ma
chère) ▷ *excl*: **~ me!** mon Dieu!; **D~ Sir/
Madam** (*in letter*) Monsieur/Madame; **D~
Mr/Mrs X** Cher Monsieur/Chère Madame X;
dearly *adv* (*love*) tendrement; (*pay*) cher
death [dɛθ] *n* mort *f*; (*Admin*) décès *m*;
death penalty *n* peine *f* de mort; **death
sentence** *n* condamnation *f* à mort
debate [dɪ'beɪt] *n* discussion *f*, débat *m* ▷ *vt*
discuter, débattre
debit ['dɛbɪt] *n* débit *m* ▷ *vt*: **to ~ a sum to
sb** *or* **to sb's account** porter une somme au
débit de qn, débiter qn d'une somme; **debit
card** *n* carte *f* de paiement
debris ['dɛbri:] *n* débris *mpl*, décombres *mpl*
debt [dɛt] *n* dette *f*; **to be in ~** avoir des
dettes, être endetté(e)
debug [di:'bʌg] *vt* (*Comput*) déboguer
debut ['deɪbju:] *n* début(s) *m(pl)*
Dec. *abbr* (= *December*) déc
decade ['dɛkeɪd] *n* décennie *f*, décade *f*
decaffeinated [dɪ'kæfɪneɪtɪd] *adj*
décaféiné(e)
decay [dɪ'keɪ] *n* (*of food, wood etc*)
décomposition *f*, pourriture *f*; (*of building*)
délabrement *m*; (*also*: **tooth ~**) carie *f*
(dentaire) ▷ *vi* (*rot*) se décomposer, pourrir;
(*teeth*) se carier
deceased [dɪ'si:st] *n*: **the ~** le (la) défunt(e)
deceit [dɪ'si:t] *n* tromperie *f*, supercherie *f*;
deceive [dɪ'si:v] *vt* tromper
December [dɪ'sɛmbər] *n* décembre *m*
decency ['di:sənsɪ] *n* décence *f*
decent ['di:sənt] *adj* (*proper*) décent(e),
convenable

deception [dɪ'sɛpʃən] *n* tromperie *f*
deceptive [dɪ'sɛptɪv] *adj* trompeur(-euse)
decide [dɪ'saɪd] *vt* (*subj: person*) décider;
(*question, argument*) trancher, régler ▷ *vi* se
décider, décider de; **to ~ to do/that** décider de
faire/que; **to ~ on** décider, se décider pour
decimal ['dɛsɪməl] *adj* décimal(e) ▷ *n*
décimale *f*
decision [dɪ'sɪʒən] *n* décision *f*
decisive [dɪ'saɪsɪv] *adj* décisif(-ive);
(*manner, person*) décidé(e), catégorique
deck [dɛk] *n* (*Naut*) pont *m*; (*of cards*) jeu
m; (*record deck*) platine *f*; (*of bus*): **top ~**
impériale *f*; **deckchair** *n* chaise longue
declaration [dɛklə'reɪʃən] *n* déclaration *f*
declare [dɪ'klɛər] *vt* déclarer
decline [dɪ'klaɪn] *n* (*decay*) déclin *m*;
(*lessening*) baisse *f* ▷ *vt* refuser, décliner ▷ *vi*
décliner; (*business*) baisser
decorate ['dɛkəreɪt] *vt* (*adorn, give a medal
to*) décorer; (*paint and paper*) peindre et
tapisser; **decoration** [dɛkə'reɪʃən] *n* (*medal
etc, adornment*) décoration *f*; **decorator** *n*
peintre *m* en bâtiment
decrease *n* ['di:kri:s] diminution *f* ▷ *vt, vi*
[di:'kri:s] diminuer
decree [dɪ'kri:] *n* (*Pol, Rel*) décret *m*; (*Law*)
arrêt *m*, jugement *m*
dedicate ['dɛdɪkeɪt] *vt* consacrer; (*book etc*)
dédier; **dedicated** *adj* (*person*) dévoué(e);
(*Comput*) spécialisé(e), dédié(e); **dedicated
word processor** station *f* de traitement de
texte; **dedication** [dɛdɪ'keɪʃən] *n* (*devotion*)
dévouement *m*; (*in book*) dédicace *f*
deduce [dɪ'dju:s] *vt* déduire, conclure
deduct [dɪ'dʌkt] *vt*: **to ~ sth (from)** déduire
qch (de), retrancher qch (de); **deduction**
[dɪ'dʌkʃən] *n* (*deducting, deducing*)
déduction *f*; (*from wage etc*) prélèvement *m*,
retenue *f*
deed [di:d] *n* action *f*, acte *m*; (*Law*) acte
notarié, contrat *m*
deem [di:m] *vt* (*formal*) juger, estimer
deep [di:p] *adj* profond(e); (*voice*) grave
▷ *adv*: **spectators stood 20 ~** il y avait 20
rangs de spectateurs; **4 metres ~** de 4
mètres de profondeur; **how ~ is the water?**
l'eau a quelle profondeur?; **deep-fry** *vt*
faire frire (dans une friteuse); **deeply** *adv*
profondément; (*regret, interested*) vivement
deer [dɪər] *n* (*pl inv*): (**red**) **~** cerf *m*; (**fallow**)
~ daim *m*; (**roe**) **~** chevreuil *m*
default [dɪ'fɔ:lt] *n* (*Comput: also*: **~ value**)
valeur *f* par défaut; **by ~** (*Law*) par défaut,
par contumace; (*Sport*) par forfait
defeat [dɪ'fi:t] *n* défaite *f* ▷ *vt* (*team,
opponents*) battre
defect *n* ['di:fɛkt] défaut *m* ▷ *vi* [dɪ'fɛkt]:
to ~ to the enemy/the West passer à
l'ennemi/l'Ouest; **defective** [dɪ'fɛktɪv] *adj*
défectueux(-euse)
defence, (*US*) **defense** [dɪ'fɛns] *n* défense *f*

defend [dɪˈfɛnd] vt défendre; **defendant** n défendeur(-deresse); (in criminal case) accusé(e), prévenu(e); **defender** n défenseur m

defense [dɪˈfɛns] n (US) = defence

defensive [dɪˈfɛnsɪv] adj défensif(-ive) ⊳ n: **on the ~** sur la défensive

defer [dɪˈfəːʳ] vt (postpone) différer, ajourner

defiance [dɪˈfaɪəns] n défi m; **in ~ of** au mépris de; **defiant** [dɪˈfaɪənt] adj provocant(e), de défi; (person) rebelle, intraitable

deficiency [dɪˈfɪʃənsɪ] n (lack) insuffisance f (: Med) carence f; (flaw) faiblesse f; **deficient** [dɪˈfɪʃənt] adj (inadequate) insuffisant(e); **to be deficient in** manquer de

deficit [ˈdɛfɪsɪt] n déficit m

define [dɪˈfaɪn] vt définir

definite [ˈdɛfɪnɪt] adj (fixed) défini(e), (bien) déterminé(e); (clear, obvious) net(te), manifeste; (certain) sûr(e); **he was ~ about it** il a été catégorique; **definitely** adv sans aucun doute

definition [dɛfɪˈnɪʃən] n définition f; (clearness) netteté f

deflate [diːˈfleɪt] vt dégonfler

deflect [dɪˈflɛkt] vt détourner, faire dévier

defraud [dɪˈfrɔːd] vt: **to ~ sb of sth** escroquer qch à qn

defriend [diːˈfrɛnd] vt (Internet) supprimer de sa liste d'amis

defrost [diːˈfrɔst] vt (fridge) dégivrer; (frozen food) décongeler

defuse [diːˈfjuːz] vt désamorcer

defy [dɪˈfaɪ] vt défier; (efforts etc) résister à; **it defies description** cela défie toute description

degree [dɪˈgriː] n degré m; (Scol) diplôme m (universitaire); **a (first) ~ in maths** (BRIT) une licence en maths; **by ~s** (gradually) par degrés; **to some ~** jusqu'à un certain point, dans une certaine mesure

dehydrated [diːhaɪˈdreɪtɪd] adj déshydraté(e); (milk, eggs) en poudre

de-icer [ˈdiːˈaɪsəʳ] n dégivreur m

delay [dɪˈleɪ] vt retarder; (payment) différer ⊳ vi s'attarder ⊳ n délai m, retard m; **to be ~ed** être en retard

delegate n [ˈdɛlɪgɪt] délégué(e) ⊳ vt [ˈdɛlɪgeɪt] déléguer

delete [dɪˈliːt] vt rayer, supprimer; (Comput) effacer

deli [ˈdɛlɪ] n épicerie fine

deliberate adj [dɪˈlɪbərɪt] (intentional) délibéré(e); (slow) mesuré(e) ⊳ vi [dɪˈlɪbəreɪt] délibérer, réfléchir; **deliberately** adv (on purpose) exprès, délibérément

delicacy [ˈdɛlɪkəsɪ] n délicatesse f; (choice food) mets fin or délicat, friandise f

delicate [ˈdɛlɪkɪt] adj délicat(e)

delicatessen [dɛlɪkəˈtɛsn] n épicerie fine

delicious [dɪˈlɪʃəs] adj délicieux(-euse)

delight [dɪˈlaɪt] n (grande) joie, grand plaisir ⊳ vt enchanter; **she's a ~ to work with** c'est un plaisir de travailler avec elle; **to take ~ in** prendre grand plaisir à; **delighted** adj: **delighted (at or with sth)** ravi(e) (de qch); **to be delighted to do sth/that** être enchanté(e) or ravi(e) de faire qch/que; **delightful** adj (person) adorable; (meal, evening) merveilleux(-euse)

delinquent [dɪˈlɪŋkwənt] adj, n délinquant(e)

deliver [dɪˈlɪvəʳ] vt (mail) distribuer; (goods) livrer; (message) remettre; (speech) prononcer; (Med: baby) mettre au monde; **delivery** n (of mail) distribution f; (of goods) livraison f; (of speaker) élocution f; (Med) accouchement m; **to take delivery of** prendre livraison de

delusion [dɪˈluːʒən] n illusion f

de luxe [dəˈlʌks] adj de luxe

delve [dɛlv] vi: **to ~ into** fouiller dans

demand [dɪˈmɑːnd] vt réclamer, exiger ⊳ n exigence f; (claim) revendication f; (Econ) demande f; **in ~** demandé(e), recherché(e); **on ~** sur demande; **demanding** adj (person) exigeant(e); (work) astreignant(e)

Be careful not to translate to demand by the French word *demander*.

demise [dɪˈmaɪz] n décès m

demo [ˈdɛməu] n abbr (inf: = demonstration) (protest) manif f; (Comput) démonstration f

democracy [dɪˈmɔkrəsɪ] n démocratie f; **democrat** [ˈdɛməkræt] n démocrate m/f; **democratic** [dɛməˈkrætɪk] adj démocratique

demolish [dɪˈmɔlɪʃ] vt démolir

demolition [dɛməˈlɪʃən] n démolition f

demon [ˈdiːmən] n démon m

demonstrate [ˈdɛmənstreɪt] vt démontrer, prouver; (show) faire une démonstration de ⊳ vi: **to ~ (for/against)** manifester (en faveur de/contre); **demonstration** [dɛmənˈstreɪʃən] n démonstration f; (Pol etc) manifestation f; **demonstrator** n (Pol etc) manifestant(e)

demote [dɪˈməut] vt rétrograder

den [dɛn] n (of lion) tanière f; (room) repaire m

denial [dɪˈnaɪəl] n (of accusation) démenti m; (of rights, guilt, truth) dénégation f

denim [ˈdɛnɪm] n jean m; **denims** npl (blue-)jeans mpl

Denmark [ˈdɛnmɑːk] n Danemark m

denomination [dɪnɔmɪˈneɪʃən] n (money) valeur f; (Rel) confession f

denounce [dɪˈnauns] vt dénoncer

dense [dɛns] adj dense; (inf: stupid) obtus(e)

density [ˈdɛnsɪtɪ] n densité f

dent [dɛnt] n bosse f ⊳ vt (also: **make a ~ in**) cabosser

dental ['dɛntl] *adj* dentaire; **dental floss** [-flɔs] *n* fil *m* dentaire; **dental surgery** *n* cabinet *m* de dentiste

dentist ['dɛntɪst] *n* dentiste *m/f*

dentures ['dɛntʃəz] *npl* dentier *msg*

deny [dɪ'naɪ] *vt* nier; (*refuse*) refuser

deodorant [diː'əudərənt] *n* déodorant *m*

depart [dɪ'pɑːt] *vi* partir; **to ~ from** (*fig: differ from*) s'écarter de

department [dɪ'pɑːtmənt] *n* (*Comm*) rayon *m*; (*Scol*) section *f*; (*Pol*) ministère *m*, département *m*; **department store** *n* grand magasin

departure [dɪ'pɑːtʃər] *n* départ *m*; **a new ~** une nouvelle voie; **departure lounge** *n* salle *f* de départ

depend [dɪ'pɛnd] *vi*: **to ~ (up)on** dépendre de; (*rely on*) compter sur; **it ~s** cela dépend; **~ing on the result ...** selon le résultat ...; **dependant** *n* personne *f* à charge; **dependent** *adj*: **to be dependent (on)** dépendre (de) ▷ *n* = **dependant**

depict [dɪ'pɪkt] *vt* (*in picture*) représenter; (*in words*) (dé)peindre, décrire

deport [dɪ'pɔːt] *vt* déporter, expulser

deposit [dɪ'pɔzɪt] *n* (*Chem, Comm, Geo*) dépôt *m*; (*of ore, oil*) gisement *m*; (*part payment*) arrhes *fpl*, acompte *m*; (*on bottle etc*) consigne *f*; (*for hired goods etc*) cautionnement *m*, garantie *f* ▷ *vt* déposer; **deposit account** *n* compte *m* sur livret

depot ['dɛpəu] *n* dépôt *m*; (*us Rail*) gare *f*

depreciate [dɪ'priːʃɪeɪt] *vi* se déprécier, se dévaloriser

depress [dɪ'prɛs] *vt* déprimer; (*press down*) appuyer sur, abaisser; (*wages etc*) faire baisser; **depressed** *adj* (*person*) déprimé(e); (*area*) en déclin, touché(e) par le sous-emploi; **depressing** *adj* déprimant(e); **depression** [dɪ'prɛʃən] *n* dépression *f*

deprive [dɪ'praɪv] *vt*: **to ~ sb of** priver qn de; **deprived** *adj* déshérité(e)

dept. *abbr* (= *department*) dép, dépt

depth [dɛpθ] *n* profondeur *f*; **to be in the ~s of despair** être au plus profond du désespoir; **to be out of one's ~** (*BRIT: swimmer*) ne plus avoir pied; (*fig*) être dépassé(e), nager

deputy ['dɛpjutɪ] *n* (*second in command*) adjoint(e); (*Pol*) député *m*; (*us: also:* **~ sheriff**) shérif adjoint ▷ *adj*: **~ head** (*Scol*) directeur(-trice) adjoint(e), sous-directeur(-trice)

derail [dɪ'reɪl] *vt*: **to be ~ed** dérailler

derelict ['dɛrɪlɪkt] *adj* abandonné(e), à l'abandon

derive [dɪ'raɪv] *vt*: **to ~ sth from** tirer qch de; trouver qch dans ▷ *vi*: **to ~ from** provenir de, dériver de

descend [dɪ'sɛnd] *vt, vi* descendre; **to ~ from** descendre de, être issu(e) de; **to ~ to**

s'abaisser à; **descendant** *n* descendant(e); **descent** *n* descente *f*; (*origin*) origine *f*

describe [dɪs'kraɪb] *vt* décrire; **description** [dɪs'krɪpʃən] *n* description *f*; (*sort*) sorte *f*, espèce *f*

desert *n* ['dɛzət] désert *m* ▷ *vt* [dɪ'zəːt] déserter, abandonner ▷ *vi* [dɪ'zəːt] (*Mil*) déserter; **deserted** [dɪ'zəːtɪd] *adj* désert(e)

deserve [dɪ'zəːv] *vt* mériter

design [dɪ'zaɪn] *n* (*sketch*) plan *m*, dessin *m*; (*layout, shape*) conception *f*, ligne *f*; (*pattern*) dessin, motif(s) *m(pl)*; (*of dress, car*) modèle *m*; (*art*) design *m*, stylisme *m*; (*intention*) dessein *m* ▷ *vt* dessiner; (*plan*) concevoir; **design and technology** *n* (*BRIT Scol*) technologie *f*

designate *vt* ['dɛzɪgneɪt] désigner ▷ *adj* ['dɛzɪgnɪt] désigné(e)

designer [dɪ'zaɪnər] *n* (*Archit, Art*) dessinateur(-trice); (*Industry*) concepteur *m*, designer *m*; (*Fashion*) styliste *m/f*

desirable [dɪ'zaɪərəbl] *adj* (*property, location, purchase*) attrayant(e)

desire [dɪ'zaɪər] *n* désir *m* ▷ *vt* désirer, vouloir

desk [dɛsk] *n* (*in office*) bureau *m*; (*for pupil*) pupitre *m*; (*BRIT: in shop, restaurant*) caisse *f*; (*in hotel, at airport*) réception *f*; **desktop** ['dɛsktɔp] *n* bureau *m*; **desktop publishing** *n* publication assistée par ordinateur, PAO *f*

despair [dɪs'pɛər] *n* désespoir *m* ▷ *vi*: **to ~ of** désespérer de

despatch [dɪs'pætʃ] *n, vt* = **dispatch**

desperate ['dɛspərɪt] *adj* désespéré(e); (*fugitive*) prêt(e) à tout; **to be ~ for sth/ to do sth** avoir désespérément besoin de qch/de faire qch; **desperately** *adv* désespérément; (*very*) terriblement, extrêmement; **desperation** [dɛspə'reɪʃən] *n* désespoir *m*; **in (sheer) desperation** en désespoir de cause

despise [dɪs'paɪz] *vt* mépriser

despite [dɪs'paɪt] *prep* malgré, en dépit de

dessert [dɪ'zəːt] *n* dessert *m*; **dessertspoon** *n* cuiller *f* à dessert

destination [dɛstɪ'neɪʃən] *n* destination *f*

destined ['dɛstɪnd] *adj*: **~ for London** à destination de Londres

destiny ['dɛstɪnɪ] *n* destinée *f*, destin *m*

destroy [dɪs'trɔɪ] *vt* détruire; (*injured horse*) abattre; (*dog*) faire piquer

destruction [dɪs'trʌkʃən] *n* destruction *f*

destructive [dɪs'trʌktɪv] *adj* destructeur(-trice)

detach [dɪ'tætʃ] *vt* détacher; **detached** *adj* (*attitude*) détaché(e); **detached house** *n* pavillon *m* maison(nette) (individuelle)

detail ['diːteɪl] *n* détail *m* ▷ *vt* raconter en détail, énumérer; **in ~** en détail; **detailed** *adj* détaillé(e)

detain [dɪ'teɪn] *vt* retenir; (*in captivity*) détenir

detect [dɪ'tɛkt] vt déceler, percevoir; (Med, Police) dépister; (Mil, Radar, Tech) détecter; **detection** [dɪ'tɛkʃən] n découverte f; **detective** n policier m; **private detective** détective privé; **detective story** n roman policier

detention [dɪ'tɛnʃən] n détention f; (Scol) retenue f, consigne f

deter [dɪ'tə:ʳ] vt dissuader

detergent [dɪ'tə:dʒənt] n détersif m, détergent m

deteriorate [dɪ'tɪərɪəreɪt] vi se détériorer, se dégrader

determination [dɪtə:mɪ'neɪʃən] n détermination f

determine [dɪ'tə:mɪn] vt déterminer; **to ~ to do** résoudre de faire, se déterminer à faire; **determined** adj (person) déterminé(e), décidé(e); **determined to do** bien décidé à faire

deterrent [dɪ'tɛrənt] n effet m de dissuasion; force f de dissuasion

detest [dɪ'tɛst] vt détester, avoir horreur de

detour ['di:tuəʳ] n détour m; (us Aut: diversion) déviation f

detox ['di:tɒks] n détox f

detract [dɪ'trækt] vt: **to ~ from** (quality, pleasure) diminuer; (reputation) porter atteinte à

detrimental [dɛtrɪ'mɛntl] adj: **~ to** préjudiciable or nuisible à

devastating ['dɛvəsteɪtɪŋ] adj dévastateur(-trice); (news) accablant(e)

develop [dɪ'vɛləp] vt (gen) développer; (disease) commencer à souffrir de; (resources) mettre en valeur, exploiter; (land) aménager ▷ vi se développer; (situation, disease: evolve) évoluer; (facts, symptoms: appear) se manifester, se produire; **can you ~ this film?** pouvez-vous développer cette pellicule?; **developing country** n pays m en voie de développement; **development** n développement m; (of land) exploitation f; (new fact, event) rebondissement m, fait(s) nouveau(x)

device [dɪ'vaɪs] n (apparatus) appareil m, dispositif m

devil ['dɛvl] n diable m; démon m

devious ['di:vɪəs] adj (person) sournois(e), dissimulé(e)

devise [dɪ'vaɪz] vt imaginer, concevoir

devote [dɪ'vəʊt] vt: **to ~ sth to** consacrer qch à; **devoted** adj dévoué(e); **to be devoted to** être dévoué(e) or très attaché(e) à; (book etc) être consacré(e) à; **devotion** n dévouement m, attachement m; (Rel) dévotion f, piété f

devour [dɪ'vauəʳ] vt dévorer

devout [dɪ'vaʊt] adj pieux(-euse)

dew [dju:] n rosée f

diabetes [daɪə'bi:ti:z] n diabète m

diabetic [daɪə'bɛtɪk] n diabétique m/f ▷ adj (person) diabétique

diagnose [daɪəg'nəʊz] vt diagnostiquer

diagnosis (pl **diagnoses**) [daɪəg'nəʊsɪs, -si:z] n diagnostic m

diagonal [daɪ'ægənl] adj diagonal(e) ▷ n diagonale f

diagram ['daɪəgræm] n diagramme m, schéma m

dial ['daɪəl] n cadran m ▷ vt (number) faire, composer

dialect ['daɪəlɛkt] n dialecte m

dialling code ['daɪəlɪŋ-], (us) **dial code** n indicatif m (téléphonique); **what's the ~ for Paris?** quel est l'indicatif de Paris?

dialling tone ['daɪəlɪŋ-], (us) **dial tone** n tonalité f

dialogue, (us) **dialog** ['daɪəlɒg] n dialogue m

diameter [daɪ'æmɪtəʳ] n diamètre m

diamond ['daɪəmənd] n diamant m; (shape) losange m; **diamonds** npl (Cards) carreau m

diaper ['daɪəpəʳ] n (us) couche f

diarrhoea, (us) **diarrhea** [daɪə'ri:ə] n diarrhée f

diary ['daɪərɪ] n (daily account) journal m; (book) agenda m

dice [daɪs] n (pl inv) dé m ▷ vt (Culin) couper en dés or en cubes

dictate vt [dɪk'teɪt] dicter; **dictation** [dɪk'teɪʃən] n dictée f

dictator [dɪk'teɪtəʳ] n dictateur m

dictionary ['dɪkʃənrɪ] n dictionnaire m

did [dɪd] pt of **do**

didn't [dɪdnt] = **did not**

die [daɪ] vi mourir; **to be dying for sth** avoir une envie folle de qch; **to be dying to do sth** mourir d'envie de faire qch; **die down** vi se calmer, s'apaiser; **die out** vi disparaître, s'éteindre

diesel ['di:zl] n (vehicle) diesel m; (also: **~ oil**) carburant m diesel, gas-oil m

diet ['daɪət] n alimentation f; (restricted food) régime m ▷ vi (also: **be on a ~**) suivre un régime

differ ['dɪfəʳ] vi: **to ~ from sth** (be different) être différent(e) de qch, différer de qch; **to ~ from sb over sth** ne pas être d'accord avec qn au sujet de qch; **difference** n différence f; (quarrel) différend m, désaccord m; **different** adj différent(e); **differentiate** [dɪfə'rɛnʃɪeɪt] vi: **to differentiate between** faire une différence entre; **differently** adv différemment

difficult ['dɪfɪkəlt] adj difficile; **difficulty** n difficulté f

dig [dɪg] vt (pt, pp **dug**) (hole) creuser; (garden) bêcher ▷ n (prod) coup m de coude; (fig: remark) coup de griffe or de patte; (Archaeology) fouille f; **to ~ one's nails into** enfoncer ses ongles dans; **dig up** vt déterrer

digest vt [dar'dʒɛst] digérer ▷ n ['daɪdʒɛst]
sommaire m, résumé m; **digestion**
[dɪ'dʒɛstʃən] n digestion f

digit ['dɪdʒɪt] n (number) chiffre m (de o à 9);
(finger) doigt m; **digital** adj (system,
recording, radio) numérique, digital(e);
(watch) à affichage numérique or digital;
digital camera n appareil m photo
numérique; **digital TV** n télévision f
numérique

dignified ['dɪgnɪfaɪd] adj digne

dignity ['dɪgnɪtɪ] n dignité f

digs [dɪgz] npl (BRIT inf) piaule f, chambre
meublée

dilemma [dar'lɛmə] n dilemme m

dill [dɪl] n aneth m

dilute [dar'luːt] vt diluer

dim [dɪm] adj (light, eyesight) faible; (memory,
outline) vague, indécis(e); (room) sombre;
(inf: stupid) borné(e), obtus(e) ▷ vt (light)
réduire, baisser; (us Aut) mettre en code,
baisser

dime [daɪm] n (US) pièce f de 10 cents

dimension [dar'mɛnʃən] n dimension f

diminish [dɪ'mɪnɪʃ] vt, vi diminuer

din [dɪn] n vacarme m

dine [daɪn] vi dîner; **diner** n (person)
dîneur(-euse); (US: eating place) petit
restaurant

dinghy ['dɪŋgɪ] n youyou m; (inflatable)
canot m pneumatique; (also: **sailing ~**)
voilier m, dériveur m

dingy ['dɪndʒɪ] adj miteux(-euse), minable

dining car ['daɪnɪŋ-] n (BRIT) voiture-
restaurant f, wagon-restaurant m

dining room ['daɪnɪŋ-] n salle f à manger

dining table ['daɪnɪŋ-] n table f de (la) salle
à manger

dinkum ['dɪŋkʌm] adj (AUST, NZ inf) vrai(e);
fair ~ vrai(e)

dinner ['dɪnəʳ] n (evening meal) dîner m;
(lunch) déjeuner m; (public) banquet m;
dinner jacket n smoking m; **dinner party**
n dîner m; **dinner time** n (evening) heure f du
dîner; (midday) heure du déjeuner

dinosaur ['daɪnəsɔːʳ] n dinosaure m

dip [dɪp] n (slope) déclivité f; (in sea)
baignade f, bain m; (Culin) ≈ sauce f ▷ vt
tremper, plonger; (BRIT Aut: lights) mettre
en code, baisser ▷ vi plonger

diploma [dɪ'pləʊmə] n diplôme m

diplomacy [dɪ'pləʊməsɪ] n diplomatie f

diplomat ['dɪpləmæt] n diplomate
m; **diplomatic** [dɪplə'mætɪk] adj
diplomatique

dipstick ['dɪpstɪk] n (BRIT Aut) jauge f de
niveau d'huile

dire [daɪəʳ] adj (poverty) extrême; (awful)
affreux(-euse)

direct [dar'rɛkt] adj direct(e) ▷ vt (tell way)
diriger, orienter; (letter, remark) adresser;
(Cine, TV) réaliser; (Theat) mettre en scène;

(order): **to ~ sb to do sth** ordonner à qn
de faire qch ▷ adv directement; **can you
~ me to ...?** pouvez-vous m'indiquer le
chemin de ...?; **direct debit** n (BRIT Banking)
prélèvement m automatique

direction [dɪ'rɛkʃən] n direction f;
directions npl (to a place) indications fpl; **~s
for use** mode m d'emploi; **sense of ~** sens m
de l'orientation

directly [dɪ'rɛktlɪ] adv (in straight line)
directement, tout droit; (at once) tout de
suite, immédiatement

director [dɪ'rɛktəʳ] n directeur m;
(Theat) metteur m en scène; (Cine, TV)
réalisateur(-trice)

directory [dɪ'rɛktərɪ] n annuaire
m; (Comput) répertoire m; **directory
enquiries**, (US) **directory assistance** n
(Tel: service) renseignements mpl

dirt [dəːt] n saleté f; (mud) boue f; **dirty** adj
sale; (joke) cochon(ne) ▷ vt salir

disability [dɪsə'bɪlɪtɪ] n invalidité f,
infirmité f

disabled [dɪs'eɪbld] adj handicapé(e);
(maimed) mutilé(e)

disadvantage [dɪsəd'vɑːntɪdʒ] n
désavantage m, inconvénient m

disagree [dɪsə'griː] vi (differ) ne pas
concorder; (be against, think otherwise):
to ~ (with) ne pas être d'accord (avec);
disagreeable adj désagréable;
disagreement n désaccord m, différend m

disappear [dɪsə'pɪəʳ] vi disparaître;
disappearance n disparition f

disappoint [dɪsə'pɔɪnt] vt décevoir;
disappointed adj déçu(e); **disappointing**
adj décevant(e); **disappointment** n
déception f

disapproval [dɪsə'pruːvəl] n
désapprobation f

disapprove [dɪsə'pruːv] vi: **to ~ of**
désapprouver

disarm [dɪs'ɑːm] vt désarmer;
disarmament [dɪs'ɑːməmənt] n
désarmement m

disaster [dɪ'zɑːstəʳ] n catastrophe
f, désastre m; **disastrous** adj
désastreux(-euse)

disbelief ['dɪsbə'liːf] n incrédulité f

disc [dɪsk] n disque m; (Comput) = **disk**

discard [dɪs'kɑːd] vt (old things) se
débarrasser de; (fig) écarter, renoncer à

discharge vt [dɪs'tʃɑːdʒ] (duties) s'acquitter
de; (waste etc) déverser; décharger;
(patient) renvoyer (chez lui); (employee,
soldier) congédier, licencier ▷ n ['dɪstʃɑːdʒ]
(Elec, Med) émission f; (dismissal) renvoi m
licenciement m

discipline ['dɪsɪplɪn] n discipline f ▷ vt
discipliner; (punish) punir

disc jockey n disque-jockey m (DJ)

disclose [dɪs'kləʊz] vt révéler, divulguer

disco ['dɪskəu] n abbr discothèque f

discoloured, (us) **discolored** [dɪs'kʌləd] adj décoloré(e), jauni(e)

discomfort [dɪs'kʌmfət] n malaise m, gêne f; (lack of comfort) manque m de confort

disconnect [dɪskə'nɛkt] vt (Elec, Radio) débrancher; (gas, water) couper

discontent [dɪskən'tɛnt] n mécontentement m

discontinue [dɪskən'tɪnjuː] vt cesser, interrompre; **"~d"** (Comm) "fin de série"

discount n ['dɪskaunt] remise f, rabais m ▷ vt [dɪs'kaunt] (report etc) ne pas tenir compte de

discourage [dɪs'kʌrɪdʒ] vt décourager

discover [dɪs'kʌvəʳ] vt découvrir; **discovery** n découverte f

discredit [dɪs'krɛdɪt] vt (idea) mettre en doute; (person) discréditer

discreet [dɪ'skriːt] adj discret(-ète)

discrepancy [dɪ'skrɛpənsɪ] n divergence f, contradiction f

discretion [dɪ'skrɛʃən] n discrétion f; **at the ~** of à la discrétion de

discriminate [dɪ'skrɪmɪneɪt] vi: **to ~ between** établir une distinction entre, faire la différence entre; **to ~ against** pratiquer une discrimination contre; **discrimination** [dɪskrɪmɪ'neɪʃən] n discrimination f; (judgment) discernement m

discuss [dɪ'skʌs] vt discuter de; (debate) discuter; **discussion** [dɪ'skʌʃən] n discussion f

disease [dɪ'ziːz] n maladie f

disembark [dɪsɪm'baːk] vt, vi débarquer

disgrace [dɪs'greɪs] n honte f; (disfavour) disgrâce f ▷ vt déshonorer, couvrir de honte; **disgraceful** adj scandaleux(-euse), honteux(-euse)

disgruntled [dɪs'grʌntld] adj mécontent(e)

disguise [dɪs'gaɪz] n déguisement m ▷ vt déguiser; **in ~** déguisé(e)

disgust [dɪs'gʌst] n dégoût m, aversion f ▷ vt dégoûter, écœurer

disgusted [dɪs'gʌstɪd] adj dégoûté(e), écœuré(e)

disgusting [dɪs'gʌstɪŋ] adj dégoûtant(e)

dish [dɪʃ] n plat m; **to do** or **wash the ~es** faire la vaisselle; **dishcloth** n (for drying) torchon m; (for washing) lavette f

dishonest [dɪs'ɔnɪst] adj malhonnête

dishtowel ['dɪʃtauəl] n (us) torchon m (à vaisselle)

dishwasher ['dɪʃwɔʃəʳ] n lave-vaisselle m

disillusion [dɪsɪ'luːʒən] vt désabuser, désenchanter

disinfectant [dɪsɪn'fɛktənt] n désinfectant m

disintegrate [dɪs'ɪntɪgreɪt] vi se désintégrer

disk [dɪsk] n (Comput) disquette f; **single-/double-sided ~** disquette une face/double face; **disk drive** n lecteur m de disquette; **diskette** n (Comput) disquette f

dislike [dɪs'laɪk] n aversion f, antipathie f ▷ vt ne pas aimer

dislocate ['dɪsləkeɪt] vt disloquer, déboîter

disloyal [dɪs'lɔɪəl] adj déloyal(e)

dismal ['dɪzml] adj (gloomy) lugubre, maussade; (very bad) lamentable

dismantle [dɪs'mæntl] vt démonter

dismay [dɪs'meɪ] n consternation f ▷ vt consterner

dismiss [dɪs'mɪs] vt congédier, renvoyer; (idea) écarter; (Law) rejeter; **dismissal** n renvoi m

disobedient [dɪsə'biːdɪənt] adj désobéissant(e), indiscipliné(e)

disobey [dɪsə'beɪ] vt désobéir à

disorder [dɪs'ɔːdəʳ] n désordre m; (rioting) désordres mpl; (Med) troubles mpl

disorganized [dɪs'ɔːgənaɪzd] adj désorganisé(e)

disown [dɪs'əun] vt renier

dispatch [dɪs'pætʃ] vt expédier, envoyer ▷ n envoi m, expédition f; (Mil, Press) dépêche f

dispel [dɪs'pɛl] vt dissiper, chasser

dispense [dɪs'pɛns] vt (medicine) préparer (et vendre); **dispense with** vt fus se passer de; **dispenser** n (device) distributeur m

disperse [dɪs'pəːs] vt disperser ▷ vi se disperser

display [dɪs'pleɪ] n (of goods) étalage m; affichage m; (Comput: information) visualisation f; (: device) visuel m; (of feeling) manifestation f ▷ vt montrer; (goods) mettre à l'étalage, exposer; (results, departure times) afficher; (pej) faire étalage de

displease [dɪs'pliːz] vt mécontenter, contrarier

disposable [dɪs'pəuzəbl] adj (pack etc) jetable; (income) disponible

disposal [dɪs'pəuzl] n (of rubbish) évacuation f, destruction f; (of property etc: by selling) vente f; (: by giving away) cession f; **at one's ~** à sa disposition

dispose [dɪs'pəuz] vi: **to ~ of** (unwanted goods) se débarrasser de, se défaire de; (problem) expédier; **disposition** [dɪspə'zɪʃən] n disposition f; (temperament) naturel m

disproportionate [dɪsprə'pɔːʃənət] adj disproportionné(e)

dispute [dɪs'pjuːt] n discussion f; (also: **industrial ~**) conflit m ▷ vt (question) contester; (matter) discuter

disqualify [dɪs'kwɔlɪfaɪ] vt (Sport) disqualifier; **to ~ sb for sth/from doing** rendre qn inapte à qch/à faire

disregard [dɪsrɪ'gaːd] vt ne pas tenir compte de

disrupt [dɪs'rʌpt] vt (plans, meeting, lesson) perturber, déranger; **disruption** [dɪs'rʌpʃən] n perturbation f, dérangement m

dissatisfaction [dɪssætɪs'fækʃən] n mécontentement m, insatisfaction f

dissatisfied [dɪs'sætɪsfaɪd] adj: ~ (with) insatisfait(e) (de)

dissect [dɪ'sɛkt] vt disséquer

dissent [dɪ'sɛnt] n dissentiment m, différence f d'opinion

dissertation [dɪsə'teɪʃən] n (Scol) mémoire m

dissolve [dɪ'zɔlv] vt dissoudre ▷ vi se dissoudre, fondre; **to ~ in(to) tears** fondre en larmes

distance ['dɪstns] n distance f; **in the ~** au loin

distant ['dɪstnt] adj lointain(e), éloigné(e); (manner) distant(e), froid(e)

distil, (US) **distill** [dɪs'tɪl] vt distiller; **distillery** n distillerie f

distinct [dɪs'tɪŋkt] adj distinct(e); (clear) marqué(e); **as ~ from** par opposition à; **distinction** [dɪs'tɪŋkʃən] n distinction f; (in exam) mention f très bien; **distinctive** adj distinctif(-ive)

distinguish [dɪs'tɪŋgwɪʃ] vt distinguer; **to ~ o.s.** se distinguer; **distinguished** adj (eminent, refined) distingué(e)

distort [dɪs'tɔːt] vt déformer

distract [dɪs'trækt] vt distraire, déranger; **distracted** adj (not concentrating) distrait(e); (worried) affolé(e); **distraction** [dɪs'trækʃən] n distraction f

distraught [dɪs'trɔːt] adj éperdu(e)

distress [dɪs'trɛs] n détresse f ▷ vt affliger; **distressing** adj douloureux(-euse), pénible

distribute [dɪs'trɪbjuːt] vt distribuer; **distribution** [dɪstrɪ'bjuːʃən] n distribution f; **distributor** n (gen, Tech) distributeur m; (Comm) concessionnaire m/f

district ['dɪstrɪkt] n (of country) région f; (of town) quartier m; (Admin) district m; **district attorney** n (US) ≈ procureur m de la République

distrust [dɪs'trʌst] n méfiance f, doute m ▷ vt se méfier de

disturb [dɪs'təːb] vt troubler; (inconvenience) déranger; **disturbance** n dérangement m; (political etc) troubles mpl; **disturbed** adj (worried, upset) agité(e), troublé(e); **to be emotionally disturbed** avoir des problèmes affectifs; **disturbing** adj troublant(e), inquiétant(e)

ditch [dɪtʃ] n fossé m; (for irrigation) rigole f ▷ vt (inf) abandonner; (person) plaquer

ditto ['dɪtəu] adv idem

dive [daɪv] n plongeon m; (of submarine) plongée f ▷ vi plonger; **to ~ into** (bag etc) plonger la main dans; (place) se précipiter dans; **diver** n plongeur m

diverse [daɪ'vəːs] adj divers(e)

diversion [daɪ'vəːʃən] n (BRIT Aut) déviation f; (distraction, Mil) diversion f

diversity [daɪ'vəːsɪtɪ] n diversité f, variété f

divert [daɪ'vəːt] vt (BRIT: traffic) dévier; (plane) dérouter; (train, river) détourner

divide [dɪ'vaɪd] vt diviser; (separate) séparer ▷ vi se diviser; **divided highway** (US) n route f à quatre voies

divine [dɪ'vaɪn] adj divin(e)

diving ['daɪvɪŋ] n plongée (sous-marine); **diving board** n plongeoir m

division [dɪ'vɪʒən] n division f; (separation) séparation f; (Comm) service m

divorce [dɪ'vɔːs] n divorce m ▷ vt divorcer d'avec; **divorced** adj divorcé(e); **divorcee** [dɪvɔː'siː] n divorcé(e)

DIY adj, n abbr (BRIT) = **do-it-yourself**

dizzy ['dɪzɪ] adj: **I feel ~** la tête me tourne, j'ai la tête qui tourne

DJ n abbr = **disc jockey**

DNA n abbr (= deoxyribonucleic acid) ADN m

🔘 **KEYWORD**

do [duː] n (inf: party etc) soirée f, fête f
▶ aux vb (pt **did**, pp **done**) **1** (in negative constructions) non traduit; **I don't understand** je ne comprends pas
2 (to form questions) non traduit; **didn't you know?** vous ne le saviez pas?; **what do you think?** qu'en pensez-vous?
3 (for emphasis, in polite expressions): **people do make mistakes sometimes** on peut toujours se tromper; **she does seem rather late** je trouve qu'elle est bien en retard; **do sit down/help yourself** asseyez-vous/ servez-vous je vous en prie; **do take care!** faites bien attention à vous!
4 (used to avoid repeating vb): **she swims better than I do** elle nage mieux que moi; **do you agree? — yes, I do/no I don't** vous êtes d'accord? — oui/non; **she lives in Glasgow — so do I** elle habite Glasgow — moi aussi; **he didn't like it and neither did we** il n'a pas aimé ça, et nous non plus; **who broke it? — I did** qui l'a cassé? — c'est moi; **he asked me to help him and I did** il m'a demandé de l'aider, et c'est ce que j'ai fait
5 (in question tags): **you like him, don't you?** vous l'aimez bien, n'est-ce pas?; **I don't know him, do I?** je ne crois pas le connaître
▶ vt (pt **did**, pp **done**) **1** (gen: carry out, perform etc) faire; (visit: city, museum) faire, visiter; **what are you doing tonight?** qu'est-ce que vous faites ce soir?; **what do you do?** (job) qu'est-ce que vous faites dans la vie?; **what can I do for you?** que puis-je faire pour vous?; **to do the cooking/washing-up** faire la cuisine/la vaisselle; **to do one's teeth/hair/nails** se brosser les dents/se coiffer/se faire les ongles

2 (*Aut etc: distance*) faire; (: *speed*) faire du; **we've done 200 km already** nous avons déjà fait 200 km; **the car was doing 100** la voiture faisait du 100 (à l'heure); **he can do 100 in that car** il peut faire du 100 (à l'heure) dans cette voiture-là
▶ vi (*pt* **did**, *pp* **done**) **1** (*act, behave*) faire; **do as I do** faites comme moi
2 (*get on, fare*) marcher; **the firm is doing well** l'entreprise marche bien; **he's doing well/badly at school** ça marche bien/mal pour lui à l'école; **how do you do?** comment allez-vous?; (*on being introduced*) enchanté(e)!
3 (*suit*) aller; **will it do?** est-ce que ça ira?
4 (*be sufficient*) suffire, aller; **will £10 do?** est-ce que 10 livres suffiront?; **that'll do** ça suffit, ça ira; **that'll do!** (*in annoyance*) ça va or suffit comme ça!; **to make do (with)** se contenter (de)
do up *vt* (*laces, dress*) attacher; (*buttons*) boutonner; (*zip*) fermer; (*renovate: room*) refaire; (: *house*) remettre à neuf
do with *vt fus* (*need*): **I could do with a drink/some help** quelque chose à boire/un peu d'aide ne serait pas de refus; **it could do with a wash** ça ne lui ferait pas de mal d'être lavé; (*be connected with*): **that has nothing to do with you** cela ne vous concerne pas; **I won't have anything to do with it** je ne veux pas m'en mêler
do without *vi* s'en passer; **if you're late for tea then you'll do without** si vous êtes en retard pour le dîner il faudra vous en passer ▶ *vt fus* se passer de; **I can do without a car** je peux me passer de voiture

dock [dɔk] *n* dock *m*; (*wharf*) quai *m*; (*Law*) banc *m* des accusés ▶ *vi* se mettre à quai; (*Space*) s'arrimer; **docks** *npl* (*Naut*) docks
doctor ['dɔktə'] *n* médecin *m*, docteur *m*; (*PhD etc*) docteur ▶ *vt* (*drink*) frelater; **call a ~!** appelez un docteur *or* un médecin!; **Doctor of Philosophy** (*degree*) doctorat *m*; (*person*) titulaire *m/f* d'un doctorat
document ['dɔkjumənt] *n* document *m*; **documentary** [dɔkju'mɛntərɪ] *adj*, *n* documentaire (*m*); **documentation** [dɔkjumən'teɪʃən] *n* documentation *f*
dodge [dɔdʒ] *n* truc *m*; combine *f* ▶ *vt* esquiver, éviter
dodgy ['dɔdʒɪ] *adj* (BRIT *inf*: *uncertain*) douteux(-euse); (: *shady*) louche
does [dʌz] *vb see* **do**
doesn't ['dʌznt] = **does not**
dog [dɔg] *n* chien(ne) ▶ *vt* (*follow closely*) suivre de près; (*fig*: *memory etc*) poursuivre, harceler; **doggy bag** ['dɔgɪ-] *n* petit sac pour emporter les restes
do-it-yourself ['du:ɪtjɔ:'sɛlf] *n* bricolage *m*
dole [dəul] *n* (BRIT: *payment*) allocation *f* de chômage; **on the ~** au chômage

doll [dɔl] *n* poupée *f*
dollar ['dɔlə'] *n* dollar *m*
dolphin ['dɔlfɪn] *n* dauphin *m*
dome [dəum] *n* dôme *m*
domestic [də'mɛstɪk] *adj* (*duty, happiness*) familial(e); (*policy, affairs, flight*) intérieur(e); (*animal*) domestique
dominant ['dɔmɪnənt] *adj* dominant(e)
dominate ['dɔmɪneɪt] *vt* dominer
domino ['dɔmɪnəu] (*pl* **dominoes**) *n* domino *m*; **dominoes** *n* (*game*) dominos *mpl*
donate [də'neɪt] *vt* faire don de, donner; **donation** [də'neɪʃən] *n* donation *f*, don *m*
done [dʌn] *pp of* **do**
dongle ['dɔŋgl] *n* (*Comput*) dongle *m*
donkey ['dɔŋkɪ] *n* âne *m*
donor ['dəunə'] *n* (*of blood etc*) donneur(-euse); (*to charity*) donateur(-trice); **donor card** *n* carte *f* de don d'organes
don't [dəunt] = **do not**
donut ['dəunʌt] (*US*) *n* = **doughnut**
doodle ['du:dl] *vi* gribouiller
doom [du:m] *n* (*fate*) destin *m* ▶ *vt*: **to be ~ed to failure** être voué(e) à l'échec
door [dɔ:'] *n* porte *f*; (*Rail, car*) portière *f*; **doorbell** *n* sonnette *f*; **door handle** *n* poignée *f* de porte; (*of car*) poignée de portière; **doorknob** *n* poignée *f* or bouton *m* de porte; **doorstep** *n* pas *m* de (la) porte, seuil *m*; **doorway** *n* (embrasure *f* de) porte *f*
dope [dəup] *n* (*inf*: *drug*) drogue *f*; (: *person*) andouille *f* ▶ *vt* (*horse etc*) doper
dormitory ['dɔ:mɪtrɪ] *n* (BRIT) dortoir *m*; (*US*: *hall of residence*) résidence *f* universitaire
DOS [dɔs] *n abbr* (= *disk operating system*) DOS *m*
dosage ['dəusɪdʒ] *n* dose *f*; dosage *m*; (*on label*) posologie *f*
dose [dəus] *n* dose *f*
dot [dɔt] *n* point *m*; (*on material*) pois *m* ▶ *vt*: **~ted with** parsemé(e) de; **on the ~** à l'heure tapante; **dotcom** *n* point com *m*, pointcom *m*; **dotted line** ['dɔtɪd-] *n* ligne pointillée; **to sign on the dotted line** signer à l'endroit indiqué *or* sur la ligne pointillée
double ['dʌbl] *adj* double ▶ *adv* (*twice*): **to cost ~ (sth)** coûter le double (de qch) *or* deux fois plus (que qch) ▶ *n* double *m*; (*Cine*) doublure *f* ▶ *vt* doubler; (*fold*) plier en deux ▶ *vi* doubler; **on the ~, at the ~** au pas de course; **double back** *vi* (*person*) revenir sur ses pas; **double bass** *n* contrebasse *f*; **double bed** *n* grand lit; **double-check** *vt, vi* revérifier; **double-click** *vi* (*Comput*) double-cliquer; **double-cross** *vt* doubler, trahir; **double-decker** *n* autobus *m* à impériale; **double glazing** *n* (BRIT) double vitrage *m*; **double room** *n* chambre *f* pour deux; **doubles** *n* (*Tennis*) double *m*; **double yellow lines** *npl* (BRIT *Aut*) double bande jaune marquant l'interdiction de stationner

doubt [daut] *n* doute *m* ▷ *vt* douter de;
no ~ sans doute; **to ~ that** douter que + *sub*;
doubtful *adj* douteux(-euse); (*person*)
incertain(e); **doubtless** *adv* sans doute,
sûrement

dough [dau] *n* pâte *f*; **doughnut**, (US)
donut *n* beignet *m*

dove [dʌv] *n* colombe *f*

Dover ['dauvər] *n* Douvres

down [daun] *n* (*fluff*) duvet *m* ▷ *adv* en bas,
vers le bas; (*on the ground*) par terre ▷ *prep*
en bas de; (*along*) le long de ▷ *vt* (*inf*: *drink*)
siffler; **to walk ~ a hill** descendre une
colline; **to run ~ the street** descendre la
rue en courant; **~ with X!** à bas X!; **down-
and-out** *n* (*tramp*) clochard(e); **downfall**
n chute *f*; ruine *f*; **downhill** *adv*: **to go
downhill** descendre; (*business*) péricliter

Downing Street ['daunɪŋ-] *n* (BRIT): **10 ~**
résidence du Premier ministre

● **DOWNING STREET**
●
● *Downing Street* est une rue de Westminster
● (à Londres) où se trouvent la résidence
● officielle du Premier ministre et celle du
● ministre des Finances. Le nom *Downing*
● *Street* est souvent utilisé pour désigner le
● gouvernement britannique.

down: download *vt* (*Comput*)
télécharger; **downloadable** *adj* (*Comput*)
téléchargeable; **downright** *adj* (*lie etc*)
effronté(e); (*refusal*) catégorique

Down's syndrome [daunz-] *n* trisomie *f*

down: downstairs *adv* (*on or to ground floor*)
au rez-de-chaussée; (*on or to floor below*) à
l'étage inférieur; **down-to-earth** *adj* terre
à terre *inv*; **downtown** *adv* en ville; **down
under** *adv* en Australie or Nouvelle Zélande;
downward ['daunwəd] *adj*, *adv* vers le bas;
downwards ['daunwədz] *adv* vers le bas

doz. *abbr* = **dozen**

doze [dəuz] *vi* sommeiller

dozen ['dʌzn] *n* douzaine *f*; **a ~ books** une
douzaine de livres; **~s of** des centaines de

Dr. *abbr* (= *doctor*) Dr; (*in street names*);
= **drive**

drab [dræb] *adj* terne, morne

draft [drɑːft] *n* (*of letter, school work*)
brouillon *m*; (*of literary work*) ébauche *f*;
(*Comm*) traite *f*; (*US Mil*: *call-up*) conscription
f ▷ *vt* faire le brouillon de; (*Mil*: *send*)
détacher; *see also* **draught**

drag [dræg] *vt* traîner; (*river*) draguer ▷ *vi*
traîner ▷ *n* (*inf*) casse-pieds *m/f*; (: *women's
clothing*): **in ~** (-en) travesti; **to ~ and drop**
(*Comput*) glisser-poser

dragonfly ['drægənflaɪ] *n* libellule *f*

drain [dreɪn] *n* égout *m*; (*on resources*)
saignée *f* ▷ *vt* (*land, marshes*) assécher;
(*vegetables*) égoutter; (*reservoir etc*) vider

▷ *vi* (*water*) s'écouler; **drainage** *n* (*system*)
système *m* d'égouts; (*act*) drainage *m*;
drainpipe *n* tuyau *m* d'écoulement

drama ['drɑːmə] *n* (*art*) théâtre *m*, art *m*
dramatique; (*play*) pièce *f*; (*event*) drame
m; **dramatic** [drə'mætɪk] *adj* (*Theat*)
dramatique; (*impressive*) spectaculaire

drank [dræŋk] *pt of* **drink**

drape [dreɪp] *vt* draper; **drapes** *npl* (US)
rideaux *mpl*

drastic ['dræstɪk] *adj* (*measures*) d'urgence,
énergique; (*change*) radical(e)

draught, (US) **draft** [drɑːft] *n* courant *m*
d'air; **on ~** (*beer*) à la pression; **draught
beer** *n* bière *f* (à la) pression; **draughts** *n*
(BRIT: *game*) (jeu *m* de) dames *fpl*

draw [drɔː] (*vb*: *pt* **drew**, *pp* **drawn**) *vt*
tirer; (*picture*) dessiner; (*attract*) attirer;
(*line, circle*) tracer; (*money*) retirer; (*wages*)
toucher ▷ *vi* (*Sport*) faire match nul ▷ *n*
match nul; (*lottery*) loterie *f*; (*picking of ticket*)
tirage *m* au sort; **draw out** *vi* (*lengthen*)
s'allonger ▷ *vt* (*money*) retirer; **draw up**
vi (*stop*) s'arrêter ▷ *vt* (*document*) établir,
dresser; (*plan*) formuler, dessiner; (*chair*)
approcher; **drawback** *n* inconvénient *m*,
désavantage *m*

drawer [drɔːʳ] *n* tiroir *m*

drawing ['drɔːɪŋ] *n* dessin *m*; **drawing
pin** *n* (BRIT) punaise *f*; **drawing room** *n*
salon *m*

drawn [drɔːn] *pp of* **draw**

dread [drɛd] *n* épouvante *f*, effroi *m* ▷ *vt*
redouter, appréhender; **dreadful** *adj*
épouvantable, affreux(-euse)

dream [driːm] *n* rêve *m* ▷ *vt*, *vi* (*pt*
dreamed, *pp* **dreamt**) rêver; **dreamer** *n*
rêveur(-euse)

dreamt [drɛmt] *pt*, *pp of* **dream**

dreary ['drɪərɪ] *adj* triste; monotone

drench [drɛntʃ] *vt* tremper

dress [drɛs] *n* robe *f*; (*clothing*) habillement
m, tenue *f* ▷ *vt* habiller; (*wound*) panser ▷ *vi*:
to get ~ed s'habiller; **dress up** *vi* s'habiller;
(*in fancy dress*) se déguiser; **dress circle** *n*
(BRIT) premier balcon; **dresser** *n* (*furniture*)
vaisselier *m* (: US) coiffeuse *f*, commode
f; **dressing** *n* (*Med*) pansement *m*; (*Culin*)
sauce *f*, assaisonnement *m*; **dressing
gown** *n* (BRIT) robe *f* de chambre; **dressing
room** *n* (*Theat*) loge *f*; (*Sport*) vestiaire *m*;
dressing table *n* coiffeuse *f*; **dressmaker**
n couturière *f*

drew [druː] *pt of* **draw**

dribble ['drɪbl] *vi* (*baby*) baver ▷ *vt* (*ball*)
dribbler

dried [draɪd] *adj* (*fruit, beans*) sec (sèche);
(*eggs, milk*) en poudre

drier ['draɪəʳ] *n* = **dryer**

drift [drɪft] *n* (*of current etc*) force *f*; direction
f; (*of snow*) rafale *f*; coulée *f* (*on ground*)
congère *f*; (*general meaning*) sens général

▷ vi (boat) aller à la dérive, dériver; (sand, snow) s'amonceler, s'entasser

drill [drɪl] n perceuse f; (bit) foret m; (of dentist) roulette f, fraise f; (Mil) exercice m ▷ vt percer; (troops) entraîner ▷ vi (for oil) faire un or des forage(s)

drink [drɪŋk] n boisson f; (alcoholic) verre m ▷ vt, vi (pt **drank**, pp **drunk**) boire; **to have a ~** boire quelque chose, boire un verre; **a ~ of water** un verre d'eau; **would you like a ~?** tu veux boire quelque chose?; **drink-driving** n conduite f en état d'ivresse; **drinker** n buveur(-euse); **drinking water** n eau f potable

drip [drɪp] n (drop) goutte f; (Med: device) goutte- à-goutte m inv; (: liquid) perfusion f ▷ vi tomber goutte à goutte; (tap) goutter

drive [draɪv] (pt **drove**, pp **driven**) n promenade f or trajet m en voiture; (also: **~way**) allée f; (energy) dynamisme m, énergie f; (push) effort (concerté) campagne f; (Comput: also: **disk ~**) lecteur m de disquette ▷ vt conduire; (nail) enfoncer; (push) chasser, pousser; (Tech: motor) actionner; entraîner ▷ vi (be at the wheel) conduire; (travel by car) aller en voiture; **left-/right-hand ~** (Aut) conduite f à gauche/droite; **to ~ sb mad** rendre qn fou (folle); **drive out** vt (force out) chasser; **drive-in** adj, n (esp US) drive-in m

driven ['drɪvn] pp of **drive**

driver ['draɪvə'] n conducteur(-trice); (of taxi, bus) chauffeur m; **driver's license** n (US) permis m de conduire

driveway ['draɪvweɪ] n allée f

driving ['draɪvɪŋ] n conduite f; **driving instructor** n moniteur m d'auto-école; **driving lesson** n leçon f de conduite; **driving licence** n (BRIT) permis m de conduire; **driving test** n examen m du permis de conduire

drizzle ['drɪzl] n bruine f, crachin m

droop [druːp] vi (flower) commencer à se faner; (shoulders, head) tomber

drop [drɔp] n (of liquid) goutte f; (fall) baisse f; (also: **parachute ~**) saut m ▷ vt laisser tomber; (voice, eyes, price) baisser; (passenger) déposer ▷ vi tomber; **drop in** vi (inf: visit): **to ~ in (on)** faire un saut (chez), passer (chez); **drop off** vi (sleep) s'assoupir ▷ vt (passenger) déposer; **drop out** vi (withdraw) se retirer; (student etc) abandonner, décrocher

drought [draut] n sécheresse f

drove [drəuv] pt of **drive**

drown [draun] vt noyer ▷ vi se noyer

drowsy ['drauzɪ] adj somnolent(e)

drug [drʌg] n médicament m; (narcotic) drogue f ▷ vt droguer; **to be on ~s** se droguer; **drug addict** n toxicomane m/f; **drug dealer** n revendeur(-euse) de drogue; **druggist** n (US) pharmacien(ne)-droguiste;

drugstore n (US) pharmacie-droguerie f, drugstore m

drum [drʌm] n tambour m; (for oil, petrol) bidon m; **drums** npl (Mus) batterie f; **drummer** n (joueur m de) tambour m

drunk [drʌŋk] pp of **drink** ▷ adj ivre, soûl(e) ▷ n (also: **~ard**) ivrogne m/f; **to get ~** se soûler; **drunken** adj ivre, soûl(e); (rage, stupor) ivrogne, d'ivrogne

dry [draɪ] adj sec (sèche); (day) sans pluie ▷ vt sécher; (clothes) faire sécher ▷ vi sécher; **dry off** vi, vt sécher; **dry up** vi (river, supplies) se tarir; **dry-cleaner's** n teinturerie f; **dry-cleaning** n (process) nettoyage m à sec; **dryer** n (tumble-dryer) sèche-linge m inv; (for hair) sèche-cheveux m inv

DSS n abbr (BRIT) = **Department of Social Security**

DTP n abbr (= desktop publishing) PAO f

dual ['djuəl] adj double; **dual carriageway** n (BRIT) route f à quatre voies

dubious ['djuːbɪəs] adj hésitant(e), incertain(e); (reputation, company) douteux(-euse)

duck [dʌk] n canard m ▷ vi se baisser vivement, baisser subitement la tête

due [djuː] adj (money, payment) dû (due); (expected) attendu(e), (fitting) qui convient ▷ adv. ~ **north** droit vers le nord; ~ **to** (because of) en raison de, (caused by) dû à; **the train is ~ at 8 a.m.** le train est attendu à 8 h; **she is ~ back tomorrow** elle doit rentrer demain; **he is ~ £10** on lui doit 10 livres; **to give sb his** or **her ~** être juste envers qn

duel ['djuəl] n duel m

duet [djuːˈɛt] n duo m

dug [dʌg] pt, pp of **dig**

duke [djuːk] n duc m

dull [dʌl] adj (boring) ennuyeux(-euse); (not bright) morne, terne; (sound, pain) sourd(e); (weather, day) gris(e), maussade ▷ vt (pain, grief) atténuer; (mind, senses) engourdir

dumb [dʌm] adj (stupid) bête

dummy ['dʌmɪ] n (tailor's model) mannequin m; (mock-up) factice m, maquette f; (BRIT: for baby) tétine f ▷ adj faux (fausse), factice

dump [dʌmp] n (also: **rubbish ~**) décharge (publique); (inf: place) trou m ▷ vt (put down) déposer; déverser; (get rid of) se débarrasser de; (Comput) lister

dumpling ['dʌmplɪŋ] n boulette f (de pâte)

dune [djuːn] n dune f

dungarees [dʌŋɡəˈriːz] npl bleu(s) m(pl); (for child, woman) salopette f

dungeon ['dʌndʒən] n cachot m

duplex ['djuːplɛks] n (US: also: **~ apartment**) duplex m

duplicate n ['djuːplɪkət] double m ▷ vt ['djuːplɪkeɪt] faire un double de; (on machine) polycopier; **in ~** en deux exemplaires, en double

durable ['djuərəbl] *adj* durable; (*clothes, metal*) résistant(e), solide
duration [djuə'reɪʃən] *n* durée *f*
during ['djuərɪŋ] *prep* pendant, au cours de
dusk [dʌsk] *n* crépuscule *m*
dust [dʌst] *n* poussière *f* ▷ *vt* (*furniture*) essuyer, épousseter; (*cake etc*): **to ~ with** saupoudrer de; **dustbin** *n* (BRIT) poubelle *f*; **duster** *n* chiffon *m*; **dustman** (*irreg*) *n* (BRIT) boueux *m*, éboueur *m*; **dustpan** *n* pelle *f* à poussière; **dusty** *adj* poussiéreux(-euse)
Dutch [dʌtʃ] *adj* hollandais(e), néerlandais(e) ▷ *n* (*Ling*) hollandais *m*, néerlandais *m* ▷ *adv*: **to go ~ or dutch** (*inf*) partager les frais; **the Dutch** *npl* les Hollandais, les Néerlandais; **Dutchman** (*irreg*) *n* Hollandais *m*; **Dutchwoman** (*irreg*) *n* Hollandaise *f*
duty ['djuːtɪ] *n* devoir *m*; (*tax*) droit *m*, taxe *f*; **on ~** de service; (*at night etc*) de garde; **off ~** libre, pas de service or de garde; **duty-free** *adj* exempté(e) de douane, hors-taxe
duvet ['duːveɪ] *n* (BRIT) couette *f*
DVD *n abbr* (= *digital versatile or video disc*) DVD *m*; **DVD burner** *n* graveur *m* de DVD; **DVD player** *n* lecteur *m* de DVD; **DVD writer** *n* graveur *m* de DVD
dwarf (*pl* **dwarves**) [dwɔːf, dwɔːvz] *n* (*pej*) nain(e) ▷ *vt* écraser
dwell (*pt, pp* **dwelt**) [dwɛl, dwɛlt] *vi* demeurer; **dwell on** *vt fus* s'étendre sur
dwelt [dwɛlt] *pt, pp of* **dwell**
dwindle ['dwɪndl] *vi* diminuer, décroître
dye [daɪ] *n* teinture *f* ▷ *vt* teindre
dying ['daɪɪŋ] *adj* mourant(e), agonisant(e)
dynamic [daɪ'næmɪk] *adj* dynamique
dynamite ['daɪnəmaɪt] *n* dynamite *f*
dyslexia [dɪs'lɛksɪə] *n* dyslexie *f*
dyslexic [dɪs'lɛksɪk] *adj* dyslexique

e

E [iː] *n* (*Mus*) mi *m*
each [iːtʃ] *adj* chaque ▷ *pron* chacun(e); **~ other** l'un l'autre; **they hate ~ other** ils se détestent (mutuellement); **they have 2 books ~** ils ont 2 livres chacun; **they cost £5 ~** ils coûtent 5 livres (la) pièce
eager ['iːgər] *adj* (*person, buyer*) empressé(e); (*keen: pupil, worker*) enthousiaste; **to be ~ to do sth** (*impatient*) brûler de faire qch; (*keen*) désirer vivement faire qch; **to be ~ for** (*event*) désirer vivement; (*vengeance, affection, information*) être avide de
eagle ['iːgl] *n* aigle *m*
ear [ɪər] *n* oreille *f*; (*of corn*) épi *m*; **earache** *n* mal *m* aux oreilles; **eardrum** *n* tympan *m*
earl [əːl] *n* comte *m*
earlier ['əːlɪər] *adj* (*date etc*) plus rapproché(e); (*edition etc*) plus ancien(ne), antérieur(e) ▷ *adv* plus tôt
early ['əːlɪ] *adv* tôt, de bonne heure; (*ahead of time*) en avance; (*near the beginning*) au début ▷ *adj* précoce, qui se manifeste (or se fait) tôt or de bonne heure; (*Christians, settlers*) premier(-ière); (*reply*) rapide; (*death*) prématuré(e); (*work*) de jeunesse; **to have an ~ night/start** se coucher/partir tôt or de bonne heure; **in the ~ or ~ in the spring/19th century** au début or commencement du printemps/19ème siècle; **early retirement** *n* retraite anticipée
earmark ['ɪəmɑːk] *vt*: **to ~ sth for** réserver or destiner qch à
earn [əːn] *vt* gagner; (*Comm: yield*) rapporter; **to ~ one's living** gagner sa vie
earnest ['əːnɪst] *adj* sérieux(-euse) ▷ *n*: **in ~** *adv* sérieusement, pour de bon
earnings ['əːnɪŋz] *npl* salaire *m*; gains *mpl*; (*of company etc*) profits *mpl*, bénéfices *mpl*
ear: earphones *npl* écouteurs *mpl*; **earplugs** *npl* boules *fpl* Quiès®; (*to keep out water*) protège-tympans *mpl*; **earring** *n* boucle *f* d'oreille

earth [ə:θ] n (gen, also BRIT Elec) terre f ▷ vt (BRIT Elec) relier à la terre; **earthquake** n tremblement m de terre, séisme m

ease [i:z] n facilité f, aisance f; (comfort) bien-être m ▷ vt (soothe: mind) tranquilliser; (reduce: pain, problem) atténuer; (: tension) réduire; (loosen) relâcher, détendre; (help pass): **to ~ sth in/out** faire pénétrer/sortir qch délicatement or avec douceur, faciliter la pénétration/la sortie de qch; **at ~** à l'aise; (Mil) au repos

easily ['i:zɪlɪ] adv facilement; (by far) de loin

east [i:st] n est m ▷ adj (wind) d'est; (side) est inv ▷ adv à l'est, vers l'est; **the E~** l'Orient m; (Pol) les pays mpl de l'Est; **eastbound** adj en direction de l'est; (carriageway) est inv

Easter ['i:stə'] n Pâques fpl; **Easter egg** n œuf m de Pâques

eastern ['i:stən] adj de l'est, oriental(e)

Easter Sunday n le dimanche de Pâques

easy ['i:zɪ] adj facile; (manner) aisé(e) ▷ adv: **to take it** or **things ~** (rest) ne pas se fatiguer; (not worry) ne pas (trop) s'en faire; **easy-going** adj accommodant(e), facile à vivre

eat (pt **ate**, pp **eaten**) [i:t, eɪt, 'i:tn] vt, vi manger; **can we have something to ~?** est-ce qu'on peut manger quelque chose?; **eat out** vi manger au restaurant

eavesdrop ['i:vzdrɔp] vi: **to ~ (on)** écouter de façon indiscrète

e-bike ['i:baɪk] n VAE m

e-book ['i:buk] n livre m électronique

e-business ['i:bɪznɪs] n (company) entreprise f électronique; (commerce) commerce m électronique

eccentric [ɪk'sɛntrɪk] adj, n excentrique m/f

echo ['ɛkəu] (pl **echoes**) n écho m ▷ vt répéter ▷ vi résonner; faire écho

e-cigarette ['i:sɪgərɛt] n cigarette f électronique

eclipse [ɪ'klɪps] n éclipse f

eco-friendly [i:kəu'frɛndlɪ] adj non nuisible à l'environnement

ecological [i:kə'lɔdʒɪkəl] adj écologique

ecology [ɪ'kɔlədʒɪ] n écologie f

e-commerce ['i:kɔmə:s] n commerce m électronique

economic [i:kə'nɔmɪk] adj économique; (profitable) rentable; **economical** adj économique; (person) économe; **economics** n (Scol) économie f politique ▷ npl (of project etc) côté m or aspect m économique

economist [ɪ'kɔnəmɪst] n économiste m/f

economize [ɪ'kɔnəmaɪz] vi économiser, faire des économies

economy [ɪ'kɔnəmɪ] n économie f; **economy class** n (Aviat) classe f touriste; **economy class syndrome** n syndrome m de la classe économique

ecstasy ['ɛkstəsɪ] n extase f; (Drugs) ecstasy m; **ecstatic** [ɛks'tætɪk] adj extatique, en extase

eczema ['ɛksɪmə] n eczéma m

edge [ɛdʒ] n bord m; (of knife etc) tranchant m, fil m ▷ vt border; **on ~** (fig) crispé(e), tendu(e)

edgy ['ɛdʒɪ] adj crispé(e), tendu(e)

edible ['ɛdɪbl] adj comestible; (meal) mangeable

Edinburgh ['ɛdɪnbərə] n Édimbourg; voir article **"Edinburgh Festival"**

edit ['ɛdɪt] vt (text, book) éditer; (report) préparer; (film) monter; (magazine) diriger; (newspaper) être le rédacteur or la rédactrice en chef de; **edition** [ɪ'dɪʃən] n édition f; **editor** n (of newspaper) rédacteur(-trice), rédacteur(-trice) en chef; (of sb's work) éditeur(-trice); (also: **film editor**) monteur(-euse); **political/foreign editor** rédacteur politique/au service étranger; **editorial** [ɛdɪ'tɔ:rɪəl] adj de la rédaction ▷ n éditorial m

educate ['ɛdjukeɪt] vt (teach) instruire; (bring up) éduquer; **educated** ['ɛdjukeɪtɪd] adj (person) cultivé(e)

education [ɛdju'keɪʃən] n éducation f; (studies) études fpl; (teaching) enseignement m, instruction f; **educational** adj pédagogique; (institution) scolaire; (game, toy) éducatif(-ive)

eel [i:l] n anguille f

eerie ['ɪərɪ] adj inquiétant(e), spectral(e), surnaturel(le)

effect [ɪ'fɛkt] n effet m ▷ vt effectuer; **effects** npl (property) effets, affaires fpl; **to take ~** (Law) entrer en vigueur, prendre effet; (drug) agir, faire son effet; **in ~** en fait; **effective** adj efficace; (actual) véritable; **effectively** adv efficacement; (in reality) effectivement, en fait

efficiency [ɪ'fɪʃənsɪ] n efficacité f; (of machine, car) rendement m

efficient [ɪ'fɪʃənt] adj efficace; (machine, car) d'un bon rendement; **efficiently** adv efficacement

effort ['ɛfət] n effort m; **effortless** adj sans effort, aisé(e); (achievement) facile
e.g. adv abbr (= exempli gratia) par exemple, p. ex.
egg [ɛg] n œuf m; **hard-boiled/soft-boiled ~** œuf dur/à la coque; **eggcup** n coquetier m; **egg plant** (us) n aubergine f; **eggshell** n coquille f d'œuf; **egg white** n blanc m d'œuf; **egg yolk** n jaune m d'œuf
ego ['i:gəu] n (self-esteem) amour-propre m; (Psych) moi m
Egypt ['i:dʒɪpt] n Égypte f; **Egyptian** [ɪ'dʒɪpʃən] adj égyptien(ne) ▷ n Égyptien(ne)
Eiffel Tower ['aɪfəl-] n tour f Eiffel
eight [eɪt] num huit; **eighteen** num dix-huit; **eighteenth** num dix-huitième; **eighth** num huitième; **eightieth** ['eɪtɪɪθ] num quatre-vingtième
eighty ['eɪtɪ] num quatre-vingt(s)
Eire ['ɛərə] n République f d'Irlande
either ['aɪðər] adj l'un ou l'autre; (both, each) chaque ▷ pron: **~ (of them)** l'un ou l'autre ▷ adv non plus ▷ conj: **~ good or bad** soit bon soit mauvais; **on ~ side** de chaque côté; **I don't like ~** je n'aime ni l'un ni l'autre; **no, I don't ~** moi non plus; **which bike do you want? — ~ will do** quel vélo voulez-vous? — n'importe lequel; **answer with ~ yes or no** répondez par oui ou par non
eject [ɪ'dʒɛkt] vt (tenant etc) expulser; (object) éjecter
elaborate adj [ɪ'læbərɪt] compliqué(e), recherché(e), minutieux(-euse) ▷ vt [ɪ'læbəreɪt] élaborer ▷ vi [ɪ'læbəreɪt] entrer dans les détails
elastic [ɪ'læstɪk] adj, n élastique (m); **elastic band** (BRIT) élastique m
elbow ['ɛlbəu] n coude m
elder ['ɛldər] adj aîné(e) ▷ n (tree) sureau m; **one's ~s** ses aînés; **elderly** adj âgé(e); **~ people** les personnes âgées
eldest ['ɛldɪst] adj, n: **the ~ (child)** l'aîné(e) (des enfants)
elect [ɪ'lɛkt] vt élire; (choose): **to ~ to do** choisir de faire ▷ adj: **the president ~** le président désigné; **election** n élection f; **electoral** adj électoral(e); **electorate** n électorat m
electric [ɪ'lɛktrɪk] adj électrique; **electrical** adj électrique; **electric blanket** n couverture chauffante; **electric fire** n (BRIT) radiateur m électrique; **electrician** [ɪlɛk'trɪʃən] n électricien m; **electricity** [ɪlɛk'trɪsɪtɪ] n électricité f; **electric shock** n choc m or décharge f électrique; **electrify** [ɪ'lɛktrɪfaɪ] vt (Rail) électrifier; (audience) électriser
electronic [ɪlɛk'trɔnɪk] adj électronique; **electronic mail** n courrier m électronique; **electronics** n électronique f
elegance ['ɛlɪgəns] n élégance f

elegant ['ɛlɪgənt] adj élégant(e)
element ['ɛlɪmənt] n (gen) élément m; (of heater, kettle etc) résistance f
elementary [ɛlɪ'mɛntərɪ] adj élémentaire; (school, education) primaire; **elementary school** n (us) école f primaire
elephant ['ɛlɪfənt] n éléphant m
elevate ['ɛlɪveɪt] vt élever
elevator ['ɛlɪveɪtər] n (in warehouse etc) élévateur m, monte-charge m inv; (us: lift) ascenseur m
eleven [ɪ'lɛvn] num onze; **eleventh** num onzième
eligible ['ɛlɪdʒəbl] adj éligible; (for membership) admissible; **an ~ young man** un beau parti; **to be ~ for sth** remplir les conditions requises pour qch
eliminate [ɪ'lɪmɪneɪt] vt éliminer
elm [ɛlm] n orme m
eloquent ['ɛləkwənt] adj éloquent(e)
else [ɛls] adv: **something ~** quelque chose d'autre, autre chose; **somewhere ~** ailleurs, autre part; **everywhere ~** partout ailleurs; **everyone ~** tous les autres; **nothing ~** rien d'autre; **where ~?** à quel autre endroit?; **little ~** pas grand-chose d'autre; **elsewhere** adv ailleurs, autre part
elusive [ɪ'lu:sɪv] adj insaisissable
email ['i:meɪl] n abbr (= electronic mail) (e-)mail m, courriel m ▷ vt: **to ~ sb** envoyer un (e-)mail or un courriel à qn; **email account** n compte m (e-)mail; **email address** n adresse f (e-)mail or électronique
embankment [ɪm'bæŋkmənt] n (of road, railway) remblai m, talus m; (of river) berge f, quai m; (dyke) digue f
embargo [ɪm'bɑ:gəu] (pl **embargoes**) n (Comm, Naut) embargo m; (prohibition) interdiction f
embark [ɪm'bɑ:k] vi embarquer ▷ vt embarquer; **to ~ on** (journey etc) commencer, entreprendre; (fig) se lancer or s'embarquer dans
embarrass [ɪm'bærəs] vt embarrasser, gêner; **embarrassed** adj gêné(e); **embarrassing** adj gênant(e), embarrassant(e); **embarrassment** n embarras m, gêne f; (embarrassing thing, person) source f d'embarras
embassy ['ɛmbəsɪ] n ambassade f
embrace [ɪm'breɪs] vt embrasser, étreindre; (include) embrasser ▷ vi s'embrasser, s'étreindre ▷ n étreinte f
embroider [ɪm'brɔɪdər] vt broder; **embroidery** n broderie f
embryo ['ɛmbrɪəu] n (also fig) embryon m
emerald ['ɛmərəld] n émeraude f
emerge [ɪ'mə:dʒ] vi apparaître; (from room, car) surgir; (from sleep, imprisonment) sortir
emergency [ɪ'mə:dʒənsɪ] n (crisis) cas m d'urgence; (Med) urgence f; **in an ~** en cas d'urgence; **state of ~** état m d'urgence;

emergency brake (US) n frein m à main;
emergency exit n sortie f de secours;
emergency landing n atterrissage forcé;
emergency room n (US Med) urgences fpl;
emergency services npl: **the emergency services** (fire, police, ambulance) les services mpl d'urgence

emigrate ['ɛmɪɡreɪt] vi émigrer,
emigration [emɪ'greɪʃən] n émigration f

eminent ['ɛmɪnənt] adj éminent(e)

emissions [ɪ'mɪʃənz] npl émissions fpl

emit [ɪ'mɪt] vt émettre

emoticon [ɪ'məʊtɪkən] n (Comput) émoticone m

emotion [ɪ'məʊʃən] n sentiment m;
emotional adj (person) émotif(-ive), très sensible; (needs) affectif(-ive); (scene) émouvant(e); (tone, speech) qui fait appel aux sentiments

emperor ['ɛmpərə'] n empereur m

emphasis (pl **emphases**) ['ɛmfəsɪs, -siːz] n accent m; **to lay** or **place ~ on sth** (fig) mettre l'accent sur, insister sur

emphasize ['ɛmfəsaɪz] vt (syllable, word, point) appuyer or insister sur; (feature) souligner, accentuer

empire ['ɛmpaɪə'] n empire m

employ [ɪm'plɔɪ] vt employer; **employee** [ɪmplɔɪ'iː] n employé(e); **employer** n employeur(-euse); **employment** n emploi m; **employment agency** n agence f or bureau m de placement

empower [ɪm'paʊə'] vt: **to ~ sb to do** autoriser or habiliter qn à faire

empress ['ɛmprɪs] n impératrice f

emptiness ['ɛmptɪnɪs] n vide m; (of area) aspect m désertique

empty ['ɛmptɪ] adj vide; (street, area) désert(e); (threat, promise) en l'air, vain(e) ▷ vt vider ▷ vi se vider; (liquid) s'écouler; **empty-handed** adj les mains vides

EMU n abbr (= European Monetary Union) UME f

emulsion [ɪ'mʌlʃən] n émulsion f; (also: **~ paint**) peinture mate

enable [ɪ'neɪbl] vt: **to ~ sb to do** permettre à qn de faire

enamel [ɪ'næməl] n émail m; (also: **~ paint**) (peinture f) laque f

enchanting [ɪn'tʃɑːntɪŋ] adj ravissant(e), enchanteur(-eresse)

encl. abbr (on letters etc: = enclosed) ci-joint(e); (: = enclosure) PJ f

enclose [ɪn'kləʊz] vt (land) clôturer; (space, object) entourer; (letter etc): **to ~ (with)** joindre (à); **please find ~d** veuillez trouver ci-joint

enclosure [ɪn'kləʊʒə'] n enceinte f

encore [ɔŋ'kɔː'] excl, n bis (m)

encounter [ɪn'kaʊntə'] n rencontre f ▷ vt rencontrer

encourage [ɪn'kʌrɪdʒ] vt encourager

encouraging [ɪn'kʌrɪdʒɪŋ] adj encourageant(e)

encyclop(a)edia [ɛnsaɪkləʊ'piːdɪə] n encyclopédie f

end [ɛnd] n fin f; (of table, street, rope etc) bout m, extrémité f ▷ vt terminer; (also: **bring to an ~, put an ~ to**) mettre fin à ▷ vi se terminer, finir; **in the ~** finalement; **on ~** (object) debout, dressé(e); **to stand on ~** (hair) se dresser sur la tête; **for hours on ~** pendant des heures (et des heures); **end up** vi: **to ~ up in** (condition) finir or se terminer par; (place) finir or aboutir à

endanger [ɪn'deɪndʒə'] vt mettre en danger; **an ~ed species** une espèce en voie de disparition

endearing [ɪn'dɪərɪŋ] adj attachant(e)

endeavour, (US) **endeavor** [ɪn'dɛvə'] n effort m; (attempt) tentative f ▷ vt: **to ~ to do** tenter or s'efforcer de faire

ending ['ɛndɪŋ] n dénouement m, conclusion f; (Ling) terminaison f

endless ['ɛndlɪs] adj sans fin, interminable

endorse [ɪn'dɔːs] vt (cheque) endosser; (approve) appuyer, approuver, sanctionner; **endorsement** n (approval) appui m, aval m; (BRIT: on driving licence) contravention f (portée au permis de conduire)

endurance [ɪn'djʊərəns] n endurance f

endure [ɪn'djʊə'] vt (bear) supporter, endurer ▷ vi (last) durer

enemy ['ɛnəmɪ] adj, n ennemi(e)

energetic [ɛnə'dʒɛtɪk] adj énergique; (activity) très actif(-ive), qui fait se dépenser (physiquement)

energy ['ɛnədʒɪ] n énergie f

enforce [ɪn'fɔːs] vt (law) appliquer, faire respecter

engaged [ɪn'ɡeɪdʒd] adj (BRIT: busy, in use) occupé(e); (betrothed) fiancé(e); **to get ~** se fiancer; **the line's ~** la ligne est occupée; **engaged tone** n (BRIT Tel) tonalité f occupé inv

engagement [ɪn'ɡeɪdʒmənt] n (undertaking) obligation f, engagement m; (appointment) rendez-vous m inv; (to marry) fiançailles fpl; **engagement ring** n bague f de fiançailles

engaging [ɪn'ɡeɪdʒɪŋ] adj engageant(e), attirant(e)

engine ['ɛndʒɪn] n (Aut) moteur m; (Rail) locomotive f

Be careful not to translate engine by the French word engin.

engineer [ɛndʒɪ'nɪə'] n ingénieur m; (BRIT: repairer) dépanneur m; (Navy, US Rail) mécanicien m; **engineering** n engineering m, ingénierie f; (of bridges, ships) génie m; (of machine) mécanique f

England ['ɪŋɡlənd] n Angleterre f

English ['ɪŋɡlɪʃ] adj anglais(e) ▷ n (Ling) anglais m; **the ~** npl les Anglais; **English**

Channel *n*: the English Channel la Manche; **Englishman** (*irreg*) *n* Anglais *m*; **Englishwoman** (*irreg*) *n* Anglaise *f*

engrave [ɪnˈɡreɪv] *vt* graver

engraving [ɪnˈɡreɪvɪŋ] *n* gravure *f*

enhance [ɪnˈhɑːns] *vt* rehausser, mettre en valeur

enjoy [ɪnˈdʒɔɪ] *vt* aimer, prendre plaisir à; (*have benefit of: health, fortune*) jouir de; (: *success*) connaître; **to ~ o.s.** s'amuser; **enjoyable** *adj* agréable; **enjoyment** *n* plaisir *m*

enlarge [ɪnˈlɑːdʒ] *vt* accroître; (*Phot*) agrandir ▷ *vi*: **to ~ on** (*subject*) s'étendre sur; **enlargement** *n* (*Phot*) agrandissement *m*

enlist [ɪnˈlɪst] *vt* recruter; (*support*) s'assurer ▷ *vi* s'engager

enormous [ɪˈnɔːməs] *adj* énorme

enough [ɪˈnʌf] *adj*: **~ time/books** assez ou suffisamment de temps/livres ▷ *adv*: **big ~** assez ou suffisamment grand ▷ *pron*: **have you got ~?** (en) avez-vous assez?; **~ to eat** assez à manger; **that's ~, thanks** cela suffit ou c'est assez, merci; **I've had ~ of him** j'en ai assez de lui; **he has not worked ~** il n'a pas assez ou suffisamment travaillé, il n'a pas travaillé assez ou suffisamment; **... which, funnily** ou **oddly** ou **strangely ~ ...** qui, chose curieuse, ...

enquire [ɪnˈkwaɪəʳ] *vt, vi* = **inquire**

enquiry [ɪnˈkwaɪərɪ] *n* = **inquiry**

enrage [ɪnˈreɪdʒ] *vt* mettre en fureur ou en rage, rendre furieux(-euse)

enrich [ɪnˈrɪtʃ] *vt* enrichir

enrol, (*US*) **enroll** [ɪnˈrəʊl] *vt* inscrire ▷ *vi* s'inscrire; **enrolment**, (*US*) **enrollment** *n* inscription *f*

en route [ɔnˈruːt] *adv* en route, en chemin

en suite [ˈɔnswiːt] *adj*: **with ~ bathroom** avec salle de bains en attenante

ensure [ɪnˈʃuəʳ] *vt* assurer, garantir

entail [ɪnˈteɪl] *vt* entraîner, nécessiter

enter [ˈɛntəʳ] *vt* (*room*) entrer dans, pénétrer dans; (*club, army*) entrer à; (*competition*) s'inscrire à ou pour; (*sb for a competition*) (faire) inscrire; (*write down*) inscrire, noter; (*Comput*) entrer, introduire ▷ *vi* entrer

enterprise [ˈɛntəpraɪz] *n* (*company, undertaking*) entreprise *f*; (*initiative*) (esprit *m* d')initiative *f*; **free ~** libre entreprise; **private ~** entreprise privée; **enterprising** *adj* entreprenant(e), dynamique; (*scheme*) audacieux(-euse)

entertain [ɛntəˈteɪn] *vt* amuser, distraire; (*invite*) recevoir (à dîner); (*idea, plan*) envisager; **entertainer** *n* artiste *m/f* de variétés; **entertaining** *adj* amusant(e), distrayant(e); **entertainment** *n* (*amusement*) distraction *f*, divertissement *m*, amusement *m*; (*show*) spectacle *m*

enthusiasm [ɪnˈθuːzɪæzəm] *n* enthousiasme *m*

enthusiast [ɪnˈθuːzɪæst] *n* enthousiaste *m/f*; **enthusiastic** [ɪnθuːzɪˈæstɪk] *adj* enthousiaste; **to be enthusiastic about** être enthousiasmé(e) par

entire [ɪnˈtaɪəʳ] *adj* (tout) entier(-ère); **entirely** *adv* entièrement

entitle [ɪnˈtaɪtl] *vt*: **to ~ sb to sth** donner droit à qch à qn; **entitled** *adj* (*book*) intitulé(e); **to be entitled to do** avoir le droit de faire

entrance *n* [ˈɛntrns] entrée *f* ▷ *vt* [ɪnˈtrɑːns] enchanter, ravir; **where's the ~?** où est l'entrée?; **to gain ~ to** (*university etc*) être admis à; **entrance examination** *n* examen *m* d'entrée ou d'admission; **entrance fee** *n* (*to museum etc*) prix *m* d'entrée; (*to join club etc*) droit *m* d'inscription; **entrance ramp** *n* (*us Aut*) bretelle *f* d'accès; **entrant** *n* (*in race etc*) participant(e), concurrent(e); (*BRIT: in exam*) candidat(e)

entrepreneur [ˈɔntrəprəˈnəːʳ] *n* entrepreneur *m*

entrust [ɪnˈtrʌst] *vt*: **to ~ sth to** confier qch à

entry [ˈɛntrɪ] *n* entrée *f*; (*in register, diary*) inscription *f*; **"no ~"** "défense d'entrer", "entrée interdite"; (*Aut*) "sens interdit"; **entry phone** *n* (*BRIT*) interphone *m* (à l'entrée d'un immeuble)

envelope [ˈɛnvələup] *n* enveloppe *f*

envious [ˈɛnvɪəs] *adj* envieux(-euse)

environment [ɪnˈvaɪərnmənt] *n* (*social, moral*) milieu *m*; (*natural world*): **the ~** l'environnement *m*; **environmental** [ɪnvaɪərnˈmɛntl] *adj* (*of surroundings*) du milieu; (*issue, disaster*) écologique; **environmentally** [ɪnvaɪərnˈmɛntlɪ] *adv*: **environmentally sound/friendly** qui ne nuit pas à l'environnement

envisage [ɪnˈvɪzɪdʒ] *vt* (*foresee*) prévoir

envoy [ˈɛnvɔɪ] *n* envoyé(e); (*diplomat*) ministre *m* plénipotentiaire

envy [ˈɛnvɪ] *n* envie *f* ▷ *vt* envier; **to ~ sb sth** envier qch à qn

epic [ˈɛpɪk] *n* épopée *f* ▷ *adj* épique

epidemic [ɛpɪˈdɛmɪk] *n* épidémie *f*

epilepsy [ˈɛpɪlɛpsɪ] *n* épilepsie *f*; **epileptic** *adj*, *n* épileptique *m/f*; **epileptic fit** *n* crise *f* d'épilepsie

episode [ˈɛpɪsəud] *n* épisode *m*

equal [ˈiːkwl] *adj* égal(e) ▷ *vt* égaler; **~ to** (*task*) à la hauteur de; **equality** [iːˈkwɔlɪtɪ] *n* égalité *f*; **equalize** *vt, vi* (*Sport*) égaliser; **equally** *adv* également; (*share*) en parts égales; (*treat*) de la même façon; (*pay*) autant; (*just as*) tout aussi

equation [ɪˈkweɪʃən] *n* (*Math*) équation *f*

equator [ɪˈkweɪtəʳ] *n* équateur *m*

equip [ɪˈkwɪp] *vt* équiper; **to ~ sb/sth with** équiper ou munir qn/qch de; **equipment** *n* équipement *m*; (*electrical etc*) appareillage *m*, installation *f*

equivalent [ɪ'kwɪvələnt] adj équivalent(e) ⊳ n équivalent m; **to be ~ to** équivaloir à, être équivalent(e) à

ER abbr (BRIT: = Elizabeth Regina) la reine Élisabeth; (US Med: = emergency room) urgences fpl

era ['ɪərə] n ère f, époque f

erase [ɪ'reɪz] vt effacer; **eraser** n gomme f

e-reader ['iːriːdə'] n liseuse f

erect [ɪ'rekt] adj droit(e) ⊳ vt construire; (monument) ériger, élever; (tent etc) dresser; **erection** [ɪ'rekʃən] n (Physiol) érection f; (of building) construction f

ERM n abbr (= Exchange Rate Mechanism) mécanisme m des taux de change

erode [ɪ'rəud] vt éroder, (metal) ronger

erosion [ɪ'rəuʒən] n érosion f

erotic [ɪ'rɔtɪk] adj érotique

errand ['ɛrnd] n course f, commission f

erratic [ɪ'rætɪk] adj irrégulier(-ière), inconstant(e)

error ['ɛrə'] n erreur f

erupt [ɪ'rʌpt] vi entrer en éruption; (fig) éclater; **eruption** [ɪ'rʌpʃən] n éruption f; (of anger, violence) explosion f

escalate ['ɛskəleɪt] vi s'intensifier; (costs) monter en flèche

escalator ['ɛskəleɪtə'] n escalier roulant

escape [ɪ'skeɪp] n évasion f, fuite f; (of gas etc) fuite f ⊳ vi s'échapper, fuir; (from jail) s'évader; (fig) s'en tirer; (leak) s'échapper ⊳ vt échapper à; **to ~ from** (person) échapper à; (place) s'échapper de; (fig) fuir; **his name ~s me** son nom m'échappe

escort vt [ɪ'skɔːt] escorter ⊳ n ['ɛskɔːt] (Mil) escorte f

especially [ɪ'speʃlɪ] adv (particularly) particulièrement; (above all) surtout

espionage ['ɛspɪənaːʒ] n espionnage m

essay ['ɛseɪ] n (Scol) dissertation f; (Literature) essai m

essence ['ɛsns] n essence f; (Culin) extrait m

essential [ɪ'sɛnʃl] adj essentiel(le); (basic) fondamental(e); **essentials** npl éléments essentiels; **essentially** adv essentiellement

establish [ɪ'stæblɪʃ] vt établir; (business) fonder, créer; (one's power etc) asseoir; affermir; **establishment** n établissement m; (founding) création f; (institution) établissement; **the Establishment** les pouvoirs établis; l'ordre établi

estate [ɪ'steɪt] n (land) domaine m, propriété f; (Law) biens mpl, succession f; (BRIT: also: **housing ~**) lotissement m; **estate agent** n (BRIT) agent immobilier; **estate car** n (BRIT) break m

estimate n ['ɛstɪmət] estimation f; (Comm) devis m ⊳ vt ['ɛstɪmeɪt] estimer

etc abbr (= et cetera) etc

eternal [ɪ'təːnl] adj éternel(le)

eternity [ɪ'təːnɪtɪ] n éternité f

ethical ['ɛθɪkl] adj moral(e); **ethics** ['ɛθɪks] n éthique f ⊳ npl moralité f

Ethiopia [iːθɪ'əupɪə] n Éthiopie f

ethnic ['ɛθnɪk] adj ethnique; (clothes, food) folklorique, exotique, propre aux minorités ethniques non-occidentales; **ethnic minority** n minorité f ethnique

e-ticket ['iːtɪkɪt] n billet m électronique

etiquette ['ɛtɪkɛt] n convenances fpl, étiquette f

EU n abbr (= European Union) UE f

euro ['juərəu] n (currency) euro m

Europe ['juərəp] n Europe f; **European** [juərə'piːən] adj européen(ne) ⊳ n Européen(ne); **European Community** n Communauté européenne; **European Union** n Union européenne

Eurostar® ['juərəustaː'] n Eurostar® m

evacuate [ɪ'vækjueɪt] vt évacuer

evade [ɪ'veɪd] vt échapper à; (question etc) éluder; (duties) se dérober à

evaluate [ɪ'væljueɪt] vt évaluer

evaporate [ɪ'væpəreɪt] vi s'évaporer; (fig: hopes, fear) s'envoler; (anger) se dissiper

eve [iːv] n: **on the ~ of** à la veille de

even ['iːvn] adj (level, smooth) régulier(-ière); (equal) égal(e); (number) pair(e) ⊳ adv même; **~ if** même si + indic; **~ though** alors même que + cond; **~ more** encore plus; **~ faster** encore plus vite; **~ so** quand même; **not ~** pas même; **~ he was there** même lui était là; **~ on Sundays** même le dimanche; **to get ~ with sb** prendre sa revanche sur qn

evening ['iːvnɪŋ] n soir m; (as duration, event) soirée f, **in the ~** le soir; **evening class** n cours m du soir; **evening dress** n (man's) tenue f de soirée, smoking m; (woman's) robe f de soirée

event [ɪ'vɛnt] n événement m; (Sport) épreuve f; **in the ~ of** en cas de; **eventful** adj mouvementé(e)

eventual [ɪ'vɛntʃuəl] adj final(e)

▌ Be careful not to translate eventual by the French word éventuel.

eventually [ɪ'vɛntʃuəlɪ] adv finalement

▌ Be careful not to translate eventually by the French word éventuellement.

ever ['ɛvə'] adv jamais; (at all times) toujours; **why ~ not?** mais enfin, pourquoi pas?; **the best ~** le meilleur qu'on ait jamais vu; **have you ~ seen it?** l'as-tu déjà vu?, as-tu eu l'occasion or t'est-il arrivé de le voir?; **~ since** (as adv) depuis; (as conj) depuis que; **~ so pretty** si joli; **evergreen** n arbre m à feuilles persistantes

⬤ **KEYWORD**

every ['ɛvrɪ] adj **1** (each) chaque; **every one of them** tous (sans exception); **every shop in town was closed** tous les magasins en ville étaient fermés

2 (all possible) tous (toutes) les; **I gave you every assistance** j'ai fait tout mon possible pour vous aider; **I have every confidence in him** j'ai entièrement or pleinement confiance en lui; **we wish you every success** nous vous souhaitons beaucoup de succès
3 (showing recurrence) tous les; **every day** tous les jours, chaque jour; **every other car** une voiture sur deux; **every other/third day** tous les deux/trois jours; **every now and then** de temps en temps; **everybody** pron = **everyone**; **everyday** adj (expression) courant(e), d'usage courant; (use) courant; (clothes, life) de tous les jours; (occurrence, problem) quotidien(ne); **everyone** pron tout le monde, tous pl; **everything** pron tout; **everywhere** adv partout; **everywhere you go you meet ...** où qu'on aille on rencontre ...

evict [ɪ'vɪkt] vt expulser
evidence ['ɛvɪdns] n (proof) preuve(s) f(pl); (of witness) témoignage m; (sign): **to show ~ of** donner des signes de; **to give ~** témoigner, déposer
evident ['ɛvɪdnt] adj évident(e); **evidently** adv de toute évidence; (apparently) apparemment
evil ['iːvl] adj mauvais(e) ▷ n mal m
evoke [ɪ'vəʊk] vt évoquer
evolution [iːvə'luːʃən] n évolution f
evolve [ɪ'vɔlv] vt élaborer ▷ vi évoluer, se transformer
ewe [juː] n brebis f
ex [ɛks] n (inf): **my ex** mon ex
ex- [ɛks] prefix ex-
exact [ɪg'zækt] adj exact(e) ▷ vt: **to ~ sth (from)** (signature, confession) extorquer qch (à); (apology) exiger qch (de); **exactly** adv exactement
exaggerate [ɪg'zædʒəreɪt] vt, vi exagérer; **exaggeration** [ɪgzædʒə'reɪʃən] n exagération f
exam [ɪg'zæm] n abbr (Scol): = **examination**
examination [ɪgzæmɪ'neɪʃən] n (Scol, Med) examen m; **to take** or **sit an ~** (BRIT) passer un examen
examine [ɪg'zæmɪn] vt (gen) examiner; (Scol, Law: person) interroger; **examiner** n examinateur(-trice)
example [ɪg'zɑːmpl] n exemple m; **for ~** par exemple
exasperated [ɪg'zɑːspəreɪtɪd] adj exaspéré(e)
excavate ['ɛkskəveɪt] vt (site) fouiller, excaver; (object) mettre au jour
exceed [ɪk'siːd] vt dépasser; (one's powers) outrepasser; **exceedingly** adv extrêmement
excel [ɪk'sɛl] vi exceller ▷ vt surpasser; **to ~ o.s.** se surpasser

excellence ['ɛksələns] n excellence f
excellent ['ɛksələnt] adj excellent(e)
except [ɪk'sɛpt] prep (also: **~ for**, **~ing**) sauf, excepté, à l'exception de ▷ vt excepter; **~ if/when** sauf si/quand; **~ that** excepté que, si ce n'est que; **exception** [ɪk'sɛpʃən] n exception f; **to take exception to** s'offusquer de; **exceptional** [ɪk'sɛpʃənl] adj exceptionnel(le); **exceptionally** [ɪk'sɛpʃənəlɪ] adv exceptionnellement
excerpt ['ɛksəːpt] n extrait m
excess [ɪk'sɛs] n excès m; **excess baggage** n excédent m de bagages; **excessive** adj excessif(-ive)
exchange [ɪks'tʃeɪndʒ] n échange m; (also: **telephone ~**) central m ▷ vt: **to ~ (for)** échanger (contre); **could I ~ this, please?** est-ce que je peux échanger ceci, s'il vous plaît?; **exchange rate** n taux m de change
excite [ɪk'saɪt] vt exciter; **excited** adj (tout) excité(e); **to get excited** s'exciter; **excitement** n excitation f; **exciting** adj passionnant(e)
exclaim [ɪk'skleɪm] vi s'exclamer; **exclamation** [ɛksklə'meɪʃən] n exclamation f; **exclamation mark**, (US) **exclamation point** n point m d'exclamation
exclude [ɪk'skluːd] vt exclure
excluding [ɪk'skluːdɪŋ] prep: **~ VAT** la TVA non comprise
exclusion [ɪk'skluːʒən] n exclusion f
exclusive [ɪk'skluːsɪv] adj exclusif(-ive); (club, district) sélect(e); (item of news) en exclusivité; **~ of VAT** TVA non comprise; **exclusively** adv exclusivement
excruciating [ɪk'skruːʃɪeɪtɪŋ] adj (pain) atroce, déchirant(e); (embarrassing) pénible
excursion [ɪk'skəːʃən] n excursion f
excuse n [ɪk'skjuːs] excuse f ▷ vt [ɪk'skjuːz] (forgive) excuser; **to ~ sb from** (activity) dispenser qn de; **~ me!** excusez-moi!, pardon!; **now if you will ~ me, ...** maintenant, si vous (le) permettez ...
ex-directory ['ɛksdɪ'rɛktərɪ] adj (BRIT) sur la liste rouge
execute ['ɛksɪkjuːt] vt exécuter; **execution** [ɛksɪ'kjuːʃən] n exécution f
executive [ɪg'zɛkjutɪv] n (person) cadre m; (managing group) bureau m; (Pol) exécutif m ▷ adj exécutif(-ive); (position, job) de cadre
exempt [ɪg'zɛmpt] adj: **~ from** exempté(e) or dispensé(e) de ▷ vt: **to ~ sb from** exempter or dispenser qn de
exercise ['ɛksəsaɪz] n exercice m ▷ vt exercer; (patience etc) faire preuve de; (dog) promener ▷ vi (also: **to take ~**) prendre de l'exercice; **exercise book** n cahier m
exert [ɪg'zəːt] vt exercer, employer; **to ~ o.s.** se dépenser; **exertion** [ɪg'zəːʃən] n effort m
exhale [ɛks'heɪl] vt exhaler ▷ vi expirer

exhaust [ɪɡˈzɔːst] n (also: ~ **fumes**) gaz mpl d'échappement; (also: ~ **pipe**) tuyau m d'échappement ▷ vt épuiser; **exhausted** adj épuisé(e); **exhaustion** [ɪɡˈzɔːstʃən] n épuisement m; **nervous exhaustion** fatigue nerveuse

exhibit [ɪɡˈzɪbɪt] n (Art) objet exposé, pièce exposée; (Law) pièce à conviction ▷ vt (Art) exposer; (courage, skill) faire preuve de; **exhibition** [ɛksɪˈbɪʃən] n exposition f

exhilarating [ɪɡˈzɪləreɪtɪŋ] adj grisant(e), stimulant(e)

exile [ˈɛksaɪl] n exil m; (person) exilé(e) ▷ vt exiler

exist [ɪɡˈzɪst] vi exister; **existence** n existence f; **existing** adj actuel(le)

exit [ˈɛksɪt] n sortie f ▷ vi (Comput, Theat) sortir; **where's the ~?** où est la sortie?; **exit ramp** n (us Aut) bretelle f d'accès

exotic [ɪɡˈzɔtɪk] adj exotique

expand [ɪkˈspænd] vt (area) agrandir; (quantity) accroître ▷ vi (trade, etc) se développer, s'accroître; (gas, metal) se dilater

expansion [ɪkˈspænʃən] n (territorial, economic) expansion f; (of trade, influence etc) développement m; (of production) accroissement m; (of population) croissance f, (of gas, metal) expansion, dilatation f

expect [ɪkˈspɛkt] vt (anticipate) s'attendre à, s'attendre à ce que + sub; (count on) compter sur, escompter; (require) demander, exiger; (suppose) supposer; (await: also baby) attendre ▷ vi: **to be ~ing** (pregnant woman) être enceinte; **expectation** [ɛkspɛkˈteɪʃən] n (hope) attente f, espérance(s) f(pl); (belief) attente

expedition [ɛkspəˈdɪʃən] n expédition f

expel [ɪkˈspɛl] vt chasser, expulser; (Scol) renvoyer, exclure

expenditure [ɪkˈspɛndɪtʃəʳ] n (act of spending) dépense f; (money spent) dépenses fpl

expense [ɪkˈspɛns] n (high cost) coût m; (spending) dépense f, frais mpl; **expenses** npl frais mpl; dépenses; **at the ~ of** (fig) aux dépens de; **expense account** (note f de) frais mpl

expensive [ɪkˈspɛnsɪv] adj cher (chère), coûteux(-euse); **it's too ~** ça coûte trop cher

experience [ɪkˈspɪərɪəns] n expérience f ▷ vt connaître; (feeling) éprouver; **experienced** adj expérimenté(e)

experiment [ɪkˈspɛrɪmənt] n expérience f ▷ vi faire une expérience; **experimental** [ɪkspɛrɪˈmɛntl] adj expérimental(e)

expert [ˈɛkspəːt] adj expert(e) ▷ n expert m; **expertise** [ɛkspəːˈtiːz] n (grande) compétence f

expire [ɪkˈspaɪəʳ] vi expirer; **expiry** n expiration f; **expiry date** n date f d'expiration; (on label) à utiliser avant …

explain [ɪkˈspleɪn] vt expliquer; **explanation** [ɛkspləˈneɪʃən] n explication f

explicit [ɪkˈsplɪsɪt] adj explicite; (definite) formel(le)

explode [ɪkˈspləud] vi exploser

exploit n [ˈɛksplɔɪt] exploit m ▷ vt [ɪkˈsplɔɪt] exploiter; **exploitation** [ɛksplɔɪˈteɪʃən] n exploitation f

explore [ɪkˈsplɔːʳ] vt explorer; (possibilities) étudier, examiner, **explorer** n explorateur(-trice)

explosion [ɪkˈspləuʒən] n explosion f; **explosive** [ɪkˈspləusɪv] adj explosif(-ive) ▷ n explosif m

export vt [ɛkˈspɔːt] exporter ▷ n [ˈɛkspɔːt] exportation f ▷ cpd [ˈɛkspɔːt] d'exportation; **exporter** n exportateur m

expose [ɪkˈspəuz] vt exposer; (unmask) démasquer, dévoiler; **exposed** adj (land, house) exposé(e); **exposure** [ɪkˈspəuʒəʳ] n exposition f; (publicity) couverture f; (Phot: speed) (temps m de) pose f, (: shot) pose; **to die of exposure** (Med) mourir de froid

express [ɪkˈsprɛs] adj (definite) formel(le), exprès(-esse); (unit: letter etc) exprès inv ▷ n (train) rapide m ▷ vt exprimer; **expression** [ɪkˈsprɛʃən] n expression f; **expressway** n (us) voie f express (à plusieurs files)

exquisite [ɛkˈskwɪzɪt] adj exquis(e)

extend [ɪkˈstɛnd] vt (visit, street) prolonger; remettre; (building) agrandir; (offer) présenter, offrir; (hand, arm) tendre ▷ vi (land) s'étendre; **extension** n (of visit, street) prolongation f; (building) annexe f; (telephone: in offices) poste m; (: in private house) téléphone m supplémentaire; **extension cable, extension lead** n (Elec) rallonge f; **extensive** adj étendu(e), vaste; (damage, alterations) considérable; (inquiries) approfondi(e)

extent [ɪkˈstɛnt] n étendue f; **to some ~** dans une certaine mesure; **to the ~ of …** au point de …; **to what ~?** dans quelle mesure?, jusqu'à quel point?; **to such an ~ that …** à tel point que …

exterior [ɛkˈstɪərɪəʳ] adj extérieur(e) ▷ n extérieur m

external [ɛkˈstəːnl] adj externe

extinct [ɪkˈstɪŋkt] adj (volcano) éteint(e); (species) disparu(e); **extinction** n extinction f

extinguish [ɪkˈstɪŋɡwɪʃ] vt éteindre

extra [ˈɛkstrə] adj supplémentaire, de plus ▷ adv (in addition) en plus ▷ n supplément m; (perk) à-côté m; (Cine, Theat) figurant(e)

extract vt [ɪkˈstrækt] extraire; (tooth) arracher; (money, promise) soutirer ▷ n [ˈɛkstrækt] extrait m

extradite [ˈɛkstrədaɪt] vt extrader

extraordinary [ɪkˈstrɔːdnrɪ] adj extraordinaire

extravagance [ɪkˈstrævəgəns] n (*excessive spending*) prodigalités fpl; (*thing bought*) folie f, dépense excessive; **extravagant** adj extravagant(e); (*in spending: person*) prodigue, dépensier(-ière); (: *tastes*) dispendieux(-euse)

extreme [ɪkˈstriːm] adj, n extrême (m); **extremely** adv extrêmement

extremist [ɪkˈstriːmɪst] adj, n extrémiste m/f

extrovert [ˈɛkstrəvəːt] n extraverti(e)

eye [aɪ] n œil m; (*of needle*) trou m, chas m ▷ vt examiner; **to keep an ~ on** surveiller; **eyeball** n globe m oculaire; **eyebrow** n sourcil m; **eye drops** npl gouttes fpl pour les yeux; **eyelash** n cil m; **eyelid** n paupière f; **eyeliner** n eye-liner m; **eye shadow** n ombre f à paupières; **eyesight** n vue f; **eye witness** n témoin m oculaire

f

F [ɛf] n (*Mus*) fa m

fabric [ˈfæbrɪk] n tissu m

fabulous [ˈfæbjuləs] adj fabuleux(-euse); (*inf: super*) formidable, sensationnel(le)

face [feɪs] n visage m, figure f; (*expression*) air m; (*of clock*) cadran m; (*of cliff*) paroi f; (*of mountain*) face f; (*of building*) façade f ▷ vt faire face à; (*facts etc*) accepter; **~ down** (*person*) à plat ventre; (*card*) face en dessous; **to lose/save ~** perdre/sauver la face; **to pull a ~** faire une grimace; **in the ~ of** (*difficulties etc*) face à, devant; **on the ~ of it** à première vue; **~ to ~** face à face; **face up to** vt fus faire face à, affronter; **face cloth** n (*BRIT*) gant m de toilette; **face pack** n (*BRIT*) masque m (de beauté)

facial [ˈfeɪʃl] adj facial(e) ▷ n soin complet du visage

facilitate [fəˈsɪlɪteɪt] vt faciliter

facilities [fəˈsɪlɪtɪz] npl installations fpl, équipement m; **credit ~** facilités de paiement

fact [fækt] n fait m; **in ~** en fait

faction [ˈfækʃən] n faction f

factor [ˈfæktəʳ] n facteur m; (*of sun cream*) indice m (de protection); **I'd like a ~ 15 suntan lotion** je voudrais une crème solaire d'indice 15

factory [ˈfæktərɪ] n usine f, fabrique f

factual [ˈfæktjuəl] adj basé(e) sur les faits

faculty [ˈfækəltɪ] n faculté f; (*US: teaching staff*) corps enseignant

fad [fæd] n (*personal*) manie f; (*craze*) engouement m

fade [feɪd] vi se décolorer, passer; (*light, sound*) s'affaiblir; (*flower*) se faner; **fade away** vi (*sound*) s'affaiblir

fag [fæg] n (*BRIT inf: cigarette*) clope f

Fahrenheit [ˈfɑːrənhaɪt] n Fahrenheit m inv

fail [feɪl] vt (*exam*) échouer à; (*candidate*) recaler; (*subj: courage, memory*) faire défaut à

▷ vi échouer; (*eyesight, health, light: also:* **be ~ing**) baisser, s'affaiblir; (*brakes*) lâcher; **to ~ to do sth** (*neglect*) négliger de or ne pas faire qch; (*be unable*) ne pas arriver or parvenir à faire qch; **without ~** à coup sûr; sans faute; **failing** n défaut m ▷ prep faute de; **failing that** à défaut, sinon; **failure** ['feɪljə'] n échec m; (*person*) raté(e); (*mechanical etc*) défaillance f

faint [feɪnt] adj faible; (*recollection*) vague; (*mark*) à peine visible ▷ n évanouissement m ▷ vi s'évanouir; **to feel ~** défaillir; **faintest** adj: **I haven't the faintest idea** je n'en ai pas la moindre idée; **faintly** adv faiblement; (*vaguely*) vaguement

fair [fɛə'] adj équitable, juste; (*hair*) blond(e); (*skin, complexion*) pâle, blanc (blanche); (*weather*) beau (belle); (*good enough*) assez bon(ne); (*sizeable*) considérable ▷ adv: **to play ~** jouer franc jeu ▷ n foire f; (BRIT: *funfair*) fête (foraine); **fairground** n champ m de foire; **fair-haired** adj (*person*) aux cheveux clairs, blond(e); **fairly** adv (*justly*) équitablement; (*quite*) assez; **fair trade** n commerce m équitable; **fairway** n (*Golf*) fairway m

fairy ['fɛəri] n fée f; **fairy tale** n conte m de fées

faith [feɪθ] n foi f; (*trust*) confiance f; (*sect*) culte m, religion f; **faithful** adj fidèle; **faithfully** adv fidèlement; **yours faithfully** (BRIT: *in letters*) veuillez agréer l'expression de mes salutations les plus distinguées

fake [feɪk] n (*painting etc*) faux m; (*person*) imposteur m ▷ adj faux (fausse) ▷ vt (*emotions*) simuler; (*painting*) faire un faux de

falcon ['fɔːlkən] n faucon m

fall [fɔːl] n chute f; (*decrease*) baisse f; (US: *autumn*) automne m ▷ vi (*pt* **fell**, *pp* **fallen**) tomber; (*price, temperature, dollar*) baisser; **falls** npl (*waterfall*) chute f d'eau, cascade f; **to ~ flat** vi (*on one's face*) tomber de tout son long; (*joke*) tomber à plat; (*plan*) échouer; **fall apart** vi (*object*) tomber en morceaux; **fall down** vi (*person*) tomber; (*building*) s'effondrer, s'écrouler; **fall for** vt fus (*trick*) se laisser prendre à; (*person*) tomber amoureux(-euse) de; **fall off** vi tomber; (*diminish*) baisser, diminuer; **fall out** vi (*friends etc*) se brouiller; (*hair, teeth*) tomber; **fall over** vi tomber (par terre); **fall through** vi (*plan, project*) tomber à l'eau

fallen ['fɔːlən] pp of **fall**

fallout ['fɔːlaut] n retombées (radioactives)

false [fɔːls] adj faux (fausse); **under ~ pretences** sous un faux prétexte; **false alarm** n fausse alerte; **false teeth** npl (BRIT) fausses dents, dentier m

fame [feɪm] n renommée f, renom m

familiar [fə'mɪliə'] adj familier(-ière); **to be ~ with sth** connaître qch; **familiarize**

[fə'mɪliəraɪz] vt: **to familiarize o.s. with** se familiariser avec

family ['fæmɪli] n famille f; **family doctor** n médecin m de famille; **family planning** n planning familial

famine ['fæmɪn] n famine f

famous ['feɪməs] adj célèbre

fan [fæn] n (*folding*) éventail m; (*Elec*) ventilateur m; (*person*) fan m, admirateur(-trice); (*Sport*) supporter m/f ▷ vt éventer; (*fire, quarrel*) attiser

fanatic [fə'nætɪk] n fanatique m/f

fan belt n courroie f de ventilateur

fan club n fan-club m

fancy ['fænsɪ] n (*whim*) fantaisie f, envie f; (*imagination*) imagination f ▷ adj (*luxury*) de luxe; (*elaborate: jewellery, packaging*) fantaisie inv ▷ vt (*feel like, want*) avoir envie de; (*imagine*) imaginer; **to take a ~ to** se prendre d'affection pour; s'enticher de; **he fancies her** elle lui plaît; **fancy dress** n déguisement m, travesti m

fan heater n (BRIT) radiateur soufflant

fantasize ['fæntəsaɪz] vi fantasmer

fantastic [fæn'tæstɪk] adj fantastique

fantasy ['fæntəsɪ] n imagination f, fantaisie f; (*unreality*) fantasme m

fanzine ['fænziːn] n fanzine m

FAQ n abbr (= frequently asked question) FAQ f inv, faq f inv

far [fɑː'] adj (*distant*) lointain(e), éloigné(e) ▷ adv loin; **the ~ side/end** l'autre côté/bout; **it's not ~ (from here)** ce n'est pas loin (d'ici); **~ away, ~ off** au loin, dans le lointain; **~ better** beaucoup mieux; **~ from** loin de; **by ~** de loin, de beaucoup; **go as ~ as the bridge** allez jusqu'au pont; **as ~ as I know** pour autant que je sache; **how ~ is it to …?** combien y a-t-il jusqu'à …?; **how ~ have you got with your work?** où en êtes-vous dans votre travail?

farce [fɑːs] n farce f

fare [fɛə'] n (*on trains, buses*) prix m du billet; (*in taxi*) prix de la course; (*food*) table f, chère f; **half ~** demi-tarif; **full ~** plein tarif

Far East n: **the ~** l'Extrême-Orient m

farewell [fɛə'wɛl] excl, n adieu m

farm [fɑːm] n ferme f ▷ vt cultiver; **farmer** n fermier(-ière); **farmhouse** n (maison f de) ferme f; **farming** n agriculture f; (*of animals*) élevage m; **farmyard** n cour f de ferme

far-reaching ['fɑː'riːtʃɪŋ] adj d'une grande portée

fart [fɑːt] (inf!) vi péter

farther ['fɑːðə'] adv plus loin ▷ adj plus éloigné(e), plus lointain(e)

farthest ['fɑːðɪst] superlative of **far**

fascinate ['fæsɪneɪt] vt fasciner, captiver

fascinating ['fæsɪneɪtɪŋ] adj fascinant(e)

fascination [fæsɪ'neɪʃən] n fascination f

fascist ['fæʃɪst] adj, n fasciste m/f

fashion ['fæʃən] n mode f; (manner) façon f, manière f ▷ vt façonner; **in ~** à la mode; **out of ~** démodé(e); **fashionable** adj à la mode; **fashion show** n défilé m de mannequins or de mode

fast [fɑːst] adj rapide; (clock): **to be ~** avancer; (dye, colour) grand or bon teint inv ▷ adv vite, rapidement; (stuck, held) solidement ▷ n jeûne m ▷ vi jeûner; **~ asleep** profondément endormi

fasten ['fɑːsn] vt attacher, fixer; (coat) attacher, fermer ▷ vi se fermer, s'attacher

fast food n fast food m, restauration f rapide

fat [fæt] adj gros(se) ▷ n graisse f; (on meat) gras m; (for cooking) matière grasse

fatal ['feɪtl] adj (mistake) fatal(e); (injury) mortel(le); **fatality** [fə'tælɪtɪ] n (road death) victime f, décès m; **fatally** adv fatalement; (injured) mortellement

fate [feɪt] n destin m; (of person) sort m

father ['fɑːðəʳ] n père m; **Father Christmas** n le Père Noël; **father-in-law** n beau-père m

fatigue [fə'tiːg] n fatigue f

fattening ['fætnɪŋ] adj (food) qui fait grossir

fatty ['fætɪ] adj (food) gras(se) ▷ n (inf) gros (grosse)

faucet ['fɔːsɪt] n (US) robinet m

fault [fɔːlt] n faute f; (defect) défaut m; (Geo) faille f ▷ vt trouver des défauts à, prendre en défaut; **it's my ~** c'est de ma faute; **to find ~ with** trouver à redire or à critiquer à; **at ~** fautif(-ive), coupable; **faulty** adj défectueux(-euse)

fauna ['fɔːnə] n faune f

favour, (US) **favor** ['feɪvəʳ] n faveur f; (help) service m ▷ vt (proposition) être en faveur de; (pupil etc) favoriser; (team, horse) donner gagnant; **to do sb a ~** rendre un service à qn; **in ~ of** en faveur de; **to find ~ with sb** trouver grâce aux yeux de qn; **favourable**, (US) **favorable** adj favorable; **favourite**, (US) **favorite** ['feɪvrɪt] adj, n favori(te)

fawn [fɔːn] n (deer) faon m ▷ adj (also: **~-coloured**) fauve ▷ vi: **to ~ (up)on** flatter servilement

fax [fæks] n (document) télécopie f; (machine) télécopieur m ▷ vt envoyer par télécopie

FBI n abbr (US: = Federal Bureau of Investigation) FBI m

fear [fɪəʳ] n crainte f, peur f ▷ vt craindre; **for ~ of** de peur que + sub or de + infinitive; **fearful** adj craintif(-ive); (sight, noise) affreux(-euse), épouvantable; **fearless** adj intrépide

feasible ['fiːzəbl] adj faisable, réalisable

feast [fiːst] n festin m, banquet m; (Rel: also: **~ day**) fête f ▷ vi festoyer

feat [fiːt] n exploit m, prouesse f

feather ['fɛðəʳ] n plume f

feature ['fiːtʃəʳ] n caractéristique f; (article) chronique f, rubrique f ▷ vt (film) avoir pour vedette(s) ▷ vi figurer (en bonne place); **features** npl (of face) traits mpl; **a (special) ~ on sth/sb** un reportage sur qch/qn; **feature film** n long métrage

Feb. abbr (= February) fév

February ['fɛbruərɪ] n février m

fed [fɛd] pt, pp of **feed**

federal ['fɛdərəl] adj fédéral(e)

federation [fɛdə'reɪʃən] n fédération f

fed up adj: **to be ~ (with)** en avoir marre or plein le dos (de)

fee [fiː] n rémunération f; (of doctor, lawyer) honoraires mpl; (of school, college etc) frais mpl de scolarité; (for examination) droits mpl

feeble ['fiːbl] adj faible; (attempt, excuse) pauvre; (joke) piteux(-euse)

feed [fiːd] n (of animal) nourriture f, pâture f; (on printer) mécanisme m d'alimentation ▷ vt (pt, pp **fed**) (person) nourrir; (BRIT: baby: breastfeed) allaiter; (: with bottle) donner le biberon à; (horse etc) donner à manger à; (machine) alimenter; (data etc): **to ~ sth into** enregistrer qch dans; **feedback** n (Elec) effet m Larsen; (from person) réactions fpl

feel [fiːl] n (sensation) sensation f; (impression) impression f ▷ vt (pt, pp **felt**) (touch) toucher; (explore) tâter, palper; (cold, pain) sentir; (grief, anger) ressentir, éprouver; (think, believe): **to ~ (that)** trouver que; **to ~ hungry/cold** avoir faim/froid; **to ~ lonely/ better** se sentir seul/mieux; **I don't ~ well** je ne me sens pas bien; **it ~s soft** c'est doux au toucher; **to ~ like** (want) avoir envie de; **feeling** n (physical) sensation f; (emotion, impression) sentiment m; **to hurt sb's feelings** froisser qn

feet [fiːt] npl of **foot**

fell [fɛl] pt of **fall** ▷ vt (tree) abattre

fellow ['fɛləu] n type m; (comrade) compagnon m; (of learned society) membre m ▷ cpd: **their ~ prisoners/students** leurs camarades prisonniers/étudiants; **fellow citizen** n concitoyen(ne); **fellow countryman** n (irreg) compatriote m; **fellow men** npl semblables mpl; **fellowship** n (society) association f; (comradeship) amitié f, camaraderie f; (Scol) sorte de bourse universitaire

felony ['fɛlənɪ] n crime m, forfait m

felt [fɛlt] pt, pp of **feel** ▷ n feutre m; **felt-tip** n (also: **felt-tip pen**) stylo-feutre m

female ['fiːmeɪl] n (Zool) femelle f; (pej: woman) bonne femme ▷ adj (Biol) femelle; (sex, character) féminin(e); (vote etc) des femmes

feminine ['fɛmɪnɪn] adj féminin(e)

feminist ['fɛmɪnɪst] n féministe m/f

fence [fɛns] n barrière f ▷ vi faire de l'escrime; **fencing** n (sport) escrime m

fend [fɛnd] vi: **to ~ for o.s.** se débrouiller (tout seul); **fend off** vt (attack etc) parer; (questions) éluder
fender ['fɛndəʳ] n garde-feu m inv; (on boat) défense f; (us: of car) aile f
fennel ['fɛnl] n fenouil m
ferment vi [fə'mɛnt] fermenter ▷ n ['fɜ:mɛnt] (fig) agitation f, effervescence f
fern [fə:n] n fougère f
ferocious [fə'rəʊʃəs] adj féroce
ferret ['fɛrɪt] n furet m
ferry ['fɛrɪ] n (small) bac m; (large: also: ~boat) ferry(-boat m) m ▷ vt transporter
fertile ['fɜ:taɪl] adj fertile; (Biol) fécond(e); **fertilize** ['fɜ:tɪlaɪz] vt fertiliser; (Biol) féconder; **fertilizer** n engrais m
festival ['fɛstɪvəl] n (Rel) fête f; (Art, Mus) festival m
festive ['fɛstɪv] adj de fête; **the ~ season** (BRIT: Christmas) la période des fêtes
fetch [fɛtʃ] vt aller chercher; (BRIT: sell for) rapporter
fête [feɪt] n fête f, kermesse f
fetus ['fi:təs] n (US) =**foetus**
feud [fju:d] n querelle f, dispute f
fever ['fi:vəʳ] n fièvre f; **feverish** adj fiévreux(-euse), fébrile
few [fju:] adj (not many) peu de ▷ pron peu; **a ~** (as adj) quelques; (as pron) quelques-uns(-unes); **quite a ~ ...** adj un certain nombre de ..., pas mal de ...; **in the past ~ days** ces derniers jours; **fewer** adj moins de; **fewest** adj le moins nombreux
fiancé [fɪ'ɑ:nseɪ] n fiancé m; **fiancée** n fiancée f
fiasco [fɪ'æskəʊ] n fiasco m
fib [fɪb] n bobard m
fibre, (US) **fiber** ['faɪbəʳ] n fibre f; **fibreglass**, (US) **Fiberglass®** n fibre f de verre
fickle ['fɪkl] adj inconstant(e), volage, capricieux(-euse)
fiction ['fɪkʃən] n romans mpl, littérature f romanesque; (invention) fiction f; **fictional** adj fictif(-ive)
fiddle ['fɪdl] n (Mus) violon m; (cheating) combine f; escroquerie f ▷ vt (BRIT: accounts) falsifier, maquiller; **fiddle with** vt fus tripoter
fidelity [fɪ'dɛlɪtɪ] n fidélité f
fidget ['fɪdʒɪt] vi se trémousser, remuer
field [fi:ld] n champ m; (fig) domaine m, champ; (Sport: ground) terrain m; **field marshal** n maréchal m
fierce [fɪəs] adj (look, animal) féroce, sauvage; (wind, attack, person) (très) violent(e); (fighting, enemy) acharné(e)
fifteen [fɪf'ti:n] num quinze; **fifteenth** num quinzième
fifth [fɪfθ] num cinquième
fiftieth ['fɪftɪɪθ] num cinquantième
fifty ['fɪftɪ] num cinquante; **fifty-fifty** adv moitié-moitié ▷ adj: **to have a fifty-fifty**

chance (of success) avoir une chance sur deux (de réussir)
fig [fɪg] n figue f
fight [faɪt] (pt, pp **fought**) n (between persons) bagarre f; (argument) dispute f; (Mil) combat m; (against cancer etc) lutte f ▷ vt se battre contre; (cancer, alcoholism, emotion) combattre, lutter contre; (election) se présenter à ▷ vi se battre; (argue) se disputer; (fig): **to ~ (for/against)** lutter (pour/contre); **fight back** vi rendre les coups; (after illness) reprendre le dessus ▷ vt (tears) réprimer; **fight off** vt repousser; (disease, sleep, urge) lutter contre; **fighting** n combats mpl; (brawls) bagarres fpl
figure ['fɪgəʳ] n (Drawing, Geom) figure f; (number) chiffre m; (body, outline) silhouette f; (person's shape) ligne f, formes fpl; (person) personnage m ▷ vt (US: think) supposer ▷ vi (appear) figurer; (US: make sense) s'expliquer; **figure out** vt (understand) arriver à comprendre; (plan) calculer
file [faɪl] n (tool) lime f; (dossier) dossier m; (folder) dossier, chemise f; (: binder) classeur m; (Comput) fichier m; (row) file f ▷ vt (nails, wood) limer; (papers) classer; (Law: claim) faire enregistrer; déposer; **filing cabinet** n classeur m (meuble)
Filipino [fɪlɪ'pi:nəʊ] adj philippin(e) ▷ n (person) Philippin(e)
fill [fɪl] vt remplir; (vacancy) pourvoir à ▷ n: **to eat one's ~** manger à sa faim; **to ~ with** remplir de; **fill in** vt (hole) boucher; (form) remplir; **fill out** vt (form, receipt) remplir; **fill up** vt remplir ▷ vi (Aut) faire le plein
fillet ['fɪlɪt] n filet m; **fillet steak** n filet m de bœuf, tournedos m
filling ['fɪlɪŋ] n (Culin) garniture f, farce f; (for tooth) plombage m; **filling station** n station-service f, station f d'essence
film [fɪlm] n film m; (Phot) pellicule f, film; (of powder, liquid) couche f, pellicule ▷ vt (scene) filmer ▷ vi tourner; **I'd like a 36-exposure ~** je voudrais une pellicule de 36 poses; **film star** n vedette f de cinéma
filter ['fɪltəʳ] n filtre m ▷ vt filtrer; **filter lane** n (BRIT Aut: at traffic lights) voie f de dégagement; (: on motorway) voie f de sortie
filth [fɪlθ] n saleté f; **filthy** adj sale, dégoûtant(e); (language) ordurier(-ière), grossier(-ière)
fin [fɪn] n (of fish) nageoire f; (of shark) aileron m; (of diver) palme f
final ['faɪnl] adj final(e), dernier(-ière); (decision, answer) définitif(-ive) ▷ n (BRIT Sport) finale f; **finals** npl (US) (Scol) examens mpl de dernière année; (Sport) finale f; **finale** [fɪ'nɑ:lɪ] n finale m; **finalist** n (Sport) finaliste m/f; **finalize** vt mettre au point; **finally** adv (eventually) enfin, finalement; (lastly) en dernier lieu

finance [faɪ'næns] n finance f ▷ vt financer;
finances npl finances fpl; **financial**
[faɪ'nænʃəl] adj financier(-ière); **financial
year** n année f budgétaire

find [faɪnd] vt (pt, pp **found**) trouver; (lost
object) retrouver ▷ n trouvaille f, découverte
f; **to ~ sb guilty** (Law) déclarer qn coupable;
find out vt se renseigner sur; (truth, secret)
découvrir; (person) démasquer ▷ vi: **to ~
out about** (make enquiries) se renseigner
sur; (by chance) apprendre; **findings** npl
(Law) conclusions fpl, verdict m; (of report)
constatations fpl

fine [faɪn] adj (weather) beau (belle);
(excellent) excellent(e); (thin, subtle, not
coarse) fin(e); (acceptable) bien inv ▷ adv
(well) très bien; (small) fin, finement ▷ n
(Law) amende f, contravention f ▷ vt (Law)
condamner à une amende; donner une
contravention à; **he's ~** il va bien; **the
weather is ~** il fait beau; **fine arts** npl
beaux-arts mpl

finger ['fɪŋgəʳ] n doigt m ▷ vt palper,
toucher; **index ~** index m; **fingernail**
n ongle m (de la main); **fingerprint** n
empreinte digitale; **fingertip** n bout m du
doigt

finish ['fɪnɪʃ] n fin f; (Sport) arrivée f; (polish
etc) finition f ▷ vt finir, terminer ▷ vi finir, se
terminer; **to ~ doing sth** finir de faire qch;
to ~ third arriver or terminer troisième;
when does the show ~? quand est-ce que
le spectacle se termine?; **finish off** vt finir,
terminer; (kill) achever; **finish up** vi, vt finir

Finland ['fɪnlənd] n Finlande f; **Finn** n
Finnois(e), Finlandais(e); **Finnish** adj
finnois(e), finlandais(e) ▷ n (Ling) finnois m

fir [fəːʳ] n sapin m

fire ['faɪəʳ] n feu m; (accidental) incendie
m; (heater) radiateur m ▷ vt (discharge): **to
~ a gun** tirer un coup de feu; (fig: interest)
enflammer, animer; (inf: dismiss) mettre à
la porte, renvoyer ▷ vi (shoot) tirer, faire feu;
~! au feu!; **on ~** en feu; **to set ~ to sth, set
sth on ~** mettre le feu à qch; **fire alarm** n
avertisseur m d'incendie; **firearm** n arme
f à feu; **fire brigade** n (régiment m de
sapeurs-)pompiers mpl; **fire engine** n (BRIT)
pompe f à incendie; **fire escape** n escalier
m de secours; **fire exit** n issue f or sortie f
de secours; **fire extinguisher** n extincteur
m; **firefighter** n pompier m; **fireplace** n
cheminée f; **fire station** n caserne f de
pompiers; **fire truck** n (US) = **fire engine**;
firewall n (Internet) pare-feu m; **firewood** n
bois m de chauffage; **fireworks** npl (display)
feu(x) m(pl) d'artifice

firm [fəːm] adj ferme ▷ n compagnie f, firme
f; **firmly** adv fermement

first [fəːst] adj premier(-ière) ▷ adv (before
other people) le premier, la première;
(before other things) en premier, d'abord;
(when listing reasons etc) en premier lieu,
premièrement; (in the beginning) au début
▷ n (person: in race) premier(-ière); (BRIT Scol)
mention f très bien; (Aut) première f;
the ~ of January le premier janvier;
at ~ au commencement, au début; **~ of
all** tout d'abord, pour commencer; **first
aid** n premiers secours or soins; **first-aid
kit** n trousse f à pharmacie; **first-class** adj
(ticket etc) de première classe; (excellent)
excellent(e), exceptionnel(le); (post)
en tarif prioritaire; **first-hand** adj de
première main; **first lady** n (US) femme f
du président; **firstly** adv premièrement, en
premier lieu; **first name** n prénom m; **first-
rate** adj excellent(e)

fiscal ['fɪskl] adj fiscal(e); **fiscal year** n
exercice financier

fish [fɪʃ] n (pl inv) poisson m ▷ vt, vi pêcher;
~ and chips poisson frit et frites;
fisherman (irreg) n pêcheur m; **fish
fingers** npl (BRIT) bâtonnets mpl de
poisson (congelés); **fishing** n pêche f; **to
go fishing** aller à la pêche; **fishing boat** n
barque f de pêche; **fishing line** n ligne f
(de pêche); **fishmonger** n (BRIT)
marchand m de poisson; **fishmonger's
(shop)** n (BRIT) poissonnerie f; **fish sticks**
npl (US) = **fish fingers**; **fishy** adj (inf)
suspect(e), louche

fist [fɪst] n poing m

fit [fɪt] adj (Med, Sport) en (bonne) forme;
(proper) convenable; approprié(e) ▷ vt (subj:
clothes) aller à; (put in, attach) installer,
poser; (equip) équiper, garnir, munir;
(suit) convenir à ▷ vi (clothes) aller; (parts)
s'adapter; (in space, gap) entrer, s'adapter
▷ n (Med) accès m, crise f; (of anger) accès;
(of hysterics, jealousy) crise; **~ to** (ready to) en
état de; **~ for** (worthy) digne de; (capable)
apte à; **to keep ~** se maintenir en forme;
this dress is a tight/good ~ cette robe
est un peu juste/(me) va très bien; **a ~ of
coughing** une quinte de toux; **by ~s and
starts** par à-coups; **fit in** vi (add up) cadrer;
(integrate) s'intégrer; (to new situation)
s'adapter; **fitness** n (Med) forme f physique;
fitted adj (jacket, shirt) ajusté(e); **fitted
carpet** n moquette f; **fitted kitchen** n
(BRIT) cuisine équipée; **fitted sheet** n
drap-housse m; **fitting** adj approprié(e) ▷ n
(of dress) essayage m; (of piece of equipment)
pose f, installation f; **fitting room** n (in
shop) cabine f d'essayage; **fittings** npl
installations fpl

five [faɪv] num cinq; **fiver** n (inf: US) billet de
cinq dollars; (: BRIT) billet m de cinq livres

fix [fɪks] vt (date, amount etc) fixer; (sort out)
arranger; (mend) réparer; (make ready: meal,
drink) préparer ▷ n: **to be in a ~** être dans le
pétrin; **fix up** vt (meeting) arranger; **to ~ sb
up with sth** faire avoir qch à qn; **fixed** adj

(*prices etc*) fixe; **fixture** *n* installation *f* (fixe); (*Sport*) rencontre *f* (au programme)

fizzy ['fɪzɪ] *adj* pétillant(e), gazeux(-euse)

flag [flæg] *n* drapeau *m*; (*also:* **~stone**) dalle *f* ▷ *vi* faiblir; fléchir; **flag down** *vt* héler, faire signe (de s'arrêter) à; **flagpole** *n* mât *m*

flair [flɛəʳ] *n* flair *m*

flak [flæk] *n* (*Mil*) tir antiaérien; (*inf*: *criticism*) critiques *fpl*

flake [fleɪk] *n* (*of rust, paint*) écaille *f*; (*of snow, soap powder*) flocon *m* ▷ *vi* (*also:* **~ off**) s'écailler

flamboyant [flæm'bɔɪənt] *adj* flamboyant(e), éclatant(e); (*person*) haut(e) en couleur

flame [fleɪm] *n* flamme *f*

flamingo [flə'mɪŋgəu] *n* flamant *m* (rose)

flammable ['flæməbl] *adj* inflammable

flan [flæn] *n* (*BRIT*) tarte *f*

flank [flæŋk] *n* flanc *m* ▷ *vt* flanquer

flannel ['flænl] *n* (*BRIT: also:* **face ~**) gant *m* de toilette; (*fabric*) flanelle *f*

flap [flæp] *n* (*of pocket, envelope*) rabat *m* ▷ *vt* (*wings*) battre (de) ▷ *vi* (*sail, flag*) claquer

flare [flɛəʳ] *n* (*signal*) signal lumineux; (*Mil*) fusée éclairante; (*in skirt etc*) évasement *m*; **flares** *npl* (*trousers*) pantalon *m* à pattes d'éléphant; **flare up** *vi* s'embraser; (*fig*: *person*) se mettre en colère, s'emporter; (*: revolt*) éclater

flash [flæʃ] *n* éclair *m*; (*also:* **news ~**) flash *m* (d'information); (*Phot*) flash ▷ *vt* (*switch on*) allumer (brièvement); (*direct*): **to ~ sth at** braquer qch sur; (*send: message*) câbler; (*smile*) lancer ▷ *vi* briller; jeter des éclairs; (*light on ambulance etc*) clignoter; **a ~ of lightning** un éclair; **in a ~** en un clin d'œil; **to ~ one's headlights** faire un appel de phares; **he ~ed by** *or* **past** il passa (devant nous) comme un éclair; **flashback** *n* flashback *m*, retour *m* en arrière; **flashbulb** *n* ampoule *f* de flash; **flashlight** *n* lampe *f* de poche

flask [flɑːsk] *n* flacon *m*, bouteille *f*; (*also:* **vacuum ~**) bouteille *f* thermos®

flat [flæt] *adj* plat(e); (*tyre*) dégonflé(e), à plat; (*beer*) éventé(e); (*battery*) à plat; (*denial*) catégorique; (*Mus*) bémol *inv* (*: voice*) faux (fausse) ▷ *n* (*BRIT: apartment*) appartement *m*; (*Aut*) crevaison *f*, pneu crevé; (*Mus*) bémol *m*; **~ out** (*work*) sans relâche; (*race*) à fond; **flatten** *vt* (*also:* **flatten out**) aplatir; (*crop*) coucher; (*house, city*) raser

flatter ['flætəʳ] *vt* flatter; **flattering** *adj* flatteur(-euse); (*clothes etc*) seyant(e)

flaunt [flɔːnt] *vt* faire étalage de

flavour, (*US*) **flavor** ['fleɪvəʳ] *n* goût *m*, saveur *f*; (*of ice cream etc*) parfum *m* ▷ *vt* parfumer, aromatiser; **vanilla-~ed** à l'arôme de vanille, vanillé(e); **what ~s do you have?** quels parfums avez-vous?;

flavouring, (*US*) **flavoring** *n* arôme *m* (synthétique)

flaw [flɔː] *n* défaut *m*; **flawless** *adj* sans défaut

flea [fliː] *n* puce *f*; **flea market** *n* marché *m* aux puces

fled [flɛd] *pt, pp of* **flee**

flee (*pt, pp* **fled**) [fliː, flɛd] *vt* fuir, s'enfuir de ▷ *vi* fuir, s'enfuir

fleece [fliːs] *n* (*of sheep*) toison *f*; (*top*) (laine *f*) polaire *f* ▷ *vt* (*inf*) voler, filouter

fleet [fliːt] *n* flotte *f*; (*of lorries, cars etc*) parc *m*; convoi *m*

fleeting ['fliːtɪŋ] *adj* fugace, fugitif(-ive); (*visit*) très bref (brève)

Flemish ['flɛmɪʃ] *adj* flamand(e) ▷ *n* (*Ling*) flamand *m*; **the ~** *npl* les Flamands

flesh [flɛʃ] *n* chair *f*

flew [fluː] *pt of* **fly**

flex [flɛks] *n* fil *m* or câble *m* électrique (souple) ▷ *vt* (*knee*) fléchir; (*muscles*) bander; **flexibility** *n* flexibilité *f*; **flexible** *adj* flexible; (*person, schedule*) souple; **flexitime**, (*US*) **flextime** *n* horaire *m* variable *or* à la carte

flick [flɪk] *n* petit coup; (*with finger*) chiquenaude *f* ▷ *vt* donner un petit coup à; (*switch*) appuyer sur; **flick through** *vt* fus feuilleter

flicker ['flɪkə] *vi* (*light, flame*) vaciller

flies [flaɪz] *npl of* **fly**

flight [flaɪt] *n* vol *m*; (*escape*) fuite *f*; (*also:* **~ of steps**) escalier *m*; **flight attendant** *n* steward *m*, hôtesse *f* de l'air

flimsy ['flɪmzɪ] *adj* peu solide; (*clothes*) trop léger(-ère); (*excuse*) pauvre, mince

flinch [flɪntʃ] *vi* tressaillir; **to ~ from** se dérober à, reculer devant

fling [flɪŋ] *vt* (*pt, pp* **flung**) jeter, lancer

flint [flɪnt] *n* silex *m*; (*in lighter*) pierre *f* (à briquet)

flip [flɪp] *vt* (*throw*) donner une chiquenaude à; (*switch*) appuyer sur; (*US: pancake*) faire sauter; **to ~ sth over** retourner qch

flip-flops ['flɪpflɔps] *npl* (*esp BRIT*) tongs *fpl*

flipper ['flɪpə] *n* (*of animal*) nageoire *f*; (*for swimmer*) palme *f*

flirt [fləːt] *vi* flirter ▷ *n* flirteur(-euse)

float [fləut] *n* flotteur *m*; (*in procession*) char *m*; (*sum of money*) réserve *f* ▷ *vi* flotter

flock [flɔk] *n* (*of sheep*) troupeau *m*; (*of birds*) vol *m*; (*of people*) foule *f*

flood [flʌd] *n* inondation *f*; (*of letters, refugees etc*) flot *m* ▷ *vt* inonder ▷ *vi* (*place*) être inondé; (*people*): **to ~ into** envahir; **flooding** *n* inondation *f*; **floodlight** *n* projecteur *m*

floor [flɔːʳ] *n* sol *m*; (*storey*) étage *m*; (*of sea, valley*) fond *m* ▷ *vt* (*knock down*) terrasser; (*baffle*) désorienter; **ground ~**, (*US*) **first ~** rez-de-chaussée *m*; **first ~**, (*US*) **second ~** premier étage; **what ~ is it on?** c'est

à quel étage?; **floorboard** n planche f
(du plancher); **flooring** n sol m; (wooden)
plancher m; (covering) revêtement m de sol;
floor show n spectacle m de variétés

flop [flɔp] n fiasco m ▷ vi (fail) faire fiasco;
(fall) s'affaler, s'effondrer; **floppy** adj lâche,
flottant(e) ▷ n (Comput: also: **floppy disk**)
disquette f

flora ['flɔ:rə] n flore f

floral ['flɔ:rl] adj floral(e); (dress) à fleurs

florist ['flɔrɪst] n fleuriste m/f; **florist's
(shop)** n magasin m or boutique f de
fleuriste

flotation [fləu'teɪʃən] n (of shares) émission
f; (of company) lancement m (en Bourse)

flour ['flauə'] n farine f

flourish ['flʌrɪʃ] vi prospérer ▷ n (gesture)
moulinet m

flow [fləu] n (of water, traffic etc) écoulement
m; (tide, influx) flux m; (of blood, Elec)
circulation f; (of river) courant m ▷ vi couler;
(traffic) s'écouler; (robes, hair) flotter

flower ['flauə'] n fleur f ▷ vi fleurir; **flower
bed** n plate-bande f; **flowerpot** n pot m
(à fleurs)

flown [fləun] pp of **fly**

fl. oz. abbr = **fluid ounce**

flu [flu:] n grippe f

fluctuate ['flʌktjueɪt] vi varier, fluctuer

fluent ['flu:ənt] adj (speech, style)
coulant(e), aisé(e); **he speaks ~ French,
he's ~ in French** il parle le français
couramment

fluff [flʌf] n duvet m; (on jacket, carpet)
peluche f; **fluffy** adj duveteux(-euse); (toy)
en peluche

fluid ['flu:ɪd] n fluide m; (in diet) liquide m
▷ adj fluide; **fluid ounce** n (BRIT) = 0.028 l;
0.05 pints

fluke [flu:k] n coup m de veine

flung [flʌŋ] pt, pp of **fling**

fluorescent [fluə'rɛsnt] adj fluorescent(e)

fluoride ['fluəraɪd] n fluor m

flurry ['flʌrɪ] n (of snow) rafale f,
bourrasque f; **a ~ of activity** un
affairement soudain

flush [flʌʃ] n (on face) rougeur f; (fig: of youth
etc) éclat m ▷ vt nettoyer à grande eau ▷ vi
rougir ▷ adj (level): **~ with** au ras de, de
niveau avec; **to ~ the toilet** tirer la chasse
(d'eau)

flute [flu:t] n flûte f

flutter ['flʌtə'] n (of panic, excitement)
agitation f; (of wings) battement m ▷ vi (bird)
battre des ailes, voleter

fly [flaɪ] (pt **flew**, pp **flown**) n (insect)
mouche f; (on trousers: also: **flies**) braguette
f ▷ vt (plane) piloter; (passengers, cargo)
transporter (par avion); (distance) parcourir
▷ vi voler; (passengers) aller en avion; (escape)
s'enfuir, fuir; (flag) se déployer; **fly away, fly
off** vi s'envoler; **fly-drive** n formule f avion

plus voiture; **flying** n (activity) aviation
f; (action) vol m ▷ adj: **flying visit** visite f
éclair inv; **with flying colours** haut la main;
flying saucer n soucoupe volante; **flyover**
n (BRIT: overpass) pont routier

FM abbr (Radio: = frequency modulation) FM

foal [fəul] n poulain m

foam [fəum] n écume f; (on beer) mousse f;
(also: **~ rubber**) caoutchouc m mousse ▷ vi
(liquid) écumer; (soapy water) mousser

focus ['fəukəs] n (pl **focuses**) foyer m;
(of interest) centre m ▷ vt (field glasses etc)
mettre au point ▷ vi: **to ~ (on)** (with camera)
régler la mise au point (sur); (with eyes)
fixer son regard (sur); (fig: concentrate)
se concentrer (sur); **out of/in ~** (picture)
flou(e)/net(te); (camera) pas au point/au
point

foetus, (us) fetus ['fi:təs] n fœtus m

fog [fɔg] n brouillard m; **foggy** adj: **it's
foggy** il y a du brouillard; **fog lamp, (us) fog
light** n (Aut) phare m anti-brouillard

foil [fɔɪl] vt déjouer, contrecarrer ▷ n
feuille f de métal; (kitchen foil) papier m
d'alu(minium); **to act as a ~ to** (fig) servir de
repoussoir à

fold [fəuld] n (bend, crease) pli m; (Agr) parc
m à moutons; (fig) bercail m ▷ vt plier; **to ~
one's arms** croiser les bras; **fold up** vi (map
etc) se plier, se replier; (business) fermer
boutique ▷ vt (map etc) plier, replier; **folder**
n (for papers) chemise f; (: binder) classeur m;
(Comput) dossier m; **folding** adj (chair, bed)
pliant(e)

foliage ['fəulɪɪdʒ] n feuillage m

folk [fəuk] npl gens mpl ▷ cpd folklorique;
folks npl (inf: parents) famille f, parents mpl;
folklore ['fəuklɔ:'] n folklore m; **folk music**
n musique f folklorique; (contemporary)
musique folk, folk m; **folk song** n chanson f
folklorique; (contemporary) chanson folk inv

follow ['fɔləu] vt suivre; (on Twitter)
s'abonner aux tweets de ▷ vi suivre; (result)
s'ensuivre; **to ~ suit** (fig) faire de même;
follow up vt (letter, offer) donner suite
à; (case) suivre; **follower** n disciple m/f,
partisan(e); **following** adj suivant(e) ▷ n
partisans mpl, disciples mpl; **follow-up** n
suite f; (on file, case) suivi m

fond [fɔnd] adj (memory, look) tendre,
affectueux(-euse); (hopes, dreams) un peu
fou (folle); **to be ~ of** aimer beaucoup

food [fu:d] n nourriture f; **food mixer** n
mixeur m; **food poisoning** n intoxication
f alimentaire; **food processor** n robot m
de cuisine; **food stamp** n (us) bon m de
nourriture (pour indigents)

fool [fu:l] n idiot(e); (Culin) mousse f de
fruits ▷ vt berner, duper; **fool about,
fool around** vi (pej: waste time) traînailler,
glandouiller; (: behave foolishly) faire l'idiot
or l'imbécile; **foolish** adj idiot(e), stupide;

(rash) imprudent(e); **foolproof** adj (plan etc) infaillible

foot (pl **feet**) [fut, fiːt] n pied m; (of animal) patte f; (measure) pied (= 30.48 cm; 12 inches) ▷ vt (bill) payer; **on ~** à pied; **footage** n (Cine: length) ≈ métrage m; (: material) séquences fpl; **foot-and-mouth (disease)** [futənd'mauθ-] n fièvre aphteuse; **football** n (ball) ballon m (de football); (sport: BRIT) football m; (: US) football américain; **footballer** n (BRIT) = **football player**; **football match** n (BRIT) match m de foot(ball); **football player** n footballeur(-euse), joueur(-euse) de football; (US) joueur(-euse) de football américain; **footbridge** n passerelle f; **foothills** npl contreforts mpl; **foothold** n prise f (de pied); **footing** n (fig) position f; **to lose one's footing** perdre pied; **footnote** n note f (en bas de page); **footpath** n sentier m; **footprint** n trace f (de pied); **footstep** n pas m; **footwear** n chaussures fpl

◯ **KEYWORD**

for [fɔːʳ] prep **1** (indicating destination, intention, purpose) pour; **the train for London** le train pour (or à destination de) Londres; **he left for Rome** il est parti pour Rome; **he went for the paper** il est allé chercher le journal; **is this for me?** c'est pour moi?; **it's time for lunch** c'est l'heure du déjeuner; **what's it for?** ça sert à quoi?; **what for?** (why?) pourquoi?; (to what end?) pour quoi faire?, à quoi bon?; **for sale** à vendre; **to pray for peace** prier pour la paix **2** (on behalf of, representing) pour; **the MP for Hove** le député de Hove; **to work for sb/sth** travailler pour qn/qch; **I'll ask him for you** je vais lui demander pour toi; **G for George** G comme Georges **3** (because of) pour; **for this reason** pour cette raison; **for fear of being criticized** de peur d'être critiqué **4** (with regard to) pour; **it's cold for July** il fait froid pour juillet; **a gift for languages** un don pour les langues **5** (in exchange for): **I sold it for £5** je l'ai vendu 5 livres; **to pay 50 pence for a ticket** payer un billet 50 pence **6** (in favour of) pour; **are you for or against us?** êtes-vous pour ou contre nous?; **I'm all for it** je suis tout à fait pour; **vote for X** votez pour X **7** (referring to distance) pendant, sur; **there are roadworks for 5 km** il y a des travaux sur or pendant 5 km; **we walked for miles** nous avons marché pendant des kilomètres **8** (referring to time) pendant; depuis; pour; **he was away for 2 years** il a été absent pendant 2 ans; **she will be away for a month** elle sera absente (pendant) un mois;

it hasn't rained for 3 weeks ça fait 3 semaines qu'il ne pleut pas, il ne pleut pas depuis 3 semaines; **I have known her for years** je la connais depuis des années; **can you do it for tomorrow?** est-ce que tu peux le faire pour demain? **9** (with infinitive clauses): **it is not for me to decide** ce n'est pas à moi de décider; **it would be best for you to leave** le mieux serait que vous partiez; **there is still time for you to do it** vous avez encore le temps de le faire; **for this to be possible … pour** que cela soit possible .. **10** (in spite of): **for all that** malgré cela, néanmoins; **for all his work/efforts** malgré tout son travail/tous ses efforts; **for all his complaints, he's very fond of her** il a beau se plaindre, il l'aime beaucoup ▶ conj (since, as: formal) car

forbid (pt **forbad** or **forbade**, pp **forbidden**) [fə'bɪd, -'bæd, -'bɪdn] vt défendre, interdire; **to ~ sb to do** défendre or interdire à qn de faire; **forbidden** adj défendu(e)

force [fɔːs] n force f ▷ vt forcer; (push) pousser (de force); **to ~ o.s. to do** se forcer à faire; **in ~** (rule, law, prices) en vigueur; (in large numbers) en force; **forced** adj forcé(e); **forceful** adj énergique

ford [fɔːd] n gué m

fore [fɔːʳ] n: **to the ~** en évidence; **forearm** n avant-bras m inv; **forecast** n prévision f; (also: **weather forecast**) prévisions fpl météorologiques, météo f ▷ vt (irreg: like **cast**) prévoir; **forecourt** n (of garage) devant m; **forefinger** n index m; **forefront** n: **in the forefront of** au premier rang or plan de; **foreground** n premier plan; **forehead** ['fɔrɪd] n front m

foreign ['fɔrɪn] adj étranger(-ère); (trade) extérieur(e); (travel) à l'étranger; **foreign currency** n devises étrangères; **foreigner** n étranger(-ère); **foreign exchange** n (system) change m; (money) devises fpl; **Foreign Office** n (BRIT) ministère m des Affaires étrangères; **Foreign Secretary** n (BRIT) ministre m des Affaires étrangères

fore: foreman (irreg) n (in construction) contremaître m; **foremost** adj le (la) plus en vue, premier(-ière) ▷ adv: **first and foremost** avant tout, tout d'abord; **forename** n prénom m

forensic [fə'rɛnsɪk] adj: **~ medicine** médecine légale

foresee (pt **foresaw**, pp **foreseen**) [fɔː'siː, -'sɔː, -'siːn] vt prévoir; **foreseeable** adj prévisible

foreseen [fɔː'siːn] pp of **foresee**

forest ['fɔrɪst] n forêt f; **forestry** n sylviculture f

forever [fə'rɛvəʳ] adv pour toujours; (fig: endlessly) continuellement

foreword ['fɔːwəːd] n avant-propos m inv
forfeit ['fɔːfɪt] vt perdre
forgave [fə'geɪv] pt of **forgive**
forge [fɔːdʒ] n forge f ▷ vt (signature)
contrefaire; (wrought iron) forger; **to
~ money** (BRIT) fabriquer de la fausse
monnaie; **forger** n faussaire m; **forgery** n
faux m, contrefaçon f
forget (pt **forgot**, pp **forgotten**) [fə'gɛt,
-'gɔt, -'gɔtn] vt, vi oublier; **I've forgotten
my key/passport** j'ai oublié ma clé/
mon passeport; **forgetful** adj distrait(e),
étourdi(e)
forgive [fə'gɪv] (pt **forgave**, pp **forgiven**) [fə'gɪv,
-'geɪv, -'gɪvn] vt pardonner; **to ~ sb for sth/
for doing sth** pardonner qch à qn/à qn de
faire qch
forgot [fə'gɔt] pt of **forget**
forgotten [fə'gɔtn] pp of **forget**
fork [fɔːk] n (for eating) fourchette f; (for
gardening) fourche f; (of roads) bifurcation f
▷ vi (road) bifurquer
forlorn [fə'lɔːn] adj (deserted)
abandonné(e); (hope, attempt) désespéré(e)
form [fɔːm] n forme f; (Scol) classe f;
(questionnaire) formulaire m ▷ vt former;
(habit) contracter; **to ~ part of sth** faire
partie de qch; **on top ~** en pleine forme
formal ['fɔːməl] adj (offer, receipt) en bonne
et due forme; (person) cérémonieux(-euse);
(occasion, dinner) officiel(le); (garden) à la
française; (clothes) de soirée; **formality**
[fɔː'mælɪtɪ] n formalité f
format ['fɔːmæt] n format m ▷ vt (Comput)
formater
formation [fɔː'meɪʃən] n formation f
former ['fɔːmə'] adj ancien(ne); (before n)
précédent(e); **the ~ ... the latter** le
premier ... le second, celui-là ... celui-ci;
formerly adv autrefois
formidable ['fɔːmɪdəbl] adj redoutable
formula ['fɔːmjulə] n formule f
fort [fɔːt] n fort m
forthcoming [fɔːθ'kʌmɪŋ] adj qui va
paraître or avoir lieu prochainement;
(character) ouvert(e), communicatif(-ive);
(available) disponible
fortieth ['fɔːtɪɪθ] num quarantième
fortify ['fɔːtɪfaɪ] vt (city) fortifier; (person)
remonter
fortnight ['fɔːtnaɪt] n (BRIT) quinzaine
f, quinze jours mpl; **fortnightly** adj
bimensuel(le) ▷ adv tous les quinze jours
fortress ['fɔːtrɪs] n forteresse f
fortunate ['fɔːtʃənɪt] adj heureux(-euse);
(person) chanceux(-euse); **it is ~ that**
c'est une chance que, il est heureux que;
fortunately adv heureusement, par
bonheur
fortune ['fɔːtʃən] n chance f; (wealth)
fortune f; **fortune-teller** n diseuse f de
bonne aventure

forty ['fɔːtɪ] num quarante
forum ['fɔːrəm] n forum m, tribune f
forward ['fɔːwəd] adj (movement, position)
en avant, vers l'avant; (not shy) effronté(e);
(in time) en avance ▷ adv (also: **~s**) en avant
▷ n (Sport) avant m ▷ vt (letter) faire suivre;
(parcel, goods) expédier; (fig) promouvoir,
favoriser; **to move ~** avancer; **forwarding
address** n adresse f de réexpédition;
forward slash n barre f oblique
fossick ['fɔsɪk] vi (AUST, NZ inf) chercher;
to ~ around for fouiner (inf) pour trouver
fossil ['fɔsl] adj, n fossile m
foster ['fɔstə'] vt (encourage) encourager,
favoriser; (child) élever (sans adopter);
foster child n enfant élevé dans une famille
d'accueil
fought [fɔːt] pt, pp of **fight**
foul [faul] adj (weather, smell, food) infect(e);
(language) ordurier(-ière) ▷ n (Football) faute
f ▷ vt (dirty) salir, encrasser; **he's got a ~
temper** il a un caractère de chien; **foul play**
n (Law) acte criminel
found [faund] pt, pp of **find** ▷ vt (establish)
fonder; **foundation** [faun'deɪʃən] n (act)
fondation f; (base) fondement m; (also:
foundation cream) fond m de teint;
foundations npl (of building) fondations fpl
founder ['faundə'] n fondateur m ▷ vi
couler, sombrer
fountain ['fauntɪn] n fontaine f; **fountain
pen** n stylo m (à encre)
four [fɔː'] num quatre; **on all ~s** à quatre
pattes; **four-letter word** n obscénité f,
gros mot; **four-poster** n (also: **four-poster
bed**) lit m à baldaquin; **fourteen** num
quatorze; **fourteenth** num quatorzième;
fourth num quatrième ▷ n (Aut: also:
fourth gear) quatrième f; **four-wheel
drive** n (Aut: car) voiture f à quatre roues
motrices
fowl [faul] n volaille f
fox [fɔks] n renard m ▷ vt mystifier
foyer ['fɔɪeɪ] n (in hotel) vestibule m; (Theat)
foyer m
fracking ['frækɪŋ] n fracturation f
hydraulique
fraction ['frækʃən] n fraction f
fracture ['fræktʃə'] n fracture f ▷ vt
fracturer
fragile ['frædʒaɪl] adj fragile
fragment ['frægmənt] n fragment m
fragrance ['freɪɡrəns] n parfum m
frail [freɪl] adj fragile, délicat(e); (person)
frêle
frame [freɪm] n (of building) charpente
f; (of human, animal) charpente, ossature
f; (of picture) cadre m; (of door, window)
encadrement m, chambranle m; (of
spectacles: also: **~s**) monture f ▷ vt (picture)
encadrer; **~ of mind** disposition f d'esprit;
framework n structure f

France [frɑːns] n la France
franchise ['fræntʃaɪz] n (Pol) droit m de
vote; (Comm) franchise f
frank [fræŋk] adj franc (franche) ▷ vt (letter)
affranchir; **frankly** adv franchement
frantic ['fræntɪk] adj (hectic) frénétique;
(distraught) hors de soi
fraud [frɔːd] n supercherie f, fraude f,
tromperie f; (person) imposteur m
fraught [frɔːt] adj (tense: person) très
tendu(e); (: situation) pénible; **~ with**
(difficulties etc) chargé(e) de, plein(e) de
fray [freɪ] vt effilocher ▷ vi s'effilocher
freak [friːk] n (eccentric person)
phénomène m; (unusual event) hasard m
extraordinaire; (pej: fanatic): **health food ~**
fana m/f or obsédé(e) de l'alimentation
saine ▷ adj (storm) exceptionnel(le);
(accident) bizarre
freckle ['frɛkl] n tache f de rousseur
free [friː] adj libre; (gratis) gratuit(e) ▷ vt
(prisoner etc) libérer; (jammed object or
person) dégager; **is this seat ~?** la place
est libre?; **~ (of charge)** gratuitement;
freedom n liberté f; **Freefone®** n numéro
vert; **free gift** n prime f; **free kick** n (Sport)
coup franc; **freelance** adj (journalist etc)
indépendant(e), free-lance inv ▷ adv en
free-lance; **freely** adv librement; (liberally)
libéralement; **Freepost®** n (BRIT) port
payé; **free-range** adj (egg) de ferme;
(chicken) fermier; **freeway** n (US) autoroute
f; **free will** n libre arbitre m; **of one's own
free will** de son plein gré
freeze [friːz] (pt **froze**, pp **frozen**) vi geler
▷ vt geler; (food) congeler; (prices, salaries)
bloquer, geler ▷ n gel m; (of prices, salaries)
blocage m; **freezer** n congélateur m;
freezing adj: **freezing (cold)** (room etc)
glacial(e); (person, hands) gelé(e), glacé(e)
▷ n: **3 degrees below freezing** 3 degrés
au-dessous de zéro; **it's freezing** il fait un
froid glacial; **freezing point** n point m de
congélation
freight [freɪt] n (goods) fret m, cargaison
f; (money charged) fret, prix m du
transport; **freight train** n (US) train m de
marchandises
French [frɛntʃ] adj français(e) ▷ n (Ling)
français m; **the ~** npl les Français; **what's
the ~ (word) for …?** comment dit-on … en
français?; **French bean** n (BRIT) haricot
vert; **French bread** n pain m français;
French dressing n (Culin) vinaigrette
f; **French fried potatoes**, **French fries**
(US) npl (pommes de terre fpl) frites fpl;
Frenchman (irreg) n; **French stick**
stick n = baguette f; **French window** n
porte-fenêtre f; **Frenchwoman** (irreg) n
Française f
frenzy ['frɛnzɪ] n frénésie f
frequency ['friːkwənsɪ] n fréquence f

frequent adj ['friːkwənt] fréquent(e)
▷ vt [frɪ'kwɛnt] fréquenter; **frequently**
['friːkwəntlɪ] adv fréquemment
fresh [frɛʃ] adj frais (fraîche); (new)
nouveau (nouvelle); (cheeky) familier(-ière),
culotté(e); **freshen** vi (wind, air) fraîchir;
freshen up vi faire un brin de toilette;
fresher n (BRIT University: inf) bizuth m,
étudiant(e) de première année; **freshly**
adv nouvellement, récemment; **freshman**
(irreg) n (US) = **fresher**; **freshwater** adj
(fish) d'eau douce
fret [frɛt] vi s'agiter, se tracasser
friction ['frɪkʃən] n friction f, frottement m
Friday ['fraɪdɪ] n vendredi m
fridge [frɪdʒ] n (BRIT) frigo m, frigidaire® m
fried [fraɪd] adj frit(e); **~ egg** œuf m sur le
plat
friend [frɛnd] n ami(e) ▷ vt (Internet)
ajouter comme ami(e); **friendly** adj
amical(e); (kind) sympathique, gentil(le);
(place) accueillant(e); (Pol: country) ami(e)
▷ n (also: **friendly match**) match amical;
friendship n amitié f
fries [fraɪz] (esp US) npl = **chips**
frigate ['frɪgɪt] n frégate f
fright [fraɪt] n peur f, effroi m; **to give sb
a ~** faire peur à qn; **to take ~** prendre peur,
s'effrayer; **frighten** vt effrayer, faire peur à;
frightened adj: **to be frightened (of)** avoir
peur (de); **frightening** adj effrayant(e);
frightful adj affreux(-euse)
frill [frɪl] n (of dress) volant m; (of shirt)
jabot m
fringe [frɪndʒ] n (BRIT: of hair) frange f;
(edge: of forest etc) bordure f
Frisbee® ['frɪzbɪ] n Frisbee® m
fritter ['frɪtə*] n beignet m
frivolous ['frɪvələs] adj frivole
fro [frəʊ] adv see **to**
frock [frɒk] n robe f
frog [frɒg] n grenouille f; **frogman** (irreg) n
homme-grenouille m

🅞 **KEYWORD**

from [frɒm] prep **1** (indicating starting place,
origin etc) de; **where do you come from?**,
where are you from? d'où venez-vous?;
where has he come from? d'où arrive-t-il?;
from London to Paris de Londres à Paris;
to escape from sb/sth échapper à qn/qch;
a letter/telephone call from my sister une
lettre/un appel de ma sœur; **to drink from
the bottle** boire à (même) la bouteille; **tell
him from me that …** dites-lui de ma part
que …
2 (indicating time) (à partir) de; **from one
o'clock to or until or till two** d'une heure
à deux heures; **from January (on)** à partir
de janvier
3 (indicating distance) de; **the hotel is one**

kilometre from the beach l'hôtel est à un kilomètre de la plage

4 (*indicating price, number etc*) de; **prices range from £10 to £50** les prix varient entre 10 livres et 50 livres; **the interest rate was increased from 9% to 10%** le taux d'intérêt est passé de 9% à 10%

5 (*indicating difference*) de; **he can't tell red from green** il ne peut pas distinguer le rouge du vert; **to be different from sb/sth** être différent de qn/qch

6 (*because of, on the basis of*): **from what he says** d'après ce qu'il dit; **weak from hunger** affaibli par la faim

front [frʌnt] *n* (*of house, dress*) devant *m*; (*of coach, train*) avant *m*; (*promenade: also*: **sea ~**) bord *m* de mer; (*Mil, Pol, Meteorology*) front *m*; (*fig: appearances*) contenance *f*, façade *f* ▷ *adj* de devant; (*seat, wheel*) avant *inv* ▷ *vi*: **in ~ (of)** devant; **front door** *n* porte *f* d'entrée; (*of car*) portière *f* avant; **frontier** ['frʌntɪə'] *n* frontière *f*; **front page** *n* première page; **front-wheel drive** *n* traction *f* avant

frost [frɔst] *n* gel *m*, gelée *f*; (*also*: **hoar~**) givre *m*; **frostbite** *n* gelures *fpl*; **frosting** *n* (*esp US*: *on cake*) glaçage *m*; **frosty** *adj* (*window*) couvert(e) de givre; (*weather, welcome*) glacial(e)

froth [frɔθ] *n* mousse *f*; écume *f*

frown [fraun] *n* froncement *m* de sourcils ▷ *vi* froncer les sourcils

froze [frəuz] *pt of* **freeze**

frozen ['frəuzn] *pp of* **freeze** ▷ *adj* (*food*) congelé(e); (*person, also assets*) gelé(e)

fruit [fruːt] *n* (*pl inv*) fruit *m*; **fruit juice** *n* jus *m* de fruit; **fruit machine** *n* (*BRIT*) machine *f* à sous; **fruit salad** *n* salade *f* de fruits

frustrate [frʌs'treɪt] *vt* frustrer; **frustrated** *adj* frustré(e)

fry (*pt, pp* **fried**) [fraɪ, -d] *vt* (faire) frire ▷ *n*: **small ~** le menu fretin; **frying pan** *n* poêle *f* (à frire)

ft. *abbr* = **foot; feet**

fudge [fʌdʒ] *n* (*Culin*) sorte de confiserie à base de sucre, de beurre et de lait

fuel [fjuəl] *n* (*for heating*) combustible *m*; (*for engine*) carburant *m*; **fuel tank** *n* (*in vehicle*) réservoir *m* de *or* à carburant

fulfil, (*US*) **fulfill** [ful'fil] *vt* (*function, condition*) remplir; (*order*) exécuter; (*wish, desire*) satisfaire, réaliser

full [ful] *adj* plein(e); (*details, hotel, bus*) complet(-ète); (*busy: day*) chargé(e); (*skirt*) ample, large ▷ *adv*: **to know ~ well that** savoir fort bien que; **I'm ~ (up)** j'ai bien mangé; **~ employment/fare** plein emploi/ tarif; **a ~ two hours** deux bonnes heures; **at ~ speed** à toute vitesse; **in ~** (*reproduce, quote, pay*) intégralement; (*write name etc*) en toutes lettres; **full-length** *adj* (*portrait*)

en pied; (*coat*) long(ue); **full-length film** long métrage; **full moon** *n* pleine lune; **full-scale** *adj* (*model*) grandeur nature *inv*; (*search, retreat*) complet(-ète), total(e); **full stop** *n* point *m*; **full-time** *adj, adv* (*work*) à plein temps; **fully** *adv* entièrement, complètement

fumble ['fʌmbl] *vi* fouiller, tâtonner; **fumble with** *vt fus* tripoter

fume [fjuːm] *vi* (*rage*) rager; **fumes** [fjuːmz] *npl* vapeurs *fpl*, émanations *fpl*, gaz *mpl*

fun [fʌn] *n* amusement *m*, divertissement *m*; **to have ~** s'amuser; **for ~** pour rire; **to make ~ of** se moquer de

function ['fʌŋkʃən] *n* fonction *f*; (*reception, dinner*) cérémonie *f*, soirée officielle ▷ *vi* fonctionner

fund [fʌnd] *n* caisse *f*, fonds *m*; (*source, store*) source *f*, mine *f*; **funds** *npl* (*money*) fonds *mpl*

fundamental [fʌndə'mɛntl] *adj* fondamental(e)

funeral ['fjuːnərəl] *n* enterrement *m*, obsèques *fpl* (*more formal occasion*); **funeral director** *n* entrepreneur *m* des pompes funèbres; **funeral parlour** *n* (*BRIT*) dépôt *m* mortuaire

funfair ['fʌnfɛə'] *n* (*BRIT*) fête (foraine)

fungus (*pl* **fungi**) ['fʌŋgəs, -gaɪ] *n* champignon *m*; (*mould*) moisissure *f*

funnel ['fʌnl] *n* entonnoir *m*; (*of ship*) cheminée *f*

funny ['fʌnɪ] *adj* amusant(e), drôle; (*strange*) curieux(-euse), bizarre

fur [fəː'] *n* fourrure *f*; (*BRIT: in kettle etc*) (dépôt *m* de) tartre *m*; **fur coat** *n* manteau *m* de fourrure

furious ['fjuəriəs] *adj* furieux(-euse); (*effort*) acharné(e)

furnish ['fəːnɪʃ] *vt* meubler; (*supply*) fournir; **furnishings** *npl* mobilier *m*, articles *mpl* d'ameublement

furniture ['fəːnɪtʃə'] *n* meubles *mpl*, mobilier *m*; **piece of ~** meuble *m*

furry ['fəːrɪ] *adj* (*animal*) à fourrure; (*toy*) en peluche

further ['fəːðə'] *adj* supplémentaire, autre; nouveau (nouvelle) ▷ *adv* plus loin; (*more*) davantage; (*moreover*) de plus ▷ *vt* faire avancer *or* progresser, promouvoir; **further education** *n* enseignement *m* postscolaire (*recyclage, formation professionnelle*); **furthermore** *adv* de plus, en outre

furthest ['fəːðɪst] *superlative of* **far**

fury ['fjuəri] *n* fureur *f*

fuse, (*US*) **fuze** [fjuːz] *n* fusible *m*; (*for bomb etc*) amorce *f*, détonateur *m* ▷ *vt, vi* (*metal*) fondre; (*BRIT Elec*): **to ~ the lights** faire sauter les fusibles *or* les plombs; **fuse box** *n* boîte *f* à fusibles

fusion ['fjuːʒən] *n* fusion *f*

fuss [fʌs] *n* (*anxiety, excitement*) chichis *mpl*, façons *fpl*; (*commotion*) tapage *m*; (*complaining, trouble*) histoire(s) *f(pl)*; **to make a ~** faire des façons (*or des histoires*); **to make a ~ of sb** dorloter qn; **fussy** *adj* (*person*) tatillon(ne), difficile, chichiteux(-euse); (*dress, style*) tarabiscoté(e)

future ['fju:tʃə'] *adj* futur(e) ▷ *n* avenir *m*; (*Ling*) futur *m*; **futures** *npl* (*Comm*) opérations *fpl* à terme; **in (the) ~** à l'avenir

fuze [fju:z] *n, vt, vi* (*US*) = **fuse**

fuzzy ['fʌzɪ] *adj* (*Phot*) flou(e); (*hair*) crépu(e)

FYI *abbr* = **for your information**

G [dʒi:] *n* (*Mus*) sol *m*

g. *abbr* (= *gram*) g

gadget ['gædʒɪt] *n* gadget *m*

Gaelic ['geɪlɪk] *adj, n* (*Ling*) gaélique (*m*)

gag [gæg] *n* (*on mouth*) bâillon *m*; (*joke*) gag *m*; ▷ *vt* (*prisoner etc*) bâillonner

gain [geɪn] *n* (*improvement*) gain *m*; (*profit*) gain, profit *m* ▷ *vt* gagner ▷ *vi* (*watch*) avancer; **to ~ from/by** gagner de/à; **to ~ on sb** (*catch up*) rattraper qn; **to ~ 3lbs (in weight)** prendre 3 livres; **to ~ ground** gagner du terrain

gal. *abbr* = **gallon**

gala ['gɑːlə] *n* gala *m*

galaxy ['gæləksɪ] *n* galaxie *f*

gale [geɪl] *n* coup *m* de vent

gall bladder ['gɔːl-] *n* vésicule *f* biliaire

gallery ['gælərɪ] *n* (*also*: **art ~**) musée *m*; (*private*) galerie; (*in theatre*) dernier balcon

gallon ['gæln] *n* gallon *m* (*Brit* = 4.543 *l*; *US* = 3.785 *l*)

gallop ['gæləp] *n* galop *m* ▷ *vi* galoper

gallstone ['gɔːlstəun] *n* calcul *m* (biliaire)

gamble ['gæmbl] *n* pari *m*, risque calculé ▷ *vt, vi* jouer; **to ~ on** (*fig*) miser sur; **gambler** *n* joueur *m*; **gambling** *n* jeu *m*

game [geɪm] *n* jeu *m*; (*event*) match *m*; (*of tennis, chess, cards*) partie *f*; (*Hunting*) gibier *m* ▷ *adj* (*willing*): **to be ~ (for)** être prêt(e) (à *or* pour); **games** *npl* (*Scol*) sport *m*; (*sport event*) jeux; **big ~** gros gibier; **games console** ['geɪmz-] *n* console *f* de jeux vidéo; **game show** *n* jeu télévisé

gammon ['gæmən] *n* (*bacon*) quartier *m* de lard fumé; (*ham*) jambon fumé *or* salé

gang [gæŋ] *n* bande *f*; (*of workmen*) équipe *f*

gangster ['gæŋstə'] *n* gangster *m*

gap [gæp] *n* trou *m*; (*in time*) intervalle *m*; (*difference*): **~ (between)** écart *m* (entre)

gape [geɪp] *vi* (*person*) être *or* rester bouche bée; (*hole, shirt*) être ouvert(e)

gap year *n* année que certains étudiants prennent pour voyager ou pour travailler avant d'entrer à l'université

garage ['gæra:ʒ] *n* garage *m*; **garage sale** *n* vide-grenier *m*

garbage ['gɑ:bɪdʒ] *n* (*US: rubbish*) ordures *fpl*, détritus *mpl*; (*inf: nonsense*) âneries *fpl*; **garbage can** *n* (*US*) poubelle *f*, boîte *f* à ordures; **garbage collector** *n* (*US*) éboueur *m*

garden ['gɑ:dn] *n* jardin *m*; **gardens** *npl* (*public*) jardin public; (*private*) parc *m*; **garden centre** (*BRIT*) *n* pépinière *f*, jardinerie *f*; **gardener** *n* jardinier *m*; **gardening** *n* jardinage *m*

garlic ['gɑ:lɪk] *n* ail *m*

garment ['gɑ:mənt] *n* vêtement *m*

garnish ['gɑ:nɪʃ] (*Culin*) *vt* garnir ▷ *n* décoration *f*

gas [gæs] *n* gaz *m*; (*US: gasoline*) essence *f* ▷ *vt* asphyxier; **I can smell ~** ça sent le gaz; **gas cooker** *n* (*BRIT*) cuisinière *f* à gaz; **gas cylinder** *n* bouteille *f* de gaz; **gas fire** *n* (*BRIT*) radiateur *m* à gaz

gasket ['gæskɪt] *n* (*Aut*) joint *m* de culasse

gasoline ['gæsəli:n] *n* (*US*) essence *f*

gasp [gɑ:sp] *n* halètement *m*; (*of shock etc*): **she gave a small ~ of pain** la douleur lui coupa le souffle ▷ *vi* haleter; (*fig*) avoir le souffle coupé

gas: gas pedal *n* (*US*) accélérateur *m*; **gas station** *n* (*US*) station-service *f*; **gas tank** *n* (*US Aut*) réservoir *m* d'essence

gastric band ['gæstrɪk-] *n* anneau *m* gastrique

gate [geɪt] *n* (*of garden*) portail *m*; (*of field, at level crossing*) barrière *f*; (*of building, town, at airport*) porte *f*

gateau (*pl* **gateaux**) ['gætəu, -z] *n* gros gâteau à la crème

gatecrash ['geɪtkræʃ] *vt* s'introduire sans invitation dans

gateway ['geɪtweɪ] *n* porte *f*

gather ['gæðəʳ] *vt* (*flowers, fruit*) cueillir; (*pick up*) ramasser; (*assemble: objects*) rassembler; (: *people*) réunir; (: *information*) recueillir; (*understand*) comprendre; (*Sewing*) froncer ▷ *vi* (*assemble*) se rassembler; **to ~ speed** prendre de la vitesse; **gathering** *n* rassemblement *m*

gauge [geɪdʒ] *n* (*instrument*) jauge *f* ▷ *vt* jauger; (*fig*) juger de

gave [geɪv] *pt of* **give**

gay [geɪ] *adj* homosexuel(le); (*colour*) gai, vif (vive)

gaze [geɪz] *n* regard *m* fixe ▷ *vi*: **to ~ at** fixer du regard

GB *abbr* = **Great Britain**

GCSE *n abbr* (*BRIT*: = *General Certificate of Secondary Education*) examen passé à l'âge de 16 ans sanctionnant les connaissances de l'élève

gear [gɪəʳ] *n* matériel *m*, équipement *m*; (*Tech*) engrenage *m*; (*Aut*) vitesse *f* ▷ *vt* (*fig: adapt*) adapter; **top** *or* (*US*) **high/low ~** quatrième (*or* cinquième)/première vitesse; **in ~** en prise; **gear up** *vi*: **to ~ up (to do)** se préparer (à faire); **gear box** *n* boîte *f* de vitesse; **gear lever** *n* levier *m* de vitesse; **gear shift** (*US*), **gear stick** (*BRIT*) *n* = **gear lever**

geese [gi:s] *npl of* **goose**

gel [dʒɛl] *n* gelée *f*

gem [dʒɛm] *n* pierre précieuse

Gemini ['dʒɛmɪnaɪ] *n* les Gémeaux *mpl*

gender ['dʒɛndəʳ] *n* genre *m*; (*person's sex*) sexe *m*

gene [dʒi:n] *n* (*Biol*) gène *m*

general ['dʒɛnərl] *n* général *m* ▷ *adj* général(e); **in ~** en général; **general anaesthetic**, (*US*) **general anesthetic** *n* anesthésie générale; **general election** *n* élection(s) législative(s); **generalize** *vi* généraliser; **generally** *adv* généralement; **general practitioner** *n* généraliste *m/f*; **general store** *n* épicerie *f*

generate ['dʒɛnəreɪt] *vt* engendrer; (*electricity*) produire

generation [dʒɛnə'reɪʃən] *n* génération *f*; (*of electricity etc*) production *f*

generator ['dʒɛnəreɪtəʳ] *n* générateur *m*

generosity [dʒɛnə'rɔsɪtɪ] *n* générosité *f*

generous ['dʒɛnərəs] *adj* généreux(-euse); (*copious*) copieux(-euse)

genetic [dʒɪ'nɛtɪk] *adj* génétique; **~ engineering** ingénierie *m* génétique; **~ fingerprinting** système *m* d'empreinte génétique; **genetically modified** *adj* (*food etc*) génétiquement modifié(e); **genetics** *n* génétique *f*

Geneva [dʒɪ'ni:və] *n* Genève

genitals ['dʒɛnɪtlz] *npl* organes génitaux

genius ['dʒi:nɪəs] *n* génie *m*

genome ['dʒi:nəum] *n* génome *m*

gent [dʒɛnt] *n abbr* (*BRIT inf*) = **gentleman**

gentle ['dʒɛntl] *adj* doux (douce); (*breeze, touch*) léger(-ère)

gentleman ['dʒɛntlmən] (*irreg*) *n* monsieur *m*; (*well-bred man*) gentleman *m*

gently ['dʒɛntlɪ] *adv* doucement

gents [dʒɛnts] *n* W.-C. *mpl* (pour hommes)

genuine ['dʒɛnjuɪn] *adj* véritable, authentique; (*person, emotion*) sincère; **genuinely** *adv* sincèrement, vraiment

geographic(al) [dʒɪə'græfɪk(l)-] *adj* géographique

geography [dʒɪ'ɔgrəfɪ] *n* géographie *f*

geology [dʒɪ'ɔlədʒɪ] *n* géologie *f*

geometry [dʒɪ'ɔmətrɪ] *n* géométrie *f*

geranium [dʒɪ'reɪnɪəm] *n* géranium *m*

geriatric [dʒɛrɪ'ætrɪk] *adj* gériatrique ▷ *n* patient(e) gériatrique

germ [dʒə:m] *n* (*Med*) microbe *m*

German ['dʒəːmən] *adj* allemand(e) ▷ *n*
Allemand(e); (*Ling*) allemand *m*; **German
measles** *n* rubéole *f*
Germany ['dʒəːmənɪ] *n* Allemagne *f*
gesture ['dʒɛstjəʳ] *n* geste *m*

⬤ **KEYWORD**

get [gɛt] (*pt, pp* **got**, (*us*) *pp* **gotten**) *vi*
1 (*become, be*) devenir; **to get old/tired**
devenir vieux/fatigué, vieillir/se fatiguer;
to get drunk s'enivrer; **to get dirty** se salir;
to get married se marier; **when do I get
paid?** quand est-ce que je serai payé?; **it's
getting late** il se fait tard
2 (*go*): **to get to/from** aller à/de; **to get
home** rentrer chez soi; **how did you get
here?** comment es-tu arrivé ici?
3 (*begin*) commencer *or* se mettre à; **to
get to know sb** apprendre à connaître
qn; **I'm getting to like him** je commence
à l'apprécier; **let's get going** *or* **started**
allons-y
4 (*modal aux vb*): **you've got to do it** il faut
que vous le fassiez; **I've got to tell the
police** je dois le dire à la police
▶ *vt* **1**: **to get sth done** (*do*) faire qch; (*have
done*) faire faire qch; **to get sth/sb ready**
préparer qch/qn; **to get one's hair cut** se
faire couper les cheveux; **to get the car
going** *or* **to go** (faire) démarrer la voiture;
to get sb to do sth faire faire qch à qn
2 (*obtain: money, permission, results*) obtenir,
avoir; (*buy*) acheter; (*find: job, flat*) trouver;
(*fetch: person, doctor, object*) aller chercher;
to get sth for sb procurer qch à qn; **get me
Mr Jones, please** (*on phone*) passez-moi Mr
Jones, s'il vous plaît; **can I get you a drink?**
est-ce que je peux vous servir à boire?
3 (*receive: present, letter*) recevoir, avoir;
(*acquire: reputation*) avoir; (*: prize*)
obtenir; **what did you get for your
birthday?** qu'est-ce que tu as eu pour ton
anniversaire?; **how much did you get for
the painting?** combien avez-vous vendu
le tableau?
4 (*catch*) prendre, saisir, attraper; (*hit: target
etc*) atteindre; **to get sb by the arm/throat**
prendre *or* saisir *or* attraper qn par le bras/à
la gorge; **get him!** arrête-le!; **the bullet got
him in the leg** il a pris la balle dans la jambe
5 (*take, move*): **to get sth to sb** faire parvenir
qch à qn; **do you think we'll get it through
the door?** on arrivera à la faire passer par
la porte?
6 (*catch, take: plane, bus etc*) prendre; **where
do I get the train for Birmingham?** où
prend-on le train pour Birmingham?
7 (*understand*) comprendre, saisir (*hear*)
entendre; **I've got it!** j'ai compris!; **I don't
get your meaning** je ne vois *or* comprends
pas ce que vous voulez dire; **I didn't get

your name** je n'ai pas entendu votre nom
8 (*have, possess*): **to have got** avoir;
how many have you got? vous en avez
combien?
9 (*illness*) avoir; **I've got a cold** j'ai le rhume;
she got pneumonia and died elle a fait une
pneumonie et elle en est morte
get away *vi* partir, s'en aller; (*escape*)
s'échapper
get away with *vt fus* (*punishment*) en être
quitte pour; (*crime etc*) se faire pardonner
get back *vi* (*return*) rentrer ▷ *vt* récupérer,
recouvrer; **when do we get back?** quand
serons-nous de retour?
get in *vi* entrer; (*arrive home*) rentrer; (*train*)
arriver
get into *vt fus* entrer dans; (*car, train etc*)
monter dans; (*clothes*) mettre, enfiler,
endosser; **to get into bed/a rage** se mettre
au lit/en colère
get off *vi* (*from train etc*) descendre; (*depart:
person, car*) s'en aller ▷ *vt* (*remove: clothes,
stain*) enlever ▷ *vt fus* (*train, bus*) descendre
de; **where do I get off?** où est-ce que je dois
descendre?
get on *vi* (*at exam etc*) se débrouiller; (*agree*):
to get on (with) s'entendre (avec); **how are
you getting on?** comment ça va? ▷ *vt fus*
monter dans; (*horse*) monter sur
get out *vi* sortir; (*of vehicle*) descendre ▷ *vt*
sortir
get out of *vt fus* sortir de; (*duty etc*)
échapper à, se soustraire à
get over *vt fus* (*illness*) se remettre de
get through *vi* (*Tel*) avoir la
communication; **to get through to sb**
atteindre qn
get up *vi* (*rise*) se lever ▷ *vt fus*
monter

getaway ['gɛtəweɪ] *n* fuite *f*
Ghana ['gɑːnə] *n* Ghana *m*
ghastly ['gɑːstlɪ] *adj* atroce, horrible
ghetto ['gɛtəu] *n* ghetto *m*
ghost [gəust] *n* fantôme *m*, revenant *m*
giant ['dʒaɪənt] *n* géant(e) ▷ *adj* géant(e),
énorme
gift [gɪft] *n* cadeau *m*; (*donation, talent*)
don *m*; **gifted** *adj* doué(e); **gift shop**, (*us*)
gift store *n* boutique *f* de cadeaux; **gift
token, gift voucher** *n* chèque-cadeau *m*
gig [gɪg] *n* (*inf: concert*) concert *m*
gigabyte ['dʒɪgəbaɪt] *n* gigaoctet *m*
gigantic [dʒaɪˈgæntɪk] *adj* gigantesque
giggle ['gɪgl] *vi* pouffer, ricaner sottement
gills [gɪlz] *npl* (*of fish*) ouïes *fpl*,
branchies *fpl*
gilt [gɪlt] *n* dorure *f* ▷ *adj* doré(e)
gimmick ['gɪmɪk] *n* truc *m*
gin [dʒɪn] *n* gin *m*
ginger ['dʒɪndʒəʳ] *n* gingembre *m*
gipsy ['dʒɪpsɪ] *n* = **gypsy**

giraffe [dʒɪˈrɑːf] n girafe f
girl [gɜːl] n fille f, fillette f; (young unmarried woman) jeune fille; (daughter) fille; **an English ~** une jeune Anglaise; **girl band** n girls band m; **girlfriend** n (of girl) amie f; (of boy) petite amie f; **Girl Guide** n (BRIT) éclaireuse f; (Roman Catholic) guide f; **Girl Scout** n (US) = **Girl Guide**
gist [dʒɪst] n essentiel m
give [gɪv] (pt **gave**, pp **given**) vt donner ▷ vi (break) céder; (stretch: fabric) se prêter; **to ~ sb sth, ~ sth to sb** donner qch à qn; (gift) offrir qch à qn; (message) transmettre qch à qn; **to ~ sb a call/kiss** appeler/embrasser qn; **to ~ a cry/sigh** pousser un cri/un soupir; **give away** vt donner; (give free) faire cadeau de; (betray) donner, trahir; (disclose) révéler; **give back** vt rendre; **give in** vi céder ▷ vt donner; **give out** vt (food etc) distribuer; **give up** vi renoncer ▷ vt renoncer à; **to ~ up smoking** arrêter de fumer; **to ~ o.s. up** se rendre
given [ˈgɪvn] pp of **give** ▷ adj (fixed: time, amount) donné(e), déterminé(e) ▷ conj: **~ the circumstances …** étant donné les circonstances …, vu les circonstances …; **~ that …** étant donné que …
glacier [ˈglæsɪə'] n glacier m
glad [glæd] adj content(e); **gladly** [ˈglædlɪ] adv volontiers
glamorous [ˈglæmərəs] adj (person) séduisant(e); (job) prestigieux(-euse)
glamour, (US) **glamor** [ˈglæmə'] n éclat m, prestige m
glance [glɑːns] n coup m d'œil ▷ vi: **to ~ at** jeter un coup d'œil à
gland [glænd] n glande f
glare [glɛə'] n (of anger) regard furieux; (of light) lumière éblouissante; (of publicity) feux mpl ▷ vi briller d'un éclat aveuglant; **to ~ at** lancer un regard or des regards furieux à; **glaring** adj (mistake) criant(e), qui saute aux yeux
glass [glɑːs] n verre m; **glasses** npl (spectacles) lunettes fpl
glaze [gleɪz] vt (door) vitrer; (pottery) vernir ▷ n vernis m
gleam [gliːm] vi luire, briller
glen [glɛn] n vallée f
glide [glaɪd] vi glisser; (Aviat, bird) planer; **glider** n (Aviat) planeur m
glimmer [ˈglɪmə'] n lueur f
glimpse [glɪmps] n vision passagère, aperçu m ▷ vt entrevoir, apercevoir
glint [glɪnt] vi étinceler
glisten [ˈglɪsn] vi briller, luire
glitter [ˈglɪtə'] vi scintiller, briller
global [ˈgləʊbl] adj (world-wide) mondial(e); (overall) global(e); **globalization** n mondialisation f; **global warming** n réchauffement m de la planète

globe [gləʊb] n globe m
gloom [gluːm] n obscurité f; (sadness) tristesse f, mélancolie f; **gloomy** adj (person) morose; (place, outlook) sombre
glorious [ˈglɔːrɪəs] adj glorieux(-euse); (beautiful) splendide
glory [ˈglɔːrɪ] n gloire f; splendeur f
gloss [glɒs] n (shine) brillant m, vernis m; (also: **~ paint**) peinture brillante
glossary [ˈglɒsərɪ] n glossaire m, lexique m
glossy [ˈglɒsɪ] adj brillant(e), luisant(e) ▷ n (also: **~ magazine**) revue f de luxe
glove [glʌv] n gant m; **glove compartment** n (Aut) boîte f à gants, vide-poches m inv
glow [gləʊ] vi rougeoyer; (face) rayonner; (eyes) briller
glucose [ˈgluːkəʊs] n glucose m
glue [gluː] n colle f ▷ vt coller
GM abbr (= genetically modified) génétiquement modifié(e)
gm abbr (= gram) g
GM crop n culture f OGM
GMO n abbr (= genetically modified organism) OGM m
GMT abbr (= Greenwich Mean Time) GMT
gnaw [nɔː] vt ronger
go [gəʊ] (pt **went**, pp **gone**) vi aller; (depart) partir, s'en aller; (work) marcher; (break) céder; (time) passer; (be sold): **to go for £10** se vendre 10 livres; (become): **to go pale/mouldy** pâlir/moisir ▷ n (pl **goes**): **to have a go (at)** essayer (de faire); **to be on the go** être en mouvement; **whose go is it?** à qui est-ce de jouer?; **he's going to do it** il va le faire, il est sur le point de le faire; **to go for a walk** aller se promener; **to go dancing/shopping** aller danser/faire les courses; **to go and see sb, to go to see sb** aller voir qn; **how did it go?** comment est-ce que ça s'est passé?; **to go round the back/by the shop** passer par derrière/devant le magasin; **…to go** (US: food) … à emporter; **go ahead** vi (take place) avoir lieu; (get going) y aller; **go away** vi partir, s'en aller; **go back** vi rentrer; revenir; (go again) retourner; **go by** vi (years, time) passer, s'écouler ▷ vt fus s'en tenir à; (believe) en croire; **go down** vi descendre; (number, price, amount) baisser; (ship) couler; (sun) se coucher ▷ vt fus descendre; **go for** vt fus (fetch) aller chercher; (like) aimer; (attack) s'en prendre à; attaquer; **go in** vi entrer; **go into** vt fus entrer dans; (investigate) étudier, examiner; (embark on) se lancer dans; **go off** vi partir, s'en aller; (food) se gâter; (milk) tourner; (bomb) sauter; (alarm clock) sonner; (alarm) se déclencher; (lights etc) s'éteindre; (event) se dérouler ▷ vt fus ne plus aimer; **the gun went off** le coup est parti; **go on** vi continuer; (happen) se passer; (lights) s'allumer ▷ vt fus: **to go on doing** continuer à faire; **go out** vi sortir;

(fire, light) s'éteindre; (tide) descendre; **to go out with sb** sortir avec qn; **go over** vi, vt fus (check) revoir, vérifier; **go past** vt fus: **go past sth** passer devant qch; **go round** vi (circulate: news, rumour) circuler; (revolve) tourner; (suffice) suffire (pour tout le monde); (visit): **to go round to sb's** passer chez qn; aller chez qn; (make a detour): **to go round (by)** faire un détour (par); **go through** vt fus (town etc) traverser; (search through) fouiller; (suffer) subir; **go up** vi monter; (price) augmenter ▷ vt fus gravir; **go with** vt fus aller avec; **go without** vt fus se passer de

go-ahead ['gəuəhɛd] adj dynamique, entreprenant(e) ▷ n feu vert

goal [gəul] n but m; **goalkeeper** n gardien m de but; **goal-post** n poteau m de but

goat [gəut] n chèvre f

gobble ['gɒbl] vt (also: ~ **down**, ~ **up**) engloutir

god [gɒd] n dieu m; **God** Dieu; **godchild** n filleul(e); **goddaughter** n filleule f; **goddess** n déesse f; **godfather** n parrain m; **godmother** n marraine f; **godson** n filleul m

goggles ['gɒglz] npl (for skiing etc) lunettes (protectrices); (for swimming) lunettes de piscine

going ['gəuɪŋ] n (conditions) état m du terrain ▷ adj: **the ~ rate** le tarif (en vigueur)

gold [gəuld] n or m ▷ adj en or; (reserves) d'or; **golden** adj (made of gold) en or; (gold in colour) doré(e); **goldfish** n poisson m rouge; **goldmine** n mine f d'or; **gold-plated** adj plaqué(e) or inv

golf [gɒlf] n golf m; **golf ball** n balle f de golf; (on typewriter) boule f; **golf club** n club m de golf; (stick) club m, crosse f de golf; **golf course** n terrain m de golf; **golfer** n joueur(-euse) de golf

gone [gɒn] pp of **go**

gong [gɒŋ] n gong m

good [gud] adj bon(ne); (kind) gentil(le); (child) sage; (weather) beau (belle) ▷ n bien m; **goods** npl marchandise f, articles mpl; ~! bon!, très bien!; **to be ~ at** être bon en; **to be ~ for** être bon pour; **it's no ~ complaining** cela ne sert à rien de se plaindre; **to make ~** (deficit) combler; (losses) compenser; **for ~** (for ever) pour de bon, une fois pour toutes; **would you be ~ enough to …?** auriez-vous la bonté or l'amabilité de …?; **is this any ~?** (will it do?) est-ce que ceci fera l'affaire?, est-ce que cela peut vous rendre service?; (what's it like?) qu'est-ce que ça vaut?; **a ~ deal (of)** beaucoup (de); **a ~ many** beaucoup (de); ~ **morning/afternoon!** bonjour!; ~ **evening!** bonsoir!; ~ **night!** bonsoir!; (on going to bed) bonne nuit!; **goodbye** excl au revoir!; **to say goodbye to sb** dire au revoir à qn; **Good**

Friday n Vendredi saint; **good-looking** adj beau (belle), bien inv; **good-natured** adj (person) qui a un bon naturel; **goodness** n (of person) bonté f; **for goodness sake!** je vous en prie!; **goodness gracious!** mon Dieu!; **goods train** n (BRIT) train m de marchandises; **goodwill** n bonne volonté

google ['gugl] vi faire une recherche Google® ▷ vt googler

goose (pl **geese**) [gu:s, gi:s] n oie f

gooseberry ['guzbərɪ] n groseille f à maquereau; **to play ~** (BRIT) tenir la chandelle

goose bumps, goose pimples npl chair f de poule

gorge [gɔ:dʒ] n gorge f ▷ vt: **to ~ o.s. (on)** se gorger (de)

gorgeous ['gɔ:dʒəs] adj splendide, superbe

gorilla [gə'rɪlə] n gorille m

gosh [gɒʃ] (inf) excl mince alors!

gospel ['gɒspl] n évangile m

gossip ['gɒsɪp] n (chat) bavardages mpl; (malicious) commérage m, cancans mpl; (person) commère f ▷ vi bavarder; cancaner, faire des commérages; **gossip column** n (Press) échos mpl

got [gɒt] pt, pp of **get**

gotten ['gɒtn] (US) pp of **get**

gourmet ['guəmeɪ] n gourmet m, gastronome m/f

govern ['gʌvən] vt gouverner; (influence) déterminer; **government** n gouvernement m; (BRIT: ministers) ministère m; **governor** n (of colony, state, bank) gouverneur m; (of school, hospital etc) administrateur(-trice); (BRIT: of prison) directeur(-trice)

gown [gaun] n robe f; (of teacher, BRIT: of judge) toge f

GP n abbr (Med) = **general practitioner**

GPS n abbr (= global positioning system) GPS m

grab [græb] vt saisir, empoigner ▷ vi: **to ~ at** essayer de saisir

grace [greɪs] n grâce f ▷ vt (honour) honorer; (adorn) orner; **5 days' ~** un répit de 5 jours; **graceful** adj gracieux(-euse), élégant(e); **gracious** ['greɪʃəs] adj bienveillant(e)

grade [greɪd] n (Comm: quality) qualité f; (: size) calibre m; (: type) catégorie f; (in hierarchy) grade m, échelon m; (Scol) note f; (US: school class) classe f; (: gradient) pente f ▷ vt classer; (by size) calibrer; **grade crossing** n (US) passage m à niveau; **grade school** n (US) école f primaire

gradient ['greɪdɪənt] n inclinaison f, pente f

gradual ['grædjuəl] adj graduel(le), progressif(-ive); **gradually** adv peu à peu, graduellement

graduate n ['grædjuɪt] diplômé(e) d'université; (US: of high school) diplômé(e) de fin d'études ▷ vi ['grædjueɪt] obtenir un diplôme d'université (or de fin d'études); **graduation** [grædju'eɪʃən] n cérémonie f de remise des diplômes

graffiti [grəˈfiːtɪ] npl graffiti mpl

graft [grɑːft] n (Agr, Med) greffe f; (bribery) corruption f ▷ vt greffer; **hard ~** (BRIT inf) boulot acharné

grain [greɪn] n (single piece) grain m; (no pl: cereals) céréales fpl; (US: corn) blé m

gram [græm] n gramme m

grammar [ˈgræməʳ] n grammaire f; **grammar school** n (BRIT) ≈ lycée m

gramme [græm] n = **gram**

gran [græn] (inf) n (BRIT) mamie f (inf), mémé f (inf)

grand [grænd] adj magnifique, splendide; (gesture etc) noble; **grandad** n (inf) = **granddad**; **grandchild** (pl **grandchildren**) n petit-fils m, petite-fille f; **grandchildren** npl petits-enfants; **granddad** n (inf) papy m (inf), papi m (inf), pépé m (inf); **granddaughter** n petite-fille f; **grandfather** n grand-père m; **grandma** n (inf) = **gran**; **grandmother** n grand-mère f; **grandpa** n (inf) = **granddad**; **grandparents** npl grands-parents mpl; **grand piano** n piano m à queue; **Grand Prix** [ˈgrɑ̃ˈpriː] n (Aut) grand prix automobile; **grandson** n petit-fils m

granite [ˈgrænɪt] n granit m

granny [ˈgrænɪ] n (inf) = **gran**

grant [grɑːnt] vt accorder; (a request) accéder à; (admit) concéder ▷ n (Scol) bourse f; (Admin) subside m, subvention f; **to take sth for ~ed** considérer qch comme acquis; **to take sb for ~ed** considérer qn comme faisant partie du décor

grape [greɪp] n raisin m

grapefruit [ˈgreɪpfruːt] n pamplemousse m

graph [grɑːf] n graphique m, courbe f; **graphic** [ˈgræfɪk] adj graphique; (vivid) vivant(e); **graphics** n (art) arts mpl graphiques; (process) graphisme m ▷ npl (drawings) illustrations fpl

grasp [grɑːsp] vt saisir ▷ n (grip) prise f; (fig) compréhension f, connaissance f

grass [grɑːs] n herbe f; (lawn) gazon m; **grasshopper** n sauterelle f

grate [greɪt] n grille f de cheminée ▷ vi grincer ▷ vt (Culin) râper

grateful [ˈgreɪtful] adj reconnaissant(e)

grater [ˈgreɪtəʳ] n râpe f

gratitude [ˈgrætɪtjuːd] n gratitude f

grave [greɪv] n tombe f ▷ adj grave, sérieux(-euse)

gravel [ˈgrævl] n gravier m

gravestone [ˈgreɪvstəun] n pierre tombale

graveyard [ˈgreɪvjɑːd] n cimetière m

gravity [ˈgrævɪtɪ] n (Physics) gravité f; pesanteur f; (seriousness) gravité f

gravy [ˈgreɪvɪ] n jus m (de viande), sauce f (au jus de viande)

gray [greɪ] adj (US) = **grey**

graze [greɪz] vi paître, brouter ▷ vt (touch lightly) frôler, effleurer; (scrape) écorcher ▷ n écorchure f

grease [griːs] n (fat) graisse f; (lubricant) lubrifiant m ▷ vt graisser; lubrifier; **greasy** adj gras(se), graisseux(-euse); (hands, clothes) graisseux

great [greɪt] adj grand(e); (heat, pain etc) très fort(e), intense; (inf) formidable; **Great Britain** n Grande-Bretagne f; **great-grandfather** n arrière-grand-père m; **great-grandmother** n arrière-grand-mère f; **greatly** adv très, grandement; (with verbs) beaucoup

Greece [griːs] n Grèce f

greed [griːd] n (also: **~iness**) avidité f; (for food) gourmandise f; **greedy** adj avide; (for food) gourmand(e)

Greek [griːk] adj grec (grecque) ▷ n Grec (Grecque); (Ling) grec m

green [griːn] adj vert(e); (inexperienced) (bien) jeune, naïf(-ive); (ecological: product etc) écologique ▷ n (colour) vert m; (on golf course) green m; (stretch of grass) pelouse f; **greens** npl (vegetables) légumes verts; **green card** n (Aut) carte verte; (US: work permit) permis m de travail; **greengage** n reine-claude f; **greengrocer** n (BRIT) marchand m de fruits et légumes; **greengrocer's (shop)** n magasin m de fruits et légumes; **greenhouse** n serre f; **the greenhouse effect** l'effet m de serre

Greenland [ˈgriːnlənd] n Groenland m

green salad n salade verte

green tax n écotaxe f

greet [griːt] vt accueillir; **greeting** n salutation f; **Christmas/birthday greetings** souhaits mpl de Noël/de bon anniversaire; **greeting(s) card** n carte f de vœux

grew [gruː] pt of **grow**

grey, (US) **gray** [greɪ] adj gris(e); (dismal) sombre; **grey-haired**, (US) **gray-haired** adj aux cheveux gris; **greyhound** n lévrier m

grid [grɪd] n grille f; (Elec) réseau m; **gridlock** n (traffic jam) embouteillage m

grief [griːf] n chagrin m, douleur f

grievance [ˈgriːvəns] n doléance f, grief m; (cause for complaint) grief m

grieve [griːv] vi avoir du chagrin; se désoler ▷ vt faire de la peine à, affliger; **to ~ for sb** pleurer qn

grill [grɪl] n (on cooker) gril m; (also: **mixed ~**) grillade(s) f(pl) ▷ vt (Culin) griller; (inf: question) cuisiner

grille [grɪl] n grillage m; (Aut) calandre f

grim [grɪm] adj sinistre, lugubre; (serious, stern) sévère

grime [graɪm] n crasse f

grin [grɪn] n large sourire m ▷ vi sourire

grind [graɪnd] (pt, pp **ground**) vt écraser; (coffee, pepper etc) moudre; (US: meat) hacher ▷ n (work) corvée f

grip [grɪp] n (handclasp) poigne f; (control) prise f; (handle) poignée f; (holdall) sac m de voyage ▷ vt saisir, empoigner; (viewer, reader) captiver; **to come to ~s with** se colleter avec, en venir aux prises avec; **to ~ the road** (Aut) adhérer à la route; **gripping** adj prenant(e), palpitant(e)

grit [grɪt] n gravillon m; (courage) cran m ▷ vt (road) sabler; **to ~ one's teeth** serrer les dents

grits [grɪts] npl (us) gruau m de maïs

groan [grəun] n (of pain) gémissement m ▷ vi gémir

grocer ['grəusə'] n épicier m; **groceries** npl provisions fpl; **grocer's (shop), grocery** n épicerie f

groin [grɔɪn] n aine f

groom [gru:m] n (for horses) palefrenier m; (also: **bride~**) marié m ▷ vt (horse) panser; (fig): **to ~ sb for** former qn pour

groove [gru:v] n sillon m, rainure f

grope [grəup] vi tâtonner; **to ~ for** chercher à tâtons

gross [grəus] adj grossier(-ière); (Comm) brut(e); **grossly** adv (greatly) très, grandement

grotesque [grə'tɛsk] adj grotesque

ground [graund] pt, pp of **grind** ▷ n sol m, terre f; (land) terrain m, terres fpl; (Sport) terrain; (reason: gen pl) raison f; (us: also: **~ wire**) terre f ▷ vt (plane) empêcher de décoller, retenir au sol; (us Elec) équiper d'une prise de terre; **grounds** npl (gardens etc.) parc m, domaine m; (of coffee) marc m; **on the ~, to the ~** par terre; **to gain/lose ~** gagner/perdre du terrain; **ground floor** n (BRIT) rez-de-chaussée m; **groundsheet** n (BRIT) tapis m de sol; **groundwork** n préparation f

group [gru:p] n groupe m ▷ vt (also: **~ together**) grouper ▷ vi (also: **~ together**) se grouper

grouse [graus] n (pl inv: bird) grouse f (sorte de coq de bruyère) ▷ vi (complain) rouspéter, râler

grovel ['grɔvl] vi (fig): **to ~ (before)** ramper (devant)

grow (pt **grew**, pp **grown**) [grəu, gru:, grəun] vi (plant) pousser, croître; (person) grandir; (increase) augmenter, se développer; (become) devenir; **to ~ rich/weak** s'enrichir/s'affaiblir ▷ vt cultiver, faire pousser; (hair, beard) laisser pousser; **grow on** vt fus: **that painting is ~ing on me** je finirai par aimer ce tableau; **grow up** vi grandir

growl [graul] vi grogner

grown [grəun] pp of **grow**; **grown-up** n adulte m/f, grande personne

growth [grəuθ] n croissance f, développement m; (what has grown) pousse f; poussée f; (Med) grosseur f, tumeur f

grub [grʌb] n larve f; (inf: food) bouffe f

grubby ['grʌbɪ] adj crasseux(-euse)

grudge [grʌdʒ] n rancune f ▷ vt: (in giving) donner qch à qn à contre-cœur; (resent) reprocher qch à qn; **to bear sb a ~ (for)** garder rancune or en vouloir à qn (de)

gruelling, (us) **grueling** ['gruəlɪŋ] adj exténuant(e)

gruesome ['gru:səm] adj horrible

grumble ['grʌmbl] vi rouspéter, ronchonner

grumpy ['grʌmpɪ] adj grincheux(-euse)

grunt [grʌnt] vi grogner

guarantee [gærən'ti:] n garantie f ▷ vt garantir

guard [gɑ:d] n garde f; (one man) garde m; (BRIT Rail) chef m de train; (safety device: on machine) dispositif m de sûreté; (also: **fire~**) garde-feu m inv ▷ vt garder, surveiller; (protect): **to ~ sb/sth (against or from)** protéger qn/qch (contre); **to be on one's ~** être sur ses gardes; **guardian** n gardien(ne); (of minor) tuteur(-trice)

guerrilla [gə'rɪlə] n guérillero m

guess [gɛs] vi deviner ▷ vt deviner; (estimate) évaluer; (us) croire, penser ▷ n supposition f, hypothèse f; **to take** or **have a ~** essayer de deviner

guest [gɛst] n invité(e); (in hotel) client(e), **guest house** n pension f, **guest room** n chambre f d'amis

guidance ['gaɪdəns] n (advice) conseils mpl

guide [gaɪd] n (person) guide m/f; (book) guide m; (also: **Girl G~**) éclaireuse f; (Roman Catholic) guide f ▷ vt guider; **is there an English-speaking ~?** est-ce que l'un des guides parle anglais?; **guidebook** n guide m; **guide dog** n chien m d'aveugle; **guided tour** n visite guidée; **what time does the guided tour start?** la visite guidée commence à quelle heure?; **guidelines** npl (advice) instructions générales, conseils mpl

guild [gɪld] n (Hist) corporation f; (sharing interests) cercle m, association f

guilt [gɪlt] n culpabilité f; **guilty** adj coupable

guinea pig ['gɪnɪ-] n cobaye m

guitar [gɪ'tɑ:'] n guitare f; **guitarist** n guitariste m/f

gulf [gʌlf] n golfe m; (abyss) gouffre m

gull [gʌl] n mouette f

gulp [gʌlp] vi avaler sa salive; (from emotion) avoir la gorge serrée, s'étrangler ▷ vt (also: **~ down**) avaler

gum [gʌm] n (Anat) gencive f; (glue) colle f; (also: **chewing-~**) chewing-gum m ▷ vt coller

gun [gʌn] n (small) revolver m, pistolet m; (rifle) fusil m, carabine f, (cannon) canon m; **gunfire** n fusillade f; **gunman** (irreg) n bandit armé; **gunpoint** n: **at gunpoint** sous la menace du pistolet (or fusil);

gunpowder n poudre f à canon; **gunshot** n coup m de feu

gush [gʌʃ] vi jaillir; (fig) se répandre en effusions

gust [gʌst] n (of wind) rafale f

gut [gʌt] n intestin m, boyau m; **guts** npl (inf: Anat) boyaux mpl; (: courage) cran m

gutter ['gʌtəʳ] n (of roof) gouttière f; (in street) caniveau m

guy [gaɪ] n (inf: man) type m; (also: **~rope**) corde f; (figure) effigie de Guy Fawkes

Guy Fawkes' Night [gaɪ'fɔːks-] n voir article **"Guy Fawkes' Night"**

- **GUY FAWKES' NIGHT**
- Guy Fawkes' Night, que l'on appelle
- également "bonfire night", commémore
- l'échec du complot (le "Gunpowder Plot")
- contre James Ier et son parlement le 5
- novembre 1605. L'un des conspirateurs,
- Guy Fawkes, avait été surpris dans les
- caves du parlement alors qu'il s'apprêtait
- à y mettre le feu. Chaque année pour
- le 5 novembre, les enfants préparent à
- l'avance une effigie de Guy Fawkes et ils
- demandent aux passants "un penny pour
- le guy" avec lequel ils pourront s'acheter
- des fusées de feu d'artifice. Beaucoup de
- gens font encore un feu dans leur jardin
- sur lequel ils brûlent le "guy".

gym [dʒɪm] n (also: **~nasium**) gymnase m; (also: **~nastics**) gym f; **gymnasium** n gymnase m; **gymnast** n gymnaste m/f; **gymnastics** n, npl gymnastique f; **gym shoes** npl chaussures fpl de gym(nastique)

gynaecologist, (us) **gynecologist** [gaɪnɪ'kɔlədʒɪst] n gynécologue m/f

gypsy ['dʒɪpsɪ] n gitan(e), bohémien(ne)

haberdashery [hæbə'dæʃərɪ] n (BRIT) mercerie f

habit ['hæbɪt] n habitude f; (costume: Rel) habit m

habitat ['hæbɪtæt] n habitat m

hack [hæk] vt hacher, tailler ⊳ n (pej: writer) nègre m; **hacker** n (Comput) pirate m (informatique)

had [hæd] pt, pp of **have**

haddock ['hædək] (pl **haddock** or **haddocks**) n églefin m; **smoked ~** haddock m

hadn't ['hædnt] = **had not**

haemorrhage, (us) **hemorrhage** ['hemərɪdʒ] n hémorragie f

haemorrhoids, (us) **hemorrhoids** ['hemərɔɪdz] npl hémorroïdes fpl

haggle ['hægl] vi marchander

Hague [heɪg] n: **The ~** La Haye

hail [heɪl] n grêle f ⊳ vt (call) héler; (greet) acclamer ⊳ vi grêler; **hailstone** n grêlon m

hair [hɛəʳ] n cheveux mpl; (of animal) pelage m; (single hair: on head) cheveu m; (: on body, of animal) poil m; **to do one's ~** se coiffer; **hairband** n (elasticated) bandeau m; (plastic) serre-tête m; **hairbrush** n brosse f à cheveux; **haircut** n coupe f (de cheveux); **hairdo** n coiffure f; **hairdresser** n coiffeur(-euse); **hairdresser's** n salon m de coiffure, coiffeur m; **hair dryer** n sèche-cheveux m, séchoir m; **hair gel** n gel m pour cheveux; **hair spray** n laque f (pour les cheveux); **hairstyle** n coiffure f; **hairy** adj poilu(e), chevelu(e); (inf: frightening) effrayant(e)

haka ['hɑːkə] n (NZ) haka m

hake [heɪk] (pl **hake** or **hakes**) n colin m, merlu m

half [hɑːf] n (pl **halves**) moitié f; (of beer: also: **~ pint**) ≈ demi m; (Rail, bus: also: **~ fare**) demi-tarif m; (Sport: of match) mi-temps f ⊳ adj demi(e) ⊳ adv (à) moitié, à demi;

~ **an hour** une demi-heure; ~ **a dozen** une demi-douzaine; ~ **a pound** une demi-livre, ≈ 250 g; **two and a** ~ deux et demi; **to cut sth in** ~ couper qch en deux; **half board** n (BRIT: in hotel) demi-pension f; **half-brother** n demi-frère m; **half day** n demi-journée f; **half fare** n demi-tarif m; **half-hearted** adj tiède, sans enthousiasme; **half-hour** n demi-heure f; **half-price** adj à moitié prix ▷ adv (also: **at half-price**) à moitié prix; **half term** n (BRIT Scol) vacances fpl (de demi-trimestre); **half-time** n mi-temps f; **halfway** adv à mi-chemin; **halfway through sth** au milieu de qch

hall [hɔ:l] n salle f; (entrance way: big) hall m; (: small) entrée f; (US: corridor) couloir m; (mansion) château m, manoir m

hallmark ['hɔ:lmɑ:k] n poinçon m; (fig) marque f

hallo [hə'ləu] excl = **hello**

hall of residence n (BRIT) pavillon m or résidence f universitaire

Hallowe'en, Halloween ['hæləu'i:n] n veille f de la Toussaint

HALLOWE'EN

● Selon la tradition, Hallowe'en est la nuit des fantômes et des sorcières. En Écosse et aux États-Unis surtout (et de plus en plus en Angleterre) les enfants, pour fêter Hallowe'en, se déguisent ce soir-là et ils vont ainsi de porte en porte en demandant de petits cadeaux (du chocolat, etc).

hallucination [həlu:sɪ'neɪʃən] n hallucination f

hallway ['hɔ:lweɪ] n (entrance) vestibule m; (corridor) couloir m

halo ['heɪləu] n (of saint etc) auréole f

halt [hɔ:lt] n halte f, arrêt m ▷ vt faire arrêter; (progress etc) interrompre ▷ vi faire halte, s'arrêter

halve [hɑ:v] vt (apple etc) partager or diviser en deux; (reduce by half) réduire de moitié

halves [hɑ:vz] npl of **half**

ham [hæm] n jambon m

hamburger ['hæmbə:gə'] n hamburger m

hamlet ['hæmlɪt] n hameau m

hammer ['hæmə'] n marteau m ▷ vt (nail) enfoncer; (fig) éreinter, démolir ▷ vi (at door) frapper à coups redoublés; **to ~ a point home to sb** faire rentrer qch dans la tête de qn

hammock ['hæmək] n hamac m

hamper ['hæmpə'] vt gêner ▷ n panier m (d'osier)

hamster ['hæmstə'] n hamster m

hamstring ['hæmstrɪŋ] n (Anat) tendon m du jarret

hand [hænd] n main f; (of clock) aiguille f; (handwriting) écriture f; (at cards) jeu m;

(worker) ouvrier(-ière) ▷ vt passer, donner; **to give sb a** ~ donner un coup de main à qn; **at** ~ à portée de la main; **in** ~ (situation) en main; (work) en cours; **to be on** ~ (person) être disponible; (emergency services) se tenir prêt(e) (à intervenir); **to** ~ (information etc) sous la main, à portée de la main; **on the one** ~ ..., **on the other** ~ d'une part ..., d'autre part; **hand down** vt passer; (tradition, heirloom) transmettre; (US: sentence, verdict) prononcer; **hand in** vt remettre; **hand out** vt distribuer; **hand over** vt remettre; (powers etc) transmettre; **handbag** n sac m à main; **hand baggage** n = **hand luggage**; **handbook** n manuel m; **handbrake** n frein m à main; **handcuffs** npl menottes fpl; **handful** n poignée f

handicap ['hændɪkæp] n handicap m ▷ vt handicaper

handkerchief ['hæŋkətʃɪf] n mouchoir m

handle ['hændl] n (of door etc) poignée f; (of cup etc) anse f; (of knife etc) manche m; (of saucepan) queue f; (for winding) manivelle f ▷ vt toucher, manier; (deal with) s'occuper de; (treat: people) prendre; **~ with care** "fragile"; **to fly off the** ~ s'énerver; **handlebar(s)** n(pl) guidon m

hand: hand luggage n bagages mpl à main; **handmade** adj fait(e) à la main; **handout** n (money) aide f, don m; (leaflet) prospectus m; (at lecture) polycopié m; **hands-free** adj (phone) mains libres inv ▷ n (also: **hands-free kit**) kit m mains libres inv

handsome ['hænsəm] adj beau (belle); (profit) considérable

handwriting ['hændraɪtɪŋ] n écriture f

handy ['hændɪ] adj (person) adroit(e); (close at hand) sous la main; (convenient) pratique

hang (pt, pp hung) [hæŋ, hʌŋ] vt accrocher; (criminal) pendre ▷ vi pendre; (hair, drapery) tomber ▷ n: **to get the** ~ **of (doing) sth** (inf) attraper le coup pour faire qch; **hang about, hang around** vi traîner; **hang down** vi pendre; **hang on** vi (wait) attendre; **hang out** vt (washing) étendre (dehors) ▷ vi (inf: live) habiter, percher; (: spend time) traîner; **hang round** vi = **hang about**; **hang up** vi (Tel) raccrocher ▷ vt (coat, painting etc) accrocher, suspendre

hanger ['hæŋə'] n cintre m, portemanteau m

hang-gliding ['hæŋglaɪdɪŋ] n vol m libre or sur aile delta

hangover ['hæŋəuvə'] n (after drinking) gueule f de bois

hankie, hanky ['hæŋkɪ] n abbr = **handkerchief**

happen ['hæpən] vi arriver, se passer, se produire; **what's ~ing?** que se passe-t-il?; **she ~ed to be free** il s'est trouvé (or se trouvait) qu'elle était libre; **as it ~s** justement

happily ['hæpɪlɪ] *adv* heureusement; (*cheerfully*) joyeusement

happiness ['hæpɪnɪs] *n* bonheur *m*

happy ['hæpɪ] *adj* heureux(-euse); ~ **with** (*arrangements etc*) satisfait(e) de; **to be** ~ **to do** faire volontiers; ~ **birthday!** bon anniversaire!

harass ['hærəs] *vt* accabler, tourmenter; **harassment** *n* tracasseries *fpl*

harbour, (*US*) **harbor** ['hɑːbər] *n* port *m* ▷ *vt* héberger, abriter; (*hopes, suspicions*) entretenir

hard [hɑːd] *adj* dur(e); (*question, problem*) difficile; (*facts, evidence*) concret(-ète) ▷ *adv* (*work*) dur; (*think, try*) sérieusement; **to look** ~ **at** regarder fixement; (*thing*) regarder de près; **no** ~ **feelings!** sans rancune!; **to be** ~ **of hearing** être dur(e) d'oreille; **to be** ~ **done by** être traité(e) injustement; **hardback** *n* livre relié; **hardboard** *n* Isorel® *m*; **hard disk** *n* (*Comput*) disque dur; **harden** *vt* durcir; (*fig*)endurcir ▷ *vi* (*substance*) durcir

hardly ['hɑːdlɪ] *adv* (*scarcely*) à peine; (*harshly*) durement; ~ **anywhere/ever** presque nulle part/jamais

hard: hardship *n* (*difficulties*) épreuves *fpl*; (*deprivation*) privations *fpl*; **hard shoulder** *n* (*BRIT Aut*) accotement stabilisé; **hard-up** *adj* (*inf*) fauché(e); **hardware** *n* quincaillerie *f*; (*Comput, Mil*) matériel *m*; **hardware shop**, (*US*) **hardware store** *n* quincaillerie *f*; **hard-working** *adj* travailleur(-euse)

hardy ['hɑːdɪ] *adj* robuste; (*plant*) résistant(e) au gel

hare [heər] *n* lièvre *m*

harm [hɑːm] *n* mal *m*; (*wrong*) tort *m* ▷ *vt* (*person*) faire du mal or du tort à; (*thing*) endommager; **out of** ~'**s way** à l'abri du danger, en lieu sûr; **harmful** *adj* nuisible; **harmless** *adj* inoffensif(-ive)

harmony ['hɑːmənɪ] *n* harmonie *f*

harness ['hɑːnɪs] *n* harnais *m* ▷ *vt* (*horse*) harnacher; (*resources*) exploiter

harp [hɑːp] *n* harpe *f* ▷ *vi*: **to** ~ **on about** revenir toujours sur

harsh [hɑːʃ] *adj* (*hard*) dur(e); (*severe*) sévère; (*unpleasant: sound*) discordant(e); (*: light*) cru(e)

harvest ['hɑːvɪst] *n* (*of corn*) moisson *f*; (*of fruit*) récolte *f*; (*of grapes*) vendange *f* ▷ *vt* moissonner; récolter; vendanger

has [hæz] *vb see* **have**

hashtag ['hæʃtæg] *n* (*on Twitter*) mot-dièse *m*, hashtag *m*

hasn't ['hæznt] = **has not**

hassle ['hæsl] *n* (*inf: fuss*) histoire(s) *f(pl)*

haste [heɪst] *n* hâte *f*, précipitation *f*; **hasten** ['heɪsn] *vt* hâter, accélérer ▷ *vi* se hâter, s'empresser; **hastily** *adv* à la hâte; (*leave*) précipitamment; **hasty** *adj* (*decision, action*) hâtif(-ive); (*departure, escape*) précipité(e)

hat [hæt] *n* chapeau *m*

hatch [hætʃ] *n* (*Naut: also:* ~**way**) écoutille *f*; (*BRIT: also:* **service** ~) passe-plats *m inv* ▷ *vi* éclore

hatchback ['hætʃbæk] *n* (*Aut*) modèle *m* avec hayon arrière

hate [heɪt] *vt* haïr, détester ▷ *n* haine *f*; **hatred** ['heɪtrɪd] *n* haine *f*

haul [hɔːl] *vt* traîner, tirer ▷ *n* (*of fish*) prise *f*; (*of stolen goods etc*) butin *m*

haunt [hɔːnt] *vt* (*subj: ghost, fear*) hanter; (*: person*) fréquenter ▷ *n* repaire *m*; **haunted** *adj* (*castle etc*) hanté(e); (*look*) égaré(e), hagard(e)

Ⓞ **KEYWORD**

have [hæv] (*pt, pp* **had**) *aux vb* **1** (*gen*) avoir; être; **to have eaten/slept** avoir mangé/dormi; **to have arrived/gone** être arrivé(e)/allé(e); **having finished** *or* **when he had finished**, **he left** quand il a eu fini, il est parti; **we'd already eaten** nous avions déjà mangé

2 (*in tag questions*): **you've done it, haven't you?** vous l'avez fait, n'est-ce pas?

3 (*in short answers and questions*): **no I haven't!/yes we have!** mais non!/mais si!; **so I have!** ah oui!, oui c'est vrai!; **I've been there before, have you?** j'y suis déjà allé, et vous?

▶ *modal aux vb* (*be obliged*): **to have (got) to do sth** devoir faire qch, être obligé(e) de faire qch; **she has (got) to do it** elle doit le faire, il faut qu'elle le fasse; **you haven't to tell her** vous n'êtes pas obligé de le lui dire; (*must not*) ne le lui dites surtout pas; **do you have to book?** il faut réserver?

▶ *vt* **1** (*possess*) avoir; **he has (got) blue eyes/dark hair** il a les yeux bleus/les cheveux bruns

2 (*referring to meals etc*): **to have breakfast** prendre le petit déjeuner; **to have dinner/lunch** dîner/déjeuner; **to have a drink** prendre un verre; **to have a cigarette** fumer une cigarette

3 (*receive*) avoir, recevoir; (*obtain*) avoir; **may I have your address?** puis-je avoir votre adresse?; **you can have it for £5** vous pouvez l'avoir pour 5 livres; **I must have it for tomorrow** il me le faut pour demain; **to have a baby** avoir un bébé

4 (*maintain, allow*): **I won't have it!** ça ne se passera pas comme ça!; **we can't have that** nous ne tolérerons pas ça

5 (*by sb else*): **to have sth done** faire faire qch; **to have one's hair cut** se faire couper les cheveux; **to have sb do sth** faire faire qch à qn

6 (*experience, suffer*) avoir; **to have a cold/flu** avoir un rhume/la grippe; **to have an operation** se faire opérer; **she had her bag**

stolen elle s'est fait voler son sac
7 (+*noun*): **to have a swim/walk** nager/se
promener; **to have a bath/shower** prendre
un bain/une douche; **let's have a look**
regardons; **to have a meeting** se réunir;
to have a party organiser une fête; **let me
have a try** laissez-moi essayer

haven ['heɪvn] *n* port *m*; (*fig*) havre *m*
haven't ['hævnt] = **have not**
havoc ['hævək] *n* ravages *mpl*
Hawaii [hə'waɪɪ] *n* (îles *fpl*) Hawaï *m*
hawk [hɔːk] *n* faucon *m*
hawthorn ['hɔːθɔːn] *n* aubépine *f*
hay [heɪ] *n* foin *m*; **hay fever** *n* rhume *m* des
foins; **haystack** *n* meule *f* de foin
hazard ['hæzəd] *n* (*risk*) danger *m*, risque
m ▷ *vt* risquer, hasarder; **hazardous** *adj*
hasardeux(-euse), risqué(e); **hazard
warning lights** *npl* (*Aut*) feux *mpl* de
détresse
haze [heɪz] *n* brume *f*
hazel [heɪzl] *n* (*tree*) noisetier *m* ▷ *adj* (*eyes*)
noisette *inv*; **hazelnut** *n* noisette *f*
hazy ['heɪzɪ] *adj* brumeux(-euse); (*idea*)
vague
he [hiː] *pron* il; **it is he who ...** c'est lui qui ...;
here **he is** le voici
head [hɛd] *n* tête *f*; (*leader*) chef *m*; (*of
school*) directeur(-trice); (*of secondary school*)
proviseur *m* ▷ *vt* (*list*) être en tête de; (*group,
company*) être à la tête de; **~s or tails** pile
ou face; **~ first** la tête la première; **~ over
heels in love** follement *or* éperdument
amoureux(-euse); **to ~ the ball** faire
une tête; **head for** *vt fus* se diriger vers,
(*disaster*) aller à; **head off** *vt* (*threat, danger*)
détourner; **headache** *n* mal *m* de tête;
to have a headache avoir mal à la tête;
heading *n* titre *m*; (*subject title*) rubrique *f*;
headlamp (BRIT) *n* = **headlight**; **headlight**
n phare *m*; **headline** *n* titre *m*; **head office**
n siège *m*, bureau *m* central; **headphones**
npl casque *m* (à écouteurs); **headquarters**
npl (*of business*) bureau *or* siège central;
(*Mil*) quartier général; **headroom** *n* (*in
car*) hauteur *f* de plafond; (*under bridge*)
hauteur limite; **headscarf** *n* foulard *m*;
headset *n* = **headphones**; **headteacher**
n directeur(-trice); (*of secondary school*)
proviseur *m*; **head waiter** *n* maître *m*
d'hôtel
heal [hiːl] *vt, vi* guérir
health [hɛlθ] *n* santé *f*; **health care** *n*
services médicaux; **health centre** *n* (BRIT)
centre *m* de santé; **health food** *n* aliment(s)
naturel(s); **Health Service** *n*: **the Health
Service** (BRIT) = la Sécurité Sociale; **healthy**
adj (*person*) en bonne santé; (*climate, food,
attitude etc*) sain(e)
heap [hiːp] *n* tas *m* ▷ *vt* (*also*: **~ up**) entasser,
amonceler; **she ~ed her plate with cakes**

elle a chargé son assiette de gâteaux; **~s
(of)** (*inf*: *lots*) des tas (de)
hear (*pt, pp* **heard**) [hɪər, həːd] *vt* entendre;
(*news*) apprendre ▷ *vi* entendre; **to ~ about**
entendre parler de; (*have news of*) avoir des
nouvelles de; **to ~ from sb** recevoir des
nouvelles de qn
heard [həːd] *pt, pp of* **hear**
hearing ['hɪərɪŋ] *n* (*sense*) ouïe *f*; (*of
witnesses*) audition *f*; (*of a case*) audience *f*;
hearing aid *n* appareil *m* acoustique
hearse [həːs] *n* corbillard *m*
heart [hɑːt] *n* cœur *m*; **hearts** *npl* (*Cards*)
cœur; **at ~** au fond; **by ~** (*learn, know*) par
cœur; **to lose/take ~** perdre/prendre
courage; **heart attack** *n* crise *f* cardiaque;
heartbeat *n* battement de cœur;
heartbroken *adj*: **to be heartbroken**
avoir beaucoup de chagrin; **heartburn** *n*
brûlures *fpl* d'estomac; **heart disease** *n*
maladie *f* cardiaque
hearth [hɑːθ] *n* foyer *m*, cheminée *f*
heartless ['hɑːtlɪs] *adj* (*person*) sans cœur,
insensible; (*treatment*) cruel(le)
hearty ['hɑːtɪ] *adj* chaleureux(-euse);
(*appetite*) solide; (*dislike*) cordial(e); (*meal*)
copieux(-euse)
heat [hiːt] *n* chaleur *f*; (*Sport: also*:
qualifying ~) éliminatoire *f* ▷ *vt* chauffer;
heat up *vi* (*liquid*) chauffer; (*room*) se
réchauffer ▷ *vt* réchauffer; **heated** *adj*
chauffé(e); (*fig*) passionné(e), échauffé(e),
excité(e); **heater** *n* appareil *m* de chauffage;
radiateur *m*; (*in car*) chauffage *m*; (*water
heater*) chauffe-eau *m*
heather ['hɛðər] *n* bruyère *f*
heating ['hiːtɪŋ] *n* chauffage *m*
heatwave ['hiːtweɪv] *n* vague *f* de chaleur
heaven ['hɛvn] *n* ciel *m*, paradis *m*; (*fig*)
paradis; **heavenly** *adj* céleste, divin(e)
heavily ['hɛvɪlɪ] *adv* lourdement;
(*drink, smoke*) beaucoup; (*sleep, sigh*)
profondément
heavy ['hɛvɪ] *adj* lourd(e); (*work, rain, user,
eater*) gros(se); (*drinker, smoker*) grand(e);
(*schedule, week*) chargé(e)
Hebrew ['hiːbruː] *adj* hébraïque ▷ *n* (*Ling*)
hébreu *m*
Hebrides ['hɛbrɪdiːz] *npl*: **the ~** les
Hébrides *fpl*
hectare ['hɛktɑːr] *n* (BRIT) hectare *m*
hectic ['hɛktɪk] *adj* (*schedule*) très chargé(e);
(*day*) mouvementé(e); (*lifestyle*) trépidant(e)
he'd [hiːd] = **he would**; **he had**
hedge [hɛdʒ] *n* haie *f* ▷ *vi* se dérober ▷ *vt*: **to
~ one's bets** (*fig*) se couvrir
hedgehog ['hɛdʒhɔg] *n* hérisson *m*
heed [hiːd] *vt* (*also*: **take ~ of**) tenir compte
de, prendre garde à
heel [hiːl] *n* talon *m* ▷ *vt* retalonner
hefty ['hɛftɪ] *adj* (*person*) costaud(e); (*parcel*)
lourd(e); (*piece, price*) gros(se)

height [haɪt] n (of person) taille f, grandeur f; (of object) hauteur f; (of plane, mountain) altitude f; (high ground) hauteur f, éminence f; (fig: of glory, fame, power) sommet m; (: of luxury, stupidity) comble m; **at the ~ of summer** au cœur de l'été; **heighten** vt hausser, surélever; (fig) augmenter

heir [ɛəʳ] n héritier m; **heiress** n héritière f

held [hɛld] pt, pp of **hold**

helicopter ['hɛlɪkɒptəʳ] n hélicoptère m

hell [hɛl] n enfer m; **oh ~!** (inf) merde!

he'll [hiːl] = **he will; he shall**

hello [hə'ləʊ] excl bonjour!; (to attract attention) hé!; (surprise) tiens!

helmet ['hɛlmɪt] n casque m

help [hɛlp] n aide f; (cleaner etc) femme f de ménage ▷ vt, vi aider; **~!** au secours!; **~ yourself** servez-vous; **can you ~ me?** pouvez-vous m'aider?; **can I ~ you?** (in shop) vous désirez?; **he can't ~ it** il n'y peut rien; **help out** vi aider ▷ vt: **to ~ sb out** aider qn; **helper** n aide m/f, assistant(e); **helpful** adj serviable, obligeant(e); (useful) utile; **helping** n portion f; **helpless** adj impuissant(e); (baby) sans défense; **helpline** n service m d'assistance téléphonique; (free) ≈ numéro vert

hem [hɛm] n ourlet m ▷ vt ourler

hemisphere ['hɛmɪsfɪəʳ] n hémisphère m

hemorrhage ['hɛmərɪdʒ] n (US) = **haemorrhage**

hemorrhoids ['hɛmərɔɪdz] npl (US) = **haemorrhoids**

hen [hɛn] n poule f; (female bird) femelle f

hence [hɛns] adv (therefore) d'où, de là; **2 years ~** d'ici 2 ans

hen night, hen party n soirée f entre filles (avant le mariage de l'une d'elles)

hepatitis [hɛpə'taɪtɪs] n hépatite f

her [həːʳ] pron (direct) la, l' + vowel or h mute; (indirect) lui; (stressed, after prep) elle ▷ adj son (sa), ses pl; see also **me, my**

herb [həːb] n herbe f; **herbal** adj à base de plantes; **herbal tea** n tisane f

herd [həːd] n troupeau m

here [hɪəʳ] adv ici; (time) alors ▷ excl tiens!, tenez!; **~!** (present) présent!; **~ is, ~ are** voici; **~ he/she is** le (la) voici

hereditary [hɪ'rɛdɪtrɪ] adj héréditaire

heritage ['hɛrɪtɪdʒ] n héritage m, patrimoine m

hernia ['həːnɪə] n hernie f

hero ['hɪərəʊ] n (pl **heroes**) n héros m; **heroic** [hɪ'rəʊɪk] adj héroïque

heroin ['hɛrəʊɪn] n héroïne f (drogue)

heroine ['hɛrəʊɪn] n héroïne f (femme)

heron ['hɛrən] n héron m

herring ['hɛrɪŋ] n hareng m

hers [həːz] pron le sien(ne), les siens (siennes); see also **mine¹**

herself [həː'sɛlf] pron (reflexive) se; (emphatic) elle-même; (after prep) elle; see also **oneself**

he's [hiːz] = **he is; he has**

hesitant ['hɛzɪtənt] adj hésitant(e), indécis(e)

hesitate ['hɛzɪteɪt] vi: **to ~ (about/to do)** hésiter (sur/à faire); **hesitation** [hɛzɪ'teɪʃən] n hésitation f

heterosexual ['hɛtərəʊ'sɛksjuəl] adj, n hétérosexuel(le)

hexagon ['hɛksəgən] n hexagone m

hey [heɪ] excl hé!

heyday ['heɪdeɪ] n: **the ~ of** l'âge m d'or de, les beaux jours de

HGV n abbr = **heavy goods vehicle**

hi [haɪ] excl salut!; (to attract attention) hé!

hibernate ['haɪbəneɪt] vi hiberner

hiccough, hiccup ['hɪkʌp] vi hoqueter ▷ n: **to have (the) ~s** avoir le hoquet

hid [hɪd] pt of **hide**

hidden ['hɪdn] pp of **hide** ▷ adj: **~ agenda** intentions non déclarées

hide [haɪd] (pt **hid**, pp **hidden**) n (skin) peau f ▷ vt cacher ▷ vi: **to ~ (from sb)** se cacher (de qn)

hideous ['hɪdɪəs] adj hideux(-euse), atroce

hiding ['haɪdɪŋ] n (beating) correction f, volée f de coups; **to be in ~** (concealed) se tenir caché(e)

hi-fi ['haɪfaɪ] adj, n abbr (= high fidelity) hi-fi f inv

high [haɪ] adj haut(e); (speed, respect, number) grand(e); (price) élevé(e); (wind) fort(e), violent(e); (voice) aigu(ë) ▷ adv haut, en haut; **20 m ~** haut(e) de 20 m; **~ in the air** haut dans le ciel; **highchair** n (child's) chaise haute; **high-class** adj (neighbourhood, hotel) chic inv, de grand standing; **higher education** n études supérieures; **high heels** npl talons hauts, hauts talons; **high jump** n (Sport) saut m en hauteur; **highlands** ['haɪləndz] npl région montagneuse; **the Highlands** (in Scotland) les Highlands mpl; **highlight** n (fig: of event) point culminant ▷ vt (emphasize) faire ressortir, souligner; **highlights** npl (in hair) reflets mpl; **highlighter** n (pen) surligneur (lumineux); **highly** adv extrêmement, très; (unlikely) fort; (recommended, skilled, qualified) hautement; **to speak highly of** dire beaucoup de bien de; **highness** n: **His/Her Highness** son Altesse f; **high-rise** n (also: **high-rise block, high-rise building**) tour f (d'habitation); **high school** n lycée m; (US) établissement m d'enseignement supérieur; **high season** n (BRIT) haute saison f; **high street** n (BRIT) grand-rue f; **high-tech** (inf) adj de pointe; **highway** n (BRIT) route f; (US) route nationale; **Highway Code** n (BRIT) code m de la route

hijack ['haɪdʒæk] vt détourner (par la force); **hijacker** n auteur m d'un détournement d'avion, pirate m de l'air

hike [haɪk] vi faire des excursions à pied
▷ n excursion f à pied, randonnée f; **hiker**
n promeneur(-euse), excursionniste m/f;
hiking n excursions fpl à pied, randonnée f
hilarious [hɪ'lɛərɪəs] adj (behaviour, event)
désopilant(e)
hill [hɪl] n colline f; (fairly high) montagne
f; (on road) côte f; **hillside** n (flanc m de)
coteau m; **hill walking** n randonnée f de
basse montagne; **hilly** adj vallonné(e),
montagneux(-euse)
him [hɪm] pron (direct) le, l' + vowel or h mute;
(stressed, indirect, after prep) lui; see also **me**;
himself pron (reflexive) se; (emphatic) lui-
même; (after prep) lui; see also **oneself**
hind [haɪnd] adj de derrière
hinder ['hɪndər] vt gêner; (delay) retarder
hindsight ['haɪndsaɪt] n: **with
(the benefit of) ~** avec du recul,
rétrospectivement
Hindu ['hɪndu:] n Hindou(e); **Hinduism** n
(Rel) hindouisme m
hinge [hɪndʒ] n charnière f ▷ vi (fig): **to ~ on**
dépendre de
hint [hɪnt] n allusion f; (advice) conseil m;
(clue) indication f ▷ vt: **to ~ that** insinuer
que ▷ vi: **to ~ at** faire une allusion à
hip [hɪp] n hanche f
hippie, hippy ['hɪpɪ] n hippie m/f
hippo ['hɪpəu] (pl **hippos**) n
hippopotame m
hippopotamus (pl **hippopotamuses**
or **hippopotami**) [hɪpə'pɔtəməs,
hɪpə'pɔtəmaɪ] n hippopotame m
hippy ['hɪpɪ] n = **hippie**
hire ['haɪər] vt (BRIT: car, equipment) louer;
(worker) embaucher, engager ▷ n location
f; **for ~** à louer; (taxi) libre; **I'd like to ~ a car**
je voudrais louer une voiture; **hire(d) car** n
(BRIT) voiture f de location; **hire purchase**
n (BRIT) achat m (or vente f) à tempérament
or crédit
his [hɪz] pron le sien(ne), les siens (siennes)
▷ adj son (sa), ses pl; **mine¹**; **my**
Hispanic [hɪs'pænɪk] adj (in US) hispano-
américain(e) ▷ n Hispano-Américain(e)
hiss [hɪs] vi siffler
historian [hɪ'stɔːrɪən] n historien(ne)
historic(al) [hɪ'stɔrɪk(l)] adj historique
history ['hɪstərɪ] n histoire f
hit [hɪt] vt (pt, pp **hit**) frapper; (reach: target)
atteindre, toucher; (collide with: car) entrer
en collision avec, heurter; (fig: affect)
toucher ▷ n coup m; (success) succès m;
(song) tube m; (to website) visite f; (on search
engine) résultat m de recherche; **to ~ it off
with sb** bien s'entendre avec qn; **hit back**
vi: **to ~ back at sb** prendre sa revanche
sur qn
hitch [hɪtʃ] vt (fasten) accrocher, attacher;
(also: **~ up**) remonter d'une saccade ▷ vi
faire de l'autostop ▷ n (difficulty) anicroche f,

contretemps m; **to ~ a lift** faire du stop;
hitch-hike vi faire de l'auto-stop;
hitch-hiker n auto-stoppeur(-euse);
hitch-hiking n auto-stop m, stop m (inf)
hi-tech ['haɪtɛk] adj de pointe
hitman ['hɪtmæn] (irreg) n (inf) tueur m à
gages
HIV n abbr (= human immunodeficiency virus)
HIV m, VIH m; **~-negative** séronégatif(-ive)
~-positive séropositif(-ive)
hive [haɪv] n ruche f
hoard [hɔːd] n (of food) provisions fpl,
réserves fpl; (of money) trésor m ▷ vt amasser
hoarse [hɔːs] adj enroué(e)
hoax [həuks] n canular m
hob [hɔb] n plaque chauffante
hobble ['hɔbl] vi boitiller
hobby ['hɔbɪ] n passe-temps favori
hobo ['həubəu] n (US) vagabond m
hockey ['hɔkɪ] n hockey m; **hockey stick**
crosse f de hockey
hog [hɔg] n porc (châtré) ▷ vt (fig)
accaparer; **to go the whole ~** aller jusqu'au
bout
Hogmanay [hɔgmə'neɪ] n réveillon m du
jour de l'An, Saint-Sylvestre f

hoist [hɔɪst] n palan m ▷ vt hisser
hold [həuld] (pt, pp **held**) vt tenir; (contain)
contenir; (meeting) tenir; (keep back) retenir;
(believe) considérer; (possess) avoir ▷ vi
(withstand pressure) tenir (bon); (be valid)
valoir; (on telephone) attendre ▷ n prise f;
(find) influence f; (Naut) cale f; **to catch or
get (a) ~ of** saisir; **to get ~ of** (find) trouver;
~ the line! (Tel) ne quittez pas!; **to ~ one's
own** (fig) (bien) se défendre; **hold back** vt
retenir; (secret) cacher; **hold on** vi tenir
bon; (wait) attendre; **~ on!** (Tel) ne quittez
pas!; **to ~ on to sth** (grasp) se cramponner
à qch; (keep) conserver or garder qch; **hold
out** vt offrir ▷ vi (resist): **to ~ out (against)**
résister (devant), tenir bon (devant); **hold
up** vt (raise) lever; (support) soutenir; (delay)
retarder (: traffic) ralentir; (rob) braquer;
holdall n (BRIT) fourre-tout m inv; **holder**
n (container) support m; (of ticket, record)
détenteur(-trice); (of office, title, passport etc)
titulaire m/f

hole [həʊl] n trou m
holiday ['hɒlədɪ] n (BRIT: vacation) vacances fpl; (day off) jour m de congé; (public) jour férié; **to be on ~** être en vacances; **I'm here on ~** je suis ici en vacances; **holiday camp** n (also: **holiday centre**) camp m de vacances; **holiday job** n (BRIT) boulot m (inf) de vacances; **holiday-maker** n (BRIT) vacancier(-ière); **holiday resort** n centre m de villégiature or de vacances
Holland ['hɒlənd] n Hollande f
hollow ['hɒləʊ] adj creux(-euse); (fig) faux (fausse) ▷ n creux m; (in land) dépression f (de terrain), cuvette f ▷ vt: **to ~ out** creuser, évider
holly ['hɒlɪ] n houx m
holocaust ['hɒləkɔːst] n holocauste m
holy ['həʊlɪ] adj saint(e); (bread, water) bénit(e); (ground) sacré(e)
home [həʊm] n foyer m, maison f; (country) pays natal, patrie f; (institution) maison ▷ adj de famille, national(e), intérieur(e); (Sport: team) qui reçoit; (: match, win) sur leur (or notre) terrain ▷ adv chez soi, à la maison; au pays natal; (right in: nail etc) à fond; **at ~** chez soi, à la maison; **to go (or come) ~** rentrer (chez soi), rentrer à la maison (or au pays); **make yourself at ~** faites comme chez vous; **home address** n domicile permanent; **homeland** n patrie f; **homeless** adj sans foyer, sans abri; **homely** adj (plain) simple, sans prétention; (welcoming) accueillant(e); **home-made** adj fait(e) à la maison; **home match** n match m à domicile; **Home Office** n (BRIT) ministère m de l'Intérieur; **home owner** n propriétaire occupant; **home page** n (Comput) page f d'accueil; **Home Secretary** n (BRIT) ministre m de l'Intérieur; **homesick** adj: **to be homesick** avoir le mal du pays; (missing one's family) s'ennuyer de sa famille; **home town** n ville natale; **homework** n devoirs mpl
homicide ['hɒmɪsaɪd] n (US) homicide m
homoeopathic, (US) **homeopathic** [həʊmɪəʊ'pæθɪk] adj (medicine) homéopathique; (doctor) homéopathe
homoeopathy, (US) **homeopathy** [həʊmɪ'ɒpəθɪ] n homéopathie f
homosexual [hɒməʊ'sɛksjuəl] adj, n homosexuel(le)
honest ['ɒnɪst] adj honnête; (sincere) franc (franche); **honestly** adv honnêtement; franchement; **honesty** n honnêteté f
honey ['hʌnɪ] n miel m; **honeymoon** n lune f de miel, voyage m de noces; **we're on honeymoon** nous sommes en voyage de noces; **honeysuckle** n chèvrefeuille m
Hong Kong ['hɒŋ'kɒŋ] n Hong Kong
honorary ['ɒnərərɪ] adj honoraire; (duty, title) honorifique; **~ degree** diplôme m honoris causa

honour, (US) **honor** ['ɒnəʳ] vt honorer ▷ n honneur m; **to graduate with ~s** obtenir sa licence avec mention; **honourable**, (US) **honorable** adj honorable; **honours degree** n (Scol) ≈ licence f avec mention
hood [hʊd] n capuchon m; (of cooker) hotte f; (BRIT Aut) capote f; (US Aut) capot m; **hoodie** ['hʊdɪ] n (top) sweat m à capuche
hoof (pl **hoofs** or **hooves**) [huːf, huːvz] n sabot m
hook [hʊk] n crochet m; (on dress) agrafe f; (for fishing) hameçon m ▷ vt accrocher; **off the ~** (Tel) décroché
hooligan ['huːlɪɡən] n voyou m
hoop [huːp] n cerceau m
hoot [huːt] vi (BRIT Aut) klaxonner; (siren) mugir; (owl) hululer
Hoover® ['huːvəʳ] (BRIT) n aspirateur m ▷ vt: **to hoover** (room) passer l'aspirateur dans; (carpet) passer l'aspirateur sur
hooves [huːvz] npl of **hoof**
hop [hɒp] vi sauter; (on one foot) sauter à cloche-pied; (bird) sautiller
hope [həʊp] vt, vi espérer ▷ n espoir m; **I ~ so** je l'espère; **I ~ not** j'espère que non; **hopeful** adj (person) plein(e) d'espoir; (situation) prometteur(-euse), encourageant(e); **hopefully** adv (expectantly) avec espoir, avec optimisme; (one hopes) avec un peu de chance; **hopeless** adj désespéré(e); (useless) nul(le)
hops [hɒps] npl houblon m
horizon [hə'raɪzn] n horizon m; **horizontal** [hɒrɪ'zɒntl] adj horizontal(e)
hormone ['hɔːməʊn] n hormone f
horn [hɔːn] n corne f; (Mus) cor m; (Aut) klaxon m
horoscope ['hɒrəskəʊp] n horoscope m
horrendous [hə'rɛndəs] adj horrible, affreux(-euse)
horrible ['hɒrɪbl] adj horrible, affreux(-euse)
horrid ['hɒrɪd] adj (person) détestable; (weather, place, smell) épouvantable
horrific [hə'rɪfɪk] adj horrible
horrifying ['hɒrɪfaɪɪŋ] adj horrifiant(e)
horror ['hɒrəʳ] n horreur f; **horror film** n film m d'épouvante
hors d'œuvre [ɔː'dəːvrə] n hors d'œuvre m
horse [hɔːs] n cheval m; **horseback**: **on horseback** adj, adv à cheval; **horse chestnut** n (nut) marron m (d'Inde); (tree) marronnier m (d'Inde); **horsepower** n puissance f (en chevaux); (unit) cheval-vapeur m (CV); **horse-racing** n courses fpl de chevaux; **horseradish** n raifort m; **horse riding** n (BRIT) équitation f
hose [həʊz] n tuyau m; (also: **garden ~**) tuyau d'arrosage; **hosepipe** n tuyau m; (in garden) tuyau d'arrosage
hospital ['hɒspɪtl] n hôpital m; **in ~** à l'hôpital; **where's the nearest ~?** où est l'hôpital le plus proche?

hospitality [hɔspɪ'tælɪtɪ] n hospitalité f
host [həust] n hôte m; (TV, Radio) présentateur(-trice); (large number): **a ~ of** une foule de; (Rel) hostie f
hostage ['hɔstɪdʒ] n otage m
hostel ['hɔstl] n foyer m; (also: **youth ~**) auberge f de jeunesse
hostess ['həustɪs] n hôtesse f; (BRIT: also: **air ~**) hôtesse de l'air; (TV, Radio) présentatrice f
hostile ['hɔstaɪl] adj hostile
hostility [hɔ'stɪlɪtɪ] n hostilité f
hot [hɔt] adj chaud(e); (as opposed to only warm) très chaud(e); (spicy) fort(e); (fig: contest) acharné(e); (topic) brûlant(e); (temper) violent(e), passionné(e); **to be ~** (person) avoir chaud; (thing) être (très) chaud; **it's ~** (weather) il fait chaud; **hot dog** n hot-dog m
hotel [həu'tɛl] n hôtel m
hotspot ['hɔtspɔt] n (Comput: also: **wireless ~**) borne f wifi, hotspot m
hot-water bottle [hɔt'wɔːtə-] n bouillotte f
hound [haund] vt poursuivre avec acharnement ▷ n chien courant
hour ['auə'] n heure f; **hourly** adj toutes les heures, (work) horaire
house n [haus] maison f; (Pol) chambre f; (Theat) salle f; auditoire m ▷ vt [hauz] (person) loger, héberger; **on the ~** (fig) aux frais de la maison; **household** n (Admin etc) ménage m; (people) famille f, maisonnée f; **householder** n propriétaire m/f; (head of house) chef m de famille; **housekeeper** n gouvernante f; **housekeeping** n (work) ménage m; **housewife** (irreg) n ménagère f, femme f au foyer; **house wine** n cuvée f maison or du patron; **housework** n (travaux mpl du) ménage m
housing ['hauzɪŋ] n logement m; **housing development, housing estate** (BRIT) n (blocks of flats) cité f; (houses) lotissement m
hover ['hɔvə'] vi planer; **hovercraft** n aéroglisseur m, hovercraft m
how [hau] adv comment; **~ are you?** comment allez-vous?; **~ do you do?** bonjour; (on being introduced) enchanté(e); **~ long have you been here?** depuis combien de temps êtes-vous là?; **~ lovely/ awful!** que or comme c'est joli/affreux!; **~ much time/many people?** combien de temps/gens?; **~ much does it cost?** ça coûte combien?; **~ old are you?** quel âge avez-vous?; **~ tall is he?** combien mesure-t-il?; **~ is school?** ça va à l'école?; **~ was the film?** comment était le film?
however [hau'ɛvə'] conj pourtant, cependant ▷ adv: **~ I do it** de quelque manière que je m'y prenne; **~ cold it is** même s'il fait très froid; **~ did you do it?** comment y êtes-vous donc arrivé?

howl [haul] n hurlement m ▷ vi hurler; (wind) mugir
H.P. n abbr (BRIT) = **hire purchase**
h.p. abbr (Aut) = **horsepower**
HQ n abbr (= headquarters) QG m
hr abbr (= hour) h
hrs abbr (= hours) h
HTML n abbr (= hypertext markup language) HTML m
hubcap [hʌbkæp] n (Aut) enjoliveur m
huddle ['hʌdl] vi: **to ~ together** se blottir les uns contre les autres
huff [hʌf] n: **in a ~** fâché(e)
hug [hʌg] vt serrer dans ses bras; (shore, kerb) serrer ▷ n: **to give sb a ~** serrer qn dans ses bras
huge [hjuːdʒ] adj énorme, immense
hull [hʌl] n (of ship) coque f
hum [hʌm] vt (tune) fredonner ▷ vi fredonner; (insect) bourdonner, (plane, tool) vrombir
human ['hjuːmən] adj humain(e) ▷ n (also: **~ being**) être humain
humane [hjuː'meɪn] adj humain(e), humanitaire
humanitarian [hjuːmænɪ'tɛərɪən] adj humanitaire
humanity [hjuː'mænɪtɪ] n humanité f
human rights npl droits mpl de l'homme
humble ['hʌmbl] adj humble, modeste
humid ['hjuːmɪd] adj humide, **humidity** [hjuː'mɪdɪtɪ] n humidité f
humiliate [hjuː'mɪlɪeɪt] vt humilier
humiliating [hjuː'mɪlɪeɪtɪŋ] adj humiliant(e)
humiliation [hjuːmɪlɪ'eɪʃən] n humiliation f
hummus ['huməs] n houm(m)ous m
humorous ['hjuːmərəs] adj humoristique
humour, (us) humor ['hjuːmə'] n humour m; (mood) humeur f ▷ vt (person) faire plaisir à; se prêter aux caprices de
hump [hʌmp] n bosse f
hunch [hʌntʃ] n (premonition) intuition f
hundred ['hʌndrəd] num cent; **~s of** des centaines de; **hundredth** ['hʌndrədθ] num centième
hung [hʌŋ] pt, pp of **hang**
Hungarian [hʌŋ'gɛərɪən] adj hongrois(e) ▷ n Hongrois(e); (Ling) hongrois m
Hungary ['hʌŋgərɪ] n Hongrie f
hunger ['hʌŋgə'] n faim f ▷ vi: **to ~ for** avoir faim de, désirer ardemment
hungry ['hʌŋgrɪ] adj affamé(e); **to be ~** avoir faim; **~ for** (fig) avide de
hunt [hʌnt] vt (seek) chercher; (Sport) chasser ▷ vi (search): **to ~ for** chercher (partout); (Sport) chasser ▷ n (Sport) chasse f; **hunter** n chasseur m; **hunting** n chasse f
hurdle ['həːdl] n (Sport) haie f; (fig) obstacle m
hurl [həːl] vt lancer (avec violence); (abuse, insults) lancer

hurrah, hurray [hu'rɑ:, hu'reɪ] *excl*
hourra!

hurricane ['hʌrɪkən] *n* ouragan *m*

hurry ['hʌrɪ] *n* hâte *f*, précipitation *f* ▷ *vi*
se presser, se dépêcher ▷ *vt* (*person*) faire
presser, faire se dépêcher; (*work*) presser; **to
be in a ~** être pressé(e); **to do sth in a ~** faire
qch en vitesse; **hurry up** *vi* se dépêcher

hurt [hə:t] (*pt, pp* **hurt**) *vt* (*cause pain to*)
faire mal à; (*injure, fig*) blesser ▷ *vi* faire mal
▷ *adj* blessé(e); **my arm ~s** j'ai mal au bras;
to ~ o.s. se faire mal

husband ['hʌzbənd] *n* mari *m*

hush [hʌʃ] *n* calme *m*, silence *m* ▷ *vt* faire
taire; **~!** chut!

husky ['hʌskɪ] *adj* (*voice*) rauque ▷ *n* chien *m*
esquimau *or* de traîneau

hut [hʌt] *n* hutte *f*; (*shed*) cabane *f*

hyacinth ['haɪəsɪnθ] *n* jacinthe *f*

hydrofoil ['haɪdrəfɔɪl] *n* hydrofoil *m*

hydrogen ['haɪdrədʒən] *n* hydrogène *m*

hygiene ['haɪdʒi:n] *n* hygiène *f*; **hygienic**
[haɪ'dʒi:nɪk] *adj* hygiénique

hymn [hɪm] *n* hymne *m*; cantique *m*

hype [haɪp] *n* (*inf*) matraquage *m*
publicitaire *or* médiatique

hyperlink ['haɪpəlɪŋk] *n* hyperlien *m*

hypermarket ['haɪpəmɑ:kɪt] (BRIT) *n*
hypermarché *m*

hyphen ['haɪfn] *n* trait *m* d'union

hypnotize ['hɪpnətaɪz] *vt* hypnotiser

hypocrite ['hɪpəkrɪt] *n* hypocrite *m/f*

hypocritical [hɪpə'krɪtɪkl] *adj* hypocrite

hypothesis (*pl* **hypotheses**) [haɪ'pɔθɪsɪs,
-si:z] *n* hypothèse *f*

hysterical [hɪ'sterɪkl] *adj* hystérique;
(*funny*) hilarant(e)

hysterics [hɪ'sterɪks] *npl*: **to be in/
have ~** (*anger, panic*) avoir une crise de
nerfs; (*laughter*) attraper un fou rire

I [aɪ] *pron* je; (*before vowel*) j'; (*stressed*) moi

ice [aɪs] *n* glace *f*; (*on road*) verglas *m* ▷ *vt*
(*cake*) glacer ▷ *vi* (*also*: **~ over**) geler; (*also*:
~ up) se givrer; **iceberg** *n* iceberg *m*; **ice
cream** *n* glace *f*; **ice cube** *n* glaçon *m*; **ice
hockey** *n* hockey *m* sur glace

Iceland ['aɪslənd] *n* Islande *f*; **Icelander** *n*
Islandais(e); **Icelandic** [aɪs'lændɪk] *adj*
islandais(e) ▷ *n* (*Ling*) islandais *m*

ice: ice lolly *n* (BRIT) esquimau *m*; **ice rink** *n*
patinoire *f*; **ice skating** *n* patinage *m* (sur
glace)

icing ['aɪsɪŋ] *n* (*Culin*) glaçage *m*; **icing
sugar** *n* (BRIT) sucre *m* glace

icon ['aɪkɔn] *n* icône *f*

ICT *n abbr* (BRIT *Scol*: = *information and
communications technology*) TIC *fpl*

icy ['aɪsɪ] *adj* glacé(e); (*road*) verglacé(e);
(*weather, temperature*) glacial(e)

I'd [aɪd] = **I would; I had**

ID card *n* carte *f* d'identité

idea [aɪ'dɪə] *n* idée *f*

ideal [aɪ'dɪəl] *n* idéal *m* ▷ *adj* idéal(e);
ideally [aɪ'dɪəlɪ] *adv* (*preferably*) dans
l'idéal; (*perfectly*): **he is ideally suited to the
job** il est parfait pour ce poste

identical [aɪ'dentɪkl] *adj* identique

identification [aɪdentɪfɪ'keɪʃən] *n*
identification *f*; **means of ~** pièce *f*
d'identité

identify [aɪ'dentɪfaɪ] *vt* identifier

identity [aɪ'dentɪtɪ] *n* identité *f*; **identity
card** *n* carte *f* d'identité; **identity theft** *n*
usurpation *f* d'identité

ideology [aɪdɪ'ɔlədʒɪ] *n* idéologie *f*

idiom ['ɪdɪəm] *n* (*phrase*) expression *f*
idiomatique; (*style*) style *m*

idiot ['ɪdɪət] *n* idiot(e), imbécile *m/f*

idle ['aɪdl] *adj* (*doing nothing*) sans
occupation, désœuvré(e); (*lazy*) oisif(-ive),
paresseux(-euse); (*unemployed*) au
chômage; (*machinery*) au repos; (*question,*

pleasures) vain(e), futile ▷ *vi* (*engine*) tourner au ralenti

idol ['aɪdl] *n* idole *f*

idyllic [ɪ'dɪlɪk] *adj* idyllique

i.e. *abbr* (= *id est: that is*) c. à d., c'est-à-dire

if [ɪf] *conj* si; **if necessary** si nécessaire, le cas échéant; **if so** si c'est le cas; **if not** sinon; **if only I could!** si seulement je pouvais!; *see also* **as; even**

ignite [ɪg'naɪt] *vt* mettre le feu à, enflammer ▷ *vi* s'enflammer

ignition [ɪg'nɪʃən] *n* (*Aut*) allumage *m*; **to switch on/off the ~** mettre/couper le contact

ignorance ['ɪgnərəns] *n* ignorance *f*

ignorant ['ɪgnərənt] *adj* ignorant(e); **to be ~ of** (*subject*) ne rien connaître en; (*events*) ne pas être au courant de

ignore [ɪg'nɔː] *vt* ne tenir aucun compte de; (*mistake*) ne pas relever; (*person: pretend to not see*) faire semblant de ne pas reconnaître; (: *pay no attention to*) ignorer

ill [ɪl] *adj* (*sick*) malade; (*bad*) mauvais(e) ▷ *n* mal *m* ▷ *adv*: **to speak/think ~ of sb** dire/penser du mal de qn; **to be taken ~** tomber malade

I'll [aɪl] = **I will; I shall**

illegal [ɪ'liːgl] *adj* illégal(e)

illegible [ɪ'lɛdʒɪbl] *adj* illisible

illegitimate [ɪlɪ'dʒɪtɪmət] *adj* illégitime

ill health *n* mauvaise santé

illiterate [ɪ'lɪtərət] *adj* illettré(e)

illness ['ɪlnɪs] *n* maladie *f*

illuminate [ɪ'luːmɪneɪt] *vt* (*room, street*) éclairer; (*for special effect*) illuminer

illusion [ɪ'luːʒən] *n* illusion *f*

illustrate ['ɪləstreɪt] *vt* illustrer

illustration [ɪlə'streɪʃən] *n* illustration *f*

I'm [aɪm] = **I am**

image ['ɪmɪdʒ] *n* image *f*; (*public face*) image de marque

imaginary [ɪ'mædʒɪnərɪ] *adj* imaginaire

imagination [ɪmædʒɪ'neɪʃən] *n* imagination *f*

imaginative [ɪ'mædʒɪnətɪv] *adj* imaginatif(-ive); (*person*) plein(e) d'imagination

imagine [ɪ'mædʒɪn] *vt* s'imaginer; (*suppose*) imaginer, supposer

imam [ɪ'mɑːm] *n* imam *m*

imbalance [ɪm'bæləns] *n* déséquilibre *m*

imitate ['ɪmɪteɪt] *vt* imiter; **imitation** [ɪmɪ'teɪʃən] *n* imitation *f*

immaculate [ɪ'mækjulət] *adj* impeccable; (*Rel*) immaculé(e)

immature [ɪmə'tjuər] *adj* (*fruit*) qui n'est pas mûr(e); (*person*) qui manque de maturité

immediate [ɪ'miːdɪət] *adj* immédiat(e); **immediately** *adv* (*at once*) immédiatement; **immediately next to** juste à côté de

immense [ɪ'mɛns] *adj* immense, énorme

immerse [ɪ'məːs] *vt* immerger, plonger; **to ~ d in** (*fig*) être plongé dans

immigrant ['ɪmɪgrənt] *n* immigrant(e); (*already established*) immigré(e); **immigration** [ɪmɪ'greɪʃən] *n* immigration *f*

imminent ['ɪmɪnənt] *adj* imminent(e)

immoral [ɪ'mɔrl] *adj* immoral(e)

immortal [ɪ'mɔːtl] *adj*, *n* immortel(le)

immune [ɪ'mjuːn] *adj*: **~ (to)** immunisé(e) (contre); **immune system** *n* système *m* immunitaire

immunize ['ɪmjunaɪz] *vt* immuniser

impact ['ɪmpækt] *n* choc *m*, impact *m*; (*fig*) impact

impair [ɪm'pɛər] *vt* détériorer, diminuer

impartial [ɪm'pɑːʃl] *adj* impartial(e)

impatience [ɪm'peɪʃəns] *n* impatience *f*

impatient [ɪm'peɪʃənt] *adj* impatient(e); **to get** *or* **grow ~** s'impatienter

impeccable [ɪm'pɛkəbl] *adj* impeccable, parfait(e)

impending [ɪm'pɛndɪŋ] *adj* imminent(e)

imperative [ɪm'pɛrətɪv] *adj* (*need*) urgent(e), pressant(e); (*tone*) impérieux(-euse) ▷ *n* (*Ling*) impératif *m*

imperfect [ɪm'pəːfɪkt] *adj* imparfait(e); (*goods etc*) défectueux(-euse) ▷ *n* (*Ling: also:* **~ tense**) imparfait *m*

imperial [ɪm'pɪərɪəl] *adj* impérial(e); (*BRIT: measure*) légal(e)

impersonal [ɪm'pəːsənl] *adj* impersonnel(le)

impersonate [ɪm'pəːsəneɪt] *vt* se faire passer pour; (*Theat*) imiter

impetus ['ɪmpɪtəs] *n* impulsion *f*; (*of runner*) élan *m*

implant [ɪm'plɑːnt] *vt* (*Med*) implanter; (*fig: idea, principle*) inculquer

implement *n* ['ɪmplɪmənt] outil *m*, instrument *m*; (*for cooking*) ustensile *m* ▷ *vt* ['ɪmplɪmɛnt] exécuter

implicate ['ɪmplɪkeɪt] *vt* impliquer, compromettre

implication [ɪmplɪ'keɪʃən] *n* implication *f*; **by ~** indirectement

implicit [ɪm'plɪsɪt] *adj* implicite; (*complete*) absolu(e), sans réserve

imply [ɪm'plaɪ] *vt* (*hint*) suggérer, laisser entendre; (*mean*) indiquer, supposer

impolite [ɪmpə'laɪt] *adj* impoli(e)

import *vt* [ɪm'pɔːt] importer ▷ *n* ['ɪmpɔːt] (*Comm*) importation *f*; (*meaning*) portée *f*, signification *f*

importance [ɪm'pɔːtns] *n* importance *f*

important [ɪm'pɔːtnt] *adj* important(e); **it's not ~** c'est sans importance, ce n'est pas important

importer [ɪm'pɔːtər] *n* importateur(-trice)

impose [ɪm'pəuz] *vt* imposer ▷ *vi*: **to ~ on sb** abuser de la gentillesse de qn; **imposing** *adj* imposant(e), impressionnant(e)

impossible [ɪmˈpɔsɪbl] *adj* impossible
impotent [ˈɪmpətnt] *adj* impuissant(e)
impoverished [ɪmˈpɔvərɪʃt] *adj* pauvre, appauvri(e)
impractical [ɪmˈpræktɪkl] *adj* pas pratique; (*person*) qui manque d'esprit pratique
impress [ɪmˈprɛs] *vt* impressionner, faire impression sur; (*mark*) imprimer, marquer; **to ~ sth on sb** faire bien comprendre qch à qn
impression [ɪmˈprɛʃən] *n* impression *f*; (*of stamp, seal*) empreinte *f*; (*imitation*) imitation *f*; **to be under the ~ that** avoir l'impression que
impressive [ɪmˈprɛsɪv] *adj* impressionnant(e)
imprison [ɪmˈprɪzn] *vt* emprisonner, mettre en prison; **imprisonment** *n* emprisonnement *m*; (*period*): **to sentence sb to 10 years' imprisonment** condamner qn à 10 ans de prison
improbable [ɪmˈprɔbəbl] *adj* improbable; (*excuse*) peu plausible
improper [ɪmˈprɔpə*] *adj* (*unsuitable*) déplacé(e), de mauvais goût; (*indecent*) indécent(e); (*dishonest*) malhonnête
improve [ɪmˈpruːv] *vt* améliorer ▷ *vi* s'améliorer; (*pupil etc*) faire des progrès; **improvement** *n* amélioration *f*; (*of pupil etc*) progrès *m*
improvise [ˈɪmprəvaɪz] *vt, vi* improviser
impulse [ˈɪmpʌls] *n* impulsion *f*; **on ~** impulsivement, sur un coup de tête; **impulsive** [ɪmˈpʌlsɪv] *adj* impulsif(-ive)

○ **KEYWORD**

in [ɪn] *prep* **1** (*indicating place, position*) dans; **in the house/the fridge** dans la maison/le frigo; **in the garden** dans le or au jardin; **in town** en ville; **in the country** à la campagne; **in school** à l'école; **in here/ there** ici/là
2 (*with place names, of town, region, country*): **in London** à Londres; **in England** en Angleterre; **in Japan** au Japon; **in the United States** aux États-Unis
3 (*indicating time: during*): **in spring** au printemps; **in summer** en été; **in May/2005** en mai/2005; **in the afternoon** (dans) l'après-midi; **at 4 o'clock in the afternoon** à 4 heures de l'après-midi
4 (*indicating time: in the space of*) en; (*: future*) dans; **I did it in 3 hours/days** je l'ai fait en 3 heures/jours; **I'll see you in 2 weeks** or **in 2 weeks' time** je te verrai dans 2 semaines
5 (*indicating manner etc*) à; **in a loud/soft voice** à voix haute/basse; **in pencil** au crayon; **in writing** par écrit; **in French** en français; **the boy in the blue shirt** le

garçon à or avec la chemise bleue
6 (*indicating circumstances*): **in the sun** au soleil; **in the shade** à l'ombre; **in the rain** sous la pluie; **a change in policy** un changement de politique
7 (*indicating mood, state*): **in tears** en larmes; **in anger** sous le coup de la colère; **in despair** au désespoir; **in good condition** en bon état; **to live in luxury** vivre dans le luxe
8 (*with ratios, numbers*): **1 in 10 households, 1 household in 10** 1 ménage sur 10; **20 pence in the pound** 20 pence par livre sterling; **they lined up in twos** ils se mirent en rangs (deux) par deux; **in hundreds** par centaines
9 (*referring to people, works*) chez; **the disease is common in children** c'est une maladie courante chez les enfants; **in (the works of) Dickens** chez Dickens, dans (l'œuvre de) Dickens
10 (*indicating profession etc*) dans; **to be in teaching** être dans l'enseignement
11 (*after superlative*) de; **the best pupil in the class** le meilleur élève de la classe
12 (*with present participle*): **in saying this** en disant ceci
▷ *adv*: **to be in** (*person: at home, work*) être là; (*train, ship, plane*) être arrivé(e); (*in fashion*) être à la mode; **to ask sb in** inviter qn à entrer; **to run/limp etc in** entrer en courant/boitant *etc*
▷ *n*: **the ins and outs (of)** (*of proposal, situation etc*) les tenants et aboutissants (de)

inability [ɪnəˈbɪlɪtɪ] *n* incapacité *f*; **~ to pay** incapacité de payer
inaccurate [ɪnˈækjurət] *adj* inexact(e); (*person*) qui manque de précision
inadequate [ɪnˈædɪkwət] *adj* insuffisant(e), inadéquat(e)
inadvertently [ɪnədˈvəːtntlɪ] *adv* par mégarde
inappropriate [ɪnəˈprəuprɪət] *adj* inopportun(e), mal à propos; (*word, expression*) impropre
inaugurate [ɪˈnɔːgjureɪt] *vt* inaugurer; (*president, official*) investir de ses fonctions
Inc. *abbr* = **incorporated**
incapable [ɪnˈkeɪpəbl] *adj*: **~ (of)** incapable (de)
incense *n* [ˈɪnsɛns] encens *m* ▷ *vt* [ɪnˈsɛns] (*anger*) mettre en colère
incentive [ɪnˈsɛntɪv] *n* encouragement *m*, raison *f* de se donner de la peine
inch [ɪntʃ] *n* pouce *m* (= 25 mm; 12 in a foot); **within an ~ of** à deux doigts de; **he wouldn't give an ~** (*fig*) il n'a pas voulu céder d'un pouce
incidence [ˈɪnsɪdns] *n* (*of crime, disease*) fréquence *f*

incident ['ɪnsɪdnt] n incident m
incidentally [ɪnsɪ'dɛntəlɪ] adv (by the way) à propos
inclination [ɪnklɪ'neɪʃən] n inclination f; (desire) envie f
incline n ['ɪnklaɪn] pente f, plan incliné ▷ vt [ɪn'klaɪn] incliner ▷ vi [ɪn'klaɪn] (surface) s'incliner; **to be ~d to do** (have a tendency to do) avoir tendance à faire
include [ɪn'kluːd] vt inclure, comprendre; **service is/is not ~d** le service est compris/ n'est pas compris; **including** prep y compris; **inclusion** n inclusion f; **inclusive** adj inclus(e), compris(e); **inclusive of tax** taxes comprises
income ['ɪnkʌm] n revenu m; (from property etc) rentes fpl; **income support** n (BRIT) ≈ revenu m minimum d'insertion, RMI m; **income tax** n impôt m sur le revenu
incoming ['ɪnkʌmɪŋ] adj (passengers, mail) à l'arrivée; (government, tenant) nouveau (nouvelle)
incompatible [ɪnkəm'pætɪbl] adj incompatible
incompetence [ɪn'kɔmpɪtns] n incompétence f, incapacité f
incompetent [ɪn'kɔmpɪtnt] adj incompétent(e), incapable
incomplete [ɪnkəm'pliːt] adj incomplet(-ète)
inconsistent [ɪnkən'sɪstnt] adj qui manque de constance; (work) irrégulier(-ière); (statement) peu cohérent(e); **~ with** en contradiction avec
inconvenience [ɪnkən'viːnjəns] n inconvénient m; (trouble) dérangement m ▷ vt déranger
inconvenient [ɪnkən'viːnjənt] adj malcommode; (time, place) mal choisi(e), qui ne convient pas; (visitor) importun(e)
incorporate [ɪn'kɔːpəreɪt] vt incorporer; (contain) contenir
incorporated [ɪn'kɔːpəreɪtɪd] adj: **~ company** (US) ≈ société f anonyme
incorrect [ɪnkə'rɛkt] adj incorrect(e); (opinion, statement) inexact(e)
increase n ['ɪnkriːs] augmentation f ▷ vi, vt [ɪn'kriːs] augmenter; **increasingly** adv de plus en plus
incredible [ɪn'krɛdɪbl] adj incroyable; **incredibly** adv incroyablement
incur [ɪn'kəː] vt (expenses) encourir; (anger, risk) s'exposer à; (debt) contracter; (loss) subir
indecent [ɪn'diːsnt] adj indécent(e), inconvenant(e)
indeed [ɪn'diːd] adv (confirming, agreeing) en effet, effectivement; (for emphasis) vraiment; (furthermore) d'ailleurs; **yes ~!** certainement!
indefinitely [ɪn'dɛfɪnɪtlɪ] adv (wait) indéfiniment

independence [ɪndɪ'pɛndns] n indépendance f; **Independence Day** n (US) fête de l'Indépendance américaine

○ **INDEPENDENCE DAY**
○
○ L'Independence Day est la fête nationale aux
○ États-Unis, le 4 juillet. Il commémore
○ l'adoption de la déclaration d'Indépendance,
○ en 1776, écrite par Thomas Jefferson et
○ proclamant la séparation des 13 colonies
○ américaines de la Grande-Bretagne.

independent [ɪndɪ'pɛndnt] adj indépendant(e); (radio) libre; **independent school** n (BRIT) école privée
index ['ɪndɛks] n (pl indexes) (in book) index m; (in library etc) catalogue m; (pl indices) (ratio, sign) indice m
India ['ɪndɪə] n Inde f; **Indian** adj Indien(ne) ▷ n Indien(ne); **(American) Indian** Indien(ne) (d'Amérique)
indicate ['ɪndɪkeɪt] vt indiquer ▷ vi (BRIT Aut): **to ~ left/right** mettre son clignotant à gauche/à droite; **indication** [ɪndɪ'keɪʃən] n indication f, signe m; **indicative** [ɪn'dɪkətɪv] adj: **to be indicative of sth** être symptomatique de qch ▷ n (Ling) indicatif m; **indicator** n (sign) indicateur m; (Aut) clignotant m
indices ['ɪndɪsiːz] npl of **index**
indict [ɪn'daɪt] vt accuser; **indictment** n accusation f
indifference [ɪn'dɪfrəns] n indifférence f
indifferent [ɪn'dɪfrənt] adj indifférent(e); (poor) médiocre, quelconque
indigenous [ɪn'dɪdʒɪnəs] adj indigène
indigestion [ɪndɪ'dʒɛstʃən] n indigestion f, mauvaise digestion
indignant [ɪn'dɪgnənt] adj: **~ (at sth/with sb)** indigné(e) (de qch/contre qn)
indirect [ɪn'rɛkt] adj indirect(e)
indispensable [ɪndɪ'spɛnsəbl] adj indispensable
individual [ɪndɪ'vɪdjuəl] n individu m ▷ adj individuel(le); (characteristic) particulier(-ière), original(e); **individually** adv individuellement
Indonesia [ɪndə'niːzɪə] n Indonésie f
indoor ['ɪndɔː] adj d'intérieur; (plant) d'appartement; (swimming pool) couvert(e); (sport, games) pratiqué(e) en salle; **indoors** [ɪn'dɔːz] adv à l'intérieur
induce [ɪn'djuːs] vt (persuade) persuader; (bring about) provoquer; (labour) déclencher
indulge [ɪn'dʌldʒ] vt (whim) céder à, satisfaire; (child) gâter ▷ vi: **to ~ in sth** (luxury) s'offrir qch, se permettre qch; (fantasies etc) se livrer à qch; **indulgent** adj indulgent(e)
industrial [ɪn'dʌstrɪəl] adj industriel(le); (injury) du travail; (dispute) ouvrier(-ière);

industrial estate n (BRIT) zone industrielle; **industrialist** n industriel m; **industrial park** n (US) zone industrielle

industry ['ɪndəstrɪ] n industrie f; (diligence) zèle m, application f

inefficient [ɪnɪ'fɪʃənt] adj inefficace

inequality [ɪnɪ'kwɒlɪtɪ] n inégalité f

inevitable [ɪn'ɛvɪtəbl] adj inévitable; **inevitably** adv inévitablement, fatalement

inexpensive [ɪnɪk'spɛnsɪv] adj bon marché inv

inexperienced [ɪnɪk'spɪərɪənst] adj inexpérimenté(e)

inexplicable [ɪnɪk'splɪkəbl] adj inexplicable

infamous ['ɪnfəməs] adj infâme, abominable

infant ['ɪnfənt] n (baby) nourrisson m; (young child) petit(e) enfant

infantry ['ɪnfəntrɪ] n infanterie f

infant school n (BRIT) classes fpl préparatoires (entre 5 et 7 ans)

infect [ɪn'fɛkt] vt (wound) infecter; (person, blood) contaminer; **infection** [ɪn'fɛkʃən] n infection f; (contagion) contagion f; **infectious** [ɪn'fɛkʃəs] adj infectieux(-euse); (also fig) contagieux(-euse)

infer [ɪn'fəːʳ] vt: **to ~ (from)** conclure (de), déduire (de)

inferior [ɪn'fɪərɪəʳ] adj inférieur(e); (goods) de qualité inférieure ▷ n inférieur(e); (in rank) subalterne m/f

infertile [ɪn'fəːtaɪl] adj stérile

infertility [ɪnfə'tɪlɪtɪ] n infertilité f, stérilité f

infested [ɪn'fɛstɪd] adj: **~ (with)** infesté(e) (de)

infinite ['ɪnfɪnɪt] adj infini(e); (time, money) illimité(e); **infinitely** adv infiniment

infirmary [ɪn'fəːmərɪ] n hôpital m; (in school, factory) infirmerie f

inflamed [ɪn'fleɪmd] adj enflammé(e)

inflammation [ɪnflə'meɪʃən] n inflammation f

inflatable [ɪn'fleɪtəbl] adj gonflable

inflate [ɪn'fleɪt] vt (tyre, balloon) gonfler; (fig: exaggerate) grossir; (: increase) gonfler; **inflation** [ɪn'fleɪʃən] n (Econ) inflation f

inflexible [ɪn'flɛksɪbl] adj inflexible, rigide

inflict [ɪn'flɪkt] vt: **to ~ on** infliger à

influence ['ɪnfluəns] n influence f ▷ vt influencer; **under the ~ of alcohol** en état d'ébriété; **influential** [ɪnflu'ɛnʃl] adj influent(e)

influenza [ɪnflu'ɛnzə] n grippe f

influx ['ɪnflʌks] n afflux m

info ['ɪnfəu] (inf) n (= information) renseignements mpl

inform [ɪn'fɔːm] vt: **to ~ sb (of)** informer or avertir qn (de) ▷ vi: **to ~ on sb** dénoncer qn, informer contre qn

informal [ɪn'fɔːml] adj (person, manner, party) simple; (visit, discussion) dénué(e) de formalités; (announcement, invitation) non officiel(le); (colloquial) familier(-ère)

information [ɪnfə'meɪʃən] n information(s) f(pl); renseignements mpl; (knowledge) connaissances fpl; **a piece of ~** un renseignement; **information office** n bureau m de renseignements; **information technology** n informatique f

informative [ɪn'fɔːmətɪv] adj instructif(-ive)

infra-red [ɪnfrə'rɛd] adj infrarouge

infrastructure ['ɪnfrəstrʌktʃəʳ] n infrastructure f

infrequent [ɪn'friːkwənt] adj peu fréquent(e), rare

infuriate [ɪn'fjuərɪeɪt] vt mettre en fureur

infuriating [ɪn'fjuərɪeɪtɪŋ] adj exaspérant(e)

ingenious [ɪn'dʒiːnjəs] adj ingénieux(-euse)

ingredient [ɪn'griːdɪənt] n ingrédient m; (fig) élément m

inhabit [ɪn'hæbɪt] vt habiter; **inhabitant** n habitant(e)

inhale [ɪn'heɪl] vt inhaler; (perfume) respirer; (smoke) avaler ▷ vi (breathe in) aspirer; (in smoking) avaler la fumée; **inhaler** n inhalateur m

inherent [ɪn'hɪərənt] adj: **~ (in or to)** inhérent(e) (à)

inherit [ɪn'hɛrɪt] vt hériter (de); **inheritance** n héritage m

inhibit [ɪn'hɪbɪt] vt (Psych) inhiber; (growth) freiner; **inhibition** [ɪnhɪ'bɪʃən] n inhibition f

initial [ɪ'nɪʃl] adj initial(e) ▷ n initiale f ▷ vt parafer; **initials** npl initiales fpl; (as signature) parafe m; **initially** adv initialement, au début

initiate [ɪ'nɪʃɪeɪt] vt (start) entreprendre; amorcer; (enterprise) lancer; (person) initier; **to ~ proceedings against sb** (Law) intenter une action à qn, engager des poursuites contre qn

initiative [ɪ'nɪʃətɪv] n initiative f

inject [ɪn'dʒɛkt] vt injecter; (person): **to ~ sb with sth** faire une piqûre de qch à qn; **injection** [ɪn'dʒɛkʃən] n injection f, piqûre f

injure ['ɪndʒəʳ] vt blesser; (damage: reputation etc) compromettre; **to ~ o.s.** se blesser; **injured** adj (person, leg etc) blessé(e); **injury** n blessure f; (wrong) tort m

injustice [ɪn'dʒʌstɪs] n injustice f

ink [ɪŋk] n encre f; **ink-jet printer** ['ɪŋkdʒɛt-] n imprimante f à jet d'encre

inland adj ['ɪnlənd] intérieur(e) ▷ adv [ɪn'lænd] à l'intérieur, dans les terres; **Inland Revenue** n (BRIT) fisc m

in-laws ['ɪnlɔːz] npl beaux-parents mpl; belle famille

inmate ['ɪnmeɪt] n (in prison) détenu(e); (in asylum) interné(e)

inn [ɪn] n auberge f

inner ['ɪnə'] adj intérieur(e); **inner-city** adj (schools, problems) de quartiers déshérités

inning ['ɪnɪŋ] n (US Baseball) tour m de batte; **innings** npl (Cricket) tour de batte

innocence ['ɪnəsns] n innocence f

innocent ['ɪnəsnt] adj innocent(e)

innovation [ɪnəu'veɪʃən] n innovation f

innovative ['ɪnəu'veɪtɪv] adj novateur(-trice); (product) innovant(e)

in-patient ['ɪnpeɪʃənt] n malade hospitalisé(e)

input ['ɪnput] n (contribution) contribution f; (resources) ressources fpl; (Comput) entrée f (de données) (: data) données fpl ▷ vt (Comput) introduire, entrer

inquest ['ɪnkwɛst] n enquête (criminelle); (coroner's) enquête judiciaire

inquire [ɪn'kwaɪə'] vi demander ▷ vt demander; **to ~ about** s'informer de, se renseigner sur; **to ~ when/where/whether** demander quand/où/si; **inquiry** n demande f de renseignements; (Law) enquête f, investigation f; **"inquiries"** "renseignements"

ins. abbr = **inches**

insane [ɪn'seɪn] adj fou (folle); (Med) aliéné(e)

insanity [ɪn'sænɪtɪ] n folie f; (Med) aliénation (mentale)

insect ['ɪnsɛkt] n insecte m; **insect repellent** n crème f anti-insectes

insecure [ɪnsɪ'kjuə'] adj (person) anxieux(-euse); (job) précaire; (building etc) peu sûr(e)

insecurity [ɪnsɪ'kjuərɪtɪ] n insécurité f

insensitive [ɪn'sɛnsɪtɪv] adj insensible

insert vt [ɪn'sə:t] insérer ▷ n ['ɪnsə:t] insertion f

inside ['ɪn'saɪd] n intérieur m ▷ adj intérieur(e) ▷ adv à l'intérieur, dedans ▷ prep à l'intérieur de; (of time): ~ **10 minutes** en moins de 10 minutes; **to go ~** rentrer; **inside lane** n (Aut: in Britain) voie f de gauche; (: in US, Europe) voie f de droite; **inside out** adv à l'envers; (know) à fond; **to turn sth inside out** retourner qch

insight ['ɪnsaɪt] n perspicacité f; (glimpse, idea) aperçu m

insignificant [ɪnsɪg'nɪfɪknt] adj insignifiant(e)

insincere [ɪnsɪn'sɪə'] adj hypocrite

insist [ɪn'sɪst] vi insister; **to ~ on doing** insister pour faire; **to ~ on sth** exiger qch; **to ~ that** insister pour que + sub; (claim) maintenir or soutenir que; **insistent** adj insistant(e), pressant(e); (noise, action) ininterrompu(e)

insomnia [ɪn'sɔmnɪə] n insomnie f

inspect [ɪn'spɛkt] vt inspecter; (BRIT: ticket) contrôler; **inspection** [ɪn'spɛkʃən] n

inspection f; (BRIT: of tickets) contrôle m; **inspector** n inspecteur(-trice); (BRIT: on buses, trains) contrôleur(-euse)

inspiration [ɪnspə'reɪʃən] n inspiration f; **inspire** [ɪn'spaɪə'] vt inspirer; **inspiring** adj inspirant(e)

instability [ɪnstə'bɪlɪtɪ] n instabilité f

install, (US) **instal** [ɪn'stɔ:l] vt installer; **installation** [ɪnstə'leɪʃən] n installation f

instalment, (US) **installment** [ɪn'stɔ:lmənt] n (payment) acompte m, versement partiel; (of TV serial etc) épisode m; **in ~s** (pay) à tempérament; (receive) en plusieurs fois

instance ['ɪnstəns] n exemple m; **for ~** par exemple; **in the first ~** tout d'abord, en premier lieu

instant ['ɪnstənt] n instant m ▷ adj immédiat(e), urgent(e); (coffee, food) instantané(e), en poudre; **instantly** adv immédiatement, tout de suite; **instant messaging** n messagerie f instantanée

instead [ɪn'stɛd] adv au lieu de cela; **~ of** au lieu de; **~ of sb** à la place de qn

instinct ['ɪnstɪŋkt] n instinct m; **instinctive** adj instinctif(-ive)

institute ['ɪnstɪtju:t] n institut m ▷ vt instituer, établir; (inquiry) ouvrir; (proceedings) entamer

institution [ɪnstɪ'tju:ʃən] n institution f; (school) établissement m (scolaire); (for care) établissement (psychiatrique etc)

instruct [ɪn'strʌkt] vt: **to ~ sb in sth** enseigner qch à qn; **to ~ sb to do** charger qn or ordonner à qn de faire; **instruction** [ɪn'strʌkʃən] n instruction f; **instructions** npl (orders) directives fpl; **instructions for use** mode m d'emploi; **instructor** n professeur m; (for skiing, driving) moniteur m

instrument ['ɪnstrəmənt] n instrument m; **instrumental** [ɪnstru'mɛntl] adj (Mus) instrumental(e); **to be instrumental in sth/in doing sth** contribuer à qch/à faire qch

insufficient [ɪnsə'fɪʃənt] adj insuffisant(e)

insulate ['ɪnsjuleɪt] vt isoler; (against sound) insonoriser; **insulation** [ɪnsju'leɪʃən] n isolation f; (against sound) insonorisation f

insulin ['ɪnsjulɪn] n insuline f

insult n ['ɪnsʌlt] insulte f, affront m ▷ vt [ɪn'sʌlt] insulter, faire un affront à; **insulting** adj insultant(e), injurieux(-euse)

insurance [ɪn'ʃuərəns] n assurance f; **fire/life ~** assurance-incendie/-vie; **insurance company** n compagnie f or société f d'assurances; **insurance policy** n police f d'assurance

insure [ɪn'ʃuə'] vt assurer; **to ~ (o.s.) against** (fig) parer à

intact [ɪn'tækt] adj intact(e)

intake ['ɪnteɪk] n (Tech) admission f;
(consumption) consommation f; (BRIT Scol):
an ~ of 200 a year 200 admissions par an
integral ['ɪntɪgrəl] adj (whole) intégral(e);
(part) intégrant(e)
integrate ['ɪntɪgreɪt] vt intégrer ▷ vi
s'intégrer
integrity [ɪn'tɛgrɪtɪ] n intégrité f
intellect ['ɪntəlɛkt] n intelligence
f; **intellectual** [ɪntə'lɛktjuəl] adj, n
intellectuel(le)
intelligence [ɪn'tɛlɪdʒəns] n intelligence f;
(Mil) informations fpl, renseignements mpl
intelligent [ɪn'tɛlɪdʒənt] adj intelligent(e)
intend [ɪn'tɛnd] vt (gift etc): **to ~ sth for**
destiner qch à; **to ~ to do** avoir l'intention
de faire
intense [ɪn'tɛns] adj intense; (person)
véhément(e)
intensify [ɪn'tɛnsɪfaɪ] vt intensifier
intensity [ɪn'tɛnsɪtɪ] n intensité f
intensive [ɪn'tɛnsɪv] adj intensif(-ive);
intensive care n: **to be in intensive care**
être en réanimation; **intensive care unit** n
service m de réanimation
intent [ɪn'tɛnt] n intention f ▷ adj
attentif(-ive), absorbé(e); **to all ~s and
purposes** en fait, pratiquement; **to be ~ on
doing sth** être (bien) décidé à faire qch
intention [ɪn'tɛnʃən] n intention
f; **intentional** adj intentionnel(le),
délibéré(e)
interact [ɪntər'ækt] vi avoir une action
réciproque; (people) communiquer;
interaction [ɪntər'ækʃən] n interaction
f; **interactive** adj (Comput) interactif,
conversationnel(le)
intercept [ɪntə'sɛpt] vt intercepter;
(person) arrêter au passage
interchange n ['ɪntətʃeɪndʒ] (exchange)
échange m; (on motorway) échangeur m
intercourse ['ɪntəkɔ:s] n: **sexual ~**
rapports sexuels
interest ['ɪntrɪst] n intérêt m; (Comm: stake,
share) participation f, intérêts mpl ▷ vt
intéresser; **interested** adj intéressé(e); **to
be interested in sth** s'intéresser à qch; **I'm
interested in going** ça m'intéresse d'y aller;
interesting adj intéressant(e); **interest
rate** n taux m d'intérêt
interface ['ɪntəfeɪs] n (Comput)
interface f
interfere [ɪntə'fɪə'] vi: **to ~ in** (quarrel)
s'immiscer dans; (other people's business)
se mêler de; **to ~ with** (object) tripoter,
toucher à; (plans) contrecarrer; (duty)
être en conflit avec; **interference** n (gen)
ingérence f; (Radio, TV) parasites mpl
interim ['ɪntərɪm] adj provisoire; (post)
intérimaire ▷ n: **in the ~** dans l'intérim
interior [ɪn'tɪərɪə'] n intérieur m ▷ adj
intérieur(e); (minister, department) de

l'intérieur; **interior design** n architecture
f d'intérieur
intermediate [ɪntə'mi:dɪət] adj
intermédiaire; (Scol: course, level) moyen(ne)
intermission [ɪntə'mɪʃən] n pause f;
(Theat, Cine) entracte m
intern vt [ɪn'tə:n] interner ▷ n ['ɪntə:n] (US)
interne m/f
internal [ɪn'tə:nl] adj interne; (dispute,
reform etc) intérieur(e); **Internal Revenue
Service** n (US) fisc m
international [ɪntə'næʃənl] adj
international(e) ▷ n (BRIT Sport)
international m
Internet [ɪntə'nɛt] n: **the ~** l'Internet m;
Internet café n cybercafé m; **Internet
Service Provider** n fournisseur m d'accès à
Internet; **Internet user** n internaute m/f
interpret [ɪn'tə:prɪt] vt interpréter ▷ vi
servir d'interprète; **interpretation**
[ɪntə:prɪ'teɪʃən] n interprétation f;
interpreter n interprète m/f; **could you
act as an interpreter for us?** pourriez-vous
nous servir d'interprète?
interrogate [ɪn'tɛrəʊgeɪt] vt interroger;
(suspect etc) soumettre à un interrogatoire;
interrogation [ɪntɛrəʊ'geɪʃən] n
interrogation f; (by police) interrogatoire m
interrogative [ɪntə'rɔgətɪv] adj
interrogateur(-trice) ▷ n (Ling)
interrogatif m
interrupt [ɪntə'rʌpt] vt, vi interrompre;
interruption [ɪntə'rʌpʃən] n
interruption f
intersection [ɪntə'sɛkʃən] n (of roads)
croisement m
interstate ['ɪntəsteɪt] (US) n autoroute f
(qui relie plusieurs États)
interval ['ɪntəvl] n intervalle m; (BRIT:
Theat) entracte m; (: Sport) mi-temps f; **at ~s**
par intervalles
intervene [ɪntə'vi:n] vi (time) s'écouler
(entre-temps); (event) survenir; (person)
intervenir
interview ['ɪntəvju:] n (Radio, TV)
interview f; (for job) entrevue f ▷ vt
interviewer, avoir une entrevue avec;
interviewer n (Radio, TV) interviewer m
intimate adj ['ɪntɪmət] intime; (friendship)
profond(e); (knowledge) approfondi(e) ▷ vt
['ɪntɪmeɪt] suggérer, laisser entendre;
(announce) faire savoir
intimidate [ɪn'tɪmɪdeɪt] vt intimider
intimidating [ɪn'tɪmɪdeɪtɪŋ] adj
intimidant(e)
into ['ɪntu] prep dans; **~ pieces/French** en
morceaux/français
intolerant [ɪn'tɔlərnt] adj: **~ (of)**
intolérant(e) (de)
intranet [ɪn'trænɛt] n intranet m
intransitive [ɪn'trænsɪtɪv] adj
intransitif(-ive)

intricate ['ɪntrɪkət] *adj* complexe, compliqué(e)
intrigue [ɪn'triːg] *n* intrigue *f* ▷ *vt* intriguer; **intriguing** *adj* fascinant(e)
introduce [ɪntrə'djuːs] *vt* introduire; (*TV show etc*) présenter; **to ~ sb (to sb)** présenter qn (à qn); **to ~ sb to** (*pastime, technique*) initier qn à; **introduction** [ɪntrə'dʌkʃən] *n* introduction *f*; (*of person*) présentation *f*; (*to new experience*) initiation *f*; **introductory** [ɪntrə'dʌktərɪ] *adj* préliminaire, introductif(-ive)
intrude [ɪn'truːd] *vi* (*person*) être importun(e); **to ~ on** *or* **into** (*conversation etc*) s'immiscer dans; **intruder** *n* intrus(e)
intuition [ɪntjuː'ɪʃən] *n* intuition *f*
inundate ['ɪnʌndeɪt] *vt*: **to ~ with** inonder de
invade [ɪn'veɪd] *vt* envahir
invalid *n* ['ɪnvəlɪd] malade *m/f*; (*with disability*) invalide *m/f* ▷ *adj* [ɪn'vælɪd] (*not valid*) invalide, non valide
invaluable [ɪn'væljuəbl] *adj* inestimable, inappréciable
invariably [ɪn'vɛərɪəblɪ] *adv* invariablement; **she is ~ late** elle est toujours en retard
invasion [ɪn'veɪʒən] *n* invasion *f*
invent [ɪn'vɛnt] *vt* inventer; **invention** [ɪn'vɛnʃən] *n* invention *f*; **inventor** *n* inventeur(-trice)
inventory ['ɪnvəntrɪ] *n* inventaire *m*
inverted commas [ɪn'vəːtɪd-] *npl* (BRIT) guillemets *mpl*
invest [ɪn'vɛst] *vt* investir ▷ *vi*: **to ~ in** placer de l'argent *or* investir dans; (*fig: acquire*) s'offrir, faire l'acquisition de
investigate [ɪn'vɛstɪgeɪt] *vt* étudier, examiner; (*crime*) faire une enquête sur; **investigation** [ɪnvɛstɪ'geɪʃən] *n* (*of crime*) enquête *f*, investigation *f*
investigator [ɪn'vɛstɪgeɪtə'] *n* investigateur(-trice); **private ~** détective privé
investment [ɪn'vɛstmənt] *n* investissement *m*, placement *m*
investor [ɪn'vɛstə'] *n* épargnant(e); (*shareholder*) actionnaire *m/f*
invisible [ɪn'vɪzɪbl] *adj* invisible
invitation [ɪnvɪ'teɪʃən] *n* invitation *f*
invite [ɪn'vaɪt] *vt* inviter; (*opinions etc*) demander; **inviting** *adj* engageant(e), attrayant(e)
invoice ['ɪnvɔɪs] *n* facture *f* ▷ *vt* facturer
involve [ɪn'vɔlv] *vt* (*entail*) impliquer; (*concern*) concerner; (*require*) nécessiter; **to ~ sb in** (*theft etc*) impliquer qn dans; (*activity, meeting*) faire participer qn à; **involved** *adj* (*complicated*) complexe; **to be involved in** (*take part*) participer à; **involvement** *n* (*personal role*) rôle *m*; (*participation*) participation *f*; (*enthusiasm*) enthousiasme *m*

inward ['ɪnwəd] *adj* (*movement*) vers l'intérieur; (*thought, feeling*) profond(e), intime ▷ *adv* = **inwards**; **inwards** *adv* vers l'intérieur
iPod® ['aɪpɔd] *n* iPod® *m*
IQ *n abbr* (= *intelligence quotient*) Q.I. *m*
IRA *n abbr* (= *Irish Republican Army*) IRA *f*
Iran [ɪ'rɑːn] *n* Iran *m*; **Iranian** [ɪ'reɪnɪən] *adj* iranien(ne) ▷ *n* Iranien(ne)
Iraq [ɪ'rɑːk] *n* Irak *m*; **Iraqi** *adj* irakien(ne) ▷ *n* Irakien(ne)
Ireland ['aɪələnd] *n* Irlande *f*
iris, irises ['aɪrɪs, -ɪz] *n* iris *m*
Irish ['aɪrɪʃ] *adj* irlandais(e) ▷ *npl*: **the ~** les Irlandais; **Irishman** (*irreg*) *n* Irlandais *m*; **Irishwoman** (*irreg*) *n* Irlandaise *f*
iron ['aɪən] *n* fer *m*; (*for clothes*) fer *m* à repasser ▷ *adj* de *or* en fer ▷ *vt* (*clothes*) repasser
ironic(al) [aɪ'rɔnɪk(l)] *adj* ironique; **ironically** *adv* ironiquement
ironing ['aɪənɪŋ] *n* (*activity*) repassage *m*; (*clothes: ironed*) linge repassé; (*: to be ironed*) linge à repasser; **ironing board** *n* planche *f* à repasser
irony ['aɪrənɪ] *n* ironie *f*
irrational [ɪ'ræʃənl] *adj* irrationnel(le); (*person*) qui n'est pas rationnel
irregular [ɪ'rɛgjulə'] *adj* irrégulier(-ière); (*surface*) inégal(e); (*action, event*) peu orthodoxe
irrelevant [ɪ'rɛləvənt] *adj* sans rapport, hors de propos
irresistible [ɪrɪ'zɪstɪbl] *adj* irrésistible
irresponsible [ɪrɪ'spɔnsɪbl] *adj* (*act*) irréfléchi(e); (*person*) qui n'a pas le sens des responsabilités
irrigation [ɪrɪ'geɪʃən] *n* irrigation *f*
irritable ['ɪrɪtəbl] *adj* irritable
irritate ['ɪrɪteɪt] *vt* irriter; **irritating** *adj* irritant(e); **irritation** [ɪrɪ'teɪʃən] *n* irritation *f*
IRS *n abbr* (US) = **Internal Revenue Service**
is [ɪz] *vb see* **be**
ISDN *n abbr* (= *Integrated Services Digital Network*) RNIS *m*
Islam ['ɪzlɑːm] *n* Islam *m*; **Islamic** [ɪz'læmɪk] *adj* islamique
island ['aɪlənd] *n* île *f*; (*also*: **traffic ~**) refuge *m* (pour piétons); **islander** *n* habitant(e) d'une île, insulaire *m/f*
isle [aɪl] *n* île *f*
isn't ['ɪznt] = **is not**
isolated ['aɪsəleɪtɪd] *adj* isolé(e)
isolation [aɪsə'leɪʃən] *n* isolement *m*
ISP *n abbr* = **Internet Service Provider**
Israel ['ɪzreɪl] *n* Israël *m*; **Israeli** [ɪz'reɪlɪ] *adj* israélien(ne) ▷ *n* Israélien(ne)
issue ['ɪʃuː] *n* question *f*, problème *m*; (*of banknotes*) émission *f*; (*of newspaper*) numéro *m*; (*of book*) publication *f*, parution *f* ▷ *vt* (*rations, equipment*) distribuer;

(orders) donner; (statement) publier, faire; (certificate, passport) délivrer; (banknotes, cheques, stamps) émettre, mettre en circulation; **at ~** en jeu, en cause; **to take ~ with sb (over sth)** exprimer son désaccord avec qn (sur qch)

IT n abbr = **information technology**

🔵 KEYWORD

it [ɪt] pron **1** (specific: subject) il (elle); (: direct object) le (la, l'); (: indirect object) lui; **it's on the table** c'est or il (or elle) est sur la table; **I can't find it** je n'arrive pas à le trouver; **give it to me** donne-le-moi
2 (after prep): **about/from/of it** en; **I spoke to him about it** je lui en ai parlé; **what did you learn from it?** qu'est-ce que vous en avez retiré?; **I'm proud of it** j'en suis fier; **in/to it** y; **put the book in it** mettez-y le livre; **I'm agreed to it** il y a consenti; **did you go to it?** (party, concert etc) est-ce que vous y êtes allé(s)?
3 (impersonal) il; ce, cela, ça; **it's Friday tomorrow** demain, c'est vendredi or nous sommes vendredi; **it's 6 o'clock** il est 6 heures; **how far is it? — it's 10 miles** c'est loin? — c'est à 10 miles; **who is it? — it's me** qui est-ce? — c'est moi; **it's raining** il pleut

Italian [ɪ'tæljən] adj italien(ne) ▷ n Italien(ne); (Ling) italien m
italics [ɪ'tælɪks] npl italique m
Italy ['ɪtəlɪ] n Italie f
itch [ɪtʃ] n démangeaison f ▷ vi (person) éprouver des démangeaisons; (part of body) démanger; **I'm ~ing to do** l'envie me démange de faire; **itchy** adj: **my back is itchy** j'ai le dos qui me démange
it'd ['ɪtd] = **it would; it had**
item ['aɪtəm] n (gen) article m; (on agenda) question f, point m; (also: **news ~**) nouvelle f
itinerary [aɪ'tɪnərərɪ] n itinéraire m
it'll ['ɪtl] = **it will; it shall**
its [ɪts] adj son (sa), ses pl
it's [ɪts] = **it is; it has**
itself [ɪt'sɛlf] pron (reflexive) se; (emphatic) lui-même (elle-même)
ITV n abbr (BRIT: = Independent Television) chaîne de télévision commerciale
I've [aɪv] = **I have**
ivory ['aɪvərɪ] n ivoire m
ivy ['aɪvɪ] n lierre m

J

jab [dʒæb] vt: **to ~ sth into** enfoncer or planter qch dans ▷ n (Med: inf) piqûre f
jack [dʒæk] n (Aut) cric m; (Cards) valet m
jacket ['dʒækɪt] n veste f, veston m; (of book) couverture f, jaquette f; **jacket potato** n pomme f de terre en robe des champs
jackpot ['dʒækpɔt] n gros lot
Jacuzzi® [dʒə'ku:zɪ] n jacuzzi® m
jagged ['dʒægɪd] adj dentelé(e)
jail [dʒeɪl] n prison f ▷ vt emprisonner, mettre en prison; **jail sentence** n peine f de prison
jam [dʒæm] n confiture f; (also: **traffic ~**) embouteillage m ▷ vt (passage etc) encombrer, obstruer; (mechanism, drawer etc) bloquer, coincer; (Radio) brouiller ▷ vi (mechanism, sliding part) se coincer, se bloquer; (gun) s'enrayer; **to be in a ~** (inf) être dans le pétrin; **to ~ sth into** (stuff) entasser or comprimer qch dans; (thrust) enfoncer qch dans
Jamaica [dʒə'meɪkə] n Jamaïque f
jammed [dʒæmd] adj (window etc) coincé(e)
janitor ['dʒænɪtər] n (caretaker) concierge m
January ['dʒænjuərɪ] n janvier m
Japan [dʒə'pæn] n Japon m; **Japanese** [dʒæpə'ni:z] adj japonais(e) ▷ n (pl inv) Japonais(e); (Ling) japonais m
jar [dʒɑ:r] n (stone, earthenware) pot m; (glass) bocal m ▷ vi (sound) produire un son grinçant or discordant; (colours etc) détonner, jurer
jargon ['dʒɑ:gən] n jargon m
javelin ['dʒævlɪn] n javelot m
jaw [dʒɔ:] n mâchoire f
jazz [dʒæz] n jazz m
jealous ['dʒɛləs] adj jaloux(-ouse); **jealousy** n jalousie f
jeans [dʒi:nz] npl jean m

Jello® ['dʒɛləu] (US) n gelée f
jelly ['dʒɛlɪ] n (dessert) gelée f; (US: jam) confiture f; **jellyfish** n méduse f
jeopardize ['dʒɛpədaɪz] vt mettre en danger or péril
jerk [dʒəːk] n secousse f, saccade f; (of muscle) spasme m; (inf) pauvre type m ▷ vt (shake) donner une secousse à; (pull) tirer brusquement ▷ vi (vehicles) cahoter
jersey ['dʒəːzɪ] n tricot m; (fabric) jersey m
Jesus ['dʒiːzəs] n Jésus
jet [dʒɛt] n (of gas, liquid) jet m; (Aviat) avion m à réaction, jet m; **jet lag** n décalage m horaire; **jet-ski** vi faire du jet-ski or scooter des mers
jetty ['dʒɛtɪ] n jetée f, digue f
Jew [dʒuː] n Juif m
jewel ['dʒuːəl] n bijou m, joyau m; (in watch) rubis m; **jeweller**, (US) **jeweler** n bijoutier(-ière), joaillier m; **jeweller's (shop)** n (BRIT) bijouterie f, joaillerie f; **jewellery**, (US) **jewelry** n bijoux mpl
Jewish ['dʒuːɪʃ] adj juif (juive)
jigsaw ['dʒɪgsɔː] n (also: ~ puzzle) puzzle m
job [dʒɔb] n (chore, task) travail m, tâche f; (employment) emploi m, poste m, place f; **it's a good ~ that ...** c'est heureux or c'est une chance que ... + sub; **just the ~!** (c'est) juste or exactement ce qu'il faut!; **job centre** (BRIT) n ≈ ANPE f, ≈ Agence nationale pour l'emploi; **jobless** adj sans travail, au chômage
jockey ['dʒɔkɪ] n jockey m ▷ vi: **to ~ for position** manœuvrer pour être bien placé
jog [dʒɔg] vt secouer ▷ vi (Sport) faire du jogging; **to ~ sb's memory** rafraîchir la mémoire de qn; **jogging** n jogging m
join [dʒɔɪn] vt (put together) unir, assembler; (become member of) s'inscrire à; (meet) rejoindre, retrouver; (queue) se joindre à ▷ vi (roads, rivers) se rejoindre, se rencontrer ▷ n raccord m; **join in** vi se mettre de la partie ▷ vt fus se mêler à; **join up** vi (meet) se rejoindre; (Mil) s'engager
joiner ['dʒɔɪnəʳ] (BRIT) n menuisier m
joint [dʒɔɪnt] n (Tech) jointure f, joint m; (Anat) articulation f, jointure; (BRIT Culin) rôti m; (inf: place) boîte f; (of cannabis) joint ▷ adj commun(e); (committee) mixte, paritaire; (winner) ex aequo; **joint account** n compte joint; **jointly** adv ensemble, en commun
joke [dʒəuk] n plaisanterie f; (also: **practical ~**) farce f ▷ vi plaisanter; **to play a ~ on** jouer un tour à, faire une farce à; **joker** n (Cards) joker m
jolly ['dʒɔlɪ] adj gai(e), enjoué(e); (enjoyable) amusant(e), plaisant(e) ▷ adv (BRIT inf) rudement, drôlement
jolt [dʒəult] n cahot m, secousse f; (shock) choc m ▷ vt cahoter, secouer
Jordan [dʒɔːdən] n (country) Jordanie f

journal ['dʒəːnl] n journal m; **journalism** n journalisme m; **journalist** n journaliste m/f
journey ['dʒəːnɪ] n voyage m; (distance covered) trajet m; **the ~ takes two hours** le trajet dure deux heures; **how was your ~?** votre voyage s'est bien passé?
joy [dʒɔɪ] n joie f; **joyrider** n voleur(-euse) de voiture (qui fait une virée dans le véhicule volé); **joy stick** n (Aviat) manche m à balai; (Comput) manche à balai, manette f (de jeu)
Jr abbr = **junior**
judge [dʒʌdʒ] n juge m ▷ vt juger; (estimate: weight, size etc) apprécier; (consider) estimer
judo ['dʒuːdəu] n judo m
jug [dʒʌg] n pot m, cruche f
juggle ['dʒʌgl] vi jongler; **juggler** n jongleur m
juice [dʒuːs] n jus m; **juicy** adj juteux(-euse)
July [dʒuːˈlaɪ] n juillet m
jumble ['dʒʌmbl] n fouillis m ▷ vt (also: **~ up, ~ together**) mélanger, brouiller; **jumble sale** n (BRIT) vente f de charité

 JUMBLE SALE

 Les jumble sales ont lieu dans les églises,
 salles des fêtes ou halls d'écoles, et l'on
 y vend des articles de toutes sortes, en
 général bon marché et surtout d'occasion,
 pour collecter des fonds pour une œuvre
 de charité, une école (par exemple, pour
 acheter des ordinateurs), ou encore une
 église (pour réparer un toit etc).

jumbo ['dʒʌmbəu] adj (also: ~ **jet**) (avion) gros porteur (à réaction)
jump [dʒʌmp] vi sauter, bondir; (with fear etc) sursauter; (increase) monter en flèche ▷ vt sauter, franchir ▷ n saut m, bond m; (with fear etc) sursaut m; (fence) obstacle m; **to ~ the queue** (BRIT) passer avant son tour
jumper ['dʒʌmpəʳ] n (BRIT: pullover) pull-over m; (US: pinafore dress) robe-chasuble f
jump leads, (US) **jumper cables** npl câbles mpl de démarrage
Jun. abbr = **June; junior**
junction ['dʒʌŋkʃən] n (BRIT: of roads) carrefour m; (of rails) embranchement m
June [dʒuːn] n juin m
jungle ['dʒʌŋgl] n jungle f
junior ['dʒuːnɪəʳ] adj, n: **he's ~ to me (by two years), he's my ~ (by two years)** il est mon cadet (de deux ans), il est plus jeune que moi (de deux ans); **he's ~ to me** (seniority) il est en dessous de moi (dans la hiérarchie), j'ai plus d'ancienneté que lui, **junior high school** n (US) ≈ collège m d'enseignement secondaire; see also **high school; junior school** n (BRIT) école f primaire

junk [dʒʌŋk] n (rubbish) camelote f; (cheap goods) bric-à-brac m inv; **junk food** n snacks vite prêts (sans valeur nutritive)

junkie ['dʒʌŋkɪ] n (inf) junkie m, drogué(e)

junk mail n prospectus mpl; (Comput) messages mpl publicitaires

Jupiter ['dʒuːpɪtə'] n (planet) Jupiter f

jurisdiction [dʒuərɪs'dɪkʃən] n juridiction f; **it falls** or **comes within/outside our** – cela est/n'est pas de notre compétence or ressort

jury ['dʒuərɪ] n jury m

just [dʒʌst] adj juste ▷ adv: **he's ~ done it/left** il vient de le faire/partir; **~ right/ two o'clock** exactement or juste ce qu'il faut/deux heures; **we were ~ going** nous partions; **I was ~ about to phone** j'allais téléphoner; **~ as he was leaving** au moment or à l'instant précis où il partait; **~ before/enough/here** juste avant/assez/ là; **it's ~ me/a mistake** ce n'est que moi/ (rien) qu'une erreur; **~ missed/caught** manqué/attrapé de justesse; **~ listen to this!** écoutez un peu ça!; **she's ~ as clever as you** elle est tout aussi intelligente que vous; **it's ~ as well that you …** heureusement que vous …; **~ a minute!, ~ one moment!** un instant (s'il vous plaît)!

justice ['dʒʌstɪs] n justice f; (us: judge) juge m de la Cour suprême

justification [dʒʌstɪfɪ'keɪʃən] n justification f

justify ['dʒʌstɪfaɪ] vt justifier

jut [dʒʌt] vi (also: ~ **out**) dépasser, faire saillie

juvenile ['dʒuːvənaɪl] adj juvénile; (court, books) pour enfants ▷ n adolescent(e)

K

K, k [keɪ] abbr (= one thousand) K

kangaroo [kæŋgə'ruː] n kangourou m

karaoke [kɑːrə'əʊkɪ] n karaoké m

karate [kə'rɑːtɪ] n karaté m

kebab [kə'bæb] n kebab m

keel [kiːl] n quille f; **on an even ~** (fig) à flot

keen [kiːn] adj (eager) plein(e) d'enthousiasme; (interest, desire, competition) vif (vive); (eye, intelligence) pénétrant(e); (edge) effilé(e); **to be ~ to do** or **on doing sth** désirer vivement faire qch, tenir beaucoup à faire qch; **to be ~ on sth/ sb** aimer beaucoup qch/qn

keep [kiːp] (pt, pp **kept**) vt (retain, preserve) garder; (hold back) retenir; (shop, accounts, promise, diary) tenir; (support) entretenir; (chickens, bees, pigs etc) élever ▷ vi (food) se conserver; (remain: in a certain state or place) rester ▷ n (of castle) donjon m; (food etc): **enough for his ~** assez pour (assurer) sa subsistance; **to ~ doing sth** (continue) continuer à faire qch; (repeatedly) ne pas arrêter de faire qch; **to ~ sb from doing/sth from happening** empêcher qn de faire or que qn (ne) fasse/que qch (n')arrive; **to ~ sb happy/a place tidy** faire que qn soit content/qu'un endroit reste propre; **to ~ sth to o.s.** garder qch pour soi, tenir qch secret; **to ~ sth from sb** cacher qch à qn; **to ~ time** (clock) être à l'heure, ne pas retarder; **for ~s** (inf) pour de bon, pour toujours; **keep away** vt: **to ~ sth/sb away from sb** tenir qch/qn éloigné de qn ▷ vi: **to ~ away (from)** ne pas s'approcher (de); **keep back** vt (crowds, tears, money) retenir; (conceal: information): **to ~ sth back from sb** cacher qch à qn ▷ vi rester en arrière; **keep off** vt (dog, person) éloigner ▷ vi: **if the rain ~s off** s'il ne pleut pas; **~ your hands off!** pas touché! (inf); **"~ off the grass"** "pelouse interdite"; **keep on** vi continuer; **to ~ on doing** continuer à faire; **don't ~ on about**

it! arrête (d'en parler)!; **keep out** vt
empêcher d'entrer ▷ vi (stay out) rester en
dehors; **"~ out"** "défense d'entrer"; **keep up**
vi (fig: in comprehension) suivre ▷ vt
continuer, maintenir; **to ~ up with sb**
(in work etc) se maintenir au même niveau
que qn; (in race etc) aller aussi vite que qn;
keeper n gardien(ne); **keep-fit** n
gymnastique f (d'entretien); **keeping** n
(care) garde f; **in keeping with** en
harmonie avec

kennel ['kɛnl] n niche f; **kennels** npl (for
boarding) chenil m

Kenya ['kɛnjə] n Kenya m

kept [kɛpt] pt, pp of **keep**

kerb [kə:b] n (BRIT) bordure f du trottoir

kerosene ['kɛrəsi:n] n kérosène m

ketchup ['kɛtʃəp] n ketchup m

kettle ['kɛtl] n bouilloire f

key [ki:] n (gen, Mus) clé f; (of piano,
typewriter) touche f; (on map) légende f
▷ adj (factor, role, area) clé inv ▷ vt (also: ~ **in**)
(text) saisir; **can I have my ~?** je peux avoir
ma clé?; **a ~ issue** un problème
fondamental; **keyboard** n clavier m;
keyhole n trou m de la serrure; **keypad** n
pavé m numérique; (of smartphone) clavier
m; **keyring** n porte-clés m

kg abbr (= kilogram) K

khaki ['kɑ:ki] adj, n kaki m

kick [kɪk] vt donner un coup de pied à
▷ vi (horse) ruer ▷ n coup m de pied; (inf:
thrill): **he does it for ~** il le fait parce que
ça l'excite, il le fait pour le plaisir; **to ~ the
habit** (inf) arrêter; **kick off** vi (Sport) donner
le coup d'envoi; **kick-off** n (Sport) coup m
d'envoi

kid [kɪd] n (inf: child) gamin(e), gosse
m/f; (animal, leather) chevreau m ▷ vi (inf)
plaisanter, blaguer

kidnap ['kɪdnæp] vt enlever, kidnapper;
kidnapping n enlèvement m

kidney ['kɪdnɪ] n (Anat) rein m; (Culin)
rognon m; **kidney bean** n haricot m rouge

kill [kɪl] vt tuer ▷ n mise f à mort; **to ~
time** tuer le temps; **killer** n tueur(-euse);
(murderer) meurtrier(-ière); **killing** n
meurtre m; (of group of people) tuerie f,
massacre m; (inf): **to make a killing** se
remplir les poches, réussir un beau coup

kiln [kɪln] n four m

kilo ['ki:ləu] n kilo m; **kilobyte** n (Comput)
kilo-octet m; **kilogram(me)** n kilogramme
m; **kilometre**, (us) **kilometer** ['kɪləmi:təʳ]
n kilomètre m; **kilowatt** n kilowatt m

kilt [kɪlt] n kilt m

kin [kɪn] n see **next-of-kin**

kind [kaɪnd] adj gentil(le), aimable ▷ n sorte
f, espèce f, (species) genre m; **to be two of
a ~** se ressembler; **in ~** (Comm) en nature;
~ of (inf: rather) plutôt; **a ~ of** une sorte de;
what ~ of ...? quelle sorte de ...?

kindergarten ['kɪndəgɑ:tn] n jardin m
d'enfants

kindly ['kaɪndlɪ] adj bienveillant(e), plein(e)
de gentillesse ▷ adv avec bonté; **will you ~ ...**
auriez-vous la bonté or l'obligeance de ...

kindness ['kaɪndnɪs] n (quality) bonté f,
gentillesse f

king [kɪŋ] n roi m; **kingdom** n royaume
m; **kingfisher** n martin-pêcheur m; **king-
size(d) bed** n grand lit (de 1,95 m de large)

kiosk ['ki:ɔsk] n kiosque m; (BRIT: also:
telephone ~) cabine f (téléphonique)

kipper ['kɪpəʳ] n hareng fumé et salé

kiss [kɪs] n baiser m ▷ vt embrasser; **to ~
(each other)** s'embrasser; **kiss of life** n
(BRIT) bouche à bouche m

kit [kɪt] n équipement m, matériel m; (set of
tools etc) trousse f; (for assembly) kit m

kitchen ['kɪtʃɪn] n cuisine f

kite [kaɪt] n (toy) cerf-volant m

kitten ['kɪtn] n petit chat, chaton m

kitty ['kɪtɪ] n (money) cagnotte f

kiwi ['ki:wi:] n (also: ~ **fruit**) kiwi m

km abbr (= kilometre) km

km/h abbr (= kilometres per hour) km/h

knack [næk] n: **to have the ~ (of doing)**
avoir le coup (pour faire)

knee [ni:] n genou m; **kneecap** n rotule f

kneel (pt, pp **knelt**) [ni:l, nɛlt] vi (also:
~ down) s'agenouiller

knelt [nɛlt] pt, pp of **kneel**

knew [nju:] pt of **know**

knickers ['nɪkəz] npl (BRIT) culotte f (de
femme)

knife (pl **knives**) [naɪf, naɪvz] n couteau
m ▷ vt poignarder, frapper d'un coup de
couteau

knight [naɪt] n chevalier m; (Chess)
cavalier m

knit [nɪt] vt tricoter ▷ vi tricoter; (broken
bones) se ressouder; **to ~ one's brows**
froncer les sourcils; **knitting** n tricot m;
knitting needle n aiguille f à tricoter;
knitwear n tricots mpl, lainages mpl

knives [naɪvz] npl of **knife**

knob [nɔb] n bouton m; (BRIT): **a ~ of butter**
une noix de beurre

knock [nɔk] vt frapper; (bump into) heurter;
(inf: fig) dénigrer ▷ vi (at door etc): **to ~ at/
on** frapper à/sur ▷ n coup m; **knock down**
vt renverser; (price) réduire; **knock off** vi
(inf: finish) s'arrêter (de travailler) ▷ vt (vase,
object) faire tomber; (inf: steal) piquer; (fig:
from price etc): **to ~ off £10** faire une remise
de 10 livres; **knock out** vt assommer;
(Boxing) mettre K.-O.; (in competition)
éliminer; **knock over** vt (object) faire
tomber; (pedestrian) renverser; **knockout**
n (Boxing) knock out m, K. O. m; **knockout
competition** (BRIT) compétition f avec
épreuves éliminatoires

knot [nɔt] n (gen) nœud m ▷ vt nouer

know [nəu] (pt **knew**, pp **known**) vt savoir;
(person, place) connaître; **to ~ that** savoir
que; **to ~ how to do** savoir faire; **to ~ how
to swim** savoir nager; **to ~ about/of sth**
(event) être au courant de qch; (subject)
connaître qch; **I don't ~** je ne sais pas; **do
you ~ where I can …?** savez-vous où je
peux …?; **know-all** n (BRIT pej) je-sais-tout
m/f; **know-how** n savoir-faire m, technique
f, compétence f; **knowing** adj (look etc)
entendu(e); **knowingly** adv (on purpose)
sciemment; (smile, look) d'un air entendu;
know-it-all n (US) = **know-all**
knowledge ['nɔlɪdʒ] n connaissance f;
(learning) connaissances, savoir m; **without
my ~** à mon insu; **knowledgeable** adj bien
informé(e)
known [nəun] pp of **know** ▷ adj (thief, facts)
notoire; (expert) célèbre
knuckle ['nʌkl] n articulation f (des
phalanges), jointure f
koala [kəu'ɑ:lə] n (also: **~ bear**) koala m
Koran [kɔ'rɑ:n] n Coran m
Korea [kə'rɪə] n Corée f; **Korean** adj
coréen(ne) ▷ n Coréen(ne)
kosher ['kəuʃəʳ] adj kascher inv
Kosovar, Kosovan ['kɔsəvɑ:ʳ, 'kɔsəvən]
adj kosovar(e)
Kosovo ['kɔsəvəu] n Kosovo m
Kuwait [ku'weɪt] n Koweït m

L abbr (BRIT Aut: = learner) signale un
conducteur débutant
l. abbr (= litre) l
lab [læb] n abbr (= laboratory) labo m
label ['leɪbl] n étiquette f; (brand: of record)
marque f ▷ vt étiqueter
labor etc ['leɪbəʳ] (US) n = **labour**
laboratory [lə'bɔrətərɪ] n laboratoire m
Labor Day n (US, CANADA) fête f du travail
(le premier lundi de septembre)

labor union n (US) syndicat m
Labour ['leɪbəʳ] n (BRIT Pol: also: **the ~
Party**) le parti travailliste, les travaillistes
mpl
labour, (US) **labor** ['leɪbəʳ] n (work) travail
m; (workforce) main-d'œuvre f ▷ vi: **to ~ (at)**
travailler dur (à), peiner (sur) ▷ vt: **to ~ a
point** insister sur un point; **in ~** (Med) en
travail; **labourer**, (US) **laborer** n
manœuvre m; **farm labourer** ouvrier m
agricole
lace [leɪs] n dentelle f; (of shoe etc) lacet m
▷ vt (shoe: also: **~ up**) lacer
lack [læk] n manque m ▷ vt manquer de;
through or **for ~ of** faute de, par manque
de; **to be ~ing** manquer, faire défaut; **to be
~ing in** manquer de
lacquer ['lækəʳ] n laque f

lacy ['leɪsɪ] adj (made of lace) en dentelle; (like lace) comme de la dentelle

lad [læd] n garçon m, gars m

ladder ['lædə'] n échelle f; (BRIT: in tights) maille filée ▷ vt, vi (BRIT: tights) filer

ladle ['leɪdl] n louche f

lady ['leɪdɪ] n dame f; "ladies and gentlemen ..." "Mesdames (et) Messieurs ..."; **young ~** jeune fille f; (married) jeune femme f; **the ladies' (room)** les toilettes fpl des dames; **ladybird**, (US) **ladybug** n coccinelle f

lag [læg] n retard m ▷ vi (also: **~ behind**) rester en arrière, traîner; (fig) rester à la traîne ▷ vt (pipes) calorifuger

lager ['lɑːgə'] n bière blonde

lagoon [lə'guːn] n lagune f

laid [leɪd] pt, pp of **lay**; **laid back** adj (inf) relaxe, décontracté(e)

lain [leɪn] pp of **lie**

lake [leɪk] n lac m

lamb [læm] n agneau m

lame [leɪm] adj (also fig) boiteux(-euse)

lament [lə'mɛnt] n lamentation f ▷ vt pleurer, se lamenter sur

lamp [læmp] n lampe f; **lamppost** n (BRIT) réverbère m; **lampshade** n abat-jour m inv

land [lænd] n (as opposed to sea) terre f (ferme); (country) pays m; (soil) terre, (piece of land) terrain m; (estate) terre(s), domaine(s) m(pl) ▷ vi (from ship) débarquer; (Aviat) atterrir; (fig: fall) (re)tomber ▷ vt (passengers, goods) débarquer; (obtain) décrocher; **to ~ sb with sth** (inf) coller qch à qn; **landing** n (from ship) débarquement m; (Aviat) atterrissage m; (of staircase) palier m; **landing card** n carte f de débarquement; **landlady** n propriétaire f, logeuse f; (of pub) patronne f; **landline** n ligne f fixe; **landlord** n propriétaire m, logeur m; (of pub etc) patron m; **landmark** n (point de m) repère m; **to be a landmark** (fig) faire date or époque; **landowner** n propriétaire foncier or terrien; **landscape** n paysage m; **landslide** n (Geo) glissement m (de terrain); (fig: Pol) raz-de-marée (électoral)

lane [leɪn] n (in country) chemin m; (Aut: of road) voie f; (: line of traffic) file f; (in race) couloir m

language ['læŋgwɪdʒ] n langue f; (way one speaks) langage m; **what ~s do you speak?** quelles langues parlez-vous?; **bad ~** grossièretés fpl, langage grossier; **language laboratory** n laboratoire m de langues; **language school** n école f de langue

lantern ['læntn] n lanterne f

lap [læp] n (of track) tour m (de piste); (of body): **in** or **on one's ~** sur les genoux ▷ vt (also: **~ up**) laper ▷ vi (waves) clapoter

lapel [lə'pɛl] n revers m

lapse [læps] n défaillance f; (in behaviour) écart m (de conduite) ▷ vi (Law) cesser d'être en vigueur; (contract) expirer; **to ~ into bad habits** prendre de mauvaises habitudes; **~ of time** laps m de temps, intervalle m

laptop (computer) ['læptɔp-] n (ordinateur m) portable m

lard [lɑːd] n saindoux m

larder ['lɑːdə'] n garde-manger m inv

large [lɑːdʒ] adj grand(e); (person, animal) gros (grosse); **at ~** (free) en liberté; (generally) en général; pour la plupart; see also **by**; **largely** adv en grande partie; (principally) surtout; **large-scale** adj (map, drawing etc) à grande échelle; (fig) important(e)

lark [lɑːk] n (bird) alouette f; (joke) blague f, farce f

larrikin ['lærɪkɪn] n (AUST, NZ inf) fripon m (inf)

laryngitis [lærɪn'dʒaɪtɪs] n laryngite f

lasagne [lə'zænjə] n lasagne f

laser ['leɪzə'] n laser m; **laser printer** n imprimante f laser

lash [læʃ] n coup m de fouet; (also: **eye~**) cil m ▷ vt fouetter; (tie) attacher; **lash out** vi: **to ~ out (at** or **against sb/sth)** attaquer violemment (qn/qch)

lass [læs] n (BRIT) (jeune) fille f

last [lɑːst] adj dernier(-ière) ▷ adv en dernier; (most recently) la dernière fois; (finally) finalement ▷ vi durer; **~ week** la semaine dernière; **~ night** (evening) hier soir; (night) la nuit dernière; **at ~** enfin; **~ but one** avant-dernier(-ière); **lastly** adv en dernier lieu, pour finir; **last-minute** adj de dernière minute

latch [lætʃ] n loquet m; **latch onto** vt fus (cling to: person, group) s'accrocher à; (: idea) se mettre en tête

late [leɪt] adj (not on time) en retard; (far on in day etc) tardif(-ive) (: edition, delivery) dernier(-ière); (dead) défunt(e) ▷ adv tard; (behind time, schedule) en retard; **to be 10 minutes ~** avoir 10 minutes de retard; **sorry I'm ~** désolé d'être en retard; **it's too ~** il est trop tard; **of ~** dernièrement; **in ~ May** vers la fin (du mois) de mai, fin mai; **the ~ Mr X** feu M. X; **latecomer** n retardataire m/f; **lately** adv récemment; **later** adj (date etc) ultérieur(e); (version etc) plus récent(e) ▷ adv plus tard; **latest** ['leɪtɪst] adj tout(e) dernier(-ière); **at the latest** au plus tard

lather ['lɑːðə'] n mousse f (de savon) ▷ vt savonner

Latin ['lætɪn] n latin m ▷ adj latin(e); **Latin America** n Amérique latine; **Latin American** adj latino-américain(e), d'Amérique latine ▷ n Latino-Américain(e)

latitude ['lætɪtjuːd] n (also fig) latitude f

latter ['lætə'] adj deuxième, dernier(-ière) ▷ n: **the ~** ce dernier, celui-ci

laugh [lɑːf] n rire m ▷ vi rire; **(to do sth) for a ~** (faire qch) pour rire; **laugh at** vt fus se moquer de; (joke) rire de; **laughter** n rire m; (of several people) rires mpl

launch [lɔːntʃ] n lancement m; (also: **motor ~**) vedette f ▷ vt (ship, rocket, plan) lancer; **launch into** vt fus se lancer dans

launder [ˈlɔːndəʳ] vt laver; (fig: money) blanchir

Launderette® [lɔːnˈdrɛt], (us) **Laundromat®** [ˈlɔːndrəmæt] n laverie f (automatique)

laundry [ˈlɔːndrɪ] n (clothes) linge m; (business) blanchisserie f; (room) buanderie f; **to do the ~** faire la lessive

lava [ˈlɑːvə] n lave f

lavatory [ˈlævətərɪ] n toilettes fpl

lavender [ˈlævəndəʳ] n lavande f

lavish [ˈlævɪʃ] adj (amount) copieux(-euse); (person: giving freely): **~ with** prodigue de ▷ vt: **to ~ sth on sb** prodiguer qch à qn; (money) dépenser qch sans compter pour qn

law [lɔː] n loi f; (science) droit m; **lawful** adj légal(e), permis(e); **lawless** adj (action) illégal(e); (place) sans loi

lawn [lɔːn] n pelouse f; **lawnmower** n tondeuse f à gazon

lawsuit [ˈlɔːsuːt] n procès m

lawyer [ˈlɔːjəʳ] n (consultant, with company) juriste m; (for sales, wills etc) ≈ notaire m; (partner, in court) ≈ avocat m

lax [læks] adj relâché(e)

laxative [ˈlæksətɪv] n laxatif m

lay [leɪ] pt of **lie** ▷ adj laïque; (not expert) profane ▷ vt (pt, pp **laid**) poser, mettre; (eggs) pondre; (trap) tendre; (plans) élaborer; **to ~ the table** mettre la table; **lay down** vt poser; (rules etc) établir; **to ~ down the law** (fig) faire la loi; **lay off** vt (workers) licencier; **lay on** vt (provide: meal etc) fournir; **lay out** vt (design) dessiner, concevoir; (display) disposer; (spend) dépenser; **lay-by** n (BRIT) aire f de stationnement (sur le bas-côté)

layer [ˈleɪəʳ] n couche f

layman [ˈleɪmən] (irreg) n (Rel) laïque m; (non-expert) profane m

layout [ˈleɪaut] n disposition f, plan m, agencement m; (Press) mise f en page

lazy [ˈleɪzɪ] adj paresseux(-euse)

lb. abbr (weight) = **pound**

lead¹ [liːd, lɛd] (pt, pp **led**) n (front position) tête f; (distance, time ahead) avance f; (clue) piste f; (Elec) fil m; (for dog) laisse f; (Theat) rôle principal m ▷ vt (guide) mener, conduire; (be leader of) être à la tête de ▷ vi (Sport) mener, être en tête; **to ~ to** (road, pipe) mener à, conduire à; (result in) conduire à; aboutir à; **to be in the ~** (Sport) (in race) mener, être en tête; (in match) mener (à la marque); **to ~ sb to do sth** amener qn à faire qch; **to ~ the way** montrer le chemin;

lead up to vt conduire à; (in conversation) en venir à

lead² [lɛd] n (metal) plomb m; (in pencil) mine f

leader [ˈliːdəʳ] n (of team) chef m; (of party etc) dirigeant(e), leader m; (Sport: in league) leader; (: in race) coureur m de tête; **leadership** n (position) direction f; **under the leadership of ...** sous la direction de ...; **qualities of leadership** qualités fpl de chef or de meneur

lead-free [ˈlɛdfriː] adj sans plomb

leading [ˈliːdɪŋ] adj de premier plan; (main) principal(e); (in race) de tête

lead singer [liːd-] n (in pop group) (chanteur m) vedette f

leaf (pl **leaves**) [liːf, liːvz] n feuille f; (of table) rallonge f; **to turn over a new ~** (fig) changer de conduite or d'existence; **leaf through** vt (book) feuilleter

leaflet [ˈliːflɪt] n prospectus m, brochure f; (Pol, Rel) tract m

league [liːg] n ligue f; (Football) championnat m; **to be in ~ with** avoir partie liée avec, être de mèche avec

leak [liːk] n (lit, fig) fuite f ▷ vi (pipe, liquid etc) fuir; (shoes) prendre l'eau; (ship) faire eau ▷ vt (liquid) répandre; (information) divulguer

lean (pt, pp **leaned** or **leant**) [liːn, lɛnt] adj maigre ▷ vt: **to ~ sth on** appuyer qch sur ▷ vi (slope) pencher; (rest): **to ~ against** s'appuyer contre; être appuyé(e) contre; **to ~ on** s'appuyer sur; **lean forward** vi se pencher en avant; **lean over** vi se pencher; **leaning** n: **leaning (towards)** penchant m (pour)

leant [lɛnt] pt, pp of **lean**

leap (pt, pp **leaped** or **leapt**) [liːp, lɛpt] n bond m, saut m ▷ vi bondir, sauter

leapt [lɛpt] pt, pp of **leap**

leap year n année f bissextile

learn (pt, pp **learned** or **learnt**) [ləːn, ləːnt] vt, vi apprendre; **to ~ (how) to do sth** apprendre à faire qch; **to ~ about sth** (Scol) étudier qch; (hear, read) apprendre qch; **learner** n débutant(e); (BRIT: also: **learner driver**) (conducteur(-trice)) débutant(e); **learning** n savoir m

learnt [ləːnt] pp of **learn**

lease [liːs] n bail m ▷ vt louer à bail

leash [liːʃ] n laisse f

least [liːst] adj: **the ~** (+ noun) le (la) plus petit(e), le (la) moindre; (smallest amount of) le moins de ▷ pron: **(the) ~** le moins ▷ adv (+ verb) le moins; (+ adj): **the ~** le (la) moins; **the ~ money** le moins d'argent; **the ~ expensive** le (la) moins cher (chère); **the ~ possible effort** le moins d'effort possible; **at ~** au moins; (or rather) du moins; **you could at ~ have written** tu aurais au moins pu écrire; **not in the ~** pas le moins du monde

leather ['lɛðə'] n cuir m
leave (pt, pp **left**) [li:v, lɛft] vt laisser; (go away from) quitter; (forget) oublier ▷ vi partir, s'en aller ▷ n (time off) congé m; (Mil, also consent) permission f; **what time does the train/bus ~?** le train/le bus part à quelle heure?; **to ~ sth to sb** (money etc) laisser qch à qn; **to be left** rester; **there's some milk left over** il reste du lait; **~ it to me!** laissez-moi faire!, je m'en occupe!; **on ~** en permission; **leave behind** vt (also fig) laisser; (forget) laisser, oublier; **leave out** vt oublier, omettre
leaves [li:vz] npl of **leaf**
Lebanon ['lɛbənən] n Liban m
lecture ['lɛktʃə'] n conférence f; (Scol) cours (magistral) ▷ vi donner des cours; enseigner ▷ vt (scold) sermonner, réprimander; **to give a ~ (on)** faire une conférence (sur), faire un cours (sur); **lecture hall** n amphithéâtre m; **lecturer** n (speaker) conférencier(-ière); (BRIT: at university) professeur m (d'université), prof m/f de fac (inf); **lecture theatre** n = **lecture hall**

Be careful not to translate lecture by the French word lecture.

led [lɛd] pt, pp of **lead¹**
ledge [lɛdʒ] n (of window, on wall) rebord m; (of mountain) saillie f, corniche f
leek [li:k] n poireau m
left [lɛft] pt, pp of **leave** ▷ adj gauche ▷ adv à gauche ▷ n gauche f; **there are two** ~ il en reste deux; **on the ~, to the ~** à gauche; **the L~** (Pol) la gauche; **left-hand** adj: **the left-hand side** la gauche, le côté gauche; **left-hand drive** n (vehicle) véhicule m avec la conduite à gauche; **left-handed** adj gaucher(-ère); (scissors etc) pour gauchers; **left-luggage locker** n (BRIT) (casier m à) consigne f automatique; **left-luggage (office)** n (BRIT) consigne f; **left-overs** npl restes mpl; **left-wing** adj (Pol) de gauche
leg [lɛg] n jambe f; (of animal) patte f; (of furniture) pied m; (Culin: of chicken) cuisse f; (of journey) étape f; **1st/2nd ~** (Sport) match m aller/retour; **~ of lamb** (Culin) gigot m d'agneau
legacy ['lɛgəsɪ] n (also fig) héritage m, legs m
legal ['li:gl] adj (permitted by law) légal(e); (relating to law) juridique; **legal holiday** (US) n jour férié; **legalize** vt légaliser; **legally** adv légalement
legend ['lɛdʒənd] n légende f; **legendary** ['lɛdʒəndərɪ] adj légendaire
leggings ['lɛgɪŋz] npl caleçon m
legible ['lɛdʒəbl] adj lisible
legislation [lɛdʒɪs'leɪʃən] n législation f
legislative ['lɛdʒɪslətɪv] adj législatif(-ive)
legitimate [lɪ'dʒɪtɪmət] adj légitime
leisure ['lɛʒə'] n (free time) temps libre, loisirs mpl; **at ~** (tout) à loisir; **at your ~** (later) à tête reposée; **leisure centre** n

(BRIT) centre m de loisirs; **leisurely** adj tranquille, fait(e) sans se presser
lemon ['lɛmən] n citron m; **lemonade** n (fizzy) limonade f; **lemon tea** n thé m au citron
lend (pt, pp **lent**) [lɛnd, lɛnt] vt: **to ~ sth (to sb)** prêter qch (à qn); **could you ~ me some money?** pourriez-vous me prêter de l'argent?
length [lɛŋθ] n longueur f; (section: of road, pipe etc) morceau m, bout m; **~ of time** durée f; **it is 2 metres in ~** cela fait 2 mètres de long; **at ~** (at last) enfin, à la fin; (lengthily) longuement; **lengthen** vt allonger, prolonger ▷ vi s'allonger; **lengthways** adv dans le sens de la longueur, en long; **lengthy** adj (très) long (longue)
lens [lɛnz] n lentille f; (of spectacles) verre m; (of camera) objectif m
Lent [lɛnt] n carême m
lent [lɛnt] pt, pp of **lend**
lentil ['lɛntl] n lentille f
Leo ['li:əʊ] n le Lion
leopard ['lɛpəd] n léopard m
leotard ['li:əta:d] n justaucorps m
leprosy ['lɛprəsɪ] n lèpre f
lesbian ['lɛzbɪən] n lesbienne f ▷ adj lesbien(ne)
less [lɛs] adj moins de ▷ pron, adv moins ▷ prep: **~ tax/10% discount** avant impôt/ moins 10% de remise; **~ than that/you** moins que cela/vous; **~ than half** moins de la moitié; **~ than ever** moins que jamais; **~ and ~** de moins en moins; **the ~ he works ...** moins il travaille ...; **lessen** vi diminuer, s'amoindrir, s'atténuer ▷ vt diminuer, réduire, atténuer; **lesser** ['lɛsə'] adj moindre; **to a lesser extent** or **degree** à un degré moindre
lesson ['lɛsn] n leçon f; **to teach sb a ~** (fig) donner une bonne leçon à qn
let (pt, pp **let**) [lɛt] vt laisser; (BRIT: lease) louer; **to ~ sb do sth** laisser qn faire qch; **to ~ sb know sth** faire savoir qch à qn, prévenir qn de qch; **~ to go** lâcher prise; **to ~ go of sth, to ~ sth go** lâcher qch; **~'s go** allons-y; **~ him come** qu'il vienne; **"to ~"** (BRIT) "à louer"; **let down** vt (lower) baisser; (BRIT: tyre) dégonfler; (disappoint) décevoir; **let in** vt laisser entrer; (visitor etc) faire entrer; **let off** vt (allow to leave) laisser partir; (not punish) ne pas punir; (firework etc) faire partir; (bomb) faire exploser; **let out** vt laisser sortir; (scream) laisser échapper; (BRIT: rent out) louer
lethal ['li:θl] adj mortel(le), fatal(e); (weapon) meurtrier(-ère)
letter ['lɛtə'] n lettre f; **letterbox** n (BRIT) boîte f aux or à lettres
lettuce ['lɛtɪs] n laitue f, salade f
leukaemia, (US) **leukemia** [lu:'ki:mɪə] n leucémie f

level ['lɛvl] *adj* (*flat*) plat(e), plan(e), uni(e); (*horizontal*) horizontal(e) ▷ *n* niveau *m* ▷ *vt* niveler, aplanir; **A ~s** *npl* (BRIT) ≈ baccalauréat *m*; **to be ~ with** être au même niveau que; **to draw ~ with** (*runner, car*) arriver à la hauteur de, rattraper; **on the ~** (*fig: honest*) régulier(-ière); **level crossing** *n* (BRIT) passage *m* à niveau

lever ['liːvər] *n* levier *m*; **leverage** *n* (*influence*): **leverage (on** *or* **with)** prise *f* (sur)

levy ['lɛvɪ] *n* taxe *f*, impôt *m* ▷ *vt* (*tax*) lever; (*fine*) infliger

liability [laɪə'bɪlətɪ] *n* responsabilité *f*; (*handicap*) handicap *m*

liable ['laɪəbl] *adj* (*subject*): **~ to** sujet(te) à, passible de; (*responsible*): **~ (for)** responsable (de); (*likely*): **~ to do** susceptible de faire

liaise [liː'eɪz] *vi*: **to ~ with** assurer la liaison avec

liar ['laɪər] *n* menteur(-euse)

libel ['laɪbl] *n* diffamation *f*; (*document*) écrit *m* diffamatoire ▷ *vt* diffamer

liberal ['lɪbərl] *adj* libéral(e); (*generous*): **~ with** prodigue de, généreux(-euse) avec ▷ *n*: **L~** (*Pol*) libéral(e); **Liberal Democrat** *n* (BRIT) libéral(e)-démocrate *m/f*

liberate ['lɪbəreɪt] *vt* libérer

liberation [lɪbə'reɪʃən] *n* libération *f*

liberty ['lɪbətɪ] *n* liberté *f*; **to be at ~** (*criminal*) être en liberté; **at ~ to do** libre de faire; **to take the ~ of** prendre la liberté de, se permettre de

Libra ['liːbrə] *n* la Balance

librarian [laɪ'brɛərɪən] *n* bibliothécaire *m/f*

library ['laɪbrərɪ] *n* bibliothèque *f*

> Be careful not to translate *library* by the French word *librairie*.

Libya ['lɪbɪə] *n* Libye *f*

lice [laɪs] *npl of* **louse**

licence, (US) **license** ['laɪsns] *n* autorisation *f*, permis *m*; (Comm) licence *f*; (Radio, TV) redevance *f*; **driving ~,** (US) **driver's license** permis *m* (de conduire)

license ['laɪsns] *n* (US) = **licence**; **licensed** *adj* (*for alcohol*) patenté(e) pour la vente des spiritueux, qui a une patente de débit de boissons; (*car*) muni(e) de la vignette; **license plate** *n* (US Aut) plaque *f* minéralogique; **licensing hours** (BRIT) *npl* heures *fpl* d'ouvertures (*des pubs*)

lick [lɪk] *vt* lécher; (*inf: defeat*) écraser, flanquer une piquette or raclée à; **to ~ one's lips** (*fig*) se frotter les mains

lid [lɪd] *n* couvercle *m*; (*eyelid*) paupière *f*

lie [laɪ] *n* mensonge *m* ▷ *vi* (*pt, pp* **lied**) (*tell lies*) mentir; (*pt, lay, pp* **lain**) (*rest*) être étendu(e) or allongé(e) or couché(e) (*: object: be situated*) se trouver, être; **to ~ low** (*fig*) se cacher, rester caché(e); **to tell ~s** mentir; **lie about, lie around** *vi* (*things*) traîner;

(BRIT: *person*) traînasser, flemmarder; **lie down** *vi* se coucher, s'étendre

Liechtenstein ['lɪktənstaɪn] *n* Liechtenstein *m*

lie-in ['laɪɪn] *n* (BRIT): **to have a ~** faire la grasse matinée

lieutenant [lɛf'tɛnənt, US luː'tɛnənt] *n* lieutenant *m*

life (*pl* **lives**) [laɪf, laɪvz] *n* vie *f*; **to come to ~** (*fig*) s'animer; **life assurance** *n* (BRIT) = **life insurance**; **lifeboat** *n* canot *m* or chaloupe *f* de sauvetage; **lifeguard** *n* surveillant *m* de baignade; **life insurance** *n* assurance-vie *f*; **life jacket** *n* gilet *m* or ceinture *f* de sauvetage; **lifelike** *adj* qui semble vrai(e) or vivant(e), ressemblant(e); (*painting*) réaliste; **life preserver** *n* (US) gilet *m* or ceinture *f* de sauvetage; **life sentence** *n* condamnation *f* à vie or à perpétuité; **lifestyle** *n* style *m* de vie; **lifetime** *n*: **in his lifetime** de son vivant

lift [lɪft] *vt* soulever, lever; (*end*) supprimer, lever ▷ *vi* (*fog*) se lever ▷ *n* (BRIT: *elevator*) ascenseur *m*; **to give sb a ~** (BRIT) emmener or prendre qn en voiture; **can you give me a ~ to the station?** pouvez-vous m'emmener à la gare?; **lift up** *vt* soulever; **lift-off** *n* décollage *m*

light [laɪt] *n* lumière *f*; (*lamp*) lampe *f*; (Aut: *rear light*) feu *m*; (*: headlamp*) phare *m*; (*for cigarette etc*): **have you got a ~?** avez-vous du feu? ▷ *vt* (*pt, pp* **lit**) (*candle, cigarette, fire*) allumer; (*room*) éclairer ▷ *adj* (*room, colour*) clair(e); (*not heavy, also fig*) léger(-ère); (*not strenuous*) peu fatigant(e); **lights** *npl* (*traffic lights*) feux *mpl*; **to come to ~** être dévoilé(e) or découvert(e); **in the ~ of** à la lumière de; étant donné; **light up** *vi* s'allumer; (*face*) s'éclairer; (*smoke*) allumer une cigarette or une pipe *etc* ▷ *vt* (*illuminate*) éclairer, illuminer; **light bulb** *n* ampoule *f*; **lighten** *vt* (*light up*) éclairer; (*make lighter*) éclaircir; (*make less heavy*) alléger; **lighter** *n* (*also*: **cigarette lighter**) briquet *m*; **light-hearted** *adj* gai(e), joyeux(-euse), enjoué(e); **lighthouse** *n* phare *m*; **lighting** *n* éclairage *m*; (*in theatre*) éclairages; **lightly** *adv* légèrement; **to get off lightly** s'en tirer à bon compte

lightning ['laɪtnɪŋ] *n* foudre *f*; (*flash*) éclair *m*

lightweight ['laɪtweɪt] *adj* (*suit*) léger(-ère) ▷ *n* (Boxing) poids léger

like [laɪk] *vt* aimer (bien) ▷ *prep* comme ▷ *adj* semblable, pareil(le) ▷ *n*: **the ~** (*pej*) (d')autres du même genre or acabit; **his ~s and dislikes** ses goûts *mpl* or préférences *fpl*; **I would ~, I'd ~** je voudrais, j'aimerais; **would you ~ a coffee?** voulez-vous du café?; **to be/look ~ sb/sth** ressembler à qn/qch; **what's he ~?** comment est-il?; **what does it look ~?** de quoi est-ce que ça a l'air?;

what does it taste ~? quel goût est-ce que ça a?; **that's just ~ him** c'est bien de lui, ça lui ressemble; **do it ~ this** fais-le comme ceci; **it's nothing ~ ...** ce n'est pas du tout comme ...; **likeable** adj sympathique, agréable

likelihood ['laɪklɪhud] n probabilité f

likely ['laɪklɪ] adj (result, outcome) probable; (excuse) plausible; **he's ~ to leave** il va sûrement partir, il risque fort de partir; **not ~!** (inf) pas de danger!

likewise ['laɪkwaɪz] adv de même, pareillement

liking ['laɪkɪŋ] n (for person) affection f; (for thing) penchant m, goût m; **to be to sb's ~** être au goût de qn, plaire à qn

lilac ['laɪlək] n lilas m

Lilo® ['laɪləu] n matelas m pneumatique

lily ['lɪlɪ] n lis m; **~ of the valley** muguet m

limb [lɪm] n membre m

limbo ['lɪmbəu] n: **to be in ~** (fig) être tombé(e) dans l'oubli

lime [laɪm] n (tree) tilleul m; (fruit) citron vert, lime f; (Geo) chaux f

limelight ['laɪmlaɪt] n: **in the ~** (fig) en vedette, au premier plan

limestone ['laɪmstəun] n pierre f à chaux; (Geo) calcaire m

limit ['lɪmɪt] n limite f ▷ vt limiter; **limited** adj limité(e), restreint(e); **to be limited to** se limiter à, ne concerner que

limousine ['lɪməziːn] n limousine f

limp [lɪmp] n: **to have a ~** boiter ▷ vi boiter ▷ adj mou (molle)

line [laɪn] n (gen) ligne f; (stroke) trait m; (wrinkle) ride f; (rope) corde f; (wire) fil m; (of poem) vers m; (row, series) rangée f; (of people) file f, queue f; (railway track) voie f; (Comm: series of goods) article(s) m(pl), ligne de produits; (work) métier m ▷ vt (subj: trees, crowd) border; **to ~ (with)** (clothes) doubler (de); (box) garnir ou tapisser (de); **to stand in ~** (us) faire la queue; **in his ~ of business** dans sa partie, dans son rayon; **to be in ~ for sth** (fig) être en lice pour qch; **in ~ with** en accord avec, en conformité avec; **in a ~** aligné(e); **line up** vi s'aligner, se mettre en rang(s); (in queue) faire la queue ▷ vt aligner; (event) prévoir; (find) trouver; **to have sb/sth ~d up** avoir qn/qch en vue or de prévu(e)

linear ['lɪnɪər] adj linéaire

linen ['lɪnɪn] n linge m (de corps or de maison); (cloth) lin m

liner ['laɪnər] n (ship) paquebot m de ligne; (for bin) sac-poubelle m

line-up ['laɪnʌp] n (us: queue) file f; (also: police ~) parade f d'identification; (Sport) (composition f de l')équipe f

linger ['lɪŋgər] vi s'attarder; traîner; (smell, tradition) persister

lingerie ['lænʒəriː] n lingerie f

linguist ['lɪŋgwɪst] n linguiste m/f; **to be a good ~** être doué(e) pour les langues; **linguistic** adj linguistique

lining ['laɪnɪŋ] n doublure f; (of brakes) garniture f

link [lɪŋk] n (connection) lien m, rapport m; (Internet) lien; (of a chain) maillon m ▷ vt relier, lier, unir; **links** npl (Golf) (terrain m de) golf m; **link up** vt relier ▷ vi (people) se rejoindre; (companies etc) s'associer

lion ['laɪən] n lion m; **lioness** n lionne f

lip [lɪp] n lèvre f; (of cup etc) rebord m; **lip-read** vi (irreg: like read) lire sur les lèvres; **lip salve** [-sælv] n pommade f pour les lèvres, pommade rosat; **lipstick** n rouge m à lèvres

liqueur [lɪˈkjuər] n liqueur f

liquid ['lɪkwɪd] n liquide m ▷ adj liquide; **liquidizer** ['lɪkwɪdaɪzər] n (BRIT Culin) mixer m

liquor ['lɪkər] n spiritueux m, alcool m; **liquor store** (us) n magasin m de vins et spiritueux

Lisbon ['lɪzbən] n Lisbonne f

lisp [lɪsp] n zézaiement m ▷ vi zézayer

list [lɪst] n liste f ▷ vt (write down) inscrire; (make list of) faire la liste de; (enumerate) énumérer

listen ['lɪsn] vi écouter; **~ to** sb/sth écouter; **listener** n auditeur(-trice)

lit [lɪt] pt, pp of **light**

liter ['liːtər] n (us) = **litre**

literacy ['lɪtərəsɪ] n degré m d'alphabétisation, fait m de savoir lire et écrire; (BRIT Scol) enseignement m de la lecture et de l'écriture

literal ['lɪtərl] adj littéral(e); **literally** adv littéralement; (really) réellement

literary ['lɪtərərɪ] adj littéraire

literate ['lɪtərət] adj qui sait lire et écrire; (educated) instruit(e)

literature ['lɪtrɪtʃər] n littérature f; (brochures etc) copie f publicitaire, prospectus mpl

litre, (us) **liter** ['liːtər] n litre m

litter ['lɪtər] n (rubbish) détritus mpl; (dirtier) ordures fpl; (young animals) portée f; **litter bin** n (BRIT) poubelle f

little ['lɪtl] adj (small) petit(e); (not much): **~ milk** peu de lait ▷ adv peu; **a ~** un peu (de); **a ~ milk** un peu de lait; **a ~ bit** un peu; **as ~ as possible** le moins possible; **~ by ~** petit à petit, peu à peu; **little finger** n auriculaire m, petit doigt

live¹ [laɪv] adj (animal) vivant(e), en vie; (wire) sous tension; (broadcast) (transmis(e)) en direct; (unexploded) non explosé(e)

live² [lɪv] vi vivre; (reside) vivre, habiter; **to ~ in London** habiter (à) Londres; **where do you ~?** où habitez-vous?; **live together** vi vivre ensemble, cohabiter; **live up to** vt fus se montrer à la hauteur de

livelihood ['laɪvlɪhud] n moyens mpl
d'existence

lively ['laɪvlɪ] adj vif (vive), plein(e)
d'entrain; (place, book) vivant(e)

liven up ['laɪvn-] vt (room etc) égayer;
(discussion, evening) animer ▷ vi s'animer

liver ['lɪvə^r] n foie m

lives [laɪvz] npl of **life**

livestock ['laɪvstɔk] n cheptel m, bétail m

living ['lɪvɪŋ] adj vivant(e), en vie ▷ n: to
earn or **make a ~** gagner sa vie; **living room**
n salle f de séjour

lizard ['lɪzəd] n lézard m

load [ləud] n (weight) poids m; (thing carried)
chargement m, charge f; (Elec, Tech) charge
▷ vt charger; (also: **~ up**): to **~ (with)** (lorry,
ship) charger (de); (gun, camera) charger
(avec); **a ~ of**, **~s of** (fig) un or des tas de,
des masses de; **to talk a ~ of rubbish** (inf)
dire des bêtises; **loaded** adj (dice) pipé(e);
(question) insidieux(-euse); (inf: rich)
bourré(e) de fric

loaf (pl **loaves**) [ləuf, ləuvz] n pain m, miche
f ▷ vi (also: **~ about**, **~ around**) fainéanter,
traîner

loan [ləun] n prêt m ▷ vt prêter; **on ~**
prêté(e), en prêt

loathe [ləuð] vt détester, avoir en horreur

loaves [ləuvz] npl of **loaf**

lobby ['lɔbɪ] n hall m, entrée f; (Pol) groupe m
de pression, lobby m ▷ vt faire pression sur

lobster ['lɔbstə^r] n homard m

local ['ləukl] adj local(e) ▷ n (BRIT: pub) pub
m or café m du coin; **the locals** npl les gens
mpl du pays or du coin; **local anaesthetic**,
(US) **local anesthetic** n anesthésie locale;
local authority n collectivité locale,
municipalité f; **local government** n
administration locale or municipale; **locally**
['ləukəlɪ] adv localement; dans les environs
or la région

locate [ləu'keɪt] vt (find) trouver, repérer;
(situate) situer; **to be ~d in** être situé à
or en

location [ləu'keɪʃən] n emplacement m;
on ~ (Cine) en extérieur

▌ Be careful not to translate location by
the French word location.

loch [lɔx] n lac m, loch m

lock [lɔk] n (of door, box) serrure f; (of canal)
écluse f; (of hair) mèche f, boucle f ▷ vt (with
key) fermer à clé ▷ vi (door etc) fermer à clé;
(wheels) se bloquer; **lock in** vt enfermer;
lock out vt enfermer dehors; (on purpose)
mettre à la porte; **lock up** vt (person)
enfermer; (house) fermer à clé ▷ vi tout
fermer (à clé)

locker ['lɔkə^r] n casier m; (in station)
consigne f automatique; **locker-room**
['lɔkə^rruːm] (US) n (Sport) vestiaire m

locksmith ['lɔksmɪθ] n serrurier m

locomotive [ləukə'məutɪv] n locomotive f

locum ['ləukəm] n (Med) suppléant(e) de
médecin etc

lodge [lɔdʒ] n pavillon m (de gardien);
(also: **hunting ~**) pavillon de chasse ▷ vi
(person): **to ~ with** être logé(e) chez, être en
pension chez; (bullet) se loger ▷ vt (appeal
etc) présenter; déposer; **to ~ a complaint**
porter plainte; **lodger** n locataire m/f; (with
room and meals) pensionnaire m/f

lodging ['lɔdʒɪŋ] n logement m

loft [lɔft] n grenier m; (apartment) grenier
aménagé (en appartement) (gén dans ancien
entrepôt ou fabrique)

log [lɔg] n (of wood) bûche f; (Naut) livre m
or journal m de bord; (of car) ≈ carte grise
▷ vt enregistrer; **log in, log on** vi (Comput)
ouvrir une session, entrer dans le système;
log off, log out vi (Comput) clore une
session, sortir du système

logic ['lɔdʒɪk] n logique f; **logical** adj logique

login ['lɔgɪn] n (Comput) identifiant m

Loire [lwaː] n: **the (River) ~** la Loire

lollipop ['lɔlɪpɔp] n sucette f; **lollipop
man/lady** (irreg) (BRIT) n contractuel(le) qui
fait traverser la rue aux enfants

lolly ['lɔlɪ] n (inf: ice) esquimau m; (: lollipop)
sucette f

London ['lʌndən] n Londres; **Londoner** n
Londonien(ne)

lone [ləun] adj solitaire

loneliness ['ləunlɪnɪs] n solitude f,
isolement m

lonely ['ləunlɪ] adj seul(e); (childhood etc)
solitaire; (place) solitaire, isolé(e)

long [lɔŋ] adj long (longue) ▷ adv
longtemps ▷ vi: **to ~ for sth/to do sth** avoir
très envie de qch/de faire qch, attendre qch
avec impatience/attendre avec impatience
de faire qch; **how ~ is this river/course?**
quelle est la longueur de ce fleuve/la durée
de ce cours?; **6 metres ~** (long) de 6 mètres;
6 months ~ qui dure 6 mois, de 6 mois; **all
night ~** toute la nuit; **he no ~er comes** il
ne vient plus; **I can't stand it any ~er** je ne
peux plus le supporter; **~ before** longtemps
avant; **before ~** (+ future) avant peu, dans
peu de temps; (+ past) peu de temps après;
don't be ~! fais vite!, dépêche-toi!; **I shan't
be ~** je n'en ai pas pour longtemps; **at ~
last** enfin; **so** or **as ~ as** à condition que
+ sub; **long-distance** adj (race) de fond;
(call) interurbain(e); **long-haul** adj (flight)
long-courrier; **longing** n désir m, envie f;
(nostalgia) nostalgie f ▷ adj plein(e) d'envie
or de nostalgie

longitude ['lɔŋgɪtjuːd] n longitude f

long: long jump n saut m en longueur;
long-life adj (batteries etc) longue durée inv;
(milk) longue conservation; **long-sighted**
adj (BRIT) presbyte; (fig) prévoyant(e); **longstanding** adj de longue date; **long-term**
adj à long terme

loo [lu:] n (BRIT inf) w.-c. mpl, petit coin
look [lʊk] vi regarder; (seem) sembler, paraître, avoir l'air; (building etc): **to ~ south/on to the sea** donner au sud/sur la mer ▷ n regard m; (appearance) air m, allure f, aspect m; **looks** npl (good looks) physique m, beauté f; **to ~ like** ressembler à; **to have a ~** regarder; **to have a ~ at sth** jeter un coup d'œil à qch; **~ (here)!** (annoyance) écoutez!; **look after** vt fus s'occuper de; (luggage etc: watch over) garder, surveiller; **look around** vi regarder autour de soi; **look at** vt fus regarder; (problem etc) examiner; **look back** vi: **to ~ back at sth/sb** se retourner pour regarder qch/ qn; **to ~ back on** (event, period) évoquer, repenser à; **look down on** vt fus (fig) regarder de haut, dédaigner; **look for** vt fus chercher; **we're ~ing for a hotel/ restaurant** nous cherchons un hôtel/ restaurant; **look forward to** vt fus attendre avec impatience; **~ing forward to hearing from you** (in letter) dans l'attente de vous lire; **look into** vt fus (matter, possibility) examiner, étudier; **look out** vi (beware): **to ~ out (for)** prendre garde (à), faire attention (à); **~ out!** attention!; **look out for** vt fus (seek) être à la recherche de; (try to spot) guetter; **look round** vt fus (house, shop) faire le tour de ▷ vi (turn) regarder derrière soi, se retourner; **look through** vt fus (papers, book) examiner (: briefly) parcourir; **look up** vi lever les yeux; (improve) s'améliorer ▷ vt (word) chercher; **look up to** vt fus avoir du respect pour; **lookout** n (tower etc) poste m de guet; (person) guetteur m; **to be on the lookout (for)** guetter
loom [lu:m] vi (also: **~ up**) surgir; (event) paraître imminent(e); (threaten) menacer
loony ['lu:nɪ] adj, n (inf) timbré(e), cinglé(e) m/f
loop [lu:p] n boucle f ▷ vt: **to ~ sth round sth** passer qch autour de qch; **loophole** n (fig) porte f de sortie; échappatoire f
loose [lu:s] adj (knot, screw) desserré(e); (clothes) vague, ample, lâche; (hair) dénoué(e), épars(e); (not firmly fixed) pas solide; (morals, discipline) relâché(e); (translation) approximatif(-ive) ▷ n: **to be on the ~** être en liberté; **~ connection** (Elec) mauvais contact; **to be at a ~ end** or (US) **at ~ ends** (fig) ne pas trop savoir quoi faire; **loosely** adv sans serrer; (imprecisely) approximativement; **loosen** vt desserrer, relâcher, défaire
loot [lu:t] n butin m ▷ vt piller
lop-sided ['lɔp'saɪdɪd] adj de travers, asymétrique
lord [lɔ:d] n seigneur m; **L~ Smith** lord Smith; **the L~** (Rel) le Seigneur; **my L~** (to noble) Monsieur le comte/le baron; (to judge) Monsieur le juge; (to bishop)

Monseigneur; **good L~!** mon Dieu!; **Lords** npl (BRIT Pol): **the (House of) Lords** la Chambre des Lords
lorry ['lɔrɪ] n (BRIT) camion m; **lorry driver** n (BRIT) camionneur m, routier m
lose (pt, pp **lost**) [lu:z, lɔst] vt perdre ▷ vi perdre; **I've lost my wallet/passport** j'ai perdu mon portefeuille/passeport; **to ~ (time)** (clock) retarder; **lose out** vi être perdant(e); **loser** n perdant(e)
loss [lɔs] n perte f; **to make a ~** enregistrer une perte; **to be at a ~** être perplexe or embarrassé(e)
lost [lɔst] pt, pp of **lose** ▷ adj perdu(e); **to get ~** vi se perdre; **I'm ~** je me suis perdu; **~ and found property** n (US) objets trouvés; **~ and found** n (US) (bureau m des) objets trouvés; **lost property** n (BRIT) objets trouvés; **lost property office** or **department** (bureau m des) objets trouvés
lot [lɔt] n (at auctions, set) lot m; (destiny) sort m, destinée f; **the ~** (everything) le tout; (everyone) tous mpl, toutes fpl; **a ~** beaucoup; **a ~ of** beaucoup de; **~s of** des tas de; **to draw ~s (for sth)** tirer (qch) au sort
lotion ['ləʊʃən] n lotion f
lottery ['lɔtərɪ] n loterie f
loud [laʊd] adj bruyant(e), sonore; (voice) fort(e); (condemnation etc) vigoureux(-euse); (gaudy) voyant(e), tapageur(-euse) ▷ adv (speak etc) fort; **out ~** tout haut; **loudly** adv fort, bruyamment; **loudspeaker** n haut-parleur m
lounge [laʊndʒ] n salon m; (of airport) salle f; (BRIT: also: **~ bar**) (salle de) café m or bar m ▷ vi (also: **~ about, ~ around**) se prélasser, paresser
louse (pl **lice**) [laʊs, laɪs] n pou m
lousy ['laʊzɪ] (inf) adj (bad quality) infect(e), moche; **I feel ~** je suis mal fichu(e)
love [lʌv] n amour m ▷ vt aimer; (caringly, kindly) aimer beaucoup; **I ~ chocolate** j'adore le chocolat; **to ~ to do** aimer beaucoup or adorer faire; **"15 ~"** (Tennis) "15 à rien or zéro"; **to be/fall in ~ with** être/ tomber amoureux(-euse) de; **to make ~** faire l'amour; **~ from Anne, ~, Anne** affectueusement, Anne; **I ~ you** je t'aime; **love affair** n liaison (amoureuse); **love life** n vie sentimentale
lovely ['lʌvlɪ] adj (pretty) ravissant(e); (friend, wife) charmant(e); (holiday, surprise) très agréable, merveilleux(-euse)
lover ['lʌvəʳ] n (person in love) amant m; (person in love) amoureux(-euse); (amateur): **a ~ of** un(e) ami(e) de, un(e) amoureux(-euse) de
loving ['lʌvɪŋ] adj affectueux(-euse), tendre, aimant(e)
low [ləʊ] adj bas (basse); (quality) mauvais(e), inférieur(e) ▷ adv bas ▷ n (Meteorology) dépression f; **to feel ~** se sentir déprimé(e); **he's very ~** (ill) il est bien bas

or très affaibli; **to turn (down)** ~ *vt* baisser; **to be** ~ **on** (*supplies etc*) être à court de; **to reach a new** *or* **an all-time** ~ tomber au niveau le plus bas; **low-alcohol** *adj* à faible teneur en alcool, peu alcoolisé(e); **low-calorie** *adj* hypocalorique

lower ['ləuə^r] *adj* inférieur(e) ▷ *vt* baisser; (*resistance*) diminuer; **to** ~ **o.s. to** s'abaisser à

low-fat ['ləu'fæt] *adj* maigre

loyal ['lɔɪəl] *adj* loyal(e), fidèle; **loyalty** *n* loyauté *f*, fidélité *f*; **loyalty card** *n* carte *f* de fidélité

L-plates ['ɛlpleɪts] *npl* (BRIT) plaques *fpl* (obligatoires) d'apprenti conducteur

Lt *abbr* (= *lieutenant*) Lt.

Ltd *abbr* (*Comm*: = *limited*) ≈ SA

luck [lʌk] *n* chance *f*; **bad** ~ malchance *f*, malheur *m*; **good** ~! bonne chance!; **bad** *or* **hard** *or* **tough** ~! pas de chance!; **luckily** *adv* heureusement, par bonheur; **lucky** *adj* (*person*) qui a de la chance; (*coincidence*) heureux(-euse); (*number etc*) qui porte bonheur

lucrative ['lu:krətɪv] *adj* lucratif(-ive), rentable, qui rapporte

ludicrous ['lu:dɪkrəs] *adj* ridicule, absurde

luggage ['lʌgɪdʒ] *n* bagages *mpl*; **our** ~ **hasn't arrived** nos bagages ne sont pas arrivés; **could you send someone to collect our** ~? pourriez-vous envoyer quelqu'un chercher nos bagages?; **luggage rack** *n* (*in train*) porte-bagages *m inv*; (*on car*) galerie *f*

lukewarm ['lu:kwɔ:m] *adj* tiède

lull [lʌl] *n* accalmie *f*; (*in conversation*) pause *f* ▷ *vt*: **to** ~ **sb to sleep** bercer qn pour qu'il s'endorme; **to be** ~**ed into a false sense of security** s'endormir dans une fausse sécurité

lullaby ['lʌləbaɪ] *n* berceuse *f*

lumber ['lʌmbə^r] *n* (*wood*) bois *m* de charpente; (*junk*) bric-à-brac *m inv* ▷ *vt* (BRIT *inf*): **to** ~ **sb with sth/sb** coller *or* refiler qch/qn à qn

luminous ['lu:mɪnəs] *adj* lumineux(-euse)

lump [lʌmp] *n* morceau *m*; (*in sauce*) grumeau *m*; (*swelling*) grosseur *f* ▷ *vt* (*also*: ~ **together**) réunir, mettre en tas; **lump sum** *n* somme globale *or* forfaitaire; **lumpy** *adj* (*sauce*) qui a des grumeaux; (*bed*) défoncé(e), peu confortable

lunatic ['lu:nətɪk] *n* fou (folle), dément(e) ▷ *adj* fou (folle), dément(e)

lunch [lʌntʃ] *n* déjeuner *m* ▷ *vi* déjeuner; **lunch break, lunch hour** *n* pause *f* de midi, heure *f* du déjeuner; **lunchtime** *n*: **it's lunchtime** c'est l'heure du déjeuner

lung [lʌŋ] *n* poumon *m*

lure [luə^r] *n* (*attraction*) attrait *m*, charme *m*; (*in hunting*) appât *m*, leurre *m* ▷ *vt* attirer *or* persuader par la ruse

lurk [lə:k] *vi* se tapir, se cacher

lush [lʌʃ] *adj* luxuriant(e)

lust [lʌst] *n* (*sexual*) désir (sexuel); (*Rel*) luxure *f*; (*fig*): ~ **for** soif *f* de

Luxembourg ['lʌksəmbə:g] *n* Luxembourg *m*

luxurious [lʌg'zjuərɪəs] *adj* luxueux(-euse)

luxury ['lʌkʃərɪ] *n* luxe *m* ▷ *cpd* de luxe

Lycra® ['laɪkrə] *n* Lycra® *m*

lying ['laɪɪŋ] *n* mensonge(s) *m(pl)* ▷ *adj* (*statement, story*) mensonger(-ère), faux (fausse); (*person*) menteur(-euse)

Lyons ['ljɔ̃] *n* Lyon

lyrics ['lɪrɪks] *npl* (*of song*) paroles *fpl*

m

m. *abbr* (= *metre*) m; (= *million*) M; (= *mile*) mi
ma [mɑː] (*inf*) *n* maman *f*
M.A. *n abbr* (*Scol*) = **Master of Arts**
mac [mæk] *n* (BRIT) imper(méable *m*) *m*
macaroni [mækə'rəunɪ] *n* macaronis *mpl*
Macedonia [mæsɪ'dəunɪə] *n* Macédoine
f; **Macedonian** [mæsɪ'dəunɪən] *adj*
macédonien(ne) ▷ *n* Macédonien(ne);
(*Ling*) macédonien *m*
machine [mə'ʃiːn] *n* machine *f* ▷ *vt* (*dress
etc*) coudre à la machine; (*Tech*) usiner;
machine gun *n* mitrailleuse *f*; **machinery**
n machinerie *f*, machines *fpl*; (*fig*)
mécanisme(s) *m(pl)*; **machine washable**
adj (*garment*) lavable en machine
macho ['mætʃəu] *adj* macho *inv*
mackerel ['mækrl] *n* (*pl inv*)
maquereau *m*
mackintosh ['mækɪntɔʃ] *n* (BRIT)
imperméable *m*
mad [mæd] *adj* fou (folle); (*foolish*)
insensé(e); (*angry*) furieux(-euse); **to be ~
(keen) about** *or* **on sth** (*inf*) être follement
passionné de qch, être fou de qch
Madagascar [mædə'gæskə'] *n*
Madagascar *m*
madam ['mædəm] *n* madame *f*
mad cow disease *n* maladie *f* des vaches
folles
made [meɪd] *pt, pp of* **make**; **made-to-
measure** *adj* (BRIT) fait(e) sur mesure;
made-up ['meɪdʌp] *adj* (*story*) inventé(e),
fabriqué(e)
madly ['mædlɪ] *adv* follement; **~ in love**
éperdument amoureux(-euse)
madman ['mædmən] (*irreg*) *n* fou *m*,
aliéné *m*
madness ['mædnɪs] *n* folie *f*
Madrid [mə'drɪd] *n* Madrid
Mafia ['mæfɪə] *n* maf(f)ia *f*
mag [mæg] *n abbr* (BRIT *inf*: = *magazine*)
magazine *m*

magazine [mægə'ziːn] *n* (*Press*) magazine
m, revue *f*; (*Radio, TV*) magazine
maggot ['mægət] *n* ver *m*, asticot *m*
magic ['mædʒɪk] *n* magie *f* ▷ *adj* magique;
magical *adj* magique; (*experience, evening*)
merveilleux(-euse); **magician** [mə'dʒɪʃən]
n magicien(ne)
magistrate ['mædʒɪstreɪt] *n* magistrat
m; juge *m*
magnet ['mægnɪt] *n* aimant *m*; **magnetic**
[mæg'nɛtɪk] *adj* magnétique
magnificent [mæg'nɪfɪsnt] *adj* superbe,
magnifique; (*splendid: robe, building*)
somptueux(-euse), magnifique
magnify ['mægnɪfaɪ] *vt* grossir; (*sound*)
amplifier; **magnifying glass** *n* loupe *f*
magpie ['mægpaɪ] *n* pie *f*
mahogany [mə'hɔgənɪ] *n* acajou *m*
maid [meɪd] *n* bonne *f*; (*in hotel*) femme *f* de
chambre; **old ~** (*pej*) vieille fille
maiden name *n* nom *m* de jeune fille
mail [meɪl] *n* poste *f*; (*letters*) courrier
m ▷ *vt* envoyer (par la poste); **by ~** par
la poste; **mailbox** *n* (US, *also Comput*)
boîte *f* aux lettres; **mailing list** *n* liste *f*
d'adresses; **mailman** (*irreg*) *n* (US) facteur
m; **mail-order** *n* vente *f* or achat *m* par
correspondance
main [meɪn] *adj* principal(e) ▷ *n* (*pipe*)
conduite principale, canalisation *f*; **the ~s**
(*Elec*) le secteur; **the ~ thing** l'essentiel *m*;
in the ~ dans l'ensemble; **main course** *n*
(*Culin*) plat *m* de résistance; **mainland** *n*
continent *m*; **mainly** *adv* principalement,
surtout; **main road** *n* grand axe, route
nationale; **mainstream** *n* (*fig*) courant
principal; **main street** *n* rue *f* principale
maintain [meɪn'teɪn] *vt* entretenir;
(*continue*) maintenir, préserver; (*affirm*)
soutenir; **maintenance** ['meɪntənəns]
n entretien *m*; (*Law: alimony*) pension *f*
alimentaire
maisonette [meɪzə'nɛt] *n* (BRIT)
appartement *m* en duplex
maize [meɪz] *n* (BRIT) maïs *m*
majesty ['mædʒɪstɪ] *n* majesté *f*; (*title*):
Your M~ Votre Majesté
major ['meɪdʒə'] *n* (*Mil*) commandant
m ▷ *adj* (*important*) important(e); (*most
important*) principal(e); (*Mus*) majeur(e) ▷ *vi*
(US *Scol*): **to ~ (in)** se spécialiser (en)
Majorca [mə'jɔːkə] *n* Majorque *f*
majority [mə'dʒɔrɪtɪ] *n* majorité *f*
make [meɪk] *vt* (*pt, pp* **made**) faire;
(*manufacture*) faire, fabriquer; (*earn*)
gagner; (*decision*) prendre; (*friend*) se faire;
(*speech*) faire, prononcer; (*cause to be*): **to
~ sb sad** *etc* rendre qn triste *etc*; (*force*):
to ~ sb do sth obliger qn à faire qch, faire
faire qch à qn; (*equal*): **2 and 2 ~ 4** 2 et 2 font
4 ▷ *n* (*manufacture*) fabrication *f*; (*brand*)
marque *f*; **to ~ the bed** faire le lit; **to ~ a**

fool of sb (*ridicule*) ridiculiser qn; (*trick*) avoir *or* duper qn; **to ~ a profit** faire un *or* des bénéfice(s); **to ~ a loss** essuyer une perte; **to ~ it** (*in time etc*) y arriver; (*succeed*) réussir; **what time do you ~ it?** quelle heure avez-vous?; **I ~ it £249** d'après mes calculs ça fait 249 livres; **to be made of** être en; **to ~ do with** se contenter de; se débrouiller avec; **make off** vi filer; **make out** vt (*write out: cheque*) faire; (*decipher*) déchiffrer; (*understand*) comprendre; (*see*) distinguer; (*claim, imply*) prétendre, vouloir faire croire; **make up** vt (*invent*) inventer, imaginer; (*constitute*) constituer; (*parcel, bed*) faire ▷ vi se réconcilier; (*with cosmetics*) se maquiller, se farder; **to be made up of** se composer de; **make up for** vt fus compenser; (*lost time*) rattraper; **makeover** ['meɪkəʊvəʳ] n (*by beautician*) soins mpl de maquillage; (*change of image*) changement m d'image; **maker** n fabricant m; (*of film, programme*) réalisateur(-trice); **makeshift** adj provisoire, improvisé(e); **make-up** n maquillage m

making ['meɪkɪŋ] n (*fig*): **in the ~** en formation *or* gestation; **to have the ~s of** (*actor, athlete*) avoir l'étoffe de

malaria [mə'lɛərɪə] n malaria f, paludisme m

Malaysia [mə'leɪzɪə] n Malaisie f

male [meɪl] n (*Biol, Elec*) mâle m ▷ adj (*sex, attitude*) masculin(e); (*animal*) mâle; (*child etc*) du sexe masculin

malicious [mə'lɪʃəs] adj méchant(e), malveillant(e)

▌ Be careful not to translate *malicious* by the French word *malicieux*.

malignant [mə'lɪgnənt] adj (*Med*) malin(-igne)

mall [mɔːl] n (*also*: **shopping ~**) centre commercial

mallet ['mælɪt] n maillet m

malnutrition [mælnjuː'trɪʃən] n malnutrition f

malpractice [mæl'præktɪs] n faute professionnelle; négligence f

malt [mɔːlt] n malt m ▷ cpd (*whisky*) pur malt

Malta ['mɔːltə] n Malte f; **Maltese** [mɔːl'tiːz] adj maltais(e) ▷ n (pl inv) Maltais(e)

mammal ['mæml] n mammifère m

mammoth ['mæməθ] n mammouth m ▷ adj géant(e), monstre

man (pl **men**) [mæn, mɛn] n homme m; (*Sport*) joueur m; (*Chess*) pièce f ▷ vt (*Naut: ship*) garnir d'hommes; (*machine*) assurer le fonctionnement de; (*Mil: gun*) servir; (*: post*) être de service à; **an old ~** un vieillard; **~ and wife** mari et femme

manage ['mænɪdʒ] vi se débrouiller; (*succeed*) y arriver, réussir ▷ vt (*business*) gérer; (*team, operation*) diriger; (*control: ship*) manier, manœuvrer; (*: person*) savoir s'y prendre avec; **to ~ to do** se débrouiller pour faire; (*succeed*) réussir à faire; **manageable** adj maniable; (*task etc*) faisable; (*number*) raisonnable; **management** n (*running*) administration f, direction f; (*people in charge: of business, firm*) dirigeants mpl, cadres mpl; (*: of hotel, shop, theatre*) direction; **manager** n (*of business*) directeur m; (*of institution etc*) administrateur m; (*of department, unit*) responsable m/f, chef m; (*of hotel etc*) gérant m; (*Sport*) manager m; (*of artist*) impresario m; **manageress** n directrice f; (*of hotel etc*) gérante f; **managerial** [mænɪ'dʒɪərɪəl] adj directorial(e); (*skills*) de cadre, de gestion; **managing director** n directeur général

mandarin ['mændərɪn] n (*also*: **~ orange**) mandarine f

mandate ['mændeɪt] n mandat m

mandatory ['mændətərɪ] adj obligatoire

mane [meɪn] n crinière f

maneuver [mə'nuːvəʳ] (*us*) n = **manoeuvre**

mangetout ['mɔnʒ'tuː] n mange-tout m inv

mango ['mæŋgəʊ] (pl **mangoes**) n mangue f

man: manhole n trou m d'homme; **manhood** n (*age*) âge m d'homme; (*manliness*) virilité f

mania ['meɪnɪə] n manie f; **maniac** ['meɪnɪæk] n maniaque m/f; (*fig*) fou (folle)

manic ['mænɪk] adj maniaque

manicure ['mænɪkjʊəʳ] n manucure f

manifest ['mænɪfɛst] vt manifester ▷ adj manifeste, évident(e)

manifesto [mænɪ'fɛstəʊ] n (*Pol*) manifeste m

manipulate [mə'nɪpjʊleɪt] vt manipuler; (*system, situation*) exploiter

man: mankind [mæn'kaɪnd] n humanité f, genre humain; **manly** adj viril(e); **man-made** adj artificiel(le); (*fibre*) synthétique

manner ['mænəʳ] n manière f, façon f; (*behaviour*) attitude f, comportement m; **manners** npl: (**good**) **~s** (bonnes) manières; **bad ~s** mauvaises manières; **all ~ of** toutes sortes de

manoeuvre, (*us*) **maneuver** [mə'nuːvəʳ] vt (*move*) manœuvrer; (*manipulate: person*) manipuler; (*: situation*) exploiter ▷ n manœuvre f

manpower ['mænpaʊəʳ] n main-d'œuvre f

mansion ['mænʃən] n château m, manoir m

manslaughter ['mænslɔːtəʳ] n homicide m involontaire

mantelpiece ['mæntlpiːs] n cheminée f

manual ['mænjuəl] adj manuel(le) ▷ n manuel m

manufacture [mænjuˈfæktʃəʳ] vt fabriquer ▷ n fabrication f; **manufacturer** n fabricant m

manure [məˈnjuəʳ] n fumier m; (artificial) engrais m

manuscript ['mænjuskrɪpt] n manuscrit m

many ['mɛnɪ] adj beaucoup de, de nombreux(-euses) ▷ pron beaucoup, un grand nombre; **a great ~** un grand nombre (de); **~ a ...** bien des .... plus d'une(e) ...

map [mæp] n carte f; (of town) plan m; **can you show it to me on the ~?** pouvez-vous me l'indiquer sur la carte?; **map out** vt tracer; (fig: task) planifier

maple ['meɪpl] n érable m

mar [mɑːʳ] vt gâcher, gâter

marathon ['mærəθən] n marathon m

marble ['mɑːbl] n marbre m; (toy) bille f

March [mɑːtʃ] n mars m

march [mɑːtʃ] vi marcher au pas; (demonstrators) défiler ▷ n marche f; (demonstration) manifestation f

mare [mɛəʳ] n jument f

margarine [mɑːdʒəˈriːn] n margarine f

margin ['mɑːdʒɪn] n marge f; **marginal** adj marginal(e); **marginal seat** (Pol) siège disputé; **marginally** adv très légèrement, sensiblement

marigold ['mærɪɡəʊld] n souci m

marijuana [mærɪˈwɑːnə] n marijuana f

marina [məˈriːnə] n marina f

marinade n [mærɪˈneɪd] marinade f

marinate ['mærɪneɪt] vt (faire) mariner

marine [məˈriːn] adj marin(e) ▷ n fusilier marin; (US) marine m

marital ['mærɪtl] adj matrimonial(e); **marital status** n situation f de famille

maritime ['mærɪtaɪm] adj maritime

marjoram ['mɑːdʒərəm] n marjolaine f

mark [mɑːk] n marque f; (of skid etc) trace f; (BRIT Scol) note f; (oven temperature): **(gas) ~ 4** thermostat m 4 ▷ vt (also Sport: player) marquer; (stain) tacher; (BRIT Scol) corriger, noter; **to ~ time** marquer le pas; **marked** adj (obvious) marqué(e), net(te); **marker** n (sign) jalon m; (bookmark) signet m

market ['mɑːkɪt] n marché m ▷ vt (Comm) commercialiser; **marketing** n marketing m; **marketplace** n place f du marché; (Comm) marché m; **market research** n étude f de marché

marmalade ['mɑːməleɪd] n confiture f d'oranges

maroon [məˈruːn] vt: **to be ~ed** être abandonné(e); (fig) être bloqué(e) ▷ adj (colour) bordeaux inv

marquee [mɑːˈkiː] n chapiteau m

marriage ['mærɪdʒ] n mariage m; **marriage certificate** n extrait m d'acte de mariage

married ['mærɪd] adj marié(e); (life, love) conjugal(e)

marrow ['mærəʊ] n (of bone) moelle f; (vegetable) courge f

marry ['mærɪ] vt épouser, se marier avec; (subj: father, priest etc) marier ▷ vi (also: **get married**) se marier

Mars [mɑːz] n (planet) Mars f

Marseilles [mɑːˈseɪ] n Marseille

marsh [mɑːʃ] n marais m, marécage m

marshal ['mɑːʃl] n maréchal m; (US: fire, police) ≈ capitaine m; (for demonstration, meeting) membre m du service d'ordre ▷ vt rassembler

martyr ['mɑːtəʳ] n martyr(e)

marvel ['mɑːvl] n merveille f ▷ vi: **to ~ (at)** s'émerveiller (de); **marvellous**, (US) **marvelous** adj merveilleux(-euse)

Marxism ['mɑːksɪzəm] n marxisme m

Marxist ['mɑːksɪst] adj, n marxiste (m/f)

marzipan ['mɑːzɪpæn] n pâte f d'amandes

mascara [mæsˈkɑːrə] n mascara m

mascot ['mæskət] n mascotte f

masculine ['mæskjulɪn] adj masculin(e) ▷ n masculin m

mash [mæʃ] vt (Culin) faire une purée de; **mashed potato(es)** n(pl) purée f de pommes de terre

mask [mɑːsk] n masque m ▷ vt masquer

mason ['meɪsn] n (also: **stone~**) maçon m; (also: **free~**) franc-maçon m; **masonry** n maçonnerie f

mass [mæs] n multitude f, masse f; (Physics) masse; (Rel) messe f ▷ cpd (communication) de masse; (unemployment) massif(-ive) ▷ vi se masser; **masses** npl: **the ~es** les masses; **~es of** (inf) des tas de

massacre ['mæsəkəʳ] n massacre m

massage ['mæsɑːʒ] n massage m ▷ vt masser

massive ['mæsɪv] adj énorme, massif(-ive)

mass media npl mass-media mpl

mass-produce ['mæsprəˈdjuːs] vt fabriquer en série

mast [mɑːst] n mât m; (Radio, TV) pylône m

master ['mɑːstəʳ] n maître m; (in secondary school) professeur m; (in primary school) instituteur m; (title for boys): **M~ X** Monsieur X ▷ vt maîtriser; (learn) apprendre à fond; **M~ of Arts/Science (MA/MSc)** n ≈ titulaire m/f d'une maîtrise (en lettres/science); **M~ of Arts/Science degree (MA/MSc)** n ≈ maîtrise f; **mastermind** n esprit supérieur ▷ vt diriger, être le cerveau de; **masterpiece** n chef-d'œuvre m

masturbate ['mæstəbeɪt] vi se masturber

mat [mæt] n petit tapis; (also: **door~**) paillasson m; (also: **table~**) set m de table ▷ adj = matt

match [mætʃ] n allumette f; (game) match m, partie f; (fig) égal(e) ▷ vt (also: **~ up**) assortir; (go well with) aller bien avec, s'assortir à; (*equal*) égaler, valoir ▷ *vi* être assorti(e); (*equal*) égaler, valoir bien assorti(e); **matchbox** *n* boîte *f* d'allumettes; **matching** *adj* assorti(e)

mate [meɪt] *n* (*inf*) copain (copine); (*animal*) partenaire *m/f*, mâle (femelle); (*in merchant navy*) second *m* ▷ *vi* s'accoupler

material [mə'tɪərɪəl] *n* (*substance*) matière *f*, matériau *m*; (*cloth*) tissu *m*, étoffe *f*; (*information, data*) données *fpl* ▷ *adj* matériel(le); (*relevant: evidence*) pertinent(e); **materials** *npl* (*equipment*) matériaux *mpl*

materialize [mə'tɪərɪəlaɪz] *vi* se matérialiser, se réaliser

maternal [mə'tə:nl] *adj* maternel(le)

maternity [mə'tə:nɪtɪ] *n* maternité *f*; **maternity hospital** *n* maternité *f*; **maternity leave** *n* congé *m* de maternité

math [mæθ] *n* (*US*: = *mathematics*) maths *fpl*

mathematical [mæθə'mætɪkl] *adj* mathématique

mathematician [mæθəmə'tɪʃən] *n* mathématicien(ne)

mathematics [mæθə'mætɪks] *n* mathématiques *fpl*

maths [mæθs] *n abbr* (*BRIT*: = *mathematics*) maths *fpl*

matinée ['mætɪneɪ] *n* matinée *f*

matron ['meɪtrən] *n* (*in hospital*) infirmière-chef *f*; (*in school*) infirmière *f*

matt [mæt] *adj* mat(e)

matter ['mætə'] *n* question *f*; (*Physics*) matière *f*, substance *f*; (*Med: pus*) pus *m* ▷ *vi* importer; **matters** *npl* (*affairs, situation*) la situation; **it doesn't ~** cela n'a pas d'importance; (*I don't mind*) cela ne fait rien; **what's the ~?** qu'est-ce qu'il y a?, qu'est-ce qui ne va pas?; **no ~ what** quoi qu'il arrive; **as a ~ of** course tout naturellement; **as a ~ of fact** en fait; **reading ~** (*BRIT*) de quoi lire, de la lecture

mattress ['mætrɪs] *n* matelas *m*

mature [mə'tjuə'] *adj* mûr(e); (*cheese*) fait(e); (*wine*) arrivé(e) à maturité ▷ *vi* mûrir; (*cheese, wine*) se faire; **mature student** *n* étudiant(e) plus âgé(e) que la moyenne; **maturity** *n* maturité *f*

maul [mɔ:l] *vt* lacérer

mauve [məuv] *adj* mauve

max *abbr* = **maximum**

maximize ['mæksɪmaɪz] *vt* (*profits etc, chances*) maximiser

maximum (*pl* **maxima**) ['mæksɪməm, -mə] *adj* maximum ▷ *n* maximum *m*

May [meɪ] *n* mai *m*

may [meɪ] (*conditional* **might**) *vi* (*indicating possibility*): **he ~ come** il se peut qu'il vienne; (*be allowed to*): **~ I smoke?** puis-je fumer?; (*wishes*): **~ God bless you!** (que) Dieu vous bénisse!; **you ~ as well go** vous feriez aussi bien d'y aller

maybe ['meɪbi:] *adv* peut-être; **~ he'll ...** peut-être qu'il ...

May Day *n* le Premier mai

mayhem ['meɪhɛm] *n* grabuge *m*

mayonnaise [meɪə'neɪz] *n* mayonnaise *f*

mayor [mɛə'] *n* maire *m*; **mayoress** *n* (*female mayor*) maire *m*; (*wife of mayor*) épouse *f* du maire

maze [meɪz] *n* labyrinthe *m*, dédale *m*

MD *n abbr* (*Comm*) = **managing director**

me [mi:] *pron* me, m' + *vowel or h mute*; (*stressed, after prep*) moi; **it's me** c'est moi; **he heard me** il m'a entendu; **give me a book** donnez-moi un livre; **it's for me** c'est pour moi

meadow ['mɛdəu] *n* prairie *f*, pré *m*

meagre, (*US*) **meager** ['mi:gə'] *adj* maigre

meal [mi:l] *n* repas *m*; (*flour*) farine *f*; **mealtime** *n* heure *f* du repas

mean [mi:n] *adj* (*with money*) avare, radin(e); (*unkind*) mesquin(e), méchant(e); (*shabby*) misérable; (*average*) moyen(ne) ▷ *vt* (*pt, pp* **meant**) (*signify*) signifier, vouloir dire; (*refer to*) faire allusion à, parler de; (*intend*): **to ~ to do** avoir l'intention de faire ▷ *n* moyenne *f*; **means** *npl* (*way, money*) moyens *mpl*; **to be ~t for** être destiné(e) à; **do you ~ it?** vous êtes sérieux?; **what do you ~?** que voulez-vous dire?; **by ~s of** (*instrument*) au moyen de; **by all ~s** je vous en prie

meaning ['mi:nɪŋ] *n* signification *f*, sens *m*; **meaningful** *adj* significatif(-ive); (*relationship*) valable; **meaningless** *adj* dénué(e) de sens

meant [mɛnt] *pt, pp of* **mean**

meantime ['mi:ntaɪm] *adv* (*also*: **in the ~**) pendant ce temps

meanwhile ['mi:nwaɪl] *adv* = **meantime**

measles ['mi:zlz] *n* rougeole *f*

measure ['mɛʒə'] *vt, vi* mesurer ▷ *n* mesure *f*; (*ruler*) règle (graduée)

measurements ['mɛʒəmənts] *npl* mesures *fpl*; **chest/hip ~** tour *m* de poitrine/hanches

meat [mi:t] *n* viande *f*; **I don't eat ~** je ne mange pas de viande; **cold ~s** (*BRIT*) viandes froides; **meatball** *n* boulette *f* de viande

Mecca ['mɛkə] *n* la Mecque

mechanic [mɪ'kænɪk] *n* mécanicien *m*; **can you send a ~?** pouvez-vous nous envoyer un mécanicien?; **mechanical** *adj* mécanique

mechanism ['mɛkənɪzəm] *n* mécanisme *m*

medal ['mɛdl] *n* médaille *f*; **medallist**, (*US*) **medalist** *n* (*Sport*) médaillé(e)

meddle ['mɛdl] *vi*: **to ~ in** se mêler de, s'occuper de; **to ~ with** toucher à

media ['mi:dɪə] *npl* media *mpl* ▷ *npl of* **medium**

mediaeval [mɛdɪ'i:vl] *adj* = **medieval**

mediate ['mi:dɪeɪt] *vi* servir d'intermédiaire

medical ['mɛdɪkl] *adj* médical(e) ▷ *n (also:* **~ examination**) visite médicale; *(private)* examen médical; **medical certificate** *n* certificat médical

medicated ['mɛdɪkeɪtɪd] *adj* traitant(e), médicamenteux(-euse)

medication [mɛdɪ'keɪʃən] *n (drugs etc)* médication *f*

medicine ['mɛdsɪn] *n* médecine *f*; *(drug)* médicament *m*

medieval [mɛdɪ'iːvl] *adj* médiéval(e)

mediocre [miːdɪ'əʊkəʳ] *adj* médiocre

meditate ['mɛdɪteɪt] *vi:* **to ~ (on)** méditer (sur)

meditation [mɛdɪ'teɪʃən] *n* méditation *f*

Mediterranean [mɛdɪtə'reɪnɪən] *adj* méditerranéen(ne); **the ~ (Sea)** la (mer) Méditerranée

medium ['miːdɪəm] *adj* moyen(ne) ▷ *n (pl* **media**) *(means)* moyen *m*, *(person)* médium *m*; **the happy ~** le juste milieu; **medium-sized** *adj* de taille moyenne; **medium wave** *n (Radio)* ondes moyennes, petites ondes

meek [miːk] *adj* doux (douce), humble

meet *(pt, pp* **met**) [miːt, mɛt] *vt* rencontrer; *(by arrangement)* retrouver, rejoindre; *(for the first time)* faire la connaissance de; *(go and fetch)*: **I'll ~ you at the station** j'irai te chercher à la gare; *(opponent, danger, problem)* faire face à; *(requirements)* satisfaire à, répondre à ▷ *vi (friends)* se rencontrer; se retrouver; *(in session)* se réunir; *(join: lines, roads)* se joindre; **nice ~ing you** ravi d'avoir fait votre connaissance; **meet up** *vi:* **to ~ up with sb** rencontrer qn; **meet with** *vt fus (difficulty)* rencontrer; **to ~ with success** être couronné(e) de succès; **meeting** *n (of group of people)* réunion *f*; *(between individuals)* rendez-vous *m*; **she's at** or **in a meeting** *(Comm)* elle est en réunion; **meeting place** *n* lieu *m* de (la) réunion; *(for appointment)* lieu de rendez-vous

megabyte ['mɛgəbaɪt] *n (Comput)* méga-octet *m*

megaphone ['mɛgəfəʊn] *n* porte-voix *m inv*

megapixel ['mɛgəpɪksl] *n* mégapixel *m*

melancholy ['mɛlənkəlɪ] *n* mélancolie *f* ▷ *adj* mélancolique

melody ['mɛlədɪ] *n* mélodie *f*

melon ['mɛlən] *n* melon *m*

melt [mɛlt] *vi* fondre ▷ *vt* faire fondre

member ['mɛmbəʳ] *n* membre *m*; **M~ of the European Parliament** eurodéputé *m*; **M~ of Parliament** *(BRIT)* député *m*; **membership** *n (becoming a member)* adhésion *f*; admission *f*; *(members)* membres *mpl*, adhérents *mpl*; **membership card** *n* carte *f* de membre

memento [mə'mɛntəu] *n* souvenir *m*

memo ['mɛməu] *n* note *f* (de service)

memorable ['mɛmərəbl] *adj* mémorable

memorandum *(pl* **memoranda**) [mɛmə'rændəm, -də] *n* note *f* (de service)

memorial [mɪ'mɔːrɪəl] *n* mémorial *m* ▷ *adj* commémoratif(-ive)

memorize ['mɛməraɪz] *vt* apprendre *or* retenir par cœur

memory ['mɛmərɪ] *n (also Comput)* mémoire *f*; *(recollection)* souvenir *m*; **in ~ of** à la mémoire de; **memory card** *n (for digital camera)* carte *f* mémoire; **memory stick** *n (Comput: flash pen)* clé *f* USB; *(: card)* carte *f* mémoire

men [mɛn] *npl of* **man**

menace ['mɛnɪs] *n* menace *f*; *(inf: nuisance)* peste *f*, plaie *f* ▷ *vt* menacer

mend [mɛnd] *vt* réparer; *(darn)* raccommoder, repriser ▷ *n:* **on the ~** en voie de guérison; **to ~ one's ways** s'amender

meningitis [mɛnɪn'dʒaɪtɪs] *n* méningite *f*

menopause ['mɛnəupɔːz] *n* ménopause *f*

men's room *(US) n:* **the ~** les toilettes *fpl* pour hommes

menstruation [mɛnstru'eɪʃən] *n* menstruation *f*

menswear ['mɛnzwɛəʳ] *n* vêtements *mpl* d'hommes

mental ['mɛntl] *adj* mental(e); **mentality** [mɛn'tælɪtɪ] *n* mentalité *f*; **mentally** *adv:* **mentally ill people** les malades *mpl* mentaux

menthol ['mɛnθɒl] *n* menthol *m*

mention ['mɛnʃən] *n* mention *f* ▷ *vt* mentionner, faire mention de; **don't ~ it!** je vous en prie, il n'y a pas de quoi!

menu ['mɛnjuː] *n (set menu, Comput)* menu *m*; *(list of dishes)* carte *f*

MEP *n abbr* = **Member of the European Parliament**

mercenary ['məːsɪnərɪ] *adj (person)* intéressé(e), mercenaire ▷ *n* mercenaire *m*

merchandise ['məːtʃəndaɪz] *n* marchandises *fpl*

merchant ['məːtʃənt] *n* négociant *m*, marchand *m*; **merchant bank** *n (BRIT)* banque *f* d'affaires; **merchant navy**, *(US)* **merchant marine** *n* marine marchande

merciless ['məːsɪlɪs] *adj* impitoyable, sans pitié

mercury ['məːkjurɪ] *n* mercure *m*

mercy ['məːsɪ] *n* pitié *f*, merci *f*; *(Rel)* miséricorde *f*; **at the ~ of** à la merci de

mere [mɪəʳ] *adj* simple; *(chance)* pur(e); **a ~ two hours** seulement deux heures; **merely** *adv* simplement, purement

merge [məːdʒ] *vt* unir; *(Comput)* fusionner, interclasser ▷ *vi (colours, shapes, sounds)* se mêler; *(roads)* se joindre; *(Comm)* fusionner; **merger** *n (Comm)* fusion *f*

meringue [mə'ræŋ] *n* meringue *f*

merit ['mɛrɪt] *n* mérite *m*, valeur *f* ▷ *vt* mériter

mermaid ['məːmeɪd] *n* sirène *f*

merry ['mɛrɪ] *adj* gai(e); **M~ Christmas!** joyeux Noël!; **merry-go-round** *n* manège *m*

mesh [mɛʃ] *n* mailles *fpl*

mess [mɛs] *n* désordre *m*, fouillis *m*, pagaille *f*; (*muddle: of life*) gâchis *m*; (: *of economy*) pagaille *f*; (*dirt*) saleté *f*; (*Mil*) mess *m*, cantine *f*; **to be (in) a ~** être en désordre; **to be/get o.s. in a ~** (*fig*) être/se mettre dans le pétrin; **mess about, mess around** (*inf*) *vi* perdre son temps; **mess up** *vt* (*inf: dirty*) salir; (*spoil*) gâcher; **mess with** (*inf*) *vt fus* (*challenge, confront*) se frotter à; (*interfere with*) toucher à

message ['mɛsɪdʒ] *n* message *m*; **can I leave a ~?** est-ce que je peux laisser un message?; **are there any ~s for me?** est-ce que j'ai des messages?

messenger ['mɛsɪndʒər] *n* messager *m*

Messrs, Messrs. ['mɛsəz] *abbr* (*on letters:* = *messieurs*) MM

messy ['mɛsɪ] *adj* (*dirty*) sale; (*untidy*) en désordre

met [mɛt] *pt, pp of* **meet**

metabolism [mɛ'tæbəlɪzəm] *n* métabolisme *m*

metal ['mɛtl] *n* métal *m* ▷ *cpd* en métal; **metallic** [mɛ'tælɪk] *adj* métallique

metaphor ['mɛtəfər] *n* métaphore *f*

meteor ['miːtɪər] *n* météore *m*; **meteorite** ['miːtɪəraɪt] *n* météorite *m/f*

meteorology [miːtɪə'rɔlədʒɪ] *n* météorologie *f*

meter ['miːtər] *n* (*instrument*) compteur *m*; (*also:* **parking ~**) parc(o)mètre *m*; (*US: unit*) = **metre** ▷ *vt* (*US Post*) affranchir à la machine

method ['mɛθəd] *n* méthode *f*; **methodical** [mɪ'θɔdɪkl] *adj* méthodique

methylated spirit ['mɛθɪleɪtɪd-] *n* (*BRIT*) alcool *m* à brûler

meticulous [mɛ'tɪkjuləs] *adj* méticuleux(-euse)

metre, (*US*) **meter** ['miːtər] *n* mètre *m*

metric ['mɛtrɪk] *adj* métrique

metro ['mɛtrəu] *n* métro *m*

metropolitan [mɛtrə'pɔlɪtən] *adj* métropolitain(e); **the M~ Police** (*BRIT*) la police londonienne

Mexican ['mɛksɪkən] *adj* mexicain(e) ▷ *n* Mexicain(e)

Mexico ['mɛksɪkəu] *n* Mexique *m*

mg *abbr* (= *milligram*) mg

mice [maɪs] *npl of* **mouse**

micro... [maɪkrəu] *prefix* micro...; **microchip** *n* (*Elec*) puce *f*; **microphone** *n* microphone *m*; **microscope** *n* microscope *m*

mid [mɪd] *adj*: **~ May** la mi-mai; **~ afternoon** le milieu de l'après-midi; **in ~ air** en plein ciel; **he's in his ~ thirties** il a dans les trente-cinq ans; **midday** *n* midi *m*

middle ['mɪdl] *n* milieu *m*; (*waist*) ceinture *f*, taille *f* ▷ *adj* du milieu; (*average*) moyen(ne); **in the ~ of the night** au milieu de la nuit; **middle-aged** *adj* d'un certain âge, ni vieux ni jeune; **Middle Ages** *npl*: **the Middle Ages** le moyen âge; **middle class(es)** *n(pl)*: **the middle class(es)** ≈ les classes moyennes; **middle-class** *adj* bourgeois(e); **Middle East** *n*: **the Middle East** le Proche-Orient, le Moyen-Orient; **middle name** *n* second prénom; **middle school** *n* (*US*) école pour les enfants de 12 à 14 ans ≈ collège *m*; (*BRIT*) école pour les enfants de 8 à 14 ans

midge [mɪdʒ] *n* moucheron *m*

midget ['mɪdʒɪt] *n* (*pej*) nain(e)

midnight ['mɪdnaɪt] *n* minuit *m*

midst [mɪdst] *n*: **in the ~ of** au milieu de

midsummer [mɪd'sʌmər] *n* milieu *m* de l'été

midway [mɪd'weɪ] *adj, adv*: **~ (between)** à mi-chemin (entre); **~ through ...** au milieu de ..., en plein(e) ...

midweek [mɪd'wiːk] *adv* au milieu de la semaine, en pleine semaine

midwife (*pl* **midwives**) ['mɪdwaɪf, -vz] *n* sage-femme *f*

midwinter [mɪd'wɪntər] *n* milieu *m* de l'hiver

might [maɪt] *vb see* **may** ▷ *n* puissance *f*, force *f*; **mighty** *adj* puissant(e)

migraine ['miːgreɪn] *n* migraine *f*

migrant ['maɪgrənt] *n* (*bird, animal*) migrateur *m*; (*person*) migrant(e) ▷ *adj* migrateur(-trice); migrant(e); (*worker*) saisonnier(-ière)

migrate [maɪ'greɪt] *vi* migrer

migration [maɪ'greɪʃən] *n* migration *f*

mike [maɪk] *n abbr* (= *microphone*) micro *m*

mild [maɪld] *adj* doux (douce); (*reproach, infection*) léger(-ère); (*illness*) bénin(-igne); (*interest*) modéré(e); (*taste*) peu relevé(e); **mildly** ['maɪldlɪ] *adv* doucement; légèrement; **to put it mildly** (*inf*) c'est le moins qu'on puisse dire

mile [maɪl] *n* mil(l)e *m* (= 1609 *m*); **mileage** *n* distance *f* en milles, ≈ kilométrage *m*; **mileometer** [maɪ'lɔmɪtər] *n* compteur *m* kilométrique; **milestone** *n* borne *f*; (*fig*) jalon *m*

military ['mɪlɪtərɪ] *adj* militaire

militia [mɪ'lɪʃə] *n* milice *f*

milk [mɪlk] *n* lait *m* ▷ *vt* (*cow*) traire; (*fig: person*) dépouiller, plumer; (: *situation*) exploiter à fond; **milk chocolate** *n* chocolat *m* au lait; **milkman** (*irreg*) *n* laitier *m*; **milky** *adj* (*drink*) au lait; (*colour*) laiteux(-euse)

mill [mɪl] *n* moulin *m*; (*factory*) usine *f*, fabrique *f*; (*spinning mill*) filature *f*; (*flour mill*) minoterie *f* ▷ *vt* moudre, broyer ▷ *vi* (*also:* **~ about**) grouiller

millennium (*pl* **millenniums** *or* **millennia**) [mɪ'lɛnɪəm, -'lɛnɪə] *n* millénaire *m*

milli... ['mɪlɪ] *prefix* milli...; **milligram(me)** *n* milligramme *m*; **millilitre**, (US) **milliliter** *n* millilitre *m*; **millimetre**, (US) **millimeter** *n* millimètre *m*

million ['mɪljən] *n* million *m*; **a ~ pounds** un million de livres sterling; **millionaire** [mɪljə'nɛəʳ] *n* millionnaire *m*; **millionth** ['mɪljənθ] *num* millionième

milometer [maɪ'lomɪtəʳ] *n* = **mileometer**

mime [maɪm] *n* mime *m* ▷ *vt, vi* mimer

mimic ['mɪmɪk] *n* imitateur(-trice) ▷ *vt, vi* imiter, contrefaire

min. *abbr* (= *minute(s)*) mn.; (= *minimum*) min.

mince [mɪns] *vt* hacher ▷ *n* (BRIT Culin) viande hachée, hachis *m*; **mincemeat** *n* hachis de fruits secs utilisés en pâtisserie; (US) viande hachée, hachis *m*; **mince pie** *n* sorte de tarte aux fruits secs

mind [maɪnd] *n* esprit *m* ▷ *vt* (attend to, look after) s'occuper de; (be careful) faire attention à; (object to): **I don't ~ the noise** je ne crains pas le bruit, le bruit ne me dérange pas; **it is on my ~** cela me préoccupe; **to change one's ~** changer d'avis; **to my ~** à mon avis, selon moi; **to bear sth in ~** tenir compte de qch; **to have sb/sth in ~** avoir qn/qch en tête; **to make up one's ~** se décider; **do you ~ if ...?** est-ce que cela vous gêne si ...?; **I don't ~** cela ne me dérange pas; (don't care) ça m'est égal; **~ you, ...** remarquez, ...; **never ~** peu importe, ça ne fait rien; (don't worry) ne vous en faites pas; **"~ the step"** "attention à la marche"; **mindless** *adj* (violence, crime) insensé(e); (boring: job) idiot(e)

mine¹ [maɪn] *pron* le (la) mien(ne), les miens (miennes); **a friend of ~** un de mes amis, un ami à moi; **this book is ~** ce livre est à moi

mine² [maɪn] *n* mine *f* ▷ *vt* (coal) extraire; (ship, beach) miner; **minefield** *n* champ *m* de mines; **miner** *n* mineur *m*

mineral ['mɪnərəl] *adj* minéral(e) ▷ *n* minéral *m*; **mineral water** *n* eau minérale

mingle ['mɪŋgl] *vi*: **to ~ with** se mêler à

miniature ['mɪnətʃəʳ] *adj* (en) miniature ▷ *n* miniature *f*

minibar ['mɪnɪbɑːʳ] *n* minibar *m*

minibus ['mɪnɪbʌs] *n* minibus *m*

minicab ['mɪnɪkæb] *n* (BRIT) taxi *m* indépendant

minimal ['mɪnɪml] *adj* minimal(e)

minimize ['mɪnɪmaɪz] *vt* (reduce) réduire au minimum; (play down) minimiser

minimum ['mɪnɪməm] *n* (pl **minima**) minimum *m* ▷ *adj* minimum

mining ['maɪnɪŋ] *n* exploitation minière

miniskirt ['mɪnɪskəːt] *n* mini-jupe *f*

minister ['mɪnɪstəʳ] *n* (BRIT Pol) ministre *m*; (Rel) pasteur *m*

ministry ['mɪnɪstrɪ] *n* (BRIT Pol) ministère *m*; (Rel): **to go into the ~** devenir pasteur

minor ['maɪnəʳ] *adj* petit(e), de peu d'importance; (Mus, poet, problem) mineur(e) ▷ *n* (Law) mineur(e)

minority [maɪ'nɔrɪtɪ] *n* minorité *f*

mint [mɪnt] *n* (plant) menthe *f*; (sweet) bonbon *m* à la menthe ▷ *vt* (coins) battre; **the (Royal) M~, the (US) M~** ≈ l'hôtel *m* de la Monnaie; **in ~ condition** à l'état de neuf

minus ['maɪnəs] *n* (also: **~ sign**) signe *m* moins ▷ *prep* moins; **12 ~ 6 equals 6** 12 moins 6 égal 6; **~ 24°C** moins 24°C

minute¹ ['mɪnɪt] *n* minute *f*; **minutes** *npl* (of meeting) procès-verbal *m*, compte rendu; **wait a ~!** (attendez) un instant!; **at the last ~** à la dernière minute

minute² [maɪ'njuːt] *adj* minuscule; (detailed) minutieux(-euse); **in ~ detail** par le menu

miracle ['mɪrəkl] *n* miracle *m*

miraculous [mɪ'rækjuləs] *adj* miraculeux(-euse)

mirage ['mɪrɑːʒ] *n* mirage *m*

mirror ['mɪrəʳ] *n* miroir *m*, glace *f*; (in car) rétroviseur *m*

misbehave [mɪsbɪ'heɪv] *vi* mal se conduire

misc. *abbr* = **miscellaneous**

miscarriage ['mɪskærɪdʒ] *n* (Med) fausse couche; **~ of justice** erreur *f* judiciaire

miscellaneous [mɪsɪ'leɪnɪəs] *adj* (items, expenses) divers(es); (selection) varié(e)

mischief ['mɪstʃɪf] *n* (naughtiness) sottises *fpl*; (playfulness) espièglerie *f*; (harm) mal *m*, dommage *m*; (maliciousness) méchanceté *f*; **mischievous** ['mɪstʃɪvəs] *adj* (playful, naughty) coquin(e), espiègle

misconception ['mɪskən'sɛpʃən] *n* idée fausse

misconduct [mɪs'kɔndʌkt] *n* inconduite *f*; **professional ~** faute professionnelle

miser ['maɪzəʳ] *n* avare *m/f*

miserable ['mɪzərəbl] *adj* (person, expression) malheureux(-euse); (conditions) misérable; (weather) maussade; (offer, donation) minable; (failure) pitoyable

misery ['mɪzərɪ] *n* (unhappiness) tristesse *f*; (pain) souffrances *fpl*; (wretchedness) misère *f*

misfortune [mɪs'fɔːtʃən] *n* malchance *f*, malheur *m*

misgiving [mɪs'gɪvɪŋ] *n* (apprehension) craintes *fpl*; **to have ~s about sth** avoir des doutes quant à qch

misguided [mɪs'gaɪdɪd] *adj* malavisé(e)

mishap ['mɪshæp] *n* mésaventure *f*

misinterpret [mɪsɪn'təːprɪt] *vt* mal interpréter

misjudge [mɪs'dʒʌdʒ] *vt* méjuger, se méprendre sur le compte de

mislay [mɪs'leɪ] *vt* (irreg: like **lay**) égarer

mislead [mɪsˈliːd] vt (irreg: like **lead**¹) induire en erreur; **misleading** adj trompeur(-euse)

misplace [mɪsˈpleɪs] vt égarer; **to be ~d** (trust etc) être mal placé(e)

misprint [ˈmɪsprɪnt] n faute f d'impression

misrepresent [mɪsreprɪˈzɛnt] vt présenter sous un faux jour

Miss [mɪs] n Mademoiselle

miss [mɪs] vt (fail to get, attend, see) manquer, rater; (regret the absence of): **I ~ him/it** il/cela me manque ⊳ vi manquer ⊳ n (shot) coup manqué; **we ~ed our train** nous avons raté notre train; **you can't ~ it** vous ne pouvez pas vous tromper; **miss out** vt (BRIT) oublier; **miss out on** vt fus (fun, party) rater, manquer; (chance, bargain) laisser passer

missile [ˈmɪsaɪl] n (Aviat) missile m; (object thrown) projectile m

missing [ˈmɪsɪŋ] adj manquant(e); (after escape, disaster: person) disparu(e); **to go ~** disparaître; **~ in action** (Mil) porté(e) disparu(e)

mission [ˈmɪʃən] n mission f; **on a ~ to sb** en mission auprès de qn; **missionary** n missionnaire m/f

misspell [mɪsˈspɛl] vt (irreg: like **spell**) mal orthographier

mist [mɪst] n brume f ⊳ vi (also: **~ over**, **~ up**) devenir brumeux(-euse); (BRIT: windows) s'embuer

mistake [mɪsˈteɪk] n erreur f, faute f ⊳ vt (irreg: like **take**) (meaning) mal comprendre; (intentions) se méprendre sur; **to ~ for** prendre pour; **by ~** par erreur, par inadvertance; **to make a ~** (in writing) faire une faute; (in calculating etc) faire une erreur; **there must be some ~** il doit y avoir une erreur, se tromper; **mistaken** pp of **mistake** ⊳ adj (idea etc) erroné(e); **to be mistaken** faire erreur, se tromper

mister [ˈmɪstə*] n (inf) Monsieur m; see **Mr**

mistletoe [ˈmɪsltəu] n gui m

mistook [mɪsˈtuk] pt of **mistake**

mistress [ˈmɪstrɪs] n maîtresse f; (BRIT: in primary school) institutrice f; (: in secondary school) professeur m

mistrust [mɪsˈtrʌst] vt se méfier de

misty [ˈmɪstɪ] adj brumeux(-euse); (glasses, window) embué(e)

misunderstand [mɪsʌndəˈstænd] vt, vi (irreg: like **stand**) mal comprendre; **misunderstanding** n méprise f, malentendu m; **there's been a misunderstanding** il y a eu un malentendu

misunderstood [mɪsʌndəˈstud] pt, pp of **misunderstand** ⊳ adj (person) incompris(e)

misuse n [mɪsˈjuːs] mauvais emploi; (of power) abus m ⊳ vt [mɪsˈjuːz] mal employer; abuser de

mitt(en) [ˈmɪt(n)] n moufle f; (fingerless) mitaine f

mix [mɪks] vt mélanger; (sauce, drink etc) préparer ⊳ vi se mélanger; (socialize): **he doesn't ~ well** il est peu sociable ⊳ n mélange m; **to ~ sth with sth** mélanger qch à qch; **cake ~** préparation f pour gâteau; **mix up** vt mélanger; (confuse) confondre; **to be ~ed up in sth** être mêlé(e) à qch or impliqué(e) dans qch; **mixed** adj (feelings, reactions) contradictoire; (school, marriage) mixte; **mixed grill** n (BRIT) assortiment m de grillades; **mixed salad** n salade f de crudités; **mixed-up** adj (person) désorienté(e), embrouillé(e); **mixer** n (for food) batteur m, mixeur m; (drink) boisson gazeuse (servant à couper un alcool); (person): **he is a good mixer** il est très sociable; **mixture** n assortiment m, mélange m; (Med) préparation f; **mix-up** n: **there was a mix-up** il y a eu confusion

ml abbr (= millilitre(s)) ml

mm abbr (= millimetre) mm

moan [məun] n gémissement m ⊳ vi gémir; (inf: complain): **to ~ (about)** se plaindre (de)

moat [məut] n fossé m, douves fpl

mob [mɔb] n foule f; (disorderly) cohue f ⊳ vt assaillir

mobile [ˈməubaɪl] adj mobile ⊳ n (Art) mobile m; (BRIT inf: phone) (téléphone m) portable m, mobile m; **mobile home** n caravane f; **mobile phone** n (téléphone m) portable m, mobile m

mobility [məuˈbɪlɪtɪ] n mobilité f

mobilize [ˈməubɪlaɪz] vt, vi mobiliser

mock [mɔk] vt ridiculiser; (laugh at) se moquer de ⊳ adj faux (fausse); **mocks** npl (BRIT Scol) examens blancs; **mockery** n moquerie f, raillerie f

mod cons [ˈmɔdˈkɔnz] npl abbr (BRIT) = **modern conveniences**; see **convenience**

mode [məud] n mode m; (of transport) moyen m

model [ˈmɔdl] n modèle m; (person: for fashion) mannequin m; (: for artist) modèle ⊳ vt (with clay etc) modeler ⊳ vi travailler comme mannequin ⊳ adj (railway: toy) modèle réduit inv; (child, factory) modèle; **to ~ clothes** présenter des vêtements; **to ~ o.s. on** imiter

modem [ˈməudɛm] n modem m

moderate adj [ˈmɔdərət] modéré(e); (amount, change) peu important(e) ⊳ vi [ˈmɔdəreɪt] se modérer, se calmer ⊳ vt [ˈmɔdəreɪt] modérer

moderation [mɔdəˈreɪʃən] n modération f, mesure f; **in ~** à dose raisonnable, pris(e) or pratiqué(e) modérément

modern [ˈmɔdən] adj moderne; **modernize** vt moderniser; **modern languages** npl langues vivantes

modest ['mɔdɪst] adj modeste; **modesty** n modestie f
modification [mɔdɪfɪ'keɪʃən] n modification f
modify ['mɔdɪfaɪ] vt modifier
module ['mɔdjuːl] n module m
mohair ['məʊhɛəʳ] n mohair m
Mohammed [mə'hæmɛd] n Mahomet m
moist [mɔɪst] adj humide, moîte; **moisture** ['mɔɪstʃəʳ] n humidité f; (on glass) buée f; **moisturizer** ['mɔɪstʃəraɪzəʳ] n crème hydratante
mold etc [məʊld] (US) n = **mould**
mole [məʊl] n (animal, spy) taupe f; (spot) grain m de beauté
molecule ['mɔlɪkjuːl] n molécule f
molest [məʊ'lest] vt (assault sexually) attenter à la pudeur de
molten ['məʊltən] adj fondu(e), (rock) en fusion
mom [mɔm] n (US) = **mum**
moment ['məʊmənt] n moment m, instant m; **at the ~** en ce moment, **momentarily** adv momentanément; (US: soon) bientôt; **momentary** adj momentané(e), passager(-ère); **momentous** [məʊ'mentəs] adj important(e), capital(e)
momentum [məʊ'mentəm] n élan m, vitesse acquise, (fig) dynamique f, **to gather ~** prendre de la vitesse; (fig) gagner du terrain
mommy ['mɔmɪ] n (US: mother) maman f
Monaco ['mɔnəkəʊ] n Monaco f
monarch ['mɔnək] n monarque m; **monarchy** n monarchie f
monastery ['mɔnəstərɪ] n monastère m
Monday ['mʌndɪ] n lundi m
monetary ['mʌnɪtərɪ] adj monétaire
money ['mʌnɪ] n argent m; **to make ~** (person) gagner de l'argent; (business) rapporter; **money belt** n ceinture-portefeuille f; **money order** n mandat m
mongrel ['mʌŋɡrəl] n (dog) bâtard m
monitor ['mɔnɪtəʳ] n (TV, Comput) écran m, moniteur m ▷ vt contrôler; (foreign station) être à l'écoute de; (progress) suivre de près
monk [mʌŋk] n moine m
monkey ['mʌŋkɪ] n singe m
monologue ['mɔnəlɔɡ] n monologue m
monopoly [mə'nɔpəlɪ] n monopole m
monosodium glutamate [mɔnə'səʊdɪəm 'ɡluːtəmeɪt] n glutamate m de sodium
monotonous [mə'nɔtənəs] adj monotone
monsoon [mɔn'suːn] n mousson f
monster ['mɔnstəʳ] n monstre m
month [mʌnθ] n mois m; **monthly** adj mensuel(le) ▷ adv mensuellement
Montreal [mɔntrɪ'ɔːl] n Montréal
monument ['mɔnjumənt] n monument m
mood [muːd] n humeur f, disposition f; **to be in a good/bad ~** être de bonne/

mauvaise humeur; **moody** adj (variable) d'humeur changeante, lunatique; (sullen) morose, maussade
moon [muːn] n lune f; **moonlight** n clair m de lune
moor [mʊəʳ] n lande f ▷ vt (ship) amarrer ▷ vi mouiller
moose [muːs] n (pl inv) élan m
mop [mɔp] n balai m à laver; (for dishes) lavette f à vaisselle ▷ vt éponger, essuyer; **~ of hair** tignasse f; **mop up** vt éponger
mope [məʊp] vi avoir le cafard, se morfondre
moped ['məʊpɛd] n cyclomoteur m
moral ['mɔrl] adj moral(e) ▷ n morale f; **morals** npl moralité f
morale [mɔ'rɑːl] n moral m
morality [mə'rælɪtɪ] n moralité f
morbid ['mɔːbɪd] adj morbide

KEYWORD

more [mɔːʳ] adj **1** (greater in number etc) plus (de), davantage (de); **more people/work (than)** plus de gens/de travail (que)
2 (additional) encore (de); **do you want (some) more tea?** voulez-vous encore du thé?; **is there any more wine?** reste-t-il du vin?; **I have no or I don't have any more money** je n'ai plus d'argent; **it'll take a few more weeks** ça prendra encore quelques semaines
▶ pron plus, davantage; **more than 10** plus de 10; **it cost more than we expected** cela a coûté plus que prévu; **I want more** j'en veux plus or davantage; **is there any more?** est-ce qu'il en reste?; **there's no more** il n'y en a plus; **a little more** un peu plus; **many/much more** beaucoup plus, bien davantage
▶ adv plus; **more dangerous/easily (than)** plus dangereux/facilement (que); **more and more expensive** de plus en plus cher; **more or less** plus ou moins; **more than ever** plus que jamais; **once more** encore une fois, une fois de plus

moreover [mɔː'rəʊvəʳ] adv de plus
morgue [mɔːɡ] n morgue f
morning ['mɔːnɪŋ] n matin m; (as duration) matinée f ▷ cpd matinal(e); (paper) du matin; **in the ~** le matin; **7 o'clock in the ~** 7 heures du matin; **morning sickness** n nausées matinales
Moroccan [mə'rɔkən] adj marocain(e) ▷ n Marocain(e)
Morocco [mə'rɔkəʊ] n Maroc m
moron ['mɔːrɔn] n (offensive) idiot(e), minus m/f
morphine ['mɔːfiːn] n morphine f
morris dancing ['mɔrɪs-] n (BRIT) danses folkloriques anglaises

Morse [mɔːs] n (also: ~ **code**) morse m
mortal ['mɔːtl] adj, n mortel(le)
mortar ['mɔːtəʳ] n mortier m
mortgage ['mɔːgɪdʒ] n hypothèque f;
(loan) prêt m (or crédit m) hypothécaire ▷ vt
hypothéquer
mortician [mɔː'tɪʃən] n (US) entrepreneur
m de pompes funèbres
mortified ['mɔːtɪfaɪd] adj mort(e) de honte
mortuary ['mɔːtjuərɪ] n morgue f
mosaic [məu'zeɪɪk] n mosaïque f
Moscow ['mɔskəu] n Moscou
Moslem ['mɔzləm] adj, n = **Muslim**
mosque [mɔsk] n mosquée f
mosquito [mɔs'kiːtəu] (pl **mosquitoes**) n
moustique m
moss [mɔs] n mousse f
most [məust] adj (majority of) la plupart
de; (greatest amount of) le plus de ▷ pron la
plupart ▷ adv le plus; (very) très,
extrêmement; **the ~** le plus; **~ fish** la
plupart des poissons; **the ~ beautiful
woman in the world** la plus belle femme du
monde; **~ of** (with plural) la plupart de; (with
singular) la plus grande partie de; **~ of them**
la plupart d'entre eux; **~ of the time** la
plupart du temps; **I saw ~** (a lot but not all)
j'en ai vu la plupart; (more than anyone else)
c'est moi qui en ai vu le plus; **at the (very) ~**
au plus; **to make the ~ of** profiter au
maximum de; **mostly** adv (chiefly) surtout,
principalement; (usually) généralement
MOT n abbr (BRIT: = Ministry of Transport): **the
~ (test)** visite technique (annuelle) obligatoire
des véhicules à moteur
motel [məu'tɛl] n motel m
moth [mɔθ] n papillon m de nuit; (in clothes)
mite f
mother ['mʌðəʳ] n mère f ▷ vt (pamper,
protect) dorloter; **motherhood** n maternité
f; **mother-in-law** n belle-mère f; **mother-
of-pearl** n nacre f; **Mother's Day** n fête f
des Mères; **mother-to-be** n future maman;
mother tongue n langue maternelle
motif [məu'tiːf] n motif m
motion ['məuʃən] n mouvement m;
(gesture) geste m; (at meeting) motion f
▷ vt, vi: **to ~ (to) sb to do** faire signe à qn
de faire; **motionless** adj immobile, sans
mouvement; **motion picture** n film m
motivate ['məutɪveɪt] vt motiver
motivation [məutɪ'veɪʃən] n motivation f

motive ['məutɪv] n motif m, mobile m
motor ['məutəʳ] n moteur m; (BRIT inf:
vehicle) auto f; **motorbike** n moto f;
motorboat n bateau m à moteur;
motorcar n (BRIT) automobile f;
motorcycle n moto f; **motorcyclist** n
motocycliste m/f; **motoring** n (BRIT)
tourisme m automobile; **motorist** n
automobiliste m/f; **motor racing** n (BRIT)
course f automobile; **motorway** n (BRIT)
autoroute f
motto ['mɔtəu] (pl **mottoes**) n devise f
mould, (US) **mold** [məuld] n moule m;
(mildew) moisissure f ▷ vt mouler, modeler;
(fig) façonner; **mouldy**, (US) **moldy** adj
moisi(e); (smell) de moisi
mound [maund] n monticule m, tertre m
mount [maunt] n (hill) mont m, montagne
f; (horse) monture f; (for picture) carton m
de montage ▷ vt monter; (horse) monter
à; (bike) monter sur; (picture) monter sur
carton ▷ vi (inflation, tension) augmenter;
mount up vi s'élever, monter; (bills,
problems, savings) s'accumuler
mountain ['mauntɪn] n montagne f ▷ cpd
de (la) montagne; **mountain bike** n VTT
m, vélo m tout terrain; **mountaineer** n
alpiniste m/f; **mountaineering** n alpinisme
m; **mountainous** adj montagneux(-euse);
mountain range n chaîne f de montagnes
mourn [mɔːn] vt pleurer ▷ vi: **to ~ for sb**
pleurer qn; **to ~ for sth** se lamenter sur
qch; **mourner** n parent(e) or ami(e) du
défunt; personne f en deuil or venue rendre
hommage au défunt; **mourning** n deuil m;
in mourning en deuil
mouse (pl **mice**) [maus, maɪs] n (also
Comput) souris f; **mouse mat** n (Comput)
tapis m de souris
moussaka [muː'sɑːkə] n moussaka f
mousse [muːs] n mousse f
moustache, (US) **mustache** [məs'tɑːʃ] n
moustache(s) f(pl)
mouth (pl **mouths**) [mauθ, mauðz] n
bouche f; (of dog, cat) gueule f; (of river)
embouchure f; (of hole, cave) ouverture
f; **mouthful** n bouchée f; **mouth organ**
n harmonica m; **mouthpiece** n (of
musical instrument) bec m, embouchure
f; (spokesperson) porte-parole m inv;
mouthwash n eau f dentifrice
move [muːv] n (movement) mouvement m;
(in game) coup m (: turn to play) tour m;
(change of house) déménagement m; (change
of job) changement m d'emploi ▷ vt
déplacer, bouger; (emotionally) émouvoir;
(Pol: resolution etc) proposer ▷ vi (gen)
bouger, remuer; (traffic) circuler; (also:
~ **house**) déménager; (in game) jouer; **can
you ~ your car, please?** pouvez-vous
déplacer votre voiture, s'il vous plaît?; **to ~
sb to do sth** pousser or inciter qn à faire qch;

to get a ~ on se dépêcher, se remuer; **move back** vi revenir, retourner; **move in** (to a house) emménager; (police, soldiers) intervenir; **move off** vi s'éloigner, s'en aller; **move on** vi se remettre en route; **move out** vi (of house) déménager; **move over** vi se pousser, se déplacer; **move up** vi avancer; (employee) avoir de l'avancement; (pupil) passer dans la classe supérieure; **movement** n mouvement m

movie ['mu:vɪ] n film m; **movies** npl: the ~s le cinéma; **movie theater** (US) n cinéma m

moving ['mu:vɪŋ] adj en mouvement; (touching) émouvant(e)

mow (pt **mowed**, pp **mowed** or **mown**) [məu, -d, -n] vt faucher; (lawn) tondre; **mower** n (also: **lawnmower**) tondeuse f à gazon

mown [məun] pp of **mow**

Mozambique [məuzəm'bi:k] n Mozambique m

MP n abbr (BRIT) = **Member of Parliament**

MP3 n mp3 m; **MP3 player** n baladeur m numérique, lecteur m mp3

mpg n abbr = **miles per gallon** (30 mpg = 9,4 l. aux 100 km)

m.p.h. abbr = **miles per hour** (60 mph = 96 km/h)

Mr, (US) **Mr.** ['mɪstəʳ] n: ~ X Monsieur X, M. X

Mrs, (US) **Mrs.** ['mɪsɪz] n: ~ X Madame X, Mme X

Ms, (US) **Ms.** [mɪz] n (Miss or Mrs): ~ X Madame X, Mme X

MSP n abbr (= Member of the Scottish Parliament) député m au Parlement écossais

Mt abbr (Geo: = mount) Mt

much [mʌtʃ] adj beaucoup de ▷ adv, n, pron beaucoup; **we don't have ~ time** nous n'avons pas beaucoup de temps; **how ~ is it?** combien est-ce que ça coûte?; **it's not ~** ce n'est pas beaucoup; **too ~** trop (de); **so ~** tant (de); **I like it very/so ~** j'aime beaucoup/tellement ça; **as ~ as** autant de; **that's ~ better** c'est beaucoup mieux

muck [mʌk] n (mud) boue f; (dirt) ordures fpl; **muck up** vt (inf: ruin) gâcher, esquinter; (dirty) salir; (exam, interview) se planter à; **mucky** adj (dirty) boueux(-euse), sale

mucus ['mju:kəs] n mucus m

mud [mʌd] n boue f

muddle ['mʌdl] n (mess) pagaille f, fouillis m; (mix-up) confusion f ▷ vt (also: ~ **up**) brouiller, embrouiller; **to get in a ~** (while explaining etc) s'embrouiller

muddy ['mʌdɪ] adj boueux(-euse)

mudguard ['mʌdgɑ:d] n garde-boue m inv

muesli ['mju:zlɪ] n muesli m

muffin ['mʌfɪn] n (roll) petit pain rond et plat; (cake) petit gâteau au chocolat ou aux fruits

muffled ['mʌfld] adj étouffé(e), voilé(e)

muffler ['mʌfləʳ] n (scarf) cache-nez m inv; (US Aut) silencieux m

mug [mʌg] n (cup) tasse f (sans soucoupe); (: for beer) chope f; (inf: face) bouille f; (: fool) poire f ▷ vt (assault) agresser; **mugger** ['mʌgəʳ] n agresseur m; **mugging** n agression f

muggy ['mʌgɪ] adj lourd(e), moite

mule [mju:l] n mule f

multicoloured, (US) **multicolored** ['mʌltɪkʌləd] adj multicolore

multimedia ['mʌltɪ'mi:dɪə] adj multimédia inv

multinational [mʌltɪ'næʃənl] n multinationale f ▷ adj multinational(e)

multiple ['mʌltɪpl] adj multiple ▷ n multiple m; **multiple choice (test)** n QCM m, questionnaire m à choix multiple, **multiple sclerosis** [-sklɪ'rəusɪs] n sclérose f en plaques

multiplex (cinema) ['mʌltɪplɛks-] n (cinéma m) multisalles m

multiplication [mʌltɪplɪ'keɪʃən] n multiplication f

multiply ['mʌltɪplaɪ] vt multiplier ▷ vi se multiplier

multistorey ['mʌltɪ'stɔ:rɪ] adj (BRIT: building) à étages; (: car park) à étages or niveaux multiples

mum [mʌm] n (BRIT) maman f ▷ adj: **to keep ~** ne pas souffler mot

mumble ['mʌmbl] vt, vi marmotter, marmonner

mummy ['mʌmɪ] n (BRIT: mother) maman f; (embalmed) momie f

mumps [mʌmps] n oreillons mpl

munch [mʌntʃ] vt, vi mâcher

municipal [mju:'nɪsɪpl] adj municipal(e)

mural ['mjuərl] n peinture murale

murder ['mə:dəʳ] n meurtre m, assassinat m ▷ vt assassiner; **murderer** n meurtrier m, assassin m

murky ['mə:kɪ] adj sombre, ténébreux(-euse); (water) trouble

murmur ['mə:məʳ] n murmure m ▷ vt, vi murmurer

muscle ['mʌsl] n muscle m; (fig) force f; **muscular** ['mʌskjuləʳ] adj musculaire; (person, arm) musclé(e)

museum [mju:'zɪəm] n musée m

mushroom ['mʌʃrum] n champignon m ▷ vi (fig) pousser comme un (or des) champignon(s)

music ['mju:zɪk] n musique f; **musical** adj musical(e); (person) musicien(ne) ▷ n (show) comédie musicale; **musical instrument** n instrument m de musique; **musician** [mju:'zɪʃən] n musicien(ne)

Muslim ['mʌzlɪm] adj, n musulman(e)

muslin ['mʌzlɪn] n mousseline f

mussel ['mʌsl] n moule f

must [mʌst] *aux vb* (*obligation*): **I ~ do it** je dois le faire, il faut que je le fasse; (*probability*): **he ~ be there by now** il doit y être maintenant, il y est probablement maintenant; (*suggestion, invitation*): **you ~ come and see me** il faut que vous veniez me voir ▷ *n* nécessité *f*, impératif *m*; **it's a ~** c'est indispensable; **I ~ have made a mistake** j'ai dû me tromper

mustache ['mʌstæʃ] *n* (*US*) = **moustache**

mustard ['mʌstəd] *n* moutarde *f*

mustn't ['mʌsnt] = **must not**

mute [mju:t] *adj* muet(te)

mutilate ['mju:tɪleɪt] *vt* mutiler

mutiny ['mju:tɪnɪ] *n* mutinerie *f* ▷ *vi* se mutiner

mutter ['mʌtər] *vt, vi* marmonner, marmotter

mutton ['mʌtn] *n* mouton *m*

mutual ['mju:tʃuəl] *adj* mutuel(le), réciproque; (*benefit, interest*) commun(e)

muzzle ['mʌzl] *n* museau *m*; (*protective device*) muselière *f*; (*of gun*) gueule *f* ▷ *vt* museler

my [maɪ] *adj* mon (ma), mes *pl*; **my house/car/gloves** ma maison/ma voiture/mes gants; **I've washed my hair/cut my finger** je me suis lavé les cheveux/coupé le doigt; **is this my pen or yours?** c'est mon stylo ou c'est le vôtre?

myself [maɪ'sɛlf] *pron* (*reflexive*) me; (*emphatic*) moi-même; (*after prep*) moi; *see also* **oneself**

mysterious [mɪs'tɪərɪəs] *adj* mystérieux(-euse)

mystery ['mɪstərɪ] *n* mystère *m*

mystical ['mɪstɪkl] *adj* mystique

mystify ['mɪstɪfaɪ] *vt* (*deliberately*) mystifier; (*puzzle*) ébahir

myth [mɪθ] *n* mythe *m*; **mythology** [mɪ'θɔlədʒɪ] *n* mythologie *f*

n/a *abbr* (= *not applicable*) n.a.

nag [næg] *vt* (*scold*) être toujours après, reprendre sans arrêt

nail [neɪl] *n* (*human*) ongle *m*; (*metal*) clou *m* ▷ *vt* clouer; **to ~ sth to sth** clouer qch à qch; **to ~ sb down to a date/price** contraindre qn à accepter *or* donner une date/un prix; **nailbrush** *n* brosse *f* à ongles; **nailfile** *n* lime *f* à ongles; **nail polish** *n* vernis *m* à ongles; **nail polish remover** *n* dissolvant *m*; **nail scissors** *npl* ciseaux *mpl* à ongles; **nail varnish** *n* (*BRIT*) = **nail polish**

naïve [naɪ'i:v] *adj* naïf(-ive)

naked ['neɪkɪd] *adj* nu(e)

name [neɪm] *n* nom *m*; (*reputation*) réputation *f* ▷ *vt* nommer; (*identify*: *accomplice etc*) citer; (*price, date*) fixer, donner; **by ~** par son nom; de nom; **in the ~ of** au nom de; **what's your ~?** comment vous appelez-vous?, quel est votre nom?; **namely** *adv* à savoir

nanny ['nænɪ] *n* bonne *f* d'enfants

nap [næp] *n* (*sleep*) (petit) somme

napkin ['næpkɪn] *n* serviette *f* (de table)

nappy ['næpɪ] *n* (*BRIT*) couche *f*

narcotics [nɑ:'kɔtɪkz] *npl* (*illegal drugs*) stupéfiants *mpl*

narrative ['nærətɪv] *n* récit *m* ▷ *adj* narratif(-ive)

narrator [nə'reɪtər] *n* narrateur(-trice)

narrow ['nærəu] *adj* étroit(e); (*fig*) restreint(e), limité(e) ▷ *vi* (*road*) devenir plus étroit, se rétrécir; (*gap, difference*) se réduire; **to have a ~ escape** l'échapper belle; **narrow down** *vt* restreindre; **narrowly** *adv*: **he narrowly missed injury/the tree** il a failli se blesser/rentrer dans l'arbre; **he only narrowly missed the target** il a manqué la cible de peu *or* de justesse; **narrow-minded** *adj* à l'esprit étroit, borné(e); (*attitude*) borné(e)

nasal ['neizl] adj nasal(e)
nasty ['nɑːstɪ] adj (person: malicious)
méchant(e); (: rude) très désagréable;
(smell) dégoûtant(e); (wound, situation)
mauvais(e), vilain(e)
nation ['neiʃən] n nation f
national ['næʃənl] adj national(e) ▷ n
(abroad) ressortissant(e); (when home)
national(e); **national anthem** n hymne
national; **national dress** n costume
national; **National Health Service** n (BRIT)
service national de santé, ≈ Sécurité Sociale;
National Insurance n (BRIT) ≈ Sécurité
Sociale; **nationalist** adj, n nationaliste m/f;
nationality [næʃə'næliti] n nationalité
f; **nationalize** vt nationaliser; **national
park** n parc national; **National Trust** n
(BRIT) ≈ Caisse f nationale des monuments
historiques et des sites

● **NATIONAL TRUST**
●
● Le National Trust est un organisme
● indépendant, à but non lucratif, dont
● la mission est de protéger et de mettre
● en valeur les monuments et les sites
● britanniques en raison de leur intérêt
● historique ou de leur beauté naturelle.

nationwide ['neiʃənwaid] adj s'étendant à
l'ensemble du pays; (problem) à l'échelle du
pays entier
native ['neitiv] n habitant(e) du
pays, autochtone m/f ▷ adj du pays,
indigène; (country) natal(e); (language)
maternel(le); (ability) inné(e); **Native
American** n Indien(ne) d'Amérique ▷ adj
amérindien(ne); **native speaker** n locuteur
natif
NATO ['neitəu] n abbr (= North Atlantic Treaty
Organization) OTAN f
natural ['nætʃrəl] adj naturel(le); **natural
gas** n gaz naturel; **natural history**
n histoire naturelle; **naturally** adv
naturellement; **natural resources** npl
ressources naturelles
nature ['neitʃə'] n nature f; **by ~** par
tempérament, de nature; **nature reserve**
n (BRIT) réserve naturelle
naughty ['nɔːti] adj (child) vilain(e), pas
sage
nausea ['nɔːsiə] n nausée f
naval ['neivl] adj naval(e)
navel ['neivl] n nombril m
navigate ['nævigeit] vt (steer) diriger,
piloter ▷ vi naviguer; (Aut) indiquer la route
à suivre; **navigation** [nævi'geiʃən] n
navigation f
navy ['neivi] n marine f
navy-blue ['neivi'bluː] adj bleu marine inv
Nazi ['nɑːtsi] n Nazi(e)
NB abbr (= nota bene) NB

near [niə'] adj proche ▷ adv près ▷ prep (also:
~ to) près de ▷ vt approcher de; **in
the ~ future** dans un proche avenir; **nearby**
[niə'bai] adj proche ▷ adv tout près, à
proximité; **nearly** adv presque; **I nearly
fell** j'ai failli tomber; **it's not nearly big
enough** ce n'est vraiment pas assez grand,
c'est loin d'être assez grand; **near-sighted**
adj myope
neat [niːt] adj (person, work) soigné(e); (room
etc) bien tenu(e) or rangé(e); (solution, plan)
habile; (spirits) pur(e); **neatly** adv avec soin
or ordre; (skilfully) habilement
necessarily ['nesisərili] adv nécessairement;
not ~ pas nécessairement or forcément
necessary ['nesisri] adj nécessaire; **if ~** si
besoin est, le cas échéant
necessity [ni'sesiti] n nécessité f; chose
nécessaire or essentielle
neck [nek] n cou m; (of horse, garment)
encolure f; (of bottle) goulot m; **~ and ~** à
égalité; **necklace** ['neklis] n collier m;
necktie ['nektai] n (esp us) cravate f
nectarine ['nektərin] n brugnon m,
nectarine f
need [niːd] n besoin m ▷ vt avoir besoin de;
to ~ to do devoir faire; avoir besoin de faire;
you don't ~ to go vous n'avez pas besoin or
vous n'êtes pas obligé de partir; **a signature
is ~ed** il faut une signature; **there's no ~ to
do ….** il n'y a pas lieu de faire …, il n'est pas
nécessaire de faire …
needle ['niːdl] n aiguille f ▷ vt (inf) asticoter,
tourmenter
needless ['niːdlis] adj inutile; **~ to say, …**
inutile de dire que
needlework ['niːdlwəːk] n (activity)
travaux mpl d'aiguille; (object) ouvrage m
needn't ['niːdnt] = **need not**
needy ['niːdi] adj nécessiteux(-euse)
negative ['negətiv] n (Phot, Elec) négatif
m; (Ling) terme m de négation ▷ adj
négatif(-ive)
neglect [ni'glekt] vt négliger; (garden)
ne pas entretenir; (duty) manquer à ▷ n
(of person, duty, garden) le fait de négliger;
(state of) ~ abandon m; **to ~ to do sth**
négliger or omettre de faire qch; **to ~ one's
appearance** se négliger
negotiate [ni'gəuʃieit] vi négocier ▷ vt
négocier; (obstacle) franchir, négocier;
to ~ with sb for sth négocier avec qn en
vue d'obtenir qch
negotiation [nigəuʃi'eiʃən] n négociation
f, pourparlers mpl
negotiator [ni'gəuʃieitə'] n
négociateur(-trice)
neighbour, (us) **neighbor** ['neibə']
n voisin(e); **neighbourhood**, (us)
neighborhood n (place) quartier m;
(people) voisinage m; **neighbouring**, (us)
neighboring adj voisin(e), avoisinant(e)

neither ['naɪðə^r] *adj, pron* aucun(e) (des deux), ni l'un(e) ni l'autre ▷ *conj*: ~ **do I** moi non plus ▷ *adv*: ~ **good nor bad** ni bon ni mauvais; ~ **of them** ni l'un ni l'autre

neon ['ni:ɔn] *n* néon *m*

Nepal [nɪ'pɔ:l] *n* Népal *m*

nephew ['nɛvju:] *n* neveu *m*

nerve [nə:v] *n* nerf *m*; (*bravery*) sang-froid *m*, courage *m*; (*cheek*) aplomb *m*, toupet *m*; **nerves** *npl* (*nervousness*) nervosité *f*; **he gets on my ~s** il m'énerve

nervous ['nə:vəs] *adj* nerveux(-euse); (*anxious*) inquiet(-ète), plein(e) d'appréhension; (*timid*) intimidé(e); **nervous breakdown** *n* dépression nerveuse

nest [nɛst] *n* nid *m* ▷ *vi* (se) nicher, faire son nid

Net [nɛt] *n* (*Comput*): **the ~** (*Internet*) le Net

net [nɛt] *n* filet *m*; (*fabric*) tulle *f* ▷ *adj* net(te) ▷ *vt* (*fish etc*) prendre au filet; **netball** *n* netball *m*

Netherlands ['nɛðələndz] *npl*: **the ~** les Pays-Bas *mpl*

nett [nɛt] *adj* = **net**

nettle ['nɛtl] *n* ortie *f*

network ['nɛtwə:k] *n* réseau *m*; **there's no ~ coverage here** (*Tel*) il n'y a pas de réseau ici

neurotic [njuə'rɔtɪk] *adj* névrosé(e)

neuter ['nju:tə^r] *adj* neutre ▷ *vt* (*cat etc*) châtrer, couper

neutral ['nju:trəl] *adj* neutre ▷ *n* (*Aut*) point mort

never ['nɛvə^r] *adv* (ne …) jamais; **I ~ went** je n'y suis pas allé; **I've ~ been to Spain** je ne suis jamais allé en Espagne; ~ **again** plus jamais; ~ **in my life** jamais de ma vie; *see also* **mind**; **never-ending** *adj* interminable; **nevertheless** [nɛvəðə'lɛs] *adv* néanmoins, malgré tout

new [nju:] *adj* nouveau (nouvelle); (*brand new*) neuf (neuve); **New Age** *n* New Age *m*; **newborn** *adj* nouveau-né(e); **newcomer** ['nju:kʌmə^r] *n* nouveau venu (nouvelle venue); **newly** *adv* nouvellement, récemment

news [nju:z] *n* nouvelle(s) *f(pl)*; (*Radio, TV*) informations *fpl*, actualités *fpl*; **a piece of ~** une nouvelle; **news agency** *n* agence *f* de presse; **newsagent** *n* (*BRIT*) marchand *m* de journaux; **newscaster** *n* (*Radio, TV*) présentateur(-trice); **newsletter** *n* bulletin *m*; **newspaper** *n* journal *m*; **newsreader** *n* = **newscaster**

newt [nju:t] *n* triton *m*

New Year *n* Nouvel An; **Happy ~!** Bonne Année!; **New Year's Day** *n* le jour de l'An; **New Year's Eve** *n* la Saint-Sylvestre

New York [-'jɔ:k] *n* New York

New Zealand [-'zi:lənd] *n* Nouvelle-Zélande *f*; **New Zealander** *n* Néo-Zélandais(e)

next [nɛkst] *adj* (*in time*) prochain(e); (*seat, room*) voisin(e), d'à côté; (*meeting, bus stop*) suivant(e) ▷ *adv* la fois suivante; la prochaine fois; (*afterwards*) ensuite; ~ **to** *prep* à côté de; ~ **to nothing** presque rien; ~ **time** *adv* la prochaine fois; **the ~ day** le lendemain, le jour suivant or d'après; ~ **year** l'année prochaine; ~ **please!** (*at doctor's etc*) au suivant!; **the week after ~** dans deux semaines; **next door** *adv* à côté ▷ *adj* (*neighbour*) d'à côté; **next-of-kin** *n* parent *m* le plus proche

NHS *n abbr* (*BRIT*) = **National Health Service**

nibble ['nɪbl] *vt* grignoter

nice [naɪs] *adj* (*holiday, trip, taste*) agréable; (*flat, picture*) joli(e); (*person*) gentil(le); (*distinction, point*) subtil(e); **nicely** *adv* agréablement; joliment; gentiment; subtilement

niche [ni:ʃ] *n* (*Archit*) niche *f*

nick [nɪk] *n* (*indentation*) encoche *f*; (*wound*) entaille *f*; (*BRIT inf*): **in good ~** en bon état ▷ *vt* (*BRIT inf: steal*) faucher, piquer; (*cut*): **to ~ o.s.** se couper; **in the ~ of time** juste à temps

nickel ['nɪkl] *n* nickel *m*; (*US*) pièce *f* de 5 cents

nickname ['nɪkneɪm] *n* surnom *m* ▷ *vt* surnommer

nicotine ['nɪkəti:n] *n* nicotine *f*

niece [ni:s] *n* nièce *f*

Nigeria [naɪ'dʒɪərɪə] *n* Nigéria *m/f*

night [naɪt] *n* nuit *f*; (*evening*) soir *m*; **at ~** la nuit; **by ~** de nuit; **last ~** (*evening*) hier soir; (*night-time*) la nuit dernière; **night club** *n* boîte *f* de nuit; **nightdress** *n* chemise *f* de nuit; **nightie** ['naɪtɪ] *n* chemise *f* de nuit; **nightlife** *n* vie *f* nocturne; **nightly** *adj* (*news*) du soir; (*by night*) nocturne ▷ *adv* (*every evening*) tous les soirs; (*every night*) toutes les nuits; **nightmare** *n* cauchemar *m*; **night school** *n* cours *mpl* du soir; **night shift** *n* équipe *f* de nuit; **night-time** *n* nuit *f*

nil [nɪl] *n* (*BRIT Sport*) zéro *m*

nine [naɪn] *num* neuf; **nineteen** [naɪn'ti:n] *num* dix-neuf; **nineteenth** [naɪn'ti:nθ] *num* dix-neuvième; **ninetieth** ['naɪntɪɪθ] *num* quatre-vingt-dixième; **ninety** *num* quatre-vingt-dix

ninth [naɪnθ] *num* neuvième

nip [nɪp] *vt* pincer ▷ *vi* (*BRIT inf*): **to ~ out/ down/up** sortir/descendre/monter en vitesse

nipple ['nɪpl] *n* (*Anat*) mamelon *m*, bout *m* du sein

nitrogen ['naɪtrədʒən] *n* azote *m*

◯ **KEYWORD**

no [nəu] *adv* (*opposite of "yes"*) non; **are you coming? — no (I'm not)** est-ce que vous venez? — non; **would you like some more? — no thank you** vous en voulez encore? — non merci

▶ *adj* (*not any*) (ne ...) pas de, (ne ...) aucun(e); **I have no money/books** je n'ai pas d'argent/de livres; **no student would have done it** aucun étudiant ne l'aurait fait; **"no smoking"** "défense de fumer", **"no dogs"** "les chiens ne sont pas admis" ▶ *n* (*pl* **noes**) non *m*

nobility [nəu'bɪlɪtɪ] *n* noblesse *f*

noble ['nəubl] *adj* noble

nobody ['nəubədɪ] *pron* (ne ...) personne

nod [nɔd] *vi* faire un signe de (la) tête (*affirmatif ou amical*); (*sleep*) somnoler ▶ *vt*: **to ~ one's head** faire un signe de (la) tête; (*in agreement*) faire signe que oui ▶ *n* signe *m* de (la) tête; **nod off** *vi* s'assoupir

noise [nɔɪz] *n* bruit *m*; **I can't sleep for the ~** je n'arrive pas à dormir à cause du bruit; **noisy** *adj* bruyant(e)

nominal ['nɔmɪnl] *adj* (*rent, fee*) symbolique; (*value*) nominal(e)

nominate ['nɔmɪneɪt] *vt* (*propose*) proposer; (*appoint*) nommer; **nomination** [nɔmɪ'neɪʃən] *n* nomination *f*; **nominee** [nɔmɪ'niː] *n* candidat agréé; personne nommée

none [nʌn] *pron* aucun(e); **~ of you** aucun d'entre vous, personne parmi vous; **I have ~ left** je n'en ai plus; **he's ~ the worse for it** il ne s'en porte pas plus mal

nonetheless ['nʌnðə'les] *adv* néanmoins

non-fiction [nɔn'fɪkʃən] *n* littérature *f* non romanesque

nonsense ['nɔnsəns] *n* absurdités *fpl*, idioties *fpl*; **~!** ne dites pas d'idioties!

non: non-smoker *n* non-fumeur *m*; **non-smoking** *adj* non-fumeur; **non-stick** *adj* qui n'attache pas

noodles ['nuːdlz] *npl* nouilles *fpl*

noon [nuːn] *n* midi *m*

no-one ['nəuwʌn] *pron* = **nobody**

nor [nɔːʳ] *conj* = **neither** ▶ *adv see* **neither**

norm [nɔːm] *n* norme *f*

normal ['nɔːml] *adj* normal(e); **normally** *adv* normalement

Normandy ['nɔːməndɪ] *n* Normandie *f*

north [nɔːθ] *n* nord *m* ▶ *adj* nord *inv*; (*wind*) du nord ▶ *adv* au *or* vers le nord; **North Africa** *n* Afrique *f* du Nord; **North African** *adj* nord-africain(e), d'Afrique du Nord ▶ *n* Nord-Africain(e); **North America** *n* Amérique *f* du Nord; **North American** *n* Nord-Américain(e) ▶ *adj* nord-américain(e), d'Amérique du Nord; **northbound** ['nɔːθbaund] *adj* (*traffic*) en direction du nord; (*carriageway*) nord *inv*; **north-east** *n* nord-est *m*; **northern** ['nɔːðən] *adj* du nord, septentrional(e); **Northern Ireland** *n* Irlande *f* du Nord; **North Korea** *n* Corée *f* du Nord; **North Pole** *n*: **the North Pole** le pôle Nord; **North Sea** *n*: **the North Sea** la mer du Nord; **north-west** *n* nord-ouest *m*

Norway ['nɔːweɪ] *n* Norvège *f*; **Norwegian** [nɔː'wiːdʒən] *adj* norvégien(ne) ▶ *n* Norvégien(ne); (*Ling*) norvégien *m*

nose [nəuz] *n* nez *m*; (*of dog, cat*) museau *m*; (*fig*) flair *m*; **nose about, nose around** *vi* fouiner *or* fureter (partout); **nosebleed** *n* saignement *m* de nez; **nosey** *adj* (*inf*) curieux(-euse)

nostalgia [nɔs'tældʒɪə] *n* nostalgie *f*

nostalgic [nɔs'tældʒɪk] *adj* nostalgique

nostril ['nɔstrɪl] *n* narine *f*; (*of horse*) naseau *m*

nosy ['nəuzɪ] (*inf*) *adj* = **nosey**

not [nɔt] *adv* (ne ...) pas; **he is ~** *or* **isn't here** il n'est pas ici; **you must ~** *or* **mustn't do that** tu ne dois pas faire ça; **I hope ~** j'espère que non; **~ at all** pas du tout; (*after thanks*) de rien; **it's too late, isn't it?** c'est trop tard, n'est-ce pas?; **~ yet/now** pas encore/maintenant; *see also* **only**

notable ['nəutəbl] *adj* notable; **notably** *adv* (*particularly*) en particulier; (*markedly*) spécialement

notch [nɔtʃ] *n* encoche *f*

note [nəut] *n* note *f*; (*letter*) mot *m*; (*banknote*) billet *m* ▶ *vt* (*also*: **~ down**) noter; (*notice*) constater; **notebook** *n* carnet *m*, (*for shorthand etc*) bloc-notes *m*; **noted** ['nəutɪd] *adj* réputé(e); **notepad** *n* bloc-notes *m*; **notepaper** *n* papier *m* à lettres

nothing ['nʌθɪŋ] *n* rien *m*; **he does ~** il ne fait rien; **~ new** rien de nouveau; **for ~** (*free*) pour rien, gratuitement; (*in vain*) pour rien; **~ at all** rien du tout; **~ much** pas grand-chose

notice ['nəutɪs] *n* (*announcement, warning*) avis *m* ▶ *vt* remarquer, s'apercevoir de; **advance ~** préavis *m*; **at short ~** dans un délai très court; **until further ~** jusqu'à nouvel ordre; **to give ~, hand in one's ~** (*employee*) donner sa démission, démissionner; **to take ~ of** prêter attention à; **to bring sth to sb's ~** porter qch à la connaissance de qn; **noticeable** *adj* visible

notice board *n* (*BRIT*) panneau *m* d'affichage

notify ['nəutɪfaɪ] *vt*: **to ~ sb of sth** avertir qn de qch

notion ['nəuʃən] *n* idée *f*; (*concept*) notion *f*; **notions** *npl* (*US: haberdashery*) mercerie *f*

notorious [nəu'tɔːrɪəs] *adj* notoire (*souvent en mal*)

notwithstanding [nɔtwɪθ'stændɪŋ] *adv* néanmoins ▶ *prep* en dépit de

nought [nɔːt] *n* zéro *m*

noun [naun] *n* nom *m*

nourish ['nʌrɪʃ] *vt* nourrir; **nourishment** *n* nourriture *f*

Nov. *abbr* (= *November*) nov

novel ['nɔvl] *n* roman *m* ▶ *adj* nouveau (nouvelle), original(e); **novelist** *n* romancier *m*; **novelty** *n* nouveauté *f*

November [nəu'vɛmbəʳ] *n* novembre *m*
novice ['nɔvɪs] *n* novice *m/f*
now [nau] *adv* maintenant ▷ *conj*: ~ (that) maintenant (que); **right ~** tout de suite; **by ~** à l'heure qu'il est; **that's the fashion just ~** c'est la mode en ce moment *or* maintenant; **~ and then, ~ and again** de temps en temps; **from ~ on** dorénavant; **nowadays** ['nauədeɪz] *adv* de nos jours
nowhere ['nəuwɛəʳ] *adv* (ne …) nulle part
nozzle ['nɔzl] *n* (*of hose*) jet *m*, lance *f*; (*of vacuum cleaner*) suceur *m*
nr *abbr* (BRIT) = **near**
nuclear ['nju:klɪəʳ] *adj* nucléaire
nucleus (*pl* **nuclei**) ['nju:klɪəs, 'nju:klɪaɪ] *n* noyau *m*
nude [nju:d] *adj* nu(e) ▷ *n* (*Art*) nu *m*; **in the ~** (tout(e)) nu(e)
nudge [nʌdʒ] *vt* donner un (petit) coup de coude à
nudist ['nju:dɪst] *n* nudiste *m/f*
nudity ['nju:dɪtɪ] *n* nudité *f*
nuisance ['nju:sns] *n*: **it's a ~** c'est (très) ennuyeux *or* gênant; **he's a ~** il est assommant *or* casse-pieds; **what a ~!** quelle barbe!
numb [nʌm] *adj* engourdi(e); (*with fear*) paralysé(e)
number ['nʌmbəʳ] *n* nombre *m*; (*numeral*) chiffre *m*; (*of house, car, telephone, newspaper*) numéro *m* ▷ *vt* numéroter; (*amount to*) compter; **a ~ of** un certain nombre de; **they were seven in ~** ils étaient (au nombre de) sept; **to be ~ed among** compter parmi; **number plate** *n* (BRIT Aut) plaque *f* minéralogique *or* d'immatriculation; **Number Ten** *n* (BRIT: 10 Downing Street) résidence du Premier ministre
numerical [nju:'mɛrɪkl] *adj* numérique
numerous ['nju:mərəs] *adj* nombreux(-euse)
nun [nʌn] *n* religieuse *f*, sœur *f*
nurse [nə:s] *n* infirmière *f*; (*also*: **~maid**) bonne *f* d'enfants ▷ *vt* (*patient, cold*) soigner
nursery ['nə:sərɪ] *n* (*room*) nursery *f*; (*institution*) crèche *f*, garderie *f*; (*for plants*) pépinière *f*; **nursery rhyme** *n* comptine *f*, chansonnette *f* pour enfants; **nursery school** *n* école maternelle; **nursery slope** *n* (BRIT Ski) piste *f* pour débutants
nursing ['nə:sɪŋ] *n* (*profession*) profession *f* d'infirmière; (*care*) soins *mpl*; **nursing home** *n* clinique *f*; (*for convalescence*) maison *f* de convalescence *or* de repos; (*for old people*) maison de retraite
nurture ['nə:tʃəʳ] *vt* élever
nut [nʌt] *n* (*of metal*) écrou *m*; (*fruit: walnut*) noix *f*; (*: hazelnut*) noisette *f*; (*: peanut*) cacahuète *f* (*terme générique en anglais*)
nutmeg ['nʌtmɛg] *n* (*noix f*) muscade *f*
nutrient ['nju:trɪənt] *n* substance nutritive

nutrition [nju:'trɪʃən] *n* nutrition *f*, alimentation *f*
nutritious [nju:'trɪʃəs] *adj* nutritif(-ive), nourrissant(e)
nuts [nʌts] (*inf*) *adj* dingue
NVQ *n abbr* (BRIT) = **National Vocational Qualification**
nylon ['naɪlɔn] *n* nylon *m* ▷ *adj* de *or* en nylon

O

oak [əuk] n chêne m ▷ cpd de or en (bois de) chêne

O.A.P. n abbr (BRIT) = **old age pensioner**

oar [ɔːʳ] n aviron m, rame f

oasis (pl **oases**) [əu'eisis, əu'eisi:z] n oasis f

oath [əuθ] n serment m; (swear word) juron m; **on** (BRIT) or **under ~** sous serment; assermenté(e)

oatmeal ['outmi:l] n flocons mpl d'avoine

oats [əuts] n avoine f

obedience [ə'bi:diəns] n obéissance f

obedient [ə'bi:diənt] adj obéissant(e)

obese [əu'bi:s] adj obèse

obesity [əu'bi:sɪti] n obésité f

obey [ə'beɪ] vt obéir à; (instructions, regulations) se conformer à ▷ vi obéir

obituary [ə'bɪtjuərɪ] n nécrologie f

object n ['ɒbdʒɪkt] objet m; (purpose) but m, objet; (Ling) complément m d'objet ▷ vi [əb'dʒɛkt]: **to ~ to** (attitude) désapprouver; (proposal) protester contre, élever une objection contre; **I ~!** je proteste!; **he ~ed that ...** il a fait valoir or a objecté que ...; **money is no ~** l'argent n'est pas un problème; **objection** [əb'dʒɛkʃən] n objection f; **if you have no objection** si vous n'y voyez pas d'inconvénient; **objective** n objectif m ▷ adj objectif(-ive)

obligation [ɒblɪ'geɪʃən] n obligation f, devoir m; (debt) dette f (de reconnaissance)

obligatory [ə'blɪgətərɪ] adj obligatoire

oblige [ə'blaɪdʒ] vt (force): **to ~ sb to do** obliger or forcer qn à faire; (do a favour) rendre service à, obliger; **to be ~d to sb for sth** être obligé(e) à qn de qch

oblique [ə'bliːk] adj oblique; (allusion) indirect(e)

obliterate [ə'blɪtəreɪt] vt effacer

oblivious [ə'blɪvɪəs] adj: **~ of** oublieux(-euse) de

oblong ['ɒblɒŋ] adj oblong(ue) ▷ n rectangle m

obnoxious [əb'nɔkʃəs] adj odieux(-euse); (smell) nauséabond(e)

oboe ['əubəu] n hautbois m

obscene [əb'siːn] adj obscène

obscure [əb'skjuəʳ] adj obscur(e) ▷ vt obscurcir; (hide: sun) cacher

observant [əb'zəːvnt] adj observateur(-trice)

observation [ɔbzə'veɪʃən] n observation f; (by police etc) surveillance f

observatory [əb'zəːvətrɪ] n observatoire m

observe [əb'zəːv] vt observer; (remark) faire observer or remarquer; **observer** n observateur(-trice)

obsess [əb'sɛs] vt obséder; **obsession** [əb'sɛʃən] n obsession f; **obsessive** adj obsédant(e)

obsolete ['ɒbsəliːt] adj dépassé(e), périmé(e)

obstacle ['ɒbstəkl] n obstacle m

obstinate ['ɒbstɪnɪt] adj obstiné(e); (pain, cold) persistant(e)

obstruct [əb'strʌkt] vt (block) boucher, obstruer; (hinder) entraver; **obstruction** [əb'strʌkʃən] n obstruction f; (to plan, progress) obstacle m

obtain [əb'teɪn] vt obtenir

obvious ['ɒbvɪəs] adj évident(e), manifeste; **obviously** adv manifestement, obviously! bien sûr!; **obviously not!** évidemment pas!, bien sûr que non!

occasion [ə'keɪʒən] n occasion f; (event) événement m; **occasional** adj pris(e) (or fait(e) etc) de temps en temps; (worker, spending) occasionnel(le); **occasionally** adv de temps en temps, quelquefois

occult [ɔ'kʌlt] adj occulte ▷ n: **the ~** le surnaturel

occupant ['ɔkjupənt] n occupant m

occupation [ɔkju'peɪʃən] n occupation f; (job) métier m, profession f

occupy ['ɔkjupaɪ] vt occuper; **to ~ o.s. with** or **by doing** s'occuper à faire

occur [ə'kəːʳ] vi se produire; (difficulty, opportunity) se présenter; (phenomenon, error) se rencontrer; **to ~ to sb** venir à l'esprit de qn; **occurrence** [ə'kʌrəns] n (existence) présence f, existence f; (event) cas m, fait m

ocean ['əuʃən] n océan m

o'clock [ə'klɔk] adv: **it is 5 ~** il est 5 heures

Oct. abbr (= October) oct

October [ɔk'təubəʳ] n octobre m

octopus ['ɔktəpəs] n pieuvre f

odd [ɔd] adj (strange) bizarre, curieux(-euse); (number) impair(e); (not of a set) dépareillé(e); **60-~** 60 et quelques; **at ~ times** de temps en temps; **the ~ one out** l'exception f; **oddly** adv bizarrement, curieusement; **odds** npl (in betting) cote f; **it makes no odds** cela n'a pas

d'importance; **odds and ends** de petites choses; **at odds** en désaccord
odometer [ɔ'dɔmɪtəʳ] n (US) odomètre m
odour, (US) **odor** [ˈəʊdəʳ] n odeur f

🔵 **KEYWORD**

of [ɔv, əv] prep **1** (gen) de; **a friend of ours** un de nos amis; **a boy of 10** un garçon de 10 ans; **that was kind of you** c'était gentil de votre part
2 (expressing quantity, amount, dates etc) de; **a kilo of flour** un kilo de farine; **how much of this do you need?** combien vous en faut-il?; **there were three of them** (people) ils étaient 3; (objects) il y en avait 3; **three of us went** 3 d'entre nous y sont allé(e)s; **the 5th of July** le 5 juillet; **a quarter of 4** (US) 4 heures moins le quart
3 (from, out of) en, de; **a statue of marble** une statue de or en marbre; **made of wood** (fait) en bois

off [ɔf] adj, adv (engine) coupé(e); (light, TV) éteint(e); (tap) fermé(e); (BRIT: food) mauvais(e), avancé(e); (: milk) tourné(e); (absent) absent(e); (cancelled) annulé(e); (removed): **the lid was ~** le couvercle était retiré or n'était pas mis; (away): **to run/ drive ~** partir en courant/en voiture ▷ prep de; **to be ~** (to leave) partir, s'en aller; **to be ~ sick** être absent pour cause de maladie; **a day ~** un jour de congé; **to have an ~ day** n'être pas en forme; **he had his coat ~** il avait enlevé son manteau; **10% ~** (Comm) 10% de rabais; **5 km ~ (the road)** à 5 km (de la route); **~ the coast** au large de la côte; **it's a long way ~** c'est loin (d'ici); **I'm ~ meat** je ne mange plus de viande; je n'aime plus la viande; **on the ~ chance** à tout hasard; **~ and on, on and ~** de temps à autre
offence, (US) **offense** [əˈfɛns] n (crime) délit m, infraction f; **to take ~ at** se vexer de, s'offenser de
offend [əˈfɛnd] vt (person) offenser, blesser; **offender** n délinquant(e); (against regulations) contrevenant(e)
offense [əˈfɛns] n (US) = **offence**
offensive [əˈfɛnsɪv] adj offensant(e), choquant(e); (smell etc) très déplaisant(e); (weapon) offensif(-ive) ▷ n (Mil) offensive f
offer [ˈɔfəʳ] n offre f, proposition f ▷ vt offrir, proposer; **"on ~"** (Comm) "en promotion"
offhand [ɔfˈhænd] adj désinvolte ▷ adv spontanément
office [ˈɔfɪs] n (place) bureau m; (position) charge f, fonction f; **doctor's ~** (US) cabinet (médical); **to take ~** entrer en fonctions; **office block**, (US) **office building** n immeuble m de bureaux; **office hours** npl heures fpl de bureau; (US Med) heures de consultation

officer [ˈɔfɪsəʳ] n (Mil etc) officier m; (also: **police ~**) agent m (de police); (of organization) membre m du bureau directeur
office worker n employé(e) de bureau
official [əˈfɪʃl] adj (authorized) officiel(le) ▷ n officiel m; (civil servant) fonctionnaire m/f; (of railways, post office, town hall) employé(e)
off: **off-licence** n (BRIT: shop) débit m de vins et de spiritueux; **off-line** adj (Comput) (en mode) autonome (: switched off) non connecté(e); **off-peak** adj aux heures creuses; (electricity, ticket) au tarif heures creuses; **off-putting** adj (BRIT) (remark) rébarbatif(-ive); (person) rebutant(e), peu engageant(e); **off-season** adj, adv hors-saison inv
offset [ˈɔfsɛt] vt (irreg: like **set**) (counteract) contrebalancer, compenser
offshore [ɔfˈʃɔːʳ] adj (breeze) de terre; (island) proche du littoral; (fishing) côtier(-ière)
offside [ˈɔfsaɪd] adj (Sport) hors jeu; (Aut: in Britain) de droite; (: in US, Europe) de gauche
offspring [ˈɔfsprɪŋ] n progéniture f
often [ˈɔfn] adv souvent; **how ~ do you go?** vous y allez tous les combien?; **every so ~** de temps en temps, de temps à autre
oh [əʊ] excl ô!, oh!, ah!
oil [ɔɪl] n huile f; (petroleum) pétrole m; (for central heating) mazout m ▷ vt (machine) graisser; **oil filter** n (Aut) filtre m à huile; **oil painting** n peinture f à l'huile; **oil refinery** n raffinerie f de pétrole; **oil rig** n derrick m; (at sea) plate-forme pétrolière; **oil slick** n nappe f de mazout; **oil tanker** n (ship) pétrolier m; (truck) camion-citerne m; **oil well** n puits m de pétrole; **oily** adj huileux(-euse); (food) gras(se)
ointment [ˈɔɪntmənt] n onguent m
O.K., okay [ˈəʊˈkeɪ] (inf) excl d'accord! ▷ vt approuver, donner son accord à ▷ adj (not bad) pas mal; **is it ~?, are you ~?** ça va?
old [əʊld] adj vieux (vieille); (person) vieux, âgé(e); (former) ancien(ne), vieux; **how ~ are you?** quel âge avez-vous?; **he's 10 years ~** il a 10 ans, il est âgé de 10 ans; **~er brother/sister** frère/sœur aîné(e); **old age** n vieillesse f; **old-age pensioner** n (BRIT) retraité(e); **old-fashioned** adj démodé(e); (person) vieux jeu inv; **old people's home** n (esp BRIT) maison f de retraite
olive [ˈɔlɪv] n (fruit) olive f; (tree) olivier m ▷ adj (also: **~-green**) (vert) olive inv; **olive oil** n huile f d'olive
Olympic® [əʊˈlɪmpɪk] adj olympique; **the ~ Games®, the ~s®** les Jeux mpl olympiques
omelet(te) [ˈɔmlɪt] n omelette f
omen [ˈəʊmən] n présage m
ominous [ˈɔmɪnəs] adj menaçant(e), inquiétant(e); (event) de mauvais augure
omit [əʊˈmɪt] vt omettre

on [ɔn] *prep* **1** (*indicating position*) sur; **on the table** sur la table; **on the wall** sur le *or* au mur; **on the left** à gauche
2 (*indicating means, method, condition etc*): **on foot** à pied; **on the train/plane** (*be*) dans le train/l'avion; (*go*) en train/avion; **on the telephone/radio/television** au téléphone/à la radio/à la télévision; **to be on drugs** se droguer; **on holiday**, (*US*) **on vacation** en vacances
3 (*referring to time*): **on Friday** vendredi; **on Fridays** le vendredi; **on June 20th** le 20 juin; **a week on Friday** vendredi en huit; **on arrival** à l'arrivée; **on seeing this** en voyant cela
4 (*about, concerning*) sur, de; **a book on Balzac/physics** un livre sur Balzac/de physique
▸ *adv* **1** (*referring to dress*): **to have one's coat on** avoir (mis) son manteau; **to put one's coat on** mettre son manteau; **what's she got on?** qu'est-ce qu'elle porte?
2 (*referring to covering*): **screw the lid on tightly** vissez bien le couvercle
3 (*further, continuously*): **to walk** *etc* **on** continuer à marcher *etc*; **from that day on** depuis ce jour
▸ *adj* **1** (*in operation: machine*) en marche; (: *radio, TV, light*) allumé(e); (: *tap, gas*) ouvert(e); (: *brakes*) mis(e); **is the meeting still on?** (*not cancelled*) est-ce que la réunion a bien lieu?; **when is this film on?** quand passe ce film?
2 (*inf*): **that's not on!** (*not acceptable*) cela ne se fait pas!; (*not possible*) pas question!

once [wʌns] *adv* une fois; (*formerly*) autrefois ▸ *conj* une fois que + *sub*; ~ **he had left/it was done** une fois qu'il fut parti/ que ce fut terminé; **at** ~ tout de suite, immédiatement; (*simultaneously*) à la fois; **all at** ~ *adv* tout d'un coup; ~ **a week** une fois par semaine; ~ **more** encore une fois; ~ **and for all** une fois pour toutes; ~ **upon a time there was …** il y avait une fois …, il était une fois …

oncoming [ˈɔnkʌmɪŋ] *adj* (*traffic*) venant en sens inverse

one [wʌn] *num* un(e); **one hundred and fifty** cent cinquante; **one by one** un(e) à *or* par un(e); **one day** un jour
▸ *adj* **1** (*sole*) seul(e), unique; **the one book which** l'unique *or* le seul livre qui; **the one man who** le seul (homme) qui
2 (*same*) même; **they came in the one car** ils sont venus dans la même voiture
▸ *pron* **1**: **this one** celui-ci (celle-ci); **that**

one celui-là (celle-là); **I've already got one/a red one** j'en ai déjà un(e)/un(e) rouge; **which one do you want?** lequel voulez-vous?
2: **one another** l'un(e) l'autre; **to look at one another** se regarder
3 (*impersonal*) on; **one never knows** on ne sait jamais; **to cut one's finger** se couper le doigt; **one needs to eat** il faut manger

one-off [wʌnˈɔf] *n* (*BRIT inf*) exemplaire *m* unique
oneself [wʌnˈsɛlf] *pron* se; (*after prep, also emphatic*) soi-même; **to hurt** ~ se faire mal; **to keep sth for** ~ garder qch pour soi; **to talk to** ~ se parler à soi-même; **by** ~ tout seul
one: one-shot [wʌnˈʃɔt] (*US*) *n* = **one-off**; **one-sided** *adj* (*argument, decision*) unilatéral(e); **one-to-one** *adj* (*relationship*) univoque; **one-way** *adj* (*street, traffic*) à sens unique
ongoing [ˈɔngəʊɪŋ] *adj* en cours; (*relationship*) suivi(e)
onion [ˈʌnjən] *n* oignon *m*
on-line [ˈɔnlaɪn] *adj* (*Comput*) en ligne (: *switched on*) connecté(e)
onlooker [ˈɔnlʊkə^r] *n* spectateur(-trice)
only [ˈəʊnlɪ] *adv* seulement ▸ *adj* seul(e), unique ▸ *conj* seulement, mais; **an** ~ **child** un enfant unique; **not** ~ **… but also** non seulement … mais aussi; **I** ~ **took one** j'en ai seulement pris un, je n'en ai pris qu'un
on-screen [ɔnˈskriːn] *adj* à l'écran
onset [ˈɔnsɛt] *n* début *m*; (*of winter, old age*) approche *f*
onto [ˈɔntu] *prep* sur
onward(s) [ˈɔnwəd(z)] *adv* (*move*) en avant; **from that time** ~ à partir de ce moment
oops [ups] *excl* houp!
ooze [uːz] *vi* suinter
opaque [əʊˈpeɪk] *adj* opaque
open [ˈəʊpn] *adj* ouvert(e); (*car*) découvert(e); (*road, view*) dégagé(e); (*meeting*) public(-ique); (*admiration*) manifeste ▸ *vt* ouvrir ▸ *vi* (*flower, eyes, door, debate*) s'ouvrir; (*shop, bank, museum*) ouvrir; (*book etc: commence*) commencer, débuter; **is it** ~ **to public?** est-ce ouvert au public?; **what time do you** ~? à quelle heure ouvrez-vous?; **in the** ~ (**air**) en plein air; **open up** *vt* ouvrir; (*blocked road*) dégager ▸ *vi* s'ouvrir; **open-air** *adj* en plein air; **opening** *n* ouverture *f*; (*opportunity*) occasion *f*; (*work*) débouché *m*; (*job*) poste vacant; **opening hours** *npl* heures *fpl* d'ouverture; **open learning** *n* enseignement universitaire à la carte, notamment par correspondance; (*distance learning*) télé-enseignement *m*; **openly** *adv* ouvertement; **open-minded** *adj* à l'esprit ouvert; **open-necked** *adj* à col ouvert; **open-plan** *adj* sans cloisons;

Open University n (BRIT) cours
universitaires par correspondance

● **OPEN UNIVERSITY**
●
● L'Open University a été fondée en 1969.
● L'enseignement comprend des cours
● (certaines plages horaires sont réservées
● à cet effet à la télévision et à la radio), des
● devoirs qui sont envoyés par l'étudiant à
● son directeur ou sa directrice d'études, et
● un séjour obligatoire en université d'été.
● Il faut préparer un certain nombre
● d'unités de valeur pendant une période
● de temps déterminée et obtenir la
● moyenne à un certain nombre d'entre
● elles pour recevoir le diplôme visé.

opera ['ɔpərə] n opéra m; **opera house** n
opéra m; **opera singer** n chanteur(-euse)
d'opéra
operate ['ɔpəreɪt] vt (machine) faire
marcher, faire fonctionner ▷ vi fonctionner;
to ~ on sb (for) (Med) opérer qn (de)
operating room n (US Med) salle f
d'opération
operating theatre n (BRIT Med) salle f
d'opération
operation [ɔpə'reɪʃən] n opération f; (of
machine) fonctionnement m; **to have an ~
(for)** se faire opérer (de); **to be in ~** (machine)
être en service; (system) être en vigueur;
operational adj opérationnel(le); (ready for
use) en état de marche
operative ['ɔpərətɪv] adj (measure) en
vigueur ▷ n (in factory) ouvrier(-ière)
operator ['ɔpəreɪtər] n (of machine)
opérateur(-trice); (Tel) téléphoniste m/f
opinion [ə'pɪnjən] n opinion f, avis m; **in
my ~** à mon avis; **opinion poll** n
sondage m d'opinion
opponent [ə'pəunənt] n adversaire m/f
opportunity [ɔpə'tjuːnɪtɪ] n occasion f;
to take the ~ to do or **of doing** profiter de
l'occasion pour faire
oppose [ə'pəuz] vt s'opposer à; **to be ~d
to sth** être opposé(e) à qch; **as ~d to** par
opposition à
opposite ['ɔpəzɪt] adj opposé(e); (house etc)
d'en face ▷ adv en face ▷ prep en face de ▷ n
opposé m, contraire m; (of word) contraire
opposition [ɔpə'zɪʃən] n opposition f
oppress [ə'prɛs] vt opprimer
opt [ɔpt] vi: **to ~ for** opter pour; **to ~ to
do** choisir de faire; **opt out** vi: **to ~ out of**
choisir de ne pas participer à or de ne pas
faire
optician [ɔp'tɪʃən] n opticien(ne)
optimism ['ɔptɪmɪzəm] n optimisme m
optimist ['ɔptɪmɪst] n optimiste m/f;
optimistic [ɔptɪ'mɪstɪk] adj optimiste
optimum ['ɔptɪməm] adj optimum

option ['ɔpʃən] n choix m, option f; (Scol)
matière f à option; **optional** adj facultatif(-ive)
or [ɔːʳ] conj ou; (with negative): **he hasn't
seen or heard anything** il n'a rien vu ni
entendu; **or else** sinon; ou bien
oral ['ɔːrəl] adj oral(e) ▷ n oral m
orange ['ɔrɪndʒ] n (fruit) orange f ▷ adj
orange inv; **orange juice** n jus m d'orange
orbit ['ɔːbɪt] n orbite f ▷ vt graviter autour de
orchard ['ɔːtʃəd] n verger m
orchestra ['ɔːkɪstrə] n orchestre m; (US:
seating) (fauteuils mpl d')orchestre
orchid ['ɔːkɪd] n orchidée f
ordeal [ɔː'diːl] n épreuve f
order ['ɔːdəʳ] n ordre m; (Comm) commande
f ▷ vt ordonner; (Comm) commander; **in ~**
en ordre; (document) en règle; **out of ~** (not
in correct order) en désordre; (machine) hors
service; (telephone) en dérangement; **a
machine in working ~** une machine en état
de marche; **in ~ to do/that** pour faire/que
+ sub; **could I ~ now, please?** je peux
commander, s'il vous plaît?; **to be on ~** être
en commande; **to ~ sb to do** ordonner à qn
de faire; **order form** n bon m de commande;
orderly n (Mil) ordonnance f; (Med) garçon
m de salle ▷ adj (room) en ordre; (mind)
méthodique; (person) qui a de l'ordre
ordinary ['ɔːdnrɪ] adj ordinaire, normal(e);
(pej) ordinaire, quelconque; **out of the ~**
exceptionnel(le)
ore [ɔːʳ] n minerai m
oregano [ɔrɪ'gɑːnəu] n origan m
organ ['ɔːgən] n organe m; (Mus) orgue
m, orgues fpl; **organic** [ɔː'gænɪk] adj
organique; (crops etc) biologique,
naturel(le); **organism** n organisme m
organization [ɔːgənaɪ'zeɪʃən] n
organisation f
organize ['ɔːgənaɪz] vt organiser;
organized ['ɔːgənaɪzd] adj (planned)
organisé(e); (efficient) bien organisé;
organizer n organisateur(-trice)
orgasm ['ɔːgæzəm] n orgasme m
orgy ['ɔːdʒɪ] n orgie f
oriental [ɔːrɪ'ɛntl] adj oriental(e)
orientation [ɔːrɪɛn'teɪʃən] n (attitudes)
tendance f; (in job) orientation f; (of building)
orientation, exposition f
origin ['ɔrɪdʒɪn] n origine f
original [ə'rɪdʒɪnl] adj original(e); (earliest)
originel(le) ▷ n original m; **originally** adv (at
first) à l'origine
originate [ə'rɪdʒɪneɪt] vi: **to ~ from** être
originaire de; (suggestion) provenir de; **to ~
in** (custom) prendre naissance dans, avoir
son origine dans
Orkney ['ɔːknɪ] n (also: **the ~s, the ~
Islands**) les Orcades fpl
ornament ['ɔːnəmənt] n ornement m;
(trinket) bibelot m; **ornamental** [ɔːnə'mɛntl]
adj décoratif(-ive); (garden) d'agrément

ornate [ɔːˈneɪt] *adj* très orné(e)

orphan [ˈɔːfn] *n* orphelin(e)

orthodox [ˈɔːθədɔks] *adj* orthodoxe

orthopaedic, (*us*) **orthopedic**
[ɔːθəˈpiːdɪk] *adj* orthopédique

osteopath [ˈɔstɪəpæθ] *n* ostéopathe *m/f*

ostrich [ˈɔstrɪtʃ] *n* autruche *f*

other [ˈʌðəʳ] *adj* autre ▷ *pron*: **the ~ (one)**
l'autre; **~s** (*other people*) d'autres ▷ *adv*: **~
than** autrement que; à part; **the ~ day**
l'autre jour; **otherwise** *adv*, *conj* autrement

Ottawa [ˈɔtəwə] *n* Ottawa

otter [ˈɔtəʳ] *n* loutre *f*

ouch [autʃ] *excl* aïe!

ought [ɔːt] *aux vb*: **I ~ to do it** je devrais le
faire, il faudrait que je le fasse; **this ~ to
have been corrected** cela aurait dû être
corrigé; **he ~ to win** (*probability*) il devrait
gagner

ounce [auns] *n* once *f* (28.35*g*; 16 *in a pound*)

our [ˈauəʳ] *adj* notre, nos *pl*; *see also* **my**;
ours *pron* le (la) nôtre, les nôtres; *see also*
mine¹; **ourselves** *pl pron* (*reflexive*, *after
preposition*) nous; (*emphatic*) nous-mêmes;
see also **oneself**

oust [aust] *vt* évincer

out [aut] *adv* dehors; (*published, not at home
etc*) sorti(e); (*light, fire*) éteint(e); **~ there**
là-bas; **he's ~** (*absent*) il est sorti; **to be ~ in
one's calculations** s'être trompé dans ses
calculs; **to run/back** *etc* **~** sortir en
courant/en reculant *etc*; **~ loud** *adv* à haute
voix; **~ of** *prep* (*outside*) en dehors de;
(*because of: anger etc*) par; (*from among*): **10 ~
of 10** 10 sur 10; (*without*): **~ of petrol** sans
essence, à court d'essence; **~ of order**
(*machine*) en panne; (*Tel: line*) en
dérangement; **outback** *n* (*in Australia*)
intérieur *m*; **outbound** *adj*: **outbound
(from/for)** en partance (de/pour);
outbreak *n* (*of violence*) éruption *f*,
explosion *f*; (*of disease*) de nombreux cas;
the outbreak of war south of the border la
guerre qui s'est déclarée au sud de la
frontière; **outburst** *n* explosion *f*, accès *m*;
outcast *n* exilé(e); (*socially*) paria *m*;
outcome *n* issue *f*, résultat *m*; **outcry** *n*
tollé (général); **outdated** *adj* démodé(e);
outdoor *adj* de or en plein air; **outdoors**
adv dehors; au grand air

outer [ˈautəʳ] *adj* extérieur(e); **outer space**
n espace *m* cosmique

outfit [ˈautfɪt] *n* (*clothes*) tenue *f*

out: **outgoing** *adj* (*president, tenant*)
sortant(e); (*character*) ouvert(e),
extraverti(e); **outgoings** *npl* (*BRIT: expenses*)
dépenses *fpl*; **outhouse** *n* appentis *m*,
remise *f*

outing [ˈautɪŋ] *n* sortie *f*, excursion *f*

out: **outlaw** *n* hors-la-loi *m inv* ▷ *vt* (*person*)
mettre hors la loi; (*practice*) proscrire;
outlay *n* dépenses *fpl*; (*investment*) mise

f de fonds; **outlet** *n* (*for liquid etc*) issue *f*,
sortie *f*; (*for emotion*) exutoire *m*; (*also*: **retail
outlet**) point *m* de vente; (*us Elec*) prise *f*
de courant; **outline** *n* (*shape*) contour *m*;
(*summary*) esquisse *f*, grandes lignes ▷ *vt*
(*fig: theory, plan*) exposer à grands traits;
outlook *n* perspective *f*; (*point of view*)
attitude *f*; **outnumber** *vt* surpasser en
nombre; **out-of-date** *adj* (*passport, ticket*)
périmé(e); (*theory, idea*) dépassé(e); (*custom*)
désuet(-ète); (*clothes*) démodé(e); **out-of-
doors** *adv* = **outdoors**; **out-of-the-way**
adj loin de tout; **out-of-town** *adj* (*shopping
centre etc*) en périphérie; **outpatient** *n*
malade *m/f* en consultation externe;
outpost *n* avant-poste *m*; **output** *n*
rendement *m*, production *f*; (*Comput*) sortie
f ▷ *vt* (*Comput*) sortir

outrage [ˈautreɪdʒ] *n* (*anger*) indignation
f; (*violent act*) atrocité *f*, acte *m* de violence;
(*scandal*) scandale *m* ▷ *vt* outrager;
outrageous [autˈreɪdʒəs] *adj* atroce;
(*scandalous*) scandaleux(-euse)

outright *adv* [autˈraɪt] complètement;
(*deny, refuse*) catégoriquement; (*ask*)
carrément; (*kill*) sur le coup ▷ *adj* [ˈautraɪt]
complet(-ète); catégorique

outset [ˈautset] *n* début *m*

outside [autˈsaɪd] *n* extérieur *m* ▷ *adj*
extérieur(e) ▷ *adv* (au) dehors, à
l'extérieur ▷ *prep* hors de, à l'extérieur
de; (*in front of*) devant; **at the ~** (*fig*) au
plus or maximum; **outside lane** *n* (*Aut:
in Britain*) voie *f* de droite; (*: in US, Europe*)
voie de gauche; **outside line** *n* (*Tel*)
ligne extérieure; **outsider** *n* (*stranger*)
étranger(-ère)

out: **outsize** *adj* énorme; (*clothes*) grande
taille *inv*; **outskirts** *npl* faubourgs *mpl*;
outspoken *adj* très franc (franche);
outstanding *adj* remarquable,
exceptionnel(le); (*unfinished: work, business*)
en suspens, en souffrance; (*debt*) impayé(e);
(*problem*) non réglé(e)

outward [ˈautwəd] *adj* (*sign, appearances*)
extérieur(e); (*journey*) (d')aller; **outwards**
adv (*esp* BRIT) = **outward**

outweigh [autˈweɪ] *vt* l'emporter sur

oval [ˈəuvl] *adj*, *n* ovale *m*

ovary [ˈəuvərɪ] *n* ovaire *m*

oven [ˈʌvn] *n* four *m*; **oven glove** *n* gant *m*
de cuisine; **ovenproof** *adj* allant au four;
oven-ready *adj* prêt(e) à cuire

over [ˈəuvəʳ] *adv* (*par-*)dessus ▷ *adj* (*finished*)
fini(e), terminé(e); (*too much*) en plus ▷ *prep*
sur; par-dessus; (*above*) au-dessus de; (*on
the other side of*) de l'autre côté de; (*more
than*) plus de; (*during*) pendant; (*about,
concerning*): **they fell out ~ money/her** ils se
sont brouillés pour des questions
d'argent/à cause d'elle; **~ here** ici; **~ there**
là-bas; **all ~** (*everywhere*) partout; **~ and ~**

(again) à plusieurs reprises; **~ and above** en plus de; **to ask sb ~** inviter qn (à passer); **to fall ~** tomber; **to turn sth ~** retourner qch

overall [əʊvər'ɔ:l] *adj* (*length*) total(e); (*study, impression*) d'ensemble ▷ *n* (*BRIT*) blouse *f* ▷ *adv* dans l'ensemble, en général; **overalls** ['əʊvərɔ:lz] *npl* (*boiler suit*) bleus *mpl* (de travail)

overboard ['əʊvəbɔːd] *adv* (*Naut*) par-dessus bord

overcame [əʊvə'keɪm] *pt of* **overcome**

overcast ['əʊvəkɑːst] *adj* couvert(e)

overcharge [əʊvə'tʃɑːdʒ] *vt*: **to ~ sb for sth** faire payer qch trop cher à qn

overcoat ['əʊvəkəʊt] *n* pardessus *m*

overcome [əʊvə'kʌm] *vt* (*irreg: like* **come**) (*defeat*) triompher de; (*difficulty*) surmonter ▷ *adj* (*emotionally*) bouleversé(e); **~ with grief** accablé(e) de douleur

over: overcrowded *adj* bondé(e); (*city, country*) surpeuplé(e); **overdo** *vt* (*irreg: like* **do**) exagérer; (*overcook*) trop cuire; **to overdo it, to overdo things** (*work too hard*) en faire trop, se surmener; **overdone** [əʊvə'dʌn] *adj* (*vegetables, steak*) trop cuit(e); **overdose** *n* dose excessive; **overdraft** *n* découvert *m*; **overdrawn** *adj* (*account*) à découvert; **overdue** *adj* en retard; (*bill*) impayé(e); (*change*) qui tarde; **overestimate** *vt* surestimer

overflow *vi* [əʊvə'fləʊ] déborder ▷ *n* ['əʊvəfləʊ] (*also:* **~ pipe**) tuyau *m* d'écoulement, trop-plein *m*

overgrown [əʊvə'grəʊn] *adj* (*garden*) envahi(e) par la végétation

overhaul *vt* [əʊvə'hɔːl] réviser ▷ *n* ['əʊvəhɔːl] révision *f*

overhead *adv* [əʊvə'hɛd] au-dessus ▷ *adj* ['əʊvəhɛd] aérien(ne); (*lighting*) vertical(e) ▷ *n* ['əʊvəhɛd] (*US*) = **overheads**; **overhead projector** *n* rétroprojecteur *m*; **overheads** *npl* (*BRIT*) frais généraux

over: overhear *vt* (*irreg: like* **hear**) entendre (par hasard); **overheat** *vi* (*engine*) chauffer; **overland** *adj, adv* par voie de terre; **overlap** *vi* se chevaucher; **overleaf** *adv* au verso; **overload** *vt* surcharger; **overlook** *vt* (*have view of*) donner sur; (*miss*) oublier, négliger; (*forgive*) fermer les yeux sur

overnight *adv* [əʊvə'naɪt] (*happen*) durant la nuit; (*fig*) soudain ▷ *adj* ['əʊvənaɪt] d'une (*or* de) nuit; soudain(e); **to stay ~ (with sb)** passer la nuit (chez qn); **overnight bag** *n* nécessaire *m* de voyage

overpass ['əʊvəpɑːs] *n* (*US: for cars*) pont autoroutier; (*for pedestrians*) passerelle *f*, pont *M*

overpower [əʊvə'paʊəʳ] *vt* vaincre; (*fig*) accabler; **overpowering** *adj* irrésistible; (*heat, stench*) suffocant(e)

over: overreact [əʊvəri:'ækt] *vi* réagir de façon excessive; **overrule** *vt* (*decision*) annuler; (*claim*) rejeter; (*person*) rejeter l'avis de; **overrun** *vt* (*irreg: like* **run**) (*Mil: country etc*) occuper; (*time limit etc*) dépasser ▷ *vi* dépasser le temps imparti

overseas [əʊvə'siːz] *adv* outre-mer; (*abroad*) à l'étranger ▷ *adj* (*trade*) extérieur(e); (*visitor*) étranger(-ère)

oversee [əʊvə'siː] *vt* (*irreg: like* **see**) surveiller

overshadow [əʊvə'ʃædəʊ] *vt* (*fig*) éclipser

oversight ['əʊvəsaɪt] *n* omission *f*, oubli *m*

oversleep [əʊvə'sliːp] *vi* (*irreg: like* **sleep**) se réveiller (trop) tard

overspend [əʊvə'spɛnd] *vi* (*irreg: like* **spend**) dépenser de trop

overt [əʊ'vəːt] *adj* non dissimulé(e)

overtake [əʊvə'teɪk] *vt* (*irreg: like* **take**) dépasser; (*BRIT Aut*) dépasser, doubler

over: overthrow *vt* (*irreg: like* **throw**) (*government*) renverser; **overtime** *n* heures *fpl* supplémentaires; **overturn** *vt* renverser; (*decision, plan*) annuler ▷ *vi* se retourner; **overweight** *adj* (*person*) trop gros(se); **overwhelm** *vt* (*subj: emotion*) accabler, submerger; (*enemy, opponent*) écraser; **overwhelming** *adj* (*victory, defeat*) écrasant(e); (*desire*) irrésistible

owe [əʊ] *vt* devoir; **to ~ sb sth, to ~ sth to sb** devoir qch à qn; **how much do I ~ you?** combien est-ce que je vous dois?; **owing to** *prep* à cause de, en raison de

owl [aʊl] *n* hibou *m*

own [əʊn] *vt* posséder ▷ *adj* propre; **a room of my ~** une chambre à moi, ma propre chambre; **to get one's ~ back** prendre sa revanche; **on one's ~** tout(e) seul(e); **own up** *vi* avouer; **owner** *n* propriétaire *m/f*; **ownership** *n* possession *f*

ox (*pl* **oxen**) [ɔks, 'ɔksn] *n* bœuf *m*

Oxbridge ['ɔksbrɪdʒ] *n* (*BRIT*) *les universités d'Oxford et de Cambridge*

oxen ['ɔksən] *npl of* **ox**

oxygen ['ɔksɪdʒən] *n* oxygène *m*

oyster ['ɔɪstəʳ] *n* huître *f*

oz. *abbr* = **ounce; ounces**

ozone ['əʊzəʊn] *n* ozone *m*; **ozone friendly** *adj* qui n'attaque pas *or* qui préserve la couche d'ozone; **ozone layer** *n* couche *f* d'ozone

P

p *abbr* (BRIT) = **penny; pence**

P.A. *n abbr* = **personal assistant; public address system**

p.a. *abbr* = **per annum**

pace [peɪs] *n* pas *m*; (*speed*) allure *f*, vitesse *f* ▷ *vi*: **to ~ up and down** faire les cent pas; **to keep ~ with** aller à la même vitesse que; (*events*) se tenir au courant de; **pacemaker** *n* (*Med*) stimulateur *m* cardiaque, (*Sport: also*: **pacesetter**) meneur(-euse) de train

Pacific [pəˈsɪfɪk] *n*: **the ~ (Ocean)** le Pacifique, l'océan *m* Pacifique

pacifier [ˈpæsɪfaɪəʳ] *n* (US: *dummy*) tétine *f*

pack [pæk] *n* paquet *m*; (*of hounds*) meute *f*; (*of thieves, wolves etc*) bande *f*; (*of cards*) jeu *m*; (US: *of cigarettes*) paquet; (*back pack*) sac *m* à dos ▷ *vt* (*goods*) empaqueter, emballer; (*in suitcase etc*) emballer; (*box*) remplir; (*cram*) entasser ▷ *vi*: **to ~ (one's bags)** faire ses bagages; **pack in** (BRIT *inf*) *vi* (*machine*) tomber en panne ▷ *vt* (*boyfriend*) plaquer; **~ it in!** laisse tomber!; **pack off** *vt*: **to ~ sb off to** expédier qn à; **pack up** *vi* (BRIT *inf*: *machine*) tomber en panne; (*person*) se tirer ▷ *vt* (*belongings*) ranger; (*goods, presents*) empaqueter, emballer

package [ˈpækɪdʒ] *n* paquet *m*; (*also*: **~ deal**) (*agreement*) marché global; (*purchase*) forfait *m*; (*Comput*) progiciel *m* ▷ *vt* (*goods*) conditionner; **package holiday** *n* (BRIT) vacances organisées; **package tour** *n* voyage organisé

packaging [ˈpækɪdʒɪŋ] *n* (*wrapping materials*) emballage *m*

packed [pækt] *adj* (*crowded*) bondé(e); **packed lunch** (BRIT) *n* repas froid

packet [ˈpækɪt] *n* paquet *m*

packing [ˈpækɪŋ] *n* emballage *m*

pact [pækt] *n* pacte *m*, traité *m*

pad [pæd] *n* bloc(-notes *m*) *m*; (*to prevent friction*) tampon *m* ▷ *vt* rembourrer; **padded** *adj* (*jacket*) matelassé(e); (*bra*) rembourré(e)

paddle [ˈpædl] *n* (*oar*) pagaie *f*; (US: *for table tennis*) raquette *f* de ping-pong ▷ *vi* (*with feet*) barboter, faire trempette ▷ *vt*: **to ~ a canoe** *etc* pagayer; **paddling pool** *n* petit bassin

paddock [ˈpædək] *n* enclos *m*; (*Racing*) paddock *m*

padlock [ˈpædlɔk] *n* cadenas *m*

paedophile, (US) **pedophile** [ˈpiːdəufaɪl] *n* pédophile *m*

page [peɪdʒ] *n* (*of book*) page *f*; (*also*: **~ boy**) groom *m*, chasseur *m*; (*at wedding*) garçon *m* d'honneur ▷ *vt* (*in hotel etc*) (faire) appeler

pager [ˈpeɪdʒəʳ] *n* bip *m* (*inf*), Alphapage® *m*

paid [peɪd] *pt, pp of* **pay** ▷ *adj* (*work, official*) rémunéré(e); (*holiday*) payé(e); **to put ~ to** (BRIT) mettre fin à, mettre par terre

pain [peɪn] *n* douleur *f*; (*inf: nuisance*) plaie *f*; **to be in ~** souffrir, avoir mal; **to take ~s to do** se donner du mal pour faire; **painful** *adj* douloureux(-euse); (*difficult*) difficile, pénible; **painkiller** *n* calmant *m*, analgésique *m*; **painstaking** [ˈpeɪnzteɪkɪŋ] *adj* (*person*) soigneux(-euse); (*work*) soigné(e)

paint [peɪnt] *n* peinture *f* ▷ *vt* peindre; **to ~ the door blue** peindre la porte en bleu; **paintbrush** *n* pinceau *m*; **painter** *n* peintre *m*; **painting** *n* peinture *f*; (*picture*) tableau *m*

pair [peəʳ] *n* (*of shoes, gloves etc*) paire *f*; (*of people*) couple *m*: **~ of scissors** (paire de) ciseaux *mpl*; **~ of trousers** pantalon *m*

pajamas [pəˈdʒɑːməz] *npl* (US) pyjama *m*

Pakistan [pɑːkɪˈstɑːn] *n* Pakistan *m*; **Pakistani** *adj* pakistanais(e) ▷ *n* Pakistanais(e)

pal [pæl] *n* (*inf*) copain (copine)

palace [ˈpæləs] *n* palais *m*

pale [peɪl] *adj* pâle; **~ blue** *adj* bleu pâle *inv*

Palestine [ˈpælɪstaɪn] *n* Palestine *f*; **Palestinian** [pælɪsˈtɪnɪən] *adj* palestinien(ne) ▷ *n* Palestinien(ne)

palm [pɑːm] *n* (*Anat*) paume *f*; (*also*: **~ tree**) palmier *m* ▷ *vt*: **to ~ sth off on sb** (*inf*) refiler qch à qn

pamper [ˈpæmpəʳ] *vt* gâter, dorloter

pamphlet [ˈpæmflət] *n* brochure *f*

pan [pæn] *n* (*also*: **sauce~**) casserole *f*; (*also*: **frying ~**) poêle *f*

pancake [ˈpænkeɪk] *n* crêpe *f*

panda [ˈpændə] *n* panda *m*

pandemic [pænˈdɛmɪk] *n* pandémie *f*

pane [peɪn] *n* carreau *m* (de fenêtre), vitre *f*

panel [ˈpænl] *n* (*of wood, cloth etc*) panneau *m*; (*Radio, TV*) panel *m*, invités *mpl*; (*for interview, exams*) jury *m*

panhandler [ˈpænhændləʳ] *n* (US *inf*) mendiant(e)

panic [ˈpænɪk] *n* panique *f*, affolement *m* ▷ *vi* s'affoler, paniquer

panorama [pænəˈrɑːmə] *n* panorama *m*

pansy [ˈpænzɪ] *n* (*Bot*) pensée *f*

pant [pænt] *vi* haleter
panther ['pænθə^r] *n* panthère *f*
panties ['pæntɪz] *npl* slip *m*, culotte *f*
pantomime ['pæntəmaɪm] *n* (BRIT) spectacle *m* de Noël

● **PANTOMIME**
●
● Une *pantomime* (à ne pas confondre avec
● le mot tel qu'on l'utilise en français),
● que l'on appelle également de façon
● familière "panto", est un genre de farce
● où le personnage principal est souvent
● un jeune garçon et où il y a toujours une
● "dame", c'est-à-dire une vieille femme
● jouée par un homme, et un méchant. La
● plupart du temps, l'histoire est basée sur
● un conte de fées comme Cendrillon ou
● Le Chat botté, et le public est encouragé
● à participer en prévenant le héros d'un
● danger imminent. Ce genre de spectacle,
● qui s'adresse surtout aux enfants, vise
● également un public d'adultes au travers
● des nombreuses plaisanteries faisant
● allusion à des faits d'actualité.

pants [pænts] *npl* (BRIT: woman's) culotte *f*, slip *m*; (: man's) slip, caleçon *m*; (US: trousers) pantalon *m*
pantyhose ['pæntɪhəʊz] *npl* (US) collant *m*
paper ['peɪpə^r] *n* papier *m*; (also: **wall~**) papier peint; (also: **news~**) journal *m*; (academic essay) article *m*; (exam) épreuve écrite ▷ adj en or de papier ▷ vt tapisser (de papier peint); **papers** *npl* (also: **identity ~s**) papiers *mpl* (d'identité); **paperback** *n* livre broché or non relié; (small) livre m de poche; **paper bag** *n* sac *m* en papier; **paper clip** *n* trombone *m*; **paper shop** *n* (BRIT) marchand de journaux; **paperwork** *n* papiers *mpl*; (pej) paperasserie *f*
paprika ['pæprɪkə] *n* paprika *m*
par [pɑː^r] *n* pair *m*; (Golf) normale *f* du parcours; **on a ~ with** à égalité avec, au même niveau que
paracetamol [pærə'siːtəmɔl] *n* (BRIT) paracétamol *m*
parachute ['pærəʃuːt] *n* parachute *m*
parade [pə'reɪd] *n* défilé *m* ▷ vt (fig) faire étalage de ▷ vi défiler
paradise ['pærədaɪs] *n* paradis *m*
paradox ['pærədɔks] *n* paradoxe *m*
paraffin ['pærəfɪn] *n* (BRIT): **~ (oil)** pétrole (lampant)
paragraph ['pærəgrɑːf] *n* paragraphe *m*
parallel ['pærəlɛl] *adj*: **~ (with or to)** parallèle (à); (fig) analogue (à) ▷ n (line) parallèle *f*; (fig, Geo) parallèle *m*
paralysed ['pærəlaɪzd] *adj* paralysé(e)
paralysis (pl **paralyses**) [pə'rælɪsɪs, -siːz] *n* paralysie *f*

paramedic [pærə'mɛdɪk] *n* auxiliaire *m/f* médical(e)
paranoid ['pærənɔɪd] *adj* (Psych) paranoïaque; (neurotic) paranoïde
parasite ['pærəsaɪt] *n* parasite *m*
parcel ['pɑːsl] *n* paquet *m*, colis *m* ▷ vt (also: **~ up**) empaqueter
pardon ['pɑːdn] *n* pardon *m*; (Law) grâce *f* ▷ vt pardonner à; (Law) gracier; **~ me!** pardon!; **~ me!** (after burping etc) excusez-moi!; **I beg your ~!** (I'm sorry) pardon!, je suis désolé!; **(I beg your) ~?**, (US) **~ me?** (what did you say?) pardon?
parent ['pɛərənt] *n* (father) père *m*; (mother) mère *f*; **parents** *npl* parents *mpl*; **parental** [pə'rɛntl] *adj* parental(e), des parents
Paris ['pærɪs] *n* Paris
parish ['pærɪʃ] *n* paroisse *f*; (BRIT: civil) ≈ commune *f*
Parisian [pə'rɪzɪən] *adj* parisien(ne), de Paris ▷ n Parisien(ne)
park [pɑːk] *n* parc *m*, jardin public ▷ vt garer ▷ vi se garer; **can I ~ here?** est-ce que je peux me garer ici?
parking ['pɑːkɪŋ] *n* stationnement *m*; **"no ~"** "stationnement interdit"; **parking lot** *n* (US) parking *m*, parc *m* de stationnement; **parking meter** *n* parc(o)mètre *m*; **parking ticket** *n* P.-V. *m*

▌ Be careful not to translate *parking* by the
▌ French word *parking*.

parkway ['pɑːkweɪ] *n* (US) route *f* express (en site vert ou aménagé)
parliament ['pɑːləmənt] *n* parlement *m*; **parliamentary** [pɑːlə'mɛntərɪ] *adj* parlementaire
Parmesan [pɑːmɪ'zæn] *n* (also: **~ cheese**) Parmesan *m*
parole [pə'rəʊl] *n*: **on ~** en liberté conditionnelle
parrot ['pærət] *n* perroquet *m*
parsley ['pɑːslɪ] *n* persil *m*
parsnip ['pɑːsnɪp] *n* panais *m*
parson ['pɑːsn] *n* ecclésiastique *m*; (Church of England) pasteur *m*
part [pɑːt] *n* partie *f*; (of machine) pièce *f*; (Theat) rôle *m*; (of serial) épisode *m*; (US: in hair) raie *f* ▷ adv = **partly** ▷ vt séparer ▷ vi (people) se séparer; (crowd) s'ouvrir; **to take ~ in** participer à, prendre part à; **to take sb's ~** prendre le parti de qn, prendre parti pour qn; **for my ~** en ce qui me concerne; **for the most ~** en grande partie; dans la plupart des cas; **in ~** en partie; **to take sth in good/bad ~** prendre qch du bon/ mauvais côté; **part with** *vt fus* (person) se séparer de; (possessions) se défaire de
partial ['pɑːʃl] *adj* (incomplete) partiel(le); **to be ~ to** aimer, avoir un faible pour
participant [pɑː'tɪsɪpənt] *n* (in competition, campaign) participant(e)
participate [pɑː'tɪsɪpeɪt] *vi*: **to ~ (in)** participer (à), prendre part (à)

particle ['pɑ:tɪkl] n particule f; (of dust) grain m

particular [pə'tɪkjulə'] adj (specific) particulier(-ière); (special) particulier, spécial(e); (fussy) difficile, exigeant(e); (careful) méticuleux(-euse); **in ~** en particulier, surtout; **particularly** adv particulièrement; (in particular) en particulier; **particulars** npl détails mpl; (information) renseignements mpl

parting ['pɑ:tɪŋ] n séparation f; (BRIT: in hair) raie f

partition [pɑ:'tɪʃən] n (Pol) partition f, division f; (wall) cloison f

partly ['pɑ:tlɪ] adv en partie, partiellement

partner ['pɑ:tnə'] n (Comm) associé(e); (Sport) partenaire m/f; (spouse) conjoint(e); (lover) ami(e); (at dance) cavalier(-ière); **partnership** n association f

partridge ['pɑ:trɪdʒ] n perdrix f

part-time ['pɑ:t'taɪm] adj, adv à mi-temps, à temps partiel

party ['pɑ:tɪ] n (Pol) parti m; (celebration) fête f; (: formal) réception f; (: in evening) soirée f; (group) groupe m; (Law) partie f

pass [pɑ:s] vt (time, object) passer; (place) passer devant; (friend) croiser; (exam) être reçu(e) à, réussir; (overtake) dépasser; (approve) approuver, accepter ▷ vi passer, (Scol) être reçu(e) or admis(e), réussir ▷ n (permit) laissez-passer m inv; (membership card) carte f d'accès or d'abonnement; (in mountains) col m; (Sport) passe f; (Scol: also: **~ mark**); **to get a ~** être reçu(e) (sans mention); **to ~ sth through sth** passer qch à qn; **could you ~ the salt/oil, please?** pouvez-vous me passer le sel/l'huile, s'il vous plaît?; **to make a ~ at sb** (inf) faire des avances à qn; **pass away** vi mourir; **pass by** vi passer ▷ vt (ignore) négliger; **pass on** vt (hand on): **to ~ on (to)** transmettre (à); **pass out** vi s'évanouir; **pass over** vt (ignore) passer sous silence; **pass up** vt (opportunity) laisser passer; **passable** adj (road) praticable; (work) acceptable

> Be careful not to translate to pass an exam by the French expression passer un examen.

passage ['pæsɪdʒ] n (also: **~way**) couloir m; (gen, in book) passage m; (by boat) traversée f

passenger ['pæsɪndʒə'] n passager(-ère)

passer-by [pɑ:sə'baɪ] n passant(e)

passing place n (Aut) aire f de croisement

passion ['pæʃən] n passion f; **passionate** adj passionné(e); **passion fruit** n fruit m de la passion

passive ['pæsɪv] adj (also: Ling) passif(-ive)

passport ['pɑ:spɔ:t] n passeport m; **passport control** n contrôle m des passeports; **passport office** n bureau m de délivrance des passeports

password ['pɑ:swɜ:d] n mot m de passe

past [pɑ:st] prep (in front of) devant; (further than) au delà de, plus loin que; après; (later than) après ▷ adv: **to run ~** passer en courant ▷ adj passé(e); (president etc) ancien(ne) ▷ n passé m; **he's ~ forty** il a dépassé la quarantaine, il a plus de or passé quarante ans; **ten/quarter ~ eight** (BRIT) huit heures dix/un or et quart; **for the ~ few/3 days** depuis quelques/3 jours; ces derniers/3 derniers jours

pasta ['pæstə] n pâtes fpl

paste [peɪst] n pâte f; (Culin: meat) pâté m (à tartiner); (: tomato) purée f, concentré m; (glue) colle f (de pâte) ▷ vt coller

pastel ['pæstl] adj pastel inv ▷ n (Art: pencil) (crayon m) pastel m; (: drawing) (dessin m au) pastel; (colour) ton m pastel inv

pasteurized ['pæstəraɪzd] adj pasteurisé(e)

pastime ['pɑ:staɪm] n passe-temps m inv, distraction f

pastor ['pɑ:stə'] n pasteur m

pastry ['peɪstrɪ] n pâte f; (cake) pâtisserie f

pasture ['pɑ:stʃə'] n pâturage m

pasty n ['pæstɪ] petit pâté (en croûte)

pasty² ['peɪstɪ] adj (complexion) terreux(-euse)

pat [pæt] vt donner une petite tape à; (dog) tapoter

patch [pætʃ] n (of material) pièce f; (eye patch) cache m; (spot) tache f; (of land) parcelle f; (on tyre) rustine f ▷ vt (clothes) rapiécer; **a bad ~** (BRIT) une période difficile; **patchy** adj inégal(e); (incomplete) fragmentaire

pâté ['pæteɪ] n pâté m, terrine f

patent ['peɪtnt, US 'pætnt] n brevet m (d'invention) ▷ vt faire breveter ▷ adj patent(e), manifeste

paternal [pə'tɜ:nl] adj paternel(le)

paternity leave [pə'tɜ:nɪtɪ-] n congé m de paternité

path [pɑ:θ] n chemin m, sentier m; (in garden) allée f; (of missile) trajectoire f

pathetic [pə'θetɪk] adj (pitiful) pitoyable; (very bad) lamentable, minable

pathway ['pɑ:θweɪ] n chemin m, sentier m; (in garden) allée f

patience ['peɪʃns] n patience f; (BRIT Cards) réussite f

patient ['peɪʃnt] n malade m/f; (of dentist etc) patient(e) ▷ adj patient(e)

patio ['pætɪəu] n patio m

patriotic [pætrɪ'ɔtɪk] adj patriotique; (person) patriote

patrol [pə'trəul] n patrouille f ▷ vt patrouiller dans; **patrol car** n voiture f de police

patron ['peɪtrən] n (in shop) client(e); (of charity) patron(ne); **~ of the arts** mécène m

patronizing ['pætrənaɪzɪŋ] adj condescendant(e)

pattern ['pætən] n (Sewing) patron m; (design) motif m; **patterned** adj à motifs

pause [pɔ:z] n pause f, arrêt m ▷ vi faire une pause, s'arrêter

pave [peɪv] vt paver, daller; **to ~ the way for** ouvrir la voie à

pavement ['peɪvmənt] n (BRIT) trottoir m; (US) chaussée f

pavilion [pə'vɪlɪən] n pavillon m; (Sport) stand m

paving ['peɪvɪŋ] n (material) pavé m

paw [pɔ:] n patte f

pawn [pɔ:n] n (Chess, also fig) pion m ▷ vt mettre en gage; **pawnbroker** n prêteur m sur gages

pay [peɪ] (pt, pp **paid**) n salaire m; (of manual worker) paie f ▷ vt payer ▷ vi payer; (be profitable) être rentable; **can I ~ by credit card?** est-ce que je peux payer par carte de crédit?; **to ~ attention (to)** prêter attention (à); **to ~ sb a visit** rendre visite à qn; **to ~ one's respects to sb** présenter ses respects à qn; **pay back** vt rembourser; **pay for** vt fus payer; **pay in** vt verser; **pay off** vt (debts) régler, acquitter; (person) rembourser ▷ vi (scheme, decision) se révéler payant(e); **pay out** vt (money) payer, sortir de sa poche; **pay up** vt (amount) payer; **payable** adj payable; **to make a cheque payable to sb** établir un chèque à l'ordre de qn; **pay-as-you-go** adj (mobile phone) à carte prépayée; **payday** n jour m de paie; **pay envelope** n (US) paie f; **payment** n paiement m; (of bill) règlement m; (of deposit, cheque) versement m; **monthly payment** mensualité f; **payout** n (from insurance) dédommagement m; (in competition) prix m; **pay packet** n (BRIT) paie f; **pay phone** n cabine f téléphonique, téléphone public; **pay raise** n (US) = **pay rise**; **pay rise** n (BRIT) augmentation f (de salaire); **payroll** n registre m du personnel; **pay slip** n (BRIT) bulletin m de paie, feuille f de paie; **pay television** n chaînes fpl payantes; **paywall** n (Comput) mur m (payant)

PC n abbr = **personal computer**; (BRIT) = **police constable** ▷ adj abbr = **politically correct**

p.c. abbr = **per cent**

pcm n abbr (= per calendar month) par mois

PDA n abbr (= personal digital assistant) agenda m électronique

PE n abbr (= physical education) EPS f

pea [pi:] n (petit) pois

peace [pi:s] n paix f; (calm) calme m, tranquillité f; **peaceful** adj paisible, calme

peach [pi:tʃ] n pêche f

peacock ['pi:kɔk] n paon m

peak [pi:k] n (mountain) pic m, cime f; (of cap) visière f; (fig: highest level) maximum m; (: of career, fame) apogée m; **peak hours** npl heures fpl d'affluence or de pointe

peanut ['pi:nʌt] n arachide f, cacahuète f; **peanut butter** n beurre m de cacahuète

pear [pɛəʳ] n poire f

pearl [pə:l] n perle f

peasant ['pɛznt] n paysan(ne)

peat [pi:t] n tourbe f

pebble ['pɛbl] n galet m, caillou m

peck [pɛk] vt (also: **~ at**) donner un coup de bec à; (food) picorer ▷ n coup m de bec; (kiss) bécot m; **peckish** adj (BRIT inf): **I feel peckish** je mangerais bien quelque chose, j'ai la dent

peculiar [pɪ'kju:lɪəʳ] adj (odd) étrange, bizarre, curieux(-euse); (particular) particulier(-ière); **~ to** particulier à

pedal ['pɛdl] n pédale f ▷ vi pédaler

pedestal ['pɛdəstl] n piédestal m

pedestrian [pɪ'dɛstrɪən] n piéton m; **pedestrian crossing** n (BRIT) passage clouté; **pedestrianized** adj: **a pedestrianized street** une rue piétonne; **pedestrian precinct**, (US) **pedestrian zone** n (BRIT) zone piétonne

pedigree ['pɛdɪgri:] n ascendance f; (of animal) pedigree m ▷ cpd (animal) de race

pedophile ['pi:dəufaɪl] (US) n = **paedophile**

pee [pi:] vi (inf) faire pipi, pisser

peek [pi:k] vi jeter un coup d'œil (furtif)

peel [pi:l] n pelure f, épluchure f; (of orange, lemon) écorce f ▷ vt peler, éplucher ▷ vi (paint etc) s'écailler; (wallpaper) se décoller; (skin) peler

peep [pi:p] n (look) coup d'œil furtif; (sound) pépiement m ▷ vi jeter un coup d'œil (furtif)

peer [pɪəʳ] vi: **to ~ at** regarder attentivement, scruter ▷ n (noble) pair m; (equal) pair, égal(e)

peg [pɛg] n (for coat etc) patère f; (BRIT: also: **clothes ~**) pince f à linge

pelican ['pɛlɪkən] n pélican m; **pelican crossing** n (BRIT Aut) feu m à commande manuelle

pelt [pɛlt] vt: **to ~ sb (with)** bombarder qn (de) ▷ vi (rain) tomber à seaux; (inf: run) courir à toutes jambes ▷ n peau f

pelvis ['pɛlvɪs] n bassin m

pen [pɛn] n (for writing) stylo m; (for sheep) parc m

penalty ['pɛnltɪ] n pénalité f; sanction f; (fine) amende f; (Sport) pénalisation f; (Football) penalty m; (Rugby) pénalité f

pence [pɛns] npl of **penny**

pencil ['pɛnsl] n crayon m; **pencil in** vt noter provisoirement; **pencil case** n trousse f (d'écolier); **pencil sharpener** n taille-crayon(s) m inv

pendant ['pɛndnt] n pendentif m

pending ['pɛndɪŋ] prep en attendant ▷ adj en suspens

penetrate ['pɛnɪtreɪt] vt pénétrer dans; (enemy territory) entrer en

pen friend n (BRIT) correspondant(e)

penguin ['pɛŋgwɪn] n pingouin m

penicillin [pɛnɪ'sɪlɪn] n pénicilline f

peninsula [pə'nɪnsjulə] n péninsule f

penis ['pi:nɪs] n pénis m, verge f

penitentiary [pɛnɪ'tɛnʃərɪ] n (US) prison f

penknife ['pɛnnaɪf] n canif m

penniless ['pɛnɪlɪs] adj sans le sou

penny (pl **pennies** or **pence**) ['pɛnɪ, 'pɛnɪz, pɛns] n (BRIT) penny m; (US) cent m

pen pal n correspondant(e)

pension ['pɛnʃən] n (from company) retraite f; **pensioner** n (BRIT) retraité(e)

pentagon ['pɛntəgən] n: **the P~** (US Pol) le Pentagone

penthouse ['pɛnthaus] n appartement m (de luxe) en attique

penultimate [pɪ'nʌltɪmət] adj pénultième, avant-dernier(-ière)

people ['pi:pl] npl gens mpl; personnes fpl; (inhabitants) population f; (Pol) peuple m ▷ n (nation, race) peuple m; **several ~ came** plusieurs personnes sont venues; **~ say that …** on dit or les gens disent que …

pepper ['pɛpə'] n poivre m; (vegetable) poivron m ▷ vt (Culin) poivrer; **peppermint** n (sweet) pastille f de menthe

per [pə:'] prep par, **~ hour** (miles etc) à l'heure; (fee) (de) l'heure; **~ kilo** etc le kilo etc; **~ day/person** par jour/personne, **~ annum** par an

perceive [pə'si:v] vt percevoir; (notice) remarquer, s'apercevoir de

per cent adv pour cent

percentage [pə'sɛntɪdʒ] n pourcentage m

perception [pə'sɛpʃən] n perception f; (insight) sensibilité f

perch [pə:tʃ] n (fish) perche f; (for bird) perchoir m ▷ vi (se) percher

percussion [pə'kʌʃən] n percussion f

perennial [pə'rɛnɪəl] n (Bot) (plante f) vivace f, plante pluriannuelle

perfect ['pə:fɪkt] adj parfait(e) ▷ n (also: **~ tense**) parfait m ▷ vt [pə'fɛkt] (technique, skill, work of art) parfaire; (method, plan) mettre au point; **perfection** [pə'fɛkʃən] n perfection f; **perfectly** ['pə:fɪktlɪ] adv parfaitement

perform [pə'fɔ:m] vt (carry out) exécuter; (concert etc) jouer, donner ▷ vi (actor, musician) jouer; **performance** n représentation f, spectacle m; (of an artist) interprétation f; (Sport: of car, engine) performance f; (of company, economy) résultats mpl; **performer** n artiste m/f

perfume ['pə:fju:m] n parfum m

perhaps [pə'hæps] adv peut-être

perimeter [pə'rɪmɪtə'] n périmètre m

period ['pɪərɪəd] n période f; (Hist) époque f; (Scol) cours m; (full stop) point m; (Med) règles fpl ▷ adj (costume, furniture) d'époque;

periodical [pɪərɪ'ɔdɪkl] n périodique m; **periodically** adv périodiquement

perish ['pɛrɪʃ] vi périr, mourir; (decay) se détériorer

perjury ['pə:dʒərɪ] n (Law: in court) faux témoignage; (breach of oath) parjure m

perk [pə:k] n (inf) avantage m, à-côté m

perm [pə:m] n (for hair) permanente f

permanent ['pə:mənənt] adj permanent(e); **permanently** adv de façon permanente; (move abroad) définitivement; (open, closed) en permanence; (tired, unhappy) constamment

permission [pə'mɪʃən] n permission f, autorisation f

permit n ['pə:mɪt] permis m

perplex [pə'plɛks] vt (person) rendre perplexe

persecute ['pə:sɪkju:t] vt persécuter

persecution [pə:sɪ'kju:ʃən] n persécution f

persevere [pə:sɪ'vɪə'] vi persévérer

Persian ['pə:ʃən] adj persan(e); **the ~ Gulf** le golfe Persique

persist [pə'sɪst] vi: **to ~ (in doing)** persister (à faire), s'obstiner (à faire); **persistent** adj persistant(e), tenace

person ['pə:sn] n personne f; **in ~** en personne; **personal** adj personnel(le); **personal assistant** n secrétaire personnel(le); **personal computer** n ordinateur individuel, PC m; **personality** [pə:sə'nælɪtɪ] n personnalité f, **personally** adv personnellement; **to take sth personally** se sentir visé(e) par qch; **personal organizer** n agenda (personnel); (electronic) agenda électronique; **personal stereo** n Walkman® m, baladeur m

personnel [pə:sə'nɛl] n personnel m

perspective [pə'spɛktɪv] n perspective f

perspiration [pə:spɪ'reɪʃən] n transpiration f

persuade [pə'sweɪd] vt: **to ~ sb to do sth** persuader qn de faire qch, amener or décider qn à faire qch

persuasion [pə'sweɪʒən] n persuasion f; (creed) conviction f

persuasive [pə'sweɪsɪv] adj persuasif(-ive)

perverse [pə'və:s] adj pervers(e); (contrary) entêté(e), contrariant(e)

pervert n ['pə:və:t] perverti(e) ▷ vt [pə'və:t] pervertir; (words) déformer

pessimism ['pɛsɪmɪzəm] n pessimisme m

pessimist ['pɛsɪmɪst] n pessimiste m/f; **pessimistic** [pɛsɪ'mɪstɪk] adj pessimiste

pest [pɛst] n animal m (or insecte m) nuisible; (fig) fléau m

pester ['pɛstə'] vt importuner, harceler

pesticide ['pɛstɪsaɪd] n pesticide m

pet [pɛt] n animal familier ▷ cpd (favourite) favori(e) ▷ vt (stroke) caresser, câliner; **teacher's ~** chouchou m du professeur; **~ hate** bête noire

petal ['petl] *n* pétale *m*
petite [pə'tiːt] *adj* menu(e)
petition [pə'tɪʃən] *n* pétition *f*
petrified ['petrɪfaɪd] *adj* (*fig*) mort(e) de peur
petrol ['petrəl] *n* (BRIT) essence *f*; **I've run out of ~** je suis en panne d'essence
  ▎ Be careful not to translate *petrol* by the French word *pétrole*.
petroleum [pə'trəʊlɪəm] *n* pétrole *m*
petrol: petrol pump *n* (BRIT: *in car, at garage*) pompe *f* à essence; **petrol station** *n* (BRIT) station-service *f*; **petrol tank** *n* (BRIT) réservoir *m* d'essence
petticoat ['petɪkəʊt] *n* jupon *m*
petty ['petɪ] *adj* (*mean*) mesquin(e); (*unimportant*) insignifiant(e), sans importance
pew [pjuː] *n* banc *m* (d'église)
pewter ['pjuːtər] *n* étain *m*
phantom ['fæntəm] *n* fantôme *m*
pharmacist ['fɑːməsɪst] *n* pharmacien(ne)
pharmacy ['fɑːməsɪ] *n* pharmacie *f*
phase [feɪz] *n* phase *f*, période *f*; **phase in** *vt* introduire progressivement; **phase out** *vt* supprimer progressivement
Ph.D. *abbr* = **Doctor of Philosophy**
pheasant ['feznt] *n* faisan *m*
phenomena [fə'nɔmɪnə] *npl of* **phenomenon**
phenomenal [fɪ'nɔmɪnl] *adj* phénoménal(e)
phenomenon (*pl* **phenomena**) [fə'nɔmɪnən, -nə] *n* phénomène *m*
Philippines ['fɪlɪpiːnz] *npl* (*also:* **Philippine Islands**): **the ~** les Philippines *fpl*
philosopher [fɪ'lɔsəfər] *n* philosophe *m*
philosophical [fɪlə'sɔfɪkl] *adj* philosophique
philosophy [fɪ'lɔsəfɪ] *n* philosophie *f*
phlegm [flem] *n* flegme *m*
phobia ['fəʊbjə] *n* phobie *f*
phone [fəʊn] *n* téléphone *m* ▷ *vt* téléphoner à ▷ *vi* téléphoner; **to be on the ~** avoir le téléphone; (*be calling*) être au téléphone; **phone back** *vt, vi* rappeler; **phone up** *vt* téléphoner à ▷ *vi* téléphoner; **phone book** *n* annuaire *m*; **phone box**, (*US*) **phone booth** *n* cabine *f* téléphonique; **phone call** *n* coup *m* de fil *or* de téléphone; **phonecard** *n* télécarte *f*; **phone number** *n* numéro *m* de téléphone
phonetics [fə'nɛtɪks] *n* phonétique *f*
phoney ['fəʊnɪ] *adj* faux (fausse), factice; (*person*) pas franc (franche)
photo ['fəʊtəʊ] *n* photo *f*; **photo album** *n* album *m* de photos; **photocopier** *n* copieur *m*; **photocopy** *n* photocopie *f* ▷ *vt* photocopier
photograph ['fəʊtəɡræf] *n* photographie *f* ▷ *vt* photographier; **photographer** [fə'tɔɡrəfər] *n* photographe *m/f*; **photography** [fə'tɔɡrəfɪ] *n* photographie *f*

phrase [freɪz] *n* expression *f*; (*Ling*) locution *f* ▷ *vt* exprimer; **phrase book** *n* recueil *m* d'expressions (pour touristes)
physical ['fɪzɪkl] *adj* physique; **physical education** *n* éducation *f* physique; **physically** *adv* physiquement
physician [fɪ'zɪʃən] *n* médecin *m*
physicist ['fɪzɪsɪst] *n* physicien(ne)
physics ['fɪzɪks] *n* physique *f*
physiotherapist [fɪzɪəʊ'θerəpɪst] *n* kinésithérapeute *m/f*
physiotherapy [fɪzɪəʊ'θerəpɪ] *n* kinésithérapie *f*
physique [fɪ'ziːk] *n* (*appearance*) physique *m*; (*health etc*) constitution *f*
pianist ['piːənɪst] *n* pianiste *m/f*
piano [pɪ'ænəʊ] *n* piano *m*
pick [pɪk] *n* (*tool: also:* **~-axe**) pic *m*, pioche *f* ▷ *vt* choisir; (*gather*) cueillir; (*remove*) prendre; (*lock*) forcer; **take your ~** faites votre choix; **the ~ of** le meilleur(e) de; **to ~ one's nose** se mettre les doigts dans le nez; **to ~ one's teeth** se curer les dents; **to ~ a quarrel with sb** chercher noise à qn; **pick on** *vt fus* (*person*) harceler; **pick out** *vt* choisir; (*distinguish*) distinguer; **pick up** *vi* (*improve*) remonter, s'améliorer ▷ *vt* ramasser; (*collect*) passer prendre; (*Aut: give lift to*) prendre; (*learn*) apprendre; (*Radio*) capter; **to ~ up speed** prendre de la vitesse; **to ~ o.s. up** se relever
pickle ['pɪkl] *n* (*also:* **~s**) (*as condiment*) pickles *mpl* ▷ *vt* conserver dans du vinaigre *or* dans de la saumure; **in a ~** (*fig*) dans le pétrin
pickpocket ['pɪkpɔkɪt] *n* pickpocket *m*
pick-up ['pɪkʌp] *n* (*also:* **~ truck**) pick-up *m inv*
picnic ['pɪknɪk] *n* pique-nique *m* ▷ *vi* pique-niquer; **picnic area** *n* aire *f* de pique-nique
picture ['pɪktʃər] *n* (*painting*) peinture *f*, tableau *m*; (*photograph*) photo(graphie) *f*; (*drawing*) dessin *m*; (*film*) film *m*; (*fig: description*) description *f* ▷ *vt* (*imagine*) se représenter; **pictures** *npl*: **the ~s** (BRIT) le cinéma; **to take a ~ of sb/sth** prendre qn/qch en photo; **would you take a ~ of us, please?** pourriez-vous nous prendre en photo, s'il vous plaît?; **picture frame** *n* cadre *m*; **picture messaging** *n* picture messaging *m*, messagerie *f* d'images
picturesque [pɪktʃə'rɛsk] *adj* pittoresque
pie [paɪ] *n* tourte *f*; (*of fruit*) tarte *f*; (*of meat*) pâté *m* en croûte
piece [piːs] *n* morceau *m*; (*item*): **a ~ of furniture/advice** un meuble/conseil ▷ *vt*: **to ~ together** rassembler; **to take to ~s** démonter
pie chart *n* graphique *m* à secteurs, camembert *m*
pier [pɪər] *n* jetée *f*

pierce [pɪəs] vt percer, transpercer; **pierced** adj (ears) percé(e)

pig [pɪg] n cochon m, porc m; (pej: unkind person) mufle m; (: greedy person) goinfre m

pigeon [ˈpɪdʒən] n pigeon m

piggy bank [ˈpɪgɪ-] n tirelire f

pigsty [ˈpɪgstaɪ] n porcherie f

pigtail [ˈpɪgteɪl] n natte f, tresse f

pike [paɪk] n (fish) brochet m

pilchard [ˈpɪltʃəd] n pilchard m (sorte de sardine)

pile [paɪl] n (pillar, of books) pile f; (heap) tas m; (of carpet) épaisseur f; **pile up** vi (accumulate) s'entasser, s'accumuler ▷ vt (put in heap) empiler, entasser; (accumulate) accumuler; **piles** npl hémorroïdes fpl; **pile-up** n (Aut) télescopage m, collision f en série

pilgrim [ˈpɪlgrɪm] n pèlerin m; voir article "Pilgrim Fathers"

■ **PILGRIM FATHERS**

● Les Pilgrim Fathers ("Pères pèlerins") sont
● un groupe de puritains qui quittèrent
● l'Angleterre en 1620 pour fuir les
● persécutions religieuses. Ayant traversé
● l'Atlantique à bord du "Mayflower", ils
● fondèrent New Plymouth en Nouvelle-
● Angleterre, dans ce qui est aujourd'hui le
● Massachusetts. Ces Pères pèlerins sont
● considérés comme les fondateurs des
● États-Unis, et l'on commémore chaque
● année, le jour de "Thanksgiving", la
● réussite de leur première récolte.

pilgrimage [ˈpɪlgrɪmɪdʒ] n pèlerinage m

pill [pɪl] n pilule f; **the ~** la pilule

pillar [ˈpɪləʳ] n pilier m

pillow [ˈpɪləʊ] n oreiller m; **pillowcase, pillowslip** n taie f d'oreiller

pilot [ˈpaɪlət] n pilote m ▷ cpd (scheme etc) pilote, expérimental(e) ▷ vt piloter; **pilot light** n veilleuse f

pimple [ˈpɪmpl] n bouton m

PIN n abbr (= personal identification number) code m confidentiel

pin [pɪn] n épingle f; (Tech) cheville f ▷ vt épingler; **~s and needles** fourmis fpl; **to ~ sb down** (fig) coincer qn; **to ~ sth on sb** (fig) mettre qch sur le dos de qn

pinafore [ˈpɪnəfɔːʳ] n tablier m

pinch [pɪntʃ] n pincement m; (of salt etc) pincée f ▷ vt pincer; (inf: steal) piquer, chiper ▷ vi (shoe) serrer; **at a ~** à la rigueur

pine [paɪn] n (also: ~ **tree**) pin m ▷ vi: **to ~ for** aspirer à, désirer ardemment

pineapple [ˈpaɪnæpl] n ananas m

ping [pɪŋ] n (noise) tintement m; **ping-pong®** n ping-pong® m

pink [pɪŋk] adj rose ▷ n (colour) rose m

pinpoint [ˈpɪnpɔɪnt] vt indiquer (avec précision)

pint [paɪnt] n pinte f (Brit = 0,57 l; US = 0,47 l); (BRIT inf) ≈ demi m, ≈ pot m

pioneer [paɪəˈnɪəʳ] n pionnier m

pious [ˈpaɪəs] adj pieux(-euse)

pip [pɪp] n (seed) pépin m; **pips** npl: **the ~s** (BRIT: time signal on radio) le top

pipe [paɪp] n tuyau m, conduite f; (for smoking) pipe f ▷ vt amener par tuyau; **pipeline** n (for gas) gazoduc m, pipeline m; (for oil) oléoduc m, pipeline; **piper** n (flautist) joueur(-euse) de pipeau; (of bagpipes) joueur(-euse) de cornemuse

pirate [ˈpaɪərət] n pirate m ▷ vt (CD, video, book) pirater

Pisces [ˈpaɪsiːz] n les Poissons mpl

piss [pɪs] vi (inf!) pisser (!); **pissed** adj (inf! BRIT: drunk) bourré(e); (: US: angry) furieux(-euse)

pistol [ˈpɪstl] n pistolet m

piston [ˈpɪstən] n piston m

pit [pɪt] n trou m, fosse f; (also: **coal ~**) puits m de mine; (also: **orchestra ~**) fosse d'orchestre; (US: fruit stone) noyau m ▷ vt: **to ~ o.s. or one's wits against** se mesurer à

pitch [pɪtʃ] n (BRIT Sport) terrain m; (Mus) ton m; (fig: degree) degré m; (tar) poix f ▷ vt (throw) lancer; (tent) dresser ▷ vi (fall): **to ~ into/off** tomber dans/de; **pitch-black** adj noir(e) comme poix

pitfall [ˈpɪtfɔːl] n piège m

pith [pɪθ] n (of orange etc) intérieur m de l'écorce

pitiful [ˈpɪtɪful] adj (touching) pitoyable, (contemptible) lamentable

pity [ˈpɪtɪ] n pitié f ▷ vt plaindre; **what a ~!** quel dommage!

pizza [ˈpiːtsə] n pizza f

placard [ˈplækɑːd] n affiche f; (in march) pancarte f

place [pleɪs] n endroit m, lieu m; (proper position, job, rank, seat) place f; (home): **at/to his ~** chez lui ▷ vt (position) placer, mettre; (identify) situer; reconnaître; **to take ~** avoir lieu; **to change ~s with sb** changer de place avec qn; **out of ~** (not suitable) déplacé(e), inopportun(e); **in the first ~** d'abord, en premier; **place mat** n set m de table; (in linen etc) napperon m; **placement** n (during studies) stage m

placid [ˈplæsɪd] adj placide

plague [pleɪg] n (Med) peste f ▷ vt (fig) tourmenter

plaice [pleɪs] n (pl inv) carrelet m

plain [pleɪn] adj (in one colour) uni(e); (clear) clair(e), évident(e); (simple) simple; (not handsome) quelconque, ordinaire ▷ adv franchement, carrément ▷ n plaine f; **plain chocolate** n chocolat m à croquer; **plainly** adv clairement; (frankly) carrément, sans détours

plaintiff [ˈpleɪntɪf] n plaignant(e)

plait [plæt] n tresse f, natte f

plan [plæn] n plan m; (scheme) projet m
▷ vt (think in advance) projeter; (prepare)
organiser ▷ vi faire des projets; **to ~ to do**
projeter de faire
plane [pleɪn] n (Aviat) avion m; (also: **~ tree**)
platane m; (tool) rabot m; (Art, Math etc)
plan m; (fig) niveau m, plan ▷ vt (with tool)
raboter
planet ['plænɪt] n planète f
plank [plæŋk] n planche f
planning ['plænɪŋ] n planification f;
family ~ planning familial
plant [plɑ:nt] n plante f; (machinery)
matériel m; (factory) usine f ▷ vt planter;
(bomb) déposer, poser; (microphone,
evidence) cacher
plantation [plæn'teɪʃən] n plantation f
plaque [plæk] n plaque f
plaster ['plɑ:stər] n plâtre m; (also: **~ of Paris**)
plâtre à mouler; (BRIT: also: **sticking ~**)
pansement adhésif ▷ vt plâtrer; (cover): **to ~
with** couvrir de; **plaster cast** n (Med) plâtre
m; (model, statue) moule m
plastic ['plæstɪk] n plastique m ▷ adj (made
of plastic) en plastique; **plastic bag** n sac m
en plastique; **plastic surgery** n chirurgie f
esthétique
plate [pleɪt] n (dish) assiette f; (sheet of
metal, on door, Phot) plaque f; (in book)
gravure f; (dental) dentier m
plateau (pl **plateaus** or **plateaux**)
['plætəu, -z] n plateau m
platform ['plætfɔ:m] n (at meeting) tribune
f; (stage) estrade f; (Rail) quai m; (Pol)
plateforme f
platinum ['plætɪnəm] n platine m
platoon [plə'tu:n] n peloton m
platter ['plætər] n plat m
plausible ['plɔ:zɪbl] adj plausible; (person)
convaincant(e)
play [pleɪ] n jeu m; (Theat) pièce f (de
théâtre) ▷ vt (game) jouer à; (team, opponent)
jouer contre; (instrument) jouer de; (part,
piece of music, note) jouer; (CD etc) passer
▷ vi jouer; **to ~ safe** ne prendre aucun
risque; **play back** vt repasser, réécouter;
play up vi (cause trouble) faire des siennes;
player n joueur(-euse); (Mus) musicien(ne);
playful adj enjoué(e); **playground** n
cour f de récréation; (in park) aire f de jeux;
playgroup n garderie f; **playing card** n
carte f à jouer; **playing field** n terrain
m de sport; **playschool** n = **playgroup**;
playtime n (Scol) récréation f; **playwright**
n dramaturge m
plc abbr (BRIT: = public limited company)
≈ SARL f
plea [pli:] n (request) appel m; (Law)
défense f
plead [pli:d] vt plaider; (give as excuse)
invoquer ▷ vi (Law) plaider; (beg): **to ~ with
sb (for sth)** implorer qn (d'accorder qch); **to**

~ guilty/not guilty plaider coupable/non
coupable
pleasant ['plɛznt] adj agréable
please [pli:z] excl s'il te (or vous) plaît ▷ vt
plaire à ▷ vi (think fit): **do as you ~** faites
comme il vous plaira; **~ yourself!** (inf)
(faites) comme vous voulez!; **pleased** adj:
pleased (with) content(e) (de); **pleased
to meet you** enchanté (de faire votre
connaissance)
pleasure ['plɛʒər] n plaisir m; **"it's a ~"**
"je vous en prie"
pleat [pli:t] n pli m
pledge [plɛdʒ] n (promise) promesse f ▷ vt
promettre
plentiful ['plɛntɪful] adj abondant(e),
copieux(-euse)
plenty ['plɛntɪ] n: **~ of** beaucoup de;
(sufficient) (bien) assez de
pliers ['plaɪəz] npl pinces fpl
plight [plaɪt] n situation f critique
plod [plɔd] vi avancer péniblement; (fig)
peiner
plonk [plɔŋk] (inf) n (BRIT: wine) pinard
m, piquette f ▷ vt: **to ~ sth down** poser
brusquement qch
plot [plɔt] n complot m, conspiration f;
(of story, play) intrigue f; (of land) lot m de
terrain, lopin m ▷ vt (mark out) tracer point
par point; (Naut) pointer; (make graph of)
faire le graphique de; (conspire) comploter
▷ vi comploter
plough, (US) **plow** [plau] n charrue f ▷ vt
(earth) labourer; **to ~ money into** investir
dans
ploy [plɔɪ] n stratagème m
pls abbr (= please) SVP m
pluck [plʌk] vt (fruit) cueillir; (musical
instrument) pincer; (bird) plumer; **to ~ one's
eyebrows** s'épiler les sourcils; **to ~ up
courage** prendre son courage à deux
mains
plug [plʌg] n (stopper) bouchon m, bonde
f; (Elec) prise f de courant; (Aut: also:
spark(ing) ~) bougie f ▷ vt (hole) boucher;
(inf: advertise) faire du battage pour,
matraquer; **plug in** vt (Elec) brancher;
plughole n (BRIT) trou m (d'écoulement)
plum [plʌm] n (fruit) prune f
plumber ['plʌmər] n plombier m
plumbing ['plʌmɪŋ] n (trade) plomberie f;
(piping) tuyauterie f
plummet ['plʌmɪt] vi (person, object)
plonger; (sales, prices) dégringoler
plump [plʌmp] adj rondelet(te), dodu(e),
bien en chair; **plump for** vt fus (inf: choose)
se décider pour
plunge [plʌndʒ] n plongeon m; (fig) chute f
▷ vt plonger ▷ vi (fall) tomber, dégringoler;
(dive) plonger; **to take the ~** se jeter à l'eau
pluperfect [plu:'pə:fɪkt] n (Ling) plus-que-
parfait m

plural ['pluərl] adj pluriel(le) ▷ n pluriel m
plus [plʌs] n (also: **~ sign**) signe m plus; (advantage) atout m ▷ prep plus; **ten/ twenty ~** plus de dix/vingt
ply [plaɪ] n (of wool) fil m ▷ vt (a trade) exercer ▷ vi (ship) faire la navette; **to ~ sb with drink** donner continuellement à boire à qn; **plywood** n contreplaqué m
P.M. n abbr (BRIT) = **prime minister**
p.m. adv abbr (= post meridiem) de l'après-midi
PMS n abbr (= premenstrual syndrome) syndrome prémenstruel
PMT n abbr (= premenstrual tension) syndrome prémenstruel
pneumatic drill [nju:'mætɪk-] n marteau-piqueur m
pneumonia [nju:'məunɪə] n pneumonie f
poach [pəutʃ] vt (cook) pocher; (steal) pêcher (or chasser) sans permis ▷ vi braconner; **poached** adj (egg) poché(e)
P.O. Box n abbr = **post office box**
pocket ['pɒkɪt] n poche f ▷ vt empocher; **to be (£5) out of ~** (BRIT) en être de sa poche (pour 5 livres); **pocketbook** n (US: wallet) portefeuille m; **pocket money** n argent m de poche
pod [pɒd] n cosse f
podcast ['pɒdkɑːst] n podcast m ▷ vi podcaster
podiatrist [pɒ'diːətrɪst] n (US) pédicure m/f
poem ['pəuɪm] n poème m
poet ['pəuɪt] n poète m; **poetic** [pəu'ɛtɪk] adj poétique; **poetry** n poésie f
poignant ['pɔɪnjənt] adj poignant(e)
point [pɔɪnt] n point m; (tip) pointe f; (in time) moment m; (in space) endroit m; (subject, idea) point, sujet m; (purpose) but m; (also: **decimal ~**): **2 ~ 3 (2.3)** 2 virgule 3 (2,3); (BRIT Elec: also: **power ~**) prise f (de courant) ▷ vt (show) indiquer; (gun etc): **to ~ sth at** braquer or diriger qch sur ▷ vi: **to ~ at** montrer du doigt; **points** npl (Rail) aiguillage m; **to make a ~ of doing sth** ne pas manquer de faire qch; **to get/miss the ~** comprendre/ne pas comprendre; **to come to the ~** en venir au fait; **there's no ~ (in doing)** cela ne sert à rien (de faire); **to be on the ~ of doing sth** être sur le point de faire qch; **point out** vt (mention) faire remarquer, souligner; **point-blank** adv (fig) catégoriquement; (also: **at point-blank range**) à bout portant; **pointed** adj (shape) pointu(e); (remark) plein(e) de sous-entendus; **pointer** n (needle) aiguille f; (clue) indication f; (advice) tuyau m; **pointless** adj inutile, vain(e); **point of view** n point m de vue
poison ['pɔɪzn] n poison m ▷ vt empoisonner; **poisonous** adj (snake) venimeux(-euse); (substance, plant) vénéneux(-euse); (fumes) toxique

poke [pəuk] vt (jab with finger, stick etc) piquer; pousser du doigt; (put): **to ~ sth in(to)** fourrer or enfoncer qch dans; **poke about** vi fureter; **poke out** vi (stick out) sortir
poker ['pəukər] n tisonnier m; (Cards) poker m
Poland ['pəulənd] n Pologne f
polar ['pəulər] adj polaire; **polar bear** n ours blanc
Pole [pəul] n Polonais(e)
pole [pəul] n (of wood) mât m, perche f; (Elec) poteau m; (Geo) pôle m; **pole bean** n (US) haricot m (à rames); **pole vault** n saut m à la perche
police [pə'liːs] npl police f ▷ vt maintenir l'ordre dans; **police car** n voiture f de police; **police constable** n (BRIT) agent m de police; **police force** n police f, forces fpl de l'ordre; **policeman** (irreg) n agent m de police, policier m; **police officer** n agent m de police; **police station** n commissariat m de police; **policewoman** (irreg) n femme-agent f
policy ['pɒlɪsɪ] n politique f; (also: **insurance ~**) police f (d'assurance)
polio ['pəulɪəu] n polio f
Polish ['pəulɪʃ] adj polonais(e) ▷ n (Ling) polonais m
polish ['pɒlɪʃ] n (for shoes) cirage m; (for floor) cire f, encaustique f; (for nails) vernis m; (shine) éclat m, poli m; (fig: refinement) raffinement m ▷ vt (put polish on: shoes, wood) cirer; (make shiny) astiquer, faire briller; **polish off** vt (food) liquider; **polished** adj (fig) raffiné(e)
polite [pə'laɪt] adj poli(e); **politeness** n politesse f
political [pə'lɪtɪkl] adj politique; **politically** adv politiquement; **politically correct** politiquement correct(e)
politician [pɒlɪ'tɪʃən] n homme/femme politique, politicien(ne)
politics ['pɒlɪtɪks] n politique f
poll [pəul] n scrutin m, vote m; (also: **opinion ~**) sondage m (d'opinion) ▷ vt (votes) obtenir
pollen ['pɒlən] n pollen m
polling station n (BRIT) bureau m de vote
pollute [pə'luːt] vt polluer
pollution [pə'luːʃən] n pollution f
polo ['pəuləu] n polo m; **polo-neck** adj à col roulé ▷ n (sweater) pull m à col roulé; **polo shirt** n polo m
polyester [pɒlɪ'ɛstər] n polyester m
polystyrene [pɒlɪ'staɪriːn] n polystyrène m
polythene ['pɒlɪθiːn] n (BRIT) polyéthylène m; **polythene bag** n sac m en plastique
pomegranate ['pɒmɪgrænɪt] n grenade f
pompous ['pɒmpəs] adj pompeux(-euse)
pond [pɒnd] n étang m; (stagnant) mare f
ponder ['pɒndər] vt considérer, peser

pony ['pəʊnɪ] n poney m; **ponytail** n
queue f de cheval; **pony trekking** n (BRIT)
randonnée f équestre or à cheval

poodle ['puːdl] n caniche m

pool [puːl] n (of rain) flaque f; (pond) mare f;
(artificial) bassin m; (also: **swimming ~**)
piscine f; (sth shared) fonds commun;
(billiards) poule f ▷ vt mettre en commun;
pools npl (football) ≈ loto sportif

poor [pʊəʳ] adj pauvre; (mediocre) médiocre,
faible, mauvais(e) ▷ npl: **the ~** les pauvres
mpl; **poorly** adv (badly) mal, médiocrement
▷ adj souffrant(e), malade

pop [pɒp] n (noise) bruit sec; (Mus) musique
f pop; (inf: drink) soda m; (US inf: father) papa
m ▷ vt (put) fourrer, mettre (rapidement)
▷ vi éclater; (cork) sauter; **pop in** vi entrer
en passant; **pop out** vi sortir; **popcorn** n
pop-corn m

pope [pəʊp] n pape m

poplar ['pɒpləʳ] n peuplier m

popper ['pɒpəʳ] n bouton-pression m

poppy ['pɒpɪ] n (wild) coquelicot m;
(cultivated) pavot m

Popsicle® ['pɒpsɪkl] n (US) esquimau m
(glace)

pop star n pop star f

popular ['pɒpjʊləʳ] adj populaire;
(fashionable) à la mode; **popularity**
[pɒpjʊ'lærɪtɪ] n popularité f

population [pɒpjʊ'leɪʃən] n population f

pop-up adj (Comput: menu, window) pop up
inv ▷ n pop up m inv, fenêtre f pop up

porcelain ['pɔːslɪn] n porcelaine f

porch [pɔːtʃ] n porche m; (US) véranda f

pore [pɔːʳ] n pore m; ▷ vi: **to ~ over**
s'absorber dans, être plongé(e) dans

pork [pɔːk] n porc m; **pork chop** n côte f
de porc; **pork pie** n pâté m de porc en
croûte

porn [pɔːn] adj (inf) porno ▷ n (inf) porno
m; **pornographic** [pɔːnə'græfɪk]
adj pornographique; **pornography**
[pɔː'nɒgrəfɪ] n pornographie f

porridge ['pɒrɪdʒ] n porridge m

port [pɔːt] n (harbour) port m; (Naut: left
side) bâbord m; (wine) porto m;
(Comput) port m, accès m; **~ of call**
(port d')escale f

portable ['pɔːtəbl] adj portatif(-ive)

porter ['pɔːtəʳ] n (for luggage) porteur m;
(doorkeeper) gardien(ne); portier m

portfolio [pɔːt'fəʊlɪəʊ] n portefeuille m; (of
artist) portfolio m

portion ['pɔːʃən] n portion f, part f

portrait ['pɔːtreɪt] n portrait m

portray [pɔː'treɪ] vt faire le portrait de;
(in writing) dépeindre, représenter; (subj:
actor) jouer

Portugal ['pɔːtjʊgl] n Portugal m

Portuguese [pɔːtjʊ'giːz] adj portugais(e)
▷ n (pl inv) Portugais(e); (Ling) portugais m

pose [pəʊz] n pose f ▷ vi poser; (pretend):
to ~ as se faire passer pour ▷ vt poser;
(problem) créer

posh [pɒʃ] adj (inf) chic inv

position [pə'zɪʃən] n position f; (job, situation)
situation f ▷ vt mettre en place or en position

positive ['pɒzɪtɪv] adj positif(-ive); (certain)
sûr(e), certain(e); (definite) formel(le),
catégorique; **positively** adv (affirmatively,
enthusiastically) de façon positive; (inf: really)
carrément

possess [pə'zɛs] vt posséder; **possession**
[pə'zɛʃən] n possession f; **possessions** npl
(belongings) affaires fpl; **possessive** adj
possessif(-ive)

possibility [pɒsɪ'bɪlɪtɪ] n possibilité f;
(event) éventualité f

possible ['pɒsɪbl] adj possible; **as big as ~**
aussi gros que possible; **possibly** adv
(perhaps) peut-être; **I cannot possibly
come** il m'est impossible de venir

post [pəʊst] n (BRIT: mail) poste f; (: letters,
delivery) courrier m; (job, situation) poste
m; (pole) poteau m; (Internet) post ▷ vt
(Internet) poster; (BRIT: send by post) poster;
(appoint): **to ~ to** affecter à; **where can I ~
these cards?** où est-ce que je peux poster
ces cartes postales?; **postage** n tarifs mpl
d'affranchissement; **postal** adj postal(e);
postal order n mandat(-poste m) m;
postbox n (BRIT) boîte f aux lettres
(publique); **postcard** n carte postale;
postcode n (BRIT) code postal

poster ['pəʊstəʳ] n affiche f

postgraduate ['pəʊst'grædjuət] n
≈ étudiant(e) de troisième cycle

postman ['pəʊstmən] (irreg) (BRIT) n
facteur m

postmark ['pəʊstmɑːk] n cachet m (de la
poste)

post-mortem [pəʊst'mɔːtəm] n autopsie f

post office n (building) poste f;
(organization): **the Post Office** les postes fpl

postpone [pəs'pəʊn] vt remettre (à plus
tard), reculer

posture ['pɒstʃəʳ] n posture f; (fig) attitude f

postwoman [pəʊst'wʊmən] (irreg) (BRIT)
n factrice f

pot [pɒt] n (for cooking) marmite f; casserole
f; (teapot) théière f; (for coffee) cafetière f;
(for plants, jam) pot m; (inf: marijuana) herbe
f ▷ vt (plant) mettre en pot; **to go to ~** (inf)
aller à vau-l'eau

potato [pə'teɪtəʊ] n (pl potatoes) pomme
f de terre; **potato peeler** n épluche-
légumes m

potent ['pəʊtnt] adj puissant(e); (drink)
fort(e), très alcoolisé(e); (man) viril

potential [pə'tɛnʃl] adj potentiel(le) ▷ n
potentiel m

pothole ['pɒthəʊl] n (in road) nid m de poule;
(BRIT: underground) gouffre m, caverne f

pot plant n plante f d'appartement

potter ['pɒtə'] n potier m ▷ vi (BRIT): **to ~ around** or **about** bricoler; **pottery** n poterie f

potty ['pɒtɪ] n (child's) pot m

pouch [pautʃ] n (Zool) poche f; (for tobacco) blague f; (for money) bourse f

poultry ['pəultrɪ] n volaille f

pounce [pauns] vi: **to ~ (on)** bondir (sur), fondre (sur)

pound [paund] n livre f (weight = 453g, 16 ounces; money = 100 ounces); (for dogs, cars) fourrière f ▷ vt (beat) bourrer de coups, marteler; (crush) piler, pulvériser ▷ vi (heart) battre violemment, taper; **pound sterling** n livre f sterling

pour [pɔː'] vt verser ▷ vi couler à flots; (rain) pleuvoir à verse; **to ~ sb a drink** verser or servir à boire à qn; **pour in** vi (people) affluer, se précipiter; (news, letters) arriver en masse; **pour out** vi (people) sortir en masse ▷ vt vider; (fig) déverser; (serve: a drink) verser; **pouring** adj: **pouring rain** pluie torrentielle

pout [paut] vi faire la moue

poverty ['pɒvətɪ] n pauvreté f, misère f

powder ['paudə'] n poudre f ▷ vt poudrer; **powdered milk** n lait m en poudre

power ['pauə'] n (strength, nation) puissance f, force f; (ability, Pol: of party, leader) pouvoir m; (of speech, thought) faculté f; (Elec) courant m; **to be in ~** être au pouvoir; **power cut** n (BRIT) coupure f de courant; **power failure** n panne f de courant; **powerful** adj puissant(e); (performance etc) très fort(e), **powerless** adj impuissant(e); **power point** n (BRIT) prise f de courant; **power station** n centrale f électrique

p.p. abbr (= per procurationem: by proxy) p. p.

PR n abbr = **public relations**

practical ['præktɪkl] adj pratique; **practical joke** n farce f; **practically** adv (almost) pratiquement

practice ['præktɪs] n pratique f; (of profession) exercice m; (at football etc) entraînement m; (business) cabinet m ▷ vt, vi (US) = **practise**; **in ~** (in reality) en pratique; **out of ~** rouillé(e)

practise, (US) **practice** ['præktɪs] vt (work at: piano, backhand etc) s'exercer à, travailler; (train for: sport) s'entraîner à; (a sport, religion, method) pratiquer; (profession) exercer ▷ vi s'exercer, travailler; (train) s'entraîner; (lawyer, doctor) exercer; **practising**, (US) **practicing** adj (Christian etc) pratiquant(e); (lawyer) en exercice

practitioner [præk'tɪʃənə'] n praticien(ne)

pragmatic [præg'mætɪk] adj pragmatique

prairie ['prɛərɪ] n savane f

praise [preɪz] n éloge(s) m(pl), louange(s) f(pl) ▷ vt louer, faire l'éloge de

pram [præm] n (BRIT) landau m, voiture f d'enfant

prank [præŋk] n farce f

prawn [prɔːn] n crevette f (rose); **prawn cocktail** n cocktail m de crevettes

pray [preɪ] vi prier; **prayer** [prɛə'] n prière f

preach [priːtʃ] vi prêcher; **preacher** n prédicateur m; (US: clergyman) pasteur m

precarious [prɪ'kɛərɪəs] adj précaire

precaution [prɪ'kɔːʃən] n précaution f

precede [prɪ'siːd] vt, vi précéder; **precedent** ['prɛsɪdənt] n précédent m; **preceding** [prɪ'siːdɪŋ] adj qui précède (or précédait)

precinct ['priːsɪŋkt] n (US: district) circonscription f, arrondissement m; **pedestrian ~** (BRIT) zone piétonnière; **shopping ~** (BRIT) centre m commercial

precious ['prɛʃəs] adj précieux(-euse)

precise [prɪ'saɪs] adj précis(e); **precisely** adv précisément

precision [prɪ'sɪʒən] n précision f

predator ['prɛdətə'] n prédateur m, rapace m

predecessor ['priːdɪsɛsə'] n prédécesseur m

predicament [prɪ'dɪkəmənt] n situation f difficile

predict [prɪ'dɪkt] vt prédire; **predictable** adj prévisible; **prediction** [prɪ'dɪkʃən] n prédiction f

predominantly [prɪ'dɒmɪnəntlɪ] adv en majeure partie; (especially) surtout

preface ['prɛfəs] n préface f

prefect ['priːfɛkt] n (BRIT: in school) élève chargé de certaines fonctions de discipline

prefer [prɪ'fəː'] vt préférer, **preferable** ['prɛfrəbl] adj préférable; **preferably** ['prɛfrəblɪ] adv de préférence; **preference** ['prɛfrəns] n préférence f

prefix ['priːfɪks] n préfixe m

pregnancy ['prɛgnənsɪ] n grossesse f

pregnant ['prɛgnənt] adj enceinte; (animal) pleine

prehistoric ['priːhɪs'tɔrɪk] adj préhistorique

prejudice ['prɛdʒudɪs] n préjugé m; **prejudiced** (person) plein(e) de préjugés; (in a matter) partial(e)

preliminary [prɪ'lɪmɪnərɪ] adj préliminaire

prelude ['prɛljuːd] n prélude m

premature ['prɛmətʃuə'] adj prématuré(e)

premier ['prɛmɪə'] adj premier(-ière), principal(e) ▷ n (Pol: Prime Minister) premier ministre; (Pol: President) chef m de l'État

premiere ['prɛmɪɛə'] n première f

Premier League n première division

premises ['prɛmɪsɪz] npl locaux mpl; **on the ~** sur les lieux; sur place

premium ['priːmɪəm] n prime f; **to be at a ~** (fig: housing etc) être très demandé(e), être rarissime

premonition [prɛmə'nɪʃən] *n*
prémonition *f*
preoccupied [pri:'ɔkjupaɪd] *adj*
préoccupé(e)
prepaid [pri:'peɪd] *adj* payé(e) d'avance
preparation [prɛpə'reɪʃən] *n* préparation *f*;
preparations *npl* (*for trip, war*)
préparatifs *mpl*
preparatory school *n* (BRIT) école
primaire privée; (US) lycée privé
prepare [prɪ'pɛəʳ] *vt* préparer ▷ *vi*: **to ~ for**
se préparer à
prepared [prɪ'pɛəd] *adj*: **~ for** préparé(e) à;
~ to prêt(e) à
preposition [prɛpə'zɪʃən] *n* préposition *f*
prep school *n* = **preparatory school**
prerequisite [pri:'rɛkwɪzɪt] *n* condition *f*
préalable
preschool ['pri:'sku:l] *adj* préscolaire;
(*child*) d'âge préscolaire
prescribe [prɪ'skraɪb] *vt* prescrire
prescription [prɪ'skrɪpʃən] *n* (*Med*)
ordonnance *f* (: *medicine*) médicament
m (obtenu sur ordonnance); **could you
write me a ~?** pouvez-vous me faire une
ordonnance?
presence ['prɛzns] *n* présence *f*; **in sb's ~** en
présence de qn; **~ of mind** présence d'esprit
present *adj* ['prɛznt] présent(e); (*current*)
présent, actuel(le) ▷ *n* ['prɛznt] cadeau
m; (*actuality*) présent *m* ▷ *vt* [prɪ'zɛnt]
présenter; (*prize, medal*) remettre; (*give*):
to ~ sb with sth offrir qch à qn; **at ~** en ce
moment; **to give sb a ~** offrir un cadeau
à qn; **presentable** [prɪ'zɛntəbl] *adj*
présentable; **presentation** [prɛzn'teɪʃən]
n présentation *f*; (*ceremony*) remise *f* du
cadeau (*or* de la médaille *etc*); **present-
day** *adj* contemporain(e), actuel(le);
presenter [prɪ'zɛntəʳ] *n* (BRIT *Radio, TV*)
présentateur(-trice); **presently** *adv* (*soon*)
tout à l'heure, bientôt; (*with verb in past*) peu
après; (*at present*) en ce moment
preservation [prɛzə'veɪʃən] *n*
préservation *f*, conservation *f*
preservative [prɪ'zə:vətɪv] *n* agent *m* de
conservation
preserve [prɪ'zə:v] *vt* (*keep safe*) préserver,
protéger; (*maintain*) conserver, garder;
(*food*) mettre en conserve ▷ *n* (*for game, fish*)
réserve *f*; (*often pl: jam*) confiture *f*
preside [prɪ'zaɪd] *vi* présider
president ['prɛzɪdənt] *n* président(e);
presidential [prɛzɪ'dɛnʃl] *adj*
présidentiel(le)
press [prɛs] *n* (*tool, machine, newspapers*)
presse *f*; (*for wine*) pressoir *m* ▷ *vt* (*push*)
appuyer sur; (*squeeze*) presser, serrer;
(*clothes: iron*) repasser; (*insist*): **to ~ sth on
sb** presser qn d'accepter qch; (*urge, entreat*):
to ~ sb to do *or* **into doing sth** pousser
qn à faire qch ▷ *vi* appuyer; **we are ~ed**

for time le temps nous manque; **to ~ for
sth** faire pression pour obtenir qch; **press
conference** *n* conférence *f* de presse;
pressing *adj* urgent(e), pressant(e); **press
stud** *n* (BRIT) bouton-pression *m*; **press-up**
n (BRIT) traction *f*
pressure ['prɛʃəʳ] *n* pression *f*; (*stress*)
tension *f*; **to put ~ on sb (to do sth)** faire
pression sur qn (pour qu'il fasse qch);
pressure cooker *n* cocotte-minute® *f*;
pressure group *n* groupe *m* de pression
prestige [prɛs'ti:ʒ] *n* prestige *m*
prestigious [prɛs'tɪdʒəs] *adj*
prestigieux(-euse)
presumably [prɪ'zju:məblɪ] *adv*
vraisemblablement
presume [prɪ'zju:m] *vt* présumer,
supposer
pretence, (US) **pretense** [prɪ'tɛns] *n*
(*claim*) prétention *f*; **under false ~s** sous des
prétextes fallacieux
pretend [prɪ'tɛnd] *vt* (*feign*) feindre, simuler
▷ *vi* (*feign*) faire semblant
pretense [prɪ'tɛns] *n* (US) = **pretence**
pretentious [prɪ'tɛnʃəs] *adj*
prétentieux(-euse)
pretext ['pri:tɛkst] *n* prétexte *m*
pretty ['prɪtɪ] *adj* joli(e) ▷ *adv* assez
prevail [prɪ'veɪl] *vi* (*win*) l'emporter,
prévaloir; (*be usual*) avoir cours; **prevailing**
adj (*widespread*) courant(e), répandu(e);
(*wind*) dominant(e)
prevalent ['prɛvələnt] *adj* répandu(e),
courant(e)
prevent [prɪ'vɛnt] *vt*: **to ~ (from
doing)** empêcher (de faire); **prevention**
[prɪ'vɛnʃən] *n* prévention *f*; **preventive** *adj*
préventif(-ive)
preview ['pri:vju:] *n* (*of film*) avant-
première *f*
previous ['pri:vɪəs] *adj* (*last*) précédent(e);
(*earlier*) antérieur(e); **previously** *adv*
précédemment, auparavant
prey [preɪ] *n* proie *f* ▷ *vi*: **to ~ on** s'attaquer
à; **it was ~ing on his mind** ça le rongeait
or minait
price [praɪs] *n* prix *m* ▷ *vt* (*goods*) fixer le prix
de; **priceless** *adj* sans prix, inestimable;
price list *n* tarif *m*
prick [prɪk] *n* (*sting*) piqûre *f* ▷ *vt* piquer;
to ~ up one's ears dresser *or* tendre l'oreille
prickly ['prɪklɪ] *adj* piquant(e),
épineux(-euse); (*fig: person*) irritable
pride [praɪd] *n* fierté *f*; (*pej*) orgueil *m* ▷ *vt*:
to ~ o.s. on se flatter de; s'enorgueillir de
priest [pri:st] *n* prêtre *m*
primarily ['praɪmərɪlɪ] *adv* principalement,
essentiellement
primary ['praɪmərɪ] *adj* primaire; (*first in
importance*) premier(-ière), primordial(e) ▷ *n*
(US: *election*) (élection *f*) primaire *f*; **primary
school** *n* (BRIT) école *f* primaire

prime [praɪm] *adj* primordial(e), fondamental(e); (*excellent*) excellent(e) ▷ *vt* (*fig*) mettre au courant ▷ *n*: **in the ~ of life** dans la fleur de l'âge; **Prime Minister** *n* Premier ministre

primitive ['prɪmɪtɪv] *adj* primitif(-ive)

primrose ['prɪmrəuz] *n* primevère *f*

prince [prɪns] *n* prince *m*

princess [prɪn'sɛs] *n* princesse *f*

principal ['prɪnsɪpl] *adj* principal(e) ▷ *n* (*head teacher*) directeur *m*, principal *m*; **principally** *adv* principalement

principle ['prɪnsɪpl] *n* principe *m*; **in ~** en principe; **on ~** par principe

print [prɪnt] *n* (*mark*) empreinte *f*; (*letters*) caractères *mpl*; (*fabric*) imprimé *m*; (*Art*) gravure *f*, estampe *f*; (*Phot*) épreuve *f* ▷ *vt* imprimer; (*publish*) publier; (*write in capitals*) écrire en majuscules; **out of ~** épuisé(e); **print out** *vt* (*Comput*) imprimer; **printer** *n* (*machine*) imprimante *f*; (*person*) imprimeur *m*; **printout** *n* (*Comput*) sortie *f* imprimante

prior ['praɪə*] *adj* antérieur(e), précédent(e); (*more important*) prioritaire ▷ *adv*: **~ to doing** avant de faire

priority [praɪ'ɔrɪtɪ] *n* priorité *f*; **to have** *or* **take ~ over sth/sb** avoir la priorité sur qch/qn

prison ['prɪzn] *n* prison *f* ▷ *cpd* pénitentiaire; **prisoner** *n* prisonnier(-ière); **prisoner of war** *n* prisonnier(-ière) de guerre

pristine ['prɪstiːn] *adj* virginal(e)

privacy ['prɪvəsɪ] *n* intimité *f*, solitude *f*

private ['praɪvɪt] *adj* (*not public*) privé(e); (*personal*) personnel(le); (*house, car, lesson*) particulier(-ière); (*quiet: place*) tranquille ▷ *n* soldat *m* de deuxième classe; **"~"** (*on envelope*) "personnelle"; (*on door*) "privé"; **in ~** en privé; **privately** *adv* en privé; (*within oneself*) intérieurement; **private property** *n* propriété privée; **private school** *n* école privée

privatize ['praɪvɪtaɪz] *vt* privatiser

privilege ['prɪvɪlɪdʒ] *n* privilège *m*

prize [praɪz] *n* prix *m* ▷ *adj* (*example, idiot*) parfait(e); (*bull, novel*) primé(e) ▷ *vt* priser, faire grand cas de; **prize-giving** *n* distribution *f* des prix; **prizewinner** *n* gagnant(e)

pro [prəu] *n* (*inf: Sport*) professionnel(le) ▷ *prep* pro; **pros** *npl*: **the ~s and cons** le pour et le contre

probability [prɔbə'bɪlɪtɪ] *n* probabilité *f*; **in all ~** très probablement

probable ['prɔbəbl] *adj* probable

probably ['prɔbəblɪ] *adv* probablement

probation [prə'beɪʃən] *n*: **on ~** (*employee*) à l'essai; (*Law*) en liberté surveillée

probe [prəub] *n* (*Med, Space*) sonde *f*; (*enquiry*) enquête *f*, investigation *f* ▷ *vt* sonder, explorer

problem ['prɔbləm] *n* problème *m*

procedure [prə'siːdʒə*] *n* (*Admin, Law*) procédure *f*; (*method*) marche *f* à suivre, façon *f* de procéder

proceed [prə'siːd] *vi* (*go forward*) avancer; (*act*) procéder; (*continue*): **to ~ (with)** continuer, poursuivre; **to ~ to do** se mettre à faire; **proceedings** *npl* (*measures*) mesures *fpl*; (*Law: against sb*) poursuites *fpl*; (*meeting*) réunion *f*, séance *f*; (*records*) compte rendu; actes *mpl*; **proceeds** ['prəusiːdz] *npl* produit *m*, recette *f*

process ['prəusɛs] *n* processus *m*; (*method*) procédé *m* ▷ *vt* traiter

procession [prə'sɛʃən] *n* défilé *m*, cortège *m*; **funeral ~** (*on foot*) cortège funèbre; (*in cars*) convoi *m* mortuaire

proclaim [prə'kleɪm] *vt* déclarer, proclamer

prod [prɔd] *vt* pousser

produce *n* ['prɔdjuːs] (*Agr*) produits *mpl* ▷ *vt* [prə'djuːs] produire; (*show*) présenter; (*cause*) provoquer, causer; (*Theat*) monter, mettre en scène; (*TV: programme*) réaliser; (: *play, film*) mettre en scène; (*Radio: programme*) réaliser; (: *play*) mettre en ondes; **producer** *n* (*Theat*) metteur *m* en scène; (*Agr, Comm, Cine*) producteur *m*; (*TV: of programme*) réalisateur *m*; (: *of play, film*) metteur en scène; (*Radio: of programme*) réalisateur, (: *of play*) metteur en ondes

product ['prɔdʌkt] *n* produit *m*; **production** [prə'dʌkʃən] *n* production *f*; (*Theat*) mise *f* en scène; **productive** [prə'dʌktɪv] *adj* productif(-ive); **productivity** [prɔdʌk'tɪvɪtɪ] *n* productivité *f*

Prof. [prɔf] *abbr* (= *professor*) Prof

profession [prə'fɛʃən] *n* profession *f*; **professional** *n* professionnel(le) ▷ *adj* professionnel(le); (*work*) de professionnel

professor [prə'fɛsə*] *n* professeur *m* (*titulaire d'une chaire*); (*us: teacher*) professeur *m*

profile ['prəufaɪl] *n* profil *m*

profit ['prɔfɪt] *n* (*from trading*) bénéfice *m*; (*advantage*) profit *m* ▷ *vi*: **to ~ (by** *or* **from)** profiter (de); **profitable** *adj* lucratif(-ive), rentable

profound [prə'faund] *adj* profond(e)

programme, (*us*) **program** ['prəugræm] *n* (*Comput*) programme *m*; (*Radio, TV*) émission *f* ▷ *vt* programmer; **programmer** *n* programmeur(-euse); **programming**, (*us*) **programing** *n* programmation *f*

progress *n* ['prəugrɛs] progrès *m(pl)* ▷ *vi* [prə'grɛs] progresser, avancer; **in ~** en cours; **progressive** [prə'grɛsɪv] *adj* progressif(-ive); (*person*) progressiste

prohibit [prə'hɪbɪt] *vt* interdire, défendre

project *n* ['prɔdʒɛkt] (*plan*) projet *m*, plan *m*; (*venture*) opération *f*, entreprise *f*; (*Scol: research*) étude *f*, dossier *m* ▷ *vt* [prə'dʒɛkt]

projeter ▷ vi [prəˈdʒɛkt] (*stick out*) faire
saillie, s'avancer; **projection** [prəˈdʒɛkʃən]
n projection f; (*overhang*) saillie f; **projector**
[prəˈdʒɛktər] n projecteur m
prolific [prəˈlɪfɪk] adj prolifique
prolong [prəˈlɒŋ] vt prolonger
prom [prɒm] n abbr = **promenade**; (*us: ball*)
bal m d'étudiants; **the P~s** série de concerts de
musique classique

● **PROM**

● En Grande-Bretagne, un *promenade*
● *concert* ou *prom* est un concert de musique
● classique, ainsi appelé car, à l'origine,
● le public restait debout et se promenait
● au lieu de rester assis. De nos jours, une
● partie du public reste debout, mais il y a
● également des places assises (plus chères).
● Les *Proms* les plus connus sont les Proms
● londoniens. La dernière séance (the
● "Last Night of the Proms") est un grand
● événement médiatique où se jouent des
● airs traditionnels et patriotiques. Aux
● États-Unis et au Canada, le *prom* ou
● *promenade* est un bal organisé par le lycée.

promenade [prɒməˈnɑːd] n (*by sea*)
esplanade f, promenade f
prominent [ˈprɒmɪnənt] adj (*standing out*)
proéminent(e); (*important*) important(e)
promiscuous [prəˈmɪskjuəs] adj (*sexually*)
de mœurs légères
promise [ˈprɒmɪs] n promesse
f ▷ vt, vi promettre; **promising** adj
prometteur(-euse)
promote [prəˈməʊt] vt promouvoir; (*new
product*) lancer; **promotion** [prəˈməʊʃən]
n promotion f
prompt [prɒmpt] adj rapide ▷ n (*Comput*)
message m (de guidage) ▷ vt (*cause*)
entraîner, provoquer; (*Theat*) souffler (son
rôle or ses répliques) à; **at 8 o'clock** ~ à
8 heures précises; **to ~ sb to do** inciter or
pousser qn à faire; **promptly** adv (*quickly*)
rapidement, sans délai; (*on time*)
ponctuellement
prone [prəʊn] adj (*lying*) couché(e) (face
contre terre); (*liable*): **~ to** enclin(e) à
prong [prɒŋ] n (*of fork*) dent f
pronoun [ˈprəʊnaʊn] n pronom m
pronounce [prəˈnaʊns] vt prononcer;
how do you ~ it? comment est-ce que ça se
prononce?
pronunciation [prənʌnsɪˈeɪʃən] n
prononciation f
proof [pruːf] n preuve f ▷ adj: **~ against** à
l'épreuve de
prop [prɒp] n support m, étai m; (*fig*) soutien
m ▷ vt (*also*: **~ up**) étayer, soutenir; **props**
npl accessoires mpl
propaganda [prɒpəˈɡændə] n propagande f

propeller [prəˈpɛlər] n hélice f
proper [ˈprɒpər] adj (*suited, right*)
approprié(e), bon (bonne); (*seemly*)
correct(e), convenable; (*authentic*) vrai(e),
véritable; (*referring to place*): **the village ~**
le village proprement dit; **properly** adv
correctement, convenablement; **proper
noun** n nom m propre
property [ˈprɒpətɪ] n (*possessions*) biens
mpl; (*house etc*) propriété f; (*land*) terres fpl,
domaine m
prophecy [ˈprɒfɪsɪ] n prophétie f
prophet [ˈprɒfɪt] n prophète m
proportion [prəˈpɔːʃən] n proportion
f; (*share*) part f; partie f; **proportions**
npl (*size*) dimensions fpl; **proportional,
proportionate** adj proportionnel(le)
proposal [prəˈpəʊzl] n proposition f, offre
f; (*plan*) projet m; (*of marriage*) demande f en
mariage
propose [prəˈpəʊz] vt proposer, suggérer
▷ vi faire sa demande en mariage; **to ~ to do**
avoir l'intention de faire
proposition [prɒpəˈzɪʃən] n proposition f
proprietor [prəˈpraɪətər] n propriétaire m/f
prose [prəʊz] n prose f; (*Scol: translation*)
thème m
prosecute [ˈprɒsɪkjuːt] vt poursuivre;
prosecution [prɒsɪˈkjuːʃən] n poursuites
fpl judiciaires; (*accusing side: in criminal
case*) accusation f; (: *in civil case*) la partie
plaignante; **prosecutor** (*lawyer*)
procureur m; (*also*: **public prosecutor**)
ministère public; (*us: plaintiff*) plaignant(e)
prospect n [ˈprɒspɛkt] perspective f; (*hope*)
espoir m, chances fpl ▷ vt, vi [prəˈspɛkt]
prospecter; **prospects** npl (*for work etc*)
possibilités fpl d'avenir, débouchés mpl;
prospective [prəˈspɛktɪv] adj (*possible*)
éventuel(le); (*future*) futur(e)
prospectus [prəˈspɛktəs] n prospectus m
prosper [ˈprɒspər] vi prospérer; **prosperity**
[prɒˈspɛrɪtɪ] n prospérité f; **prosperous** adj
prospère
prostitute [ˈprɒstɪtjuːt] n prostituée f;
male ~ prostitué m
protect [prəˈtɛkt] vt protéger; **protection**
[prəˈtɛkʃən] n protection f; **protective** adj
protecteur(-trice); (*clothing*) de protection
protein [ˈprəʊtiːn] n protéine f
protest n [ˈprəʊtɛst] protestation f ▷ vi
[prəˈtɛst]: **to ~ against/about** protester
contre/à propos de; **to ~ (that)** protester
que
Protestant [ˈprɒtɪstənt] adj, n
protestant(e)
protester, protestor [prəˈtɛstər] n (*in
demonstration*) manifestant(e)
protractor [prəˈtræktər] n (*Geom*)
rapporteur m
proud [praʊd] adj fier(-ère); (*pej*)
orgueilleux(-euse)

prove [pruːv] *vt* prouver, démontrer ▷ *vi*:
to ~ correct *etc* s'avérer juste *etc*; **to ~ o.s.**
montrer ce dont on est capable

proverb ['prɔvəːb] *n* proverbe *m*

provide [prə'vaɪd] *vt* fournir; **to ~ sb with**
sth fournir qch à qn; **provide for** *vt fus*
(*person*) subvenir aux besoins de; (*future*
event) prévoir; **provided** *conj*: **provided**
(that) à condition que + *sub*; **providing**
[prə'vaɪdɪŋ] *conj* à condition que + *sub*

province ['prɔvɪns] *n* province *f*; (*fig*)
domaine *m*; **provincial** [prə'vɪnʃəl] *adj*
provincial(e)

provision [prə'vɪʒən] *n* (*supplying*)
fourniture *f*; approvisionnement *m*;
(*stipulation*) disposition *f*; **provisions**
npl (*food*) provisions *fpl*; **provisional** *adj*
provisoire

provocative [prə'vɔkətɪv] *adj*
provocateur(-trice), provocant(e)

provoke [prə'vəuk] *vt* provoquer

prowl [praul] *vi* (*also*: **~ about, ~ around**)
rôder

proximity [prɔk'sɪmɪtɪ] *n* proximité *f*

proxy ['prɔksɪ] *n*: **by ~** par procuration

prudent ['pruːdnt] *adj* prudent(e)

prune [pruːn] *n* pruneau *m* ▷ *vt* élaguer

pry [praɪ] *vi*: **to ~ into** fourrer son nez dans

PS *n abbr* (= *postscript*) PS *m*

pseudonym ['sjuːdənɪm] *n* pseudonyme *m*

PSHE *n abbr* (*BRIT Scol*: = *personal, social and*
health education) cours d'éducation personnelle,
sanitaire et sociale préparant à la vie adulte

psychiatric [saɪkɪ'ætrɪk] *adj*
psychiatrique

psychiatrist [saɪ'kaɪətrɪst] *n* psychiatre
m/f

psychic ['saɪkɪk] *adj* (*also*: **~al**)
(*méta*)psychique; (*person*) doué(e) de
télépathie *or* d'un sixième sens

psychoanalysis (*pl* **psychoanalyses**)
[saɪkəuə'nælɪsɪs, -siːz] *n* psychanalyse *f*

psychological [saɪkə'lɔdʒɪkl] *adj*
psychologique

psychologist [saɪ'kɔlədʒɪst] *n*
psychologue *m/f*

psychology [saɪ'kɔlədʒɪ] *n* psychologie *f*

psychotherapy [saɪkəu'θerəpɪ] *n*
psychothérapie *f*

pt *abbr* = **pint; pints; point; points**

PTO *abbr* (= *please turn over*) TSVP

PTV *abbr* (*US*) = **pay television**

pub [pʌb] *n abbr* (= *public house*) pub *m*

puberty ['pjuːbətɪ] *n* puberté *f*

public ['pʌblɪk] *adj* public(-ique) ▷ *n* public
m; **in ~** en public; **to make ~** rendre public

publication [pʌblɪ'keɪʃən] *n* publication *f*

public: public company *n* société *f*
anonyme; **public convenience** *n* (*BRIT*)
toilettes *fpl*; **public holiday** *n* (*BRIT*) jour
férié; **public house** *n* (*BRIT*) pub *m*

publicity [pʌb'lɪsɪtɪ] *n* publicité *f*

publicize ['pʌblɪsaɪz] *vt* (*make known*) faire
connaître, rendre public; (*advertise*) faire de
la publicité pour

public: public limited company *n*
= société *f* anonyme (SA) (*cotée en Bourse*);
publicly *adv* publiquement, en public;
public opinion *n* opinion publique; **public**
relations *n or npl* relations publiques (RP);
public school *n* (*BRIT*) école privée; (*US*)
école publique; **public transport** (*US*)
public transportation *n* transports *mpl*
en commun

publish ['pʌblɪʃ] *vt* publier; **publisher** *n*
éditeur *m*; **publishing** *n* (*industry*) édition *f*

pub lunch *n* repas *m* de bistrot

pudding ['pudɪŋ] *n* (*BRIT: dessert*) dessert
m, entremets *m*; (*sweet dish*) pudding *m*,
gâteau *m*

puddle ['pʌdl] *n* flaque *f* d'eau

puff [pʌf] *n* bouffée *f* ▷ *vt* (*also*: **~ out**: *sails,*
cheeks) gonfler ▷ *vi* (*pant*) haleter; **puff**
pastry, (*US*) **puff paste** *n* pâte feuilletée

pull [pul] *n* (*tug*): **to give sth a ~** tirer sur qch
▷ *vt* tirer; (*trigger*) presser; (*strain: muscle,*
tendon) se claquer ▷ *vi* tirer; **to ~ to pieces**
mettre en morceaux; **to ~ one's punches**
(*also fig*) ménager son adversaire; **to ~ one's**
weight y mettre du sien; **to ~ o.s. together**
se ressaisir; **to ~ sb's leg** (*fig*) faire marcher
qn; **pull apart** *vt* (*break*) mettre en pièces,
démantibuler; **pull away** *vi* (*vehicle: move*
off) partir; (*draw back*) s'éloigner; **pull back**
vt (*lever etc*) tirer sur; (*curtains*) ouvrir ▷ *vi*
(*refrain*) s'abstenir; (*Mil: withdraw*) se retirer;
pull down *vt* baisser, abaisser; (*house*)
démolir; **pull in** *vi* (*Aut*) se ranger; (*Rail*)
entrer en gare; **pull off** *vt* enlever, ôter; (*deal*
etc) conclure; **pull out** *vi* démarrer, partir;
(*Aut: come out of line*) déboîter ▷ *vt* (*from bag,*
pocket) sortir; (*remove*) arracher; **pull over**
vi (*Aut*) se ranger; **pull up** *vi* (*stop*) s'arrêter
▷ *vt* remonter; (*uproot*) déraciner, arracher

pulley ['pulɪ] *n* poulie *f*

pullover ['puləuvəʳ] *n* pull-over *m*, tricot *m*

pulp [pʌlp] *n* (*of fruit*) pulpe *f*; (*for paper*) pâte
f à papier

pulpit ['pulpɪt] *n* chaire *f*

pulse [pʌls] *n* (*of blood*) pouls *m*; (*of*
heart) battement *m*; **pulses** *npl* (*Culin*)
légumineuses *fpl*

puma ['pjuːmə] *n* puma *m*

pump [pʌmp] *n* pompe *f*; (*shoe*) escarpin *m*
▷ *vt* pomper; **pump up** *vt* gonfler

pumpkin ['pʌmpkɪn] *n* potiron *m*,
citrouille *f*

pun [pʌn] *n* jeu *m* de mots, calembour *m*

punch [pʌntʃ] *n* (*blow*) coup *m* de poing;
(*tool*) poinçon *m*; (*drink*) punch *m* ▷ *vt* (*make*
a hole in) poinçonner, perforer; (*hit*): **to ~ sb/**
sth donner un coup de poing à qn/sur qch;
punch-up *n* (*BRIT inf*) bagarre *f*

punctual ['pʌŋktjuəl] *adj* ponctuel(le)

punctuation [pʌŋktjuˈeɪʃən] n
ponctuation f
puncture [ˈpʌŋktʃəʳ] n (BRIT) crevaison f
▷ vt crever
punish [ˈpʌnɪʃ] vt punir; **punishment** n
punition f, châtiment m
punk [pʌŋk] n (person: also: ~ **rocker**) punk
m/f; (music: also: ~ **rock**) le punk; (US inf:
hoodlum) voyou m
pup [pʌp] n chiot m
pupil [ˈpjuːpl] n élève m/f; (of eye) pupille f
puppet [ˈpʌpɪt] n marionnette f, pantin m
puppy [ˈpʌpɪ] n chiot m, petit chien
purchase [ˈpəːtʃɪs] n achat m ▷ vt acheter
pure [pjuəʳ] adj pur(e); **purely** adv
purement
purify [ˈpjuərɪfaɪ] vt purifier, épurer
purity [ˈpjuərɪtɪ] n pureté f
purple [ˈpəːpl] adj violet(te); (face)
cramoisi(e)
purpose [ˈpəːpəs] n intention f, but m;
on ~ exprès
purr [pəːʳ] vi ronronner
purse [pəːs] n (BRIT: for money) porte-
monnaie m inv; (US: handbag) sac m (à main)
▷ vt serrer, pincer
pursue [pəˈsjuː] vt poursuivre
pursuit [pəˈsjuːt] n poursuite f; (occupation)
occupation f, activité f
pus [pʌs] n pus m
push [puʃ] n poussée f ▷ vt pousser; (button)
appuyer sur; (fig: product) mettre en avant,
faire de la publicité pour ▷ vi pousser; **to ~
for** (better pay, conditions) réclamer; **push
in** vi s'introduire de force; **push off** vi (inf)
filer, ficher le camp; **push on** vi (continue)
continuer; **push over** vt renverser; **push
through** vi (in crowd) se frayer un chemin;
pushchair n (BRIT) poussette f; **pusher** n
(also: **drug pusher**) revendeur(-euse) (de
drogue), ravitailleur(-euse) (en drogue);
push-up n (US) traction f
pussy(-cat) [ˈpusɪ-] n (inf) minet m
put (pt, pp **put**) [put] vt mettre; (place)
poser, placer; (say) dire, exprimer; (a
question) poser; (case, view) exposer,
présenter; (estimate) estimer; **put aside** vt
mettre de côté; **put away** vt (store) ranger;
put back vt (replace) remettre, replacer;
(postpone) remettre; **put by** vt (money)
mettre de côté, économiser; **put down**
vt (parcel etc) poser, déposer; (in writing)
mettre par écrit, inscrire; (suppress: revolt
etc) réprimer, écraser; (attribute) attribuer;
(animal) abattre; (cat, dog) faire piquer;
put forward vt (ideas) avancer, proposer;
put in vt (complaint) soumettre; (time,
effort) consacrer; **put off** vt (postpone)
remettre à plus tard, ajourner; (discourage)
dissuader; **put on** vt (clothes, lipstick, CD)
mettre; (light etc) allumer; (play etc) monter;
(weight) prendre; (assume: accent, manner)

prendre; **put out** vt (take outside) mettre
dehors; (one's hand) tendre; (light etc)
éteindre; (person: inconvenience) déranger,
gêner; **put through** vt (Tel: caller) mettre
en communication; (: call) passer; (plan)
faire accepter; **put together** vt mettre
ensemble; (assemble: furniture) monter,
assembler; (: meal) préparer; **put up** vt
(raise) lever, relever, remonter; (hang)
accrocher; (build) construire, ériger;
(increase) augmenter; (accommodate) loger;
put up with vt fus supporter
putt [pʌt] n putt m; **putting green** n
green m
puzzle [ˈpʌzl] n énigme f, mystère m; (game)
jeu m, casse-tête m; (jigsaw) puzzle m; (also:
crossword ~) mots croisés ▷ vt intriguer,
rendre perplexe ▷ vi: **to ~ over** chercher
à comprendre; **puzzled** adj perplexe;
puzzling adj déconcertant(e), inexplicable
pyjamas [pɪˈdʒɑːməz] npl (BRIT) pyjama m
pylon [ˈpaɪlən] n pylône m
pyramid [ˈpɪrəmɪd] n pyramide f
Pyrenees [pɪrəˈniːz] npl Pyrénées fpl

q

quack [kwæk] n (of duck) coin-coin m inv; (pej: doctor) charlatan m

quadruple [kwɔ'dru:pl] vt, vi quadrupler

quail [kweɪl] n (Zool) caille f ▷ vi: **to ~ at** or **before** reculer devant

quaint [kweɪnt] adj bizarre; (old-fashioned) désuet(-ète); (picturesque) au charme vieillot, pittoresque

quake [kweɪk] vi trembler ▷ n abbr = **earthquake**

qualification [kwɔlɪfɪ'keɪʃən] n (often pl: degree etc) diplôme m; (training) qualification(s) f(pl); (ability) compétence(s) f(pl); (limitation) réserve f, restriction f

qualified ['kwɔlɪfaɪd] adj (trained) qualifié(e); (professionally) diplômé(e); (fit, competent) compétent(e), qualifié(e); (limited) conditionnel(le)

qualify ['kwɔlɪfaɪ] vt qualifier; (modify) atténuer, nuancer ▷ vi: **to ~ (as)** obtenir son diplôme (de); **to ~ (for)** remplir les conditions requises (pour); (Sport) se qualifier (pour)

quality ['kwɔlɪtɪ] n qualité f

qualm [kwɑ:m] n doute m; scrupule m

quantify ['kwɔntɪfaɪ] vt quantifier

quantity ['kwɔntɪtɪ] n quantité f

quarantine ['kwɔrnti:n] n quarantaine f

quarrel ['kwɔrl] n querelle f, dispute f ▷ vi se disputer, se quereller

quarry ['kwɔrɪ] n (for stone) carrière f; (animal) proie f, gibier m

quart [kwɔ:t] n ≈ litre m

quarter ['kwɔ:tə^r] n quart m; (of year) trimestre m; (district) quartier m; (US, CANADA: 25 cents) (pièce f de) vingt-cinq cents mpl ▷ vt partager en quartiers or en quatre; (Mil) caserner, cantonner; **quarters** npl logement m; (Mil) quartiers mpl, cantonnement m; **a ~ of an hour** un quart d'heure; **quarter final** n quart m de finale;

quarterly adj trimestriel(le) ▷ adv tous les trois mois

quartet(te) [kwɔ:'tɛt] n quatuor m; (jazz players) quartette m

quartz [kwɔ:ts] n quartz m

quay [ki:] n (also: **~side**) quai m

queasy ['kwi:zɪ] adj: **to feel ~** avoir mal au cœur

Quebec [kwɪ'bɛk] n (city) Québec; (province) Québec m

queen [kwi:n] n (gen) reine f; (Cards etc) dame f

queer [kwɪə^r] adj étrange, curieux(-euse); (suspicious) louche ▷ n (offensive) homosexuel m

quench [kwɛntʃ] vt: **to ~ one's thirst** se désaltérer

query ['kwɪərɪ] n question f ▷ vt (disagree with, dispute) mettre en doute, questionner

quest [kwɛst] n recherche f, quête f

question ['kwɛstʃən] n question f ▷ vt (person) interroger; (plan, idea) mettre en question or en doute; **beyond ~** sans aucun doute; **out of the ~** hors de question; **questionable** adj discutable; **question mark** n point m d'interrogation; **questionnaire** [kwɛstʃə'nɛə^r] n questionnaire m

queue [kju:] (BRIT) n queue f, file f ▷ vi (also: **~ up**) faire la queue

quiche [ki:ʃ] n quiche f

quick [kwɪk] adj rapide; (mind) vif (vive); (agile) agile, vif (vive) ▷ n: **cut to the ~** (fig) touché(e) au vif; **be ~!** dépêche-toi!; **quickly** adv (fast) vite, rapidement; (immediately) tout de suite

quid [kwɪd] n (pl inv: BRIT inf) livre f

quiet ['kwaɪət] adj tranquille, calme; (voice) bas(se); (ceremony, colour) discret(-ète) ▷ n tranquillité f, calme m; (silence) silence m; **quietly** adv tranquillement; (silently) silencieusement; (discreetly) discrètement

quilt [kwɪlt] n édredon m; (continental quilt) couette f

quirky ['kwɜ:kɪ] adj singulier(-ère)

quit [kwɪt] (pt, pp **quit** or **quitted**) vt quitter ▷ vi (give up) abandonner, renoncer; (resign) démissionner

quite [kwaɪt] adv (rather) assez, plutôt; (entirely) complètement, tout à fait; **~ a few of them** un assez grand nombre d'entre eux; **that's not ~ right** ce n'est pas tout à fait juste; **~ (so)!** exactement!

quits [kwɪts] adj: **~ (with)** quitte (envers); **let's call it ~** restons-en là

quiver ['kwɪvə^r] vi trembler, frémir

quiz [kwɪz] n (on TV) jeu-concours m (télévisé); (in magazine etc) test m de connaissances ▷ vt interroger

quota ['kwəʊtə] n quota m

quotation [kwəʊ'teɪʃən] *n* citation *f*; (*estimate*) devis *m*; **quotation marks** *npl* guillemets *mpl*

quote [kwəʊt] *n* citation *f*; (*estimate*) devis *m* ▷ *vt* (*sentence, author*) citer; (*price*) donner, soumettre ▷ *vi*: **to ~ from** citer; **quotes** *npl* (*inverted commas*) guillemets *mpl*

r

rabbi ['ræbaɪ] *n* rabbin *m*

rabbit ['ræbɪt] *n* lapin *m*

rabies ['reɪbiːz] *n* rage *f*

RAC *n abbr* (BRIT: = *Royal Automobile Club*) ≈ ACF *m*

rac(c)oon [rə'kuːn] *n* raton *m* laveur

race [reɪs] *n* (*species*) race *f*; (*competition, rush*) course *f* ▷ *vt* (*person*) faire la course avec ▷ *vi* (*compete*) faire la course, courir; (*pulse*) battre très vite; **race car** *n* (US) = **racing car**; **racecourse** *n* champ *m* de courses; **racehorse** *n* cheval *m* de course; **racetrack** *n* piste *f*

racial ['reɪʃl] *adj* racial(e)

racing ['reɪsɪŋ] *n* courses *fpl*; **racing car** *n* (BRIT) voiture *f* de course; **racing driver** *n* (BRIT) pilote *m* de course

racism ['reɪsɪzəm] *n* racisme *m*; **racist** ['reɪsɪst] *adj, n* raciste *m/f*

rack [ræk] *n* (*for guns, tools*) râtelier *m*; (*for clothes*) portant *m*; (*for bottles*) casier *m*; (*also*: **luggage ~**) filet *m* à bagages; (*also*: **roof ~**) galerie *f*; (*also*: **dish ~**) égouttoir *m* ▷ *vt* tourmenter; **to ~ one's brains** se creuser la cervelle

racket ['rækɪt] *n* (*for tennis*) raquette *f*; (*noise*) tapage *m*, vacarme *m*; (*swindle*) escroquerie *f*

racquet ['rækɪt] *n* raquette *f*

radar ['reɪdɑːʳ] *n* radar *m*

radiation [reɪdɪ'eɪʃən] *n* rayonnement *m*; (*radioactive*) radiation *f*

radiator ['reɪdɪeɪtəʳ] *n* radiateur *m*

radical ['rædɪkl] *adj* radical(e)

radio ['reɪdɪəʊ] *n* radio *f* ▷ *vt* (*person*) appeler par radio; **on the ~** à la radio; **radioactive** *adj* radioactif(-ive); **radio station** *n* station *f* de radio

radish ['rædɪʃ] *n* radis *m*

RAF *n abbr* (BRIT) = **Royal Air Force**

raffle ['ræfl] *n* tombola *f*

raft [rɑːft] *n* (*craft: also*: **life ~**) radeau *m*; (*logs*) train *m* de flottage

rag [ræg] n chiffon m; (pej: newspaper) feuille f, torchon m; (for charity) attractions organisées par les étudiants au profit d'œuvres de charité; **rags** npl haillons mpl

rage [reɪdʒ] n (fury) rage f, fureur f ▷ vi (person) être fou (folle) de rage; (storm) faire rage, être déchaîné(e); **it's all the ~** cela fait fureur

ragged ['rægɪd] adj (edge) inégal(e), qui accroche; (clothes) en loques; (appearance) déguenillé(e)

raid [reɪd] n (Mil) raid m; (criminal) hold-up m inv; (by police) descente f, rafle f ▷ vt faire un raid sur or un hold-up dans or une descente dans

rail [reɪl] n (on stair) rampe f; (on bridge, balcony) balustrade f; (of ship) bastingage m; (for train) rail m; **railcard** n (BRIT) carte f de chemin de fer; **railing(s)** n(pl) grille f, **railway**, (US) **railroad** n chemin m de fer; (track) voie f ferrée; **railway line** n (BRIT) ligne f de chemin de fer; (track) voie ferrée; **railway station** n (BRIT) gare f

rain [reɪn] n pluie f ▷ vi pleuvoir; **in the ~** sous la pluie; **it's ~ing** il pleut; **rainbow** n arc-en-ciel m; **raincoat** n imperméable m; **raindrop** n goutte f de pluie; **rainfall** n chute f de pluie; (measurement) hauteur f des précipitations; **rainforest** n forêt tropicale; **rainy** adj pluvieux(-euse)

raise [reɪz] n augmentation f ▷ vt (lift) lever, hausser; (increase) augmenter; (morale) remonter; (standards) améliorer; (a protest, doubt) provoquer, causer; (a question) soulever; (cattle, family) élever; (crop) faire pousser; (army, funds) rassembler; (loan) obtenir; **to ~ one's voice** élever la voix

raisin ['reɪzn] n raisin sec

rake [reɪk] n (tool) râteau m; (person) débauché m ▷ vt (garden) ratisser

rally ['rælɪ] n (Pol etc) meeting m, rassemblement m; (Aut) rallye m; (Tennis) échange m ▷ vt rassembler, rallier; (support) gagner ▷ vi (sick person) aller mieux; (Stock Exchange) reprendre

RAM [ræm] n abbr (Comput: = random access memory) mémoire vive

ram [ræm] n bélier m ▷ vt (push) enfoncer; (crash into: vehicle) emboutir; (: lamppost etc) percuter

Ramadan [ræmə'dæn] n Ramadan m

ramble ['ræmbl] n randonnée f ▷ vi (walk) se promener, faire une randonnée; (pej: also: ~ **on**) discourir, pérorer; **rambler** n promeneur(-euse), randonneur(-euse); **rambling** adj (speech) décousu(e); (house) plein(e) de coins et de recoins; (Bot) grimpant(e)

ramp [ræmp] n (incline) rampe f; (Aut) dénivellation f; (in garage) pont m; **on/off** ~ (US Aut) bretelle f d'accès

rampage ['ræmpeɪdʒ] n: **to be on the ~** se déchaîner

ran [ræn] pt of **run**

ranch [rɑːntʃ] n ranch m

random ['rændəm] adj fait(e) or établi(e) au hasard; (Comput, Math) aléatoire ▷ n: **at ~** au hasard

rang [ræŋ] pt of **ring**

range [reɪndʒ] n (of mountains) chaîne f; (of missile, voice) portée f; (of products) choix m, gamme f; (also: **shooting ~**) champ m de tir; (also: **kitchen ~**) fourneau m (de cuisine) ▷ vt (place) mettre en rang, placer ▷ vi: **to ~ over** couvrir; **to ~ from ... to** aller de ... à

ranger ['reɪndʒəʳ] n garde m forestier

rank [ræŋk] n rang m; (Mil) grade m; (BRIT: also: **taxi ~**) station f de taxis ▷ vi: **to ~ among** compter or se classer parmi ▷ adj (smell) nauséabond(e); **the ~ and file** (fig) la masse, la base

ransom ['rænsəm] n rançon f; **to hold sb to ~** (fig) exercer un chantage sur qn

rant [rænt] vi fulminer

rap [ræp] n (music) rap m ▷ vt (door) frapper sur or à; (table etc) taper sur

rape [reɪp] n viol m; (Bot) colza m ▷ vt violer

rapid ['ræpɪd] adj rapide; **rapidly** adv rapidement; **rapids** npl (Geo) rapides mpl

rapist ['reɪpɪst] n auteur m d'un viol

rapport [ræ'pɔːʳ] n entente f

rare [rɛəʳ] adj rare; (Culin: steak) saignant(e), **rarely** adv rarement

rash [ræʃ] adj imprudent(e), irréfléchi(e) ▷ n (Med) rougeur f, éruption f; (of events) série f (noire)

rasher ['ræʃəʳ] n fine tranche (de lard)

raspberry ['rɑːzbərɪ] n framboise f

rat [ræt] n rat m

rate [reɪt] n (ratio) taux m, pourcentage m; (speed) vitesse f, rythme m; (price) tarif m ▷ vt (price) évaluer, estimer; (people) classer; **rates** npl (BRIT: property tax) impôts locaux; **to ~ sb/sth as** considérer qn/qch comme

rather ['rɑːðəʳ] adv (somewhat) assez, plutôt; (to some extent) un peu; **it's ~ expensive** c'est assez cher; (too much) c'est un peu cher; **there's ~ a lot** il y en a beaucoup; **I would** or **I'd ~ go** j'aimerais mieux or je préférerais partir; **or ~** (more accurately) ou plutôt

rating ['reɪtɪŋ] n (assessment) évaluation f; (score) classement m; (Finance) cote f; **ratings** npl (Radio) indice(s) m(pl) d'écoute; (TV) Audimat® m

ratio ['reɪʃɪəu] n proportion f; **in the ~ of 100 to 1** dans la proportion de 100 contre 1

ration ['ræʃən] n ration f ▷ vt rationner; **rations** npl (food) vivres mpl

rational ['ræʃənl] adj raisonnable, sensé(e); (solution, reasoning) logique; (Med: person) lucide

rat race n foire f d'empoigne

rattle ['rætl] n (of door, window) battement m; (of coins, chain) cliquetis m; (of train, engine) bruit m de ferraille; (for baby) hochet m ▷ vi cliqueter; (car, bus): **to ~ along** rouler en faisant un bruit de ferraille ▷ vt agiter (bruyamment); (inf: disconcert) décontenancer

rave [reɪv] vi (in anger) s'emporter; (with enthusiasm) s'extasier; (Med) délirer ▷ n (inf: party) rave f, soirée f techno

raven ['reɪvən] n grand corbeau

ravine [rə'viːn] n ravin m

raw [rɔː] adj (uncooked) cru(e); (not processed) brut(e); (sore) à vif, irrité(e); (inexperienced) inexpérimenté(e); **~ materials** matières premières

ray [reɪ] n rayon m; **~ of hope** lueur f d'espoir

razor ['reɪzəʳ] n rasoir m; **razor blade** n lame f de rasoir

Rd abbr = **road**

RE n abbr (BRIT: = religious education) instruction religieuse

re [riː] prep concernant

reach [riːtʃ] n portée f, atteinte f; (of river etc) étendue f ▷ vt atteindre, arriver à; (conclusion, decision) parvenir à ▷ vi s'étendre; **out of/within ~** (object) hors de/à portée; **reach out** vt tendre ▷ vi: **to ~ out (for)** allonger le bras (pour prendre)

react [riː'ækt] vi réagir; **reaction** [riː'ækʃən] n réaction f; **reactor** [riː'æktəʳ] n réacteur m

read (pt, pp **read**) [riːd, rɛd] vi lire ▷ vt lire; (understand) comprendre, interpréter; (study) étudier; (meter) relever; (subj: instrument etc) indiquer, marquer; **read out** vt lire à haute voix; **reader** n lecteur(-trice)

readily ['rɛdɪlɪ] adv volontiers, avec empressement; (easily) facilement

reading ['riːdɪŋ] n lecture f; (understanding) interprétation f; (on instrument) indications fpl

ready ['rɛdɪ] adj prêt(e); (willing) prêt, disposé(e); (available) disponible ▷ n: **at the ~** (Mil) prêt à faire feu; **when will my photos be ~?** quand est-ce que mes photos seront prêtes?; **to get ~** (as vi) se préparer; (as vt) préparer; **ready-cooked** adj précuit(e); **ready-made** adj tout(e) faite(e)

real [rɪəl] adj (world, life) réel(le); (genuine) véritable; (proper) vrai(e) ▷ adv (us inf: very) vraiment; **real ale** n bière traditionnelle; **real estate** n biens fonciers or immobiliers; **realistic** [rɪə'lɪstɪk] adj réaliste; **reality** [riː'ælɪtɪ] n réalité f; **reality TV** n téléréalité f

realization [rɪəlaɪ'zeɪʃən] n (awareness) prise f de conscience; (fulfilment, also: of asset) réalisation f

realize ['rɪəlaɪz] vt (understand) se rendre compte de, prendre conscience de; (a project, Comm: asset) réaliser

really ['rɪəlɪ] adv vraiment; **~?** vraiment?, c'est vrai?

realm [rɛlm] n royaume m; (fig) domaine m

realtor ['rɪəltɔːʳ] n (us) agent immobilier

reappear [riːə'pɪəʳ] vi réapparaître, reparaître

rear [rɪəʳ] adj de derrière, arrière inv; (Aut: wheel etc) arrière ▷ n arrière m ▷ vt (cattle, family) élever ▷ vi (also: **~ up**: animal) se cabrer

rearrange [riːə'reɪndʒ] vt réarranger

rear: rear-view mirror n (Aut) rétroviseur m; **rear-wheel drive** n (Aut) traction f arrière

reason ['riːzn] n raison f ▷ vi: **to ~ with sb** raisonner qn, faire entendre raison à qn; **it stands to ~ that** il va sans dire que; **reasonable** adj raisonnable; (not bad) acceptable; **reasonably** adv (behave) raisonnablement; (fairly) assez; **reasoning** n raisonnement m

reassurance [riːə'ʃuərəns] n (factual) assurance f, garantie f; (emotional) réconfort m

reassure [riːə'ʃuəʳ] vt rassurer

rebate ['riːbeɪt] n (on tax etc) dégrèvement m

rebel n ['rɛbl] rebelle m/f ▷ vi [rɪ'bɛl] se rebeller, se révolter; **rebellion** [rɪ'bɛljən] n rébellion f, révolte f; **rebellious** [rɪ'bɛljəs] adj rebelle

rebuild [riː'bɪld] vt (irreg: like **build**) reconstruire

recall vt [rɪ'kɔːl] rappeler; (remember) se rappeler, se souvenir de ▷ n ['riːkɔl] rappel m; (ability to remember) mémoire f

receipt [rɪ'siːt] n (document) reçu m; (for parcel etc) accusé m de réception; (act of receiving) réception f; **receipts** npl (Comm) recettes fpl; **can I have a ~, please?** je peux avoir un reçu, s'il vous plaît?

receive [rɪ'siːv] vt recevoir; (guest) recevoir, accueillir; **receiver** n (Tel) récepteur m, combiné m; (Radio) récepteur m; (of stolen goods) receleur m; (for bankruptcies) administrateur m judiciaire

recent ['riːsnt] adj récent(e); **recently** adv récemment

reception [rɪ'sɛpʃən] n réception f; (welcome) accueil m, réception; **reception desk** n réception f; **receptionist** n réceptionniste m/f

recession [rɪ'sɛʃən] n (Econ) récession f

recharge [riː'tʃɑːdʒ] vt (battery) recharger

recipe ['rɛsɪpɪ] n recette f

recipient [rɪ'sɪpɪənt] n (of payment) bénéficiaire m/f; (of letter) destinataire m/f

recital [rɪ'saɪtl] n récital m

recite [rɪ'saɪt] vt (poem) réciter

reckless ['rɛkləs] adj (driver etc) imprudent(e); (spender etc) insouciant(e)

reckon ['rɛkən] vt (count) calculer, compter; (consider) considérer, estimer; (think): **I ~ (that)** ... je pense (que) ..., j'estime (que) ...

reclaim [rɪ'kleɪm] vt (land: from sea) assécher; (demand back) réclamer (le remboursement or la restitution de); (waste materials) récupérer

recline [rɪ'klaɪn] vi être allongé(e) or étendu(e)

recognition [rɛkəg'nɪʃən] n reconnaissance f; **transformed beyond ~** méconnaissable

recognize ['rɛkəgnaɪz] vt: **to ~ (by/as)** reconnaître (à/comme étant)

recollection [rɛkə'lɛkʃən] n souvenir m

recommend [rɛkə'mɛnd] vt recommander; **can you ~ a good restaurant?** pouvez-vous me conseiller un bon restaurant? **recommendation** [rɛkəmɛn'deɪʃən] n recommandation f

reconcile ['rɛkənsaɪl] vt (two people) réconcilier; (two facts) concilier, accorder; **to ~ o.s. to** se résigner à

reconsider [ri:kən'sɪdə'] vt reconsidérer

reconstruct [ri:kən'strʌkt] vt (building) reconstruire; (crime, system) reconstituer

record n ['rɛkɔːd] rapport m, récit m; (of meeting etc) procès-verbal m; (register) registre m; (file) dossier m; (Comput) article m, (also: **police ~**) casier m judiciaire; (Mus: disc) disque m; (Sport) record m ▷ adj ['rɛkɔːd] record inv ▷ vt ['rɪ'kɔːd] (set down) noter; (Mus: song etc) enregistrer; **public ~s** archives fpl; **in ~ time** dans un temps record; **recorded delivery** n (BRIT Post): **to send sth recorded delivery** = envoyer qch en recommandé; **recorder** n (Mus) flûte f à bec; **recording** n (Mus) enregistrement m; **record player** n tourne-disque m

recount [rɪ'kaʊnt] vt raconter

recover [rɪ'kʌvə'] vt récupérer ▷ vi (from illness) se rétablir; (from shock) se remettre; **recovery** n récupération f; rétablissement m; (Econ) redressement m

recreate [ri:krɪ'eɪt] vt recréer

recreation [rɛkrɪ'eɪʃən] n (leisure) récréation f, détente f; **recreational drug** n drogue récréative; **recreational vehicle** n (US) camping-car m

recruit [rɪ'kruːt] n recrue f ▷ vt recruter; **recruitment** n recrutement m

rectangle ['rɛktæŋgl] n rectangle m; **rectangular** [rɛk'tæŋgjulə'] adj rectangulaire

rectify ['rɛktɪfaɪ] vt (error) rectifier, corriger

rector ['rɛktə'] n (Rel) pasteur m

recur [rɪ'kə:'] vi se reproduire; (idea, opportunity) se retrouver; (symptoms) réapparaître; **recurring** adj (problem) périodique, fréquent(e); (Math) périodique

recyclable [ri:'saɪkləbl] adj recyclable

recycle [ri:'saɪkl] vt, vi recycler

recycling [ri:'saɪklɪŋ] n recyclage m

red [rɛd] n rouge m; (Pol: pej) rouge m/f ▷ adj rouge; (hair) roux (rousse); **in the ~** (account) à découvert; (business) en déficit; **Red Cross** n Croix-Rouge f; **redcurrant** n groseille f (rouge)

redeem [rɪ'diːm] vt (debt) rembourser; (sth in pawn) dégager; (fig, also Rel) racheter

red: red-haired adj roux (rousse); **redhead** n roux (rousse); **red-hot** adj chauffé(e) au rouge, brûlant(e); **red light** n: **to go through a red light** (Aut) brûler un feu rouge; **red-light district** n quartier mal famé

red meat n viande f rouge

reduce [rɪ'djuːs] vt réduire; (lower) abaisser; **"~ speed now"** (Aut) "ralentir"; **to ~ sb to tears** faire pleurer qn; **reduced** adj réduit(e); **"greatly reduced prices"** "gros rabais"; **at a reduced price** (goods) au rabais; (ticket etc) à prix réduit; **reduction** [rɪ'dʌkʃən] n réduction f; (of price) baisse f; (discount) rabais m; réduction; **is there a reduction for children/students?** y a-t-il une réduction pour les enfants/les étudiants?

redundancy [rɪ'dʌndənsɪ] n (BRIT) licenciement m, mise f au chômage

redundant [rɪ'dʌndnt] adj (BRIT: worker) licencié(e), mis(e) au chômage; (detail, object) superflu(e); **to be made ~** (worker) être licencié, être mis au chômage

reed [riːd] n (Bot) roseau m

reef [riːf] n (at sea) récif m, écueil m

reel [riːl] n bobine f; (Fishing) moulinet m; (Cine) bande f; (dance) quadrille écossais ▷ vi (sway) chanceler

ref [rɛf] n abbr (inf: = referee) arbitre m

refectory [rɪ'tɛktərɪ] n réfectoire m

refer [rɪ'fə:'] vt: **to ~ sb to** (inquirer, patient) adresser qn à; (reader: to text) renvoyer qn à ▷ vi: **to ~ to** (allude to) parler de, faire allusion à; (consult) se reporter à; (apply to) s'appliquer à

referee [rɛfə'riː] n arbitre m; (BRIT: for job application) répondant(e) ▷ vt arbitrer

reference ['rɛfrəns] n référence f, renvoi m; (mention) allusion f, mention f; (for job application: letter) références; lettre f de recommandation; **with ~ to** en ce qui concerne; (Comm: in letter) me référant à; **reference number** n (Comm) numéro m de référence

refill vt [ri:'fɪl] remplir à nouveau; (pen, lighter etc) recharger ▷ n ['ri:fɪl] (for pen etc) recharge f

refine [rɪ'faɪn] vt (sugar, oil) raffiner; (taste) affiner; (idea, theory) peaufiner; **refined** adj (person, taste) raffiné(e); **refinery** n raffinerie f

reflect [rɪ'flɛkt] vt (light, image) réfléchir, refléter ▷ vi (think) réfléchir, méditer; **it ~s**

badly on him cela le discrédite; **it ~s well on him** c'est tout à son honneur; **reflection** [rɪ'flɛkʃən] n réflexion f; (image) reflet m; **on reflection** réflexion faite

reflex ['riːflɛks] adj, n réflexe (m)

reform [rɪ'fɔːm] n réforme f ⊳ vt réformer

refrain [rɪ'freɪn] vi: **to ~ from doing** s'abstenir de faire ⊳ n refrain m

refresh [rɪ'frɛʃ] vt rafraîchir; (subj: food, sleep etc) redonner des forces à; **refreshing** adj (drink) rafraîchissant(e); (sleep) réparateur(-trice); **refreshments** npl rafraîchissements mpl

refrigerator [rɪ'frɪdʒəreɪtəʳ] n réfrigérateur m, frigidaire m

refuel [riː'fjuəl] vi se ravitailler en carburant

refuge ['rɛfjuːdʒ] n refuge m; **to take ~ in** se réfugier dans; **refugee** [rɛfju'dʒiː] n réfugié(e)

refund n ['riːfʌnd] remboursement m ⊳ vt [rɪ'fʌnd] rembourser

refurbish [riː'fəːbɪʃ] vt remettre à neuf

refusal [rɪ'fjuːzəl] n refus m; **to have first ~ on sth** avoir droit de préemption sur qch

refuse[1] ['rɛfjuːs] n ordures fpl, détritus mpl

refuse[2] [rɪ'fjuːz] vt, vi refuser; **to ~ to do sth** refuser de faire qch

regain [rɪ'geɪn] vt (lost ground) regagner; (strength) retrouver

regard [rɪ'ɡɑːd] n respect m, estime f, considération f ⊳ vt considérer; **to give one's ~s to** transmettre ses amitiés à; **"with kindest ~s"** "bien amicalement"; **as ~s, with ~ to** en ce qui concerne; **regarding** prep en ce qui concerne; **regardless** adv quand même; **regardless of** sans se soucier de

regenerate [rɪ'dʒɛnəreɪt] vt régénérer ⊳ vi se régénérer

reggae ['rɛɡeɪ] n reggae m

regiment ['rɛdʒɪmənt] n régiment m

region ['riːdʒən] n région f; **in the ~ of** (fig) aux alentours de; **regional** adj régional(e)

register ['rɛdʒɪstəʳ] n registre m; (also: **electoral ~**) liste électorale ⊳ vt enregistrer, inscrire; (birth) déclarer; (vehicle) immatriculer; (letter) envoyer en recommandé; (subj: instrument) marquer ⊳ vi s'inscrire; (at hotel) signer le registre; (make impression) être (bien) compris(e); **registered** adj (BRIT: letter) recommandé(e); **registered trademark** n marque déposée

registrar ['rɛdʒɪstrɑːʳ] n officier m de l'état civil

registration [rɛdʒɪs'treɪʃən] n (act) enregistrement m; (of student) inscription f; (BRIT Aut: also: **~ number**) numéro m d'immatriculation

registry office ['rɛdʒɪstrɪ-] n (BRIT) bureau m de l'état civil; **to get married in a ~** ≈ se marier à la mairie

regret [rɪ'ɡrɛt] n regret m ⊳ vt regretter; **regrettable** adj regrettable, fâcheux(-euse)

regular ['rɛɡjuləʳ] adj régulier(-ière), (usual) habituel(le), normal(e); (soldier) de métier; (Comm: size) ordinaire ⊳ n (client etc) habitué(e); **regularly** adv régulièrement

regulate ['rɛɡjuleɪt] vt régler; **regulation** [rɛɡju'leɪʃən] n (rule) règlement m; (adjustment) réglage m

rehabilitation ['riːəbɪlɪ'teɪʃən] n (of offender) réhabilitation f; (of addict) réadaptation f

rehearsal [rɪ'həːsəl] n répétition f

rehearse [rɪ'həːs] vt répéter

reign [reɪn] n règne m ⊳ vi régner

reimburse [riːɪm'bəːs] vt rembourser

rein [reɪn] n (for horse) rêne f

reincarnation [riːɪnkɑː'neɪʃən] n réincarnation f

reindeer ['reɪndɪəʳ] n (pl inv) renne m

reinforce [riːɪn'fɔːs] vt renforcer; **reinforcements** npl (Mil) renfort(s) m(pl)

reinstate [riːɪn'steɪt] vt rétablir, réintégrer

reject n ['riːdʒɛkt] (Comm) article m de rebut ⊳ vt [rɪ'dʒɛkt] refuser; (idea) rejeter; **rejection** [rɪ'dʒɛkʃən] n rejet m, refus m

rejoice [rɪ'dʒɔɪs] vi: **to ~ (at or over)** se réjouir (de)

relate [rɪ'leɪt] vt (tell) raconter; (connect) établir un rapport entre ⊳ vi: **to ~ to** (connect) se rapporter à; **to ~ to sb** (interact) entretenir des rapports avec qn; **related** adj apparenté(e); **related to** (subject) lié(e) à; **relating to** prep concernant

relation [rɪ'leɪʃən] n (person) parent(e); (link) rapport m, lien m; **relations** npl (relatives) famille f; **relationship** n rapport m, lien m; (personal ties) relations fpl, rapports; (also: **family relationship**) lien de parenté; (affair) liaison f

relative ['rɛlətɪv] n parent(e) ⊳ adj relatif(-ive); (respective) respectif(-ive); **relatively** adv relativement

relax [rɪ'læks] vi (muscle) se relâcher; (person: unwind) se détendre ⊳ vt relâcher; (mind, person) détendre; **relaxation** [riːlæk'seɪʃən] n relâchement m; (of mind) détente f; (recreation) détente, délassement m; **relaxed** adj relâché(e); détendu(e); **relaxing** adj délassant(e)

relay ['riːleɪ] n (Sport) course f de relais ⊳ vt (message) retransmettre, relayer

release [rɪ'liːs] n (from prison, obligation) libération f; (of gas etc) émission f; (of film etc) sortie f; (new recording) disque m ⊳ vt (prisoner) libérer; (book, film) sortir; (report, news) rendre public, publier; (gas etc) émettre, dégager; (free: from wreckage etc) dégager; (Tech: catch, spring etc) déclencher; (let go: person, animal) relâcher; (: hand, object) lâcher; (: grip, brake) desserrer

relegate ['rɛləgeɪt] vt reléguer; (BRIT Sport): **to be ~d** descendre dans une division inférieure

relent [rɪ'lɛnt] vi se laisser fléchir; **relentless** adj implacable; (non-stop) continuel(le)

relevant ['rɛləvənt] adj (question) pertinent(e); (corresponding) approprié(e); (fact) significatif(-ive); (information) utile

reliable [rɪ'laɪəbl] adj (person, firm) sérieux(-euse), fiable; (method, machine) fiable; (news, information) sûr(e)

relic ['rɛlɪk] n (Rel) relique f; (of the past) vestige m

relief [rɪ'liːf] n (from pain, anxiety) soulagement m; (help, supplies) secours m(pl); (Art, Geo) relief m

relieve [rɪ'liːv] vt (pain, patient) soulager; (fear, worry) dissiper; (bring help) secourir; (take over from: gen) relayer; (: guard) relever; **to ~ sb of sth** débarrasser qn de qch; **to ~ o.s.** (euphemism) se soulager, faire ses besoins; **relieved** adj soulagé(e)

religion [rɪ'lɪdʒən] n religion f

religious [rɪ'lɪdʒəs] adj religieux(-euse); (book) de piété; **religious education** n instruction religieuse

relish ['rɛlɪʃ] n (Culin) condiment m; (enjoyment) délectation f ▷ vt (food etc) savourer; **to ~ doing** se délecter à faire

relocate [riːləʊ'keɪt] vt (business) transférer ▷ vi se transférer, s'installer or s'établir ailleurs

reluctance [rɪ'lʌktəns] n répugnance f

reluctant [rɪ'lʌktənt] adj peu disposé(e), qui hésite; **reluctantly** adv à contrecœur, sans enthousiasme

rely on [rɪ'laɪ-] vt fus (be dependent on) dépendre de; (trust) compter sur

remain [rɪ'meɪn] vi rester; **remainder** n reste m, (Comm) fin f de série; **remaining** adj qui reste; **remains** npl restes mpl

remand [rɪ'mɑːnd] n: **on ~** en détention préventive ▷ vt: **to be ~ed in custody** être placé(e) en détention préventive

remark [rɪ'mɑːk] n remarque f, observation f ▷ vt (faire) remarquer, dire; **remarkable** adj remarquable

remarry [riː'mærɪ] vi se remarier

remedy ['rɛmədɪ] n: **~ (for)** remède m (contre or à) ▷ vt remédier à

remember [rɪ'mɛmbər] vt se rappeler, se souvenir de; (send greetings): **~ me to him** saluez-le de ma part; **Remembrance Day** [rɪ'mɛmbrəns-] n (BRIT) ≈ (le jour de) l'Armistice m, ≈ le 11 novembre

● mondiale a officiellement pris fin. Il rend
● hommage aux victimes des deux guerres
● mondiales. À cette occasion, on observe
● deux minutes de silence à 11h, heure de la
● signature de l'armistice avec l'Allemagne
● en 1918; certaines membres de la famille
● royale et du gouvernement déposent des
● gerbes de coquelicots au cénotaphe de
● Whitehall, et des couronnes sont placées
● sur les monuments aux morts dans toute
● la Grande-Bretagne; par ailleurs, les
● gens portent des coquelicots artificiels
● fabriqués et vendus par des membres de
● la légion britannique blessés au combat,
● au profit des blessés de guerre et de leur
● famille.

remind [rɪ'maɪnd] vt: **to ~ sb of sth** rappeler qch à qn; **to ~ sb to do** faire penser à qn à faire, rappeler à qn qu'il doit faire; **reminder** n (Comm: letter) rappel m; (note etc) pense-bête m; (souvenir) souvenir m

reminiscent [rɛmɪ'nɪsnt] adj: **~ of** qui rappelle, qui fait penser à

remnant ['rɛmnənt] n reste m, restant m; (of cloth) coupon m

remorse [rɪ'mɔːs] n remords m

remote [rɪ'məʊt] adj éloigné(e), lointain(e); (person) distant(e); (possibility) vague; **remote control** n télécommande f; **remotely** adv au loin; (slightly) très vaguement

removal [rɪ'muːvəl] n (taking away) enlèvement m; suppression f; (BRIT: from house) déménagement m; (from office: dismissal) renvoi m; (of stain) nettoyage m, (Med) ablation f; **removal man** (irreg) n (BRIT) déménageur m; **removal van** n (BRIT) camion m de déménagement

remove [rɪ'muːv] vt enlever, retirer; (employee) renvoyer; (stain) faire partir; (abuse) supprimer; (doubt) chasser

Renaissance [rɪ'neɪsɑ̃s] n: **the ~** la Renaissance

rename [riː'neɪm] vt rebaptiser

render ['rɛndər] vt rendre

rendezvous ['rɒndɪvuː] n rendez-vous m inv

renew [rɪ'njuː] vt renouveler; (negotiations) reprendre; (acquaintance) renouer; **renewable** adj (energy) renouvelable

renovate ['rɛnəveɪt] vt rénover; (work of art) restaurer

renowned [rɪ'naʊnd] adj renommé(e)

rent [rɛnt] n loyer m ▷ vt louer; **rental** n (for television, car) (prix m de) location f

reorganize [riː'ɔːgənaɪz] vt réorganiser

rep [rɛp] n abbr (Comm) = **representative**

repair [rɪ'pɛər] n réparation f ▷ vt réparer; **in good/bad ~** en bon/mauvais état; **where can I get this ~ed?** où est-ce que je peux faire réparer ceci?; **repair kit** n trousse f de réparations

repay [riː'peɪ] vt (irreg: like **pay**)
(money, creditor) rembourser; (sb's
efforts) récompenser; **repayment** n
remboursement m

repeat [rɪ'piːt] n (Radio, TV) reprise f ▷ vt
répéter; (promise, attack, also Comm: order)
renouveler; (Scol: a class) redoubler ▷ vi
répéter; **can you ~ that, please?** pouvez-
vous répéter, s'il vous plaît?; **repeatedly**
adv souvent, à plusieurs reprises; **repeat
prescription** n (BRIT): **I'd like a repeat
prescription** je voudrais renouveler mon
ordonnance

repellent [rɪ'pɛlənt] adj repoussant(e) ▷ n:
insect ~ insectifuge m

repercussions [riːpə'kʌʃənz] npl
répercussions fpl

repetition [rɛpɪ'tɪʃən] n répétition f

repetitive [rɪ'pɛtɪtɪv] adj (movement, work)
répétitif(-ive); (speech) plein(e) de redites

replace [rɪ'pleɪs] vt (put back) remettre,
replacer; (take the place of) remplacer;
replacement n (substitution)
remplacement m; (person) remplaçant(e)

replay ['riːpleɪ] n (of match) match rejoué,
(of tape, film) répétition f

replica ['rɛplɪkə] n réplique f, copie exacte

reply [rɪ'plaɪ] n réponse f ▷ vi répondre

report [rɪ'pɔːt] n rapport m; (Press etc)
reportage m; (BRIT: also: **school ~**) bulletin
m (scolaire); (of gun) détonation f ▷ vt
rapporter, faire un compte rendu de; (Press
etc) faire un reportage sur; (notify: accident)
signaler; (: culprit) dénoncer ▷ vi (make a
report) faire un rapport; **I'd like to ~ a theft**
je voudrais signaler un vol; **to ~ (to sb)**
(present o.s.) se présenter (chez qn); **report
card** n (US, SCOTTISH) bulletin m (scolaire);
reportedly adv: **she is reportedly living
in Spain** elle habiterait en Espagne; **he
reportedly told them to …** il leur aurait dit
de …; **reporter** n reporter m

represent [rɛprɪ'zɛnt] vt représenter;
(view, belief) présenter or expliquer; (describe):
to ~ sth as présenter or décrire qch comme;
representation [rɛprɪzɛn'teɪʃən] n
représentation f; **representative** n
représentant(e); (US Pol) député m ▷ adj
représentatif(-ive), caractéristique

repress [rɪ'prɛs] vt réprimer; **repression**
[rɪ'prɛʃən] n répression f

reprimand ['rɛprɪmɑːnd] n réprimande f
▷ vt réprimander

reproduce [riːprə'djuːs] vt reproduire
▷ vi se reproduire; **reproduction**
[riːprə'dʌkʃən] n reproduction f

reptile ['rɛptaɪl] n reptile m

republic [rɪ'pʌblɪk] n république f;
republican adj, n républicain(e)

reputable ['rɛpjutəbl] adj de
bonne réputation; (occupation) honorable

reputation [rɛpju'teɪʃən] n réputation f

request [rɪ'kwɛst] n demande f; (formal)
requête f ▷ vt: **to ~ (of or from sb)**
demander (à qn); **request stop** n (BRIT: for
bus) arrêt facultatif

require [rɪ'kwaɪəʳ] vt (need: subj: person)
avoir besoin de; (: thing, situation)
nécessiter, demander; (want) exiger; (order):
to ~ sb to do sth/sth of sb exiger que qn
fasse qch/qch de qn; **requirement** n (need)
exigence f; besoin m; (condition) condition
f (requise)

resat [riː'sæt] pt, pp of **resit**

rescue ['rɛskjuː] n (from accident) sauvetage
m; (help) secours mpl ▷ vt sauver

research [rɪ'sɜːtʃ] n recherche(s) f(pl) ▷ vt
faire des recherches sur

resemblance [rɪ'zɛmbləns] n
ressemblance f

resemble [rɪ'zɛmbl] vt ressembler à

resent [rɪ'zɛnt] vt être contrarié(e)
par; **resentful** adj irrité(e), plein(e)
de ressentiment; **resentment** n
ressentiment m

reservation [rɛzə'veɪʃən] n (booking)
réservation f; **to make a ~ (in a hotel/a
restaurant/on a plane)** réserver or retenir
une chambre/une table/une place;
reservation desk n (US: in hotel) réception f

reserve [rɪ'zɜːv] n réserve f; (Sport)
remplaçant(e) ▷ vt (seats etc) réserver,
retenir; **reserved** adj réservé(e)

reservoir ['rɛzəvwɑːʳ] n réservoir m

reshuffle [riː'ʃʌfl] n: **Cabinet ~** (Pol)
remaniement ministériel

residence ['rɛzɪdəns] n résidence f;
residence permit n (BRIT) permis m de
séjour

resident ['rɛzɪdənt] n (of country)
résident(e); (of area, house) habitant(e);
(in hotel) pensionnaire ▷ adj résidant(e);
residential [rɛzɪ'dɛnʃəl] adj de résidence;
(area) résidentiel(le); (course) avec
hébergement sur place

residue ['rɛzɪdjuː] n reste m; (Chem, Physics)
résidu m

resign [rɪ'zaɪn] vt (one's post) se démettre
de ▷ vi démissionner; **to ~ o.s. to** (endure)
se résigner à; **resignation** [rɛzɪg'neɪʃən]
n (from post) démission f; (state of mind)
résignation f

resin ['rɛzɪn] n résine f

resist [rɪ'zɪst] vt résister à; **resistance** n
résistance f

resit vt [riː'sɪt] (irreg: like **sit**) (BRIT: exam)
repasser ▷ n ['riːsɪt] deuxième session f
(d'un examen)

resolution [rɛzə'luːʃən] n résolution f

resolve [rɪ'zɔlv] n résolution f ▷ vt (problem)
résoudre; (decide): **to ~ to do** résoudre or
décider de faire

resort [rɪ'zɔːt] n (seaside town) station
f balnéaire; (for skiing) station de ski;

(*recourse*) recours *m* ▷ vi: **to ~ to** avoir
recours à; **in the last ~** en dernier ressort
resource [rɪ'sɔːs] *n* ressource *f*;
resourceful *adj* ingénieux(-euse),
débrouillard(e)
respect [rɪs'pɛkt] *n* respect *m* ▷ vt
respecter; **respectable** *adj* respectable;
(*quite good: result etc*) honorable; **respectful**
adj respectueux(-euse); **respective**
adj respectif(-ive); **respectively** *adv*
respectivement
respite ['rɛspaɪt] *n* répit *m*
respond [rɪs'pɔnd] *vi* répondre; (*react*)
réagir; **response** [rɪs'pɔns] *n* réponse *f*;
(*reaction*) réaction *f*
responsibility [rɪspɔnsɪ'bɪlɪtɪ] *n*
responsabilité *f*
responsible [rɪs'pɔnsɪbl] *adj* (*liable*):
~ (for) responsable (de); (*person*) digne
de confiance; (*job*) qui comporte des
responsabilités; **responsibly** *adv* avec
sérieux
responsive [rɪs'pɔnsɪv] *adj* (*student,
audience*) réceptif(-ive); (*brakes, steering*)
sensible
rest [rɛst] *n* repos *m*; (*stop*) arrêt *m*, pause *f*;
(*Mus*) silence *m*; (*support*) support *m*, appui
m; (*remainder*) reste *m*, restant *m* ▷ vi se
reposer; (*be supported*): **to ~ on** appuyer or
reposer sur ▷ vt (*lean*): **to ~ sth on/against**
appuyer qch sur/contre; **the ~ of them** les
autres
restaurant ['rɛstərɔŋ] *n* restaurant *m*;
restaurant car *n* (BRIT *Rail*) wagon-
restaurant *m*
restless ['rɛstlɪs] *adj* agité(e)
restoration [rɛstə'reɪʃən] *n* (*of building*)
restauration *f*; (*of stolen goods*) restitution *f*
restore [rɪ'stɔː] *vt* (*building*) restaurer; (*sth
stolen*) restituer; (*peace, health*) rétablir; **to ~
to** (*former state*) ramener à
restrain [rɪs'treɪn] *vt* (*feeling*) contenir;
(*person*): **to ~ (from doing)** retenir (de
faire); **restraint** *n* (*restriction*) contrainte *f*;
(*moderation*) retenue *f*; (*of style*) sobriété *f*
restrict [rɪs'trɪkt] *vt* restreindre, limiter;
restriction [rɪs'trɪkʃən] *n* restriction *f*,
limitation *f*
rest room *n* (US) toilettes *fpl*
restructure [riː'strʌktʃəʳ] *vt* restructurer
result [rɪ'zʌlt] *n* résultat *m* ▷ vi: **to ~ in**
aboutir à, se terminer par; **as a ~ of** à la
suite de
resume [rɪ'zjuːm] *vt* (*work, journey*)
reprendre ▷ vi (*work etc*) reprendre
résumé ['reɪzjuːmeɪ] *n* (*summary*) résumé
m; (US: *curriculum vitae*) curriculum vitae
m inv
resuscitate [rɪ'sʌsɪteɪt] *vt* (*Med*) réanimer
retail ['riːteɪl] *adj* de or au détail ▷ *adv* au
détail; **retailer** *n* détaillant(e)
retain [rɪ'teɪn] *vt* (*keep*) garder, conserver

retaliation [rɪtælɪ'eɪʃən] *n* représailles *fpl*,
vengeance *f*
retire [rɪ'taɪəʳ] *vi* (*give up work*) prendre sa
retraite; (*withdraw*) se retirer, partir; (*go to
bed*) (aller) se coucher; **retired** *adj* (*person*)
retraité(e); **retirement** *n* retraite *f*
retort [rɪ'tɔːt] *vi* riposter
retreat [rɪ'triːt] *n* retraite *f* ▷ vi battre en
retraite
retrieve [rɪ'triːv] *vt* (*sth lost*) récupérer;
(*situation, honour*) sauver; (*error, loss*)
réparer; (*Comput*) rechercher
retrospect ['rɛtrəspɛkt] *n*: **in ~**
rétrospectivement, après coup;
retrospective [rɛtrə'spɛktɪv] *adj*
rétrospectif(-ive); (*law*) rétroactif(-ive) ▷ *n*
(*Art*) rétrospective *f*
return [rɪ'təːn] *n* (*going or coming back*)
retour *m*; (*of sth stolen etc*) restitution *f*;
(*Finance: from land, shares*) rapport *m* ▷ cpd
(*journey*) de retour; (BRIT: *ticket*) aller et
retour; (*match*) retour ▷ vi (*person etc:
come back*) revenir; (: *go back*) retourner
▷ vt rendre; (*bring back*) rapporter; (*send
back*) renvoyer; (*put back*) remettre; (*Pol:
candidate*) élire; **returns** *npl* (*Comm*) recettes
fpl; (*Finance*) bénéfices *mpl*; **many happy
~s (of the day)!** bon anniversaire!; **by ~ (of
post)** par retour (du courrier); **in ~ (for)** en
échange (de); **a ~ (ticket) for ...** un billet
aller et retour pour ...; **return ticket** *n* (*esp
BRIT*) billet *m* aller-retour
retweet [riː'twiːt] *vt* (*on Twitter*) retweeter
reunion [riː'juːnɪən] *n* réunion *f*
reunite [riːjuː'naɪt] *vt* réunir
revamp [riː'væmp] *vt* (*house*) retaper; (*firm*)
réorganiser
reveal [rɪ'viːl] *vt* (*make known*) révéler;
(*display*) laisser voir; **revealing** *adj*
révélateur(-trice); (*dress*) au décolleté
généreux or suggestif
revel ['rɛvl] *vi*: **to ~ in sth/in doing** se
délecter de qch/à faire
revelation [rɛvə'leɪʃən] *n* révélation *f*
revenge [rɪ'vɛndʒ] *n* vengeance *f*; (*in game
etc*) revanche *f* ▷ vt venger; **to take ~ (on)** se
venger (sur)
revenue ['rɛvənjuː] *n* revenu *m*
Reverend ['rɛvərənd] *adj*: **the ~ John
Smith** (*Anglican*) le révérend John Smith;
(*Catholic*) l'abbé (John) Smith; (*Protestant*) le
pasteur (John) Smith
reversal [rɪ'vəːsl] *n* (*of opinion*) revirement
m; (*of order*) renversement *m*; (*of direction*)
changement *m*
reverse [rɪ'vəːs] *n* contraire *m*, opposé
m; (*back*) dos *m*, envers *m*; (*of paper*) verso
m; (*of coin*) revers *m*; (*Aut: also*: **~ gear**)
marche *f* arrière ▷ *adj* (*order, direction*)
opposé(e), inverse ▷ vt (*order, position*)
changer, inverser; (*direction, policy*) changer
complètement de; (*decision*) annuler;

(roles) renverser ▷ vi (BRIT Aut) faire marche arrière; **reversing lights** npl (BRIT Aut) feux mpl de marche arrière or de recul

revert [rɪˈvəːt] vi: **to ~** revenir à, retourner à

review [rɪˈvjuː] n revue f; (of book, film) critique f; (of situation, policy) examen m, bilan m; (us: examination) examen ▷ vt passer en revue; faire la critique de; examiner

revise [rɪˈvaɪz] vt réviser, modifier; (manuscript) revoir, corriger ▷ vi (study) réviser; **revision** [rɪˈvɪʒən] n révision f

revival [rɪˈvaɪvəl] n reprise f; (recovery) rétablissement m; (of faith) renouveau m

revive [rɪˈvaɪv] vt (person) ranimer; (custom) rétablir; (economy) relancer; (hope, courage) raviver, faire renaître; (play, fashion) reprendre ▷ vi (person) reprendre connaissance (: from ill health) se rétablir; (hope etc) renaître; (activity) reprendre

revolt [rɪˈvəult] n révolte f ▷ vi se révolter, se rebeller ▷ vt révolter, dégoûter; **revolting** adj dégoûtant(e)

revolution [rɛvəˈluːʃən] n révolution f; (of wheel etc) tour m, révolution; **revolutionary** adj, n révolutionnaire (m/f)

revolve [rɪˈvɔlv] vi tourner

revolver [rɪˈvɔlvəʳ] n revolver m

reward [rɪˈwɔːd] n récompense f ▷ vt: **to ~ (for)** récompenser (de); **rewarding** adj (fig) qui (en) vaut la peine, gratifiant(e)

rewind [riːˈwaɪnd] vt (irreg: like **wind²**) (tape) réembobiner

rewritable [riːˈraɪtəbl] adj (CD, DVD) réinscriptible

rewrite [riːˈraɪt] (irreg: like **write**) vt récrire

rheumatism [ˈruːmətɪzəm] n rhumatisme m

Rhine [raɪn] n: **the (River) ~** le Rhin

rhinoceros [raɪˈnɔsərəs] n rhinocéros m

rhubarb [ˈruːbɑːb] n rhubarbe f

rhyme [raɪm] n rime f; (verse) vers mpl

rhythm [ˈrɪðm] n rythme m

rib [rɪb] n (Anat) côte f

ribbon [ˈrɪbən] n ruban m; **in ~s** (torn) en lambeaux

rice [raɪs] n riz m; **rice pudding** n riz m au lait

rich [rɪtʃ] adj riche; (gift, clothes) somptueux(-euse); **to be ~ in sth** être riche en qch

rid [rɪd] (pt, pp **rid**) vt: **to ~ sb of** débarrasser qn de; **to get ~ of** se débarrasser de

ridden [ˈrɪdn] pp of **ride**

riddle [ˈrɪdl] n (puzzle) énigme f ▷ vt: **to be ~d with** être criblé(e) de; (fig) être en proie à

ride [raɪd] (pt **rode**, pp **ridden**) n promenade f, tour m; (distance covered) trajet m ▷ vi (as sport) monter (à cheval), faire du cheval; (go somewhere: on horse, bicycle) aller (à cheval or bicyclette etc); (travel: on bicycle, motor cycle,

bus) rouler ▷ vt (a horse) monter; (distance) parcourir, faire; **to ~ a horse/bicycle** monter à cheval/à bicyclette; **to take sb for a ~** (fig) faire marcher qn; (cheat) rouler qn; **rider** n cavalier(-ière); (in race) jockey m; (on bicycle) cycliste m/f; (on motorcycle) motocycliste m/f

ridge [rɪdʒ] n (of hill) faîte m; (of roof, mountain) arête f; (on object) strie f

ridicule [ˈrɪdɪkjuːl] n ridicule m; dérision f ▷ vt ridiculiser, tourner en dérision; **ridiculous** [rɪˈdɪkjuləs] adj ridicule

riding [ˈraɪdɪŋ] n équitation f; **riding school** n manège m, école f d'équitation

rife [raɪf] adj répandu(e); **~ with** abondant(e) en

rifle [ˈraɪfl] n fusil m (à canon rayé) ▷ vt vider, dévaliser

rift [rɪft] n fente f, fissure f; (fig: disagreement) désaccord m

rig [rɪg] n (also: **oil ~**: on land) derrick m; (: at sea) plate-forme pétrolière ▷ vt (election etc) truquer

right [raɪt] adj (true) juste, exact(e); (correct) bon (bonne); (suitable) approprié(e), convenable; (just) juste, équitable; (morally good) bien inv; (not left) droit(e) ▷ n (moral good) bien m; (title, claim) droit m; (not left) droite f ▷ adv (answer) correctement; (treat) bien, comme il faut; (not on the left) à droite ▷ vt redresser ▷ excl bon!; **do you have the ~ time?** avez-vous l'heure juste or exacte?; **to be ~** (person) avoir raison; (answer) être juste or correct(e); **by ~s** en toute justice; **on the ~** à droite; **to be in the ~** avoir raison; **~ in the middle** en plein milieu; **~ away** immédiatement; **right angle** n (Math) angle droit; **rightful** adj (heir) légitime; **right-hand** adj: **the right-hand side** la droite; **right-hand drive** n conduite f à droite; (vehicle) véhicule m avec la conduite à droite; **right-handed** (person) droitier(-ière); **rightly** adv bien, correctement; (with reason) à juste titre; **right of way** n (on path etc) droit m de passage; (Aut) priorité f; **right-wing** adj (Pol) de droite

rigid [ˈrɪdʒɪd] adj rigide; (principle, control) strict(e)

rigorous [ˈrɪgərəs] adj rigoureux(-euse)

rim [rɪm] n bord m; (of spectacles) monture f; (of wheel) jante f

rind [raɪnd] n (of bacon) couenne f; (of lemon etc) écorce f, zeste m; (of cheese) croûte f

ring [rɪŋ] n anneau m; (on finger) bague f; (also: **wedding ~**) alliance f; (of people, objects) cercle m; (of spies) réseau m; (of smoke etc) rond m; (arena) piste f, arène f; (for boxing) ring m; (sound of bell) sonnerie f ▷ vi (pt **rang**, pp **rung**) (telephone, bell) sonner; (person: by telephone) téléphoner; (ears) bourdonner; (also: **~ out**: voice, words) retentir ▷ vt (also: **~ up**) téléphoner à, appeler; **to ~ the bell** sonner; **to give sb a ~** (Tel) passer un coup de téléphone or de fil à qn; **ring back** vt, vi (BRIT Tel) rappeler; **ring off** vi (BRIT Tel) raccrocher; **ring up** vt (BRIT Tel) téléphoner à, appeler; **ringing tone** n (BRIT Tel) tonalité f d'appel; **ringleader** n (of gang) chef m, meneur m; **ring road** n (BRIT) rocade f; (motorway) périphérique m; **ringtone** n (on mobile) sonnerie f (de téléphone portable)

rink [rɪŋk] n (also: **ice ~**) patinoire f

rinse [rɪns] n rinçage m ▷ vt rincer

riot ['raɪət] n émeute f, bagarres fpl ▷ vi (demonstrators) manifester avec violence; (population) se soulever, se révolter; **to run ~** se déchaîner

rip [rɪp] n déchirure f ▷ vt déchirer ▷ vi se déchirer; **rip off** vt (inf: cheat) arnaquer; **rip up** vt déchirer

ripe [raɪp] adj (fruit) mûr(e); (cheese) fait(e)

rip-off ['rɪpɔf] n (inf): **it's a ~!** c'est du vol manifeste!, c'est de l'arnaque!

ripple ['rɪpl] n ride f, ondulation f; (of applause, laughter) cascade f ▷ vi se rider, onduler

rise [raɪz] n (slope) côte f, pente f; (hill) élévation f; (increase: BRIT) augmentation f; (: in prices, temperature) hausse f, augmentation; (fig: to power etc) ascension f ▷ vi (pt **rose**, pp **risen**) s'élever, monter; (prices, numbers) augmenter, monter; (waters, river) monter; (sun, wind, person: from chair, bed) se lever; (also: **~ up**: tower, building) s'élever; (: rebel) se révolter, se rebeller; (in rank) s'élever; **to give ~ to** donner lieu à; **to ~ to the occasion** se montrer à la hauteur; **risen** ['rɪzn] pp of **rise**; **rising** adj (increasing: number, prices) en hausse; (tide) montant(e); (sun, moon) levant(e)

risk [rɪsk] n risque m ▷ vt risquer; **to take** or **run the ~ of doing** courir le risque de faire; **at ~** en danger; **at one's own ~** à ses risques et périls; **risky** adj risqué(e)

rite [raɪt] n rite m; **the last ~s** les derniers sacrements

ritual ['rɪtjuəl] adj rituel(le) ▷ n rituel m

rival ['raɪvl] n rival(e); (in business) concurrent(e) ▷ adj rival(e); qui fait concurrence ▷ vt (match) égaler; **rivalry** n rivalité f; (in business) concurrence f

river ['rɪvəʳ] n rivière f; (major: also fig) fleuve m ▷ cpd (port, traffic) fluvial(e); **up/down~** en amont/aval; **riverbank** n rive f, berge f

rivet ['rɪvɪt] n rivet m ▷ vt (fig) river, fixer

Riviera [rɪvɪ'eərə] n: **the (French) ~** la Côte d'Azur

road [rəud] n route f; (in town) rue f; (fig) chemin, voie f ▷ cpd (accident) de la route; **major/minor ~** route principale or à priorité/voie secondaire; **which ~ do I take**

for ...? quelle route dois-je prendre pour aller à ...?; **roadblock** n barrage routier; **road map** n carte routière; **road rage** n comportement très agressif de certains usagers de la route; **road safety** n sécurité routière; **roadside** n bord m de la route, bas-côté m; **road sign** n panneau m de signalisation; **road tax** n (BRIT Aut) taxe f sur les automobiles; **roadworks** npl travaux mpl (de réfection des routes)

roam [rəum] vi errer, vagabonder

roar [rɔːʳ] n rugissement m; (of crowd) hurlements mpl; (of vehicle, thunder, storm) grondement m ▷ vi rugir; hurler; gronder; **to ~ with laughter** rire à gorge déployée

roast [rəust] n rôti m ▷ vt (meat) (faire) rôtir; (coffee) griller, torréfier; **roast beef** n rôti m de bœuf, rosbif m

rob [rɔb] vt (person) voler; (bank) dévaliser; **to ~ sb of sth** voler or dérober qch à qn; (fig: deprive) priver qn de qch; **robber** n bandit m, voleur m; **robbery** n vol m

robe [rəub] n (for ceremony etc) robe f; (also: **bath~**) peignoir m, (US: rug) couverture f ▷ vt revêtir (d'une robe)

robin ['rɔbɪn] n rouge-gorge m

robot ['rəubɔt] n robot m

robust [rəu'bʌst] adj robuste; (material, appetite) solide

rock [rɔk] n (substance) roche f, roc m; (boulder) rocher m, roche; (US: small stone) caillou m; (BRIT: sweet) = sucre m d'orge ▷ vt (swing gently: cradle) balancer; (: child) bercer; (shake) ébranler, secouer ▷ vi se balancer, être ébranlé(e) or secoué(e); **on the ~s** (drink) avec des glaçons; (marriage etc) en train de craquer; **rock and roll** n rock (and roll) m, rock'n'roll m; **rock climbing** n varappe f

rocket ['rɔkɪt] n fusée f; (Mil) fusée, roquette f; (Culin) roquette

rocking chair ['rɔkɪŋ-] n fauteuil m à bascule

rocky ['rɔkɪ] adj (hill) rocheux(-euse); (path) rocailleux(-euse)

rod [rɔd] n (metallic) tringle f; (Tech) tige f; (wooden) baguette f; (also: **fishing ~**) canne f à pêche

rode [rəud] pt of **ride**

rodent ['rəudnt] n rongeur m

rogue [rəug] n coquin(e)

role [rəul] n rôle m; **role-model** n modèle m à émuler

roll [rəul] n rouleau m; (of banknotes) liasse f; (also: **bread ~**) petit pain; (register) liste f; (sound: of drums etc) roulement m ▷ vt rouler; (also: **~ up**) (string) enrouler; (: also: **~ out**: pastry) étendre au rouleau, abaisser ▷ vi rouler; **roll over** vi se retourner; **roll up** vi (inf: arrive) arriver, s'amener ▷ vt (carpet, cloth, map) rouler; (sleeves) retrousser; **roller** n rouleau m; (wheel) roulette f; (for road)

rouleau compresseur; (*for hair*) bigoudi *m*;
roller coaster *n* montagnes *fpl* russes;
roller skates *npl* patins *mpl* à roulettes;
roller-skating *n* patin *m* à roulettes; **to go
roller-skating** faire du patin à roulettes;
rolling pin *n* rouleau *m* à pâtisserie
ROM [rɔm] *n abbr* (*Comput:* = *read-only
memory*) mémoire morte, ROM *f*
Roman ['rəumən] *adj* romain(e) ▷ *n*
Romain(e); **Roman Catholic** *adj, n*
catholique (*m/f*)
romance [rə'mæns] *n* (*love affair*) idylle
f; (*charm*) poésie *f*; (*novel*) roman *m* à l'eau
de rose
Romania [rəu'meɪnɪə] *n* = **Rumania**
Roman numeral *n* chiffre romain
romantic [rə'mæntɪk] *adj* romantique;
(*novel, attachment*) sentimental(e)
Rome [rəum] *n* Rome
roof [ruːf] *n* toit *m*; (*of tunnel, cave*) plafond *m*
▷ *vt* couvrir (d'un toit); **the ~ of the mouth**
la voûte du palais; **roof rack** *n* (*Aut*) galerie *f*
rook [ruk] *n* (*bird*) freux *m*; (*Chess*) tour *f*
room [ruːm] *n* (*in house*) pièce *f*; (*also:* **bed~**)
chambre *f* (à coucher); (*in school etc*) salle
f; (*space*) place *f*; **roommate** *n* camarade
m/f de chambre; **room service** *n* service
m des chambres (*dans un hôtel*); **roomy** *adj*
spacieux(-euse); (*garment*) ample
rooster ['ruːstə'] *n* coq *m*
root [ruːt] *n* (*Bot, Math*) racine *f*; (*fig: of
problem*) origine *f*, fond *m* ▷ *vi* (*plant*)
s'enraciner
rope [rəup] *n* corde *f*; (*Naut*) cordage *m* ▷ *vt*
(*tie up or together*) attacher; (*climbers: also:
~ together*) encorder; (*area: also: ~ off*)
interdire l'accès de; (*: divide off*) séparer;
to know the ~s (*fig*) être au courant,
connaître les ficelles
rort [rɔːt] *n* (*AUST, NZ inf*) arnaque *f* (*inf*) ▷ *vt*
escroquer
rose [rəuz] *pt of* **rise** ▷ *n* rose *f*; (*also:* **~bush**)
rosier *m*
rosé ['rəuzeɪ] *n* rosé *m*
rosemary ['rəuzmərɪ] *n* romarin *m*
rosy ['rəuzɪ] *adj* rose; **a ~ future** un bel
avenir
rot [rɔt] *n* (*decay*) pourriture *f*; (*fig: pej:
nonsense*) idioties *fpl*, balivernes *fpl* ▷ *vt, vi*
pourrir
rota ['rəutə] *n* liste *f*, tableau *m* de service
rotate [rəu'teɪt] *vt* (*revolve*) faire tourner;
(*change round: crops*) alterner; (*: jobs*) faire à
tour de rôle ▷ *vi* (*revolve*) tourner
rotten ['rɔtn] *adj* (*decayed*) pourri(e);
(*dishonest*) corrompu(e); (*inf: bad*)
mauvais(e), moche; **to feel ~** (*ill*) être mal
fichu(e)
rough [rʌf] *adj* (*cloth, skin*) rêche,
rugueux(-euse); (*terrain*) accidenté(e);
(*path*) rocailleux(-euse); (*voice*) rauque,
rude; (*person, manner: coarse*) rude, fruste;

(*: violent*) brutal(e); (*district, weather*)
mauvais(e); (*sea*) houleux(-euse); (*plan*)
ébauché(e); (*guess*) approximatif(-ive) ▷ *n*
(*Golf*) rough *m* ▷ *vt*: **to ~ it** vivre à la dure; **to
sleep ~** (*BRIT*) coucher à la dure; **roughly**
adv (*handle*) rudement, brutalement; (*speak*)
avec brusquerie; (*make*) grossièrement;
(*approximately*) à peu près, en gros
roulette [ruː'lɛt] *n* roulette *f*
round [raund] *adj* rond(e) ▷ *n* rond *m*, cercle
m; (*BRIT: of toast*) tranche *f*; (*duty: of police
officer, milkman etc*) tournée *f*; (*: of doctor*)
visites *fpl*; (*game: of cards, in competition*)
partie *f*; (*Boxing*) round *m*; (*of talks*) série
f ▷ *vt* (*corner*) tourner ▷ *prep* autour de
▷ *adv*: **right ~, all ~** tout autour; **~ of
ammunition** cartouche *f*; **~ of applause**
applaudissements *mpl*; **~ of drinks** tournée
f; **the long way ~** (*par*) le chemin le plus
long; **all (the) year ~** toute l'année; **it's just
~ the corner** (*fig*) c'est tout près; **to go ~ to
sb's (house)** aller chez qn; **go ~ the back**
passez par derrière; **enough to go ~** assez
pour tout le monde; **she arrived ~ (about)
noon** (*BRIT*) elle est arrivée vers midi; **~ the
clock** 24 heures sur 24; **round off** *vt* (*speech
etc*) terminer; **round up** *vt* rassembler;
(*criminals*) effectuer une rafle de; (*prices*)
arrondir (au chiffre supérieur); **roundabout**
n (*BRIT: Aut*) rond-point *m* (à sens giratoire);
(*: at fair*) manège *m* (de chevaux de bois)
▷ *adj* (*route, means*) détourné(e); **round trip**
n (*voyage m*) aller et retour *m*; **roundup** *n*
rassemblement *m*; (*of criminals*) rafle *f*
rouse [rauz] *vt* (*wake up*) réveiller; (*stir
up*) susciter, provoquer; (*interest*) éveiller;
(*suspicions*) susciter, éveiller
route [ruːt] *n* itinéraire *m*; (*of bus*) parcours
m; (*of trade, shipping*) route *f*
router *n* (*Comput*) routeur *m*
routine [ruː'tiːn] *adj* (*work*) ordinaire,
courant(e); (*procedure*) d'usage ▷ *n* (*habits*)
habitudes *fpl*; (*pej*) train-train *m*; (*Theat*)
numéro *m*
row¹ [rəu] *n* (*line*) rangée *f*; (*of people, seats,
Knitting*) rang *m*; (*behind one another: of cars,
people*) file *f* ▷ *vi* (*in boat*) ramer; (*as sport*)
faire de l'aviron ▷ *vt* (*boat*) faire aller à la
rame *or* à l'aviron; **in a ~** (*fig*) d'affilée
row² [rau] *n* (*noise*) vacarme *m*; (*dispute*)
dispute *f*, querelle *f*; (*scolding*) réprimande *f*,
savon *m* ▷ *vi* (*also:* **to have a ~**) se disputer,
se quereller
rowboat ['rəubəut] *n* (*US*) canot *m* (à
rames)
rowing ['rəuɪŋ] *n* canotage *m*; (*as sport*)
aviron *m*; **rowing boat** *n* (*BRIT*) canot *m* (à
rames)
royal ['rɔɪəl] *adj* royal(e); **royalty** *n* (*royal
persons*) (membres *mpl* de la) famille royale;
(*payment: to author*) droits *mpl* d'auteur; (*: to
inventor*) royalties *fpl*

rpm *abbr* (= *revolutions per minute*) t/mn (= *tours/minute*)

R.S.V.P. *abbr* (= *répondez s'il vous plaît*) RSVP

Rt. Hon. *abbr* (BRIT: = *Right Honourable*) titre donné aux députés de la Chambre des communes

rub [rʌb] *n*: **to give sth a ~** donner un coup de chiffon *or* de torchon à qch ▷ *vt* frotter; (*person*) frictionner; (*hands*) se frotter; **to ~ sb up** (BRIT) *or* **to ~ sb** (US) **the wrong way** prendre qn à rebrousse-poil; **rub in** *vt* (*ointment*) faire pénétrer; **rub off** *vi* partir; **rub out** *vt* effacer

rubber ['rʌbəʳ] *n* caoutchouc *m*; (BRIT: *eraser*) gomme *f* (à effacer); **rubber band** *n* élastique *m*; **rubber gloves** *npl* gants *mpl* en caoutchouc

rubbish ['rʌbɪʃ] *n* (*from household*) ordures *fpl*; (*fig*: *pej*) choses *fpl* sans valeur; camelote *f*; (*nonsense*) bêtises *fpl*, idioties *fpl*; **rubbish bin** *n* (BRIT) boîte *f* à ordures, poubelle *f*; **rubbish dump** *n* (BRIT: *in town*) décharge publique, dépotoir *m*

rubble ['rʌbl] *n* décombres *mpl*; (*smaller*) gravats *mpl*; (*Constr*) blocage *m*

ruby ['ruːbɪ] *n* rubis *m*

rucksack ['rʌksæk] *n* sac *m* à dos

rudder ['rʌdəʳ] *n* gouvernail *m*

rude [ruːd] *adj* (*impolite*: *person*) impoli(e), (*: word, manners*) grossier(-ière); (*shocking*) indécent(e), inconvenant(e)

ruffle ['rʌfl] *vt* (*hair*) ébouriffer; (*clothes*) chiffonner; (*fig*: *person*): **to get ~d** s'énerver

rug [rʌg] *n* petit tapis; (BRIT: *blanket*) couverture *f*

rugby ['rʌgbɪ] *n* (*also*: **~ football**) rugby *m*

rugged ['rʌgɪd] *adj* (*landscape*) accidenté(e); (*features, character*) rude

ruin ['ruːɪn] *n* ruine *f* ▷ *vt* ruiner; (*spoil*: *clothes*) abîmer; (*: event*) gâcher; **ruins** *npl* (*of building*) ruine(s)

rule [ruːl] *n* règle *f*, (*regulation*) règlement *m*, (*government*) autorité *f*, gouvernement *m* ▷ *vt* (*country*) gouverner; (*person*) dominer; (*decide*) décider ▷ *vi* commander; **as a ~** normalement, en règle générale; **rule out** *vt* exclure; **ruler** *n* (*sovereign*) souverain(e); (*leader*) chef *m* (d'État); (*for measuring*) règle *f*; **ruling** *adj* (*party*) au pouvoir; (*class*) dirigeant(e) ▷ *n* (*Law*) décision *f*

rum [rʌm] *n* rhum *m*

Rumania [ruːˈmeɪnɪə] *n* Roumanie *f*; **Rumanian** *adj* roumain(e) ▷ *n* Roumain(e); (*Ling*) roumain *m*

rumble ['rʌmbl] *n* grondement *m*; (*of stomach, pipe*) gargouillement *m* ▷ *vi* gronder; (*stomach, pipe*) gargouiller

rumour, (US) **rumor** ['ruːməʳ] *n* rumeur *f*, bruit *m* (qui court) ▷ *vt*: **it is ~ed that** le bruit court que

rump steak *n* romsteck *m*

run [rʌn] (*pt* **ran**, *pp* **run**) *n* (*race*) course *f*, (*outing*) tour *m or* promenade *f* (en voiture);

(*distance travelled*) parcours *m*, trajet *m*; (*series*) suite *f*, série *f*; (*Theat*) série de représentations; (*Ski*) piste *f*; (*Cricket, Baseball*) point *m*; (*in tights, stockings*) maille filée, échelle *f* ▷ *vt* (*business*) diriger; (*competition, course*) organiser; (*hotel, house*) tenir; (*race*) participer à; (*Comput*: *program*) exécuter; (*to pass*: *hand, finger*): **to ~ sth over** promener *or* passer qch sur; (*water, bath*) faire couler; (*Press*: *feature*) publier ▷ *vi* courir; (*pass*: *road etc*) passer; (*work*: *machine, factory*) marcher; (*bus, train*) circuler; (*continue*: *play*) se jouer, être à l'affiche; (*: contract*) être valide *or* en vigueur; (*flow*: *river, bath, nose*) couler; (*colours, washing*) déteindre; (*in election*) être candidat, se présenter; **at a ~** au pas de course; **to go for a ~** aller courir *or* faire un peu de course à pied; (*in car*) faire un tour *or* une promenade (en voiture); **there was a ~ on** (*meat, tickets*) les gens se sont rués sur; **in the long ~** à la longue; **on the ~** en fuite; **I'll ~ you to the station** je vais vous emmener *or* conduire à la gare; **to ~ a risk** courir un risque; **run after** *vt fus* (*to catch up*) courir après; (*chase*) poursuivre; **run away** *vi* s'enfuir; **run down** *vt* (*Aut*: *knock over*) renverser; (BRIT: *reduce*: *production*) réduire progressivement; (*: factory/shop*) réduire progressivement la production/l'activité de; (*criticize*) critiquer, dénigrer; **to be ~ down** (*tired*) être fatigué(e) *or* à plat; **run into** *vt fus* (*meet*: *person*) rencontrer par hasard; (*: trouble*) se heurter à; (*collide with*) heurter; **run off** *vi* s'enfuir ▷ *vt* (*water*) laisser s'écouler; (*copies*) tirer; **run out** *vi* (*person*) sortir en courant; (*liquid*) couler; (*lease*) expirer; (*money*) être épuisé(e); **run out of** *vt fus* se trouver à court de; **run over** *vt* (*Aut*) écraser ▷ *vt fus* (*revise*) revoir; **run through** *vt fus* (*recap*) reprendre, revoir; (*play*) répéter; **run up** *vi*: **to ~ up against** (*difficulties*) se heurter à; **runaway** *adj* (*horse*) emballé(e); (*truck*) fou (folle); (*person*) fugitif(-ive); (*child*) fugueur(-euse)

rung [rʌŋ] *pp* of **ring** ▷ *n* (*of ladder*) barreau *m*

runner ['rʌnəʳ] *n* (*in race*: *person*) coureur(-euse); (*: horse*) partant *m*; (*on sledge*) patin *m*; (*for drawer etc*) coulisseau *m*; **runner bean** *n* (BRIT) haricot *m* (à rames); **runner-up** *n* second(e)

running ['rʌnɪŋ] *n* (*in race etc*) course *f*; (*of business, organization*) direction *f*, gestion *f* ▷ *adj* (*water*) courant(e); (*commentary*) suivi(e); **6 days ~** 6 jours de suite; **to be in/out of the ~ for sth** être/ne pas être sur les rangs pour qch

runny ['rʌnɪ] *adj* qui coule

run-up ['rʌnʌp] *n* (BRIT): **~ to sth** période *f* précédant qch

runway ['rʌnweɪ] *n* (Aviat) piste *f* (d'envol *or* d'atterrissage)

rupture ['rʌptʃə'] *n* (Med) hernie *f*

rural ['ruərl] *adj* rural(e)

rush [rʌʃ] *n* (of crowd, Comm: sudden demand) ruée *f*; (hurry) hâte *f*; (of anger, joy) accès *m*; (current) flot *m*; (Bot) jonc *m* ▷ *vt* (hurry) transporter *or* envoyer d'urgence ▷ *vi* se précipiter; **to ~ sth off** (do quickly) faire qch à la hâte; **rush hour** *n* heures *fpl* de pointe *or* d'affluence

Russia ['rʌʃə] *n* Russie *f*; **Russian** *adj* russe ▷ *n* Russe *m/f*; (Ling) russe *m*

rust [rʌst] *n* rouille *f* ▷ *vi* rouiller

rusty ['rʌstɪ] *adj* rouillé(e)

ruthless ['ruːθlɪs] *adj* sans pitié, impitoyable

RV *n abbr* (US) = **recreational vehicle**

rye [raɪ] *n* seigle *m*

Sabbath ['sæbəθ] *n* (Jewish) sabbat *m*; (Christian) dimanche *m*

sabotage ['sæbətɑːʒ] *n* sabotage *m* ▷ *vt* saboter

saccharin(e) ['sækərɪn] *n* saccharine *f*

sachet ['sæʃeɪ] *n* sachet *m*

sack [sæk] *n* (bag) sac *m* ▷ *vt* (dismiss) renvoyer, mettre à la porte; (plunder) piller, mettre à sac; **to get the ~** être renvoyé(e) *or* mis(e) à la porte

sacred ['seɪkrɪd] *adj* sacré(e)

sacrifice ['sækrɪfaɪs] *n* sacrifice *m* ▷ *vt* sacrifier

sad [sæd] *adj* (unhappy) triste; (deplorable) triste, fâcheux(-euse); (inf: pathetic: thing) triste, lamentable; (: person) minable

saddle ['sædl] *n* selle *f* ▷ *vt* (horse) seller; **to be ~d with sth** (inf) avoir qch sur les bras

sadistic [sə'dɪstɪk] *adj* sadique

sadly ['sædlɪ] *adv* tristement; (unfortunately) malheureusement; (seriously) fort

sadness ['sædnɪs] *n* tristesse *f*

s.a.e. *n abbr* (BRIT: = stamped addressed envelope) enveloppe affranchie pour la réponse

safari [sə'fɑːrɪ] *n* safari *m*

safe [seɪf] *adj* (out of danger) hors de danger, en sécurité; (not dangerous) sans danger; (cautious) prudent(e); (sure: bet) assuré(e) ▷ *n* coffre-fort *m*; **~ and sound** sain(e) et sauf; **(just) to be on the ~ side** pour plus de sûreté, par précaution; **safely** *adv* (assume, say) sans risque d'erreur; (drive, arrive) sans accident; **safe sex** *n* rapports sexuels protégés

safety ['seɪftɪ] *n* sécurité *f*; **safety belt** *n* ceinture *f* de sécurité; **safety pin** *n* épingle *f* de sûreté *or* de nourrice

saffron ['sæfrən] *n* safran *m*

sag [sæg] *vi* s'affaisser, fléchir; (hem, breasts) pendre

sage [seɪdʒ] *n* (herb) sauge *f*; (person) sage *m*

Sagittarius [sædʒɪ'tɛərɪəs] *n* le Sagittaire

Sahara [sə'hɑːrə] n: the ~ (Desert) le (désert du) Sahara m

said [sɛd] pt, pp of **say**

sail [seɪl] n (on boat) voile f; (trip): **to go for a ~** faire un tour en bateau ▷ vt (boat) manœuvrer, piloter ▷ vi (travel: ship) avancer, naviguer; (set off) partir, prendre la mer; (Sport) faire de la voile; **they ~ed into Le Havre** ils sont entrés dans le port du Havre; **sailboat** n (US) bateau m à voiles, voilier m; **sailing** n (Sport) voile f; **to go sailing** faire de la voile; **sailing boat** n bateau m à voiles, voilier m; **sailor** n marin m, matelot m

saint [seɪnt] n saint(e)

sake [seɪk] n: **for the ~ of** (out of concern for) pour (l'amour de), dans l'intérêt de; (out of consideration for) par égard pour

salad ['sæləd] n salade f; **salad cream** (BRIT) (sorte f de) mayonnaise f; **salad dressing** n vinaigrette f

salami [sə'lɑːmɪ] n salami m

salary ['sælərɪ] n salaire m, traitement m

sale [seɪl] n vente f; (at reduced prices) soldes mpl; **sales** npl (total amount sold) chiffre m de ventes; **"for ~"** "à vendre"; **on ~** en vente; **sales assistant**, (US) **sales clerk** n vendeur(-euse); **salesman** (irreg) n (in shop) vendeur m; **salesperson** (irreg) n (in shop) vendeur(-euse); **sales rep** n (Comm) représentant(e) m/f; **saleswoman** (irreg) n (in shop) vendeuse f

saline ['seɪlaɪn] adj salin(e)

saliva [sə'laɪvə] n salive f

salmon ['sæmən] n (pl inv) saumon m

salon ['sælɔn] n salon m

saloon [sə'luːn] n (US) bar m; (BRIT Aut) berline f; (ship's lounge) salon m

salt [sɔːlt] n sel m ▷ vt saler; **saltwater** adj (fish etc) (d'eau) de mer; **salty** adj salé(e)

salute [sə'luːt] n salut m; (of guns) salve f ▷ vt saluer

salvage ['sælvɪdʒ] n (saving) sauvetage m; (things saved) biens sauvés or récupérés ▷ vt sauver, récupérer

Salvation Army [sæl'veɪʃən-] n Armée f du Salut

same [seɪm] adj même ▷ pron: **the ~** le (la) même, les mêmes; **the ~ book as** le même livre que; **at the ~ time** en même temps; (yet) néanmoins; **all** or **just the ~** tout de même, quand même; **to do the ~** faire de même, en faire autant; **to do the ~ as sb** faire comme qn; **and the ~ to you!** et à vous de même!; (after insult) toi-même!

sample ['sɑːmpl] n échantillon m; (Med) prélèvement m ▷ vt (food, wine) goûter

sanction ['sæŋkʃən] n approbation f, sanction f ▷ vt cautionner, sanctionner; **sanctions** npl (Pol) sanctions

sanctuary ['sæŋktjuərɪ] n (holy place) sanctuaire m; (refuge) asile m; (for wildlife) réserve f

sand [sænd] n sable m ▷ vt (also: ~ **down**: wood etc) poncer

sandal ['sændl] n sandale f

sand: sandbox n (US: for children) tas m de sable; **sand castle** n château m de sable; **sand dune** n dune f de sable; **sandpaper** n papier m de verre; **sandpit** n (BRIT: for children) tas m de sable; **sands** npl plage f (de sable); **sandstone** ['sændstəun] n grès m

sandwich ['sændwɪtʃ] n sandwich m ▷ vt (also: ~ **in**) intercaler; **~ed between** pris en sandwich entre; **cheese/ham ~** sandwich au fromage/jambon

sandy ['sændɪ] adj sablonneux(-euse); (colour) sable inv, blond roux inv

sane [seɪn] adj (person) sain(e) d'esprit; (outlook) sensé(e), sain(e)

sang [sæŋ] pt of **sing**

sanitary towel, (US) **sanitary napkin** ['sænɪtərɪ-] n serviette f hygiénique

sanity ['sænɪtɪ] n santé mentale; (common sense) bon sens

sank [sæŋk] pt of **sink**

Santa Claus [sæntə'klɔːz] n le Père Noël

sap [sæp] n (of plants) sève f ▷ vt (strength) saper, miner

sapphire ['sæfaɪə'] n saphir m

sarcasm ['sɑːkæzm] n sarcasme m, raillerie f

sarcastic [sɑː'kæstɪk] adj sarcastique

sardine [sɑː'diːn] n sardine f

SASE n abbr (US: = self-addressed stamped envelope) enveloppe affranchie pour la réponse

sat [sæt] pt, pp of **sit**

Sat. abbr (= Saturday) sa

satchel ['sætʃl] n cartable m

satellite ['sætəlaɪt] n satellite m; **satellite dish** n antenne f parabolique; **satellite navigation system** n système m de navigation par satellite; **satellite television** n télévision f par satellite

satin ['sætɪn] n satin m ▷ adj en or de satin, satiné(e)

satire ['sætaɪə'] n satire f

satisfaction [sætɪs'fækʃən] n satisfaction f

satisfactory [sætɪs'fæktərɪ] adj satisfaisant(e)

satisfied ['sætɪsfaɪd] adj satisfait(e); **to be ~ with sth** être satisfait de qch

satisfy ['sætɪsfaɪ] vt satisfaire, contenter; (convince) convaincre, persuader

Saturday ['sætədɪ] n samedi m

sauce [sɔːs] n sauce f; **saucepan** n casserole f

saucer ['sɔːsə'] n soucoupe f

Saudi Arabia ['saudɪ-] n Arabie f Saoudite

sauna ['sɔːnə] n sauna m

sausage ['sɔsɪdʒ] n saucisse f; (salami etc) saucisson m; **sausage roll** n friand m

sautéed ['səuteɪd] adj sauté(e)

savage ['sævɪdʒ] adj (cruel, fierce) brutal(e), féroce; (primitive) primitif(-ive), sauvage ▷ n sauvage m/f ▷ vt attaquer férocement

save [seɪv] vt (person, belongings) sauver; (money) mettre de côté, économiser; (time) (faire) gagner; (keep) garder; (Comput) sauvegarder; (Sport: stop) arrêter; (avoid: trouble) éviter ▷ vi (also: **~ up**) mettre de l'argent de côté ▷ n (Sport) arrêt m (du ballon); ▷ prep sauf, à l'exception de

saving ['seɪvɪŋ] n économie f; **savings** npl économies fpl

savings account n compte m d'épargne

savings and loan association (us) n ≈ société f de crédit immobilier

savoury, (us) **savory** ['seɪvərɪ] adj savoureux(-euse); (dish: not sweet) salé(e)

saw [sɔ:] pt of **see** ▷ n (tool) scie f ▷ vt (pt **sawed**, pp **sawed** or **sawn**) scier; **sawdust** n sciure f

sawn [sɔ:n] pp of **saw**

saxophone ['sæksəfəun] n saxophone m

say [seɪ] vt (pt, pp **said**) dire ▷ n: **to have one's ~** dire ce qu'on a à dire; **to have a ~** avoir voix au chapitre; **could you ~ that again?** pourriez-vous répéter ce que vous venez de dire?; **to ~ yes/no** dire oui/non; **my watch ~s 3 o'clock** ma montre indique 3 heures, il est 3 heures à ma montre; **that is to ~** c'est-à-dire; **that goes without ~ing** cela va sans dire, cela va de soi; **saying** n dicton m, proverbe m

scab [skæb] n croûte f; (pej) jaune m

scaffolding ['skæfəldɪŋ] n échafaudage m

scald [skɔ:ld] n brûlure f ▷ vt ébouillanter

scale [skeɪl] n (of fish) écaille f; (Mus) gamme f; (of ruler, thermometer etc) graduation f, échelle (graduée); (of salaries, fees etc) barème m; (of map, also size, extent) échelle ▷ vt (mountain) escalader; **scales** npl balance f; (larger) bascule f; (also: **bathroom ~s**) pèse-personne m inv; **~ of charges** tableau m des tarifs; **on a large ~** sur une grande échelle, en grand

scallion ['skæljən] n (us: salad onion) ciboule f

scallop ['skɔləp] n coquille f Saint-Jacques; (Sewing) feston m

scalp [skælp] n cuir chevelu ▷ vt scalper

scalpel ['skælpl] n scalpel m

scam [skæm] n (inf) arnaque f

scampi ['skæmpɪ] npl langoustines (frites), scampi mpl

scan [skæn] vt (examine) scruter, examiner; (glance at quickly) parcourir; (TV, Radar) balayer ▷ n (Med) scanographie f

scandal ['skændl] n scandale m; (gossip) ragots mpl

Scandinavia [skændɪ'neɪvɪə] n Scandinavie f; **Scandinavian** adj scandinave ▷ n Scandinave m/f

scanner ['skænər] n (Radar, Med) scanner m, scanographe m; (Comput) scanner

scapegoat ['skeɪpgəut] n bouc m émissaire

scar [skɑ:ʳ] n cicatrice f ▷ vt laisser une cicatrice or une marque à

scarce [skɛəs] adj rare, peu abondant(e); **to make o.s. ~** (inf) se sauver; **scarcely** adv à peine, presque pas

scare [skɛəʳ] n peur f, panique f ▷ vt effrayer, faire peur à; **to ~ sb stiff** faire une peur bleue à qn; **bomb ~** alerte f à la bombe; **scarecrow** n épouvantail m; **scared** adj: **to be scared** avoir peur

scarf (pl **scarves**) [skɑ:f, skɑ:vz] n (long) écharpe f; (square) foulard m

scarlet ['skɑ:lɪt] adj écarlate

scarves [skɑ:vz] npl of **scarf**

scary ['skɛərɪ] adj (inf) effrayant(e); (film) qui fait peur

scatter ['skætəʳ] vt éparpiller, répandre; (crowd) disperser ▷ vi se disperser

scenario [sɪ'nɑ:rɪəu] n scénario m

scene [si:n] n (Theat, fig etc) scène f; (of crime, accident) lieu(x) m(pl), endroit m; (sight, view) spectacle m, vue f; **scenery** n (Theat) décor(s) m(pl); (landscape) paysage m; **scenic** adj offrant de beaux paysages or panoramas

scent [sɛnt] n parfum m, odeur f; (fig: track) piste f

sceptical, (us) **skeptical** ['skɛptɪkl] adj sceptique

schedule ['ʃɛdju:l, us 'skɛdju:l] n programme m, plan m; (of trains) horaire m; (of prices etc) barème m, tarif m ▷ vt prévoir; **on ~** à l'heure (prévue); à la date prévue; **to be ahead of/behind ~** avoir de l'avance/du retard; **scheduled flight** n vol régulier

scheme [ski:m] n plan m, projet m; (plot) complot m, combine f; (arrangement) arrangement m, classification f; (pension scheme etc) régime m ▷ vt, vi comploter, manigancer

schizophrenic [skɪtsə'frɛnɪk] adj schizophrène

scholar ['skɔlər] n érudit(e); (pupil) boursier(-ère); **scholarship** n érudition f; (grant) bourse f (d'études)

school [sku:l] n (gen) école f; (secondary school) collège m; lycée m; (in university) faculté f; (us: university) université f ▷ cpd scolaire; **schoolbook** n livre m scolaire or de classe; **schoolboy** n écolier m; (at secondary school) collégien m; lycéen m; **schoolchildren** npl écoliers mpl; (at secondary school) collégiens mpl; lycéens mpl; **schoolgirl** n écolière f; (at secondary school) collégienne f; lycéenne f; **schooling** n instruction f, études fpl; **schoolteacher** n (primary) instituteur(-trice); (secondary) professeur m

science ['saɪəns] n science f; **science fiction** n science-fiction f; **scientific** [saɪən'tɪfɪk] adj scientifique; **scientist** n scientifique m/f; (eminent) savant m

sci-fi ['saɪfaɪ] n abbr (inf: = science fiction) SF f
scissors ['sɪzəz] npl ciseaux mpl; **a pair of ~** une paire de ciseaux
scold [skəʊld] vt gronder
scone [skɔn] n sorte de petit pain rond au lait
scoop [sku:p] n pelle f (à main); (for ice cream) boule f à glace; (Press) reportage exclusif or à sensation
scooter ['sku:tə'] n (motor cycle) scooter m; (toy) trottinette f
scope [skəʊp] n (capacity: of plan, undertaking) portée f, envergure f; (: of person) compétence f, capacités fpl; (opportunity) possibilités fpl
scorching ['skɔːtʃɪŋ] adj torride, brûlant(e)
score [skɔː'] n score m, décompte m des points; (Mus) partition f ▷ vt (goal, point) marquer; (success) remporter; (cut: leather, wood, card) entailler, inciser ▷ vi marquer des points; (Football) marquer un but; (keep score) compter les points; **on that ~** sur ce chapitre, à cet égard; **a ~ of** (twenty) vingt; **~s of** (fig) des tas de; **to ~ 6 out of 10** obtenir 6 sur 10; **score out** vt rayer, barrer, biffer; **scoreboard** n tableau m; **scorer** n (Football) auteur m du but; buteur m; (keeping score) marqueur m
scorn [skɔːn] n mépris m, dédain m
Scorpio ['skɔːpɪəʊ] n le Scorpion
scorpion ['skɔːpɪən] n scorpion m
Scot [skɔt] n Écossais(e)
Scotch [skɔtʃ] n whisky m, scotch m
Scotch tape® (US) n scotch® m, ruban adhésif
Scotland ['skɔtlənd] n Écosse f
Scots [skɔts] adj écossais(e); **Scotsman** (irreg) n Écossais m; **Scotswoman** (irreg) n Écossaise f; **Scottish** ['skɔtɪʃ] adj écossais(e); **the Scottish Parliament** le Parlement écossais
scout [skaʊt] n (Mil) éclaireur m; (also: **boy ~**) scout m; **girl ~** (US) guide f
scowl [skaʊl] vi se renfrogner; **to ~ at** regarder de travers
scramble ['skræmbl] n (rush) bousculade f, ruée f ▷ vi grimper/descendre tant bien que mal; **to ~ for** se bousculer or se disputer pour (avoir); **to go scrambling** (Sport) faire du trial; **scrambled eggs** npl œufs brouillés
scrap [skræp] n bout m, morceau m; (fight) bagarre f; (also: **~ iron**) ferraille f ▷ vt jeter, mettre au rebut; (fig) abandonner, laisser tomber ▷ vi se bagarrer; **scraps** npl (waste) déchets mpl; **scrapbook** n album m
scrape [skreɪp] vt, vi gratter, racler ▷ n: **to get into a ~** s'attirer des ennuis; **scrape through** vi (exam etc) réussir de justesse
scrap paper n papier m brouillon
scratch [skrætʃ] n égratignure f, rayure f; (on paint) éraflure f; (from claw) coup m de griffe ▷ vt (rub) (se) gratter, (paint etc) érafler; (with claw, nail) griffer ▷ vi (se)

gratter; **to start from ~** partir de zéro; **to be up to ~** être à la hauteur; **scratch card** n carte f à gratter
scream [skri:m] n cri perçant, hurlement m ▷ vi crier, hurler
screen [skri:n] n écran m; (in room) paravent m; (fig) écran, rideau m ▷ vt masquer, cacher; (from the wind etc) abriter, protéger; (film) projeter; (candidates etc) filtrer; **screening** n (of film) projection f; (Med) test m (or tests) de dépistage; **screenplay** n scénario m; **screen saver** n (Comput) économiseur m d'écran; **screenshot** n (Comput) capture f d'écran
screw [skru:] n vis f ▷ vt (also: **~ in**) visser; **screw up** vt (paper etc) froisser; **to ~ up one's eyes** se plisser les yeux; **screwdriver** n tournevis m
scribble ['skrɪbl] n gribouillage m ▷ vt gribouiller, griffonner
script [skrɪpt] n (Cine etc) scénario m, texte m; (writing) (écriture f) script m
scroll [skrəʊl] n rouleau m ▷ vt (Comput) faire défiler (sur l'écran)
scrub [skrʌb] n (land) broussailles fpl ▷ vt (floor) nettoyer à la brosse; (pan) récurer; (washing) frotter
scruffy ['skrʌfɪ] adj débraillé(e)
scrum(mage) ['skrʌm(ɪdʒ)] n mêlée f
scrutiny ['skru:tɪnɪ] n examen minutieux
scuba diving ['sku:bə-] n plongée sous-marine
sculptor ['skʌlptə'] n sculpteur m
sculpture ['skʌlptʃə'] n sculpture f
scum [skʌm] n écume f, mousse f; (pej: people) rebut m, lie f
scurry ['skʌrɪ] vi filer à toute allure; **to ~ off** détaler, se sauver
sea [si:] n mer f ▷ cpd marin(e), de (la) mer, maritime; **by** or **beside the ~** (holiday, town) au bord de la mer; **by ~** par mer, en bateau; **out to ~** au large; **(out) at ~** en mer; **to be all at ~** (fig) nager complètement; **seafood** n fruits mpl de mer; **sea front** n bord m de mer; **seagull** n mouette f
seal [si:l] n (animal) phoque m; (stamp) sceau m, cachet m ▷ vt sceller; (envelope) coller (: with seal) cacheter; **seal off** vt (forbid entry to) interdire l'accès de
sea level n niveau m de la mer
seam [si:m] n couture f; (of coal) veine f, filon m
search [sə:tʃ] n (for person, thing, Comput) recherche(s) f(pl); (of drawer, pockets) fouille f; (Law: at sb's home) perquisition f ▷ vt fouiller; (examine) examiner minutieusement; scruter ▷ vi: **to ~ for** chercher; **in ~ of** à la recherche de; **search engine** n (Comput) moteur m de recherche; **search party** n expédition f de secours
sea: seashore n rivage m, plage f, bord m de (la) mer; **seasick** adj: **to be seasick** avoir

le mal de mer; **seaside** n bord m de mer; **seaside resort** n station f balnéaire

season ['si:zn] n saison f ▷ vt assaisonner, relever; **to be in/out of ~** être/ne pas être de saison; **seasonal** adj saisonnier(-ière); **seasoning** n assaisonnement m; **season ticket** n carte f d'abonnement

seat [si:t] n siège m; (in bus, train: place) place f; (buttocks) postérieur m; (of trousers) fond m ▷ vt faire asseoir, placer; (have room for) avoir des places assises pour, pouvoir accueillir; **to be ~ed** être assis; **seat belt** n ceinture f de sécurité; **seating** n sièges fpl, places assises

sea: sea water n eau f de mer; **seaweed** n algues fpl

sec. abbr (= second) sec

secluded [sɪ'klu:dɪd] adj retiré(e), à l'écart

second ['sɛkənd] num deuxième, second(e) ▷ adv (in race etc) en seconde position ▷ n (unit of time) seconde f; (Aut: also: ~ **gear**) seconde; (Comm: imperfect) article m de second choix; (BRIT Scol) ≈ licence f avec mention ▷ vt (motion) appuyer; **seconds** npl (inf: food) rab m (inf); **secondary** adj secondaire; **secondary school** n (age 11 to 15) collège m; (age 15 to 18) lycée m; **second-class** adj de deuxième classe; (Rail) de seconde (classe); (Post) au tarif réduit; (pej) de qualité inférieure ▷ adv (Rail) en seconde; (Post) au tarif réduit; **secondhand** adj d'occasion; (information) de seconde main; **secondly** adv deuxièmement; **second-rate** adj de deuxième ordre, de qualité inférieure; **second thoughts** npl: **to have second thoughts** changer d'avis; **on second thoughts** or (US) **thought** à la réflexion

secrecy ['si:krəsɪ] n secret m

secret ['si:krɪt] adj secret(-ète) ▷ n secret m; **in ~** adv en secret, secrètement, en cachette

secretary ['sɛkrətrɪ] n secrétaire m/f; **S~ of State (for)** (Pol) ministre m (de)

secretive ['si:krətɪv] adj réservé(e); (pej) cachottier(-ière), dissimulé(e)

secret service n services secrets

sect [sɛkt] n secte f

section ['sɛkʃən] n section f; (Comm) rayon m; (of document) section, article m, paragraphe m; (cut) coupe f

sector ['sɛktəʳ] n secteur m

secular ['sɛkjuləʳ] adj laïque

secure [sɪ'kjuəʳ] adj (free from anxiety) sans inquiétude, sécurisé(e); (firmly fixed) solide, bien attaché(e) (or fermé(e) etc); (in safe place) en lieu sûr, en sûreté ▷ vt (fix) fixer, attacher; (get) obtenir, se procurer

security [sɪ'kjuərɪtɪ] n sécurité f, mesures fpl de sécurité; (for loan) caution f, garantie f; **securities** npl (Stock Exchange) valeurs fpl, titres mpl; **security guard** n garde

chargé de la sécurité; (transporting money) convoyeur m de fonds

sedan [sə'dæn] n (US Aut) berline f

sedate [sɪ'deɪt] adj calme; posé(e) ▷ vt donner des sédatifs à

sedative ['sɛdɪtɪv] n calmant m, sédatif m

seduce [sɪ'dju:s] vt séduire; **seductive** [sɪ'dʌktɪv] adj séduisant(e); (smile) séducteur(-trice); (fig: offer) alléchant(e)

see [si:] (pt **saw**, pp **seen**) vt (gen) voir; (accompany): **to ~ sb to the door** reconduire or raccompagner qn jusqu'à la porte ▷ vi voir; **to ~ that** (ensure) veiller à ce que + sub, faire en sorte que + sub, s'assurer que; **~ you soon/later/tomorrow!** à bientôt/ plus tard/demain!; **see off** vt accompagner (à l'aéroport etc); **see out** vt (take to door) raccompagner à la porte; **see through** vt mener à bonne fin ▷ vt fus voir clair dans; **see to** vt fus s'occuper de, se charger de

seed [si:d] n graine f; (fig) germe m; (Tennis etc) tête f de série; **to go to ~** (plant) monter en graine; (fig) se laisser aller

seeing ['si:ɪŋ] conj: **~ (that)** vu que, étant donné que

seek [si:k] (pt, pp **sought**) vt chercher, rechercher

seem [si:m] vi sembler, paraître; **there ~s to be ...** il semble qu'il y a ..., on dirait qu'il y a ...; **seemingly** adv apparemment

seen [si:n] pp of **see**

seesaw ['si:sɔ:] n (jeu m de) bascule f

segment ['sɛgmənt] n segment m; (of orange) quartier m

segregate ['sɛgrɪgeɪt] vt séparer, isoler

Seine [seɪn] n: **the (River) ~** la Seine

seize [si:z] vt (grasp) saisir, attraper; (take possession of) s'emparer de; (opportunity) saisir

seizure ['si:ʒəʳ] n (Med) crise f, attaque f; (of power) prise f

seldom ['sɛldəm] adv rarement

select [sɪ'lɛkt] adj choisi(e), d'élite; (hotel, restaurant, club) chic inv, sélect inv ▷ vt sélectionner, choisir; **selection** n sélection f, choix m; **selective** adj sélectif(-ive); (school) à recrutement sélectif

self (pl **selves**) [sɛlf, sɛlvz] n: **the ~** le moi inv ▷ prefix auto-; **self-assured** adj sûr(e) de soi, plein(e) d'assurance; **self-catering** adj (BRIT: flat) avec cuisine, où l'on peut faire sa cuisine; (: holiday) en appartement (or chalet etc) loué; **self-centred**, (US) **self-centered** adj égocentrique; **self-confidence** n confiance f en soi; **self-confident** adj sûr(e) de soi, plein(e) d'assurance; **self-conscious** adj timide, qui manque d'assurance; **self-contained** adj (BRIT: flat) avec entrée particulière, indépendant(e); **self-control** n maîtrise f de soi; **self-defence**, (US) **self-defense** n autodéfense f; (Law) légitime défense f;

self-drive adj (BRIT): **self-drive car** voiture f
de location; **self-employed** adj qui travaille
à son compte; **self-esteem** n amour-
propre m; **self-harm** vi s'automutiler;
self-indulgent adj qui ne se refuse rien;
self-interest n intérêt personnel; **selfish**
adj égoïste; **self-pity** n apitoiement m sur
soi-même; **self-raising** [sɛlfˈreɪzɪŋ], (US)
self-rising [sɛlfˈraɪzɪŋ] adj: **self-raising
flour** farine f pour gâteaux (avec levure
incorporée); **self-respect** n respect m de soi,
amour-propre m; **self-service** adj, n libre-
service (m), self-service (m)

selfie [sɛlfi] n selfie m

sell (pt, pp **sold**) [sɛl, səuld] vt vendre ▷ vi
se vendre; **to ~ at** or **for 10 euros** se vendre
10 euros; **sell off** vt liquider; **sell out** vi:
to ~ out (of sth) (use up stock) vendre tout
son stock (de qch); **sell-by date** n date f
limite de vente; **seller** n vendeur(-euse),
marchand(e)

Sellotape® [ˈsɛləuteɪp] n (BRIT) scotch® m

selves [sɛlvz] npl of **self**

semester [sɪˈmɛstəʳ] n (esp US) semestre m

semi... [ˈsɛmɪ] prefix semi-, demi-; à demi,
à moitié; **semicircle** n demi-cercle m;
semidetached (house) n (BRIT) maison
jumelée or jumelle; **semi-final** n demi-
finale f

seminar [ˈsɛmɪnɑːʳ] n séminaire m

semi-skimmed [ˈsɛmɪˈskɪmd] adj demi-
écrémé(e)

senate [ˈsɛnɪt] n sénat m; (US): **the S~** le
Sénat; **senator** n sénateur m

send (pt, pp **sent**) [sɛnd, sɛnt] vt envoyer;
send back vt renvoyer; **send for** vt fus
(by post) se faire envoyer, commander
par correspondance; **send in** vt (report,
application, resignation) remettre; **send off**
vt (goods) envoyer, expédier; (BRIT Sport:
player) expulser or renvoyer du terrain; **send
on** vt (BRIT: letter) faire suivre; (luggage etc:
in advance) (faire) expédier à l'avance; **send
out** vt (invitation) envoyer (par la poste);
(emit: light, heat, signal) émettre; **send
up** vt (person, price) faire monter; (BRIT:
parody) mettre en boîte, parodier; **sender**
n expéditeur(-trice); **send-off** n: **a good
send-off** des adieux chaleureux

senile [ˈsiːnaɪl] adj sénile

senior [ˈsiːnɪəʳ] adj (high-ranking) de haut
niveau; (of higher rank): **to be ~ to sb** être le
supérieur de qn; **senior citizen** n personne
f du troisième âge; **senior high school** n
(US) ≈ lycée m

sensation [sɛnˈseɪʃən] n sensation
f; **sensational** adj qui fait sensation;
(marvellous) sensationnel(le)

sense [sɛns] n sens m; (feeling) sentiment m;
(meaning) sens, signification f; (wisdom) bon
sens ▷ vt sentir, pressentir; **it makes ~** c'est
logique; **senseless** adj insensé(e), stupide;

(unconscious) sans connaissance; **sense of
humour**, (US) **sense of humor** n sens m de
l'humour

sensible [ˈsɛnsɪbl] adj sensé(e),
raisonnable; (shoes etc) pratique

▌ Be careful not to translate sensible by the
French word sensible.

sensitive [ˈsɛnsɪtɪv] adj: **~ (to)** sensible (à)

sensual [ˈsɛnsjuəl] adj sensuel(le)

sensuous [ˈsɛnsjuəs] adj
voluptueux(-euse), sensuel(le)

sent [sɛnt] pt, pp of **send**

sentence [ˈsɛntns] n (Ling) phrase f; (Law:
judgment) condamnation f, sentence f;
(: punishment) peine f ▷ vt: **to ~ sb to death/
to 5 years** condamner qn à mort/à 5 ans

sentiment [ˈsɛntɪmənt] n sentiment m;
(opinion) opinion f, avis m; **sentimental**
[sɛntɪˈmɛntl] adj sentimental(e)

separate adj [ˈsɛprɪt] séparé(e);
(organization) indépendant(e); (day, occasion,
issue) différent(e) ▷ vt [ˈsɛpəreɪt] séparer;
(distinguish) distinguer ▷ vi [ˈsɛpəreɪt]
se séparer; **separately** adv séparément;
separates npl (clothes) coordonnés mpl;
separation [sɛpəˈreɪʃən] n séparation f

September [sɛpˈtɛmbəʳ] n septembre m

septic [ˈsɛptɪk] adj (wound) infecte(e);
septic tank n fosse f septique

sequel [ˈsiːkwl] n conséquence f; séquelles
fpl; (of story) suite f

sequence [ˈsiːkwəns] n ordre m, suite f; (in
film) séquence f; (dance) numéro m

sequin [ˈsiːkwɪn] n paillette f

Serb [səːb] adj, n = **Serbian**

Serbia [ˈsəːbɪə] n Serbie f

Serbian [ˈsəːbɪən] adj serbe ▷ n Serbe m/f;
(Ling) serbe m

sergeant [ˈsɑːdʒənt] n sergent m; (Police)
brigadier m

serial [ˈsɪərɪəl] n feuilleton m; **serial killer** n
meurtrier m tuant en série; **serial number**
n numéro m de série

series [ˈsɪəriz] n série f; (Publishing)
collection f

serious [ˈsɪərɪəs] adj sérieux(-euse);
(accident etc) grave; **seriously** adv
sérieusement; (hurt) gravement

sermon [ˈsəːmən] n sermon m

servant [ˈsəːvənt] n domestique m/f; (fig)
serviteur (servante)

serve [səːv] vt (employer etc) servir, être
au service de; (purpose) servir à; (customer,
food, meal) servir; (subj: train) desservir;
(apprenticeship) faire, accomplir; (prison
term) faire; purger ▷ vi (Tennis) servir; (be
useful): **to ~ as/for/to do** servir de/à/à
faire ▷ n (Tennis) service m; **it ~s him right**
c'est bien fait pour lui; **server** n (Comput)
serveur m

service [ˈsəːvɪs] n (gen) service m; (Aut)
révision f; (Rel) office m ▷ vt (car etc) réviser;

services *npl* (*Econ: tertiary sector*) (secteur *m*) tertiaire *m*, secteur des services; (*BRIT: on motorway*) station-service *f*; (*Mil*): **the S~s** *npl* les forces armées; **to be of ~ to sb, to do sb a ~** rendre service à qn; **~ included/not included** service compris/non compris; **service area** *n* (*on motorway*) aire *f* de services; **service charge** *n* (*BRIT*) service *m*; **serviceman** (*irreg*) *n* militaire *m*; **service station** *n* station-service *f*

serviette [sə:vɪˈɛt] *n* (*BRIT*) serviette *f* (de table)

session [ˈsɛʃən] *n* (*sitting*) séance *f*; **to be in ~** siéger, être en session *or* en séance

set [sɛt] (*pt, pp* set) *n* série *f*, assortiment *m*; (*of tools etc*) jeu *m*; (*Radio, TV*) poste *m*; (*Tennis*) set *m*; (*group of people*) cercle *m*, milieu *m*; (*Cine*) plateau *m*; (*Theat: stage*) scène *f*; (: *scenery*) décor *m*; (*Math*) ensemble *m*; (*Hairdressing*) mise *f* en plis ▷ *adj* (*fixed*) fixe, déterminé(e); (*ready*) prêt(e) ▷ *vt* (*place*) mettre, poser, placer; (*fix, establish*) fixer (: *record*) établir; (*assign: task, homework*) donner; (*exam*) composer; (*adjust*) régler; (*decide: rules etc*) fixer, choisir ▷ *vi* (*sun*) se coucher; (*jam, jelly, concrete*) prendre; (*bone*) se ressouder; **to be ~ on doing** être résolu(e) à faire; **to ~ to music** mettre en musique; **to ~ on fire** mettre le feu à; **to ~ free** libérer; **to ~ sth going** déclencher qch; **to ~ sail** partir, prendre la mer; **set aside** *vt* mettre de côté; (*time*) garder; **set down** *vt* (*subj: bus, train*) déposer; **set in** *vi* (*infection, bad weather*) s'installer; (*complications*) survenir, surgir; **set off** *vi* se mettre en route, partir ▷ *vt* (*bomb*) faire exploser; (*cause to start*) déclencher; (*show up well*) mettre en valeur, faire valoir; **set out** *vi*: **to ~ out (from)** partir (de) ▷ *vt* (*arrange*) disposer; (*state*) présenter, exposer; **~ out to do** entreprendre de faire; avoir pour but *or* intention de faire; **set up** *vt* (*organization*) fonder, créer; **setback** *n* (*hitch*) revers *m*, contretemps *m*; **set menu** *n* menu *m*

settee [sɛˈtiː] *n* canapé *m*

setting [ˈsɛtɪŋ] *n* cadre *m*; (*of jewel*) monture *f*; (*position: of controls*) réglage *m*

settle [ˈsɛtl] *vt* (*argument, matter, account*) régler; (*problem*) résoudre; (*Med: calm*) calmer ▷ *vi* (*bird, dust etc*) se poser; **to ~ for sth** accepter qch, se contenter de qch; **to ~ on sth** opter *or* se décider pour qch; **settle down** *vi* (*get comfortable*) s'installer; (*become calmer*) se calmer; se ranger; **settle in** *vi* s'installer; **settle up** *vi*: **to ~ up with sb** régler (ce que l'on doit à) qn; **settlement** *n* (*payment*) règlement *m*; (*agreement*) accord *m*; (*village etc*) village *m*, hameau *m*

setup [ˈsɛtʌp] *n* (*arrangement*) manière *f* dont les choses sont organisées; (*situation*) situation *f*, allure *f* des choses

seven [ˈsɛvn] *num* sept; **seventeen** *num* dix-sept; **seventeenth** [sɛvnˈtiːnθ] *num* dix-septième; **seventh** *num* septième; **seventieth** [ˈsɛvntɪɪθ] *num* soixante-dixième; **seventy** *num* soixante-dix

sever [ˈsɛvəʳ] *vt* couper, trancher; (*relations*) rompre

several [ˈsɛvərl] *adj, pron* plusieurs *pl*; **~ of us** plusieurs d'entre nous

severe [sɪˈvɪəʳ] *adj* (*stern*) sévère, strict(e); (*serious*) grave, sérieux(-euse); (*plain*) sévère, austère

sew (*pt* sewed, *pp* sewn) [səu, səud, səun] *vt, vi* coudre

sewage [ˈsuːɪdʒ] *n* vidange(s) *f(pl)*

sewer [ˈsuːəʳ] *n* égout *m*

sewing [ˈsəuɪŋ] *n* couture *f*; (*item(s)*) ouvrage *m*; **sewing machine** *n* machine *f* à coudre

sewn [səun] *pp of* sew

sex [sɛks] *n* sexe *m*; **to have ~ with** avoir des rapports (sexuels) avec; **sexism** [ˈsɛksɪzəm] *n* sexisme *m*; **sexist** *adj* sexiste; **sexual** [ˈsɛksjuəl] *adj* sexuel(le); **sexual intercourse** *n* rapports sexuels; **sexuality** [sɛksjuˈælɪtɪ] *n* sexualité *f*; **sexy** *adj* sexy *inv*

shabby [ˈʃæbɪ] *adj* miteux(-euse); (*behaviour*) mesquin(e), méprisable

shack [ʃæk] *n* cabane *f*, hutte *f*

shade [ʃeɪd] *n* ombre *f*; (*for lamp*) abat-jour *m inv*; (*of colour*) nuance *f*, ton *m*; (*US: window shade*) store *m*; (*small quantity*): **a ~ of** un soupçon de ▷ *vt* abriter du soleil, ombrager; **shades** *npl* (*US: sunglasses*) lunettes *fpl* de soleil; **in the ~** à l'ombre; **a ~ smaller** un tout petit peu plus petit

shadow [ˈʃædəu] *n* ombre *f* ▷ *vt* (*follow*) filer; **shadow cabinet** *n* (*BRIT Pol*) cabinet parallèle formé par le parti qui n'est pas au pouvoir

shady [ˈʃeɪdɪ] *adj* ombragé(e); (*fig: dishonest*) louche, véreux(-euse)

shaft [ʃɑːft] *n* (*of arrow, spear*) hampe *f*; (*Aut, Tech*) arbre *m*; (*of mine*) puits *m*; (*of lift*) cage *f*; (*of light*) rayon *m*, trait *m*

shake [ʃeɪk] (*pt* shook, *pp* shaken) *vt* secouer; (*bottle, cocktail*) agiter; (*house, confidence*) ébranler ▷ *vi* trembler; **to ~ one's head** (*in refusal etc*) dire *or* faire non de la tête; (*in dismay*) secouer la tête; **to ~ hands with sb** serrer la main à qn; **shake off** *vt* secouer; (*pursuer*) se débarrasser de; **shake up** *vt* secouer; **shaky** *adj* (*hand, voice*) tremblant(e); (*building*) branlant(e), peu solide

shall [ʃæl] *aux vb*: **I ~ go** j'irai; **~ I open the door?** j'ouvre la porte?; **I'll get the coffee, ~ I?** je vais chercher le café, d'accord?

shallow [ˈʃæləu] *adj* peu profond(e); (*fig*) superficiel(le), qui manque de profondeur

sham [ʃæm] *n* frime *f*

shambles ['ʃæmblz] n confusion f, pagaïe f, fouillis m

shame [ʃeɪm] n honte f ▷ vt faire honte à; **it is a ~ (that/to do)** c'est dommage (que + sub/de faire); **what a ~!** quel dommage!; **shameful** adj honteux(-euse), scandaleux(-euse); **shameless** adj éhonté(e), effronté(e)

shampoo [ʃæm'puː] n shampo(o)ing m ▷ vt faire un shampo(o)ing à

shandy ['ʃændɪ] n bière panachée

shan't [ʃɑːnt] = **shall not**

shape [ʃeɪp] n forme f ▷ vt façonner, modeler; (sb's ideas, character) former; (sb's life) déterminer ▷ vi (also: ~ **up**: events) prendre tournure; (: person) faire des progrès, s'en sortir; **to take ~** prendre forme or tournure

share [ʃɛəʳ] n part f; (Comm) action f ▷ vt partager; (have in common) avoir en commun; **to ~ out (among** or **between)** partager (entre); **shareholder** n (BRIT) actionnaire m/f

shark [ʃɑːk] n requin m

sharp [ʃɑːp] adj (razor, knife) tranchant(e), bien aiguisé(e); (point, voice) aigu(ë); (nose, chin) pointu(e); (outline, increase) net(te); (cold, pain) vif (vive); (taste) piquant(e), âcre; (Mus) dièse; (person: quick-witted) vif (vive), éveillé(e); (: unscrupulous) malhonnête ▷ n (Mus) dièse m ▷ adv: **at 2 o'clock ~** à 2 heures pile or tapantes; **sharpen** vt aiguiser; (pencil) tailler; (fig) aviver; **sharpener** n (also: **pencil sharpener**) taille-crayon(s) m inv; **sharply** adv (turn, stop) brusquement; (stand out) nettement; (criticize, retort) sèchement, vertement

shatter ['ʃætəʳ] vt briser, (fig: upset) bouleverser; (: ruin) briser, ruiner ▷ vi voler en éclats, se briser; **shattered** adj (overwhelmed, grief-stricken) bouleversé(e); (inf: exhausted) éreinté(e)

shave [ʃeɪv] vt raser ▷ vi se raser ▷ n: **to have a ~** se raser; **shaver** n (also: **electric shaver**) rasoir m électrique

shaving cream n crème f à raser

shaving foam n mousse f à raser

shavings ['ʃeɪvɪŋz] npl (of wood etc) copeaux mpl

shawl [ʃɔːl] n châle m

she [ʃiː] pron elle

sheath [ʃiːθ] n gaine f, fourreau m, étui m; (contraceptive) préservatif m

shed [ʃɛd] n remise f, resserre f ▷ vt (pt, pp **shed**) (leaves, fur etc) perdre; (tears) verser, répandre; (workers) congédier

she'd [ʃiːd] = **she had**; **she would**

sheep [ʃiːp] n (pl inv) mouton m; **sheepdog** n chien m de berger; **sheepskin** n peau f de mouton

sheer [ʃɪəʳ] adj (utter) pur(e), pur et simple; (steep) à pic, abrupt(e); (almost transparent) extrêmement fin(e) ▷ adv à pic, abruptement

sheet [ʃiːt] n (on bed) drap m; (of paper) feuille f; (of glass, metal etc) feuille, plaque f

sheik(h) [ʃeɪk] n cheik m

shelf (pl **shelves**) [ʃɛlf, ʃɛlvz] n étagère f, rayon m

shell [ʃɛl] n (on beach) coquillage m; (of egg, nut etc) coquille f; (explosive) obus m; (of building) carcasse f ▷ vt (peas) écosser; (Mil) bombarder (d'obus)

she'll [ʃiːl] = **she will**; **she shall**

shellfish ['ʃɛlfɪʃ] n (pl inv: crab etc) crustacé m; (: scallop etc) coquillage m ▷ npl (as food) fruits mpl de mer

shelter ['ʃɛltəʳ] n abri m, refuge m ▷ vt abriter, protéger; (give lodging to) donner asile à ▷ vi s'abriter, se mettre à l'abri; **sheltered** adj (life) retiré(e), à l'abri des soucis; (spot) abrité(e)

shelves ['ʃɛlvz] npl of **shelf**

shelving ['ʃɛlvɪŋ] n (shelves) rayonnage(s) m(pl)

shepherd ['ʃɛpəd] n berger m ▷ vt (guide) guider, escorter; **shepherd's pie** n ≈ hachis m Parmentier

sheriff ['ʃɛrɪf] (US) n shérif m

sherry ['ʃɛrɪ] n xérès m, sherry m

she's [ʃiːz] = **she is**; **she has**

Shetland ['ʃɛtlənd] n (also: **the ~s, the ~ Isles** or **Islands**) les îles fpl Shetland

shield [ʃiːld] n bouclier m; (protection) écran m de protection ▷ vt: **to ~ (from)** protéger (de or contre)

shift [ʃɪft] n (change) changement m; (work period) période f de travail; (of workers) équipe f, poste m ▷ vt déplacer, changer de place; (remove) enlever ▷ vi changer de place, bouger

shin [ʃɪn] n tibia m

shine [ʃaɪn] n éclat m, brillant m ▷ vi (pt, pp **shone**) briller ▷ vt (pt, pp **shined**) (polish) faire briller or reluire; **to ~ sth on sth** (torch) braquer qch sur qch

shingles ['ʃɪŋglz] n (Med) zona m

shiny ['ʃaɪnɪ] adj brillant(e)

ship [ʃɪp] n bateau m; (large) navire m ▷ vt transporter (par mer); (send) expédier (par mer); **shipment** n cargaison f; **shipping** n (ships) navires mpl; (traffic) navigation f; (the industry) industrie navale; (transport) transport m; **shipwreck** n épave f; (event) naufrage m ▷ vt: **to be shipwrecked** faire naufrage; **shipyard** n chantier naval

shirt [ʃəːt] n chemise f; (woman's) chemisier m; **in ~ sleeves** en bras de chemise

shit [ʃɪt] excl (inf!) merde (!)

shiver ['ʃɪvəʳ] n frisson m ▷ vi frissonner

shock [ʃɔk] n choc m; (Elec) secousse f, décharge f; (Med) commotion f, choc ▷ vt (scandalize) choquer, scandaliser; (upset) bouleverser; **shocking** adj (outrageous)

choquant(e), scandaleux(-euse); (*awful*)
épouvantable

shoe [ʃuː] n chaussure f, soulier m; (*also:*
horse~) fer m à cheval ▷ vt (pt, pp **shod**)
(*horse*) ferrer; **shoelace** n lacet m (de
soulier); **shoe polish** n cirage m; **shoeshop**
n magasin m de chaussures

shone [ʃɔn] pt, pp of **shine**

shonky [ˈʃɔŋkɪ] adj (AUST, NZ inf:
untrustworthy) louche

shook [ʃuk] pt of **shake**

shoot [ʃuːt] n (*on branch,
seedling*) pousse f ▷ vt (*game: hunt*) chasser;
(: *aim at*) tirer; (: *kill*) abattre; (*person*)
blesser/tuer d'un coup de fusil (or de
revolver); (*execute*) fusiller; (*arrow*) tirer;
(*gun*) tirer un coup de; (*Cine*) tourner ▷ vi
(*with gun, bow*): **to ~ (at)** tirer (sur); (*Football*)
shooter, tirer; **shoot down** vt (*plane*)
abattre; **shoot up** vi (*fig: prices etc*) monter
en flèche; **shooting** n (*shots*) coups mpl de
feu; (*attack*) fusillade f; (*murder*) homicide m
(*à l'aide d'une arme à feu*); (*Hunting*) chasse f

shop [ʃɔp] n magasin m; (*workshop*)
atelier m ▷ vi (*also:* **go ~ping**) faire ses
courses or ses achats; **shop assistant** n
(BRIT) vendeur(-euse); **shopkeeper** n
marchand(e), commerçant(e); **shoplifting** n
vol m à l'étalage; **shopping** n (*goods*)
achats mpl, provisions fpl; **shopping bag** n
sac m (à provisions); **shopping centre**, (US)
shopping center n centre commercial;
shopping mall n centre commercial;
shopping trolley n (BRIT) Caddie® m; **shop
window** n vitrine f

shore [ʃɔːʳ] n (*of sea, lake*) rivage m, rive f ▷ vt:
to ~ (up) étayer; **on ~** à terre

short [ʃɔːt] adj (*not long*) court(e); (*soon
finished*) court, bref (brève); (*person, step*)
petit(e); (*curt*) brusque, sec (sèche);
(*insufficient*) insuffisant(e) ▷ n (*also:* **~ film**)
court métrage; (*Elec*) court-circuit m; **to
be ~ of sth** être à court de or manquer de
qch; **in ~** bref; en bref; **~ of doing** à moins
de faire; **everything ~ of** tout sauf; **it is ~
for** c'est l'abréviation or le diminutif de; **to
cut ~** (*speech, visit*) abréger, écourter; **to fall
~ of** ne pas être à la hauteur de; **to run ~ of**
arriver à court de, venir à manquer de; **to
stop ~** s'arrêter net; **to stop ~ of** ne pas aller
jusqu'à; **shortage** n manque m, pénurie
f; **shortbread** n ≈ sablé m; **shortcoming**
n défaut m; **short(crust) pastry** n (BRIT)
pâte brisée; **shortcut** n raccourci m;
shorten vt raccourcir; (*text, visit*) abréger;
shortfall n déficit m; **shorthand** n (BRIT)
sténo(graphie) f; **shortlist** n (BRIT: *for job*)
liste f des candidats sélectionnés; **short-
lived** adj de courte durée; **shortly** adv
bientôt, sous peu; **shorts** npl: **(a pair of)
shorts** un short; **short-sighted** adj (BRIT)
myope; (*fig*) qui manque de clairvoyance;

short-sleeved adj à manches courtes;
short story n nouvelle f; **short-tempered**
adj qui s'emporte facilement; **short-term**
adj (*effect*) à court terme

shot [ʃɔt] pt, pp of **shoot** ▷ n coup m (de feu);
(*try*) coup, essai m; (*injection*) piqûre f; (*Phot*)
photo f; **to be a good/poor ~** (*person*) tirer
bien/mal; **like a ~** comme une flèche; (*very
readily*) sans hésiter; **shotgun** n fusil m de
chasse

should [ʃud] aux vb: **I ~ go now** je devrais
partir maintenant; **he ~ be there now** il
devrait être arrivé maintenant; **I ~ go if I
were you** si j'étais vous j'irais; **I ~ like to**
volontiers, j'aimerais bien

shoulder [ˈʃəuldəʳ] n épaule f ▷ vt (*fig*)
endosser, se charger de; **shoulder blade** n
omoplate f

shouldn't [ˈʃudnt] = **should not**

shout [ʃaut] n cri m ▷ vt crier ▷ vi crier,
pousser des cris

shove [ʃʌv] vt pousser; (*inf: put*): **to ~ sth in**
fourrer or ficher qch dans ▷ n poussée f

shovel [ˈʃʌvl] n pelle f ▷ vt pelleter, enlever
(or enfourner) à la pelle

show [ʃəu] (pt **showed**, pp **shown**) n (*of
emotion*) manifestation f, démonstration
f; (*semblance*) semblant m, apparence f;
(*exhibition*) exposition f, salon m; (*Theat, TV*)
spectacle m; (*Cine*) séance f ▷ vt montrer;
(*film*) passer; (*courage etc*) faire preuve de,
manifester; (*exhibit*) exposer ▷ vi se voir,
être visible; **can you ~ me where it is,
please?** pouvez-vous me montrer où c'est?;
to be on ~ être exposé(e); **it's just for ~** c'est
juste pour l'effet; **show in** vt faire entrer;
show off vi (*pej*) crâner ▷ vt (*display*) faire
valoir; (*pej*) faire étalage de; **show out** vt
reconduire à la porte; **show up** vi (*stand
out*) ressortir; (*inf: turn up*) se montrer ▷ vt
(*unmask*) démasquer, dénoncer; (*flaw*) faire
ressortir; **show business** n le monde du
spectacle

shower [ˈʃauəʳ] n (*for washing*) douche f;
(*rain*) averse f; (*of stones etc*) pluie f, grêle f;
(US: *party*) réunion organisée pour la remise
de cadeaux ▷ vi prendre une douche, se
doucher ▷ vt: **to ~ sb with** (*gifts etc*)
combler qn de; **to have** or **take a ~** prendre
une douche, se doucher; **shower cap** n
bonnet m de douche; **shower gel** n gel m de
douche

showing [ˈʃəuɪŋ] n (*of film*) projection f

show jumping [-dʒʌmpɪŋ] n concours m
hippique

shown [ʃəun] pp of **show**

show: show-off n (*inf: person*)
crâneur(-euse), m'as-tu-vu(e); **showroom**
n magasin m or salle f d'exposition

shrank [ʃræŋk] pt of **shrink**

shred [ʃrɛd] n (*gen pl*) lambeau m, petit
morceau m; (*fig: of truth, evidence*) parcelle

f ▷ *vt* mettre en lambeaux, déchirer;
(*documents*) détruire; (*Culin: grate*) râper;
(: *lettuce etc*) couper en lanières

shrewd [ʃruːd] *adj* astucieux(-euse),
perspicace; (*business person*) habile

shriek [ʃriːk] *n* cri perçant *or* aigu,
hurlement *m* ▷ *vt*, *vi* hurler, crier

shrimp [ʃrɪmp] *n* crevette grise

shrine [ʃraɪn] *n* (*place*) lieu *m* de pèlerinage

shrink (*pt* **shrank**, *pp* **shrunk**) [ʃrɪŋk,
ʃræŋk, ʃrʌŋk] *vi* rétrécir; (*fig*) diminuer;
(*also*: **~ away**) reculer ▷ *vt* (*wool*) (faire)
rétrécir ▷ *n* (*Inf, pej*) psychanalyste *m/f*; **to ~
from (doing) sth** reculer devant (la pensée
de faire) qch

shrivel ['ʃrɪvl], **shrivel up** *vt* ratatiner,
flétrir ▷ *vi* se ratatiner, se flétrir

shroud [ʃraud] *n* linceul *m* ▷ *vt*: **~ed in
mystery** enveloppé(e) de mystère

Shrove Tuesday ['ʃrəuv-] *n* (le) Mardi gras

shrub [ʃrʌb] *n* arbuste *m*

shrug [ʃrʌg] *n* haussement *m* d'épaules
▷ *vt*, *vi*: **to ~ (one's shoulders)** hausser les
épaules; **shrug off** *vt* faire fi de

shrunk [ʃrʌŋk] *pp of* **shrink**

shudder ['ʃʌdəʳ] *n* frisson *m*, frémissement
m ▷ *vi* frissonner, frémir

shuffle ['ʃʌfl] *vt* (*cards*) battre; **to ~ (one's
feet)** traîner les pieds

shun [ʃʌn] *vt* éviter, fuir

shut (*pt*, *pp* **shut**) [ʃʌt] *vt* fermer ▷ *vi*
(se) fermer; **shut down** *vt* fermer
définitivement ▷ *vi* fermer définitivement;
shut up *vi* (*inf: keep quiet*) se taire ▷ *vt* (*close*)
fermer; (*silence*) faire taire; **shutter** *n* volet
m; (*Phot*) obturateur *m*

shuttle ['ʃʌtl] *n* navette *f*; (*also*: **~ service**)
(service *m* de) navette *f*; **shuttlecock** *n*
volant *m* (de badminton)

shy [ʃaɪ] *adj* timide

siblings ['sɪblɪŋz] *npl* (*formal*) frères et
sœurs *mpl* (de mêmes parents)

Sicily ['sɪsɪlɪ] *n* Sicile *f*

sick [sɪk] *adj* (*ill*) malade; (*BRIT: humour*)
noir(e), macabre; (*vomiting*): **to be ~** vomir;
to feel ~ avoir envie de vomir, avoir mal
au cœur; **to be ~ of** (*fig*) en avoir assez
de; **sickening** *adj* (*fig*) écœurant(e),
révoltant(e), répugnant(e); **sick leave**
n congé *m* de maladie; **sickly** *adj*
maladif(-ive), souffreteux(-euse); (*causing
nausea*) écœurant(e); **sickness** *n* maladie *f*;
(*vomiting*) vomissement(s) *m(pl)*

side [saɪd] *n* côté *m*; (*of lake, road*) bord *m*;
(*of mountain*) versant *m*; (*fig: aspect*) côté,
aspect *m*; (*team: Sport*) équipe *f*; (*TV: channel*)
chaîne *f* ▷ *adj* (*door, entrance*) latéral(e)
▷ *vi*: **to ~ with sb** prendre le parti de qn, se
ranger du côté de qn; **by the ~ of** au bord
de; **~ by ~** côte à côte; **to rock from ~ to ~**
se balancer; **to take ~s (with)** prendre parti
(pour); **sideboard** *n* buffet *m*; **sideboards**,

(US) **sideburns** *npl* (*whiskers*) pattes *fpl*;
side effect *n* effet *m* secondaire; **sidelight**
n (*Aut*) veilleuse *f*; **sideline** *n* (*Sport*) (ligne
f de) touche *f*; (*fig*) activité *f* secondaire;
side order *n* garniture *f*; **side road** *n* petite
route, route transversale; **side street** *n* rue
transversale; **sidetrack** *vt* (*fig*) faire dévier
de son sujet; **sidewalk** *n* (US) trottoir *m*;
sideways *adv* de côté

siege [siːdʒ] *n* siège *m*

sieve [sɪv] *n* tamis *m*, passoire *f* ▷ *vt* tamiser,
passer (au tamis)

sift [sɪft] *vt* passer au tamis *ou* au crible; (*fig*)
passer au crible

sigh [saɪ] *n* soupir *m* ▷ *vi* soupirer, pousser
un soupir

sight [saɪt] *n* (*faculty*) vue *f*; (*spectacle*)
spectacle *m* ▷ *vt* apercevoir; **in ~** visible; (*fig*)
en vue; **out of ~** hors de vue; **sightseeing**
n tourisme *m*; **to go sightseeing** faire du
tourisme

sign [saɪn] *n* (*gen*) signe *m*; (*with hand etc*)
signe, geste *m*; (*notice*) panneau *m*,
écriteau *m*; (*also*: **road ~**) panneau de
signalisation ▷ *vt* signer; **where do I ~?** où
dois-je signer?; **sign for** *vt fus* (*item*) signer
le reçu pour; **sign in** *vi* signer le registre (en
arrivant); **sign on** *vi* (BRIT: *as unemployed*)
s'inscrire au chômage; (*enrol*) s'inscrire ▷ *vt*
(*employee*) embaucher; **sign over** *vt*: **to ~
sth over to sb** céder qch par écrit à qn;
sign up *vi* (*Mil*) s'engager; (*for course*)
s'inscrire

signal ['sɪgnl] *n* signal *m* ▷ *vi* (*Aut*) mettre
son clignotant ▷ *vt* (*person*) faire signe à;
(*message*) communiquer par signaux

signature ['sɪgnətʃəʳ] *n* signature *f*

significance [sɪgˈnɪfɪkəns] *n* signification
f; importance *f*

significant [sɪgˈnɪfɪkənt] *adj*
significatif(-ive); (*important*) important(e),
considérable

signify ['sɪgnɪfaɪ] *vt* signifier

sign language *n* langage *m* par signes

signpost ['saɪnpəust] *n* poteau indicateur

Sikh [siːk] *adj*, *n* Sikh *m/f*

silence ['saɪlns] *n* silence *m* ▷ *vt* faire taire,
réduire au silence

silent ['saɪlnt] *adj* silencieux(-euse); (*film*)
muet(te); **to keep** *or* **remain ~** garder le
silence, ne rien dire

silhouette [sɪluˈet] *n* silhouette *f*

silicon chip ['sɪlɪkən-] *n* puce *f*
électronique

silk [sɪlk] *n* soie *f* ▷ *cpd* de *ou* en soie

silly ['sɪlɪ] *adj* stupide, sot(te), bête

silver ['sɪlvəʳ] *n* argent *m*; (*money*) monnaie
f (en pièces d'argent); (*also*: **~ware**)
argenterie *f* ▷ *adj* (*made of silver*) d'argent, en
argent; (*in colour*) argenté(e); **silver-plated**
adj plaqué(e) argent

SIM card ['sɪm-] *abbr* (*Tel*) carte *f* SIM

similar ['sɪmɪlə^r] *adj*: ~ **(to)** semblable (à);
similarity [sɪmɪ'lærɪtɪ] *n* ressemblance *f*,
similarité *f*; **similarly** *adv* de la même façon,
de même

simmer ['sɪmə^r] *vi* cuire à feu doux, mijoter

simple ['sɪmpl] *adj* simple; **simplicity**
[sɪm'plɪsɪtɪ] *n* simplicité *f*; **simplify**
['sɪmplɪfaɪ] *vt* simplifier; **simply** *adv*
simplement; (*without fuss*) avec simplicité;
(*absolutely*) absolument

simulate ['sɪmjʊleɪt] *vt* simuler, feindre

simultaneous [sɪməl'teɪnɪəs] *adj*
simultané(e); **simultaneously** *adv*
simultanément

sin [sɪn] *n* péché *m* ▷ *vi* pécher

since [sɪns] *adv, prep* depuis ▷ *conj* (*time*)
depuis que; (*because*) puisque, étant donné
que, comme; ~ **then, ever** ~ depuis ce
moment-là

sincere [sɪn'sɪə^r] *adj* sincère; **sincerely**
adv sincèrement; **yours sincerely** (*at
end of letter*) veuillez agréer, Monsieur (*or*
Madame) l'expression de mes sentiments
distingués *or* les meilleurs

sing (*pt* **sang**, *pp* **sung**) [sɪŋ, sæŋ, sʌŋ] *vt,
vi* chanter

Singapore [sɪŋgə'pɔː^r] *n* Singapour *m*

singer ['sɪŋə^r] *n* chanteur(-euse)

singing ['sɪŋɪŋ] *n* (*of person, bird*) chant *m*

single ['sɪŋgl] *adj* seul(e), unique;
(*unmarried*) célibataire; (*not double*)
simple ▷ *n* (BRIT: *also*: ~ **ticket**) aller *m*
(simple); (*record*) 45 tours *m*; **singles** *npl*
(*Tennis*) simple *m*; **every** ~ **day** chaque
jour sans exception; **single out** *vt* choisir;
(*distinguish*) distinguer; **single bed** *n* lit *m*
d'une personne *or* à une place; **single file**
n: **in single file** en file indienne; **single-
handed** *adv* tout(e) seul(e), sans (aucune)
aide; **single-minded** *adj* résolu(e),
tenace; **single parent** *n* parent unique (*or*
célibataire); **single-parent family** famille
monoparentale; **single room** *n* chambre *f* à
un lit *or* pour une personne

singular ['sɪŋgjʊlə^r] *adj* singulier(-ière);
(*odd*) singulier, étrange; (*outstanding*)
remarquable; (*Ling*) (au) singulier, du
singulier ▷ *n* (*Ling*) singulier *m*

sinister ['sɪnɪstə^r] *adj* sinistre

sink [sɪŋk] (*pt* **sank**, *pp* **sunk**) *n* évier *m*;
(*washbasin*) lavabo *m* ▷ *vt* (*ship*) (faire)
couler, faire sombrer; (*foundations*) creuser
▷ *vi* couler, sombrer; (*ground etc*) s'affaisser;
to ~ into sth (*chair*) s'enfoncer dans qch;
sink in *vi* (*explanation*) rentrer (*inf*), être
compris

sinus ['saɪnəs] *n* (*Anat*) sinus *m inv*

sip [sɪp] *n* petite gorgée ▷ *vt* boire à petites
gorgées

sir [sə^r] *n* monsieur *m*; **S~ John Smith** sir
John Smith; **yes ~** oui Monsieur

siren ['saɪərn] *n* sirène *f*

sirloin ['sə:lɔɪn] *n* (*also*: ~ **steak**) aloyau *m*

sister ['sɪstə^r] *n* sœur *f*; (*nun*) religieuse *f*,
(bonne) sœur; (BRIT: *nurse*) infirmière *f* en
chef; **sister-in-law** *n* belle-sœur *f*

sit (*pt, pp* **sat**) [sɪt, sæt] *vi* s'asseoir; (*be
sitting*) être assis(e); (*assembly*) être en
séance, siéger; (*for painter*) poser ▷ *vt*
(*exam*) passer, se présenter à; **sit back** *vi* (*in
seat*) bien s'installer, se carrer; **sit down** *vi*
s'asseoir; **sit on** *vt fus* (*jury, committee*) faire
partie de; **sit up** *vi* s'asseoir; (*straight*) se
redresser; (*not go to bed*) rester debout, ne
pas se coucher

sitcom ['sɪtkɔm] *n abbr* (*TV*: = *situation
comedy*) sitcom *f*, comédie *f* de situation

site [saɪt] *n* emplacement *m*, site *m*; (*also*:
building ~) chantier *m*; (*Internet*) site *m* web
▷ *vt* placer

sitting ['sɪtɪŋ] *n* (*of assembly etc*) séance *f*;
(*in canteen*) service *m*; **sitting room** *n*
salon *m*

situated ['sɪtjʊeɪtɪd] *adj* situé(e)

situation [sɪtju'eɪʃən] *n* situation *f*; "~s
vacant/wanted" (BRIT) "offres/demandes
d'emploi"

six [sɪks] *num* six; **sixteen** *num* seize;
sixteenth *num* seizième; **sixth**
['sɪksθ] *num* sixième; **sixth form** (BRIT)
≈ classes *fpl* de première et de terminale;
sixth-form college *n* lycée n'ayant que des
classes de première et de terminale; **sixtieth**
['sɪkstɪɪθ] *num* soixantième; **sixty** *num*
soixante

size [saɪz] *n* dimensions *fpl*; (*of person*) taille
f; (*of clothing*) taille; (*of shoes*) pointure *f*; (*of
problem*) ampleur *f*; (*glue*) colle *f*; **sizeable**
adj assez grand(e); (*amount, problem,
majority*) assez important(e)

sizzle ['sɪzl] *vi* grésiller

skate [skeɪt] *n* patin *m*; (*fish: pl inv*) raie *f*
▷ *vi* patiner; **skateboard** *n* skateboard *m*,
planche *f* à roulettes; **skateboarding** *n*
skateboard *m*; **skater** *n* patineur(-euse);
skating *n* patinage *m*; **skating rink** *n*
patinoire *f*

skeleton ['skɛlɪtn] *n* squelette *m*; (*outline*)
schéma *m*

skeptical ['skɛptɪkl] (US) *adj* = **sceptical**

sketch [skɛtʃ] *n* (*drawing*) croquis *m*,
esquisse *f*; (*outline plan*) aperçu *m*; (*Theat*)
sketch *m*, saynète *f* ▷ *vt* esquisser, faire
un croquis *or* une esquisse de; (*plan etc*)
esquisser

skewer ['skjuːə^r] *n* brochette *f*

ski [skiː] *n* ski *m* ▷ *vi* skier, faire du ski; **ski
boot** *n* chaussure *f* de ski

skid [skɪd] *n* dérapage *m* ▷ *vi* déraper

ski: skier *n* skieur(-euse); **skiing** *n* ski *m*;
to go skiing (aller) faire du ski

skilful, (US) **skillful** ['skɪlful] *adj* habile,
adroit(e)

ski lift *n* remonte-pente *m inv*

skill [skɪl] n (ability) habileté f, adresse f, talent m; (requiring training) compétences fpl; **skilled** adj habile, adroit(e); (worker) qualifié(e)

skim [skɪm] vt (soup) écumer; (glide over) raser, effleurer ▷ vi: **to ~ through** (fig) parcourir; **skimmed milk**, (US) **skim milk** n lait écrémé

skin [skɪn] n peau f ▷ vt (fruit etc) éplucher; (animal) écorcher; **skinhead** n skinhead m; **skinny** adj maigre, maigrichon(ne)

skip [skɪp] n petit bond or saut; (BRIT: container) benne f ▷ vi gambader, sautiller, (with rope) sauter à la corde ▷ vt (pass over) sauter

ski: ski pass n forfait-skieur(s) m; **ski pole** n bâton m de ski

skipper ['skɪpər] n (Naut, Sport) capitaine m; (in race) skipper m

skipping rope ['skɪpɪŋ-], (US) **skip rope** n corde f à sauter

skirt [skəːt] n jupe f ▷ vt longer, contourner

skirting board ['skəːtɪŋ-] n (BRIT) plinthe f

ski slope n piste f de ski

ski suit n combinaison f de ski

skull [skʌl] n crâne m

skunk [skʌŋk] n mouffette f

sky [skaɪ] n ciel m; **skyscraper** n gratte-ciel m inv

slab [slæb] n (of stone) dalle f; (of meat, cheese) tranche épaisse

slack [slæk] adj (loose) lâche, desserré(e); (slow) stagnant(e); (careless) négligent(e), peu sérieux(-euse) or consciencieux(-euse); **slacks** npl pantalon m

slain [sleɪn] pp of **slay**

slam [slæm] vt (door) (faire) claquer, (throw) jeter violemment, flanquer; (inf: criticize) éreinter, démolir ▷ vi claquer

slander ['slɑːndər] n calomnie f; (Law) diffamation f

slang [slæŋ] n argot m

slant [slɑːnt] n inclinaison f; (fig) angle m, point m de vue

slap [slæp] n claque f, gifle f; (on the back) tape f ▷ vt donner une claque or une gifle (or une tape) à ▷ adv (directly) tout droit, en plein; **to ~ on** (paint) appliquer rapidement

slash [slæʃ] vt entailler, taillader; (fig: prices) casser

slate [sleɪt] n ardoise f ▷ vt (fig: criticize) éreinter, démolir

slaughter ['slɔːtər] n carnage m, massacre m; (of animals) abattage m ▷ vt (animal) abattre; (people) massacrer; **slaughterhouse** n abattoir m

Slav [slɑːv] adj slave

slave [sleɪv] n esclave m/f ▷ vi (also: **~ away**) trimer, travailler comme un forçat; **slavery** n esclavage m

slay (pt **slew**, pp **slain**) [sleɪ, sluː, sleɪn] vt (literary) tuer

sleazy ['sliːzɪ] adj miteux(-euse), minable

sled [slɛd] (US) n = **sledge**

sledge [slɛdʒ] n luge f

sleek [sliːk] adj (hair, fur) brillant(e), luisant(e); (car, boat) aux lignes pures or élégantes

sleep [sliːp] n sommeil m ▷ vi (pt, pp **slept**) dormir; **to go to ~** s'endormir; **sleep in** vi (oversleep) se réveiller trop tard; (on purpose) faire la grasse matinée; **sleep together** vi (have sex) coucher ensemble; **sleeper** n (person) dormeur(-euse); (BRIT Rail: on track) traverse f, (: train) train-couchettes m; (: berth) couchette f; **sleeping bag** ['sliːpɪŋ-] n sac m de couchage; **sleeping car** n wagon-lits m, voiture-lits f; **sleeping pill** n somnifère m; **sleepover** n nuit f chez un copain or une copine; **we're having a sleepover at Jo's** nous allons passer la nuit chez Jo; **sleepwalk** vi marcher en dormant; **sleepy** adj (fig) endormi(e)

sleet [sliːt] n neige fondue

sleeve [sliːv] n manche f; (of record) pochette f; **sleeveless** adj (garment) sans manches

sleigh [sleɪ] n traîneau m

slender ['slɛndər] adj svelte, mince; (fig) faible, ténu(e)

slept [slɛpt] pt, pp of **sleep**

slew [sluː] pt of **slay**

slice [slaɪs] n tranche f, (round) rondelle f; (utensil) spatule f; (also: **fish ~**) pelle f à poisson ▷ vt couper en tranches (or en rondelles)

slick [slɪk] adj (skilful) bien ficelé(e); (salesperson) qui a du bagout ▷ n (also: **oil ~**) nappe f de pétrole, marée noire

slide (pt, pp **slid**) [slaɪd, slɪd] n (in playground) toboggan m; (Phot) diapositive f; (BRIT: also: **hair ~**) barrette f; (in prices) chute f, baisse f ▷ vt (faire) glisser ▷ vi glisser; **sliding** adj (door) coulissant(e)

slight [slaɪt] adj (slim) mince, menu(e); (frail) frêle; (trivial) faible, insignifiant(e); (small) petit(e), léger(-ère) before n ▷ n offense f, affront m ▷ vt (offend) blesser, offenser; **not in the ~est** pas le moins du monde, pas du tout; **slightly** adv légèrement, un peu

slim [slɪm] adj mince ▷ vi maigrir; (diet) suivre un régime amaigrissant; **slimming** n amaigrissement m ▷ adj (diet, pills) amaigrissant(e), pour maigrir; (food) qui ne fait pas grossir

slimy ['slaɪmɪ] adj visqueux(-euse), gluant(e)

sling [slɪŋ] n (Med) écharpe f; (for baby) porte-bébé m; (weapon) fronde f, lance-pierre m ▷ vt (pt, pp **slung**) lancer, jeter

slip [slɪp] n faux pas; (mistake) erreur f, bévue f; (underskirt) combinaison f; (of paper) petite feuille, fiche f ▷ vt (slide) glisser

▷ vi (slide) glisser; (decline) baisser; (move smoothly): **to ~ into/out of** se glisser or se faufiler dans/hors de; **to ~ sth on/off** enfiler/enlever qch; **to give sb the ~** fausser compagnie à qn; **a ~ of the tongue** un lapsus; **slip up** vi faire une erreur, gaffer

slipped disc [slɪpt-] n déplacement m de vertèbre

slipper ['slɪpə^r] n pantoufle f

slippery ['slɪpərɪ] adj glissant(e)

slip road n (BRIT: to motorway) bretelle f d'accès

slit [slɪt] n fente f; (cut) incision f ▷ vt (pt, pp **slit**) fendre; couper, inciser

slog [slɔg] n (BRIT: effort) gros effort; (work) tâche fastidieuse ▷ vi travailler très dur

slogan ['sləugən] n slogan m

slope [sləup] n pente f, côte f; (side of mountain) versant m; (slant) inclinaison f ▷ vi: **to ~ down** être or descendre en pente; **to ~ up** monter; **sloping** adj en pente, incliné(e); (handwriting) penché(e)

sloppy ['slɔpɪ] adj (work) peu soigné(e), bâclé(e); (appearance) négligé(e), débraillé(e)

slot [slɔt] n fente f ▷ vt: **to ~ sth into** encastrer or insérer qch dans; **slot machine** n (BRIT: vending machine) distributeur m (automatique), machine f à sous; (for gambling) appareil m or machine à sous

Slovakia [sləu'vækɪə] n Slovaquie f

Slovene [sləu'vi:n] adj slovène ▷ n Slovène m/f; (Ling) slovène m

Slovenia [sləu'vi:nɪə] n Slovénie f; **Slovenian** adj, n = **Slovene**

slow [sləu] adj lent(e); (watch): **to be ~** retarder ▷ adv lentement ▷ vt, vi ralentir; **"~" (road sign)** "ralentir"; **slow down** vi ralentir; **slowly** adv lentement; **slow motion** n: **in slow motion** au ralenti

slug [slʌg] n limace f; (bullet) balle f; **sluggish** adj (person) mou (molle), lent(e); (stream, engine, trading) lent(e)

slum [slʌm] n (house) taudis m; **slums** npl (area) quartiers mpl pauvres

slump [slʌmp] n baisse soudaine, effondrement m; (Econ) crise f ▷ vi s'effondrer, s'affaisser

slung [slʌŋ] pt, pp of **sling**

slur [slə:^r] n (smear): **~ (on)** atteinte f (à); insinuation f (contre) ▷ vt mal articuler

slush [slʌʃ] n neige fondue

sly [slaɪ] adj (person) rusé(e); (smile, expression, remark) sournois(e)

smack [smæk] n (slap) tape f; (on face) gifle f ▷ vt donner une tape à; (on face) gifler; (on bottom) donner la fessée à ▷ vi: **to ~ of** avoir des relents de, sentir

small [smɔ:l] adj petit(e); **small ads** npl (BRIT) petites annonces; **small change** n petite or menue monnaie

smart [smɑ:t] adj élégant(e), chic inv; (clever) intelligent(e); (quick) vif (vive),

prompt(e) ▷ vi faire mal, brûler; **smart card** n carte f à puce; **smart phone** n smartphone m

smash [smæʃ] n (also: **~-up**) collision f, accident m; (Mus) succès foudroyant ▷ vt casser, briser, fracasser; (opponent) écraser; (Sport: record) pulvériser ▷ vi se briser, se fracasser; s'écraser; **smashing** adj (inf) formidable

smear [smɪə^r] n (stain) tache f; (mark) trace f; (Med) frottis m ▷ vt enduire; (make dirty) salir; **smear test** n (BRIT Med) frottis m

smell [smɛl] (pt, pp **smelt** or **smelled**) n odeur f; (sense) odorat m ▷ vt sentir ▷ vi (pej) sentir mauvais; **smelly** adj qui sent mauvais, malodorant(e)

smelt [smɛlt] pt, pp of **smell**

smile [smaɪl] n sourire m ▷ vi sourire

smirk [smə:k] n petit sourire suffisant or affecté

smog [smɔg] n brouillard mêlé de fumée

smoke [sməuk] n fumée f ▷ vt, vi fumer; **do you mind if I ~?** ça ne vous dérange pas que je fume?; **smoke alarm** n détecteur m de fumée; **smoked** adj (bacon, glass) fumé(e); **smoker** n (person) fumeur(-euse); (Rail) wagon m fumeurs; **smoking** n: **"no smoking"** (sign) "défense de fumer"; **smoky** adj enfumé(e); (taste) fumé(e)

smooth [smu:ð] adj lisse; (sauce) onctueux(-euse); (flavour, whisky) moelleux(-euse); (movement) régulier(-ière), sans à-coups or heurts; (flight) sans secousses; (pej: person) doucereux(-euse), mielleux(-euse) ▷ vt (also: **~ out**) lisser, défroisser; (creases, difficulties) faire disparaître

smother ['smʌðə^r] vt étouffer

SMS n abbr (= short message service) SMS m; **SMS message** n (message m) SMS m

smudge [smʌdʒ] n tache f, bavure f ▷ vt salir, maculer

smug [smʌg] adj suffisant(e), content(e) de soi

smuggle ['smʌgl] vt passer en contrebande or en fraude; **smuggling** n contrebande f

snack [snæk] n casse-croûte m inv; **snack bar** n snack(-bar) m

snag [snæg] n inconvénient m, difficulté f

snail [sneɪl] n escargot m

snake [sneɪk] n serpent m

snap [snæp] n (sound) claquement m, bruit sec; (photograph) photo f, instantané m ▷ adj subit(e), fait(e) sans réfléchir ▷ vt (fingers) faire claquer; (break) casser net ▷ vi se casser net or avec un bruit sec; (speak sharply) parler d'un ton brusque; **to ~ open/ shut** s'ouvrir/se refermer brusquement; **snap at** vt fus (subj: dog) essayer de mordre; **snap up** vt sauter sur, saisir; **snapshot** n photo f, instantané m

snarl [snɑ:l] vi gronder

snatch [snætʃ] n ▷ vt saisir (d'un geste vif); (steal) voler; **to ~ some sleep** arriver à dormir un peu

sneak [sni:k] (US: pt, pp **snuck**) vi: **to ~ in/out** entrer/sortir furtivement or à la dérobée ▷ n (inf: pej: informer) faux jeton; **to ~ up on sb** s'approcher de qn sans faire de bruit; **sneakers** npl tennis mpl, baskets fpl

sneer [snɪəʳ] vi ricaner; **to ~ at sb/sth** se moquer de qn/qch avec mépris

sneeze [sni:z] vi éternuer

sniff [snɪf] vi renifler ▷ vt renifler, flairer; (glue, drug) sniffer, respirer

snigger ['snɪgəʳ] vi ricaner

snip [snɪp] n (cut) entaille f; (BRIT inf: bargain) (bonne) occasion or affaire f ▷ vt couper

sniper ['snaɪpəʳ] n tireur embusqué

snob [snɔb] n snob m/f

snooker ['snu:kəʳ] n sorte de jeu de billard

snoop [snu:p] vi: **to ~ about** fureter

snooze [snu:z] n petit somme ▷ vi faire un petit somme

snore [snɔːʳ] vi ronfler ▷ n ronflement m

snorkel ['snɔ:kl] n (of swimmer) tuba m

snort [snɔ:t] n grognement m ▷ vi grogner; (horse) renâcler

snow [snəu] n neige f ▷ vi neiger; **snowball** n boule f de neige; **snowdrift** n congère f; **snowman** (irreg) n bonhomme m de neige; **snowplough**, (US) **snowplow** n chasse-neige m inv; **snowstorm** n tempête f de neige

snub [snʌb] vt repousser, snober ▷ n rebuffade f

snuck [snʌk] (US) pt, pp of **sneak**

snug [snʌg] adj douillet(te), confortable; (person) bien au chaud

---

🄚 **KEYWORD**

so [səu] adv **1** (thus, likewise) ainsi, de cette façon; **if so** si oui; **so do** or **have I** moi aussi; **it's 5 o'clock — so it is!** il est 5 heures — en effet! or c'est vrai!; **I hope/think so** je l'espère/le crois; **so far** jusqu'ici, jusqu'à maintenant; (in past) jusque-là

2 (in comparisons etc: to such a degree) si, tellement; **so big (that)** si or tellement grand (que); **she's not so clever as her brother** elle n'est pas aussi intelligente que son frère

3: **so much** adj, adv tant (de); **I've got so much work** j'ai tant de travail; **I love you so much** je vous aime tant; **so many** tant (de)

4 (phrases): **10 or so** à peu près or environ 10; **so long!** (inf: goodbye) au revoir!, à un de ces jours!; **so (what)?** (inf) (bon) et alors?, et après?

▶ conj **1** (expressing purpose): **so as to do** pour faire, afin de faire; **so (that)** pour que or afin que + sub

2 (expressing result) donc, par conséquent; **so that's the reason!** c'est donc (pour) ça!; **so you see, I could have gone** alors tu vois, j'aurais pu y aller

soak [səuk] vt faire or laisser tremper; (drench) tremper ▷ vi tremper; **soak up** vt absorber; **soaking** adj (also: **soaking wet**) trempé(e)

so-and-so ['səuənsəu] n (somebody) un(e) tel(le)

soap [səup] n savon m; **soap opera** n feuilleton télévisé (quotidienneté réaliste ou embellie); **soap powder** n lessive f, détergent m

soar [sɔːʳ] vi monter (en flèche), s'élancer; (building) s'élancer

sob [sɔb] n sanglot m ▷ vi sangloter

sober ['səubəʳ] adj qui n'est pas (or plus) ivre; (serious) sérieux(-euse), sensé(e); (colour, style) sobre, discret(-ète); **sober up** vi se dégriser

so-called ['səu'kɔ:ld] adj soi-disant inv

soccer ['sɔkəʳ] n football m

sociable ['səuʃəbl] adj sociable

social ['səuʃl] adj social(e); (sociable) sociable ▷ n (petite) fête; **socialism** n socialisme m; **socialist** adj, n socialiste (m/f); **socialize** vi: **to socialize with** (meet often) fréquenter; (get to know) lier connaissance or parler avec; **social life** n vie sociale; **socially** adv socialement, en société; **social media** npl médias mpl sociaux; **social networking** n réseaux mpl sociaux; **social networking site** n site m de réseautage; **social security** n aide sociale; **social services** npl services sociaux; **social work** n assistance sociale; **social worker** n assistant(e) sociale(e)

society [sə'saɪətɪ] n société f; (club) société, association f; (also: **high ~**) (haute) société, grand monde

sociology [səusɪ'ɔlədʒɪ] n sociologie f

sock [sɔk] n chaussette f

socket ['sɔkɪt] n cavité f; (Elec: also: **wall ~**) prise f de courant

soda ['səudə] n (Chem) soude f; (also: **~ water**) eau f de Seltz; (US: also: **~ pop**) soda m

sodium ['səudɪəm] n sodium m

sofa ['səufə] n sofa m, canapé m; **sofa bed** n canapé-lit m

soft [sɔft] adj (not rough) doux (douce); (not hard) doux, mou (molle); (not loud) doux, léger(-ère); (kind) doux, gentil(le); **soft drink** n boisson non alcoolisée; **soft drugs** npl drogues douces; **soften** ['sɔfn] vt (r)amollir; (fig) adoucir ▷ vi se ramollir; (fig) s'adoucir; **softly** adv doucement; (touch) légèrement; (kiss) tendrement; **software** n (Comput) logiciel m, software m

soggy ['sɔgɪ] adj (clothes) trempé(e); (ground) détrempé(e)

soil [sɔɪl] *n* (*earth*) sol *m*, terre *f* ⊳ *vt* salir; (*fig*) souiller

solar ['səʊləʳ] *adj* solaire; **solar power** *n* énergie *f* solaire; **solar system** *n* système *m* solaire

sold [səʊld] *pt, pp of* **sell**

soldier ['səʊldʒəʳ] *n* soldat *m*, militaire *m*

sold out *adj* (*Comm*) épuisé(e)

sole [səʊl] *n* (*of foot*) plante *f*; (*of shoe*) semelle *f*; (*fish: pl inv*) sole *f* ⊳ *adj* seul(e), unique; **solely** *adv* seulement, uniquement

solemn ['sɔləm] *adj* solennel(le); (*person*) sérieux(-euse), grave

solicitor [sə'lɪsɪtəʳ] *n* (*BRIT: for wills etc*) ≈ notaire *m*; (: *in court*) ≈ avocat *m*

solid ['sɔlɪd] *adj* (*not liquid*) solide; (*not hollow: mass*) compact(e); (: *metal, rock, wood*) massif(-ive) ⊳ *n* solide *m*

solitary ['sɔlɪtərɪ] *adj* solitaire

solitude ['sɔlɪtjuːd] *n* solitude *f*

solo ['səʊləʊ] *n* solo *m* ⊳ *adv* (*fly*) en solitaire; **soloist** *n* soliste *m/f*

soluble ['sɔljubl] *adj* soluble

solution [sə'luːʃən] *n* solution *f*

solve [sɔlv] *vt* résoudre

solvent ['sɔlvənt] *adj* (*Comm*) solvable ⊳ *n* (*Chem*) (dis)solvant *m*

sombre, (*US*) **somber** ['sɔmbəʳ] *adj* sombre, morne

⬤ **KEYWORD**

some [sʌm] *adj* **1** (*a certain amount or number of*): **some tea/water/ice cream** du thé/de l'eau/de la glace; **some children/apples** des enfants/pommes; **I've got some money but not much** j'ai de l'argent mais pas beaucoup

2 (*certain: in contrasts*): **some people say that ...** il y a des gens qui disent que ...; **some films were excellent, but were mediocre** certains films étaient excellents, mais la plupart étaient médiocres

3 (*unspecified*): **some woman was asking for you** il y avait une dame qui vous demandait; **he was asking for some book (or other)** il demandait un livre quelconque; **some day** un de ces jours; **some day next week** un jour la semaine prochaine

▶ *pron* **1** (*a certain number*) quelques-un(e)s, certain(e)s; **I've got some** (*books etc*) j'en ai (quelques-uns); **some (of them) have been sold** certains ont été vendus

2 (*a certain amount*) un peu; **I've got some** (*money, milk*) j'en ai (un peu); **would you like some?** est-ce que vous en voulez?, en voulez-vous?; **could I have some of that cheese?** pourrais-je avoir un peu de ce fromage?; **I've read some of the book** j'ai lu une partie du livre

▶ *adv*: **some 10 people** quelque 10 personnes, 10 personnes environ;

somebody ['sʌmbədɪ] *pron* = **someone**;

somehow *adv* d'une façon ou d'une autre; (*for some reason*) pour une raison ou une autre; **someone** *pron* quelqu'un;

someplace *adv* (*US*) = **somewhere**;

something *pron* quelque chose *m*; **something interesting** quelque chose d'intéressant; **something to do** quelque chose à faire; **sometime** *adv* (*in future*) un de ces jours, un jour ou l'autre; (*in past*): **sometime last month** au cours du mois dernier; **sometimes** *adv* quelquefois, parfois; **somewhat** *adv* quelque peu, un peu; **somewhere** *adv* quelque part; **somewhere else** ailleurs, autre part

son [sʌn] *n* fils *m*

song [sɔŋ] *n* chanson *f*; (*of bird*) chant *m*

son-in-law ['sʌnɪnlɔː] *n* gendre *m*, beau-fils *m*

soon [suːn] *adv* bientôt; (*early*) tôt; **~ afterwards** peu après; *see also* **as**; **sooner** *adv* (*time*) plus tôt; (*preference*): **I would sooner do that** j'aimerais autant *or* je préférerais faire ça; **sooner or later** tôt ou tard

soothe [suːð] *vt* calmer, apaiser

sophisticated [sə'fɪstɪkeɪtɪd] *adj* raffiné(e), sophistiqué(e); (*machinery*) hautement perfectionné(e), très complexe

sophomore ['sɔfəmɔːʳ] *n* (*US*) étudiant(e) de seconde année

soprano [sə'prɑːnəʊ] *n* (*singer*) soprano *m/f*

sorbet ['sɔːbeɪ] *n* sorbet *m*

sordid ['sɔːdɪd] *adj* sordide

sore [sɔːʳ] *adj* (*painful*) douloureux(-euse), sensible ⊳ *n* plaie *f*

sorrow ['sɔrəʊ] *n* peine *f*, chagrin *m*

sorry ['sɔrɪ] *adj* (*condition, excuse, tale*) triste, déplorable; **~!** pardon!, excusez-moi!; **~?** pardon?; **to feel ~ for sb** plaindre qn

sort [sɔːt] *n* genre *m*, espèce *f*, sorte *f*; (*make: of coffee, car etc*) marque *f* ⊳ *vt* (*also: ~ out: select which to keep*) trier; (*classify*) classer; (*tidy*) ranger; **sort out** *vt* (*problem*) résoudre, régler

SOS *n* SOS *m*

so-so ['səʊsəʊ] *adv* comme ci comme ça

sought [sɔːt] *pt, pp of* **seek**

soul [səʊl] *n* âme *f*

sound [saʊnd] *adj* (*healthy*) en bonne santé, sain(e); (*safe, not damaged*) solide, en bon état; (*reliable, not superficial*) sérieux(-euse), solide; (*sensible*) sensé(e) ⊳ *adv*: **~ asleep** profondément endormi(e) ⊳ *n* (*noise, volume*) son *m*; (*louder*) bruit *m*; (*Geo*) détroit *m*, bras *m* de mer ⊳ *vt* (*alarm*) sonner ⊳ *vi* sonner, retentir; (*fig: seem*) sembler (être); **to ~ like** ressembler à; **sound bite** *n* phrase toute faite (*pour être citée dans les médias*); **soundtrack** *n* (*of film*) bande *f* sonore

soup [suːp] *n* soupe *f*, potage *m*

sour ['sauə^r] adj aigre; **it's ~ grapes** c'est du dépit
source [sɔːs] n source f
south [sauθ] n sud m ▷ adj sud inv; (wind) du sud ▷ adv au sud, vers le sud; **South Africa** n Afrique f du Sud; **South African** adj sud-africain(e) ▷ n Sud-Africain(e); **South America** n Amérique f du Sud; **South American** adj sud-américain(e) ▷ n Sud-Américain(e); **southbound** adj en direction du sud; (carriageway) sud inv; **south-east** n sud-est m; **southern** ['sʌðən] adj (du) sud; méridional(e), **South Korea** n Corée f du Sud; **South of France** n: **the South of France** le Sud de la France, le Midi; **South Pole** n: **the South Pole** le Pôle Sud; **southward(s)** adv vers le sud; **south-west** n sud-ouest m
souvenir [suːvə'nɪə^r] n souvenir m (objet)
sovereign ['sɔvrɪn] adj, n souverain(e)
sow[1] (pt **sowed**, pp **sown**) [sau, saud, saun] vt semer
sow[2] n [sau] truie f
soya ['sɔɪə], (US) **soy** [sɔɪ] n: **~ bean** graine f de soja; **~ sauce** sauce f au soja
spa [spaː] n (town) station thermale; (US: also: **health ~**) établissement m de cure de rajeunissement
space [speɪs] n (gen) espace m; (room) place f, espace; (length of time) laps m de temps ▷ cpd spatial(e) ▷ vt (also: **~ out**) espacer; **spacecraft** n engin or vaisseau spatial; **spaceship** n = **spacecraft**
spacious ['speɪʃəs] adj spacieux(-euse), grand(e)
spade [speɪd] n (tool) bêche f, pelle f; (child's) pelle; **spades** npl (Cards) pique m
spaghetti [spə'gɛtɪ] n spaghetti mpl
Spain [speɪn] n Espagne f
spam [spæm] n (Comput) pourriel m
span [spæn] n (of bird, plane) envergure f; (of arch) portée f; (in time) espace m de temps, durée f ▷ vt enjamber, franchir; (fig) couvrir, embrasser
Spaniard ['spænjəd] n Espagnol(e)
Spanish ['spænɪʃ] adj espagnol(e), d'Espagne ▷ n (Ling) espagnol m; **the Spanish** npl les Espagnols
spank [spæŋk] vt donner une fessée à
spanner ['spænə^r] n (BRIT) clé f (de mécanicien)
spare [spɛə^r] adj de réserve, de rechange; (surplus) de or en trop, de reste ▷ n (part) pièce f de rechange, pièce détachée ▷ vt (do without) se passer de; (afford to give) donner, accorder, passer; (not hurt) épargner; **to ~** (surplus) en surplus, de trop; **spare part** n pièce f de rechange, pièce détachée; **spare room** n chambre f d'ami; **spare time** n moments mpl de loisir; **spare tyre**, (US) **spare tire** n (Aut) pneu m de rechange; **spare wheel** n (Aut) roue f de secours

spark [spaːk] n étincelle f
sparkle ['spaːkl] n scintillement m, étincellement m, éclat m ▷ vi étinceler, scintiller
sparkling ['spaːklɪŋ] adj (wine) mousseux(-euse), pétillant(e); (water) pétillant(e), gazeux(-euse)
spark plug n bougie f
sparrow ['spærəu] n moineau m
sparse [spaːs] adj clairsemé(e)
spasm ['spæzəm] n (Med) spasme m
spat [spæt] pt, pp of **spit**
spate [speɪt] n (fig): **~ of** avalanche f or torrent m de
spatula ['spætjulə] n spatule f
speak (pt **spoke**, pp **spoken**) [spiːk, spəuk, 'spəukn] vt (language) parler; (truth) dire ▷ vi parler; (make a speech) prendre la parole; **to ~ to sb/of or about sth** parler à qn/de qch; **I don't ~ French** je ne parle pas français; **do you ~ English?** parlez-vous anglais?; **can I ~ to ...?** est-ce que je peux parler à ...?; **speaker** n (in public) orateur m; (also: **loudspeaker**) haut-parleur m; (for stereo etc) baffle m, enceinte f; (Pol): **the Speaker** (BRIT) le président de la Chambre des communes or des représentants; (US) le président de la Chambre
spear [spɪə^r] n lance f ▷ vt transpercer
special ['spɛʃl] adj spécial(e); **special delivery** n (Post): **by special delivery** en express; **special effects** npl (Cine) effets spéciaux; **specialist** n spécialiste m/f; **speciality** [spɛʃɪ'ælɪtɪ] n (BRIT) spécialité f; **specialize** vi: **to specialize (in)** se spécialiser (dans); **specially** adv spécialement, particulièrement; **special needs** npl (BRIT) difficultés fpl d'apprentissage scolaire; **special offer** n (Comm) réclame f; **special school** n (BRIT) établissement m d'enseignement spécialisé; **specialty** n (US) = **speciality**
species ['spiːʃiːz] n (pl inv) espèce f
specific [spə'sɪfɪk] adj (not vague) précis(e), explicite; (particular) particulier(-ière); **specifically** adv explicitement, précisément; (intend, ask, design) expressément, spécialement
specify ['spɛsɪfaɪ] vt spécifier, préciser
specimen ['spɛsɪmən] n spécimen m, échantillon m; (Med: of blood) prélèvement m; (: of urine) échantillon m
speck [spɛk] n petite tache, petit point; (particle) grain m
spectacle ['spɛktəkl] n spectacle m; **spectacles** npl (BRIT) lunettes fpl; **spectacular** [spɛk'tækjulə^r] adj spectaculaire
spectator [spɛk'teɪtə^r] n spectateur(-trice)
spectrum (pl **spectra**) ['spɛktrəm, -rə] n spectre m; (fig) gamme f
speculate ['spɛkjuleɪt] vi spéculer; (ponder): **to ~ about** s'interroger sur

sped [spɛd] *pt, pp of* **speed**

speech [spiːtʃ] *n* (*faculty*) parole *f*; (*talk*) discours *m*, allocution *f*; (*manner of speaking*) façon *f* de parler, langage *m*; (*enunciation*) élocution *f*; **speechless** *adj* muet(te)

speed [spiːd] *n* vitesse *f*; (*promptness*) rapidité *f* ▷ *vi* (*pt, pp* **sped**) (*Aut: exceed speed limit*) faire un excès de vitesse; **at full** *or* **top ~** à toute vitesse *or* allure; **speed up** (*pt, pp* **speeded up**) *vi* aller plus vite, accélérer ▷ *vt* accélérer; **speedboat** *n* vedette *f*, hors-bord *m inv*; **speed camera** *n* (*Aut*) radar *m* (automatique); **speeding** *n* (*Aut*) excès *m* de vitesse; **speed limit** *n* limitation *f* de vitesse, vitesse maximale permise; **speedometer** [spɪˈdɔmɪtər] *n* compteur *m* (de vitesse); **speedy** *adj* rapide, prompt(e)

spell [spɛl] *n* (*also:* **magic ~**) sortilège *m*, charme *m*; (*period of time*) (courte) période ▷ *vt* (*pt, pp* **spelled** *or* **spelt**) (*in writing*) écrire, orthographier; (*aloud*) épeler; (*fig*) signifier; **to cast a ~ on sb** jeter un sort à qn; **he can't ~** il fait des fautes d'orthographe; **spell out** *vt* (*explain*): **to ~ sth out for sb** expliquer qch clairement à qn; **spellchecker** [ˈspɛltʃɛkər] *n* (*Comput*) correcteur *m or* vérificateur *m* orthographique; **spelling** *n* orthographe *f*

spelt [spɛlt] *pt, pp of* **spell**

spend (*pt, pp* **spent**) [spɛnd, spɛnt] *vt* (*money*) dépenser; (*time, life*) passer; (*devote*) consacrer; **spending** *n*: **government spending** les dépenses publiques

spent [spɛnt] *pt, pp of* **spend** ▷ *adj* (*cartridge, bullets*) vide

sperm [spəːm] *n* spermatozoïde *m*; (*semen*) sperme *m*

sphere [sfɪər] *n* sphère *f*; (*fig*) sphère, domaine *m*

spice [spaɪs] *n* épice *f* ▷ *vt* épicer

spicy [ˈspaɪsɪ] *adj* épicé(e), relevé(e); (*fig*) piquant(e)

spider [ˈspaɪdər] *n* araignée *f*

spike [spaɪk] *n* pointe *f*; (*Bot*) épi *m*

spill (*pt, pp* **spilt** *or* **spilled**) [spɪl, -t, -d] *vt* renverser; répandre ▷ *vi* se répandre; **spill over** *vi* déborder

spilt [spɪlt] *pt, pp of* **spill**

spin [spɪn] (*pt, pp* **spun**) *n* (*revolution of wheel*) tour *m*; (*Aviat*) (chute *f* en) vrille *f*; (*trip in car*) petit tour, balade *f*; (*on ball*) effet *m* ▷ *vt* (*wool etc*) filer; (*wheel*) faire tourner ▷ *vi* (*turn*) tourner, tournoyer

spinach [ˈspɪnɪtʃ] *n* épinards *mpl*

spinal [ˈspaɪnl] *adj* vertébral(e), spinal(e); **spinal cord** *n* moelle épinière

spin doctor *n* (*inf*) personne employée pour présenter un parti politique sous un jour favorable

spin-dryer [spɪnˈdraɪər] *n* (*BRIT*) essoreuse *f*

spine [spaɪn] *n* colonne vertébrale; (*thorn*) épine *f*, piquant *m*

spiral [ˈspaɪərl] *n* spirale *f* ▷ *vi* (*fig: prices etc*) monter en flèche

spire [ˈspaɪər] *n* flèche *f*, aiguille *f*

spirit [ˈspɪrɪt] *n* (*soul*) esprit *m*, âme *f*; (*ghost*) esprit, revenant *m*; (*mood*) esprit, état *m* d'esprit; (*courage*) courage *m*, énergie *f*; **spirits** *npl* (*drink*) spiritueux *mpl*, alcool *m*; **in good ~s** de bonne humeur

spiritual [ˈspɪrɪtjuəl] *adj* spirituel(le); (*religious*) religieux(-euse)

spit [spɪt] *n* (*for roasting*) broche *f*; (*spittle*) crachat *m*; (*saliva*) salive *f* ▷ *vi* (*pt, pp* **spat**) cracher; (*sound*) crépiter; (*rain*) crachiner

spite [spaɪt] *n* rancune *f*, dépit *m* ▷ *vt* contrarier, vexer; **in ~ of** en dépit de, malgré; **spiteful** *adj* malveillant(e), rancunier(-ière)

splash [splæʃ] *n* (*sound*) plouf *m*; (*of colour*) tache *f* ▷ *vt* éclabousser ▷ *vi* (*also:* **~ about**) barboter, patauger; **splash out** *vi* (*BRIT*) faire une folie

splendid [ˈsplɛndɪd] *adj* splendide, superbe, magnifique

splinter [ˈsplɪntər] *n* (*wood*) écharde *f*; (*metal*) éclat *m* ▷ *vi* (*wood*) se fendre; (*glass*) se briser

split [splɪt] (*pt, pp* **split**) *n* fente *f*, déchirure *f*; (*fig: Pol*) scission *f* ▷ *vt* fendre, déchirer; (*party*) diviser; (*work, profits*) partager, répartir ▷ *vi* (*break*) se fendre, se briser; (*divide*) se diviser; **split up** *vi* (*couple*) se séparer, rompre; (*meeting*) se disperser

spoil (*pt, pp* **spoiled** *or* **spoilt**) [spɔɪl, -d, -t] *vt* (*damage*) abîmer; (*mar*) gâcher; (*child*) gâter

spoilt [spɔɪlt] *pt, pp of* **spoil** ▷ *adj* (*child*) gâté(e); (*ballot paper*) nul(le)

spoke [spəuk] *pt of* **speak** ▷ *n* rayon *m*

spoken [ˈspəukn] *pp of* **speak**

spokesman [ˈspəuksmən] (*irreg*) *n* porte-parole *m inv*

spokesperson [ˈspəukspəːsn] (*irreg*) *n* porte-parole *m inv*

spokeswoman [ˈspəukswumən] (*irreg*) *n* porte-parole *m inv*

sponge [spʌndʒ] *n* éponge *f*; (*Culin: also:* **~ cake**) ≈ biscuit *m* de Savoie ▷ *vt* éponger ▷ *vi*: **to ~ off** *or* **on** vivre aux crochets de; **sponge bag** *n* (*BRIT*) trousse *f* de toilette

sponsor [ˈspɔnsər] *n* (*Radio, TV, Sport*) sponsor *m*; (*for application*) parrain *m*, marraine *f*; (*BRIT: for fund-raising event*) donateur(-trice) ▷ *vt* sponsoriser; parrainer; faire un don à; **sponsorship** *n* sponsoring *m*; parrainage *m*; dons *mpl*

spontaneous [spɔnˈteɪnɪəs] *adj* spontané(e)

spooky [ˈspuːkɪ] *adj* (*inf*) qui donne la chair de poule

spoon [spuːn] *n* cuiller *f*; **spoonful** *n* cuillerée *f*

sport [spɔːt] *n* sport *m*; (*person*) chic type *m*/chic fille *f* ▷ *vt* (*wear*) arborer; **sport**

jacket n (US) = **sports jacket**; **sports car** n voiture f de sport; **sports centre** (BRIT) n centre sportif; **sports jacket** n (BRIT) veste f de sport; **sportsman** (irreg) n sportif m; **sports utility vehicle** n véhicule m de loisirs (de type SUV); **sportswear** n vêtements mpl de sport; **sportswoman** (irreg) n sportive f; **sporty** adj sportif(-ive)

spot [spɔt] n tache f; (dot: on pattern) pois m; (pimple) bouton m; (place) endroit m, coin m ▷ vt (notice) apercevoir, repérer; **on the ~** sur place, sur les lieux; (immediately) sur le champ; **spotless** adj immaculé(e); **spotlight** n projecteur m; (Aut) phare m auxiliaire

spouse [spauz] n époux (épouse)

sprain [spreɪn] n entorse f, foulure f ▷ vt: **to ~ one's ankle** se fouler or se tordre la cheville

sprang [spræŋ] pt of **spring**

sprawl [sprɔːl] vi s'étaler

spray [spreɪ] n jet m (en fines gouttelettes); (from sea) embruns mpl; (aerosol) vaporisateur m, bombe f; (for garden) pulvérisateur m; (of flowers) petit bouquet ▷ vt vaporiser, pulvériser; (crops) traiter

spread [sprɛd] (pt, pp **spread**) n (distribution) répartition f; (Culin) pâte f à tartiner; (inf: meal) festin m ▷ vt (paste, contents) étendre, étaler; (rumour, disease) répandre, propager; (wealth) répartir ▷ vi s'étendre; se répandre; se propager; (stain) s'étaler; **spread out** vi (people) se disperser; **spreadsheet** n (Comput) tableur m

spree [spriː] n: **to go on a ~** faire la fête

spring [sprɪŋ] (pt **sprang**, pp **sprung**) n (season) printemps m; (leap) bond m, saut m; (coiled metal) ressort m; (of water) source f ▷ vi bondir, sauter; **spring up** vi (problem) se présenter, surgir; (plant, buildings) surgir de terre; **spring onion** n (BRIT) ciboule f, cive f

sprinkle ['sprɪŋkl] vt: **to ~ water** etc on, **~ with water** etc asperger d'eau etc; **to ~ sugar** etc **on, ~ with sugar** etc saupoudrer de sucre etc

sprint [sprɪnt] n sprint m ▷ vi courir à toute vitesse; (Sport) sprinter

sprung [sprʌŋ] pp of **spring**

spun [spʌn] pt, pp of **spin**

spur [spəːʳ] n éperon m; (fig) aiguillon m ▷ vt (also: **~ on**) éperonner aiguillonner; **on the ~ of the moment** sous l'impulsion du moment

spurt [spəːt] n jet m; (of blood) jaillissement m; (of energy) regain m, sursaut m ▷ vi jaillir, gicler

spy [spaɪ] n espion(ne) ▷ vi: **to ~ on** espionner, épier ▷ vt (see) apercevoir

Sq. abbr (in address) = **square**

sq. abbr (Math etc) = **square**

squabble ['skwɔbl] vi se chamailler

squad [skwɔd] n (Mil, Police) escouade f, groupe m; (Football) contingent m

squadron ['skwɔdrn] n (Mil) escadron m; (Aviat, Naut) escadrille f

squander ['skwɔndəʳ] vt gaspiller, dilapider

square [skwɛəʳ] n carré m; (in town) place f ▷ adj carré(e) ▷ vt (arrange) régler; arranger; (Math) élever au carré; (reconcile) concilier; **all ~** quitte; à égalité; **a ~ meal** un repas convenable; **2 metres ~** (de) 2 mètres sur 2; **1 ~ metre** 1 mètre carré; **square root** n racine carrée

squash [skwɔʃ] n (BRIT Sport) squash m; (US: vegetable) courge f; (drink): **lemon/orange ~** citronnade f/orangeade f ▷ vt écraser

squat [skwɔt] adj petit(e) et épais(se), ramassé(e) ▷ vi (also: **~ down**) s'accroupir; **squatter** n squatter m

squeak [skwiːk] vi (hinge, wheel) grincer; (mouse) pousser un petit cri

squeal [skwiːl] vi pousser un or des cri(s) aigu(s) or perçant(s); (brakes) grincer

squeeze [skwiːz] n pression f ▷ vt presser; (hand, arm) serrer

squid [skwɪd] n calmar m

squint [skwɪnt] vi loucher

squirm [skwəːm] vi se tortiller

squirrel ['skwɪrəl] n écureuil m

squirt [skwəːt] vi jaillir, gicler ▷ vt faire gicler

Sr abbr = **senior**

Sri Lanka [srɪˈlæŋkə] n Sri Lanka m

St abbr = **saint; street**

stab [stæb] n (with knife etc) coup m (de couteau etc); (of pain) lancée f; (inf: try): **to have a ~ at (doing) sth** s'essayer à (faire) qch ▷ vt poignarder

stability [stəˈbɪlɪtɪ] n stabilité f

stable ['steɪbl] n écurie f ▷ adj stable

stack [stæk] n tas m, pile f ▷ vt empiler, entasser

stadium ['steɪdɪəm] n stade m

staff [stɑːf] n (work force) personnel m; (BRIT Scol: also: **teaching ~**) professeurs mpl, enseignants mpl, personnel enseignant ▷ vt pourvoir en personnel

stag [stæg] n cerf m

stage [steɪdʒ] n scène f; (platform) estrade f; (point) étape f, stade m; (profession): **the ~** le théâtre ▷ vt (play) monter, mettre en scène; (demonstration) organiser; **in ~s** par étapes, par degrés

▎Be careful not to translate stage by the French word stage.

stagger ['stægəʳ] vi chanceler, tituber ▷ vt (person: amaze) stupéfier; (hours, holidays) étaler, échelonner; **staggering** adj (amazing) stupéfiant(e), renversant(e)

stagnant ['stægnənt] adj stagnant(e)

stag night, stag party n enterrement m de vie de garçon

stain [steɪn] n tache f; (colouring) colorant m ▷ vt tacher; (wood) teindre; **stained**

glass n (decorative) verre coloré; (in church) vitraux mpl; **stainless steel** n inox m, acier m inoxydable

staircase ['stɛəkeɪs] n = **stairway**

stairs [stɛəz] npl escalier m

stairway ['stɛəweɪ] n escalier m

stake [steɪk] n pieu m, poteau m; (Comm: interest) intérêts mpl; (Betting) enjeu m ▷ vt risquer, jouer; (also: ~ **out**: area) marquer, délimiter; **to be at** ~ être en jeu

stale [steɪl] adj (bread) rassis(e); (food) pas frais (fraîche); (beer) éventé(e); (smell) de renfermé; (air) confiné(e)

stalk [stɔːk] n tige f ▷ vt traquer

stall [stɔːl] n (in street, market etc) éventaire m, étal m; (in stable) stalle f ▷ vt (Aut) caler; (fig: delay) retarder ▷ vi (Aut) caler; (fig) essayer de gagner du temps; **stalls** npl (BRIT: in cinema, theatre) orchestre m

stamina ['stæmɪnə] n vigueur f, endurance f

stammer ['stæməʳ] n bégaiement m ▷ vi bégayer

stamp [stæmp] n timbre m; (also: **rubber** ~) tampon m; (mark: also fig) empreinte f; (on document) cachet m ▷ vi (also: ~ **one's foot**) taper du pied ▷ vt (letter) timbrer; (with rubber stamp) tamponner; **stamp out** vt (fire) piétiner; (crime) éradiquer; (opposition) éliminer; **stamped addressed envelope** n (BRIT) enveloppe affranchie pour la réponse

stampede [stæm'piːd] n ruée f; (of cattle) débandade f

stance [stæns] n position f

stand [stænd] (pt, pp **stood**) n (position) position f; (for taxis) station f (de taxis); (Comm) étalage m, stand m; (Sport: also: ~**s**) tribune f; (also: **music** ~) pupitre m ▷ vi être or se tenir (debout); (rise) se lever, se mettre debout; (be placed) se trouver; (remain: offer etc) rester valable ▷ vt (place) mettre, poser; (tolerate, withstand) supporter; (treat, invite) offrir, payer; **to make a** ~ prendre position; **to** ~ **for parliament** (BRIT) se présenter aux élections (comme candidat à la députation); **I can't** ~ **him** je ne peux pas le voir; **stand back** vi (move back) reculer, s'écarter; **stand by** vi (be ready) se tenir prêt(e) ▷ vt fus (opinion) s'en tenir à; (person) ne pas abandonner, soutenir; **stand down** vi (withdraw) se retirer; **stand for** vt fus (signify) représenter, signifier; (tolerate) supporter, tolérer; **stand in for** vt fus remplacer; **stand out** vi (be prominent) ressortir; **stand up** vi (rise) se lever, se mettre debout; **stand up for** vt fus défendre; **stand up to** vt fus tenir tête à, résister à

standard ['stændəd] n (norm) norme f, étalon m; (level) niveau m (voulu); (criterion) critère m; (flag) étendard m ▷ adj (size etc) ordinaire, normal(e); (model, feature) standard inv; (practice) courant(e); (text)

de base; **standards** npl (morals) morale f, principes mpl; **standard of living** n niveau m de vie

stand-by ticket n (Aviat) billet m stand-by

standing ['stændɪŋ] adj debout inv; (permanent) permanent(e) ▷ n réputation f, rang m, standing m; **of many years'** ~ qui dure or existe depuis longtemps; **standing order** n (BRIT: at bank) virement m automatique, prélèvement m bancaire

stand: standpoint n point m de vue; **standstill** n: **at a standstill** à l'arrêt; (fig) au point mort; **to come to a standstill** s'immobiliser, s'arrêter

stank [stæŋk] pt of **stink**

staple ['steɪpl] n (for papers) agrafe f ▷ adj (food, crop, industry etc) de base principal(e) ▷ vt agrafer

star [stɑːʳ] n étoile f; (celebrity) vedette f ▷ vt (Cine) avoir pour vedette; **stars** npl: **the** ~**s** (Astrology) l'horoscope m

starboard ['stɑːbəd] n tribord m

starch [stɑːtʃ] n amidon m; (in food) fécule f

stardom ['stɑːdəm] n célébrité f

stare [stɛəʳ] n regard m fixe ▷ vi: **to** ~ **at** regarder fixement

stark [stɑːk] adj (bleak) désolé(e), morne ▷ adv: ~ **naked** complètement nu(e)

start [stɑːt] n commencement m, début m; (of race) départ m; (sudden movement) sursaut m; (advantage) avance f, avantage m ▷ vt commencer; (cause: fight) déclencher; (rumour) donner naissance à; (fashion) lancer; (found: business, newspaper) lancer, créer; (engine) mettre en marche ▷ vi (begin) commencer; (begin journey) partir, se mettre en route; (jump) sursauter; **when does the film** ~? à quelle heure est-ce que le film commence?; **to** ~ **doing** or **to do sth** se mettre à faire qch; **start off** vi commencer; (leave) partir; **start out** vi (begin) commencer; (set out) partir; **start up** vi commencer; (car) démarrer ▷ vt (fight) déclencher; (business) créer; (car) mettre en marche; **starter** n (Aut) démarreur m; (Sport: official) starter m; (BRIT Culin) entrée f; **starting point** n point m de départ

startle ['stɑːtl] vt faire sursauter; donner un choc à; **startling** adj surprenant(e), saisissant(e)

starvation [stɑː'veɪʃən] n faim f, famine f

starve [stɑːv] vi mourir de faim ▷ vt laisser mourir de faim

state [steɪt] n état m; (Pol) État m ▷ vt (declare) déclarer, affirmer; (specify) indiquer, spécifier; **States** npl: **the S~s** les États-Unis; **to be in a** ~ être dans tous ses états; **stately home** ['steɪtlɪ-] n manoir m or château m (ouvert au public); **statement** n déclaration f; (Law) déposition f; **state school** n école publique; **statesman** (irreg) n homme m d'État

static ['stætɪk] n (Radio) parasites mpl; (also: **~ electricity**) électricité f statique ▷ adj statique

station ['steɪʃən] n gare f; (also: **police ~**) poste m or commissariat m (de police) ▷ vt placer, poster

stationary ['steɪʃnərɪ] adj à l'arrêt, immobile

stationer's (shop) n (BRIT) papeterie f

stationery ['steɪʃnərɪ] n papier m à lettres, petit matériel de bureau

station wagon n (US) break m

statistic [stə'tɪstɪk] n statistique f;
statistics n (science) statistique f

statue ['stætjuː] n statue f

stature ['stætʃər] n stature f; (fig) envergure f

status ['steɪtəs] n position f, situation f; (prestige) prestige m; (Admin, official position) statut m; **status quo** [-'kwəʊ] n: **the status quo** le statu quo

statutory ['stætjutrɪ] adj statutaire, prévu(e) par un article de loi

staunch [stɔːntʃ] adj sûr(e), loyal(e)

stay [steɪ] n (period of time) séjour m ▷ vi rester; (reside) loger; (spend some time) séjourner; **to ~ put** ne pas bouger; **to ~ the night** passer la nuit; **stay away** vi (from person, building) ne pas s'approcher; (from event) ne pas venir; **stay behind** vi rester en arrière; **stay in** vi (at home) rester à la maison; **stay on** vi rester; **stay out** vi (of house) ne pas rentrer; (strikers) rester en grève; **stay up** vi (at night) ne pas se coucher

steadily ['stɛdɪlɪ] adv (regularly) progressivement; (firmly) fermement; (walk) d'un pas ferme; (fixedly: look) sans détourner les yeux

steady ['stɛdɪ] adj stable, solide, ferme; (regular) constant(e), régulier(-ière); (person) calme, pondéré(e) ▷ vt assurer, stabiliser; (nerves) calmer; **a ~ boyfriend** un petit ami

steak [steɪk] n (meat) bifteck m, steak m; (fish, pork) tranche f

steal (pt **stole**, pp **stolen**) [stiːl, stəʊl, 'stəʊln] vt, vi voler; (move) se faufiler, se déplacer furtivement; **my wallet has been stolen** on m'a volé mon portefeuille

steam [stiːm] n vapeur f ▷ vt (Culin) cuire à la vapeur ▷ vi fumer; **steam up** vi (window) se couvrir de buée; **to get ~ed up about sth** (fig: inf) s'exciter à propos de qch; **steamy** adj humide; (window) embué(e); (sexy) torride

steel [stiːl] n acier m ▷ cpd d'acier

steep [stiːp] adj raide, escarpé(e); (price) très élevé(e), excessif(-ive) ▷ vt (faire) tremper

steeple ['stiːpl] n clocher m

steer [stɪər] vt diriger; (boat) gouverner; (lead: person) guider, conduire ▷ vi tenir le gouvernail; **steering** n (Aut) conduite f; **steering wheel** n volant m

stem [stɛm] n (of plant) tige f; (of glass) pied m ▷ vt contenir, endiguer; (attack, spread of disease) juguler

step [stɛp] n pas m; (stair) marche f; (action) mesure f, disposition f ▷ vi: **to ~ forward/back** faire un pas en avant/arrière, avancer/reculer; **steps** npl (BRIT) = **stepladder**; **to be in/out of ~ (with)** (fig) aller dans le sens (de)/être déphasé(e) (par rapport à); **step down** vi (fig) se retirer, se désister; **step in** vi (fig) intervenir; **step up** vt (production, sales) augmenter; (campaign, efforts) intensifier; **stepbrother** n demi-frère m; **stepchild** (pl **stepchildren**) n beau-fils m, belle-fille f; **stepdaughter** n belle-fille f; **stepfather** n beau-père m; **stepladder** n (BRIT) escabeau m; **stepmother** n belle-mère f; **stepsister** n demi-sœur f; **stepson** n beau-fils m

stereo ['stɛrɪəʊ] n (sound) stéréo f; (hi-fi) chaîne f stéréo ▷ adj (also: **~phonic**) stéréo(phonique)

stereotype ['stɪərɪətaɪp] n stéréotype m ▷ vt stéréotyper

sterile ['stɛraɪl] adj stérile; **sterilize** ['stɛrɪlaɪz] vt stériliser

sterling ['stɜːlɪŋ] adj (silver) de bon aloi, fin(e) ▷ n (currency) livre f sterling inv

stern [stɜːn] adj sévère ▷ n (Naut) arrière m, poupe f

steroid ['stɪərɔɪd] n stéroïde m

stew [stjuː] n ragoût m ▷ vt, vi cuire à la casserole

steward ['stjuːəd] n (Aviat, Naut, Rail) steward m; **stewardess** n hôtesse f

stick [stɪk] n (pt, pp **stuck**) n bâton m; (for walking) canne f; (of chalk etc) morceau m ▷ vt (glue) coller; (thrust): **to ~ sth into** piquer or planter or enfoncer qch dans; (inf: put) mettre, fourrer; (: tolerate) supporter ▷ vi (adhere) tenir, coller; (remain) rester; (get jammed: door, lift) se bloquer; **stick out** vi dépasser, sortir; **stick up** vi dépasser, sortir; **stick up for** vt fus défendre; **sticker** n auto-collant m; **sticking plaster** n sparadrap m, pansement adhésif; **stick insect** n phasme m; **stick shift** n (US Aut) levier m de vitesses

sticky ['stɪkɪ] adj poisseux(-euse); (label) adhésif(-ive); (fig: situation) délicat(e)

stiff [stɪf] adj (gen) raide, rigide; (door, brush) dur(e); (difficult) difficile, ardu(e); (cold) froid(e), distant(e); (strong, high) fort(e), élevé(e) ▷ adv: **to be bored/scared/frozen ~** s'ennuyer à mourir/être mort(e) de peur/froid

stifling ['staɪflɪŋ] adj (heat) suffocant(e)

stigma ['stɪɡmə] n stigmate m

stiletto [stɪ'lɛtəʊ] n (BRIT: also: **~ heel**) talon m aiguille

still [stɪl] *adj* immobile ▷ *adv* (*up to this time*) encore, toujours; (*even*) encore; (*nonetheless*) quand même, tout de même

stimulate ['stɪmjʊleɪt] *vt* stimuler

stimulus (*pl* **stimuli**) ['stɪmjʊləs, 'stɪmjʊlaɪ] *n* stimulant *m*; (*Biol, Psych*) stimulus *m*

sting [stɪŋ] *n* piqûre *f*; (*organ*) dard *m* ▷ *vt, vi* (*pt, pp* **stung**) piquer

stink [stɪŋk] *n* puanteur *f* ▷ *vi* (*pt* **stank**, *pp* **stunk**) puer, empester

stir [stəːʳ] *n* agitation *f*, sensation *f* ▷ *vt* remuer ▷ *vi* remuer, bouger; **stir up** *vt* (*trouble*) fomenter, provoquer; **stir-fry** *vt* faire sauter ▷ *n*: **vegetable stir-fry** légumes sautés à la poêle

stitch [stɪtʃ] *n* (*Sewing*) point *m*; (*Knitting*) maille *f*; (*Med*) point de suture; (*pain*) point de côté ▷ *vt* coudre, piquer; (*Med*) suturer

stock [stɔk] *n* réserve *f*, provision *f*; (*Comm*) stock *m*; (*Agr*) cheptel *m*, bétail *m*; (*Culin*) bouillon *m*; (*Finance*) valeurs *fpl*, titres *mpl*; (*descent, origin*) souche *f* ▷ *adj* (*fig: reply etc*) classique ▷ *vt* (*have in stock*) avoir, vendre; **in ~** en stock, en magasin; **out of ~** épuisé(e); **to take ~** (*fig*) faire le point; **~s and shares** valeurs (mobilières), titres; **stockbroker** ['stɔkbrəʊkəʳ] *n* agent *m* de change; **stock cube** *n* (*BRIT Culin*) bouillon-cube *m*; **stock exchange** *n* Bourse *f* (des valeurs); **stockholder** ['stɔkhəʊldəʳ] *n* (*US*) actionnaire *m/f*

stocking ['stɔkɪŋ] *n* bas *m*

stock market *n* Bourse *f*, marché financier

stole [stəʊl] *pt of* **steal** ▷ *n* étole *f*

stolen ['stəʊln] *pp of* **steal**

stomach ['stʌmək] *n* estomac *m*; (*abdomen*) ventre *m* ▷ *vt* supporter, digérer; **stomachache** *n* mal *m* à l'estomac *or* au ventre

stone [stəʊn] *n* pierre *f*; (*pebble*) caillou *m*, galet *m*; (*in fruit*) noyau *m*; (*Med*) calcul *m*; (*BRIT: weight*) = 6.348 kg; 14 pounds ▷ *cpd* de or en pierre ▷ *vt* (*person*) lancer des pierres sur, lapider; (*fruit*) dénoyauter

stood [stʊd] *pt, pp of* **stand**

stool [stuːl] *n* tabouret *m*

stoop [stuːp] *vi* (*also*: **have a ~**) être voûté(e); (*also*: **~ down**: *bend*) se baisser, se courber

stop [stɔp] *n* arrêt *m*; (*in punctuation*) point *m* ▷ *vt* arrêter; (*break off*) interrompre; (*also*: **put a ~ to**) mettre fin à; (*prevent*) empêcher ▷ *vi* s'arrêter; (*rain, noise etc*) cesser, s'arrêter; **to ~ doing sth** cesser *or* arrêter de faire qch; **to ~ sb (from) doing sth** empêcher qn de faire qch; **~ it!** arrête!; **stop by** *vi* s'arrêter (au passage); **stop off** *vi* faire une courte halte; **stopover** *n* halte *f*; (*Aviat*) escale *f*; **stoppage** *n* (*strike*) arrêt *m* de travail; (*obstruction*) obstruction *f*

storage ['stɔːrɪdʒ] *n* emmagasinage *m*

store [stɔːʳ] *n* (*stock*) provision *f*, réserve *f*; (*depot*) entrepôt *m*; (*BRIT: large shop*) grand magasin; (*US: shop*) magasin *m* ▷ *vt* emmagasiner; (*information*) enregistrer; **stores** *npl* (*food*) provisions; **who knows what is in ~ for us?** qui sait ce que l'avenir nous réserve *or* ce qui nous attend?;

storekeeper *n* (*US*) commerçant(e)

storey, (*US*) **story** ['stɔːrɪ] *n* étage *m*

storm [stɔːm] *n* tempête *f*; (*thunderstorm*) orage *m* ▷ *vi* (*fig*) fulminer ▷ *vt* prendre d'assaut; **stormy** *adj* orageux(-euse)

story ['stɔːrɪ] *n* histoire *f*; (*Press: article*) article *m*; (*US*) = **storey**

stout [staʊt] *adj* (*strong*) solide; (*fat*) gros(se), corpulent(e) ▷ *n* bière brune

stove [stəʊv] *n* (*for cooking*) fourneau *m*; (*: small*) réchaud *m*; (*for heating*) poêle *m*

straight [streɪt] *adj* droit(e); (*hair*) raide; (*frank*) honnête, franc (franche); (*simple*) simple ▷ *adv* (*tout*) droit; (*drink*) sec, sans eau; **to put** *or* **get ~** mettre en ordre, mettre de l'ordre dans; (*fig*) mettre au clair; **~ away, ~ off** (*at once*) tout de suite; **straighten** *vt* ajuster; (*bed*) arranger; **straighten out** *vt* (*fig*) débrouiller; **straighten up** *vi* (*stand up*) se redresser; **straightforward** *adj* simple; (*frank*) honnête, direct(e)

strain [streɪn] *n* (*Tech*) tension *f*; pression *f*; (*physical*) effort *m*; (*mental*) tension (nerveuse); (*Med*) entorse *f*; (*breed: of plants*) variété *f*; (*: of animals*) race *f* ▷ *vt* (*fig: resources etc*) mettre à rude épreuve, grever; (*hurt: back etc*) se faire mal à; (*vegetables*) égoutter; **strains** *npl* (*Mus*) accords *mpl*, accents *mpl*; **strained** *adj* (*muscle*) froissé(e); (*laugh etc*) forcé(e), contraint(e); (*relations*) tendu(e); **strainer** *n* passoire *f*

strait [streɪt] *n* (*Geo*) détroit *m*; **straits** *npl*: **to be in dire ~s** (*fig*) avoir de sérieux ennuis

strand [strænd] *n* (*of thread*) fil *m*, brin *m*; (*of rope*) toron *m*; (*of hair*) mèche *f* ▷ *vt* (*boat*) échouer; **stranded** *adj* en rade, en plan

strange [streɪndʒ] *adj* (*not known*) inconnu(e); (*odd*) étrange, bizarre; **strangely** *adv* étrangement, bizarrement; *see also* **enough**; **stranger** *n* (*unknown*) inconnu(e); (*from somewhere else*) étranger(-ère)

strangle ['stræŋgl] *vt* étrangler

strap [stræp] *n* lanière *f*, courroie *f*, sangle *f*; (*of slip, dress*) bretelle *f*

strategic [strə'tiːdʒɪk] *adj* stratégique

strategy ['strætɪdʒɪ] *n* stratégie *f*

straw [strɔː] *n* paille *f*; **that's the last ~!** ça c'est le comble!

strawberry ['strɔːbərɪ] *n* fraise *f*

stray [streɪ] *adj* (*animal*) perdu(e), errant(e); (*scattered*) isolé(e) ▷ *vi* s'égarer; **~ bullet** balle perdue

streak [striːk] *n* bande *f*, filet *m*; (*in hair*) raie *f* ▷ *vt* zébrer, strier

stream [striːm] n (brook) ruisseau m; (current) courant m, flot m; (of people) défilé ininterrompu, flot ▷ vt (Scol) répartir par niveau ▷ vi ruisseler; **to ~ in/out** entrer/ sortir à flots

street [striːt] n rue f; **streetcar** n (us) tramway m; **street light** n réverbère m; **street map, street plan** n plan m des rues

strength [strɛŋθ] n force f; (of girder, knot etc) solidité f; **strengthen** vt renforcer; (muscle) fortifier; (building, Econ) consolider

strenuous ['strɛnjuəs] adj vigoureux(-euse), énergique; (tiring) ardu(e), fatigant(e)

stress [strɛs] n (force, pressure) pression f; (mental strain) tension (nerveuse), stress m; (accent) accent m; (emphasis) insistance f ▷ vt insister sur, souligner; (syllable) accentuer; **stressed** adj (tense) stressé(e); (syllable) accentué(e); **stressful** adj (job) stressant(e)

stretch [strɛtʃ] n (of sand etc) étendue f ▷ vi s'étirer; (extend): **to ~ to or as far as** s'étendre jusqu'à ▷ vt tendre, étirer; (fig) pousser (au maximum); **at a ~** d'affilée; **stretch out** vi s'étendre ▷ vt (arm etc) allonger, tendre; (to spread) étendre

stretcher ['strɛtʃə'] n brancard m, civière f

strict [strɪkt] adj strict(e); **strictly** adv strictement

stridden ['strɪdn] pp of **stride**

stride [straɪd] n grand pas, enjambée f ▷ vi (pt **strode**, pp **stridden**) marcher à grands pas

strike [straɪk] (pt, pp **struck**) n grève f; (of oil etc) découverte f; (attack) raid m ▷ vt frapper; (oil etc) trouver, découvrir; (make: agreement, deal) conclure ▷ vi faire grève; (attack) attaquer; (clock) sonner; **to go on** or **come out on ~** se mettre en grève, faire grève; **to ~ a match** frotter une allumette; **striker** n gréviste m/f; (Sport) buteur m; **striking** adj frappant(e), saisissant(e); (attractive) éblouissant(e)

string [strɪŋ] n ficelle f, fil m; (row: of beads) rang m; (Mus) corde f ▷ vt (pt, pp **strung**): **to ~ out** échelonner; **to ~ together** enchaîner; **the strings** npl (Mus) les instruments mpl à cordes; **to pull ~s** (fig) faire jouer le piston

strip [strɪp] n bande f; (Sport) tenue f ▷ vt (undress) déshabiller; (paint) décaper; (fig) dégarnir, dépouiller; (also: **~ down**) (machine) démonter ▷ vi se déshabiller; **strip off** vt (paint etc) décaper ▷ vi (person) se déshabiller

stripe [straɪp] n raie f, rayure f; (Mil) galon m; **striped** adj rayé(e), à rayures

stripper ['strɪpə'] n strip-teaseuse f

strip-search ['strɪpsəːtʃ] vt: **to ~ sb** fouiller qn (en le faisant se déshabiller)

strive (pt **strove**, pp **striven**) [straɪv, strəuv, 'strɪvn] vi: **to ~ to do/for sth** s'efforcer de faire/d'obtenir qch

strode [strəud] pt of **stride**

stroke [strəuk] n coup m; (Med) attaque f; (Swimming: style) (sorte f de) nage f ▷ vt caresser; **at a ~** d'un (seul) coup

stroll [strəul] n petite promenade ▷ vi flâner, se promener nonchalamment; **stroller** n (us: for child) poussette f

strong [strɒŋ] adj (gen) fort(e); (healthy) vigoureux(-euse); (heart, nerves) solide; **they are 50 ~** ils sont au nombre de 50; **stronghold** n forteresse f, fort m; (fig) bastion m; **strongly** adv fortement, avec force; vigoureusement; solidement

strove [strəuv] pt of **strive**

struck [strʌk] pt, pp of **strike**

structure ['strʌktʃə'] n structure f; (building) construction f

struggle ['strʌɡl] n lutte f ▷ vi lutter, se battre

strung [strʌŋ] pt, pp of **string**

stub [stʌb] n (of cigarette) bout m, mégot m; (of ticket etc) talon m ▷ vt: **to ~ one's toe (on sth)** se heurter le doigt de pied (contre qch); **stub out** vt écraser

stubble ['stʌbl] n chaume m; (on chin) barbe f de plusieurs jours

stubborn ['stʌbən] adj têtu(e), obstiné(e), opiniâtre

stuck [stʌk] pt, pp of **stick** ▷ adj (jammed) bloqué(e), coincé(e)

stud [stʌd] n (on boots etc) clou m; (collar stud) bouton m de col; (earring) petite boucle d'oreille; (of horses: also: **~ farm**) écurie f, haras m; (also: **~ horse**) étalon m ▷ vt (fig): **~ded with** parsemé(e) or criblé(e) de

student ['stjuːdənt] n étudiant(e) ▷ adj (life) estudiantin(e), étudiant(e), d'étudiant; (residence, restaurant) universitaire; (loan, movement) étudiant; **student driver** n (us) (conducteur(-trice)) débutant(e); **students' union** n (brit: association) ≈ union f des étudiants; (: building) ≈ foyer m des étudiants

studio ['stjuːdɪəu] n studio m, atelier m; (TV etc) studio; **studio flat**, (us) **studio apartment** n studio m

study ['stʌdɪ] n étude f; (room) bureau m ▷ vt étudier; (examine) examiner ▷ vi étudier, faire ses études

stuff [stʌf] n (gen) chose(s) f(pl), truc m; (belongings) affaires fpl, trucs; (substance) substance f ▷ vt rembourrer; (Culin) farcir; (inf: push) fourrer; **stuffing** n bourre f, rembourrage m; (Culin) farce f; **stuffy** adj (room) mal ventilé(e) or aéré(e); (ideas) vieux jeu inv

stumble ['stʌmbl] vi trébucher; **to ~ across** or on (fig) tomber sur

stump [stʌmp] n souche f; (of limb) moignon m ▷ vt: **to be ~ed** sécher, ne pas savoir que répondre

stun [stʌn] vt (blow) étourdir; (news) abasourdir, stupéfier

stung [stʌŋ] *pt, pp of* **sting**

stunk [stʌŋk] *pp of* **stink**

stunned [stʌnd] *adj* assommé(e); (*fig*) sidéré(e)

stunning ['stʌnɪŋ] *adj* (*beautiful*) étourdissant(e); (*news etc*) stupéfiant(e)

stunt [stʌnt] *n* (*in film*) cascade *f*, acrobatie *f*; (*publicity*) truc *m* publicitaire ▷ *vt* retarder, arrêter

stupid ['stju:pɪd] *adj* stupide, bête; **stupidity** [stju:'pɪdɪtɪ] *n* stupidité *f*, bêtise *f*

sturdy ['stə:dɪ] *adj* (*person, plant*) robuste, vigoureux(-euse); (*object*) solide

stutter ['stʌtə'] *n* bégaiement *m* ▷ *vi* bégayer

style [staɪl] *n* style *m*; (*distinction*) allure *f*, cachet *m*, style; (*design*) modèle *m*; **stylish** *adj* élégant(e), chic *inv*; **stylist** *n* (*hair stylist*) coiffeur(-euse)

sub... [sʌb] *prefix* sub..., sous-; **subconscious** *adj* subconscient(e)

subdued [səb'dju:d] *adj* (*light*) tamisé(e); (*person*) qui a perdu de son entrain

subject *n* ['sʌbdʒɪkt] sujet *m*; (*Scol*) matière *f* ▷ *vt* [səb'dʒɛkt]: **to ~ to** soumettre à; **to be ~ to** (*law*) être soumis(e) à; **subjective** [səb'dʒɛktɪv] *adj* subjectif(-ive); **subject matter** *n* (*content*) contenu *m*

subjunctive [səb'dʒʌŋktɪv] *n* subjonctif *m*

submarine [sʌbmə'ri:n] *n* sous-marin *m*

submission [səb'mɪʃən] *n* soumission *f*

submit [səb'mɪt] *vt* soumettre ▷ *vi* se soumettre

subordinate [sə'bɔ:dɪnət] *adj* (*junior*) subalterne; (*Grammar*) subordonné(e) ▷ *n* subordonné(e)

subscribe [səb'skraɪb] *vi* cotiser; **to ~ to** (*opinion, fund*) souscrire à; (*newspaper*) s'abonner à; être abonné(e) à

subscription [səb'skrɪpʃən] *n* (*to magazine etc*) abonnement *m*

subsequent ['sʌbsɪkwənt] *adj* ultérieur(e), suivant(e); **subsequently** *adv* par la suite

subside [səb'saɪd] *vi* (*land*) s'affaisser; (*flood*) baisser; (*wind, feelings*) tomber

subsidiary [səb'sɪdɪərɪ] *adj* subsidiaire; accessoire; (*BRIT Scol: subject*) complémentaire ▷ *n* filiale *f*

subsidize ['sʌbsɪdaɪz] *vt* subventionner

subsidy ['sʌbsɪdɪ] *n* subvention *f*

substance ['sʌbstəns] *n* substance *f*

substantial [səb'stænʃl] *adj* substantiel(le); (*fig*) important(e)

substitute ['sʌbstɪtju:t] *n* (*person*) remplaçant(e); (*thing*) succédané *m* ▷ *vt*: **to ~ sth/sb for** substituer qch/qn à, remplacer par qch/qn; **substitution** *n* substitution *f*

subtitles ['sʌbtaɪtlz] *npl* (*Cine*) sous-titres *mpl*

subtle ['sʌtl] *adj* subtil(e)

subtract [səb'trækt] *vt* soustraire, retrancher

suburb ['sʌbə:b] *n* faubourg *m*; **the ~s** la banlieue; **suburban** [sə'bə:bən] *adj* de banlieue, suburbain(e)

subway ['sʌbweɪ] *n* (*BRIT: underpass*) passage souterrain; (*US: railway*) métro *m*

succeed [sək'si:d] *vi* réussir ▷ *vt* succéder à; **to ~ in doing** réussir à faire

success [sək'sɛs] *n* succès *m*; réussite *f*; **successful** *adj* (*business*) prospère, qui réussit; (*attempt*) couronné(e) de succès; **to be successful (in doing)** réussir (à faire); **successfully** *adv* avec succès

succession [sək'sɛʃən] *n* succession *f*

successive [sək'sɛsɪv] *adj* successif(-ive)

successor [sək'sɛsə'] *n* successeur *m*

succumb [sə'kʌm] *vi* succomber

such [sʌtʃ] *adj* tel (telle); (*of that kind*): **~ a book** un livre de ce genre *or* pareil, un tel livre; (*so much*): **~ courage** un tel courage ▷ *adv* si; **~ a long trip** un si long voyage; **~ a lot of** tellement *or* tant de; **~ as** (*like*) tel (telle) que, comme; **as ~** *adv* en tant que tel (telle), à proprement parler; **such-and-such** *adj* tel ou tel (telle ou telle)

suck [sʌk] *vt* sucer; (*breast, bottle*) téter

Sudan [su'dɑ:n] *n* Soudan *m*

sudden ['sʌdn] *adj* soudain(e), subit(e); **all of a ~** soudain, tout à coup; **suddenly** *adv* brusquement, tout à coup, soudain

sudoku [su'dəuku:] *n* sudoku *m*

sue [su:] *vt* poursuivre en justice, intenter un procès à

suede [sweɪd] *n* daim *m*, cuir suédé

suffer ['sʌfə'] *vt* souffrir, subir; (*bear*) tolérer, supporter, subir ▷ *vi* souffrir; **to ~ from** (*illness*) souffrir de, avoir; **suffering** *n* souffrance(s) *f(pl)*

suffice [sə'faɪs] *vi* suffire

sufficient [sə'fɪʃənt] *adj* suffisant(e)

suffocate ['sʌfəkeɪt] *vi* suffoquer; étouffer

sugar ['ʃugə'] *n* sucre *m* ▷ *vt* sucrer

suggest [sə'dʒɛst] *vt* suggérer, proposer; (*indicate*) sembler indiquer; **suggestion** *n* suggestion *f*

suicide ['suɪsaɪd] *n* suicide *m*; **~ bombing** attentat *m* suicide; *see also* **commit**; **suicide bomber** *n* kamikaze *m/f*

suit [su:t] *n* (*man's*) costume *m*, complet *m*; (*woman's*) tailleur *m*, ensemble *m*; (*Cards*) couleur *f*; (*lawsuit*) procès *m* ▷ *vt* (*subj: clothes, hairstyle*) aller à; (*be convenient for*) convenir à; (*adapt*): **to ~ sth to** adapter *or* approprier qch à; **well ~ed** (*couple*) faits l'un pour l'autre, très bien assortis; **suitable** *adj* qui convient; approprié(e), adéquat(e); **suitcase** *n* valise *f*

suite [swi:t] *n* (*of rooms, also Mus*) suite *f*; (*furniture*): **bedroom/dining room ~** (ensemble *m* de) chambre *f* à coucher/ salle *f* à manger; **a three-piece ~** un salon (canapé et deux fauteuils)

sulfur ['sʌlfə'] (*US*) *n* = **sulphur**

sulk [sʌlk] *vi* bouder
sulphur, (*us*) **sulfur** [ˈsʌlfər] *n* soufre *m*
sultana [sʌlˈtɑːnə] *n* (*fruit*) raisin (sec) de Smyrne
sum [sʌm] *n* somme *f*; (*Scol etc*) calcul *m*; **sum up** *vt* résumer ▷ *vi* résumer
summarize [ˈsʌməraiz] *vt* résumer
summary [ˈsʌməri] *n* résumé *m*
summer [ˈsʌmər] *n* été *m* ▷ *cpd* d'été, estival(e); **in (the) ~** en été, pendant l'été; **summer holidays** *npl* grandes vacances; **summertime** *n* (*season*) été *m*
summit [ˈsʌmit] *n* sommet *m*; (*also*: **~ conference**) (conférence *f* au) sommet *m*
summon [ˈsʌmən] *vt* appeler, convoquer; **to ~ a witness** citer or assigner un témoin
sun [sʌn] *n* soleil *m*
Sun. *abbr* (= *Sunday*) dim
sun: sunbathe *vi* prendre un bain de soleil; **sunbed** *n* lit pliant; (*with sun lamp*) lit à ultra-violets; **sunblock** *n* écran *m* total; **sunburn** *n* coup *m* de soleil; **sunburned**, **sunburnt** *adj* bronzé(e), hâlé(e); (*painfully*) brûlé(e) par le soleil
Sunday [ˈsʌndi] *n* dimanche *m*
sunflower [ˈsʌnflauər] *n* tournesol *m*
sung [sʌŋ] *pp of* **sing**
sunglasses [ˈsʌnɡlɑːsiz] *npl* lunettes *fpl* de soleil
sunk [sʌŋk] *pp of* **sink**
sun: sunlight *n* (lumière *f* du) soleil *m*; **sun lounger** *n* chaise longue; **sunny** *adj* ensoleillé(e); **it is sunny** il fait (du) soleil, il y a du soleil; **sunrise** *n* lever *m* du soleil; **sun roof** *n* (*Aut*) toit ouvrant; **sunscreen** *n* crème *f* solaire; **sunset** *n* coucher *m* du soleil; **sunshade** *n* (*over table*) parasol *m*; **sunshine** *n* (lumière *f* du) soleil *m*; **sunstroke** *n* insolation *f*, coup *m* de soleil; **suntan** *n* bronzage *m*; **suntan lotion** *n* lotion *f* or lait *m* solaire; **suntan oil** *n* huile *f* solaire
super [ˈsuːpər] *adj* (*inf*) formidable
superb [suːˈpəːb] *adj* superbe, magnifique
superficial [suːpəˈfiʃəl] *adj* superficiel(le)
superintendent [suːpərinˈtendənt] *n* directeur(-trice); (*Police*) ≈ commissaire *m*
superior [suˈpiəriər] *adj* supérieur(e); (*smug*) condescendant(e), méprisant(e) ▷ *n* supérieur(e)
superlative [suˈpəːlətiv] *n* (*Ling*) superlatif *m*
supermarket [ˈsuːpəmɑːkit] *n* supermarché *m*
supernatural [suːpəˈnætʃərəl] *adj* surnaturel(le) ▷ *n*: **the ~** le surnaturel
superpower [ˈsuːpəpauər] *n* (*Pol*) superpuissance *f*
superstition [suːpəˈstiʃən] *n* superstition *f*
superstitious [suːpəˈstiʃəs] *adj* superstitieux(-euse)
superstore [ˈsuːpəstɔːr] *n* (*BRIT*) hypermarché *m*, grande surface

supervise [ˈsuːpəvaiz] *vt* (*children etc*) surveiller; (*organization, work*) diriger; **supervision** [suːpəˈviʒən] *n* surveillance *f*; (*monitoring*) contrôle *m*; (*management*) direction *f*; **supervisor** *n* surveillant(e); (*in shop*) chef *m* de rayon
supper [ˈsʌpər] *n* dîner *m*; (*late*) souper *m*
supple [ˈsʌpl] *adj* souple
supplement *n* [ˈsʌplimənt] supplément *m* ▷ *vt* [sʌpliˈment] ajouter à, compléter
supplier [səˈplaiər] *n* fournisseur *m*
supply [səˈplai] *vt* (*provide*) fournir; (*equip*): **to ~ (with)** approvisionner or ravitailler (en); fournir (en) ▷ *n* provision *f*, réserve *f*; (*supplying*) approvisionnement *m*; **supplies** *npl* (*food*) vivres *mpl*; (*Mil*) subsistances *fpl*
support [səˈpɔːt] *n* (*moral, financial etc*) soutien *m*, appui *m*; (*Tech*) support *m*, soutien *m* ▷ *vt* soutenir, supporter; (*financially*) subvenir aux besoins de; (*uphold*) être pour, être partisan de, appuyer; (*Sport: team*) être pour; **supporter** *n* (*Pol etc*) partisan(e); (*Sport*) supporter *m*
suppose [səˈpəuz] *vt, vi* supposer; imaginer; **to be ~d to do/be** être censé(e) faire/être; **supposedly** [səˈpəuzidli] *adv* soi-disant; **supposing** *conj* si, à supposer que + *sub*
suppress [səˈpres] *vt* (*revolt, feeling*) réprimer; (*information*) faire disparaître; (*scandal, yawn*) étouffer
supreme [suˈpriːm] *adj* suprême
surcharge [ˈsəːtʃɑːdʒ] *n* surcharge *f*
sure [ʃuər] *adj* (*gen*) sûr(e); (*definite, convinced*) sûr, certain(e); **~!** (*of course*) bien sûr!; **~ enough** effectivement; **to make ~ of sth/that** s'assurer de qch/que, vérifier qch/que; **surely** *adv* sûrement; certainement
surf [səːf] *n* (*waves*) ressac *m* ▷ *vt*: **to ~ the Net** surfer sur Internet, surfer sur le Net
surface [ˈsəːfis] *n* surface *f* ▷ *vt* (*road*) poser un revêtement sur ▷ *vi* remonter à la surface; (*fig*) faire surface; **by ~ mail** par voie de terre; (*by sea*) par voie maritime
surfboard [ˈsəːfbɔːd] *n* planche *f* de surf
surfer [ˈsəːfər] *n* (*in sea*) surfeur(-euse); **web** *or* **Net ~** internaute *m/f*
surfing [ˈsəːfiŋ] *n* (*in sea*) surf *m*
surge [səːdʒ] *n* (*of emotion*) vague *f* ▷ *vi* déferler
surgeon [ˈsəːdʒən] *n* chirurgien *m*
surgery [ˈsəːdʒəri] *n* chirurgie *f*; (*BRIT: room*) cabinet *m* (de consultation); (*also*: **~ hours**) heures *fpl* de consultation
surname [ˈsəːneim] *n* nom *m* de famille
surpass [səːˈpɑːs] *vt* surpasser, dépasser
surplus [ˈsəːpləs] *n* surplus *m*, excédent *m* ▷ *adj* en surplus, de trop; (*Comm*) excédentaire
surprise [səˈpraiz] *n* (*gen*) surprise *f*; (*astonishment*) étonnement *m* ▷ *vt* surprendre, étonner; **surprised** *adj* (*look,*

smile) surpris(e), étonné(e); **to be surprised** être surpris; **surprising** *adj* surprenant(e), étonnant(e); **surprisingly** *adv* (*easy, helpful*) étonnamment, étrangement; **(somewhat) surprisingly, he agreed** curieusement, il a accepté

surrender [sə'rɛndə^r] *n* reddition *f*, capitulation *f* ▷ *vi* se rendre, capituler

surround [sə'raund] *vt* entourer; (*Mil etc*) encercler; **surrounding** *adj* environnant(e); **surroundings** *npl* environs *mpl*, alentours *mpl*

surveillance [sə:'veɪləns] *n* surveillance *f*

survey *n* ['sə:veɪ] enquête *f*, étude *f*; (*in house buying etc*) inspection *f*, (*rapport m* d')expertise *f*; (*of land*) levé *m* ▷ *vt* [sə:'veɪ] (*situation*) passer en revue; (*examine carefully*) inspecter; (*building*) expertiser; (*land*) faire le levé de; (*look at*) embrasser du regard; **surveyor** *n* (*of building*) expert *m*; (*of land*) (arpenteur *m*) géomètre *m*

survival [sə'vaɪvl] *n* survie *f*

survive [sə'vaɪv] *vi* survivre; (*custom etc*) subsister ▷ *vt* (*accident etc*) survivre à, réchapper de; (*person*) survivre à; **survivor** *n* survivant(e)

suspect *adj, n* ['sʌspɛkt] suspect(e) ▷ *vt* [səs'pɛkt] soupçonner, suspecter

suspend [səs'pɛnd] *vt* suspendre; **suspended sentence** *n* (*Law*) condamnation *f* avec sursis; **suspenders** *npl* (*BRIT*) jarretelles *fpl*; (*US*) bretelles *fpl*

suspense [səs'pɛns] *n* attente *f*, incertitude *f*; (*in film etc*) suspense *m*; **to keep sb in ~** tenir qn en suspens, laisser qn dans l'incertitude

suspension [səs'pɛnʃən] *n* (*gen, Aut*) suspension *f*; (*of driving licence*) retrait *m* provisoire; **suspension bridge** *n* pont suspendu

suspicion [səs'pɪʃən] *n* soupçon(s) *m(pl)*; **suspicious** *adj* (*suspecting*) soupçonneux(-euse), méfiant(e); (*causing suspicion*) suspect(e)

sustain [səs'teɪn] *vt* soutenir; (*subj: food*) nourrir, donner des forces à; (*damage*) subir; (*injury*) recevoir

SUV *n abbr* (*esp US*: = *sports utility vehicle*) SUV *m*, véhicule *m* de loisirs

swallow ['swɔləu] *n* (*bird*) hirondelle *f* ▷ *vt* avaler; (*fig: story*) gober

swam [swæm] *pt of* **swim**

swamp [swɔmp] *n* marais *m*, marécage *m* ▷ *vt* submerger

swan [swɔn] *n* cygne *m*

swap [swɔp] *n* échange *m*, troc *m* ▷ *vt*: **to ~ (for)** échanger (contre), troquer (contre)

swarm [swɔ:m] *n* essaim *m* ▷ *vi* (*bees*) essaimer; (*people*) grouiller; **to be ~ing with** grouiller de

sway [sweɪ] *vi* se balancer, osciller ▷ *vt* (*influence*) influencer

swear [swɛə^r] (*pt* **swore**, *pp* **sworn**) *vt, vi* jurer; **swear in** *vt* assermenter; **swearword** *n* gros mot, juron *m*

sweat [swɛt] *n* sueur *f*, transpiration *f* ▷ *vi* suer

sweater ['swɛtə^r] *n* tricot *m*, pull *m*

sweatshirt ['swɛtʃə:t] *n* sweat-shirt *m*

sweaty ['swɛtɪ] *adj* en sueur, moite *or* mouillé(e) de sueur

Swede [swi:d] *n* Suédois(e)

swede [swi:d] *n* (*BRIT*) rutabaga *m*

Sweden ['swi:dn] *n* Suède *f*; **Swedish** ['swi:dɪʃ] *adj* suédois(e) ▷ *n* (*Ling*) suédois *m*

sweep [swi:p] (*pt, pp* **swept**) *n* (*curve*) grande courbe; (*also: chimney ~*) ramoneur *m* ▷ *vt* balayer; (*subj: current*) emporter

sweet [swi:t] *n* (*BRIT: pudding*) dessert *m*; (*candy*) bonbon *m* ▷ *adj* doux (douce); (*not savoury*) sucré(e); (*kind*) gentil(le); (*baby*) mignon(ne); **sweetcorn** *n* maïs doux; **sweetener** ['swi:tnə^r] *n* (*Culin*) édulcorant *m*; **sweetheart** *n* amoureux(-euse); **sweetshop** *n* (*BRIT*) confiserie *f*

swell [swɛl] (*pt* **swelled**, *pp* **swollen** *or* **swelled**) *n* (*of sea*) houle *f* ▷ *adj* (*us inf: excellent*) chouette ▷ *vt* (*increase*) grossir, augmenter ▷ *vi* (*increase*) grossir, augmenter; (*sound*) s'enfler; (*Med: also: ~ up*) enfler; **swelling** *n* (*Med*) enflure *f* (*: lump*) grosseur *f*

swept [swɛpt] *pt, pp of* **sweep**

swerve [swə:v] *vi* (*to avoid obstacle*) faire une embardée *or* un écart; (*off the road*) dévier

swift [swɪft] *n* (*bird*) martinet *m* ▷ *adj* rapide, prompt(e)

swim [swɪm] (*pt* **swam**, *pp* **swum**) *n*: **to go for a ~** aller nager *or* se baigner ▷ *vi* nager; (*Sport*) faire de la natation; (*fig: head, room*) tourner ▷ *vt* traverser (à la nage); **to ~ a length** nager une longueur; **swimmer** *n* nageur(-euse); **swimming** *n* nage *f*, natation *f*; **swimming costume** *n* (*BRIT*) maillot *m* (de bain); **swimming pool** *n* piscine *f*; **swimming trunks** *npl* maillot *m* de bain; **swimsuit** *n* maillot *m* (de bain)

swine flu ['swaɪn-] *n* grippe *f* A

swing [swɪŋ] (*pt, pp* **swung**) *n* (*in playground*) balançoire *f*; (*movement*) balancement *m*, oscillations *fpl*; (*change in opinion etc*) revirement *m* ▷ *vt* balancer, faire osciller; (*also: ~ round*) tourner, faire virer ▷ *vi* se balancer, osciller; (*also: ~ round*) virer, tourner; **to be in full ~** battre son plein

swipe card ['swaɪp-] *n* carte *f* magnétique

swirl [swə:l] *vi* tourbillonner, tournoyer

Swiss [swɪs] *adj* suisse ▷ *n* (*pl inv*) Suisse(-esse)

switch [swɪtʃ] *n* (*for light, radio etc*) bouton *m*; (*change*) changement *m*, revirement *m* ▷ *vt* (*change*) changer; **switch off** *vt* éteindre; (*engine, machine*) arrêter; **could**

you ~ off the light? pouvez-vous éteindre la lumière?; **switch on** vt allumer; (engine, machine) mettre en marche; **switchboard** n (Tel) standard m

Switzerland ['swɪtsələnd] n Suisse f

swivel ['swɪvl] vi (also: ~ **round**) pivoter, tourner

swollen ['swəulən] pp of **swell**

swoop [swu:p] n (by police etc) rafle f, descente f ▷ vi (bird: also: ~ **down**) descendre en piqué, piquer

swop [swɔp] n, vt = **swap**

sword [sɔ:d] n épée f; **swordfish** n espadon m

swore [swɔ:ʳ] pt of **swear**

sworn [swɔ:n] pp of **swear** ▷ adj (statement, evidence) donné(e) sous serment; (enemy) juré(e)

swum [swʌm] pp of **swim**

swung [swʌŋ] pt, pp of **swing**

syllable ['sɪləbl] n syllabe f

syllabus ['sɪləbəs] n programme m

symbol ['sɪmbl] n symbole m; **symbolic(al)** [sɪm'bɔlɪk(l)] adj symbolique

symmetrical [sɪ'mɛtrɪkl] adj symétrique

symmetry ['sɪmɪtrɪ] n symétrie f

sympathetic [sɪmpə'θɛtɪk] adj (showing pity) compatissant(e); (understanding) bienveillant(e), compréhensif(-ive); ~ towards bien disposé(e) envers

> Be careful not to translate sympathetic by the French word sympathique.

sympathize ['sɪmpəθaɪz] vi: to ~ with sb plaindre qn; (in grief) s'associer à la douleur de qn; to ~ with sth comprendre qch

sympathy ['sɪmpəθɪ] n (pity) compassion f

symphony ['sɪmfənɪ] n symphonie f

symptom ['sɪmptəm] n symptôme m; indice m

synagogue ['sɪnəgɔg] n synagogue f

syndicate ['sɪndɪkɪt] n syndicat m, coopérative f; (Press) agence f de presse

syndrome ['sɪndrəum] n syndrome m

synonym ['sɪnənɪm] n synonyme m

synthetic [sɪn'θɛtɪk] adj synthétique

Syria ['sɪrɪə] n Syrie f

syringe [sɪ'rɪndʒ] n seringue f

syrup ['sɪrəp] n sirop m; (BRIT: also: **golden ~**) mélasse raffinée

system ['sɪstəm] n système m; (Anat) organisme m; **systematic** [sɪstə'mætɪk] adj systématique; méthodique; **systems analyst** n analyste-programmeur m/f

ta [tɑ:] excl (BRIT inf) merci!

tab [tæb] n (label) étiquette f; (on drinks can etc) languette f; **to keep ~s on** (fig) surveiller

table ['teɪbl] n table f ▷ vt (BRIT: motion etc) présenter; **to lay** or **set the ~** mettre le couvert or la table; **tablecloth** n nappe f; **table d'hôte** [tɑ:bl'dəut] adj (meal) à prix fixe; **table lamp** n lampe décorative or de table; **tablemat** n (for plate) napperon m, set m; (for hot dish) dessous-de-plat m inv; **tablespoon** n cuiller f de service; (also: **tablespoonful**: as measurement) cuillerée f à soupe

tablet ['tæblɪt] n (Med) comprimé m; (Comput) tablette f (tactile); (of stone) plaque f

table tennis n ping-pong m

tabloid ['tæblɔɪd] n (newspaper) quotidien m populaire

taboo [tə'bu:] adj, n tabou (m)

tack [tæk] n (nail) petit clou; (fig) direction f ▷ vt (nail) clouer; (sew) bâtir ▷ vi (Naut) tirer un or des bord(s); **to ~ sth on to (the end of) sth** (of letter, book) rajouter qch à la fin de qch

tackle ['tækl] n matériel m, équipement m; (for lifting) appareil m de levage; (Football, Rugby) plaquage m ▷ vt (difficulty, animal, burglar) s'attaquer à; (person: challenge) s'expliquer avec; (Football, Rugby) plaquer

tacky ['tækɪ] adj collant(e); (paint) pas sec (sèche); (pej: poor-quality) minable; (: showing bad taste) ringard(e)

tact [tækt] n tact m; **tactful** adj plein(e) de tact

tactics ['tæktɪks] npl tactique f

tactless ['tæktlɪs] adj qui manque de tact

tadpole ['tædpəul] n têtard m

taffy ['tæfɪ] n (us) (bonbon m au) caramel m

tag [tæg] n étiquette f

tail [teɪl] n queue f; (of shirt) pan m ▷ vt (follow) suivre, filer; **tails** npl (suit) habit m; see also **head**

tailor ['teɪlə'] n tailleur m (artisan)
Taiwan ['taɪ'wɑːn] n Taïwan (no article);
  Taiwanese [taɪwə'niːz] adj taïwanais(e)
  ▷ n inv Taïwanais(e)
take [teɪk] (pt **took**, pp **taken**) vt prendre;
  (gain: prize) remporter; (require: effort,
  courage) demander; (tolerate) accepter,
  supporter; (hold: passengers etc) contenir;
  (accompany) emmener, accompagner;
  (bring, carry) apporter, emporter; (exam)
  passer, se présenter à; (drawer
  etc) prendre qch dans; (person) prendre
  qch à; **I - it that** je suppose que; **to be
  ~n ill** tomber malade; **it won't - long** ça
  ne prendra pas longtemps; **I was quite
  ~n with her/it** elle/cela m'a beaucoup
  plu; **take after** vt fus ressembler à; **take
  apart** vt démonter; **take away** vt (carry
  off) emporter; (remove) enlever; (subtract)
  soustraire; **take back** vt (return) rendre,
  rapporter; (one's words) retirer; **take down**
  vt (building) démolir; (letter etc) prendre,
  écrire; **take in** vt (deceive) tromper, rouler;
  (understand) comprendre, saisir; (include)
  couvrir, inclure; (lodger) prendre; (dress,
  waistband) reprendre; **take off** vi (Aviat)
  décoller ▷ vt (remove) enlever; **take on** vt
  (work) accepter, se charger de; (employee)
  prendre, embaucher; (opponent) accepter
  de se battre contre; **take out** vt sortir;
  (remove) enlever; (invite) sortir avec; **to ~
  sth out of** (out of drawer etc) prendre qch
  dans; **to ~ sb out to a restaurant** emmener
  qn au restaurant; **take over** vt (business)
  reprendre ▷ vi: **to ~ over from sb** prendre
  la relève de qn; **take up** vt (one's story)
  reprendre; (dress) raccourcir; (occupy: time,
  space) prendre, occuper; (engage in: hobby
  etc) se mettre à; (accept: offer, challenge)
  accepter; **takeaway** (BRIT) adj (food) à
  emporter ▷ n (shop, restaurant) ≈ magasin
  m qui vend des plats à emporter; **taken**
  pp of **take**; **takeoff** n (Aviat) décollage m;
  takeout adj, n (US) = **takeaway**; **takeover**
  n (Comm) rachat m; **takings** npl (Comm)
  recette f
talc [tælk] n (also: **~um powder**) talc m
tale [teɪl] n (story) conte m, histoire f;
  (account) récit m; **to tell ~s** (fig) rapporter
talent ['tælnt] n talent m, don m; **talented**
  adj doué(e), plein(e) de talent
talk [tɔːk] n (a speech) causerie f, exposé
  m; (conversation) discussion f; (interview)
  entretien m; (gossip) racontars mpl (pej) ▷ vi
  parler; (chatter) bavarder; **talks** npl (Pol etc)
  entretiens mpl; **to ~ about** parler de; **to ~
  sb out of/into doing** persuader qn de ne
  pas faire/de faire; **to ~ shop** parler métier
  or affaires; **talk over** vt discuter (de); **talk
  show** n (TV, Radio) émission-débat f
tall [tɔːl] adj (person) grand(e); (building, tree)
  haut(e); **to be 6 feet ~** ≈ mesurer 1 mètre 80

tambourine [tæmbə'riːn] n tambourin m
tame [teɪm] adj apprivoisé(e); (fig: story,
  style) insipide
tamper ['tæmpə'] vi: **to ~ with** toucher à
  (en cachette ou sans permission)
tampon ['tæmpən] n tampon m
  hygiénique or périodique
tan [tæn] n (also: **sun~**) bronzage m ▷ vt, vi
  bronzer, brunir ▷ adj (colour) marron clair inv
tandem ['tændəm] n tandem m
tangerine [tændʒə'riːn] n mandarine f
tangle ['tæŋgl] n enchevêtrement m; **to
  get in(to) a ~** s'emmêler
tank [tæŋk] n réservoir m; (for fish)
  aquarium m; (Mil) char m d'assaut, tank m
tanker ['tæŋkə'] n (ship) pétrolier m, tanker
  m; (truck) camion-citerne m
tanned [tænd] adj bronzé(e)
tantrum ['tæntrəm] n accès m de colère
Tanzania [tænzə'nɪə] n Tanzanie f
tap [tæp] n (on sink etc) robinet m; (gentle
  blow) petite tape ▷ vt frapper or taper
  légèrement; (resources) exploiter, utiliser;
  (telephone) mettre sur écoute; **on ~** (fig:
  resources) disponible; **tap dancing** n
  claquettes fpl
tape [teɪp] n (for tying) ruban m; (also:
  magnetic ~) bande f (magnétique);
  (cassette) cassette f; (sticky) Scotch® m ▷ vt
  (record) enregistrer (au magnétoscope or
  sur cassette); (stick) coller avec du Scotch®;
  tape measure n mètre m à ruban; **tape
  recorder** n magnétophone m
tapestry ['tæpɪstrɪ] n tapisserie f
tar [tɑː] n goudron m
target ['tɑːgɪt] n cible f; (fig: objective)
  objectif m
tariff ['tærɪf] n (Comm) tarif m; (taxes) tarif
  douanier
tarmac ['tɑːmæk] n (BRIT: on road)
  macadam m; (Aviat) aire f d'envol
tarpaulin [tɑː'pɔːlɪn] n bâche goudronnée
tarragon ['tærəgən] n estragon m
tart [tɑːt] n (Culin) tarte f; (BRIT inf: pej:
  prostitute) poule f ▷ adj (flavour) âpre,
  aigrelet(te)
tartan ['tɑːtn] n tartan m ▷ adj écossais(e)
tartar(e) sauce ['tɑːtə-] n sauce f tartare
task [tɑːsk] n tâche f; **to take to ~** prendre
  à partie
taste [teɪst] n goût m; (fig: glimpse, idea) idée
  f, aperçu m ▷ vt goûter ▷ vi: **to ~ of** (fish etc)
  avoir le or un goût de; **you can ~ the garlic
  (in it)** on sent bien l'ail; **to have a ~ of sth**
  goûter (à) qch; **can I have a ~?** je peux
  goûter?; **to be in good/bad** or **poor ~** être
  de bon/mauvais goût; **tasteful** adj de bon
  goût; **tasteless** adj (food) insipide; (remark)
  de mauvais goût; **tasty** adj
  savoureux(-euse), délicieux(-euse)
tatters ['tætəz] npl: **in ~** (also: **tattered**) en
  lambeaux

tattoo [tə'tu:] n tatouage m; (spectacle) parade f militaire ▷ vt tatouer

taught [tɔ:t] pt, pp of **teach**

taunt [tɔ:nt] n raillerie f ▷ vt railler

Taurus ['tɔ:rəs] n le Taureau

taut [tɔ:t] adj tendu(e)

tax [tæks] n (on goods etc) taxe f; (on income) impôts mpl, contributions fpl ▷ vt taxer; imposer; (fig: patience etc) mettre à l'épreuve; **tax disc** n (BRIT Aut) vignette f (automobile); **tax-free** adj exempt(e) d'impôts

taxi ['tæksɪ] n taxi m ▷ vi (Aviat) rouler (lentement) au sol; **taxi driver** n chauffeur m de taxi; **taxi rank**, (US) **taxi stand** n station f de taxis

tax payer [-peɪəʳ] n contribuable m/f

tax return n déclaration f d'impôts or de revenus

TB n abbr = **tuberculosis**

tbc abbr = **to be confirmed**

tea [ti:] n thé m; (BRIT: snack: for children) goûter m; **high ~** (BRIT) collation combinant goûter et dîner; **tea bag** n sachet m de thé; **tea break** n (BRIT) pause-thé f

teach (pt, pp **taught**) [ti:tʃ, tɔ:t] vt: **to ~ sb sth, to ~ sth to sb** apprendre qch à qn; (in school etc) enseigner qch à qn ▷ vi enseigner; **teacher** n (in secondary school) professeur m; (in primary school) instituteur(-trice); **teaching** n enseignement m; **teaching assistant** n aide-éducateur(-trice)

tea: teacup n tasse f à thé; **tea leaves** npl feuilles fpl de thé

team [ti:m] n équipe f; (of animals) attelage m; **team up** vi: **to ~ up (with)** faire équipe (avec)

teapot ['ti:pɔt] n théière f

tear¹ ['tɪəʳ] n larme f; **in ~s** en larmes

tear² [tɛəʳ] (pt **tore**, pp **torn**) n déchirure f ▷ vt déchirer ▷ vi se déchirer; **tear apart** vt (also fig) déchirer; **tear down** vt (building, statue) démolir; (poster, flag) arracher; **tear off** vt (sheet of paper etc) arracher; (one's clothes) enlever à toute vitesse; **tear up** vt (sheet of paper etc) déchirer, mettre en morceaux or pièces

tearful ['tɪəful] adj larmoyant(e)

tear gas ['tɪə-] n gaz m lacrymogène

tearoom ['ti:ru:m] n salon m de thé

tease [ti:z] vt taquiner; (unkindly) tourmenter

tea: teaspoon n petite cuiller; (also: **teaspoonful**: as measurement) ≈ cuillerée f à café; **teatime** n l'heure f du thé; **tea towel** n (BRIT) torchon m (à vaisselle)

technical ['tɛknɪkl] adj technique

technician [tɛk'nɪʃən] n technicien(ne)

technique [tɛk'ni:k] n technique f

technology [tɛk'nɔlədʒɪ] n technologie f

teddy (bear) ['tɛdɪ-] n ours m (en peluche)

tedious ['ti:dɪəs] adj fastidieux(-euse)

tee [ti:] n (Golf) tee m

teen [ti:n] adj = **teenage** ▷ n (US) = **teenager**

teenage ['ti:neɪdʒ] adj (fashions etc) pour jeunes, pour adolescents; (child) qui est adolescent(e); **teenager** n adolescent(e)

teens [ti:nz] npl: **to be in one's ~** être adolescent(e)

teeth [ti:θ] npl of **tooth**

teetotal ['ti:'təutl] adj (person) qui ne boit jamais d'alcool

telecommunications ['tɛlɪkəmju:nɪ'keɪʃənɪz] n télécommunications fpl

telegram ['tɛlɪgræm] n télégramme m

telegraph pole ['tɛlɪgrɑ:f-] n poteau m télégraphique

telephone ['tɛlɪfəun] n téléphone m ▷ vt (person) téléphoner à; (message) téléphoner; **to be on the ~** (be speaking) être au téléphone; **telephone book** n = **telephone directory**; **telephone box**, (US) **telephone booth** n cabine f téléphonique; **telephone call** n appel m téléphonique; **telephone directory** n annuaire m (du téléphone); **telephone number** n numéro m de téléphone

telesales ['tɛlɪseɪlz] npl télévente f

telescope ['tɛlɪskəup] n télescope m

televise ['tɛlɪvaɪz] vt téléviser

television ['tɛlɪvɪʒən] n télévision f; **on ~** à la télévision; **television programme** n (BRIT) émission f de télévision

tell (pt, pp **told**) [tɛl, təuld] vt dire, (relate: story) raconter; (distinguish): **to ~ sth from** distinguer qch de ▷ vi (talk): **to ~ of** parler de; (have effect) se faire sentir, se voir; **to ~ sb to do** dire à qn de faire; **to ~ the time** (know how to) savoir lire l'heure; **tell off** vt réprimander, gronder; **teller** n (in bank) caissier(-ière)

telly ['tɛlɪ] n abbr (BRIT inf: = television) télé f

temp [tɛmp] n (BRIT: = temporary worker) intérimaire m/f ▷ vi travailler comme intérimaire

temper ['tɛmpəʳ] n (nature) caractère m; (mood) humeur f; (fit of anger) colère f ▷ vt (moderate) tempérer, adoucir; **to be in a ~** être en colère; **to lose one's ~** se mettre en colère

temperament ['tɛmprəmənt] n (nature) tempérament m; **temperamental** [tɛmprə'mɛntl] adj capricieux(-euse)

temperature ['tɛmprətʃəʳ] n température f; **to have** or **run a ~** avoir de la fièvre

temple ['tɛmpl] n (building) temple m; (Anat) tempe f

temporary ['tɛmpərərɪ] adj temporaire, provisoire; (job, worker) temporaire

tempt [tɛmpt] vt tenter; **to ~ sb into doing** induire qn à faire; **temptation** n tentation f; **tempting** adj tentant(e); (food) appétissant(e)

ten [tɛn] *num* dix

tenant ['tɛnənt] *n* locataire *m/f*

tend [tɛnd] *vt* s'occuper de ▷ *vi*: **to ~ to do** avoir tendance à faire; **tendency** ['tɛndənsɪ] *n* tendance *f*

tender ['tɛndəʳ] *adj* tendre; (*delicate*) délicat(e); (*sore*) sensible ▷ *n* (*Comm: offer*) soumission *f*; (*money*): **legal ~** cours légal ▷ *vt* offrir

tendon ['tɛndən] *n* tendon *m*

tenner ['tɛnəʳ] *n* (BRIT *inf*) billet *m* de dix livres

tennis ['tɛnɪs] *n* tennis *m*; **tennis ball** *n* balle *f* de tennis; **tennis court** *n* (court *m* de) tennis *m*; **tennis match** *n* match *m* de tennis; **tennis player** *n* joueur(-euse) de tennis; **tennis racket** *n* raquette *f* de tennis

tenor ['tɛnəʳ] *n* (*Mus*) ténor *m*

tenpin bowling ['tɛnpɪn-] *n* (BRIT) bowling *m* (*à 10 quilles*)

tense [tɛns] *adj* tendu(e) ▷ *n* (*Ling*) temps *m*

tension ['tɛnʃən] *n* tension *f*

tent [tɛnt] *n* tente *f*

tentative ['tɛntətɪv] *adj* timide, hésitant(e); (*conclusion*) provisoire

tenth [tɛnθ] *num* dixième

tent: **tent peg** *n* piquet *m* de tente; **tent pole** *n* montant *m* de tente

tepid ['tɛpɪd] *adj* tiède

term [təːm] *n* terme *m*; (*Scol*) trimestre *m* ▷ *vt* appeler; **terms** *npl* (*conditions*) conditions *fpl*; (*Comm*) tarif *m*; **in the short/ long ~** à court/long terme; **to come to ~s with** (*problem*) faire face à; **to be on good ~s with** bien s'entendre avec, être en bons termes avec

terminal ['təːmɪnl] *adj* (*disease*) dans sa phase terminale; (*patient*) incurable ▷ *n* (*Elec*) borne *f*; (*for oil, ore etc, also* Comput) terminal *m*; (*also*: **air ~**) aérogare *f*; (BRIT: *also*: **coach ~**) gare routière

terminate ['təːmɪneɪt] *vt* mettre fin à; (*pregnancy*) interrompre

termini ['təːmɪnaɪ] *npl of* **terminus**

terminology [təːmɪ'nɔlədʒɪ] *n* terminologie *f*

terminus (*pl* **termini**) ['təːmɪnəs, 'təːmɪnaɪ] *n* terminus *m inv*

terrace ['tɛrəs] *n* terrasse *f*; (BRIT: *row of houses*) rangée *f* de maisons (*attenantes les unes aux autres*); **the ~s** (BRIT Sport) les gradins *mpl*; **terraced** *adj* (*garden*) en terrasses; (*in a row: house*) attenant(e) aux maisons voisines

terrain [tɛ'reɪn] *n* terrain *m* (*sol*)

terrestrial [tɪ'rɛstrɪəl] *adj* terrestre

terrible ['tɛrɪbl] *adj* terrible, atroce; (*weather, work*) affreux(-euse), épouvantable; **terribly** *adv* terriblement; (*very badly*) affreusement mal

terrier ['tɛrɪəʳ] *n* terrier *m* (*chien*)

terrific [tə'rɪfɪk] *adj* (*very great*) fantastique, incroyable, terrible; (*wonderful*) formidable, sensationnel(le)

terrified ['tɛrɪfaɪd] *adj* terrifié(e); **to be ~ of sth** avoir très peur de qch

terrify ['tɛrɪfaɪ] *vt* terrifier; **terrifying** *adj* terrifiant(e)

territorial [tɛrɪ'tɔːrɪəl] *adj* territorial(e)

territory ['tɛrɪtərɪ] *n* territoire *m*

terror ['tɛrəʳ] *n* terreur *f*; **terrorism** *n* terrorisme *m*; **terrorist** *n* terroriste *m/f*; **terrorist attack** *n* attentat *m* terroriste

test [tɛst] *n* (*trial, check*) essai *m*; (*of courage etc*) épreuve *f*; (*Med*) examen *m*; (*Chem*) analyse *f*; (*Scol*) interrogation *f* de contrôle; (*also*: **driving ~**) (examen du) permis *m* de conduire ▷ *vt* essayer; mettre à l'épreuve; examiner; analyser; faire subir une interrogation à

testicle ['tɛstɪkl] *n* testicule *m*

testify ['tɛstɪfaɪ] *vi* (*Law*) témoigner, déposer; **to ~ to sth** (*Law*) attester qch

testimony ['tɛstɪmənɪ] *n* (*Law*) témoignage *m*, déposition *f*

test: **test match** *n* (*Cricket, Rugby*) match international; **test tube** *n* éprouvette *f*

tetanus ['tɛtənəs] *n* tétanos *m*

text [tɛkst] *n* texte *m*; (*on mobile phone*) SMS *m inv*, texto® *m* ▷ *vt* (*inf*) envoyer un SMS or texto® à; **textbook** *n* manuel *m*

textile ['tɛkstaɪl] *n* textile *m*

text message *n* SMS *m inv*, texto® *m*

text messaging [-'mɛsɪdʒɪŋ] *n* messagerie textuelle

texture ['tɛkstʃəʳ] *n* texture *f*; (*of skin, paper etc*) grain *m*

Thai [taɪ] *adj* thaïlandais(e) ▷ *n* Thaïlandais(e)

Thailand ['taɪlænd] *n* Thaïlande *f*

Thames [tɛmz] *n*: **the (River) ~** la Tamise

than [ðæn, ðən] *conj* que; (*with numerals*): **more ~ 10/once** plus de 10/d'une fois; **I have more/less ~ you** j'en ai plus/moins que toi; **she has more apples ~ pears** elle a plus de pommes que de poires; **it is better to phone ~ to write** il vaut mieux téléphoner (plutôt) qu'écrire; **she is older ~ you think** elle est plus âgée que tu le crois

thank [θæŋk] *vt* remercier, dire merci à; **thanks** *npl* remerciements *mpl*; **~s!** merci!; **~ you (very much)** merci (beaucoup); **~ God** Dieu merci; **~s to** *prep* grâce à; **thankfully** *adv* (*fortunately*) heureusement; **Thanksgiving (Day)** *n* jour *m* d'action de grâce

• THANKSGIVING (DAY)

> •
> • *Thanksgiving (Day)* est un jour de congé
> • aux États-Unis, le quatrième jeudi du
> • mois de novembre, commémorant la
> • bonne récolte que les Pèlerins venus

- de Grande-Bretagne ont eue en 1621;
- traditionnellement, c'était un jour où
- l'on remerciait Dieu et où l'on organisait
- un grand festin. Une fête semblable,
- mais qui n'a aucun rapport avec les Pères
- Pèlerins, a lieu au Canada le deuxième
- lundi d'octobre.

 KEYWORD

that [ðæt] adj (demonstrative) ce, cet + vowel
or h mute, cette f; **that man/woman/book**
cet homme/cette femme/ce livre, (not this)
cet homme-là/cette femme-là/ce livre-là;
that one celui-là (celle-là)
▶ pron 1 (demonstrative) ce; (: not this one)
cela, ça; (: that one) celui (celle); **who's that?**
qui est-ce?; **what's that?** qu'est-ce que
c'est?; **is that you?** c'est toi?; **I prefer this to
that** je préfère ceci à cela or ça; **that's what
he said** c'est or voilà ce qu'il a dit; **will you
eat all that?** tu vas manger tout ça?; **that is
(to say)** c'est-à-dire, à savoir
2 (relative: subject) qui; (: object) que; (: after
prep) lequel (laquelle), lesquels (lesquelles)
pl; **the book that I read** le livre que j'ai lu;
the books that are in the library les livres
qui sont dans la bibliothèque; **all that I
have** tout ce que j'ai; **the box that I put
it in** la boîte dans laquelle je l'ai mis; **the
people that I spoke to** les gens auxquels or
à qui j'ai parlé
3 (relative: of time) où; **the day that he
came** le jour où il est venu
▶ conj que; **he thought that I was ill** il
pensait que j'étais malade
▶ adv (demonstrative): **I don't like it that
much** ça ne me plaît pas tant que ça; **I didn't
know it was that bad** je ne savais pas que
c'était si or aussi mauvais; **it's about that
high** c'est à peu près de cette hauteur

thatched [θætʃt] adj (roof) de chaume;
~ cottage chaumière f

thaw [θɔː] n dégel m ▶ vi (ice) fondre; (food)
dégeler ▶ vt (food) (faire) dégeler

 KEYWORD

the [ðiː, ðə] def art 1 (gen) le, la f, l' + vowel or h
mute, les pl (NB: à + le(s) = **au(x)**; de + le =
du; de + les = **des**); **the boy/girl/ink** le garçon/
la fille/l'encre; **the children** les enfants;
the history of the world l'histoire du
monde; **give it to the postman** donne-le
au facteur; **to play the piano/flute** jouer
du piano/de la flûte
2 (+ adj to form n) le, la f, l' + vowel or h mute,
les pl; **the rich and the poor** les riches et les
pauvres; **to attempt the impossible** tenter
l'impossible
3 (in titles): **Elizabeth the First** Elisabeth

première; **Peter the Great** Pierre le Grand
4 (in comparisons): **the more he works, the
more he earns** plus il travaille, plus il gagne
de l'argent

theatre, (US) **theater** ['θɪətər] n théâtre m;
(Med: also: **operating ~**) salle f d'opération
theft [θɛft] n vol m (larcin)
their [ðɛər] adj leur, leurs pl; see also **my**;
theirs pron le (la) leur, les leurs; see also
mine[1]
them [ðɛm, ðəm] pron (direct) les; (indirect)
leur; (stressed, after prep) eux (elles); **give
me a few of ~** donnez m'en quelques uns (or
quelques unes); see also **me**
theme [θiːm] n thème m; **theme park** n
parc m à thème
themselves [ðəm'sɛlvz] pl pron (reflexive)
se; (emphatic, after prep) eux-mêmes (elles-
mêmes), **between ~** entre eux (elles); see
also **oneself**
then [ðɛn] adv (at that time) alors, à ce
moment-là; (next) puis, ensuite; (and also)
et puis ▷ conj (therefore) alors, dans ce cas
▷ adj: **the ~ president** le président d'alors
or de l'époque; **by ~** (past) à ce moment-là;
(future) d'ici là; **from ~ on** dès lors; **until ~**
jusqu'à ce moment-là, jusque-là
theology [θɪ'ɒlədʒɪ] n théologie f
theory ['θɪərɪ] n théorie f
therapist ['θɛrəpɪst] n thérapeute m/f
therapy ['θɛrəpɪ] n thérapie f

 KEYWORD

there [ðɛər] adv 1: **there is, there are** il y a;
there are 3 of them (people, things) il y en a
3; **there is no-one here/no bread left** il n'y
a personne/il n'y a plus de pain; **there has
been an accident** il y a eu un accident
2 (referring to place) là, là-bas; **it's there** c'est
là(-bas); **in/on/up/down there** là-dedans/
là-dessus/là-haut/en bas; **he went there
on Friday** il y est allé vendredi; **I want that
book there** je veux ce livre-là; **there he is!**
le voilà!
3: **there, there!** (esp to child) allons, allons!

there: thereabouts adv (place) par là,
près de là; (amount) environ, à peu près;
thereafter adv par la suite; **thereby** adv
ainsi; **therefore** adv donc, par conséquent
there's ['ðɛəz] = **there is; there has**
thermal ['θɜːml] adj thermique;
~ underwear sous-vêtements mpl en
Thermolactyl®
thermometer [θə'mɒmɪtər] n
thermomètre m
thermostat ['θɜːməustæt] n thermostat m
these [ðiːz] pl pron ceux-ci (celles-ci) ▷ pl adj
ces, (not those): **books** ces livres-ci
thesis (pl **theses**) ['θiːsɪs, 'θiːsiːz] n thèse f

they [ðeɪ] *pl pron* ils (elles); (*stressed*) eux (elles); ~ **say that ...** (*it is said that*) on dit que ...; **they'd = they had; they would; they'll = they shall; they will; they're = they are; they've = they have**

thick [θɪk] *adj* épais(se); (*stupid*) bête, borné(e) ▷ *n*: **in the ~ of** au beau milieu de, en plein cœur de; **it's 20 cm ~** ça a 20 cm d'épaisseur; **thicken** *vi* s'épaissir ▷ *vt* (*sauce etc*) épaissir; **thickness** *n* épaisseur *f*

thief (*pl* **thieves**) [θi:f, θi:vz] *n* voleur(-euse)

thigh [θaɪ] *n* cuisse *f*

thin [θɪn] *adj* mince; (*skinny*) maigre; (*soup*) peu épais(se); (*hair, crowd*) clairsemé(e) ▷ *vt* (*also*: ~ **down**: *sauce, paint*) délayer

thing [θɪŋ] *n* chose *f*; (*object*) objet *m*; (*contraption*) truc *m*; **things** *npl* (*belongings*) affaires *fpl*; **the ~ is ...** c'est que ...; **the best ~ would be to** le mieux serait de; **how are ~s?** comment ça va?; **to have a ~ about** (*be obsessed by*) être obsédé(e) par; (*hate*) détester; **poor ~!** le (*or* la) pauvre!

think (*pt, pp* **thought**) [θɪŋk, θɔ:t] *vi* penser, réfléchir ▷ *vt* penser, croire; (*imagine*) s'imaginer; **what did you ~ of them?** qu'avez-vous pensé d'eux?; **to ~ about sth/ sb** penser à qch/qn; **I'll ~ about it** je vais y réfléchir; **to ~ of doing** avoir l'idée de faire; **I ~ so/not** je crois *or* pense que oui/non; **to ~ well of** avoir une haute opinion de; **think over** *vt* bien réfléchir à; **think up** *vt* inventer, trouver

third [θə:d] *num* troisième ▷ *n* (*fraction*) tiers *m*; (*Aut*) troisième (vitesse) *f*; (*BRIT Scol: degree*) ≈ licence *f* avec mention passable; **thirdly** *adv* troisièmement; **third party insurance** *n* (*BRIT*) assurance *f* au tiers; **Third World** *n*: **the Third World** le Tiers-Monde

thirst [θə:st] *n* soif *f*; **thirsty** *adj* qui a soif, assoiffé(e); (*work*) qui donne soif; **to be thirsty** avoir soif

thirteen [θə:'ti:n] *num* treize; **thirteenth** [θə:'ti:nθ] *num* treizième

thirtieth ['θə:tɪɪθ] *num* trentième

thirty ['θə:tɪ] *num* trente

KEYWORD

this [ðɪs] *adj* (*demonstrative*) ce, cet + *vowel or h mute*, cette *f*; **this man/woman/book** cet homme/cette femme/ce livre; (*not that*) cet homme-ci/cette femme-ci/ce livre-ci; **this one** celui-ci (celle-ci)

▶ *pron* (*demonstrative*) ce (: *not that one*) celui-ci (celle-ci), ceci; **who's this?** qui est-ce?; **what's this?** qu'est-ce que c'est?; **I prefer this to that** je préfère ceci à cela; **this is where I live** c'est ici que j'habite; **this is what he said** voici ce qu'il a dit; **this is Mr Brown** (*in introductions*) je vous présente Mr Brown; (*in photo*) c'est Mr Brown; (*on telephone*) ici Mr Brown

▶ *adv* (*demonstrative*): **it was about this big** c'était à peu près de cette grandeur *or* grand comme ça; **I didn't know it was this bad** je ne savais pas que c'était si *or* aussi mauvais

thistle ['θɪsl] *n* chardon *m*

thorn [θɔ:n] *n* épine *f*

thorough ['θʌrə] *adj* (*search*) minutieux(-euse); (*knowledge, research*) approfondi(e); (*work, person*) consciencieux(-euse); (*cleaning*) à fond; **thoroughly** *adv* (*search*) minutieusement; (*study*) en profondeur; (*clean*) à fond; (*very*) tout à fait

those [ðəuz] *pl pron* ceux-là (celles-là) ▷ *pl adj* ces; (*not these*): ~ **books** ces livres-là

though [ðəu] *conj* bien que + *sub*, quoique + *sub* ▷ *adv* pourtant

thought [θɔ:t] *pt, pp of* **think** ▷ *n* pensée *f*; (*idea*) idée *f*; (*opinion*) avis *m*; **thoughtful** *adj* (*deep in thought*) pensif(-ive); (*serious*) réfléchi(e); (*considerate*) prévenant(e); **thoughtless** *adj* qui manque de considération

thousand ['θauzənd] *num* mille; **one ~** mille; **two ~** deux mille; **~s of** des milliers de; **thousandth** *num* millième

thrash [θræʃ] *vt* rouer de coups; (*inf: defeat*) donner une raclée à (*inf*)

thread [θrɛd] *n* fil *m*; (*of screw*) pas *m*, filetage *m* ▷ *vt* (*needle*) enfiler

threat [θrɛt] *n* menace *f*; **threaten** *vi* (*storm*) menacer ▷ *vt*: **to threaten sb with sth/to do** menacer qn de qch/de faire; **threatening** *adj* menaçant(e)

three [θri:] *num* trois; **three-dimensional** *adj* à trois dimensions; **three-piece suite** *n* salon *m* (canapé et deux fauteuils); **three-quarters** *npl* trois-quarts *mpl*; **three-quarters full** aux trois-quarts plein

threshold ['θrɛʃhəuld] *n* seuil *m*

threw [θru:] *pt of* **throw**

thrill [θrɪl] *n* (*excitement*) émotion *f*, sensation forte; (*shudder*) frisson *m* ▷ *vt* (*audience*) électriser; **thrilled (with)** ravi(e) de; **thriller** *n* film *m* (*or* roman *m or* pièce *f*) à suspense; **thrilling** *adj* (*book, play etc*) saisissant(e); (*news, discovery*) excitant(e)

thriving ['θraɪvɪŋ] *adj* (*business, community*) prospère

throat [θrəut] *n* gorge *f*; **to have a sore ~** avoir mal à la gorge

throb [θrɔb] *vi* (*heart*) palpiter; (*engine*) vibrer; **my head is ~bing** j'ai des élancements dans la tête

throne [θrəun] *n* trône *m*

through [θru:] *prep* à travers; (*time*) pendant, durant; (*by means of*) par, par l'intermédiaire de; (*owing to*) à cause de ▷ *adj* (*ticket, train, passage*) direct(e) ▷ *adv* à travers; **(from) Monday ~ Friday** (*US*)

de lundi à vendredi; **to put sb ~ to sb** (*Tel*)
passer qn à qn; **to be ~** (*BRIT Tel*) avoir la
communication; (*esp US: have finished*) avoir
fini; "**no ~ traffic**" (*US*) "passage interdit";
"**no ~ road**" (*BRIT*) "impasse"; **throughout**
prep (*place*) partout dans; (*time*) durant
tout(e) le ▷ *adv* partout

throw [θrəʊ] *n* jet *m*; (*Sport*) lancer *m*
▷ *vt* (*pt* **threw**, *pp* **thrown**) lancer, jeter;
(*Sport*) lancer; (*rider*) désarçonner; (*fig*)
décontenancer; **to ~ a party** donner une
réception; **throw away** *vt* jeter; (*money*)
gaspiller; **throw in** *vt* (*Sport: ball*) remettre
en jeu; (*include*) ajouter; **throw off** *vt* se
débarrasser de; **throw out** *vt* jeter; (*reject*)
rejeter; (*person*) mettre à la porte; **throw
up** *vi* vomir

thrown [θrəʊn] *pp of* **throw**
thru [θru:] (*US*) *prep* = **through**
thrush [θrʌʃ] *n* (*Zool*) grive *f*
thrust [θrʌst] *vt* (*pt, pp* **thrust**) pousser
brusquement; (*push in*) enfoncer
thud [θʌd] *n* bruit sourd
thug [θʌg] *n* voyou *m*
thumb [θʌm] *n* (*Anat*) pouce *m* ▷ *vt*: **to ~ a
lift** faire de l'auto-stop, arrêter une voiture;
thumbtack *n* (*US*) punaise *f* (*clou*)
thump [θʌmp] *n* grand coup; (*sound*) bruit
sourd ▷ *vt* cogner sur ▷ *vi* cogner, frapper
thunder ['θʌndər] *n* tonnerre *m* ▷ *vi*
tonner; (*train etc*): **to ~ past** passer dans
un grondement or un bruit de tonnerre;
thunderstorm *n* orage *m*
Thursday ['θɜːzdɪ] *n* jeudi *m*
thus [ðʌs] *adv* ainsi
thwart [θwɔːt] *vt* contrecarrer
thyme [taɪm] *n* thym *m*
Tibet [tɪ'bet] *n* Tibet *m*
tick [tɪk] *n* (*sound: of clock*) tic-tac *m*; (*mark*)
coche *f*; (*Zool*) tique *f* ▷ *vi* faire tic-tac ▷ *vt*
(*item on list*) cocher; **in a ~** (*BRIT inf*) dans
un instant; **tick off** *vt* (*item on list*) cocher;
(*person*) réprimander, attraper
ticket ['tɪkɪt] *n* billet *m*; (*for bus, tube*) ticket
m; (*in shop, on goods*) étiquette *f*; (*for library*)
carte *f*; (*also*: **parking ~**) contravention
f, p.-v. *m*; **ticket barrier** *n* (*BRIT Rail*)
portillon *m* automatique; **ticket collector**
n contrôleur(-euse); **ticket inspector** *n*
contrôleur(-euse); **ticket machine** *n*
billetterie *f* automatique; **ticket office** *n*
guichet *m*, bureau *m* de vente des billets
tickle ['tɪkl] *vi* chatouiller ▷ *vt* chatouiller;
ticklish *adj* (*person*) chatouilleux(-euse);
(*problem*) épineux(-euse)
tide [taɪd] *n* marée *f*; (*fig: of events*) cours *m*
tidy ['taɪdɪ] *adj* (*room*) bien rangé(e); (*dress,
work*) net (nette), soigné(e); (*person*)
ordonné(e), qui a de l'ordre ▷ *vt* (*also*: **~ up**)
ranger
tie [taɪ] *n* (*string etc*) cordon *m*; (*BRIT: also*:
neck~) cravate *f*; (*fig: link*) lien *m*; (*Sport:*

draw) égalité *f* de points match nul ▷ *vt*
(*parcel*) attacher; (*ribbon*) nouer ▷ *vi* (*Sport*)
faire match nul; finir à égalité de points;
to ~ sth in a bow faire un nœud à or avec
qch; **to ~ a knot in sth** faire un nœud à
qch; **tie down** *vt*: **to ~ sb down to** (*fig*)
contraindre qn à accepter; **to feel ~d down**
(*by relationship*) se sentir coincé(e); **tie
up** *vt* (*parcel*) ficeler; (*dog, boat*) attacher;
(*prisoner*) ligoter; (*arrangements*) conclure;
to be ~d up (*busy*) être pris(e) or occupé(e)
tier [tɪər] *n* gradin *m*; (*of cake*) étage *m*
tiger ['taɪgər] *n* tigre *m*
tight [taɪt] *adj* (*rope*) tendu(e), raide;
(*clothes*) étroit(e), très juste; (*budget,
programme, bend*) serré(e); (*control*)
strict(e), sévère; (*inf: drunk*) ivre, rond(e)
▷ *adv* (*squeeze*) très fort; (*shut*) à bloc,
hermétiquement; **hold ~!** accrochez-vous
bien!; **tighten** *vt* (*rope*) tendre; (*screw*)
resserrer; (*control*) renforcer ▷ *vi* se tendre;
se resserrer; **tightly** *adv* (*grasp*) bien, très
fort; **tights** *npl* (*BRIT*) collant *m*
tile [taɪl] *n* (*on roof*) tuile *f*; (*on wall or floor*)
carreau *m*
till [tɪl] *n* caisse (enregistreuse) ▷ *prep, conj*
= **until**
tilt [tɪlt] *vt* pencher, incliner ▷ *vi* pencher,
être incliné(e)
timber ['tɪmbər] *n* (*material*) bois *m* de
construction
time [taɪm] *n* temps *m*; (*epoch: often pl*)
époque *f*, temps; (*by clock*) heure *f*; (*moment*)
moment *m*; (*occasion, also Math*) fois *f*;
(*Mus*) mesure *f* ▷ *vt* (*race*) chronométrer;
(*programme*) minuter; (*visit*) fixer; (*remark
etc*) choisir le moment de; **a long ~** un long
moment, longtemps; **four at a ~** quatre à la
fois; **for the ~ being** pour le moment; **from
~ to ~** de temps en temps; **at ~s** parfois, **in ~**
(*soon enough*) à temps; (*after some time*) avec
le temps, à la longue; (*Mus*) en mesure; **in a
week's ~** dans une semaine; **in no ~** en un
rien de temps; **any ~** n'importe quand; **on ~**
à l'heure; **5 ~s 5** 5 fois 5; **what ~ is it?** quelle
heure est-il?; **what ~ is the museum/
shop open?** à quelle heure ouvre le musée/
magasin?; **to have a good ~** bien s'amuser;
time limit *n* limite *f* de temps, délai *m*;
timely *adj* opportun(e); **timer** *n* (*in kitchen*)
compte-minutes *m inv*; (*Tech*) minuteur
m; **time-share** *n* maison *f*/appartement
m en multipropriété; **timetable** *n* (*Rail*)
(indicateur *m*) horaire *m*; (*Scol*) emploi *m* du
temps; **time zone** *n* fuseau *m* horaire
timid ['tɪmɪd] *adj* timide; (*easily scared*)
peureux(-euse)
timing ['taɪmɪŋ] *n* (*Sport*) chronométrage
m; **the ~ of his resignation** le moment
choisi pour sa démission
tin [tɪn] *n* étain *m*; (*also*: **~ plate**) fer-blanc *m*;
(*BRIT: can*) boîte *f* (*de conserve*); (*for baking*)

moule *m* (à gâteau); (*for storage*) boîte *f*;
tinfoil *n* papier *m* d'étain *or* d'aluminium
tingle ['tɪŋgl] *vi* picoter; (*person*) avoir des
picotements
tinker ['tɪŋkər]: **tinker with** *vt fus* bricoler,
rafistoler
tinned [tɪnd] *adj* (*BRIT: food*) en boîte, en
conserve
tin opener [-'əupnər] *n* (*BRIT*) ouvre-
boîte(s) *m*
tinsel ['tɪnsl] *n* guirlandes *fpl* de Noël
(*argentées*)
tint [tɪnt] *n* teinte *f*; (*for hair*)
shampo(o)ing colorant; **tinted** *adj* (*hair*)
teint(e); (*spectacles, glass*) teinté(e)
tiny ['taɪnɪ] *adj* minuscule
tip [tɪp] *n* (*end*) bout *m*; (*gratuity*) pourboire
m; (*BRIT: for rubbish*) décharge *f*; (*advice*)
tuyau *m* ▷ *vt* (*waiter*) donner un pourboire
à; (*tilt*) incliner; (*overturn: also: ~ over*)
renverser; (*empty: also: ~ out*) déverser;
how much should I ~? combien de
pourboire est-ce qu'il faut laisser?; **tip off** *vt*
prévenir, avertir
tiptoe ['tɪptəu] *n*: **on ~** sur la pointe des pieds
tire ['taɪər] *n* (*US*) = **tyre** ▷ *vt* fatiguer ▷ *vi* se
fatiguer; **tired** *adj* fatigué(e); **to be tired
of** en avoir assez de, être las (lasse) de; **tire
pressure** (*US*) *n* = **tyre pressure**; **tiring** *adj*
fatigant(e)
tissue ['tɪʃuː] *n* tissu *m*, (*paper handkerchief*)
mouchoir *m* en papier, kleenex® *m*; **tissue
paper** *n* papier *m* de soie
tit [tɪt] *n* (*bird*) mésange *f*; **to give ~ for tat**
rendre coup pour coup
title ['taɪtl] *n* titre *m*
T-junction ['tiː'dʒʌŋkʃən] *n* croisement
m en T
TM *n abbr* = **trademark**

KEYWORD

to [tuː, tə] *prep* (*with noun/pronoun*)
1 (*direction*) à; (: *towards*) vers; envers; **to go
to France/Portugal/London/school** aller
en France/au Portugal/à Londres/à l'école;
to go to Claude's/the doctor's aller chez
Claude/le docteur; **the road to Edinburgh**
la route d'Édimbourg
2 (*as far as*) (jusqu')à; **to count to 10**
compter jusqu'à 10; **from 40 to 50 people**
de 40 à 50 personnes
3 (*with expressions of time*): **a quarter to 5**
5 heures moins le quart; **it's twenty to 3**
il est 3 heures moins vingt
4 (*for, of*) de; **the key to the front door** la
clé de la porte d'entrée; **a letter to his wife**
une lettre (adressée) à sa femme
5 (*expressing indirect object*) à; **to give
sth to sb** donner qch à qn; **to talk to sb**
parler à qn; **to be a danger to sb** être
dangereux(-euse) pour qn

6 (*in relation to*) à; **3 goals to 2** 3 (buts) à 2;
30 miles to the gallon ≈ 9,4 litres aux
cent (km)
7 (*purpose, result*): **to come to sb's aid** venir
au secours de qn, porter secours à qn; **to
sentence sb to death** condamner qn à
mort; **to my surprise** à ma grande surprise
▶ *prep* (*with vb*) **1** (*simple infinitive*): **to go/
eat** aller/manger
2 (*following another vb*): **to want/try/start
to do** vouloir/essayer de/commencer à
faire
3 (*with vb omitted*): **I don't want to** je ne
veux pas
4 (*purpose, result*) pour; **I did it to help you**
je l'ai fait pour vous aider
5 (*equivalent to relative clause*): **I have things
to do** j'ai des choses à faire; **the main thing
is to try** l'important est d'essayer
6 (*after adjective etc*): **ready to go** prêt(e)
à partir; **too old/young to ...** trop vieux/
jeune pour ...
▶ *adv*: **push/pull the door to** tirez/poussez
la porte

toad [təud] *n* crapaud *m*; **toadstool** *n*
champignon (vénéneux)
toast [təust] *n* (*Culin*) pain grillé, toast *m*;
(*drink, speech*) toast ▷ *vt* (*Culin*) faire griller;
(*drink to*) porter un toast à; **toaster** *n* grille-
pain *m inv*
tobacco [tə'bækəu] *n* tabac *m*
toboggan [tə'bɔgən] *n* toboggan *m*;
(*child's*) luge *f*
today [tə'deɪ] *adv*, *n* (*also fig*) aujourd'hui (*m*)
toddler ['tɔdlər] *n* enfant *m/f* qui
commence à marcher, bambin *m*
toe [təu] *n* doigt *m* de pied, orteil *m*; (*of
shoe*) bout *m* ▷ *vt*: **to ~ the line** (*fig*) obéir, se
conformer; **toenail** *n* ongle *m* de l'orteil
toffee ['tɔfɪ] *n* caramel *m*
together [tə'gɛðər] *adv* ensemble; (*at same
time*) en même temps; **~ with** *prep* avec
toilet ['tɔɪlət] *n* (*BRIT: lavatory*) toilettes
fpl, cabinets *mpl*; **to go to the ~** aller
aux toilettes; **where's the ~?** où sont les
toilettes?; **toilet bag** *n* (*BRIT*) nécessaire
m de toilette; **toilet paper** *n* papier *m*
hygiénique; **toiletries** *npl* articles *mpl* de
toilette; **toilet roll** *n* rouleau *m* de papier
hygiénique
token ['təukən] *n* (*sign*) marque *f*,
témoignage *m*; (*metal disc*) jeton *m* ▷ *adj* (*fee,
strike*) symbolique; **book/record ~** (*BRIT*)
chèque-livre/-disque *m*
Tokyo ['təukjəu] *n* Tokyo
told [təuld] *pt, pp of* **tell**
tolerant ['tɔlərnt] *adj*: **~ (of)** tolérant(e)
(à l'égard de)
tolerate ['tɔləreɪt] *vt* supporter
toll [təul] *n* (*tax, charge*) péage *m* ▷ *vi* (*bell*)
sonner; **the accident ~ on the roads** le

nombre des victimes de la route; **toll call** n (US Tel) appel m (à) longue distance; **toll-free** adj (US) gratuit(e) ▷ adv gratuitement

tomato [tə'mɑːtəu] (pl **tomatoes**) n tomate f; **tomato sauce** n sauce f tomate

tomb [tuːm] n tombe f; **tombstone** n pierre tombale

tomorrow [tə'mɔrəu] adv, n (also fig) demain (m); **the day after ~** après-demain; **a week ~** demain en huit; **~ morning** demain matin

ton [tʌn] n tonne f (Brit: = 1016 kg; US = 907 kg; metric = 1000 kg); **~s of** (inf) des tas de

tone [təun] n ton m; (of radio, BRIT Tel) tonalité f ▷ vi (also: **~ in**) s'harmoniser; **tone down** vt (colour, criticism) adoucir

tongs [tɔnz] npl pinces fpl; (for coal) pincettes fpl; (for hair) fer m à friser

tongue [tʌn] n langue f; **~ in cheek** adv ironiquement

tonic [ˈtɔnɪk] n (Med) tonique m; (also: **~ water**) Schweppes® m

tonight [təˈnaɪt] adv, n cette nuit; (this evening) ce soir

tonne [tʌn] n (BRIT: metric ton) tonne f

tonsil [ˈtɔnsl] n amygdale f; **tonsillitis** [tɔnsɪ'laɪtɪs] n: **to have tonsillitis** avoir une angine or une amygdalite

too [tuː] adv (excessively) trop, (also) aussi; **~ much** (as adv) trop; (as adj) trop de; **~ many** adj trop de

took [tuk] pt of **take**

tool [tuːl] n outil m; **tool box** n boîte f à outils; **tool kit** n trousse f à outils

tooth (pl **teeth**) [tuːθ, tiːθ] n (Anat, Tech) dent f; **to brush one's teeth** se laver les dents; **toothache** n mal m de dents; **to have toothache** avoir mal aux dents; **toothbrush** n brosse f à dents; **toothpaste** n (pâte f) dentifrice m; **toothpick** n cure-dent m

top [tɔp] n (of mountain, head) sommet m; (of page, ladder) haut m; (of box, cupboard, table) dessus m; (lid: of box, jar) couvercle m; (: of bottle) bouchon m; (toy) toupie f; (Dress: blouse etc) haut m; (: of pyjamas) veste f ▷ adj du haut; (in rank) premier(-ière); (best) meilleur(e) ▷ vt (exceed) dépasser; (be first in) être en tête de; **from ~ to bottom** de fond en comble; **on ~ of** sur; (in addition to) en plus de; **over the ~** (inf) (behaviour etc) qui dépasse les limites; **top up**, (US) **top off** vt (bottle) remplir; (salary) compléter; **to ~ up one's mobile (phone)** recharger son compte; **top floor** n dernier étage; **top hat** n haut-de-forme m

topic [ˈtɔpɪk] n sujet m, thème m; **topical** adj d'actualité

topless [ˈtɔplɪs] adj (bather etc) aux seins nus

topping [ˈtɔpɪn] n (Culin) couche de crème, fromage etc qui recouvre un plat

topple [ˈtɔpl] vt renverser, faire tomber ▷ vi basculer; tomber

top-up [ˈtɔpʌp] n (for mobile phone) recharge f, minutes fpl; **top-up card** n (for mobile phone) recharge f

torch [tɔːtʃ] n torche f; (BRIT: electric) lampe f de poche

tore [tɔː'] pt of **tear²**

torment n [ˈtɔːmɛnt] tourment m ▷ vt [tɔːˈmɛnt] tourmenter; (fig: annoy) agacer

torn [tɔːn] pp of **tear²**

tornado [tɔːˈneɪdəu] (pl **tornadoes**) n tornade f

torpedo [tɔːˈpiːdəu] (pl **torpedoes**) n torpille f

torrent [ˈtɔrnt] n torrent m; **torrential** [tɔˈrɛnʃl] adj torrentiel(le)

tortoise [ˈtɔːtəs] n tortue f

torture [ˈtɔːtʃə'] n torture f ▷ vt torturer

Tory [ˈtɔːrɪ] adj, n (BRIT Pol) tory m/f, conservateur(-trice)

toss [tɔs] vt lancer, jeter; (BRIT: pancake) faire sauter; (head) rejeter en arrière ▷ vi: **to ~ up for sth** (BRIT) jouer qch à pile ou face; **to ~ a coin** jouer à pile ou face; **to ~ and turn** (in bed) se tourner et se retourner

total [ˈtəutl] adj total(e) ▷ n total m ▷ vt (add up) faire le total de, additionner; (amount to) s'élever à

totalitarian [təutælɪ'tɛərɪən] adj totalitaire

totally [ˈtəutəlɪ] adv totalement

touch [tʌtʃ] n contact m, toucher m; (sense, skill: of pianist etc) toucher ▷ vt (gen) toucher; (tamper with) toucher à; **a ~ of** (fig) un petit peu de; une touche de; **to get in ~ with** prendre contact avec; **to lose ~** (friends) se perdre de vue; **touch down** vi (Aviat) atterrir; (on sea) amerrir; **touchdown** n (Aviat) atterrissage m; (on sea) amerrissage m; (US Football) essai m; **touched** adj (moved) touché(e), **touching** adj touchant(e), attendrissant(e); **touchline** n (Sport) (ligne f de) touche f; **touch-sensitive** adj (keypad) à effleurement; (screen) tactile

tough [tʌf] adj dur(e); (resistant) résistant(e), solide; (meat) dur, coriace; (firm) inflexible; (task, problem, situation) difficile

tour [ˈtuə'] n voyage m; (also: **package ~**) voyage organisé; (of town, museum) tour m, visite f; (by band) tournée f ▷ vt visiter; **tour guide** n (person) guide m/f

tourism [ˈtuərɪzm] n tourisme m

tourist [ˈtuərɪst] n touriste m/f ▷ cpd touristique; **tourist office** n syndicat m d'initiative

tournament [ˈtuənəmənt] n tournoi m

tour operator n (BRIT) organisateur m de voyages, tour-opérateur m

tow [təʊ] vt remorquer; (caravan, trailer) tracter; "**on ~**", (US) "**in ~**" (Aut) "véhicule en remorque"; **tow away** vt (subj: police) emmener à la fourrière; (: breakdown service) remorquer

toward(s) [təˈwɔːd(z)] prep vers; (of attitude) envers, à l'égard de; (of purpose) pour

towel ['taʊəl] n serviette f (de toilette); **towelling** n (fabric) tissu-éponge m

tower ['taʊəʳ] n tour f; **tower block** n (BRIT) tour f (d'habitation)

town [taʊn] n ville f; **to go to ~** aller en ville; (fig) mettre le paquet; **town centre** n (BRIT) centre m de la ville, centre-ville m; **town hall** n ≈ mairie f

tow truck n (US) dépanneuse f

toxic ['tɔksɪk] adj toxique

toy [tɔɪ] n jouet m; **toy with** vt fus jouer avec; (idea) caresser; **toyshop** n magasin m de jouets

trace [treɪs] n trace f ▷ vt (draw) tracer, dessiner; (follow) suivre la trace de; (locate) retrouver

tracing paper ['treɪsɪŋ-] n papier-calque m

track [træk] n (mark) trace f; (path: gen) chemin m, piste f; (: of bullet etc) trajectoire f; (: of suspect, animal) piste f; (Rail) voie ferrée, rails mpl; (Comput, Sport) piste f; (on CD) piste f; (on record) plage f ▷ vt suivre la trace ou la piste de; **to keep ~ of** suivre; **track down** vt (prey) trouver et capturer; (sth lost) finir par retrouver; **tracksuit** n survêtement m

tractor ['træktəʳ] n tracteur m

trade [treɪd] n commerce m; (skill, job) métier m ▷ vi faire du commerce ▷ vt (exchange): **to ~ sth (for sth)** échanger qch (contre qch); **to ~ with/in** faire du commerce avec/le commerce de; **trade in** vt (old car etc) faire reprendre; **trademark** n marque f de fabrique; **trader** n commerçant(e), négociant(e); **tradesman** (irreg) (shopkeeper) commerçant m; **trade union** n syndicat m

trading ['treɪdɪŋ] n affaires fpl, commerce m

tradition [trə'dɪʃən] n tradition f; **traditional** adj traditionnel(le)

traffic ['træfɪk] n trafic m; (cars) circulation f ▷ vi: **to ~ in** (pej: liquor, drugs) faire le trafic de; **traffic circle** n (US) rond-point m; **traffic island** n refuge m (pour piétons); **traffic jam** n embouteillage m; **traffic lights** npl feux mpl (de signalisation); **traffic warden** n contractuel(le)

tragedy ['trædʒədɪ] n tragédie f

tragic ['trædʒɪk] adj tragique

trail [treɪl] n (tracks) trace f, piste f; (path) chemin m, piste; (of smoke etc) traînée f ▷ vt (drag) traîner, tirer; (follow) suivre ▷ vi traîner; (in game, contest) être en retard;

trailer n (Aut) remorque f; (US: caravan) caravane f; (Cine) bande-annonce f

train [treɪn] n train m; (in underground) rame f; (of dress) traîne f; (BRIT: series): **~ of events** série f d'événements ▷ vt (apprentice, doctor etc) former; (Sport) entraîner; (dog) dresser; (memory) exercer; (point: gun etc): **to ~ sth on** braquer qch sur ▷ vi recevoir sa formation; (Sport) s'entraîner; **one's ~ of thought** le fil de sa pensée; **what time does the ~ from Paris get in?** à quelle heure arrive le train de Paris?; **is this the ~ for ...?** c'est bien le train pour ...?; **trainee** [treɪ'niː] n stagiaire m/f; (in trade) apprenti(e); **trainer** n (Sport) entraîneur(-euse); (of dogs etc) dresseur(-euse); **trainers** npl (shoes) chaussures fpl de sport; **training** n formation f; (Sport) entraînement m; (of dog etc) dressage m; **in training** (Sport) à l'entraînement; (fit) en forme; **training course** n cours m de formation professionnelle; **training shoes** npl chaussures fpl de sport

trait [treɪt] n trait m (de caractère)

traitor ['treɪtəʳ] n traître m

tram [træm] n (BRIT: also: **~car**) tram(way) m

tramp [træmp] n (person) vagabond(e), clochard(e); (inf, pej: woman): **to be a ~** être coureuse

trample ['træmpl] vt: **to ~ (underfoot)** piétiner

trampoline ['træmpəliːn] n trampoline m

tranquil ['træŋkwɪl] adj tranquille; **tranquillizer**, (US) **tranquilizer** n (Med) tranquillisant m

transaction [træn'zækʃən] n transaction f

transatlantic ['trænzət'læntɪk] adj transatlantique

transcript ['trænskrɪpt] n transcription f (texte)

transfer n ['trænsfəʳ] (gen, also Sport) transfert m; (Pol: of power) passation f; (of money) virement m; (picture, design) décalcomanie f (: stick-on) autocollant m ▷ vt [træns'fəː'] transférer; passer; virer; **to ~ the charges** (BRIT Tel) téléphoner en P.C.V.

transform [træns'fɔːm] vt transformer; **transformation** n transformation f

transfusion [træns'fjuːʒən] n transfusion f

transit ['trænzɪt] n: **in ~** en transit

transition [træn'zɪʃən] n transition f

transitive ['trænzɪtɪv] adj (Ling) transitif(-ive)

translate [trænz'leɪt] vt: **to ~ (from/into)** traduire (du/en); **can you ~ this for me?** pouvez-vous me traduire ceci?; **translation** [trænz'leɪʃən] n traduction f; (Scol: as opposed to prose) version f; **translator** n traducteur(-trice)

transmission [trænz'mɪʃən] n transmission f

transmit [trænz'mɪt] vt transmettre; (Radio, TV) émettre; **transmitter** n émetteur m

transparent [træns'pærnt] adj transparent(e)

transplant ['trænsplɑ:nt] n (Med) transplantation f

transport n ['trænspɔ:t] transport m ▷ vt [træns'pɔ:t] transporter; **transportation** [trænspɔ:'teɪʃən] n (moyen m de) transport m

transvestite [trænz'vɛstaɪt] n travesti m

trap [træp] n (snare, trick) piège m; (carriage) cabriolet m ▷ vt prendre au piège; (confine) coincer

trash [træʃ] n (inf: pej: goods) camelote f; (: nonsense) sottises fpl; (us: rubbish) ordures fpl; **trash can** n (us) poubelle f

trauma ['trɔ:mə] n traumatisme m; **traumatic** [trɔ:'mætɪk] adj traumatisant(e)

travel ['trævl] n voyage(s) m(pl) ▷ vi voyager; (news, sound) se propager ▷ vt (distance) parcourir; **travel agency** n agence f de voyages; **travel agent** n agent m de voyages; **travel insurance** n assurance-voyage f; **traveller**, (us) **traveler** n voyageur(-euse); **traveller's cheque**, (us) **traveler's check** n chèque m de voyage; **travelling**, (us) **traveling** n voyage(s) m(pl); **travel-sick** adj: **to get travel-sick** avoir le mal de la route (or de mer or de l'air); **travel sickness** n mal m de la route (or de mer or de l'air)

tray [treɪ] n (for carrying) plateau m; (on desk) corbeille f

treacherous ['trɛtʃərəs] adj traître(sse); (ground, tide) dont il faut se méfier

treacle ['tri:kl] n mélasse f

tread [trɛd] n (step) pas m; (sound) bruit m de pas; (of tyre) chape f, bande f de roulement ▷ vi (pt trod, pp trodden) marcher; **tread on** vt fus marcher sur

treasure ['trɛʒər] n trésor m ▷ vt (value) tenir beaucoup à; **treasurer** n trésorier(-ière)

treasury ['trɛʒərɪ] n: **the T~**, (us) **the T~ Department** ≈ le ministère des Finances

treat [tri:t] n petit cadeau, petite surprise ▷ vt traiter; **to ~ sb to sth** offrir qch à qn; **treatment** n traitement m

treaty ['tri:tɪ] n traité m

treble ['trɛbl] adj triple ▷ vt, vi tripler

tree [tri:] n arbre m

trek [trɛk] n (long walk) randonnée f; (tiring walk) longue marche, trotte f

tremble ['trɛmbl] vi trembler

tremendous [trɪ'mɛndəs] adj (enormous) énorme; (excellent) formidable, fantastique

trench [trɛntʃ] n tranchée f

trend [trɛnd] n (tendency) tendance f; (of events) cours m; (fashion) mode f; **trendy** adj (idea, person) dans le vent; (clothes) dernier cri inv

trespass ['trɛspəs] vi: **to ~ on** s'introduire sans permission dans; **"no ~ing"** "propriété privée", "défense d'entrer"

trial ['traɪəl] n (Law) procès m, jugement m; (test: of machine etc) essai m; **trials** npl (unpleasant experiences) épreuves fpl; **trial period** n période f d'essai

triangle ['traɪæŋgl] n (Math, Mus) triangle m

triangular [traɪ'æŋgjulər] adj triangulaire

tribe [traɪb] n tribu f

tribunal [traɪ'bju:nl] n tribunal m

tribute ['trɪbju:t] n tribut m, hommage m; **to pay ~ to** rendre hommage à

trick [trɪk] n (magic) tour m; (joke, prank) tour, farce f; (skill, knack) astuce f; (Cards) levée f ▷ vt attraper, rouler; **to play a ~ on sb** jouer un tour à qn; **that should do the ~** (inf) ça devrait faire l'affaire

trickle ['trɪkl] n (of water etc) filet m ▷ vi couler en un filet or goutte à goutte

tricky ['trɪkɪ] adj difficile, délicat(e)

tricycle ['traɪsɪkl] n tricycle m

trifle ['traɪfl] n bagatelle f; (Culin) ≈ diplomate m ▷ adv: **a ~ long** un peu long

trigger ['trɪgər] n (of gun) gâchette f

trim [trɪm] adj (house, garden) bien tenu(e); (figure) svelte ▷ n (haircut etc) légère coupe; (on car) garnitures fpl ▷ vt (cut) couper légèrement; (Naut: a sail) gréer; (decorate): **to ~ (with)** décorer (de)

trio ['tri:əu] n trio m

trip [trɪp] n voyage m; (excursion) excursion f; (stumble) faux pas ▷ vi faire un faux pas, trébucher; **trip up** vi trébucher ▷ vt faire un croc-en-jambe à

triple ['trɪpl] adj triple

triplets ['trɪplɪts] npl triplés(-ées)

tripod ['traɪpɔd] n trépied m

triumph ['traɪʌmf] n triomphe m ▷ vi: **to ~ (over)** triompher (de); **triumphant** [traɪ'ʌmfənt] adj triomphant(e)

trivial ['trɪvɪəl] adj insignifiant(e); (commonplace) banal(e)

trod [trɔd] pt of **tread**

trodden ['trɔdn] pp of **tread**

troll [trɔl] n (Comput) troll m, trolleur(-euse) m/f

trolley ['trɔlɪ] n chariot m

trombone [trɔm'bəun] n trombone m

troop [tru:p] n bande f, groupe m; **troops** npl (Mil) troupes fpl (: men) hommes mpl, soldats mpl

trophy ['trəufɪ] n trophée m

tropical ['trɔpɪkl] adj tropical(e)

trot [trɔt] n trot m ▷ vi trotter; **on the ~** (BRIT fig) d'affilée

trouble ['trʌbl] n difficulté(s) f(pl), problème(s) m(pl); (worry) ennuis mpl, soucis mpl; (bother, effort) peine f; (Pol)

conflit(s) m(pl), troubles mpl; (Med):
stomach etc ~ troubles gastriques etc ▷ vt
(disturb) déranger, gêner; (worry) inquiéter
▷ vi: **to ~ to do** prendre la peine de faire;
troubles npl (Pol etc) troubles; (personal)
ennuis, soucis; **to be in ~** avoir des ennuis;
(ship, climber etc) être en difficulté; **to have
~ doing sth** avoir du mal à faire qch; **it's no
~!** je vous en prie!; **the ~ is ...** le problème,
c'est que ...; **what's the ~?** qu'est-ce qui ne
va pas?; **troubled** adj (person) inquiet(-ète);
(times, life) agitée(e); **troublemaker** n
élément perturbateur, fauteur m de
troubles; **troublesome** adj (child)
fatigant(e), difficile; (cough) gênant(e)
trough [trɔf] n (also: **drinking ~**) abreuvoir
m; (also: **feeding ~**) auge f; (depression)
creux m
trousers ['trauzəz] npl pantalon m; **short ~**
(BRIT) culottes courtes
trout [traut] n (pl inv) truite f
truant ['truənt] n: **to play ~** (BRIT) faire
l'école buissonnière
truce [truːs] n trêve f
truck [trʌk] n camion m; (Rail) wagon m à
plate-forme; **truck driver** n camionneur m
true [truː] adj vrai(e); (accurate) exact(e);
(genuine) vrai, véritable; (faithful) fidèle; **to
come ~** se réaliser
truly ['truːlɪ] adv vraiment, réellement; (for
truthfully) sans mentir; **yours ~** (in letter) je
vous prie d'agréer, Monsieur (or Madame
etc), l'expression de mes sentiments
respectueux
trumpet ['trʌmpɪt] n trompette f
trunk [trʌŋk] n (of tree, person) tronc m; (of
elephant) trompe f; (case) malle f; (US Aut)
coffre m; **trunks** npl (also: **swimming ~s**)
maillot m or slip m de bain
trust [trʌst] n confiance f; (responsibility): **to
place sth in sb's ~** confier la responsabilité
de qch à qn; (Law) fidéicommis m ▷ vt (rely
on) avoir confiance en; **to ~ sth
to sb** confier qch à qn; (hope): **to ~ (that)**
espérer (que); **to take sth on ~** accepter
qch les yeux fermés; **trusted** adj en qui l'on
a confiance; **trustworthy** adj digne de
confiance
truth [truːθ, truːðz] n vérité f; **truthful** adj
(person) qui dit la vérité; (answer) sincère
try [traɪ] n essai m, tentative f; (Rugby) essai
▷ vt (attempt) essayer, tenter; (test: sth new:
also: ~ **out**) essayer, tester; (Law: person)
juger; (strain) éprouver ▷ vi essayer; **to ~
to do** essayer de faire; (seek) chercher à
faire; **try on** vt (clothes) essayer; **trying** adj
pénible
T-shirt ['tiːʃəːt] n tee-shirt m
tub [tʌb] n cuve f; (for washing clothes)
baquet m; (bath) baignoire f
tube [tjuːb] n tube m; (BRIT: underground)
métro m; (for tyre) chambre f à air

tuberculosis [tjubə:kjuˈləusɪs] n
tuberculose f
tube station n (BRIT) station f de métro
tuck [tʌk] vt (put) mettre; **tuck away** vt
cacher, ranger; (money) mettre de côté;
(building): **to be ~ed away** être caché(e);
tuck in vt rentrer; (child) border ▷ vi (eat)
manger de bon appétit; attaquer le repas
tucker ['tʌkəʳ] n (AUST, NZ inf) bouffe f (inf)
tuck shop n (BRIT Scol) boutique f à
provisions
Tuesday ['tjuːzdɪ] n mardi m
tug [tʌg] n (ship) remorqueur m ▷ vt tirer
(sur)
tuition [tjuːˈɪʃən] n (BRIT: lessons) leçons fpl;
(: private) cours particuliers; (US: fees) frais
mpl de scolarité
tulip ['tjuːlɪp] n tulipe f
tumble ['tʌmbl] n (fall) chute f, culbute f
▷ vi tomber, dégringoler; **to ~ to sth** (inf)
réaliser qch; **tumble dryer** n (BRIT) séchoir
m (à linge) à air chaud
tumbler ['tʌmblə'] n verre (droit),
gobelet m
tummy ['tʌmɪ] n (inf) ventre m
tumour, (US) **tumor** ['tjuːmə'] n tumeur f
tuna ['tjuːnə] n (pl inv: also: ~ **fish**) thon m
tune [tjuːn] n (melody) air m ▷ vt (Mus)
accorder; (Radio, TV, Aut) régler, mettre au
point; **to be in/out of ~** (instrument) être
accordé/désaccordé; (singer) chanter juste/
faux; **tune in** vi (Radio, TV): **to ~ in (to)** se
mettre à l'écoute (de); **tune up** vi (musician)
accorder son instrument
tunic ['tjuːnɪk] n tunique f
Tunis ['tjuːnɪs] n Tunis
Tunisia [tjuːˈnɪzɪə] n Tunisie f
Tunisian [tjuːˈnɪzɪən] adj tunisien(ne) ▷ n
Tunisien(ne)
tunnel ['tʌnl] n tunnel m; (in mine) galerie f
▷ vi creuser un tunnel (or une galerie)
turbulence ['təːbjuləns] n (Aviat)
turbulence f
turf [təːf] n gazon m; (clod) motte f (de
gazon) ▷ vt gazonner
Turk [təːk] n Turc (Turque)
Turkey ['təːkɪ] n Turquie f
turkey ['təːkɪ] n dindon m, dinde f
Turkish ['təːkɪʃ] adj turc (turque) ▷ n (Ling)
turc m
turmoil ['təːmɔɪl] n trouble m,
bouleversement m
turn [təːn] n tour m; (in road) tournant
m; (tendency: of mind, events) tournure
f; (performance) numéro m; (Med) crise
f, attaque f ▷ vt tourner; (collar, steak)
retourner; (age) atteindre; (change): **to ~
sth into** changer qch en ▷ vi (object, wind,
milk) tourner; (person: look back) se (re)
tourner; (reverse direction) faire demi-tour;
(become) devenir; **to ~ into** se changer en, se
transformer en; **a good ~** un service;

it gave me quite a ~ ça m'a fait un coup;
"no left ~" (*Aut*) "défense de tourner à
gauche"; **~ left/right at the next junction**
tournez à gauche/droite au prochain
carrefour; **it's your ~** c'est (à) votre tour;
in ~ à son tour; à tour de rôle; **to take
~s** se relayer; **turn around** *vi* (*person*) se
retourner ▷ *vt* (*object*) tourner; **turn away**
vi se détourner, tourner la tête ▷ *vt* (*reject:
person*) renvoyer; (: *business*) refuser; **turn
back** *vi* revenir, faire demi-tour; **turn
down** *vt* (*refuse*) rejeter, refuser; (*reduce*)
baisser; (*fold*) rabattre; **turn in** *vi* (*inf: go
to bed*) aller se coucher ▷ *vt* (*fold*) rentrer;
turn off *vi* (*from road*) tourner ▷ *vt* (*light,
radio etc*) éteindre; (*tap*) fermer; (*engine*)
arrêter; **I can't ~ the heating off** je n'arrive
pas à éteindre le chauffage; **turn on** *vt*
(*light, radio etc*) allumer; (*tap*) ouvrir; (*engine*)
mettre en marche; **I can't ~ the heating
on** je n'arrive pas à allumer le chauffage;
turn out *vt* (*light, gas*) éteindre; (*produce*)
produire ▷ *vi* (*voters, troops*) se présenter;
to ~ out to be ... s'avérer ..., se révéler ...;
turn over *vi* (*person*) se retourner ▷ *vt*
(*object*) retourner; (*page*) tourner; **turn
round** *vi* faire demi-tour; (*rotate*) tourner;
turn to *vt fus*: **to ~ to sb** s'adresser à qn;
turn up *vi* (*person*) arriver, se pointer (*inf*),
(*lost object*) être retrouvé(e) ▷ *vt* (*collar*)
remonter; (*radio, heater*) mettre plus fort;
turning *n* (*in road*) tournant *m*; **turning
point** *n* (*fig*) tournant *m*, moment décisif
turnip ['tə:nɪp] *n* navet *m*
turn: turnout *n* (*of voters*) taux *m* de
participation; **turnover** *n* (*Comm: amount
of money*) chiffre *m* d'affaires; (: *of goods*)
roulement *m*; (*of staff*) renouvellement *m*,
changement *m*; **turnstile** *n* tourniquet
m (*d'entrée*); **turn-up** *n* (*BRIT: on trousers*)
revers *m*
turquoise ['tə:kwɔɪz] *n* (*stone*) turquoise *f*
▷ *adj* turquoise *inv*
turtle ['tə:tl] *n* tortue marine; **turtleneck
(sweater)** *n* pullover *m* à col montant
tusk [tʌsk] *n* défense *f* (*d'éléphant*)
tutor ['tju:təʳ] *n* (*BRIT Scol: in college*)
directeur(-trice) d'études; (*private teacher*)
précepteur(-trice); **tutorial** [tju:'tɔ:rɪəl] *n*
(*Scol*) (séance *f* de) travaux *mpl* pratiques
tuxedo [tʌk'si:dəu] *n* (*US*) smoking *m*
TV [ti:'vi:] *n abbr* (= *television*) télé *f*, TV *f*
tweed [twi:d] *n* tweed *m*
tweet [twi:t] (*on Twitter*) *n* tweet *m* ▷ *vt, vi*
tweeter
tweezers ['twi:zəz] *npl* pince *f* à épiler
twelfth [twɛlfθ] *num* douzième
twelve [twɛlv] *num* douze; **at ~ (o'clock)** à
midi; (*midnight*) à minuit
twentieth ['twɛntɪɪθ] *num* vingtième
twenty ['twɛntɪ] *num* vingt; **in ~ fourteen**
en deux mille quatorze

twice [twaɪs] *adv* deux fois; **~ as much** deux
fois plus
twig [twɪg] *n* brindille *f* ▷ *vt, vi* (*inf*) piger
twilight ['twaɪlaɪt] *n* crépuscule *m*
twin [twɪn] *adj, n* jumeau(-elle) ▷ *vt*
jumeler; **twin-bedded room** *n* = **twin
room**; **twin beds** *npl* lits *mpl* jumeaux
twinkle ['twɪŋkl] *vi* scintiller; (*eyes*) pétiller
twin room *n* chambre *f* à deux lits
twist [twɪst] *n* torsion *f*, tour *m*; (*in wire,
flex*) tortillon *m*; (*bend: in road*) tournant
m; (*in story*) coup *m* de théâtre ▷ *vt* tordre;
(*weave*) entortiller; (*roll around*) enrouler;
(*fig*) déformer ▷ *vi* (*road, river*) serpenter;
to ~ one's ankle/wrist (*Med*) se tordre la
cheville/le poignet
twit [twɪt] *n* (*inf*) crétin(e)
twitch [twɪtʃ] *n* (*pull*) coup sec, saccade *f*;
(*nervous*) tic *m* ▷ *vi* se convulser; avoir un tic
two [tu:] *num* deux; **to put ~ and ~
together** (*fig*) faire le rapprochement
type [taɪp] *n* (*category*) genre *m*, espèce *f*;
(*model*) modèle *m*; (*example*) type *m*; (*Typ*)
type, caractère *m* ▷ *vt* (*letter etc*) taper (à la
machine); **typewriter** *n* machine *f* à écrire
typhoid ['taɪfɔɪd] *n* typhoïde *f*
typhoon [taɪ'fu:n] *n* typhon *m*
typical ['tɪpɪkl] *adj* typique,
caractéristique; **typically** ['tɪpɪklɪ] *adv* (*as
usual*) comme d'habitude; (*characteristically*)
typiquement
typing ['taɪpɪŋ] *n* dactylo(graphie) *f*
typist ['taɪpɪst] *n* dactylo *m/f*
tyre, (*US*) **tire** ['taɪəʳ] *n* pneu *m*; **tyre
pressure** *n* (*BRIT*) pression *f* (de gonflage)

U

UFO ['juːfəu] *n abbr* (= *unidentified flying object*) ovni *m*

Uganda [juːˈgændə] *n* Ouganda *m*

ugly ['ʌglɪ] *adj* laid(e), vilain(e); (*fig*) répugnant(e)

UHT *adj abbr* (= *ultra-heat treated*): **~ milk** lait *m* UHT *or* longue conservation

UK *n abbr* = **United Kingdom**

ulcer ['ʌlsəʳ] *n* ulcère *m*; **mouth ~** aphte *f*

ultimate ['ʌltɪmət] *adj* ultime, final(e); (*authority*) suprême; **ultimately** *adv* (*at last*) en fin de compte; (*fundamentally*) finalement; (*eventually*) par la suite

ultimatum (*pl* **ultimatums** *or* **ultimata**) [ʌltɪˈmeɪtəm, -tə] *n* ultimatum *m*

ultrasound ['ʌltrəsaund] *n* (*Med*) ultrason *m*

ultraviolet ['ʌltrəˈvaɪəlɪt] *adj* ultraviolet(te)

umbrella [ʌmˈbrɛlə] *n* parapluie *m*; (*for sun*) parasol *m*

umpire ['ʌmpaɪəʳ] *n* arbitre *m*; (*Tennis*) juge *m* de chaise

UN *n abbr* = **United Nations**

unable [ʌnˈeɪbl] *adj*: **to be ~ to** ne (pas) pouvoir, être dans l'impossibilité de; (*not capable*) être incapable de

unacceptable [ʌnəkˈsɛptəbl] *adj* (*behaviour*) inadmissible; (*price, proposal*) inacceptable

unanimous [juːˈnænɪməs] *adj* unanime

unarmed [ʌnˈɑːmd] *adj* (*person*) non armé(e); (*combat*) sans armes

unattended [ʌnəˈtɛndɪd] *adj* (*car, child, luggage*) sans surveillance

unattractive [ʌnəˈtræktɪv] *adj* peu attrayant(e); (*character*) peu sympathique

unavailable [ʌnəˈveɪləbl] *adj* (*article, room, book*) (qui n'est) pas disponible; (*person*) (qui n'est) pas libre

unavoidable [ʌnəˈvɔɪdəbl] *adj* inévitable

unaware [ʌnəˈwɛəʳ] *adj*: **to be ~ of** ignorer, ne pas savoir, être inconscient(e) de; **unawares** *adv* à l'improviste, au dépourvu

unbearable [ʌnˈbɛərəbl] *adj* insupportable

unbeatable [ʌnˈbiːtəbl] *adj* imbattable

unbelievable [ʌnbɪˈliːvəbl] *adj* incroyable

unborn [ʌnˈbɔːn] *adj* à naître

unbutton [ʌnˈbʌtn] *vt* déboutonner

uncalled-for [ʌnˈkɔːldfɔːʳ] *adj* déplacé(e), injustifié(e)

uncanny [ʌnˈkænɪ] *adj* étrange, troublant(e)

uncertain [ʌnˈsəːtn] *adj* incertain(e); (*hesitant*) hésitant(e); **uncertainty** *n* incertitude *f*, doutes *mpl*

unchanged [ʌnˈtʃeɪndʒd] *adj* inchangé(e)

uncle ['ʌŋkl] *n* oncle *m*

unclear [ʌnˈklɪəʳ] *adj* (qui n'est) pas clair(e) *or* évident(e); **I'm still ~ about what I'm supposed to do** je ne sais pas encore exactement ce que je dois faire

uncomfortable [ʌnˈkʌmfətəbl] *adj* inconfortable, peu confortable; (*uneasy*) mal à l'aise, gêné(e); (*situation*) désagréable

uncommon [ʌnˈkɔmən] *adj* rare, singulier(-ière), peu commun(e)

unconditional [ʌnkənˈdɪʃənl] *adj* sans conditions

unconscious [ʌnˈkɔnʃəs] *adj* sans connaissance, évanoui(e); (*unaware*): **~ (of)** inconscient(e) (de) ▷ *n*: **the ~** l'inconscient *m*

uncontrollable [ʌnkənˈtrəuləbl] *adj* (*child, dog*) indiscipliné(e); (*temper, laughter*) irrépressible

unconventional [ʌnkənˈvɛnʃənl] *adj* peu conventionnel(le)

uncover [ʌnˈkʌvəʳ] *vt* découvrir

undecided [ʌndɪˈsaɪdɪd] *adj* indécis(e), irrésolu(e)

undeniable [ʌndɪˈnaɪəbl] *adj* indéniable, incontestable

under ['ʌndəʳ] *prep* sous; (*less than*) (de) moins de; au-dessous de; (*according to*) selon, en vertu de ▷ *adv* au-dessous; en dessous; **~ there** là-dessous; **~ the circumstances** étant donné les circonstances; **~ repair** en (cours de) réparation; **undercover** *adj* secret(-ète), clandestin(e); **underdone** *adj* (*Culin*) saignant(e); (: *pej*) pas assez cuit(e); **underestimate** *vt* sous-estimer, mésestimer; **undergo** *vt* (*irreg: like* **go**) subir; (*treatment*) suivre; **undergraduate** *n* étudiant(e) (qui prépare une licence); **underground** *adj* souterrain(e); (*fig*) clandestin(e) ▷ *n* (*BRIT: railway*) métro *m*; (*Pol*) clandestinité *f*; **undergrowth** *n* broussailles *fpl*, sous-bois *m*; **underline** *vt* souligner; **undermine** *vt* saper, miner; **underneath** [ʌndəˈniːθ] *adv* (en) dessous ▷ *prep* sous, au-dessous de; **underpants** *npl* caleçon *m*, slip *m*; **underpass** *n* (*BRIT: for pedestrians*) passage souterrain; (: *for cars*) passage inférieur; **underprivileged** *adj* défavorisé(e); **underscore** *vt* souligner; **undershirt** *n* (*US*) tricot *m* de corps; **underskirt** *n* (*BRIT*) jupon *m*

understand [ʌndə'stænd] *vt, vi* (*irreg: like* **stand**) comprendre; **I don't ~** je ne comprends pas; **understandable** *adj* compréhensible; **understanding** *adj* compréhensif(-ive) ▷ *n* compréhension *f*; (*agreement*) accord *m*

understatement ['ʌndəsteitmənt] *n*: **that's an ~** c'est (bien) peu dire, le terme est faible

understood [ʌndə'stud] *pt, pp of* **understand** ▷ *adj* entendu(e); (*implied*) sous-entendu(e)

undertake [ʌndə'teik] *vt* (*irreg: like* **take**) (*job, task*) entreprendre; (*duty*) se charger de; **to ~ to do sth** s'engager à faire qch

undertaker ['ʌndəteikəʳ] *n* (*BRIT*) entrepreneur *m* des pompes funèbres, croque-mort *m*

undertaking ['ʌndəteikiŋ] *n* entreprise *f*; (*promise*) promesse *f*

under: underwater *adv* sous l'eau ▷ *adj* sous-marin(e); **underway** *adj*: **to be underway** (*meeting, investigation*) être en cours; **underwear** *n* sous-vêtements *mpl*; (*women's only*) dessous *mpl*; **underwent** *pt of* **undergo**; **underworld** *n* (*of crime*) milieu *m*, pègre *f*

undesirable [ʌndi'zaiərəbl] *adj* peu souhaitable; (*person, effect*) indésirable

undisputed ['ʌndis'pju:tid] *adj* incontesté(e)

undo [ʌn'du:] *vt* (*irreg: like* **do**) défaire

undone [ʌn'dʌn] *pp of* **undo** ▷ *adj*: **to come ~** se défaire

undoubtedly [ʌn'dautidli] *adv* sans aucun doute

undress [ʌn'dres] *vi* se déshabiller

unearth [ʌn'ə:θ] *vt* déterrer; (*fig*) dénicher

uneasy [ʌn'i:zi] *adj* mal à l'aise, gêné(e); (*worried*) inquiet(-ète); (*feeling*) désagréable; (*peace, truce*) fragile

unemployed [ʌnim'plɔid] *adj* sans travail, au chômage ▷ *n*: **the ~** les chômeurs *mpl*

unemployment [ʌnim'plɔimənt] *n* chômage *m*; **unemployment benefit**, (*US*) **unemployment compensation** *n* allocation *f* de chômage

unequal [ʌn'i:kwəl] *adj* inégal(e)

uneven [ʌn'i:vn] *adj* inégal(e); (*quality, work*) irrégulier(-ière)

unexpected [ʌnik'spektid] *adj* inattendu(e), imprévu(e); **unexpectedly** *adv* (*succeed*) contre toute attente; (*arrive*) à l'improviste

unfair [ʌn'fɛəʳ] *adj*: **~ (to)** injuste (envers)

unfaithful [ʌn'feiθful] *adj* infidèle

unfamiliar [ʌnfə'miliəʳ] *adj* étrange, inconnu(e); **to be ~ with sth** mal connaître qch

unfashionable [ʌn'fæʃnəbl] *adj* (*clothes*) démodé(e); (*place*) peu chic *inv*

unfasten [ʌn'fɑ:sn] *vt* défaire; (*belt, necklace*) détacher; (*open*) ouvrir

unfavourable, (*US*) **unfavorable** [ʌn'feivrəbl] *adj* défavorable

unfinished [ʌn'finiʃt] *adj* inachevé(e)

unfit [ʌn'fit] *adj* (*physically: ill*) en mauvaise santé; (: *out of condition*) pas en forme; (*incompetent*): **~ (for)** impropre (à); (*work, service*) inapte (à)

unfold [ʌn'fəuld] *vt* déplier ▷ *vi* se dérouler

unforgettable [ʌnfə'getəbl] *adj* inoubliable

unfortunate [ʌn'fɔ:tʃnət] *adj* malheureux(-euse); (*event, remark*) malencontreux(-euse); **unfortunately** *adv* malheureusement

unfriend [ʌn'frend] *vt* (*Internet*) supprimer de sa liste d'amis

unfriendly [ʌn'frendli] *adj* peu aimable, froid(e)

unfurnished [ʌn'fə:niʃt] *adj* non meublé(e)

unhappiness [ʌn'hæpinis] *n* tristesse *f*, peine *f*

unhappy [ʌn'hæpi] *adj* triste, malheureux(-euse); (*unfortunate: remark etc*) malheureux(-euse); (*not pleased*): **~ with** mécontent(e) de, peu satisfait(e) de

unhealthy [ʌn'hɛlθi] *adj* (*gen*) malsain(e); (*person*) maladif(-ive)

unheard-of [ʌn'hə:dɔv] *adj* inouï(e), sans précédent

unhelpful [ʌn'hɛlpful] *adj* (*person*) peu serviable; (*advice*) peu utile

unhurt [ʌn'hə:t] *adj* indemne, sain(e) et sauf

unidentified [ʌnai'dentifaid] *adj* non identifié(e); *see also* **UFO**

uniform ['ju:nifɔ:m] *n* uniforme *m* ▷ *adj* uniforme

unify ['ju:nifai] *vt* unifier

unimportant [ʌnim'pɔ:tənt] *adj* sans importance

uninhabited [ʌnin'hæbitid] *adj* inhabité(e)

unintentional [ʌnin'tenʃənəl] *adj* involontaire

union ['ju:njən] *n* union *f*; (*also:* **trade ~**) syndicat *m* ▷ *cpd* du syndicat, syndical(e); **Union Jack** *n* drapeau du Royaume-Uni

unique [ju:'ni:k] *adj* unique

unisex ['ju:niseks] *adj* unisexe

unit ['ju:nit] *n* unité *f*; (*section: of furniture etc*) élément *m*, bloc *m*; (*team, squad*) groupe *m*, service *m*; **kitchen ~** élément de cuisine

unite [ju:'nait] *vt* unir ▷ *vi* s'unir; **united** *adj* uni(e); (*country, party*) unifié(e); (*efforts*) conjugué(e); **United Kingdom** *n*

Royaume-Uni *m*; **United Nations (Organization)** *n* (Organisation *f* des) Nations unies; **United States (of America)** *n* États-Unis *mpl*

unity ['juːnɪtɪ] *n* unité *f*

universal [juːnɪ'vəːsl] *adj* universel(le)

universe ['juːnɪvəːs] *n* univers *m*

university [juːnɪ'vəːsɪtɪ] *n* université *f* ▷ *cpd* (*student, professor*) d'université; (*education, year, degree*) universitaire

unjust [ʌn'dʒʌst] *adj* injuste

unkind [ʌn'kaɪnd] *adj* peu gentil(le), méchant(e)

unknown [ʌn'nəʊn] *adj* inconnu(e)

unlawful [ʌn'lɔːful] *adj* illégal(e)

unleaded [ʌn'lɛdɪd] *n* (*also*: **~ petrol**) essence *f* sans plomb

unleash [ʌn'liːʃ] *vt* (*fig*) déchaîner, déclencher

unless [ʌn'lɛs] *conj*: **~ he leaves** à moins qu'il (ne) parte; **~ otherwise stated** sauf indication contraire

unlike [ʌn'laɪk] *adj* dissemblable, différent(e) ▷ *prep* à la différence de, contrairement à

unlikely [ʌn'laɪklɪ] *adj* (*result, event*) improbable; (*explanation*) invraisemblable

unlimited [ʌn'lɪmɪtɪd] *adj* illimité(e)

unlisted ['ʌn'lɪstɪd] *adj* (*us Tel*) sur la liste rouge

unload [ʌn'ləʊd] *vt* décharger

unlock [ʌn'lɔk] *vt* ouvrir

unlucky [ʌn'lʌkɪ] *adj* (*person*) malchanceux(-euse); (*object, number*) qui porte malheur; **to be ~** (*person*) ne pas avoir de chance

unmarried [ʌn'mærɪd] *adj* célibataire

unmistak(e)able [ʌnmɪs'teɪkəbl] *adj* indubitable; qu'on ne peut pas ne pas reconnaître

unnatural [ʌn'nætʃrəl] *adj* non naturel(le); (*perversion*) contre nature

unnecessary [ʌn'nɛsəsərɪ] *adj* inutile, superflu(e)

UNO ['juːnəʊ] *n abbr* = **United Nations Organization**

unofficial [ʌnə'fɪʃl] *adj* (*news*) officieux(-euse), non officiel(le); (*strike*) ≈ sauvage

unpack [ʌn'pæk] *vi* défaire sa valise ▷ *vt* (*suitcase*) défaire; (*belongings*) déballer

unpaid [ʌn'peɪd] *adj* (*bill*) impayé(e); (*holiday*) non-payé(e), sans salaire; (*work*) non rétribué(e)

unpleasant [ʌn'plɛznt] *adj* déplaisant(e), désagréable

unplug [ʌn'plʌg] *vt* débrancher

unpopular [ʌn'pɔpjuləʳ] *adj* impopulaire

unprecedented [ʌn'prɛsɪdɛntɪd] *adj* sans précédent

unpredictable [ʌnprɪ'dɪktəbl] *adj* imprévisible

unprotected ['ʌnprə'tɛktɪd] *adj* (*sex*) non protégé(e)

unqualified [ʌn'kwɔlɪfaɪd] *adj* (*teacher*) non diplômé(e), sans titres; (*success*) sans réserve, total(e); (*disaster*) total(e)

unravel [ʌn'rævl] *vt* démêler

unreal [ʌn'rɪəl] *adj* irréel(le); (*extraordinary*) incroyable

unrealistic ['ʌnrɪə'lɪstɪk] *adj* (*idea*) irréaliste; (*estimate*) peu réaliste

unreasonable [ʌn'riːznəbl] *adj* qui n'est pas raisonnable

unrelated [ʌnrɪ'leɪtɪd] *adj* sans rapport; (*people*) sans lien de parenté

unreliable [ʌnrɪ'laɪəbl] *adj* sur qui (*or* quoi) on ne peut pas compter, peu fiable

unrest [ʌn'rɛst] *n* agitation *f*, troubles *mpl*

unroll [ʌn'rəʊl] *vt* dérouler

unruly [ʌn'ruːlɪ] *adj* indiscipliné(e)

unsafe [ʌn'seɪf] *adj* (*in danger*) en danger; (*journey, car*) dangereux(-euse)

unsatisfactory ['ʌnsætɪs'fæktərɪ] *adj* peu satisfaisant(e)

unscrew [ʌn'skruː] *vt* dévisser

unsettled [ʌn'sɛtld] *adj* (*restless*) perturbé(e); (*unpredictable*) instable; incertain(e); (*not finalized*) non résolu(e)

unsettling [ʌn'sɛtlɪŋ] *adj* qui a un effet perturbateur

unsightly [ʌn'saɪtlɪ] *adj* disgracieux(-euse), laid(e)

unskilled [ʌn'skɪld] *adj*: **~ worker** manœuvre *m*

unspoiled ['ʌn'spɔɪld], **unspoilt** ['ʌn'spɔɪlt] *adj* (*place*) non dégradé(e)

unstable [ʌn'steɪbl] *adj* instable

unsteady [ʌn'stɛdɪ] *adj* mal assuré(e), chancelant(e), instable

unsuccessful [ʌnsək'sɛsful] *adj* (*attempt*) infructueux(-euse); (*writer, proposal*) qui n'a pas de succès; **to be ~** (*in attempting sth*) ne pas réussir; ne pas avoir de succès; (*application*) ne pas être retenu(e)

unsuitable [ʌn'suːtəbl] *adj* qui ne convient pas, peu approprié(e); (*time*) inopportun(e)

unsure [ʌn'ʃʊəʳ] *adj* pas sûr(e); **to be ~ of o.s.** ne pas être sûr de soi, manquer de confiance en soi

untidy [ʌn'taɪdɪ] *adj* (*room*) en désordre; (*appearance, person*) débraillé(e); (*person: in character*) sans ordre, désordonné(e); (*work*) peu soigné(e)

untie [ʌn'taɪ] *vt* (*knot, parcel*) défaire; (*prisoner, dog*) détacher

until [ən'tɪl] *prep* jusqu'à; (*after negative*) avant ▷ *conj* jusqu'à ce que + *sub*; (*in past, after negative*) avant que + *sub*; **~ he comes** jusqu'à ce qu'il vienne, jusqu'à son arrivée; **~ now** jusqu'à présent, jusqu'ici; **~ then** jusque-là

untrue [ʌn'truː] *adj* (*statement*) faux (fausse)

unused¹ [ʌnˈjuːzd] adj (new) neuf (neuve)

unused² [ʌnˈjuːst] adj: **to be ~ to sth/to doing sth** ne pas avoir l'habitude de qch/de faire qch

unusual² [ʌnˈjuːʒuəl] adj insolite, exceptionnel(le), rare; **unusually** adv exceptionnellement, particulièrement

unveil [ʌnˈveɪl] vt dévoiler

unwanted [ʌnˈwɒntɪd] adj (child, pregnancy) non désiré(e); (clothes etc) à donner

unwell [ʌnˈwɛl] adj souffrant(e); **to feel ~** ne pas se sentir bien

unwilling [ʌnˈwɪlɪŋ] adj: **to be ~ to do** ne pas vouloir faire

unwind [ʌnˈwaɪnd] vt (irreg: like **wind²**) dérouler ▷ vi (relax) se détendre

unwise [ʌnˈwaɪz] adj imprudent(e), peu judicieux(-euse)

unwittingly [ʌnˈwɪtɪŋlɪ] adv involontairement

unwrap [ʌnˈræp] vt défaire; ouvrir

unzip [ʌnˈzɪp] vt ouvrir (la fermeture éclair de); (Comput) dézipper

○ **KEYWORD**

up [ʌp] prep: **he went up the stairs/the hill** il a monté l'escalier/la colline; **the cat was up a tree** le chat était dans un arbre; **they live further up the street** ils habitent plus haut dans la rue; **go up that road and turn left** remontez la rue et tournez à gauche
▶ adv **1** en haut; en l'air; (upwards, higher): **up in the sky/the mountains** (là-haut) dans le ciel/les montagnes; **put it a bit higher up** mettez-le un peu plus haut; **to stand up** (get up) se lever, se mettre debout; (be standing) être debout; **up there** là-haut; **up above** au-dessus

2: **to be up** (out of bed) être levé(e); (prices) avoir augmenté or monté; (finished): **when the year was up** à la fin de l'année

3: **up to** (as far as) jusqu'à; **up to now** jusqu'à présent

4: **to be up to** (depending on): **it's up to you** c'est à vous de décider; (equal to): **he's not up to it** (job, task etc) il n'en est pas capable; (inf: be doing): **what is he up to?** qu'est-ce qu'il peut bien faire?
▶ n: **ups and downs** hauts et bas mpl

up-and-coming [ʌpəndˈkʌmɪŋ] adj plein(e) d'avenir or de promesses

upbringing [ˈʌpbrɪŋɪŋ] n éducation f

update [ʌpˈdeɪt] vt mettre à jour

upfront [ʌpˈfrʌnt] adj (open) franc (franche) ▷ adv (pay) d'avance; **to be ~ about sth** ne rien cacher de qch

upgrade [ʌpˈɡreɪd] vt (person) promouvoir; (job) revaloriser; (property, equipment) moderniser

upheaval [ʌpˈhiːvl] n bouleversement m; (in room) branle-bas m; (event) crise f

uphill [ʌpˈhɪl] adj qui monte; (fig: task) difficile, pénible ▷ adv (face, look) en amont, vers l'amont; **to go ~** monter

upholstery [ʌpˈhəʊlstərɪ] n rembourrage m; (cover) tissu m d'ameublement; (of car) garniture f

upload [ˈʌpləʊd] vt (Comput) télécharger

upmarket [ʌpˈmɑːkɪt] adj (product) haut de gamme inv; (area) chic inv

upon [əˈpɒn] prep sur

upper [ˈʌpə*] adj supérieur(e); du dessus ▷ n (of shoe) empeigne f; **upper-class** adj de la haute société, aristocratique; (district) élégant(e), huppé(e); (accent, attitude) caractéristique des classes supérieures

upright [ˈʌpraɪt] adj droit(e); (fig) droit, honnête

uprising [ˈʌpraɪzɪŋ] n soulèvement m, insurrection f

uproar [ˈʌprɔː*] n tumulte m, vacarme m; (protests) protestations fpl

upset n [ˈʌpsɛt] dérangement m ▷ vt [ʌpˈsɛt] (irreg: like **set**) (glass etc) renverser; (plan) déranger; (person: offend) contrarier; (: grieve) faire de la peine à; bouleverser ▷ adj [ʌpˈsɛt] contrarié(e); peiné(e); **to have a stomach ~** (BRIT) avoir une indigestion

upside down [ˈʌpsaɪd-] adv à l'envers; **to turn sth ~** (fig: place) mettre sens dessus dessous

upstairs [ʌpˈstɛəz] adv en haut ▷ adj (room) du dessus, d'en haut ▷ n: **the ~** l'étage m

up-to-date [ˈʌptəˈdeɪt] adj moderne; (information) très récent(e)

upward [ˈʌpwəd] adj ascendant(e); vers le haut ▷ adv = **upwards**

upwards adv vers le haut; (more than): **~ of** plus de

uranium [jʊəˈreɪnɪəm] n uranium m

Uranus [jʊəˈreɪnəs] n Uranus f

urban [ˈɜːbən] adj urbain(e)

urge [ɜːdʒ] n besoin (impératif), envie (pressante) ▷ vt (person): **to ~ sb to do** exhorter qn à faire, pousser qn à faire, recommander vivement à qn de faire

urgency [ˈɜːdʒənsɪ] n urgence f; (of tone) insistance f

urgent [ˈɜːdʒənt] adj urgent(e); (plea, tone) pressant(e)

urinal [ˈjʊərɪnl] n (BRIT: place) urinoir m

urinate [ˈjʊərɪneɪt] vi uriner

urine [ˈjʊərɪn] n urine f

URL abbr (= uniform resource locator) URL f

US n abbr = **United States**

us [ʌs] pron nous; see also **me**

USA n abbr = **United States of America**

USB stick n clé f USB

use n [juːs] emploi m, utilisation f; (usefulness) utilité f ▷ vt [juːz] se servir de, utiliser, employer; **in ~** en usage; **out of ~**

hors d'usage; **to be of ~** servir, être utile;
it's no ~ ça ne sert à rien; **to have the ~
of** avoir l'usage de; **she ~d to do it** elle le
faisait (autrefois), elle avait coutume de
le faire; **to be ~d to** avoir l'habitude de,
être habitué(e) à; **use up** vt finir, épuiser;
(food) consommer; **used** [ju:zd] adj (car)
d'occasion; **useful** adj utile; **useless**
adj inutile; (inf: person) nul(le); **user** n
utilisateur(-trice), usager m; **user-friendly**
adj convivial(e), facile d'emploi; **username**
n (Comput) nom m d'utilisateur
usual ['ju:ʒʊəl] adj habituel(le); **as ~**
comme d'habitude; **usually** adv d'habitude,
d'ordinaire
ute [ju:t] n (AUST, NZ) pick-up m inv
utensil [ju:'tɛnsl] n ustensile m; **kitchen ~s**
batterie f de cuisine
utility [ju:'tɪlɪtɪ] n utilité f; (also: **public ~**)
service public
utilize ['ju:tɪlaɪz] vt utiliser; (make good use
of) exploiter
utmost ['ʌtməʊst] adj extrême, le plus
grand(e) ▷ n: **to do one's ~** faire tout son
possible
utter ['ʌtəʳ] adj total(e), complet(-ète) ▷ vt
prononcer, proférer; (sounds) émettre;
utterly adv complètement, totalement
U-turn ['ju:'tə:n] n demi-tour m; (fig) volte-
face f inv

v. abbr = **verse**; (= vide) v.; (= versus) vs;
(= volt) V
vacancy ['veɪkənsɪ] n (job) poste
vacant; (room) chambre f disponible; "**no
vacancies**" "complet"
vacant ['veɪkənt] adj (post) vacant(e); (seat
etc) libre, disponible; (expression) distrait(e)
vacate [və'keɪt] vt quitter
vacation [və'keɪʃən] n (esp US) vacances
fpl; **on ~** en vacances; **vacationer**, (US)
vacationist n vacancier(-ière)
vaccination [væksɪ'neɪʃən] n
vaccination f
vaccine ['væksi:n] n vaccin m
vacuum ['vækjum] n vide m; **vacuum
cleaner** n aspirateur m
vagina [və'dʒaɪnə] n vagin m
vague [veɪg] adj vague, imprécis(e);
(blurred: photo, memory) flou(e)
vain [veɪn] adj (useless) vain(e); (conceited)
vaniteux(-euse); **in ~** en vain
Valentine's Day ['væləntaɪnz-] n Saint-
Valentin f
valid ['vælɪd] adj (document) valide, valable;
(excuse) valable
valley ['vælɪ] n vallée f
valuable ['væljuəbl] adj (jewel) de grande
valeur; (time, help) précieux(-euse);
valuables npl objets mpl de valeur
value ['vælju:] n valeur f ▷ vt (fix price)
évaluer, expertiser; (appreciate) apprécier;
values npl (principles) valeurs fpl
valve [vælv] n (in machine) soupape f; (on
tyre) valve f; (Med) valve, valvule f
vampire ['væmpaɪəʳ] n vampire m
van [væn] n (Aut) camionnette f
vandal ['vændl] n vandale m/f; **vandalism**
n vandalisme m; **vandalize** vt saccager
vanilla [və'nɪlə] n vanille f
vanish ['vænɪʃ] vi disparaître
vanity ['vænɪtɪ] n vanité f
vapour, (US) **vapor** ['veɪpəʳ] n vapeur f;
(on window) buée f

variable ['vɛərɪəbl] *adj* variable; (*mood*) changeant(e)

variant ['vɛərɪənt] *n* variante *f*

variation [vɛərɪ'eɪʃən] *n* variation *f*; (*in opinion*) changement *m*

varied ['vɛərɪd] *adj* varié(e), divers(e)

variety [və'raɪətɪ] *n* variété *f*; (*quantity*) nombre *m*, quantité *f*

various ['vɛərɪəs] *adj* divers(e), différent(e); (*several*) divers, plusieurs

varnish ['vɑːnɪʃ] *n* vernis *m* ▷ *vt* vernir

vary ['vɛərɪ] *vt, vi* varier, changer

vase [vɑːz] *n* vase *m*

Vaseline® ['væsɪliːn] *n* vaseline *f*

vast [vɑːst] *adj* vaste, immense; (*amount, success*) énorme

VAT [væt] *n abbr* (BRIT: = *value added tax*) TVA *f*

vault [vɔːlt] *n* (*of roof*) voûte *f*; (*tomb*) caveau *m*; (*in bank*) salle *f* des coffres; chambre forte ▷ *vt* (*also:* **~ over**) sauter (d'un bond)

VCR *n abbr* = **video cassette recorder**

VDU *n abbr* = **visual display unit**

veal [viːl] *n* veau *m*

veer [vɪər] *vi* tourner; (*car, ship*) virer

vegan ['viːgən] *n* végétalien(ne)

vegetable ['vɛdʒtəbl] *n* légume *m* ▷ *adj* végétal(e)

vegetarian [vɛdʒɪ'tɛərɪən] *adj, n* végétarien(ne); **do you have any ~ dishes?** avez-vous des plats végétariens?

vegetation [vɛdʒɪ'teɪʃən] *n* végétation *f*

vehicle ['viːɪkl] *n* véhicule *m*

veil [veɪl] *n* voile *m*

vein [veɪn] *n* veine *f*; (*on leaf*) nervure *f*

Velcro® ['vɛlkrəu] *n* velcro® *m*

velvet ['vɛlvɪt] *n* velours *m*

vending machine ['vɛndɪŋ-] *n* distributeur *m* automatique

vendor ['vɛndər] *n* vendeur(-euse); **street ~** marchand ambulant

Venetian blind [vɪ'niːʃən-] *n* store vénitien

vengeance ['vɛndʒəns] *n* vengeance *f*; **with a ~** (*fig*) vraiment, pour de bon

venison ['vɛnɪsn] *n* venaison *f*

venom ['vɛnəm] *n* venin *m*

vent [vɛnt] *n* conduit *m* d'aération; (*in dress, jacket*) fente *f* ▷ *vt* (*fig: one's feelings*) donner libre cours à

ventilation [vɛntɪ'leɪʃən] *n* ventilation *f*, aération *f*

venture ['vɛntʃər] *n* entreprise *f* ▷ *vt* risquer, hasarder ▷ *vi* s'aventurer, se risquer; **a business ~** une entreprise commerciale

venue ['vɛnjuː] *n* lieu *m*

Venus ['viːnəs] *n* (*planet*) Vénus *f*

verb [vəːb] *n* verbe *m*; **verbal** *adj* verbal(e)

verdict ['vəːdɪkt] *n* verdict *m*

verge [vəːdʒ] *n* bord *m*; **"soft ~s"** (BRIT) "accotements non stabilisés"; **on the ~ of doing** sur le point de faire

verify ['vɛrɪfaɪ] *vt* vérifier

versatile ['vəːsətaɪl] *adj* polyvalent(e)

verse [vəːs] *n* vers *mpl*; (*stanza*) strophe *f*; (*in Bible*) verset *m*

version ['vəːʃən] *n* version *f*

versus ['vəːsəs] *prep* contre

vertical ['vəːtɪkl] *adj* vertical(e)

very ['vɛrɪ] *adv* très ▷ *adj*: **the ~ book which** le livre même que; **the ~ last** le tout dernier; **at the ~ least** au moins; **~ much** beaucoup

vessel ['vɛsl] *n* (*Anat, Naut*) vaisseau *m*; (*container*) récipient *m*; *see also* **blood vessel**

vest [vɛst] *n* (BRIT: *underwear*) tricot *m* de corps; (US: *waistcoat*) gilet *m*

vet [vɛt] *n abbr* (BRIT: = *veterinary surgeon*) vétérinaire *m/f*; (US: = *veteran*) ancien(ne) combattant(e) ▷ *vt* examiner minutieusement

veteran ['vɛtərn] *n* vétéran *m*; (*also:* **war ~**) ancien combattant

veterinary surgeon ['vɛtrɪnərɪ-] (BRIT) *n* vétérinaire *m/f*

veto ['viːtəu] *n* (*pl* **vetoes**) veto *m* ▷ *vt* opposer son veto à

via ['vaɪə] *prep* par, via

viable ['vaɪəbl] *adj* viable

vibrate [vaɪ'breɪt] *vi*: **to ~ (with)** vibrer (de)

vibration [vaɪ'breɪʃən] *n* vibration *f*

vicar ['vɪkər] *n* pasteur *m* (*de l'Église anglicane*)

vice [vaɪs] *n* (*evil*) vice *m*; (*Tech*) étau *m*; **vice-chairman** (*irreg*) *n* vice-président(e)

vice versa ['vaɪsɪ'vəːsə] *adv* vice versa

vicinity [vɪ'sɪnɪtɪ] *n* environs *mpl*, alentours *mpl*

vicious ['vɪʃəs] *adj* (*remark*) cruel(le), méchant(e); (*blow*) brutal(e); (*dog*) méchant(e), dangereux(-euse); **a ~ circle** un cercle vicieux

victim ['vɪktɪm] *n* victime *f*

victor ['vɪktər] *n* vainqueur *m*

Victorian [vɪk'tɔːrɪən] *adj* victorien(ne)

victorious [vɪk'tɔːrɪəs] *adj* victorieux(-euse)

victory ['vɪktərɪ] *n* victoire *f*

video ['vɪdɪəu] *n* (*video film*) vidéo *f*; (*also:* **~ cassette**) vidéocassette *f*; (*also:* **~ cassette recorder**) magnétoscope *m* ▷ *vt* (*with recorder*) enregistrer; (*with camera*) filmer; **video camera** *n* caméra *f* vidéo *inv*; **video game** *n* jeu *m* vidéo *inv*; **videophone** *n* vidéophone *m*; **video recorder** *n* magnétoscope *m*; **video shop** *n* vidéoclub *m*; **video tape** *n* bande *f* vidéo *inv*; (*cassette*) vidéocassette *f*

vie [vaɪ] *vi*: **to ~ with** lutter avec, rivaliser avec

Vienna [vɪ'ɛnə] *n* Vienne

Vietnam, Viet Nam ['vjɛt'næm] *n* Viêt-nam *or* Vietnam *m*; **Vietnamese** [vjɛtnə'miːz] *adj* vietnamien(ne) ▷ *n* (*pl inv*) Vietnamien(ne)

view [vju:] *n* vue *f*; (*opinion*) avis *m*, vue ▷ *vt* voir, regarder; (*situation*) considérer; (*house*) visiter; **on ~** (*in museum etc*) exposé(e); **in full ~ of sb** sous les yeux de qn; **in my ~** à mon avis; **in ~ of the fact that** étant donné que; **viewer** *n* (*TV*) téléspectateur(-trice); **viewpoint** *n* point *m* de vue

vigilant ['vɪdʒɪlənt] *adj* vigilant(e)
vigorous ['vɪgərəs] *adj* vigoureux(-euse)
vile [vaɪl] *adj* (*action*) vil(e); (*smell, food*) abominable; (*temper*) massacrant(e)
villa ['vɪlə] *n* villa *f*
village ['vɪlɪdʒ] *n* village *m*; **villager** *n* villageois(e)
villain ['vɪlən] *n* (*scoundrel*) scélérat *m*; (BRIT: *criminal*) bandit *m*; (*in novel etc*) traître *m*
vinaigrette [vɪneɪ'grɛt] *n* vinaigrette *f*
vine [vaɪn] *n* vigne *f*
vinegar ['vɪnɪgəʳ] *n* vinaigre *m*
vineyard ['vɪnjɑːd] *n* vignoble *m*
vintage ['vɪntɪdʒ] *n* (*year*) année *f*, millésime *m* ▷ *cpd* (*car*) d'époque; (*wine*) de grand cru
vinyl ['vaɪnl] *n* vinyle *m*
viola [vɪ'əulə] *n* alto *m*
violate ['vaɪəleɪt] *vt* violer
violation [vaɪə'leɪʃən] *n* violation *f*; **in ~ of** (*rule, law*) en infraction à, en violation de
violence ['vaɪələns] *n* violence *f*
violent ['vaɪələnt] *adj* violent(e)
violet ['vaɪələt] *adj* (*colour*) violet(te) ▷ *n* (*plant*) violette *f*
violin [vaɪə'lɪn] *n* violon *m*
VIP *n abbr* (= *very important person*) VIP *m*
viral ['vaɪərəl] *adj* (*also Comput*) viral(e)
virgin ['vɜːdʒɪn] *n* vierge *f*
Virgo ['vɜːgəu] *n* la Vierge
virtual ['vɜːtjuəl] *adj* (*Comput, Physics*) virtuel(le); (*in effect*): **it's a ~ impossibility** c'est quasiment impossible; **virtually** *adv* (*almost*) pratiquement; **virtual reality** *n* (*Comput*) réalité virtuelle
virtue ['vɜːtju:] *n* vertu *f*; (*advantage*) mérite *m*, avantage *m*; **by ~ of** en vertu or raison de
virus ['vaɪərəs] *n* virus *m*
visa ['viːzə] *n* visa *m*
vise [vaɪs] *n* (US Tech) = **vice**
visibility [vɪzɪ'bɪlɪtɪ] *n* visibilité *f*
visible ['vɪzəbl] *adj* visible
vision ['vɪʒən] *n* (*sight*) vue *f*, vision *f*; (*foresight, in dream*) vision
visit ['vɪzɪt] *n* visite *f*; (*stay*) séjour *m* ▷ *vt* (*person*: US: *also*: **~ with**) rendre visite à; (*place*) visiter; **visiting hours** *npl* heures *fpl* de visite; **visitor** *n* visiteur(-euse); (*to one's house*) invité(e); **visitor centre**, (US) **visitor center** *n* hall *m* or centre *m* d'accueil
visual ['vɪzjuəl] *adj* visuel(le); **visualize** *vt* se représenter
vital ['vaɪtl] *adj* vital(e); **of ~ importance (to sb/sth)** d'une importance capitale (pour qn/qch)

vitality [vaɪ'tælɪtɪ] *n* vitalité *f*
vitamin ['vɪtəmɪn] *n* vitamine *f*
vivid ['vɪvɪd] *adj* (*account*) frappant(e), vivant(e); (*light, imagination*) vif (vive)
V-neck ['viːnɛk] *n* décolleté *m* en V
vocabulary [vəu'kæbjulərɪ] *n* vocabulaire *m*
vocal ['vəukl] *adj* vocal(e); (*articulate*) qui n'hésite pas à s'exprimer, qui sait faire entendre ses opinions
vocational [vəu'keɪʃənl] *adj* professionnel(le)
vodka ['vɔdkə] *n* vodka *f*
vogue [vəug] *n*: **to be in ~** être en vogue or à la mode
voice [vɔɪs] *n* voix *f* ▷ *vt* (*opinion*) exprimer, formuler; **voice mail** *n* (*system*) messagerie *f* vocale, boîte *f* vocale; (*device*) répondeur *m*
void [vɔɪd] *n* vide *m* ▷ *adj* (*invalid*) nul(le); (*empty*): **~ of** vide de, dépourvu(e) de
volatile ['vɔlətaɪl] *adj* volatil(e); (*fig: person*) versatile; (: *situation*) explosif(-ive)
volcano [vɔl'keɪnəu] (*pl* **volcanoes**) *n* volcan *m*
volleyball ['vɔlɪbɔːl] *n* volley(-ball) *m*
volt [vəult] *n* volt *m*; **voltage** *n* tension *f*, voltage *m*
volume ['vɔljuːm] *n* volume *m*; (*of tank*) capacité *f*
voluntarily ['vɔləntrɪlɪ] *adv* volontairement
voluntary ['vɔləntərɪ] *adj* volontaire; (*unpaid*) bénévole
volunteer [vɔlən'tɪəʳ] *n* volontaire *m/f* ▷ *vt* (*information*) donner spontanément ▷ *vi* (*Mil*) s'engager comme volontaire; **to ~ to do** se proposer pour faire
vomit ['vɔmɪt] *n* vomissure *f* ▷ *vt*, *vi* vomir
vote [vəut] *n* vote *m*, suffrage *m*; (*votes cast*) voix *f*, vote; (*franchise*) droit *m* de vote ▷ *vt* (*chairman*) élire; (*propose*): **to ~ that** proposer que + *sub* ▷ *vi* voter; **~ of thanks** discours *m* de remerciement; **voter** *n* électeur(-trice); **voting** *n* scrutin *m*, vote *m*
voucher ['vautʃəʳ] *n* (*for meal, petrol, gift*) bon *m*
vow [vau] *n* vœu *m*, serment *m* ▷ *vi* jurer
vowel ['vauəl] *n* voyelle *f*
voyage ['vɔɪɪdʒ] *n* voyage *m* par mer, traversée *f*
vulgar ['vʌlgəʳ] *adj* vulgaire
vulnerable ['vʌlnərəbl] *adj* vulnérable
vulture ['vʌltʃəʳ] *n* vautour *m*

W

waddle ['wɒdl] vi se dandiner

wade [weɪd] vi: **to ~ through** marcher dans, patauger dans; (*fig: book*) venir à bout de

wafer ['weɪfə'] n (*Culin*) gaufrette f

waffle ['wɒfl] n (*Culin*) gaufre f ▷ vi parler pour ne rien dire; faire du remplissage

wag [wæg] vt agiter, remuer ▷ vi remuer

wage [weɪdʒ] n (*also*: **~s**) salaire m, paye f ▷ vt: **to ~ war** faire la guerre

wag(g)on ['wægən] n (*horse drawn*) chariot m; (*BRIT Rail*) wagon m (de marchandises)

wail [weɪl] n gémissement m; (*of siren*) hurlement m ▷ vi gémir; (*siren*) hurler

waist [weɪst] n taille f, ceinture f; **waistcoat** n (*BRIT*) gilet m

wait [weɪt] n attente f ▷ vi attendre; **to ~ for sb/sth** attendre qn/qch; **to keep sb ~ing** faire attendre qn; **~ for me, please** attendez-moi, s'il vous plaît; **I can't ~ to ...** (*fig*) je meurs d'envie de ...; **to lie in ~ for** guetter; **wait on** vt fus servir; **waiter** n garçon m (de café), serveur m; **waiting list** n liste f d'attente; **waiting room** n salle f d'attente; **waitress** ['weɪtrɪs] n serveuse f

waive [weɪv] vt renoncer à, abandonner

wake [weɪk] (*pt* **woke** *or* **waked**, *pp* **woken** *or* **waked**) vt (*also*: **~ up**) réveiller ▷ vi (*also*: **~ up**) se réveiller ▷ n (*for dead person*) veillée f mortuaire; (*Naut*) sillage m

Wales [weɪlz] n pays m de Galles; **the Prince of ~** le prince de Galles

walk [wɔːk] n promenade f; (*short*) petit tour; (*gait*) démarche f; (*path*) chemin m; (*in park etc*) allée f ▷ vi marcher; (*for pleasure, exercise*) se promener ▷ vt (*distance*) faire à pied; (*dog*) promener; **10 minutes' ~ from** à 10 minutes de marche de; **to go for a ~** se promener; faire un tour; **from all ~s of life** de toutes conditions sociales; **walk out** vi (*go out*) sortir; (*as protest*) partir (en signe de protestation); (*strike*) se mettre en grève; **to ~ out on sb** quitter qn; **walker** n (*person*) marcheur(-euse); **walkie-talkie** ['wɔːkɪ'tɔːkɪ] n talkie-walkie m; **walking** n marche f à pied; **walking shoes** npl chaussures fpl de marche; **walking stick** n canne f; **Walkman®** n Walkman® m; **walkway** n promenade f, cheminement piéton

wall [wɔːl] n mur m; (*of tunnel, cave*) paroi f

wallet ['wɒlɪt] n portefeuille m; **I can't find my ~** je ne retrouve plus mon portefeuille

wallpaper ['wɔːlpeɪpə'] n papier peint ▷ vt tapisser

walnut ['wɔːlnʌt] n noix f; (*tree, wood*) noyer m

walrus ['wɔːlrəs] (*pl* **walrus** *or* **walruses**) n morse m

waltz [wɔːls] n valse f ▷ vi valser

wand [wɒnd] n (*also*: **magic ~**) baguette f (magique)

wander ['wɒndə'] vi (*person*) errer, aller sans but; (*thoughts*) vagabonder ▷ vt errer dans

want [wɒnt] vt vouloir; (*need*) avoir besoin de ▷ n: **for ~ of** par manque de, faute de; **to ~ to do** vouloir faire; **to ~ sb to do** vouloir que qn fasse; **wanted** adj (*criminal*) recherché(e) par la police

war [wɔː'] n guerre f; **to make ~ (on)** faire la guerre (à)

ward [wɔːd] n (*in hospital*) salle f; (*Pol*) section électorale; (*Law: child: also*: **~ of court**) pupille m/f

warden ['wɔːdn] n (*BRIT: of institution*) directeur(-trice); (*of park, game reserve*) gardien(ne); (*BRIT: also*: **traffic ~**) contractuel(le)

wardrobe ['wɔːdrəub] n (*cupboard*) armoire f; (*clothes*) garde-robe f

warehouse ['wɛəhaus] n entrepôt m

warfare ['wɔːfɛə'] n guerre f

warhead ['wɔːhɛd] n (*Mil*) ogive f

warm [wɔːm] adj chaud(e); (*person, thanks, welcome, applause*) chaleureux(-euse); **it's ~** il fait chaud; **I'm ~** j'ai chaud; **warm up** vi (*person, room*) se réchauffer; (*athlete, discussion*) s'échauffer ▷ vt (*food*) (faire) réchauffer; (*water*) (faire) chauffer; (*engine*) faire chauffer; **warmly** adv (*dress*) chaudement; (*thank, welcome*) chaleureusement; **warmth** n chaleur f

warn [wɔːn] vt avertir, prévenir; **to ~ sb (not) to do** conseiller à qn de (ne pas) faire; **warning** n avertissement m; (*notice*) avis m; **warning light** n avertisseur lumineux

warrant ['wɒrnt] n (*guarantee*) garantie f; (*Law: to arrest*) mandat m d'arrêt; (: *to search*) mandat de perquisition ▷ vt (*justify, merit*) justifier

warranty ['wɒrəntɪ] n garantie f

warrior ['wɒrɪə'] n guerrier(-ière)

Warsaw ['wɔːsɔː] n Varsovie

warship ['wɔːʃɪp] n navire m de guerre
wart [wɔːt] n verrue f
wartime ['wɔːtaɪm] n: **in ~** en temps de
guerre
wary ['wɛərɪ] adj prudent(e)
was [wɒz] pt of **be**
wash [wɒʃ] vt laver ▷ vi se laver; (sea): **to ~
over/against** sth inonder/baigner qch ▷ n
(clothes) lessive f; (washing programme)
lavage m; (of ship) sillage m; **to have a ~** se
laver, faire sa toilette; **wash up** vi (BRIT)
faire la vaisselle; (US: have a wash) se
débarbouiller; **washbasin** n lavabo m;
washer n (Tech) rondelle f, joint m;
washing n (BRIT: linen etc: dirty) linge m;
(: clean) lessive f; **washing line** n (BRIT)
corde f à linge; **washing machine** n
machine f à laver; **washing powder** n
(BRIT) lessive f (en poudre)
Washington ['wɒʃɪŋtən] n Washington m
wash: **washing-up** n (BRIT) vaisselle f;
washing-up liquid n (BRIT) produit m pour
la vaisselle; **washroom** n (US) toilettes fpl
wasn't ['wɒznt] = **was not**
wasp [wɒsp] n guêpe f
waste [weɪst] n gaspillage m; (of time) perte
f; (rubbish) déchets mpl; (also: **household ~**)
ordures fpl ▷ adj (land, ground: in city) à
l'abandon; (leftover): **~ material** déchets
▷ vt gaspiller; (time, opportunity) perdre;
waste ground n (BRIT) terrain m vague;
wastepaper basket n corbeille f à papier
watch [wɒtʃ] n montre f; (act of watching)
surveillance f; (guard: Mil) sentinelle f;
(: Naut) homme m de quart; (Naut: spell
of duty) quart m ▷ vt (look at) observer
(: match, programme) regarder; (spy on, guard)
surveiller; (be careful of) faire attention à
▷ vi regarder; (keep guard) monter la garde;
to keep ~ faire le guet; **watch out** vi faire
attention; **watchdog** n chien m de garde;
(fig) gardien(ne); **watch strap** n bracelet m
de montre
water ['wɔːtəʳ] n eau f ▷ vt (plant, garden)
arroser ▷ vi (eyes) larmoyer; **in British ~s**
dans les eaux territoriales Britanniques; **to
make sb's mouth ~** mettre l'eau à la bouche
de qn; **water down** vt (milk etc) couper avec
de l'eau; (fig: story) édulcorer; **watercolour**,
(US) **watercolor** n aquarelle f; **watercress**
n cresson m (de fontaine); **waterfall** n
chute f d'eau; **watering can** n arrosoir m;
watermelon n pastèque f; **waterproof**
adj imperméable; **water-skiing** n ski m
nautique
watt [wɒt] n watt m
wave [weɪv] n vague f; (of hand) geste m,
signe m; (Radio) onde f; (in hair) ondulation
f; (fig) vague ▷ vi faire signe de la main;
(flag) flotter au vent; (grass) ondoyer
▷ vt (handkerchief) agiter; (stick) brandir;
wavelength n longueur f d'ondes

waver ['weɪvəʳ] vi vaciller; (voice) trembler;
(person) hésiter
wavy ['weɪvɪ] adj (hair, surface) ondulé(e);
(line) onduleux(-euse)
wax [wæks] n cire f; (for skis) fart m ▷ vt
cirer; (car) lustrer; (skis) farter ▷ vi (moon)
croître
way [weɪ] n chemin m, voie f; (distance)
distance f; (direction) chemin, direction f;
(manner) façon f, manière f; (habit) habitude
f, façon; **which ~? — this ~/that ~** par où or
de quel côté? — par ici/par là; **to lose one's
~** perdre son chemin; **on the ~ (to)** en route
(pour); **to be on one's ~** être en route; **to
be in the ~** bloquer le passage; (fig) gêner;
it's a long ~ away c'est loin d'ici; **to go out
of one's ~ to do** (fig) se donner beaucoup de
mal pour faire; **to be under ~** (work, project)
être en cours; **in a ~** dans un sens; **by the ~**
à propos; **"~ in"** (BRIT) "entrée"; **"~ out"**
(BRIT) "sortie"; **the ~ back** le chemin du
retour; **"give ~"** (BRIT Aut) "cédez la priorité";
no ~! (inf) pas question!
W.C. n abbr (BRIT: = water closet) w.-c. mpl,
waters mpl
we [wiː] pl pron nous
weak [wiːk] adj faible; (health) fragile; (beam
etc) peu solide; (tea, coffee) léger(-ère);
weaken vi faiblir ▷ vt affaiblir; **weakness** n
faiblesse f, (fault) point m faible
wealth [wɛlθ] n (money, resources)
richesse(s) f(pl); (of details) profusion f;
wealthy adj riche
weapon ['wɛpən] n arme f; **~s of mass
destruction** armes fpl de destruction
massive
wear [wɛəʳ] (pt **wore**, pp **worn**) n (use)
usage m; (deterioration through use) usure
f ▷ vt (clothes) porter; (put on) mettre;
(damage: through use) user ▷ vi (last) faire
de l'usage; (rub etc through) s'user; **sports/
baby~** vêtements mpl de sport/pour bébés;
evening ~ tenue f de soirée; **wear off** vi
disparaître; **wear out** vt user; (person,
strength) épuiser
weary ['wɪərɪ] adj (tired) épuisé(e);
(dispirited) las (lasse); abattu(e) ▷ vi: **to ~ of**
se lasser de
weasel ['wiːzl] n (Zool) belette f
weather ['wɛðəʳ] n temps m ▷ vt (storm: lit,
fig) essuyer; (crisis) survivre à; **under the ~**
(fig: ill) mal fichu(e); **weather forecast** n
prévisions fpl météorologiques, météo f
weave (pt **wove**, pp **woven**) [wiːv, wəuv,
'wəuvn] vt (cloth) tisser; (basket) tresser
web [wɛb] n (of spider) toile f; (on duck's
foot) palmure f; (fig) tissu m; (Comput): **the
(World-Wide) W~** le Web; **web address**
n adresse f Web; **webcam** n webcam f;
webinar ['wɛbɪnɑːʳ] n (Comput) séminaire
m en ligne; **web page** n (Comput) page f
Web; **website** n (Comput) site m Web

wed [wɛd] (pt, pp **wedded**) vt épouser ▷ vi se marier

we'd [wi:d] = **we had; we would**

wedding ['wɛdɪŋ] n mariage m; **wedding anniversary** n anniversaire m de mariage; **silver/golden wedding anniversary** noces fpl d'argent/d'or; **wedding day** n jour m du mariage; **wedding dress** n robe f de mariée; **wedding ring** n alliance f

wedge [wɛdʒ] n (of wood etc) coin m; (under door etc) cale f; (of cake) part f ▷ vt (fix) caler; (push) enfoncer, coincer

Wednesday ['wɛdnzdɪ] n mercredi m

wee [wi:] adj (SCOTTISH) petit(e); tout(e) petit(e)

weed [wi:d] n mauvaise herbe ▷ vt désherber; **weedkiller** n désherbant m

week [wi:k] n semaine f; **a ~ today/ on Tuesday** aujourd'hui/mardi en huit; **weekday** n jour m de semaine; (Comm) jour ouvrable; **weekend** n week-end m; **weekly** adv une fois par semaine, chaque semaine ▷ adj, n hebdomadaire (m)

weep [wi:p] (pt, pp **wept**) vi (person) pleurer

weigh [weɪ] vt, vi peser; **to ~ anchor** lever l'ancre; **weigh up** vt examiner

weight [weɪt] n poids m; **to put on/ lose ~** grossir/maigrir; **weightlifting** n haltérophilie f

weir [wɪər] n barrage m

weird [wɪəd] adj bizarre; (eerie) surnaturel(le)

welcome ['wɛlkəm] adj bienvenu(e) ▷ n accueil m ▷ vt accueillir; (also: **bid ~**) souhaiter la bienvenue à; (be glad of) se réjouir de; **you're ~!** (after thanks) de rien, il n'y a pas de quoi

weld [wɛld] vt souder

welfare ['wɛlfɛər] n (wellbeing) bien-être m; (social aid) assistance sociale; **welfare state** n État-providence m

well [wɛl] n puits m ▷ adv bien ▷ adj: **to be ~** aller bien ▷ excl eh bien!; (relief also) bon!; (resignation) enfin!; **~ done!** bravo!; **get ~ soon!** remets-toi vite!; **to do ~** bien réussir; (business) prospérer; **as ~** (in addition) aussi, également; **as ~ as** aussi bien que or de; en plus de

we'll [wi:l] = **we will; we shall**

well: well-behaved adj sage, obéissant(e); **well-built** adj (person) bien bâti(e); **well-dressed** adj bien habillé(e), bien vêtu(e); **well-groomed** ['-'gru:md] adj très soigné(e)

wellies ['wɛlɪz] npl (BRIT inf) = **wellingtons**

wellingtons ['wɛlɪŋtənz] npl (also: **wellington boots**) bottes fpl en caoutchouc

well: well-known adj (person) bien connu(e); **well-off** adj aisé(e), assez riche; **well-paid** [wɛl'peɪd] adj bien payé(e)

Welsh [wɛlʃ] adj gallois(e) ▷ n (Ling) gallois m; **the Welsh** npl (people) les Gallois; **Welshman** (irreg) n Gallois m; **Welshwoman** (irreg) n Galloise f

went [wɛnt] pt of **go**

wept [wɛpt] pt, pp of **weep**

were [wə:r] pt of **be**

we're [wɪər] = **we are**

weren't [wə:nt] = **were not**

west [wɛst] n ouest m ▷ adj (wind) d'ouest; (side) ouest inv ▷ adv à or vers l'ouest; **the W~** l'Occident m, l'Ouest; **westbound** ['wɛstbaund] adj en direction de l'ouest; (carriageway) ouest inv; **western** adj occidental(e), de or à l'ouest ▷ n (Cine) western m; **West Indian** adj antillais(e) ▷ n Antillais(e); **West Indies** [-'ɪndɪz] npl Antilles fpl

wet [wɛt] adj mouillé(e); (damp) humide; (soaked. also: **~ through**) trempé(e); (rainy) pluvieux(-euse); **to get ~** se mouiller; **"~ paint"** "attention peinture fraîche"; **wetsuit** n combinaison f de plongée

we've [wi:v] = **we have**

whack [wæk] vt donner un grand coup à

whale [weɪl] n (Zool) baleine f

wharf (pl **wharves**) [wɔ:f, wɔ:vz] n quai m

⊙ **KEYWORD**

what [wɔt] adj **1** (in questions) quel(le); **what size is he?** quelle taille fait-il?; **what colour is it?** de quelle couleur est-ce?; **what books do you need?** quels livres vous faut-il?

2 (in exclamations): **what a mess!** quel désordre!; **what a fool I am!** que je suis bête!

▶ pron **1** (interrogative) que; de/à/en etc quoi; **what are you doing?** que faites-vous?, qu'est-ce que vous faites?; **what is happening?** qu'est-ce qui se passe?, que se passe-t-il?; **what are you talking about?** de quoi parlez-vous?; **what are you thinking about?** à quoi pensez-vous?; **what is it called?** comment est-ce que ça s'appelle?; **what about me?** et moi?; **what about doing …?** et si on faisait …?

2 (relative: subject) ce qui; (: direct object) ce que; (: indirect object) ce à quoi, ce dont; **I saw what you did/was on the table** j'ai vu ce que vous avez fait/ce qui était sur la table; **tell me what you remember** dites-moi ce dont vous vous souvenez; **what I want is a cup of tea** ce que je veux, c'est une tasse de thé

▶ excl (disbelieving) quoi!, comment!

whatever [wɔt'ɛvər] adj: **take ~ book you prefer** prenez le livre que vous préférez, peu importe lequel; **~ book you take** quel que soit le livre que vous preniez ▷ pron·

do ~ is necessary faites (tout) ce qui est nécessaire; ~ happens quoi qu'il arrive; no reason ~ or whatsoever pas la moindre raison; nothing ~ or whatsoever rien du tout

whatsoever [wɒtsəu'ɛvəʳ] adj see **whatever**

wheat [wiːt] n blé m, froment m

wheel [wiːl] n roue f; (Aut: also: **steering ~**) volant m; (Naut) gouvernail m ▷ vt (pram etc) pousser, rouler ▷ vi (birds) tournoyer; (also: **~ round**: person) se retourner, faire volte-face; **wheelbarrow** n brouette f; **wheelchair** n fauteuil roulant; **wheel clamp** n (Aut) sabot m (de Denver)

wheeze [wiːz] vi respirer bruyamment

🅞 **KEYWORD**

when [wen] adv quand; **when did he go?** quand est-ce qu'il est parti?
▶ conj 1 (at, during, after the time that) quand, lorsque; **she was reading when I came in** elle lisait quand or lorsque je suis entré
2 (on, at which): **on the day when I met him** le jour où je l'ai rencontré
3 (whereas) alors que; **I thought I was wrong when in fact I was right** j'ai cru que j'avais tort alors qu'en fait j'avais raison

whenever [wɛn'ɛvəʳ] adv quand donc ▷ conj quand; (every time that) chaque fois que

where [wɛəʳ] adv, conj où; **this is ~** c'est là que; **whereabouts** adv où donc ▷ n: **nobody knows his whereabouts** personne ne sait où il se trouve; **whereas** conj alors que; **whereby** adv (formal) par lequel (or laquelle etc); **wherever** adv où donc ▷ conj où que + sub; **sit wherever you like** asseyez-vous (là) où vous voulez

whether ['wɛðəʳ] conj si; **I don't know ~ to accept or not** je ne sais pas si je dois accepter ou non; **it's doubtful ~** il est peu probable que + sub; **~ you go or not** que vous y alliez ou non

🅞 **KEYWORD**

which [wɪtʃ] adj 1 (interrogative, direct, indirect) quel(le); **which picture do you want?** quel tableau voulez-vous?; **which one?** lequel (laquelle)?
2: **in which case** auquel cas; **we got there at 8pm, by which time the cinema was full** quand nous sommes arrivés à 20h, le cinéma était complet
▶ pron 1 (interrogative) lequel (laquelle), lesquels (lesquelles) pl; **I don't mind which** peu importe lequel; **which (of these) are yours?** lesquels sont à vous?; **tell me which**

you want dites-moi lesquels or ceux que vous voulez
2 (relative: subject) qui; (: object) que; sur/vers etc lequel (laquelle) (NB: à + lequel = **auquel**; de + lequel = **duquel**); **the apple which you ate/which is on the table** la pomme que vous avez mangée/qui est sur la table; **the chair on which you are sitting** la chaise sur laquelle vous êtes assis; **the book of which you spoke** le livre dont vous avez parlé; **he said he knew, which is true/I was afraid of** il a dit qu'il le savait, ce qui est vrai/ce que je craignais; **after which** après quoi

whichever [wɪtʃ'ɛvəʳ] adj: **take ~ book you prefer** prenez le livre que vous préférez, peu importe lequel; **~ book you take** quel que soit le livre que vous preniez

while [waɪl] n moment m ▷ conj pendant que; (as long as) tant que; (as, whereas) alors que; (though) bien que + sub, quoique + sub; **for a ~** pendant quelque temps; **in a ~** dans un moment

whilst [waɪlst] conj = **while**

whim [wɪm] n caprice m

whine [waɪn] n gémissement m; (of engine, siren) plainte stridente ▷ vi gémir, geindre, pleurnicher; (dog, engine, siren) gémir

whip [wɪp] n fouet m; (for riding) cravache f; (Pol: person) chef m de file (assurant la discipline dans son groupe parlementaire) ▷ vt fouetter; (snatch) enlever (or sortir) brusquement; **whipped cream** n crème fouettée

whirl [wəːl] vi tourbillonner; (dancers) tournoyer ▷ vt faire tourbillonner; faire tournoyer

whisk [wɪsk] n (Culin) fouet m ▷ vt (eggs) fouetter, battre; **to ~ sb away** or **off** emmener qn rapidement

whiskers ['wɪskəz] npl (of animal) moustaches fpl; (of man) favoris mpl

whisky, (IRISH, US) **whiskey** ['wɪskɪ] n whisky m

whisper ['wɪspəʳ] n chuchotement m ▷ vt, vi chuchoter

whistle ['wɪsl] n (sound) sifflement m; (object) sifflet m ▷ vi siffler ▷ vt siffler, siffloter

white [waɪt] adj blanc (blanche); (with fear) blême ▷ n blanc m; (person) blanc (blanche); **White House** n (US): **the White House** la Maison-Blanche; **whitewash** n (paint) lait m de chaux ▷ vt blanchir à la chaux; (fig) blanchir

whiting ['waɪtɪŋ] n (pl inv: fish) merlan m

Whitsun ['wɪtsn] n la Pentecôte

whittle ['wɪtl] vt: **to ~ away, to ~ down** (costs) réduire, rogner

whizz [wɪz] vi aller (or passer) à toute vitesse

who [hu:] *pron* qui
whoever [hu:ˈevəʳ] *pron*: ~ finds it celui
(celle) qui le trouve (, qui que ce soit),
quiconque le trouve; **ask ~ you like**
demandez à qui vous voulez; ~ **he marries**
qui que ce soit *or* quelle que soit la
personne qu'il épouse; ~ **told you that?**
qui a bien pu vous dire ça?, qui donc vous
a dit ça?
whole [həul] *adj* (*complete*) entier(-ière),
tout(e); (*not broken*) intact(e), complet(-ète)
▷ *n* (*entire unit*) tout *m*; (*all*): **the ~ of** la
totalité de, tout(e) le; **the ~ of the town**
la ville tout entière; **on the ~, as a ~** dans
l'ensemble; **wholefood(s)** *n(pl)* aliments
complets; **wholeheartedly** [həulˈhɑːtɪdlɪ]
adv sans réserve; **to agree wholeheartedly**
être entièrement d'accord; **wholemeal** *adj*
(BRIT: *flour, bread*) complet(-ète); **wholesale**
n (vente *f* en) gros *m* ▷ *adj* (*price*) de gros;
(*destruction*) systématique; **wholewheat**
adj = **wholemeal**; **wholly** *adv* entièrement,
tout à fait

KEYWORD

whom [hu:m] *pron* **1** (*interrogative*) qui;
whom did you see? qui avez-vous vu?; **to
whom did you give it?** à qui l'avez-vous
donné?
2 (*relative*) que à/de *etc* qui; **the man whom
I saw/to whom I spoke** l'homme que j'ai
vu/à qui j'ai parlé

whore [hɔːʳ] *n* (*inf: pej*) putain *f*

KEYWORD

whose [hu:z] *adj* **1** (*possessive, interrogative*):
whose book is this?, whose is this book?
à qui est ce livre?; **whose pencil have you
taken?** à qui est le crayon que vous avez
pris?, c'est le crayon de qui que vous avez
pris?; **whose daughter are you?** de qui
êtes-vous la fille?
2 (*possessive, relative*): **the man whose son
you rescued** l'homme dont or de qui vous
avez sauvé le fils; **the girl whose sister
you were speaking to** la fille à la sœur de
qui or de laquelle vous parliez; **the woman
whose car was stolen** la femme dont la
voiture a été volée
▷ *pron* à qui; **whose is this?** à qui est ceci?;
I know whose it is je sais à qui c'est

KEYWORD

why [waɪ] *adv* pourquoi; **why not?**
pourquoi pas?
▷ *conj*: **I wonder why he said that** je me
demande pourquoi il a dit ça; **that's not
why I'm here** ce n'est pas pour ça que je suis

là; **the reason why** la raison pour laquelle
▷ *excl* eh bien!, tiens!; **why, it's you!** tiens,
c'est vous!; **why, that's impossible!**
voyons, c'est impossible!

wicked [ˈwɪkɪd] *adj* méchant(e);
(*mischievous: grin, look*) espiègle,
malicieux(-euse); (*crime*) pervers(e); (*inf:
very good*) génial(e) (*inf*)
wicket [ˈwɪkɪt] *n* (*Cricket: stumps*) guichet
m; (: *grass area*) espace compris entre les
deux guichets
wide [waɪd] *adj* large; (*area, knowledge*)
vaste, très étendu(e); (*choice*) grand(e)
▷ *adv*: **to open ~** ouvrir tout grand; **to
shoot ~** tirer à côté; **it is 3 metres ~** cela
fait 3 mètres de large; **widely** *adv*
(*different*) radicalement; (*spaced*) sur une
grande étendue; (*believed*) généralement;
(*travel*) beaucoup; **widen** *vt* élargir ▷ *vi*
s'élargir; **wide open** *adj* grand(e)
ouvert(e); **widespread** *adj* (*belief etc*) très
répandu(e)
widow [ˈwɪdəu] *n* veuve *f*; **widower** *n*
veuf *m*
width [wɪdθ] *n* largeur *f*
wield [wi:ld] *vt* (*sword*) manier; (*power*)
exercer
wife (*pl* **wives**) [waɪf, waɪvz] *n* femme *f*,
épouse *f*
Wi-Fi [ˈwaɪfaɪ] *n* wifi *m*
wig [wɪg] *n* perruque *f*
wild [waɪld] *adj* sauvage; (*sea*) déchaîné(e);
(*idea, life*) fou (folle); (*behaviour*) déchaîné(e),
extravagant(e); (*inf: angry*) hors de soi,
furieux(-euse) ▷ *n*: **the ~** la nature;
wilderness [ˈwɪldənɪs] *n* désert *m*, région
f sauvage; **wildlife** *n* faune *f* (et flore *f*);
wildly *adv* (*behave*) de manière déchaînée;
(*applaud*) frénétiquement; (*hit, guess*) au
hasard; (*happy*) follement

KEYWORD

will [wɪl] *aux vb* **1** (*forming future tense*): **I will
finish it tomorrow** je le finirai demain;
I will have finished it by tomorrow je
l'aurai fini d'ici demain; **will you do it?** —
yes I will/no I won't le ferez-vous? —
oui/non
2 (*in conjectures, predictions*): **he will** or **he'll
be there by now** il doit être arrivé à l'heure
qu'il est; **that will be the postman** ça doit
être le facteur
3 (*in commands, requests, offers*): **will you
be quiet!** voulez-vous bien vous taire!;
will you help me? est-ce que vous pouvez
m'aider?; **will you have a cup of tea?**
voulez-vous une tasse de thé?; **I won't put
up with it!** je ne le tolérerai pas!
▷ *vt* (*pt, pp* **willed**): **to will sb to do**
souhaiter ardemment que qn fasse;

he willed himself to go on par un suprême effort de volonté, il continua
▶ *n* 1 volonté *f*; **against one's will** à contre-cœur
2 (*document*) testament *m*

willing ['wɪlɪŋ] *adj* de bonne volonté, serviable; **he's ~ to do it** il est disposé à le faire, il veut bien le faire; **willingly** *adv* volontiers
willow ['wɪləʊ] *n* saule *m*
willpower ['wɪl'paʊə'] *n* volonté *f*
wilt [wɪlt] *vi* dépérir
win [wɪn] (*pt, pp* **won**) *n* (*in sports etc*) victoire *f* ▶ *vt* (*battle, money*) gagner; (*prize, contract*) remporter; (*popularity*) acquérir ▶ *vi* gagner; **win over** *vt* convaincre
wince [wɪns] *vi* tressaillir
wind¹ [wɪnd] *n* (*also Med*) vent *m*; (*breath*) souffle *m* ▶ *vt* (*take breath away*) couper le souffle à; **the ~(s)** (*Mus*) les instruments *mpl* à vent
wind² (*pt, pp* **wound**) [waɪnd, waʊnd] *vt* enrouler; (*wrap*) envelopper; (*clock, toy*) remonter ▶ *vi* (*road, river*) serpenter; **wind down** *vt* (*car window*) baisser; (*fig: production, business*) réduire progressivement; **wind up** *vt* (*clock*) remonter; (*debate*) terminer, clôturer
windfall ['wɪndfɔːl] *n* coup *m* de chance
wind farm *n* ferme *f* éolienne
winding ['waɪndɪŋ] *adj* (*road*) sinueux(-euse); (*staircase*) tournant(e)
windmill ['wɪndmɪl] *n* moulin *m* à vent
window ['wɪndəʊ] *n* fenêtre *f*; (*in car, train: also:* **~pane**) vitre *f*; (*in shop etc*) vitrine *f*; **window box** *n* jardinière *f*; **window cleaner** *n* (*person*) laveur(-euse) de vitres; **window pane** *n* vitre *f*, carreau *m*; **window seat** *n* (*on plane*) place *f* côté hublot; **windowsill** *n* (*inside*) appui *m* de la fenêtre; (*outside*) rebord *m* de la fenêtre
windscreen ['wɪndskriːn] *n* pare-brise *m inv*; **windscreen wiper** *n* essuie-glace *m inv*
windshield ['wɪndʃiːld] (*US*) *n* = **windscreen**
windsurfing ['wɪndsəːfɪŋ] *n* planche *f* à voile
wind turbine [-təːbaɪn] *n* éolienne *f*
windy ['wɪndɪ] *adj* (*day*) de vent, venteux(-euse); (*place, weather*) venteux; **it's ~** il y a du vent
wine [waɪn] *n* vin *m*; **wine bar** *n* bar *m* à vin; **wine glass** *n* verre *m* à vin; **wine list** *n* carte *f* des vins; **wine tasting** *n* dégustation *f* (de vins)
wing [wɪŋ] *n* aile *f*; **wings** *npl* (*Theat*) coulisses *fpl*; **wing mirror** *n* (*BRIT*) rétroviseur latéral
wink [wɪŋk] *n* clin *m* d'œil ▶ *vi* faire un clin d'œil; (*blink*) cligner des yeux
winner ['wɪnə'] *n* gagnant(e)

winning ['wɪnɪŋ] *adj* (*team*) gagnant(e); (*goal*) décisif(-ive); (*charming*) charmeur(-euse)
winter ['wɪntə'] *n* hiver *m* ▶ *vi* hiverner; **in ~** en hiver; **winter sports** *npl* sports *mpl* d'hiver; **wintertime** *n* hiver *m*
wipe [waɪp] *n*: **to give sth a ~** donner un coup de torchon/de chiffon/d'éponge à qch ▶ *vt* essuyer; (*erase: tape*) effacer; **to ~ one's nose** se moucher; **wipe out** *vt* (*debt*) éteindre, amortir; (*memory*) effacer; (*destroy*) anéantir; **wipe up** *vt* essuyer
wire ['waɪə'] *n* fil *m* (de fer); (*Elec*) fil électrique; (*Tel*) télégramme *m* ▶ *vt* (*house*) faire l'installation électrique de; (*also:* **~ up**) brancher; (*person: send telegram to*) télégraphier à
wireless ['waɪəlɪs] *adj* sans fil; **wireless technology** *n* technologie *f* sans fil
wiring ['waɪərɪŋ] *n* (*Elec*) installation *f* électrique
wisdom ['wɪzdəm] *n* sagesse *f*; (*of action*) prudence *f*; **wisdom tooth** *n* dent *f* de sagesse
wise [waɪz] *adj* sage, prudent(e); (*remark*) judicieux(-euse)
wish [wɪʃ] *n* (*desire*) désir *m*; (*specific desire*) souhait *m*, vœu *m* ▶ *vt* souhaiter, désirer, vouloir; **best ~es** (*on birthday etc*) meilleurs vœux; **with best ~es** (*in letter*) bien amicalement; **to ~ sb goodbye** dire au revoir à qn; **he ~ed me well** il m'a souhaité bonne chance; **to ~ to do/sb to do** désirer *or* vouloir faire/que qn fasse; **to ~ for** souhaiter
wistful ['wɪstful] *adj* mélancolique
wit [wɪt] *n* (*also:* **~s**: *intelligence*) intelligence *f*, esprit *m*; (*presence of mind*) présence *f* d'esprit; (*wittiness*) esprit; (*person*) homme/femme d'esprit
witch [wɪtʃ] *n* sorcière *f*

🅞 **KEYWORD**

with [wɪð, wɪθ] *prep* 1 (*in the company of*) avec; (*: at the home of*) chez; **we stayed with friends** nous avons logé chez des amis; **I'll be with you in a minute** je suis à vous dans un instant
2 (*descriptive*): **a room with a view** une chambre avec vue; **the man with the grey hat/blue eyes** l'homme au chapeau gris/aux yeux bleus
3 (*indicating manner, means, cause*): **with tears in her eyes** les larmes aux yeux; **to walk with a stick** marcher avec une canne; **red with anger** rouge de colère; **to shake with fear** trembler de peur; **to fill sth with water** remplir qch d'eau
4 (*in phrases*): **I'm with you** (*I understand*) je vous suis; **to be with it** (*inf: up to-date*) être dans le vent

withdraw [wɪθ'drɔː] vt (irreg: like **draw**) retirer ▷ vi se retirer; **withdrawal** n retrait m; (Med) état m de manque; **withdrawn** pp of **withdraw** ▷ adj (person) renfermé(e)

withdrew [wɪθ'druː] pt of **withdraw**

wither ['wɪðəʳ] vi se faner

withhold [wɪθ'həuld] vt (irreg: like **hold**) (money) retenir; (decision) remettre; **to ~ (from)** (permission) refuser (à); (information) cacher (à)

within [wɪð'ɪn] prep à l'intérieur de ▷ adv à l'intérieur; **~ his reach** à sa portée; **~ sight of** en vue de; **~ a mile of** à moins d'un mille de; **~ the week** avant la fin de la semaine

without [wɪð'aut] prep sans; **~ a coat** sans manteau; **~ speaking** sans parler; **to go** or **do ~ sth** se passer de qch

withstand [wɪθ'stænd] vt (irreg: like **stand**) résister à

witness ['wɪtnɪs] n (person) témoin m ▷ vt (event) être témoin de; (document) attester l'authenticité de; **to bear ~ to sth** témoigner de qch

witty ['wɪtɪ] adj spirituel(le), plein(e) d'esprit

wives [waɪvz] npl of **wife**

wizard ['wɪzəd] n magicien m

wk abbr = **week**

wobble ['wɔbl] vi trembler; (chair) branler

woe [wəu] n malheur m

woke [wəuk] pt of **wake**

woken ['wəukn] pp of **wake**

wolf (pl **wolves**) [wulf, wulvz] n loup m

woman (pl **women**) ['wumən, 'wimin] n femme f ▷ cpd **~ doctor** femme f médecin; **~ teacher** professeur m femme

womb [wuːm] n (Anat) utérus m

women ['wimin] npl of **woman**

won [wʌn] pt, pp of **win**

wonder ['wʌndəʳ] n merveille f, miracle m; (feeling) émerveillement m ▷ vi. **to ~ whether/why** se demander si/pourquoi; **to ~ at** (surprise) s'étonner de; (admiration) s'émerveiller de; **to ~ about** songer à; **it's no ~ that** il n'est pas étonnant que + sub; **wonderful** adj merveilleux(-euse)

won't [wəunt] = **will not**

wood [wud] n (timber, forest) bois m; **wooden** adj en bois; (fig: actor) raide; (: performance) qui manque de naturel; **woodwind** n: **the woodwind** les bois mpl; **woodwork** n menuiserie f

wool [wul] n laine f; **to pull the ~ over sb's eyes** (fig) en faire accroire à qn; **woollen**, (US) **woolen** adj de or en laine; **woolly**, (US) **wooly** adj laineux(-euse); (fig: ideas) confus(e)

word [wəːd] n mot m; (spoken) mot, parole f; (promise) parole, (news) nouvelles fpl ▷ vt rédiger, formuler; **in other ~s** en d'autres termes; **to have a ~ with sb** toucher un mot à qn; **to break/keep one's ~** manquer à sa parole/tenir (sa) parole; **wording** n termes mpl, langage m; (of document) libellé m; **word processing** n traitement m de texte; **word processor** n machine f de traitement de texte

wore [wɔːʳ] pt of **wear**

work [wəːk] n travail m; (Art, Literature) œuvre f ▷ vi travailler; (mechanism) marcher, fonctionner; (plan etc) marcher; (medicine) agir ▷ vt (clay, wood etc) travailler; (mine etc) exploiter; (machine) faire marcher or fonctionner; (miracles etc) faire; **works** n (BRIT: factory) usine f; **how does this ~?** comment est-ce que ça marche?; **the TV isn't ~ing** la télévision est en panne or ne marche pas; **to be out of ~** être au chômage or sans emploi; **to ~ loose** se défaire, se desserrer; **work out** vi (plans etc) marcher; (Sport) s'entraîner ▷ vt (problem) résoudre; (plan) élaborer; **it ~s out at £100** ça fait 100 livres; **worker** n travailleur(-euse), ouvrier(-ière); **work experience** n stage m; **workforce** n main-d'œuvre f; **working class** n classe ouvrière ▷ adj: **working-class** ouvrier(-ière), de la classe ouvrière; **working week** n semaine f de travail; **workman** (irreg) n ouvrier m; **work of art** n œuvre f d'art; **workout** n (Sport) séance f d'entraînement; **work permit** n permis m de travail; **workplace** n lieu m de travail; **worksheet** n (Scol) feuille f d'exercices; **workshop** n atelier m; **work station** n poste m de travail; **work surface** n plan m de travail; **worktop** n plan m de travail

world [wəːld] n monde m ▷ cpd (champion) du monde; (power, war) mondial(e); **to think the ~ of sb** (fig) ne jurer que par qn; **World Cup** n: **the World Cup** (Football) la Coupe du monde; **world-wide** adj universel(le); **World-Wide Web** n: **the World-Wide Web** le Web

worm [wəːm] n (also: **earth~**) ver m

worn [wɔːn] pp of **wear** ▷ adj usé(e); **worn-out** adj (object) complètement usé(e); (person) épuisé(e)

worried ['wʌrɪd] adj inquiet(-ète); **to be ~ about sth** être inquiet au sujet de qch

worry ['wʌrɪ] n souci m ▷ vt inquiéter ▷ vi s'inquiéter, se faire du souci; **worrying** adj inquiétant(e)

worse [wəːs] adj pire, plus mauvais(e) ▷ adv plus mal ▷ n pire m; **to get ~** (condition, situation) empirer, se dégrader; **a change for the ~** une détérioration; **worsen** vt, vi empirer; **worse off** adj moins à l'aise financièrement; (fig): **you'll be worse off this way** ça ira moins bien de cette façon

worship ['wəːʃɪp] n culte m ▷ vt (God) rendre un culte à; (person) adorer

worst [wəːst] adj le (la) pire, le (la) plus mauvais(e) ▷ adv le plus mal ▷ n pire m; **at ~** au pis aller

worth [wə:θ] n valeur f ▷ adj: **to be ~** valoir; **it's ~ it** cela en vaut la peine, ça vaut la peine; **it is ~ one's while (to do)** ça vaut le coup (inf) (de faire); **worthless** adj qui ne vaut rien; **worthwhile** adj (activity) qui en vaut la peine; (cause) louable

worthy ['wə:ðɪ] adj (person) digne; (motive) louable; **~ of** digne de

KEYWORD

would [wud] aux vb **1** (conditional tense): **if you asked him he would do it** si vous le lui demandiez, il le ferait; **if you had asked him he would have done it** si vous le lui aviez demandé, il l'aurait fait

2 (in offers, invitations, requests): **would you like a biscuit?** voulez-vous un biscuit?; **would you close the door please?** voulez-vous fermer la porte, s'il vous plaît?

3 (in indirect speech): **I said I would do it** j'ai dit que je le ferais

4 (emphatic): **it WOULD have to snow today!** naturellement il neige aujourd'hui!, il fallait qu'il neige aujourd'hui!

5 (insistence): **she wouldn't do it** elle n'a pas voulu or elle a refusé de le faire

6 (conjecture): **it would have been midnight** il devait être minuit; **it would seem so** on dirait bien

7 (indicating habit): **he would go there on Mondays** il y allait le lundi

wouldn't ['wudnt] = **would not**
wound¹ [wu:nd] n blessure f ▷ vt blesser
wound² [waund] pt, pp of **wind²**
wove [wəuv] pt of **weave**
woven ['wəuvn] pp of **weave**
wrap [ræp] vt (also: **~ up**) envelopper; (parcel) emballer; (wind) enrouler; **wrapper** n (on chocolate etc) papier m; (BRIT: of book) couverture f; **wrapping** n (of sweet, chocolate) papier m; (of parcel) emballage m; **wrapping paper** n papier m d'emballage; (for gift) papier cadeau
wreath [ri:θ] n couronne f
wreck [rɛk] n (sea disaster) naufrage m; (ship) épave f; (vehicle) véhicule accidentée; (pej: person) loque (humaine) ▷ vt démolir; (fig) briser, ruiner; **wreckage** n débris mpl; (of building) décombres mpl; (of ship) naufrage m
wren [rɛn] n (Zool) troglodyte m
wrench [rɛntʃ] n (Tech) clé f (à écrous); (tug) violent mouvement de torsion; (fig) déchirement m ▷ vt tirer violemment sur, tordre; **to ~ sth from** arracher qch à qn (violemment) à or de
wrestle ['rɛsl] vi: **to ~ (with sb)** lutter (avec qn); **wrestler** n lutteur(-euse); **wrestling** n lutte f; (BRIT: also: **all-in wrestling**) catch m
wretched ['rɛtʃɪd] adj misérable

wriggle ['rɪgl] vi (also: **~ about**) se tortiller
wring (pt, pp **wrung**) [rɪŋ, rʌŋ] vt tordre; (wet clothes) essorer; (fig): **to ~ sth out of** arracher qch à
wrinkle ['rɪŋkl] n (on skin) ride f; (on paper etc) pli m ▷ vt rider, plisser ▷ vi se plisser
wrist [rɪst] n poignet m
write (pt **wrote**, pp **written**) [raɪt, rəut, 'rɪtn] vt, vi écrire; (prescription) rédiger; **write down** vt noter; (put in writing) mettre par écrit; **write off** vt (debt) passer aux profits et pertes; (project) démolir complètement; **write out** vt écrire; (copy) recopier; **write-off** n perte totale; **the car is a write-off** la voiture est bonne pour la casse; **writer** n auteur m, écrivain m
writing ['raɪtɪŋ] n écriture f; (of author) œuvres fpl; **in ~** par écrit; **writing paper** n papier m à lettres
written ['rɪtn] pp of **write**
wrong [rɒŋ] adj (incorrect) faux (fausse); (incorrectly chosen: number, road etc) mauvais(e); (not suitable) qui ne convient pas; (wicked) mal; (unfair) injuste ▷ adv mal ▷ n tort m ▷ vt faire du tort à, léser; **you are ~ to do it** tu as tort de le faire; **you are ~ about that, you've got it ~** tu te trompes; **what's ~?** qu'est-ce qui ne va pas?; **what's ~ with the car?** qu'est-ce qu'elle a, la voiture?; **to go ~** (person) se tromper; (plan) mal tourner; (machine) se détraquer; **I took a ~ turning** je me suis trompé de route; **wrongly** adv à tort; (answer, do, count) mal, incorrectement; **wrong number** n (Tel): **you have the wrong number** vous vous êtes trompé de numéro
wrote [rəut] pt of **write**
wrung [rʌŋ] pt, pp of **wring**
WWW n abbr = **World-Wide Web**

XL *abbr* (= *extra large*) XL
Xmas ['ɛksməs] *n abbr* = **Christmas**
X-ray ['ɛksreɪ] *n* (*ray*) rayon *m* X; (*photograph*) radio(graphie) *f* ▷ *vt* radiographier
xylophone ['zaɪləfəun] *n* xylophone *m*

yacht [jɔt] *n* voilier *m*; (*motor, luxury yacht*) yacht *m*; **yachting** *n* yachting *m*, navigation *f* de plaisance
yard [jɑːd] *n* (*of house etc*) cour *f*; (*us: garden*) jardin *m*; (*measure*) yard *m* (= 914 mm; 3 *feet*); **yard sale** *n* (*us*) brocante *f* (dans son propre jardin)
yarn [jɑːn] *n* fil *m*; (*tale*) longue histoire
yawn [jɔːn] *n* bâillement *m* ▷ *vi* bâiller
yd. *abbr* = **yard; yards**
yeah [jɛə] *adv* (*inf*) ouais
year [jɪəʳ] *n* an *m*, année *f*; (*Scol etc*) année; **to be 8 ~s old** avoir 8 ans; **an eight-~-old child** un enfant de huit ans; **yearly** *adj* annuel(le) ▷ *adv* annuellement; **twice yearly** deux fois par an
yearn [jəːn] *vi*: **to ~ for sth/to do** aspirer à qch/à faire
yeast [jiːst] *n* levure *f*
yell [jɛl] *n* hurlement *m*, cri *m* ▷ *vi* hurler
yellow ['jɛləu] *adj*, *n* jaune (*m*); **Yellow Pages®** *npl* (*Tel*) pages *fpl* jaunes
yes [jɛs] *adv* oui; (*answering negative question*) si ▷ *n* oui *m*; **to say ~ (to)** dire oui (à)
yesterday ['jɛstədɪ] *adv*, *n* hier (*m*); **~ morning/evening** hier matin/soir; **all day ~** toute la journée d'hier
yet [jɛt] *adv* encore; (*in questions*) déjà ▷ *conj* pourtant, néanmoins; **it is not finished ~** ce n'est pas encore fini *or* toujours pas fini; **have you eaten ~?** vous avez déjà mangé?; **the best ~** le meilleur jusqu'ici *or* jusque-là; **as ~** jusqu'ici, encore
yew [juː] *n* if *m*
Yiddish ['jɪdɪʃ] *n* yiddish *m*
yield [jiːld] *n* production *f*, rendement *m*; (*Finance*) rapport *m* ▷ *vt* produire, rendre, rapporter; (*surrender*) céder ▷ *vi* céder; (*us Aut*) céder la priorité
yob(bo) ['jɔb(əu)] *n* (*BRIT inf*) loubar(d) *m*
yoga ['jəugə] *n* yoga *m*

yog(h)urt ['jɔgət] *n* yaourt *m*
yolk [jəuk] *n* jaune *m* (d'œuf)

KEYWORD

you [ju:] *pron* **1** (*subject*) tu; (: *polite form*)
vous; (: *plural*) vous; **you are very kind**
vous êtes très gentil; **you French enjoy
your food** vous autres Français, vous aimez
bien manger; **you and I will go** toi et moi
or vous et moi, nous irons; **there you are!**
vous voilà!
2 (*object: direct, indirect*) te, t' + *vowel*; vous;
I know you je te *or* vous connais; **I gave it
to you** je te l'ai donné, je vous l'ai donné
3 (*stressed*) toi; vous; **I told you to do it** c'est
à toi *or* vous que j'ai dit de le faire
4 (*after prep, in comparisons*) toi; vous;
it's for you c'est pour toi *or* vous; **she's
younger than you** elle est plus jeune que
toi *or* vous
5 (*impersonal: one*) on; **fresh air does you
good** l'air frais fait du bien; **you never
know** on ne sait jamais; **you can't do that!**
ça ne se fait pas!

you'd [ju:d] = **you had; you would**
you'll [ju:l] = **you will; you shall**
young [jʌŋ] *adj* jeune ▷ *npl* (*of animal*)
petits *mpl*; **the ~** (*people*) les jeunes, la
jeunesse; **my ~er brother** mon frère cadet;
youngster *n* jeune *m/f*; (*child*) enfant *m/f*
your [jɔ:ʳ] *adj* ton (ta), tes *pl*; (*polite form, pl*)
votre, vos *pl*; *see also* **my**
you're [juəʳ] = **you are**
yours [jɔ:z] *pron* le (la) tien(ne), les tiens
(tiennes); (*polite form, pl*) le (la) vôtre, les
vôtres; **is it ~?** c'est à toi (*or* à vous)?; **a
friend of ~** un(e) de tes (*or* de vos) amis; *see
also* **faithfully; mine¹; sincerely**
yourself [jɔ:'sɛlf] *pron* (*reflexive*) te; (: *polite
form*) vous; (*after prep*) toi; vous; (*emphatic*)
toi-même; vous-même; *see also* **oneself**;
yourselves *pl pron* vous; (*emphatic*) vous-
mêmes; *see also* **oneself**
youth [ju:θ] *n* jeunesse *f*; (*young man*)
jeune homme *m*; **youth club** *n* centre *m*
de jeunes; **youthful** *adj* jeune; (*enthusiasm
etc*) juvénile; **youth hostel** *n* auberge *f* de
jeunesse
you've [ju:v] = **you have**
Yugoslav ['ju:gəuslɑ:v] *adj* (*Hist*)
yougoslave ▷ *n* Yougoslave *m/f*
Yugoslavia [ju:gəu'slɑ:viə] *n* (*Hist*)
Yougoslavie *f*

Z

zeal [zi:l] *n* (*revolutionary etc*) ferveur *f*;
(*keenness*) ardeur *f*, zèle *m*
zebra ['zi:brə] *n* zèbre *m*; **zebra crossing** *n*
(*BRIT*) passage clouté *or* pour piétons
zero ['zɪərəu] *n* zéro *m*
zest [zɛst] *n* entrain *m*, élan *m*; (*of lemon etc*)
zeste *m*
zigzag ['zɪgzæg] *n* zigzag *m* ▷ *vi* zigzaguer,
faire des zigzags
Zimbabwe [zɪm'bɑ:bwɪ] *n* Zimbabwe *m*
zinc [zɪŋk] *n* zinc *m*
zip [zɪp] *n* (*also*: **~ fastener**) fermeture *f*
éclair® *or* à glissière ▷ *vt* (*file*) zipper; (*also*:
~ up) fermer (avec une fermeture éclair®);
zip code *n* (*US*) code postal; **zip file** *n*
(*Comput*) fichier *m* zip *inv*; **zipper** *n* (*US*) = **zip**
zit [zɪt] (*inf*) *n* bouton *m*
zodiac ['zəudɪæk] *n* zodiaque *m*
zone [zəun] *n* zone *f*
zoo [zu:] *n* zoo *m*
zoology [zu:'ɔlədʒɪ] *n* zoologie *f*
zoom [zu:m] *vi*: **to ~ past** passer en
trombe; **zoom lens** *n* zoom *m*
zucchini [zu:'ki:nɪ] *n* (*US*) courgette *f*